Expert Oracle9*i* Database Administration

SAM R. ALAPATI

Expert Oracle9i Database Administration
Copyright © 2003 by Sam R. Alapati

ISBN (pbk): 1-59059-022-8
Printed and bound in the United States of America 12345678910

Trademarked names may appear in this book. Rather than use a trademark symbol with every occurrence of a trademarked name, we use the names only in an editorial fashion and to the benefit of the trademark owner, with no intention of infringement of the trademark.

Technical Reviewer: Kee Heng Tiow

Editorial Directors: Dan Appleman, Gary Cornell, Simon Hayes, Martin Streicher, Karen Watterson, John Zukowski

Assistant Publisher: Grace Wong

Project Manager: Alexa Stuart

Development Editor: Tracy Brown Collins

Copy Editor: Nicole LeClerc

Production Editor: Laura Cheu

Compositor: Diana Van Winkle, Van Winkle Design Group

Indexer: Julie Kawabata

Artist and Cover Designer: Kurt Krames

Production Manager: Kari Brooks

Manufacturing Manager: Tom Debolski

Distributed to the book trade in the United States by Springer-Verlag New York, Inc., 175 Fifth Avenue, New York, NY, 10010 and outside the United States by Springer-Verlag GmbH & Co. KG, Tiergartenstr. 17, 69112 Heidelberg, Germany.

In the United States: phone 1-800-SPRINGER, email orders@springer-ny.com, or visit http://www.springer-ny.com. Outside the United States: fax +49 6221 345229, email orders@springer.de, or visit http://www.springer.de.

For information on translations, please contact Apress directly at 2560 Ninth Street, Suite 219, Berkeley, CA 94710. Phone 510-549-5930, fax 510-549-5939, email info@apress.com, or visit http://www.apress.com.

To my mother,
Swarna Kumari,
And my father,
Appa Rao,
For all the love, affection, and sacrifice.

To the memory of my sister,
Usha Rani,
Your words of praise still ring in my ears.

To my wife,
Valerie,
For your selfless support and help.

Contents at a Glance

Contents

Part Three
Database Creation, Connectivity,
and User Management

Chapter 11 User Management and Database Security 469

Part Four
Data Loading, Backup, and Recovery

Chapter 12 Loading and Transforming Data

Part Five
Managing the Operational Oracle Database 721

Part Six
Performance Tuning and Troubleshooting
the Production Database

Chapter 18 Improving Database Performance: SQL Query Optimization

About the Author

Sam R. Alapati is an experienced Oracle DBA who holds the Oracle OCP DBA certification and the Hewlett-Packard UNIX System Administrator certification. He currently manages Oracle databases at the Boy Scouts of America's national office in Los Colinas, Texas. Previously, Alapati worked for AMR Holdings (Sabre) and the Blanch Company in Dallas. Alapati was a senior principal consultant for Oracle Corporation in New York and worked at NBC and Lehman Brothers on behalf of Oracle. Alapati's other DBA experience, which includes Sybase and DB2 databases, consists of assignments with Lewco Securities and AT&T in New Jersey.

About the Technical Reviewer

Kee Heng Tiow is a consultant at Procase Consulting Inc., taking the role of technical project manager at workopolis.com, the biggest job site in Canada. Prior to joining Procase Consulting Inc., Kee Heng worked in different Oracle Corporation Canada departments, including Oracle Consulting and Oracle University. He was involved in various consulting projects for many clients using Oracle products, primarily the Oracle database, Oracle Designer/Developer/Discoverer, and PL/SQL. Currently, Kee Heng is an instructor for Oracle technology training courses at Learning Tree International. He graduated with a bachelor's degree (with honors) in computer science from the University of Toronto, Canada.

Acknowledgments

I HAVE HAD THE IDEA of writing a book such as this for a long time, and the book would have remained just that—an idea—but for two people: my father, Dr. Appa Rao, who encouraged me to go ahead with the plan and explained why it was a good idea, and my wife, Valerie, who not only supported the idea, but also backed it up with a lot of sacrifice over the last year. I'm grateful to both for helping make my idea a reality.

This book has benefited from the suggestions of several good technical reviewers. Sheldon Barry reviewed the first half of the book and Martin Reid reviewed some of the early chapters. Thanks to both of you, Sheldon and Martin. The reviewer who spent the most time on this book, however, was Kee Heng Tiow. Kee, thank you for your painstaking technical reviews and your great suggestions for improving the content. You were on the mark all the time, and I'm grateful for your conscientious effort.

Karen Watterson, editorial director at Apress, has been instrumental in bringing this book about, and I'm grateful for her suggestions and support throughout the writing process. Karen, thanks also for reviewing the entire book and for your enormous patience and the grace you have shown throughout.

Several people at Apress have contributed significantly to the book. I've had the great fortune of having a most unique and talented team work on this book. Alexa Stuart, the book's project manager, showed tremendous organizational skill in shepherding the book through to publication. It's simply amazing how she kept up with the monumental task of keeping everything moving in an orderly fashion. The book has benefited tremendously from great developmental editing by Tracy Brown Collins. Tracy's graceful handling of many difficult issues made the developmental review process a lot of fun. The magical touch of "copy editor extraordinaire" Nicole LeClerc made the book far better than it was in its original form. I'm simply astonished at how Nicole could time and again improve a highly technical sentence or paragraph without changing its meaning. Alexa, Tracy, and Nicole, I'm grateful for the extraordinary work and care you devoted to my book.

My thanks to Apress's marketing director, Simon Hayes, who helped with several issues dealing with the publication of this book. Laura Cheu, the book's production editor, displayed tremendous skill in dealing with the minutiae while keeping the production process moving along. Production manager Kari Brooks took over as production editor toward the very end, and thanks to you, Kari, for seeing the project through. Diana Van Winkle of the Van Winkle Design Group has been a most skillful and fast compositor. Although I didn't deal with them directly, Grace Wong, Apress's assistant publisher, and Gary Cornell, Apress's publisher, helped the project at critical times with answers to important questions about the publication process. Apress's manufacturing manager, Tom Debolski, helped tremendously several times by providing fast and accurate answers to difficult questions. Thanks to all of you for your help.

Several people have indirectly played a role in the publication of this book because of the role they have played in my life. Thanks to Brother Roberts of All Saints High School for lending all those books to me. I'm grateful to Professor Janardhana Reddy for helping me come to the United States when it wasn't easy to do so. Thanks to Madan Mohan Rao for helping me when I first came to the United States and for years after that, in so many ways. I thank Eddie Colon of New Brunswick, New Jersey, from the bottom of my heart for helping me when I really needed it. I wouldn't have been an Oracle DBA but for Jayesh Patel's help—thank you, Jayesh, for all you've done for me. I wish to thank Yuri for helping me learn the UNIX operating system and unravel the mysteries of databases. My thanks to Anil Sinha and J. Ram for their help while I worked with them. I owe a special debt of gratitude to my good friend Rajanna (Rajeshwara Rao) for explaining why ideas are so important. Yes, Bishop Berkeley did have a point.

Several colleagues at the Boy Scouts of America were helpful during the course of writing this book. My colleague Mark Potts has helped me in several ways, including letting me use his PC when I was having problems with mine. Thanks, Mark, for all the help at work and outside. My thanks also to Stan Galbraith, who somehow managed to provide space on the server for the Oracle9*i* test databases. Thanks to Lance Parkes, who helped with some questions I had during the installation process. I'm also thankful to Rob Page for all the kindness and help at work. I wish to thank my friend Don Rios for helping me with answers to several difficult Oracle programming questions. I'm appreciative of Dan Nelson's encouragement and support for my endeavors. I'm thankful to Linda Almanza for her consistent support and help in various matters at work. I'm extremely grateful for having two remarkable people, David Jeffress and Dave Campbell, as my managers at the Boy Scouts of America. David's wide technical knowledge coupled with his exquisite sense of humor helps us keep our perspective and stay on top of things. My thanks to Dave, whose compassion for people coupled with his technical savvy is a source of inspiration for our group. Information Systems Division Director Nathan O. Langston encourages us to strive for higher goals and shows the way by leading from the front. By focusing relentlessly on efficient customer service, Nate helps us understand the true mission of an information technology professional.

I would like to thank my mother and father for all they have done for their children. No parents have been more loving or more giving than you, and I'm grateful for everything. I'm grateful for the kindness and affection shown throughout my life by my two brothers, Hari and Bujji. I'm also appreciative of the affection shown by my sisters-in-law, Aruna and Vanaja. I'm lucky to have wonderful nieces like Aparna and Neelima and loving nephews like Ashwini and Teja. Special thanks to Shannon, my "number one" son, for all the love and affection. Thanks also to Keith, Shawn, and Dale for their love and support. I know you can't read this yet, but a whole lot of thanks to you, our magical twins, Nina and Nicholas, for all the fun, love, and cheer. I promise to make up for all the time I spent writing this book! Once again, thanks to my wife, Valerie, for all the support, encouragement, and sacrifice, which made this book possible.

Introduction

GRATIANO

. . . As who should say 'I am Sir Oracle,

And when I ope my lips, let no dog bark!'

—The Merchant of Venice, *act 1, scene 1*

Oracle Corporation used to print the preceding quotation from Shakespeare at the beginning of one of its chapters in the Oracle database administrator (DBA) manual (the early versions). I always thought the quote was interesting. If you proceed a little further in the play, you'll find this quotation:

BASSANIO

Gratiano speaks an infinite deal of nothing, more

than any man in all Venice. His reasons are as two

grains of wheat hid in two bushels of chaff: you

shall seek all day ere you find them . . .

—The Merchant of Venice, *act 1, scene 1*

Bassanio counters that, in truth, Gratiano speaks too much: From two bushels of chaff, two grains of wheat may be recovered. And that's the raison d'être for this book: to separate the wheat from the chaff. This second part of the quotation is more apt when you consider the difficulty of extracting the right database management procedures from the tons of material available on the Oracle9*i* Release 2 database. Oracle Corporation publishes copious material to help you manage its increasingly complex databases. Oracle Corporation also conducts several in-person and Web-based classes to explain the vast amount of subject matter that you need to understand to effectively work with the Oracle database today. Yet users will have a good deal of difficulty finding the essential material that they need to perform their jobs if they rely exclusively on Oracle's voluminous (albeit well-written) material in the form of the aforementioned manuals, class notes, videos, and so on.

How to Become an Oracle DBA

Currently, you have several ways to become a proficient Oracle DBA. First, you can take the whole series of Oracle classes, each of which lasts between 3 and 5 working days. You have to take all of these classes just to be able to perform the basic DBA duties. In addition, you need to peruse the Oracle manuals—there's an entire library of books that Oracle gives away freely on CD and on its Web site. Lastly, you may also wish to purchase books published by private publishers that impart various pieces of the knowledge it takes to become an accomplished Oracle DBA. Oh, and don't forget, you'll also need to acquire the necessary operating system knowledge somewhere. Because most of the large databases using Oracle are based on the UNIX (or Linux) operating system, you'll need to have a reasonably good understanding of UNIX. You can gain this understanding either by attending a class or two from the leading UNIX system vendors such as Hewlett-Packard and Sun Microsystems or by reading manuals and/or books about UNIX published by independent companies.

As many of the new entrants to the Oracle9*i* database field find out, the Oracle DBA world is exhilarating, but alas, it's also exhaustive in its reach and scope. It isn't uncommon for many DBAs to have an entire shelf full of books, all explaining various facets of the DBA profession—for example, modeling books, UNIX texts, DBA handbooks, backup and recovery guides, performance tuning manuals, and networking and troubleshooting books. The amazing thing is, even after you run through the whole gauntlet of courses and books, you aren't really assured of success in the sense of being fully prepared to handle complex, day-to-day database administration chores. There are many, many people who have taken all the requisite classes to become an Oracle DBA who won't or can't be competent Oracle DBAs based solely on their training. The reason? Refer back to that quotation from Shakespeare at the beginning of this introduction: You need to separate the grain from the chaff, and all the coursework and manuals, while excellent in their content, can serve to muddy the waters further.

The experienced Oracle DBA can well find his or her way through this baffling amount of material. But what about the newly initiated? That's where this book comes in. This text will not only educate you in the theory and principles involved in managing relational databases, but it will also help you in actually translating that theory into the useful, practical knowledge that will enable you to manage real-life databases with real-life data and real-life problems.

Why Read This Oracle9*i* Book?

What sets this book apart from the others on the market is the constant adherence to the practical side of the DBA's work life. What does a new DBA need to know to begin work? How much and what SQL does the prospective candidate need to know? What UNIX, Windows Server, and Windows commands and utilities does the new DBA need to know? How does a DBA perform the basic UNIX system administration tasks? How does a DBA install the Oracle RDBMS software from scratch? This book provides the conceptual background and operational details for all the necessary topics a DBA needs to be familiar with. The following sections outline other reasons to choose this Oracle9*i* book.

Delivers a One-Volume Reference

This book's specific purpose is to serve as a one-volume handbook for professional Oracle DBAs, a book with both the theory and practice of what DBAs need to know to learn their craft and practice it on a daily basis. As I mentioned before, most newcomers to the field are intimidated and bewildered by the sheer amount of material they're confronted with and the great number of administrative commands they need to have at their fingertips. Well, everything you need to know to run your databases efficiently is right here in this one book.

How did I manage to achieve the difficult feat of providing comprehensive instruction in just one book? Well, although there's a lot of terrain to cover if you want to learn all the DBA material, you must learn to separate the critical from the trivial so you can identify what matters most and what you merely need to be aware of, at least in the beginning. I discuss how this book is organized and how you should read it in later sections of this introduction.

I'm definitely not suggesting that this one book will supplant all of the Oracle material that you need to know. I strongly recommend that inquisitive readers make it a habit to refer to Oracle's documentation set for the 9*i* database, which is available on a CD bundled with most Oracle software. Optionally, you can obtain this documentation on the Web by getting a free membership to the Oracle Technology Network (OTN), which you can access through the Oracle Web site at `http://technet.oracle.com`.

Reading the Oracle Manuals

Whether you use this or some other DBA handbook, you still need to refer to the Oracle database manuals frequently to get the full details of complex database operations. I can't overemphasize the importance of mastering the fundamentals of the Oracle9*i* database that are presented in the "Oracle Concepts" manual. Mastering this volume is critical to understanding many advanced DBA procedures.

The Oracle manuals are invaluable if you need an extreme amount of detail. For example, the chapters on backup and recovery are good starting points in your attempt to master the Oracle procedures in those areas. Oracle recommends a total of no less than five manuals to cover their backup and recovery material. Once you finish the two relevant chapters (Chapters 14 and 15) in this book, you'll find going through those five manuals a pretty easy task, because you'll already have a good understanding of all the important concepts. This book provides a foundation on which you can build using the Oracle manuals and other online help available from Oracle.

In addition to the online manuals, Oracle provides an excellent set of tutorials that contain step-by-step instructions on how to perform many useful Oracle9*i* database tasks. You can access these tutorials, the "Oracle9*i* by Example Series," by going to `http://otn.oracle.com/products/oracle9i/htdocs/9iobe/OBE9i-Public/`.

Emphasizes New Methods and When to Use Them

One of the fundamental difficulties for a neophyte in this field is the ambiguity involved in adopting the right strategy for managing databases. Although the essential tasks of database management are pretty similar in Oracle9*i* Release 2 compared to earlier versions of the software, the database contains several innovative techniques that make a number of routine tasks easier to perform. Oracle Corporation, however, has shied away from firmly recommending the adoption of the new methods and techniques to manage databases. The reason for this is twofold. First, Oracle rarely discards current techniques abruptly between versions; features advertised as destined for obsolescence are made obsolete only after the passage of many years. Thus, old and new ways of performing similar tasks coexist in the same version. Second, Oracle isn't very effective in clearly communicating its guidelines regarding the choice between contending methods. Thus, you as a DBA have to exercise caution when you select the appropriate methods to use, when more than one method exists for performing a task.

In this book, I clearly emphasize the newer features of Oracle that have been refined in the last 3 to 4 years and encourage you to move away from traditional techniques when the new innovations are clearly superior. I help you in formulating a solid strategy regarding the proper course to take when multiple choices are offered.

Covers UNIX, SQL, PL/SQL, and Data Modeling

Some people who are motivated to become Oracle DBAs are stymied in their initial efforts to do so by their lack of training in UNIX and SQL. Also, sometimes DBAs are confused by the whole set of data modeling and the "logical DBA" techniques. This book is unique in that it covers all the essential UNIX, SQL, PL/SQL, and data modeling that a DBA ought to know to perform his or her job well.

As a DBA, you need to be able to use a number of UNIX tools and utilities to administer an Oracle database. Unfortunately, up until now, many books haven't included coverage of these vital tools. This book remedies this neglect by carefully covering tools such as telnet, ftp, and the crontab. Many developers and managers want to have a better understanding of the UNIX system, including the use of the vi file editor, file manipulation, and basic shell script writing techniques. This book enables you to start using the UNIX operating system right away and shows you how to write solid shell scripts to perform various tasks. Of course, you can take a specialized class or study a separate book in each of the previous areas, but that's exactly what you're trying to avoid by using this book.

In addition to learning all the UNIX you need to start working with the UNIX operating system right away, you can get a good working knowledge of SQL and PL/SQL from a DBA's perspective in this book. Of course, I strongly recommend further study of both UNIX and SQL for strengthening your skills as an Oracle DBA as you progress in your career.

NOTE *understand that some of you may not really need the UNIX back-*
ground or the introduction to SQL and PL/SQL (presented in the Appendix).
If this is the case, please skip those chapters and get to the main database
management chapters.

Offers Hands-on Administrative Experience

Although a number of books have been published in the last decade on the subject
of database administration, there has been a surprising lack of the blending of the
concepts of Oracle with the techniques needed to perform several administrative
tasks. A glaring example is the area of backup and recovery, where it's difficult to
find discussions of the conceptual underpinnings of the backup and recovery
process. Consequently, many DBAs end up learning backup and recovery techniques without having a solid grasp of the underlying principles of backup and
recovery. As you can imagine, this dichotomy of theory and practice proves
expensive in the middle of a recovery operation, where fuzziness on the concepts
could lead to simple mistakes.

The success of a DBA is directly related to the amount of hands-on experience
he or she has in conjunction with an understanding of the concepts behind the
operation of the database. Readers can practice all the commands from this book
on a UNIX-based or a Windows-based Oracle9*i* database. Oracle9*i* Release 2 is
loaded with features that make it the cutting-edge database in the relational
database market. This book covers all the new additions and modifications to
database administration contained in the Oracle9*i* version. Although it's a lot of
fun for an experienced DBA to have the opportunity to use all the wonderful features of the new database, beginning- and intermediate-level DBAs will have *more*
fun, because they're embarking on the great endeavor that is the mastery of Oracle
database management.

Focuses on the Oracle9i Release 2 Database

This book was written entirely with the Oracle9*i* Release 2 database in mind—it
doesn't contain just an addition of Oracle9*i* features to a book written for earlier
versions. The book was written for the express purpose of taking advantage of
Oracle9*i*'s new powerful features for database administration and making them an
integral part of a working DBA's toolkit. Unlike the current practice in the market,
this book takes a clear stand when alternative methods exist to perform the same
task and advocates the use of the newer Oracle9*i* methods consistently. I consider
it superfluous to continue to teach the old methods along with the more sophisticated new techniques. If you're a DBA who is currently managing Oracle 8.*x*
databases, or if you've never managed databases and intend to master the management of the new Oracle9*i* databases, you can do so with the help of this book.

Who Should Read This Book?

This book is primarily intended for beginning- and intermediate-level Oracle9*i* DBAs. Prior experience with Oracle databases isn't assumed. Oracle8*i* DBAs can also benefit from this book, but as I mentioned earlier in this introduction, this book isn't an Oracle8*i* book with a smattering of Oracle9*i* features. Consequently, you may not find any worthwhile discussion of some 8*i* features that have been supplanted by better methods in the Oracle9*i* version. More precisely, the audience for this book will fall into the following categories:

- Beginning Oracle DBAs who are just starting out

- Oracle developers and UNIX/NT administrators who intend to learn Oracle DBA skills

- Managers who intend to get a hands-on feel for database management

- Anybody who wants to learn how to become a proficient Oracle DBA on his or her own

A Note About UNIX

I personally like the UNIX operating system and use it at work. I'm familiar with the Windows platform and I happen to think it's a good operating system for small enterprises. But my favorite operating system remains UNIX, which stands out for its reliability, scalability, and speed. For medium and large organizations, the UNIX system offers wonderful features and ease of use. As a result, you'll find this book heavily oriented toward the use of Oracle on UNIX systems. If you happen to admire the Linux system, there isn't a new learning curve involved, as most of the operating system commands will work the same way in the UNIX and Linux systems. For those of you who need to find out how to use the Oracle9*i* database on a Windows platform, here's some interesting news for you: The commands and methods work exactly the same way in both the UNIX and Windows environments. There are minor changes in syntax in a very few cases. Chapter 22 summarizes these differences and covers basic Windows system administration as it pertains to Oracle9*i* database management.

How This Book Is Organized

I have organized the contents of this book with the new DBA in mind. My goal is to provide you with a decent background in data modeling, SQL, and UNIX, while providing a thorough course in the essentials of Oracle9*i* database management skills. I know it's unusual to provide UNIX and SQL background in an Oracle DBA book. But the inclusion is in line with the goal I set when I decided to write this book: There ought be a single book or manual that has all the necessary background for a reader to start working as an Oracle9*i* DBA.

I strove to write the chapters to mirror real-life practical training. For example, it's advisable to understand basic database modeling and UNIX learning to manage Oracle databases. I therefore start with a discussion of database modeling and UNIX first (in Part One of the book). You'll also first install the Oracle database software before you create an actual database (Part Two). After you install the software, you can create databases, create users, and establish connectivity (Part Three). You can load and back up data only after the database is created (Part Four). As you can see, the chapters follow a logical progression similar to the real-life precedence of the tasks covered by them.

I advise beginning DBAs to start at the beginning of the book and keep going. A more experienced user, on the other hand, can pick the topics in any sequence he or she desires. The scripts that accompany the book will keep a DBA in good stead during routine operation of the database and during crisis situations when information needs to be communicated through paging. There's no reason why you can't keep the pager from going off during those early morning hours if you adopt the preventive maintenance scripts included in this book.

I've tried throughout the book to provide detailed, step-by-step, tested examples to illustrate the use of several data connects and features of Oracle9*i*. I strongly recommend that you set up an Oracle9*i* database server on your PC and practice these how-to sections. Following along with these examples will teach you the relevant commands and help you build great confidence in your skill level. Plus, the examples are a whole lot of fun! The following sections briefly summarize the contents of the book.

Part One: Database Basics, Data Modeling, and UNIX/Linux

Part One provides a background on the Oracle DBA profession and offers an intro-duction to data modeling and the UNIX operating system. I discuss the role of the Oracle DBA in the organization, and I offer some advice on improving your skill set as a DBA. I then discuss the basics of relational databases. The data modeling chapter (Chapter 2) provides an introduction to both logical and physical database design, including the use of entity-relationship diagrams. You'll learn about the Oracle Flexible Architecture (OFA) with regard to disk layout. You'll then learn the basic UNIX commands and how to use the vi text processing commands. You'll also explore the essential UNIX system administration tasks for Oracle DBAs. This part finishes with coverage on disks and storage systems, including the popular RAID systems.

Part Two: The Oracle RDBMS

Part Two covers installing the Oracle server and Oracle SQL and PL/SQL. You'll first learn how to install the new Oracle9*i* server software. You'll also learn about the processes and memory that constitute the Oracle server architecture. You'll then move on to cover the conceptual foundations of the Oracle database. The chapter covering schema management in Oracle9*i* (Chapter 7) contains a quick review of the important types of Oracle objects and shows you how to manage them. The chapter on Oracle transaction processing (Chapter 8) provides you with a good understanding of how Oracle databases conduct transaction processing.

Part Three: Database Creation, Connectivity, and User Management

Part Three covers the creation of actual databases, connectivity issues, and user management. You'll go through a step-by-step discussion of database creation and then learn how to configure Oracle networking. You'll also learn how to create users and manage them.

Part Four: Data Loading, Backup, and Recovery

Part Four deals with loading data and performing backups and recovery. You'll learn how to use SQL*Loader and the export and import utilities to perform data loading and data exports from the Oracle9*i* database. The important topic of database backup comes next, and the final chapter in this section details the recovery of databases.

Part Five: Managing the Operational Oracle Database

Part Five covers managing the operational Oracle9*i* database. Chapter 16 shows you how to manage data files, tablespaces, and Oracle redo logs, and how to perform undo management. Chapter 17 describes how to use Oracle Enterprise Manager (OEM).

Part Six: Performance Tuning and Troubleshooting the Production Database

Part Six covers Oracle9*i* performance tuning and troubleshooting issues. You'll first learn the basics of writing efficient SQL queries and then you'll see how to optimize the use of Oracle's memory and the operating system itself. The importance of mastering the Oracle data dictionary is discussed next, followed by an explanation of using the excellent packages supplied by Oracle. The final chapter of this section covers the management of Oracle9*i* databases on Windows and Linux systems.

Salud!

I truly enjoy the Oracle database for its amazing range of capabilities and the intricate challenges it throws my way as I explore its wide-ranging capabilities. I hope you derive as much satisfaction and fulfillment from the Oracle database as I do. I leave you with the following section that I paraphrased from the introduction to the famous textbook by Paul A. Samuelson, the great economist and Nobel Laureate:[1]

> *I envy you, the beginning Oracle DBA, as you set out to explore the exciting world of Oracle9i database management for the first time. This is a thrill that, alas, you can experience only once in a lifetime. So, as you embark, I wish you bon voyage!*

---

1. Samuelson, Paul A. and William D. Nordhaus. *Economics, Seventeenth Edition.* New York: McGraw-Hill, 1998.

Part One

Database Basics, Data Modeling, and UNIX/Linux

The Oracle DBA's World

THIS CHAPTER DISCUSSES the nature and role of the Oracle database administrator (DBA) in most organizations, as well as the training that Oracle DBAs typically need to receive to be successful. There are many types of Oracle databases, and there are many types of Oracle DBAs. In this chapter, you'll look at the daily routine of a typical DBA, which will give you an idea of what to expect if you're new to the field. This chapter also covers ways you can improve your skill level as an Oracle DBA and prepare for the optimal performance of the databases under your stewardship. Toward the end of the chapter, you'll find a list of resources and organizations that will help you in your quest to become a top-notch DBA.

The Oracle DBA's Role

The main responsibility of a DBA is to make corporate data available to the end users and the decision makers of an organization. All other DBA tasks are subordinate and in support of that single issue, and almost everything DBAs do on a day-to-day basis is aimed toward meeting that single target. Without access to data, many companies and organizations would simply cease to function.

NOTE *Just think of the chaos that would ensue if a company such as Amazon.com no longer had access to their customer database, even for a short time. The entire company could cease to function. At a minimum, they would lose perhaps thousands of online orders. Business data should be viewed as a company asset, and as such, it has a monetary value. As a DBA, you have the keys to the safe, and your job is to protect the data.*

That's not to say that availability of data is the only thing DBAs have to worry about. DBAs are also responsible for other areas, such as

- *Security:* Ensuring that the data and access to the data are secure

- *Backup:* Ensuring that the database can be restored in the event of either human or systems failure

- *Performance:* Ensuring that the database and its subsystems are optimized for performance

- *Design:* Ensuring that the design of the database meets the needs of the organization

- *Implementation:* Ensuring proper implementation of new database systems and applications

In addition to their standard roles, many DBAs are responsible for the accuracy of the actual data. However, in some organizations, this responsibility is relegated to the data owners and end users themselves, putting the onus on them to ensure that the data being input to the system is correct. Job responsibilities for Oracle DBAs do vary across organizations. In a small organization, a DBA could be managing the entire information technology (IT) infrastructure, including the databases, whereas in a large organization, a DBA could be one of a number of DBAs, each charged with managing a particular area of the system. However, there is a *fundamental set* of tasks that a DBA is expected to perform, whatever the organization type or size. The three most vital DBA tasks are as follows:

- Ensuring frequent backups are made (so data isn't lost)

- Securing the database from unauthorized use

- Minimizing downtime

These tasks are definitely not the only ones that matter. I've emphasized these particular tasks only because a failure in any of these areas could prevent a firm or organization from carrying out its mission.

The following sections discuss what you could consider the bare minimum level of performance expected of a DBA. Although this list seems long and daunting, it's really not that difficult in practice if you follow certain guidelines. Proper planning and testing as well as automating most of the routine tasks keep the drudgery to a minimum. All you're left with to do on a daily basis, then, are the really enjoyable things such as performance tuning or whatever else may appeal to you.

You can put the tasks you'll perform as an Oracle DBA in the following three roles or categories:

- Security role

- System management role

- Database design role

I discuss each of these broad roles in more detail in the following sections.

The DBA's Security Role

As a DBA, you'll be involved in many different areas of system security, mainly focusing on the database and its data but not restricted to this single area. *Several* potential security loopholes are possible when you implement a new Oracle system out of the box, and you need to know how to plug these security loopholes thoroughly before the databases go live in a production environment. In Chapter 11, which deals with user management, you'll find a fuller discussion of standard

Oracle security guidelines, as well as other Oracle security related issues. Oracle regularly issues Oracle Security Alerts for its databases, and you need to keep up with these as part of your job.

Protecting the Database

For an Oracle DBA, no job requirement is more fundamental and critical than the protection of the database itself. The Oracle DBA is definitely the person the information departments entrust with safeguarding the organization's data. This involves timely and effective backups of the production data to keep it from being lost due to hardware problems, sabotage, or a natural disaster. The other aspect of the DBA's job as the keeper of the data is the security of the database itself, which involves preventing unauthorized use and access of the database. The DBA has several means to ensure the database's security, and based on the company's security guidelines, he or she needs to come up with and/or maintain the database security policy. A more complex issue is the authorization of users' actions within the database itself, after access has already been granted. I address this topic in depth in a later chapter.

NOTE *Some organizations don't have a general security policy in place. This is particularly true of smaller companies. In that case, it's usually up to the DBA to come up with the security policy and then enforce it within the database.*

Monitoring the System

Once a database is actually in production, the DBA is expected to monitor the system to ensure uninterrupted service. The tasks involved in monitoring the system include the following:

- Monitoring space in the database to ensure it is sufficient for the system

- Checking that batch jobs are finishing as expected

- Monitoring log files for evidence of any errors or any unusual performance issues.

Creating and Managing Users

Every database has users, and it's the DBA's job to create them based on requests from the appropriate people. A DBA is expected to help the users with the use of the database and ensure the database's security by using proper authorization schemes, roles, and privileges. Of course, when users are locked out of the database because of password expiration and related issues, the DBA needs to take care of them. Ultimately, the DBA's job is a service job, and by providing efficient service to the database servers, a DBA indirectly provides service to the customers of his or her applications.

The DBA's System Management Role

Another of the DBA's major roles is the day-to-day management of the database and its subsystems. This daily monitoring is not really limited to the database itself. As a DBA, you need to be aware of how the system as a whole is performing. You need to monitor the performance of the servers that hosts the database and the network that enables connections to the database. The following sections describe the various facets of the system management part of the Oracle DBA's job.

Troubleshooting

One of the Oracle DBA's main job responsibilities is troubleshooting the database to fix problems. "Troubleshooting" is a catchall term, and it could consist of several parts of the job that I discuss in the following sections. Two important aspects of troubleshooting are knowing how to get the right kind of help from Oracle support personnel and how to use other Oracle resources to help you fix problems quickly.

Ensuring Performance Tuning

Performance tuning is an omnipresent issue. It's a part of the design stage, the implementation stage, the testing stage, and the production stage. In fact, performance tuning is an ongoing task that constantly requires the attention of a good Oracle DBA. Depending on the organizational setup, the DBA may need to perform either database tuning or application tuning, or sometimes both. Generally, the DBA performs database tuning him- or herself and assists in the testing and implementation of the application tuning performed by the application developers.

Performance requirements change for a living database constantly, and the DBA needs to continuously monitor the performance by applying the right indicators. For example, after my firm migrated from Oracle8*i* to the new Oracle9*i*, I found that several large batch programs weren't completing within the allotted time. After much frustration, I realized that this was because some of the code was using cost-based optimizer "hints" that were no longer optimal under the new version. A quick revision of those "hints" improved the performance of the programs dramatically. The moral of the story: Make sure you test all the code under the new version before you switch over to it.

Minimizing Downtime

Providing uninterrupted service by eliminating (or at least minimizing) downtime is an important criterion by which you can judge a DBA's performance. Of course, if the downtime is the result of a faulty disk, the company's service level agreements (SLAs), if any, will determine how fast the disk is replaced. DBAs may or may not have control over the maximum time for service provided in the SLAs. For their part, however, DBAs are expected to be proactive and prevent avoidable downtimes (for example, due to a process running out of space).

Estimating Requirements

Only the DBA can estimate the operating system, disk, and memory requirements for a new project. The DBA is also responsible for coming up with growth estimates for the databases he or she is managing and the consequent increase in resource requirements. Although some of the decisions regarding physical equipment, such as the number of CPUs per machine and the type of UNIX server, may be made independently by system administrators and managers, the DBA can help during the process by providing good estimates of the database requirements.

In addition to estimating initial requirements, the DBA is responsible for planning for future growth and potential changes in the applications. This is known as *capacity planning*, and the DBA's estimates will be the basis for funding requests by department managers.

Developing Backup and Recovery Strategies

This is arguably the most important part of a DBA's job. The DBA needs to back up databases on a regular basis in order for those databases to survive a disaster, and the DBA is expected to test and implement a sound backup strategy. Further, the DBA is in charge of periodic recovery testing to ensure that the backup strategy will actually work.

Adequate backups can prevent the catastrophic loss of an organization's vital business data. The Oracle DBA needs to come up with a proper backup strategy and test the backups for corruption. The DBA also needs to have recovery plans in place, and the best way to do this is to simulate several types of data loss. Proper testing of backup and recovery plans is a sorely neglected topic in many companies, in spite of its critical importance for the company.

Loss of business data could not only lead to immediate monetary damage in the form of lost profits, but also cost customer goodwill in the long run. Unplanned database downtime due to a myriad of reasons reflects poorly on the firm's technical prowess and the competency of the management. A good example of this is the repeated stoppage of the successful online auction firm eBay during 1998 and 1999, which lost the company millions of dollars in revenue and cost them considerable embarrassment.

When disasters or technical malfunctions keep the database from functioning, the DBA can fall back on backed-up copies of the database to resume functioning at peak efficiency. The DBA is responsible for the formulation, implementation, and testing of fail-safe backup and restore policies for the organization. In fact, no other facet of the DBA's job is as critical as the successful and speedy restoration of the company's database in an emergency. I've personally seen careers made or broken based on one backup- and recovery-related emergency; an emergency can test the true mettle of an Oracle DBA like no other job requirement can.

During those times when disaster strikes, the seasoned DBA is the one who is confident that he or she has the necessary technical skills and is quite calm in his or her actions. This calmness is really the outcome of years of painstaking study and testing of the theoretical principles and the operational commands necessary to perform sensitive tasks such as the restoration and recovery of damaged databases.

Loading Data

After the DBA has created the database objects, schemas, and users, the DBA needs to load the data, usually from older legacy systems or sometimes from a data warehouse. The DBA has to choose the best method of data loading and implement it. If the data loads need to be done on a periodic basis, the DBA needs to design, test, and implement the appropriate loading programs.

Change Management

Every application needs to go through changes over time to improve features and fix known bugs in the software. There is a constant cycle of development, testing, and implementation, and the DBA plays an important role in that cycle. *Change management* is the process of proper migration of new code, and the Oracle DBA needs to understand the process that's in place in his or her organization.

The DBA's Database Design Role

Many Oracle DBAs spend at least part of their time helping design new databases. The DBA's role may include helping create entity-relationship diagrams and suggesting dependencies and candidates for primary keys. In fact, active involvement of the DBA in designing new databases will have a direct bearing on the performance of the databases down the road. It's a well-known fact that an improperly designed database thwarts all attempts to tune its performance.

Designing the Database

Although designing databases is probably not the first thing that comes to mind when you think of a DBA's responsibilities, design issues (whether initial design or design change issues) are a fundamental part of the Oracle DBA's job duties. Remember that I'm talking in pretty broad terms here—if you're hired as a DBA and you're entrusted with just backing up databases 8 hours a day (or night), you're not going to have much design work in your daily list of tasks. Administrators who are particularly skilled in the logical design of databases can be crucial members of the team that's designing and building brand-new databases. A talented DBA can keep the design team from making poor choices during the design process.

Installing and Upgrading Software

The Oracle DBA plays an important role in evaluating the features of alternative products. The DBA is the person who installs the Oracle Database Server software in most organizations. The UNIX system administrator may also handle the actual installation process. Prior to actual installation, the DBA is responsible for listing all the memory and disk requirements, so the Oracle software and databases, as well as the system itself, can perform adequately. If the DBA wants the system administrator to reconfigure the UNIX kernel so it can support the Oracle installation, the DBA is responsible for providing the necessary information. Besides installing the Oracle Database Server software, the DBA is also called upon to install any "middleware," such as the Oracle9*i* Application Server, and Oracle client software on client machines.

 TIP *Although they're optional, always set the parameters for Oracle licensing in the initialization file or the new SPFILE, both of which I discuss in detail in Chapter 4. The first licensing parameter, license_sessions_warning, will warn you about the impending license limits. The second parameter, license_max_sessions, will limit the number of concurrent sessions in accordance with your Oracle licensing. Use of the licensing parameters ensures that you're always in compliance with Oracle licensing requirements.*

Creating Databases

The DBA is responsible for the creation of databases. Initially, he or she may create a test database and later, after satisfactory testing, move the database to a production version. The DBA plans the logical design of the database structures, such as tablespaces, and implements them by creating the structures after the database is created. As the DBA has a part in the new database creation, he or she needs to work with the application team closely to come up with proper sizing estimates of the database objects, such as tables and indexes.

Creating Database Objects

An empty database doesn't do anyone a whole lot of good, so the DBA needs to create the various objects of the database, such as tables, indexes, and so on. Here, the developers and the DBA work together closely, with the developers providing the tables and indexes to be created and the DBA making sure that the objects are designed soundly. The DBA may also make suggestions and modifications to the objects to improve their performance. Through proper evaluation, the DBA can come up with alternative access methods for selecting data, which can improve performance.

 NOTE *As a DBA, you can contribute significantly to your organization by explaining all the alternatives your application team has in designing an efficient database. For example, if you explain to the application team the Oracle Partitioning option, including the various partitioning schemes and strategies, the team can make smarter choices at the design stage. You can't expect the application team to know the intricacies of many such Oracle options and features, especially in the new Oracle9i software.*

Finally, remember that the organization will look to the DBA for many aspects of information management. The DBA may be called upon to not only assist in the design of the databases, but also provide strategic guidance as to the right types of databases (OLTP, DSS, and so forth) and the appropriate architecture for implementing the organization's database-driven applications.

Different DBA Job Classifications

Given the diverse nature of business, a DBA's job description is not exactly the same in all organizations. There are several variations in the job classification and duties across organizations. Of course, the nature of the job is based to a large extent on the size of the firm. In a small firm, a single DBA might be the UNIX or NT administrator and the network administrator as well as the Oracle DBA, with all job functions rolled into one. A large company might have a dozen or more Oracle DBAs, each in charge of a certain database or a certain set of tasks (e.g., backups and so forth).

Sometimes you'll hear the terms "production DBA" and "development" (or "logical") DBA. *Production DBA* refers to database administrators in charge of production databases. Because the database is already in production (i.e., serving the business functions), such DBAs aren't required to have design or other such developmental skills. DBAs who are involved in the preproduction design and development of databases are usually called *development* or *logical* DBAs. Ideally, you should strive to acquire the relevant skill sets from both sides of the field, development as well as production, but reality demands that you usually are doing more of one thing than the other at any given time.

Individual preference, the availability of financial and technical resources, and the necessary skill sets determine whether a DBA is doing production or development work. In general, because large establishments usually have a number of DBAs, they can afford to assign specialized tasks to their personnel. If you work for a small organization, chances are you'll be doing a little bit of everything. A DBA who comes up from the developer ranks or who's happiest coding is usually more likely to be a development or logical DBA. This same person also may not really want to carry a pager day and night and be woken up in the dead of night to perform a database recovery.

On the other hand, a person who likes to do production work and work with business analysts to understand their needs is less likely to enjoy programming in SQL or in any other language.

Although all of the above is true, both development and production DBAs are well advised to cross-train and learn more aspects of the "other" side of Oracle database administration. Too often, people who characterize themselves as production DBAs do not do much more beyond performing backups and restores and implementing the physical layout of databases. Similarly, development DBAs, due to their preference for the programming and design aspects of the job, may not be fully cognizant of the operational aspects of database management, such as storage and memory requirements.

Types of Databases

In many organizations, as a DBA you can face on a daily basis the possibility of working with different types of databases and, as a result, different types of data and management requirements. You may find yourself working on simple SQL queries with users and simultaneously wrestling with decision-support systems for management. Databases perform a variety of functions, but you can group all of those functions into two broad categories: online transaction processing (OLTP) and decision support system (DSS) (which is sometimes also called online analytical processing [OLAP]). Let's take a quick look at some of the basic classifications of Oracle databases.

Online Transaction Processing and Decision Support System Databases

The *online transaction processing* (OLTP) category of databases represents the bread and butter of most consumer- and supplier-oriented databases. This category includes order entry, billing, customer, supplier, and supply-chain databases. These databases are characterized by rapid transactions and a need to be online continuously, which today (given the use of the Internet to access such systems) means 24/7/365 availability, short maintenance intervals, and low tolerance for breakdowns in the system.

Decision support systems (DSSs) range from small databases to large data warehouses. These are typically not 24/7 operations and they can easily manage with regularly scheduled downtime and maintenance windows. The extremely large size of some of these data warehouses necessitates the use of special techniques both to load and to use the data.

There isn't a whole lot of difference between the administration of a DSS-oriented data warehouse and a transaction-oriented OLTP system from the DBA's perspective. The backup and recovery methodology is essentially the same, and database security and other related issues are also very similar. The big difference between the two types of databases occurs at the design and implementation stages. DSS systems usually involve a different optimization strategy for queries and different physical storage strategies. Oracle9*i* provides you a choice between using an OLTP database and a DSS database using the same database server software.

Performance design considerations that may work well with one type of database may be entirely inappropriate for another type of database. For example, a large number of indexes can help you query a typical data warehouse efficiently while you are getting some reports out of that database. If you have the same number of indexes on a live OLTP system with a large number of concurrent users, you may see a substantial slowing down of the database, because the many updates, inserts, and deletes on the OLTP system require more work on the part of the database. So, know what you are trying to achieve with your new system and design accordingly in terms of choosing indexes, index types, and space parameters for the various objects in your database.

Development, Test, and Production Databases

Oracle databases can generally be grouped into three categories: development, test, and production. Applications are developed, tested, and put into production. A firm usually has all three database versions in use at any given time, although for smaller companies, the test and development versions of the database may be integrated in one database.

Development databases are usually owned by the development team, which has full privileges to access and modify data and objects in those databases. The test databases are designed to simulate actual production databases and are used to test the functionality of code after it comes out of the development databases. No new code is usually implemented in the production or the "real" databases of the company unless it has been successfully tested in the test databases.

When a new application is developed, tested, and put into actual business use (production), the development and production cycle does not end. Application software is always being modified, for two reasons: to fix bugs and to improve the functionality of the application. Although most applications go through several layers of testing before they move into production, coding errors and the pressure to meet deadlines contribute to actual errors in software, which are sometimes caught later when the application is already in use. In addition, users continually request (or, more appropriately, *demand*) modifications in the software to improve the functionality of the application. Consequently, application code does not remain static; rather, developers and testers are always working on it.

Background and Training

Your strength as an Oracle DBA is directly related to the amount of effort you put into understanding the conceptual underpinnings of the Oracle9*i* database. As you're assimilating the concepts, it's vital to implement the various techniques to see if they work as advertised and if a particular backup or recovery technique, for example, is suitable for your organization.

 TIP *There's no substitute for hands-on "playing" with the database. Download the most recent Oracle9i server software, install it, buy some good Oracle DBA books, access the Oracle manuals on one of the Internet sites, and just start experimenting. Of course, you shouldn't experiment on production databases. Create your own small test databases. Destroy them, bring them back to life, but above all have fun. I had great trainers who lived and breathed databases; they made it fun to learn and always had the time to show me new techniques and correct my errors. You'll find database experts willing to share knowledge and skills freely both in the workplace and on the Internet.*

In this section I discuss the help and services that professional organizations and other resources can provide to enhance your credentials.

Background and Training for an Oracle DBA

Oracle DBAs come from a variety of backgrounds. There's no "ideal" background for a DBA, but it's highly desirable that a DBA have a real interest in the hardware side, with a decent knowledge of operating systems, UNIX and NT servers, and disk and memory issues. It also helps tremendously to have a programming or development background because you'll be working with developers frequently. The most common operating system for the Oracle database is UNIX, with the Hewlett-Packard (HP) and Sun Microsystems (Sun) versions being the ones commonly adopted. IBM supplies the AIX variant of the UNIX operating system, but it has its own proprietary database, the DB2 Universal Database.

There is no one common career path for Oracle DBAs, although most start out by taking the introductory courses offered by the Oracle Corporation in SQL and database management. Some DBAs take the entire set of courses, which includes networking, backup/recovery, and performance-tuning classes. It is somewhat rare for a person to take the complete set of Oracle courses before he or she actually begins work as a DBA. Most companies that promote from within do so by asking their new hires to work as DBAs while they are training. Usually, the new hires work alongside a senior DBA or a consultant. This turns to be an excellent arrangement, because database administration is certainly a field where you learn by doing. Concepts do not become completely clear until you actually implement them in real databases. Newly minted DBAs acquire the necessary confidence and expertise by actually working in the field while they are taking the Oracle classes.

If you're taking classes from Oracle or another provider to become a full-fledged Oracle9*i* DBA, you need to take four separate courses. If your firm uses Oracle Real Application Clusters or distributed databases, you need to take additional, specialized courses. If your firm uses the UNIX operating system and you don't have experience using it, you may be better off taking a basic class in UNIX as well. Here's a typical course list to take on the road to becoming an Oracle9*i* DBA:

- *"Introduction to Oracle9i: SQL," from Oracle Corporation:* Provides an introduction to SQL and Oracle PL/SQL programming.

- *"Oracle9i DBA Fundamentals I," from Oracle Corporation:* Covers topics such as creating databases and maintaining their various components.

- *"Oracle9i DBA Fundamentals II," from Oracle Corporation:* Covers backup and recovery of databases as well as Oracle networking and connectivity.

- *"Oracle9i Performance Tuning," from Oracle Corporation:* Focuses on tuning the performance of the database through database management techniques and proper design and coding of applications.

- *Introduction to UNIX (or Linux) course from HP, Sun, or another vendor:* You don't need to take this course for Oracle DBA certification purposes, but it sure will help you if you're new to the UNIX or Linux environment. Of course, if your databases are going to use the Windows environment, you may get away without a long and formal course in managing Windows.

Consider the preceding list a bare minimum set of courses you'll need. I've known several professionals who took the whole set of courses in quick succession but were still frustrated at their inability to master the fundamental tasks of the job. The reason for this seems to be that in order to get the most out of the classes, you should be working with the database itself in parallel. This may seem a bit strange, but believe me, it works. A lot of the techniques you learn in class seem dry and remote until you perform them at your job site and start understanding the concepts and the implications of the different choices you can make in designing and maintaining the system.

NOTE *Remember that Oracle Corporation is not the only source of Oracle classes. Although Oracle University is a large entity with fine courses, other, private vendors offer courses that are just as good or better than those Oracle University offers. As with other classes you may have taken, the quality of the teaching depends directly on the teacher's experience and communication skills. Also, remember that you really don't have to go anywhere to take a class; you can take all the courses online. In addition, you can get certified online. If you're planning to take the Oracle courses, make sure you're also working on a server with an actual database. Oracle supplies some very well-designed sample schemas that you can use to sharpen your SQL skills, whether your database is a development version on a UNIX server or a free downloaded Windows version of Oracle9i Enterprise Server on your desktop computer. You'll go further in a shorter time with this approach.*

Once you get started as an Oracle9*i* DBA, you will find that the real world of Oracle databases is much wider and a lot more complex than that shown to you in the various courses you attend. Once you get into real-world databases, each with its own unique personality, you will find that your learning has only begun. As each new facet of the database is revealed, you may find that you are digging more and more into the heart of the software, why it works, and sometimes why it doesn't work. It is here that you will learn the most about the database and the software used to manage it. If you really have read everything that Oracle and other private parties have to offer, do not worry—there are always new versions coming out, with new features and new approaches, that will practically guarantee an endless supply of interesting new information.

After the first year or two of your DBA journey, you'll know enough to competently administrate the databases and troubleshoot typical problems that occur. If you've also worked on your programming skills during this time (mainly UNIX shell scripting and PL/SQL), you should be able to write sophisticated scripts to monitor and tune your databases. At this stage, if you dig deeper, you'll find out a lot more about your database software that can enhance your knowledge and thereby your contribution to your organization.

TIP *As part of your learning efforts, you can take advantage of the many Oracle Corporation online study programs and online seminars. You can access the Oracle9i Database Daily Features site at* http://otn.oracle.com/products/oracle9i/daily/content.html *for an explanation of the new features you can implement in your databases.*

Oracle is constantly coming up with new features that you can adopt to improve the performance of your production databases. Although the developers, testers, and administrators are also striving mightily in the organization's cause, it is you, the Oracle DBA, who will ultimately lead the way to new and efficient ways of using the new features of the database.

Certification

In many IT fields, certification by approved authorities is a required credential for advancement and, sometimes, even for initial hiring. Oracle has had the Oracle Certification Program (OCP) in effect for a number of years now. The OCP is divided into three levels: Associate, Professional, and Master. The brand-new Master-level certification, the highest certification level issued by Oracle, involves a lab test besides other requirements (at the time of this writing, all the details are not yet out for the Master-level certification). Traditionally, certification has never been a big issue with most organizations, especially in the face of the severe shortages in the field for many years. There is no question, though, that certification will help tremendously in underlining your qualifications for the job in today's more balanced job market.

My views on certification are really more practical: Preparing for certification will force you to learn all the little details that you've been ignoring for some reason or another, and it will clarify your thinking regarding many concepts. Also, the need to certify will compel you to learn some aspects of database administration that you either don't like for some reason or currently don't use in your organization. So, if you're not already certified, by all means start on that path. You can get all the information you need by going to Oracle's certification Web site at `http://www.oracle.com/education/certification`. Believe me, that certificate does look nice hanging in your cubicle, and it's a symbol of the vast amount of knowledge you've acquired in the field over time. You can rightfully take pride in obtaining OCP-certified DBA status!

···

System Administration and the Oracle DBA

There's a clear and vital connection between the Oracle DBA's functions and those of the UNIX (or Windows) administrator in your organization. Your database and the database software will be running on a physical UNIX (or Windows/Linux) server and will be run on a UNIX (or Windows/Linux) operating system. Depending on the size of your organization and your role within it, you may need anywhere from a basic to a thorough understanding of UNIX system administration. In small firms where there's no separate UNIX system administrator position, you may need to know how to configure the UNIX server itself before you actually install and manage an Oracle server and the data on it. Fortunately, this situation is very rare, and most organizations have one or more UNIX administrators in charge of managing the UNIX servers and the data storage systems. Smaller entities usually adopt Windows as an operating system, as it isn't quite as complex to manage as the UNIX operating system.

Although the system administrators usually are very helpful to you, it's in your best interest to acquire as much skill in this field as you can. This will help you in more ways than you can imagine. It will help you in working effectively with the UNIX administrator because you can both speak the same language when it comes to fancy topics such as the logical volume manager and subnet masks. More important, a good understanding of the UNIX disk structure will help you make the proper choice of disks when you do the physical layout of your database. By understanding concepts such as UNIX disk volumes and the usage of system memory, you can improve the performance of your databases and avoid bottlenecks that slow down databases. You can also write excellent monitoring scripts by being well steeped in the UNIX shell scripting and the related awk and sed programming languages.

You'll find that UNIX is a fun operating system, with interesting commands and scripting languages that can contribute to your being a highly effective Oracle DBA. One of the marks of an accomplished Oracle DBA is his or her expertise in the way the operating system works. By acquiring system administration skills, you'll become a well-rounded professional who can contribute significantly to your organization's IT needs. Many excellent books are available on UNIX system administration for beginning- and intermediate-level candidates, and I highly recommend the following two books:

- *Essential System Administration*, by Æleen Frisch (O'Reilly & Associates, Inc., 2002), is a wonderful introduction to administering all flavors of UNIX.

- *Inside UNIX*, by Chris Hare, Emmett Dulaney, and George Eckel (New Riders, 1996), not only covers system administration in detail, but it's also is an excellent introduction to the entire UNIX operating system, including the vi text editor and the use of important commands. In addition, this book provides a good introduction to the awk and sed programming languages.

Resources and Organizations for Oracle DBAs

As you progress in your career as an Oracle DBA, you'll need to refer to various sources for troubleshooting information and general knowledge enhancement. I have a couple of recommendations of organizations you may want to make a part of your professional DBA practice. The first organization is very useful and, even better, it's totally free! In fact, it's so important that I'll highlight it in the following Note.

NOTE *The Oracle Technology Network (OTN) at* http://otn.oracle.com *and* http://technet.oracle.com *is highly useful for DBAs and Oracle developers. You'll find everything from online documentation to copies of all Oracle software available freely for download on the OTN. The site offers a complete set of Oracle documentation.*

The other organization I'd like to recommend is the International Oracle Users Group (IOUG), which you can find on the Web at http://www.ioug.org/. Membership to this organization will set you back $80 or so currently, an expenditure that most organizations will reimburse their DBAs for. The IOUG holds annual conventions where practitioners in the field present literally hundreds of extremely useful papers. IOUG makes these articles available to its members, and the organization also publishes a monthly magazine. In addition to the international group, there are several regional Oracle user groups, where users meet in their hometowns and discuss relevant DBA topics. For example, the group located in Dallas, Texas, is known as the Dallas Oracle Users Group (http://www.doug.org/).

There are dozens of sites on the Web today where you can find all kinds of useful information and scripts for managing your databases, as well as help in certifying yourself as an OCP DBA. Just go to your favorite search engine, type in the relevant keywords, and you'll be amazed at the amount of help you can get online in seconds. Before the proliferation of DBA-related Web sites, DBAs had to rely on printed materials or telephone conversations with experts for resolving several day-to-day issues, but that's not the case anymore.

Although the Web is a great source of material for troubleshooting and learning about concepts you didn't know about, there's still no substitute for a good reading of the Oracle manuals if you want to become a top-notch Oracle DBA. The manuals are well written and provide the relevant background and in-depth treatment that you need to really master the many complex areas of Oracle database management.

A great way to enhance your knowledge is to maintain a network of other practicing Oracle DBAs. It's amazing how useful these contacts can be in the long run, as they provide a good way to compare notes on new releases and difficult troubleshooting issues that crop up from time to time. There's really no need to reinvent the wheel every time you encounter a problem, and chances are that most of the problems you face have already been fixed by someone else. Especially when you're starting out, during many a dark night, your friendly Oracle DBA contacts will help you avoid disasters and get you (and your databases) out of harm's way.

When it comes to the tools you use to perform your daily tasks, you'll find that you have plenty of choices. The set of tools you select for your administration depends on your organization's financial resources, your training, and your personal preferences. You can achieve a high level of performance by using the standard set of utilities that come bundled with Oracle, including the basic database management software called Oracle Enterprise Manager. You can also use UNIX and SQL scripts to automate standard tasks, as well as to send you alerts and prepare performance reports. If you aren't keen on writing and maintaining scripts, you can use the GUI tools such as Enterprise Manager. If your firm is willing to spend extra money, a number of fine third-party products are available that will help you perform your job efficiently. In addition, excellent third-party GUI tools from companies such as Quest Software (http://www.quest.com/) can provide you with "lights off" database management capabilities and sophisticated tools that aid database performance tuning.

You can find many excellent resources on the Internet to help you when you're stuck or when you need to learn about new features and new concepts. The Oracle DBA community has always been a very helpful and cooperative group, and you'll probably learn over time that you can resolve many troublesome issues by getting on the Internet and visiting DBA-related sites. You can write a script to perform a backup by yourself, but why reinvent the wheel? You can find hundreds of useful scripts on the Internet, and you're invited to partake in them. The following is a brief list of excellent sites for Oracle DBAs. Of course, any omissions from this list are purely unintentional. My sincere apologies to any other great sites that I either don't know about yet or have just plain forgotten momentarily. These sites just happen to be some of the ones that I visit often.

Hotsos (http://www.hotsos.com/): The redoubtable Carey Milsap, well-known creator of the Optimal Flexible Architecture (OFA) guidelines, is the person behind the Hotsos site. Visit this site for sophisticated, cutting-edge discussions of performance tuning and other issues.

Ixora (http://www.ixora.com.au): The great Oracle internals expert Steve Adams is the main force behind this site. Ixora offers first-rate discussion of many Oracle and UNIX performance issues.

OraPub (http://www.orapub.com/): This is another top-notch site led by an ex-Oracle employee. It provides consistently high-grade white papers on key database administration topics.

DBAsupport.com (http://www.dbasupport.com/): Another useful site that offers many scripts and a "how-to" series of articles on a variety of topics.

Burleson Oracle Consulting (http://www.dba-oracle.com/): Popular Oracle writer and editor Don Burleson runs this Web site. This site is packed with terrific articles covering a broad range of DBA topics, and Burleson's style makes the papers fun to read. Don't miss this site.

The Pipelines (http://www.quest-pipelines.com/): Quest Software maintains this highly useful site aimed not only at Oracle databases, but also at the DB2 and SQL Server databases. The Pipelines has excellent white papers, scripts, and other goodies. Well-known authors, including the prolific writer and Oracle PL/SQL expert Steven Feuerstein, contribute great papers on this site.

Oracle FAQ (http://www.orafaq.com/): This site provides a lot of question-and-answer–type discussions of relevant topics.

DBACLICK.com (http://www.dbaclick.com/): This site has plenty of good DBA scripts for all your needs, as well as DBA forums for questions and answers.

Managing High-Performance Databases

The DBA's chief preoccupation, once a database is put into production, is how well the database is performing. Is the database running fast enough? Are batch jobs, usually run in off-hours, finishing successfully and on time? Are customers complaining that they are having problems connecting to or maintaining their connections with the database?

If performance parameters are explicitly laid down (for example, so many transactions within a set period of time), the DBA should strive to meet those performance guidelines. If the database seems to be running slowly, the DBA needs to come up with the correct explanation of the problem and propose remedies for it. Does the solution require a minor adjustment in the memory allocated to the database, or does it need massive changes in the hardware itself based on the new requirements of the organization? Does the Oracle software need to be upgraded to a more recent release to fix the problem?

To ensure proper performance, it's vital to follow a systematic (rather than a shotgun) approach. When you're beset by a performance problem on your production machine, sometimes it's very hard to see where the problem might be occurring. Following a planned course of action is usually better in the end. The following database performance best practices checklist can help you ensure your database is running optimally. In later chapters on performance tuning, you'll learn in great detail how to actually perform these tasks.

- Always maintain historical data to enable you to compare performance as a benchmark.

- Track the time taken to perform standard batch jobs over time.

- Use the Oracle-provided utility Statspack to create and store data pertaining to performance.

- Test code not only for syntax and privileges, but also for performance implications.

- Use tools such as Oracle's explain plan and the trace facility to track execution plans of queries and resource usage.

- Don't rely on the traditional measures of performance such as examining hit ratios. Adopt new measures of performance, such as analyzing the wait ratios in the database.

- Always explore the potential and the implications of using new Oracle techniques by constantly testing new features. You may enhance performance tremendously by adopting the latest Oracle9*i* database administration features as well as new SQL and PL/SQL features.

Improving Your Troubleshooting Skills

Troubleshooting is the area that really sets newcomers apart from accomplished Oracle DBAs. When a database crashes and your phone starts ringing, the last thing you want to do is panic. Inexperienced DBAs tend to panic initially because they may not have sufficient confidence in their abilities and knowledge to get the database up and running again in time. Along with experience comes self-assurance because you have truly learned your craft. There are two aspects to troubleshooting: the subjective issue of your mental attitude and your mastery of the concepts and commands necessary to perform various tasks. As a rule, the first aspect is directly dependent on the second. That is, the more well versed you become in the conceptual underpinnings of how your database system works, the more confidence you will have when a disaster occurs and you are called upon to rescue all or part of a database.

In my view, if you adhere to a few basic principles, you'll avoid many embarrassing moments or even a total disaster. First, always be aware of the complete consequences of any step you might take and any command you may issue. In other words, don't actually issue a command to the database unless you know without any doubt what that command will do to the database. If I'm not completely certain of the possible effects of any command on a production database, I do one of two things: I refer to an authoritative manual or I consult with an expert who may be sitting in the next cubicle, 2,000 miles away in New York, or at Oracle Worldwide Support. In any case, you should refrain from giving directives to the database that may cause unintended or unknown results and further complicate the situation.

Second, understand that there are some steps you may take during troubleshooting that, although technically correct, can't be undone. These steps are what I call "one-way commands" and ideally, you should use them only after considerable deliberation and consultation. "Measure twice, cut once" should be your motto for such operations on a production database.

Third and most important, help yourself by not waiting until disaster strikes to learn how to use a new feature or a new command. You're likely to make mistakes because you've never used this feature before, or the feature may simply not work as intended due to a software bug. In either case, you'll be wise to test the feature and learn how to use it well before a disastrous event occurs in real life. Although it's completely normal to consult your manuals during a troubleshooting session, it may not be the ideal setting for actually learning about a feature or a set of commands. I strongly recommend that you set up the Oracle server on your own PC or a small workstation that can serve as your lab for learning and testing purposes. You'll be amazed at the improvement in your troubleshooting skills as well as your confidence when you do this.

When you buy the Oracle server software and licenses from Oracle, you can choose among various levels of service support. Support that requires a quick response and round-the-clock attention costs more. Years ago, the only way to get Oracle Worldwide Support to help you was by calling them and talking to an analyst by phone. Once an analyst was assigned to your technical assistance request (TAR), you and the analyst would try to resolve the issue over the phone. If the analyst couldn't fix the problem right away, there would be a delay until the analyst found a solution to the problem.

For the last several years, Oracle has promoted the use of a Web-based service called MetaLink to help resolve TARs from customers. The MetaLink service is of enormous importance to the working DBA, as it not only facilitates the exchange of important files and other troubleshooting information through the File Transfer Protocol (FTP), but it also provides access to the actual database of previous customer issues and the solutions provided by Oracle for similar problems. Thus, in many cases where you are dealing with problems of a small to medium degree of complexity, you can just log onto the MetaLink Web site (http://metalink.oracle.com/) and completely resolve your problem in minutes by looking up information based on keywords or the Oracle error number. All this, of course, saves a bundle of money for Oracle, but more important, from the DBA's point of view, it saves a tremendous amount of time the DBA would otherwise have to spend resolving garden-variety troubleshooting issues.

The Daily Routine of a Typical Oracle DBA

Many of the daily tasks DBAs perform on a database involve monitoring for problems. This can mean running monitoring scripts or using the Oracle built-in tools such as Enterprise Manager to keep track of what's actually happening with the database.

A good example of something you'll want to monitor closely is space in the database. If you run out of space on a disk where a database table resides, you can't insert any more new data into the table, and the transactions will fail. Of course, you can fix the problem by adding the requisite amount of space and rerunning the transaction. But if you were properly monitoring the database, you would have been alerted through a page and/or an e-mail that the particular table was in danger of running out of space, and you could have easily avoided the subsequent Oracle errors.

You'll normally check the reports generated by your monitoring scripts on a daily basis to make sure no problems are developing with regard to disk space, memory allocation, or input/output from the disks. Enterprise Manager is a handy tool for getting a quick, visual idea about various issues such as memory allocation and other resource usage. The monitoring scripts, on the other hand, can provide summarized information over a lengthy period of time; for example, they can provide interval-based information for an entire night.

It's also worthwhile to study the *alert log* (the log that Oracle databases maintain to capture significant information about database activity) on a regular basis to see if it's trapping any errors reported by Oracle. You may do this alert log monitoring directly by perusing the log itself, or you could put in place a script that monitors and reports any errors soon after they appear in the alert log. You need to take some action to fix the reported Oracle errors. Based on the nature of the error, you may change some parameters, add some space, or perform an administrative task to fix the problem. If the problem has no fix that you are aware of, you may search the MetaLink database and then open a new TAR with Oracle Worldwide Support to get help as soon as you can.

Oracle, like every other software company, is constantly improving its software by releasing upgraded versions, which usually have newer and more sophisticated features. It's your responsibility as a DBA to be on top of these changes and plan the appropriate time for switching over to new versions. Some of these switches might be to completely upgraded versions of software and may require changes in both the applications and the DBA's configuration parameters. Again, the right approach would be to allow plenty of time for testing the new software to avoid major interruptions in serving your customers following the switch over to a major new release.

Some General Advice

As you progress in your journey as an Oracle DBA, you'll have many satisfying experiences as well as some very frustrating and nerve-racking moments. I want to make some suggestions that will help you when you are going through the latter. In the following sections, I briefly discuss three important suggestions that will serve you well in the long run.

Know When You Need Help

Although it's always nice to figure out how to improve performance or recover an almost lost production database on your own, always know when to call for help. It doesn't matter how much experience you gain, there will always be times when you're better off seeking advice and help from someone else. I've seen people lose data as well as prolong their service disruption when they didn't know what they didn't know. It's easy, and it could happen to anyone. You can't manage production databases with your decisions based on incomplete knowledge or insufficient information.

Remember You Are Not Alone

I don't mean this in any philosophical way—I just want to remind you that as an Oracle DBA, you're but one of the people who have the responsibility for supporting the applications that run on your databases. You usually work within a group that may consist of UNIX and Windows administrators, network administrators, storage experts, and application developers. Sometimes, the solution to a problem may lie in your domain, and at other times, it may not. You can't take all the credit for your application running well, just as you don't deserve all the blame every time database performance tanks. Today's enterprises use very sophisticated servers, storage systems, and networks. You need the help of experts in all these areas to make your database deliver the goods. Oracle isn't always the answer for your problems—sometimes the system administrator or the network expert can fix your problems in a hurry for you.

Think Outside the Box

Good DBAs constantly seek to find ways to improve performance, especially when users perceive that the database response may be slow. Sometimes, all the tinkering in the world with your initialization parameters won't help you. You have to step back at times like this and ask yourself the following question: Am I trying to fix today's problems with yesterday's solutions? There's no guarantee that things that worked well for you once upon a time will serve you equally well now. Databases aren't static—data changes over time, users' expectations change, load factors increase with time, and so on. As a DBA, it pays for you not to sit on your laurels when things are going fine; rather, you should always be looking at new database features that you can take advantage of. You can't constantly increase memory or CPU in order to fix a performance problem. For example, you may have a situation where memory usage is very high, response times are slow, and the user count is going up steadily. Maybe you should rethink your architectural strategies at times like this—how about replacing the dedicated server approach with the Oracle Multithreaded Server? It's a big switch in terms of the way clients connect to your database, but if the new strategy has great potential, the effort will pay off big.

The new Oracle9*i* database has loads of features that could improve database performance in many different ways. Keep up with the advances—it's a terrible waste not to use as many of the features as possible instead of sticking to old ways, comfortable as they are.

Summary

This chapter provided a quick review of the typical set of tasks you can expect to perform as an Oracle database administrator (DBA). You got a good sense of the DBA's job requirements from the discussion, irrespective of the specific needs of an organization. In this chapter, I discussed what I consider to be the fundamental tasks of the DBA: ensuring frequent database backups are made, securing the database from unauthorized use, and minimizing downtime. Do understand that your job as a DBA only starts with satisfying the minimum criteria for success. To be an effective DBA, you should eventually be fully proficient in the entire range of tasks that you may be called upon to perform at some time or other during your career (usually sooner than you might think!).

In this chapter, I also discussed the Oracle Certification Program (OCP). I strongly urge all Oracle DBAs to invest the additional resources necessary to get certified as an OCP DBA. This will show your commitment to the profession, and it will reward you immensely in terms of the additional knowledge you'll gain in the certification process. The database performance best practices checklist at the end of the chapter provided an outline for the detailed discussion to come in the following chapters.

Relational Database Modeling and Database Design

A GOOD DATABASE is the bedrock on which you can create a good application. To create a sound database, you need to learn conceptual modeling skills. Database modeling and design are areas in which not all database administrators (DBAs) are uniformly proficient. Other than dealing with tables and the queries that are based on them, many DBAs don't have a detailed understanding of areas such as normalization, functional dependency, and entity-relationship modeling.

The ability to design a database is particularly useful to DBAs working in smaller organizations where they'll need to know how to do everything from work with the UNIX file system to resolve networking issues. Even if designing databases isn't a part of your job description, understanding database design will help you when performance tuning the database.

Because the needs of organizations differ, you can't take a "one size fits all" approach. This makes database design one of the most interesting and challenging areas available to you when working with databases, particularly large corporate systems. Someone in the organization needs to first model the needs of the organization on a conceptual level and then use this conceptual design to physically design and build the database. Even though it's not absolutely necessary that you, as a DBA, be an expert in database design, your knowledge as a competent Oracle DBA isn't complete until you learn at least the rudiments of database modeling and design.

In this chapter, you'll first learn the conceptual basis of a relational database, which is what an Oracle9*i* database is. Oracle Corporation refers to its databases as "object-relational," and you'll look at this nomenclature issue in more detail toward the end of this chapter. After you explore the basic elements of the relational database life cycle, you'll learn how to perform conceptual or logical data modeling. The topic of data normalization is very important when dealing with relational databases, and this chapter discusses normalization in detail. Finally, you'll learn how to translate the logical data model into a design you can physically implement. The chapter concludes with a brief discussion of object-relational databases.

Relational Databases: A Brief Introduction

Oracle9*i* is a leading example of a relational database management system (RDBMS), although Oracle prefers to call its database an object-relational database management system (ORDBMS). As you'll see toward the end of this chapter, you derive the object-relational model by combining object-oriented design with the traditional relational model. Relational databases have become the pervasive model of organizing data in the last three decades, and they have revolutionized the management of data by companies. The powerful and easy-to-understand relational databases are indeed the mainstay of a vast majority of organizations in today's world economy.

> **NOTE** *The very ease with which you can create a database sometimes contributes to poorly designed databases. Thanks to the many RDBMS wizards that walk users step by step through the database creation process, even novices can set up a database. My own general rule of thumb is that if database design isn't your forte, find a person who is good at database design to help you. Good design up front will pay rich dividends later on.*

The relational model's domination of the database market is expected to continue into the foreseeable future given the massive investment many large organizations have made in both the databases themselves and the staff required to manage them.

Relational databases are based on the precepts laid down by E. F. Codd in the 1970s, when he was working for IBM Corporation. D. L. Childs presented a similar set-oriented relational model in 1968, but it is Codd's exposition that made relational databases popular. There have been (and there still are) database models that preceded the relational model that are nonrelational in nature—specifically, the hierarchical and the network models. Typically, both the network model and the hierarchical model use actual data links called *pointers* to process queries issued by users. Both of these models, although powerful as far as performance goes, lead to a very complex database, which has prevented their adoption by most organizations. You can call relational databases second-generation database management systems, with the traditional network and hierarchical flat-file databases being the first-generation database management systems.

The Relational Database Model

A basic feature of relational databases is that all the data is stored in the form of two-dimensional tables. Tables store the data and the *metadata* (the data about the data). Furthermore, the data has interrelationships among its many components.

> **NOTE** *The capability of a relational database to describe itself, through the use of metadata, is one of its most interesting features. Even desktop databases such as Microsoft Access maintain system tables that describe the data and the relationships among the data.*

Three key terms are used extensively in relational database models: relations, attributes, and domains. A *relation* is a table with columns and rows. The named columns of the relation are called the *attributes*, and the *domain* is the set of values the attributes are allowed to take. The basic data structure of the relational model is the table, where information about the particular entity (say, an employee) is depicted in the form of columns and rows (also called *tuples*). Thus, the "relation" in "relational database" refers to the various tables in the database. The columns enumerate the various attributes of the entity, and the rows are actual instances of the entity (employee) that is represented by the relation. As a result, each tuple of the employee table represents various attributes of a single employee.

All relations (tables) in a relational database have to adhere to some basic rules to qualify as such. Let's review the important requirements for a relational model. First, the ordering of the columns is immaterial in a table. Second, there can't be identical tuples or rows in the table. Each tuple will contain a single value for each of its attributes. (Remember that you can order the tuples and columns in any way you wish.)

Tables can have a single attribute or a set of attributes that can act as a "key." You can then use the key to uniquely identify each tuple in the table. Keys serve many important functions. They are commonly used to join or combine data from two or more tables. Keys are also critical in the creation of indexes, which facilitate fast retrieval of data from large tables. Although you can use as many columns as you wish as part of the key, it is easier to handle small keys that are (ideally) based on just one or two attributes.

Oracle databases (and many other relational databases) use *schemas*, which generally consist of a set of related tables and other database objects. I discuss database schemas in detail in the next section.

Database Schemas

The database schema is a fundamental concept in relational databases, and it is part of the logical database structure of an Oracle database. A schema is always associated with a user, and it can be defined as a named collection of objects owned by a user. That is why the terms "user" and "schema" are used almost synonymously in Oracle databases. A relational database schema consists of the definition of all relations with their specific attribute names as well as a primary key. The schema further includes the definition of all the domains, which are the ranges of values the attributes can take.

Data Definition and Data Manipulation Languages

All work on a relational database is essentially performed through the use of a database language called *Structured Query Language* (SQL). SQL is an English-like language that enables you to manipulate data in a database. SQL statements can be divided into two major categories: data definition language (DDL) and data manipulation language (DML). DDL statements are used to build and alter database structures such as tables. Database schemas are defined and constructed using DDL statements. DML statements are used to manipulate data in the database tables. With DML statements, you can delete, update, and insert tuples that are part of a relation. Appendix A provides a quick introduction to the Oracle9*i* SQL language.

Relational Algebra

Relational databases are founded on basic mathematical principles (set theory). The very first line of E. F. Codd's seminal paper that laid out the outlines of the relational database model makes this clear:

> *"This paper is concerned with the application of elementary relation theory to systems which provide shared access to large banks of formatted data."*[1]

Relational algebra consists of a set of operations to manipulate relations. The operations work on one or more relations without changing the original relation. You can perform a set of operations on a relational database using relational algebra. The following are the basic operations that you can perform on a relation. These are also called *unary* operations, because they involve the manipulation of tuples in one relation.

- *Selection:* Selection involves the extraction of a set of tuples from a relation based on the values of the attributes of the relation.
- *Projection:* A projection operation extracts a specified set of columns of a relation.

Besides these basic operations, relational algebra supports other operations called *binary* or *set* operations to manipulate the relations themselves. (Remember, relations are akin to sets.) The set operations are as follows:

- *Union* combines two relations to produce a new, larger relation.
- *Intersection* creates a new relation that has only the common tuples in two relations.
- *Difference* creates a new relation that has only the noncommon tuples in two relations.
- *Cartesian product* creates a new relation that concatenates every tuple in relation A with every tuple in relation B. The Cartesian product is just one example of a join operation. *Join operations* combine two or more relations to derive a new relation based on certain conditions. A join involves combining tuples from one or more relations. The resulting relation of course would be a Cartesian product, *if you include all the tuples in both the relations*. However, in reality, you usually need only a part of this Cartesian product. This subset is based on all tuples in both tuples that share a common value for the identical join column, which has the same value in both the tuples.

---

1. E. F. Codd, "A Relational Model of Data for Large Shared Data Banks," *Communications of the ACM, Vol. 13, No. 6,* (1970): 377–387.

NOTE *When you join two relations, the term "create" doesn't really refer to the actual creation of a new relation. It only refers to the result set derived by the concerned operation. For example, in an order-processing relation (table), a result set would be all customers and the orders placed by them within a specific timeframe.*

Well, it looks like relational algebra, which is based on set theory principles, should be sufficient to retrieve information from relational databases, which are also based on set theory. Why don't you use relational algebra to do all your database querying? The problem with relational algebra is that though it's based on correct mathematical principles, it relies on a mathematical procedural language. So, if you want to use it for anything but the simplest database queries, you're apt to run into quite complex, messy mathematical operations. Only highly skilled professional programmers can use such a database.

To avoid the complexity of relational algebra and to focus on the queries without worrying about the procedural techniques, you need to use relational calculus. In the following sections, I explain how relational calculus helps simplify database queries.

Relational Calculus

Relational calculus does not involve the mathematical complexity of relational algebra, because it focuses only on what the database is being queried for, rather than how to conduct the query. In other words, it is a declarative language. You focus on the results you expect and the conditions to be satisfied in the process and ignore the sequencing of the relational algebra concepts. Relational calculus is based on a part of mathematical logic called *propositional calculus* or, more precisely, *first-order predicate calculus*. Relational calculus involves the use of quantifies such as AND and OR to manipulate relations in logical expressions.

SQL and Relational Theory

Relational calculus is far easier to use than relational algebra, but it still is based on the principles of logic and it is not easy for most people to use. You thus need an easy-to-use implementation of relational calculus. Structured Query Language (SQL) is one such implementation, and it has become hugely popular as the predominant and almost official language for the relational database model. SQL is considered a "relationally complete" language, in the sense that it can express any query that is supported by relational calculus.

Using SQL, you can derive any relation that can be derived using relational calculus. You can formulate queries in easy-to-format structures, which are then processed by sophisticated database servers into complex forms to get the queried data. Its intuitive appeal, ease of use, and tremendous power and sophistication has made SQL the language of choice when working with any relational database.

Another thing that has made SQL so popular—particularly with end users — is the explosion of high-end graphical tools such as Oracle Discoverer (you can download it from http://www.oracle.com/) and other excellent third-party developer tools, such as the free TOAD software and other sophisticated development and diagnostic software available from Quest Software (http://www.quest.com/), which make the creation of complex statements fairly simple.

SQL has become the standard language for RDBMSs, although not all implementations adhere completely to the official standards. SQL is also termed a *transform-oriented language* because it transforms inputs in the form of relations into outputs. Oracle has its own implementation of SQL, which is very close to the American National Standards Institute (ANSI) standard (visit http://www.ansi.org/ for more information). You can use SQL as both a DDL and a DML. That is, not only can you select and modify data from tables in the database, but you can also create tables and other objects using SQL. Appendix A provides an overview of SQL and PL/SQL as used with Oracle. PL/SQL is Oracle's procedural extension to standard SQL, and provides you with the power of traditional programming languages, along with SQL's ease of use.

Relational Database Life Cycle

You can follow a number of methodologies to construct a relational database. In essence, all of them involve similar core steps, with some variations. The essential steps involved in a typical relational database life cycle are as follows:

1. Requirements gathering and analysis

2. Logical database design

3. Physical database design

4. Production implementation

You will examine each of these stages in detail in the rest of this chapter. Keep in mind that several different methodologies are in use. You could, of course, forget about using any methodology and design your database any way you want, create the structures, load the data, and be in business. However, improper database design has serious long-term performance implications, and you risk your database proving inadequate or simply wrong for your company's information and analysis needs.

One thing to bear in mind is to always try and factor in some future proofing for the database. Databases tend to grow, and the better the database, the bigger it tends to get as more and more users rely on it. In addition, it won't take long for your application developers to begin to expand upon the core data, especially with today's requirements to put as much data as possible on the Web.

Requirements Gathering and Analysis

The requirements gathering stage is the first step in designing a new database. You first find out, through an iterative process, the requirements of the organization vis-à-vis the database. The preliminary stage of the database life cycle addresses questions of this nature:

- Why is this new database necessary?

- What objective is this database going to help achieve?

- What current systems is the database going to replace?

- What systems (if any) will the database have to interact with?

- Who are the target users of the database?

The design team should evaluate the data that will go into the database and the expected output of the database at this stage. Requirements analysis for the firm involves extensive interviewing of users and management. This stage should yield a clear idea of the expectations of all the concerned parties regarding the new system to be supported by the yet-to-be-created database.

It's common practice to use graphical representations of the application systems to better understand the flow of data through the system. Data flow diagrams (DFDs) or process models are commonly used at this stage to capture the data processes within and outside the application.

So how do you capture the processes of a system? Let's use an educational institution as an example to demonstrate the identification of the processes. Say that a college has four processes: Manage Student Records, Manage Course Information, Manage Enrollment, and Manage Class Schedules. The Manage Student Records process maintains all student records and updates that information as necessary. The Manage Course Information process takes care of collecting all future course information from the various departments of the college. It is also responsible for making changes in the course list when departments add or drop courses for any reason.

The Manage Enrollment process is more complex than others, of course, because it receives inputs from several processes. For example, when a student requests enrollment in a new course, the Manage Enrollment process needs to first verify from the Manage Student Records process whether the student is in good status. Next, it has to find out from the Manage Course Information process if the course is indeed being offered. In the next step, the Manage Enrollment process will enter this new student/course information in its part of the data flow. Only after all the successful completion of all these processes can the Manage Class Schedules process send the new schedule out to the student.

As complex as the brief description of data flows and business processes sounds, the use of sophisticated tools such as Oracle Designer makes it easy to come up with fancy DFDs and process models with a minimum of frustration.

Logical Database Design

Database design is both an art and a science. The science part comes in the form of adherence to certain rules and conditions such as normalization (more about this later). Database design is also an art, because you need to model relationships using your understanding of the real-world functioning of the entity. You can formally define *logical database design* as the process of creating a model of the real world for the database, independent of an actual database system or other physical considerations. Accuracy and completeness are the keys with this activity.

One of the best things about design is that it's easy to take the design, roll it up, and toss it away and start again or simply amend it. It's a whole lot easier to tinker in this way at the design stage than to deal with the production headaches of an already implemented database that isn't designed well.

The logical design stage is sometimes broken up into a conceptual part and a logical part, but that's merely a distinction based on nomenclature. Logical design involves conceptually modeling the database and ensuring that data in the tables passes integrity checks and isn't redundant. To satisfy these requirements, you need to implement data normalization principles, as you'll see shortly.

Entity-relationship modeling (ERM) is a widely used methodology to logically represent and analyze the components of the business system. The entity-relationship models are easy to construct, and their graphical emphasis makes them very easy to understand. The entity-relationship model is commonly used to model the enterprise after the requirements analysis is completed. The entity-relationship model is built on the basis of the relationships among the various entities in the organization. However, you can't build a real-life RDBMS using the entity-relationship model of an enterprise. The entity-relationship model's utility lies in *designing* databases, not *implementing* databases. The reason is that the entity-relationship model can't form the basis of a high-level data manipulation language like SQL. The model that designers build using the ERM approach is translated to the relational model for implementation. By converting the abstract entity-relationship design into a *relational database schema,* the relational model helps convert the entity-relationship design into a relational DBMS.

It is also customary to use constructs called *process models* (processes are akin to individual business tasks) and data flow diagrams (DFDs) to help in analyzing the interrelationships among the various parts of the business organization. You'll study the important concept of ERM modeling in more detail in the next section.

Entity-Relationship Modeling

Before you can proceed to the actual creation of databases, you need to conceptually model the organization's information system so you can easily see the interrelationships among the various components of the system. Data models are simple representations of complex real-world data structures. The models help you depict not only the data structures, but also the relationships among the components and any constraints that exist. Conceptual modeling of the enterprise leads to clear indications regarding the tables to be built later on and the relationships that should exist between those tables. An entity-relationship model is the most commonly used conceptual model for designing databases. ERM involves the creation of valid models of the business, using standard entity-relationship diagrams (ERDs). Notice that the conceptual model is always independent of both software and hardware considerations.

You may think that the purpose of conceptual modeling is to help you build your physical database. Well, that is indeed true, but conceptual modeling serves an even larger purpose. You can use the conceptual model of your organization as a communications tool to facilitate cooperative work among your database designers, application programmers, and end users. You can resolve the differing conceptions of data among these groups by using good conceptual models. Conceptual models help define the constraints that your organization imposes on the data and clarify data processing needs, thus helping to create sound databases.

ERM was originally proposed by Peter Chen in 1976, and it is now the most widely used technique for database design. You can download Chen's original proposal document from `http://bit.csc.lsu.edu/~chen/pdf/erd.pdf`. Several design methodologies other than ERM are available for you to use. For a number of years, researchers have struggled to model the real world more realistically by using *semantic data models,* which try to go beyond the traditional ERM methodology.

NOTE *The World Wide Web Consortium (W3C) is working on a specification related to data representation on the Internet. The general idea is to try and bring some meaning to the massive amount of data and information available. Information on the Web is designed for and presented to humans. On the semantic Web, data and information will be designed so that it can be understood and manipulated by computers as well as humans. On the semantic Web, you will use software agents to go off in search of data and information on your behalf.*

An excellent article on this new and exciting approach is available at `http://www.scientificamerican.com/article.cfm?articleID=00048144-10D2-1C70-84A9809EC588EF21&catID=2.`

In practice, though, it is still the ERM methodology, in spite of its limited modeling capabilities, that is used for most database design even today. One of the great benefits to ERM is that you can explain the topic easily to a nontechnical user. You can take a diagram of the business process and walk users through it, explaining the outline and business rules to them through images. The old saying "A picture is worth a thousand words" is particularly true when it comes to modeling data in this fashion.

ERM views all objects of the business area being modeled as entities that have certain attributes. An *entity* is anything of interest to the system that exists in the business world. An entity can be real (e.g., a student) or it can be conceptual (e.g., a student enrollment). A student enrollment does not actually exist until the entity's student and course are combined when the student signs up for a particular course. Conceptual entities are generally the hardest to discover, but ERM, as you shall see, assists in their discovery.

Attributes of entities are simply some properties of the entities that are of interest to you. For example, a student entity may have attributes such as Student ID, Address, Phone Number, and so on.

ERM further describes the *relationships* among these business entities. Relationships describe how the different entities are connected (or related) to one another. For example, an employee is an entity that possesses attributes such as Name and Address, and he or she is, or may be, related to another entity in the model called Department through the fact that the employee *works* in that department. In this case, "works" is the relationship between the employee and the department.

Cardinality of a relationship shows how many instances of one entity can be related to an instance of another entity. Cardinality in ERM expresses the number of occurrences of one entity in relation to another entity. Entity relationships can be one-to-one, one-to-many, many-to-many, or some other type. The most common relationships are the following:

- *One-to-one (1:1) relationship:* For example, an employee works in only one department. A department employs one and only one employee. It is very unusual to find a true one-to-one relationship in the real world, and they are normally used to split tables for security reasons.

- *One-to-many (1:M) relationship:* For example, an entity called Customer can check out many books from a library. One and only one Customer can borrow each book. So, the entity Customer and the entity Book have a one-to-many relationship. Of course, the relationship may not exist if you have a Customer who has not yet borrowed a Book. So the relation is actually "one Customer *may* borrow none, one, or many Books."

- *Many-to-many (M:M) relationship:* As an example, let's take an entity called Movie Star and an entity called Movie. Each Movie Star can star in several Movies, and each Movie may have several Movie Stars. In real life, a many-to-many relationship is broken down usually into a simpler one-to-many relationship, which happens to be the predominant form of "cardinality" in the relationships between entities.

Candidate Keys and Unique Identifiers

Candidate keys are those attributes that can uniquely identify an instance—for example, a row in a table. Of course, any whole row itself could serve as a candidate key, because by definition a relational model can't have any duplicate tuples. The *primary key* is the candidate key that's chosen to serve as the unique identifier (UID) for that entity (or table). You should always strive to select a single-attribute-based key rather than a multiple-attribute-based key, for simplicity and efficiency purposes. Keys are vital when you come to the point of physical building of the entity models, and it's from among the attributes of the entity that you choose a primary key.

NOTE *A natural primary key is one that you can select from the data items or entity attributes, whereas a* surrogate *key is simply made up and generated by the database. Later in this chapter I provide you with some guidelines about selecting keys (primary keys in particular).*

Almost all modern relational databases, including Oracle, provide simple system numbers or sequenced numbers generated and maintained by the RDBMS as an alternative to a natural key. Such keys are often referred to as *surrogate* or *artificial* primary keys. Whatever method you choose, either a data item or a surrogate key, certain rules apply:

- The primary key value must be unique.

- The primary key can't be null (i.e., blank).

- The primary key can't be changed (i.e., it must remain stable over the life of the entity).

- The primary key must be as concise as possible.

The opposite of the primary key is the foreign key. Simply put, a *foreign key* is an attribute that relates back to the primary key in the entity at the "one" side of a one-to-many relationship. You use a foreign key to implement the relationship between entities and eventually tables. Each entity can have one or more foreign keys, depending on its relationships.

Step-by-Step: Building an Entity-Relationship Diagram

In this section, you'll build a simple entity-relationship diagram describing a university using entities called Student, Class, and Professor. You'll use a rectangle to depict an entity and a diamond shape to show relationships (per common practice), although you could use different notations.

....

The Changing Nature of Relationships

Let's assume the following relationship between two entities, Student and Class:

- A Student can enroll in one and only one Class.

- A Class has one or more Students enrolled.

What if a Student has to complete one Class before moving on to another? In other words, what if the Student can only be enrolled in a single Class at a time and must complete that Class before he or she can enroll in any other Class? Things start getting interesting at this point. That's why data modeling is so much fun. It starts out easy and then rapidly gets complex, as you begin to ask questions and discover the various rules and constraints that need to be enforced.

....

The following are the general steps to follow to create the university entity-relationship diagram:

1. Define all the entities: Student, Class, and Professor.

> **NOTE** *Entity names are usually singular nouns. Some designers get slightly confused by the use of singular nouns when they first start creating diagrams because they tend to concentrate on the big picture. At this point, just worry about one student and the relationships that the student data has with other entities in the diagram.*

2. Draw the entities using a rectangle to represent each one (the rectangles usually have rounded corners).

3. For each of the entities in turn, look at its relationship with the others. It doesn't matter which entity you begin with. For example, look at the Student and the Professor. Is there a relationship between these entities? Well, a Professor teaches a class and a student attends a class. So, at first glance, there is a relationship between these entities. But in this case, it is an indirect relationship via the Class entity.

CAUTION *It is quite common to be misled by indirect relationships such as this and build an incorrect model.*

4. Examine the Student and Class entities. Is there a relationship? Yes. A Student may attend one or more Classes. One or more Students may attend a Class. This is a many-to-many relationship. However, you need to be careful, as the business rules specific to the organization dictate the actual relationship.

5. Now look at the Class and Professor entities. The relationship between Class and Professor is straightforward. One Professor teaches a Class and each Professor can teach many Classes. However, if a Professor was absent (due to illness, for example), would you need to record the fact that a different Professor taught his or her Class on that occasion? What about if two Professors teach the same Class? Do you need to record that information? As a modeler, you need to address all questions of this nature, so your model is realistic and will serve you well.

6. Assign the following attributes to the various entities:

   Student: student_id, first_name, last_name, address, year

   Professor: staff_id, social_security_number, first_name, last_name, office_address, phone_number

   Class: class_id, classroom, textbook, credit_hours, class_fee

   Look at the textbook attribute in the Class entity. You can use this attribute to illustrate an important point. As the entity stands right now, you could record only one textbook per Class. This could be the case again depending on the business rules involved. What do you do if you want to record the fact that there are several textbooks recommended for each Class? The current model would not permit you to do this unless you stored multiple data items in a single field. To resolve this, you could add a new entity called Textbooks. This entity could then be related to the Class entity. This way, you could associate many different Textbooks with each Class.

7. The cardinality of a relationship, as you saw earlier, dictates whether a relationship is one-to-one, one-to-many, many-to-many, or something else. Define the cardinality of the system at this point. Assign the one-to-many or many-to-one cardinality indicators. Break down any many-to-many relationships to simpler relationships (e.g., two one-to-many relationships). For example:

    A Student can enroll in one or more Classes.

    Each Class can have many Students enrolled.

    This is a many-to-many relationship, which you must break down by using a link table. In this case, the link table turns out to be an entity in its own right. This new entity contains the individual enrollment record for each Class attended by a single Student.

8. Translate the relationships into an actual entity-relationship diagram by using the appropriate symbols, which depend on the notation or tools in use. For example, you can use rectangles for entities, diamonds for relationships, and ovals for the attributes of the entities.

9. Test the functionality of the entity-relationship diagram by stepping through and navigating the diagram. Your entity-relationship diagram should be able to address all the functional requirements of the database in order for it to be adopted as a valid model.

In this case study, sequence numbers are used as candidate keys for each entity. The three different relationships in this example represent only part of the story. There are other relationships available to you, but it is unlikely you will see them on a regular basis. One such relationship is the *recursive* relationship, which comes about when data within an entity has a relationship to itself. For example, in a staff table, a member of the staff may report to another member of the staff of a higher grade. If this is the case, then the table is said to have a recursive relationship with itself.

I have barely scratched the surface of ERM, which is in itself an art—one at which you will improve with practice. As with anything else, the more time you spend actually practicing data modeling, the more proficient you will get at it.

 TIP *The Internet is a great source for both simple and complex case studies you can use to try out your modeling skills. On the Web, you can find anything from simple order processing databases to fully-fledged personnel systems. One of the best resources I've found is the Web sites of major universities. Find the descriptions of computer science courses and pay special attention to the contents of database design courses, many of which have tutorials on creating entity-relationship diagrams.*

Normalization

Once you translate the logical model into tables, you are still not finished with logical modeling. You need to make sure that the tables you have mapped out are normalized. ERM will allow you to model entities and the relationships between them. *Normalization* deals with the entity attributes that are not covered using ERM.

NOTE *I would also argue that a correctly designed entity-relationship model should already be in the third normal form (3NF). (I discuss 3NF later in this chapter.) In fact, many of the high-end design tools permit you to generate the database creation scripts directly based on the entity-relationship model produced by the software.*

Normalization is the elimination procedure through which you break down and simplify the relations (tables) in a database in an appropriate way to achieve efficiency in retrieving and maintaining data. The most common reason for normalizing table data is to avoid redundancy, which reduces data storage needs and leads to more efficient queries. Another need that prompts normalization of data is the need to avoid data anomalies, which you'll learn about in detail in the section "Data Anomalies" later in this chapter.

Why Normalize?

You've probably heard discussions about normalization that range from treating it like the Holy Grail to viewing it as a feature that adversely affects performance. What is it about normalization that gets people going so? You can put all your data somewhere in a table, and as long as you can write SQL code to retrieve the necessary data and you have a good RDBMS running on a machine with plenty of fast processors, you shouldn't have a slow performing database, right? The truth is that bad design of relations and the tables in that database can have serious effects, not only on the efficacy of your database, but also on the validity of the data itself.

Let's look at an example of an ordering system in a warehouse. Imagine a simple table with each customer's information contained in a single tuple or row. Well, what if customer A has 1,000 transactions or customer B has only one or two transactions? In each case, you may not be able to cater to the customer, or if you do, you may waste a tremendous amount of space in the database. Simple queries would turn into terrible resource wasters under this design.

You can try another variation on the previous design by creating a much more compact table (in terms of the length of rows) by allowing repeatable values of the attributes. That is, for each transaction, each customer's complete information would be repeated. Well, now you have just traded one set of problems for another. With repeated groups, when you perform updates, you have to make sure to update all occurrences of the particular customer's data or you end up with an inconsistent set of data.

Data Anomalies

You can see on an intuitive level that designing without a solid design strategy based on sound mathematical principles will lead to several problems. Although it is easy to see the inefficiency involved in the consumption of storage space and longer query execution times, other, more serious problems occur with off-the-cuff design of tables in a database. These other kinds of problems are the so-called data anomaly problems. Three types of data anomalies could result from improperly designed databases:

- *The update anomaly.* In this well-known anomaly, you could fail to update all the occurrences of a certain attribute because of the repeating values problem.

- *The insertion anomaly.* In this anomaly, you are prevented from inserting certain data because you are missing other pieces of information. For example, you cannot insert a customer's data because that customer has not bought a product from your warehouse yet.

- *The deletion anomaly.* In this anomaly, you could end up losing data inadvertently because you are trying to remove some duplicate attributes from a customer's data. Let's look at an example of a data anomaly caused by non-normalized data. Table 2-1 shows the kind of data that could lead to such problems.

Table 2-1. Example of a Non-Normalized Table

CUSTOMER ID	NAME	CITY	PHONE	PRODUCT ID
212	Thomas	Manhattan	932-795-2627	236789
212	Thomas	Manhattan	932-795-2627	487218
524	Copeland	Kansas City	675-938-9256	186308

You can see that the details for the customer Thomas had to be repeated completely because he bought different products. If he buys 1,000 products over time, you end up with 1,000 rows just for one customer! You can't remove any of the multiple rows belonging to Thomas, because you'll then lose the order information. What if the Product ID is part of the primary key, which is used to uniquely identify a tuple? Well, because a primary key can't be null (absent) in a row by definition, you can't enter any new information for a new customer until that customer has actually bought a specific product. Non-normalized tables can thus lead to redundancy, inefficiency, and potential update, delete, and insertion anomalies.

NOTE *The debate between database developers and designers continues over denormalization. Many believe it's OK to break almost all design rules and denormalize for performance gains. However, others believe that this isn't correct and the act of denormalization reduces the integrity of the database by removing the controls that lie at the heart of RDBMS design. A good paper on this process is available at* http://dlib2.computer.org/conferen/hicss/0981/pdf/09813013.pdf.

The Normal Forms

Before you embark on the normalization process, it's a good idea to understand the concept of *functional dependence,* which is defined as follows:

Given a relation (table) R, a set of attributes B is functionally dependent on attribute A if at any given time each value of attribute A is associated with a given value of B.

In simple terms, functional dependency is denoted symbolically as A -> B (meaning that entity A determines the value of entity B) and it turns out to be crucial in understanding the normalization process.

Normalization is nothing more than the simplification of tables into progressively simpler forms to get rid of undesirable properties such as data anomalies and data redundancy, without sacrificing any information in the process. E. F. Codd laid out the normalization requirements succinctly by requiring the elimination of nonsimple domains and then the removal of partial and indirect dependencies. As the tables are taken through simpler *normal forms,* the preceding problems are eliminated. You can take a table through several levels of simplification. These simpler forms are called the first normal form (1NF), second normal form (2NF), third normal form (3NF), Boyce-Codd normal form (BCNF), fourth normal form (4NF), and fifth normal form (5NF). Note that each successively higher stage of the normalization process eliminates a particular type of an undesirable dependency that you saw earlier in this section. For most database needs, a simplification to the level of the 3NF is deemed sufficient. Therefore, I only cover the first three normal forms in detail in the following discussion.

First Normal Form (1NF)

A table is said to be in the 1NF if it doesn't contain any repeating groups; that is, no column should have multiple values for any given row. Table 2-2 shows a table with repeating groups.

Table 2-2. Table with Repeating Groups

CUSTOMER ID	NAME	CITY	PHONE
212	Thomas	Manhattan	932-795-2627
—	—	—	972-239-7869
524	Copeland	Kansas City	675-938-9256

Table 2-2 shows a table with multiple column values or repeating groups. The way to simplify this table into a 1NF table is to break it down so there are only single, atomic values for each attribute or column. Table 2-3 shows the resulting decomposition of Table 2-2.

Table 2-3. Table in the 1NF

CUSTOMER ID	NAME	CITY	PHONE
212	Thomas	Manhattan	932-795-2627
212	Thomas	Manhattan	932-239-7869
524	Copeland	Kansas City	675-938-9256

Second Normal Form (2NF)

A table is said to be in the 2NF if it is already in the 1NF and every nonkey attribute is fully functionally dependent on the primary key.

First, I illustrate a case where a table is in the 1NF but not in the 2NF. Table 2-4 shows such a relationship.

Table 2-4. Table in the 1NF But Not in the 2NF

CUSTOMER ID	NAME	CITY	PHONE	PART NUMBER	DATE	QUANTITY
212	Thomas	Manhattan	932-795-2627	1111	2-2-2002	10
212	Thomas	Manhattan	932-795-2627	2222	3-3-2002	5
524	Copeland	Kansas City	675-938-9256	3333	2-2-2002	8

Let's say the primary key of Table 2-4 is the composite key consisting of three attributes: Customer ID, Part Number, and Date. That is, given the values of this key, you can pick any unique tuple in the preceding relation. You can also see that Table 2-4 is already in the 1NF because there are no repeating groups. The attribute quantity is fully functionally dependent on the primary key of the relation. The quantity bought of a commodity is entirely dependent on the amount a particular customer bought of that product on a particular day. How about the name of the customer? Well, Name has nothing to do with the Part Number and the Date; it only depends on the Customer ID component of the primary key. These are called *partial dependencies*, and they would lead to data anomalies.

For example, it is possible to introduce an update anomaly by only updating one row belonging to the customer Thomas when his phone number changes. You can't put in any new customer information unless you have an actual Part Number for that customer because Part Number is part of the primary key and it needs to be always populated. If a customer cancels an order and you delete that transaction from Table 2-4, you lose all of that customer's information.

The way to get rid of these anomalies is to break down the table into simpler versions where you completely get rid of any partial key dependencies. That is, all nonkey attributes should be fully functionally dependent on the primary key. Tables 2-5 and 2-6 illustrate this decomposition of the Sales table into two tables, Customer and Parts, in the 2NF.

Table 2-5. The Customer Table (a 2NF Table)

CUSTOMER ID	NAME	CITY	PHONE
212	Thomas	Manhattan	932-795-2627
524	Copeland	Kansas City	675-938-9256

Table 2-6. The Parts Table (a 2NF Table)

CUSTOMER ID	PART NUMBER	DATE	QUANTITY
212	1111	2-2-2002	10
212	2222	3-3-2002	5
524	3333	2-2-2002	8

Now you can see clearly that customers can exist in your database without any corresponding part numbers. You can delete any information about parts that were ordered but canceled later on without losing customer information. Most important, you won't need 1,000 virtually similar rows for Thomas in the customer table if he does place 1,000 different orders!

Third Normal Form (3NF)

A table is said to be in the 3NF if it is already in the 2NF and every nonkey attribute is fully and *directly* dependent on the primary key.

Right now, you have two tables in the 2NF in this example. Let's add another column attribute called Manager to the two tables and see how that changes things. Each manager attends to one or more customers. So, the Customer ID attribute will determine the Name, the City, the Phone, and the Manager who takes care of this customer. The resulting Customer table is shown in Table 2-7. ·

Table 2-7. The Customer Table with the New Manager Attribute Added

CUSTOMER ID	NAME	CITY	PHONE	MANAGER
212	Thomas	Manhattan	932-795-2627	Patel
524	Copeland	Kansas City	675-938-9256	Colon

What if you happen to lose the customer Copeland for some reason? If you remove the row with Copeland's information, you also lose information about Colon and the fact that Colon manages the Kansas City accounts. The problem here is that there's a *transitive*, or indirect, relationship between the primary key, Customer ID, and the Manager attribute. Manager directly depends on the City attribute and the City attribute depends on the Customer ID attribute. To remove the resulting anomalies, you need to simplify this table, which is already in the 2NF, by breaking it down in the manner shown in Tables 2-8 and 2-9.

Table 2-8. The Customer Table After Taking Out the Manager Attribute

CUSTOMER ID	NAME	CITY	PHONE
212	Thomas	Manhattan	932-795-2627
524	Copeland	Kansas City	675-938-9256

Table 2-9. The New Manager Table Formed from the Original Customer Table

CUSTOMER ID	CITY	MANAGER
212	Manhattan	Patel
524	Kansas City	Colon

When you look at Tables 2-8 and 2-9, you can see that Copeland's removal from the Customer database doesn't mean you'll lose manager Colon's information, because the Manager attribute directly depends on the primary key, which is Customer ID.

If all of the preceding information seems a bit confusing to you initially, don't lose heart. The following is an easier way to remember and understand this whole process of putting a relation in the 3NF:

> *A relation is said to be in the third normal form if all the nonkey attributes are fully dependent on the primary key, the whole primary key, and nothing but the primary key.*

Although there are more advanced forms of normalization, it is commonly accepted that normalization up to the 3NF is adequate for most business needs. For completeness, a brief discussion of the other popular normal forms is presented in the next sections.

Boyce-Codd Normal Form (BCNF)

The Boyce-Codd normal form (BCNF) is based on the functional dependencies that exist in the relation. The BCNF is based on candidate keys.

A relation is said to be in BCNF if, and only if, every determinant is a primary key. A BCNF is a more strongly defined relationship than the 3NF. BCNF requires that if A determines B, then A must be a candidate key.

Fourth Normal Form (4NF)

The 4NF is designed to take care of a special type of dependency called the *multivalued dependency*. A multivalued dependency exists between attributes X, Y, and Z if X determines more than one value of both Y and Z, and the values of Y and Z are independent of each other.

A relationship is defined as being in the 4NF if it is in the BCNF and contains no nontrivial, multivalued dependencies.

Fifth Normal Form (5NF)

When a relation is decomposed into several relations, and then the subrelations are joined back again, you are not supposed to lose any tuples. This property is defined as a *lossless-join dependency*.

5NF is defined as a relation that has no join dependency.

....

Denormalization

Should you always work toward normalizing all your tables to reduce redundancy and avoid data anomalies? Well, theoretically yes, but in reality, you don't always have to be obsessed with the normalization process. When it comes to actual practice, you'll find that larger databases can easily deal with redundancy. In fact, the normalization process could lead to inefficient query processing in very large databases such as warehouses, because there will be more tables that need to be joined in order to retrieve information. Also, operations such as updates take more time when you have a completely normalized table structure. You thus end up having to decide between potential data anomalies and performance criteria.

You can find an excellent article on the problems you may encounter with denormalization at `http://www.dmreview.com/master.cfm?NavID=193&EdID=5251`.

....

ERM Tools: The Oracle Designer

Many tools are available to assist you in modeling the database. In addition, some tools actually generate DDL scripts that you can use to create the database itself. There are several excellent tools that you can utilize to help you in your data modeling efforts. Oracle provides the Oracle9*i* Designer as part of its software, and in this section, I provide a quick overview of how you can use the powerful features of this tool.

You can find detailed information about the Oracle9*i* Designer tool at `http://otn.oracle.com/products/designer/content.html`. Although you can design the basics of a system without the help of any tools per se, for most real-world systems, it is better to use a modeling and designing tool. ERwin, which is now marketed by Computer Associates, was at one time the leading modeling tool on the market. Powersoft's Power Designer is also a well-known tool, as is ER/Studio from Embarcadero Technologies. As mentioned earlier in this chapter, Quest Software produces many useful tools, both for Oracle developers and DBAs.

Oracle9*i* Designer is an extremely capable, but complex, tool. For modeling purposes, however, you need to learn just a few of its basic features, and it's really easy to get proficient in short order. The Oracle9*i* Designer toolset helps both in identifying the business process model and in designing the database. You can use Oracle9*i* Designer from the requirements stage to the implementation stage. And because it's geared toward Oracle's own software, Oracle9*i* Designer is extremely useful when you work with Oracle9*i* databases.

Once you install Oracle9*i* Designer from the CD, you are asked whether you want to create a repository or not. Choose the repository option, as it gives you plenty of options later on to use all the capabilities of Oracle9*i* Designer. The repository is also essential if you expect several modelers and developers to generate complete systems ready for implementation at the same time.

Using Oracle9*i* Designer, you can define your entities and the relationships among them. You can then take the resulting entity-relationship diagram and create the table definitions. Oracle9*i* Designer will do the mapping between the entities and the database tables. You can then proceed to create the DDL, which will actually help create the database tables. If you are satisfied with your design, you can execute the DDL through Oracle9*i* Designer.

Tools like Oracle9*i* Designer can provide tremendous help in designing and building your databases. Contrary to popular opinion, they are not very hard to use and after a little trial and error, you will become quite adept at using the tools. As with most other software, when you're working with Oracle software, it's in your best interest to try to ensure that whenever possible the entire toolset is provided by the same vendor. No one knows how to build software to interact with an Oracle database like Oracle Corporation does, and you can be fairly sure that Oracle's design tools, although perhaps missing the functionality of some other tools, will work together well.

The following list summarizes how you can use Oracle9*i* Designer's various components during your design and implementation phase:

- The Dataflow Diagrammer helps you create DFDs.

- The Process Modeler enables you to create process maps.

- The Function Hierarchy Diagrammer helps you see the hierarchical relationships among functions and subfunctions.

- The Entity Relationship Diagrammer, as its name implies, helps you create entity-relationship diagrams.

- The Database Design Transformer enables you to convert your entity-relationship models to physical database designs.

Physical Database Design

After you finalize the logical model, you can get to down to the design of the database itself. You now start reviewing the logical data model and decide which data elements you'll need for your physical database. Next, you create a first-cut physical data model from your logical data model using a tool such as ERwin or Oracle9*i* Designer. You can then work on tuning this initial physical model for performance considerations later on.

Transformation of Entities and Relationships

In this first stage of the physical design process, you transform the entity-relationship diagrams into relational tables. For example, you convert an entity into a table. You create the tables based on the different groups or types of information that you have in the database. For example, you may create a table called People to hold information about the members of an organization, a table called Payments to track membership payments, and so on.

What if you want to ensure that the data in your tables is unique, which is a basic assumption in most cases? How about establishing relationships among tables that hold related information? You can use primary keys and foreign keys to ensure uniqueness, and accurate and valid relationships in your database. You'll examine these two types of keys in detail in the following sections.

Primary Keys

A *primary key* is a field or a combination of fields (columns, to be accurate) that uniquely identifies each record (or row) in a table. It is common to use social security numbers as primary keys because it's obvious that every person has a unique social security number. If there is no appropriate field you can choose as a primary key, you can use system-generated numbers to uniquely identify your rows. A primary key must be unique and present in every row of the table to maintain the validity of the data.

You must select the primary keys from among the list of candidate keys for all the tables in your database. If you are using software to model the data, it is likely that you will already have defined and created all the keys for each entity. The application team determines the best candidates for the primary keys.

Foreign Keys

Suppose you have two tables, Employees and Department, with the simple requirement that every employee must be a member of a department. The way to do ensure this is to check that all employees have a Department column in the Employees table. Let's say the Department table has a primary key named dept_id. You need to have this primary key column in the Employees table. Remember that the Employees table will have its own primary key—for example, Soc_Sec_No. However, the values of the column dept_id in the Employees table must all be present in the Department table. This dept_id field in the Employees table is the primary key in the Department table, and you refer to it as a *foreign key*. Foreign keys ensure that only valid data is entered in your tables.

If you have a one-to-many relationship, you take the primary key of the entity that has the one-sided relationship and make it the foreign key on the other side. You can create the primary key of this table by using the primary keys of each entity on the "one" side of the relationship being used as the foreign key in the other entity on the "many" side. If you wish, you can use a *sequence number,* which is an Oracle database object that increments automatically, to create a surrogate primary key.

Designing Different Types of Tables

You should determine which of your tables are going to be your main data tables and which will be your lookup tables. A *lookup table* generally contains static data, such as a Department table. Usually, when you have a foreign key in a table, the table from which the foreign key comes will be your lookup table.

One of the ways to ensure good performance later on is to spend a lot of time at the design stage thinking about how your users are going to use the database. For example, whereas normalization may be a technically correct way to design a database, it may lead to the need to read more tables for a single query. The increase in the number of tables that you need to join for any query will, of course, lead to a higher CPU and memory usage, which may hurt database performance.

If you perform the appropriate amount of due diligence at this stage, you can depict your organization's process flow accurately while you design your tables. When you consider the cost and frustration involved in tuning poorly written SQL later on, it's clear that careful choice of tables and fields should occupy a primary place in your database design efforts.

Table Structures and Naming Conventions

Table structures and naming conventions to be followed should be finalized at this stage. However, in many organizations, these elements are predetermined and you may need to use a standard convention. It is important to use short, meaningful names when you name tables. This will save you a lot of grief later when you need to maintain the tables.

Column Specifications and Choosing Data Types

You should now have a good idea about the exact nature of the columns in all your tables. You should also now determine which data types you'll use for your column specification. For example, you need to specify whether the column data is going to be integers, characters, or something else.

Business Rules and Data Integrity

Good database design should adhere faithfully to the company's business rules. The design should also ensure data integrity through the proper use of various constraints provided by the RDBMS. Business rules help you model information that is usually not captured by your diagramming techniques.

The following four methods are commonly used to enforce business rules in the entity-relationship model:

- You can use the primary keys to enforce uniqueness of data in the tables. Note that the primary key values should be *unique* as well as *non-null*. The primary key should also not change its value over the life of the entity instance.

- You can use foreign keys to enforce referential integrity, thus guaranteeing the integrity and consistency of data. *Referential integrity* refers to maintaining correct dependency relationships between two tables. *Declarative referential integrity* refers to ensuring data integrity by defining the relationship between two different tables.

- You can ensure the validity and meaningfulness of data by enforcing domain constraints such as check constraints. *Domain constraints* ensure valid values for certain entities. For example, in a banking related database, you could have a constraint that states that the withdrawal amount in any transaction is always less than or equal to the total balance of the account holder.

- You can use *database triggers*, which will perform certain operations automatically when predetermined actions occur, to ensure the validity of data.

You will learn about all of the constraints and triggers in the preceding list in detail in Chapter 7. The entity-relationship model provides you with an opportunity to note these constraints and plan ahead.

Implementation of the Physical Design

Implementation of the physical design involves creating the new database itself and allocating proper space for it. It also involves creating all tables, indexes, and stored program code (such as triggers, procedures, and packages) to be stored on the server.

Database Sizing and Database Storage

You need to estimate the size of your tables, indexes, and other database objects at this stage so you can allocate the proper space for them. You can follow some basic rules of thumb or fairly elaborate sizing algorithms to size your database.

Storage decisions refer to the choice of the type of storage. Although most systems today are based on hard disks, you have several choices to make with regard to disk configuration and other issues—all of which could have a significant impact on the database's performance down the road.

Implementing Database Security

Before you actually implement your new system, you need to make sure you have a security policy in place. There are several layers and levels of security, and you need to ultimately ensure that the system is indeed secure at all these levels. Normally, you need to worry about security at the system and network levels, and you will usually entrust the system/network administrators with this type of security. You need to ensure security at the database level, which includes locking up passwords and so forth. Finally, in consultation with the application designers, you also have to come up with the right application security scheme. This involves controlling the privileges and roles of the users of the database.

Moving to the New System

During this final implementation stage, you establish exact timings for the actual "cut over" to the new business system. You may be replacing an older system or you may be implementing a brand-new business system. In either case, you need to have a checklist of the detailed steps to be undertaken to ensure a smooth transition to the new system. This checklist should also include fallback options if things don't go quite as planned. You may run ad hoc queries at this stage to fine-tune your system and to find out where bottlenecks, if any, lie.

Reverse Engineering a Database

This chapter has provided you with an introduction to the art of database design and normalization. This will help you when you are designing and implementing a database from scratch. However, what do you do when you walk into a company to manage its databases and you have no idea of the underlying physical data model and/or entity-relationship diagrams? Not to worry, you can use any of the data modeling tools discussed earlier in the chapter to reverse engineer the underlying database model.

The process of generating a logical model from an actual physical database is called *reverse engineering*. By contrast, the generating of the physical database structure from the logical data model is called *forward engineering*. By using the reverse engineering feature in say, the Power Designer or the Oracle9*i* Designer tool, you can quickly generate the physical model and or the entity-relationship model of your database.

Reverse engineering a database can help you understand the underlying model. It can also serve to provide documentation that may be missing in situations where the DBA or the lead developer has left, the entity-relationship diagram must be somewhere, and nobody can find it. Developers can make good use of the entity-relationship diagrams when making improvements to the application. Reverse engineering diagrams prove to be crucial in tracking the foreign key relationships in the data model.

 CAUTION *You need to be careful with the diagrams produced by many of the tools you'll use. Most tools use primary/foreign key relationships to create the diagram. If you use other methods in addition to primary/ foreign key pairs, you may find that not all the relationships have been created.*

Object-Relational and Object Databases

The discussion in this chapter has dealt with the relational model of databases, where all the data is stored in the form of tables. Relational databases have been accepted as the superior model for storing most kinds of "simple" data—for example, ordinary accounting data. For modeling complex data relationships, a different model, the object database management system (ODBMS), has been put forward as being more appropriate.

ODBMSs are still not at the point where they can seriously compete with traditional relational databases, for several reasons. The relational model and the object model refer to two different extremes in data modeling, and a newer extension of the relational model has come forth to bridge the gap between the two. This new model is the object-relational database management system (ORDBMS), and Oracle has adopted this ORDBMS model since the Oracle 8 version of its server software.

Oracle defines the 9i version (as well as the 8i version) of its database server as an ORDBMS. The following sections compare and contrast the three database management system categories: relational, object, and object-relational.

The Relational Model

The relational model has several limitations. One of the biggest problems with the relational model is its limited capability to represent real-world entities, which are much more complex than what can be represented in tuples and relations. The model is especially weak when it comes to distinguishing between different kinds of relationships between entities. You can't represent and manipulate complex data in traditional relational databases. The set of operations you can perform in relational models isn't adequate for many real-world applications that include objects with non-numerical attributes.

The limitations of the traditional relational model in modeling several real-world entities led to research into semantic data models and the so-called extended relational data models. Two data models now compete for the mantle of successor to the relational model: the object-oriented data model and the object-relational data model. Databases based on the first model are called object-oriented database management systems (OODBMSs) and databases based on the second model are called object-relational database management systems (ORDBMSs).

The Object Model

Object (or object-oriented) databases are based primarily on object-oriented programming languages such as C++, Java, and Smalltalk. ODBMSs are created by combining database capabilities with the functionality of object-oriented programming languages. In this sense, you can view an ODBMS as an extension of the object-oriented language with data concurrency and data recovery capabilities added on to it. Both application development and data storage are done through the use of the object-oriented language. Object-oriented languages are used to create objects, which are the basic components of the ODBMS.

Objects are defined as entities containing the attributes of a real-world object and its associated actions. *Methods* are functions in the object world, and they define the behavior of the object. Objects communicate by means of *messages*. A *class* is a grouping of objects that have the same attributes. *Instances* are the actual objects in the class. Classes can be divided into *subclasses*, with the parent class being called the *superclass*. The following three concepts are fundamental to understanding object-oriented systems:

1. *Data abstraction* refers to the simplification of data to its core representation.

2. *Encapsulation* refers to the inclusion of behavior with the object instances. Thus, code and data are packaged together. Encapsulation includes the definition of methods for a class of objects. Methods perform the behavior of the object instances. For example, if a person is an object in the model and there is a method to calculate the person's annual salary, then the code (or method) for calculating the salary is "encapsulated" with the instance object, which is the person.

3. *Inheritance* is the way you define one class in terms of another class. For example, the object Student is a type of Person (a subclass).

Although the pure object methodology is appealing, in terms of actual practice, it is quite difficult to implement. The data model Object Definition Language (ODL) is classified as an object-oriented model by the Object Data Management Group (ODMG).

The Object-Relational Model

ORDBMSs strive to combine the best that relational models have to offer while adding as much of the object-oriented methodology as possible. The fundamental tabular form of the relational model is retained. As Oracle views it, its ORDBMS model seeks to put complex business data in the basic relational database. The basis for Oracle's (and other vendor's) ORDBMS offerings is the SQL standard named SQL-99 (SQL:1999).

The ORDBMS is somewhat of a hybrid between the traditional relational and the pure object-oriented databases. It doesn't quite achieve the implementation of all the key precepts of an object-oriented database, such as encapsulation. The ORDBMS is really the relational model with a few object-oriented features added on. You can choose to ignore the object-oriented features completely and use the database as a purely traditional relational database. All the database information is still in the form of tables. ORDBMSs mainly depend on abstract types to bring object-oriented methodology to relational databases. Objects are simplified abstractions of real-world objects and encompass both the structure of the data and the methods of operating on data. So, using object types, you are not limited to the traditional data types anymore. An object type consists of its name, attributes, and methods, which can be stored within the database or outside of it. Two more object-oriented features, type inheritance and polymorphism, are also enabled in the new Oracle9*i* ORDBMS.

Database vendors such as Informix have maintained for a while now that they have really merged the relational and object-oriented databases and come up with an integral ORDBMS. This claim is motivated mostly by marketing concerns and isn't based on true technical criteria. Real object-oriented databases are still far from becoming commercially viable on a large scale. For the foreseeable future, the relational or the object-enhanced relational model (e.g., Oracle's ORDBMS) will hold sway as an efficient, well-developed, and proven product. You can also expect further developments with the addition of more and more object-oriented features to databases.

There is a continuing debate today over the merits of the relational database system versus the object-oriented database system. It is accepted by all parties that relational databases do certain chores extremely well—for example, the business applications they are currently used for. Object-oriented databases, though they are more realistic than relational databases, are quite hard to implement and are many years away from being operationally as mature and sophisticated as relational databases. Object-oriented databases have been increasing in popularity over the years, although their market share is still miniscule. The real question is this: Can object-oriented databases supplant relational databases?

Well, it seems unlikely in the near future that the object-oriented databases can become as powerful as well-established RDBMSs in performing most business operations. It seems more practical for relational databases to be extended to make them closer to the real world. ORDBMSs attempt to bridge the gap between the relational and pure object-oriented systems by incorporating object-oriented features such as encapsulation, inheritance, user-defined data types, and polymorphism into the relational model. Business processing involves a lot of data processing and the new hybrid would continue to support these activities while also serving the more complex data modeling needs. ORDBMSs seem like a smart way to progress into the object-oriented world, because their adoption doesn't involve abandoning the tremendous amount of RDBMS know-how developed over the last 25 years or so. All that knowledge could be enhanced to incorporate more of the object-oriented data model. In other words, you can get both higher operational efficiency and the benefits of realistic object type modeling by using ORDBMSs.

Oracle9*i* is an ORDBMS. It evolved over the years from a traditional pure relational system to one with increasingly object-oriented features. Oracle uses the following set of object-oriented features:

- *User-defined data types:* Oracle supports both object types and collections. Oracle provides a built-in data type called REF to model relationships between row objects belonging to the same type.

- *Methods:* Oracle implements methods in PL/SQL or Java.

- *Collection types:* The collection types include array types known as *varrays* and table types known as *nested tables*.

- *Large objects:* Oracle supports the used of binary large objects (BLOBs) and character large objects (CLOBs).

The newest frontier in data models is the emphasis on "semistructured" data models. Semistructured data models are much more flexible than traditional relational and object-relational models. This inherent flexibility ensures a more realistic representation of the complex real-world phenomena DBAs deal with every day. The use of Extensible Markup Language (XML) is but one of the new implementations of the semistructured data models. Oracle includes excellent XML capabilities that are better than those of any other commercial database in its latest version of the Oracle9*i* database.

Summary

This chapter introduced you to the concept of a relational database. Oracle's databases are called object relational database management systems (ORDBMSs) because they have several object constructs in their database engines, but essentially they are based on the relational database model. I covered the concepts of relational algebra and relational calculus to help you understand the relational database model. Then I explained the conceptual, logical, and physical designing stages. The key thing you should take away from his chapter besides the main relational concepts is the fact that the physical design of a database is the culmination of a long and important process of conceptual and logical database design.

As a DBA, it is important that you understand logical and conceptual modeling as well. In the last part of the chapter, I compared relational databases to the newer object-oriented and object-relational databases. Although object orientation is increasingly becoming an important part of the database world, the databases based on the relational data model are here to stay, not only because they perform valuable services in the real world, but also because the newer models are not yet operationally sophisticated enough for most types of applications.

CHAPTER 3

Essential UNIX (and Linux) for the Oracle DBA

IF THE ONLY thing you needed to learn about was Oracle database administration, your life would be so much easier. However, to ensure that your database perform efficiently, to it fullest, you will also need to have some understanding of the underlying operating system. In this chapter, you will examine the UNIX operating system.

The first part of the chapter shows you the most important UNIX commands that you need to know. You'll learn about files and directories and how to manage them, as well as UNIX processes and how to monitor them. You'll then learn how to edit files using the vi text editor, and you'll go on to discover how to write shell scripts.

As an Oracle database administrator (DBA), you'll need to know how to use UNIX utilities such as the File Transfer Protocol (FTP), telnet, and the remote login and remote copy services. The chapter provides you with an introduction to these useful features. You'll also learn the key UNIX administrative tools to perform system backups and monitor system performance. A discussion of the basics of RAID systems and the use of the Logical Volume Manager (LVM) to manage disk systems is part of the chapter. Toward the end of the chapter, you'll find a discussion of the important topics of data storage arrays and new techniques to enhance availability and performance.

Overview of the UNIX Operating System

UNIX became the leading operating system for commercial enterprises during the 1980s and 1990s. Although IBM mainframes still perform well for extremely large (multiterabyte) databases, most medium to large firms have moved to UNIX for its economy, versatility, power, and stability.

UNIX has a rich history. It progressed through several versions before reaching its current popular place in the operating system market. I could spend quite a bit of time discussing the history and the variants of the UNIX system, but I'll simplify the discussion by stating that in reality, the UNIX system variant a DBA uses doesn't make much difference.

NOTE *If you're interested in the story of the UNIX operating system, you can learn more at* http://www.bell-labs.com/history/UNIX *and* http://cm.bell-labs.com/cm/cs/who/dmr/hist.html.

The differences between the UNIX variants are very superficial from an operational point of view. The basic commands don't vary much, and the different flavors mainly distinguish themselves on the basis of the utilities that come packaged with them. UNIX has become well known as a multitasking, multiuser system and it is currently the most popular platform for major Oracle implementations.

The most popular UNIX flavors on the market as of this writing are Sun Solaris, HP-UX, and the IBM AIX versions. Linux is similar to the UNIX system in many ways, and users could transition easily from UNIX to Linux and vice versa. Contrary to what newcomers to the field might imagine, UNIX is an easy operating system to learn and use. What might put off many developers and others who were weaned on the Windows GUI framework are the terse and cryptic commands commonly associated with the UNIX operating system. Take heart, though, in the knowledge that the set of commands necessary to perform well are limited in number and you can become proficient in a very short time.

Sun Microsystems (Sun), Hewlett-Packard (HP), and IBM sell the leading UNIX servers—the machines that run each firm's variation of the Berkeley UNIX system V. Sun's product offerings include the Sun Enterprise series, which includes the 64-processor Sun Enterprise 10000 and the Sun Fire 15K, which can have as many as 106 1.05 GHz processors. Hewlett-Packard's top current series is the HP Super Dome Series, with up to 64 processors per machine at the high end. Currently, Sun uses the Solaris 9 version and HP uses the HP-UX 11 version as the software to run their servers. IBM is also a big UNIX supplier with its AIX server. Sun and HP currently run the vast majority of UNIX-based Oracle installations.

NOTE *Of course I can't ignore the arrival of Microsoft in the server environment and the consequent tussle between Microsoft and Oracle Corporation for dominance of the database market for the Windows platform. Chapter 22 looks at running Oracle on the Windows operating system. The majority of Oracle installations are currently UNIX based, though; hence the focus on the UNIX operating system throughout this book.*

Linux and UNIX

Linux is similar in many ways to the main UNIX operating systems. Developed by Linus Torvalds, Linux is constantly under development because it is released under the GPU license and is freely available for download from the Internet. Many users prefer using Linux because more programs and drivers are available,

it's free (or close to free, as the commercial versions are fairly cheap), and bug fixes are released very quickly. A version of Oracle9*i* for Linux is available for download at
`http://otn.oracle.com/software/products/oracle9i/content.html`.

Oracle was the first company to offer a commercially available database for the Linux operating system. Oracle even offers a cluster file system for Linux, which will make it possible to use Oracle's Real Application Clusters (ORAC) on Linux without the more costly and complex raw file systems. Even Sun Microsystems has bitten the bullet and announced plans for its first computers running the Linux operating system.

Do all these moves toward the Linux operating system foreshadow the demise of the UNIX operating system? The market for UNIX systems has dropped 17 percent in terms of revenue in 2001, according to International Data Corporation. You have to interpret these figures cautiously, as most of the movement toward the Linux operating system is intended for low-end machines that serve network and other desktop applications. For the foreseeable future, UNIX-based systems will continue to rule the roost when it comes to large, companywide servers that are useful for running large and complex databases such as the new Oracle9*i* software.

Understanding the UNIX Shell(s)

In UNIX systems, any commands you issue to the operating system are passed through a command interpreter called the *shell*. When you initially log in, you are communicating with this shell. The shell is a layer around the kernel. The *kernel* is the part of UNIX that actually interacts with the hardware to ensure the proper completion of tasks such as writing data to disk and printing to a printer. The shell translates your simple English language commands into a form the kernel can understand and returns the results to you. Therefore, any commands you issue as a user are *shell commands* and any scripts (small programs of grouped commands) that you write are *shell scripts.*

The UNIX shell has many variants, but they are fundamentally the same, and you can easily migrate from one to another with hardly any difficulty. Currently, the most common shells on UNIX installations are the Korn shell, the Bourne shell, and the C shell. For consistency purposes, I use the Korn shell throughout this book. Most of the basic commands I discuss in the following sections are the same in all the shells. Note that most of the UNIX systems can run several shells; that is, you can choose whether you want to run your session or your programs in a particular shell, and you can easily switch among the shells.

 NOTE *Some commands may not work, or may work differently, in different shells. You need to remember this when you switch among shells.*

The Korn shell (as well as the other popular types of shells) acts as both a command interpreter and a high-level UNIX programming language. As a command interpreter, the Korn shell processes user commands entered interactively. As a programming language, the Korn shell processes commands that are stored in shell scripts.

Accessing the UNIX System

You can manage the Oracle databases that run on UNIX systems in several ways:

- Directly from the server hosting the database itself

- Via a UNIX workstation

- Through a Windows NT Server front end

Most DBAs use the last approach, preferring to use their regular PC for managing the databases. Again, you have several choices here as to how exactly you interact with the databases running on the remote server. You can directly log into the server through the telnet service or a display framework such as Hummingbird or Reflection, both of which have the look and feel of a UNIX workstation. Many Oracle DBAs connect to their databases through a GUI-based management console such as the Oracle-supplied Oracle Enterprise Manager (OEM) or through a similar third-party tool sold by vendors such as BMC Software (http://www.bmc.com/) or Quest Software (http://www.quest.com/).

Regardless of the method you choose to log into the UNIX box, through the server or another interface, the first thing you will need is an account and the appropriate privileges to enable you to log in and actually get something done. The UNIX system administrator, with whom you should become very friendly, is the person who will perform this task and give you your password. The system administrator will also assign you a *home directory,* a location where you will land inside the UNIX file system when you log in initially.

Logging Into and Logging Out of UNIX

You can log into a UNIX machine in several ways. Of course, you can always log into the server directly by using the terminal attached to the machine itself. However, this is not a commonly used option for day-to-day work. One of the common ways to work with UNIX is through your own PC by using what's called a *terminal emulator,* which will enable your screen to mimic a UNIX terminal screen. Several vendors, including Hummingbird (http://www.hummingbird.com/) and WRQ (http://www.wrq.com/), produce the popular emulators Hummingbird and Reflections, respectively, which offer an easy way to communicate with your UNIX machine. These emulators, also called X Window emulators, emulate the X Window System, which is the standard GUI for UNIX systems. The emulators use special display protocols that will let you use your Windows terminal as an X terminal to access a UNIX server.

The general idea behind many of these interfaces is to try and make working with UNIX as easy as possible by providing what is to many today a familiar GUI. Figure 3-1 shows a basic X Window session connected to the UNIX operating system.

You can also use telnet, which you'll learn about later on in this chapter. Let's assume you are equipped with a terminal emulator, such as Reflection, which will let you log into your UNIX machine. You need to know a couple of things before you can log in and use the system.

First, you need to know the machine name, which can be in either symbolic or numerical form.

```
 ┌──────────────────────────── Terminal ──────────────────────┐
 │  Window   Edit   Options                            Help    │
 │                                                             │
 │    oracle 25272 25258  0  Jan 17   ?      0:06 oracleremorse (DESCRIPTION=(LOCA │
 │  L=YES)(ADDRESS=(PROTOCOL=beq                                │
 │    oracle 10758     1  0  Jan 13   ?      3:26 ora_smon_monitor │
 │    oracle  1801  1097  3 19:16:45 pts/3   0:00 grep oracle   │
 │    oracle 10754     1  0  Jan 13   ?      7:49 ora_lgwr_monitor │
 │    oracle 25258  4557  0  Jan 17  pts/1   0:00 sqlplus /nolog │
 │    oracle 10763     1  0  Jan 13   ?      6:16 ora_cjq0_monitor │
 │    oracle 26803     1  0  Jan  8   ?      5:02 ora_pmon_pfnd │
 │    oracle  4558  4548  0  Jan 17  pts/2   0:00 /usr/bin/ksh │
 │    oracle 10760     1  0  Jan 13   ?      0:01 ora_reco_monitor │
 │    oracle 20876  4558  0  Jan 17  pts/2   0:00 vi alert_remorse.log │
 │    oracle  3447  6181  0  Jan  9   ?      0:27 /a08/app/oracle/product/oas9i/Ap │
 │  ache/Apache/bin/httpd -d /a0                               │
 │    oracle 26879     1  0  Jan  8   ?      0:02 ora_reco_pfnd │
 │    oracle  9378     1  0  Jan 17   ?      0:00 ora_reco_remorse │
 │    oracle 15933  6181  0  Jan 15   ?      0:08 /a08/app/oracle/product/oas9i/Ap │
 │  ache/Apache/bin/httpd -d /a0                               │
 │    oracle 25446 25258  0  Jan 17  pts/1   0:00 /usr/bin/ksh │
 │    oracle 14587  8797  0  Jan 17  pts/1   0:00 /usr/bin/ksh │
 │    oracle 26929  6052  0  Jan 17   ?      0:12 f60webm webfile=5,531,PID6052 │
 │    oracle  4555  4547  0  Jan 17  pts/0   0:00 /usr/bin/ksh │
 │                                                             │
 │  oracle@hp50.netbsa.org    [/u01/app/oracle]               │
 │  [remorse] $ ▊                                              │
 └─────────────────────────────────────────────────────────────┘
```

Figure 3-1. X Window session

 NOTE *All UNIX machines (also called also called UNIX boxes or UNIX servers) have an Internet Protocol (IP) address, usually in a form like this: 162.15.155.17. Each IP address is guaranteed to be unique. By using a special system file (etc/hosts), the UNIX administrator can give what's called a* symbolic name *to the machine. For example, the machine with the IP address 162.15.155.17 can be called prod1, for simplicity. In this case, you can connect by using either the IP address or the symbolic name.*

Next, the system will ask you for your password. Once the UNIX system verifies your password, it will let you into the system. A message and the subsequent command prompt indicate a successful login. The command prompt will be a dollar sign ($) if you are using the Bourne shell or the Korn shell. The C shell uses the percent sign (%) as its command prompt. Once you log into the system, you are said to be working in a UNIX *session*. Also, note that when you log in you are automatically working in your home directory. You can end your session by typing the word **exit** at the prompt, as follows:

```
$ exit
```

Overview of Basic UNIX Commands

Once you are authorized to use UNIX, you have hundreds of commands you can execute at the command prompt. Don't get overwhelmed just yet, though: Of the many commands available to you, you'll find that you'll use a minority of them on a day-to-day basis. This section covers the basic commands you'll need to operate in the UNIX environment.

Getting Help in UNIX

The UNIX *man pages* refer to manual-like command explanations and examples provided to the user. The man pages are easy to use, and better still, they're free! To use the man pages, just type **man** at the command prompt, along with the name of the topic you're trying to get help with. For example, if you type in the expression **man date**, you'll receive information about the *date* command, examples of its use, and a lot of other good stuff.

As I go into the details of using UNIX commands, remember that I can only touch on a few interesting topics here. If you want to explore a topic further, the man pages are an excellent means of furthering your knowledge in the UNIX field.

Figure 3-2 shows the partial output of a *man* command, which seeks to get information about the *date* command.

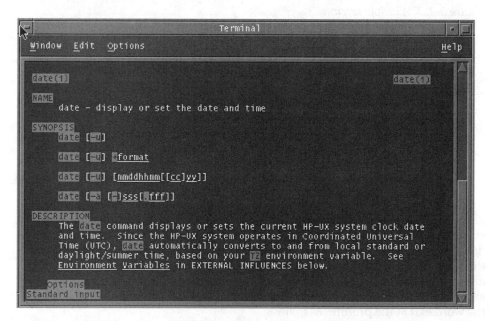

Figure 3-2. Output of the UNIX man command

The UNIX shell has a few simple, built-in commands. The other commands are all in the form of executable files that are stored in a special directory called *bin* (short for "binary"). Table 3-1 presents some of the more important UNIX commands that you'll need to know to carry out daily activities on UNIX. The UNIX commands tend to be cryptic, but some commands should be familiar to Windows users. The commands *cd* and *mkdir* in Windows, for example, have the same meaning in UNIX.

Table 3-1. Basic UNIX Commands

COMMAND	DESCRIPTION

cd	The *cd* command enables you to change directories. The format is *cd new location*. The example in the Example column takes you from the directory /u01/app/oracle to the directory /tmp.
	EXAMPLE
	`$ cd /tmp`
	`$ pwd`
	`/tmp`
	`$`

date	The *date* command gives you the time and date.
	EXAMPLE
	`$ date`
	`Sun Nov 11   10:06:57   CST   2001`
	`$`

echo	With the *echo* command, you can display text on your screen.
	EXAMPLE
	`$ echo Buenos Dias`
	`Buenos Dias`
	`$`

grep	The *grep* command is a pattern-recognition command. It enables you to see if a certain word or set of words occurs in a file or the output of any other command. In the example in the Example column, the grep command is checking to see if the word alapati occurs anywhere in the file test.txt. (The answer is yes.) *Grep* is a very useful command when you need to search large file structures to see if they contain specific information.
	EXAMPLE
	`$grep alapati test.txt`
	`alapati`
	`$`

history	The *history* command gives you the commands entered previously by you or other users. To see the last three commands, type **history –3**. The default number of commands shown depends on the specific operating system, but it is usually between 15 and 20.
	EXAMPLE
	`$ history -3`
	`23 vi abc.txt`
	`24 cd /a01/app/oracle`
	`25 sqlplus repadm`

(Continued)

Table 3-1. Basic UNIX Commands (Continued)

COMMAND	DESCRIPTION

passwd	When you are first assigned an account, you'll get a username/password combination. You are free to change your password using the passwd command.
	EXAMPLE
	`$ passwd`
	`Changing password for salapatiOld password:`
	`New password:`

pwd	Use the pwd command to find out your present working directory or simply confirm your current location in the file system. **EXAMPLE** `$ pwd/u01/app/oracle$`

uname	In the instance shown in the Example column, the command tells you that the machine's symbolic name is prod1 and it's an HP-UX machine. The –a option is asking UNIX to give all the details of the system. If you had omitted the –a option, UNIX would just respond with HP-UX.
	EXAMPLE
	`$ uname  -aHP-UX  prod5    B.11.00  A    9000/800    190    two-`
	`user license$`

whereis	As the name of this command indicates, whereis will give you the exact location of the executable file for the utility in question. **EXAMPLE** `$ whereis whowho:  /usr/bin/who  /usr/share/man/man1.z/who.1$`
which	The which command enables you to find out which version (of possibly multiple versions) of a command the shell is using. You run this command when you see somewhat different results than you expect when you run a common command such as cat. The which command helps you verify if you are indeed using the correct version of the command. **EXAMPLE** `/bin/cat$$ which cat`

who	If you are curious about who else besides you is slogging away on the system, you can find out by typing **who**. This command provides you with a list of all the users currently logged into the system.
	EXAMPLE
	`$ whosalapati        pts/0        Nov 8  08:31rhudson`
	`pts/1        Nov 8  09:04lthomas        pts/3        Nov 9`
	`15:54dcampbel        pts/7        Nov 8  16:27dfarrell`
	`pts/16        Nov 5  07:00`

whoami	The whoami command indicates who you are logged in as. This may seem trivial, but as a DBA, there are instances when you could be logged into the system using any one of several user names. It's good to know who exactly you are at a given point in time in order to prevent the execution of commands that may not be appropriate, such as deleting files or directories. The example in the Example column shows that you are logged in as user Oracle, who is the owner of Oracle software running on the UNIX system. **EXAMPLE** `$ whoamioracle$`

TIP *Many UNIX commands have additional options or switches (just like their MS-DOS counterparts) that extend the basic functionally of the command. Table 3-1 shows the most useful command switches. It is also worthwhile to always check that you are where you're supposed to be before you press the Enter key to avoid running any destructive commands. The following commands will help you control your input at the command line. Under the Korn shell, to retrieve the previous command all you have to do is press the Esc key followed by the letter k. If you want an older command, continue typing the letter k and you'll keep going back in the command sequence. If you have typed a long sequence of commands and wish to edit it, press the Esc key followed by the letter h to go back and press the letter l to go forward on the typed command line.*

You need to know a number of other commands, but these will make more sense if you try them out after you learn some essential features of UNIX, such as the management of file and directory systems and using the vi text editor.

Introducing the UNIX Environment

When you first log into the UNIX system, you must make several bits of information available to the shell. For example, the home directory into which you are placed when you first connect, the type of editor you prefer to use for editing text, and the type of prompt you want the system to display while your session is active.

Fortunately, you don't have to manually set up this operating environment every time you log into the system. There is a file usually named /etc/profile that's owned and managed by the system administrator that is used to automatically set the environment variables for all users at login time. The environment is defined by the set of environment variables. When you log in, the shell will look in the /etc/profile file, which contains your basic setup actions. The shell will also look in your home directory as an alternative location for environment information, and you can keep your personalized environment preferences in a special file called the .profile file, which is located in your home directory. (You can think of the home directory as a sort of a default directory for a user. You'll learn more about it later on in this chapter.)

There are two kinds of UNIX variables. Those set by the shell itself are called *shell variables*. The shell inherits these variables from the system when the user logs in. HOME and PROMPT are examples of commonly used shell variables. There are also other variables that you, the user, can create and assign values to. You may also export these variables to make them accessible to other shells you may start during your session.

NOTE *Remember that UNIX is a case-sensitive environment. The files Life.txt and life.txt are two entirely different things.*

The following example is typical of a /etc/profile file:

```
Set file creation mask unmask 022
MAIL=/usr/mail/$LOGNAME
TERM=vt100
PATH=/usr/bin:/usr/ccs/bin:/usr/contrib./bin
Stty erase ^H
HISTSIZE=100
SHELL=/usr/bin/ksh
```

Simply put, the /etc/profile file will have generic environment variables listed, including the path for the UNIX executables themselves. The $HOME/profile file, on the other hand, is used to include the variables that are pertinent to the specific user or group. These environment variables are exported into the environment as soon as the user logs on. When you are working within a UNIX shell, you may start a child process (within a new shell) after you log into the system. This new shell will not have access to the variables that are declared in your login shell. You have to use the *export* command, as mentioned previously, to make the variables accessible to the new shells that you started.

The following is an example of a $HOME/.profile file customized for a typical Oracle user, the generic user called oracle, under whose login you usually install the Oracle software on UNIX systems. If the variables you see here look strange, don't worry. Right now, they may not mean anything to you, but you'll learn about these and other Oracle environment variables in detail in Chapter 4.

```
export ORACLE_HOME=/u01/app/oracle/product/9.7.2.1.0
export ORACLE_SID=prod1
export TNS_ADMIN=/u01/app/oracle/product/network
export TMPDIR=/TMP
export ORACLE_BASE=/u01/app/oracle
```

NOTE *The Interactive mode and the Batch mode are two entirely different ways of executing programs or a series of commands. Interactive mode is when you log in and type in your commands directly to the screen. Batch mode refers to running your commands or an entire program at once, usually by using executable shell scripts in the form of UNIX text files.*

Displaying the Environment

What environment variables are in force when you first log in? You don't have to examine either of the profile files I discussed in the preceding section to find out. All you have to do is type **env** at the prompt, and your entire set of environment variables will scroll by on the screen. For example:

```
$ env
 PATH=/usr/bin:/usr/ccs/bin:/user/config/bin
 ORACLE_PATH=/u01/app/oracle/admin/dba/sql
 ORACLE_HOME=/u01/app/oracle/product/9.2.0.1.0
 ORACLE_SID=prod1
```

```
TNS_ADMIN=/u01/app/oracle/product/network
TERM=vt100
$
```

To see the value of a single environment variable at a time, rather than the entire set of environment variables each time (the list could be fairly long in a real-world production system), you can just ask the shell to print the individual environment variable's value to the screen by using the *echo* command:

```
$ echo $ORCLE_HOME
/u01/app/oracle/product/9.2.0.1.0
$
```

Working with Shell Variables

When you log in, your environment will be defined by a set of environment variables, as explained earlier. In addition, the shell (whether it's a Bourne shell or a Korn shell) comes with its own set of variables. Some common shell variables are PS1, which indicates the shell prompt; the PATH variable, which consists of all directories that will be searched for executable commands; and the HISTSIZE variable, which sets a limit to the number of commands retrieved by the *history* command.

Modifying the Environment

If you want to change or add new variables to the operating environment (Bourne shell or Korn shell), you can do so by using the *export* command:

```
$ export ORACLE_SID=prod2
```

Note that in the case of the C shell, you'll use the *setenv* command rather than the *export* command:

```
$ setenv  ORACLE_SID=prod2
```

When the shell starts a program, the environment variables are used for the new program. Any other variables that were explicitly defined in the shell, called *local variables,* are not automatically sent to the child program from the parent shell. To make the child program see the local variables, you can use the *export* command.

Input and Output in UNIX

When you type in your commands and when you view UNIX's output, you mostly do so through the terminal screen itself, but you can also use files to perform the input and output of data. The keyboard is the standard way to input a command to the shell and the terminal is the standard location for the output of the commands. Any resulting errors are called *standard errors* and are usually displayed on the screen itself. When you are using a UNIX window on your PC or you are using a UNIX workstation, the results of the commands and programs that you type in will display on your screen.

Your monitor automatically shows the output of any command you issue. However, that's only one way to route the output. UNIX can also "redirect" the output to a specified file or, under some circumstances, to a special location called /dev/null, which really means that UNIX sends the output to nowhere at all. It's common to use the terms *standard input, standard output,* and *standard error* to refer to the standard input and output locations in the UNIX shell.

How about if you don't want to type in commands on the keyboard directly or see the results on the screen directly? Can you send input from a previously written file and also have UNIX send the output to a file instead of the screen? Yes, you can, and this process of routing your input and output through files is called *input and output redirection.*

The two basic redirection operators are the less than (<) and greater than (>) symbols. The operator < passes the input to a command, and the operator > sends the output of a command to a file. There is another operator, >>, that appends the results of a command to a file. Table 3-2 summarizes the key redirection operators in most versions of UNIX.

Table 3-2. Input/Output Redirection in UNIX

COMMAND	DESCRIPTION
<	Redirects standard input
>	Redirects standard output
>>	Appends standard output to a file
<<	Appends standard input to a file
2 >	Redirects standard error

In the following example, the *date* command's output is stored in file1, and file2 in turn gets the output of file1:

```
$ date > file1.txt
$ file1 < file2.txt
```

You can achieve the same result with the use of the UNIX pipe (|):

```
$ date | file2
```

The pipe command, shown by the pipe symbol (|), instructs the shell to take the output of the command *before* the | symbol and make it the input for the command *after* the | symbol.

Navigating Files and Directories in UNIX

In this section, you'll learn all about the UNIX file system and directory structure. As you might have inferred, files and directories in UNIX hold pretty much the same meaning as they do in the Windows system. You'll also learn what the important UNIX directories are and some important file-handling commands.

Files in the UNIX System

A *file* is a sequence of characters stored on a disk. Files are the basic data storage unit on most computer systems. Keep this in mind: In Oracle, everything is in a *table* somewhere, and in UNIX, everything is in a *file* somewhere. The UNIX file system is hierarchical, with an inverted, treelike structure. At the base of this tree is the root directory, denoted simply by a forward slash (/).

You use files to store text, for example, user lists or some other data. You also use them to store data. Files are where you write and store the shell programs or shell scripts that you'll learn more about later in this chapter.

Types of Files

Files in a typical UNIX system can belong to the following three types:

- *Ordinary files:* These files can contain text, data, or programs. A file cannot contain another file.

- *Directories:* Directories contain files. Directories can also contain other directories because of the UNIX tree directory structure.

- *Special files:* These files are not really for ordinary users to input their data or text; rather, they are for the use of input/output devices such as printers and terminals. The special files are called *character* special files if they have streams of characters, and they are called *block* special files if they work with large blocks of data.

Linking Files

A *symbolic link* is a pointer to another file. That is, you can create a new file as a link to an existing file. You use the *link* command to create this additional pointer to an existing file. When you do this, you aren't actually creating a new file; you are pointing a new filename to the existing file. There are two types of links: *Hard* links are pointers to an existing file, and *symbolic* links are indirect pointers. You can create hard links between files in the same directory, whereas you can create symbolic links for any file residing in any directory. Thus, symbolic links are more useful to the Oracle DBA than hard links, because they are more general in nature.

In the following example, you create a link to uptime.ksh. After you create the link, you can access the file from either its original location or the new location to which the link command is creating the symbolic link. In this example, the *link* command enables you to access the uptime.sql from either the /u01/app/oracle directory or the /u01/app/oracle/admin/dba/sql directory. Thus, the *link* command gives you a virtual copy of the original by pointing to it.

```
$ pwd
$ /u01/app/oracle
$ ln -s  uptime.sql  /u01/app/oracle/admin/dba/sql
$ cd /u01/app/oracle/admin/dba/sql
$ ls -al up*
$ lrwxr-xr-x      1     oracle     dba    6     Feb 24 10:45  up.sql  -> up.sql
$
```

Managing Files

The following code sample shows you how to list files in a directory. The command *ls* lists all the files within a directory. The command ls -al (or *ll*) provides a long listing of all the files, with permissions and so forth. The command *ls – altr* gives you an ordered list of all the files, with the newest or most recently edited files at the bottom.

```
$ ls
catalog.dbf1     tokill.ksh     consumer
$ ll
total 204818
-rw-rw-r---  1 oracle  dba  104867572      Nov 19  13:23  catalog.dbf1
-rw-r------     1 oracle  dba            279         Jan   04  1999     tokill.ksh
drwrxr-xr-x  1 oracle  dba          1024        Sep  17   1:29     consumer
$ ls –altr
-rw-r------     1 oracle  dba  279                Jan   04    1999      tokill.ksh
drwrxr-xr-x  1 oracle  dba  1024            Sep 17    11:29     consumer
-rw-rw-r---  1 oracle  dba  04867572  Nov 19    13:23     catalog.dbf1
$
```

You can view the contents of a file by using the *cat* command, as shown in the following code snippet. Later on, you'll learn how to use the vi editor to view and modify files.

```
$ cat test.txt
This is a test file.
This file shows how to use the cat command.
Bye!
$
```

What if the file you want to view is very large? The contents would fly by on the screen in an instant. You can use the *more* command in this case, as follows. This will enable you to see the contents of a long file one page at a time. To advance to the next page, simply press the spacebar.

```
$ cat abc.txt | more
```

You can copy a file to a different location by using the *cp* command.

```
$ pwd
$ /u10/oradata
$cp test.txt  /u09/app/oracle/data
```

The *mv* command enables you to move the original file to a different location, change the file's name, or both.

```
$ mv test.txt abc.txt
$ ls
abc.txt catalog.txt sysinfo.txt
```

If you want to get rid of a file for whatever reason, you use the *rm* command. Watch out—the *rm* command could be lethal! To stay on the safe side, you may want to use the *rm* command with the *–i* option, which gives you a warning before the file is permanently obliterated.

```
$ ls
abc.txt  careful.txt  catalog.txt  sysinfo.txt
$ rm abc.txt
$ rm -i careful.txt
careful.txt: ? (y/n) y
$ ls
$catalog.txt   sysinfo.txt
```

Permissions: Reading from or Writing to Files in UNIX

Can you read from or write to any file on the UNIX system? It depends on the permissions that have been granted on that file by the owner of the file or directory. Note that the user who creates a file is the owner of that file. Every file has that information specified clearly.

Permission Types in UNIX

Every file and directory comes with three types of permissions: read, write, and execute. The read permission on a file lets you view the contents of the file only; you don't have the power to modify or delete the file. Read permission on a directory will let you list the directory's contents. Write permission on a file will let you change the contents of the file, and the write permission on a directory will let you create, modify, or delete files from that directory. Finally, the execute permission on a file will let you execute (i.e., run) the file if the file contains an executable program (script). Note that the read permission is the most basic permission. Even if you have the execute permission, without the read permission, it is of no use to you. You can't execute a file if you can't read it in the first place.

Determining File Permissions

How can you tell what the file permissions are? If you use the *ls* command, you can list all the files in a directory. If you use the *ls –l* command, you can list the file permissions along with the filenames in a directory. For example, look at the (partial) output of the following command:

```
$ ls -al /u01/app/oracle
-rwxrwxrwx 1 oracle    dba 320   Jan 23   09:00    test.ksh
-rw-r---r-- 1 oracle dba 152   Jul 18   13:38    updown.ksh
-rw-r-r-- 1 oracle dba 70    Nov 22   01:30   tokill.ksh
$
```

If you look carefully, you'll notice that each file listed could have a maximum of ten different letters or a combination of ten letters and the blank sign (-) at the very beginning of its line. The first letter could be a blank or the letter *d*. If it is the letter *d*, then it's a directory. If it's a blank, it's a regular file. The next nine spaces are grouped into three sets of letters: rwx. The rwx group refers to the read, write, and execute permissions on that file. The first set of rwx refers to the permissions assigned to the owner of the file. The second set of rwx refers to the permissions assigned to the group the user belongs to. The last set of rwx refers to the permissions on that file granted to all the other users of that system.

For example, how would you read the access permissions on the following file?

```
$ -rwxr-x--r 1 oracle dba Nov 11 2001 test.ksh
```

Because the first character is a dash (-), this is a file, not a directory. The next three characters, rwx, indicate that the owner of the file has all three permissions (read, write, and execute) on the file test.ksh. The next three characters, r-x, show that all the users who are in the same group as the owner have read and execute permissions, but not write permissions. In other words, they cannot change the contents of the file. The last set of characters, --r,indicates that all other users on the system can read the file, but they cannot execute or modify it.

Setting and Modifying File Permissions

Any file that you create will first have the permissions set to -rw-r--r--. That is, everybody has read permissions and no user has any permissions to execute the file. If you happen to put an executable program inside the file, you'll want to grant folks the permission to execute the file. In this case, you can set the permissions on the file by using the *chmod* command in one of two ways.

First, you can use the *symbolic notation,* with the letter *u* standing for owner, *g* for group, and *o* for other users on the system. If you want to add any permission, you need to use the plus sign (+) followed the appropriate permission. For example, the notation go +x *test.ksh* grants both the owner's group and all the other users of the system execute permission on the test.ksh file you just created:

```
$ chmod go+x  test.ksh
```

Second, you can use the *octal numbers method* to change file permissions. In this method, each permission carries different numeric "weights." Read carries a weight of 4, write a weight of 2, and execute a weight of 1. Therefore, the highest number that can be associated with each of the three different entities—owner, group, and all the others—is the number 7, which is the same as having read, write, and execute permissions on the file. For example, consider the following:

```
$ ls
$ -rw-r—r--  1  oracle dba     102   Nov  11  15:20  test.txt
$ chmod 777 test.txt
$ls
$-rwxrwxrwx  1  oracle dba     102   Nov  11  15:20  test.txt
```

The command *chmod 777* assigned full permissions (read, write, and execute) to all three entities: owner, group, and all the others. If you want to change this back to where only the owner has complete rights and all the others have no permissions at all, set the octal number to 700 (read, write, and execute for the owner and nothing for the group and others) and use the *chmod* command as follows:

```
$ chmod 700 test.txt
```

Table 3-3 provides a short summary of the commands you can use to change file permissions.

Table 3-3. UNIX Symbolic and Octal Numbers

SYMBOLIC PRIVILEGE	OCTAL NUMBER PRIVILEGE	DESCRIPTION
---	0	No privileges
--x	1	Execute only
-w-	2	Write only
-wx	3	Write and execute, no read
r--	4	Read only
r-x	5	Read and execute, no write
rw-	6	Read and write, no execute
rwx	7	Read, write, and execute (full privileges)

By default, all files come with read and write privileges assigned, and directories come with read, write, and execute privileges turned on. UNIX provides a feature called *umask* that enables you to change the default permissions on new files. For example, an umask with the value 022 means all new files will by default have the write permission denied to the group and others in the system (note that "2" refers to the write permission under the octal numbers scheme). As an illustration of how umask can change default permissions, look at the results of the following changes to the umask. First, the umask is set to 002 and the file test is created, using the *touch* command. The umask is set to 022 next, and a new file test1.txt is created. Notice the difference in file permissions between the two files.

```
$umask 002
$touch test.txt
$umask 022
$touch test1.txt
$ls -altr
total 24
drwxrwxrwx  10 oracle    pasdev    12288 Nov  1 11:02 ..
-rw-rw-r--   1 oracle    dba           0 Nov  1 11:03 test.txt
drwxr-xr-x   2 oracle    dba          96 Nov  1 11:04 .
-rw-r--r--   1 oracle    dba           0 Nov  1 11:04 test1.txt
$
```

UNIX Directory Structure

The UNIX directory structure is a hierarchy-based tree structure. The directory structure, which looks like an inverted tree, starts with the root directory, which is owned by the UNIX system administrator. From the root, you have several directories and files going downward in all directions. These directories and files include the system files, which are static in nature, and user files. As a DBA, you are concerned both with the Oracle software files and your database files, which are also somewhere in the directory structure.

From the moment you are logged in, you are somewhere in the file system. Let's say you are in the directory /u01/app/oracle when you log in. You may want to refer to, or execute, a program that's inside a file that is located in the /u01/app/oracle/admin/dba/script directory. To let the UNIX system know which location you are specifying in the hierarchy, you must give it a *path*. If you want, you can give the complete path from the root directory, as in /u01/app/oracle/admin/dba/script. This is called the *absolute path*, because it starts with the root directory itself. You can also specify a *relative path*, which is a path that starts from your current location only. In this case, the relative path for the file you need is admin/dba/script.

The following two examples demonstrate the difference between using a relative path and an absolute path.

```
$ pwd
/test01/app/oracle/9.0.1.0.0
$ cd bin
$pwd
/test01/app/oracle/9.0.1.0.0
$ cd /
$pwd
/
$cd /test01/app/oracle/9.0.1.0.0
$pwd
$ /test01/app/oracle/9.0.1.0.0
$
```

When you were in the /test01/app/oracle/9.0.1.0.0 directory, all you had to do was type **cd bin** to go to the /test01/app/oracle/9.0.1.0.0/bin directory. This shows the use of a relative path: You want to go to the /test01/app/oracle/9.0.1.0.0/bin directory, which is one directory below where you currently are. On the other hand, when you were in the root directory, /, you had to use the complete absolute path, /test01/app/oracle/9.0.1.0.0/bin, to get to where you wanted to go.

Directory Management

In this section, you'll learn some important directory management commands. You're interested in commands that will enable you to create, move, and delete directories.

The *mkdir* command lets you create a new directory:

```
$ mkdir newdir
```

The *rmdir* command removes a directory. If the directory has files in it, you have to use the command with the *–r* option, as in *rm –r filename*.

```
$ rmdir newdir
$ rmdir -r newdir
```

To move around the UNIX hierarchical directory structure, you use the command *cd*, which stands for "change directory." First, you need to understand the command *pwd*, which stands for "present working directory":

```
$ pwd
/u01/app/oracle
$ cd   /u01/app/oracle/admin
$ cd   /u01/app/oracle
$ cd admin
$ pwd
/u01/app/oracle/admin
$
```

Notice that you can use the *cd* command with the complete path (absolute path) or just the short path relative to the present working directory (/u01/app/oracle).

Important UNIX Directories

You should understand well some important directories in UNIX. Table 3-4 briefly describes the directories here that you'll come across these quite often when you're using the UNIX system as a DBA.

Table 3-4. UNIX Directories

DIRECTORY	DESCRIPTION
/etc	The /etc directory is where the system administrator keeps the system configuration files. Important files here pertain to passwords (etc/passwd) and information concerning hosts (etc/hosts).
/dev	The /dev directory has device files for example printer configuration files.
/tmp	The /tmp directory is where the system keeps temporary files, including maybe the log files of your programs. Usually you'll have access to write to this directory.
/home	The home directory is the directory assigned to you by your UNIX administrator when he or she creates your initial account. This is where you'll land first when you log in. You own this directory and have the right to create any files you want here. To create files in other directories, or even to read files, you have to be given express permission by the owners of those directories.
root	The root directory, denoted simply by a forward slash (/), is owned by the system administrator and is at the very top level of the treelike directory structure.

Writing Files with the vi Editor

The vi editor is commonly used to write and edit files in the UNIX system. To the novice, the vi editor looks very cryptic and intimidating. Yes, it is cryptic, but it need not be intimidating at all. In this section, you'll learn how to navigate through the vi editor and create and save files. You'll find that vi really is a simple text editor, with many interesting and powerful features.

Creating and Modifying Files Using vi

First, you start vi by typing just **vi** or, better yet, **vi filename**. This will start up the vi editor and show the file contents on the screen. If the file doesn't exist, it allocates a memory buffer for the file, which you can later save into a new file. Let's assume you want to create and edit a new file called test.txt. When you type the command **vi test.txt**, the cursor will blink, but you can't start to enter any text yet, because you aren't in the input mode. All you have to do to enter the input mode is type the letter **i**, which of course denotes the "insert" or "input" mode. You can start typing now just like you would in a normal text processor.

You have many cursor movement commands available to you in UNIX, and as you advance, you can arm yourself with more and more of them. For now, just know the commands in Table 3-5 to enable you to navigate your way through the vi editor. Table 3-5 shows some of the most basic vi navigation commands. These commands enable you to move around, write files, and save files.

Table 3-5. Basic vi Navigation Commands

SYMBOL	DESCRIPTION
h	Move a character to the left.
l	Move a character to the right.
j	Move a line down.
k	Move a line up.
w	Go to the beginning of the next word.
b	Go to the beginning of the last word.
$	Go to the end of the current line.
^	Go to the start of the current line.
Shift-G	Go to the end of the file.
Shift-:1	Go to the top of the file.

There are numerous vi text manipulation commands, but unless you are a full-time system administrator or a UNIX developer, you can get by nicely with the text commands summarized in Table 3-6.

Table 3-6. Important vi Text Manipulation Commands

COMMAND	DESCRIPTION
i	Start inserting from the current character.
a	Start inserting from the next character.
o	Start inserting from a new line below.
O	Start inserting from a new line above.
x	Delete the character where the cursor is.
dd	Delete the line where the cursor is.
r	Replace the character where the cursor is.
/text	Search for a test string.
:s/old/new/g	Substitute a text string with a new string.
yy	Copy a the line where the cursor is.
p	Paste a copied line after the current cursor.
P	Paste a copied line before the current cursor.
Shift-/:wq	Save and quit
Shift-/:q	Exit and discard changes

Once you get familiar with the cursor movement, it is time to learn the interesting text-processing features of vi. Again, remember that the commands given are sufficient for most daily needs. If you need more specialized information down the road, you can always look up a vi reference.

Using the Head and Tail Commands

The *head* and *tail* commands help you get the top or bottom portion of a file. By default, they will show you the first and last ten lines of the file, but you can specify a different number if you so desire. The following simple example shows the use of the *head* command:

```
$ head -5 /etc/group
$ root::0:root
$ other::1:root
$ bin::2:root,bin
$ sys::3:root,uucp
$ adm::4:root
```

The preceding sample shows the use of the *head* command, and it displays the first ten lines of the file /etc/passwd. The *tail* command works in a similar fashion on the last few lines of any file.

What if you want only the first field of the /etc/passwd file? To do this, you can use the *cut* command, as follows:

```
$ cut -d : -f 1 /etc/passwd
```

This command gives you only the first field of the /etc/passwd file. It doesn't actually cut any part of the original file—it only displays selected fields of the file to you.

Other Editors

In addition to the UNIX vi editor, you have several other alternatives available to use, including pico, sed, and Emacs. Most are simple text editors that you can use in addition to the more popular vi editor. Windows users have other alternatives. It's worth noting that Emacs also works well in graphical mode when you use X Window. There are also specific editors for X Window—for example, dtpad. Some brief but useful information on the various UNIX editors is available at http://www.helpdesk.umd.edu/systems/wam/general/1235/.

Shell Scripting

Although the preceding commands and features are useful for day-to-day work with UNIX, the real power of this operating system comes from the ability to create shell scripts. In this section, you'll start slowly by building a simple shell program, and you'll proceed to build up your confidence and skill level as you move along into branching, looping, and all that good stuff.

A shell script is a file with a set of commands. The shell script looks just like any regular UNIX file, the main difference lying in the fact that it contains commands that can be executed by the shell. Although you'll learn mostly about Korn shell programming, Bourne and C shell programming are similar in many ways. If you want to make the Korn shell your default shell, ask your system administrator to set it up by changing the shell entry for your username in the /etc/passwd file.

Creating a Simple UNIX Shell Program

Before you begin creating the shell program, you should understand this basic fact: Shell programs don't contain any special commands that you can't use at the command prompt level. In fact, you can type any command in any shell script at the command level to achieve the same result. All the shell program or shell script does for you is eliminate the drudgery involved in retyping every time you need to perform a set of commands together. Shell programs also are easy to schedule on a regular basis.

Using Shell Variables

You learned about the use of environmental variables earlier. It's common to set variables within shell programs, and these variables will hold their values only for the duration of the execution of the shell program. There's an important reason why you may want to set shell variables. If you're running the shell program manually, you can set the variables in the session you're using, and there's really no need for separate specification of shell variables. However, you can't always run a shell program manually—that kind of defeats of purpose of using shell programs in the first place. If the shell program is run as part of the cron job, it could be run from a session that doesn't have all the environmental variables set right. That's why you need to use shell variables—to make sure you're using the right values for key variables such as PATH, ORACLE_SID, and ORACLE_HOME.

Changing the Prompt

The default prompt for the Korn shell is the dollar sign ($). You may easily change it to something else by changing the value of the PS1 shell variable. Change your default prompt to finance1> as follows:

```
$ echo PS1
$
$ export PS1='finance1 >'
finance1 >
```

> **TIP** *The ability to change the prompt is useful if you're managing many different databases via UNIX. You can amend the prompt to reflect the database you're working on at any given time. For example, when you're working in an inventory system, the prompt can display Invent>. That way, you won't delete daily orders by mistake.*

Executing Shell Programs with Command-Line Arguments

It's common to use arguments to specify parameters to shell programs. For example, you can run the shell program example.ksh as *example.ksh prod1 system.* Here, example.ksh is, of course, your shell script, and the command-line arguments are prod1, the database name, and system, which is the usernam in the database. There will be two arguments inside the shell script referred to as $1 and $2, and these arguments will correspond to prod1 and system. How do you know which variable inside is being passed on which argument?

It's simple. UNIX uses a *positional system,* meaning the first argument after the shell script's name is the variable $1, the second argument is the value of the variable $2, and so on. Thus, whenever there's a reference made to $1 inside the shell script, you know the variable is referring to prod1, the database name. Now you can see how the use of command-line arguments enables the reuse of the script for several database/username combinations. You don't have to change any of the script. The same script could be run with different command-line arguments in each case.

Analyzing a Shell Script

Let's analyze a simple database monitoring shell script, example.ksh. This script will look for a certain file and let you know if it fails to find it. The script uses one command-line argument, prod1, which is the name of the database. You therefore expect to find a $1 variable inside, which will be passed the value prod1. When the shell program is created, UNIX has no way of knowing it's an executable program. You make your little program an executable shell script by using the *chmod* command.

```
$ ll example.ksh
-rw-rw-rw-  1  salapati   dba   439   feb  02   16:51  example.ksh
$ chmod 766 example.ksh
$ ll example.ksh
4-rwxrw-rw-  1  salapati   dba   439   feb  02   16:52  example.ksh
$
```

You can see that when the script was first created, it wasn't executable, because it didn't have the execution permissions set for anyone. Using the *chmod* command, the execution permission is granted to the owner of the program, user oracle, and now the program is an executable shell script.

```
#!/bin/ksh
ORACLE_SID=$1Export ORACLE_SID
PATH=/usr/bin:/usr/local/bin:/usr/contrib./bin:$PATH
export PATH
ORACLE_BASE=${ORACLE_HOME}/../..;
export ORACLE_BASE
export CURRDATE='date +%m%dY_%H%M'
export LOGFILE=/tmp/dba/dba.log
test -s $ORACLE_HOME/dbs/test${ORACLE_SID}.dbf
if [ 'echo $?' -ne 0 ]
then
    echo   "$File not found!"
mailx  -s ""Critical: Test file not found!
$ORACLE_SID    $CURRDATE"
page.dba@bankone.com   <  $LOGFILE
fi
```

The first line in the program announces that this is a program that will use the Korn shell—that's what $#$!/bin/ksh indicates. This is a standard line in all shell programs.

CAUTION *Always check to make sure that your Korn shell executables are actually located in /usr/bin/ksh and not in some other directory.*

Next, you see the $1 variable being assigned the value ORACLE_SID. That is, the first parameter you pass with the shell program at the time of execution will be the value of the argument $1. In this case, ORALE_SID will be given a value of prod1. Next, you'll notice that the program exports the values of three environmental variables: PATH, CURRDATE, and LOGFILE. Then the script uses the file testing command, *test*, to check for the existence of the file testprod1.dbf (where *prod1* is the ORACLE_SID) in a specific location. In UNIX, success of a command is indicated by 0 and failure is indicated by 1. Remember that *echo* $?*variable_name* will print the value of the variable on the screen, and that will be a 0 or a 1, based on the success or failure of the immediately preceding statement. Therefore, the next line, if ['echo $? ' ne 0], literally means "if the result of the above test command is negative" (i.e., if the file doesn't exist, then do the following).

The then statement sends out a page to the concerned person saying that the required file is missing. All you have to do to run or execute your shell script is simply type the name of the script at the command prompt. For this simple method to work, however, you must be in the Korn shell at the time you run the script. The file must also have the executable bit set by using the *chmod* command, because by default the script files do not have execute permissions turned on. By setting the execution bit, you are making the file executable as well as denoting who can execute the file (owner, group, or public).

Now that you've learned the basics of creating shell scripts, you'll move on to learn some powerful but still easy techniques that will help you write more powerful shell programs.

Control Flow Structures in Korn Shell Programming

The Korn shell provides several control flow structures similar to the ones found in regular programming languages such as C or Java. Important among these are the conditional structures that use if statements and the iterative statements that use while and for statements to loop through several steps based on certain conditions being satisfied. Besides these control flow structures, you can use special commands to interrupt or get out of loops when necessary.

Looping

In real-world programming, you may want to execute a command several times based on some condition. UNIX provides you several loop constructs to enable this, the main ones being the *while-do-done* loop, which executes a command while a condition is true; the *for-do-done* loop, which executes a command for a set number of times; and the *until-do-done* loop, which performs the same command until some condition becomes true.

The next sections examine each of the three loop structures in more detail with the help of simple examples.

A while-do-done Loop

The while-do-done loop tests a condition each time before executing the commands within the loop. If the test is successful, the command is executed. If the test is never successful, the command isn't executed even once. Thus, the loop ensures that the command inside the loop gets executed "while" a certain condition remains true. Here's the syntax for the while-do-loop:

```
while condition
do
    commands
done
```

An example of the while-do-done loop follows. Note that this loop ensures the command inside executes 99 times:

```
#! /usr/bin/sh
VAR1=1
while ((var1 < 100))
do
        print "value of VAR1 is: $VAR1"
        ((VAR1 =VAR1 +1))
done
```

A *for-do-done* Loop

You can use the for-do-done loop when you have to process a "list" of items. For each item in the list, the loop executes the command within it. Processing will continue until the list elements are exhausted. The syntax of the for-do-done loop is as follows:

```
for var in list
do
    commands
done
```

Here's an example of a for-do-done loop:

```
#!/usr/bin/sh
##  this loop gives you a list of all files (not directories
## in a specified directory.
for F in /u01/app/oracle
do
    if [ -f  $F]
    then
            ls     $F
    fi
done
```

An *until-do-done* Loop

An until-do-done loop executes the commands inside the loop "until" a certain condition becomes true. The loop executes as long as the condition remains false. Here's the general syntax for the until-do-done loop:

```
until condition
do
    commands
done
```

Here's an example of the until-do-done loop:

```
#! /usr/bin/sh
VAR1=1
while ((var1 < 100))
do
        print "value of VAR1 is: $VAR1"
        ((VAR1 =VAR1 done
+1))
```

Conditional Branching

Branching constructs enable you to instruct the shell program to perform alternative tasks based on whether a certain fact is true or not. For example, a snippet of code tells the program to execute the command if a certain file exists. If the file does not exist, the code instructs the shell to issue an error message. You can also use the case structure to branch to different statements in the program depending on the specific value a variable holds. In the following sections, you'll look at an example that shows the use of a simple conditional branching expression, and you'll look at another example that uses the *case* command.

The if-then-else Control Structure

The most common form of conditional branching in all types of programming, of course, is the *if-then-else-fi* structure. This conditional structure will perform one of two or more actions, depending on the results of a test. The syntax for the if-then-else-fi structure is as follows:

```
if  condition
then
        Action a
else
        Action b
fi
```

Here's an example of the if-then-else-fi structure:

```
#!/usr/bin/sh
LOGFILE= /tmp/dba/error.log
if [ -s $LOGFILE ]
then
      mail salapati@netbsa.org "Production Error - batch Job Failed"
else
    mail salapati@netbsa.org "Nightly batch job successful"
  fi
```

Using the Case Command

The *case* structure is quite different from all the other conditional statements. This structure lets the program branch to a segment of the program based on the value of a certain variable. A variable's value is checked against several patterns. When the patterns match, the command(s) associated with the pattern will be executed. Here's the general syntax of the *case* command:

```
case var in
pattern1)
          commands
           ;;
pattern2)
          commands
          ;
...
patternn)
          commands
           ;;
esac
```

Here's a simple example that illustrates the use of the *case* command:

```
#!/usr/bin/sh
echo " Enter b to see the list of books"
echo " Enter t  to see the library timings"
echo " Enter e to exit the menu"
echo
echo "Please enter a choice": \c"
read VAR
case $VAR in
b/B) book.sh
      ;;
t/T) times.sh
      ;;
e/E) logout.sh
      ;;
*)    echo " "wrong Key entry: Please choose again"
esac
```

Dealing with UNIX Processes

When you execute your shell program, UNIX creates an active instance of your program called the *process*. UNIX also assigns your process a unique identification number called the *process ID* (PID). As a DBA, you need to know how to track the processes that pertain to your programs and the database instance that you are managing. The *ps* command, with its many options, is what you'll use to gather information about the currently running processes on your system. The *ps –ef* command will let you know the process ID, the user, the program the user is executing, and the length of the program's execution.

In the following example of the *ps* command's use, you issue the command *ps –ef* to see the list of processes, but because the list is going to be very long, you use the pipe command to filter the results. The *grep* command ensures that the list displays only those processes that contain the word "pmon". You'll find out later on that pmon is an essential process that needs to be running in order for the Oracle database to function. The output indicates that three different Oracle databases are currently running:

```
$ ps -ef | grep   pmon
oracle 10703        1   0   09:05:39  ?        0.00   ora_pmon_test
oracle 18655        1   0   09:24:00  ?        0.00   ora_pmon_prod1
oracle 10984        1   0   09:17:50  ?        0.00   ora_pmon_finance
$
```

Running Programs in the Background with Nohup

Sometimes, you may want to run a program from a terminal from which you need to disconnect later on. To keep the programs you are executing from terminating abruptly when you disconnect from the UNIX server, you can run your shell programs with the *nohup* option, which means "no hang up." You can then disconnect, but your program will continue to run on the main server. In addition, sometimes you will want to run a program in the background. The way to do this is to specify the & parameter after the program name.

In the following example, you can see how to run a program in the background, along with the *nohup* command:

```
$ example.ksh & nohup
[1]    23286
$
```

Terminating Processes with the Kill Command

Sometimes you'll need to terminate a process because it's a runaway or because you realize you ran the wrong program. To bring your UNIX process to an abrupt stop, you can use the *kill* command. When you use the *kill* command, you are sending a "signal" to the shell. In this case, the signal is to terminate the session before its conclusion. Needless to say, mistakes in the use of the *kill* command can prove to be disastrous.

In Chapter 7, you'll learn how to terminate a session in an Oracle database. Although you can always kill an unwanted user or a process directly from UNIX itself, you're better off always using Oracle's methods for terminating database sessions. There are a couple of reasons for this. First, you may accidentally wipe out the wrong session when you terminate from the UNIX operating system. Second, when you're using the Oracle shared server method, a process may have spawned off several other processes, in which case killing the operating system session could end up wiping out more sessions than you had intended.

There is more than one *kill* signal you can issue to terminate any particular process. The general format of the *kill* command is as follows:

```
kill -[signal] PID
```

where n is the number of the signal used and PID refers to the process ID of the process to be killed. To kill a process gracefully, you send a SIGTERM signal to the process. You can do this in either of the following ways to kill the process with the process ID (PID) 21427:

```
$ Kill -SIGTERM  21427
$ Kill -15  21427
```

If your SIGTERM signal, which is intended to terminate a process gracefully, doesn't succeed in terminating the session, you can send a signal that will *force* the process to die. This signal uses the *kill -9* signal, as shown in the following example:

```
$ kill -9 233456
```

UNIX System Administration and the Oracle DBA

It isn't necessary for you to be an accomplished system administrator to be able to manage your database, but it doesn't hurt to know as much as you can about what system administration entails. Most organizations hire UNIX system administrators to manage their systems, and as an Oracle DBA, you'll need to interact closely with those UNIX system administrators. Although the networking and other aspects of the system administrator's job may not be your kettle of fish, you do need to know quite a bit about disk management, process control, and backup operations. UNIX system administrators are your best source of information and guidance regarding these issues.

UNIX Backup and Restore Utilities

Several utilities in UNIX make copies or restore files from copies. Of these, the *dd* command pertains mainly to the so-called raw files. Most of the time, you'll be dealing with UNIX file systems, and you'll need to be familiar with two sets of commands to perform backups and restores. Other methods such as *fbackup/ frecover*, *dump/ restore*, and *xdump/ vxrestore* are available in UNIX to perform backups and restores, but those methods are mainly of interest to UNIX administrators. It is common practice on UNIX to use the *tar* and *cpio* commands to perform backups. For example:

```
$ tar -cvf /dev/rmt/0m  /u10/oradata/data/data01.dbf
```

will compress the file data01.dbf and copy it to a tape named /dev/rmt/0m. *-cvf* creates a new archive.

This utility will copy each file separately, without compressing it:

```
$ cpio
```

The following command will extract the backed up files from the tape to the specified directory:

```
$ tar -xvf/dev/rmt/0m  /u20/oradata/data/data01.dbf
```

The following command will copy the contents of the entire directory (all the files) to the tape named /dev/rmt/0m:

```
$ ls | cpio -O > /dev/rmt/0m
```

The *cpio* command with the *–i* option restores all the contents of the tape named /dev/rmt/0m to the current directory:

```
$ cpio -i < /dev/rmt/0m
```

The Crontab and Automation of Scripts

Most DBAs will have to schedule their shell programs and other data loading programs for regular execution by the UNIX system. UNIX provides the cron table, or crontab, to schedule database tasks. In this section, you'll learn how you can schedule jobs using this wonderful, easy-to-use utility offered by UNIX.

You can invoke the crontab by typing in **crontab –l**. This will give you a listing of the contents of crontab. To add programs to the schedule or make scheduling changes, you need to invoke crontab in the following way:

```
$ crontab -e
```

Each line in the crontab is an entry for a regularly scheduled job or program, and the way you edit the crontab is the same way you edit any normal vi-based file. There are specific files in each line in the crontab, and they stand for different time and day indicators. Here's the standard format for a line in the crontab:

```
#-------------------------------------------------------------------------
minute hour     date    month   day of week    command
30     18        *       *        1-6           analyze.ksh
#-------------------------------------------------------------------------
```

The preceding code indicates that the program analyze.ksh will be run Monday through Saturday at 6:30 P.M. (In cron, 0 stands for Sunday, 1 for Monday, and so on.) Once you edit the crontable and input the preceding line, you can exit out of cron by pressing Shift-wq, just as you would in a regular vi file. You now have "cronned" your job, and it will run without any manual intervention every day from now on.

It's common practice for DBAs to put most of their monitoring and daily data load jobs in the crontab for automatic execution. If crontab comes back with an error when you first try to edit it, you need to talk your UNIX system administrator and have permissions granted to use the crontab.

Using Telnet

Telnet is a facility that lets you log into UNIX servers from your PC or from another UNIX server or workstation. You can remotely log into a UNIX system with telnet. You just need to ensure that your machine is connected to the target machine through a network and that you have a valid user account to access it. To use telnet on your PC, for example, go to the DOS prompt and simply type **telnet**. At the telnet prompt, just type in either your machine's IP address or its symbolic name, and your machine will connect to the UNIX server. Unless you are doing a lot of file editing and so on, telnet is all you need to connect and work with a UNIX server most of the time, in the absence of a terminal emulator.

A session that connects you to and disconnects you from a server named hp50 would look like the following. Of course, what you can do on the server hp50 would depend on the privileges you have on that machine.

```
$ telnet hp50
Trying...
Connected to hp50.netbsa.org.
Escape character is '^]'.
Local flow control on
Telnet TERMINAL-SPEED option ON
login: oracle
Password:
Last    successful login for oracle: Tue Nov  5 09:39:45
CST6CDT 2002 on tty
Last unsuccessful login for oracle: Thu Oct 24 09:31:17
CST6CDT 2002 on tty
Please wait...checking for disk quotas
…
You have mail.
TERM = (dtterm)
oracle@hp50[/u01/app/oracle]
$
```

Once you log in, you can do everything you are able to do when you log directly into the server without using telnet. You log out from your telnet session in the following way:

```
$ exit
logout
Connection closed by foreign host.
$
```

Remote Login and Remote Copy

Using the *rlogin* command, you can log into a remote system, just as you would using the telnet service. Here is how you can use the *rlogin* command for remotely logging into the server hp5:

```
$ rlogin hp5
```

To copy files from a server on the network, you don't necessarily have to log into that machine or even use the FTP service. You can simply use the *rcp* command to copy the files. For example, to copy a file named /etc/oratab from the server hp5 to your client machine (or a different server), you use the *rcp* command as follows (note that the dot in the command indicates that the copy should be placed in your current location):

```
$ rcp hp5:/etc/oratab/  .
```

To copy a file called /test.txt to the /etc directory of the server hp50, you would use the rcp command as follows:

```
$ rcp /test/txt hp5:/etc/
```

Using ssh, the Secure Shell

Like *rlogin*, ssh is a program that enables remote logins to a system. The big difference between ssh and *rlogin*, of course, is that ssh is a secure way to communicate with remote servers. Ssh uses encrypted communications to connect two untrusted hosts over an insecure network. Ssh intends eventually to replace *rlogin* as a way to connect to remote servers. Here's an example of using the ssh protocol to connect to the hp0 server:

```
$ ssh hp0
oracle's password:
Authentication successful.Last login: Tue Dec 31 2002
    18:00:00 -0600

$
```

Using FTP to Send and Receive Files

FTP, which stands for *File Transfer Protocol*, is a popular way to transmit files between UNIX servers or between a UNIX server and your PC. It's a simple and fast way to send files back and forth.

The following is a sample FTP session between my PC and a UNIX server on my network. I am getting a file from the UNIX server called hp5 using the *ftp get* command. If, instead, I want to place a file from my machine on the UNIX server I connected to, I would use the put command, as in *put analyze.ksh*. Note that the default mode of data transmission is the ASCII character text mode. If you want binary type data transmission, just type in the word **binary** before you use the *get* or *put* command.

```
$ ftp prod5
connected to prod_5
ready.
User (prod_5:-(none)): oracle
331 Password required for oracle.
Password:
User oracle logged in.
ftp> pwd
'//u01/app/oracle" is the current directory.
ftp>  cd admin/dba/test
CWD command successful.
ftp> get analyze.ksh
200  PORT command successful.
150  Opening ASCII mode data connection for analyze.ksh
 (3299 bytes).
226 Transfer complete.
ftp: 3440 bytes received in 0.00Seconds  3440000.00Lbytes/sec.
ftp> bye
221 Goodbye.
$
```

Of course, GUI-based FTP clients are an increasingly popular choice. If you have access to one of those, transferring files is usually simply a case of dragging and dropping files from the server to the client, similar to the way you move files in Windows Explorer.

UNIX System Performance Monitoring Tools

Several tools are available to monitor the performance of the UNIX system. These tools check on the memory and disk utilization of the host system and let you know of any performance bottlenecks. In this section, you'll explore the main UNIX-based monitoring tools and you'll discover how these tools can help you monitor the performance of your system.

In Chapter 19, which deals with tuning the instance performance, you'll learn how to use these kinds of monitoring tools in detail. Remember that a "slow" system could be the result of a bottleneck in processing (CPU), disk, memory, or network resources. System monitoring tools help you to clearly identify the bottlenecks causing poor performance.

The vmstat utility helps you monitor memory usage, among other things. This utility offers you statistics about processes, page faults, and memory. It also provides you information regarding the CPUs, but you'll ignore that in the following example. The VM section refers to the virtual memory part of the output, with avm standing for "active virtual memory" and free referring to "free memory." Page and faults items provide detailed information on page reclaims, pages paged in and out, and device interrupt rates. The vmstat utility gives you an idea about whether the memory on the system is a bottleneck during peak times. The po ("page outs") variable under Pages should ideally be 0, indicating that there is no swapping (i.e., the system is pushing the pages to swap disk devices, because it needs to free up that memory for other processes).

```
$ vmstat
procs                              memory
r     b     w          avm      free  re    at
18    10    0          642258  970267 580   143
      page faults                    cpu
pi    po    fr    de    sr    in    sy    cs    us    sy id
15    3     748   0     0     9089  50770 5309  15    12 72
$
```

In the trace of the vmstat utility, the *r* in the first column refers to the run queue. If your system has 24 CPUs and your run queue shows 20, that means 20 processes are waiting in the queue for a turn on the CPUs, and it is definitely not a bad thing. If the same *r* of 24 occurs on a two-CPU machine, it indicates a serious problem with the system CPU bound, where a large number of processes are waiting for CPU time. The id column at the very end, under the CPU category, indicates that 79 percent of the system is idle, which means this server is not being stressed with a heavy workload at the moment.

The iostat utility is another useful UNIX monitor for Oracle DBAs. It gives you input/output statistics for all the disks on your system. The bps column refers to kilobytes transferred back and forth from the machine. The sps column indicates the number of seeks per second, and msps shows the average seek time in milliseconds.

```
$ iostat 4 5
      device      bps      sps      msps
      c2t6d0      234      54.9     1.0
      c5t6d0      198      42.6     1.0
      c0t1d1      708      27.7     1.0
      c4t3d1      608      19.0     1.0
      c0t1d2      961      46.6     1.0
      c4t3d2      962      46.1     1.0
      c0t1d3      731      91.3     1.0
      c4t3d3      760      93.5     1.0
      c0t1d4       37       7.0     1.0
$
```

The *iostat* command shown previously will display its output every 4 seconds, for a total of five times. In the output, the following are what the four columns stand for:

- *Device:* The disk device whose performance iostat is measuring

- *Bps:* Kilobytes transferred from the device per second

- *Sps:* Number of disk seeks per second

- *Msps:* The time in milliseconds per average seek

From the preceding output, you can see that the disks c0t1d2 and c4t3d2 are the most heavily used disks on the system.

The UNIX *sar* command is a very powerful way to analyze how the read/write operations are occurring from disk to buffer cache and from the buffer cache to disk. By using the various options of the *sar* command, you can monitor disk and CPU activity in addition to buffer cache activity. Here's the output of a typical *sar* command (*–b* asks for buffer cache activity on the system, and *1 10* tells *sar* to print the output to screen every second, for a total of ten times):

```
[finance1] $ sar -b 1 10
HP-UX finance1 B.11.00 A 9000/800     01/19/03
14:29:36 bread/s lread/s %rcache bwrit/s lwrit/s %wcache
14:29:37    2230   21706      90     271     768      65
14:29:38    1807   24084      92      98     489      80
14:29:39    1546   30456      95     166     400      58
14:29:40    1679   26356      94     188     692      73
14:29:41    1540   25571      94     121     344      65
14:29:42    1685   21248      92      84     269      69
14:29:43    1920   27471      93     213     256      17
14:29:44    1182   16334      93     237     446      47
14:29:45    1790   16430      89     109     488      78
14:29:46    1992   24791      92     129     417      69
Average     1736   23432      93     162     457      65
oracle@finance1.com    [/u01/app/oracle]
[finance1] $
```

In the preceding example, the columns have the following meaning:

- *bread/s:* Read operations per second from disk to the buffer cache
- *lread/s:* Read operations per second from the buffer cache
- *%rcache:* Cache hit ratio for read requests
- *bwrit/s:* Write operations per second from disk to the buffer cache
- *lwrit/s:* Write operations per second to the buffer cache
- *%wcache:* Cache hit ratio for write requests

The *top* command is another commonly used performance-monitoring tool. The *top* command shows you the top CPU and memory utilization processes. It shows you the percentage of CPU time used by the top processes and the memory utilization.

Here's an example of typical output of the *top* command, this time with a four-processor UNIX machine. The top part of the output (not shown here) shows the resource usage for each processor in the system. The second part of the *top* command's output, shown in the following snippet, gives you information about the heaviest users of your system.

```
$ top
CPU  PID   USER   PRI NI   SIZE    RES   TIME   %CPU COMMAND
21   2713  nsuser 134  0   118M   104M 173:31  49.90 ns-httpd
23   28611 oracle 241 20 40128K  9300K   2:20  46.60 oraclepasprod
20   6951  oracle 241 20 25172K 19344K   3:45  44.62 rwrun60
13   9334  oracle 154 20 40128K  9300K   1:31  37.62 oraclepasprod
22   24517 oracle  68 20 36032K  5204K   0:55  36.48 oraclepasprod
22   13166 oracle 241 20 40128K  9300K   0:41  35.19 oraclepasprod
12   14097 oracle 241 20 40128K  9300K   0:29  33.75 oraclepasprod
$
```

In the preceding output, the various columns stand for the following:

- *CPU* stands for the processor.

- *PID* is the process ID.

- *User* is the owner of the process.

- *Pri* is the priority value of the process.

- *Ni* is the nice value.

- *Size* is the total size of the process in memory.

- *Res* is the resident size of the process.

- *Time* is the CPU used up by the process.

- *%CPU* is the CPU usage as a percentage of total CPU.

- *Command* is the command that started the process.

Several UNIX operating systems have their own system monitoring tools. For example, on the HP-UX operating system, glanceplus is a package that is commonly used by system administrators and DBAs to monitor memory, disk I/O and CPU performance. Figure 3-3 shows a typical glanceplus session in text mode. Glanceplus also has an attractive and highly useful GUI interface, which you can invoke by using the command *gpm*. Note that this session shows memory usage in detail because glanceplus was invoked with the *–m* option (*glance –c* would give you a report on CPU usage, and *glance –d* would give you a disk usage report).

```
$ glance -m
```

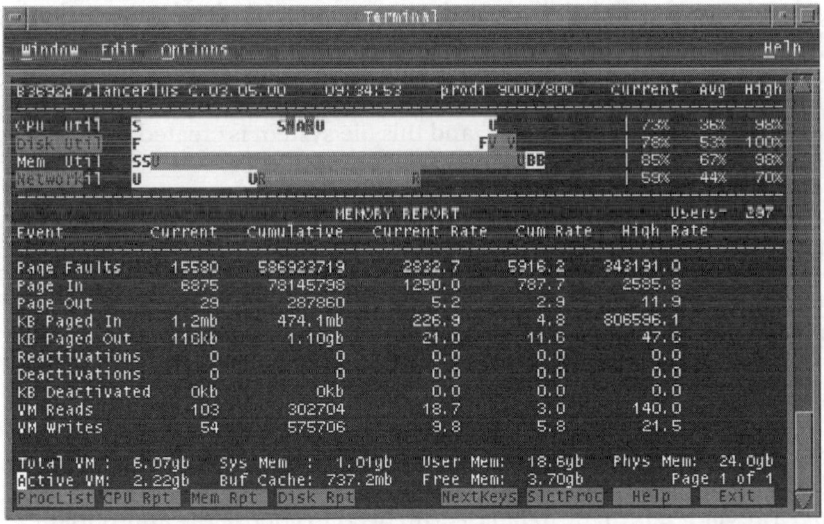

Figure 3-3. Typical glanceplus session

In Figure 3-3, the CPU, memory, disk, and swap usage is summarized in the top section. The middle part gives you a detailed memory report, and at the bottom of the screen, you can see a short summary of memory usage again.

Besides monitoring the CPU and memory on the system, you need to monitor the network to make sure there are no serious traffic bottlenecks. The netstat utility comes in handy for measuring the activity on the network. The *netstat* command works the same way as it does on the Windows servers. The following is an example of using the netstat utility. On my machine, the server prod1 is associated with the network name lan3, so the *netstat* command includes this information:

```
$ netstat -I lan3
Name    Mtu     Network
lan3    1500    172.16.0.0
Name        Address          Ipkts      Opkts
lan3    prod1.company.org   259378416  291282027
$
```

In the preceding trace of netstat, the number of packets sent and received is provided, which gives you an idea of how busy the network is right now. You can also compare the ratio of collisions to the number of output packets, which indicates network congestion.

Disks and Storage in UNIX

The topic of physical storage and using the disk system in UNIX is extremely important from the DBA's point of view. The DBA's choice of disk configuration has a profound impact on the availability and the performance of the database. Some Oracle databases benefit by using "raw" disk storage instead of disks controlled by the UNIX operating system. The Oracle Real Application Clusters (ORAC) can only use the raw devices; they can't use the regular UNIX-formatted disks. All the UNIX files on a system make up its file system, and this file system is created on a disk partition, which is the "slice" of a disk, the basic storage device.

Disk Storage Configuration Choices

The choices you make regarding disk storage configuration will have a major impact on the performance and the uptime protection of your database. It's not a good idea to make storage device decisions in a vacuum; rather, you should base these decisions on the expectations regarding your database applications and the type of database that is going to be located on the storage systems.

For example, if have a data warehouse, you may want your system administrator to use larger striping sizes for the disks. If you are going to have large numbers of writes or reads to the database, you need to choose the appropriate disk configuration strategy. Compared to the technologies of only a few years ago, today's ultrasophisticated storage technologies afford you the possibility to have both a high level of performance and a high availability of data simultaneously. Still, you have plenty of choices that will have an impact on performance and availability. The nature of the I/Os, database caches, read/write ratios, and other issues are fundamentally different in OLTP and DSS systems. Also, response time expectations are significantly different between OLTP and DSS systems. Thus, a storage design that is excellent for one type of database may be a terrible choice for another type. So, learn more about the operational needs of your application at the physical design stage to make smart choices in this extremely critical area.

Monitoring Disk Usage

It is common for a UNIX system administrator to allocate you a certain amount of physical space on the disk storage system. Typically, you will make a formal request to the system administrator for physical space based on your sizing estimates and growth expectations for the database. Once the general space request is approved by the system administrator, he or she will give you the location of the mount points on which your space is located. *Mount points* are directories on the system to which the file systems are mounted. You will then create all the necessary directories prior to the installation of the Oracle software and the creation of the database itself.

Once space is assigned for your software and databases, it's your responsibility to keep track of its usage. If you seem to be running out of space, you will need to request more space from the system administrator. Ideally, you should always have a cushion in terms of some free disk space on the mount points assigned to you, so you can allocate space to your database files if the need arises. A couple of commands are very useful in checking your disk space and seeing what has been used up and what is still left free for future use.

The *df* ("disk free") command indicates the total allocation for any mount point and how much of it is currently being used. The *df–k* option gives you the same information in more useful kilobyte terms. The following examples show the usage of the *df* command. The second example shows the use of the command with the –*k* option. It shows that out of a total of 7.9GB allocated to the /finance09 mount point, about 5.35GB is currently allocated to various files and about 1.74GB of space is still free.

```
$df
$df -k /finance09
/finance09 ( /dev/vgxp1_0f038/lvol1) :
7093226 total allocated Kb
1740427 free allocated (Kb)
5352799 used allocated Kb
75% allocation used
$
```

Another related command to find out how the disks are being used is the *du* command. The *du* command indicates, in bytes, the amount of space being used by the mount point.

```
$ du -k /finance09
         /finance09/lost+found
         /finance09/ffacts/home
. . .
5348701    /finance09
$
```

As you can see from the preceding code, the *du* command indicates the space (in bytes) used by the various files and directories of mountpoint /finance09 and the total space used up by it. I prefer the *df –k* command over the *du –k* command, because I can see at a glance the percentages of free space and used space.

Disk Storage, Performance, and Availability

The one thing you can be sure of when you use disk-based storage systems is that a disk will fail at some point. All disks come with a Mean Time Between Failure (MTBF) rating, which could run into hundreds of thousands of hours. Therefore, you can expect an average disk of a certain high rating to last for many years. As we all know, averages can be dangerous in situations like this, because an individual disk can fail at any given time, regardless of its high MTBF rating. Disk controllers manage the disks, and a controller failure can doom your system operations.

Performance is also an issue when you are considering the configuration of your storage devices. In systems with highly intensive simultaneous reads and writes, you could quickly end up with disk bottlenecks, unless you planned the disk configuration smartly from the beginning.

The preceding two considerations, availability and performance, lie at the heart of all disk configuration strategies. It is common now to build redundancy into your disks (as well as other key components of the entire system) to provide continuous availability. To improve performance, the common strategy employed is *disk striping,* which is fundamental to the concept of redundant disk strategies. Striping enables you to create a single logical unit from several physical disks. The single logical unit is composed of alternating stripes from each disk in the set. Data is divided into equally sized blocks and written in stripes to each disk. Reads are done in a same way, with the simultaneous use of all the disks. Thus, you can enhance I/O operations dramatically, because you are now using the I/O capacity of a set of disks to do your processing at once.

Disk Striping

It's important to realize that you could place the file system on a single physical disk or across several physical disks. In the latter case, although the file system is placed on several disks, the user will see the files as one so-called logical volume. You can use logical volumes, also known as *striped disks,* for performance or protection purposes. You can increase performance using striped disks because input and output rates can be speeded up if the read/write operations can be done simultaneously to several physical disks at one time, using parallel operations.

UNIX systems offer several ways of combining multiple disks into single logical volumes. One way to create a logical device on many UNIX systems is to use a utility known as the Logical Volume Manager (LVM). Using a LVM, you can take, let's say, eight physical disks of 4GB each and create one 32GB logical disk. Thus, you can see that disk striping can also enable you to create a much larger logical disk, which can handle a larger file system. File systems can't traverse disks, and therefore logical disks offer an easy way to create large volumes.

Raw Files vs. UNIX File Systems

Oracle has always recommended the use of raw files, which bypass the UNIX buffer caches, for its Oracle Real Application Cluster (ORAC) architectures. Otherwise, Oracle has not expressed any preference for raw files. Raw devices, because they by pass the UNIX buffer cache, are inherently faster than UNIX-based files, but that advantage is probably nullified by several disadvantages that accompany their use. These disadvantages include limitations with regard to file sizes and the inability of raw files to be backed up as flexibly as UNIX-based files.

Logical Volumes and the Logical Volume Manager

Let's briefly look at the two basic methods of configuring physical disks. Although you may never have to do this yourself, it's a good idea to have a basic under-standing of how disks are managed by system administrators. You can configure disks as whole disks or as logical volumes. Whole disks are exactly what their name implies: Each physical disk is taken as a whole and a single file system is created on each disk. You can neither extend nor shrink the file system at a later stage.

Logical volumes, on the other hand, use the sophisticated Logical Volume Manager (LVM) to combine physical disks. This gives you a way to change file sizes easily as the system grows. A set of physical disks is combined into a volume group. This volume group is sliced up by the LVM into smaller logical volumes. Most modern systems use the LVM approach because it is an extremely flexible and easy way to manage disk space.

You have a number of ways to organize disk storage, which is the most common form of data storage. These include the traditional whole disks and the modern RAID-based storage arrays. There has been a revolution in the storage area in the last half-dozen years or so. You can still use individual disks, commonly referred to as Just a Bunch of Disks (JOBs), that the operating system on the host machine can address directly. You can store these disks in a separate, external cabinets, and they can talk to the host through a host-based controller. There is no redundancy or striping (usually) on these drives.

RAID Systems

A popular way to configure large logical disks from a set of smaller disks is provided by redundant array of independent disks (RAID) devices. If disks in a RAID system fail, you can immediately and automatically reconstruct the data on the failed disk from the rest of the devices. RAID systems are ubiquitous and most Oracle databases employ them for the several benefits they provide with regard to performance and safeguarding data. Traditionally, data was stored on single-disk systems, but there were severe performance limitations with these systems; hence, the impetus toward multidisk solutions. Today, disk arrays are the standard storage mechanisms in organizations. Disk arrays provide both higher performance and redundancy, a key factor in safeguarding the data. The basic idea behind the RAID systems is to harness the power of several small and cheap storage drives to surpass the performance of expensive, traditional single-disk systems. In the process, because RAID systems have multiple disks, there is built-in redundancy that contributes to higher reliability.

Aggregating smaller disks into a RAID system makes sense for many reasons. The disk capacity and transfer rates are higher. Input and output rates are significantly better than those possible with single disks.

When it comes to the performance of disk systems, two factors are of interest to you: the transfer rate and the I/O operations per second. *Transfer rate* refers to the efficiency with which data can move through the disk system's controller. *I/O operations* refers to the number of I/O operations that the disk system can handle in a specified period.

The other reason for employing storage arrays of disks is the reliability factor. Compared to traditional disks, which had an MTBF of tens of thousands of hours, disk arrays have an MTBF of millions of hours. Even when a disk in a RAID system fails, the array itself continues to operate successfully. Most modern arrays automatically start using one of the spare disks called *hot spares*, to which the data from the failed drive is transferred. Most disk arrays also enable the replacement of failed disks online—that is, without bringing the system itself down (also known as *hot swapping*).

RAID Levels

The inherent tradeoff in RAID systems is between performance and reliability. You can employ two fundamental techniques, striping and mirroring the disk arrays, to improve disk performance and to enhance reliability. Note that mirroring schemes involve complete—that is, 100 percent—duplication. Most of the non-mirrored RAID systems also involve redundancy, though it is not as high as in the mirrored systems. The redundancy in nonmirrored RAID systems is due the fact that they store the necessary parity information need for reconstruction of disks in case there is a malfunction in the array of disks. Note that array management software is used to make the striped and mirrored disks appear as one virtual disk to the operating system and applications that use the arrays. The following list presents the most commonly used RAID classifications. Note that except RAD 0, all the levels offer redundancy in your disk storage system.

> *RAID 0:* Striping. The data is broken into chunks and placed across several disks that make up the disk array. The stripe here refers to the set of all the chunks. Because input and output are spread across multiple disks and disk controllers, the throughput of RAID 0 systems is quite high. For example, to write a 800KB file over a RAID set of eight disks with a stripe size of 100KB means that you could do so in roughly 1/8 of the time it would take to do the same operation on a single disk. However, because there is no built-in redundancy, the loss of a single drive could result in the loss of all the data, as data is stored sequentially on the chunks. So, RAID 0 is all about performance, with little attention paid to protection.

RAID 1: Mirroring. In RAID 1, all the data is duplicated, or "mirrored," on one or more disks. The performance of a RAID 1 system is slower than a RAID 0 system, because input transactions are completed only when all the mirrored disks are successfully written to. The reliability of mirrored arrays is high, though, because the failure of one disk in the set doesn't lead to any data loss. The system continues operation under such circumstances, and you'll have time to regenerate the contents of the lost disks by copying data from the surviving disks. To conclude, RAID 1 is geared toward protecting the data, with performance taking a back seat when compared to a RAID 0 setup. But, of all the redundant RAID arrays, RAID 1 still offers the best performance. Understand that RAID 1, or mirroring, means that you will pay for n number of disks but you get to allocate only $n/2$ number of disks for your system, because all the disks are duplicated.

RAID 2: Striping with error detection and correction. RAID 2 uses striping, with additional error detection and correction capabilities built in. The striping part guarantees high performance, and error correction methods are supposed to ensure reliability. But the mechanism used to correct errors is bulky and takes up a lot of the disk space for itself. So, this is a costly and inefficient storage system.

RAID 3: Striping with dedicated parity. RAID 3 systems are also striped systems, with an additional parity disk, which holds the necessary information for correcting errors for the stripe. Parity involves the use of algorithms to derive values that allow the lost data on a disk to be reconstructed on other disks. Input and output are slower than pure striped systems such as RAID 1, because information has to be written to the parity disk also. Nevertheless, RAID 3 is a more sophisticated system than RAID 2, and it involves less overhead than RAID 2. You'll only need one extra disk drive in addition to your drives that hold the data. If you have ten data drives, you'll only need one extra disk to hold the parity information needed for error correction. However, RAID 3 systems can only process one I/O request at a time. If a single disk fails, the array continues to operate successfully, with the failed drive being reconstructed with the help of the stored error correcting parity information on the extra parity drive. RAID 5 arrays with small stripes can provide better performance than RAID 3 disk arrays.

RAID 4: Modified striping with dedicated parity. The stripes are done in much larger chunks than in RAID 3 systems, which allows the system to process multiple I/O requests simultaneously. In RAID 4 systems, the individual disks can be independently accessed, unlike in RAID 3 systems. This leads to much higher performance when it comes to reading the data from the disks. Writes are a different story, however, under this setup. Every time you need to perform a write operation, the parity data for the relevant disk must be updated before the new data can be written. Thus, writes become very slow and the parity disk could become a bottleneck.

RAID 5: Modified striping with interleaved parity. Under this disk array setup, both the data and the parity information are interleaved across the disk array. Writes under RAID 5 tend to be slower, but not as slow as under RAID 4 systems, because it can handle multiple concurrent write requests.

Several vendors improve the write performance by using special techniques such as nonvolatile memory for logging the writes. RAID 5 gives you virtually all the benefits of striping (high read rates), while providing the redundancy needed for reliability, which RAID 0 striping does not offer.

RAID 0+1: Striping and mirroring. These RAID systems provide the benefits of striped and mirrored disks. They tend to achieve a high degree of performance because of the striping while offering high reliability due to the fact that all disks are mirrored (duplicated). You just have to be prepared to request double the number of disks you need for your data, because you are mirroring the disks.

Choosing the Ideal Disk Configuration

You can draw the following basic conclusions about the various RAID systems that you explored in the preceding section.

- RAID 0 offers high read and write performance.

- RAID 0 is cheap but not very reliable (no redundancy).

- RAID 1 offers high reliability but is expensive.

- RAID 1 provides 100 percent redundancy, but all writes must be duplicated.

- RAID 2, 3, and 4 are high-cost solutions.

- RAID 2 wastes a lot of space for overhead.

- RAID 2 is not commercially viable because of special disk needs.

- RAID 3 has poor random access performance.

- RAID 4 leads to degraded write performance as well as a potential parity bottleneck.

- RAID 5 offers high reliability.

- RAID 5 involves a write penalty, although it is smaller than in RAID 4 systems.

- RAID 0+1 is expensive (due to the mirroring of the disks).

- RAID 0+1 offers great random access performance as well as high transfer rates.

- RAID levels 3, 4, and 5 provide the ability to reconstruct data when only one disk fails. If two disks fail at the same time, there will be data loss.

There is no one ideal disk configuration that every organization can use for all its databases. You'll have to weigh factors such as safety and speed with the cost of the system under consideration. It's important to understand the benefits and costs of the main types of disk configuration that are available to you. Mirroring offers complete security and integrity of the data in cases where damaged disks or disk controllers affect part of your database. Mirroring involves duplicating a whole disk on another "mirrored" disk. The obvious drawback of mirroring is that you need twice as much disk storage space as your requirements. But mirroring also provides you solid protection during a problem involving disks. Striping gives you faster input and output capabilities, because the operations can be run in parallel across several physical disks, but it doesn't provide safeguarding of the data like mirroring does. RAID 5 systems provide safety because the data on any disk can be reconstructed quickly from the parity information that is saved, but the writes to a RAID 5 disk are slower, because of the so-called write penalty of RAID 5 systems caused by the extra time taken to compute the parity information. RAID 5 is highly cost-effective when it comes to protecting the data. However, the performance of a RAID 5 is not as good as a RAID 0 disk array.

What's the best strategy in terms of disk configuration? You, the DBA, and your system administrator should discuss your data needs, management's business objectives, the impact and cost of downtime, and available resources. The more complex the configuration, the more money needs to be spent on the hardware, the software, and the training of personnel to manage the system. The choice essentially depends upon the needs of your organization. If your database needs the very highest possible performance and reliability at the same time, you may want to go first class and adopt the RAID 0+1 system. Note that this is an expensive way to go, although several companies in critical data-processing areas such as airline reservations systems have adopted this as a company standard for data storage. If data protection is your primary concern, however, and you can live with a moderate throughput performance, you can go with the RAID 5 configuration and save a lot of money in the process. This is especially true if read operations constitute the bulk of the work done by your database. If you want complete redundancy and the resulting data protection, you can choose to use the RAID 1 configuration. If you are concerned purely with performance and your data is not critical, but it can be reproduced easily, then you'll be better off just using a plain vanilla RAID 0 configuration. To make the right choice, find out the exact response time expectations for your databases.

CAUTION *Once you configure a certain RAID level on your disk, you can't easily switch to a different configuration. You have to completely reload all your applications and the databases if you decide to change configurations midstream.*

You configuration choice will depend on finances, the nature of your applications, availability requirements, performance expectations, and growth patterns. In general, the following guidelines will serve you well when you are considering the RAID configuration for your disks:

- RAID 5 offers you many advantages over the other levels of RAID. The traditional complaint about the "write penalty" should be discounted because of sophisticated advances in write caches and other strategies that make RAID 5 much more efficient than in the past. The RAID 5 implementations using specialized controllers are far more efficient than software-based RAID or RAID 5 implementations based on the server itself. Write cache usage in RAID 5 level systems improves the overall write performance significantly.

- Allow for a lot more raw disk space than what you figure is the amount you'll need. This includes your expansion estimates for storage space. Fault tolerance needs more disks under RAID systems. If you need 400GB of disk space and you are using a RAID 5 configuration, then you would need seven disks, each with 72GB of space. One of the eight drives is needed for writing parity information. If you want to use a hot spare on the system itself, you would then need eight disks (eight times 72GB).

- Stripe widths depend on your database applications. If you are using OLTP applications, you need smaller stripe sizes, up to 128KB per stripe. Data warehouses benefit from much larger stripe sizes.

- Striping across a large number of disks will certainly improve performance, but you can't carry it too far.

- Know your application. Having a good idea about what you are trying to achieve with the databases you are managing will help you decide among competing alternatives.

- Always have at least one or two hot spares ready on the storage systems.

Redundant Disk Controllers

If you have a RAID 5 configuration along with mirroring, you are still vulnerable to a malfunction of the disk controllers. To avoid this, you can configure your systems in a couple of different ways. First, you can mirror the disks on different controllers. Alternatively, you can use redundant pairs of disk controllers, where the second controller takes over automatically by using an alternative path when the first controller fails for some reason.

RAID and Backups

Suppose you have a RAID 0+1 or a RAID 5 data storage array, which more or less assures that you are protected adequately against disk failure. Do you still need database backups? Of course you do! RAID systems protect against mainly one kind of failure involving disks or their controllers. How about human error? If you or your developers wipe out data accidentally, no amount of disk mirroring is going to help you—you need those backups with the good data on them. Similarly, when a disaster such as a fire destroys your entire computer room, you need to fall back upon reliable and up-to-date backups. So, do not neglect the correct and timely backing up of data, even though you may be using the latest disk storage array solution.

RAID systems, it must be understood, do not guarantee nonstop access to your mission-critical data. The way to ensure that would be to go beyond the basic RAID architecture and build a system that is disaster tolerant.

RAID and Oracle

Oracle uses several different kinds of files as part of its database. You may need a combination of several of the RAID configurations explained previously to optimize the performance of your database while keeping the total cost of the disk arrays reasonable. An important thing to remember here is that when you use a RAID 3 or RAID 5 system, there is no one-to-one correspondence between the physical disks in the array and the logical disks, or logical unit numbers (LUNs), that are used by your system administrator to create logical volumes, which are in turn mounted for creating your file systems. Advise your system administrator to try and create as many logical volumes on each LUN as there are physical drives in the LUN. This way, the Oracle optimizer will have a more realistic idea as to the physical disk set up that the database is using. Logical volumes are deceptive and could mislead the optimizer.

Implementing RAID

You can implement RAID in a number of ways. You could make a fundamental distinction between software-based and hardware based RAID arrays. Software RAID implementation is done through the host server's CPU and memory to send RAID instructions and I/O commands to the arrays. Hardware RAID is implemented by using a special RAID controller, which is usually externally based. Host-based controllers can also be used to provide RAID functionality to a bunch of disks, but they are not as efficient as externally based RAID controllers. Software RAID implementations impose an extra burden on the host CPU. When disks fail, the disks with the operating system may not be able to boot if you are using a software-based RAID system.

Storage Technologies

Today's storage technologies are vastly superior to the technologies of even 5 years ago. Disk drives themselves have gotten faster—it is not difficult to find disks with 10000 RPMS and 15000 RPMS spindle speeds today. These disks have seek speeds of about 3.5 milliseconds. In addition, advance SCSI interfaces and the increasing use of fiber channel interfaces between servers and storage devices have increased data transfer rates to 100MB per second and faster. The capacity of individual disks has also risen considerably, with 180GB disks being fairly common today. The average MTBF for these new-generation disks is also very high—sometimes more than a million hours. New technological architectures for data storage take advantage of all the previous factors to provide excellent storage support to today's Oracle databases. Two such storage architectures are Storage Area Networks (SANs) and Network Attached Storage Systems (NAS). Let's take a closer look at these storage architectures.

Storage Area Networks

Today, large databases are ubiquitous, with terabyte (100GB) databases not being a rarity any longer. Organizations tend to not only have several large databases for their OLTP work, but also use huge data warehouses and data marts for supporting management decision making. "Consolidation" and "centralization" of data are buzzwords in the information technology area today. Storage area networks (SANs) use high performance fiber channel connecting technology and RAID storage techniques to achieve the high performance and reliability that today's information organizations demand.

Modern data centers use SANs to optimize performance and reliability. SANs can be very small or extremely large, and they lend themselves to the latest technologies in disk storage and network communications. Traditionally, storage devices were hooked to the host computer through a SCSI device. SANs enable the servers to connect to them via high-speed fiber channel technology, with the help of switches and hubs. You can adapt legacy SCSI-based devices to use a SAN, or you can use entirely new devices specially designed for the SAN. Core infrastructure for building a SAN is enabled by the use of fiber channel switches called *brocade switches*. Using hubs will let you use SANs that are as far as 10 kilometers away from your host servers.

So chances are if you are not on one already, you'll be soon on a SAN in the very near future. SANs offer many benefits to an organization. They allow data to be stored independently of the servers that run the databases and other applications. They enable backups that do not impact the performance of the network. SANs also facilitate data sharing among applications. SANs are usually preconfigured as far as the RAID level is concerned. Depending on your company's policy, they could come mirrored or as a RAID 5 configuration. The individual disks in the SANs are not directly controllable by the UNIX system administrator. The system administrator will have control over the logical units (ldevs in HP systems), which are denoted by LUNs. Each of the LUNs that the system administrator accesses from the storage network can consist of 8 or 16 physical hard disk drives. The system administrator will only see the LUN as a single disk. The storage array's controllers map the LUNs to the underlying physical disks. The administrator can use LVMs to create file systems on these LUNS after incorporating them into volume groups first.

When you use RAID-based storage arrays, the RAID controllers on the SAN will send the server I/O requests to the various physical drives, depending on the mirroring and/or parity level chosen.

Networked Attached Storage

Put simply, NAS is a black box connected to your network and it provides additional storage. The size of a NAS box can range from as small as 2GB up to terabytes of storage capacity. The main difference between a NAS and a SAN is that it is usually easier to scale up a SAN's base storage system using the software provided by your supplier. For example, you can easily combine several disks into a single volume. NAS is set up with its own address, thus moving the storage facilities away from the servers onto the NAS box. The NAS communicates with and transfers data to client servers using protocols such as the Network File System

(NFS). The NAS architecture is really not very suitable for large OLTP type databases. One of the approaches now being recommended by many large storage vendors for general storage as well as some databases is to combine the SAN and NAS technologies to have the best of both worlds.

> **NOTE** *A good paper comparing the RAID and SAN technologies is available at* http://www.netapp.com/tech_library/3105.html. *This article is slightly dated, as the article's authors used Oracle8 for the tests, but it still provides a useful comparison of the technologies.*

InfiniBand

One of the latest and greatest network technologies is InfiniBand. One of the driving forces behind network storage is to reduce the I/O bottlenecks between the CPU and the disks. InfiniBand takes another approach and works between a host channel controller on the server and a special adapter on the storage machines or device, thereby not requiring an I/O bus. A single link can operate at 2.5 gigabits per second. You can find a full discussion of this new technology at http://www.infinibandta.org/ibta/. Given the high-profile companies involved in developing this concept, you can expect to see considerable push in the storage area. Microsoft, IBM, Sun, HP, and some of the main storage vendors are all involved in the development of InfiniBand technology.

Oracle and Storage System Compatibility

Oracle Corporation actively works with vendors to ensure that the storage arrays and other technologies are compatible with its own architectural requirements. Oracle manages a vendor-oriented certification program called the Oracle Storage Compatibility Program (OSCP). The OSCP is designed to facilitate the development of storage solutions for Oracle databases. As part of the OSCP program, Oracle provides test suites for vendors to ensure their products' compatibility with the Oracle9i database. As part of this certification program, vendors normally test their storage systems on several platforms, including several variants of the UNIX operating system, Linux, and the Windows operating system.

Oracle has also been responsible for the Hardware Assisted Resilient Data (HARD) Initiative. HARD's primary goal is to prevent data corruption and thus ensure data integrity. The program also includes other measures to prevent the loss of data by validating the data in the storage devices. Availability and protection of data are enhanced because data integrity is ensured through the entire pipeline, from the database to the hardware. Oracle does have its own corruption-detecting features, but the HARD Initiative is designed to prevent data corruption that could occur as you move data between various operating system and storage layers. For example, EMC Corporation's solution to comply with the HARD Initiative involves checking the checksums of data when they reach their storage devices with the Oracle's checksums. Data will be written to disk only if the two checksums are identical.

NOTE *New technologies have come to the fore in recent years that enable business continuance on a 24/7 basis as well as data protection. Backup windows are considerably reduced by the use of these new technologies, which enable nondisruptive backup operations. These technologies include the* clone *or* snapshot *techniques, which enable a quick copy of the production on to a different server. Compaq's SANworks Enterprise Volume Manager, Hewlett-Packard's Business Copy, Fujitsu's Remote Equivalent Copy, and Sun's Instant Image all allow data copying between Oracle databases at a primary site to databases at remote locations. The key thing to remember is that these techniques take snapshots of live data in dramatically short time periods. So, these techniques can be used for backup purposes as well as for disaster recovery.*

Summary

You can't be an effective Oracle DBA on UNIX systems if you don't master the basics of vi and shell scripting, as well as the basic set of UNIX commands. This chapter provided broad coverage of UNIX issues and reviewed all the important UNIX commands you'll need to use in your daily work life. The basic primer on vi should enable you to start using vi as an editor on UNIX-based systems. You learned the essentials of shell scripting, which will enable you to write scripts with increasing fluency and confidence as you master the usage of more commands. The discussion of RAID, storage arrays, and possible configurations of disk systems is not really part of the Oracle DBA's job description, but it's nice to know how changes in configurations will impact the performance of your application. A good source for a lot of very useful material regarding RAID systems in general is the Web site maintained by the industry group called The Raid Advisory Group. For useful papers on storage systems, visit `http://www.bitpipe.com` and `http://www.storage.com`.

This is a time of tremendous technical change in the storage and networking arenas, with the evolution of new techniques that promise both increased availability and higher performance of Oracle9*i* databases. You, as an Oracle DBA, might not be responsible for the management of any these storage technologies, but it is very helpful for you to know as much as you can about the interrelationships between your databases and the storage technologies. This will enable you to take advantage of the sophisticated techniques available today for preventing data corruption and performing nonintrusive data backups.

Part Two

The Oracle RDBMS

CHAPTER 4

Installing the Oracle9*i* RDBMS

THIS CHAPTER'S GOAL is to give you a good understanding of the requirements for the correct installation of the Oracle9*i* server software. This chapter deals with an actual installation on a UNIX server. Chapter 22 contains a discussion of Oracle installation on Windows servers. There are some variations of the installation steps for the different flavors of UNIX such as Sun's Solaris, Hewlett Packard's HP-UX, IBM's AIX, and so on, but the essential steps are the same. You need to follow these steps and incorporate the necessary changes suggested by the Oracle installation manuals for your operating system. Several steps need to be performed before and after the installation of the software, by you and the UNIX system administrator, and this chapter explains those steps. It is necessary to install the software according to a sensible plan, and this chapter shows you how to install Oracle by following the well-known Optimal Flexible Architecture (OFA) guidelines.

Note that you'll be going through the main features of generic Oracle installation in this chapter. It's important that you have access to the Oracle installation manuals for your specific operating system before you begin installing the Oracle9*i* software. The installation manuals are all available on the Oracle site at http://technet.oracle.com/docs/products/oracle9i/content.html.

There are minor differences in some of the steps, and the manuals go into great detail regarding all those different steps. However, Oracle software installation itself is no different from any other software installation, and if you follow all the preinstallation procedures, there's no reason you can't have a clean installation in a couple of hours or less on even the most complex machines. Of course, if you're configuring Oracle Real Application Clusters (ORAC) or some such advanced architecture, you'll need more time to finish the installation. Complex as the Oracle9*i* database server software is, the actual time you need to install the software is trivial compared to the time you need to spend to ensure that all the preinstallation steps have been completed correctly. If you follow all the recommended steps, the installation process should work the first time around.

Installing Oracle on UNIX Systems

When it comes to the mechanics of the process, installing the Oracle server software is really a simple affair. Installation of all the software for Oracle9*i* will probably not take you more than a couple of hours. All the real effort goes into the proper planning of the installation. This planning will involve consultations with the UNIX systems administrator regarding the physical space and memory allocation you need as well as configuring the operating system itself, UNIX, for the optimal functioning of your Oracle databases.

Although the software and the databases managed by it will function even if they're installed on a single disk or a set of disks without any organization as such, you'll lose performance and endanger the safety of the databases if you don't follow a well-thought-out strategy regarding disk allocation. Oracle strongly recommends a disk layout methodology formally called the *Optimal Flexible Architecture* (OFA), for efficiency as well as many other reasons. Before you start any installation of the Oracle software itself, it is absolutely necessary for you to know what the OFA recommendations are regarding proper disk layout.

NOTE *This chapter deals with the installation of Oracle server software on UNIX systems. Installing the Oracle client is a much simpler task. When you invoke the Oracle Installer, simply choose the client installation option instead of the server installation option.*

I'm assuming that you or your organization has bought the necessary software from Oracle Corporation. If that's the case, you'll have the software CDs sent to you by Oracle. If you just want to try the Oracle9*i* software, you don't have to purchase a thing. You can download the Oracle9*i* server software freely from the Oracle Technology Network (OTN) Web site at http://technet.oracle.com/. The OTN site has complete enterprise versions of the server software for all UNIX flavors, as well as Linux, and Windows servers. In addition, you can check out the operating system installation and administration manuals at the OTN site.

NOTE *Although the general methodology is the same, there may be slight differences in the installation procedures among the various operating systems. Treat the following discussion as a set of generic installation procedures, and read the installation manual for your operating system before you proceed toward an installation of the software.*

Reviewing the Documentation

You can save yourself a lot of grief during the installation process by carefully reviewing the operating system–specific Oracle installation manuals. These manuals are very clear and specific, and provide you with a detailed roadmap of the installation process. You'll need to review three sets of installation documents:

- *Oracle Installation Guide for your operating system:* This document will provide you with information about the system requirements, UNIX users and groups, and other requirements, and step you through the installation and postinstallation processes.

- *Release Notes and Release Notes Addendums:* The Release Notes are very important, and they cover the most recent changes to the installation and upgrade procedures for many components of the Oracle9*i* server and client.

The last-minute changes that are covered in the Release Notes may make the difference between a successful installation of the various components and an error-prone installation.

- *README files:* The README files are usually in the \doc\readmes directory on the first product CD-ROM.

The Release Notes and the README files inform you about any potential restrictions, limitations concerning the installation, and the use of new Oracle9*i* software.

NOTE *The Installation Guides and the Release Notes are available at the OTN site, or you can access them by going to either* http://docs.oracle.com/ *or* http://tahiti.oracle.com/.

Determining Disk and Memory Requirements

You should focus on two key resources when you are planning a new Oracle installation: disk storage and the amount of memory (RAM) that your systems need on the server machine. The amount of total physical space (disk storage) will depend on the size of your application(s). The Oracle software itself would take about 3GB–5GB of file system space, depending on the operating system. Now you do have to run one or more databases with this software, so the total space you'd need would depend on the requirements for all the databases considered together. You need to find out the table and index sizes, and the number of stored procedures you will have in the database. You also need to find out as much as you can about the growth expectations for the data that your databases are supposed to store over time. If you have a database that you anticipate will grow quickly, you need to make allowances for that. Plan ahead of time, because disk space is something that needs to be budgeted for, and you may find yourself scrambling for space if you are way off the mark.

TIP *For larger databases, the size of the tables and indexes would be the predominant component of total database size. Fortunately, you can easily find out your database's size by using* database-sizing spreadsheets. *One such sizing spreadsheet is available from* http://bhtech.com/. *Although the spreadsheet is for an older version of Oracle, the idea behind it remains the same, and you can derive meaningful estimates of the size of the tables and indexes using this spreadsheet.*

Chapter 5 discusses the components of Oracle9*i* memory, but the total amount of memory that you need will really depend on the size and nature of your application. Oracle does provide a rule of thumb for your memory requirements, and you can follow this rule when you are in the initial stages of planning your system. Later on, you can adjust these initial estimates.

The minimum requirement that Oracle imposes for memory is 256MB, but this amount is not enough for most serious applications. In addition, Oracle requires that you allocate a swap space of the server that is at least twice your Oracle RAM or 400MB, whichever is greater. The requirements of the applications that your system will be running determine the total memory you need. Of course, everybody would love to have a system that will "run fast," but you'll have to be more precise than that. At the least, your system shouldn't be memory bound. Inadequate amounts of memory for Oracle leads to excessive swapping and paging, and your system could slow down to a crawl.

In Chapter 5, you'll find out how to determine the size of the various components of Oracle's memory allocation. In Chapter 19, you'll learn how to monitor memory usage and know when you may need to increase its size.

Following the Optimal Flexible Architecture

The Optimal Flexible Architecture (OFA), a set of recommendations from Oracle Corporation, is aimed at simplifying management of complex software and databases often running under multiple versions of software. The OFA essentially imposes a standardized way of naming the different physical components of Oracle as well as placing them on the file system according to a logically thought-out plan.

Laying out the UNIX directories according to the OFA guidelines leads to a clear and efficient distribution of Oracle's various files, even with several databases simultaneously running under different Oracle versions.

The OFA guidelines were formulated at Oracle Corporation under the authorship of Cary Milsap in 1990 in the way of an internal paper. Milsap published the guidelines as a paper in 1991 and revised it in 1995.

 NOTE *Milsap's 1995 paper is titled "The OFA Standard—Oracle for Open Systems." You can find this paper and many other excellent white papers at* http://www.hotsos.com/.

You can view the OFA guidelines as a set of best practices regarding two important issues, disk layout and naming conventions, based on extensive field experience by Oracle professionals. Originally intended for internal Oracle use, the OFA is now the standard by which all Oracle installations should be measured.

The OFA guidelines are only Oracle's recommendations, and by no means do you have to follow them in their entirety. The whole premise behind OFA is the need to support large, complex Oracle databases with a minimum of maintenance. The main goals that OFA was designed to achieve are to minimize disk contention, provide for operating more than one database without administrative confusion and, finally, to improve database performance.

Suppose you're using a half a dozen production databases on your UNIX server. How do you manage to keep track of the many administrative files if you don't properly organize them? Let's assume you're already organizing them according to your own naming conventions. What if your organization hires another DBA to help with several databases that are already in production? How does the new DBA know where the different log and configuration files are on the system in the absence of detailed documentation? If you've ever walked into an organization and taken over a database installation that had files stored all over the place, you'll immediately recognize the benefits of the OFA. If the previous DBA has adhered to the OFA guidelines, any new hire can easily go the standard directories and look for various types of information.

If your database is growing and needs more space, following the OFA guidelines will ensure that space will be added in the right directories with the standard naming convention. The standardization of directory and file placement as well as naming leads to minimal administrative overhead and helps create more efficient databases. The usefulness of the OFA guidelines becomes particularly clear when you are trying to manage a bunch of databases on the same server.

First I'll define some terms before plunging into a detailed discussion of the OFA concepts and the implementation details:

Mount points are directories in the UNIX file system that are used to access mounted file systems.

Product files refer to the many sets of configuration and binary executable files that come with the Oracle software.

Versions may refer to entirely different releases or just point upgrades (patch upgrades). For example, 8.0.1.0.0, 8.1.7.1.0, and 9.2.0.1.0 are different versions of the server software.

Oracle *data files* refer to the UNIX files that will hold Oracle table and index data.

Oracle *administrative files* include the database log files, error logs, and so forth.

The term *tablespace* (which I discuss in detail in Chapter 8) refers to the logical allocation of space within Oracle. The sum of the space in all the tablespaces is equal to the total size of an Oracle database.

Let's now examine the main OFA guidelines and see exactly how they help you attain several necessary goals in terms of avoiding contention and providing for growth.

You can enhance administrative simplicity through the use of the structured OMF system for maintaining your files. Creating new databases won't pose any problems, because each database is separated into its own directories, simplifying user administration and the creation of new databases. The OFA guidelines contribute to database reliability, because your hard drive failures won't propagate to whole applications. The OFA guidelines help in balancing the load efficiently across the disk drives, thereby enhancing performance and minimizing contention. The OFA guidelines also promote the efficient separation of administrative files from several databases by using standard naming conventions.

TIP *If you are using NFS file systems, know that these can't guarantee that writes always complete successfully, leaving open the possibility of file corruption. Unless your storage vendor appears in the Oracle Storage Compatibility Program (OSCP) member list, don't install the software on NFS file systems.*

Mount Points

Mount points are the directory names under which file systems are mounted by the UNIX operating system. Oracle recommends that all your Oracle mount points be named according to the convention /*pm*, where *p* is a string constant to distinguish itself from other mount points, and *m* refers to a two-digit number. This means you can name your mount points /u01, /u02, /u03, and so on. Keep the mount point names simple and don't include any hardware-related information in the mount point name. That way, changing your disk system hardware will not affect the mount point names.

Oracle recommends that you have four mount points to fully comply with the OFA guidelines. The first of these are for locating the Oracle software itself, and the other three are for placing the database files. In such a case, the three mount points designated for the data files could be more clearly named as follows: /u01/oradata/prod1, /u02/oradata/prod2, and /u03/oradata/prod3.

This nomenclature has several benefits. First, by using the /unn/oradata convention, you are making it clear that these file systems are meant for Oracle databases. Second, the /unn/oradata/database_name model helps in separating data from several databases. For example, in the previously described four-disk structure (three disks for database files), you can have the mount points /u02/oradta/prod1 and /u03/oradata/prod2. This type of naming will help separate data files belonging to several databases, which is good from a maintenance and a performance point of view.

Directory and File Naming Conventions

All home directories should follow the convention /*pm*/*h*/*u*, where *pm* refers to the mount point name, *h* is a standard directory name, and *u* refers to the directory owner. For example, you can have a specific directory named /u02/app/oracle and another named /u03/financials/finmanager. This entire home directory for each user (e.g., /u01/app/oracle) may be denoted by the letter *h* for your purposes in the following discussion.

Directory Structure

At the root of the Oracle directory structure is the directory called the Oracle Base, which is usually in the form of /*pm*/*app*/*oracle* (e.g., /u01/app/oracle). The Oracle Installer will take this as the default Oracle Base and install all the software under this base directory. The Oracle home directory is a very important directory, with the structure /*pm*/*app*/*oracle*/*product*/*product_release_number*. An example of the

Oracle home directory is /u01/app/oracle/product/9.2.0.1.0 It is under this directory that the Oracle Installer will place all Oracle-supplied executable code and other key configuration files for the server software. Some key subdirectories under the Oracle home directory are the bin, dbs, and network directories. The dbs directory holds the configuration files and the bin directory holds the executables for the Oracle products. The network directory holds the Oracle Net services files.

Administrative Files

Every Oracle database contains several administrative files associated with it. Among these files are configuration files, core dump files, trace files, export files, and other related log files. You need to store these files under separate directories for ease of maintenance. Assuming you have about ten or so of these directories for each database, you can see why it's imperative that you have a simple means of organizing these files. Oracle recommends the following directory structure for clarity: */h/admin/d/a*, where *h* is your home directory (e.g., /u01/app/oracle), *admin* indicates that this directory holds administration-related files, *d* refers to the specific database, and *a* refers to the directories. For example, /u01/app/oracle/admin/prod1/exp will have all the export files pertaining to the prod1 database.

Table 4-1 is a list of the standard administrative directories that you'll need in most cases. Of course, you may add to the recommended list or modify it to fit your circumstances.

Table 4-1. Typical Administrative Directories

DIRECTORY	CONTENTS
adhoc	Contains ad hoc SQL files
adump	Contains any audit files
bdump	Contains background process trace files
cdump	Contains core dumps
create	Contains files you use to create the database
exp	Contains export files
pfile	Contains instance parameter files (e.g., init.ora)
udump	Contains SQL trace files for user processes

So, if you follow the OFA guidelines, you'll end up with the following directories for your administrative files for a database called prod1:

```
$ pwd
/u01/app/oracle/admin/prod1
$ ls
adhoc adump bdump cdump create exp pfile udump
$
```

Product Files

The whole idea behind properly naming and placing the product files is to be able to implement multiple versions of the Oracle server software simultaneously. Why would you need to run different versions in the same time frame? When you migrate between versions, it is normal to retain the older software versions until you make the "cut over" into the new version.

Also, different applications on the system may have different time frames within which they want to migrate to the new version. Consequently, in most cases, you'll end up having to support multiple versions of the Oracle server software simultaneously. Oracle recommends that you keep each version of the software in a separate directory named used the convention */h/product/v*, where *h* is the home directory, *product* indicates that the software versions are under this directory, and *v* refers to the version of the product. For example, I have a directory on my server called /u01/app/oracle/product/8.1.7.0, under which I save all the Oracle server software subdirectories during installation. If I decide to install the 9.2.0.1.01.0.0 version, I'll do so under the directory /u01/app/oracle/product/9.2.0.1.0. You can see that this type of naming convention makes it very easy to install and manage multiple versions of the Oracle software.

Database Files

The administrative and product files you looked at earlier are generic files. Oracle databases contain another set of key files called *database files*. These include the data files, which contain the data for the specific database and certain operational files called control files and redo log files. *Control files* are crucial to the operation of the database and *redo log files* hold information necessary to recover the database during an instance crash and similar situations. The OFA recommendation for the database files is to follow the conventions */pm/q/d/control.ctl* and */pm/q/d/redo0n.log* for control and redo files, respectively. In this notation, *pm* refers to the mount point; *q* refers to an indicator such as "oradata," which hints about what the files contain; and *d* refers to the database name.

Oracle recommends that all tablespaces be named with no more than eight characters, with the format */tn.dbf*, where *t* refers to the descriptive name of the tablespace and *n* denotes a two-digit number. For data files, the recommended notation is */pm/q/d/tn.dbf*, where *t* refers to the tablespace that contains this data file and *n* refers to an integer. Thus, a typical data file under the OFA guidelines would have the following structure: /u01/app/oracle/oradta/prod1/system01.dbf, which refers to a data file under the system tablespace.

Table 4-2 clearly shows how an OFA-compliant database enables you to easily manage files pertaining to several databases and even several database versions. When you realize that in real life, you may sometimes have several databases, possibly running under several software versions, you can understand why you need to follow the simple, commonsense recommendations of the OFA approach.

Table 4-2. An OFA-Compliant Oracle Database

DIRECTORY FORMAT	DESCRIPTION
/u01/app/oracle	Oracle Base (also home for the Oracle software owner)
/u01/app/oracle/product/9.1.0.1	Oracle home directory
/u01/app/oracle/admin	Directory for the Oracle administrative files
/u01/app/oracle/admin/prod1	Directory for the Oracle administrative files for the prod1 database
/u01/app/oracle/admin/prod2	Directory for the Oracle administrative files for the prod2 database
/u01/app/oracle/product	Oracle software files directory
/u01/app/oracle/product/8.1.7.1	Software distribution for the 8.1.7.1 version databases
/u01/app/oracle/product/9.1.0.0	Software distribution for the 9.1.0.0 version databases
/u01/oradata	Directory tree for the Oracle data files
/u01/oradata/prod1	Directory for the prod1 data files
/u01/oradata/prod2	Directory for the prod2 data files

Performing Preinstallation Tasks

The installation of the Oracle software, as I mentioned earlier, is a fairly straightforward exercise. Most of your work is done before the installation. Your crucial partner at this stage (and later on) is the UNIX system administrator. It is your responsibility to find out what the needs are for your system in terms of physical disk space, memory requirements, and directory structures that need to be created and communicate this to the system administrator. You can always have more memory and physical space allocated later on, but it is always nice to get the allocation done up front.

To estimate the total disk space you need, you have to add the space required for the Oracle9i installation itself. For example, for an Oracle9i installation on the HP UNIX system, Oracle recommends you allocate around 2GB of space on your system for your software. You can also figure out the estimated memory by following some basic guidelines: Most small online transaction processing (OLTP) systems require about 500MB, medium installations require about 1GB, and larger installations require around 1.5GB. More important with regard to the software installation is that you allocate enough swap space for your system. The Oracle Installer requires huge amounts of memory to perform its tasks and the real memory on your system may not be adequate sometimes during the installation process.

At this stage, you'll need to prepare an installation requirements document with the amount of resources you'll require along with the preferred layout of the disks. In return, the system administrator will give you the allocated memory and disk space. The system administrator will also give you the location of all your mount points, which are the file systems under which the disk space is mounted. The preinstallation tasks depend on the operating system, but the steps are fairly similar. In this discussion, I assume you are using an HP-UX 11 operating system. You need to consult your specific documentation from Oracle for exact installation procedures for your operating system.

Before you install the Oracle software, you need to complete several steps.

NOTE *The Oracle Universal Installer, which comes with the software distribution, will let you install a seed database, but you won't have to install this database. You're better off configuring your own database for your needs and creating it. It's fairly easy (and fun) to create a new database. However, for a complete beginner, the seed database provides a good basis for learning.*

UNIX System Administrator's Tasks

The UNIX system administrator needs to perform several steps before you can install your Oracle software. First of all, the system administrator should make sure that the latest operating system patch sets are applied as per Oracle's installation recommendations. The most important tasks are creating separate mount points for the Oracle software, reconfiguring the kernel (if necessary), creating the necessary users and groups on the UNIX server, and making sure that the Oracle users have the right file and directory permissions. I cover these system administrator tasks in some detail in the following sections.

Installing Required Operating System Patches

The UNIX administrator must ensure that all required operating system patches are installed before undertaking the Oracle software installation. Oracle's operating system-specific guides will provide you with the required and recommended patches for your operating system.

Creating Mount Points for the Installation

Oracle recommends at least two mount points: one for the software and the other for the database files. However, you actually need a lot more than that. A minimum OFA-compatible installation requires four mount points: one for the Oracle software and three for the various database files. The number of mount points you need depends on your total space requirements. If your computations indicate that you need around 200GB of total space and each of your mount points support 7GB each, you would need roughly 30 mount points for your applications.

It is also important that the UNIX administrator names the mount points in accordance with the OFA guidelines discussed earlier in this chapter. That is, the disks should be named /prod01, /prod02, and so on.

Reconfiguring the UNIX Kernel

The system administrator for your system should also look into the possibility of reconfiguring the UNIX kernel, which, in essence, is the UNIX operating system. Oracle requires huge amounts of shared memory segments, which are not configured by default with the UNIX operating systems. Therefore, there is a good possibility that the system administrator will need to change certain kernel parameters. The kernel parameters that UNIX administrators need to change are the ones dealing with memory and *semaphores,* which are structures that control access to UNIX memory.

It is extremely important for the kernel to be reconfigured at the outset. If enough memory resources aren't configured per Oracle's guidelines, either your installation will not succeed or you will encounter an error when you try to create a database after the installation of the Oracle software. The kernel reconfiguration is a very simple task for the administrator. All he or she has to do is change the kernel configuration file and regenerate a new kernel file using the appropriate UNIX command. The system administrator then needs to restart the UNIX system with the new kernel file replacing the older version. Table 4-3 shows a typical set of UNIX memory parameters that need to be modified in the kernel configuration file to meet Oracle's requirements.

Table 4-3. UNIX Kernel Parameters for Oracle

KERNEL PARAMETER	ORACLE'S REQUIREMENT	COMMENT
SHHMAX	4294967295	Maximum size of a shared memory segment
SHMMIN	1	Minimum size of a shared memory segment
SHMMNI	100	Maximum number of shared memory segments
SHMSEG	10	Maximum number of shared memory segments a process can have
SEMMNS	2000	Maximum number of semaphores
SEMMSL	1000	Maximum number of semaphores per set
SEMMNI	100	Maximum number of semaphore sets

To reconfigure the parameters in Table 4-3, the system administrator needs to add the following lines to the kernel configuration file. If your system doesn't provide enough shared memory and semaphores, later on you may not be able to start your instance or your system may be unable to handle a large number of processes. After you reconfigure your kernel parameter settings (if necessary), the system administrator must reboot the system for the new settings to take effect.

```
set shmsys:shminfo_shmmax=4294967295
set shmsys:shminfo_shmmin=1
set shmsys:shminfo_shmmni=100
set shmsys:shminfo_shmseg=10
set semsys:seminfo_semmns=2000
set semsys:seminfo_semmsl=1000
set semsys:seminfo_semmni=100
set semsys:seminfo_semopm=100
set semsys:seminfo_semvmx=32767
```

NOTE *Oracle uses the shared memory segments of the operating system to share data among its various processes. It uses semaphores to handle locking.*

Creating Necessary UNIX Groups

The UNIX administrator needs to create a couple of important UNIX groups. UNIX groups, as you are aware, consist of set of users who perform related tasks and have similar privileges. The creation of two special groups, OSDBA and OSOPER, will facilitate the authentication of users, as you'll see later on. Note that the HP UNIX system, which is what I'm basing this discussion on, would require the granting of the RTSCHED, RTPRIO, and MLOCK privileges to these two groups by the system administrator. Other systems may have similar requirements, which you can ascertain by referring to the system-specific Oracle manuals.

In addition to the OSDBA and OSOPER groups, it is necessary to create another group called the ORAINVENTORY group. For the UNIX systems, Oracle in general requires only the OSDBA group for installing the software. The OSOPER and the ORAINVENTORY groups are recommended but not required. In addition, Oracle recommends the creation of an APACHE group for most operating systems. The ORAINVENTORY group will be the owner of the ORAINVENTORY subdirectory under which all the Oracle installation products are kept. All new installations and upgrades are supposed to be performed by users belonging to the ORAINVENTORY group.

NOTE *Users belonging to the ORAINVENTORY group must be given read, write, and execute privileges on the ORAINVENTORY directory. The group should not be given write permissions for any other directories.*

Creating Necessary UNIX Users

After the system administrator has created the necessary UNIX groups, he or she needs to create the all-important user usually named "oracle" (you can choose any name, but "oracle" is usually used by convention). The user oracle is the owner of the Oracle software, and this user's default group will be the newly created ORAINVENTORY directory group. The oracle user's secondary group should be the

OSDBA group. The oracle user will have a home directory like all the other users (usually something like /u01/app/oracle), under which you'll create the rest of the directory structure for holding the Oracle9*i* software.

> **CAUTION** *Don't use the root account to install or modify Oracle software. Only the user oracle should perform any Oracle software installation operations.*

Under an HP UNIX system, for example, you can use the administrative tool SAM to create the users, but assuming the system administrator wants to create the users manually, here is the command to create the oracle user:

```
$ useradd -d /home/oracle -g orainventory -G OSDBA -m -s /usr/bin/sh  oracle
```

The *passwd* command is then used to set the password for the oracle user. Please refer to Chapter 3 for more details about the *passwd* command. Note that the default home directory of the oracle user should be similar to that of the normal users of the system. The ORACLE_HOME directory is not meant for the oracle user; it's the location of the Oracle software binaries and similar files.

> **NOTE** *The user oracle should be given read, write, and execute privileges on all files and directories that are part of the Oracle9i installation.*

Setting File Permissions

The next step the system administrator needs to perform is to set the correct default UNIX file permissions. To do this, the system administrator must first check the existing default permissions by simply issuing the command *umask*. If the umask is set to anything but 022, change it to 022 by issuing the command *umask 022*. As you saw in Chapter 3, the default permissions for a newly created file system are denoted by 666 under the octal notation. That is, everyone would be able read and write any file. By using a default file permission of 644 (by using the umask of 022), you are granting any users other than the user oracle only a read permission on the file systems.

Only two users, the oracle user (who owns the Oracle software) and the ORAINVENTORY group, should have any write privileges in the system by default. The oracle user, of course, should have complete privileges (read, write, and execute) on all the directories in the Oracle9*i* installation. The ORAINVENTORY group should have similar privileges on the directories in the ORAINVENTORY group. Of course, privilege levels will vary between production and development servers. On a development machine, the administrator should allow developers to create trace files in the udump directory, for example.

The UNIX administrator must ensure the existence of a local bin director~~~ example, /user/local/bin or /opt/bin. The administrator must further e~~~ this directory is included in the PATH of the user oracle and ensure th~~~ oracle has execute permissions on this directory.

The system administrator must also create a directory with the name /var/opt/oracle that is owned by the user oracle. This directory will contain files that describe various components of the Oracle9*i* software installation. The following commands will create the directory and assign it the necessary privileges:

```
$ mkdir /var/opt/oracle
$ chown oracle:dba /var/opt/oracle
$ chmod 755 /var/opt/oracle
```

Oracle Owner's Tasks

You have to ask the system administrator to create an account for the "owner" of the Oracle software. Usually, this is an account with the name "oracle." The oracle owner—in our case, user oracle—needs to perform the following set of actions before the installation of the software.

Setting the Environment Variables

The oracle owner needs to log in and set the following environment variables. Although all of the following variables can be set manually, you are better off editing the .profile file in the home directory of the user oracle, which will ensure that the environment will always be set the desired way each time the user oracle logs in.

NOTE *Your environment variables may be slightly different from the ones listed here, depending on your operating system and its version. Always check the operating system–specific installation guides—it's well worth the effort to read them. I am using an HP 11 version operating system for the Oracle software installation.*

- *ORACLE_BASE variable:* The ORACLE_BASE variable is the starting directory for all Oracle installations. All the software files and other files are placed in directories underneath the ORACLE_BASE directory. In this case, the directory is /test02/app/oracle.

- *ORACLE_HOME variable:* The ORACLE_HOME variable should be set to the $ORACLE_BASE/product/release. In this case, it is test02/app/oracle/product/9.0.1.0.0. This is the directory under which all the other directories are created for the user oracle, including the Oracle binaries and the database administrative files. The Oracle Installer gives you the opportunity to select the ORACLE_HOME variable during installation of the software.

- *PATH variable:* The PATH variable should be set to the following:

```
$ exportPATH=$ORACLE_HOME/bin:/usr/bin:/usr/ccs/bin:
/etc:/usr/binx11:/usr/local/bin
```

- *DISPLAY variable:* The environment variable DISPLAY should be set to the following, assuming the symbolic name of your server is prod1. If you want to use the IP address instead of the symbolic machine for your machine, you can get it by typing **ipconfig** at the command prompt in DOS.

```
$ export DISPLAY=prod1:0:0
```

- *TNS_ADMIN variable:* The TNS_ADMIN variable is used to set the location of the Oracle Net configuration files.

- *ORACLE_SID variable:* The important ORACLE_SID variable need not be set if you are not planning to create a database right now. Because you are not planning to create a database with your installation of Oracle Server software, you can ignore this for now.

- *ORAENV_ASK variable:* In addition to the environment variables in the .profile file, you also need to add another line so all user sessions will automatically read the oraenv file upon logging in as the oracle software user. The oraenv file will basically prompt the user oracle for the correct SID of the database he or she wants to use. On a system with several database instances, the oraenv file comes in handy in making this choice as soon as you log in.

  On my HP server, for example, this is how I can make the system ask me for the database SID when I log in. I need to include the following line in the user oracle's profile file:

```
. /usr/local/bin/oraenv
```

  If you set the value of the ORAENV_ASK variable to NO, the current value ORACLE_SID will be assumed to be the SID you want to use.

Sometimes, you'll run into problems when you are trying to read the CD-ROM with the Oracle software, because of display issues. For example, you may get the error "Cannot open display." You may then have to use the following command to get rid of the problems:

```
$ xhost +prod1
```

TIP *It may be a good idea to incorporate as many of the environment variables as possible in the .profile file in the user oracle's home directory. This way, when you log in as the user oracle, the variables will already be in force in your shell.*

Setting Other Variables

You will need to set some other variables. The ORA_NLS33 variable specifies the location for files defining languages, territories, and other related settings. This directory should be set to $ORACLE_HOME/ocommon/nls/admin/data. The ORACLE_BASE variable refers to the root directory for all Oracle software and administrative files, and in this case you should set it to /prod1/app/oracle.

A Final Checklist for the Installation

To ensure that your Oracle9*i* installation won't abort in the middle, make sure you satisfy the following requirements:

- Make sure you have enough temporary space. Temporary space on most UNIX servers is usually a small amount, something like 100MB or so. If your system is like this, your Oracle9*i* installation will fail midway through, because Oracle uses the temp directory on the server heavily during the installation process. You have two ways to get around this problem. You can either ask your system administrator to increase the size of the temporary directory on the server or just change the environment variable for the temporary directory. Usually, you do this by setting the environment variable TEMPDIR to something other than /tmp and making sure that there is at least 400MB of space under this "temporary" directory. Here's how I "changed" my temporary space during the Oracle installation:

```
$ export TMPDIR=/test01/app/oracle/tmp
$ export    TMP=/test01/app/oracle/tmp
```

- Make sure the swap space is set to a high amount, at the minimum satisfying Oracle's requirements specified in the operating system–specific installation guide. Although Oracle recommends that swap be about three times your RAM, you don't literally have to follow this recommendation on systems with large Oracle RAM allocation. Make sure you allocate about 500MB to avoid any swapping or paging problems on the server.

- Make sure your Oracle kernel is modified to meet your installation requirements. Even if you install the server software correctly, if the kernel parameters such as SHMMAX and SEMMNS are not set high enough, your database creation will fail if you have a large number of processes in your initialization file.

- Set the DISPLAY variable properly so the Oracle Installer will come up correctly. If you're installing the Oracle software directly on the server, then you need to change the DISPLAY variable on the server. If you're installing remotely from a client, you need to set the variable on the client. In most cases, a command such as the following would do the trick in terms of setting up your display correctly. (Note that the "0.0" at the end of the line follows the IP address of your sever or client machine.)

```
$ export DISPLAY=< Your IP address>:0.0
```

- Sometimes when you are working on workstation, you will be unable to use the X Window emulation on the machine, which means the Oracle Universal Installer cannot function in the GUI mode. In these circumstances, use the *xhost* command in a window on the workstation. Here's an example:

```
$ xhost  +workstation_name
```

- Make sure that you mount the installation CD-ROM correctly. Just follow your operating system–specific installation guide for the correct CD-ROM installation commands. For example, on a Linux system, the following command will install the CD-ROM:

```
$ su root
$ mkdir /cdrom
$ mount -t is9660 /dev/cdrom/cdrom
$ exit
```

Installing the Oracle Software

Once you have finished all the preinstallation work, you are ready to install the
Oracle9*i* software on your machine. You can install directly from the Oracle
software distribution or you can install from your hard drive. I find it easy to install
from the CD-ROM itself. Your system administrator should be able to mount the
CD-ROM easily for you. A standard mount point such as /cdrom/cdrom0 is
advisable. Once the CD-ROM is mounted, you can see the files on it under
the CD-ROM mount point at which it was mounted on your system. You can
install the Oracle9*i* software from the software CD directly, but Oracle recommends that you perform the installation from a directory on your system. In
several versions of UNIX, the CD-ROMs load automatically, but sometimes you
may have to use an explicit command such as the following to mount the CD-ROM:

```
$ mount -r -F hsfs  device_name/cdrom
```

In the installation example that follows, I used an HP UNIX–specific Oracle9*i*
version 9.2.0.1.0 software that I downloaded from the Oracle Web site. The
download site gives clear instructions on how to download and install the software
on different operating systems, including Windows versions. Once you have
downloaded the software, you need to use either the gunzip (gzip) utility on UNIX
or the WinZip utility on Windows before you can install the software. Usually, the
downloaded files for most UNIX systems have to be unzipped using a utility such
as gunzip, and then you can unpack the distribution using the cpio utility. I omit
the specific steps involved in uncompressing and unzipping the installation files,
but the download window tells you exactly what to do to get the installation
started. After you have unzipped the downloaded files or after you have mounted
the CD-ROM to the appropriate directory, go to the $MOUNT_POINT/Disk1
directory. You'll see a directory structure similar to the following:

```
oracle@finance1  [/test01/app/oracle/load/Disk1]
[finance1] $ ls -altr
total 26
-rwxr-xr-x  1 oracle    dba          651 Mar 13  2001 runInstaller
drwxr-xr-x  2 oracle    dba           96 May  6  2001 lsm
drwxr-xr-x  4 oracle    dba           96 May 23  2001 install
drwxr-xr-x  2 oracle    dba         1024 May 30  2001 response
drwxr-xr-x  7 oracle    dba         1024 Jun  1  2001 stage
drwxrwxr-x  2 oracle    dba           96 Jun  1  2001 oidupgrade
-rwxrwxr-x  1 oracle    dba         5921 Jun  1  2001 index.htm
drwxrwxr-x  5 oracle    dba         1024 Jun  4  2001 doc
drwxr-xr-x  5 oracle    dba         1024 Mar 21 09:06 ..
drwxr-xr-x  8 oracle    dba         1024 Mar 23 12:06 .
```

You need to execute the runInstaller script to bring up the Oracle Universal Installer GUI, which will enable you to install the Oracle software. You can use the runInstaller and the Oracle Universal Installer not only for this initial installation of the Oracle9*i* software, but also for modifications and additions to the initial software configuration. Always ensure your system administrator is nearby to help you out, because you may need help with setting the DISPLAY for the Installer GUI, or you may run into unforeseen space or file privilege problems. You'll also need the administrator to run the root.sh script toward the end as the root user.

TIP *Make sure you have enough space in the temporary directory, as the Oracle Installer creates a lot of files in this directory installation. Your installation may stop in the middle and you'll have to restart it if this happens. About 400MB to 500MB of space in the /tmp directory should be available for the Oracle Installer's use during the installation process.*

Then, as the user oracle, run the following set of commands:

```
$ cd /cdrom_mountpoint_directory
$  ./runInstaller
```

At this point, assuming there are no problems with the DISPLAY variable settings, the GUI version of the Oracle Universal Installer should show up. If the GUI doesn't show up on your screen, you probably have to adjust your DISPLAY variable. If you need to abort the installation and start over fresh, you need to first go to your temporary directory and remove all files that were created by the Oracle Universal Installer. Only then will you be able to reinvoke the Oracle Universal Installer. The following is the series of screens and prompts during a typical Oracle9*i* installation:

1. When the Welcome screen appears, as shown in Figure 4-1, click Next. If this is not a fresh release of Oracle software, the installer will give you the opportunity to uninstall some of the installed software.

2. The File Locations window appears next, as shown in Figure 4-2. There are two directories that you are required to select now. The first one is called the Source, which is the location of the installation files. If you're installing from the CD-ROM, as you're doing now, the Source window will display the full path of your CD-ROM mount point and you don't have to do anything. The second directory is the Destination directory. Here, you select the full path of the ORACLE_HOME that you chose earlier. In your case, it will be /test01/app/oracle/product/9.2.0.1.0. Click Next. You'll see a small rectangular bar filling up in the upper-right corner. This indicates that the Installer is loading the product list. This will take about 3 or 4 minutes. When the product list is loaded, click Next.

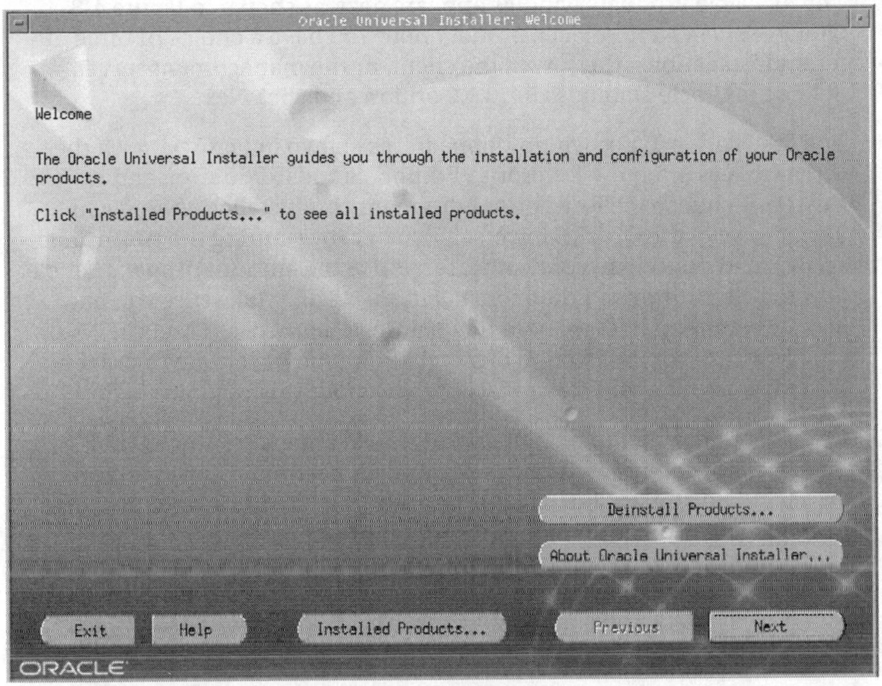

Figure 4-1. The Welcome screen

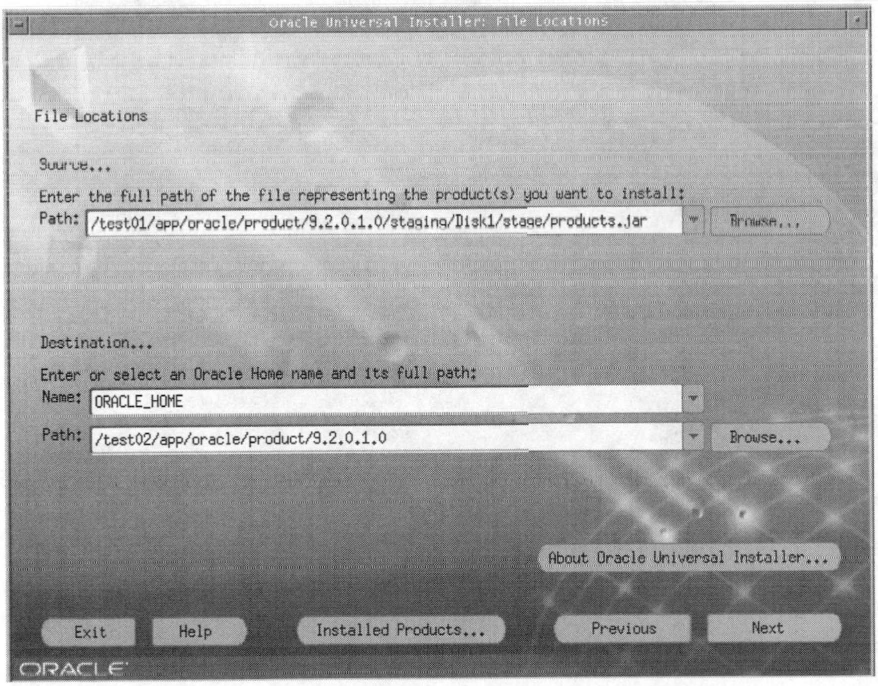

Figure 4-2. The File Locations window

3. The Available Products window appears next, as shown in Figure 4-3. Oracle wants you to select a product now. You have a choice of three different installations: the server, the client, or the management server. Select the Oracle Database 9.2.0.1.0 option and click Next.

4. The Installation Types window appears, as shown in Figure 4-4. Of the three choices offered—Enterprise Edition, Standard Edition, and Custom—choose the Enterprise Edition for this installation. You can always invoke the Oracle Universal Installer (by running the runInstaller script), and customize your software. Notice the amount of space Oracle lists for the Enterprise Edition installation: 3.7GB. Make sure you have at least this amount of disk space free before you proceed. Then click Next. Oracle will do some selection of installation types internally, a process that takes about a minute or so. Click Next once this is completed.

5. Next, the Component Locations window will appear, as shown in Figure 4-5. This window simply shows you where the components of the Oracle9i software will be installed and lets you provide alternative locations for the installation of these components.

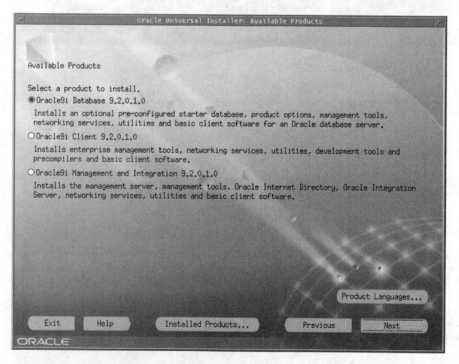

Figure 4-3. The Available Products window

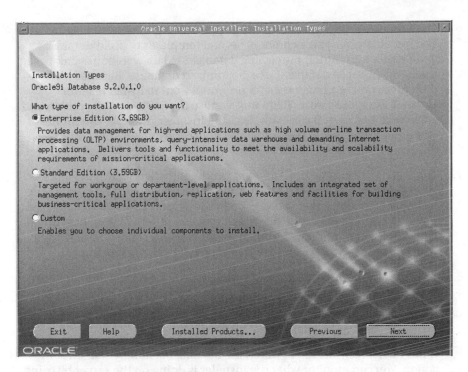

Figure 4-4. The Installation Types window

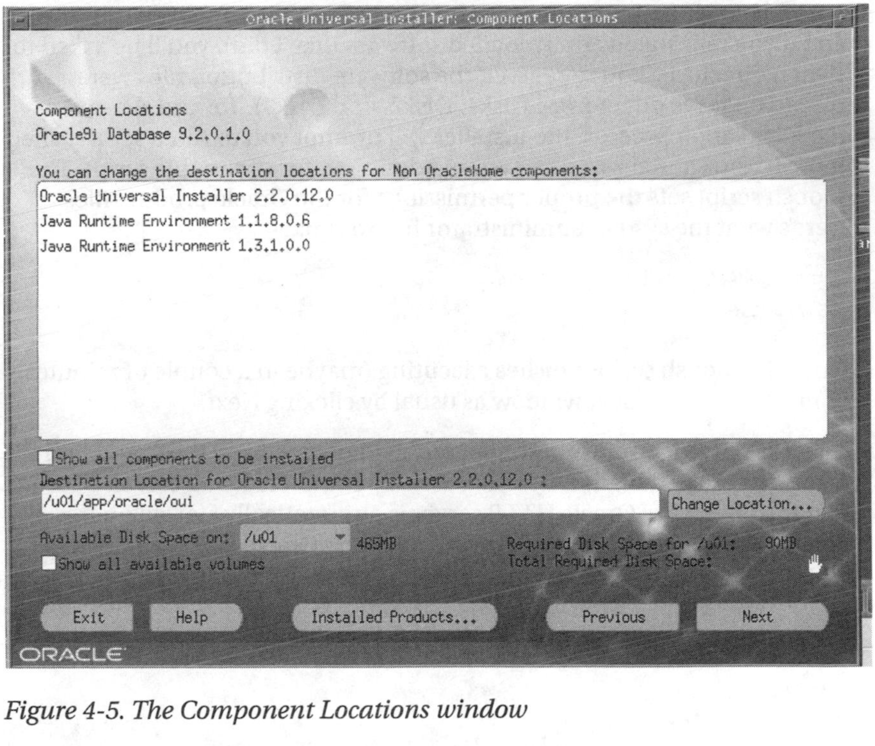

Figure 4-5. The Component Locations window

6. The Database Configuration window appears next, as shown in Figure 4-6. The Installer gives you a choice of several templates to build a starter database: a transaction processing database, a data warehouse database, a general-purpose database, or a customized database. Because it's not difficult to create a database later on, you'll want to install just the Oracle9i Server software. To do this, choose the Software Only option and click Next. Before you can click Next, the Installer prompts you for the location for the Oracle JDK software. I chose the default /opt/java1.3 directory on my server for this location.

7. The Installer brings up the Summary window, which is shown in Figure 4-7. Here, you can see a list of all the products that will be installed (and uninstalled) during the Oracle Enterprise Edition installation. Notice that the Installer again presents the estimated space requirement and how much free space you have in the installation directory you chose earlier. After you verify that you have enough free space, click the Install button.

8. The Install window appears, as shown in Figure 4-8. The window shows the components as each one is installed on your server. On the bottom of this screen, you'll also find the directory name where the installation log is being written to. For example, on my HP server, the installation log was written to the /u01/app/oracle/orainventory/logs directory. It can sometimes be nerve-wracking to watch the Installer seemingly stall on some action. You can monitor what the Installer is doing on the server by using the *tail* command and monitoring the previously mentioned log file in a separate window. This process will run for about an hour and a half or two hours. You will be prompted for the other CDs in the Oracle distribution, and if you're installing downloaded software (like I did), you'll be asked to switch directories (on my server, the software distribution files were placed on three directories: Disk1, Disk2, and Disk3). Toward the end of the installation process, the Installer will prompt you to run a script called root.sh. You should ask your system administrator to run this script. The root.sh script sets the proper permissions for the Oracle product files. Here's what the system administrator has to run:

```
$ cd $ORACLE_HOME
$ ./root.sh
```

9. Once the root.sh script finishes executing (maybe in a couple of minutes at most), go to the next window as usual by clicking Next.

10. The final installation window appears, as shown in Figure 4-9, and indicates that the installation was successfully completed. You can also see in Figure 4-9 that the Oracle HTTP server is automatically started on the default port settings. At this point, you exit the Oracle Universal Installer. Your Oracle server installation is now complete.

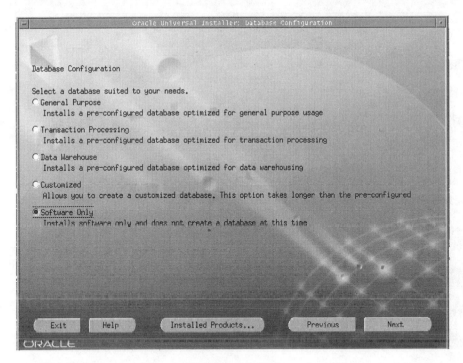

Figure 4-6. The Database Configuration window

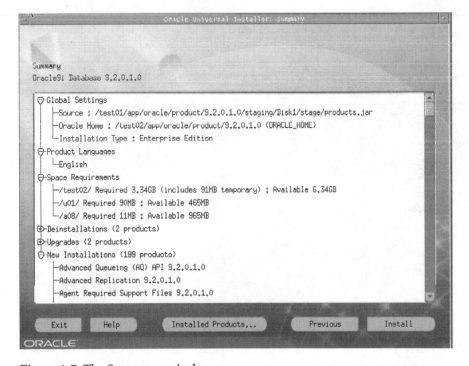

Figure 4-7. The Summary window

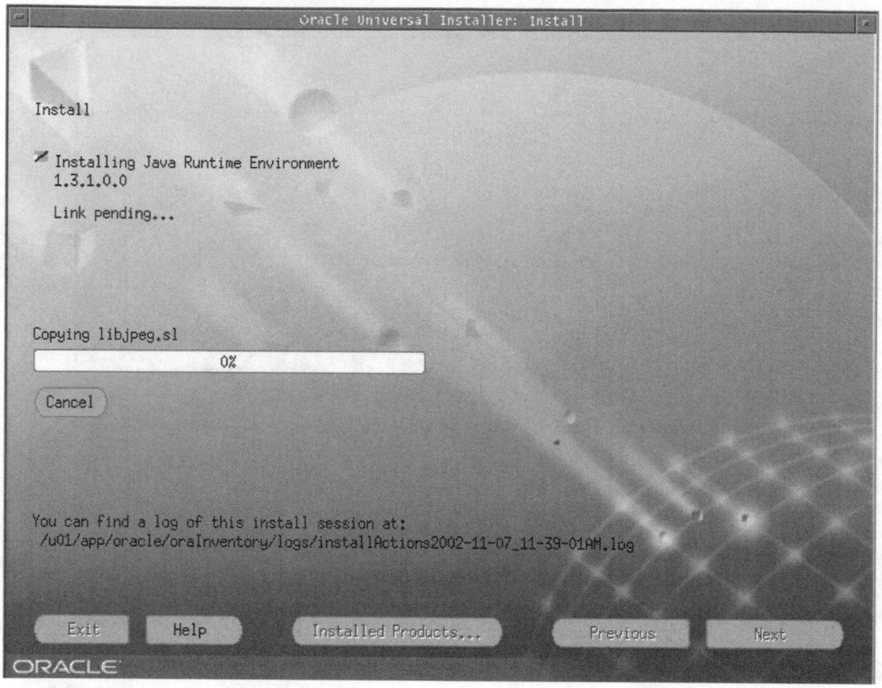

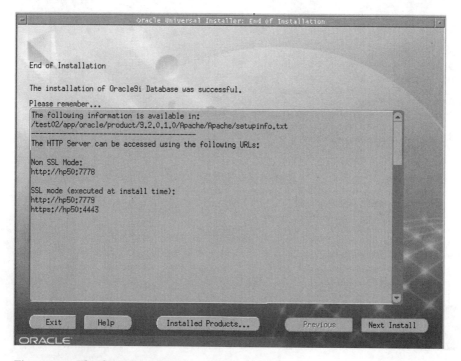

Figure 4-8. The Install window

Figure 4-9. The final installation window

Running the Installer in "Silent" Mode

You can also perform an Oracle installation in the so-called silent mode—that is, in a mode that doesn't require any response or input from the person who is installing the software. Why would you want to do this? Well, there may be a situation where you can't be there for an installation physically. In such circumstances, you can create a *response file,* which will let you perform the installation in a noninteractive mode. The response file will contain the responses to the questions asked by the Oracle Installer. Response files could be very useful for client installations, where you can't physically visit and install the software on all the different client servers.

If you're doing multiple installations of the same product(s), the "silent" installation approach will ensure uniformity and consistency in the product installation. This is particularly useful when you're working in an organization that has multiple geographical locations and client installations are required, but perhaps there are no skilled database personnel at a specific location. Oracle supplies different response files for the installation of various types of software. In the test installation that I describe in this sidebar, Oracle installed the response files in the following directory: /test01/app/oracle/product/9.2.0.1.0/staging/Disk1/response. Here's a list of some of the important response files Oracle provides:

- *Enterprise.rsp:* Oracle9*i* Enterprise version

- *Standard.rsp:* Oracle9*i* Standard version

- *Oid.rsp:* Oracle Internet Directory installation

- *Clientruntime.rsp:* Oracle9*i* client software installation

- *Netca.rsp:* Oracle Net Configuration Assistant

- *Emca.rsp:* Oracle Enterprise Manager Configuration

The response file for the Enterprise edition installation is copied from the CD-ROM during installation, along with the other files and scripts. It's located in a separate directory called response, which is located in the same directory as the runInstaller executable file. You need to copy the response file to a directory on your own system and edit it according to your needs. The editing of the response file may take some time, but it's well worth it if you're planning multiple installations.

Once you've edited the response file, you can start the automatic silent installation by using the following command. Make sure you set your DISPLAY variable correctly before using the silent mode for installation.

```
$ cd $CDROM_mount_directory
$ ./runInstaller -silent -responseFile <response file name>
```

This command will run the Oracle Installer in the silent automatic mode. It will use all the configuration choices you selected by modifying the response file.

When Oracle finishes the silent installation, it will display the following message on the screen:

```
The installation of Oracle9i database was successful.
Please check /u01/app/oracle/oraInventory/logs
/silentInstall.log for more details.
```

At this point, you need to manually run the root.sh script, just as you would in the normal manual installation procedure. You'll find the root.sh script in the /u01/app/oracle/product/9.2.0.1.0 directory. After the root.sh script runs successfully, you're done with the silent installation of Oracle. Of course, you still have to create the database(s) and configure the networking components.

Oracle provides a whole set of response files for several types of installations, including server and client installations. You may have occasions when you need to instruct someone to install the software in a remote location. The response file will basically enable you to automate the installation, with very little human intervention. In reality, you'll probably use the Oracle client response file more frequently, because it makes it unnecessary for you to physically visit all the client stations that need to have their client installations done. Here's the Oracle 9.0.1.0.0 Enterprise response file, with all the options listed:

```
###########################################################
##    Oracle9i Enterprise Edition Install Response File Template    ##
## Copyright(c) Oracle Corporation 1998,2000. All rights reserved.##
## Specify values for the variables listed below to customize      ##
## your installation.
## Each variable is associated with a comment. The comment         ##
## identifies the variable type.
## Please specify the values in the following format
##         Type          Example
##         String        "Sample Value"
##         Boolean       True or False
##         Number        1000
##         StringList    {"String value 1","String Value 2"}       ##
## The values that are given as <Value Required> need to be        ##
## specified for a silent installation to be successful.
## This response file is generated by Oracle Software
## Packager.
##########################################[General]
RESPONSEFILE_VERSION=1.7.0
[SESSION]
Name:  UNIX_GROUP_NAME
# Datatype      : String
# Description   : UNIX group which will have write permissions on the
#                 installer inventory directory
# Valid values  : Any UNIX group to which the current user belongs
# Example value : "oinstall"
# Default value : None
# Mandatory     : No
```

```
UNIX_GROUP_NAME=<Value Unspecified>
# Name          : FROM_LOCATION
# Datatype      : String
# Description   : Complete path of the products.jar file from the staging area
#                 containing products to install
# Valid values  : Full path ending in "products.jar"
# Example value : "/cdrom/oracle9i/stage/products.jar"
# Default value : "../stage/products.jar"
# Mandatory     : No
FROM_LOCATION_CD_LABEL=<Value Unspecified>
NEXT_SESSION_RESPONSE=<Value Unspecified>
ORACLE_HOME=<Value Required>
TOPLEVEL_COMPONENT={"oracle.server","9.0.1.0.0"}
SHOW_SPLASH_SCREEN=false
SHOW_WELCOME_PAGE=false
SHOW_COMPONENT_LOCATIONS_PAGE=false
SHOW_CUSTOM_TREE_PAGE=false
SHOW_SUMMARY_PAGE=true
SHOW_INSTALL_PROGRESS_PAGE=true
SHOW_REQUIRED_CONFIG_TOOL_PAGE=true
SHOW_OPTIONAL_CONFIG_TOOL_PAGE=false
SHOW_RELEASE_NOTES=false
SHOW_ROOTSH_CONFIRMATION=true
SHOW_END_SESSION_PAGE=false
SHOW_EXIT_CONFIRMATION=false
NEXT_SESSION=false
NEXT_SESSION_ON_FAIL=false
CD images to the hard disk.
LOCATION_FOR_DISK2=<Value Required>
LOCATION_FOR_DISK3=<Value Required>
INSTALL_TYPE="Enterprise Edition"
s_cfgtyperet=<Value Unspecified>
sl_userNodeList=<Value Unspecified>
sl_dbaOperGroups=<Value Unspecified>
s_rawDeviceName=<Value Unspecified>
s_jservPort=<Value Unspecified>
s_apachePort=<Value Unspecified>
b_autoStartApache=<Value Unspecified>
OPTIONAL_CONFIG_TOOLS={"dbca"}
s_globalDBName=<Value Required>
s_dbSid=<Value Required>
s_mountPoint=<Value Unspecified>
sample value : "Use Unicode (UTF8) as the character set"
s_dbRetChoice=<Value Unspecified>
OPTIONAL_CONFIG_TOOLS={"netca"}
s_responseFileName=<Value Unspecified>
```

....

After the Installation

After you've installed the Oracle Server software, you still have some chores left to do. You need to perform these postinstallation steps carefully to make sure that the software functions correctly. As in the case of the installation procedures, the system administrator and the user oracle are responsible for various tasks. Let's look at the important tasks that the system administrator and the user oracle must perform after the server software installation is finished.

UNIX Post-Installation Tasks

The UNIX administrator has to perform the following tasks after the installation of Oracle software is complete.

Shutdown and Start-up Scripts

The Oracle software comes with sample automatic start-up and shutdown scripts, which are located in the $ORACLE_HOME/bin directory. The automatic start-up and shutdown of the Oracle database upon the booting up and shutting down of the server ensures that the database is always closed cleanly and you don't have to manually bring up the database after system crashes.

In most versions of UNIX, the contents of the file /etc/oratab will determine whether your database will automatically start-up or shutdown each time the server starts up and shuts down. The /etc/oratab file is simply a list of the databases running on a server, each with a yes or no indicator for automatic start-up/shutdown. If you're creating a new database finance1 and you want to automate the start-up/shutdown for it, here's what you need to add to the oratab file:

```
finance1:/a03/app/oracle/product/9.2.0.1.0:Y
```

The entry in the /etc/oratab file has three components: the database name, the Oracle home location, and whether the database should be automatically started up (and shutdown). If you want automatic start-up/shutdown, you specify *Y* at the end of the line; otherwise, you specify *N*.

The UNIX administrator must add the database start-up and shutdown script to the system start-up and shutdown scripts. For example, on a HP UNIX system, the rc scripts (in the /sbin directory) are run automatically whenever the system moves from one run level to the other. When the system moves to run level 0 (shutdown), the rc script halts the UNIX system by stopping certain daemons and server processes. Similarly, when the run level changes from 0 to 1, the rc script starts the system by starting the necessary daemons and server processes. The system administrator has to include Oracle-related information in the /sbin/rc script to automate the shutdown and start-up of the Oracle databases whenever the UNIX server stops and starts for any reason. Listings 4-1 and 4-2 show some examples of the information that the system administrator needs to add to the rc script. The script will determine whether to use the start-up or shutdown scripts after testing the system run levels.

Listing 4-1. Start-up Information

```
/u01/app/oracle/product/9.2.0.1.0/bin/dbstart_finance1
/u01/app/oracle/product/9.2.0.1.0/bin/lsnrctl start
```

Listing 4-2. Shutdown Information

```
/u01/app/oracle/product/9.2.0.1.0/bin/dbstop_finance1
/u01/app/oracle/product/9.2.0.1.0/bin/lsnrctl start
```

Creating Additional UNIX Accounts

After the installation is complete, the UNIX system administrator must create any other necessary user accounts. All the DBA users must be part of the OSDBA group.

User Oracle Post-Installation Tasks

The user oracle (the username you used to install the Oracle software under) has a set of tasks to perform after the server software installation is complete. These include setting the correct environment, applying any necessary Oracle patches, and setting the initialization parameters. Let's look at the user oracle's post-installation tasks in more detail in the following sections.

Setting the Environment

Your installation tasks are not yet over when you complete the installation of the server software. Before you can create a database on your system, you need to set some environment variables. The most important environment variables that you need to set are the ORACLE_HOME, ORACLE_SID, TNS_ADMIN, CLASS_PATH, TWO_TASK, and LD_LIBRARY_PATH variables. Please refer to your operating system–specific guidelines before you set these and other environmental variables.

As the user oracle, you also need to initialize the oraenv script (the coraenv script if you're using the C shell). This script lets you ensure a common environment for all Oracle users. The oraenv script is initialized by including it in the .login or .profile file. For example, for a single-instance database in the Korn shell, this is what you need to add to your .login or .profile file:

```
ORAENV_ASK=NO
. /usr/local/bin/oraenv
```

Miscellaneous Tasks

You need to perform some additional tasks as the user oracle. After the installation of the Oracle9*i* server software is complete, make sure you check the patch directory on your CD-ROM and apply any available patches. You also need to ensure that your databases are a part of the /etc/oratab file, so they can be automatically started up and shut down. Back up the root.sh script, as it may be overwritten during additional Oracle product installations.

The Oratab File

The oratab file, which is usually located in the /etc directory on UNIX systems, is useful for several reasons. First, you can use this file to specify whether you want automatic start/stop procedures in place for your databases. Second, oraenv reads the contents of the /etc/oratab file during the setting of the environment variables. The oratab file is also very handy when you have multiple Oracle instances on your server. For example, if you want to back up all the databases on the server in sequence, you can use the oratab file to provide a list of all the databases the backup script must include.

Setting Initialization Parameters

You, of course, have to edit the sample initialization file and modify it for your needs. After you create the database, make sure you create an SPFILE, which is a more sophisticated way of managing your initialization parameters than the traditional init.ora file.

Configuring Oracle Net

To enable connectivity to the database, you must configure Oracle Net. Configuration tasks include starting the listener process or, if the listener is already running on the server, making sure your databases are registered with it. Note that in Oracle9*i*, when you create a database, it automatically registers with the listener. Because you have not yet created any databases on your server, you don't have to configure the network connections. You'll learn all about connectivity in Chapter 11, when you deal with Oracle Net.

Uninstalling Oracle

Sometimes, your installation process may get messed up in the middle, or a lack of disk space may force you to abort the installation abruptly. What do you do? The best thing would be to simply uninstall all the components that you have already installed. You can install again from scratch when you are ready. Here are the simple steps you need to follow to uninstall the Oracle software:

1. Run the Oracle Universal Installer and select the Deinstall Products option. Click all product headings that the Installer presents you in the Inventory screen. Click the Remove button.

2. Remove all the directories under the Oracle home directory.

You need to take a few additional steps for a Windows uninstall, including making changes to the Windows Registry. You'll learn about these changes in Chapter 22, after I discuss Oracle9*i* installation on Windows systems.

Summary

This chapter took you through an Oracle9*i* server software installation exercise. The amazing thing is, whether it is a 1-user Oracle Windows database or a 1,000-user multiterabyte OLTP behemoth, the software is installed in exactly the same way and the installation process takes just about the same amount of time. Of course, large installations require significantly more planning.

Your system administrator is an invaluable ally in the installation process. Be sure to bring your system administrator into the picture early on, and make your configuration needs clear to him or her so the installation is a smooth process. The response files are not heavily used for server installations, but I gave you an example of how to use them so you know they're available to you as a valid option for some types of installations.

I hope that one of the main points you take away from this chapter is that a successful Oracle installation depends on adequate preparation *before* you install the software. Do make sure you carefully read the Oracle installation manuals as well as the README notes for the specific version you are installing. The post-installation tasks are vital for proper functioning of both the software and the databases that you'll create later. Time spent doing these postinstallation tasks carefully will pay off later on when you're using the databases.

Introduction to the Oracle9*i* Architecture

IN THIS CHAPTER, you'll learn about the fundamental structures of the Oracle9*i* database. I explain in detail the various logical and physical components of the Oracle database and introduce the basic building blocks of the Oracle database: extents, segments, and tablespaces. I also explain the conceptual underpinnings of the Oracle database management system. You'll learn the difference between an Oracle database and an Oracle instance, and you'll understand the way Oracle uses memory. You'll also discover how the Oracle server performs transaction processing, and you'll cover the concepts behind many of the key Oracle database features.

To understand how the Oracle database works, you need to understand several concepts, including transaction processing, undo management, optimization of SQL queries, and the importance of the data dictionary. This chapter introduces several of these important topics. Later chapters build on the general ideas introduced in this chapter.

Oracle Database Structures

Before you delve deep into the logical and physical structures that make up an Oracle database, I would like to clarify the difference between an Oracle instance and an Oracle database. It is very common for people to use the terms interchangeably, but they refer to different things altogether.

An *Oracle database* consists of not only your data files, but also many other files. You can see right away that your data will be of no use to you unless you can access it, change it, and add to it. You interact with these files with the help of the operating system. The operating system provides you with processing capabilities and resources, such as memory, to enable you to manipulate the data on the disk drives. When you combine the specific set of processes created by Oracle on the server with the memory allocated to it by the operating system, you get the *Oracle instance*.

Many times, you'll hear people remarking that the database is "up," though what they really mean is that the instance is "up." The database itself, in the form of the set of physical files it's composed of, is of no use if the instance is not up and running. The instance performs all the necessary work for the database.

Three major components on a server machine are relevant to the performance of an Oracle database: the central processing unit (CPU), the disk storage system, and random access memory (RAM). (The network that connects users and the server is also important, but that's not a part of the server, per se.)

Although an Oracle database's performance depends on all three operating system components, most of the time you'll be tuning the database performance by tuning the memory and disk storage components. There isn't a whole lot to tune in terms of the CPU. You make your initial decisions based on your organization's needs and the available finances, and purchase the server with the requisite number of processors (24 Intel 1.05 GHz processors, for example). Once you buy the CPU, you're pretty much done as far as tweaking and adjusting it, unless you realize there's a CPU bottleneck and you upgrade the number and/or the speed of your processors. The other two components, disk space and memory, are a different ballgame altogether. You will often face the need to tune and adjust several configuration parameters related to these two components.

You can approach the structures of the Oracle databases based on the distinction between physical and logical structures. You don't take all the data belonging to the tables of an Oracle database and just put it on disk somewhere on the operating system storage system. Oracle uses a sophisticated logical view of the internal database structures that help in storing and managing data properly on the physical data files. This logical defining of Oracle's database structure has another fundamental motive behind it. By organizing space into logical structures and assigning these logical entities to users of the database, Oracle databases achieve the logical separation of users (owners of the database objects, such as tables) of the database from the physical manifestations of the database in terms of data files and so forth. The next section covers how Oracle logically partitions its databases and maps these logical parts to the physical components of the database.

The Logical Structures

Oracle9*i* uses a set of logical database storage structures to use disk space, whether the database uses operating system files or "raw" database files. These logical structures, which primarily include tablespaces, segments, extents, and blocks, control the allocation and use of the "physical" space allocated to the Oracle database. Note that Oracle database objects such as tables, indexes, views, sequences, and others are also logical entities. These logical objects make up the relational design of the database, which I discuss in detail later on.

You can look at the logical composition of Oracle databases from either a top-down viewpoint or a bottom-up viewpoint. Let's use the bottom-up approach by first looking at the smallest logical components of an Oracle database and progressively move up to the largest entities. Before you begin learning about the logical components, remember that Oracle database objects such as tables, indexes, and packaged SQL code are actually logical entities. Taken together, a set of related database logical objects is called a *schema*. Dividing a database's objects among various schemas promotes ease of management and a higher level of security.

The Oracle *data block* is the foundation of the database storage hierarchy. The Oracle data block is the basis of all database storage in an Oracle database. Two or more contiguous Oracle data blocks form an *extent*. A set of extents that you allocate to a table or an index (or some other object) is termed a *segment*. A *tablespace* is a set of one or more data files, and it usually consists of related segments. The following sections explore each of these logical database structures in detail.

Data Blocks

The smallest logical component of an Oracle database is a *data block*. Data blocks are defined in terms of operating system bytes, and they are the smallest unit of space allocation in an Oracle database. For example, you can size an Oracle data block in units of 2KB, 4KB, 8KB, 16KB, or 32KB (or ever larger chunks). It is common to refer to the data blocks as *Oracle blocks*.

The storage disks on which the Oracle blocks reside are themselves divided into *disk blocks*, which are areas of contiguous storage containing a certain number of bytes—for example, 4096 or 32768 bytes (4KB or 32KB, because each kilobyte has 1024 bytes). Note that if the Oracle block size is smaller than the operating system file system buffer size, you may be wasting the capacity of the operating system to read and write larger chunks of data for each I/O. Ideally, the Oracle block size should be a multiple of the operating system block size. On an HP-UX system, for example, if you set your Oracle block size to a multiple of the operating system block size, you gain 5 percent in performance.

How Big Should the Block Size Be?

You, as the DBA, have to make the decision on how big your Oracle block should be by providing the value for the *db_block size* parameter in your Oracle initialization file (called the *init.ora file*). If you choose the common Oracle block size of 8KB, that means your block has 8192 bytes. Note that your UNIX system may very well have its own block size, usually about 64KB or so. Think of the block size as the minimum unit for conducting Oracle's business of updating, selecting, or inserting data. In Chapter 9, which discusses the creation of Oracle databases, you'll learn a lot more about the Oracle database block size and the criteria for choosing the appropriate block size.

NOTE *The Oracle database block size depends what you're going to do with your database. For example, a small block size is useful if you're working with small rows where you're doing a lot of index lookups. However, the downside to a small block size is that the number of concurrent changes can be limited. Larger block sizes are useful in report applications when you're doing large table scans. Those coming to Oracle from SQL Server can think of a block as being the same as the page size.*

You allocate space to new databases in the form of operating system data files, which you will assign to specific tablespaces. When you run out of space or you are about to reach the space limits, you add more space to your database in units of operating system bytes. Note that although you add space in terms of bytes, Oracle itself uses the concept of Oracle blocks to manage the space within the data files. When a user selects data from a table, the select operation will "read," or fetch, data from the database files in units of Oracle blocks. The Oracle blocks usually are a multiple of the operating system block size. All data blocks can be divided into two main parts: the row data portion and the free space portion. (There are other, smaller areas such as overhead and header space for maintenance purposes also.)

The *row data* section of data blocks consists of the data pertaining to the tables or their indexes. The *free space* section is the free space left in the Oracle block for insertion of new data or for extension of rows that are already placed in the block.

Oracle9*i* lets you use either a manual or an automatic mode to manage the free space available in the data blocks. Note that it's important for the Oracle database server to manage the free space in the data blocks, so it doesn't waste a great deal of space in the Oracle blocks in all the different types of segments.

Multiple Oracle Block Sizes

The initialization parameter *db_size* determines the size of the Oracle data block in the database. Unlike previous Oracle database versions, Oracle9*i* lets you specify up to four additional *nonstandard* block sizes in addition to the *standard* block size. Thus, you can have a total of five different block sizes in an Oracle9*i* database. For example, you can have 2KB, 4KB, 8KB, 16KB, and 32KB block sizes all within the same database. If you choose to configure multiple Oracle block sizes, you must also configure corresponding subcaches in the buffer cache of the System Global Area (SGA, Oracle's memory allocation), as you'll see shortly. Multiple data block sizes aren't always necessary, and you'll do just fine with one standard Oracle block size.

The use of multiple Oracle block sizes in a database means that you can create tablespaces with different block sizes in the database. When you create a tablespace, you can specify the block size for that tablespace. The System tablespace will always have the standard block size. Chapter 7 shows you how to create tablespaces.

What's Inside a Data Block?

Sometimes it may be useful to find out exactly what data is on a particular block or to find out which block has a particular piece of data. Can you actually "see" what's inside a data block? You sure can, by "dumping" the block contents. Oracle blocks can be dumped at the operating system level (referred to as *binary dumps*), and you can also perform Oracle-formatted block dumps.

The most common reason for performing a block dump, of course, is to investigate *block corruption*, which may be caused by operating system or Oracle software errors, hardware defects, and memory and I/O caching problems. Oracle does have tools that can help you restore data from corrupted data blocks. In addition, you can adopt several other strategies to recover from data block corruption; you'll learn about these strategies in Chapter 15.

Let's look at an example that shows how to see what's actually in an Oracle data block. First, find out which data file and data block you want to dump. Listing 5-1 shows the query that enables you to find out the file and block IDs.

Listing 5-1. Query to Find Out the File and Block IDs

```
SQL> SELECT  SEGMENT_NAME,
2       FILE_ID,
3       BLOCK_ID
4       FROM  DBA_EXTENTS
5     WHERE  OWNER = 'OE'
6*    AND  SEGMENT_NAME LIKE 'ORDERS%'
SQL> /
SEGMENT_NAME                    FILE_ID   BLOCK_ID
----------------------- ---------- ----------
ORDERS                        5        345
SQL>
```

Next, issue the following command to get a dump of the file and block you need:

```
SQL> alter system dump datafile 5 block 345;
System altered.
SQL>
```

This command will produce the block dump shown in Listing 5-2 in the default trace directory of the Oracle database. Listing 5-2 shows the (partial) output of the block dump command.

Listing 5-2. A Sample Block Dump

```
*** 2002-11-13 06:41:15.000
*** SESSION ID:(10.3503) 2002-11-13 06:41:15.000
Start dump data blocks tsn: 5 file#: 5 minblk 345 maxblk 345
buffer tsn: 5 rdba: 0x01400159 (5/345)
scn: 0x0000.00026940 seq: 0x04 flg: 0x04 tail: 0x69402004
frmt: 0x02 chkval: 0x665e type: 0x20=FIRST LEVEL BITMAP BLOCK
Dump of First Level Bitmap Block
```

Extents

When you combine several contiguous data blocks, you get an *extent*. Remember that you can allocate an extent only if you can find enough contiguous data blocks. Your choice of tablespace type will determine how the Oracle database allocates the extents. The traditional dictionary-managed tablespaces allow you to specify both the beginning allocation of space and further increments as needed.

All database objects are allocated an initial amount of space, called the *initial extent*, when they are created. When you create an object, you specify the size of the next and subsequent extents as well as the maximum number of extents for that object, in the object creation statement. Once allocated to a table or index, the extents remain allocated to the particular object, unless you drop the object from the database, at which time the space will revert to the pool of allocatable free space in the database.

The locally managed tablespaces (explained later in this chapter) use the simpler method of allocating a uniform extent size, which is chosen automatically by the database. Therefore, you don't have to worry about setting the actual sizes for future allocation of extents to any particular tablespace.

Segments

A set of extents forms the next higher unit of data storage, the *segment*. In an Oracle database you can store different kinds of objects, such as tables and indexes, as you'll see in the next few chapters. Oracle calls all the space allocated to any particular database object a segment. That is, if you have a table called customer, you simply refer to the space you allocate to it as the "customer segment."

Each object in the database has its own segment. For example, the customer table is associated with the customer segment. When you create a table called customer, Oracle will create a new segment named customer also and allocate a certain number of extents to it based on the table creation specifications for the customer table. When you create an index, it will have its own segment named after the index name.

You can have several types of segments, with the most common being the *data segment* and the *index segment*. Any space you allocate to these two types of segments will remain intact even if you *truncate* (remove all rows) a table, for example, as long as the object is part of the database. However, as you'll see later on, there's something called a *temporary tablespace* in Oracle, and Oracle deallocates the temporary segments as soon the transactions or sessions that are using the segments are completed.

Tablespaces

A *tablespace* is defined as the combination of a set of related segments. For example, all the data segments belonging to the out-of-town sales team can be grouped into a tablespace called out_of_town_sales. You can have other segments belonging to other types of data in the same tablespace, but usually you try to keep related information together in the same tablespace. Note that the tablespace is a purely logical construct, and it is the primary logical structure of an Oracle database. All tablespaces need not be of the same size within a database. For example, it is quite common to have tablespaces that are 100GB in size coexisting in the same database with tablespaces as small as 1GB. The size of the tablespace depends on the current and expected size of the objects included in the various segments of the tablespace.

As you have already seen, Oracle9*i* lets you have multiple block sizes, in addition to the default block size. Because tablespaces ultimately consist of data blocks, this means that you can have tablespaces with different block sizes in the same database. This is a great new feature, and it gives you the opportunity to pick the right block size for a tablespace based on the data structure of the tables within that tablespace. This customization of the block size for tablespaces provides several benefits:

Optimal disk I/O: Remember that the Oracle server has to read the table data from mechanical disks into the buffer cache area for processing. One of your primary goals as a DBA is to optimize the expensive I/O involved in the reads and writes to disk. If you have tables that have very long rows, you're better off with a larger block size. Each read, for example, will fetch more data than with a smaller block size, and you'll need fewer read operations to get the same amount of data. Tables with large object (LOB) data will also benefit from a very high block size. Similarly, tables with small row lengths can have a small block size as the building block for the tablespace. If you have large indexes in your database, you need to have a large block size for their tablespace, so each read will fetch a larger number of index pointers for the data.

Optimal caching of data: The Oracle9i feature of separate pools for the various block sizes leads to a better use of the buffer cache area.

Easier to transport tablespaces: If you have tablespaces with multiple block sizes, it's easier to use the "transport tablespaces" feature. In Chapter 13, you'll find examples showing you how to transport tablespaces between databases.

Each Oracle tablespace consists of one or more operating system (or *raw*) files called *data files*, and a data file can only belong to one tablespace. An Oracle database can have any number of tablespaces in it. You could manage a database with ten or several hundred tablespaces, all sized differently. However, for every Oracle database, you'll need a minimum of two tablespaces: the System tablespace and the temporary tablespace. Later on, you can add and drop tablespaces as you wish, but you can't drop the System tablespace. At database creation time, the only tablespace you *must* have is the System tablespace, which contains Oracle's data dictionary. However, users need a temporary location to perform certain activities such as sorting, and if you don't provide a default temporary tablespace for them, they end up doing the temporary sorting in the System tablespace.

When you consider the importance of the System tablespace, which contains the data dictionary tables along with other important information, it quickly becomes obvious why you *must* have a temporary tablespace. Oracle9i allows you to create this temporary tablespace at database creation time, and all users will automatically have this tablespace as their default temporary tablespace. In addition, if you choose the Oracle-recommended Automatic Undo Management over the traditional manual rollback segment management mode, you'll also need to create the undo tablespace at database creation time. Thus, although only the System tablespace is absolutely required by Oracle, your database should have at least the System, temporary, and undo tablespaces when you initially create it.

NOTE *The only tablespace that Oracle creates automatically is the System tablespace, which is created when you create the database. However, you still have to provide the location of the data file so Oracle can create the System tablespace.*

All the tablespaces together make up the total space within a database. You can find out the total size of any Oracle database by simply adding up the sizes of the tablespaces in that database.

Tablespaces store all the usable data of the database. The data files that are part of each tablespace together constitute the total amount of physical space assigned to a particular database. If you're running out of space due to the addition of new data, you need to create more tablespaces with new data files, add new data files to existing tablespaces, or make the existing data files of a tablespace larger. You'll see an example of how to do each of these tasks in Chapter 7.

Why Tablespaces?

Tablespaces perform a number of key functions in an Oracle database. The concept of a tablespace is not common to all relational databases. For instance, the Microsoft SQL Server database doesn't use this concept at all. Here's a brief list of the benefits of using tablespaces:

- Tablespaces make it easier to allocate space quotas to various users in the database.

- Tablespaces enable you to perform only a partial backup or recovery based on the tablespace as a unit.

- Because a large object can be spread over several tablespaces, you can increase performance by spanning the tablespace over several disks and controllers.

- You can take a tablespace offline for several reasons, without having to bring down the entire database.

- Tablespaces are an easy way to allocate database space.

- You can import or export specific application data by using the import and export utilities at the tablespace level.

Physical Database Structures

The Oracle database consists of several types of operating system files, which it uses to manage itself. Although you call these files *physical files* to distinguish them from the logical entities they contain, understand that from an operating system point of view, even these files are not really physical, but rather logical components of the physical disk storage supported by the operating system.

Oracle Data Files

Data files are the way Oracle allocates space to the tablespaces that make up the logical database. Remember that in the previous section, I pointed out that the total size of any Oracle database is the same as the total space allocated to its tablespaces. The data files are the way Oracle maps the logical tablespaces to the physical disks. Each tablespace consists of one or more data files, which in turn belong to an operating system file system. Therefore, the total space allocated to all the data files in an Oracle database will give you the total size of that database.

When you create your database, your system administrator assigns you a certain amount of disk space based on your initial database sizing estimates. All you have at this point are the mount points of the various disks you are assigned (e.g., /prod01, /prod02, /prod03, and so on). You then need to create your directory structure on the various files. After you install your software and create the Oracle administrative directories, you can use the remaining file system space for storing database objects such as tables and indexes. The Oracle data files make up the largest part of the physical storage of your database. However, other files are also part of the Oracle physical storage, as you'll see in the following sections.

The Control File

Control files are key files that the Oracle DBMS maintains about the state of the database. They are a bit like a database within a database, and they include, for example, the names and locations of the data files and the all-important System Change Number (SCN), which indicates the most recent version of committed changes in the database. Control files are key to the functioning of the database, and recovery is difficult without access to an up-to-date control file. Oracle creates the control files during the initial database creation process.

Due to its obvious importance, Oracle recommends that you keep multiple copies of the control file. If you lose all your control files, you won't be able to bring up your database without re-creating the control file using special commands. You specify the name, location, and the number of copies of the control file in the initialization file (init.ora). Oracle highly recommends that you provide for more than one control file in the initialization file. Here's a brief list of the key information captured by the Oracle control file:

- Checkpoint progress records
- Redo thread records
- Log file records
- Data file records
- Tablespace records
- Log file history records
- Archived log records
- Backup set and data file copy records

Control files are vital during the time the Oracle instance is operating and during database recovery. During the normal operation of the database, the control file is consulted periodically for necessary information on data files and other things. Note that the Oracle server process continually updates the control file during the operation of the database. During recovery, it's the control file that has the data file information necessary to bring the database up to a stable mode.

The Redo Log Files

The Oracle *redo log files* are vital during the recovery of a database. The redo log files record all the changes made to the database. In case you need to restore your database from a backup, you can recover the latest change made to the database from the redo log files.

Redo log files consist of *redo records,* which are groups of *change vectors,* each referring to a distinct atomic change made to a data block in the Oracle database. Note that a single transaction may have more than one redo record. If your database comes down without warning, the redo log helps you determine if all transactions were committed before the crash or if some were still incomplete. Initially, the contents of the log will be in the *redo log buffer* (a memory area), but they will be transferred to disk very quickly.

Oracle redo log files contain the following information regarding database changes made by transactions:

- Indicators to let you know when the transaction started

- Name of the transaction

- Name of the data object (e.g., an application table) that was being updated

- The "before image" of the transaction (i.e., the data as it was before the changes were made)

- The "after image" of the transaction (i.e., the data after the transaction changed the data)

- Commit indicators that let you know if and when the transaction completed

When a database crashes, for example, all transactions that are shown as having been committed by the redo log files have to be applied to the data files belonging to the database. This is done by applying the "after image" records to the database. Any transactions that did not commit when the crash occurred must not affect the state of the database in any way. These incomplete transactions must be "undone" and the database restored to its original state. This is done by using the "before image" records in the redo logs. To put all this in simpler terms, all redo log transactions that have both a begin and a commit entry must be "redone," and all transactions that began but have no commit entries must be "undone." "Redoing" in this context simply means that you apply the information in the redo log files to the database; you do not rerun the transaction itself. In any case, either all changes occur or no changes occur at all; there is no in-between alternative. As you can see from this discussion, redo log files are an essential part of database management, and they are one of the main ways you enforce database consistency at all times.

Oracle requires that every database have at least two redo log files. Because of the critical importance of the redo log files in helping recover from database crashes, Oracle recommends *multiplexing* the redo log files (i.e., maintaining simultaneous copies of the changes being made to the database). Losing a redo log file could mean a point of single failure for the database. Oracle also recommends that you archive the filled-up redo log files, so you can maintain a complete record of all the changes made to the database since the last backup.

The Initialization Files: Init.ora and SPFILE

When you create a new database, you specify the initialization parameters for the Oracle instance in a special file called the *init.ora file* or, even better, the new *server parameter file* (SPFILE). Typically, you specify the memory limits for the instance, the locations of the control files, whether and where the archived logs are saved, and a whole bunch of other settings that determine the behavior of the Oracle database server.

You can operate the database with either type of initialization parameter file, but Oracle recommends using the newer SPFILE. The init.ora file is simpler to use than the SPFILE, but it doesn't give you the flexibility that the SPFILE provides. The usual naming convention for the init.ora file is init_*dbname*.ora (where *dbname* is the name of your database). Oracle provides a template of this file, which is placed by default in the ORACLE_HOME/dbs directory in UNIX systems and the ORACLE_HOME/database directory in Windows systems. The ORACLE_HOME directory is the standard location for the Oracle executables.

Oracle allows you to change a number of the initialization parameters after you start up the instance; these are called *dynamic initialization parameters*. The rest of the parameters aren't dynamically changeable and you'll have to restart your instance if you need to modify any of those parameters. You can use the *alter system* or *alter session* command to change the dynamic initialization parameters. Once you change a parameter's value in this manner, the change is in force only for the duration of the instance if you're using the traditional init.ora file. When you restart the instance, it will come up with the old values for the parameter.

Quite often, you'll find that you've managed to fix a performance problem by altering an initialization parameter dynamically (while the instance is operating). The right thing to do in this case, of course, is to go and change your init.ora file to reflect the newly discovered optimal values for the changed parameters. Often, DBAs forget to take this extra step, and when they shut the database down for some maintenance window (e.g., for a scheduled backup), Oracle "forgets" the dynamically modified changes and comes up with the old parameter values instead. If you use the SPFILE, you have the option of making all the dynamically changed parameters a part of the permanent initialization file. This, in fact, is the most important benefit of using the SPFILE over the traditional init.ora file.

Listing 5-3 shows how to create an SPFILE from your existing Oracle init.ora file. It also shows you how to create the init.ora file from the SPFILE.

Listing 5-3. Creating the SPFILE from the Init.ora File and Vice Versa

```
SQL> create spfile='/test01/app/oracle/product/9.2.0.1.0/dbs/spfilefinance1.ora'
     fFrom pfile = '/test01/app/oracle/product/9.2.0.1.0/dbs/initfinance1.ora';
fFile created.
SQL>
Alternately,
You can create the init.ora file from a SPFILE as follows:
SQL> create pfile='test01/app/oracle/product/9.2.0.1.0/dbs/finance1.ora'
From spfile = '/test01/app/oracle/product/9.2.0.1.0/dbsspfilefinance1.ora';
SQL>
```

NOTE *It's well worth the extra effort to create and maintain the SPFILE parameter configuration file. The SPFILE gives you a lot more flexibility compared to the traditional init.ora initialization file. When you want to retain the new values of dynamic parameters after changing them, the SPFILE ensures you don't forget to incorporate the changes in the initialization file.*

Checking Current Initialization Parameters

You can use the V$PARAMETER data dictionary view to find out the values for the various initialization parameters that you have explicitly set for your database. The analogous view if you are using the SPFILE to store your initialization parameters is the V$SPPARAMETER view. In addition to the parameter values you chose through the init.ora file or the SPFILE, the V$PARAMETER table contains other variables that take certain default values set by Oracle. The following query enables you see what the default parameters and their values are:

```
SQL> select name,value, isdefault from V$Parameter where isdefault = 'TRUE';
```

The preceding query provides you with a long list of all the default initialization parameters. However, you can change several initialization parameters on the fly while the instance is running with the *alter system* command or the *alter session* command, as in the following example:

```
SQL> alter session set max_dump_file_size=100000;
        Session altered.
SQL>
```

The *show parameter* command will show all the parameter settings, whether they are part of your init.ora file or they are set by Oracle as default values. If you issue the *show parameter* command with a keyword, you can get the value of a specified class of parameters, as shown in Listing 5-4.

Listing 5-4. Using the Show Parameter Command

```
SQL> show parameter dump
NAME                          TYPE         VALUE
----------------------------- ----------   ------------------------------
background_core_dump          string       partial
background_dump_dest          string       C:\oracle\admin\mark1\bdump
core_dump_dest                string       C:\oracle\admin\mark1\cdump
max_dump_file_size            string       UNLIMITED
shadow_core_dump              string       partial
user_dump_dest                string       C:\oracle\admin\mark1\udump
SQL>
```

CAUTION *Sometimes you'll see references to undocumented or hidden Oracle parameters. These parameters usually have an underscore (_) prefix. Don't use them unless you're requested to do so by Oracle support experts or other trustworthy sources.*

The Password File

The *password file* is an optional file that you may maintain, in which you can specify the names of people who have the SYSDBA privilege to log into the system. Oracle provides a special utility called *orapwd* to create the password file. In addition, some operating systems enable you to create the password file during installation. Chapter 11 shows you how to create and maintain the password file.

The Alert Log File

Every Oracle database has an *alert log* with the standard naming convention alert*db_name*.log (where *db_name* is the name of the database). This file will register major changes, events, and errors that occur during the running of the Oracle instance. The alert log captures events including log switches, any Oracle-related errors, warnings, and other messages. In addition, every time you start up the Oracle instance, Oracle will list all your initialization parameters in the alert log, along with the complete sequence of the start-up process. You can also use the alert log to automatically keep track of all tablespace creation as well as the addition and resizing of data files. The alert log could come in handy during troubleshooting and it is usually the first place you would want to check to get an idea about what was happening inside the database when a problem occurred. In fact, Oracle support may ask you for a copy of the pertinent sections of the alert log during their analysis of problems occurring within the database.

By default, the Oracle alert log is always written to the Oracle *background_dump_destination* directory. For example, on my system this is the /u01/app/oracle/admin/finance1/bdump directory. If you don't specify a value for the *background_dump_destination* parameter, the file will be placed in a default location. For example, on HP-UX machines, the default location for the alert log is $ORACLE_HOME/rdbms/log (the same location is used for *user_dump_* *destination*). To find out where the alert log is located on my Windows system, I issue the following command:

```
SQL> show parameter background dump
NAME                              TYPE    VALUE
background_core_dump      string    partial
background_dump_dest      string    C:\oracle\admin\real\bdump
```

To see if there are any Oracle-related errors in your alert log, simply issue the following command (assuming you are in your background dump directory):

```
$ grep ORA- alert_finance1.log
ORA-1503 signalled during: CREATE CONTROLFILE SET DATABASE "FINANCE1" RESETLOGS...
ORA-1109 signalled during: ALTER DATABASE CLOSE NORMAL...
ORA-00600: internal error code, arguments:[12333], [0], [0], [0], [], [], [], []
```

As you can see, several Oracle errors are listed in the alert log for the database fiannce1. A regular scan of your database for all kinds of Oracle errors, including the serious "internal" errors, should be one of your daily database management tasks. You can easily schedule a script to scan the alert log for you and e-mail you the results.

Trace Files

Oracle requires that you specify three different trace file directories in your initialization file. Of these, the *background dump directory*, of course, has the alert log file for the database instance. In addition, the background dump directory is used for any trace files generated by the Oracle background processes. The other two dump directories are the core dump directory and the user dump directory. The *core dump directory* holds any "core" files generated during the occurrence of major errors such as the ORA-600 internal Oracle software errors. The *user dump directory* holds all trace files for any errors during the execution of the Oracle server processes.

Data Files and Tablespaces

As you learned in the earlier sections of this chapter, the database is simply the sum of all its constituent tablespaces. You also learned that tablespaces are merely logical entities consisting of one or more data files each. You can also look at a database from a physical disk point of view as the aggregation of all the data files allocated to it. If you're talking to other DBAs, you'll make perfect sense if you speak entirely in terms of tablespaces. If, on the other hand, you're discussing space issues with your UNIX administrator, you won't make much headway unless you speak in terms of file systems and file sizes.

How do you add space to a database? Well, logically speaking, you'll either add more tablespaces or enlarge some of the existing tablespaces. However, from a practical point of view, you have just two ways to make the database larger: enlarge the size of one or more data files or add a new data file to a tablespace. The new files that you add may belong to an existing tablespace or they may be a part of a new tablespace.

To be able to use the disk storage for storing your data, you first need to have directories and a file system created for you by the system administrator. You also have to make sure you have all the proper rights to read from and write to these directories and files. When you create a tablespace, you assign it these data files. For example, you may want to create a tablespace called customer01 and add two data files, each about 500MB in size. As you load more data into your database, Oracle will allocate new extents to the database tables and extents out of these data files that are part of the customer01 tablespace. Although the data itself is placed on actual data files, there is no direct link between tables and indexes and the data files they are placed on. The objects are linked directly to the logical tablespace that the data files are part of. Thus, Oracle maintains a separation between the logical objects (such as tables) and the physical data files. A table could easily be moved to a different tablespace directly, but not to a data file.

Locally Managed and Dictionary Managed Tablespaces

Every database needs to have a minimum of one tablespace (the System tablespace) and every tablespace can have a minimum of one data file. You have a choice between two kinds of tablespaces: *dictionary managed* tablespaces and *locally managed* tablespaces. Locally managed tablespaces are the default format for Oracle9i databases. Here's the essential difference between the two types of tablespaces: Dictionary managed tablespace management means that every time a table or other object needs to grow, Oracle has to check its data dictionary to ensure there's free space and then update its free space information following the allocation of the extent to the objects. In addition to activity in the data dictionary, there's also activity in the rollback segments when these requests for additional extents are made. Occasionally this enhanced activity could lead to a performance slowdown when an object is trying to grow. When new extents are allocated to an object, the update activity in the data dictionary tables needs to be recorded in the rollback segments, and this could potentially cause a further deterioration in performance, because the rollback segments may need to extend.

Locally managed databases keep the space management information in the data files themselves and automatically track adjacent free space. The information about the free and used space is kept in *bitmaps* within the data file headers. Because any space allocation (or deallocation) is managed by these local entities, these tablespaces are called locally managed tablespaces. Bitmaps contain bits, each of which tracks the space in a block or a group of blocks. Remember that when an object needs to grow in size, Oracle will assign new space not in data block units, but will allocate new extents to the object. When a new extent needs to be allocated to an object, Oracle will first select a data file and look up its bitmap to see if it has enough free contiguous data blocks. Oracle will then change the bitmap in that data file to show the new used status of the blocks in the extent. During this process, the data dictionary is not used in any way; therefore, recursive SQL operations (operations that occur when you consult the data dictionary) are significantly reduced. Rollback information is not generated during this updating of the bitmaps in the data files. Thus, the usage of the bitmaps leads to performance gains when compared to the data dictionary managed tablespaces.

Temporary tablespaces illustrate the advantage in using locally managed tablespaces. Temporary tablespaces have high extent allocation and deallocation needs due to frequent sorting in the tablespace. A locally managed temporary tablespace would perform much more efficiently than a traditional dictionary managed tablespace. Another important benefit of using locally managed tablespaces is the fact that these tablespaces avoid the notorious tablespace fragmentation problem that you encounter with most dictionary managed tablespaces. Tablespace fragmentation problems occur when Oracle can't find enough contiguous free space in a tablespace to allocate to an object. When Oracle is looking for free space, especially for the larger extents, if it can't find enough contiguous space, it has to perform a coalescing of the tablespace to create enough adjacent free space. This coalescing of the tablespace can also be performed automatically by the PMON process, or you can manually coalesce tablespaces by using the *alter tablespace ... coalesce* command. Locally managed tablespaces avoid the tablespace fragmentation problem and thus give you one more strong reason to choose them. Fragmentation of tablespaces is a major problem with many traditional databases that have dictionary managed tablespaces. To eliminate fragmentation, most DBAs have to schedule time-consuming "tablespace reorg(anization)s." Locally managed tablespaces free you from the tablespace fragmentation headaches and, according to Oracle, 97 percent of the users who adopted locally managed tablespaces reported that fragmentation wasn't an issue.

TIP *Create locally managed tablespaces to take advantage of their superior space management abilities compared to the traditional data dictionary managed tablespaces. The benefits are especially significant if your database is an OLTP database with numerous inserts, deletes, and updates on a continuous basis. Locally managed tablespaces will enable you to use the automatic space management features of Oracle9i and eliminate the need to worry about configuring the PCTUSED and FREELIST parameters. When you create these locally managed tablespaces, choose the* auto *option for segment space management and not the* default *manual* option. *This will enable the locally managed tablespaces to use the bitmaps in the data files to keep track of the free space in the data blocks of the extents, rather than use the data dictionary.*

Automatic vs. Manual Segment Space Management

Oracle9*i* provides you a new and efficient way to manage space within the database. The traditional way to manage free space allocation in the Oracle data blocks involved the use of a pair of storage parameters called *PCTFREE* and *PCTUSED*. Before I go any further, I'd like to remind you that you can use the free space in an Oracle block for only two purposes: inserting fresh data or updating existing data in the blocks.

The PCTFREE parameter lets you reserve a percentage of space in each data block for future updates to already existing data. For example, you may have some data on a person's address in a certain block. If you update that address later to a much larger size in terms of the space it takes up, there should ideally be room in the existing block for enlarging the address. This is exactly what the PCTFREE parameter provides: room for growth of the existing rows. The PCTUSED parameter, on the other hand, deals with the threshold below which the used space must fall before new data can be placed in the blocks. For example, if the PCTUSED parameter is set at 40, Oracle can't insert new data into the block until the amount of free space falls below this threshold level.

You can see easily how the PCTFREE and PCTUSED parameters together optimize the use of the space within an Oracle block. Suppose 80 percent of the space in a block is filled with data. This will be the maximum amount of data that you can insert inside the block, of course, if the PCTFREE parameter is 20 percent. That is, you have to leave 20 percent free for future updates of existing data. Now, if some deletes take place in this block, there will be potential room to insert new rows. However, here is where Oracle uses the PCTUSED parameter in a clever way to keep any newly available free space from being automatically used up for new inserts. The crucial point to understand here is that Oracle will incur an overhead when it tries to use the newly available free space in the data blocks due to the deletes. If every time a row deletion occurs, you try and insert a new row into that empty space, Oracle has to do too much housekeeping work, nullifying your efforts to efficiently use all the free space. So Oracle essentially tells the block, "Let me know when your used space falls below a certain level (denoted by the PCTUSED parameter)." Until then, although there may be free spaces in blocks, Oracle ignores them and goes to new data blocks to insert data.

How does Oracle keep track of how much free space is in its data blocks? This information is provided by the maintenance of *FREELISTS* by Oracle. Every table and index maintains a list of all its data blocks with free space greater than PCTUSED. That is, FREELISTS contain the list of all blocks eligible for data insertion. Oracle first checks the FREELIST before any insertion into tables or indexes. For efficiency purposes, you can have multiple FREELISTS. You can supply a value for the FREELIST parameter when you create a table or an index. As you can imagine, the Oracle database has to do a lot of work to maintain the FREELISTS, as blocks reach their PCTUSED threshold after insertions and fall below the threshold due to deletions. Later on, you'll see how you can choose an easier mode of managing space, letting Oracle do all the work, without your having to juggle a number of tuning parameters.

The parameters PCTFREE and PCTUSED and the use of the FREELISTS have been the standard way to manage space within Oracle segments for many years now. You can consider this method a manual way of checking for space, because you are making Oracle continually check for blocks with the right amount of free space. In a database with heavy updates, inserts, and deletes, this could lead to a slowdown of your transactions. Oracle9i lets you make the choice as to whether you want to *automate space allocation*. If you choose to create your tablespaces as *locally managed* instead of *dictionary managed*, you can reap the benefits of this new automatic space management feature.

Once you create a tablespace as local, you can specify exactly how the tablespace manages free and used space within the segments. Remember that all Oracle objects, such as tables and indexes, are referred to as *segments* (a segment being a collection of extents). You can choose between the *manual* and *auto* options to tell Oracle how to manage segment space. Under manual segment space-management, the database will use the traditional FREELISTS, FREELIST

GROUPS, and PCTUSED storage parameters to manage space. Before Oracle can add data to a segment, it first consults the FREELIST(S) in that object. Remember that a data block can be used for new data only if it has free space below the PCTUSED parameter. When the space utilization in a block reaches the PCTFREE parameter value, as you saw earlier, the block comes off the FREELIST. If you have configured your database objects with the default single FREELIST, or even if you have multiple FREELISTS for an object, sometimes the sheer volume and frequency of inserts and updates can overwhelm the Oracle's capability to handle the overhead inherent in taking blocks off and putting them back on the FREELISTS. When the FREELISTS cannot keep up with the updating of the free space usage within a segment, severe performance degradation will result. All your careful tuning of the FREELISTS and the PCTUSED parameter will have come to naught in this case.

Oracle9*i* helps you avoid all these problems regarding the tracking of free space within segments by making the whole process automatic. If you choose the Automatic Segment Space Management feature by using the *auto* option for segment management when creating a database, Oracle uses bitmaps to track free space availability in a segment. For example, a bitmap, which is contained in a bitmap block, indicates whether free space in a data block is below 25 percent, between 50 percent and 75 percent, or above 75 percent. For an index block, the bitmaps can tell you whether the blocks are empty or formatted. Oracle points out that automatic segment management is scalable as well as efficient when it comes to using space. The gains are even more striking if the database objects have a varying row size.

Maintenance of these bitmaps will consume space, but it is less than 1 percent for most large size objects. Oracle also claims that the automatic management of segment space leads to a gain of about 20 percent to 25 percent in SQL*Loader operations because of the way unformatted blocks are allowed below the high-water mark. The performance degradation you see in heavily used OLTP applications due to the overhead of managing free space will not occur when you use automatic space management. Of course, the biggest argument in favor of using the automatic space management option is that you do not have to endlessly tune the space-related parameters (FREELISTS and PCTUSED). Leave it to Oracle!

Allocating the Extent Size: Autoallocate vs. Uniform

If you create your database with a locally managed System tablespace, any tablespaces that you create later on must also be locally managed tablespaces. When you create the locally managed tablespaces, you have two options as to how to manage the extent sizes.

Recall that a tablespace consists of extents, and any time the tablespace needs to grow, it will do in terms of data extents. If you choose the *autoallocate* option, Oracle will manage the extent sizes for you. Depending on the size of the object, Oracle will figure out the best size to allocate. Oracle uses extent sizes varying from 64KB to 64MB, and it automatically decides what size the new extent size for an object should be. Note an interesting point here: Oracle will *increase* the extent size for an object automatically as the object grows in size! The minimum size of an autoallocated object is 64KB. *Autoallocate* is especially useful if you aren't sure about the growth rate of an object and you would like Oracle to deal with it.

When you do know the growth rate of an object, you can choose the other option, *uniform,* to determine the extent size. Anytime an object within a tablespace needs to grow, it will be assigned a new extent specified by the *uniform size* clause when the tablespace is created. All extents will be of the same size, hence the name uniform size. Choosing the *uniform size* option means that you, not Oracle, will determine the size of new extents that are allocated to database objects when they grow.

> **TIP** *Oracle recommends that unless all the objects in a table are of the same size, you should use the* autoallocate *feature. In addition to the simplicity of management,* autoallocate *can potentially save you a significant amount of disk space, compared to the uniform extent size option.*

Creating a Tablespace

The preceding discussion of locally managed and dictionary managed tablespaces, the *autoallocate* and *uniform size* parameters, and the *manual* versus *auto* segment storage parameters can be a little overwhelming at first. Chapter 7 presents several examples of how to create various types of tablespaces, which makes it very easy understand how to use all the new terms relating to the Oracle9*i* tablespaces.

Migrating from Dictionary Managed to Locally Managed Tablespaces

It is easy to migrate tablespaces from a dictionary managed configuration to a locally managed one. Oracle provides the DBMS_SPACE_ADMIN package, which enables you to perform the tablespace migration. There is a procedure in this package that does the actual migration. You need to first migrate all the other tablespaces to a local management mode before you migrate the System tablespace.

Automatic Undo Management

When you make a change to a table, you should have the chance to undo or roll back the change if necessary. The necessary information to undo or roll back changes in transactions is called "undo" (the change vectors) and is stored in *undo records.* When you issue a *rollback* command, Oracle uses these undo records to replace the changed data with the original version. As Chapter 8 explains in detail, the undo records are vital during database recovery when the database needs to discard all "unfinished" or uncommitted transactions to make the database consistent.

In previous versions of the Oracle database, it was the DBAs job to manage what are known as *rollback segments* by explicitly allocating a regular, permanent tablespace for these segments. In fact, the management of the rollback segments used to be a vexing and time-consuming part of the job for many DBAs who managed large databases, especially if they had frequent, long-running transactions. Oracle writes to the rollback segments in a circular fashion, and it's not uncommon to find that information needed by a transaction to ensure "read consistency" has been overwritten by a newer transaction.

Many DBAs find the sizing of the rollback segments a tricky issue. If you have several small rollback segments, a large transaction may fail. If you have a small number of very large rollbacks segments, your transactions may encounter contention for the rollback segment "transaction tables."

Oracle9*i* will still let you manage the undo information in traditional rollback segments if you wish. This "manual" mode of undo management is called *Rollback Segment Undo* (RBU) mode. However, Oracle strongly recommends the use of the new *Automatic Undo Management* (AUM) feature, whereby the Oracle server itself will maintain and manage the undo (rollback) segments. All you need to do is provide a dedicated undo tablespace and specify the length of time for which Oracle should retain the undo information using an initialization parameter called the *undo retention* parameter, and Oracle will take care of the rest. It will create the necessary number of undo segments, which are structurally similar to the traditional rollback segments, and size and extend them according to the transaction needs of your database. Thus, the DBA is spared from the rigors of traditional rollback segment creation and management. Chapter 8 shows you in detail how to create and manage undo tablespaces, and Chapter 16 provides further information about the AUM feature.

 NOTE *The use of AUM doesn't mean that the rollback segments are going to go away from the Oracle database. Rollback segments still exist, but now they are referred to as "undo segments" and created and maintained by Oracle. The old system rollback segment is still created in the System tablespace.*

Because AUM means that Oracle will do the sizing of the individual undo segments for you, the big decision you have to make regards the sizing of the undo tablespace. Remember that your undo tablespace should not only be able to accommodate all the long-running transactions, but it also has to be big enough for the Flashback Query feature of Oracle9*i*. The Flashback Query feature lets you query data from a time in the past. (You'll learn more about how to implement this feature in Chapters 8 and 15.) You can use Oracle Enterprise Manager (OEM) to help you figure out the ideal size for your undo tablespaces. Using the current undo space consumption statistics, you can estimate future undo generation rates for the instance. OEM can then depict the estimated rollback size in an *undo space estimate* graph. The undo space estimate graphs will come in handy for administrators in figuring out the right size for the undo tablespace.

Oracle Managed Files

Oracle has introduced a new file management feature in the 8*i* server version that is designed to help DBAs manage file systems easily. The *Oracle Managed Files* (OMF) feature aims at relieving DBAs from their traditional file-management tasks. All you need to do is to state in your initialization file where you want the files (e.g., data files, log files, and control files) to be created, and Oracle automatically creates them. The initialization parameter that you need to specify is *db_create_file_dest*. OMF files have a default size of 100MB.

When you use the OMF feature, you don't have to worry about the physical files. Instead, you can focus on the objects you're creating. Oracle will automatically create and delete the files on the UNIX or Windows server as needed. OMF seems like a great new feature, but it has several limitations. You lose the flexibility necessary to maintain large databases if you rely exclusively on the OMF feature. The OMF-based files are ideal for test and small databases. If you have a terabyte-sized database with a large number of archived logs and redo logs, you need flexibility, which the OMF file system can't provide. If you want to use OMF files for your database, read the discussion of OMF in Chapter 16, where you'll learn how to create and manage OMF-based files.

NOTE *Unless you have a very small database or you're using a test database, the OMF feature is not suitable for your database. Stick to the traditional operating system–level file management methods for better control over your file system.*

Oracle Processes

Oracle server processes running on the operating system perform all the database operations, such as inserting and deleting data. These Oracle processes, together with the memory structures allocated to Oracle by the operating system, form the working Oracle instance. There is a set of mandatory Oracle processes that need to be up and running for the database to function at all. In addition, other processes exist that are necessary only if you are using certain specialized features of the Oracle databases (e.g., replicated databases). This section's focus is on the set of mandatory processes that every Oracle instance uses to perform database activities.

Processes are essentially a connection or thread to the operating system that performs a task or job. The Oracle processes you'll encounter in this section are continuous, in the sense that they come up when the instance starts, and they stay up for the duration of the instance's life. Thus, they act like Oracle's "hooks" into the operating system resources. Note that what I call a *process* on a UNIX system is analogous to a *thread* on a Windows system.

> **NOTE** *The following discussion mostly pertains to Oracle databases on UNIX systems. The Windows Oracle installations use the terms "Oracle instance" and "process" somewhat differently. Please refer to the discussion on managing Oracle on Windows systems in Chapter 22 for a full explanation of Windows-based systems.*

Oracle instances need two different types of processes to perform various types of database activities. This distinction is made for efficiency purposes and the need to keep client processes separate from the database server's tasks. The first set of processes is called *user processes*. These processes are responsible for running the application that connects the user to the database instance. The second and more important set of processes is called the *Oracle processes*. These processes perform the Oracle server's tasks, and you can divide the Oracle processes into two major categories: the *server processes* and the *background processes*. Together, these processes perform all the actual work of the database, from managing connections to writing to the logs and data files to monitoring the user processes.

Interaction Between the User and Oracle Processes

User processes execute program code of application programs and that of Oracle tools such as SQL*Plus. The user processes communicate with the server processes through the user interface. These processes request that the Oracle server processes perform work on their behalf. Oracle responds by using its server processes to service the user processes' requests.

When you connect to an Oracle database, you have to use software such as SQL Net, which is Oracle's proprietary networking tool. Regardless of how you connect and establish a session with the database instance, Oracle has to manage these connections. The Oracle server creates server processes to manage the user connections. It's the job of the server processes to monitor the connection, accept requests for data, and so forth from the database, and hand the results back from the database itself. All selects, for example, involve reading data from the database, and it's the server processes that bring the output of the *select* statement back to the users.

You'll examine the two types of Oracle processes, the server processes and the background processes, in detail in the following sections.

The Server Process

The *server process* is the process that services the user process. The server process is responsible for all interaction between the user and the database. When the user submits requests to select data, for example, the server process checks the syntax of the code and executes the SQL code. It will then read the data from the data files into the memory blocks. If another user intends to read the same data, the new user's server process will read it not from disk again, but from Oracle's memory, where it usually remains for a while. Finally, the server process is also responsible for returning the requested data to the user.

The most common configuration for the server process is where you assign each user a dedicated server process. However, Oracle provides for a more sophisticated means of servicing several users through the same server process called the *shared server architecture*, which enables you to service a large number of users efficiently. A shared server process enables a large number of simultaneous connections using fewer server processes, thereby conserving critical system resources such as memory.

The Background Processes

The *background processes* are the real workhorses of the Oracle instance. These processes enable large numbers of users to use the information that is stored in the database files. By being continuously hooked into the operating system, these processes relieve Oracle software from having to constantly start numerous, separate processes for each task that needs to be done on the operating system server. Table 5-1 lists the mandatory background processes that run in all types of Oracle databases. Note that there are some specialized background processes that you'll need to use only if you're implementing certain advanced features.

Table 5-1. Key Oracle Background Processes

BACKGROUND PROCESS	PROCESS FUNCTION
Database writer	Writes modified data from buffer cache to disk (data files)
Log writer	Writes redo log buffer contents to online redo log files
Checkpoint	Signals database to flush its contents to disk
Process monitor	Cleans up after finished and failed processes
System monitor	Performs crash recovery and coalesces extents
Archiver	Archives filled online redo log files
Recoverer	Used only in distributed databases
Dispatcher	Used only in shared server configurations
Coordination job	Coordinates job queues to expedite job processes queue process

I discuss in detail the main Oracle background processes in the following sections.

The Database Writer

The *database writer* (DBW) process is responsible for writing data from the memory areas known as *database buffers* to the actual data files on disk. It is the database writer process's job to monitor the usage of the database buffer cache and help manage it. For example, if the free space in the database buffer area is getting low, the database writer process has to make room there by writing some of the data in the buffers to the disk files. The database writer process uses an algorithm called *least recently used* (LRU), which basically writes data to the data files on disk based on how long it has been since someone asked for it. If the data has been sitting in the buffers for a very long time, chances are it is "dated" and the database writer process clears that portion of the database buffers by writing the data to disk.

 NOTE *Just because a user commits a transaction, it is not made "permanent" by the database writer process with an immediate write of the committed transaction to the database files. Oracle conserves physical I/O by waiting to perform a more efficient write of "batches" of committed transactions at once.*

For very large databases or for databases performing intensive operations, a single database writer process may be inadequate to perform all the writing to the database files. Oracle provides for the use of multiple database writer processes to share heavy workloads. You can have as many as nine database writer processes (DBW9) in addition to the default single database writer process (DBW1). Oracle recommends using multiple database writer processes, provided you have multiple processors. You can specify the additional database writer processes by using the *db_writer_process* parameter in the init.ora configuration file. Note that Oracle further recommends that you first ensure that your system is using asynchronous I/O. Even when a system is capable of asynchronous I/O, that feature may not be enabled. If your database writer can't keep up with the amount of work even after asynchronous I/O is enabled, you should consider increasing the number of database writers from the default of one. Check with your system administrator to see whether your system supports asynchronous I/O. Oracle suggests that you may not need multiple database writer processes if your operating system supports asynchronous I/O.

The Log Writer

The job of the *log writer* (LGWR) process is to transfer the contents of the redo log buffer to disk. Whenever you make a change to a database table in the form of an insert, update, or delete of data, Oracle writes the change to memory buffers first. The log writer process is in charge of the process of transferring these changes to files on disk (the redo log files). The redo log files, as you learned earlier, are vital during the recovery of an Oracle database from a lost or damaged disk (or disks).

The Checkpoint

The *checkpoint* (CKPT) process is charged with signaling the database writer process when exactly to write the "dirty" or modified data in the memory buffers to disk. After telling the database writer process to write the changed data, the checkpoint process updates the data file headers and the control file to indicate when the checkpoint was performed.

The purpose of the checkpoint process is to synchronize the buffer cache information with the information on the database disks. When the database writer process writes the dirty or modified blocks from the buffer cache to the disks, Oracle synchronizes the data blocks on the disk with the data blocks in the buffer cache. Each checkpoint record consists of a list of all active transactions and the address of the most recent log record for those transactions. Checkpoints are taken at specified intervals by Oracle and involve the following steps:

1. Flush the contents of the redo log buffers to the redo log files.

2. Write a checkpoint record to the redo log file.

3. Flush the contents of the database buffers cache to disk.

4. Update the data file headers and the control files after the checkpoint completes.

There is a close connection between how often Oracle checkpoints and the length of the recovery time after a database crash. Because database writer processes write all modified blocks to disk at checkpoints, the more frequent the checkpoints, the less data needs to be recovered when the instance crashes. The checkpoint process frequency is based on the following factors:

- *The frequency with which redo log files fill:* Each time there is a log switch, upon filling up an online redo log file Oracle performs an automatic checkpoint. Database administrators can manually checkpoint the database by using the following command:

```
SQL>Alter system checkpoint;
       System altered.
SQL>
```

- *The checkpoint timeout parameter:* The checkpoint interval can be set in terms of time (seconds) by forcing checkpoints after a specified amount of time elapses. This ensures that checkpointing is being done even if the redo log files aren't being filled completely.

Checkpointing Frequency and Recovery Time

When a checkpoint occurs, as you saw earlier, Oracle flushes the dirty data blocks in the buffer cache to the database disks. At the same time, the control file records the checkpoint location by using a checkpoint *redo byte address* (RBA). When the database is recovering from an instance crash, Oracle checks the control file to see what the checkpoint RBA is. The database needs to recover only from the checkpoint RBA onward, because at checkpoints the data blocks in memory will be written to disk and there is no need to recover these data blocks. The more advanced the RBA is, the less data there will be to recover.

The more frequently you checkpoint, the more advanced the RBA will be in the control file. But checkpointing doesn't come without a price. A performance overhead is associated with checkpointing because you're forcing the database writer process to write to disk, even though it may not be an optimal time to do so.

The frequent checkpointing keeps the CPUs on your system from doing other work if they're frequently assisting the database writer process in flushing the data blocks to disk. If the checkpoint interval is increased, the recovery time may not increase very much compared to a regimen of more frequent checkpointing.

Fast Start Time–Based Recovery Limit

When Oracle starts its recovery process, it needs to read the log files first and determine from which point it needs to recover the data blocks. Oracle also needs to open the redo log files and write the necessary data blocks to data files on disk, to synchronize the database again. Sometimes the time it takes to do all this may be beyond what is acceptable for your organization's service level needs. Oracle9*i* provides a very convenient initialization parameter, the *fast_start_mttr_target* (FSMT) parameter, which sets an upper limit for the recovery process to complete. The way it does this, of course, is by ensuring that the checkpoint process is done frequently enough so recovery never takes more time than the target time you specify with the FSMT parameter. The FSMT parameter can take a value between 0 and 3,600 seconds.

So, what is an ideal value for the FSMT parameter? Well, you have to decide this number based on several factors, such as the size of your database, the size of your buffer cache, the number of transactions in your database, your service level agreement (SLA), and the potential performance hit you will take if you set the FSMT parameter too low. A value for the parameter that's too small will, of course, ensure that you can recover your database very quickly, but this also means that the database will perform frequent and unnecessary checkpoints to keep advancing the checkpoint RBA. After a period of trial and error with varying the workloads, you can arrive at an ideal value for the FSMT parameter.

How Oracle Uses the FSMT Targets

The FSMT uses two other settings, the *fast_start_io_target* and *log_checkpoint_interval* parameters, to figure out how fast it should perform the database checkpoints. You can define the two parameters as follows:

- *fast_start_io_target:* Determines the number of data blocks the database needs to recover. Oracle will determine the maximum number of I/Os needed to recover the database. The database writer process will automatically flush the dirty blocks when this target is hit.

- *log_checkpoint_interval:* States the maximum number of redo records that could exist between the checkpoint position and the end of the redo log. This interval determines how many blocks the log writer process can write to the online redo log files before Oracle triggers a checkpoint.

You can set the two parameters explicitly in the init.ora file, in which case they will override the FSMT parameter. But it is more efficient to set the FSMT target and let Oracle determine the appropriate values for the two parameters.

NOTE *You can monitor Oracle's checkpointing using the V$INSTANCE_RECOVERY view.*

The Process Monitor

The *process monitor* (PMON) process cleans up after failed user processes and the server processes. Essentially, when processes die, the PMON process ensures that the database frees up the resources that the dead processes were using. For example, when a user process dies while holding certain table locks, the PMON process would release those locks, so other users could use them without any interference from the dead process. In addition, the PMON process restarts failed server processes. The PMON process sleeps most of the time, waking up to see if it is needed. Other processes will also wake up the PMON process if necessary.

In Oracle9*i*, the PMON process automatically performs dynamic service registration. When you create a new database instance, the PMON process registers the instance information with the listener. (The *listener* is the entity that manages requests for database connections. Chapter 10 discusses the listener in detail.) This *dynamic service registration* eliminates the need to register the new service information in the listener.ora file, which is the configuration file for the listener.

The System Monitor

The *system monitor* (SMON) process, as its name indicates, performs system monitoring tasks for the Oracle instance. The SMON process performs crash recovery upon the restarting of an instance that crashed. The SMON process determines if the database is consistent following a restart after an unexpected shutdown. This process is also responsible for coalescing free extents if you happen to use dictionary managed tablespaces. Coalescing free extents will enable you to assign larger contiguous free areas on disk to your database objects. In addition, the SMON process cleans up unnecessary temporary segments. Like the PMON process, the SMON process sleeps most of the time, waking up to see if it is needed. Other processes will also wake up the SMON process if they detect a need for it.

The Archiver

The *archiver* (ARCH) process is used when the system is being operated in an *archive log mode*—that is, the changes logged to the redo log files are being saved and not being overwritten by new changes. The archiver process will archive the redo log files to a specified location, assuming you chose the automatic archiving option in the init.ora file. If a huge number of changes are being made to your database, and consequently your logs are filling up at a very rapid pace, you can use multiple archiver processes up to a maximum of ten. The parameter *log_archive_maximum_processes* in the initialization file will determine how many archiver processes Oracle will invoke. If the log writer process is writing logs faster than the default single archiver process can archive them, it will be necessary to enable more than one archiver process.

Note that besides the processes discussed here, there are other Oracle background processes that perform specialized tasks that may be running in your system. For example, if you use Oracle Real Application Clusters (ORAC), you'll see a background process called the *lock* (LCKn) process, which is responsible for performing interinstance locking. If you use the Oracle Advanced Replication Option, you'll notice the background process called *recoverer* (RECO), which recovers terminated transactions in a distributed database environment.

Oracle Memory Structures

Oracle uses a part of its memory allocation to hold both program code and data to make processing much faster than if it had to fetch data from the disks constantly. It is the use of these memory structures that enables Oracle to share executable code among several users, without having to go through all the pre-execution processing every time a user invokes a piece of code. The Oracle server doesn't always write changes to disk directly. It writes database changes to the memory area, and when it's convenient, it writes the changes to disk. Because accessing memory is many times faster (memory access is in terms of nanoseconds, whereas disk access is in terms of milliseconds) than reading and writing to physical disks, Oracle is able to overcome the I/O limitations of the disk system. The more your database performs its work in memory rather than in the physical disk storage system, the faster the response will be. Of course, as physical I/O decreases, CPU usage will also decrease, thus leading to a more efficient system.

....

The High Cost of Disk I/O

Although secondary storage (usually magnetic disks) is significantly larger than main memory, it's also significantly slower. The Oracle server never reads from or writes to the disk drives directly. It always transfers data from the disk to memory first. A disk I/O involves either moving a data block from disk to memory (*disk read*) or writing a data block to disk from memory (*disk write*). Typically, it takes about 10–40 milliseconds (0.01–0.04 seconds) to perform a single disk I/O. If your update transaction involves 25 I/Os, in this case, you could spend up to 1 second just waiting to read or write data. Well, in that 1 second, your CPUs could perform millions of instructions. The update takes a negligible amount of time compared to the disk reads and disk writes. If, on the other hand, you already have the necessary data in Oracle's memory, the retrieval time would be much faster, as memory read/writes take only a few *nanoseconds* and use only a few thousandths of machine instructions. This is why avoiding or minimizing disk I/Os plays such a big role in providing high performance in Oracle databases.

....

An important part of the information Oracle stores in its memory areas is the program code that is executing currently or has been executed recently. If a new user process needs to use the same code, it's available in memory in a compiled form, thereby making the processing time a whole lot faster. If some users are "locking" certain objects such as data tables, the memory areas will hold that information, thereby helping different sessions communicate effectively. Most important, perhaps, the memory areas help in processing data that's stored in permanent disk storage. Oracle doesn't make changes directly to the data on disk: Data is always read from the disks, held in memory, and changed right there, before being transferred back to disk.

It's common to use the term *buffers* to refer to units of memory. Memory buffers are page-sized areas of memory into which Oracle transfers the contents of the disk blocks. If Oracle intends to just read (select) or update data, it copies the relevant blocks from disk to the memory buffers. After it makes any necessary changes, Oracle will transfer the contents of the memory buffers to disk.

Oracle uses two kinds of memory structures, one shared and the other process-specific. The *System Global Area* (SGA) is the part of total memory that all server processes (as well as the background processes) share. The process-specific part of the memory is known as the *Program Global Area* (PGA), or *process-private memory*. Although both structures may sound equally important, for configuration and tuning purposes, you'll mainly deal with the SGA. Although the PGA sizing and management has important consequences relating to the performance of the database, the SGA is much more instrumental in the proper performance of the database. Besides, the SGA lends itself to much more detailed calibration than the PGA components. The following sections examine the two components of Oracle's memory in more detail.

Oracle System Global Area (SGA)

The SGA is the most important memory component in an Oracle instance. In large OLTP databases, especially, the SGA turns out to be a much larger and more important memory area than the PGA. When DBAs and system administrators are discussing Oracle memory, it's the SGA that they're referring to. The SGA's purpose is to speed up query performance and to enable a high amount of concurrent database activity. When you start an instance in Oracle, the instance takes a certain amount of memory from the operating system RAM based on the size of the SGA component in the initialization file. When the instance is shut down, the memory taken by SGA goes back to the host system.

Because processing in memory is much faster than disk I/O, the size of the SGA is one of the more important configuration issues when you're tuning the database for optimal performance. Is there any limit to the size of the SGA you can use for your database? Of course, you're constrained by the amount of memory available on the server as a whole. The system administrator can advise you on the maximum amount you may take for your Oracle database. There are no hard-and-fast rules regarding the size of the SGA and its components. You use certain performance criteria to decide whether your allocations are optimal and adjust accordingly. You'll have a chance to study SGA allocation and tuning in more detail in Chapter 19, which deals with tuning Oracle instance performance.

The SGA isn't a homogeneous entity; rather, it's a combination of several memory structures. The main components of the SGA are the database buffer cache, the shared pool, the redo log buffer, the Java pool, and the optional large pool.

Only the log buffer and the Java pool values remain static after you start up the instance. You can reconfigure the sizes of the other components dynamically while the instance is running (using the *alter system* command). Oracle requires that you assign memory to the buffer cache, shared pool, large pool, and Java pool in *granules*, which are units of contiguous memory allocation. The size of a granule is operating system dependent. On UNIX systems, here's how to determine the size of a granule:

- A granule is 4MB if the SGA size is less than 128MB.

- A granule is 16MB if the SGA size is greater than 128MB.

The minimum amount of SGA you can allocate to an Oracle instance is three granules: one granule for the buffer cache; one for the shared pool; and one for the fixed SGA, redo log buffers, and other miscellaneous components. In the Oracle initialization file, the parameter *sga_max_size* determines the maximum amount of memory you can allocate to the SGA. You can dynamically increase or reduce the memory allocation to the various components of the SGA using the *alter system* command, and Oracle will take your new size, round it up to the nearest multiple of the granule size (4MB or 16 MB), and increase or reduce the total granules so the SGA is as close as possible to your target size. Note that initially the sum of the memory allocated to all components can be less than or equal to your *sga_max_size* value.

When you dynamically raise or lower memory allocations for the various components of the SGA, you can reduce memory allocated to one component in order to increase the allocation to another component. Oracle will exchange the memory from one dynamically sizable memory component such as the shared pool to another dynamically configurable component such as the buffer cache. For example, if your statistics indicate your buffer cache hit ratio is low, you can increase the memory assigned to the buffer cache by taking it from the shared pool, for example, or vice versa. If you have certain jobs run only at specified times of the day, you can write a simple script that runs before the job executes and modifies the allocation of memory among the various components. After the job completes, you can have another script run that will change the memory allocation back to the original settings. However, the *sga_max_size* parameter sets the limit for the total memory allocation. If your total memory allocation is already at the *sga_max_size* limit, you can't increase memory to any component without decreasing some other component's memory allocation.

 NOTE *To increase the* sga_max_size *parameter, you have to shut down the instance, change the parameter's value in the init.ora file, and restart the instance. You can't dynamically change the value of the* sga_max_size *parameter. If you don't specify the* sga_max_size *parameter explicitly, it defaults to the total SGA size.*

Let's look at how the DBA can manage the important components of the SGA in the following sections.

Locking the SGA

When you start the Oracle instance, Oracle allocates only a virtual address space equivalent to the value of the *sga_max_size* parameter, not physical memory. Sometimes experts advocate the locking of the SGA in physical memory to guarantee that none of the SGA ever pages out. You can use the initialization parameter *lock_sga* to "lock" or pin Oracle SGA in physical memory. Some operating systems may even lock the SGA implicitly. When the SGA is thus locked, the entire memory specified by the *sga_max_size* is unavailable to the operating system. Only Oracle can use the free memory over and above the current SGA size. If your current SGA level is significantly smaller than your *sga_max_size*, this would lead to a significant waste of memory from the system's point of view. Oracle recommends that you *not* use the *lock_sga* parameter.

The Database Buffer Cache

The *database buffer cache* refers to the memory buffers that the database can use to hold the data that the server process reads from the data files on disk in response to user's requests. The buffer cache is designed to hold the more frequently accessed data in the memory buffers, as the alternative is to read the data constantly from the slower disk storage. The buffer cache contains both original blocks from disk and changed blocks that may be written back to disk. The database buffer cache holds the most recently used data blocks. You can group the memory buffers in the database buffer cache into three components. *Free buffers* are empty buffers that the database can use to place new data it reads from disk. *Dirty buffers* contain data that was read and modified later. *Pinned buffers* are data buffers that are currently in active use. Oracle maintains a least recently used (LRU) list that contains a list of all free, pinned, and dirty buffers in memory.

If a user requests data from a table, Oracle will first search the database buffer cache to see if the data is already there. If it isn't, Oracle will go get the data from disk. Ideally, you would want to retain data as long as possible in memory to reduce access times. However, because the total memory is usually smaller than the database size, as the number of Oracle blocks read into memory rises, free space eventually is exhausted. It's the database writer process's job to make sure there are free buffers available at all times in the database buffer cache. The database writer process makes room in the database cache by writing the changed dirty buffers to disk. To determine which dirty blocks get written to disk, Oracle uses a modified LRU algorithm to decide the optimal buffers to write out to disk. Obviously, if you write data that isn't being currently requested to disk, you'll enhance the performance of the database. The LRU algorithm ensures that only the most recently accessed data is retained in the buffer cache.

Sizing the buffer cache is very important for the proper performance of your database. The larger the size of the buffer cache, the fewer the number of disk reads and writes and the better the performance of the database. Of course, carrying this principle to its extremes can hurt you, because you may end up taking more memory than your needs warrant and contribute directly to paging and swapping on your server.

Multiple Buffer Pools

Assigning one general database cache for all the database objects is not particularly efficient. Different objects and various types of data may have different requirements as to the duration of their retention in the data cache. Oracle gives you flexibility in the use of the buffer cache by allowing you to use *multiple buffer pools* for your database. You need to assign the specific buffer pool for an object when you create the object. You can also use the *alter table* or *alter index* command to modify the type of buffer pool to use for a database object. Table 5-2 shows the main types of buffer pools that you can configure.

Table 5-2. Main Buffer Pool Types

BUFFER POOL	INITIALIZATION PARAMETER	DESCRIPTION
Keep buffer pool	*db_keep_cache_size*	Always keeps the data blocks in memory. For example, you may have small tables that are frequently accessed. To prevent them from being aged out of the database buffer cache, you can assign them to the keep buffer cache when the tables are created.
Recycle buffer pool	*db_recycle_cache_size*	Removes data from the cache immediately after use. You need to use this buffer pool carefully, if you decide to use it at all. The recycle buffer pool will cycle out the object from the cache as soon as the transaction is over. Obviously, you would need to use the recycle buffer pool for only those large tables that are infrequently accessed and do not need to be retained in the buffer cache indefinitely.
Default buffer pool	*db_cache_size*	Contains all data and objects that are not assigned to the keep and recycle buffer pools.

Remember that the main goal in assigning objects to multiple buffer pools is to minimize the misses in the data cache and thus minimize your disk I/O. In fact, all buffer caching strategies have this as their main goal. If you aren't sure which objects in your database belong to the different types of buffer caches, just let the database run for a while with some best-guess multiple cache sizes and query the data dictionary view V\$DB_CACHE_ADVICE to get some advice from Oracle itself. You'll see how to use the V\$DB_CACHE_ADVICE view later in this chapter.

Multiple Buffer Block Sizes

As you saw earlier, Oracle9*i* allows you to have more than one block size for your database. You have to choose a standard block size first and then you can choose up to four other nonstandard cache sizes. The *db_block_size* parameter in your init.ora file determines the size of your *standard* block size in the database. The *db_cache_size* parameter in your init.ora file determines the size of the buffer cache with the standard block size buffers. Notice that you don't set the number of database buffers; rather, you *specify the size of the buffer cache* itself using the *db_cache_size* parameter. If you have two other block sizes that you are using in your database, you can set two other parameters in your initialization file to create two more buffer cache areas using the two nonstandard buffer block sizes. Oracle allows you to have up to a total of five buffer block sizes (four nonstandard plus one standard block size denoted by the *db block size* parameter), and you can specify these by using the initialization parameter *db_nK_cache_size*, where *n* is the block size and can take a value of 2, 4, 8, 16, or 32.

Determining Total Buffer Cache Size

The previous description of multiple buffer pools and multiple buffer block sizes can tend to be a little confusing. First, allow me to summarize the buffer cache discussion: The database buffer cache can be divided into three pools: the default, keep, and recycle buffer pools. The total size of the buffer cache is the sum of memory blocks assigned to all the components of the database buffer cache. Of the three components, the keep and recycle buffer pools can only be created with the standard block size. You can use up to five different nonstandard block sizes to configure different (default pool) *db_cache_size* components. Each *db_nK_cache_size* parameter shows the size of the buffer cache for the corresponding *nK* block size. Here's a simple example to clarify the discussion:

```
Db_Keep_Cache_Size      =    48 MB
Db_Recyle_Cache_Size    =    24 MB
Db_Cache_Size (default)    =  128 MB (standard 4K block size)
DB_2k_Cache_Size           =   48 MB  (2K  non-standard block size)
DB_8K_Cache_Size           =  192 MB  (8K non-standard block size)
DB_16k_Cache_Size          =  384 MB  (16K non-standard block size)
Total Buffer Cache Size = 824 MB
```

The Buffer Cache Hit Ratio

Buffer reads are much faster than reads from disk because I/O transactions are infinitely slower than memory reads. The all-important principle in the appropriate sizing of the buffer cache is to "touch as few blocks as possible." An important indicator of performance is the buffer cache *hit ratio*, which measures the percentage of time users accessed the data they needed from the buffer cache. You derive the buffer cache hit ratio in the following way:

```
Hit rate = (1 - (physical reads)/(logical reads)) * 100
```

Note that the physical reads and the logical reads, which include both the reads from memory and the reads from disk, are accumulated from the start of the Oracle instance. So, if you calculate the preceding ratio on Monday morning, after a restart on Sunday night for a backup, it will show a very low hit ratio. As the week progresses, the hit ratio could increase dramatically, because as more read requests come in, Oracle satisfies them with the data that is already in memory. Unfortunately, Oracle does not give you any reliable rules or guidelines to indicate how much memory you should allocate for your SGA. Some trial and error with data loads should give you a good idea about the right size.

In Chapter 19, I present much more information on the proper tuning of the buffer block size. A high hit ratio does not always correlate with superior database performance. It is entirely possible for your database to have a very high hit ratio—say, in the high 90s—and still have a performance problem. Note that if your total logical reads are extremely high, although the hit ratio is high, your SQL queries may be inefficient.

For OLTP systems with large numbers of users, the sizing of the database buffer cache is critical, as it increases response times by retaining needed data blocks in memory, thereby reducing time-consuming disk I/O.

The Shared Pool

The shared pool is a very important part of the Oracle SGA, and properly tuning it has major implications for your system performance. Unlike the database buffer cache, which holds actual data blocks, the shared pool holds executable PL/SQL code and SQL statements, as well as information regarding the data dictionary tables. The *data dictionary* is a set of key tables that Oracle maintains, and it contains crucial metadata about the database tables, users, privileges, and so forth.

Proper sizing of the shared pool area benefits you in more than one way. First, your response times are going to be better because you're reducing processing time. Second, more users can use the system because the reuse of code makes it possible for the database to serve more users with the same resources. Both the I/O rates and the CPU usage time will diminish when your database uses its shared pool memory effectively. Let's take a detailed look at the individual components of the shared pool.

The Library Cache

The *library cache* component of the shared pool memory is used or shared by all the users of the database. When you issue a SQL statement, Oracle will first parse the SQL statement (check it for syntax, among other things) before executing it. Each time you issue a new SQL statement, Oracle first checks the library cache to see if there is an already parsed and ready-to-execute form of the statement in there. If there is, the processing time is reduced considerably, because you don't have to go through the complicated process again. If Oracle doesn't find the execution-ready version of the SQL code in the library cache, it has to allocate memory from the shared pool. If there isn't enough free memory in the shared pool, Oracle will jettison older code from the shared pool to make room for your new code.

All application code, whether it is pure SQL code or code embedded in the form of PL/SQL program units such as procedures and packages, is parsed first and executed later. If the new code that comes in does not find an already parsed and execution-ready version in the shared pool, the executable has to be built fresh. This is called a *hard parse*, as opposed to a *soft parse*, which occurs when Oracle finds a previously compiled executable. Because all hard parses involve the use of critical system resources such as processing power and internal Oracle structures such as latches, you must make every attempt to reduce their occurrence. High hard parse counts will lead to resource contention, as you will see later, and a consequent slowdown of the database when responding to user requests.

You make library cache sizing decisions based on the statistics regarding the hit and miss ratios on the library cache. Chapter 19 shows you how to use various ratios for measuring the performance of the shared pool. If your system is showing more than the normal amount of misses (i.e., needed code is being reparsed and/or re-executed often), it is time to raise the library cache memory. The way to do this is to raise the total memory allocated to the shared pool.

The Data Dictionary Cache

The *data dictionary cache* component of the shared pool primarily contains object definitions, usernames, roles, privileges, and other such information. When you run a segment of SQL code, Oracle has to first ascertain if you have the privileges to perform the planned operation. It checks the dictionary cache to see if the pertinent information is present there. If it is not, Oracle has to read in the information from the data dictionary into the dictionary cache. Obviously, the more hits you get, the shorter the processing time will be, especially because the data dictionary cache misses tend to be more expensive than library cache hits.

There is no direct way to adjust the data dictionary cache size. You have to increase or decrease the shared pool size to increase or decrease the data dictionary cache size. Therefore, the solution to a low data dictionary cache hit ratio or a low library cache hit ratio is the same: Increase the shared pool size.

TIP *A cache miss on either the data dictionary cache or the library cache component of the shared pool has more impact on database performance than a cache miss on the buffer pool cache. For example, a drop in the data dictionary cache hit ratio from 99 percent to 89 percent leads to a much more substantial deterioration in performance as compared to a similar drop in the buffer cache hit ratio.*

The Redo Log Buffer

The redo log buffer, though it is nowhere near the size of the database buffer cache and the shared pool cache, is nonetheless a crucial component of the SGA. When a server process changes data in the data buffer cache (via an insert, a delete, or an update), it generates redo data, which is recorded in the redo log buffer. The log writer process is in charge of writing redo information from the log buffer in memory to the redo log files on disk. Proper sizing of redo log buffers is important to keep Oracle from writing too often or too infrequently to the buffer. You use the initialization parameter *log_buffer* to set the size of the redo log buffer, and it stays fixed for the duration of the instance. That is, you can't adjust the redo log buffer size dynamically, unlike the other components of the SGA.

The log writer process writes the contents of the redo log buffer to disk under any of the following circumstances:

- The redo log buffer is one-third full.

- Users commit a transaction.

- The database buffer cache is running low on free space and needs to write changed data to the redo log. The database writer instructs the log writer process to make room for the new data by first flushing the log buffer's contents to disk.

The redo log buffer is a "circular" buffer—as the log writer process writes the redo entries from the redo log buffer to the redo log files, server processes will write new redo log entries that will write over the entries that have been already written to the redo log files. You need to have only a small redo log buffer, about 1MB or so. The log writer process usually writes very fast to the redo log files, even when its workload is quite heavy. You'll run into more problems with a too-small buffer size than with a too-large buffer size. A log buffer that is too small will keep the log writer process excessively busy; the log writer process will be constantly writing to disk. Furthermore, if the log buffer is set too small, frequently it will run out of space to accommodate new redo entries. Oracle provides an option called *nologging* that lets you bypass the redo logs almost completely and thus avoid contention during certain operations (e.g., a large data load). You can also batch the commits in a long job, thus enabling a more efficient writing of the redo log entries by the log writer process.

The Large Pool and the Java Pool

The large pool is a purely optional memory pool, and Oracle manages it quite differently from the shared pool. A modified LRU algorithm isn't used to age out entries in the large pool. Oracle uses the large pool area mostly for accommodating the Recovery Manager (RMAN) operations. You set the value of this pool in the initialization file by using the parameter *large_pool_size*. The large pool memory component is important if you're running the shared server architecture.

The Java pool is designed for databases that contain a lot of Java code, so the regular SGA doesn't have to be allocated to components using Java-based objects. Java pool memory is reserved for both the Java Virtual Machine (JVM) and your code for Java-based applications. The default size for this memory pool is 20MB, but if you're deploying Enterprise JavaBeans or using CORBA, you could potentially be looking at Java pool sizes greater than 1GB.

The Program Global Area (PGA)

Of the two major components of the total system memory assigned to the Oracle database and its users, the SGA is clearly the most commonly talked about and tuned component. I must qualify this statement by stating that the nature of the database's transactions determines the size of the PGA relative to the SGA. For most OLTP databases, where transactions are very short, the PGA usage is quite low. On the other hand, complex, long-running queries, which are more typical of a DSS environment, require a larger amount of PGA.

The PGA contains data and control information for server processes. Oracle creates a PGA area for each user (in a dedicated server configuration) when the user starts a session. This area holds data and control information for the dedicated server process that Oracle creates for each individual user. Note that a session's logon information and persistent information, such as bind variable information and data type conversion, are still a part of the SGA (for dedicated server processes). However, the runtime area that is used while SQL statements are executing is located in the PGA. For example, a user's process may have some cursors (handles to memory areas where you store the values for some variables) associated with it. Because these are the user's cursors, they are not shareable by other users automatically, and the PGA is a good location to save those private values.

The runtime area of the PGA is used for all DML and DDL operations, but not for queries. For queries, the runtime area of the SQL execution memory resides in the SGA. However, for complex SQL queries that involve sorts, hash joins, and bitmap merges, the PGA holds the runtime area of the SQL execution memory.

CAUTION *Many Oracle manuals provide the guideline that you can allocate up to half of the total system memory for the Oracle SGA. This guideline assumes that the PGA memory will be fairly small. However, if the number of users is very large and the queries are complex, your PGA component may end up being even higher than the SGA. You should estimate the total memory requirements by projecting both SGA and PGA needs.*

Another major use of the PGA is for performing memory-intensive SQL operations that involve sorting, such as code involving *order by* and *group by* clauses. These sort operations need a working area and the PGA provides that memory area. You could tune the size of these private work areas, but it is a hit-or-miss approach that involves weighing a number of complex Oracle configuration parameters. The parameters that you needed to manually configure include *sort_area_size, hash_area_size, bitmap_area_size,* and others. In Oracle9*i*, you have, for the first time, the option of automating the allocation of the PGA memory to user's work areas. This automation of the allocation of the PGA memory is also called *automatic SQL execution memory management.* Let's see how you can automate this very important component of Oracle's memory to help enhance database query performance.

NOTE *Use the Oracle9i automatic PGA memory management feature to avoid problems in the manual configuration of the PGA.*

Automatic SQL Execution Memory Management

To automate the management of the PGA, you should first configure the initialization parameter *pga_aggregate_target.* You can set the *pga_aggregate_target* parameter to a predetermined amount, say 300MB. In addition, you need to set the *workarea_size_policy* parameter to *auto.* The default on Oracle9*i* for this parameter is *auto.* Here's an example that shows how to set the two initialization parameters to automate the management of the PGA:

```
Workarea_size_policy = AUTO
Pga_aggregate_target = 50000k
```

Once you specify the maximum amount of memory available to your instance by setting the *pga_aggregate_target* parameter, the Oracle server automatically allocates this memory among the queries currently executing in the database. You can set the target to an initial number and later on change it dynamically. Here's an example that shows how you can dynamically alter the amount of memory that can be allocated to the PGA:

```
SQL> alter system set pga_aggregate_target=500m;
```

Oracle9*i* provides the following guidelines to calculate the size of the *pga_aggregate_target* parameter. For an OLTP system, Oracle recommends using 20 percent of the system memory allocated to Oracle for allocation to the *pga_aggregate_target* parameter. For a DSS system, which usually runs complex queries, Oracle recommends using as much as 70 percent of the total memory allocation for Oracle, leaving 30 percent for the SGA. If you have a mixed environment, Oracle recommends using 60 percent of the memory for the SGA and the rest for the PGA. In any case, try avoiding PGA targets that are too small, as the database will have to resort to a large number of inefficient multipass sorts.

PGA Size and Query Efficiency

To reduce response time, ideally, all the sorts that you are performing in the PGA should be performed completely in the "cache" of the work area. Failing this, you should at least try to do it on a one-pass basis. This will eliminate multiple passes over the same set of data, even if this is not a practical goal in all circumstances (you may have a total system memory of 2GB and the table that needs to be sorted consists of 10GB worth of data). Multiple passes over the same data will mean that your queries will take longer to complete. Thus, there is a direct correlation between the PGA size and query performance.

How does the Oracle server know how to automatically configure the optimal work size areas for all the user sessions that are executing SQL operations? Each SQL operation, upon its start, registers its *work area profile* with the Oracle server. The work profiles show the type of operation (e.g., a hash join) and the minimum one-pass and cache memory requirements. As long as the SQL operation is active, the operation's profile is continuously undated and stored in the SGA. A server background process calculates a "global" limit on the PGA every few seconds. A local memory manager process uses the global limit (or memory bound) and the latest work profiles to determine how much PGA memory to allocate to a work area. To prevent a single work area from taking up most of the allocated PGA memory, a single work area is prevented from using more than 5 percent of the total PGA global limit.

Automatic SQL execution memory management, through the use of the *pga_aggregate_target* parameter, helps you use the memory allocated to your database in an efficient manner. The feature performs especially well when you have varying workloads, because it is dynamically adjusting its available memory bounds and the work profiles on a continuous basis. Manual management of PGA could easily lead to either too little or too much memory being allocated, which causes performance problems.

NOTE *In a manual management mode, any PGA memory that isn't being used isn't automatically returned to the system. Every session that logs into the database is allocated a specific amount of PGA memory, which it holds until it logs off, no matter if it's performing SQL operations or not. Under automatic SQL execution memory management, the Oracle server returns all unused PGA memory to the operating system. On a busy system, this makes a huge difference in terms of database and system performance.*

Note that you can still configure the PGA manually by using several init.ora parameters (e.g., *sort_area_size*). Oracle9*i* enables the manual management of the PGA mainly for backward compatibility reasons. Manual management of the PGA includes setting several initialization parameters such as *sort_area_size*, *hash_area_size, bitmap_merge_area_size*, and *create_bitmap_area_size*. When you choose automatic management of the PGA by Oracle, you don't have to use the preceding parameters. This should save you a considerable amount of effort, because prior to Oracle9*i*, you had no choice but to play with several settings for all these parameters, and it was always difficult to determine the exact values for the various components of the PGA. If you don't set a value for the *pga_aggregate_target* parameter, you'll be using the manual mode. Or, you can activate the manual mode by setting the *workarea_size_policy* parameter to *manual*. Oracle strongly recommends the new automatic PGA management because it enables a much more efficient use of memory. For the users, this means a better throughput, in addition to a faster response time for queries in general. You can use automatic PGA management in your database provided you aren't using the Oracle shared server option.

Monitoring Memory Allocation

How do you know how much memory there is in the SGA and what its various components are? To perform a simple check of your SGA allocation, you can issue the *show sga* command, as shown in Listing 5-6.

Listing 5-6. Using the Show Sga Command

```
SQL> show sga
Total System Global Area   147615836 bytes
Fixed Size                 282716 bytes
Variable Size              113246208 bytes
Database Buffers           33554432 bytes
Redo Buffers               532480 bytes
```

The query in Listing 5-6 shows that out of a total of 147MB of memory allocated to the SGA, about 113MB has been allocated to the component variable size, which includes the shared pool, Java pool, large pool, and free memory. The size of the buffer cache is about 33MB. Notice the relatively tiny size of the redo log buffer at about half of a megabyte. The fixed size component of the SGA, which is a little over one-quarter of a megabyte, is a fixed overhead and consists of the instance and database information that the various database processes need.

Although the query in Listing 5-6 gives you the total SGA allocation through the initialization parameters, you really don't get any idea of how the database instance is *currently* distributing the memory among the various processes. To see the current usage of the SGA that has been allocated to your instance, you need to run the query shown in Listing 5-7. It gives you much more information than you really need, but it has several important uses.

You can check the current usage of the SGA by querying the V$SGASTAT dynamic performance view, as shown in Listing 5-7.

Listing 5-7. The Current Usage of the SGA

```
SQL> select * from v$sgastat
POOL    NAME                                  BYTES
----------  -------------------------  --------------------------- ---------
fixed_sga                                     282716
db_block_buffers                              33554432
log_buffer                                    524288
shared pool 1M buffer                         1049088
shared pool Checkpoint queue                  141152
shared pool DML lock                          100408
shared pool FileIdentificatonBlock            323292
shared pool FileOpenBlock                     695504
shared pool KGK heap                          3756
shared pool KGLS heap                         194000
shared pool KSXR pending messages que         226636
shared pool KSXR pending reply queue          90292
shared pool KSXR receive buffers              1060000
shared pool PL/SQL DIANA                      533096
shared pool PL/SQL MPCODE                     106504
shared pool PLS non-lib hp                    2068
shared pool VIRTUAL CIRCUITS                  266120
shared pool character set object              315704
shared pool db_handles                        93000
shared pool dictionary cache                  569332
shared pool enqueue                           171860
shared pool errors                            37896
shared pool event statistics per sess         1356600
shared pool fixed allocation callback         60
shared pool free memory                       31323188
shared pool joxlod: in ehe                    304952
shared pool joxlod: in phe                    114816
shared pool joxs heap init                    4220
shared pool ksm_file2sga region               148652
shared pool library cache                     2337944
shared pool message pool freequeue            772672
shared pool miscellaneous                     2218744
shared pool parameters                        4176
shared pool processes                         127800
shared pool sessions                          395760
shared pool simulator trace entries           98304
shared pool sql area                          764712
shared pool transaction                       182376
shared pool trigger defini                    1520
shared pool trigger inform                    1024
shared pool trigger source                    116
java pool   free memory                       49283072
java pool   memory in use                     5242880
```

As you can see, the output shows the usage of the memory by the SQL area, processes, sessions, library cache, dictionary cache, Java pool, and so on. It also gives you highly useful information about the amount of free memory left in the shared pool. If this memory is consistently getting very low, you need to enlarge the size of your shared pool memory area. On the other hand, if you always see a little bit of memory in the free pool, but not a whole lot, it is an indication that your shared pool memory allocation is appropriate for your instance.

Determining PGA Usage

You can use the V$PROCESS view to determine how the PGA memory is being used by various Oracle processes. Note that these processes will include both the user sessions connected to the database and the Oracle background processes. Thus, you have, for the first time, a way of looking inside the memory allocation for the key Oracle processes such as the log writer and the database writer. Listing 5-8 shows the output from a query using the V$PROCESS dictionary view that lets you know how the PGA memory is being used by various Oracle processes of a database.

Listing 5-8. The Current Usage of the PGA Memory

```
SQL> select
  2    program ,pga_used_mem ,pga_alloc_mem ,pga_max_mem
  3    from
  4    v$process
  5* order by pga_used_mem desc;
```

PROGRAM	PGA_USED_MEM	PGA_ALLOC MEM	PGA_MAX MEM
oracle@hp50 (TNS V1-V3)	16,898,541	21,887,509	29,876,525
oracle@hp50 (LGWR)	4,372,917	4,736,853	4,736,853
oracle@hp50 (D000)	1,287,341	1,616,333	1,616,333
oracle@hp50 (QMN0)	442,261	750,893	763,317
oracle@hp50 (SMON)	240,709	672,325	672,325
oracle@hp50 (DBW0)	169,341	544,557	544,557
oracle@hp50 (CKPT)	163,133	914,285	931,341
oracle@hp50 (DBW1)	159,349	492,141	492,141
oracle@hp50 (RECO)	156,525	483,973	483,973
oracle@hp50 (PMON)	148,109	475,373	475,373
oracle@hp50 (CJQ0)	146,309	475,373	475,373
oracle@hp50 (S000)	70,717	420,293	420,293
PSEUDO	0	0	0

```
13 rows selected.
SQL>
```

As you can see from the output of the query, the log writer and database writer processes take up significant amounts of the total PGA memory.

To check how the total PGA is being allocated by the instance, you need to query the V$PGASTAT dynamic view. Listing 5-9 shows how you can use the

V$PGASTAT view to find out the aggregate *pga_auto* target, the current amount of PGA in use, and how the total PGA allocation stacks up against the estimated PGA needed for optimal and one-pass execution of sort operations.

Listing 5-9. Using the V$PGASTAT View

```
SQL> select * from v$pgastat;
NAME                                                  VALUE
---------------------------------------------------   ----------
aggregate PGA auto target                             912052224
global memory bound                                   51200
total expected memory                                 262144
total PGA in use                                      35444736
total PGA allocated                                   53967872
maximum PGA allocated                                 66970624
total PGA used for auto workareas                     262144
maximum PGA used for auto workareas                   5292032
total PGA used for manual workareas                   0
maximum PGA used for manual workareas                 0
estimated PGA memory for optimal                      262144
maximum PGA memory for optimal                        500123520
estimated PGA memory for one pass                     262144
maximum PGA memory for one-pass                       70123520
14 rows selected.
SQL >
```

The *aggregate PGA auto target,* which is a little over 912MB, is determined by the init.ora parameter *pga_aggregate_target.* This is the total memory that all Oracle connections can have in this instance. The *total PGA in use* component is about 35MB as compared to the *total PGA allocated* (currently) component of about 54MB. The *maximum PGA allocated* value of about 66MB is the highest amount of PGA memory allocated at any time since the instances started. You can see that the estimated PGA memory requirements for optimal and one-pass operations are well below the *pga_aggregate_target,* indicating that the PGA memory is more than enough to prevent inefficient multipass sorting of data in the PGA. Remember that a shortage in the *maximum PGA memory for optimal* and *maximum PGA memory for one-pass* components of the PGA would lead Oracle to invoke mutipass sorting. High multipass executions are a clear indication that you should be increasing the *pga_aggregate_target* size. If the value of *estimated PGA memory for one-pass* exceeds the *pga_aggregate_target,* then you should bump up the latter.

Dynamically Modifying the SGA

What can you do if you find out in the middle of a very busy day that you're running low on free memory? Well, not a whole lot—until recently. The Oracle9*i* version has made it possible to dynamically adjust most of the key components of the SGA. This is good from the DBA's point of view, as you don't have to request a downtime window to modify the necessary initialization parameters. Oracle sometimes refers to the SGA as *dynamic SGA* now, because of its new capability to dynamically adjust memory size on the fly. You can adjust the sizes of the database buffer cache, shared pool, redo log buffer, and the large pool by using the *alter system* command.

Here's how you would adjust the SGA dynamically without having to stop your instance. Let's say you want to increase your *db_cache* size and simultaneously decrease your shared pool size to better allocate the memory you have on your system. Listing 5-10 shows how you can dynamically reconfigure the SGA to achieve this goal. In the listing, the *alter system* command first reduces the shared pool size and then increases the *db_cache* size. The total SGA size remains the same, but now the shared pool and *db_cache* sizes are different.

Listing 5-10. Dynamically Changing the SGA

```
SQL> sho sga
Total System Global Area   147615836 bytes
Fixed Size                       282716 bytes
Variable Size                 113246208 bytes
Database Buffers              33554432 bytes
Redo Buffers                     532480 bytes
SQL> alter system set shared_pool_size=20000000;
System altered.
SQL> alter system set db_cache_size = 50000000;
System altered.
SQL> show sga
Total System Global Area   147615836 bytes
Fixed Size                       282716 bytes
Variable Size                  96468992 bytes
Database Buffers              50331648 bytes
Redo Buffers                     532480 bytes
SQL>
```

The ability to adjust Oracle's memory allocation on the fly without having to incur any downtime means that you can adjust the memory for your shared pool and other components as needed. For example, batch jobs and OLTP daytime processing have widely disparate needs for memory. You could run a shell script that alters the shared pool memory before the batch jobs run and sets it back to its original OLTP levels after the batch jobs complete. Similarly, if your database has clearly definable peak activity times, you could arrange for a larger amount of memory to be available to the instance during the peak periods, without having to shut down the instance. You can use the dynamic management of the SGA to improve database performance. If your monitoring of the instance tells you that your library cache hit ratio or the data dictionary hit ratio is below a critical threshold, you can increase the shared pool size to bring up these hit ratios. If there is contention for the redo log buffer, you may want to increase the size of the redo log buffer dynamically. Chapter 16 contains detailed examples of how you can take advantage of this new dynamic memory management feature of the Oracle9*i* database.

To track the progress of an ongoing SGA dynamic resizing operation, you can use the view V$SGA_CURRENT_RESIZE_OPS. The view has the columns initial_size, current_size, and target_size, through which you can see how the resizing operation is progressing. The closely related V$SGA_RESIZE_OPS view maintains history for about the last 100 SGA resize operations. In addition, you can look in the alert log for your instance, for information regarding all *alter system* commands that have been issued to resize any SGA components.

Using Oracle's SGA and PGA Advisories

What if you aren't quite sure about the correct size of your buffer cache or the shared pool size, and you want Oracle's help in figuring it out? Well, Oracle9*i* provides you with a comprehensive set of advisories for the key components of the SGA and the PGA. The V$ view V$STATISTICS_LEVEL stores the information necessary for Oracle to simulate the improvements in various factors such as physical reads when you change the various components of Oracle's memory. In other words, you get to see the future without risking an actual change. The "what if" scenarios make it easier for you to pick a higher or lower allocation for the component of Oracle's memory. What do you have to do in order for you to start using these wonderful advisories? Nothing, as Oracle will automatically load the dynamic views necessary for using all the sizing advisories by default. The initialization parameter *statistics_level* must be set to TYPICAL in order to populate the various dynamic views that are the basis of the advisories, and the default value for the *statistics_level* parameter happens to be TYPICAL.

The V$STATISTICS_LEVEL view lists all the advisories that you can use in the database. The following query shows the various advisories currently available in the database:

```
SQL> select statistics_view_name from
  2  v$statistics_level;
STATISTICS_VIEW_NAME
-------------------------------------------
V$DB_CACHE_ADVICE
V$MTTR_TARGET_ADVICE
/*this column is for 'timed statistics'*/
/*this column is for 'timed OS statistics'*/
V$SEGSTAT
V$PGA_TARGET_ADVICE
V$SQL_PLAN_STATISTICS
V$SHARED_POOL_ADVICE
8 rows selected.
SQL>
```

In the following sections, you'll learn how you can use the various sizing advisories to predict the effect of altering individual components of the SGA: the buffer cache and the shared pool, as well as the SQL execution memory, the PGA.

The Buffer Cache Advisory

The *Buffer Cache Advisory* uses the data dictionary view V$DB_CACHE_ADVICE to advise you about the proper sizing of the buffer cache. Oracle takes your current workload and estimates through simulation how your cache hits would change if you changed your database cache to a different size. The column estimated_physical_read_factor enables Oracle to correlate physical reads and the buffer cache size. The Buffer Cache Advisory feature eliminates the traditional trial-and-error method of calibrating the SGA, which potentially could hurt database performance. You can use the advisory to see if any increases in the buffer cache would lead to a significant drop in the physical reads.

The following query asks Oracle to conduct various simulations of the estimated physical reads for different buffer cache levels:

```
SQL> select size_for_estimate,
  2  buffers_for_estimate,
  3  estd_physical_read_factor,
  4  estd_physical_reads
  5  from v$db_cache_advice
  6  where name = 'DEFAULT'
  7* AND block_size = 4096
SQL>
```

The V$DB_CACHE_ADVICE view will simulate a change in the buffer cache at 20 different levels, starting from 10 percent of the current buffer cache to a high of 200 percent of the current cache. It will give you the misses on the cache and the resulting I/O activity for each simulated buffer cache level. Based on the values in the output in the select_size_for_estimate and buffers_for_estimate columns, you can decide if you need to adjust the *db_cache* in the default pool.

The Shared Pool Advisory

The Shared Pool Advisory uses the V$SHARED_POOL_ADVICE view to provide you with information about the library cache component of the shared pool. The view shows you simulation results of estimated parse-time savings for different sizes of the shared pool. *Parse-time savings* refer to the reduction in total processing time of a SQL statement because a parsed version of it is already in the shared pool. Oracle performs the simulation for 50 percent to 200 percent of the current size of the shared pool. The following listing shows the V$SHARED_POOL_ADVICE view:

```
SQL> desc v$shared pool advice
            Name                        Null?    Type
 ------------------------------------- -------- ---------------------
 SHARED_POOL_SIZE_FOR_ESTIMATE                   NUMBER
 SHARED_POOL_SIZE_FACTOR                         NUMBER
 ESTD_LC_SIZE                                    NUMBER
 ESTD_LC_MEMORY_OBJECTS                          NUMBER
 ESTD_LC_TIME_SAVED                              NUMBER
 ESTD_LC_TIME_SAVED_FACTOR                       NUMBER
 ESTD_LC_MEMORY_OBJECT_HITS                      NUMBER
SQL>
```

The PGA Advisory

You can use the V$PGA_TARGET_ADVICE and V$PGA_TARGET_ADVICE_HIS-TOGRAM views to help you determine the ideal size for your PGA memory size. Oracle simulates the workload history for several values of the *pga_aggregate_target* parameter. Ideally, you should increase the PGA memory allocation as long as the simulations show that it is contributing to a drop in the inefficient multipass executions. The following listing shows the V$PGA_TARGET_ADVICE view:

```
SQL> desc v$pga_target_advice
Name                                    Null?    Type
--------------------------------------- -------- ------------------------
 PGA_TARGET_FOR_ESTIMATE                          NUMBER
 PGA_TARGET_FACTOR                                NUMBER
 ADVICE_STATUS                                    VARCHAR2(3)
 BYTES_PROCESSED                                  NUMBER
 ESTD_EXTRA_BYTES_RW                              NUMBER
 ESTD_PGA_CACHE_HIT_PERCENTAGE                    NUMBER
 ESTD_OVERALLOC_COUNT                             NUMBER
SQL>
```

Managing Memory Parameters with Oracle Enterprise Manager

Oracle 9*i* provides you with new memory management features through Oracle Enterprise Manager (OEM). Chapter 17 covers OEM in detail, including the installation and setup process. In this section, you'll briefly look at how you can use OEM to manage memory allocations to the various components of the SGA. Instead of using the V$DB_CACHE_ADVICE view and the Buffer Cache Advisory manually, for example, you can quickly get an estimate of ideal memory configuration through OEM. From the OEM console, select Databases and click the Instances icon. Next, choose the Configuration option. From here, you can choose to modify memory and other database configuration parameters. Figure 5-1 shows you the initial memory configuration screen for my test database, finance1, running on a Windows server.

In Figure 5-1, you can see the current amount of memory allocated to the buffer cache, shared pool, large pool, and Java pool. Notice that the Shared Pool, Buffer Cache, and Aggregate PGA Target options have an Advice button next to them. When you click the Advice button for a specific component, you can easily get Oracle's recommendations concerning potential changes in memory allocations to the various components of the SGA.

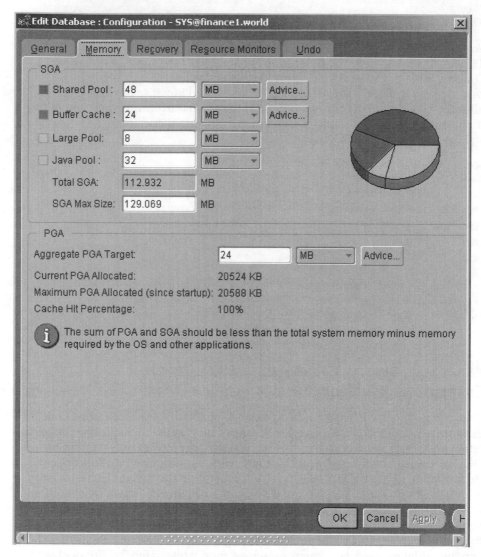

Figure 5-1. The Oracle Enterprise Manager memory configuration screen

 NOTE *One of the main themes of this book is that Oracle database administration can be made easier and less manually driven by using many of the Oracle9i features to simplify day-to-day management. The use of OEM is an important part of this modern approach to Oracle database management. You are much better off using OEM to configure memory allocation.*

You can use OEM to decide whether you should change your memory settings for the shared pool, buffer cache, and the PGA. Figure 5-2 shows you how to use OEM to get buffer cache size advice from Oracle. Because my database doesn't have many transactions, being a mere test database, you can't really see a difference in the physical reads for various buffer cache settings, but you can see the essential idea using either the graph or the table below it. Both the graph and table information clearly show whether you're benefiting by increasing the buffer size. In a similar way, you can get advice on the shared pool size and the PGA aggregate target.

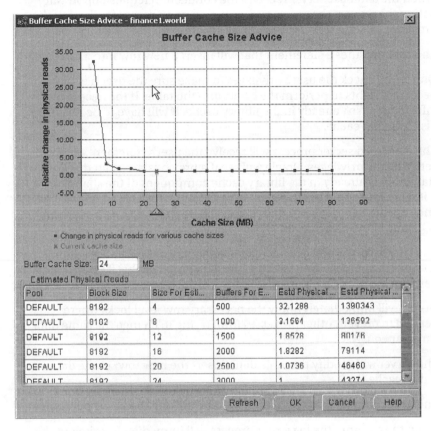

Figure 5-2. Using OEM to get buffer cache size advice

A Simple Oracle Database Transaction

So far, you've been looking at all the components of the Oracle database system: the necessary files and memory allocation, and how you can adjust them. It's time now to look into how Oracle actually operates, in terms of processing users' queries and the mechanics of how it makes changes to data. It's important to understand the mechanics of SQL transaction processing, because all interaction with an Oracle database occurs in the form of either SQL queries that read data or

SQL operations that modify, insert, or delete data. Generally speaking, slow processing is the result of the database not processing your queries and transactions at an optimal speed by the database due to some as-yet unknown reason.

The following is a simplified example of how Oracle processes transactions in general:

1. A user requests a connection to the Oracle server through a 3-tier or an n-tier Web-based client.

2. When the database server receives the connection request, upon validating the request the server starts a new server process for that user's process.

3. The user executes a statement that will insert a new row into a table.

4. Oracle will check the user's privileges to make sure the user has the necessary rights to perform the insert into the table. If the necessary information isn't already in the library cache, it will have to be read from disk into that cache.

5. The dedicated server process will receive the user's statement. After verifying the privileges, Oracle will see if a previously executed SQL statement is already in the library cache component of the shared pool. If it is, Oracle will execute this version of the SQL. If it isn't, Oracle will parse and execute the user's SQL statement. Oracle will then create a private SQL area in the user session's PGA.

6. The Oracle server process will read the data from the data files. If the relevant data blocks are already in the data buffer cache, it doesn't have to perform the previous step.

7. Oracle will immediately apply the necessary row level locks where needed to prevent other processes from trying to change the same data simultaneously.

8. The server will modify the table data (insert the new row) in the data buffer cache first.

9. The user commits the transaction, thereby making the insert permanent.

10. Upon the commit, the log writer process will immediately write out the changed data to the online redo log file.

11. The server process sends a message to the client process to indicate the successful completion of the insert operation. It will send a message indicating the failure of the operation if it can't complete the request successfully.

12. Changes made to the table by the insertion may not be written to disk right away. The database writer process writes the changes in batches, so it may be some time before the inserted information is actually written permanently to the database files on disk.

Transaction Processing in Oracle

A *transaction* is defined as a discrete unit of work in Oracle and consists of at least one SQL statement. The transaction completes when it is completely made permanent or *committed*, or it is completely undone or *rolled back*. Note that either the user executing the transaction or a malfunction of the database (e.g., due to inadequate space in a table) can roll back a SQL statement. If the user does the rollback, it is done explicitly using the *rollback* statement. The user, similarly, performs a commit by using the *commit* statement. In addition to the *commit* and *rollback* statements, users can use the *save point* statement, which will commit the results of a long transaction until a certain intermediate point only. If a program successfully completes and the user exists gracefully from SQL*Plus, the results are implicitly committed, even without the *commit* command.

Data Consistency and Data Concurrency

Databases aren't very useful if a large number of users can't access and modify data simultaneously. *Data concurrency* refers to the capability of the database to handle this concurrent usage of the database by many users. How do you know that another user is not changing the data you're modifying right now, simultaneously? To provide consistent results, the database needs a mechanism within it that ensures users don't step on each other's changes. *Data consistency* refers to the ability of a user to get a meaningful and consistent view of the data, including the changes made to it by all the other users.

Oracle uses special structures called *undo segments* to ensure data consistency. Suppose you're reading in a set of data for a transaction. What if some of the data set shows changes made by one transaction and some of the data shows changes made by another transaction? Oracle ensures that the data you read is *transaction-set consistent;* that is, it guarantees that the data you see reflects a single set of committed transactions. Oracle also provides *read consistency* of data, meaning all the data selected by your queries comes from a single point in time.

Oracle uses locking mechanisms to ensure data concurrency. Locking of individual rows or entire tables by one user ensures the exclusive use of the table by that user for updating purposes, for example. An important feature of Oracle locking mechanisms is that they are, for the most part, automatic. You don't need to concern yourself with the details of how to lock the objects you want to modify—Oracle will take care of it for you behind the scenes. This implicit locking by Oracle is based on the principle of the "least restrictive" level of locking.

Oracle uses two basic modes of locking. The *exclusive mode* is used for updates and the *share lock mode* is used for select operations on tables. The share lock mode enables several users to simultaneously read the same rows in a table. The exclusive mode, because it involves updates to the table, can only allow one user at any given time to employ it. Oracle locking is complex and you'll learn about it in detail in Chapter 8. Oracle releases the locks it holds on the tables and other internal resources automatically after the issue of a *commit, save point,* or *rollback* command. Chapter 8 also discusses how Oracle ensures data consistency and data concurrency.

The Database Writer and the Write Ahead Protocol

The database writer, as you saw earlier, is responsible for writing all modified buffers in the database buffer cache to the data files. Further, it has the responsibility of ensuring there is free space in the buffer cache, so the server process can read in new data from the data files when necessary. However, the database writer has to make sure at all times that the redo records in the redo log buffer associated with the changed data in the data buffer cache must first be written to the redo log data files. This is called the (log) *write ahead protocol.* The enormous importance of the redo log contents makes it imperative that Oracle write its contents to permanent storage ahead of its writes to the database files on disk.

The write ahead protocol prevents a committed transaction from being written in the database records, without recording it first in the redo log files. When users commit their transactions, the log writer process immediately writes only a single commit record to the redo log files. The entire set of records affected by the committed transaction may not be written simultaneously to the data files. This is called the *fast commit mechanism.* The write ahead protocol and the fast commit mechanism ensure that the database is not waiting for all the physical writes to be completed after each transaction. As you can well imagine, a huge OLTP database with numerous changes throughout the day cannot function optimally if it has to write to disk after every committed data change.

NOTE *If there are a large number of transactions and, therefore, a large number of commit requests, the log writer process may not write each transaction's commit record immediately to the redo log. It may batch multiple commit requests if it is busy writing previously issued commit records to the redo log. This writing of multiple records at once is known as group commits.*

The System Change Number

The *System Change Number* (SCN) is an important quantifier that the Oracle database uses to keep track of its state at any given point in time. When you read (select) the data in the tables, you don't affect the state of the database. When you modify, insert, or delete a row, the state of the database is different from what it was before. How is Oracle to know what the current state of the database is? It uses the convenient device of the SCN to keep track of all the changes made to the database over time. The SCN indicates the committed version of the database at that point in time. You can regard the SCN as an internal Oracle timestamp. The SCN is *a logical time stamp* that is used by Oracle to order events that occur within the database. The SCN is very important for several reasons, not the least of which is the recovery of the database after a crash. SCNs are like an increasing sequence of numbers, and Oracle increments them in the SGA.

When a transaction modifies or inserts data, Oracle first writes a new SCN to the rollback segment. The log writer process writes the commit record of the transaction immediately to the redo log. This commit record will have the unique SCN of the new transaction. In fact, the writing of this SCN to the redo log file denotes a committed transaction in an Oracle database. SCNs help Oracle implement data concurrency and transaction consistency. SCNs are also used by Oracle in ordering redo records, and as you'll learn in Chapter 15, they play a critical role during database recovery. Oracle determines how far back you should apply the archived redo logs during a recovery based on the SCN.

The SCN helps Oracle determine if a crash recovery is needed after a sudden termination of the database instance or after a *shutdown abort* command is issued. Every time the database checkpoints, Oracle writes a *start SCN* command to the data file headers. The control file maintains an SCN value for each data file, called the *stop SCN*. The *stop SCN* is usually set to infinity, and every time the instance is stopped normally (e.g., with the *shutdown normal* or *shutdown immediate* command), Oracle copies the *start SCN* number in the data file headers to the *stop SCN* numbers for the data files in the control file. When you restart the database after a graceful shutdown, there is thus no need for any kind of recovery, because the SCNs in the data files and the control files match. On the other hand, abrupt instance termination does not leave time for this matching of SCNs, and instance recovery is usually required because of the varying SCN numbers in data files on the one hand and the control file on the other.

The Central Role of the Oracle Control File

The control file is probably the single most important file in the Oracle database. The control file is a small file that Oracle updates continuously throughout its operation. The control file has information relating to the names and locations of data files and redo log files, as well as the current log sequence numbers—information that is not accessible by the users for even reading purposes. Only Oracle can write the information to the control file.

The control file is created automatically by Oracle at the time the database is created. You need to specify the location for the control file in the initialization file. The instance can run with a single control file, but Oracle recommends at least two control files on separate disks, because of their critical importance. When you turn the instance on, Oracle reads the control file for the location of the data and log files. From that point on, the database checks the control file anytime it needs to verify the existence of a file.

The control file is also important in verifying the integrity of the database and during database recovery. As you recall, the checkpoint process instructs the database writer to write data to the disk. The control file notes all checkpoint information from the online redo log files; this information comes in handy during a recovery process. During a recovery, the checkpoint information in the control file enables Oracle to decide from how far back it should recover from the online redo log files. As the checkpoint indicates the SCN up to which the data files are already written back to the data files, the recovery process will disregard all the information in the online redo log files before the checkpoint noted in the control file.

The Oracle Data Dictionary and the Dynamic Performance Views

Oracle provides a huge number of internal tables to aid you in tracking changes to database objects and to fix problems that will occur from time to time. Mastering these key internal tables is vital if you want to become a savvy Oracle9*i* DBA. All the GUI tools such as OEM depend on these key internal tables (and views) to gather information for monitoring Oracle databases. Although you may want to rely on GUI tools to perform your database administration tasks, do learn as much as you can about these internal tables. Knowledge of these tables gives you valuable information about what is actually happening within the database. Just doing a basic describe of these views will give you insight into the type of information that lies within these tables and will help you write your own monitoring scripts.

You can divide the internal tables into two broad types: the static data dictionary tables and the dynamic performance tables. You won't access these tables directly; rather, you'll access the information through views based on these tables. Chapter 21 is dedicated to a discussion of these views. You can get a complete list of all the data dictionary views in the meantime by issuing the following simple query:

```
SQL > select * from dict;
```

The following sections examine the role of these two important types of views.

The Oracle Data Dictionary

How do you know how many users are in your database and what their roles and privileges are? How about the total number of tables and the columns within those tables? Fortunately, you don't have to keep records on all these important types of information—Oracle does it all for you. Oracle maintains a set of tables within the database called the *data dictionary*. The data dictionary is one of the most important components of the Oracle database.

The data dictionary is a set of static tables that Oracle maintains in the database. The data that the data dictionary maintains is also known as *metadata*. DBAs and developers depend heavily on the data dictionary for information about the various components of the database. These tables contain information such as the list of tables, table columns, users, user privileges, file and tablespace names, and so on. A simple query such as the following necessitates several calls to the data dictionary before Oracle can execute it. Oracle needs to verify from the data dictionary tables that the table employee and the column city exist, as well as confirm that the user has the rights to execute that statement. As you can imagine, a heavily used OLTP database will require numerous queries on the data dictionary tables during the course of a day.

```
SQL> select  employee_name from emp
        where city = 'NEW York';
```

It's important to note that the data dictionary tables don't report on the running instance at all. The data dictionary only holds information about the database, and another set of views called the *dynamic performance views* records important information about the instance. The data dictionary tables describe the entire database: its logical and physical structure, its space usage, its object descriptions and constraints on them, and user information. You really can't access the data dictionary tables directly; instead, you're given access to views built on them. You also can't change any of the information in the data dictionary tables yourself, because they're tables you can *only select* from. Only Oracle has the capability to change data in the data dictionary tables. A common data dictionary table, for example, is the dba_users table, which contains all the names, roles, and profiles of the users in the database.

The Oracle superuser SYS owns most of the data dictionary tables (some are created under the system username), and they are stored in the System tablespace, which is a mandatory tablespace in Oracle databases. DBAs and developers use the data dictionary views to find out details about various items in the database. Often, a DBA can find out quite a bit about a database that has been newly assigned to her or him by making a few simple queries based on the data dictionary views. Oracle also uses the data dictionary heavily during routine SQL processing.

Before you can update any table, for example, Oracle has to first verify that the table in fact exists and that you have the privilege to execute the *update* statement. In a busy OLTP database, therefore, the data dictionary needs to be consulted frequently during transactions. Oracle maintains the data dictionary cache, which is apart of the SGA, to query the data dictionary efficiently. The data dictionary cache keeps the most recently accessed data dictionary tables in cache to avoid constant disk searches for the tables and the consequent increase in physical I/O, all of which leads to a deterioration in performance.

The Dynamic Performance (V$) Views

In addition to the data dictionary, Oracle maintains a set of important tables called the *V$* or *dynamic performance tables*. These tables maintain information about the current instance, and Oracle continuously updates these tables. This is why they are called "dynamic," as opposed to the "static" data dictionary tables. The V$ views are the foundation of all Oracle database performance tuning. If you wish to "master" the Oracle9*i* database, you must master the V$ dynamic views because they are the wellspring of so much knowledge about the Oracle instance.

As in the case of the data dictionary tables, there's a set of base tables that act as the source for the V$ views. Oracle maintains a set of virtual dynamic tables called the X$ tables. The dynamic views, which start with the prefix "V$," are created from the X$ tables. Oracle doesn't allow you to refer to the X$ tables directly; rather, Oracle creates views on all these tables and then creates synonyms for these views, all starting with the prefix V$. That's the reason why the dynamic views are also referred to simply as *V$ views*. It is these V$ views, rather than the actual dynamic tables, that you'll be accessing to get information about various aspects of a running instance.

The dynamic performance views, like the data dictionary views, are read-only tables and so only Oracle can update them. Also, remember that the dynamic performance tables are only populated for the duration of the course and are cleaned out when you shut down the instance. Some of the tables capture sessionwide information, and some of them capture systemwide information. You'll find the dynamic views extremely useful in session management, backup operations and, most important, in performance tuning.

Listing 5-11 shows a simple example using the V$SESSION dynamic view, which lets you find out all the currently active users' usernames and the SQL they are executing in the database.

Listing 5-11. Using Some Key Dynamic Views

```
SQL> select a.username,
  2  s.sql_text
  3  from v$session a,v$sqltext s
  4  where a.sql_address = s.address
  5  and a.sql_hash_value = s.hash_value
  6  AND A.STATUS='ACTIVE'
  7* order by a.username,a.sid,s.piece
SQL> /
USERNAME                         SQL_TEXT
-----------------------------------------------------------------
10 SYSTEM      select a.sid,a.username, s.sql_text from
                         v$session a,v$sqltext s where
                         a.sql_address = s.address and
                         a.sql_hash_value = s.hash_v
                     AND A.STATUS='ACTIVE'
                         order by a.username,a.sid,s.piece
SYS               Select f.file#, f.block#, f.ts#,
                         f.length from fet$ f, ts$ t
                         where t.ts#=f.ts# and
                         t.dflextpct!=0 and t.bitmapped=0

SQL>
```

The Oracle Optimizer

The *optimizer* is a component of all relational DBMSs that ensures that the database uses the most efficient method to process queries. All databases based on the SQL language will need to have an optimizer to choose the best way to access the data objects and process the SQL statements. The job of the optimizer is to suggest an "optimal" (not always the "best") way to process a query. In most cases, when users issue a query against the database, there's more than one way to access the tables and retrieve the data. Thus, because there are many ways to execute the same statement, Oracle uses an optimizer to choose the best execution plan for queries based on the cost of the query in terms of resource use. That's why it's called the *cost-based optimizer* (CBO). You can also use the so-called rule-based optimizer that Oracle also provides, but the CBO is the more efficient and consequently the more popular optimizer. Query optimizing is at the heart of modern relational databases and is an essential part of how Oracle conducts its operations. The query optimizer is transparent to the users and Oracle will automatically apply the best access and join methods to your queries before it starts processing.

How does Oracle figure out the best execution strategy for a query? To aid in choosing the best execution plans, Oracle uses statistics on tables and indexes, which include counts of the number of rows and the data distribution or "data skew" in the tables within the database. The physical storage statistics and the data distribution statistics for all database tables and indexes, columns, and partitions are stored in various tables that are part of the Oracle data dictionary. Armed with this information, the optimizer usually succeeds in finding the best path to access and execute complex queries, especially ones involving multitable joins. Oracle also lets you use *hints* to override the optimizer's choice of an execution path. This is because in some instances the application developer's knowledge of the data enables him or her to use more efficient execution plans than what the optimizer can came up with based on its statistics.

Oracle Enterprise Manager

Oracle Enterprise Manager (OEM) is Oracle's GUI based management tool that lets you manage multiple databases efficiently. OEM enables security management, backups, and routine user and object management. Because OEM is GUI based, you don't have to know a lot of SQL to use the tool. However, understanding the V$ and dynamic performance tables will enhance your knowledge about how the database works, and OEM will be an even more powerful tool in your hands after you master the management of the database using the data dictionary–based and dynamic performance table–based SQL queries. Oracle has really improved OEM in its most recent versions, and all serious practitioners of the trade should master the use of the tool both for daily database management and "lights out" database operation administration and troubleshooting. Chapter 17 explains the configuration and use of the OEM tool set.

You can invoke OEM from your Windows desktop by installing the OEM software on your machine. You can also start the OEM console from your UNIX session by invoking the oemapp executable.

OEM is most definitely not the only GUI tool for managing Oracle databases. Several other excellent third-party tools are available, some with smarter features than OEM. The big advantages to using OEM are that it comes free with the Oracle9i server software and that Oracle has devoted considerable effort to improving the quality of this monitoring and management tool over the years.

Summary

This chapter's goal was to merely cover the terrain lightly and familiarize you with the various components that help Oracle databases perform their complex workloads. I cover many of this chapter's topics exhaustively in later chapters in the book.

In this chapter, you learned that the difference between the logical view and the physical view of the database is very important. The logical view simplifies the complex physical layouts of the database for database developers and DBAs alike.

You also learned about the key database files, including the init.ora file and other administrative files you'll deal with on a daily basis as a DBA. The discussion of the main Oracle processes helped you understand how Oracle performs its work. The discussion of SGA and its components will help you tune the Oracle9*i* database for optimum performance later on. Concepts such as concurrency, consistency, the write ahead protocol, and others are key to understanding the theory behind Oracle's transaction processing.

Be patient if the coverage seems sketchy at times—you'll surely encounter all of these components in more detail during the relevant discussions later on in this book.

CHAPTER 6

Using SQL*Plus and *i*SQL*Plus

YOU CAN CONNECT to and work with the Oracle9*i* database in many ways. Chances are, though, that you'll spend a lot of time using the Oracle SQL*Plus interface and a set of commands known as SQL*Plus commands. SQL*Plus is the Oracle user interface for interacting with a database. You can perform all database administration tasks, including starting and stopping the instance, through this single interface. Thus, the importance of this utility has grown even further in the Oracle9*i* version.

Before the release of Oracle9*i*, administrators did most of their database administration work from the Server Manager interface. SQL*Plus was used for some database administration tasks, but DBAs still couldn't start or stop the instance from it. Administrators had to use the two utilities, SQL*Plus and Server Manager, together to do their job. Oracle9*i* dispenses with the Server Manager utility completely.

In this chapter, I start off by discussing how to use the SQL*Plus utility to perform typical database administration tasks. I begin with an overview of how to start, conduct, and end a SQL*Plus session. You'll get a chance to learn the important SQL*Plus commands, if you aren't already familiar with them, during this overview.

This chapter also includes a brief discussion on building reports using SQL*Plus. Although you probably won't use the SQL*Plus interface to produce a lot of reports, it's nice to know how to work with its many report-building features.

Later in this chapter, I show you how to install, configure, and use the *i*SQL*Plus utility, which enables you to connect to the Oracle9*i* database through a Web browser and use most of the standard SQL*Plus commands.

SQL*Plus for the DBA

The SQL*Plus interface provides you with a window into the Oracle database. Oracle developers use the interface extensively to create SQL and PL/SQL program units. The interface is a valuable tool for Oracle DBAs for several reasons: You can use it to run SQL queries and PL/SQL (Oracle's Procedural Language extension to SQL) code blocks and receive the results; it helps you issue database administration commands and automate jobs; it enables you start up and shut down the database; and it provides you with a convenient way to create database administration reports.

SQL*Plus is included with your Oracle9*i* server software, and you can access it in three different ways: through the command line, through a Windows client interface, or through a Web browser–based interface. The Oracle9*i* client software also contains the SQL*Plus executables. Once you ascertain that the SQL*Plus software is installed on your server or client machine, it's a straightforward process to log into the SQL*Plus environment. You can use either a GUI from a client machine or the command line from the server to log into SQL*Plus. You can access SQL*Plus from the command line by typing **sqlplus** at the operating system prompt. If you are using the SQL*Plus GUI on a Windows client, click the SQL*Plus icon and the interface prompts you for your username, password, and the instance name. As long as your connectivity to the database is established through the proper entries in the tnsnames.ora file (see Chapter 11 for more information on this file), you are all set to use the SQL*Plus interface.

NOTE *On UNIX servers, be sure to type in lowercase letters. On Windows, the interface is not case sensitive. Other than this minor detail, the SQL*Plus command line interface works the same way on Windows and all variants of the UNIX and Linux platforms.*

When you invoke SQL*Plus by typing **sqlplus** at the operating system prompt, the interface will prompt you for your username and password. As a DBA, you should log in with one of your administrative accounts. You can also type in the username/password combination when you invoke SQL*Plus, but your password will be visible to others when you do this. If you have the SYSDBA privileges, you can log into SQL*Plus as follows:

```
sqlplus sys/password as sysdba.
```

Certain operations such as start-up and shutdown are permitted only if you log into SQL*Plus with SYSDBA credentials.

Using SQL*Plus in Interactive and Noninteractive Modes

You can use the SQL*Plus utility in both manual and scripted noninteractive modes. It stands to reason that you would want to perform sensitive administration tasks such as database recovery in an interactive mode. On the other hand, you can automate routine processing of SQL using scripts, and your SQL commands will then run noninteractively. In either case, the commands are the same—it is just the mode in which you issue the commands that is different.

SQL*Plus Commands and SQL Commands

Remember that the SQL*Plus interface lets you interact with the Oracle database. You can use two basic types of commands in SQL*Plus. The first type are called *local commands*, and these are executed locally with SQL*Plus. For example, commands such as *copy*, *compute*, and *set linesize* are local commands. These SQL*Plus commands all end with a new line, and they don't need a command terminator as such. All other commands, including the SQL commands *create table* and *insert* and PL/SQL code that is enclosed in *Begin* and *End* statements, are called *server-executed commands*. Note that all SQL-type commands end in a semicolon (;) or a slash (/). All PL/SQL-type commands end with a slash (/).

SQL*Plus Security

Oracle provides an additional security mechanism for using the SQL*Plus interface, beyond the mandatory username/password requirement. This security mechanism involves the use of a special table called product_user_profile, which is owned by the user System, who is one of the two superusers of the Oracle database. Using the product_user_profile table, you can limit access to SQL*Plus and SQL commands, as well as PL/SQL statements. When a user logs into the SQL*Plus session, SQL*Plus will check this table to see what restrictions are supposed to be applied to the user in the SQL*Plus session. How Oracle administers this security layer is a little bit tricky: The user may have an insert or delete privilege in the database, but because the SQL*Plus privileges override this privilege, Oracle may deny the user the right to exercise the privilege.

After you create a database, you should run a special script, pupbld.sql, which is used to support SQL*Plus security. This script, which is located in the $ORACLE_HOME/sql/admin directory, should be run as the user System. This script will build the product_user_profile table, which is then used to limit the user's privileges in a SQL*Plus session. Note that the product_user_profile table is actually a synonym for the table sqlplus_product_user_profile. Listing 6-1 shows the format of the product_user_profile table.

Listing 6-1. The Product_user_profile Table

```
SQL> desc product_user_profile
Name                              Null?     Type
------------------------------    --------  --------------------------
PRODUCT                           NOT NULL  VARCHAR2(30)
USERID                                      VARCHAR2(30)
ATTRIBUTE                                   VARCHAR2(240)
 SCOPE                                      VARCHAR2(240)
NUMERIC_VALUE                               NUMBER(15,2)
CHAR_VALUE                                  VARCHAR2(240)
DATE_VALUE                                  DATE
LONG_VALUE                                  LONG
SQL>
```

NOTE *By default, SQL*Plus imposes no restrictions on any users, so when the product_user_profile table is first created, there are no rows in it. The user system has to explicitly insert rows into the product_user_profile table if some users need to be restricted in SQL*Plus. You can choose to restrict a user from executing the following commands:* alter, begin connect, declare exec, execute, grant, host, insert, select, *and* update.

Listing 6-2 shows how you can use the product_user_profile table to prevent the user OE from deleting, inserting, or updating any data in the database.

Listing 6-2. Using the Product_user_profile Table

```
Sql> insert into product_user_profile
2  values
3* ('SQL*PLUS','OE','INSERT',NULL,NULL,NULL,NULL,NULL);
1 row created.
Sql> insert into product_user_profile
2  values
3* ('SQL*PLUS','OE','DELETE',NULL,NULL,NULL,NULL,NULL);
1 row created.
SQL> insert into product_user_profile
values
3* ('SQL*PLUS','OE','UPDATE',NULL,NULL,NULL,NULL,NULL);
1 row created.
market1 > COMMIT;
Commit complete.
market1 >
```

You can see the entries pertaining to user OE by querying the product_user_profile table in the following way:

```
market1 > select product,attribute from
  2  product_user_profile where userid='OE';
PRODUCT                       ATTRIBUTE
----------------------------------------------
SQL*PLUS                      INSERT
SQL*PLUS                      DELETE
SQL*PLUS                      UPDATE
market1 >
```

If the user OE tries to delete data from a table, the result would be the following error, even though the table orders belongs to the oe schema:

```
SQL> connect oe/oe
Connected.
SQL> delete from oe.orders;
SP2-0544: invalid command: delete
SQL>
```

If you want to grant to user OE the right to delete data through SQL*Plus, you can do so by *deleting* the relevant line from the product_user_profile table, as follows:

```
market1 > delete from product_user_profile
  2  where userid='OE' and attribute = 'DELETE';
1 row deleted.
market1 > COMMIT;
Commit complete.
market1 >
```

The *alter, begin, declare, execute,* and *grant* commands are data definition language (DDL) and PL/SQL commands. The *insert, select,* and *update* commands are, of course, data manipulation language (DML) commands, except the *host* attribute, which I explain later in this chapter. The *host* command is used in SQL*Plus to access the operating system and issue operating system commands. You really don't want your users to be able to issue operating system commands by simply using the *host* command. For example, if you want to deny user salapati this dangerous privilege, this is what you have to do to the product_user_profile table:

```
SQL> insert into product_user_profile
  2  (product,userid,attribute)
  3  values
  4  ('SQL*Plus','salapati','HOST')
  /
1 row created.
SQL>
```

If you want to restore to user salapati the right to use the *host* command, you can do so by deleting the row you just inserted. For example, in this case, you need to issue the following command to restore the *host* privilege to user salapati:

```
SQL> delete from product_user_profile where userid='SALAPATI';
```

NOTE *Remember that users will retain any privileges you grant them, even though they can't exercise the privileges in the SQL*Plus session. This way, you can grant application owners privileges on the data objects when they are using packages and procedures that are stored and executed in the database, while denying them these same privileges when they log into SQL*Plus.*

Controlling Security Through the Set Role Command

As you probably know, it is better to grant and revoke database privileges through the use of roles, rather than grant the privileges directly, for several reasons. The use of roles, however, carries with it a potential security issue, because any user can change his or her role to a specific role by simply using the *set role* command in SQL*Plus. You can shut down this security loophole by using the product_user_profile table to disable any user's ability to use the *set role* command.

Using the Restrict Command to Disable Commands

You can also use the *restrict* command to prevent users from using certain operating system commands. The net effect is the same as using the product_user_profile table, with the difference being that the *restrict* command disables the commands even where there are no connections to the server.

You can use the *restrict* command in three levels. The following example illustrates the use of the command at level 1:

```
$ sqlplus -restrict 1
```

Table 6-1 shows the commands that are disabled by using the *restrict* command and the differences between the three restriction levels.

Table 6-1. The Three Restriction Levels for SQL*Plus

COMMAND	LEVEL 1	LEVEL 2	LEVEL 3
edit	Disabled	Disabled	Disabled
get			Disabled
host	Disabled	Disabled	Disabled
save		Disabled	Disabled
spool		Disabled	Disabled
start	@,@@		Disabled
store		Disabled	Disabled

TIP *By using* iSQL*Plus *instead of the traditional SQL*Plus interface, you remove the ability of the users to issue operating system commands such as* host *and* spool. *In the* iSQL*Plus *environment, the users never access the intermediate operating system.*

Setting the SQL*Plus Environment with the Set Command

Of all the commands that you can use in SQL*Plus, the *set* command is probably the most fundamental command, because it enables you to set the all-important environment for your SQL*Plus sessions. Environment settings include the number of lines per page of output, width of the numeric data in the output, titles for reports, and HTML formatting, all of which are enabled, disabled, or modified with the *set* command. The *set* command is but one of the commands that you can use in SQL*Plus, and you can see the entire list of available commands by typing **help index** at the SQL prompt, as shown in Listing 6-3.

Listing 6-3. Using the Help Index Command to Show Help Topics

```
SQL> help index
Enter Help [topic] for help.
 @              COPY        PAUSE        SHUTDOWN
 @@             DEFINE      PRINT        SPOOL
 /              DEL         PROMPT       SQL*PLUS
 ACCEPT         DESCRIBE    QUIT         START
```

APPEND	DISCONNECT	RECOVER	STARTUP
ARCHIVE LOG	EDIT	REMARK	STORE
ATTRIBUTE	EXECUTE	REPFOOTER	TIMING
BREAK	EXIT	REPHEADER	TTITLE
BTITLE	GET	RESERVED WORDS ()	
CHANGE	HELP	RESERVED WORDS (PL/SQL)	
CLEAR	HOST	RUN	LIST
COLUMN	COLUMN	INPUT	SAVE
CONNECT	PASSWORD	SHOW	COMPUTE
SETWHENEVER	OSERROR	WHENEVER	SQLERROR
UNDEFINE	VARIABLE		

As you can see in Listing 6-3, the *set* command is listed as one of the available commands. If you want to see all the environment variables that you can control through using the *set* command, type **help set**. For performing your day-to-day tasks in SQL*Plus, you need to be familiar with several of these commands, which I explain briefly in the next section.

Setting Common SQL*Plus Variables

Variables are values of key attributes that you can change while using SQL*Plus. Table 6-2 summarizes the most common variables you need to know. Practice with the variables will enhance your comfort level and help you become a skilled practitioner of SQL*Plus in a relatively short time. To save space, I'm not providing examples of the use of these variables, so it's important you actually try them out in your SQL*Plus session.

*Table 6-2. Common SQL*Plus Environment Variables*

VARIABLE	FUNCTION	USAGE
Array[size]	Sets the batch of rows fetched from database at one time	set array 50
Auto[commit]	Sets the commits of transactions to automatic or manual	set auto on
Colsep	Sets any text that you want printed in between column values	set colsep
Copyc[ommit]	Sets the frequency of commits when using the *copy* command	set copy 10000
Def[ine]{&/c/on/off}	Sets the prefix character during variable substitutions	set define on
Echo {off/on}	If you have echo on, the command file listing will be shown onscreen	set echo on
Edit filename	Sets the default filename when you use your default editor	set editfile draft.sql

(Continued)

Table 6-2. *Common SQL*Plus Environment Variables (Continued)*

VARIABLE	FUNCTION	USAGE
Feed[back] {off/on}	Shows the number of records returned by your query	`set feedback off`
Hea[ding] {off/on}	Sets whether the column headers are printed or not	`set head off`
line[esize] {80\n}	Sets the number of characters displayed per line	`set linesize 40`
long {80/n}	Sets the maximum width of the LONG, CLOB, NCLOB, and XMLType values	`set long 10000`
newp[age] {1/n/none}	Sets the number of blank lines at the top of each new page	`set newpage 0`
num[width] {10/n}	Sets the format for displaying numbers	`num`
pages[ize] {24/n}	Sets the number of lines in each page	`set pagesize 60`
pau[se] {off/on}/text}	Sets the amount of output that is printed to the screen	`set pause on`
serverout[put] { off/on}[size n]	Sets whether output of PL/SQL code is shown	`set serveroutput on`
sqlp[rompt] {sql> \text}	Sets the command prompt for SQL*Plus sessions	`set sqlprompt 'salapati >'`
term[out] {off/on}	Determines whether command file output is displayed or not	`set termout off`
ti[me] {off/on}	Displays time if set to on	`set time off`
timi[ng] {off/on}	Controls the display of timing for SQL commands	`set timing off`
ver[ify] {off/on}	Determines whether SQL text is displayed after variable substitution	`set verify off`

NOTE *Table 6-2 doesn't represent a complete list of environment variables that you can control using the* set *command. Refer to the Oracle SQL*Plus manuals for a complete listing of and usage guidelines for all the variables.*

If there is text inside the square brackets ([]) next to the variable, it means that the command listed before the square brackets commence is the abbreviation for the complete variable name. Either version will work the same way.

The options inside the curly brackets ({}) show you the possible options you can choose and the default values. The value listed first inside the curly brackets for a variable is its default value. You can either leave it as is by not doing anything, or you can change it to the other possible values by using the *set variable value* notation.

You can have all your preferred session settings stored in a file, which you can execute like any other SQL file whenever you want to change a bunch of variable values at once. You can also have several of these files saved for different tasks if your job involves a lot of reporting using the SQL*Plus interface.

You can change the environment variables for your session by using the Options menu and choosing Environment. You are shown all the current environment variables for your session, and you can modify them as long as you stay within the limits. This option is available to you only if you are using the Oracle SQL*Plus GUI interface on Windows. If you are logged into SQL*Plus on a UNIX server, unfortunately you lose this nice option of easily changing values of your environment variables.

Specifying Variable Preferences with the glogin.sql File

Do you have to manually adjust your environment each time you log into SQL*Plus if the values of the default variables don't meet your needs? Fortunately, you don't have to do this, because Oracle allows you to specify your preferences for all variable values in the glogin.sql file. During the server software installation, this file is placed in the $ORACLE_HOME/sqlplus/admin directory. Listing 6-4 shows a sample glogin.sql file, which is read by Oracle every time you log into SQL*Plus.

Listing 6-4. A Sample Glogin.sql File

```
-- Copyright (c) Oracle Corporation 1988, 2000.  All Rights Reserved.
-- NAME
--   glogin.sql
-- DESCRIPTION
--   SQL*Plus global login startup file.
--   Add any SQL*Plus commands here that are to be executed when a user
--   starts SQL*Plus on your system
-- USAGE
--   This script is automatically run when SQL*Plus starts
-- For backward compatibility
SET PAGESIZE 14
SET SQL*PLUSCOMPATIBILITY 8.1.7
-- Used by Trusted Oracle
COLUMN ROWLABEL FORMAT A15
-- Used for the SHOW ERRORS command
COLUMN LINE/COL FORMAT A8
COLUMN ERROR     FORMAT A65  WORD_WRAPPED
-- Used for the SHOW SGA command
COLUMN name_col_plus_show_sga FORMAT a24
-- Defaults for SHOW PARAMETERS
COLUMN name_col_plus_show_param FORMAT a36 HEADING NAME
COLUMN value_col_plus_show_param FORMAT a30 HEADING VALUE
-- Defaults for SET AUTOTRACE EXPLAIN report
```

```
COLUMN id_plus_exp FORMAT 990 HEADING i
COLUMN parent_id_plus_exp FORMAT 990 HEADING p
COLUMN plan_plus_exp FORMAT a60
COLUMN object_node_plus_exp FORMAT a8
COLUMN other_tag_plus_exp FORMAT a29
COLUMN other_plus_exp FORMAT a44
```

NOTE *The glogin.sql file applies to all the users of the system, and therefore it is called a* site profile. *So, if you want all SQL*Plus sessions to have some special variable values each time you log in, all you have to do is edit the glogin.sql file.*

Specifying Default Preferences with the .login File

What if individual users wish to set their own particular preferences for variables as the default for their sessions? The .login file is another file that is checked by Oracle to set your individual SQL*Plus environment. This file is usually located in your home directory. Because the .login file helps set individual user variables, it is also known as the user profile for SQL*Plus. The following is a sample .login file:

```
set time on
col user_id new_value user_id
col user_name new_value user_name
select user_id, lower(username) user_name from user_users where username=user;
col db_name new_value db_name
col db new_value db
select distinct(machine) db from v$session where type='BACKGROUND';
select name db_name from v$database;
set sqlprompt "&db_name@&db:SQL> "
```

NOTE *All SQL*Plus variable values you specify in the .login file will override the settings in the glogin.sql file. Any changes you make in the session itself will override everything else and last for the duration of that session only.*

SQL*Plus Command Line Arguments

As you have seen, you can start a new SQL*Plus session by merely typing in **sqlplus** at the command prompt. However, you can specify several command line arguments to customize the SQL*Plus session. The following sections cover the command line arguments you can use when you start a SQL*Plus session.

The Silent Argument -s

If you invoke SQL*Plus with the –s argument, the session will run silently; there won't be any output on the screen. When would you use this argument? When you're running batch jobs and you have no need to see the output of the SQL*Plus session, you can start the session in the silent mode. The silent option is very helpful when you're producing reports because the banner, version, and other information is suppressed.

The "No Prompt" Logon Argument -L

If you invoke SQL*Plus with the –L argument, it won't prompt you for a new username and password if you fail to log in the first time. Again, this is an option that's handy during the execution of SQL batch jobs through the operating system.

The Restrict Option -R

You've already seen how you can use the SQL*Plus –R option (at three different levels) to disable certain operating system commands in SQL*Plus. Please refer to the section "Using the Restrict Command to Disable Comments" earlier in this chapter for more information.

The Markup Option -M

You can generate complete Web pages from your SQL*Plus sessions by invoking SQL*Plus with the –M option (more on the *markup* command later in this chapter).

Removing Settings with the Clear Command

The *clear* command removes the current setting of several things, including columns and the SQL*Plus buffer. You use the *clear* command to make sure that settings no longer needed are not in force in the current session of SQL*Plus. Listing 6-5 shows sample output of the *clear* command.

Listing 6-5. Using the Clear Command

```
SQL> clear breaks
breaks cleared
SQL> clear buffer
buffer cleared
SQL> clear
SQL> clear breaks
breaks cleared
SQL> clear buffer
buffer cleared
SQL> clear columns
columns cleared
```

```
SQL> clear sql
sql cleared
SQL> clear timing
SQL>
```

The *clear* command by itself clears your screen without affecting any of the settings of SQL*Plus. The *clear buffer* and *clear sql* commands achieve the same effect: They remove the SQL in the memory buffer of SQL*Plus. The *clear columns* and the *clear break* commands remove any column definitions and breaks. The *clear timing* command deactivates all timers.

The Store Command

During a given SQL*Plus session, it's likely that you'll need to change your environment settings in order to run a specific SQL script or command. If you want to preserve these settings for future use, you can do so with the help of the *store* command. The following example shows how to use the *store* command to save your SQL*Plus environment settings. Once you store your favorite environment variables, you can easily reuse them anytime you want by simply executing the mySQL*Plus.sql script. (I explain the execution of SQL scripts in the following sections.)

```
SQL> store set mySQLPlus.sql
Created file mySQLPlus.sql
SQL>
```

The Show Command

How can you find out what your present environment variables are set to? You can use the *show* command to find out variable values. To get the values for all variables, you use the *show all* command. To find out the individual values, you type in the specific variable's name, as shown in the following example:

```
SQL> show ttitle
ttitle ON and is the following 49 characters:
Annual Financial Report for the Ladies Club, 2001
SQL>
```

Exiting SQL*Plus

You exit a SQL*Plus session by simply typing **exit** in lowercase letters or caps. You may also type in **quit** to exit to the operating system.

 CAUTION *If you make a graceful exit from SQL*Plus by typing in the command **exit** (or **quit**), your transactions will all be committed immediately. If you don't intend to commit the transactions, check and make sure you issue the* rollback *command before you exit.*

Key SQL*Plus "Performing" Commands

All the work you do in SQL*Plus, whether you are issuing simple commands or elaborate scripts to gather information from the database, involves knowing how to use two kinds of parameters. The commands in the first group are those that actually *do* something—for example, the *recover* command recovers a database.

The commands in the second group are formatting commands, which will help you get clean output from your queries. You'll learn about the most important of both kinds of commands next. In this section you'll look at the commands that "do something," and you'll leave the "formatting commands" for study later on in this chapter.

The Sqlprompt Command

As a DBA, you'll more than likely be working on several databases throughout the day. When you're performing multiple tasks during the day, it's very easy to forget which database you're connected to from a particular SQL*Plus session. Is there any way to easily figure out which database you're logged into? Yes, there is: To avoid committing blunders (such as dropping production tables instead of development or testing tables), you should always set your environment so the instance name shows up on your prompt every time, reminding you where exactly you are currently.

You can use the following command, which uses the DEFINE variable called CONNECT_IDENTIFIER, to help you set your SQL*Plus prompt to show the database name. Notice how the *set* command changes your prompt immediately in the SQL*Plus interface. When you use this command, your prompt will no longer be the generic SQL > prompt—it will instead be the more meaningful DBNAME> prompt, which will always remind you which database you are in without your having to make any dangerous guesses.

```
SQL> set SQLPROMPT '&_CONNECT_IDENTIFIER > '
market1 >
```

If you wish, you can incorporate the preceding line in your glogin.sql file, which will set your session values at the user level.

The Describe Command

The *describe* command describes or lists the columns and the column specifications of a table. It also enables you to describe an Oracle package or procedure. The *describe* command is immensely useful when you're performing routine DBA activities. If, for example, you aren't sure what column to select in a particular table, but you're sure what table you should be querying, the *describe* command helps out by giving you all the column names. Because you can describe even the metadata (the data dictionary), it's very easy to get familiar with and use table and column information that is critical for the database.

Listing 6-6 shows how the *describe* command enables you to find out the columns and the column types for a table.

Listing 6-6. Using the Describe Command

```
SQL> desc employees
 Name                                    Null?       Type
 --------------------------------------  --------    --------------------------------------
 EMPLOYEE_ID                             NOT NULL    NUMBER(6)
 FIRST_NAME                                          VARCHAR2(20)
 LAST_NAME                               NOT NULL    VARCHAR2(25)
 EMAIL                                   NOT NULL    VARCHAR2(25)
 PHONE_NUMBER                                        VARCHAR2(20)
 HIRE_DATE                               NOT NULL    DATE
 JOB_ID                                  NOT NULL    VARCHAR2(10)
 SALARY                                              NUMBER(8,2)
 COMMISSION_PCT                                      NUMBER(2,2)
 MANAGER_ID                                          NUMBER(6)
 DEPARTMENT_ID                                       NUMBER(4)
SQL>
```

The Host Command

The *host* command enables you to use operating system commands from within SQL*Plus. You may, for example, want to see if a file exists in a certain directory, or you may want to use the *cp* or *tar* commands at the UNIX level and return to your SQL*Plus session to resume interaction with the Oracle database. Here is an example showing how to use the *host* command:

```
SQL> host cp /u01/app/oracle/new.sql  /tmp
```

The *host* command in this example will help you copy the file new.sql from the specified directory to the tmp directory. Just about any command you can use at the operating system level you can execute using the *host* command. You can replace the *host* command with *!* (bang, or exclamation point) to run operating system commands from within SQL*Plus, as in the following example:

```
Sql> ! cp /u01/app/oracle/new.sql  /tmp
```

Note that if you just type the command by itself, as in **host** or **!**, you'll be transported to the operating system directory from which you logged into the SQL*Plus session. When you're done with your operating system task, just type in **exit** and you'll return to the SQL*Plus session you just left. Here's the command to do so:

```
SQL > host
Prod1    [/u01/app/oracle/admin/finance/sql]
[finance] $ exit
SQL >
```

The Spool Command

What if your SQL query provides you with a voluminous report that you want to refer to later on? The *spool* command enables you to save the output of one or more SQL statements to an operating system file in both UNIX and Windows:

```
SQL> set linesize 180
SQL> spool employee
SQL>  select  emp_id, last_name,salary, manager from employee;
SQL> spool off;
```

By default, spooled text files are saved as *filename*.lst by default. Spooling files is very useful when you use SQL itself to help you write SQL scripts, and you can see examples in the review of SQL in Appendix A of this book. If you are using simple statements that, for example, are inserting just a row at a time, there is no need to build a formal script—just type the commands in.

The Accept and Prompt Commands

The *accept* command is used to read user input from the screen and save it in a variable. You can either specify the variable or let SQL*Plus create one. The *accept* command is typically used to read user input in response to prompts from the SQL*Plus interface.

The *prompt* command comes in handy when you're creating interactive scripts. The command sends a message from SQL*Plus to the screen. It's commonly used to elicit user input. The *accept* and *prompt* commands are usually together in a SQL script, typically to request user input and save the input in variables that can be used later in the program.

The following example illustrates the use of the *accept* and *prompt* commands:

```
SQL> prompt 'Please enter your last name'
'Please enter your last name'
SQL> accept lastname char format a20
Alapati
```

The Execute Command

When you use scripts that invoke PL/SQL code in the form of procedures and packages, you need to use the *execute* command to actually fire off the package or procedure. Here is an example of using this command:

```
Sql> execute .insert_into_fintables
PL/SQL procedure successfully completed
Sql>
```

The *execute* command is frequently used in SQL scripts to run batch jobs.

The Pause Command

Often, you'll be executing scripts that generate output that doesn't fit on one screen. The output just zips past you on the screen, and it's gone before you can actually read it. You can use the *spool* command to capture the entire output, but it's a waste to do this constantly, because you'll be creating files all day long just so you can look at the output of your scripts. SQL*Plus provides you with the *pause* command to pause after every full screen of output. You press the Enter key to see the next full screen.

The following example shows how to use the *pause* command to slow down the output displayed on your terminal:

```
SQL> show pause
PAUSE is OFF
SQL> set pause on
SQL> show pause
PAUSE is ON and set to ""
SQL> select username,profile
  2  from dba_users;
```

When you execute this command, the cursor will blink, but there won't be the usual printing of the output to the screen right away. When you run your queries with the *pause* command set, you need to, in most cases, press the Enter key an extra time to see the first screen of output.

Creating Command Files in SQL*Plus

Instead of using a single command each time, you can use a set of commands together by writing them to a file and running the file at once. When you do this, all the SQL commands included in the file will be executed sequentially. You can create a spool file containing SQL commands in one of two ways: in your text file or with your editor.

You can type the commands in a text file, save the file, and execute it. Note that if you log into SQL*Plus and type the word **edit**, you'll be automatically taken into your default editor.

The *SQL>ed* command will bring up your editor. In UNIX, it will be the vi editor, and in Windows it will be Notepad. The *ed* command will invoke the appropriate editor. To get into edit mode, simply type **SQL> ed**.

In either case, you can save your commands and name your saved file something meaningful, so you can execute the commands later on. You set the default editor's name, usually the vi editor in UNIX, in either your glogin.sql file or your .login file. Of course, you can also set the default editor after you log into SQL*Plus.

 TIP *If the SQL you intend to execute is complex or long, you can also input the commands and then use the* save *command to create a command file you can execute later.*

Saving SQL Commands to a File

Many times when you're writing fairly complex scripts, it would be nice if you could take the output of your SQL*Plus session and save it directly to a file. You could then retrieve the file for use later on or, if you wish, use it for an automated execution. Here's a simple example of how you can save your SQL code to a file:

```
SQL> select username,process,sid,serial#
from v$session
where status = 'ACTIVE'
.
SQL> SAVE status.sql
Created file status.sql
SQL>
```

> **NOTE** *After you've typed in the first three lines, you just type the dot (.) character on line 4. This indicates that you're finished with writing the block of SQL. When you type in the* save filename *command, your most recent SQL statement is saved as a file with the assigned name—in this case, status.sql.*

Executing SQL*Plus Scripts

If you want to execute a SQL script, you have two choices:

- If you don't intend to make any changes before execution, just invoke the script by using the at sign (@).

- If the status.sql file in the previous example is in the same directory as the directory from which you started SQL*Plus, all you have to do is list the name of the file.

If the command file is in a different directory, then you have to give the complete absolute path of the file's location in order to run it in SQL*Plus.

On UNIX systems, you can configure an environment variable called ORACLE_PATH to tell SQL*Plus where to look for a script. This way, you can put all your routine SQL scripts in one location and you don't need to specify the complete path for the file location each time you want to execute an already existing script. On my UNIX servers, for example, this is how I can set the variable:

```
Export $ORACLE_PATH=/u01/app/oracle/admin/dba/sql
```

On Windows systems, you can edit the Windows Registry to specify the ORACLE_PATH variable.

Executing a SQL*Plus Command Script

Executing SQL scripts is easy: All you have to do is specify the name of the script from within a SQL session. You don't have to be in the directory where the script is saved. If you're executing from a different directory, you have to provide the full path of the script's location. The at sign (@) will help you run any SQL script, as shown in the following example.

In Listing 6-7, the status.sql script happens to be in the same directory from which SQL*Plus was invoked. You can run a script located in a different directory by entering the complete path of the script's location, as in @/u0-1/app/oracle/admin/dba/sql/status.sql. The following output shows how to use the @ command to execute a script.

Listing 6-7. Using the At (@) Command to Execute a Script

```
SQL> @status.sql
USERNAME            STATUS    PROCESS    SID    SERIAL#
------------------------------ -------- --------- ---------- ----------
                    ACTIVE    2076       1      1
                    ACTIVE    2080       2      1
                    ACTIVE    2084       3      1
                    ACTIVE    2088       4      1
                    ACTIVE    2092       5      1
                    ACTIVE    2096       6      1
SYSTEM              ACTIVE    1856:444   8      58
7 rows selected.
SQL>
```

The status.sql script is run without any path information, because it is located in the same directory from which you logged into SQL*Plus.

You can also execute the preceding script by just typing the command **run status.sql**. The *run* command will execute the contents of the specified file. If your SQL commands are actually listed on the screen or are in the buffer, you can use the / command to execute the SQL code. Look at Listing 6-8, which shows the use of the / command.

Listing 6-8. Using the / Command

```
SQL>  select username,status,process,sid,serial#
  2  from v$session
  3* where status = 'ACTIVE'
SQL> /
USERNAME                       STATUS    PROCESS         SID    SERIAL#
------------------------------ -------- --------- ---------- ----------
                               ACTIVE    2076        1      1
                               ACTIVE    2080        2      1
                               ACTIVE    2084        3      1
                               ACTIVE    2088        4      1
                               ACTIVE    2092        5      1
                               ACTIVE    2096        6      1
SYSTEM                         ACTIVE    1856:444    8      58
7 rows selected.
SQL>
```

Note that when you use the /command to execute a script, the commands aren't listed again. Instead, the /command executes the script right away. You could also have used the *run* command instead of the /command and your SQL would have been executed the same way. You can use the *run* command to execute a SQL script as follows:

```
SQL> run test1
  1  select username,status
  2* from v$session
USERNAME                        STATUS
------------------------------ --------
                                ACTIVE
                                ACTIVE
                                ACTIVE
                                ACTIVE
                                ACTIVE
                                ACTIVE
SYSTEM                          ACTIVE
7 rows selected.
SQL>
```

CAUTION *When you invoke a script with the* run *command, the SQL is shown on the screen before it's executed. On the other hand, the /command won't show the SQL, but executes it right away. Because of this, you have to exercise extreme caution when you use the /command. After all, you may not realize that the script in the buffer isn't what you want to run.*

Creating a Windows Batch Script

You can easily create a batch script in a Windows system to run your SQL'Plus commands. For instance, say you have a script called startup.sql to start up the database.

If you want to schedule this script to run at a specified time, you must first create a Windows batch file that invokes the start-up script. You can then use the Windows at (@) command, if you wish, to schedule the batch script. The following samples show two examples of this.

For startup.sql:

```
Connect sys/password@market1 as sysdba;
Startup pfile =$ORACLE HOME\database\initmarket1.ora
```

For runstart.bat (Windows script):

```
set ORACLE_SID=market1
@startup.sql
```

The Define and Undefine Commands

During the course of writing and using SQL scripts, sometimes you need to specify variables and their values. The *define* command enables you to create your own variables (user variables). The variables will continue to hold the values you specify for the duration of the SQL*Plus session or until you use the *undefine* command and unset the variable's definition. Here is an example demonstrating the use of the *define* and *undefine* commands:

```
Sql> define dept = finance
Sql> undefine dept
```

This example is straightforward. In SQL*Plus, however, you'll often use the *define* command in scripts to substitute values for variables. You typically do this by using the *define* command with a substitution variable instead of a user variable. A substitution variable is represented by adding an ampersand (&) to the user variable, as in &*variable*.

Listing 6-9 presents a simple example to illustrate the use of the *define* command, using a substitution variable.

Listing 6-9. Using the Define Command

```
SQL>col segment_name for a27
define owner = '&1'
select segment_name,segment_type,extents
from dba_segments
where owner = upper ('&owner)
and extents > 10
and segment_name not like 'TMP%'
order by segment_type,extetns desc
SQL> @extents.sql
Enter value for 1: system
SEGMENT_NAME              SEGMENT_TYPE        EXTENTS
HELP_TOPIC_SEQ            INDEX               18
PRODUCT_PROFILE           TABLE               22
SQL>
```

TIP *In the extents.sql script, you define the owner variable, but instead of giving it a hard-coded single value, you let it take on any substituted value provided for the user. Thus, this same script can be run for any user in the database. All you need to do is plug in a different name for the schema owner each time you run the script.*

Using Comments in SQL*Plus

Often, you'll need to use nonexecutable comments in your SQL*Plus scripts and reports. You have several ways to incorporate comments in SQL*Plus. Here's a brief description of the commenting features available in SQL*Plus:

- *The /*...*/ delimiters:* You can enclose one or more lines in your script with these delimiters to indicate that those lines are merely comments.

- *The -- notation:* You can preface the line(s) you want commented by a pair of hyphens.

- *The* remark *command:* The *remark* command before the beginning of a line indicates that the line is not to be executed.

Listing Your SQL Commands

SQL*Plus stores your most recently issued SQL statement in an area in memory called the *SQL buffer*. Unfortunately, SQL*Plus lets you save only the last command you issued in the buffer. Every new statement that you enter will replace the older statement in the buffer. If you want to see the last command you issued, type in the word **list** or just the letter **l.**

```
SQL>   l
  1   select username,status,process,sid,serial#
  2   from v$session
  3*  where status = 'ACTIVE'
SQL>
```

If you want to see what's in your SQL script before you execute it, then first load it from the operating system into the SQL buffer by using the *get* command, as follows:

```
SQL> get status.sql
  1   select username,status,process,sid,serial#
  2   from v$session
  3*  where status = 'ACTIVE'
SQL>
```

CAUTION *If you just enter the command slash (/) in your SQL*Plus session, you'll execute the last command you entered, which is always stored in the SQL buffer. It's a very good idea to always use the* list *command to first see what you're actually executing.*

Sometimes you may want to execute several SQL command scripts consecutively. You can specify all the scripts you want to run in one main script and just run that main script. All the included scripts will run consecutively. Here's an example of how you can embed several SQL scripts into one main file:

```
SQL> get one_script.sql
  1  @check.sql
  2  @create_table.sql
  3  @insert_table.sql
  4* @create_constraint.sql
SQL>
```

When you run the script one_script.sql, its four constituent scripts will run one after the other. You can see that this is an efficient way to execute scripts, especially when you're creating and populating a new database, provided you have already tested the individual scripts individually.

NOTE *You can also use the @@commandfile notation, as in @@one_script.sql, to run command files that include several command files. The use of the @@ notation ensures that Oracle looks for the individual files in the same path as the command file.*

Editing Within SQL*Plus

Often you'll want to make minor changes in the SQL code you're using. It isn't necessary to resort to your editor for minor changes. SQL*Plus comes with its own change commands. The general pattern for changing SQL text is *c/old/new*, where *c* stands for change, *old* stands for the actual SQL you intend to change, and *new* stands for the SQL text replacing the old text. Listing 6-10 shows how to use pattern matching to replace text in a SQL*Plus session.

Listing 6-10. Changing Text Using Pattern Matching

```
sql> l
  1  select username,status,process,sid,serial
  2  from v$session
  3* where status = 'ACTIVE'
SQL> /
select username,status,process,sid,serial
                                         *
ERROR at line 1:
ORA-00904: invalid column name
SQL> 1
  1* select username,status,process,sid,serial
SQL> c/serial/serial#
  1* select username,status,process,sid,serial#
```

```
SQL> l
  1  select username,status,process,sid,serial#
  2  from v$session
  3* where status = 'ACTIVE'
SQL> /
USERNAME                         STATUS   PROCESS        SID    SERIAL#
------------------------------   -------- ---------  ---------- ----------
                                 ACTIVE   2076            1          1
                                 ACTIVE   2080            2          1
                                 ACTIVE   2084            3          1
                                 ACTIVE   2088            4          1
                                 ACTIVE   2092            5          1
                                 ACTIVE   2096            6          1
SYSTEM                           ACTIVE   1856:444        8         58
7 rows selected.
SQL>
```

Pattern matching is used to modify SQL*Plus command lines. Therefore, you can add or modify a word or a part of a word by just replacing an existing pattern with a new one. If you have a complicated script, making changes using pattern matching as shown in Listing 6-8 can quickly get hairy! Use the runtime editor instead to make your changes conveniently in an editor. Saving the changes will bring you into the SQL*Plus interface automatically, and you should execute your edited SQL there.

> **NOTE** *In UNIX, the usual editor is the vi editor, which you invoke by typing* **ed** *at the SQL*Plus command line. In Windows, the usual editor is Notepad, which you also invoke by typing in* **ed**.

Inserting and Deleting Lines in SQL*Plus

You can always remove or add a line to your SQL text by merely invoking the editor and making the changes there. The SQL*Plus interface also offers you easy ways to add and delete lines. The following output shows how to use the *insert* command (you just type in the letter **i** to insert new text) to insert a new line at the end of a SQL script:

```
SQL> l
  1  select username,status,process,sid,serial#
  2  from v$session
  3* where status = 'ACTIVE'
SQL> i
  4  and username = 'HR'
  5  .
SQL> /
```

```
USERNAME      STATUS    PROCESS     SID    SERIAL#
------------------------------ -------- --------- ---------- -----------
HR            ACTIVE    1856:444    8      64
SQL>
```

The following example shows how to insert a line in the middle of a SQL script:

```
SQL> select username,status,process,sid,serial#
  2  from v$session
  3  where status='ACTIVE'
  4  .
SQL> 1
  1* select username,status,process,sid,serial#
SQL> i
  2i ,logon_time,terminal
  3i .
SQL> l
  1  select username,status,process,sid,serial#
  2  ,logon_time,terminal
  3  from v$session
  4* where status='ACTIVE'
SQL>
```

In the first example, you added a line using the *insert* command, denoted by the letter *i*. If you want to insert a line not at the end of a script but somewhere in the middle, you can do that too, as shown in the second example. Just print the line on the screen by using the *list* command and then add the new line afterward using the *input* command. Similarly, you can delete lines by using the *delete* command *d* (or *del*), accompanied by the line number, as shown in Listing 6-11.

*Listing 6-11. Deleting Text in SQL*Plus*

```
SQL> l
  1  select username,status,process,sid,serial#
  2  from v$session
  3  where status = 'ACTIVE'
  4* and username='HR'
SQL> del4
SQL> l
  1  select username,status,process,sid,serial#
  2  from v$session
  3* where status = 'ACTIVE'
SQL>
```

The *del* command will delete the specified line number. Using the *del* command without a line number will remove the last line of the SQL you have in the buffer.

Adding to Text

Sometimes, you need to add a word or two to a particular line. Instead of invoking the editor, you can just use the *append* command to accomplish this, as shown in Listing 6-12.

Listing 6-12. Using the Append Command

```
SQL> select username,profile
  2  from dba_users
  3  .
SQL> 1
  1* select username,profile
SQL> append ,created_date
  1* select username,profile,created_date
SQL> l
  1  select username,profile,created_date
  2* from dba_users
SQL>
```

Incorporating Comments with the Remark Command

The *remark* command is straightforward. It enables you to incorporate comments in your SQL scripts. It is not meant to be considered for execution.

```
SQL> get user_report.sql
1 REM This script gives you the usernames and their profiles
2 REM Author: sam alapati
3 REM Date: March 20,2003
4 Select username,profile from dba_users;
SQL>
```

Copying Tables with the Copy Command

Sometimes you need to copy large tables by using the *create table as select * from* (CTAS) technique. On large tables, you tend to get into trouble doing this, because Oracle does not commit in between the inserts, and in the meantime, the rollback segments may run out of space. You are also limited to non-LONG data types when you use this technique. The *copy* command gives you a way to easily copy all types of tables, and it avoids many of the problems of using the CTAS statement because it does commit while it's copying the data from the source table. You'll see the *copy* command's full functionality in Chapter 12.

Listing 6-13 shows how to use the very useful *copy* command. Note that the hyphen (-) lets you break up long SQL statements into the next line.

Listing 6-13. Using the Copy Command

```
SQL> copy from sysadm/sysadm1@financ e1-
> create test02 -
> using select * from test_table

Array fetch/bind size is 15. (arraysize is 15)
Will commit when done. (copycommit is 0)
Maximum long size is 80. (long is 80)
Table TEST02 created.

   4954 rows selected from sysadm@finance1
      4954 rows inserted into TEST02.
 4954 rows committed into TEST02 at DEFAULT HOST connection.
SQL>
```

Making DML Changes Permanent with SQL*Plus

When you use SQL*Plus, you can enter data manipulation statements or DML either separately or as part of a named or anonymous block of PL/SQL code. Of course, you can always choose when exactly you want the changes committed or made permanent, but there are other, less obvious ways to make the changes permanent, and you should be aware of them. Here are the different ways in which DML changes are made permanent:

- You can commit the results of a transaction by using the keyword *commit* at the end of the transaction.

- You can set the autocommit setting to ON in your SQL*Plus session, which will ensure that changes being made in the session are committed periodically on an automatic basis.

- You may issue a DDL command, such as *drop index*, that will also automatically commit all the transactions pending either a commit or a rollback within the session.

- You can exit gracefully from SQL*Plus by typing in **exit** or **quit**. When you issue the *exit* command, Oracle will automatically commit all changes you made in that session, even if you never issued a commit request, or even if the autocommit flag has been set to OFF.

Creating Web Pages Using SQL*Plus

You can easily create a compelling Web page from within a SQL*Plus session by using the *markup* command. When you embed SQL*Plus in program scripts, you can use the *markup* command in the following way to produce HTML output. Before executing any SQL commands, it outputs the HTML and BODY tags.

```
SQLPLUS -MARKUP "HTML ON"
```

If you want to output a HTML page that can be embedded in an existing Web page, you can use the *markup* command in the following way:

```
SQL >SET MARKUP HTML ON SPOOL ON
SQL> commands here …
SQL> SET MARKUP HTML ON SPOOL OFF
```

Key SQL*Plus Database Administration Commands

Although you may use every SQL*Plus command in the course of database administration, some specific commands in SQL*Plus exist for the sole use of the Oracle9*i* DBA. Previous editions of the Oracle database allowed you to run these commands in alternative DBA interfaces such as the Server Manager utility. In Oracle9*i*, the Server Manager tool is finally obsolete and therefore SQL*Plus is the only interface for all manual commands for administering databases. The list of SQL*Plus commands for the DBA is short, but the commands in the list are very powerful. Let's take a quick look at the important database administration commands in SQL*Plus.

The Recover Command

The *recover* command, as you can imagine, is used during a recovery of the database or one of its files or tablespaces after a database failure. To be able to run this command, you need to have the OSOPER or the OSDBA role. You can perform manual or automatic recovery, and in either case, you're responsible for first restoring all the necessary data files so you can recover your database. The *recover* command is complex and critical, and you'll examine it in great detail in Chapter 15, which deals with database recovery.

The Start and Shutdown Commands

The *start* and *shutdown* commands are used to start up and shut down your Oracle9*i* instance. Again, these are pretty complex commands and you'll explore them in detail in later chapters.

The Archivelog Command

Archive logs are the archived or stored redo logs, and they play a critical role in database recovery. The *archivelog* command can be used by anyone with an OSDBA or OSOPER privilege. It enables you to list manually archived logs as well as start and stop the archiving of redo log files. You'll learn much more about this command in Chapters 14 and 15.

Commands for Formatting SQL*Plus Output and Creating Reports

Using the regular SQL*Plus commands coupled with some formatting commands, you can add structure to the output of your queries and create rudimentary reports. Although your firm may have sophisticated software that will keep you from having to use SQL*Plus's cumbersome formatting and reporting capabilities, chances are that you'll want to know how to use SQL*Plus's many formatting features to make your output look pretty and, at times, even to make it legible to you! The formatting capabilities may be somewhat primitive, but they get the job done in most cases, because most of your reports will be for database management purposes.

The Break Command

The *break* command controls how and when a report's format should be changed. You can use the *break* command on a column, a row, an action, or the report. Here's an example of the *break* command:

```
BREAK ON DEPARTMENT_ID SKIP 1 ON JOB_ID SKIP 1 DUPLICATES
COMPUTE SUM OF SALARY ON DEPARTMENT_ID
COMPUTE AVG OF SALARY ON JOB_ID
SELECT DEPARTMENT_ID, JOB_ID, LAST_NAME, SALARY
FROM EMP_DETAILS_VIEW
WHERE JOB_ID IN ('_CLERK', '_MANAGER')
AND DEPARTMENT_ID IN (10,20)
ORDER BY DEPARTMENT_ID, JOB_ID;
```

The Column Command

The *column* command shows various properties of any specified column in a table. Once issued, the settings for column format put in place by this command can be used by all the SQL commands used in this session. Therefore, if you're running similar reports all the time, you may find it beneficial to include the *column* command specifications in a file using the *store set* command sequence. You could use a number of options for the *column* command, but here's a simple example of how to use the command:

```
SQL> column dept format a15 heading 'Department'
SQL> column cost format $9,999,999.99
```

In the first *column* command, the dept column is specified to be up to 15 characters in length. Longer names will be truncated. It further specifies a meaningful heading under which the department names should be listed. The second *column* command shows you how SQL*Plus formats dollar values, in this case, in millions of dollars, including decimal values.

The Compute Command

As its name indicates, the *compute* command is used for several types of computations, including averages, standard deviations, and so on. Here's an example of how to use this command:

```
SQL> Compute avg of sales on district
SQL> select  region,district,sales
2     From total_sales
3     Where district = 'NORTH';
SQL>
```

The Repfooter Command

The *repfooter* command prints specified footer text at the bottom of a report. Here's an example:

```
SQL> repfooter page right 'END OF THE 1ST QUARTER RESULTS REPORT'
```

The Repheader Command

The *repheader* command is similar to the *repfooter* command, but instead of placing a footer at the bottom of your report, it places a header at the top of your report according to your specifications. The following example prints the report header in the top center of the first page of your report:

```
SQL> repheader page center '1st QUARTER RESULTS REPORT FOR 2002'
```

The Btitle and Ttitle Commands

The *ttitle* command places a title at the top of each page of your report and the *btitle* command does the same at the bottom of each page. Here are some examples to illustrate their use:

```
SQL> ttitle 'Annual Financial Report for the Ladies Club, 2001'
SQL> btitle '2001 Report'
```

CAUTION *After you use the* btitle *and* title *commands, as well as many other SQL*Plus commands, you have to manually turn them off to avoid all the ensuing SQL commands in that session from inheriting those settings. For example, if you don't turn the title off after you create a report, all the subsequent output for any command will have the same title printed at the top of the first page.*

Using SQL to Generate SQL

There will be occasions when you have to write a SQL script that involves a number of similar lines. A good example would be a script where you have to assign a set of privileges to a bunch of users. You can, of course, execute separate SQL statements for each user, but it will be a waste of time to do so, besides being a mind-numbing exercise. Fortunately, you can use SQL to generate a script with all the SQL statements that need to be executed. Using SQL to generate SQL essentially involves using the output of one SQL statement as input to another SQL statement.

It is very easy to write SQL code that generates more SQL code as output. First, you write the SQL to generate the SQL. Next, you start spooling a file, where the output of this first SQL script will be captured. Then you stop the spooling, which will give you a script with the final set of commands you are interested in. Finally, you execute the spooled output. Listing 6-14 shows an example that you are likely to be familiar with.

 CAUTION *Always make sure you set the heading off, echo off, and feedback off. This will give you a clean, spooled output script, which you can execute directly without any changes.*

Listing 6-14. Using SQL to Generate SQL Scripts

```
Step 1. Set the environment variables.
SQL> set echo off heading off feedback off
Step 2. Name a spool file, to which the output
of the first script will be written
SQL> spool test.txt
Step 3.  Execute the following SQL:
SQL> select 'grant connect, resource to '||username||';' from dba_users;
The following is the  output of the above command:
GRANT CONNECT, RESOURCE TO DBA1;
GRANT CONNECT, RESOURCE TO ODSCOMMON;
GRANT CONNECT, RESOURCE TO JEFFRESS;
GRANT CONNECT, RESOURCE TO CAMPBELL;
GRANT CONNECT, RESOURCE TO GALBRAITH;
GRANT CONNECT, RESOURCE TO DIXON;
GRANT CONNECT, RESOURCE TO BOGAVELLI;
SQL> spool off
Step 4. The spooled script, test.txt, will have captured the above
commands. Now run the test.txt script
SQL> @ test.txt
Grant succeeded.
Grant succeeded.
Grant succeeded.
Grant succeeded.
Grant succeeded.
Grant succeeded.
Grant succeeded.
SQL>
```

As you can see, if you had to run this command for 100 users, the effort would be the same as it is for one user. You can easily adapt the preceding technique to reverse engineer the schema in your database. For example, you can query the data dictionary to find out the storage and parameters for tables and indexes. This is a very useful little technique to have in your arsenal. You'll find many uses for it in performing your administrative tasks.

Introducing the Oracle9*i* *i*SQL*Plus Interface

Oracle9*i* *i*SQL*Plus is really not very different from the traditional SQL*Plus interface. You can run most of the normal SQL*Plus commands through *i*SQL*Plus. The big difference, however, is that *i*SQL*Plus is browser based; therefore, once you have access to a machine that has an Internet browser, all you need is the URL of the HTTP server to log into the database from anywhere, security considerations permitting. You can do the same things in *i*SQL*Plus that you can in SQL*Plus, including running queries, either manually or with the help of scripts, and administering the database itself.

The *i*SQL*Plus interface comes bundled with the Oracle9*i* server as a component of the SQL*Plus software. You can use any Web server with the Oracle9*i* *i*SQL*Plus interface, but Oracle bundles an Apache Web server with its software that you can install on your Windows server and get going in a very short time.

The *i*SQL*Plus interface's architecture is based on a middle tier, which includes the Web server, communicating with the database on one side and the client on the other. The middle tier also holds the *i*SQL server, which manages the communication between the client and the Oracle9*i* database server. As usual, Oracle uses Oracle Net to conduct the user and database interaction, but the new addition is the middleware, which runs the Web server and the *i*SQL*Plus server.

The *i*SQL*Plus interface involves minimal configuration, and in some cases, you may be able to use it right out of the box. However, it may take some time for you to feel completely comfortable with *i*SQL*Plus. There are some limitations with regard to using *i*SQL*Plus, besides the extra work needed to configure it. Some of the common SQL*Plus commands are either redundant or can't be used in it. You might wonder if it's worth all the effort to configure and get used to the way this new interface works. Install it anyway and get good at using it, because it does provide some interesting reporting facilities, especially HTML-formatted reports.

NOTE *Because the* iSQL*Plus *interface requires the HTTP server, you need the Oracle9i server in order to use* iSQL*Plus—*the normal Oracle client software will not enable you to use* iSQL*Plus. *I have all three tiers of* iSQL*Plus *running on my Windows server, but it is more common to have the database on a different server. Oracle has started shipping the* iSQL*Plus *interface with its UNIX-based server software, so it's possible that you can use a UNIX server to host your* iSQL *engine. If* iSQL*Plus *is installed on a common server, clients can log into the* iSQL*Plus *environment and access all the databases, without* any *Oracle software on the client machines.*

Installing the iSQL*Plus Software

Really, there isn't much to installing the *i*SQL*Plus interface, as its installation is part of the Oracle9*i* server software installation. The Apache HTTP server software is also installed during that time. If for some reason you need to install a different Web server instead of Apache, you can do so.

Configuring iSQL*Plus

Because you have three components in the *i*SQL*Plus architecture, you need to configure all of them. Although the configuration of any one of the three components is not really difficult, you may have to deal with certain issues at each level, depending on your system configuration and your Internet or intranet architecture. The following sections examine each of these three components in detail.

Client Tier

The client tier consists of the Web-browser-based *i*SQL*Plus user interface, and it is easy to configure. All you have to do is ensure you have installed Microsoft Internet Explorer 5.0 or later, or Netscape Navigator 4.7 or later. In most cases, you are not required to make any changes in your browser settings, as long as you are set to accept cookies and run JavaScript. In addition, on some Internet browsers, you may have to set up new application extensions for files or add a proxy server exception for your Web server running in the middle tier. You can make all these changes by selecting Preferences from the Edit menu in Netscape or by selecting Internet Options from the Tools menu in Microsoft Internet Explorer.

Middle Tier

As you recall, the two important components of *i*SQL*Plus in the middle tier are the HTTP Web server and the Oracle *i*SQL*Plus server itself. Both of these components get installed automatically, and the HTTP server is preconfigured to run the Oracle *i*SQL*Plus server. In addition, you may regard Oracle Net as part of the middle tier, because it facilitates database connectivity. Chances are, you will be able to start using *i*SQL*Plus without making any changes to the configuration of any of the middle tier components. You should familiarize yourself, however, with the configuration issues for them just so you can troubleshoot and modify parameters when the occasion arises.

Oracle bundles the Apache HTTP Web server with your Oracle9*i* software. This is the only HTTP server that *i*SQL*Plus is certified to run on. The Apache software is located in the $ORACLE_HOME/Apache directory. On my Windows server, it is in the $ORACLE_HOME\Apache directory, for example. The Apache Web server has a configuration file called httpd.conf that is located in the $ORACLE_HOME/Apache/Apache/conf directory. You can make changes in this configuration file before you start the Web server or even while the Web server is running, in which case you restart the server dynamically for the configuration changes to take effect. Let's actually test and start the Web server.

First, go the directory where the Apache server is located and test the server configuration, as follows:

```
C:\Oracle9i\Apache\Apache> apache -t
c:/oracle9i/apache/apache/conf/httpd.conf: Syntax OK
C:\Oracle9i\Apache\Apache>
   If the syntax is NOT OK, then you need to check the
 httpd.conf mfile and make the necessary changes.
To start the apache server:
C:\Oracle9i\Apache\Apache> apache -k start
To stop the apache server:
C:\Oracle9i\Apache\Apache> apache -k shutdown
To restart a running apache server after making changes in the httpd.conf file:
C:\Oracle9i\Apache\Apache> apache -k restart
```

 CAUTION *On my Windows server, when I start my Apache server I sometimes get an error message that says that the httpd.PID file has been overwritten. The message contains the words "fatal error" and looks alarming, but don't worry about it. Your server will start regardless.*

The configuration file for the HTTP server, httpd.conf, refers to the Oracle9*i* configuration file, which will enable you to customize certain parameters to fit your needs. For example, at the very end of my Apache configuration file, there is a directive to read the Oracle9*i* configuration file:

```
# Include the Oracle configuration file for custom settings
include "c:\oracle9i\Apache\Apache\conf\oracle_apache.conf"
```

The Oracle_apache.conf file in the httpd.conf file is changed if you need to enable Oracle HTTP server authentication at the user privilege level. The Oracle_apache.conf file reads the *i*SQL*Plus configuration file, which is called isqlplus.conf, as shown in the following line:

```
#
include "c:\oracle9i\SQL*Plus\admin\isqlplus.conf"
#
```

The *i*SQL*Plus server merely refers to the *i*SQL*Plus software component installed with your Oracle9*i* database in the SQL*Plus directories. You can change the isqlplus.conf file in the $ORACLE_HOME/sqlplus/admin directory to modify the default settings of the *i*SQL*Plus server. You should probably edit the isqlplus.conf file to change the default *i*SQL*Plus session timeout limit of 60 minutes. The *i*SQL*Plus timeout parameter will enable you to do this. You can also change the standard style sheets provided by Oracle for the *i*SQL*Plus interface by modifying the isqlplus.conf file.

NOTE *Remember to edit the tnsnames.ora file in your $ORACLE_HOME/ network/admin directory and include the network information for the database server. Oracle Net will make the connection between the iSQL*Plus module and the Oracle9i database.*

Database Tier

All you have to do on the database side is ensure that the Oracle9*i* database is running. There are no configuration requirements for *i*SQL*Plus, as the *i*SQL*Plus server automatically starts running when the database starts.

Using the iSQL*Plus Interface

In the following sections, you'll learn how to log in and use the *i*SQL*Plus interface. It's somewhat of a novel experience to log into the *i*SQL*Plus interface for those who are used to the monitor-based SQL*Plus surface, but the rewards in terms of well-formatted output, the ability to run saved scripts from the interface, and great reporting abilities make the learning curve well worth the effort.

To bring up the *i*SQL*Plus interface and log into it, you need to perform the following steps:

1. Invoke your Internet browser and type in the Web address of your server and the port number that the Oracle HTTP server is using, after you confirm that the HTTP server is configured correctly. On my Windows computer, for example, I enter the URL **http://alapati_sam:3339/isqlplus/**, where alapati_sam is the symbolic name of my computer. If your computer's DNS doesn't support the symbolic name, you can replace it with the actual IP address for your machine. You can find out your IP address by typing **ipconfig** at the DOS command prompt. Press Enter to get the *i*SQL*Plus Login screen.

2. You can use the *i*SQL*Plus interface to log into a database in two different modes. You can either log in as a regular user or, if you intend to perform database administration, you can log in as a user with the SYSDBA or SYSOPER privilege. Bt default, you can log in as a regular user only and all SYSDBA connections have to be authenticated by the HTTP server. The HTTP server maintains a password file and in this case, it will be located in the $ORACLE_HOME\sqlplus\admin\iplusdba.pw directory.

3. Figure 6-1 shows the initial login screen of the *i*SQL*Plus interface. Enter your Oracle database username and password in the username and password boxes. If you are logging into the default database, you can leave the Connection Identifier field blank. Otherwise, specify the database connection identifier, as specified in your tnsnames.ora file. Once you click the Login button, you'll see the *i*SQL*Plus work screen. To log out of your *i*SQL*Plus session, click the Logout button, which will be located in the at the top right of the work screen that will appear once you successfully log in.

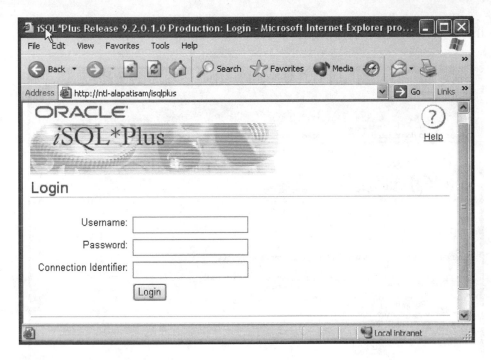

Figure 6-1. The iSQL*Plus *login screen*

Invoking iSQL*Plus from a Web Address (URL)

It is very easy to start an iSQL*Plus session and pass SQL scripts to it as URL variables. The iSQL*Plus interface will execute the scripts that you supply it, and then pass and exhibit the results in your browser window. The examples in the following sections show how to start an iSQL*Plus session and how to pass a script as a URL variable.

Logging into iSQL*Plus

To log into iSQL*Plus on my machine, for example, I enter the following statement, where *system* is the username and *manager* is the password:

```
http://ntl-alapatisam:3339/isqlplus?userid=system/manager
```

Executing Scripts

If you just want to pass a script to the database through iSQL*Plus without giving out your username and password, you can do so in the following way:

```
http://ntl-alapatisam:3339/isqlplus?script="select username
 from v$session;"&type=text&action=load
```

Figure 6-2 illustrates passing a script through a URL. You specify the script in the URL, and *i*SQL*Plus prompts you for the username and password.

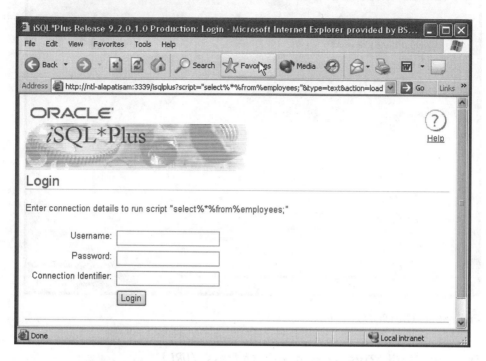

Figure 6-2. Passing a script through a URL

The *i*SQL*Plus Work Screen

Once you log into the *i*SQL*Plus interface successfully, you'll see the *i*SQL*Plus work screen. The work screen lets you enter SQL commands for execution. In addition, you can use the work screen to navigate to the following areas:

- *History:* You can save and reuse recently executed SQL scripts through the History screen.

- *Preferences:* The Preferences screen lets you change your password, set system variables, and set the interface options (size of screen and so forth) for your *i*SQL*Plus sessions. Figure 6-3 shows how you can use the Preferences screen to set values for various system variables.

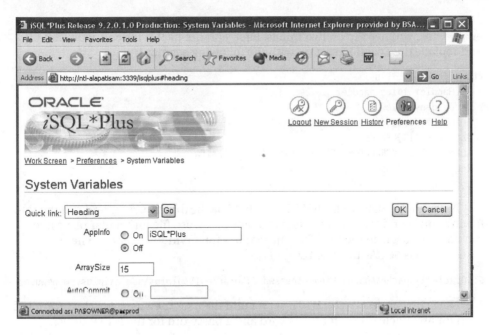

Figure 6-3. The iSQL*Plus Preferences screen*

NOTE *If you exit the* iSQL*Plus session by typing in the word **exit**, you'll still be connected to the database. The* exit *command in* iSQL*Plus only stops any scripts you may be currently executing, but it leaves your database connection intact. You need to click the Logout icon to completely exit the* iSQL*Plus interface.*

Authentication Levels

You can log into an *i*SQL*Plus session in two different ways. If you are logging in as a normal user, all you have to do is submit your database username/password combination. If you are logging in as a DBA with the SYSDBA or SYSOPER privilege, you have to go through an extra layer of authentication. In addition to database authentication, the HTTP server also needs to authenticate privileged users. The mandatory SYSOPER and SYSDBA role authentication by the HTTP server actually means that there are two sets of usernames and passwords that you need to use to gain entry into the Oracle database as a DBA using the *i*SQL*Plus interface. You need to first log into the *i*SQL*Plus interface with a slightly different Web address to log in as a DBA.

For example, on my server, this is what I need to enter as the Web address: **http://ntl-alapatisam:3339/isqlplusdba**. I then see a username/password box, which will let the HTTP server check my authentication first. Once my HTTP server credentials are confirmed, I see another box asking me to enter my database username/password and the database connection details.

If you wish, you can have the HTTP server also authentic regular users. To enable this, you need to do two things. First, edit the *i*SQL*Plus configuration file and replace the Location section with the following segment:

```
<Location /iSQL*Plus>
  SetHandler iplus-handler
  Order deny,allow
  AuthType Basic
  AuthName 'iSQL*Plus'
  AuthUserFile %ORACLE_HOME%\sqlplus\admin\iplus.pw
  Require valid-user
</Location>
```

Next, go the $ORACLE_HOME\Apache\Apache\bin directory and run the following command from there to create a new password file for regular users and include new users in the file. The command is for a Windows server, where *C:\Oracle 9i* is $ORACLE_HOME:

```
C:\Oracle9i\Apache\Apache\bin> htpasswd C:\oracle9i\sqlplus\admin\iplus.pw newuser
```

Now you can restart the HTTP server and the user "newuser" will be prompted both for an Oracle username/password and a password for the HTTP server.

 CAUTION *If you are a member of groups such as dba (UNIX) or ORA_DBA (Windows), the operating system automatically authenticates the iSQL*Plus DBA URL. Therefore, you need to start the HTTP server as an ordinary user who doesn't have any of the operating system authenticated groups like the ones mentioned here.*

---

*iSQL*Plus* Security

The *i*SQL*Plus interface uses the security model of the *restrict* option, which you saw earlier in the chapter. Thus, you can't execute commands such as *host*, *@*, and *spool* from *i*SQL*Plus. This means that you can't reference the local file system using an *i*SQL*Plus interface.

Note that *i*SQL*Plus does not use a login.sql file, like the SQL*Plus interface does. When you first log in, only the global login file, .glogin, is read. This file is usually located in the $ORACLE_HOME/sqlplus/admin directory. Users thus cannot customize the environment for their use, as they can in SQL*Plus.

You can further restrict access to the *i*SQL*Plus server to a set of authorized users by using Oracle's HTTP server authentication, as shown in the previous section. To enhance security, you can use the HTTPS (SSL)–type connection to the *i*SQL*Plus server.

A final note of caution: Because of possible HTTP network timeouts, Oracle recommends that you stick to using the traditional SQL*Plus interface for running time-consuming DBA operations (for example, analyzing on a huge table).

Executing Statements

The *i*SQL*Plus interface provides several buttons to facilitate the entry and execution of your SQL commands. You use the Load Script and Save Script buttons to load and save SQL scripts, respectively. When you execute the entered statements by clicking the Execute button, the results are shown at the bottom of the *i*SQL*Plus screen.

Figure 6-4 shows the results of executing a simple SQL query. Note the difference in the output of the *i*SQL*Plus and the SQL*Plus interfaces. The *i*SQL*Plus interface enables you to turn out smart-looking reports without any of the formatting that is needed in SQL*Plus scripts. Of course, you can save the SQL queries to a directory and reuse them from there later on.

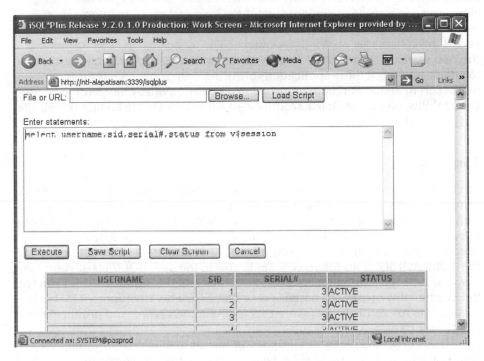

Figure 6-4. Executing a SQL query in iSQL*Plus

Inapplicable SQL*Plus Commands in *i*SQL*Plus

For several reasons, including redundancy, several of the regular SQL*Plus commands do not work in the *i*SQL*Plus environment. The following are some of the important commands that you can't use in the *i*SQL*Plus environment:

```
Append,delete,change,edit,input,exit,quit,get,host,save,spool,Store,
 flush,newpage,pause,sqlprompt, tab,termout,trimouttrimspool
```

Although you may be disappointed to see so many of your old standby SQL*Plus commands unavailable, the *i*SQL*Plus environment does give you a better display and capabilities for Web reporting, which compensate for the drawbacks. You may find yourself using both interfaces, depending on the kinds of tasks you are performing.

A Security Warning for iSQL*Plus

David Lichfield, a cofounder of Next Generation Security Software (http://www.nextgenss.com/), found a serious security flaw in *i*SQL*Plus. A malicious user can provide a username that is too long and cause an internal buffer overflow. This enables the user to run code as the oracle user on UNIX systems and as the system user on Windows systems. The malicious user can further use the Web server to launch attacks. Any Web-based Oracle application is susceptible to attack, but only if those applications are using *i*SQL*Plus—SQL*Plus is immune to this sort of attack. For more information on this potentially dangerous security vulnerability, please see Oracle security alert #46 on the Oracle MetaLink Web site (http://metalink.oracle.com/).

Summary

All Oracle DBAs need to be familiar with the SQL*Plus, interface, which provides a window into the Oracle database. This chapter was aimed toward administrators without a whole lot of experience with writing SQL statements using the SQL*Plus interface. Although the chapter dealt with SQL*Plus commands first and introduced the *i*SQL*Plus interface afterward, note that just about every command in the traditional SQL*Plus interface is applicable in the new *i*SQL*Plus environment. The new *i*SQL*Plus environment is easy to install and use, and it provides you with the functionality of browser-based access. The *i*SQL*Plus environment makes it easy for you to execute scripts scored on your Windows server and produce easy HTML reports.

There are several types of SQL*Plus commands, including formatting, database administration, and other types. If you use manual commands, you'll be spending most of your time in the SQL*Plus environment. Even if you primarily depend on a GUI-based tool to manage your databases, you still need to understand the intricacies of SQL*Plus and *i*SQL*Plus commands, especially those dealing with security and authentication. Become proficient at using this interface. It will enhance your productivity and enable you to create scripts and prepare useful database administration reports.

#### CHAPTER 7

Schema Management in Oracle9*i*

THIS CHAPTER STARTS with a review of the different types of SQL statements used in Oracle9*i*. Although you need to know all the different types of SQL statements well, an important part of the Oracle DBA's job is to support developers in creating database objects and, later on, manage these objects after implementing them in production systems. This chapter will give you a thorough understanding of the nature of objects such as tables, indexes, views, sequences, and triggers, which will help you not only assist the development process, but also troubleshoot problems during data loads and other situations.

To create a table, index, or other object, you first need to create tablespaces in your databases. The first part of this chapter devotes considerable attention to creating and managing tablespaces. The newer local extent management is preferable to the traditional dictionary extent management because it's more efficient and leads to less contention in the data dictionary. I explain Oracle's automatic segment management in this context.

Next, I describe the creation and management of various types of Oracle9*i* tables. Several special tables, such as the temporary tables and the newer external tables, are very useful to the DBA in performing specialized tasks. Both of these special tables as well as index organized tables and clusters are discussed in detail in this chapter. I follow this discussion with coverage of index creation and management. You'll find more information on index management in the performance tuning chapters later on. Creating the right indexes has significant bearing on the performance of database queries, and I provide basic guidelines for creating Oracle indexes. Managing database constraints during data loading and troubleshooting problems caused by table constraints are important parts of an Oracle DBA's task list, and I provide a summary of all the major types of constraints, constraint states, and their implications. I also explain how to create partitioned tables and partitioned indexes.

The management of other database objects such as views, sequences, and synonyms form an important part of the Oracle DBA's skill set. I explore these topics in detail before concluding the chapter with an in-depth discussion of creating and managing materialized views, which are a powerful feature of the Oracle9*i* database.

Types of SQL Statements in Oracle

Structured Query Language (SQL) is now the most common relational database access language. It is well known for its ease of use and its many powerful data-manipulation features. SQL is certified as the standard language for relational database systems by the American National Standards Institute (ANSI) and International Organization for Standardization (ISO) groups. ANSI introduced the first industry SQL standard in 1986.

There are several versions of the SQL language. Oracle conforms to the *SQL-99* core specification (often called *SQL:99*), which is the current minimum level for conforming to official SQL standards. Oracle extends the basic ANSI/ISO standard in several ways, making its own "Oracle SQL" language far more powerful than the minimum acceptable SQL standards for the relational database industry.

Relational database principles underlie the SQL language, which is a nonprocedural language, thereby making it extremely easy to use. You only need to instruct the language "what to do," not "how to do" it. No matter which tool you use to access the Oracle database, ultimately you'll be using the Oracle SQL language to perform your transactions. Your application program or the Oracle tool you use may allow you access to the database without using SQL, but the tools and applications have to use SQL to process your requests.

Oracle9*i* Release 2 (9.2.0.1.0) integrates XML query, storage, and update functionality in the database engine. Oracle has made several XML-centric extensions to its SQL language. Oracle9*i* now supports XML schema and XPath, using the SQLX standard extensions to the SQL language. In addition to traditional relational data, Oracle's new SQL enables you to manage XML, full text, multimedia, and objects. No matter which tool you use to access the Oracle database, you'll be using the Oracle SQL language to perform your transactions.

The SQL language includes commands for data modeling, data definition, data access, data security, and data administration. SQL statements used by Oracle can be broadly divided into several groups based on whether they change the table data, the table structures, or some other session or instance characteristic. The SQL statement types are as follows:

- System control
- Session control
- Data manipulation
- Transaction control
- Data definition

The following sections examine each of these broad types of SQL statements in detail.

System Control Statements

You can use the system control statement *alter system* to alter the properties of a running database instance. For example, you can use the *alter system* statement to modify certain initialization parameters such as the shared pool component of the System Global Area (SGA). At present, the *alter system* command is the only system control SQL statement in Oracle. Here's an example of the *alter system* command:

```
Sql> alter system kill session '25,9192';
Session killed
Sql>
```

Session Control Statements

Session control statements dynamically alter the properties of an individual user's session. For example, if you intend to trace what your SQL session is doing in the database, you can use the *alter session set sql trace = true* SQL statement to trace your session alone. The session control statements also come in handy when you're changing several initialization parameters just for your session. Note that PL/SQL doesn't support session control statements.

Common session control statements include the *alter session* and *set role* commands. Here's a common example of the use of the *alter session* statement:

```
SQL> alter session set nls_date_format = 'MM-DD-YYYY HH:MI:SS';
Session altered.
SQL>
```

Data Manipulation Statements

The data manipulation language (DML) statements are statements that either query (retrieve) or manipulate (change) data in a table. For the most part, DML statements modify the data in the schema objects. In most online transaction processing systems (OLTPs), the bulk of Oracle's work consists of accepting requests from users that contain DML statements and bringing them back the results of the particular DML statement.

You'll deal with four important DML statements most of the time: *select, insert, update,* and *delete*. Note that in addition to these four common DML statements, there are other DML statements such as *call, lock table, explain plan,* and *merge*. Most of these *other* DML statements facilitate the execution of the four basic DML statements. For example, the *merge* statement deals with conditional inserts and deletes, and the *lock table* statement is used to prevent other transactions from modifying the same data while a transaction is still running.

Select Statements

Select statements are queries that retrieve data from a table or a set of tables (or views). Oracle provides set operators such as *union, minus,* and *intersection* that enable you to combine the results of several queries to get one final result set of data. You can use the *order by* command to sort the results provided by Oracle; otherwise, the results will not be in any particular order. When you need data that has to reference several tables, you need to join the tables in your *select* statements. When you join tables, you need to provide a join condition, which will limit the result set.

You can also use subqueries as part of the main or top query. A subquery that is used in the *where* clause of a *select* statement is called a *nested subquery*. A subquery that is part of the *from* clause of a *select* statement is called an *inline view*. Appendix A provides examples of subqueries, nested subqueries, and inline views.

Insert, Delete, and Update Statements

The *insert* statement inserts new rows into existing tables and the *delete* statement removes entire rows from tables. The *update* SQL command modifies one or more columns of a single row or multiple rows within a table. As an Oracle DBA, it's the amount and type of these three DML activities that you'll be mostly concerned with on a day-to-day basis. Although optimizing the writing of *select* statements that address large tables is an important part of performance tuning, it's the data manipulation SQL statements per se that could cause more frustration for the typical DBA dealing with an OLTP database. A data warehouse, on the other hand, in general caters mostly to users' queries. Designing the data objects properly is important to be able to efficiently process a large number of concurrent inserts, deletes, and updates to tables.

Transaction Control Statements

You use transaction control statements to control the changes made when you issue data manipulation SQL statements such as *insert, update*, and *delete*.

The four transaction control statements are *commit, rollback, save point*, and *set transaction*. Table 7-1 defines these four types of transaction control statements.

Table 7-1. Transaction Control Statements

STATEMENT	DEFINITION
commit	When it follows a set of DML statements, this statement will make the changes permanent.
rollback	When it follows one or more DML statements, this statement will undo the statements made by the preceding statements.
save point	This statement allows flexibility in your transactions, helping you set intermediate points in the transaction to which you can roll back or undo your transactions.
set transaction	This rarely used statement denotes the start of a transaction. Its use is optional in Oracle, and it's mostly used for specifying a particular rollback segment for use by a transaction. Of course, if you're using automatic undo management, as this book strongly advocates, you won't have any rollback segments to manage, and you thus won't have a need to use this statement.

Data Definition Statements

Data definition language (DDL) statements enable you to *define* the database. DDL is what enables you to create and manage objects in Oracle. DDL statements define the structure of the various schema objects in Oracle. They can also alter the structure of the objects and drop the objects from the database. The following list presents some of the main uses of the DDL statements:

- Creating tables, indexes, and other similar schema objects

- Creating and modifying procedures, functions, and packages

- Dropping and modifying database objects

- Creating and managing users of the database

- Granting privileges on objects to users and revoking privileges on objects from users

- Analyzing the data within a table or index

- Creating and altering tablespaces

- Creating and modifying database links

Oracle Schema Management

In Oracle, a *schema* is defined as a logical collection of objects, although it is used mostly as a synonym for a user (specifically, an application owner). Thus, the accounting schema within a company database would have all the tables and code pertaining to the accounting department. In addition to containing tables, a schema contains other database objects such as PL/SQL procedures, functions and packages, views, sequences, synonyms, and clusters. This separation of the objects within the database on a logical basis allows you considerable flexibility in managing and securing your Oracle databases.

Although you can use the *create schema* statement to create a specific schema, more often the application owner creates the database objects and therefore is referred to as the *schema owner*. The user who creates the objects owns database objects such as tables, views, procedures, functions, and triggers. The owner of the object has to explicitly assign specific rights such as select or update to other users. In addition, the owner has to create synonyms for the various objects if the other users are to access the objects.

Although all the various types of SQL statements are important, as a DBA your main preoccupation will be with the DDL statements concerning schema objects, because they enable you to directly control schema management. There are many types of schema objects, and you'll be dealing with the following important types of schema objects in this chapter:

- Tables

- Indexes

- Views

- Materialized views

- Procedures, functions, and packages

- Object tables and object types

- Database triggers

- Database links

Oracle is an object-relational database and, as such, it allows users to define several types of data other than the standard relational data types. These user-defined data types include the following:

- *Object types:* These complex types are an abstraction of real-world entities.

- *Array types:* These types are used to create ordered sets of data elements of the same type.

- *Table types:* These types are used to create an unordered set of data elements of the same data type.

- *XML schema:* This is a new object type that is used to create types and storage elements for XML documents based on the XML schema.

Appendix A provides examples of how to create various kinds of user-defined object types. In this chapter, the focus is on the traditional relational type of objects. In the following sections, you'll learn how Oracle DBAs manage the schema objects. Before you start looking at the various schema objects, first you'll need to learn how to manage the all-important Oracle tablespaces.

....

What's the Dual Table?

The *dual table* belongs to the sys schema and is created automatically when the data dictionary is created. The dual table has one column called "dummy" and one row. The dual table enables you to use the Oracle *select* command to compute a constant expression. As you can see, everything in Oracle has to be in a table somewhere. Even if something isn't, for example, the evaluation of an arithmetical expression, a query that intends to retrieve those results needs to use a table. The dual table serves as a catchall table for those expressions. For example, to compute the product of 9 and 24567, you can issue the following SQL command: *select 9*24567 from dual.*

....

Creating and Managing Tablespaces

Before you can create tables or indexes, you must create tablespaces. As you learned in Chapter 5, *tablespaces* are logical entities that facilitate the management of an Oracle database. Tablespaces consist of one or more files. Although your data and objects reside in operating system files, the organization of these files into Oracle tablespaces makes it easy for you to group related information.

NOTE *Tablespaces are not unique to Oracle. The DB2 databases also have tablespaces, although Microsoft SQL Server databases don't use tablespaces. For example, in a SQL Server database, the tempdb database corresponds to the temporary tablespace in an Oracle database.*

Locally and Dictionary Managed Tablespaces

As you learned in Chapter 5, you can create two basic types of tablespaces in Oracle9*i*: locally managed and dictionary managed. *Locally managed* tablespaces maintain all extent information "locally," within the tablespace itself. *Dictionary managed* tablespaces, on the other hand, keep the information in the data dictionary. Unless your database has LOBs or columns that are of type LONG, use the Locally Managed Tablespaces (LMT) option available in Oracle9*i*. Locally managed tablespaces free you from the usual worries of setting the PCTUSED and FREELIST parameters when you are creating new tables and indexes. In Oracle9*i*, the System tablespace is automatically created when you create the database and it is always a locally managed tablespace.

As mentioned earlier, locally managed tablespaces don't rely on the data dictionary for extent management purposes. In a way, these tablespaces manage extent allocation on their own, without recourse to the data dictionary. They manage extents by referring to the bitmaps kept in each data file of a tablespace for all the blocks within that data file. The bitmaps indicate whether the blocks are free or occupied. If, for example, Oracle needs to allocate an extent to an object, the bitmap values are updated to show the latest status of the availability of data blocks. This takes the burden of free-space management for the extents off the data dictionary.

Locally managed tablespaces have several advantages over the traditional dictionary managed tablespaces. Dictionary managed tablespaces have to constantly check the data dictionary during the course of extent management. Whenever an extent is allocated to an object or reclaimed from an object, Oracle will update the relevant tables in the data dictionary. If you have an OLTP system with heavy inserts and deletes, this could lead to contention for the data dictionary objects used to manage extents. Locally managed tablespaces also save the DBA the headaches of free-space fragmentation, which makes it harder to allocate extents to objects. Table 7-2 presents a comparison of locally and dictionary managed tablespaces.

Table 7-2. Comparison of Locally and Dictionary Managed Tablespaces

LOCALLY MANAGED TABLESPACES	DICTIONARY MANAGED TABLESPACES
Default tablespace type in Oracle9*i*	Nondefault tablespace type
Offers better performance due to reduction	Performance is slower due to more recursive operations in recursive queries on the data dictionary
Reduced contention for enqueue and other resources	Higher contention for resources
Faster operations	Slower operations because of free space checks in the data dictionary
Automatic extent size selection using *autoallocate*	Manual extent size selection

(Continued)

Table 7-2. Comparison of Locally and Dictionary Managed Tablespaces (Cont.)

LOCALLY MANAGED TABLESPACES	DICTIONARY MANAGED TABLESPACES
Easy segment space management using the *auto* option	Manual segment space management using the parameters PCUSED, PCTINCREASE, and FREELISTS
No need to coalesce free extents	Free extents need to be coalesced to avoid fragmentation
Easy-to-use resumable statements feature	Potential problems under some circumstances with resumable statements
Can't use default storage settings	Can use default storage settings
Can use DBMS_SPACE_ADMIN for troubleshooting	Can't use DBMS_SPACE_ADMIN

Creating Locally Managed Tablespaces

Although it is possible to create dictionary managed tablespaces in Oracle9*i*, in the discussion that follows I only cover locally managed tablespaces because of their clear superiority to the traditional tablespaces. If your database is created with a locally managed tablespace, you can only create all the other tablespaces as locally managed. Please see the database creation script shown in Listing 9-8 in Chapter 9 to learn how you can specify the System tablespace as locally managed.

 NOTE *In Oracle9i version 2 (9.2), if you create your System tablespace as locally managed, all other tablespaces will be locally managed by default. In fact, you can't create any traditional dictionary managed tablespaces in this tablespace.*

Before you can create your tablespaces, you need to decide how you're going to manage two important storage features of tablespaces. The first deals with extent management. Each time an object in a tablespaces grows in size, it's allocated a new extent. As you saw in Chapter 5, you can have Oracle manage the extent sizing, or you can do it yourself. The second storage feature relates to segment space management. Here again, you have two choices: manual or automatic management of segment space. The next section briefly covers making the choice between these two storage features of tablespaces.

Choosing the Extent Management Type

You can create locally managed tablespaces with either uniform extent sizes or variable extent sizes. If you want uniform extent sizes, you need to specify the clause *extent management uniform size*. If you want Oracle to allocate the extents, you have to specify the keyword *autoallocate* during the creation of the locally managed tablespaces. When the tablespace needs to grow by acquiring extents, Oracle will decide on the size of the new extent. The extents that Oracle will create are multiples of 64KB. By using the *uniform* keyword, however, you can choose the size of the extents yourself. Oracle's default extent size is 1MB, but you can choose a much larger uniform extent size if you wish.

A good practice is to create locally managed tablespaces with the *uniform* allocation clause so you don't blindly rely on Oracle for sizing the extents. The *uniform* allocation clause tells Oracle to create new extents of a specified size and not according to the Oracle default size. For example, say you know your largest tables will consume a lot of space and therefore need a very high extent size. Just create a tablespace with a very large uniform size for such tables. From both a performance and a space utilization point of view, locally managed tablespaces should be used for all heavy-duty databases. If you have a database with potentially widely different table and index sizes, create your locally managed tablespaces using the *uniform size* option for extent management.

NOTE *The default for tablespace extent management is the* autoallocate *option.*

Segment Space Management

As you learned in Chapter 5, one of the biggest advantages when you use locally managed tablespaces is that they enable you to specify that Oracle take care of your segment space management needs. Traditionally, the DBA had to manually manage segment space management, which deals with how Oracle objects manage free space within segments.

In Oracle9i, you have two choices regarding segment space management: *manual* and *auto*. The manual method is the traditional manual management, which uses FREELISTS to manage free space. The second, newer automatic management of free space by Oracle uses *bitmaps* to monitor free space. The choice of *auto* for segment space management tells Oracle to manage the free space in the data blocks that are part of the segments. Chapter 5 explains how automatic segment space management by Oracle will keep you from worrying about the PCTUSED, FREELISTS, and FREELIST GROUPS parameters to specify how free space is managed for the objects you create in a tablespace.

Listing 7-1 shows you how to create a locally managed tablespace with different extent management and space management options. Again, remember that the default for the extent management is *autoallocate*, and the default for segment space management is *manual*.

Listing 7-1. Creating Locally Managed Tablespaces

```
Example 1.
SQL>  create tablespace test01
  2        datafile '/test01/app/oracle/oradata/remorse/test01.dbf'
  3*       size 100M;
Tablespace created.
SQL>
Note: Extent allocation : autoallocate (default)
        Segment space  : manual (default)
Example 2
SQL> create tablespace test02
  2        datafile '/test01/app/oracle/oradata/remorse/test02.dbf'
  3      size 100M
  4*     autoallocate;
Tablespace created.
SQL>
Note: Extent allocation: autoallocate (explicitly chosen option)
        Segment space : manual (default)
Example 3
SQL>  create tablespace test03
  2  datafile '/test01/app/oracle/oradata/remorse/test03.dbf'
  3  size 100M
  4* segment space management auto;
Tablespace created.
SQL>
Note: Extent allocation : autoallocate (default)
        Segment space  : automatic
Example 4
SQL>  create tablespace test04
  2        datafile '/test01/app/oracle/oradata/remorse/test04.dbf'
  3      size 100M
  4*     uniform size 2m;
Tablespace created.
SQL>
Note: Extent allocation : uniform size 2m
        Segment space  : manual (default)
Example 5
SQL>
SQL>  create tablespace test05
  2  datafile '/test01/app/oracle/oradata/remorse/test05.dbf'
  3  size 100M
  4  uniform size 2m
  5* segment space management auto;
Tablespace created.
SQL>
Note: Extent allocation : uniform size 2m
        Segment space  : auto
```

Notes on the Create Tablespace Commands

Let me briefly explain the various parts of the create tablespace commands that I used in Listing 7-1 to create the new tablespaces.

The *create tablespace* segment of the command indicates that I'm creating a tablespace. Because my test database was created with a locally managed System tablespace, I can only create locally managed tablespaces in this database. If I had a non-locally-managed System tablespace, I could use an *extent management dictionary* clause to specify a dictionary managed tablespace. All tablespaces have to be created in one or more data files, specified by the *datafile* clause.

The *uniform size* parameter indicates to Oracle that I want this tablespace's extents to be managed with uniform extents of the size specified. If you don't want uniform extent allocation, you can leave it out and Oracle will use the default *autoallocate* option, with a minimum of 64KB for the extent size. If you're going to include objects of different extent sizes in the same tablespace, then it's better to let Oracle do the allocation of extents automatically. If you want to explicitly allocate the extent size, you can choose the *uniform size* option.

The *segment space management* option tells Oracle how to manage the free and used space within the segment. If you choose *auto*, you don't have to worry about specifying conditions under which Oracle should pick new data blocks for data insertion, for example. Oracle will do all that for you. When you insert data into Oracle blocks, you can use some guidelines to tell Oracle how far to fill each data block. You also want to reserve some space in each data block in case the row values increase in the future. The amount of space you want Oracle to reserve for the expansion of existing rows in a data block is called the *PCTFREE* parameter.

 NOTE *Suppose the PCTFREE parameter is 20 percent. You can then fill up the block with new data up to the remaining 80 percent of the data block. When data gets deleted from the blocks, you don't want Oracle to right away use up every morsel of free space for inserting new data. This is because there's an overhead associated with keeping the lists of free blocks available for Oracle to check free space. These lists, called FREELISTS, are stored in the headers of data blocks and have to be constantly maintained by Oracle.*

To avoid this constant overhead, Oracle provides you with another parameter called *PCTUSED*. The PCTUSED parameter specifies how much of the data in a block should get deleted before it can be considered for insertion of fresh data. If the PCTUSED parameter is 60, for example, and the PCTFREE parameter is 10, the block can be filled up to the remaining 90 percent with new data. Thereafter, if there are deletions, the percent of used space has to come down to 60 before Oracle will allow insertions again into that data block. If the *auto* option is chosen for the segment space management parameter, you don't have to worry about setting the PCTUSED, FREELISTS, or PCTINCREASE parameter values. Oracle will automatically manage all these for you.

If you choose the *auto* option for segment space management, you don't have to specify the usual storage parameters PCTINCREASE, minextents, and maxextents during the creation of locally managed tablespaces. The default for the segment space management parameter is *manual*. If you choose to do this, you may have to set the FREELISTS, PCTINCREASE, and PCTUSED parameters for the objects in the tablespace.

 NOTE *Default storage parameters for a tablespace imply that any objects created in that tablespace inherited those storage specifications (PCTFREE, PCTUSED, and so forth) by default. Locally managed tablespaces don't allow you to specify default storage settings.*

Listing 7-2 shows how you can use the DBA_TABLESPACES data dictionary view to find out how the tablespaces in your database are being managed.

Listing 7-2. Determining Space and Extent Management of Tablespaces

```
SQL> select tablespace_name,
  2  initial_extent,
  3  next_extent,
  4  extent_management,
  5  allocation_type,
  6  segment_space_management
  7* from dba_tablespaces;
```

TABLESPACE	INITIAL EXTENT	NEXT -EXTENT	EXTENT --MNAGMNT---	ALLOCATIO TYPE-----	SEGMENT -SPACE-
SYSTEM	65536		LOCAL	SYSTEM	MANUAL
UNDOTBS	65536		LOCAL	SYSTEM	MANUAL
TEMPTBS1	1048576	1048576	LOCAL	UNIFORM	MANUAL
USERS	65536		LOCAL	SYSTEM	MANUAL
TEST01	65536		LOCAL	SYSTEM	MANUAL
TEST02	65536		LOCAL	SYSTEM	MANUAL
TEST03	65536		LOCAL	SYSTEM	AUTO
TEST04	2097152	2097152	LOCAL	UNIFORM	MANUAL
TEST05	2097152	2097152	LOCAL	UNIFORM	AUTO

```
9 rows selected.
SQL>
```

In Listing 7-2 the various columns stand for the following things:

- *Tablespace_Name:* This is the name of the tablespace.

- *Initial_Extent and Next_Extent:* These columns denote the size of the first and second extents. For tablespaces test01, test02, and test03, it's about 64KB, which is Oracle's minimum extent allocation size. Remember that these three tablespaces were created with the *autoallocate* option. For tablespaces test04 and test05, the initial and next extents are 2097152 bytes, because the *uniform size* was 2MB for these tablespaces.

- *Extent_Management:* This column could show a value of local or dictionary, but because your System tablespace is locally managed, all your tablespaces are locally managed as well.

- *Allocation_Type:* This column refers to the extent allocation, which is uniform for the last two databases and system (*autoallocate*) for the first three.

- *Segment_Space_Management:* Tablespaces test03 and test05 show the *auto* segment space management option, which is how they were created. The other three show the default *manual* segment space management mode.

Creating Tablespaces with Multiple Block Sizes

You have the option in Oracle9i of creating tablespaces with varying block sizes. This way, you can customize a tablespace for the types of objects it contains. For example, you can allocate a large table that requires a large number of reads and writes to a tablespace with a large block size. Similarly, you can place smaller tables in tablespaces with a smaller block size. Note that if you don't create tablespaces with multiple block sizes, you can't take advantage of Oracle multiple buffer pool feature. The following are some of the important points to remember about the multiple block size feature for tablespaces:

- As you recall from Chapter 5, multiple buffer pools enable you to configure up to a total of five different pools in the buffer cache, each with a different block size.

- The System tablespace always has to be created with the *standard* block size specified by the *db_block_size* parameter in the init.ora file.

- You can have up to four *nonstandard* block sizes.

- You specify the block size for tablespaces in the *create tablespace* statement by using the *blocksize* clause.

- The nonstandard block sizes must be 2KB, 4KB, 8KB, 16KB, or 32KB. One of these sizes, of course, will have to be chosen as the standard block size by using the *db_block_size* parameter in the init.ora file.

- If you're transporting tablespaces between databases, using multiple block size tablespaces makes it easier to transport tablespaces of different block sizes.

- If you're planning on configuring multiple buffer pools in your buffer cache, you must plan on creating tablespaces with multiple block sizes.

- You can use the online table redefinition feature of Oracle9i to migrate tables from one tablespace to another, without having to export and import the table data.

Creating Temporary Tablespaces

Oracle uses temporary tablespaces to perform sort operations for users and operations such as sorting done during the process of creating indexes. Oracle doesn't allow users to create objects in a temporary tablespace for permanent use in the database. You do, however, have the option of using the dictionary managed option or the locally managed option to create your temporary tablespace. You should create locally managed temporary tablespaces because they provide superior performance and are far easier to manage than dictionary managed tablespaces. Instead of the regular data files, locally managed temporary tablespaces use what are known as *tempfiles*. Tempfiles have little or no redo associated with them.

Creating temporary tablespaces is very similar to creating regular, permanent tablespaces. Just make sure you use the *tempfile* parameter instead of *datafile* when you allocate space in the file system. Chapter 9 shows how you can create a default temporary tablespace during database creation. If you want to create other temporary tablespaces, use the following statement:

```
1  create temporary tablespace temptbs02i
2  tempfile
3  '/test01/app/oracle/oradata/remorse/temp02.dbf'
4* size 100M;
Tablespace created.
SQL>
```

Removing Tablespaces

Sometimes you may want to get rid of a tablespace. You may want to rename a tablespace or remove a tablespace entirely because of some modifications in your application. You can remove a tablespace from the database by issuing this simple command:

```
SQL> Drop tablespace test01;
```

If test01 includes tables or indexes, you'll get an error. You can either move the objects to a different tablespace or, if the objects are dispensable, use this command:

```
SQL> Drop tablespace test01 including contents;
```

which will drop the tablespace regardless of the fact that it has some data objects residing in it.

However, the data files that you assigned to the tablespace test01 are still not released back to the operating system file system. To do so, you have to either manually remove the data files that were a part of the test01 tablespace or issue the following command to remove both the objects and the physical data files at once. The one tablespace you can't drop, of course, is the System tablespace.

```
SQL> Drop tablespace test01 including contents and datafiles;
```

The preceding statement would *automatically drop the data files* along with the tablespace. If referential integrity constraints are present in other tables that refer to the tables in the tablespace you intend to drop, you need to use the following command:

```
SQL> drop tablespace test01 cascade constraints;
```

Adding Space to a Tablespace

When your tablespace is filling up with table and index data, you need to expand its size. You do this by adding more physical file space in the following manner:

```
SQL> Alter tablespace finan_data01
Add datafile '/finance10/app/oracle/finance/finan_01.dbf' size 1000M;
```

You can also increase or decrease the size of the tablespace by increasing or decreasing the size of the tablespace's data files. You can increase or decrease the size of the data files using the *resize* command. You usually use the *resize* command to correct data file sizing errors. Note that you can't decrease a data file's size beyond the space that is already occupied by objects in the data file. The following is an example of manually resizing a data file. Originally, the file had 250MB. The following operation doubles the size of the file to 500MB. Note that you need to use the *alter database* command, not the *alter tablespace* command, to resize a data file.

```
SQL> Alter database datafile '/finance10/oradata/data_09.dbf'
Resize 500m;
```

Automatic Data File Extension

You can use the *autoextend* provision when you create a tablespace or when you add data files to a tablespace to tell Oracle to automatically extend the size of the data files in the tablespace. That is, if the tablespace is nearing a saturation point with regard to space usage in its data files, Oracle will automatically extend the size of the data files up to a specified maximum. This alternative was attractive when DBAs ran the risk of failed programs due to lack of space. Oracle9i has the new *Resumable Space Allocation* feature, which makes the use of the *autoextend* feature less attractive. You can use the Resumable Space Allocation feature, as you'll see in Chapter 8, to suspend operations that might otherwise fail on account of a space problem and resume those operations after more space is added to the database object. Here is the command syntax for using the *autoextend* feature for automatically extending your data files when necessary:

```
SQL> ALTER TABLESPACE data01
      ADD DATAFILE '/finance10/oradata/data01.dbf' SIZE 200M
      AUTOEXTEND ON
      NEXT 1M
      MAXSIZE 1000M;
SQL>
```

251

Renaming a Data File

Sometimes you may need to rename a data file. The process is straightforward. Here are the steps you need to follow:

1. Take the data file offline by taking the tablespace that contains the data file offline by using the following command:

```
SQL> alter tablespace test01 offline normal;
Tablespace altered.
SQL>
```

2. Rename the file using an operating system utility such as cp/mv in UNIX or copy in Windows.

```
cp  /test01/app/oracle/admin/remorse/test01.dbf
        /test02/app/oracle/admin/remorse/test01.dbf
```

3. Rename the data file in the database by using the following command:

```
SQL>  alter tablespace test01
  2  rename
  3  datafile '/test01/app/oracle/oradata/remorse/test01.dbf'
  4  to
  5* '/test02/app/oracle/admin/remorse/test01.dbf';
Tablespace altered.
SQL>
```

Taking Tablespaces Offline

An Oracle database consists of several tablespaces, including the System tablespace. Except for the System tablespace, you can take any or all the other tablespaces *offline*—that is, you make them temporarily unavailable to users. You usually need to take tablespaces offline when a data file within a tablespace contains some errors or you are changing code in an application that accesses one of the tablespaces being taken offline.

Four modes of "offlining" are possible with Oracle tablespaces: normal, temporary, immediate, and for recover. Except the normal mode, which is the default mode of taking tablespaces offline, all the other modes of taking the tablespaces offline may involve recovery of the included data files or the tablespace itself. You'll see the usage of these nondefault offlining methods in Chapter 15. For now, know that you can take any tablespace offline with no harm using the following command:

```
SQL> Alter tablespace index_01 offline normal;
```

Oracle will ensure the checkpointing of all the data files in the index_01 tablespace before it takes the tablespace offline. Thus, there is no need for recovery when you later bring the tablespace back online. To bring the tablespace online, use the following command:

```
SQL> Alter tablespace index_01 online;
```

Read-Only Tablespaces

By default, all Oracle tablespaces are both readable and writable when created. However, you can specify that a tablespace cannot be written to by making it a read-only tablespace. The command to do so is simple:

```
SQL> Alter tablespace test01 read only;
```

If you want to make this tablespace writable again, you use the following command:

```
SQL> Alter tablespace test01 read write;
```

Oracle Managed Files

The Oracle9*i* database enables you to use Oracle Managed Files (OMF), which enable Oracle to manage the creation and deletion of data files. The previous discussion dealt with manual management of data files, where you, the DBA, will have to manually create, delete, and manage the data files. As you know, tablespaces are logical units of storage that are made up of data files. OMF files offer a simpler way of managing the file system, but they come with some disadvantages. If you choose to use the OMF way of managing files, you don't have to worry about specifying the filenames when you're creating tablespaces or redo log groups or even control files. Here's what you have to do to be able to use OMF files in your database.

First, you need to tell Oracle where it can create the files for the various types of files you want to use the OMF files for. You need to specify the file locations for the following two parameters in the init.ora file:

```
db_create_file_dest=/finance10/oradata/data/finance_10.dbf
db_create_online_log_dest_n=/finance20/oradta/logs/finance_20.dbf
```

The first parameter specifies the location for OMF data files and temporary files, and the second parameter specifies the location for the online redo log files and control files.

You can also specify the OMF directories dynamically by using the *alter system* command as follows:

```
Alter system
set db_create_file_dest='/finance10/oradata/
data/finance_10.dbf'
            OR
Alter system
Set db_create_online_log_dest_n=
'/finance20/oradta/logs/finance_20.dbf'
```

When you want to create a tablespace or add data files using OMF files, you don't have to give a location for the data files. Oracle will automatically create the file in the location you specified for that type of file in the init.ora file. Here are some examples:

```
SQL> create tablespace finance01;
alter tablespace finance01 add datafile 501M;
```

When you want drop a tablespace, you issue the following command and the OMF data files are automatically removed by Oracle, along with the tablespace definition:

```
SQL> drop tablespace finance01;
```

The OMF files are definitely easier to manage than the traditional manually created operating system files. However, there are several reasons why OMF files may not be very useful in real life:

- Oracle limits the OMF files to 100MB. What if you're running a large database and you need much larger files?

- OMF files can't be used on raw devices, which offer superior performance to operating system files for certain applications (e.g., Oracle Real Application Clusters [ORAC]).

- All the OMF files for data files have to be created in one directory. It's hard to envision a large database fitting into this one file system.

- You can't choose your own names for the data files created under OMF files. Oracle will use a naming convention that includes the database name and unique character strings to name the data files.

- Oracle itself recommends OMF files for small and test databases.

Because of these reasons, although OMF files are definitely an interesting innovation from Oracle, they are not really feasible for any kind of large, real-world database. The traditional way of managing data files is far superior to the OMF way. If you want to learn more about administering the OMF files, you can find a lengthier discussion of this topic in Chapter 16.

Data Dictionary Views for Managing Tablespaces

This section presents the key dictionary views you will want to get familiar with for administrating tablespaces in Oracle9*i*.

DBA_DATA_FILES

The DBA_DATA_FILES dictionary view contains useful information to determine the size of the data files. You can get the name of the data files, the tablespaces they belong to, the size in bytes, and the status of the data file (online or offline) from the DBA_DATA_FILES table.

Listing 7-3 shows the structure of the DBA_DATA_FILES view.

Listing 7-3. *The DBA_DATA_FILES View*

```
SQL> desc dba_data_files
 Name                    Null?    Type
 ----------------------- -------- ---------------
 FILE_NAME                        VARCHAR2(513)
 FILE_ID                          NUMBER
 TABLESPACE_NAME                  VARCHAR2(30)
 BYTES                            NUMBER
 BLOCKS                           NUMBER
 STATUS                           VARCHAR2(9)
 RELATIVE_FNO                     NUMBER
 AUTOEXTENSIBLE                   VARCHAR2(3)
 MAXBYTES                         NUMBER
 MAXBLOCKS                        NUMBER
 INCREMENT_BY                     NUMBER
 USER_BYTES                       NUMBER
 USER_BLOCKS                      NUMBER
```

DBA_TABLESPACES

The DBA_TABLESPACES view is a very important dictionary view that you can use to help manage tablespaces. Listing 7-4 shows a small query using the DBA_TABLESPACES view.

Listing 7-4. *Using the DBA_TABLESPACES View*

```
Sql> select tablespace_name,status,extent_management from       dba_tablespaces
TABLESPACE_NAME                     STATUS    EXTENT MAN
----------------------------------- --------- ----------
SYSTEM                              ONLINE    DICTIONARY
UNDOTBS                             ONLINE    LOCAL
CWMLITE                             ONLINE    LOCAL
DRSYS                               ONLINE    LOCAL
EXAMPLE                             ONLINE    LOCAL
INDX                                ONLINE    LOCAL
TEMP                                ONLINE    LOCAL
TOOLS                               ONLINE    LOCAL
USERS                               ONLINE    LOCAL
9 rows selected.
SQL>
```

DBA_FREE_SPACE

The main columns of interest in the DBA_FREE_SPACE table are the tablespace_name and bytes (of free space) in each tablespace. For example, you can use the query shown in Listing 7-5 to see what the free space is in each tablespace of your database.

Listing 7-5. The DBA_FREE_SPACE View

```
SQL>  SELECT TABLESPACE_NAME,sum(bytes)
  2  from dba_free_space
  3* group by tablespace_name
TABLESPACE_NAME      SUM(BYTES)
------------------ ----------
CWMLITE            14680064
DRSYS              12845056
EXAMPLE            196608
INDX               26148864
SYSTEM             89100288
TOOLS              4390912
UNDOTBS            208338944
USERS              26148864
8 rows selected.
SQL>
```

DBA_SEGMENTS

The DBA_SEGMENTS data dictionary view shows the segment name and type, and the tablespace the segment belongs to, among other things. For example, the following query shows that there are no permanent objects being created in the temporary tablespace TEMP:

```
SQL> L
  1  select segment_name,segment_type,tablespace_name
  2  from dba_segments
  3* where tablespace_name='TEMP'
SQL> /
no rows selected
SQL>
```

Creating a Simple Table

Before you create a new table, it's a good idea to get some kind of an estimate of the size of the table, both the size you expect now and the size you expect in the future. Knowing the size of the table allows you to make the right kind of space allocation decisions.

Algorithms are available for finding out the potential size of tables and indexes. The formulas basically take the row size in bytes and multiply it by the estimated number of rows in the table. Estimation of table size is more an art than a precise science, and you don't need to agonize over coming up with "accurate" figures. Just use common sense and make sure you are not wildly off the mark.

NOTE *The following discussion on table operations deals with the "normal" or "regular" Oracle tables. The normal tables are formally called* heap-organized tables, *whose rows are stored in the order they are inserted into the table. Most of the table operations are common to all types of tables discussed here, but with some syntax modifications or limitations.*

Listing 7-6 gives the syntax for creating a simple table. The first thing you do is specify a tablespace for the table creation. If you don't, the table will be created in the user's default tablespace. Unless you really want to create the tables in a user's default tablespace, always specify the tablespace name when you create a table.

Listing 7-6. Creating a Simple Table

```
SQL> CREATE TABLE       employee
(
        empno      NUMBER(5) PRIMARY KEY,
        ename      VARCHAR2(15) NOT NULL,
        job        VARCHAR2(10),
        mgr        NUMBER(5),
        hiredate   DATE DEFAULT sysdate,
        sal        NUMBER(7,2),
        comm       NUMBER(7,2),
        deptno     NUMBER(3) NOT NULL)
                       TABLESPACE finan_data01
;
Table created
SQL1>
```

You can see that the use of the locally managed tablespace frees you from having to specify a large number of parameters at table creation time.

The employee table is created within the tablespace finan_data01. Let's assume the finan_data01 tablespace was created as a locally managed tablespace, with the segment space management *auto* parameter. The employee table automatically inherits all the default storage parameters from the finan_data01 tablespace. If you want to, you can specify all the storage parameters manually at table creation time, as shown in Listing 7-7.

Listing 7-7. Specifying Explicit Storage Parameters for a Table

```
SQL> CREATE TABLE          employee
     (
        empno        NUMBER(5) PRIMARY KEY,
        employee_name      VARCHAR2(15) NOT NULL,
        job          VARCHAR2(10),
        manager           NUMBER(5),
        hire_date    DATE DEFAULT (sysdate),
        salary       NUMBER(7,2),
        commission        NUMBER(7,2),
        department_no      NUMBER(3) NOT NULL
        )
   PCTFREE 10
   PCTUSED 40
   TABLESPACE users
   STORAGE ( INITIAL 50K
           NEXT 50K
           MAXEXTENTS 10
               PCTINCREASE  25  );
Table created
SQL>
```

Altering Tables

If you realize you incorrectly estimated the size parameters and the table really needs to have a different set of table storage parameters than what it inherited from the finan_data01 tablespace, you can use the DDL SQL command *alter table … move* to fix things, as shown in the following example:

```
SQL> Alter table emp move
Storage (initial 2m
        Next extent 2m
        Minextents 2
        Maxextents 40);
Table altered
SQL>
```

You can use *alter table … move* command to change the tablespace in which a table is located. In the following example, table emp is moved from its current tablespace to the users tablespace.

```
SQL> alter table emp move
  2  tablespace users;
Table altered.
SQL>
```

Note that you can use the *alter table … move* command with either the storage clause or the tablespace clause, or both, in the same statement.

Adding a Column to a Table

Adding a column to a table is a very straightforward operation. You can use the *alter table* option to add a column to a table. The following listing provides a simple example of adding a column to a table:

```
SQL> Alter table emp
Add (retired char(1));
Table altered.
SQL>
```

Dropping a Column from a Table

Prior to Oracle8, you couldn't drop a column from a table. If you wanted to get rid of a column, you had to re-create the table without the unneeded column. Now you can drop an existing column from a table by using the following command:

```
Sql> alter table emp
Drop (retired);
Table altered.
Sql>
```

NOTE *You have several options if you have a large amount of data in the column you're about to drop and it's not absolutely necessary for the data to be removed at the present time. If you can wait for the actual removal of data in the column, you can use the* drop column deferrable *option, and Oracle will drop the column at a later, more opportune time.*

Renaming a Table Column

You can easily rename columns in Oracle9i using the *rename column* command. For example, the following command will rename the column "retired" in the employee table to "non-active". Note that you can also rename the column constraints, if you wish.

```
Sql> alter table emp
Rename column retired to non-active;
Table altered.
Sql>
```

Renaming a Table

On occasion, an application developer may want to rename a table. Renaming a table is straightforward, as shown by the following listing:

```
SQL> Alter table employee
Rename to emp;
Table altered.
SQL>
```

Removing All the Data from a Table

To remove all the rows from a table, you need to use the *truncate* command. The *truncate* command, contrary to its name, doesn't abbreviate or shorten anything—it summarily removes all the rows very quickly. *Truncate* is a DDL command, and therefore it can't be undone by using the *rollback* command. You can also remove all the rows in the table with the *delete * from table* command, and because this is a DML command, you can roll back the deletion if you desire. However, because the *delete* command writes all changes to the rollbacks segments, it takes a much longer time to execute. Because the *truncate* command doesn't have to bother with the rollback segments, it executes in a few seconds, even for the largest tables. Here's an example of the *truncate* command in action:

```
SQL> select count (*) from test;
  COUNT(*)
      31
SQL> truncate table test;
Table truncated.
SQL> select count(*) from test;
  COUNT(*)
       0
SQL>
```

Creating a New Table with the CTAS Option

To create a new table identical to an existing table, or to create a new table that includes only some rows and columns of another table, you can use the *create table as select * from* (CTAS) command. You can use the CTAS command to load a portion of an existing table into a new table by using *where* conditions, or you can load all the data of the old table into the newly created table by simply using *select **, as shown in the following code snippet:

```
SQL> create table employee_new
  2  as
  3  select * from employees;
Table created.
SQL>
```

But what if the table has millions of rows and your window of time is too narrow for using the simple CTAS method shown here? Fortunately, you have a couple of ways to speed up the creation of new tables that contain large amounts of data. If the table you're creating is empty, you don't need to be concerned with the speed with which it's created; it's created immediately. But if you're using an existing table to load the new table from, you can benefit from using the *parallel* and *nologging* options. The *nologging* and *parallel* options dramatically speed up the loading of large tables. The *parallel* option enables you to do your data loading in parallel by several processes, and the *nologging* option instructs Oracle not to bother logging the changes to the redo log files and rollback segments (except the very minimum necessary for housekeeping purposes). Here's an example:

```
SQL> create table employee_new
  2  as select * from employees
  3  parallel degree 4
  4* nologging;
Table created.
SQL>
```

The other method you can use when you're trying to save time during table creation is to simply move a table from one tablespace to another. You can take advantage of the moving operation to change any storage parameters if you wish. Here's an example of the *alter table ... move* command, which enables you to move tables between tablespaces rapidly. In this example, the table employee is moved from its present tablespace to the new tablespace:

```
SOL> Alter table employee move new_tablespace;
```

Special Oracle Tables

The simple tables you saw in the previous sections satisfy most of the data needs of an application, but these aren't the only kinds of tables Oracle allows you to create. You can create several kinds of specialized tables, such as temporary tables, external tables, and index-organized tables. In the following sections you'll examine the important types of tables you can create in Oracle9i.

Temporary Tables

Oracle9i allows you to create temporary tables to hold data just for the duration of a session or even a transaction. After the session or the transaction ends, the table is truncated (i.e., the rows are automatically removed). Temporary tables are handy when you are dealing with complex queries or transactions that require transitory row information before inserting or updating a permanent table.

The data in temporary tables cannot be backed up like other permanent tables. No data or index segments are automatically allotted to temporary tables or indexes upon their creation, such as in the case of permanent tables and indexes. Space is allocated in temporary segments for the temporary tables only after the first *insert* command is used for the tables.

As I mentioned, temporary tables are a great way to increase the performance of transactions that involve complex queries. One of the traditional responses to complex queries is to use a view to make the complex queries simpler to handle. Unfortunately, the view needs to execute each time you access it, thereby negating its benefits in such cases. Temporary tables are an excellent solution for cases like this, because they can be created as the product of complex *select* statements used for the particular session or transaction, and the data is automatically removed after the session.

NOTE *Although Oracle doesn't analyze the temporary table data to gather the data distribution, that's not a problem for efficient query processing, because the temporary tables can keep constantly accessed join and other information in one handy location. You can just repeatedly access this table rather than having to repeatedly execute complex queries.*

Temporary tables are created in the user's temporary tablespace and are assigned temporary segments only after the first *insert* statement is issued for the temporary table. They are deallocated after the completion of the transaction or the end of the session, depending on how the temporary tables were defined.

Here are some attractive features of temporary tables from the Oracle9*i* DBA's point of view:

- They drastically reduce the amount of redo activity generated by transactions. Redo logs don't fill up fast if temporary tables are used extensively during complex transactions.

- They can be indexed to improve performance.

- Sessions can update, insert, and delete data just like in normal permanent tables.

- The data is automatically removed after a session or a transaction.

- Table constraints can be defined on temporary tables.

- Different users can access the same temporary table, with each user seeing only his or her session data.

- They provide efficient data access because complex queries need not be executed repeatedly.

- The minimal amount of locking of temporary tables means more efficient query processing.

- The structure of the table persists after the data is removed, so future use is facilitated.

Here's another interesting thing about temporary tables: The rows inserted by a specific user are visible only to that user. The data will be in the table as long as the session is open or as long as the transaction is not completed if the *on commit delete rows* option is chosen. Each user sees the same temporary table structure, but each user's instantiation of the table will be different. That is, each user will have a separate instance of that temporary table for his or her session or transaction usage.

You can create two types of temporary tables in Oracle. The first type of temporary table lasts for the duration of an entire session and the other type lasts for the duration of a transaction.

Creating a Session Temporary Table

The following is an example of a temporary table that lasts for an entire session. The table is used for storing temporary information for the duration of an OLTP ticketing transaction.

```
SQL> CREATE GLOBAL TEMPORARY  TABLE  flight_status
(
(destination  varchar2(30),
startdate date,
return_date date,
ticket_price number
)
on commit preserve rows;
```

The *on commit preserve rows* option in the preceding example indicates that the table data is saved for the course of the entire session, not just for the length of the transaction.

Creating a Transaction Temporary Table

Unlike session temporary tables, transaction temporary tables are specific to a single transaction. As soon as the transaction is committed or rolled back, the data is deleted from the temporary tables. Here's how you create a transaction-specific temporary table:

```
SQL> CREATE GLOBAL TEMPORARY TABLE  sales_info
(
(customer_name varchar2(30),
transaction_no  number,
transaction_date date
)
on commit delete rows;
```

The *on commit delete rows* option makes it clear that the data in this table should be retained only for the duration of the transaction that used this temporary table.

Index-Organized Tables

Index-organized tables (IOTs) are somewhat of a hybrid, because they possess features of both indexes and tables. IOTs are tables in which the data is stored in the form of a B-tree index structure. They are unlike a regular or heap-organized table because regular tables do not order data. They are unlike regular indexes because indexes consist of only the indexed columns. IOTs contain the primary key and no indexed columns. So, although you can perform normal SQL operations on IOTs, Oracle uses the B-tree index structures to store and manipulate values in the tables.

When you update the table, it is the index structure that really gets updated. Data access is much faster because you only have to perform one I/O to access the index/table. There is no need to access the real table and index separately, as is the case with traditional B-tree–based indexes. The actual row data, and not merely the ROWID, is held in the index leaf block along with the indexed column value. IOTs are especially well suited for cases where you need to query based on the values of the primary key. IOTs are very convenient for very large databases (VLDBs) and OLTPs. IOTs can be reorganized without rebuilding the indexes separately, which means that the reorganization window is smaller than if you used regular heap-based tables.

The major differences between the normal tables in Oracle9*i* and IOTs are shown in Table 7-3.

Table 7-3. Differences Between Regular Oracle Tables and IOTs

REGULAR ORACLE TABLES	IOTS
Logical ROWIDs	Physical ROWIDs
Uniquely identified by primary key	Uniquely identified by ROWID
Unique constraints not allowed	Unique constraints allowed
Can't contain LONG data	Can contain LONG and LOB data
Not allowed in table clusters	Allowed in table clusters
Larger space requirements	Small space requirements
Slow data access	Fast data access

Listing 7-8 shows the syntax for creating an IOT.

Listing 7-8. Creating an Index-Organized Table

```
SQL> CREATE TABLE employee_new (
EMPLOYEE_ID number,
DEPT_ID number,
NAME varchar230),
ADDRESS varchar2(120),
CITY varchar2(30),
STATE char(2),
PHONE_NUMBER number,
CONSTRAINT PK_EMPLOYEE_NEW primary_key (employee_ID))
ORGANIZATION INDEX TABLESPACE EMPINDEX_01
PCTTHRESHOLD 25
OVERFLOW TBLESPACE OVERFLOW TABLES;
```

A few keywords in the previous *create* statement are worth reviewing carefully. The key phrase *organization index* indicates that this table is an IOT rather than a regular B-tree table. The *pctthreshold* keyword indicates the percentage of space reserved in the index blocks for the IOT employee_new. Any part of a row in the table that does not fit the 25 percent threshold value in each data block would be saved in an overflow area. The *create* statement assigns the tablespace overflow_tables to hold the overflow of data from the index blocks.

Remember that index entries in IOTs tend to be large sometimes because they contain not just a key value, but the whole row values. So IOTs do not have all of their data necessarily stored in the index blocks. It is quite possible for the key and part of the row to be saved in the index blocks and the rest in some other table-space. If the *pctthreshold* parameter is too low, there is a risk of a chaining problem in which parts of the row reside in different data blocks, leading to a slowdown of your queries.

External Tables

Databases in general, and data warehouses in particular, need to regularly extract data from various sources and transform the data into a more useful form. For example, a data warehouse may collect data from the OLTP data sources, and extract and transform the data according to some business rules to make it useful for decision support by management.

Traditionally, the way to load a data warehouse has been to first load staging tables with the raw data where the data would be eventually transformed and loaded to the final data warehouse tables. Of course, sometimes the data would be transformed outside of the database and loaded directly in one pass to the warehouse tables. No matter which method is used, the process is usually very cumbersome, even when you use state-of-the-art extraction and transformation tools or custom-made scripts.

Oracle9i allows the use of *external tables*—that is, tables that use data in external operating system files (see http://otn.oracle.com/products/oracle9i/daily/sept19.html). Contrary to what their name indicates, external tables aren't real tables and they don't need any storage in terms of extents in the database like the regular tables. The definition of an external table merely makes an entry in the data dictionary, which will enable you to load data into other normal database tables from the external tables. For example, if you drop an external table, you'll only be removing its definition from the data dictionary—the data itself remains safe in the external source files. External tables enable you to view externally stored data as if it were inside a table in the database. You can perform any kind of queries and joins on external tables, but you can't update, insert, or delete from these tables; no DML operations are permissible on external tables.

External tables are commonly used as intermediate staging tables during data transformations. The Oracle-provided SQL*Loader utility contains the necessary drivers to read from any external table and load into a regular Oracle table. Note that you really don't have to load the external data, which could reside in a comma-delimited text file, for example, and not in a table form. You pass Oracle the table structure for reading the data, the location of the operating system text file with the data, and the type parameter, which indicates to Oracle what kind of access driver to use, and the database does the rest.

Usually, the ORACLE_LOADER driver is specified as the access driver. The ORACLE_LOADER driver's data-mapping capabilities are a subset of the

SQL*Loader control file syntax. Consequently, the external table creation statement looks very similar to a SQL*Loader control file, because it uses the same technique to load data from the operating system flat files into Oracle tables. To load the external data into a predefined table, you need to create the external table, as shown in Listing 7-9.

Listing 7-9. Creating an External Table

```
SQL> create table employee_ext
  (
      employee_no         NUMBER(4),
      emplyee_name        VARCHAR2(10),
      job         VARCHAR2(9),
      manager             NUMBER(4),
      hire_date     DATE,
      salary          NUMBER(7,2),
      commission          NUMBER(7,2),
      department_no       NUMBER(2)
  )
      ORGANIZATION EXTERNAL
      (
      TYPE ORACLE_LOADER
      DEFAULT DIRECTORY load_dir
        (
          records delimited by newline
          badfile bad_dir:'employee_ext.bad'
          logfile log_dir:'employee_ext..log'
          fields terminated by ','
          ( empno, ename, job
          )
        )
        LOCATION ('test.dat')
      )
      REJECT LIMIT UNLIMITED;
```

Test.dat is the operating system flat file, with data listed in a comma-delimited style as follows:

```
20001,Campbell,Director
20002,Jeffries,Manager
20003,Nelson,,Manager
20004,Langston,CIO
```

When you finish running the preceding statement successfully, what you have is an empty table that's ready to be loaded in a manner very similar to the load process employed by the familiar SQL*Loader utility. (You'll learn more about this utility in Chapter 12.) You can query the table employee.ext as you would a regular table. You can drop the table if you wish, but only the definition of the table will be dropped—the external data file will remain intact.

Like Oracle's new OMF files, external tables are a nice addition to Oracle's repertoire. External tables are especially useful for data loading and transformation operations in large data warehouses. However, external tables aren't very useful for day-to-day operations because of the following limitations:

- You cannot have update, delete, or insert operations on external tables. They are strictly read-only tables.

- Large external tables can be a problem for queries, because you can't index them.

- Regular tables are just as easy to load and offer a bunch of advantages.

NOTE *Chapter 12 provides a detailed example of using the external tables feature.*

Partitioned Tables

When you have extremely large tables, query times slow down and DML operations take more time due to the sheer number of rows in the columns. Managing the tables also becomes unwieldy, because you always have to have the entire table online.

Partitioning is a way of logically dividing a large table in to smaller chunks to facilitate query processing, DML operations, and database management. All the partitions share the same logical definition, column definitions, and constraints. Improvements in query response times are startling when you partition a 500-million-row table into a dozen or more partitions. Partitioning leads directly to better query performance, because the database needs to search only the relevant partitions of the table during a query. Each query will have only a small portion of the table to contend with, because Oracle will automatically search only the relevant partition for each query you make against the table. This elimination of unnecessary partitions from a query is called *partition pruning*. Availability of one partition is independent of the availability of the other partitions. You can also copy single partition data using the export utility, thereby reducing export and import times dramatically when you only need part of the entire data set. Data I/O is enhanced because you can keep the partitions of a heavily accessed table on different disk drives. If you are using the Oracle parallel DML features, partitioned tables provide you with better performance.

In addition to faster query performance in large tables, partitioning a table also provides *partition independence*, meaning, among other things, that you can perform your backup and recovery operations, data loading, and index creation on partitions of a large table instead of the whole table. The ability to perform tasks on partitions instead of entire tables, of course, means that your database downtime will be cut drastically.

NOTE *Although partitioned tables improve query performance in very large tables in general, they aren't a panacea for poor coding or other design problems in the application. Partitioning also carries a price in terms of additional work to maintain the partitions and their indexes.*

Partitioning tables also provides an effective way of purging and/or archiving older data that is not currently needed. It is very common for large data warehouses to archive data that is older than a certain date. Archiving data also poses several problems in most organizations, and it is usually a tedious process. Partitioned tables make archiving easy. For example, each quarter you can drop the oldest partition and replace it with a new partition. The partitioned table in this case will end up having roughly the same amount of data, and it will cover the same length of time (say, a quarterly collection of company data for 3 years will always have 12 partitions in the table). In addition, large table exports can be performed within a much smaller window of time when you partition the table into smaller chunks and partition each chunk separately.

Oracle9*i* offers five different ways to partition your table data: range, hash, list, composite hash-range, and composite hash-list. Let's examine each of these five types of partitioning briefly, using a simple example for the first four types. The last method, hash-list, is very similar conceptually to the hash-range method, and consequently, I can skip an example for this type of partitioning.

Range Partitioning

Range partitioning is a popular way to partition Oracle table data, and it is the first type of partitioning introduced in an Oracle database. Range partitioning is used for data that can be separated based on some criterion into ranges. Ranges can include time, a sequence number, or a part number.

The range-partitioning technique is usually used for data based on time (e.g., monthly or quarterly data). Let's say you need to create a table for an application, which will hold quarterly sales data for a period of 3 years for a major airline. Quarterly sales data for 3 years for a major airline could add up to several hundreds of million transactions. If you partition the sales table by a range of quarters and decide to hold no more than 3 years' worth of data at any given time, you'll have 12 partitions in the table, partitioned by quarters. Each time you enter a new quarter, you can archive the oldest quarter's data (see the following discussion on dropping and renaming partitions), thus keeping the number of partitions constant, if you so desire. By partitioning the huge table, which has a total of, let's say, 480 million rows, any queries you run have to deal with only 1/12 of the table— that is, about 40 million rows—which makes a big difference. Partitioning thus provides you with a "divide and conquer" technique to deal efficiently with massive amounts of data in tables.

Listing 7-10 shows the DDL for creating a range-partitioned table.

Listing 7-10. Creating a Range-Partitioned Table

```
SQL> Create table ticket_sales
(
transaction_no          number,
year                          date,
month                        number,
destination_city          char(3),
source_city                char(3),
ticket_price               number
)
   storage (initial 10m nezt 5m) logging
partition by range (year, month)
(
partition sales_quarter1 values less than (2000, 03)
 tablespace fightsales_01,
partition sales_quarter2 values less than (2000, 06)
 tablespace fightsales_01,
partition sales_quarter3 values less than (2000, 09)
 tablespace fightsales_01,
partition salcs_quartcr4 valucs lcss than (2000, 12)
 tablespace fightsales_01)
enable row movement;
```

Notice how the partitions are made based on date ranges. The first partition, salcs_quartcr1, will includc all transactions that took placc in the first 3 months (one quarter) of the year 1999. The second quarter, sales_quarter2, would include transactions that occurred between April and June (months 4, 5, and 6 of the year) of 1999 and so on. It is also common in range-partitioned tables to use a catchall partition as the very last one. When this is the case, the last partition will contain values less than a value called *maxvalue*, which is simply any value higher than the values in the second-to-last partition. When a query requests data from the table for January 1999, the query zooms in on partition lightsales_01. So, the query has a much smaller table it has to work with. As a result, query time is inevitably reduced, oftentimes dramatically, when you use partitioned tables when there is a large amount of data in your tables (usually a 100 million rows or so). The last clause, *enable row movement*, indicates that if updates to a key value place it in a different location, the affected rows are allowed to migrate to the new partition.

Hash Partitioning

Suppose the transaction data in the previous example is not evenly distributed among the quarters. What if, due to business and cyclical reasons, an over-whelming amount of sales occurred just in the last two quarters, with the earlier quarters contributing relatively negligible amounts of sales? Well, your parti-tioning scheme will only be good in theory, because the last two quarters could end up with almost half each of the original nonpartitioned table's data.

In such cases where the data might be unevenly spread among partitions if you choose range-portioning schemes, it's better to use the hash-partitioning scheme. All you have to do is decide on the number of partitions and Oracle's hashing algorithms will assign a hash value to each row's partitioning key and place it in the appropriate partition. You don't have to know anything about the distribution of the data in the table, other than the fact that the data doesn't fall into some easily determined ranges. All you need to do is provide a partition key, which in the hash-partitioning scheme shown in Listing 7-11 is the transaction_no column.

Listing 7-11. Creating a Hash-Partitioned Table

```
SQL> Create table ticket_sales
   (
transaction_no          number,
year                        date,
month                       number,
destination_city        char(3),
source_city              char(3),
ticket_price                number
   )
   storage initial (1m)
 partition by hash(transaction_no)

(partition p1 tablespace tocketsales_01,
 partition p2 tablespace tocketsales_02,
 partition p3 tablespace tocketsales_03,
 partition p4 tablespace tocketsales_04,
 partition p5 tablespace tocketsales_05,
 partition p6 tablespace tocketsales_06,
);
```

List Partitioning

There may be times when you'll want to partition the data not on the basis of a time range or evenly distributed hashing scheme, but rather by known values such as city, territory, or some such attribute. List partitioning is preferable to range or hash partitioning when your data distribution follows discrete values. For example, you may want to group a company's sales data according to regions rather than quarters. List partitioning enables you to group your data on the same lines as real-world groupings of data, not arbitrary ranges of time or some such criterion. For example, when you're dealing with statewide totals in the United States, you'll be dealing with 50 different sets of data. It makes more sense in this situation to partition your data into four or five regions, rather than use the range method to partition the data alphabetically. Listing 7-12 shows how to use list partitioning to partition the table ticket_sales.

Listing 7-12. Creating a List-Partitioned Table

```
SQL> Create table ticket_sales
   (
transaction_no         number,
year                          date,
month                         number,
destination_city       char(3),
start_city                  char(3),
ticket_price                  number
   )
partition by LIST (start_city)
(
partition northeast_sales  values (NYC,BOS,PEN) tablespace ticketsales_01,
partition southwest_sales values (DFW,ORL,HOU) tablespace ticketsales 02,
partition pacificwest_sales values (SAN,LOS,WAS) tablespace ticketsales_03,
partition  southeast_sales values (MIA,CHA,ATL)  tablespace ticketsales_04);
```

Composite Partitioning

Oracle offers you two types of composite partitioning. In the first type, you can partition a table range-wise and later on subpartition each of those partitions using a hash scheme. This is called the *composite range-hash partitioning* method. In the other method, you first partition range-wise and then use list partitioning to do the subpartitioning. This second type of partitioning is called the composite *list-hash composite partitioning* method.

In the following example, you'll see how to use the composite range-hash partitioning scheme. As mentioned earlier, because the two partitioning schemes use essentially similar strategies for partitioning, except that one uses range partitioning and the other uses list partitioning initially, you're going to see an example of just the first composite type here. At times you may partition a table range-wise, but the distribution may not be very equal. You can make this a better partitioning scheme by hash partitioning after the range partitioning is done.

In this example, the ticket_sales table is first partitioned by range on the transaction_no column. The subpartitioning is done on the first partitions using a hash-partitioning scheme, with the results stored in hash partitions. This will allow you to store the data more efficiently, although it becomes more complex to manage. Composite range-hash partitioning combines the best of the range and hash partitioning schemes. Range partitioning, as you've already seen, is easy to implement, and hash partitioning provides you benefits such as striping and parallelism. The SQL script in Listing 7-13 shows how to partition a table using the composite range-hash partitioning scheme.

Listing 7-13. Creating a Range-Hash Partitioned Table

```
SQL> create table ticket_sales
(
transaction_no          number,
year                        date,
month                       number,
destination_city        char(3),
start_city              char(3),
ticket_price                number
    )
tablespace test
partition by range (transaction_no) subpartition by hash(start_city)
subpartitions 12
store in
(ticketsales_01,ticketsales_02,ticketsales_03,ticketsales_04,
ticketsales_05,ticketsales_06)
 (partition t1 values less than (200000),
 partition t2  values less than  (maxvalue)
store in
(ticketsales_07,ticket_sales_08));
```

Partition Maintenance Operations

After you initially create partitioned tables, you can perform a number of maintenance operations on the partitions to meet your data requirements. For example,
you can add and drop partitions if you are maintaining a fixed number of partitions based on a quarterly time period. That is, if you want to maintain quarterly
data for 3 years, each quarter you need to add a new partition after dropping the
oldest partition.

In this section, I illustrate the use of these maintenance operations by
assuming a range-partitioning scheme. The following maintenance operations
apply to all five types of partitioning schemes, with the following exceptions:

- Range and list partitions can't be coalesced.

- Hash partitions can't be dropped, split, or merged.

- Only list partitions allow the modification of partitions by adding and
  dropping the partition values.

Adding Partitions

You can add a new partition to the ticket_sales table to include a new quarter as
follows:

```
SQL> alter table ticket_sales
Add partition sales_quarter5 values less than (2001, 4)
Tablespace ticket_sales05;
```

Splitting a Partition

The *add partition* statement will add partitions only to the upper end of the existing table. In this example, you add the new quarterly partition for the first quarter of the year 2001, which comes after the last quarter in the original table. What if you need to insert some new data into the middle of a table? What if an existing partition becomes too large and you would rather have smaller partitions? The splitting partition takes the data in an existing partition and distributes it between two partitions. The existing partition is split up into two partitions, with all column values lower than the column value specified by the split column going into one partition and the rest going into a different partition. You can use the *split* clause to break up a partition, as shown here:

```
SQL> alter table ticket_sales
Split partition ticket_sales01 at (2000) into
(partition ticket_sales01A,ticket_sales01B);
```

Merging Partitions

You can use the *merge partition* command to combine the contents of two adjacent partitions. For example, you can merge the first two partitions of the ticket_sales table in the following way:

```
Alter table ticket_sales
Merge partitions ticket_sales01,ticket_sales02 into partition flight_sales02;
```

Renaming Partitions

You rename partitions in the same way you rename a table. For example:

```
SQL> Alter table
Rename partition fight_sales01 to quarterly_sales01;
```

Exchanging Partitions

The *exchange partition* command enables you to convert a regular nonpartitioned table into a partition of a partitioned table. Here's an example:

```
SQL> ALTER TABLE stocks
EXCHANGE PARTITION p3 WITH stock_table_3;
```

Dropping Partitions

Dropping partitions is fairly easy if you don't have any data in the partitions. If you do have data in the partitions you intend to drop, you need to be careful to use the additional update global indexes parameter with the following drop partition syntax. Otherwise, all globally created indexes will be invalidated. Local indexes will still be OK because they're mapped directly to the affected partitions only. Here's an example:

```
SQL> Alter table ticket_sales
Drop partition ticket_sales01;
```

Coalescing Partitions

The hash-partitioned and list-partitioned tables enable you to coalesce their partitions, which amounts to shrinking the number of partitions. Here's an example of coalescing a hash-partitioned table, which will reduce the number of partitions by one:

```
SQL> Alter table ticket_sales
Coalesce partition ;
```

Data Dictionary Views for Managing Tables

You can use several data dictionary views to help you manage Oracle tables. The most important one is the DBA_TABLES view. The DBA_TABLES view gives you the owner, the number of rows, the tablespace name, space information, and a number of other details about all the tables in the database. Listing 7-14 shows a sample query.

Listing 7-14. Using the DBA_TABLES View

```
SQL>   select tablespace_name,table_name,num_rows
  2   from dba_tables
  3* where owner='HR'
SQL> /
TABLESPACE_NAME        TABLE_NAME      NUM_ROWS
---------------------------- --------------
EXAMPLE               DEPARTMENTS      27
EXAMPLE               EMPLOYEES        107
EXAMPLE               JOBS             19
EXAMPLE               JOB_HISTORY      10
EXAMPLE               LOCATIONS        23
EXAMPLE               REGIONS          4
6 rows selected.
SQL>
```

The DBA_TAB_COLUMNS view is another useful dictionary view that provides you a lot of information about table columns. Listing 7-15 shows a simple query using the DBA_TAB_COLUMNS view.

Listing 7-15. Using the DBA_TAB_COLUMNS View

```
SQL>   select column_name,data_type,
  2   nullable
  3   from dba_tab_columns
  4   where owner='HR'
  5* and table_name='EMPLOYEES'
```

```
SQL> /
COLUMN_NAME      DATA_TYPE           NULLABLE
EMPLOYEE_ID      NUMBER              N
FIRST_NAME       VARCHAR2            Y
LAST_NAME        VARCHAR2            N
EMAIL            VARCHAR2            N
PHONE_NUMBER     VARCHAR2            Y
HIRE_DATE        DATE                N
JOB_ID           VARCHAR2            N
SALARY           NUMBER              Y
8 rows selected.
SQL>
```

Of course, you could have obtained this information easily by using the *describe* command. Listing 7-16 shows how to use the *describe* command.

Listing 7-16. Using the Describe Command

```
SQL> describe hr.employees
 Name                  Null?           Type
 -------------------- --------- ---------------
 EMPLOYEE_ID          NOT NULL        NUMBER(6)
 FIRST_NAME           NOT NULL        VARCHAR2(20)
 LAST_NAME            NOT NULL        VARCHAR2(25)
 EMAIL                NOT NULL        VARCHAR2(25)
 PHONE_NUMBER                         VARCHAR2(20)
 HIRE_DATE            NOT NULL        DATE
 JOB_ID               NOT NULL        VARCHAR2(10)
 SALARY                               NUMBER(8,2)
SQL>
```

Extracting Object DDL Using the DBMS_METADATA Package

What if you want to get the DDL used to create the employee table under the HR schema? Often, you'll want to create the same table or a similar table in a different database, and it would be nice to have the DDL for the original table handy. Well, if you're using a third-party tool such as the SQL Navigator of TOAD, all you have to do is click a few buttons to have your table DDL statements shown on the screen.

But what commands can you use to get the *create* statement that created the employee table? You can get the information from the DBA_TABLES and DBA_TAB_COLUMNS views, but you would have to write lengthy SQL statements to do so. Alternatively, you can use the Oracle-supplied package DBMS_METADATA to quickly get the DDL statements for your tables and indexes. Let's get the DDL for the employee table using this package. The following listing shows the output of the package execution:

```
SQL> set long 10000
SQL> select dbms_metadata.get_ddl('TABLE','EMPLOYEE')
            2* from dual
SQL> /
DBMS_METADATA.GET_DDL('TABLE','EMPLOYEE')
--------------------------------------------------------------------------------
CREATE TABLE "HR"."EMPLOYEES"
   (    "EMPLOYEE_ID" NUMBER(6,0),
        "FIRST_NAME" VARCHAR2(20),
        "LAST_NAME" VARCHAR2(25) CONSTRAINT "EMP_LAST_NAME_NN" NOT NULL ENABLE,
        "EMAIL" VARCHAR2(25) CONSTRAINT "EMP_EMAIL_NN" NOT NULL ENABLE,
        "PHONE_NUMBER" VARCHAR2(20),
        "HIRE_DATE" DATE CONSTRAINT "EMP_HIRE_DATE_NN" NOT NULL ENABLE,
        "JOB_ID" VARCHAR2(10) CONSTRAINT "EMP_JOB_NN" NOT NULL ENABLE,
        "SALARY" NUMBER(8,2),
        "COMMISSION_PCT" NUMBER(2,2),
        "MANAGER_ID" NUMBER(6,0),
        "DEPARTMENT_ID" NUMBER(4,0),
         CONSTRAINT "EMP_SALARY_MIN" CHECK (salary > 0) ENABLE NOVALIDATE,
         CONSTRAINT "EMP_EMAIL_UK" UNIQUE ("EMAIL")
  USING INDEX PCTFREE 10 INITRANS 2 MAXTRANS 255
STORAGE(INITIAL 65536 NEXT 1048576
MINEXTENTS 1  MAXEXTENTS 2147483645 PCTINCREASE 0
  FREELISTS 1 FREELIST GROUPS 1 BUFFER_POOL DEFAULT) TABLESPACE "EXAMPLE"  ENABLE,
         CONSTRAINT "EMP_EMP_ID_PK" PRIMARY KEY ("EMPLOYEE_ID")
  USING INDEX PCTFREE 10 INITRANS 2 MAXTRANS 255
  STORAGE(INITIAL 65536 NEXT 1048576 MINEXTENTS 1 MAXEXTENTS
2147483645 PCTINCREASE 0
  FREELISTS 1 FREELIST GROUPS 1 BUFFER_POOL DEFAULT) TABLESPACE
"EXAMPLE"  ENABLE,
         CONSTRAINT "EMP_DEPT_FK" FOREIGN KEY ("DEPARTMENT_ID")
  REFERENCES "HR"."DEPARTMENTS" ("DEPARTMENT_ID") ENABLE NOVALIDATE,
         CONSTRAINT "EMP_JOB_FK" FOREIGN KEY ("JOB_ID")
  REFERENCES "HR"."JOBS" ("JOB_ID") ENABLE NOVALIDATE,
         CONSTRAINT "EMP_MANAGER_FK" FOREIGN KEY ("MANAGER_ID")
  REFERENCES "HR"."EMPLOYEES" ("EMPLOYEE_ID") ENABLE NOVALIDATE
   ) PCTFREE 10 PCTUSED 40 INITRANS 1 MAXTRANS 255 LOGGING
DBMS_METADATA.GET_DDL('TABLE','EMPLOYEES')
  STORAGE(INITIAL 65536 NEXT 1048576 MINEXTENTS 1 MAXEXTENTS
2147483645 PCTINCREASE 0
  FREELISTS 1 FREELIST GROUPS 1 BUFFER_POOL DEFAULT) TABLESPACE "EXAMPLE"
```

 TIP *The output of the* get_ddl *procedure in the DBMS_METADATA package spits out its DDL text in long format. If you don't have the LONG variable set in your SQL*Plus session, you may not see the entire DDL statement.*

This is the most elegant and the easiest way to get the DDL for your tables and indexes, assuming you aren't using TOAD or Oracle Enterprise Manager (OEM). Later, in Chapter 13, you'll come across another method whereby you can extract the DDL, but that's a clumsier way to get the same information. You should use the DBMS_METADATA package to get the DDL statements for your database objects.

Clusters

You can use clusters to organize the storing of tables that have common columns and are usually used together. For example, if two tables have an identical column and you frequently need to join the two tables, it is advantageous to store the common column values in the same data block. The goal is to reduce disk I/O and thereby increase access speed when you join related tables. *Clusters* are two or more tables that are physically stored together to take advantage of similar columns between the tables. However, clusters will reduce the performance of your *insert* statements, because more blocks are needed to store a clustered table's data because the data of multiple tables needs to be stored in each block.

Hash Clusters

You can create a *hash cluster* and store tables in the cluster. Retrieval of rows is done according to the results of a hash function. To find any row value, all you need to do is find the hash value for a cluster's key value, which you can get by using the hash function. The hash values point to data blocks in the hash cluster. Thus, a single I/O will get you the row data and lead to more efficient performance.

Oracle Indexes

Oracle indexes provide speedy access to table rows by sorting specified column values and looking up the rows pertaining to the specified index row value. Indexes enable you to find a row with a certain column value without your having to look at more than a small fraction of the total rows in a table. Thus, the proper usage of indexes will reduce your expensive disk I/Os to a bare minimum.

If you don't have an index on a table, you have to read *all* the table's data to find what you're looking for. You can use indexes to improve the performance of queries and to enforce database integrity. They're purely optional database structures and they're maintained completely by Oracle.

Using an index involves a tradeoff between speedy retrieval of query results and slower updates and insertions. Why is this so? The first part of the tradeoff, the speedy execution of queries, is quite apparent: If you look up a sorted index rather than perform a full table scan, your queries will be faster. But every time you update or insert a row on a table with indexes, the indexes have to be updated and deleted as well. This makes the update and delete processes more time consuming on a table with indexes. In addition, don't forget that large tables will have large indexes in terms of size, and you need a large disk space to accommodate these indexes in addition to the table data.

In general, if your tables are mostly used for reading (selecting) data, as in a data warehouse, you are better off with indexes. If your database is more of an OLTP type, with heavy inserts, updates, and deletes, you are better off with fewer indexes.

Unless you need to access most of the rows of a table, indexed queries often provide results much faster than queries that do not use indexes. There is no limit to the number of indexes you can have on a single Oracle table, but you should understand that there are performance implications if you include a lot of indexes. Each time you insert or delete data from the table, the indexes also have to be inserted and deleted. This will increase the activity in your database and may slow down transactions if you have a very active OLTP database.

An index is completely transparent to the user—that is, the user's SQL does not have to be changed when you create any indexes. However, it is incumbent upon application developers to be well versed in the subject of indexes and how they work, in order to build efficient queries.

NOTE *You'll find a detailed discussion on an appropriate indexing strategy in Chapter 19.*

Regardless of the particular index scheme—for example, bitmapped or function-based—Oracle indexes can be of several types, the most important of which are listed here:

- *Unique and nonunique keys:* Unique keys are those based on a unique column, usually something like the social security number of an employee. Although you can explicitly create unique indexes, Oracle recommends that you not do so. Oracle advises you to use unique constraints instead. Unique constraints, when placed on a table's column, will automatically have unique indexes created on them by Oracle.

- *Primary and secondary indexes:* Primary indexes are the unique indexes in a table that must always possess a value; they can't be null. Secondary indexes are other indexes in the same table that may not be unique.

- *Composite indexes:* Composite indexes are indexes that contain two or more columns from the same table. They're also known as *concatenated indexes.* Composite indexes are especially useful for enforcing uniqueness in a table's columns in cases where there's no single column that can uniquely identify a row.

Guidelines for Creating Indexes

Although it is well known that indexes will enhance database performance, you will need to understand how to make them work well for you. Placing unnecessary or inappropriate indexes on your table may prove to be detrimental to performance. Here are some guidelines for creating efficient indexes for your Oracle tables:

- Index only if you need to access no more than 10 or 15 percent of the data in a table. The alternative to using an index to access row data in a table is to read the entire table sequentially from top to bottom, an activity that is termed a *full table scan*. Full table scans are better for queries that require a high percentage of the data in a table. Remember that using indexes to retrieve rows requires *two* reads: an index read followed by a table read.

- Avoid indexes on relatively small tables. Full table scans are just fine for small tables. There's no need to store both table and index data for small tables.

- Create primary keys for all relations. When you designate a column as a primary key, Oracle automatically creates an index on the column.

- Index the columns that are involved in multitable join operations.

- Index columns that are used frequently in *where* clauses.

- Index the columns that are involved in *order by* and *group by* operations, or other operations such as *union* and *distinct* that involve sorting. Because indexes are already sorted, the sorting necessary to perform the previously mentioned operations will be considerably reduced.

- Columns that consist of long character strings are usually poor candidates for indexing.

- Columns that are frequently updated should ideally not be indexes because of the overhead involved.

- Index tables with high selectivity only. That is, choose to index tables where few rows have similar values.

- Limit the number of indexes to a small number.

- Composite indexes may need to be used where single-column values may not be unique by themselves. In composite indexes, the driving or the first column should be the most selective column.

Before you proceed to the next section on the various Oracle index schemes, remember the *golden rule* of indexing a table: The index on a table should be based on the types of queries you expect to occur against the table's columns. You can create more than one index on a table; you can choose to create an index on column X or column Y, or on both. You may also create a composite index on both column X and column Y. You make the right decisions about which index to create by thinking about the most frequent types of queries involving the table's data.

Oracle Index Schemes

Oracle9*i* provides several indexing schemes to suit various kings and queens of applications. During the design phase, you select the right index type after you conduct a careful analysis of the particular requirements of your application.

The data structure called the B-tree (or the B+ tree) underlies the mostly commonly used indexes in Oracle9*i*. Oracle uses its own variation on the B-tree called the B*tree for implementing B-tree indexes. These are the regular default indexes created when you use a *create index* statement in Oracle9*i*. You don't normally use the term "B*tree index" to refer to Oracle regular indexes—you just call them "indexes."

The B-tree indexes are structured in the form of an inverse tree, with top-level blocks called *branch blocks* and lower level blocks called *leaf blocks*. In the hierarchy of nodes, all nodes except the top or root node have one *parent node* and may have zero or more nodes beneath them called *child nodes*. If the depth of the tree structure—that is, the number of levels—is the same from each leaf block to the root node, the tree is called a *balanced tree* or *B-tree*.

B-trees automatically maintain the necessary level of index for the size of the table. B-trees also ensure that the index blocks are always between half used and full. B-trees permit select, insert, update, and delete operations with very few I/Os per statement. Most B-trees have only three or fewer levels. When you use a B-tree, you need to only read the B-tree blocks, so the number of disk I/Os will be the number of B-tree levels (say, three) plus the I/Os for performing an update or delete (two: one to read and one to write). To search through a B-tree, you would only need three or fewer disk I/Os.

Oracle's implementation of the B-tree, the B*tree, keeps the tree always balanced. The leaf blocks contain two items: the indexed column values and the corresponding ROWID for the row that contains the particular column value. The ROWID is a unique Oracle pointer that identifies the physical location of the row in question. The ROWID is the fastest way to access a row in an Oracle database. Scanning the index will quickly get you the ROWID of the row, and from there it's a quick hop to the row itself. If the query just wanted the value of the indexed column itself, of course, the latter step is omitted because you don't have to fetch any more data for the query.

Creating a Simple Index

You create an index using the *create index* statement, as follows:

```
SQL> CREATE INDEX  employee_id on employee(employee_id)
     Tablespace emp_index_01;
```

Again, notice that you don't have to specify any storage parameters if you use an assigned locally managed tablespace with the automatic extent management. In the case where you're creating the index in a regular dictionary managed tablespace and you don't want the index to take on the default storage parameters of the tablespace in which it's being created, you can use the following index creation SQL statement:

```
SQL> CREATE INDEX employee_id on employee(employee_id)
     Tablespace emp_index_10;
```

Bitmap Indexes

Bitmap indexes use bitmaps to indicate the value of the column being indexed. This is an ideal index for a column with a low cardinality and a large table size. These indexes are not usually appropriate for tables with heavy updates and are well suited for data warehouse applications. Bitmap indexes consist of a bit stream (0 or 1) for each column in the index. Bitmap indexes are very efficient for low cardinality columns and are very compact in size compared to the normal B-tree indexes. Table 7-4 presents a comparison of B-tree indexes and bitmap indexes.

Table 7-4. B-tree Indexes vs. Bitmap Indexes

B-TREE INDEXES	BITMAP INDEXES
Good for high-cardinality data	Good for low-cardinality data
Good for OLTP databases	Good for warehousing applications
Use a large amount of space	Are a compact size
Easy to update	Difficult to update

To create a bitmap index, you use the *create index* statement with the *bitmap* keyword added to it:

```
SQL> CREATE BITMAP INDEX  gender_idx on employee(gender)
     Tablespace em_index_05;
```

I've seen query performance significantly improve when bitmap indexes replaced ordinary B*tree indexes in some very large tables. However, if the table involves a large number of inserts, deletes, or updates, bitmap indexes may not be the most appropriate choice. Each bitmap index entry covers a large number of rows in the table. Consequently, when data is updated, inserted, or deleted in the table, the necessary bitmap index updates would be very large, and the index could quite literally "blow up" in size. The only way around this increase in bitmap index size and consequent drop in performance is to "maintain" the bitmap index by regular rebuilds of the index. Or, you may decide that the bitmap index is not a smart alternative to tables, which involve large number of inserts, deletes, and updates.

Reverse Key Indexes

These indexes are fundamentally same as the B-tree indexes, except that the bytes of key column data are reversed during indexing. The column order is kept intact; only the bytes are reversed. The biggest advantage to using reverse key indexes is that they tend to avoid "hot spots" when doing sequential insertion of values into the index. Here's how to create one:

```
SQL> CREATE INDEX reverse_idx on employee(emp_id) reverse;
```

Function-Based Indexes

These indexes precompute functions on a given column and store it in an index. Rather than the value of the column itself, it is the transformed values of columns that are stored in the index. When *where* clauses include functions, function-based indexes are an ideal way to index the column. Here's how to create a function-based index:

```
SQL> CREATE INDEX  lastname on employee (lower(l_name));
```

Partitioned Indexes

Partitioned indexes are used to index partitioned tables. Oracle provides two types of indexes for partitioned tables: local and global. The essential difference is that local indexes are based on the underlying table partitions. If the table is partitioned 12 ways using date ranges, the indexes are also ranged over the same 12 partitions. There is a one-to-one correspondence, in other words, between data partitions and index partitions. There is no such one-to-one correspondence between global indexes and the underlying table partitions—a global index is partitioned independently of the base tables. The following sections cover the important differences between managing globally partitioned indexes and locally partitioned indexes.

Globally Partitioned Indexes

Global indexes on a partitioned table can be either partitioned or nonpartitioned. The globally nonpartitioned indexes are similar to the regular Oracle indexes for nonpartitioned tables. You just use the regular *create index* syntax to create these globally nonpartitioned indexes. Globally partitioned indexes are always partitioned by range, although you can use them for any type of partitioned table.

Here's an example of a global index on the table ticket_sales:

```
SQL> Create index ticketsales_idx on ticket_sales(month)
     Global partition by range(month)
 (  PARTITION ticketsales1_idx  VALUES LESS THAN (3)
    PARTITION ticketsales2_idx  VALUES LESS THAN (6)
    PARTITION ticketsales3_idx  VALUES LESS THAN (9)
    PARTITION ticketsales4_idx  VALUES LESS THAN (MAXVALUE)
 )
 ;
```

Note that there's substantial maintenance involved in the management of globally partitioned indexes. Whenever there is DDL activity on a partitioned table, its global indexes need to be rebuilt. DDL activity on the underlying table will mark the associated global indexes as "unusable." By default, any table maintenance operation on a partitioned table will invalidate (mark as unusable) global indexes. Let's use the ticket_sales table an example to see why this is so. When a partition belonging to the ticket_sales table gets dropped, the global indexes could be invalidated, because some of the data the index is pointing to isn't there anymore. To prevent this invalidation due to the dropping of an index, you have to use the *update global indexes* option along with your *drop partition* statement, as shown here:

```
SQL> Alter table flight_data
Drop partition sales_quarter01
Update global indexes;
```

> **NOTE** *If you don't include the* update global indexes *statement, the entire global index will be invalidated. You can also use the* update global index *option when you add, coalesce, exchange, merge, move, split, or truncate partitioned tables. Of course, you can use the* alter index ... rebuild *option to rebuild any index that becomes "unusable," but this option also involves additional time and maintenance.*

Locally Partitioned Indexes

Locally partitioned indexes, unlike globally partitioned indexes, have a one-to-one correspondence with the table partitions. You can create locally partitioned indexes to match partitions or even subpartitions. Any time you modify the underlying table partition, the index partition is maintained automatically. This is probably the biggest advantage to using locally partitioned indexes compared to globally partitioned indexes: Oracle will automatically rebuild the locally partitioned indexes whenever a partition gets dropped or any other DDL activity occurs on a partition. Here is a simple example of creating a locally partitioned index on a partitioned table:

```
SQL> Create index ticket_noticket_noticket_nox on ticket_sales(ticket__no)  LOCAL
    Tablespace localidx_01;
```

Monitoring Index Usage

How do you know how well your indexes on a certain table are being used? Oracle offers you the tools explain plan and SQL Trace, using which you can see the path followed by your queries on the way to their execution. Chapter 18 covers explain plan and SQL Trace in detail. You can use the explain plan output or the results of a SQL Trace to see what the execution path of the query looks like and thus determine if your indexes are being used. Oracle9*i* provides an easier way to monitor index usage in your database. If you are doubtful as to the usefulness of a particular index, you can ask Oracle to *monitor* the index usage. This way, if the index turns out to be redundant, you can drop it and save the storage space and the overhead during DML operations.

Here's what you have to do to monitor index usage in your database. Assume you're trying to find out if the index pkey_sales is being used by certain queries on the sales table. Be sure you are logging in as the owner of the index pkey_sales.

```
SQL> alter index pkey_sales monitoring usage;
Index altered.
SQL>
```

Now, run some queries on the sales table. End the monitoring by using the following command:

```
SQL> alter index pkey_sales nomonitoring usage;
Index altered.
SQL>
```

You can now query the V$OBJECT_USAGE dictionary view to find out if the index pkey_sales is being used. As the results confirm, the index is indeed being used:

```
SQL> select * from v$object_usage
  2* where index_name='PKEY_SALES'
SQL> /
INDEX TABLE MON    USED     START_MONIT         END_MONITORING
PKEY_ SALES NO     YES    04/07/2003 16:19:54   04/07/2003 16:21:26
```

Once you execute the *alter index – monitoring* query, run some queries that you think will use the index in question. When you execute your *select* statement from the V$OBJECT_USAGE view at the end of the monitoring session, Oracle will place a YES value in the USED column of the output if the index was used while the monitoring session was on. If the index was ignored during the monitoring period, the column will contain NO instead.

Index Maintenance

Index data constantly changes due to the underlying table's DML activity. Indexes often become too large if there are many deletions, as the space used by the deleted values is not reused automatically by the index. You use the *rebuild* command on a periodic basis to reorganize indexes to make them more compact and thus more efficient. You can also use the *rebuild* command to alter the storage parameters you used during the initial creation of the index. Here's an example:

```
Sql>Alter index pkey_sales rebuild;
Index altered
Sql>
```

Rebuilding indexes is better than dropping and re-creating a bad index, because users will continue to have access to the index while you're rebuilding it. But indexes in the process of rebuilding do impose many limits on users' actions during the process. An even more efficient way to perform the rebuilding of indexes is to do them *online*, as shown in the following example. You can perform all DML operations, but not any DDL operations, while the online rebuild of the index is going on.

```
SQL>Alter index pkey_sales rebuild online;
Index altered.
SQL>
```

Database Integrity Constraint Management

Integrity constraints in relational databases enable easy and automatic enforcement of important business rules in the database tables. For example, in a human resources–related table, you can't have an employee without assigning him or her to a supervisor. When you create the relevant tables, you declare the necessary integrity constraints, which must be satisfied each time data is entered or modified in the table. You can also use application logic to enforce business rules. Integrity constraints are usually simpler to enforce than application logic, and they usually do their job by making sure that inserts, updates, and deletes of table data conform to certain rules. Application logic has the advantage that it can reject or approve data without having to check the entire table's contents. Thus, you have to determine which method you'll use to enforce the business rules—application logic or integrity constraints—based on the needs of your application. In any case, integrity constraints are so fundamental to the operation of relational databases that you are bound to use them in your database.

By default, Oracle allows null values in all columns. If null values are not permissible for some columns in table, you need to use the NOT NULL constraint when specifying the column during table creation time. Note that you can impose the database constraints on tables in two different ways: You can either specify them at table creation time or impose them later by using the *alter table* command. Of course, the latter choice is much harder to implement under some circumstances.

Obviously, if you already have null columns or duplicate data, it is not possible to alter the table and impose the NOT NULL or unique constraint on the table. You can enforce several types of constraints in an Oracle table. For simplicity's sake, you can divide the constraints into five different types:

- Primary key constraints

- Not null constraints

- Check constraints

- Unique constraints

- Referential integrity constraints

I discuss each of these types of constraints in the following sections.

Primary Key Constraints

The primary key is a very important kind of constraint on a table. When you want a column's values to be identified uniquely, you can do this by creating a primary key on the column value. A column on which a primary key has been defined has to be *unique as well as not null.*

A table can have only one primary key. You can create a primary key in either of the two ways, as shown in the following example:

```
SQL> Create table department(
     Dept_id        number(9)        PRIMARY KEY);
```

or

```
SQL> Alter table department
     Add primary key (dept_id);
```

or (with an explicit constraint name)

```
 SQL> alter table emp
  2    add constraint
  3*   department_pk PRIMARY KEY (dept_id);
Table altered.
SQL>
```

Note that if the primary key will have more than one column in it (a composite key), then you can't specify the primary key designation against the column name during table creation. You have to specify the primary key columns as a separate item at the end of the *create table* command, after listing all the columns.

NOTE *In both of the preceding examples, Oracle automatically creates an index on the column you designate as the primary key.*

Not Null Constraints

A table usually has one or more columns that can't be allowed to be left *null*—that is, with no values. A good example is the last_name column in the employee table. You would hope that all employees' names are listed in the employee table. You can force the table to always put a value in this column at table creation time by using the NOT NULL option for the column you don't want to be null:

```
SQL> Create table employee
    ( last_name  varchar2(30)    NOT NULL);
```

If the table has already been created and you want to modify a column from a nullable to a non-nullable constraint, you can use the following statement:

```
SQL> Alter table employee MODIFY last_name NOT NULL;
```

Check Constraints

You use check constraints to ensure that data in a column is within some parameters that you specify. For example, say the salary for an employee in a firm can't exceed $100,000 under any circumstance. You can enforce this condition by using the following statement:

```
SQL> Create table employee
    ( employee_id      number,
     last_name         varchar2(30),
     first_name        varchar2(30),
     department_id     number,
     salary            number CHECK(salary < 100000));
```

Unique Constraints

Unique constraints are very common in relational databases. These constraints ensure the uniqueness of the rows in a relational table. You may have more than one unique constraint on a table. For example, a unique constraint on the employee_id column ensures that no employee is listed twice in the employee table. In the following example, the first statement specifies a unique constraint on the combination of the dept_name and location columns:

```
SQL> create table department (
    Dept_no  NUMBER(3),
    Dept_name   VARCHAR2(15),
    Location    VARCHAR2(25),
    CONSTRAINT Dept_name_ukey UNIQUE (Dept_Name,Location);
```

You can also create a unique constraint on the department table using the *alter table* syntax:

```
SQL> alter table department
  2* add  constraint depart_idx unique (dept_no);
Table altered.
SQL>
```

Referential Integrity Constraints

Referential integrity constraints ensure that values for certain important columns make sense. Suppose you have a parent table that refers to values in another table, as in the case of the department and employee tables. You shouldn't be able to assign an employee to a department in the employee table if the department doesn't exist in the first place in the department table.

Oracle ensures the existence of a valid department through the enforcement of the referential integrity constraint. In this case, the department_id column in the department table is its primary key and the department_id column in the employee table, which refers to the corresponding column in the department table, is called the *foreign key*. The table containing the foreign key is usually referred to as the *child table* and the table containing the referenced key is called the *parent table*. As with all the other types of constraint, the referential integrity constraint can be created at table creation time or later on, with the help of the *alter table* command:

```
SQL> Create table employee (
Employee_id    number (7),
Last_name      varchar2(30),
First_name     varcahr2(30),
Job            varchar2(15),
Department_id  number (3) NOT NULL
               Constraint dept_fkey REFERENCES department(dept_id) );
```

The department_id column of this employee table has been designated as a foreign key because it refers to the department_id column in the department table. Note that for a column to serve as the referenced column, it must be unique or be a primary key in the reference table.

Integrity Constraint States

As you saw in the previous section, integrity constraints are defined on tables to ensure that data that violates preset rules doesn't enter the tables. However, during times like data loading, you can't keep the integrity constraints in a valid state, as this will lead to certain problems. Oracle lets you disable constraints when necessary and enable them when you want. Oracle DBAs spend a lot of time during data loading, for example, pondering over the enabling and disabling of various constraints on tables. Let's examine the various ways you can alter the states of table constraints.

Disabling Integrity Constraints

During large data loads, using either the SQL*Loader or the import utility, it may take a considerably longer time to load the data if you have to check for integrity violations for each row inserted into the tale. A better strategy would be to disable the constraint, load the data, and worry about any possible insertion of "bad data" later on. After the load is completed, the constraints are brought into effect again by "enabling" them.

NOTE *The* enabled *state is Oracle's default constraint state.*

You can disable constraints in two ways: you can specify either the *disable validate* or the *disable no validate* constraint state, using the command *disable validate* or *disable no validate*, respectively. The next sections briefly discuss these two ways of disabling constraints.

Disable Validate State

When you use the *disable validate* command, you're doing the following two things at once. First, by using the *validate* command, you're ensuring that all the data in the table satisfies the constraint. Second, by using the *disable* command, you're doing away with the requirements of maintaining the constraint. Oracle drops the index on the constraint, but keeps it valid. Here's an example:

```
SQL> Alter table sales_data
     Add constraint quantity_unique
     UNIQUE (prod_id,customer_id) DISABLE VALIDATE;
```

When you issue the preceding SQL statement, Oracle ensures that only unique combinations of the unique key prod_id and customer_id exist in the table, but it will *not* maintain a unique index. Note that because I have chosen to keep the constraint in a *disabled* state, no DML is possible against the table. This option is really ideal for large data warehouse tables, which are normally used only for querying purposes.

Disable No Validate State

Under the *disable no validate* constraint state, the constraint is disabled and there is no guarantee of the data meeting the constraint requirements, because Oracle does not perform constraint validation. This is essentially the same as a *disable* constraint command.

Enable Validate State

This constraint state will have an enabled constraint that ensures that all data is checked to ensure compliance with the constraint. This state is exactly the same as the plain enabled state. The following example shows the usage of this state:

```
SQL>  ALTER TABLE sales_data  ADD CONSTRAINT sales_region_fk
FOREIGN KEY (sales_region) REFERENCES region (region_id)
ENABLE VALIDATE;
```

Enable No Validate State

Under this constraint state, all new inserts and updates will be checked for compliance. Because the existing data won't be checked for compliance, there's no assurance that the data already in the table meets the constraint requirements. You'll usually use this option when you're loading large tables and you have reason to believe that the data will satisfy the constraint. Here's an example:

```
SQL>  ALTER TABLE sales ADD CONSTRAINT sales_region_fk
FOREIGN KEY (sales_region_id) REFERENCES time (time_id)
ENABLE NOVALIDATE;
```

Rely Constraints

Data *Extraction, Transformation, Loading* (ETL) steps are usually undertaken before loading data into data warehouse tables. If you have reason to believe that the data is good, you can save time during loading by disabling and not validating the constraints. You can use the *alter table* command to disable the constraints with the *rely disable novalidate* option, as shown in the following example:

```
SQL>  ALTER TABLE sales        ADD CONSTRAINT sales_region_fk
      FOREIGN KEY (sales_region_id) REFERENCES time (region_id)
      RELY DISABLE NOVALIDATE;
```

Deferrable and Immediate Constraints

In addition to the specification of the type of validation of a constraint, you can specify *when* exactly this constraint is checked during the loading process. If you want the constraint to be checked immediately after each data modification occurs, you choose the *not deferrable* option, which is, in fact, the default behavior in Oracle databases. If you want a one-time check of a constraint after the whole transaction is committed, you choose the *deferrable* option. All constraints and foreign keys may be declared *deferrable* or *not deferrable*. If you choose the *deferrable* option, you have two further options. You can specify that the *deferrable* constraint may be either *initially deferred* or *initially immediate*. In the former case, the database will defer checking until the transaction completes. If you choose the *initially immediate* option, the database checks the constraint before any data is changed. The following example shows how to specify this kind of constraint in the employee table:

```
SQL> Create table employee
     Employee_id   number,
     Last_name     varchar2 (30),
     First_name    varchar2 (30),
     Department    varchar2(30) unique
     References    department(dept_name)
     Deferrable    initially deferred;
SQL>
```

Oracle also provides a way of changing a deferrable constraint from *imme-diate* to *deferred* or vice versa with the following statements:

```
SQL> set constraint constraint_name deferred;
SQL> set constraint constraint_name immediate;
```

Using Synonyms

Synonyms are aliases for objects in the database and are used mainly for security purposes. Synonyms hide the underlying object's identity and can be either private or public, with *public* synonyms being accessible by all the users in the database. *Private* synonyms are part of the individual user's schema, and access rights have to be individually granted to specific users before they can use the private synonyms. Oracle9i synonyms can be created for tables, views, materialized views, and stored code such as packages and procedures.

Synonyms are very powerful from the point of view of allowing users access to objects that do not lie within their schemas. All synonyms have to be created explicitly with the *create synonym* command, and the underlying objects could be located in the same database or in other databases that are connected through the use of database links.

The two major uses of synonyms are *object transparency* and *location trans-parency*. Synonyms can be created to keep the original object transparent to the user. Synonyms are used for location transparency when they are created as aliases for tables and other objects that belong to a database other than the local database.

 NOTE *Keep in mind that even if you know the synonym for a schema table, you can't access it. You must also have been granted the necessary privileges on the table for you to be able to access the table.*

When you create a table or procedure, it is created in your schema and other users can access it only by using your schema name as a prefix to the object's name. Listing 7-17 shows a couple of examples that illustrate this point.

Listing 7-17. Using Schema Names to Access Tables

```
SQL> show user
USER is "SYSTEM"
SQL> describe employees
ERROR:
ORA-04043: object employees does not exist
SQL> desc hr.employees
 Name                    Null?    Type
 ----------------------- -------- -------------
 EMPLOYEE_ID             NOT NULL NUMBER(6)
 FIRST_NAME                       VARCHAR2(20)
 LAST_NAME               NOT NULL VARCHAR2(25)
 EMAIL                   NOT NULL VARCHAR2(25)
 PHONE_NUMBER                     VARCHAR2(20)
 HIRE_DATE               NOT NULL DATE
 JOB_ID                  NOT NULL VARCHAR2(10)
 SALARY                           NUMBER(8,2)
 COMMISSION_PCT                   NUMBER(2,2)
 MANAGER_ID                       NUMBER(6)
 DEPARTMENT_ID                    NUMBER(4)
SQL>
```

As you can see, when the user system tried to describe the table without the schema prefix, Oracle issued an error. When system used the schema.tableschema.table notation, the employee table could be described. Now, what if you know the table name, but you don't know the schema name? Again, Oracle will issue an error stating that the "table does not exist" when you do this. The way around this is for the schema owner to create a synonym with the same name as the table name. Oracle provides for both private synonyms that specified users can use and public synonyms that all users can use. In the following sections, you'll learn how to create both types of synonyms.

Creating a Public Synonym

Public synonyms are owned by a special schema in the Oracle database called PUBLIC. As mentioned earlier, public synonyms can be referenced by all users in the database. Public synonyms are usually created by the application owner for tables and other objects such as procedures and packages, so the users of the application can "see" the objects. The following code shows how to create a public synonym for the employee table. After you create the public synonym, any user in the database can refer to the employee table directly, without specifying the schema name.

```
SQL> create public synonym employees for hr.employees;
Synonym created.
SQL>
```

Now any user can see the table by just typing the original table name. If you wish, you could, of course, provide a different name for the table in the *create synonym* statement. Remember that the DBA should explicitly grant the *create public synonym* privilege to user hr before hr can create any public synonyms.

Just because you can "see" a table through a public (or private) synonym doesn't mean that you can also perform select, insert, update, or delete operations on the table. To be able to perform those operations, a user needs specific privileges, either directly or through roles, from the application owner. The topic of granting privileges and roles is discussed exhaustively in Chapter 11.

Creating a Private Synonym

Private synonyms, unlike public synonyms, can be referenced only by the schema that owns the table or object. You may want to create private synonyms when you want to refer to the same table by different aliases in different contexts. You create private synonyms the same way you create public synonyms, but you omit the keyword *public* in the *create* statement.

Listing 7-18 shows how to create a private synonym called addresses for the table locations. Note that once you create the private synonym, you can refer to the synonym exactly as you would the original table.

Listing 7-18. Creating a Private Synonym

```
Sql> create synonym addresses for hr.locations;
Synonym created.
SQL> desc addresses
 Name                            Null?          Type
 --------------------------------------------- -------- ------------------
 LOCATION_ID                     NOT NULL       NUMBER(4)
 STREET_ADDRESS                                 VARCHAR2(40)
 POSTAL_CODE                                    VARCHAR2(12)
 CITY                            NOT NULL       VARCHAR2(30)
 STATE_PROVINCE                                 VARCHAR2(25)
 COUNTRY_ID                                     CHAR(2)
SQL>
```

Synonyms, both private and public, are dropped in the same manner by using the *drop synonym* command, but there is one important difference. If you are dropping a public synonym, you need to add the keyword *public*, as shown in the following examples.

Here's an example of dropping a private synonym:

```
SQL> drop synonym addresses;
Synonym dropped.
SQL>
```

Here's an example of dropping a public synonym:

```
SQL> drop public synonym addresses;
Synonym dropped.
SQL>
```

Viewing Information on Synonyms

The table DBA_SYNONYMS gives you all the necessary information to manage synonyms for database objects. Here is how you query the view to find information about the synonyms owned by user HR:

```
SQL> select synonym_name,table_name from dba_synonyms
  2* where owner='HR';
SYNONYM_NAME                       TABLE_NAME
--------------------------------   ----------------------
EMP                                EMPLOYEES
SQL>
```

Using Sequences

Oracle uses a sequence generator to automatically generate a unique sequence of numbers that users can use in their operations. If users were to use programmatically created sequence numbers instead, Oracle would have to constantly lock and unlock records holding the maximum value of those sequences to ensure an orderly incrementing of the sequence. This locking would lead users to wait serially for the next value of the sequence to be issued to their transactions. Oracle sequences are generated automatically internally. This automatic generation of sequences increases database concurrency. Sequences are commonly used to create a unique number to generate a unique primary key for a column.

In this section I discuss how to use an Oracle sequence during a data insert. You have several options to choose from to create the sequence. This sequence is a plain vanilla sequence, which starts at 10,000 and is incremented by 1 each time. The sequence is never recycled or reused, because you want distinct sequence numbers for each employee.

 NOTE *There are two pseudo-columns called currval and nextval that you can use to query sequence values. The currval pseudo-column provides you the current value of the sequence, and the nextval pseudo-column gets you the new or next sequence number.*

First, create a sequence as shown in the following example. This is usually the way you use a sequence to generate a unique primary key for a column.

```
SQL> create sequence employee_seq
  2  start with 10000
  3  increment by 1
  4  no maxvalue
  5* no cycle
SQL> /
Sequence created.
SQL>
```

Second, select the current sequence number by using the following statement:

```
SQL> select  employee_seq.currval from dual;
```

Third, insert a new row into the employee table using nextval from the sequence employee_seq:

```
SQL>   insert into employees(employee_id,first_name,last_name,email,
  2  phone_number,hire_date,)
  3  values
  4* (employee_seq.nextval,'sam','alapati','salapati.tnt.org'
,345-555-5555,to_char('21-JUN-2000')
SQL> /
1 row created.
SQL> commit;
Commit complete.
```

Finally, check to make sure the employee_id column is being populated by the employee_seq sequence:

```
SQL>   select employee_id,first_name,last_name from employees
  2* where last_name='alapati'
SQL> /
EMPLOYEE_ID FIRST_NAME      LAST_NAME
----------- --------------- --------------------------
      10011 sam             alapati
SQL>
```

 TIP *When you use sequences, make sure that you drop them before performing a table import to avoid inconsistent data.*

Note that you can have an Oracle sequence that is incremented continuously, but there may be occasional gaps in the sequence numbers. This is because Oracle always keeps about 20 values (by default) in memory, and that's where it gets its nextval from. If there should be a database crash, the numbers stored in memory will be "lost," and there will be a gap in that particular sequence.

Using Triggers

Oracle triggers are similar to PL/SQL procedures with the difference being that they are automatically fired by the database based on an event. Triggers are commonly used in databases to perform an action based on whether some event occurs. For DBAs, triggers come in handy in performing audit- and security-related tasks. Besides the standard Oracle triggers, which fire before or after DML statements, there are powerful triggers based on system events such as the database start-up and shutdown, and the user logon and logoff events. Chapter 11 shows you how to use triggers to enhance database security.

Using Views

A *view* is a specific representation of a table or a set of tables. Views are defined by using a *select* statement. A view does not physically "exist," like regular tables, as part of a tablespace. Because a view is the product of a query, only the view definition is stored in the data dictionary. When you export the database, for example, you'll see the statement *exporting views*, but that's referring to only the view definitions and not to any physical objects such as tables and indexes.

Views are used in applications for several reasons, including the following:

- Reducing complexity

- Improving security

- Increasing convenience

- Renaming table columns

- Customizing the data for users

- Protecting data integrity

You create views by using a SQL statement that describes the composition of the view. When you invoke the view, the query on which the view is defined is executed and the results are presented to you. A query on a view looks identical to a regular query, but the database converts the query on the view into an identical query on the underlying tables(s). Defining a query on a table or a set of tables is at the heart of creating a view. In the following example, you create and drop a view called my_employees, which gives a specific manager the information on all the employees managed by her directly:

```
SQL> create view my_employees as
  2  select employee_id,first_name,last_name,salary
  3  from employees
  4* where manager_id=122
SQL> /
View created.
SQL> drop view my_employees;
View dropped.
SQL>
```

Now the manager with the ID 122 can query the my_employees view just as she would a normal table, but it gives her information on her employees only:

```
SQL> select * from my_employees;
EMPLOYEE_ID FIRST_NAME  LAST_NAME    SALARY
----------- ----------- ------------ ----------
        133 Jason        Mallin         3300
        134 Michael      Rogers         2900
        135 Ki           Gee            2400
        136 Hazel        Philtanker     2200
        188 Kelly        Chung          3800
        189 Jennifer     Dilly          3600
        190 Timothy      Gates          2900
        191 Randall      Perkins        2500
rows selected
SQL>
```

Although you use views mostly for querying purposes, under some circumstances you can also insert, delete, and update views. For example, you can perform a DML operation on a view if it doesn't have any *group by, start with,* and *connect by* clauses, or any subqueries in its *select* clause. If a view really doesn't "exist," like a table does, how do you update its values? Well, when you update a view, Oracle will update the underlying base table's rows. Appendix A shows you how to perform DML operations with views.

Using Materialized Views

Every time you need to access a view, Oracle must execute the query that defines the view in question and get you the results. This process of "populating" the view is called *view resolution*, and it must be done afresh each time a user refers to the view. If you're dealing with views with multiple joins and *group by*s, this process of view resolution could take a very long time. If you need to access a view frequently, then it is very inefficient to have to constantly resolve the view by performing the expensive operations each time you issue a query that involves the view.

There must be a better way to do these things, and Oracle's materialized view facility offers a way out of this predicament. You can think of *materialized views* as specialized views that have a physical representation unlike normal views—they occupy space and need storage just like your regular tables.

 NOTE *A view is always computed on the fly and its data isn't stored separately from the tables on which it's defined. Thus, queries using views, by definition, guarantee that the latest, up-to-the-minute data will be returned. Any change in the source tables on which the view is defined will be reflected by the view instantaneously. Materialized views, on the other hand, are static objects that derive their data from the underlying base tables. If you refresh your materialized views infrequently, the data in them may be at odds with the data in the underlying tables.*

Traditionally, data warehousing and other similar large databases have needed summary tables or aggregate tables to perform their work. It was a complex task to define these summary tables and constantly maintain them. Anytime you add data to the underlying "detail" table, you have to manually update all the summary tables and their indexes. Oracle's materialized views are a way to simplify summary management in large databases. The beauty of Oracle's materialized view facility is that once the views are created, they are automatically updated by the database whenever there are changes in the underlying base tables on which the view is defined. The materialized views are completely transparent to the users. If users write queries using the underlying table, Oracle will automatically rewrite those queries to use the materialized views. The Oracle Optimizer will automatically decide to use the materialized view rather than the underlying tables and views if it would be more efficient to do so. Complex joins involve a lot of overhead and the use of the materialized views will avoid incurring this cost each time you need to perform such joins. Because the materialized views already have the summary information precomputed in them, your queries will run much faster.

You can also partition materialized views and create indexes on them if necessary. A major problem with the aggregate or summary tables is their maintenance, which involves keeping the tables in accord with the base tables that are being constantly modified. If you aren't sure about which materialized views to create, you can take advantage of Oracle's Summary Advisor, which can make specific recommendations based on its use of the DBMS_OLAP package. The next section covers the Oracle Summary Advisor in detail.

Using the Summary Advisor

As a DBA, you may not be in the best position to come up with the right materialized view, especially if you don't know your application thoroughly. Oracle provides the Summary Advisor component to help you find out which materialized views are worth creating, and if you already have some, which ones are worth keeping. You can use the Summary Advisor through OEM or manually through Oracle-supplied packages and procedures. The Summary Advisor will populate certain tables with its recommendations and advice. You can also have the Summary Advisor print out a report for your analysis. In the following sections, you'll run through the manual use of the Summary Advisor.

Collecting Statistics

The first step in using the Summary Advisor is the collection of the statistics to aid the Advisor in making its recommendations. You'll need to take the following steps to enable the collection of the statistics.

First, make sure you have analyzed all the tables that are part of the queries you are considering as candidates for materialized views. Then analyze whether the *analyze table* commands or the use of the DBMS_STATS package will provide the necessary data distribution statistics to the Summary Advisor when it is considering the efficacy of the materialized view you are evaluating. In this case, you have two tables that are involved in the queries, and you can analyze them as follows:

```
Sql> analyze table sales compute statistics;
Table analyzed.
Sql> analyze table products compute statistics;
Table analyzed.
Sql>
```

Next, grant the necessary privileges. The system user should provide the user who is running the materialized views analysis the following privileges so the user can access the necessary data dictionary tables:

```
CONNECT system/manager
GRANT SELECT ON mview_recommendations to sam;
GRANT SELECT ON mview_workload to sam;
GRANT SELECT ON mview_filter to sam;
```

Providing the Workload

For best results, Oracle advises you to provide the Summary Advisor some typical workloads (queries). Although the materialized views are used during queries, they are also used during insert operations. You can provide the workload to the Advisor in three different ways:

- You can provide the workload as typical queries that you use and store these queries in a special table so the Summary Advisor can access them.

- You can ask the Summary Advisor to get the queries from the SQL cache.

- You can ask the Summary Advisor to use the queries collected by Oracle Trace if it is available in your database.

In this example, you will use the user-defined workload method to provide the candidate queries. First, create the table to load the proposed queries. Listing 7-19 shows the creation of a simple table to do this.

Listing 7-19. Creating a Table to Load the Queries

```
CONNECT sam/sam;
SQL> l
  1  CREATE TABLE user_workload(
  2    query         VARCHAR2(400),
  3    owner         VARCHAR2(40),
  4    application   VARCHAR2(30),
  5    frequency     NUMBER,
  6    lastuse       DATE,
  7    priority      NUMBER,
  8    responsetime  NUMBER,
  9    resultsize    NUMBER
 10* )
SQL> /
Table created.
```

Next, load the table you just created with a set of sample queries that you want considered as candidates for a materialized view. Listing 7-20 shows how to load the sample queries.

Listing 7-20. Loading the Queries into the User_Workload Table

```
SQL> INSERT INTO user_workload values
  2  (
  3    'SELECT SUM(s.quantity_sold)
  4     FROM sales s, products p
  5     WHERE s.prod_id = p.prod_id and p.prod_category = ''Boys''
  6     GROUP BY p.prod_category',  'SH', 'app1', 10, NULL, 5, NULL, NULL
  7  )
  8  /
1 row created.
SQL> INSERT INTO user_workload values
  2  (
  3    'SELECT SUM(s.amount)
  4     FROM sales s, products p
  5     WHERE s.prod_id = p.prod_id AND
  6       p.prod_category = ''Girls''
  7     GROUP BY p.prod_category',
  8    'SH', 'app1', 10, NULL, 6, NULL, NULL
  9  )
 10  /
1 row created.
SQL> INSERT INTO user_workload values
  2  (
  3    'SELECT SUM(quantity_sold)
  4     FROM sales s, products p
  5     WHERE s.prod_id = p.prod_id and
  6       p.prod_category = ''Men''
  7     GROUP BY p.prod_category
  8    ',
  9    'SH', 'app1', 11, NULL, 3, NULL, NULL
 10  )
 11  /
1 row created.
SQL> INSERT INTO user_workload VALUES
  2  (
  3    'SELECT SUM(quantity_sold)
  4     FROM sales s, products p
  5     WHERE s.prod_id = p.prod_id and
  6       p.prod_category in (''Women'', ''Men'')
  7     GROUP BY p.prod_category  ', 'SH', 'app1', 1, NULL, 8, NULL, NULL
  8  )
  9  /
1 row created.
SQL> commit;
Commit complete.
```

Loading the User-Defined Workload into the Workload Definition

Using the DBMS_OLAP package, load the workload you have saved in the user_workload table into the workload collection after you create a unique identifier for your workload, as shown here:

```
SQL> VARIABLE WORKLOAD_ID NUMBER;
SQL> EXECUTE DBMS_OLAP.CREATE_ID(:workload_id);
PL/SQL procedure successfully completed.
SQL> EXECUTE DBMS_OLAP.LOAD_WORKLOAD_USER(:workload_id,-
> DBMS_OLAP.WORKLOAD_NEW,-
> DBMS_OLAP.FILTER_NONE, 'SALAPATI', 'USER_WORKLOAD');
PL/SQL procedure successfully completed.
```

Filtering the Contents of the Workload

The Summary Advisor need not use all the contents of the workload it is examining. You can use filtering to limit the Summary Advisor to certain parts of the workload. In the example shown here, two filter items, frequency and priority, are chosen. Frequency is the number of times the query is run and priority is a user-chosen priority value.

```
SQL> VARIABLE filter_id NUMBER;
SQL> EXECUTE DBMS_OLAP.CREATE_ID(:filter_id);
PL/SQL procedure successfully completed.
SQL> EXECUTE DBMS_OLAP.ADD_FILTER_ITEM(:filter_id, 'PRIORITY',-
> NULL, 5, NULL, NULL, NULL);
PL/SQL procedure successfully completed.
SQL> EXECUTE DBMS_OLAP.ADD_FILTER_ITEM(:filter_id, 'FREQUENCY',  NULL,-
> NULL, 10, NULL, NULL);
PL/SQL procedure successfully completed.
```

Using the Advisor to Get Materialized View Recommendations

Now you can execute the procedure recommend_mview_strategy to get recommendations on the materialized views. Here's how:

```
SQL> VARIABLE RUN_ID NUMBER;
SQL> EXECUTE DBMS_OLAP.CREATE_ID(:run_id);
PL/SQL procedure successfully completed
.SQL> EXECUTE DBMS_OLAP.
RECOMMEND_MVIEW_STRATEGY
(:run_id, :workload_id, :filter_id, 100000, 100,
 NULL, NULL);
PL/SQL procedure successfully completed.
SQL>
```

Reporting the Recommendations

You can choose to either query the view recommend_mview_strategy or use the following procedure to easily produce an HTML report that gives the recommendations in an easily readable format. Here's the code:

```
SQL> EXECUTE DBMS_OLAP.GENERATE_MVIEW_REPORT('c:\temp\output1.html', :run_id, -
> DBMS_OLAP.RPT_RECOMMENDATION);
PL/SQL procedure successfully completed.
```

TIP *You may want to save these material view recommendations so you can compare them to recommendations you may generate later.*

Cleaning Up the Workload and Filtering Information

Finally, you run a set of procedures that will clean up after you and also empty the workload table you created for helping the Summary Advisor perform the analysis. Here's how to do it:

```
SQL> EXECUTE DBMS_OLAP.PURGE_RESULTS(:run_id);
PL/SQL procedure successfully completed.
SQL> EXECUTE DBMS_OLAP.PURGE_FILTER(:filter_id);
PL/SQL procedure successfully completed.
SQL> EXECUTE DBMS_OLAP.PURGE_WORKLOAD(:workload_id);
PL/SQL procedure successfully completed.
SQL> DROP TABLE user_workload;
Table dropped.
SQL>
```

Recommendations of the Summary Advisor

The Summary Advisor's recommendations provide a lot of information as to the value of the proposed materialized view. For example, in the test case, the information includes the several criteria such as the gain due to the use of the materialized view and the savings in storage space. Listing 7-21 shows an excerpt from the Summary Advisor's recommendation report.

Listing 7-21. The Summary Advisor's Recommendation Report

```
Rank: 1
Action: Create
Storage: 800 Kilo Bytes
Gain: 100.00%
Fact Tables: Sales
Grouping Levels: Products_Dim_category
Query:  SELECT sh.products.prod_category, sum (sh.sales.quantity_sold), count
```

```
(sh.sales.quantity_sold), count(*)
     FROM sh.sales, sh.products
     WHERE sh.products.prod_id = sh.sales.prod_id
     AND sh.products.prod_category <= 'Women'
     AND sh.products.prod_category >= 'Boys'
     GROUP BY sh.products.prod_category
```

 NOTE *The report advises you not only on the creation of new materialized views, but also on the removal or continuance of existing materialized views.*

The Rank entry represents the materialized view's rank among all the materialized views. The Action keyword presents the actual Summary Advisor recommendation, in this case, to create the materialized view in question. The Summary Advisor reports that the proposed view will only take about 800KB in storage. A 100 percent improvement in performance is indicated by the value of the Gain parameter. The Query section gives you the query to be used in creating the recommended materialized view. You can also have the report itself prepare the materialized view creation statement.

Creating Materialized Views

You have to follow several steps to get the materialized views going, although the creation itself is simple.

Making the Necessary Grants

The user who is creating the materialized view needs to have the necessary privileges granted as follows:

```
SQL> grant create materialized view to salapati;
Grant succeeded.
SQL> grant query rewrite to salapati;
Grant succeeded.
SQL>
```

Creating the Materialized View Log

When you create the materialized log, you need a mechanism to propagate the changes in the base tables to the materialized view. You have several ways to do this, and you'll be using the fast refresh mechanism in the next section. Using the fast refresh option means that at periodic intervals, the database will send all the changes made to the tables to the materialized views created upon those views. If you don't do a periodic fast refresh, you'll have to re-execute the entire materialized view query to populate the materialized view. The materialized view log is a table based on the associated materialized view. Each of the tables involved in the join in the materialized view needs its own materialized view log to capture changes to the tables. Here's how you create the materialized log:

```
SQL> create materialized view log on products;
Materialized view log created.
SQL> create materialized view log on sales;
Materialized view log created.
SQL>
```

 CAUTION *If the tables on which you're creating the materialized view logs don't have any primary keys defined on them, you can't create the log. Make sure you have the primary keys in place before you try to create the materialized logs.*

Creating the Materialized View

Now you can go ahead and create the materialized view in your schema. If you have an aggregate table already in your database, you can use the *create materialize view* statement with the *on prebuilt table* clause to register the existing summary table as a materialized view.

Remember that you need to update a materialized view to keep it in sync with the underlying tables. You have three options to do this: a *fast refresh* will add only the changes to the tables, a *complete refresh* will fully refresh the view, and the *on commit* option will update the materialized view whenever a change is made to the underlying tables. The example shown in Listing 7-22 uses the *refresh complete* option for simplicity.

Listing 7-22. Creating a Materialized View

```
SQL> create materialized view test_mv
  2  build immediate
  3  refresh complete
  4  next sysdate + 1
  5  enable query rewrite
  6  as
  7  SELECT sh.products.prod_category,
  8  sum(sh.sales.quantity_sold),
  9  count(sh.sales.quantity_sold),
 10  count(*)
 11  FROM sh.sales, sh.products
 12  WHERE sh.products.prod_id = sh.sales.prod_id
 13  AND sh.products.prod_category <= 'Women'
 14  AND sh.products.prod_category >= 'Boys'
 15  GROUP BY sh.products.prod_category
 /
Materialized view created.
SQL>
```

Let's look at some of the important parts of the *create materialized view* statement:

- *Build immediate* will populate the materialized view right away and is the default option. The alternative is to use the *build deferred* option, which will load the materialized view at a specified time.

- *Refresh complete* specifies that the materialized view's data should be refreshed completely, not incrementally.

- The *next* parameter specifies when the next refresh will be done.

- *Enable query rewrite* means that the Oracle database will force queries to use the newly created materialized views.

- The *as* clause specifies the query that underlies the materialized view, and it is similar to how you create a normal Oracle view.

Query Rewrite

The query rewrite capability of Oracle is a query optimization technique whereby Oracle will decide to use the materialized views, even though the user specifies the query in terms of the regular tables. The rewrite is automatic, and thus completely transparent to the user. The query rewrite works even when there is no exact match between the user's queries and the materialized views.

You enable query rewrite by specifying *query rewrite* when you create the materialized view itself (as in the preceding example) or by specifying the option after the materialized view is created. Listing 7-23 shows how to do this.

Listing 7-23. Using the Query Rewrite Feature

```
SQL> alter session set query_rewrite_enabled=true;
Session altered.
To test whether the query rewrite is working,
let's execute the following the following
PL/SQL code block query first:
SQL> DECLARE
 querytxt varchar2(500) :=
'SELECT sh.products.prod_category, sum
(sh.sales.quantity_sold),
count(sh.sales.quantity_sold),
                count(*)
        FROM sh.sales, sh.products
        WHERE sh.products.prod_id = sh.sales.prod_id
            AND sh.products.prod_category <= ''Women''
            AND sh.products.prod_category >= ''Boys''
        GROUP BY sh.products.prod_category';
 begin
 dbms_mview.Explain_Rewrite(querytxt,null,'ID2');
 end;
 /
SQL>
```

Next, you can query the explain plan or query the rewrite_table as follows:

```
SQL> select message from rewrite_table;
MESSAGE
-----------------------------------------
QSM-01009: materialized view, TEST_MV, matched query text
QSM-01033: query rewritten with materialized view
TEST_MV
```

Alternatively, you can use the explain plan tool to see the proposed execution plan for the query. Your explain plan should not show any references to the underlying base tables. It should show that the materialized view is being referred to instead, to convince you that the query rewrite is indeed working in forcing queries to use the new materialized view.

Estimating the Size of Materialized Views

You can use the DBMS_OLAP package to get a quick estimate of the estimated size of a materialized view that you have decided to create. Listing 7-24 shows you the code to do so.

Listing 7-24. Using the DBMS_OLAP Package to Size a Materialized View

```
SQL> declare
  2    no_of_rows number;
  3    mv_size    number;
  4    begin
  5    dbms_olap.estimate_summary_size('MV 1',
  6    'SELECT sh.products.prod_category, sum(sh.sales.quantity_sold), count(s
  7              count(*)
  8          FROM sh.sales, sh.products
  9          WHERE sh.products.prod_id = sh.sales.prod_id
 10            AND sh.products.prod_category <= ''Women''
 11            AND sh.products.prod_category >= ''Boys''
 12          GROUP BY sh.products.prod_category',
 13          no_of_rows,mv_size);
 14* end;
dbms_out.put_line ('estimated number of rows:  '||no_of_rows);
dbms_out.put_line ('estimated size in bytes    : '||mv_size);
estimated number of rows: 245504
estimated size in bytes      :21604352
```

Summary

This chapter was mainly devoted to the subject of managing schema objects in the Oracle9*i* database. First, you learned how to create and manage simple tables. You then explored more advanced table structures such as partitioned tables, index-organized tables (IOTs), and clusters.

A large part of the DBA's job involves troubleshooting code errors, whether in a development or testing database or even a production server. To troubleshoot well, you need to not only know SQL and PL/SQL well, but also understand how Oracle manages its tables, indexes, and other objects internally. The chapter provided guidelines for creating optimal indexes. Constraints are a common source of puzzlement for both developers and DBAs. Constraint state is an important topic, and you might want to practice several scenarios on a test database. Knowing how to use synonyms, sequences, and views well will enhance your capabilities as a DBA.

I discussed the topic of materialized views in detail toward the end of the chapter. Materialized views primarily address the problems inherent in managing data warehouses, but they can also be very helpful to any database that involves complex joins and summarization of data.

CHAPTER 8

Oracle Transaction Management

A *TRANSACTION* IS a logical unit of work consisting of one or more SQL statements. Transactions may encompass all of your program or just a part of it. A transaction may perform one operation or an entire series of operations on the database objects. You can execute transactions interactively or as part of a program. Transactions are begun implicitly whenever data is read or written, and they are ended by the *commit* or *rollback* statement.

To manage a database efficiently, you first need to understand how the database conducts, or manages, its transactions. Transaction management is at the heart of database processing. In order for a large number of users to concurrently run transactions, the DBMS must manage the transactions with the least amount of conflict while ensuring the consistency of the database. Transaction management ensures that a database is accessible to many users simultaneously, and that users can't undo each other's work.

In this chapter, I take you through the basics of transaction management. I start the chapter with an explanation of a transaction in the context of a relational database. I then explain the standard transaction isolation levels standards (ISO) and how Oracle complies with them.

The concept of serializability is crucial in transaction processing. Concurrency of usage gives relational databases their great strength, and serializability conditions ensure the concurrency of database transactions. In this chapter, I explain how Oracle uses the twin techniques of transaction locking and multiversion concurrency control using undo records to enforce serializability in transactions.

Undo space management is an important part of transaction management, and in this chapter you'll learn about the new automatic management of undo. The other component in Oracle's transaction management is its locking feature, which helps Oracle increase concurrency.

In this chapter, you'll take a good look at Oracle's locking strategies and how to use them to improve concurrency. Longer transactions pose many problems, including the possibility of failing to complete due to space errors. You'll learn how to use Oracle's new Resumable Space Allocation feature to resume transactions that have suspended due to space-related errors. You'll also learn how to use the Oracle Workspace Manager feature, which enables you to version-control table data. In addition, you'll discover how to use Oracle's powerful Flashback Query feature, which allows you to go back to a point in time without having to perform a complicated data recovery.

Transactions

Note that DDL statements issued by a DBA aren't very complex to process. The DDL commands alter the schema (amounting to changing the data dictionary), which contains object definitions and other related metadata for the database. DML language (also called *query language*) operations are a different kettle of fish altogether. The majority of DML statements retrieve data from the database (queries), and the rest modify or insert new data. DML transaction processing involves compiling and executing the SQL statements in the most efficient manner, with the least amount of contention among multiple transactions, while preserving the consistency of the database.

A *transaction* consists of one or more SQL data manipulation statements that together perform a logical unit of work. Transactions must be executed separately and in isolation from other transactions. A transaction starts implicitly when the first executable SQL statement begins and continues to process all following SQL statements until one of the following four events occurs:

- *Commit:* If a transaction encounters a *commit* statement, all the changes made until that point are made permanent in the database.

- *Rollback:* If a transaction encounters a *rollback* statement, all changes made up to that point are cancelled.

- *Normal program conclusion:* If a program ends without errors, all changes are implicitly committed by the database.

- *Abnormal program failure:* If the program crashes or is terminated, all changes made by it are implicitly rolled back by the database.

All SQL transactions in Oracle go through certain predefined steps before actually being executed by the server. The SQL statements are first checked for syntax, and then the user issuing the statement must make sure he or she has the necessary privileges on the objects. Next, Oracle determines if the query should be parsed fresh or if a preparsed version already exists in memory.

If the executed version is in memory, execution may not be necessary. In fact, you can put all your data in memory without using any physical disks at all. This type of database is known as an *in-memory database* (IMDB) or a *main memory database* (MMDB).

NOTE *In-memory databases can be useful for certain specific applications such as set-top boxes and networking gear. Traditional database requirements are too expensive for such price-sensitive applications. Main memory databases are a good solution in cases where you need an on-device database. For one such example, visit* http://www.mcobject.com, *where you can learn more about an IMDB called eXtremeDB.*

Anatomy of a SQL Transaction

SQL statements pass through several stages before they're executed. In the following sections, I discuss these stages. Note that Oracle automatically opens a cursor for the statement you're executing. A *cursor* is a name for a private SQL area. Oracle uses cursors to store parsed statements and other information relating to the statements it's currently processing. Oracle automatically opens a cursor for all SQL statements.

Parsing

During the parsing stage, Oracle does several things to check your SQL statements. Oracle checks that your statements are syntactically correct. The data dictionary needs to be consulted to see if the tables and column specifications are correct. After this, Oracle ensures that you have the privileges to perform the actions you are attempting through your SQL statements.

Once it makes all these semantic and syntactic checks, Oracle draws up the *execution plan* for the statement, which involves selecting the best access methods for the objects in the statement. Oracle also checks whether there is a parsed representation of the statement in memory already. If there is, the user can execute this parsed representation without going through the parsing process all over again.

After the parsing operation is complete, Oracle allots a shared SQL area for the statement. Other users can access this parsed version as long as it is retained in memory.

Soft Parsing

After it checks the privileges, Oracle assigns a number called the *SQL hash value* to the SQL statement for identification purposes. If the SQL hash value already exists in memory, Oracle will look for the execution plan for the statement, which details the way the objects are to be accessed, among other things. Oracle will proceed straight to the actual execution of the statement using the execution plan it found. The preceding process is called a *soft parse*, and it is the preferred technique in statement SQL processing. Because it uses previously formed execution plans, soft parsing is fast and efficient.

Hard Parsing

The opposite of a soft parse is a *hard parse*, and Oracle has to perform this type of parse when it doesn't find the SQL hash value in memory for the statement it wants to execute. Hard parses are tough on system memory and other resources. Oracle has to create a fresh execution plan, which means the numerous possibilities have to be evaluated by Oracle and it must choose the best plan. During this process, Oracle needs to access the library cache and dictionary cache numerous times to check the data dictionary. Each time it accesses these commonly used areas, Oracle needs to use *latches*, which can be seen as low-level serialization control mechanisms to protect shared data structures in the System Global Area (SGA). Thus, hard parsing contributes to an increase in latch contention.

Anytime there's a severe contention for resources during statement processing, the execution time will increase. Remember that if identical SQL hash values aren't being frequently found in shared memory, it means many hard parses, which will lead to a fragmentation of the shared pool, which will in turn make your contention problem worse.

Binding

During the binding stage, Oracle retrieves the values for the variables used in the parsing stage. The execution of the statement can't proceed until Oracle obtains these values for the variables used in the parsing stage.

Execution

Once Oracle completes the parsing and binding stages, it executes the statement; that is, it performs either the query or the DML operations in the SQL statement. It's during the execution phase that the database gets the data from the disk into the memory buffers (if it doesn't find the data there already). The database also administers all the necessary locks and ensures that any changes made during the SQL execution are logged. After the execution of the SQL statement, Oracle automatically closes the cursors.

 NOTE *It's important for you as a DBA to fully understand the nature of transactions in relational databases. A good reference is the book by Jim Gray (along with Andreas Reuter), a leading expert on database and transaction processing, called* Transaction Processing: Concepts and Techniques *(Morgan Kaufmann Publishers, 1993).*

Transaction Properties

Transactions in RDBMSs must possess four important properties. These properties are symbolized by the ACID acronym, which stands for *atomicity, consistency, isolation,* and *durability* of transactions. Transaction management in general means supporting database transactions so the ACID properties are maintained. Let's look at the transaction properties in more detail:

- *Atomicity:* Either a transaction should be performed entirely or none of it should be performed. That is, you can't have the database performing parts of a transaction. For example, if you issue a SQL statement that should delete 1,000 records, your entire transaction should abort (roll back) if your database crashes after the transaction deletes 999 records.

- *Consistency:* The database is supposed to ensure that it's always in a consistent state. For example, in a banking transaction that involves debits from your savings account and credits to your checking account, the database can't just credit your checking account and stop. This will lead to inconsistent data, and the consistency property of transactions ensures that the database doesn't perform partial transactions. All transactions must preserve the consistency of the database. For example, if you wish to delete a department ID from the table Department, the database shouldn't permit your action if some employees in the Employees table belong to the department you're planning on eliminating.

- *Isolation:* Isolation means that although there's concurrent access to the database by multiple transactions, each transaction must appear to be executing in isolation. The isolation property of transactions ensures that a transaction is kept from viewing changes made by another transaction before the first transaction commits or is rolled back. The isolation property is upheld by the database's concurrency control mechanisms, as you'll see in the following sections. For example, a lock on an object will prevent more than one transaction from accessing that object the same way, leading to a disastrous impact on data. Although concurrent access is a hallmark of the relational database, isolation techniques make it *appear* as though users are executing transactions *serially*, one after another.

    This chapter discusses how Oracle implements *concurrency control*, the assurance of atomicity and isolation of individual transactions in a concurrently accessed database.

- *Durability:* The last ACID property, durability, ensures that the database saves committed transactions permanently. Once a transaction completes, the database should ensure that the transaction's changes are not lost. This property is enforced by the database recovery mechanisms, which make sure that all committed transactions are retrieved. As you saw in Chapter 5, Oracle uses the write ahead protocol, which ensures that all changes are first written to the redo logs on disk before they're transferred to the database files on disk. In Chapters 14 and 15 of this book, you'll learn more about how Oracle enforces the durability property of transactions using its recovery mechanism.

 NOTE *Users can name a transaction to help monitor it, and there are several advantages to giving a meaningful name to a long-running transaction. For example, using the LogMiner utility, you can look for details of the exact transaction you're interested in. Chapter 15 shows how to use the LogMiner utility to help undo DML changes. Assigning names to transactions also makes it easier for the user to query the transaction details using the name column of the V$TRANSACTION view.*

Transaction Concurrency Control

Transaction concurrency is the process of managing simultaneous work by users without any interference among them. Improper interactions among transactions can cause the database to become inconsistent. The database needs to control the actions of the different transactions. If you're the only user of the database, you don't need to worry about concurrency control of transactions. However, in most cases, databases enable thousands of users to conduct transactions simultaneously. Users will access and perform simultaneous select, update, insert, and delete transactions against the same table. How can some users select meaningful data from tables, for example, while others are deleting data from the very same table? Should the select users wait on the delete users?

One solution is to lock the entire table for duration of the delete. But this would mean that the access to the table is severely reduced. As you'll see, Oracle does use locking mechanisms to keep the data consistent among users, but the locking is done in the least restrictive fashion. Concurrency will no doubt increase the throughput of an RDBMS, but it brings along its own special set of problems, as you'll learn in the next section.

Concurrency Problems

Concurrent access to the database by users introduces several problems into transaction processing. The following sections detail the most important problems encountered in concurrent transaction processing.

The Dirty Read Problem

A *dirty read* occurs when a transaction reads data that is updated but not committed permanently to the database. If a transaction is allowed to view the results of an ongoing transaction before it commits, you may end up with a dirty read problem. For example, say transaction B is reading the intermediate data from transaction A. Transaction A has just updated the value of a column, which is now read by transaction B. What if transaction A rolls back its transaction, whether intentionally or because it aborts for some reason? The value of the updated column will also be rolled back as a result. Unfortunately, transaction B has already read the new value of the column, which is now really incorrect because of the rolling back of transaction A.

TIP *As you can see, the problem described in this section could have been avoided by imposing a simple rule: Don't let any transaction read the intermediate results of another transaction before the other transaction is either committed or rolled back. This way, the reads are guaranteed to be consistent.*

The Phantom Read Problem

Say you're reading data from a table. You execute your query after some time elapses, and in the meantime, some other user has inserted new data into the table. Because your second query will come up with extra rows that weren't in the first read, they're referred to as "phantom" reads, and the problem is termed a *phantom read*. Phantom read problems are caused by the appearance of new data in between two database operations in a transaction.

The Lost Update Problem

The *lost update* problem is caused by transactions trying to read data while it is being updated by other transactions. If transaction A is reading a table's data while it is being updated by transaction B, transaction B completes successfully and is committed. If transaction A has read the data before transaction B has fully completed, it might end up with intermediate data and you might be left with inconsistent data in the end. Allowing transactions to read and update a table before the completion of another transaction causes the problem in this case.

The Nonrepeatable Read Problem

When a transaction finds that data it has read previously has been modified by some other transaction, you have a *nonrepeatable read* problem. Suppose you access a table's data at a certain point in time, and then you try to access the same data a little later, only to find that the data is different the second time around. This problem of inconsistent data during the same transaction is a nonrepeatable read problem.

Schedules and Serializability

You can safely assume that a transaction executed in isolation will always leave the database in a consistent state when the transaction completes. If the database permits concurrent access (i.e., several transactions running simultaneously), then you need to consider the cumulative effect of all the transactions on database consistency. To do this, you use a concept called a *schedule*. A schedule is a sequence of operations from one or more transactions. If all the transactions executed serially, one after another, the schedule will also be *serial*. If you can produce a schedule that is equivalent in its effect to a serial schedule, even though it may be derived from a set of concurrent transactions, it is called a *serializable schedule*. The serializable schedule consists of a series of intermingled database operations drawn from several transactions, and the final outcome of a serializable sequence is a consistent database.

The ISO Transaction Standard

The ISO (http://www.iso.ch) standard for transactions rests on the two key transaction-ending statements: *commit* and *rollback*. All transactions, according to the ISO standard, begin with a *select, update, insert,* or *delete* statement. No transaction can view another transaction's intermediate results. Results of a second transaction are available to the first transaction only after the second transaction completes.

All transactions must ensure that they preserve database consistency. A database is consistent before a transaction begins, and it must be left in a consistent state at the end of the transaction. If you can devise a method to avoid the problems mentioned in the previous section, you can ensure a high degree of concurrent interactions among transactions in the database. There is a price to pay for this, however: Attempts to reduce the anomalies will result in reduced concurrency. The ISO transaction standards are meant to ensure the compliance of transactions with the atomic and isolation properties, and avoid the concurrency problems explained in the previous section.

Of course, you can avoid the problems described in the previous section and thus ensure database consistency at all times by imposing this simple rule: You can't start a new transaction until the current transaction is committed or rolled back. However, this defeats the whole purpose of having a multiuser database, as you'll have to completely eliminate the idea of concurrency in accessing the database. It's the database's job to ensure that concurrently run transactions preserve the consistency of the database, just as a transaction run in isolation would.

Consistency can be achieved by enforcing a serial usage of the database, but it's impractical. Therefore, the practical goal is to find those types of concurrent transactions that don't interfere with each other—in other words, transactions that guarantee a serializable schedule. As long as you have concurrent updates or a mix of read and write transactions going on in the database, proper ordering of the transactions becomes very important, unless they're all read-only transactions.

Oracle Transaction Management

An Oracle transaction begins with the first executable SQL statement and ends when the transaction encounters a *commit* or *rollback* statement. The transaction can also end when a user disconnects gracefully from Oracle or when a user process fails (i.e., terminates abnormally). When a transaction begins, Oracle will assign a rollback segment to the transaction to record the original data wherever data is modified by an update or delete. The first statement after the completion of a transaction will mark the beginning of a new transaction. In the sections that follow, you'll look at the important Oracle transaction controls statements in detail.

Commit

The *commit* statement ends a transaction successfully. All changes made by all SQL statements since the transaction began are recorded permanently in the database. Before the *commit* statement is issued, the changes may not be visible to other transactions. You can commit a transaction by using either of the following commands, both of which result in making the changes permanent:

```
Sql> commit;
Sql> commit work;
```

Before Oracle can issue a *commit* statement, the following things happen in the database:

- Oracle generates rollback records in the SGA rollback segment buffers area. As you know, the rollback records contain the "old" values of the updated and deleted table rows.

- Oracle generates redo log entries in the redo log buffer area of the SGA.

- Oracle modifies the database buffers in the SGA.

> **NOTE** *The modified database buffers may be written to the disk before a* commit *statement is issued. Similarly, the redo log entries may be written to the redo logs before a* commit *statement is ever issued.*

When an Oracle transaction is committed, the following three things happen:

1. The transaction tables in the redo records are tagged with the unique System Change Number (SCN) of the committed transaction.

2. The log writer writes the redo log information for the transaction from the redo log buffer to the redo log files on disk, along with the transaction's SCN. This is the point at which a commit is considered complete in Oracle.

3. Any locks that Oracle holds are released and Oracle marks the transaction as complete.

> **NOTE** *If you set the SQL*Plus variable* autocommit *to on, Oracle will automatically commit transactions, even without an explicit* commit *statement.*

Rollback

The *rollback* statement aborts or terminates a transaction unsuccessfully. None of the changes made to the tables by SQL statements since the transaction began are recorded to the database permanently. The *rollback* statement reverses the changes made by the transaction. You can roll back all the changes made during the transaction, or if you use *save points* in the transaction, you can roll back only up to the last *save point* command in the transaction, as shown in the following examples. The *save point* statement acts like a bookmark for the uncommitted statements in the transaction. In the second example, the rollback is only up to point A in the transaction. Everything before point A is still committed.

```
Sql> rollback;
Sql> rollback to savepoint pointA;
```

Oracle uses the undo records in the undo tablespace to roll back the transactions after a *rollback* command. It also releases any locks that are held and marks the transaction as complete. If the rollback is to a save point, instead of the transaction, the transaction is deemed incomplete, and you can continue the transaction.

Oracle's Isolation Levels

The ISO transaction standards use the term *isolation level* to indicate the extent to which a database allows interaction among transactions. Isolation of transactions keeps concurrently executing database transactions from viewing incomplete results of other transactions. There are several isolation levels based on how they avoid the consistency problems. The concept of *serializability* helps explain how transaction isolation will help reduce the impact of the data problems introduced by concurrent access to the database by many transactions. If the database allows transactions only in serial order (i.e., no concurrent transactions at all), then the data problems you saw earlier would, of course, disappear. A completely serialized operation mode will avoid all three problems, but it is not feasible from a practical point of view.

Practical, real-world databases need a compromise between concurrency access and serializable modes of operation. The key issue here is this: By specifying a high degree of isolation, you can keep one transaction from affecting another, but at the cost of a significant deterioration in database performance. On the other side, a low level of transaction isolation will introduce the data problems you saw in the previous section, but it leads to better performance. A transaction running at a serializable isolation level will appear as if it's running in isolation—it's as if all the other concurrent transactions run before or after this transaction. Three of the four main ISO isolation levels allow for some deviation from the theoretical concept of serializable transactions. Table 8-1 shows the extent to which each of the four main levels of isolation avoids the concurrency problems listed earlier.

Table 8-1. ISO Standard for Isolation Levels

LEVEL	DIRTY READ	NONREPEATABLE READ	PHANTOM READ
Read uncommitted	Yes	Yes	Yes
Read committed	No	Yes	Yes
Repeatable read	No	No	Yes
Serializable	No	No	No

As you can see, the last isolation level, *serializable,* avoids all three of the concurrency problems. Under the serializable level of isolation, the transaction will lock all the tables it is accessing, thereby preventing other transactions from updating any of the tables underneath it until it has completed its transaction by using a *commit* or *rollback* command.

The *repeatable read* isolation level guarantees read consistency—a transaction that reads the data twice from a table at two different points in time will find the same values each time. You avoid both the dirty read problem and the nonrepeatable read problem through this level of isolation.

The *read uncommitted* level, which allows a transaction to read another transaction's intermediate values before it commits, will result in the occurrence of all three problems of concurrent usage.

Oracle's default isolation level is the *read committed* level of isolation level at the statement level. Oracle queries see only the data that was committed at the beginning of the query. Because the isolation level is at the statement level, each statement is allowed to see only the data that was committed before the commencement of the statement. The read committed level of isolation guarantees that the row data won't change while you're accessing a particular row in an Oracle table.

 NOTE *If you're in the process of updating a row that you fetched into a cursor, you can rest assured no one else is updating the same row simultaneously. However, if you're executing your query, you may get different values each time if other transactions have updated data successfully in between your queries. Remember that Oracle only guarantees statement-level isolation here, not transaction-level isolation.*

The default read committed isolation level for Oracle described previously will get rid of the dirty read and the lost update problems. You won't have the dirty read problem because your queries will read only data that was committed at the beginning of the query, thereby avoiding reading data that may later be rolled back by a different transaction. In addition, you'll avoid the lost update problem because transactions can't read data that's currently being modified until the updates have been completed.

Oracle doesn't force you to lock a table when you insert data into it. If one transaction is in the process of writing to a table, other processes aren't kept from reading the data. Users can read all committed data in the database—that's why Oracle's transaction level is called the "read committed" transaction level. Because transactions can only read committed data, Oracle avoids the problems of both dirty reads and repeatable reads. Dirty reads, as you learned earlier, occur when transactions read data that's being changed by another transaction. By definition, a dirty read can't occur in Oracle, because you can't read uncommitted data in Oracle. Repeatable reads occur when you get different data from reads at different points within the same transaction.

Changing the Default Isolation Level

As you can see, Oracle's default isolation level doesn't guarantee the avoidance of the nonrepeatable read problem. This is because Oracle guarantees only statement-level, not transaction-level, read consistency. However, Oracle allows you to explicitly set the isolation level of transactions. If you wish, you can implement a read-only isolation level or a serializable isolation level in your database. You can modify the default isolation level with the *set transaction* command at the beginning of a transaction or with the *alter session* command if you wish to change the isolation level for the entire session. You'll examine these two nondefault isolation levels in the following sections.

The Read-Only Isolation Level

The *read-only isolation* level permits transactions to see only data that was committed before the transaction started. You specify read-only transactions when you want transaction-level read consistency. Note that your transactions can't be involved in any inserts, deletes, or updates if you want to use the read-only isolation level. You can set this isolation level at the session level by using the following command:

```
SQL> alter session set isolation level read only;
```

If you want to set the isolation level just for a transaction, use the following command at the beginning of your transaction:

```
SQL> Set transaction read only;
```

Because you can't modify data under this isolation level, it's a restrictive one and it isn't very useful for most applications.

The Serializable Isolation Level

You can set the *serializable isolation* level of isolation using the *alter session* or *set transaction* statement. Here is the syntax for both the alternatives (you can also change the serializable parameter to *true* from the default value of *false* in the init.ora file, but Oracle discourages the use of this method):

To set serialization for the entire session, use this command:

```
SQL> alter session set isolation level serializable;
```

To set serialization at the transaction level, use this command:

```
SQL> set transaction isolation level serializable;
```

The Read Committed vs. the Serializable Level of Isolation

Oracle's read committed level of isolation provides protection against dirty reads and lost updates because queries read data only after the *commit* statement is executed. The transactions are all consistent on a per-statement basis. Readers will not block writers of transactions and vice versa. The *read committed* level provides a great deal of concurrency and consistency in the database. However, this mode does not provide transaction-level consistency. Because it's a statement-level isolation, changes made in between statements in a transaction may not be seen by a query, and this is the reason you'll continue to have the nonrepeatable read problem; you simply can't be guaranteed the same results if you repeat your queries. The phantom read problem also still lurks because the model doesn't prevent other transactions from updating tables in between your queries.

By using either the *set transaction* command or the *alter session* command, as shown in the previous examples, you can change the isolation level to the serializable level to avoid the concurrency problems. A serializable level of isolation is suited for databases where multiple consistent queries need to be issued during an update transaction. Actually, the serializable mode provides the same consistency as the read-only mode of isolation, with the one difference being that in a serialized mode, you can also perform DML operations. However, serialization is not a simple choice, because it seriously reduces your concurrency. Following are some of the problems involved in setting the serializable isolation level:

- Serialization involves locking tables for exclusive use by transactions, thereby slowing down transaction concurrency.

- You have to set the parameter INITTRANS for tables at creation time to at least 3 in order for the serialization level of isolation to take effect. The parameter INITTRANS determines the number of concurrent transactions on a table.

- Throughput is much lower than in the read committed isolation level, especially in high concurrency databases with many transactions accessing the same tables for updates.

- You must incorporate error-checking code in the application if you want to use the serializable mode of isolation.

- You can always use explicit locks to get a repeatable read if that's your objective in using a serializable isolation level.

- Serializable transactions are more prone to *deadlocks*, a situation in which transactions are stuck in situations where they're waiting for each other to release locks over data objects. Deadlocks lead to costly rollbacks of transactions.

So, in general, it's safest to stick with Oracle's default read committed level of transaction isolation, although it isn't perfect. If queries are executed multiple times, it's possible to run into nonrepeatable reads and phantom rows. The read committed transaction level provides a good tradeoff between data concurrency and data consistency. The throughput is much higher with this mode of isolation than with the "purer" serialization mode. For standard OLTP applications in particular, which are high-volume, concurrent, short-lived transactions, with few transactions likely to conflict with each other, this mode is ideal from a performance point of view. Very few transactions in an OLTP database issue the same query multiple times, so phantom reads and nonrepeatable reads are rare. Serializable modes of concurrency are more appropriate for databases with mostly read-only transactions that run for a long time.

Implementing Oracle's Concurrency Control

A database may use one or more ways to implement concurrency of use. These methods include locking mechanisms to guarantee exclusive use of a table by a transaction, timestamping methods that enable serialization of transactions, and the validation-based scheduling of transactions. Locking methods are called *pessimistic,* because they assume that transactions will violate the serializable schedules unless they're prevented explicitly from doing so. The timestamping and the validation methods, on the other hand, are called *optimistic* because they don't assume that transactions are bound to violate the serializable schedules. As you may sense, locking methods cause more delays, because they keep conflicting transactions waiting for access to the locked database objects.

On the positive side, locking methods don't have to abort transaction because they prevent potentially conflicting transactions from interacting with other trans- actions. The optimistic methods have to usually abort transactions when they might violate a serializable schedule. Locking methods prevent unserializable schedules by keeping more than one transaction from accessing the same data elements. Timestamping methods assign timestamps to each transaction and enforce serializability by ensuring that the transaction timestamps match the schedule for the transactions. Validation methods maintain a record of transaction activity. Before committing a transaction, the changed data is "validated" against the changed items of all currently active transactions to eliminate any unserialized schedules. Oracle uses a combination of the available methods. It uses locks along with what is called the *multiversion concurrency control system* (a variation of the timestamping method) to manage concurrency.

Locking methods provide serializability by forcing transactions to wait for other transactions to complete. Locks are designed to prevent destructive inter- action between transactions for the same resources. These resources could be objects such as tables and indexes or shared memory structures in the SGA. Oracle does its locking implicitly; you don't have to worry about which table to lock or how to lock it, as Oracle will automatically place locks on your transaction's behalf when necessary. By default, Oracle uses *row-level locking,* which involves the least restrictive amount of locking, thus guaranteeing the highest amount of concur- rency. By default, Oracle stores the locked row information in the data blocks. Also, Oracle never uses *lock escalation*—that is, it doesn't go from row-level to table- level locking levels.

As mentioned previously, Oracle uses a multiversion concurrency control system, which is a variation of the timestamp-ordering approach to concurrency control. Multiversion timestamping maintains older versions of table data to ensure that any transaction can read the original data even after it has been changed by other transactions. Unlike locking, no waits are involved here; transactions use different versions of the same table instead of waiting for other transactions to complete. How do the transactions have access to different ver- sions of the same table? This is where Oracle undo segments come in. When transactions want to update a row, Oracle will first write the original "before image" to an undo segment (or a rollback segment, if you are using the manual undo management mode). Thus, queries will have a consistent view of the data, which provides read consistency. The multiversion concurrency control system used by Oracle is the reason you can get by with the read committed mode of isolation instead of having to use the slower but safer serializable isolation level.

Using its undo segments, Oracle guarantees statement-level read consistency. This means that the query only sees data from a single point in time. Using the same mechanism, Oracle is also capable of providing transaction-level read consistency, meaning all the separate statements in a transaction see data from a single point in time. To enforce transaction-level read consistency, you must run the database in the nondefault serializable mode.

Following are some important features of Oracle locking:

- Oracle implements locks by setting a bit in the data item being locked. The locking information is stored in the data block where the row lives.

- Locks are held for the entire length of a transaction and are released when a *commit* or a *rollback* statement is issued.

- Oracle does not use lock escalation. Oracle doesn't need to escalate locks, as it stores the locking information in the individual data blocks. Lock escalation—for example, an escalation from the row level to the table level—reduces concurrency.

- Oracle does use *lock conversion,* which involves changing the restrictiveness of a lock while keeping the granularity of the lock the same. For example, a row share table lock is converted into a more restrictive row exclusive table lock when a *select for update* statement starts updating the previously locked rows in the table.

In the next few sections, you'll study the locking methods and lock types of Oracle's concurrency control mechanism in detail.

Oracle Locking Methods

Oracle uses locks to control access to two broad types of objects: user objects, which include tables, and system objects, which may include shared memory structures and data dictionary objects. Locking strategies can be guided by two broad approaches: optimistic and pessimistic. Optimistic approaches are based on the premise that conflicts generally don't happen, so they're interested in checking for conflicts, preferring to wait for the end of the transactions to do so. Pessimistic approaches look for potential conflicts and will block some transactions from interfering with others to avoid conflicts between concurrent transactions.

Granularity, in the context of locking, is the size of the data unit used by the locking mechanism. Oracle uses row-level granularity to lock objects, which is the least restrictive level of granularity (exclusive table locking is the most restrictive level). Several databases, including Microsoft SQL Server, provide only page-level, not row-level, locking. Page-level (a *page* is somewhat similar to an Oracle data block, each of which can have a bunch of rows) locking means that during an update, several rows, in addition to the affected rows, are locked. Of course, if other users need the locked rows that are not part of the update, they have to wait for the lock on the page (block) to be released. For example, if your block or page size is 8KB, and the average row length in a table is 100 bytes, about 80 rows can fit in that one block. If one of the rows is being updated, a block-level lock limits access to the other 79 rows in the block. All this means that locking at a level larger than the row level would reduce data concurrency, which is one of the key functions of a relational database.

 NOTE *Remember, the more restrictive the locking granularity, the more serializable the transactions, and thus the fewer the concurrency anomalies. The flip side of this is that the more restrictive the granularity level, the lower the concurrency level. Oracle locks don't prevent other users from reading a table's data and queries never place locks on tables.*

How long does Oracle hold a lock? All locks acquired by statements in a transaction are held by Oracle until the transaction completes. When an explicit or implicit *commit* or *rollback* is issued by a transaction, Oracle will release any locks the statements within the transaction have been holding. If Oracle rolls back to a save point, it releases any locks acquired after the save point.

In the following section, I discuss the lock types used by Oracle in more detail.

Oracle Lock Types

Locks, as you have seen, prevent destructive interaction between transactions by allowing orderly access to resources. These resources could be database objects such as tables or other shared database structures in memory. Based on the type of object locked, Oracle locks can be broadly divided into the following types: DML locks, DDL locks, latches, internal locks, and distributed locks. I describe these lock types in the following sections.

DML Locks

DML locks are locks placed by Oracle to protect data in tables and indexes. Whenever a DML statement seeks to modify data in a table, Oracle automatically places a row-level lock on rows in the table being modified. Every transaction that is performing a DML operation such as an *insert, update, delete*, or a *select for update* will acquire an exclusive DML lock on each row that is involved in the DML operation.

You can place DML locks at the row level or table level. Row-level DML locks guarantee that readers of data don't wait for writers of data and vice versa. Writers will have to wait when they want to update the same rows that are being modified currently by other transactions.

Any query a transaction issues won't interfere with any other transaction, because all they do is read data—they don't modify it. Queries in this regard will include not only transactions using the *select* statement, but also transactions such as insert, update, and delete, all of which use an implicit *select* statement. Queries never need locks, and they never need to wait for any other locks to be released.

Any *insert, delete, update,* or *select for update* statements will automatically issue an exclusive row-level lock on the rows affected by the transaction. This exclusive row-level lock means that other transactions can't modify the concerned rows until the original transaction commits or rolls back, thereby releasing the exclusive locks that were placed on the rows. In addition, an exclusive table lock is placed on the table that contains the rows set for modification.

In summary, all the locks implicitly applied by Oracle during DML transactions are row-level locks, and Oracle doesn't escalate these locks to a more restrictive form (e.g., a table lock). This low-granularity-type locking by Oracle affords a high degree of concurrency.

DDL Locks

Oracle automatically places DDL locks on tables that are in the process of having some of their rows modified by a transaction. Note that even though a transaction my just hold row-level locking for its DML operations, it simultaneously also holds a table-level DDL lock on the table, which will prevent other transactions from altering or dropping the table from underneath it while its DML transactions aren't yet completed. You can also place DDL locks on tables for conducting a purely DDL operation without any accompanying DML transaction.

Latches, Internal Locks, and Distributed Locks

Latches are internal mechanisms that protect shared data structures in the SGA. For example, data dictionary entries are accessed in the buffer by many processes. Latches control access to these memory structures by the processes. For example, the data structures that list the blocks currently in memory are frequently consulted during the running of the Oracle instance. Server and background processes that need to change or read the data in critical data structures such as these would acquire a very short lock (called a latch in this instance) on the object.

The implementation of latches, including the specification of how long a process will wait for it, is usually operating system–specific. *Data dictionary locks* are used by Oracle whenever the dictionary objects are being modified. *Distributed locks* are specialized locking mechanisms used in a distributed database system or in the Oracle Real Application Clusters (ORAC) environment. Oracle uses *internal locks* to protect access to structures such as data files, tablespaces, and rollback segments.

Oracle Lock Modes

Oracle employs several types of locking mechanisms. The mechanism used depends on the kind of resources that need to be locked and the manner in which they should be locked. You can make a fundamental distinction between Oracle locking modes based on whether they are exclusive or shared. An *exclusive* locking mode is always obtained to modify data. A transaction that acquires an exclusive lock on a table, for example, is the only transaction that can modify data in the table until it releases the lock. A *shared* lock allows several transactions to simultaneously access a resource, usually for reading data rather than modifying it. If you want to modify a table row(s), you must have an exclusive lock on that row(s). Table 8-2 shows the main table locking modes available in Oracle9*i*.

Table 8-2. Oracle's Table Locking Modes

LOCK TYPE	ALLOWABLE OPERATIONS
Row share (RS) table lock	Least restrictive mode of locking. Others can use RS locks on same table.
Row exclusive (RX) table lock	No share mode locking permitted. Used for updates, deletes, and inserts.
Share (S) table lock	Other transactions can only query the data. Multiple share locks can be issued.
Share row exclusive (SRX) table lock	Allows only queries on the locked rows.
Exclusive (X) table lock	Only queries are allowed by other transactions.

In this section, you'll learn more about the various locking modes available in the Oracle9*i* database. Before I explain the various types of Oracle locking modes described in Table 8-2, you should understand the difference between the two basic types of Oracle locks: row-level locks (TX) and table locks (TM).

Oracle automatically acquires *row locks* in the exclusive mode to perform updates. Each active transaction requires one lock. A row that is modified will always be locked exclusively to prevent other transactions from modifying the data until the first transaction either commits or rolls back (this makes it impossible, for example, for a bank of booking clerks to sell the "last" ticket to more than one customer). When a transaction acquires an exclusive row lock, it always automatically acquires a table lock on the table itself. This table lock prevents conflicting DDL operations by other transactions.

NOTE *The fine-grained row-level locking and the use of multiversion concurrency control in Oracle means that for all practical purposes, the only real conflict will be between transactions that want to update the same rows simultaneously. Readers of data don't wait for writers, because the undo segments provide a read consistent view of data. Writers of data don't wait on readers either.*

A *table lock* is held for operations that include the *insert, update, delete,* and the *select for update* DML operations. DML operations need table locks to ensure that some other transaction isn't changing the table definition while modifying data. This means that a table can't be altered or dropped while an uncommitted transaction is still holding a table lock on the table. Table locks could range from a very restrictive to a minimally restrictive mode. The following sections describe some of the main modes in which Oracle can deploy table-level locks.

Row Share (RS) Table Lock

The *row share table lock* is the least restrictive of the table-level locks. Other transactions are allowed to select, update, insert, and delete from the row share locked table concurrently. Other transactions are only prevented from exclusive write access to the tables that are locked in this mode. Either of the following statements can issue the row share lock (one implicitly and the other explicitly):

```
SQL> select * from accounts for update;
SQL> lock table accounts in row share mode;
Table(s) Locked.
```

A row share table lock means that the transaction placing this lock has locked one or more rows in the table, with an intention to update them. This lock permits other transactions to select, insert, update, delete, or lock rows in the table while this transaction holds the table lock. Other transactions, however, can't lock the table in an exclusive mode.

Row Exclusive (RX) Table Lock

The *row exclusive table lock* indicates that a transaction holding the lock has updated one or more rows in the table. This is a slightly more restrictive lock than the table locks. Other transactions are allowed to select, insert, update, delete, or lock rows in the same table concurrently. However, other transactions can't lock the table exclusively for their own reads or writes. All *insert*, *update*, and *delete* statements impose row exclusive locks, and you can also explicitly impose this lock in the following way:

```
SQL> lock table accounts in row exclusive mode;
Table(s) Locked.
SQL>
```

Share (S) Table Lock

The *share table lock* is more restrictive than the two previously described locking modes. Other transactions can basically only issue *select* statements against a table locked in the share lock mode. Other transactions can, however, reserve some rows for future updates by issuing the *select for update* statement. Other transactions are also allowed to issue their own share locks against this table. When more than one transaction issues a share lock on a table, no table is allowed to update rows in that table, of course. Here's how you explicitly acquire this lock:

```
SQL> lock table accounts in share mode;
Table(s) Locked.
```

Share Row Exclusive (SRX) Table Lock

The *share row exclusive table lock* is more restrictive than the share table lock. The difference between the share row exclusive lock and the share table lock is that a share row exclusive lock can be held only by the first transaction that issues it. Like the share table locks, share row exclusive locks disallow updates to the rows by other transactions, allowing only select operations. Here's an example:

```
SQL> lock table accounts in row exclusive mode;
Table(s) Locked.
```

Exclusive (X) Table Lock

An *exclusive table lock* is the most restrictive lock mode, and it prevents any other transaction from performing any DML operations or acquiring any kind of locks on the same table. The transaction issuing the exclusive table lock is the only one that can write to the table; all other transactions can only read (select) the data in the table.

Explicit Locking in Oracle

Oracle automatically applies the necessary locks to the tables and other objects based on the transactions that are coded in the applications. Oracle's locking mechanism works automatically to ensure statement-level read consistency and concurrency. For the most part, Oracle's default, behind-the-scenes locking operations should suffice, but there may be some situations when you will be better off manually locking tables. Sometimes when the transaction needs to see consistent data across many joined tables, it may do an explicit locking. In other cases, a transaction may not want to wait for the completion of other transactions. In addition, when you don't want the data values changed during long transactions, it may be necessary to apply explicit locks.

Oracle provides explicit locking features to facilitate the overriding of the implicit locks placed by Oracle on behalf of transactions. You can override Oracle's default locking mechanism at the transaction level or the session level. If you want to override all Oracle's default locking mechanisms, you can do so by using the *set transaction isolation level* statement at the session level. The same statement will also override the default locking modes at the transaction level. In addition, you have several other means of overriding the default locking at the transaction level. In the following sections, you'll explore these manual locking techniques.

An Exclusive Table Lock

The following statement locks the table Customers in an exclusive mode, further specifying that it will not wait for a lock on the Customers table by using the *nowait* option when requesting the lock. The following SQL command will lock a table in the exclusive mode:

```
SQL> LOCK TABLE  Customers
     In exclusive mode nowait;
   Table(s) Locked.
SQL>
```

Once you lock a table in exclusive mode in this manner, no other session can perform any DML operations on the table until the lock is released by your session. Obviously, this is a highly restrictive type of lock, which can bring down the concurrency level quite dramatically.

A Select for Update

You can also use the *select for update* statement to override Oracle's default locking mechanism. The *select for update* command will lock all the rows covered by the *select* statement for an update later on. The lock is removed after the update is completed by using the *commit* or *rollback* statement. The following SQL statements show how to use *select for update* command:

In the following example, Oracle will lock only one row (rownum < 2) until the update completes:

```
SQL> select * from sales
  2* where rownum <2 for update
SQL> /
PROD_ID   CUST_ID  TIME_ID    PROMO_ID   NUM_SOLD
--------- -------- --------- - --------- ------------
9465      37290    01-JAN-98  S9999      18
SQL>
```

A For Update Select with Nowait

The *select for update* statement could be used in a more restrictive mode, by using the *nowait* option. This statement forces Oracle to either grant an lock on the requested object or issue an error but not keep the requesting session waiting for that lock. Here's a simple example:

```
SQL>Select * from employees
Where manager_id=2349
For update of employee_name nowait;
SQL>
```

In the preceding example, all the rows in the table corresponding to the manager_id of 2349 are locked for a future update. The *for update of employee_name* part specifies that employee_name is the column you're interested in updating, and the *nowait* keyword indicates that you don't want this statement to wait until other current locks are released on the table. So, if there are locks currently on the same table, the statement will return an error rather than wait. If other transactions now issue an *update* or *select for update* statement, they won't be successful. The second transaction will get an error because of the locks imposed by the *select for update* statement issued by the first statement.

Managing Oracle Locks

As I mentioned in the previous sections, locking in Oracle is usually done implicitly by Oracle itself, at the least restrictive level. Users can override Oracle's default locking behavior, but in general, you won't find too many cases where you'll be dealing with user-managed locks. Most of your lock management on a live database will be to see if any active locks are being held that are actually blocking users from conducting their DML operations. Oracle provides a script called utllockt.sql that gives you a lock wait-for graph in a tree-structured form about sessions that are holding locks that are affecting other sessions. Using this script, you can see what locks a session may be waiting for and the session that's holding the lock. The script is located in the $ORACLE_HOME/rdbms/admin directory. Here's a sample execution of the utllockt.sql script to identify locking information in the database:

```
SQL> @C:\oracle\oracle92\rdbms\admin\utllockt.sql
Session Waiting Type  Mode requested  Mode Held  Lock Id1
682             NONE   None            None        0
363             TX     Share (S)       Exclusive (X)
```

The session ID on the left side, 682, is what session 363 is waiting for. The information printed next to each session shows the lock information for the lock it's waiting for. Thus, session 682, although it's holding a lock, doesn't show anything (shows None) in the lock information columns, because it isn't waiting for any lock. Session 363, however, tells you that it has requested a share (S) lock and is waiting for session 682 to release its exclusive (X) lock on the table.

NOTE *The data dictionary tables that you need to look at to find locking information are the DBA_LOCKS, DBA_BLOCKERS, and DBA_WAITERS views. If for some reason you don't see the DBA_BLOCKERS view, run the $ORACLE_HOME/rdbms/admin/catproc.sql script to create it.*

You should be familiar with two special types of Oracle locking situations: blocking locks and deadlocks.

Blocking Locks

A *blocking lock* occurs when a lock on an object by a user prevents or blocks other users from accessing the same object(s). The DBA_BLOCKERS table is useful in getting this information. The DBA_BLOCKERS table tells you which sessions are currently holding locks on objects for which some other object is presently waiting. By combining the information in the DBA_BLOCKERS table with that in the V$SESSION tables, you can find out who is holding the blocking session by using the following SQL statement:

```
SQL> select a.username, a.program, a.sid, a.serial#
  2  from v$session a, dba_blockers b
  3  where a.sid = b.holding_session;
SQL>
```

When you do find a blocking session, you may have to terminate the user's session by using the *alter system kill session* command if the session is blocking another session from doing its job. If the process or the session still won't go away, go the operating system level and kill the process or the thread that spawned the Oracle session.

Deadlocks

Deadlocks occur in any RDBMS when two sessions block each other while waiting for the resource that the other session is holding currently. This is a catch-22 situation, because the stalemate can't be broken by either session unilaterally. In such circumstances, Oracle steps in, kills one of the sessions, and rolls back its transaction. Oracle quickly recognizes that two sessions are deadlocked and terminates the transaction that holds the most recently applied lock. This will release the object locks the other session is waiting for. Therefore, you don't really need to do anything when there are deadlocks, although you'll see messages in your dump directory that deadlocks are currently in the database.

When Oracle encounters a deadlock between transactions, it provides in the trace file (udump directory) the session IDs involved, the SQL statement issued in the transactions, and the specific object name and the rows on which locks are held in each session involved in the deadlock. Oracle further informs you that the deadlock is not an Oracle error, but is due to errors in application design or a result of issuing ad-hoc SQL. Application designers must write exception handlers in the code to roll back the aborted transaction and restart it. You can avoid dead locks by paying attention in the design phase to ensure proper locking order of the objects. Given that writers block other writers, deadlocks in Oracle are a rare phenomenon.

NOTE *Be prepared to wait for a very long time when you run most of the locking scripts. It's smarter to schedule these scripts using your crontab or Oracle Enterprise Manager (OEM) and arranging for alerts when there are problem locks in the system so you can take action to fix the problem.*

Using OEM to Manage Session Locks

You can use either OEM's Lock Manager or TopSessions to see what locks currently exist within your instance. Either method gives you a tremendous amount of locking information for sessions, including information concerning lock types, username, session ID, and the object names. Most of the locks you see in the Lock Manager or the TopSessions view are harmless; they are routine locks Oracle uses to maintain concurrency.

To see locks that are causing contention in your system, you need to select Drilldown ➤ Blocking/Waiting Locks Chart from the menu in the Lock Manager screen. If this screen shows no information, it generally means that no blocking locks are currently in the instance. Once you confirm that a session is blocking some other session, the Lock Manager tool allows you to kill the offending session easily by choosing the Drilldown ➤ Kill Session option from the top menu. Figure 8-1 shows how you can identify blocking/waiting locks using the OEM Lock Manager and even remove the blocks by killing one of the sessions involved in the locking situation. The figure shows that the user salapati is blocking the user tester from getting an exclusive lock on the table test_emp.

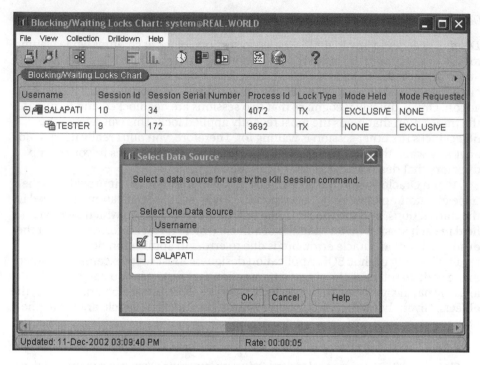

Figure 8-1. Using the OEM Lock Manager to identify blocking/waiting sessions

Using Undo Records to Provide Read Consistency

Oracle uses special structures called *undo records* to help provide statement-level and transaction-level read consistency. *Read consistency* means that all the data a query sees is from a single point in time. So, if a transaction is modifying data, Oracle will write a "before image" of the table data in its undo records. You can use this same "before image" to perform a rollback if necessary and you can also use it to perform database recovery. Oracle's undo records are located in the undo space specified at database creation time (you can optionally create them after the database is created, if you choose manual rollback management). The undo space in the undo tablespace will always hold the "before image" of table data for users if some other transaction is also updating it concurrently.

Oracle uses the SCN to enforce read consistency based on information recorded in the rollback segments. The SCN gives you the order in which transactions occurred in the database. Thus, when you issue a query, Oracle will read all the data that was committed at the time you issued the query. It uses the SCN that is present at that time to see which transactions have committed after the query began. If the SCNs are more recent than the beginning SCN, Oracle goes to the undo records to read the old data that existed prior to the change. Any changes that are made to the table data since the query began are ignored, so the viewer can get a consistent read of the data. Undo records help Oracle avoid application deadlocks due to read locks.

> **NOTE** *Although you can use manual undo management using rollback segments in Oracle9i, Oracle recommends using the new Automatic Undo Management (AUM) feature using undo tablespaces. Besides freeing you from the traditional chores of undo space management, use of the AUM feature is necessary to make several very useful Oracle9i features (including the Flashback Query feature), which you'll see later in this chapter and in more detail in Chapter 15.*

Automatic Undo Management

Oracle9*i* provides you two ways of allocating and managing undo (rollback) space among the various transactions occurring in the database. If you want to control the undo space *manually*, you can do so by creating traditional rollback segments. However, it is much more efficient and easier to let Oracle worry about managing the undo space by choosing *Automatic Undo Management* (AUM). AUM takes the entire issue of sizing and allocation of undo segments from the DBA and makes it Oracle's responsibility. As the DBA, all you have to do is to create an adequately sized tablespace (the undo tablespace) for storing undo information. Oracle will dynamically create undo (rollback) segments to meet the instance workload requirements.

Advantages of AUM

There are many advantages to using AUM, including facilitating the Oracle Flashback Query feature and avoiding many of the vexing errors associated with rollback segments. Traditionally, DBAs had to contend with regular ORA_1555 errors (snapshot too old), due to the rollback segments being written over with new information too quickly for some transactions. When a DBA uses traditional rollback segments, the DBA has the responsibility of monitoring the rollback segments for contention, and he or she may need to change the number and size of the rollback segments when necessary. AUM eliminates most of the undo block and consistent read contention.

Traditional rollback segments would sometimes be slow to relinquish the space they occupied, even after their transactions completed. Undo segments use space much more efficiently by exchanging space dynamically with other segments. Oracle will create, bring online, and take offline the undo segments automatically as needed. When the undo segments are no longer necessary, Oracle will reclaim the space used by the segments.

It is common practice for DBAs to assign a transaction to a specific rollback segment using the *set transaction* command. AUM removes the need to do this manual assignment of rollback segments. Oracle manages all undo space allocation automatically behind the scenes.

Setting Up AUM

To enable the automatic management of your undo space, you first need to specify the automatic undo mode in the init.ora file. Second, ideally at database creation time, you need to create a dedicated tablespace to hold the undo information. This will guarantee that you don't end up storing the undo in the system tablespace, which isn't a great idea.

If you want to choose AUM when you create a new database, you need to perform the following steps:

1. Make sure you specify *Automatic Undo Management* in the init.ora file (and the SPFILE).

2. Create an undo tablespace to store the undo records. To specify AUM, add the following line to your init.ora file (and the SPFILE). Remember that automatic management of undo means that you don't have to specify any rollback segments in your initialization file.

    Undo_management=auto

3. After you specify AUM in the initialization file, create an undo tablespace when you create the database. The undo tablespace will be a locally managed tablespace, and Oracle will manage its extent sizes. Users can't create application tables in this tablespace. The following database creation statement shows how to create the undo tablespace to hold your undo segments:

    SQL> CREATE DATABASE cust_prod
      ...
    undo tablespace undotbs_01 datafile
    '/cutprod10/oradata/data/undotbs_0101.dbf'
      size 500M;

 NOTE *If you use the Oracle Database Creation Agent (DBCA) to create your databases or create a default database when you install the Oracle9i software, Oracle will use AUM by default.*

Database creation time is not the only time you can create an undo tablespace. You may choose not to create the undo tablespace when you create the database. Even if you create an undo tablespace at database creation time, you may choose to add another undo tablespace later on. The following command shows you how to create the undo tablespace:

```
SQL> create undo tablespace undo02
  2  datafile 'C:\ORACLE9I\ORADATA\REMORSE\undotbs02.dbf' size 50M;
Tablespace created.
SQL>
```

You can always specify a new undo tablespace after database creation, without having to bring the instance down. You can create several undo tablespaces for your database, but the instance can use a single undo tablespace at any given time. The following *alter system* command will dynamically change the undo tablespace for your database:

```
SQL> Alter system set undo_tablespace = undotbs_5;
```

If you want Oracle to continue to use the new undo tablespace you just created, undotbs_5, you need to specify this in the init.ora file, as follows. Otherwise, Oracle will always use the default undo tablespace, which is the tablespace you specified for the *undo_tablespace* parameter in the database creation statement.

You can switch the undo tablespace when you think it is necessary by simply using the following *alter system* command:

```
SQL> ALTER SYSTEM SET UNDO_TABLESPACE = undotbs_11;
```

In the example, you created the undo02 tablespace for undo. How about the undo segments? Who creates them? If you now look at the very end of your alert log (alertremorse.ora), as shown in Listing 8-1, you'll see the creation of undo segments.

Listing 8-1. The Alert Log Showing the Creation of the Undo Segments

```
Sun Dec 01 16:44:54 2002
create undo tablespace undo02
datafile 'C:\ORACLE9I\ORADATA\REMORSE\undotbs02.dbf' size 50M
Sun Dec 01   16:45:02 2002
Created Undo Segment _SYSSMU11$
Created Undo Segment _SYSSMU12$
Created Undo Segment _SYSSMU13$
Created Undo Segment _SYSSMU14$
Created Undo Segment _SYSSMU15$
Created Undo Segment _SYSSMU16$
Created Undo Segment _SYSSMU17$
Created Undo Segment _SYSSMU18$
Created Undo Segment _SYSSMU19$
Created Undo Segment _SYSSMU20$
Completed: create undo tablespace undo02
datafile 'C:\ORACLE9i
```

The undo segments you see in Listing 8-1 are structurally similar to the traditional rollback segments. The big difference, of course, is that Oracle will automatically create them and drop them as necessary. Oracle creates a predetermined number of undo segments when you create the undo tablespace, and it may bring all or some of them online when you start up the instance. Oracle will always try to assign each transaction its own undo segment, and it will create more undo segments if necessary based on the transactions in the database.

If the *undo_management* parameter is set to *auto* and you fail to create a specific undo tablespace for storing undo information, Oracle will still create undo records in a default tablespace called *undotbs* with a default size of around 200MB, as shown in Listing 8-2.

Listing 8-2. Querying the DBA_ROLLBACK_SEGS View

```
SQL>  select segment_name,tablespace_name from
  2* dba_rollback_segs;
SEGMENT_NAME            TABLESPACE_NAME
------------------------------ ------------------------------
   SYSTEM                      SYSTEM
_SYSSMU1$                      UNDOTBS
_SYSSMU2$                      UNDOTBS
_SYSSMU3$                      UNDOTBS
_SYSSMU4$                      UNDOTBS
_SYSSMU5$                      UNDOTBS
_SYSSMU6$                      UNDOTBS
_SYSSMU7$                      UNDOTBS
_SYSSMU8$                      UNDOTBS
_SYSSMU9$                      UNDOTBS
_SYSSMU10$                     UNDOTBS
11 rows selected
SQL>.
```

The following SQL script will tell you the location and size of the undo tablespace in your database:

```
SQL> select file_name,bytes
  2  from dba_data_files
  3  where tablespace_name='UNDOTBS';
FILE_NAME                 BYTES
C:\ORACLE9I\ORADATA\
REMORSE\UNDOTBS01.DBF     209715200
SQL>
```

You can add data files to undo tablespaces, drop or rename them, or take them offline or bring them online just as you would in the case of normal tablespaces.

Setting the Undo Retention Time Period

If transactions are long in nature, then there is a possibility of them being over-written by other, newer transactions and you could get an error message from the database indicating that the original "before image" of the transaction has been overwritten. The *committed* undo records can normally be written over by new transaction information. However, your long-running transaction may fail because the older images of data blocks it needs have been overwritten.
To prevent this, Oracle provides you a configuration parameter called the *undo_retention* parameter, which you can set to the interval you wish. For each undo extent in an undo segment, Oracle will determine if the difference between the current commit time and the last commit time is greater than the undo retention period. If it is, Oracle will mark the segment *expired*.

All other extents are marked *unexpired*, even though they may not have an active current transaction using them. Note that setting the *undo_retention* interval is *not a guarantee* that Oracle will always retain undo for at least that time period. If there is no free space left in the undo tablespace for a new transaction, Oracle will use an unexpired undo extent—a transaction can't be stopped, after all. Even though this is a last-resort event, be aware of this possibility. The key is to size the undo tablespace big enough so it can support your undo retention interval, thus helping Oracle retain undo for the specified period. You can set the undo retention size by specifying it in the initialization file as follows:

```
Undo_retention=500  -- (in seconds)
```

If you wish to change the amount of time the undo information should be retained by the database, you can dynamically change the *undo_retention* parameter in the following way:

```
SQL>alter system set undo_retention = 100;
SQL>
```

 TIP *You can avoid the familiar "snapshot too old" error in Oracle9i by choosing the appropriate* undo_retention *interval. Up until now, DBAs didn't have the option of determining how long Oracle retained undo information.*

There is no one ideal *undo_retention* time interval. The default is 900 seconds, and your retention time interval will depend on how long you estimate your longest transactions may run. Based on the information about the transaction length in your database, you can arrive at an approximate number to assign for the *undo_retention* parameter. The V$UNDOSTAT table provides an indicator for helping figure out the undo retention interval. Query the V$UNDOSTAT view as follows:

```
SQL> select max(maxquerylen) from v$undostat;
MAX(MAXQUERYLEN)
----------------
     210
```

The maxquerylen column of the V$UNDOSTAT view tells you what the length of the longest executed query was during the past 24 hours. Your *undo_retention* time parameter should at least be as large as the value provided by the max-querylen column. This will ensure that your longest transactions will have read consistency guaranteed through the use of the undo tablespace.

Oracle provides the following guidelines for setting the undo retention interval for a new database:

- OLTP: 15 minutes

- Mixed: 1 hour

- DSS: 3 hours

- For Flashback Query: 24 hours

Sizing the Undo Tablespace

There is one other size issue that you need to worry about besides the undo_retention parameter time period, and that is the question of how big your undo tablespace should be. Well, the answer depends on two things:

- How long is your undo_retention_time period?

- How many undo blocks are generated per time period in your system?

The V$UNDOSTAT table, among other things, is also very helpful in sizing your undo tablespace size. Here is a simple example of how to size the undo table-space:

```
Size of Undo tablespace = No. of undo Blocks * Undo_retention Period + overhead
So, if No. of undo Blocks (from V$undostat) = 780,
Undo_retention_period = 1440 seconds
Overhead = 4K (Derived by the formula AVG(undoblks/(10*60))
Size of  undo tablespace =  780 * 1440  * 4000 = 4,492,800,000  (4.49 Gigabytes).
```

You can also use OEM to help you figure out the right size of the undo tablespace for various undo retention periods. OEM's Undo Table Advisory will determine the space required for your undo tablespace based on average and peak level undo generation rates. Of course, as you increase your undo retention period in the Advisory, the recommended size of the undo tablespace will be larger. Figure 8-2 shows the OEM Undo Tablespace Advisory.

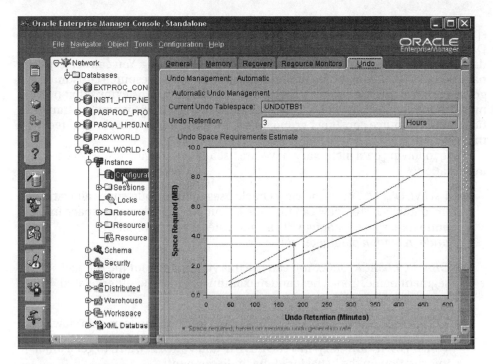

Figure 8-2. Using the OEM Undo Tablespace Advisory

Managing Undo Tablespaces

Managing undo tablespaces is similar to managing regular tablespaces in your database. You can add space to an undo tablespace by adding a data file, and you can decrease the size of an undo tablespace by reducing the size of the data file(s) in it using the *alter database datafile …resize* command. To drop an undo tablespace, you use the normal *drop tablespace* command. Thus, if you wish to switch undo tablespaces for some reason, you can drop the old one after you create the new undo tablespace.

Managing Undo Space Information

You can use the *show parameter undo* command in SQL*Plus to see what the configured options are for undo space management, as shown here:

```
SQL> show  parameter undo
NAME                                    TYPE         VALUE
--------------------------------------- ------------ ----------------------
undo_management                         string       AUTO
undo_retention                          integer      900
undo_suppress_errors                    boolean      FALSE
undo_tablespace                         string       UNDOTBS
SQL>
```

How do you prevent a single transaction from taking up most of the undo space, thus hindering new transactions from acquiring undo space? If you use the Database Resource Manager to create consumer groups (see Chapter 11) in your database, you can easily keep such an event from happening. You can set a special parameter called *undo_pool* to limit the maximum undo a resource consumer group can use. Once this *undo_pool* limit is reached, any transactions that need more undo room will error out. Only after some of the currently running transactions in the resource consumer group finish can more undo space be granted to that group.

The following data dictionary views are useful in managing undo space information:

- *V$UNDOSTAT:* This is the view Oracle uses to tune undo space allocation in the database. This view can indicate if your current allocation space in the undo tablespace is enough. It also indicates if you have set the *undo_retention* parameter correctly.

- *DBA_ROLLBACK_SEGS:* You can use this view to find out the rollback segment name, initial, next and maximum extents, and other related information.

- *V$TRANSACTION:* You can get transaction information from this view.

- *V$ROLLSTAT:* You can join V$ROLLSTAT and V$ROLLNAME to get a lot of information on the behavior of the undo segments.

- *DBA_UNDO_EXTENTS:* This view provides you with detailed information on the undo extents within the undo tablespace.

Querying Old Data with Oracle Flashback

It is common for an application to need older data for analysis purposes. A company's sales force, for example, may need older sales data but find that it has been modified already. Even more important, sometimes a user error or faulty application code may force the restoration of older data. Right now, the most common way to go back in time is by the DBA performing a laborious and time-consuming point-in-time database recovery, which may involve some disruption in service and a loss of critical business data. The Oracle9*i* Flashback Query feature provides you an easy way to query data at a point in time.

Oracle provides a special package called DBMS_FLASHBACK that enables you to execute your application on a chosen version of the database. The package allows you to see a consistent version of the database at a time (or SCN) that you specify. Note that manual undo management doesn't allow you to use the Flashback Query feature; instead, you must use AUM. This is one more good reason for using the option if you aren't convinced already.

The ability to see unsaved, old data enables you to query the database for some highly useful types of information. For example, you can write queries that give you the number of new customer accounts created during the last 2 hours by using two instances of the same table from two different time periods. You can also see the running totals for transactions from a past period using this feature. In addition, you can develop reports from two different sets of data. Although it provides all this new functionality, the Flashback Query feature makes it unnecessary for the application to store some time-based data separately.

Using the Flashback Query feature, users can re-create table rows they deleted accidentally. You can choose the older version of the database based either on the SCN or on a specific time in the past. Behind the scenes, Oracle simply creates a snapshot of how the database was at the specified time period or SCN using the undo space. Remember that Oracle's version-based read consistency mechanism saves older images of data in undo segments before any modifications are made. When a user rolls back a statement, for example, Oracle uses the undo information to re-create the original data. Oracle uses the same undo segments to support the Flashback Query feature. Oracle uses the undo segments to create an image of the table data that existed at an earlier point in time.

The Flashback Query feature is amazingly flexible, and it provides you several ways to access older data stored in the undo segments. The Flashback Query feature enables you to

- See deleted rows

- Replace current column values with older values

- Select the difference between two times

Use the DBMS_FLASHBACK package to execute a Flashback Query. You can also execute a Flashback Query using the *as of* clause of a *select* statement instead of using the DBMS_FLASHBACK package.

Use a Flashback Query inside an *insert table as select* or a *create table as select* statement to restore past data.

You have complete control over how far back data can be queried by using the *undo_retention* initialization parameter. Of course, your undo tablespace should be sized large enough so it can store all the undo information for the time specified by the *undo_retention* parameter. As you saw in the previous section, the parameter *undo_retention_time* specifies how long Oracle will retain undo information. So, the period the Flashback Query can go back in time is based on the *undo_retention_time* parameter specified for your undo records.

In essence, the Flashback Query feature gives you a sort of versioning capability with which you can query the database as of a specific point in time. You can generate this new version of the database based on either time or the SCN. The use of the SCN gives you pinpoint control over the transactions you want to start with. If you can't be precise, you can always choose a system time point, and Oracle will flash back to a SCN that occurred within 5 minutes of the specified system time. The SMON process takes the system time you specify and converts it into the closest SCN number.

NOTE *The Flashback Query functionality only applies to DML transactions; it doesn't apply to DDL transactions. The data retrieved is for read-only purposes only. Similarly, packages, procedures, and functions don't come under the umbrella of the Flashback Query functionality.*

Implementing Flashback Query

The Flashback Query methodology depends on Oracle's undo management functionality. Before you can invoke the Flashback Query feature, make sure you have the following things configured:

- Your database should be running in the automatic undo space management mode. This means that your undo space tablespace should be assigned already, and the init.ora undo space management parameter should be set to *auto*.

- The *undo_retention* parameter should be set to an hour, because that is how far you want to go back in your database to get old data. The following command will set the *undo_retention* interval to an hour:

```
SQL> Alter system set undo_retention = 3600 ;
```

Next, set up a test table to illustrate the use of the Flashback Query feature. The test table is named test_emp.

```
SQL> create table test_emp
  2  (
  3  employee_no        number(5) primary key,
  4  employee_name      varchar2(30),
  5  employee_manager   number(5),
  6  salary             number,
  7  hiredate           date
  8* )
SQL> /
Table created.
```

Insert some values into your test table as follows:

```
SQL> insert into test_emp values (34234,'sam alapati',88888,50000,sysdate);
1 row created.
SQL> insert into test_emp values (34235,'rob page'
,88888,50000,sysdate);
1 row created.
SQL> insert into test_emp values (34236,'lance parkes',88888,50000,sysdate);
1 row created.
SQL> insert into test_emp values (34237,'mark potts'
,88888,50000,sysdate);
1 row created.
SQL> insert into test_emp values (34238,'stan galbraith',88888,50000,sysdate);
1 row created.SQL> commit;
Commit complete.
SQL>
```

Execute the following query to ensure that the table has all five rows that you just inserted:

```
SQL> select * from test_emp;
EMPLOYEE_NO EMPLOYEE   EMPLOYEE     SALARY    HIREDATE
            NAME       MANAGER
----------- ------------------------------- ----------
34234   sam_alapati    88888        50000     11-DEC-02
34235   rob page       88888        50000     11-DEC-02
34236   lance parkes   88888        50000     11-DEC-02
34237   mark potts     88888        50000     11-DEC-02
34238   stan galbraith 88888        50000     11-DEC-02
SQL>Now, go ahead and delete 2 rows from our table and verify the deletion:
SQL> delete  from test_emp
  2* where employee_name in ('sam_alapati','rob page')
SQL> /
2 rows deleted.
SQL> commit;
Commit complete.
SQL> select * from test_emp;
EMPLOYEE  EMPLOYEE       EMPLOYEE    SALARY   HIREDATE
NO        NAME           MANAGER              _
--------- ------------------------------- ----------------- ---------- --------
34236   lance parkes    88888        50000     11-DEC-02
34237   mark potts      88888        50000     11-DEC-02
34238   stan galbraith  88888        50000     11-DEC-02

SQL>
```

You can implement the Flashback Query feature by using the DBMS_FLASHBACK package. You can also implement it by using the as of time-stamp construct. In the following sections you'll explore how you can implement the Flashback Query feature with both these methods.

Flashback Using the DBMS_FLASHBACK Package

Say you want to retrieve a deleted employee's information in order to run some query pertaining to the employee. You can specify either a timestamp or an SCN number as the starting point for your Flashback Query. In the example that follows, you'll see how you can query for the number of rows that existed in a table before they were deleted permanently (committed) from the test table. First, invoke the DBMS_FLASHBACK package as follows to perform your query:

```
SQL>  execute dbms_flashback.enable_at_time(TO_TIMESTAMP '11-DEC-2002:10:00:00',
- 'DD-MON-YYYY:hh24:MI:SS'));
PL/SQL procedure successfully completed.
```

Now that you enabled the Flashback Query, you can go back to a time in the past, 10:00 A.M. in this case. Execute the following query:

```
SQL> select * from test_emp;
  COUNT(*)
       5
SQL> execute dbms_flashback.disable();
PL/SQL procedure successfully completed.
SQL>
```

Enabling the Flashback Query feature in the preceding example allowed you to see how many rows were in the table at a time in the past. You found out from your simple query that the table test_emp had five rows at some time in the recent past (that you specified) and not the three rows it's currently showing. You can use cursors to retrieve the accidentally deleted data and insert it into the test_emp table. In Chapter 15, you'll see detailed examples of how to use the Flashback Query feature to perform effortless recovery of old data, without resorting to complex measures such as tablespace point-in-time recovery.

Flashback Using the As Of Clause

Note that using the DBMS_FLASHBACK package isn't the only way to generate and use flashback information. You can use the *as of* clause of the *select* statement to see and use data from a past point in time, without ever using the DBMS_FLASHBACK package. Using the *as of* clause gives you flexibility because you can use this technique in joins, views, and subqueries. The *as of* technique also lets you incorporate Flashback Queries in *insert* statements.

A user needs to have the privilege to issue a Flashback Query on a table if the user isn't the owner of the table. Note that you don't need this privilege to execute the DBMS_FLASHBACK package or any of its component procedures. Here's how the DBA can grant the object privileges to enable a user to issue Flashback Queries:

```
SQL> grant flashback on salapati.test_emp to tester
Grant succeeded.
OR,
SQL> grant flashback any table to tester;
Grant succeeded.
SQL>
```

 NOTE *You can grant the Flashback Query object privilege (e.g.,* grant flashback any table*) on a table, view, or a materialized view.*

Let's look at a simple demonstration using the *as of* clause that shows the power of the Flashback Query feature. Recall that in the previous example, two of the five rows in table test_emp were permanently deleted from the table. You now realize you removed the two employees by mistake a few minutes ago (it could be a few hours ago or a few days ago, in practice). How do you go about retrieving the accidentally deleted employee information? Very easily, as you'll see shortly. Let's say you realized soon after your deletes that you might have made a mistake. The following query will let you see the data in the table from a time in the past (5 minutes ago, in this case):

```
SQL> select * from test_emp
  2  AS OF TIMESTAMP sysdate - 5/1440;
EMP_ EMP_NAME    EMP_       SALARY HIREDATE
--NO--------- ---------Manager-------------------- ----------
34234 sam_alapati        88888      50000 11-DEC-02
34235 rob page           88888      50000 11-DEC-02
34236 lance parkes       88888      50000 11-DEC-02
34237 mark potts         88888      50000 11-DEC-02
34238 stan galbraith     88888      50000 11-DEC-02
SQL>
```

If this is a table in which the user is the only person in charge of modifying data, then the following *create tables as select * from* (CTAS) command will help you get all the deleted rows back quickly. Otherwise, you can use an *insert* command to reinsert the accidentally deleted data into the test_emp table. If you use the CTAS method, you will follow these steps:

1. Create a new table, new_test_emp, from the old test_emp table, which you can select from, thanks to the Flashback Query feature:

    ```
    SQL> create table new_test_emp as
         select * from test_emp AS OF timestamp
    2            sysdate - 5/1440; /* 5 minutes ago */
    Table created.
    SQL> select * from new_test_emp;
    EMP_ EMP_NAME        EMP_       SALARY HIREDATE
    NO--------- ---Manager-------------------- ----------
    34234 sam_alapati    88888      50000 11-DEC-02
    34235 rob page       88888      50000 11-DEC-02
    34236 lance parkes   88888      50000 11-DEC-02
    34237 mark potts     88888      50000 11-DEC-02
    34238 stan galbraith 88888      50000 11-DEC-02
    SQL>
    ```

2. Now drop the current test_emp table and rename the new_test_emp table to test_emp. You have all your original data in the test_emp table.

    ```
    SQL> drop table test_emp;
    Table dropped.
    SQL>
    SQL> rename new_test_emp to test_emp;
    Table renamed.
    SQL>
    ```

The great benefit of using the Flashback Query feature is that it enables you to read committed data from a previous time, if necessary. You can use the Flashback Query capability to correct errors and compare current table data with the data that existed at a previous point in time, essentially enabling you compare different versions of the same table. Oracle allows you to go back as far as 5 days using the Flashback Query feature. You can recover lost or wrongly deleted data using this method very easily. You can recover lost data using other methods, as you will see in Chapter 15. However, the Flashback Query feature gives you a chance to just analyze or verify old data, even in cases where you are not interested in restoring old data.

Discrete Transactions

To enhance the speed of transactions, Oracle enables the explicit use of *discrete transactions*. When you specify a transaction as a discrete transaction, Oracle skips certain routine processing overhead such as writing the undo records, thereby speeding up the transaction. Oracle doesn't modify the data blocks until the transaction commits.

You use the *begin_discrete_transaction* procedure supplied by Oracle to implement the discrete transaction strategy. Short transactions run faster when you use this procedure. However, if discrete transactions occur during the course of long queries, there could be problems if the queries request data modified by the discrete transactions. Because discrete transactions skip the undo writing process, it isn't possible for the long-running query to get a consistent view of the data. Why doesn't a discrete transaction need to record undo data? Oracle doesn't generate undo records for discrete transactions because the data blocks aren't modified until the discrete transaction commits.

NOTE *Discrete transaction management doesn't imply the elimination of redo information. Oracle doesn't write the redo information to the redo log buffers—it writes it straight to the redo logs after the transactions commit. Oracle applies the changes to the database blocks directly, thus saving time.*

Autonomous Transactions

A transaction could run as part of another transaction. In such cases, the parent transaction is called the *main* transaction and the independent child transaction is called the *autonomous* transaction. An autonomous transaction is formally defined as an independent transaction that can be called from another transaction. Notice that although the child transaction is called from the parent transaction, it is independent of the parent transaction. Packages, procedures, functions, and triggers could all include transactions marked as autonomous. You have to include a directive in the main transaction so Oracle will know you intend to use an autonomous transaction within the main transaction. The autonomous transaction can have its own *rollback* and *commit* statements just like normal transactions. The main transaction, by using an autonomous transaction, can pause its transactions, execute the autonomous transaction, and continue from where it stopped. In other words, you leave the calling transaction context, execute SQL statements that are part of the autonomous transaction, either commit or roll back your transaction, and resume the parent transaction upon returning to the calling transaction's context. Note that the autonomous transaction does not share transaction resources such as locks with the parent transaction.

Autonomous transactions provide developers with the ability to create more fine-grained transactions, where a transaction will not be an all-or-nothing affair. You can have the nested autonomous transactions commit or roll back their transactions independent of the calling parent transaction.

NOTE *If you don't use an autonomous transaction, all the changes in your session will be committed or rolled back at once (when you issue a* commit *or* rollback *statement). The autonomous transactions give you the ability to commit or roll back the subprogram's changes independent of the main program. Also note that if you don't commit or roll back an autonomous transaction, Oracle will issue an error message.*

Listing 8-3 shows provides a simple example of an autonomous transaction. Note that the *pragma* (a compiler directive) *autonomous transaction* statement is instructing Oracle to mark the attached piece of code, the function Loans, as autonomous.

Listing 8-3. A Simple Autonomous Transaction

```
CREATE OR REPLACE PACKAGE Lending AS
    FUNCTION Loans (User_id INTEGER) RETURN REAL;
    -- add additional functions and/or packages
END Banking;
CREATE OR REPLACE PACKAGE BODY Lending AS
    FUNCTION Loans (User_id INTEGER) RETURN REAL IS
        PRAGMA AUTONOMOUS_TRANSACTION;
        Loan_bal REAL;
    BEGIN
        --the code goes here
    END;
    -- any additional functions and/or packages go here
END Lending;
```

Autonomous transactions provide you with a lot of flexibility. You can suspend the main transaction, run the autonomous transaction, and resume the processing of the main transaction. The autonomous transaction's committed changes are visible to the main transaction, because the default isolation level in Oracle is read committed, meaning a transaction will see all the committed data. There can be many uses for autonomous transactions—for example, you can use the transactions to send error logging messages. You can have a single procedure that will write error messages to an error log table and invoke this procedure as an autonomous transaction from the usual transaction processing procedures. Listing 8-4 shows how to write error messages to a table.

Listing 8-4. Writing Error Messages to a Table

```
Procedure error_log(error__msg in varchar2,
     Procedure_name  in varchar2)
is
   PRAGMA AUTONOMOUS_TRANSACTION;
   Begin
       Insert into log_table (error_msg, procedure_name, …)
       Values (error_msg, procedure_name));
       Commit;
   Exception
    When others then rollback;   …
   end;
END;
```

Autonomous transactions can serve purposes in the Oracle9*i* database, including enabling the handling of nonstandard PL/SQL coding issues such as using DDL statements in triggers. Autonomous transactions also are useful in performing an audit of database queries and failed (unauthorized) database activity. For example, Listing 8-5 shows how you can use the autonomous transaction feature to audit (presumably) unauthorized update activity. Even when a user is unsuccessful in the update attempt, the user's name can be successfully logged into an audit table if you code a simple pair of triggers that use the autonomous transaction feature.

Listing 8-5. Using an Autonomous Transaction to Audit Database Activity

```
SQL> create or replace trigger audit_trig
Before insert on employees for each row
Declare
 PRAGMA AUTONOMOUS TRANSACTION
Begin
Insert into audit_employee values (
  :new.username, 'before insert', sysdate);
 commit;
end;
SQL> create or replace trigger audit_trig
After insert on employees for each row
Declare
 PRAGMA AUTONOMOUS TRANSACTION
Begin
Insert into audit_employee values (
  :new.username, 'after insert', sysdate);
 commit;
end;
SQL>
```

Note that you can't always use just a pair of normal triggers to audit database activity. This is because auditing data provided by the triggers won't be recorded if the triggering statement is rolled back.

Resumable Storage Allocation

Imagine you're running a very long batch job and it runs out of space for some reason, whether as the result of an unexpected amount of data or just a failure to notice that the space was running out for the objects involved in the DML transactions. Or, you could have programs aborting in midstream for other reasons, such as the "maximum number of extents reached" error. What are your options when this sort of thing happens (as it inevitably will)?

Most of the time, the procedure involves correcting the space or other condition that caused the problem in the first place and then restarting your transactions. More often than not, you will roll back the whole operation, which will take up quite a bit of time. Sometimes, you have to start at the very beginning of the program all over again, which is a waste of time. In any case, your actions as a DBA are limited to playing catch up after the fact to rectify the error and redo the operation. The Resumable Space Allocation feature will come in handy when you're trying to ensure that key batch jobs or data loads run within the window of operation they are allotted when they encounter space-related issues.

NOTE *To take full advantage of the Resumable Space Allocation feature, you should be using locally managed tablespaces coupled with the Automatic Undo Management option.*

You can choose to use the Resumable Space Allocation feature to avoid the time-consuming rerunning and or rolling back of entire operations. You can explicitly make operations run in the Resumable Space Allocation mode by using the *alter session* command. The Resumable Space Allocation will just suspend operations until the problem is fixed (say, by you going in and adding a data file to extend space) and resume automatically after that.

Resumable Operations

Unfortunately, you can't resume every type of operation when space-related errors stop them from completing. The following types of database operations are resumable:

- *Queries:* These operations can always be resumed after they run out of temporary space needed for sorting.

- *DML operations:* Insert, update, and delete operations can be resumed after an error is issued.

- *DDL operations:* Index operations involving creating, rebuilding, and altering as well as the *create table as select* operations are resumable, in addition to several other DDL operations.

- *Import and export operations:* Resumable Space Allocation will suspend imports when the target tablespace runs out of room.

Common Resumable Errors

You can resume operations after fixing any of the following types of errors during the execution of any operation:

- *Out of space errors:* Typically, operations fail when you can't add space to your tables or indexes by adding extents because the tablespace is full. You need to add a data file to your tablespace to enable the objects to throw a new extent and continue to grow. The typical error message is ORA-01653.

- *Maximum extents errors:* When the table or a rollback segment reaches the maximum extents specified, it can't grow any further, even if you have space in the tablespace. You end up with errors such as ORA-01628.

- *User's space quota–related errors:* If the user's quota on a tablespace is exceeded, your operations on that tablespace will come to a halt. The typical Oracle error is ORA-01536.

Using the Resumable Space Allocation Feature

To use the Resumable Space Allocation feature, first ensure that the user who needs to use the Resumable Space Allocation feature has the appropriate privileges:

```
SQL> grant resumable to salapati;
Grant succeeded.
SQL>
When you wish to revoke the privilege, use the following command:
SQL> revoke resumable from salapati;
Revoke succeeded.
SQL>
```

Next, ensure that the *timeout* parameter is set correctly for the resumable operations. The *timeout* parameter gives you a time interval within which you need to fix the problem that caused the operation to suspend. If you don't respond within the allotted time interval, the program will error out with the ORA-30032 error ("the statement has timed out") and you can't resume it from where it stopped initially. In the following example, the *timeout* parameter is set to 18,000 seconds, which is equal to 5 hours. The Oracle default timeout is set for 7,200 seconds. If you think you don't want to change the default timeout period, all you have to do is issue the simpler *alter session enable resumable* command.

```
SQL> alter session enable resumable timeout 18000;
Session altered.
SQL>
```

You can also set the timeout interval in the following manner. The first number in the parentheses, 7, is the SID of the session, which you can get from looking at the V$SESSION table. You can omit the SID if you're setting the timeout for the current session only.

```
SQL> execute dbms_resumable.set_session_timeout(7,18000);
PL/SQL procedure successfully completed.
SQL>
```

You can then *name* the operation you want to make resumable if it encounters any of the space problems you saw earlier:

```
SQL>  alter session enable resumable
  2* name 'test of resumable space'
SQL> /
Session altered.
SQL>
```

The *name* parameter is optional and you want to give it a meaningful name to help track the operation later on. The *name* parameter has no real operational significance otherwise.

CAUTION *If an operation is suspended, any locks that are held by Oracle on various database objects will not be released automatically. The locks and other resources will be released only after the transaction either completes successfully upon resumption or ends after throwing an exception (if you set the DBMS_RESUMABLE.abort procedure).*

Notification of Suspended Operations

Once the Resumable Space Allocation mode is in place, any space-related problems will cause the operation to be suspended rather than aborted. Upon suspension, Oracle will automatically generate an AFTER SUSPEND event. You can write a trigger that will be automatically set off by this event if you want to be notified, as shown in Listing 8-6. (Note that the trigger must always be declared as an autonomous transaction.)

Listing 8-6. Sending Notifications of Suspended Operations

```
SQL> l
  1   create or replace trigger page_dba
  2   after suspend on database
  3   declare
  4   pragma autonomous_transaction;
  5   begin
  6   /* Page the DBA */
  7   commit;
  8*  end;
SQL> /
Trigger created.
SQL>
```

Monitoring Resumable Space Allocation

You can monitor Resumable Space Allocation by using the data dictionary view DBA_RESUMABLE. The DBA_RESUMABLE view provides the name of the operation, the user's SID, the start time of the statement, the error message encountered, the suspend time and the resume time, and the text and current status of the SQL statement(s). The DBMS_RESUMABLE package contains procedures to help you manage suspended sessions. The *set_session_timeout* procedure, for example, allows you to specify the time a suspended session will wait before failing.

Managing Long Transactions

Suppose you're running transactions in your database that are extremely long, maybe even as long as a whole day. How does Oracle manage this sort of transaction? Well, it manages it the same way it manages any regular short-lived transaction. It uses locks as the primary weapon to ensure concurrency and atomicity. Locks on a long-running transaction can reduce concurrency dramatically because the other users are forced to wait for the long-running transaction to complete. Long transactions could take many hours sometimes to complete. Clearly, any locking method will cause severe concurrency problems.

Fortunately, Oracle provides the Workspace Manager, a feature you can use to version-enable tables, so different users can maintain different versions of the data. During long-running transactions, changes are made to the same table in different workspaces and are finally reconciled and the results stored permanently in the original table. You can think of a *workspace* as a virtual environment shared by several users making changes to the same data. In addition to facilitating long transactions, the Workspace Manager enables you to create multiple data scenarios for what-if analyses. The Workspace Manager also helps you to track the history of all the changes to a set of tables you're interested in tracking. The feature is especially useful in collaborative projects because it allows teams to share content.

The Workspace Manager enables simultaneous read and write access to production data during long transactions. The goals of concurrency and consistency are served by the Workspace Manager. The long-running transaction will be implemented with the help of other short-term transactions and multiple versions of tables, thus enabling concurrency. Consistency is guaranteed because the final, permanent version will not have any conflicts within the data. All the users see their own virtual version of the database—that is, different versions of the rows in the same tables. But the versions each user sees from his or her workspace are guaranteed to be transactionally consistent; the user's versions will have the original data the user started with plus all the changes he or she made to the original data.

Benefits of Using the Workspace Manager

As mentioned previously, besides helping improve concurrency during long-term transactions, the Workspace Manager enables you to try out various scenarios (e.g., different marketing campaigns) before you finally settle on one acceptable version of data that you can make permanent by merging all the virtual versions of the table data. Merging, in effect, incorporates the child workspace data with the original (parent workspace) data. If, after analysis, you decide to nullify all the workspace data, you can do so by rolling it back, just like you would roll back a transaction under normal circumstances.

NOTE *Although the Workspace Manager provides you with the capability to create multiple versions of one table, or even all the tables in your database, it doesn't impose a severe storage cost, because only the changed rows in each workspace are versioned, and these new versions are saved in the original table (and the original tablespace). In other words, you don't need to make any special storage allocations for the database tables that belong to different versions.*

Here's a brief summary of the features provided by the Workspace Manager:

- The Workspace Manager is implemented as a series of short transactions.

- You can maintain multiple versions of data, which you can keep or discard as necessary.

- Multiple users can simultaneously access and modify the same data.

- The updates made by several users over time are isolated in workspaces until they're merged into the production database.

- Conflicts between multiple versions are resolved automatically by the Workspace Manager.

Table Versioning and Workspaces

The concepts of *table versioning* and *workspaces* are the foundations of the Workspace Manager feature. Table versioning enables you to have different sets of rows sharing the same table name. The amazing thing about table versioning is that users can continue to change data through DML operations on a day-to-day basis. The Workspace Manager maintains the structure of the versioned tables using views based on the original production table. This ability to version-enable even production tables makes the Workspace Manager very powerful in performing what-if analyses. You can use the tables WM$VERSIONED_TABLES and WM$VERSION_TABLE to find out details about the versioned tables. The WMSYS schema owns both of these tables, so first make sure that you have the WMSYS schema in your database.

Workspaces enable users to make changes to multiple versions of a table. The workspaces isolate the versioned tables until they're finally discarded or merged with the original table. This ability of the workspaces to save the versioned tables means that access to the tables involved isn't impeded. Each workspace can be assigned to one or several users and they can see a consistent view of the database, including the rows in their versions of the tables in the workspace, plus all the other tables at the time the workspaces were either created or refreshed, whichever one comes later.

Workspaces help manage updates for multiple projects that are part of a master project. They are excellent for creating multiple scenarios and projections so you can perform what-if analyses. All updates made by users of a workspace affect only their own version of the tables. Thus, workspaces provide you the ability to enable several users to work on the *same rows* of a table concurrently. Note that when versioned tables are created in a database, the original table is renamed tableName_LT. Oracle also creates a new table called table_Name_AUX and a view with an identical name as the original table. When users log in, they are placed by default in the *LIVE* workspace. All other workspaces that exist in the database are children of the LIVE workspace. Whenever you refresh your workspace, you can see the latest changes made in the parent workspace, which also include any changes merged from other child workspaces. The merging of a workspace with the parent LIVE tablespace makes the changes in the child workspace public. The *merge* statement follows the resolution of any conflicts.

Installing the Workspace Manager

The Workspace Manager feature is provided with the Oracle9.2 version software, but the feature won't be automatically installed in a database that you create manually. If you use the DBCA to create a new database, you let Oracle create a seed database as part of the Oracle software installation, and the Workspace Manager feature is automatically installed. An easy way to find out if the Workspace Manager is already installed is to look for the user WMSYS using the DBA_USERS view. WMSYS is the user that owns the Workspace Manager tables, and if the user is already there, you can skip the rest of this section and go on to using the feature. You'll need to perform the following steps to install the Oracle Workspace Manager in your database:

1. First, go the $ORACLE_HOME/rdbms/admin directory:

   ```
   $ cd  $ORACLE_HOME/rdbms/admin
   ```

2. Log in as the user SYS:

   ```
   SQL> connect sys/username as sysdba;
   ```

3. Run the following script, which will install the entire WMSYS schema:

   ```
   SQL> @owminst.plb
   ```

4. Verify that the Workspace Manager schema owner WMSYS has been created, and change the account status of this user by using the following statements:

```
SQL> select username,account_status from
2*     dba_users where username like '%WM%';
USERNAME                    ACCOUNT_STATUS
WMSYS                       EXPIRED & LOCKED
SQL> alter user wmsys account unlock;
User altered.
SQL> alter user wmsys identified by wmsys1;
User altered.
SQL>
```

Privileges Needed to Use the Workspace Manager

To enable users to implement the Workspace Manager's features, you need to grant them certain special privileges. The DBA is automatically granted the privilege Wm_Admin_Role, which includes all the Workspace Manager privileges. You can grant individual users either this role or, if you want to be more careful, specific components of the Wm_Admin_Role privilege. You can specifically grant users Workspace Manager privileges such as the following:

- *Create_Workspace:* Enables users to create a child workspace

- *Remove_Workspace:* Enables users to remove a specified workspace

- *Access_Workspace:* Grants users the right to go to a specified workspace

- *Merge_Workspace:* Allows users to merge the child workspace with the parent workspace

- *Rollback_Workspace:* Allows users to undo the changes in a specified workspace

The following is a simple example to demonstrate the use of the Workspace Manager. You invoke and manage the Workspace Manager with the Oracle package DBMS_WM. You execute various PL/SQL procedures from this package to manage the Workspace Manager facility. By default, all users are placed in the topmost workspace, the LIVE workspace.

You can create a hierarchy of workspaces underneath the LIVE database workspace. After you create your own workspaces, you can enter the workspace by using the *gotoworkspace* procedure from the DBMS_WM package and make your changes. Later on, you can choose to merge or rescind the changes you made in your workspace.

Granting the Workspace User the Necessary Privileges

The first thing you have to do is grant the user—in this case, salapati—the necessary privileges. You do this with the following code:

```
SQL> execute dbms_wm.GrantSystemPriv('ACCESS_ANY_WORKSPACE,-
 MERGE_ANY_WORKSPACE,-CREATE_ANY_WORKSPACE,-
 REMOVE_ANY_WORKSPACE,-
 ROLLBACK_ANY_WORKSPACE','salapati','YES');
PL/SQL procedure successfully completed.
SQL>
```

Note that you could have given all the preceding privileges (and more) with the following grant:

```
SQL> grant wm_admin_role to salapati;
Grant succeeded.
```

Invoking the DBMS_WM Package

The next step is to create a table you want to use with the Workspace Manager, and version-enable the table by invoking the DBMS_WM package. In order for a table to be eligible for version enabling, the table must have a primary key and it must not be owned by the user SYS. Any user can version-enable a table in his or her schema, and any user with the Wm_Admin_Role can also do so. By using the *history* option while you create the versioned tables, you can choose to record all changes or just the latest changes made to a version-enabled table. The *history* option also allows you to create a timestamped copy of the table for each change or just one table incorporating the latest changes.

The following example shows how to create a versioned table using the DBMS_WM package. When changes to the version-enabled table are completed, you can disable versioning using the same package.

```
SQL> create table foreign_aid
  2  (country_id          char(2) primary key,
  3  country_name        varchar2(40),
  4  region_id           number,
  5  foreign_aid         number
  6  );
Table created.
SQL> EXECUTE DBMS_WM.EnableVersioning ('foreign_aid','VIEW_WO_OVERWRITE');
PL/SQL procedure successfully completed.
SQL>
```

Inserting Test Values

After you create the table for the Workspace Manager and version it, you need to populate the table. The following SQL statements insert some test values into the table foreign_aid:

```
SQL> insert into foreign_aid values (21,'republic of China',3,430000000);
1 row created.
SQL> insert into foreign_aid values (22,'Mongolia',4,1000000);
1 row created.
SQL> insert into foreign_aid values (23,'republic of Vietnam',3,30000000);
1 row created.
SQL> insert into foreign_aid values (24,'Bulgaria',3,2000000);
1 row created.
SQL> commit;
Commit complete.
SQL>
```

Creating Workspaces

In this step, you'll create a couple of sample workspaces. Name the first one state_dept and the second one defense_dept.

```
SQL> EXECUTE DBMS_WM.CreateWorkspace ('state_dept');
PL/SQL procedure successfully completed.
SQL> EXECUTE DBMS_WM.CreateWorkspace ('defense_dept');
PL/SQL procedure successfully completed.
SQL>
```

After you create the workspaces, go to the first workspace (state_dept), modify the row values of your versioned table foreign_aid, and save the changes, as shown in Listing 8-7.

Listing 8-7. Modifying Table Values Using the First Workspace

```
SQL> EXECUTE DBMS_WM.GotoWorkspace('state_dept');
PL/SQL procedure successfully completed.
SQL> update foreign_aid
  2  set foreign_aid='50000000'
  3  where country_name in ('Bulgaria','Mongolia');
2 rows updated.
SQL> commit;
Commit complete.
SQL> select * from foreign_aid;
CO COUNTRY_NAME          REGION_ID          FOREIGN_AID
-- ------------------------------------- ---------- -----------
21 republic of China       3                430000000
22 Mongolia                4                 50000000
23 republic of Vietnam     3                 30000000
24 Bulgaria                3                 50000000
```

Freeze the changes in the workspace you are currently in, state_dept. To do this successfully, first you have to move to the parent workspace, the LIVE workspace.

```
SQL> EXECUTE DBMS_WM.GotoWorkspace ('LIVE');
PL/SQL procedure successfully completed.
SQL> EXECUTE DBMS_WM.FreezeWorkspace('state_dept');
PL/SQL procedure successfully completed.
SQL>
```

Using the second workspace, defense_dept, again modify some other values in the versioned table foreign_aid, and save the changes. Listing 8-8 shows how to do this.

Listing 8-8. Modifying Table Values Using the Second Workspace

```
SQL> EXECUTE DBMS_WM.GotoWorkspace('defense_dept');
PL/SQL procedure successfully completed.
SQL> update foreign_aid
  2  set foreign_aid=0
  3  where country_name in ('Bulgaria','Mongolia');
2 rows updated.
SQL> commit;
Commit complete.
SQL> select * from foreign_aid;
CO COUNTRY_NAME       REGION_ID    FOREIGN_AID
-- ----------------------------------------- ---------- -----------
21 republic of China      3        430000000
22 Mongolia               4        0
23 republic of Vietnam    3        30000000
24 Bulgaria               3        0
SQL>
```

Again, go back to the LIVE workspace and freeze the workspace defense_dept:

```
SQL> EXECUTE DBMS_WM.GotoWorkspace ('LIVE');
PL/SQL procedure successfully completed.
SQL> EXECUTE DBMS_WM.GotoWorkspace ('defense_dept');
PL/SQL procedure successfully completed.
SQL>
```

Suppose there is a tussle between the State Department and Defense Department as to what the size of foreign aid for some countries should be. Let's assume the State Department won the battle, and the government wants to *finalize* foreign_aid according to the State Department's figures (state_dept workspace). Merging a workspace will make the data in its versioned tables (all rows in a table or only some, according to the need) part of the real table in the production database. You need to first remove the other workspace, defense_dept, and then merge the state_dept workspace with the original data, as shown in Listing 8-9.

Listing 8-9. Merging the Workspaces

```
SQL> EXECUTE DBMS_WM.GotoWorkspace ('LIVE');
PL/SQL procedure successfully completed.
SQL> EXECUTE DBMS_WM.UnfreezeWorkspace ('defense_dept')
PL/SQL procedure successfully completed.
SQL> EXECUTE DBMS_WM.RemoveWorkspace ('defense_dept');
PL/SQL procedure successfully completed.
SQL> EXECUTE DBMS_WM.MergeWorkspace ('state_dept');
PL/SQL procedure successfully completed.
SQL> select * from foreign_aid;
CO   COUNTRY_NAME          REGION_ID     FOREIGN_AID
--   ------------------------------------------------
21   Republic of China        3          430000000
23   Republic of Vietnam      3          30000000
22   Mongolia                 4          50000000
24   Bulgaria                 3          50000000
SQL>
```

NOTE *The final data in the table foreign_aid is the same as the data in the committed version of the workspace state_dept.*

Managing the Workspace Manager

Managing the Workspace Manager really means managing the workspaces that you created in the database. You have several data dictionary views you can consult to help manage the Workspace Manager, including DBA_WM_VER-SIONED_TABLES, DBA_WORKSPACES, and others. Here are a couple of examples of the usage of two of the key tables for helping managing workspaces:

```
SQL> select table_name,owner from dba_wm_versioned_tables
/
TABLE_NAME                      OWNER
------------------------------  -------------------
FOREIGN_AID                     SALAPATI
SQL> l
  1 select workspace, parent_workspace,
  2 owner, createtime,freeze_status from
  3* dba_workspaces
SQL> /
WORKSPACE    PARENT      OWNER        CREATE        FREEZE
----------   WORKSPACE   -----------  TIME ---- --- STATUS----
state_dept   LIVE        SALAPATI     06-DEC-02     UNFROZEN
LIVE                     SYS                        UNFROZEN
SQL>
```

The easiest way to manage the workspaces, however, is through OEM. OEM lets you create and manage workspaces, as well as enable and disable table versioning. The OEM GUI tool is also effective in reconciling conflicts between child and parent workspaces.

Summary

This chapter focused on Oracle transaction management in detail. Oracle, as any RDBMS, adheres to a set of transaction isolation level standards, and it uses various techniques to enforce the isolation levels so that transactions can conform to serializable schedules. Oracle uses transaction-locking mechanisms and a multiversion concurrency control mechanism to maintain transaction concurrency. In this chapter you learned how Oracle uses various types of locking mechanisms to help the database implicitly control transactions and avoid conflicts among users seeking to use the same resources. The concept of undo tablespaces and undo records is an important part of Oracle transaction management, and this chapter covered the concepts of Automatic Undo Management (AUM) in detail. Because this book takes the stand that AUM is vastly superior to manual undo management, only the former type of undo management was discussed.

Newer concepts such as discrete transactions and autonomous transactions give developers and DBAs more control over transactions. In this chapter you learned how to use both transaction types. Nothing is more frustrating than an important batch job failing merely because you ran out of room on a disk drive. Oracle's new Resumable Space Allocation feature ensures that your transactions don't fail for simple space-related reasons. You can use this feature to provide yourself a safety cushion while running long transactions.

The autonomous transaction feature of Oracle9*i* was also illustrated in this chapter. The Oracle Flashback Query feature enables you to reclaim accidentally deleted data and perform what-if database analyses. You learned how to use the *as of* query clause to "see" old data and to recover it if necessary. In Chapter 15 you will find more complex examples of how you can use the Flashback Query facility to recover lost data. Features such as the Workspace Manager go a long way in helping Oracle9*i* DBAs support large-scale concurrent usage of databases, and this chapter introduced you to the use of this valuable tool.

Part Three

Database Creation, Connectivity, and User Management

CHAPTER 9

Creating an Oracle Database

IN THIS CHAPTER, you'll create a database from scratch. Oracle9*i* comes with a starter database in both Windows and UNIX versions, and it provides several templates for database creation, including the decision support systems (DSS) and online transaction processing (OLTP) templates. You can also invoke the Oracle Database Configuration Assistant (DBCA), a GUI tool, to guide you through the installation process.

Until you become very well versed in the installation of databases, however, you may be better off using the seemingly tedious but more flexible manual mode to create databases. You can type all your database creation commands in a script and simply execute the script. (I recommend that you manually type in the creation statements line by line rather than running a script; this will give you insight into the various steps involved and the potential problems at every stage.) Later on, you can just run the whole script to create other databases, or just use the DBCA, after you're completely comfortable with how the script works.

This chapter begins with a review of the steps you need to take before you start creating an Oracle database. These steps include ensuring that you have the right permissions, checking that the file structures are in place, and determining if you have enough memory and other resources allocated to your new database.

Next, the chapter provides a summary of all the important Oracle9*i* configuration (initialization) parameters, with guidelines for their use. One of the strong points of Oracle9*i* is that it allows DBAs to tune a high number of the internal parameters, so this is a valuable section.

This chapter also helps you determine the ideal configuration of the key parameters for your Oracle9*i* database. Databases can be geared primarily toward OLTP or DSS. The two types of databases have different requirements for configuration, and in general you should configure these databases differently.

You'll need to take several steps after you create a new database, and I explain these steps in detail in this chapter. These steps include running the necessary post–database creation scripts, changing the passwords, and configuring the database for archive logging. In this chapter I also introduce the SPFILE, a server-based alternative to the traditional Oracle init.ora configuration file, and show you how to create it. You'll see why the SPFILE is a superior choice as an initialization parameter file and how to implement it in your new database.

After you learn how to create a database, I discuss how to start and stop a database. You can stop a database in several ways, and you need to understand the implications of the alternative methods. You'll also learn how to restrict access to just the DBAs when necessary. Finally, you'll explore two new features, quiescing and suspending a database, which improve an Oracle9*i* DBA's ability to efficiently manage his or her databases.

Getting Ready to Create the Database

You can create a new database either manually (using scripts) or by using the Oracle Database Configuration Assistant (DBCA). DBCA is configured to appear immediately after the installation of the Oracle9*i* software to assist you in creating a database. You can also invoke DBCA later on to help you create a database.

DBCA has several benefits, including the provision of templates for creating DSS, OLTP, or hybrid databases. You can run the tool in an interactive or "silent" mode. The biggest benefit to using DBCA is that for DBAs with little experience, it lets Oracle set all the configuration parameters and start up a new database quickly without errors. Finally, DBCA also automatically creates all its file systems based on the highly utilitarian Oracle Flexible Architecture (OFA) standard.

DBCA is an excellent tool that will help you create a new database quickly without your having to type in any database creation commands or use any scripts. The tool helps you create both small and large databases very easily, and it even allows you to register a new database automatically with Oracle Internet Directory (OID). However, I recommend strongly that you use the manual approach initially, so you can get a good idea of what initialization parameters to pick and how the database is created step by step. Once you gain sufficient confidence, of course, DBCA is without a doubt the best choice for creating an Oracle database of any size and complexity.

Whether you create a database manually or let Oracle create one for you at software installation, a configuration file called the *init.ora* file or its newer equivalent, the *SPFILE*, holds all the database configuration details. After the initial creation of the database, you can always change the behavior of the database by changing the init.ora file parameters. You can also change the behavior of the database for brief periods or during some sessions by using the *alter system* and *alter session* commands to temporarily modify some parameter values.

 NOTE *If you are migrating from an Oracle8 or Oracle8i version to the Oracle9i version, please refer to the relevant documents on MetaLink (*http://metalink.oracle.com*) for the complete Oracle9i migration procedures.*

You need to perform certain steps before you can create a database. Among other things, you need to make sure you have the necessary software and the memory and storage resources to successfully create the database. The next few sections run down the brief list of preliminary steps.

Installing the Software

Before you can create a database, you must first install the Oracle9*i* software. If you currently have other Oracle9*i* databases running on your system, then of course you are already set and can proceed to the creation of the database itself.

If you are going to create the first database on the server, you have to first install the Oracle9*i* software. Chapter 4 covers in detail how to install the Oracle9*i* software on UNIX systems and Chapter 22 covers the same for Windows-based systems.

Creating the File System for the Database

Planning your file systems is an important task you need to complete before you get down to creating the database. The location of the various files such as the redo log files and archive log files has to be carefully thought out beforehand. Similarly, the placement of the table and index data has serious implications for performance down the road. Two issues you need to focus on with regard to your file system are its size and location. Let's look at both of these issues in some detail.

Sizing the File System

It is a good idea to systematically figure out how big your database is going to be in terms of the total space required. Your overall space estimate should include estimates for the following:

- *Space for the tables:* Table data is the biggest component of the physical database. You need to first estimate the size of all the tables by getting information regarding the columns included in the tables. You also need row estimates for all the major tables. You don't need accurate numbers here; roughly accurate figures should suffice.

- *Space for the indexes:* There are formulas you can use to figure out the space required by the indexes in your database. First, though, you must know the indexes needed by your application. You also need to know the type of indexes you're going to create, as this has a major bearing on the physical size of the indexes.

- *Space for the undo tablespace:* The space that needs to be allocated to the undo tablespace depends on the size of your database and the nature of your transactions. If you anticipate a lot of large transactions or you need to plan for large batch jobs, you will require a fairly large undo tablespace.

- *Space for the temporary tablespace:* The temporary tablespace size also depends on the nature of your application and the transaction pattern. If the queries involve a lot of sorting operations, you're better off with a larger temporary tablespace in general. Note that you'll be creating the temporary tablespace with the *create temporary tablespace* command. This temporary tablespace will be designated during the creation of the database as the *default temporary tablespace* for the users in the database.

Choosing the Location for the Files

If you've been following the OFA guidelines you learned about in Chapter 2, you'll place the various files of the database such as the system, redo log, and archive log files so you can benefit from the OFA guidelines. The following list summarizes the benefits of using the OFA guidelines for file placement in your database. OFA-based files will

- Make it easy for you to locate and identify the various files such as the database files, control files, and redo log files

- Make it easy to administer multiple Oracle databases and multiple Oracle software versions

- Improve database performance by minimizing contention between competing types of files

---

TIP *In addition to laying out the files in the OFA format, you need to put the data and index files on different drives for performance reasons. If you're going to have several data files, it's a good idea to stripe them across several spindles. This will improve the I/O performance in your database. Chapter 19, which discusses instance tuning, explains striping and other disk-related issues in detail.*

Sizing the Redo Log Files

Redo log files are critical for the functioning of a database, and they're key components when you're trying to recover the database without any loss in committed data. Here are some other points about redo log files:

- Oracle recommends a minimum of two redo log groups (each group can have one or more members). Redo log files need to be *multiplexed*—that is, you should have more than a single redo log file in each group, because they're a critical part of the database and they're a single point of failure in the database.

- The size of the redo log file will depend on how fast your database is writing to the log. If you have a lot of DML operations in your database and the redo logs seem to be filling up very fast, you may want to increase the size of the log file. You can't increase the size of an existing redo log file, though—what I mean here is that you can create larger files and drop the smaller redo log files. The redo log files are written in a circular fashion, and your goal should be to size the log files such that no more than two to three redo log files are filled up every hour. The fundamental conflict here is between performance and recovery time. A very large redo log file will be efficient because there won't be many log switches and associated checkpoints, all of which impose a performance overhead on the database. However, when you need to perform recovery, larger redo logs take more time to recover from because you have more data to recover due to infrequent checkpointing.

If you have followed the OFA guidelines while installing your software, you should be in good shape regarding the way your files are physically laid out.

Ensuring Enough Memory Is Allocated

If you don't have enough memory on the system to satisfy the requirements of your database, your database instance will fail to start. Even if it does start, there will be a severe penalty to be paid by the system in the form of memory paging and swapping, which will slow your database down. Memory cost is such a small part of enterprise computing costs these days that you're better off getting a large amount of memory for the server on which you plan to install the Oracle database.

NOTE *See the discussion of the various memory-related initialization parameters in the "Important Oracle9i Initialization Parameters" section later in this chapter, to get an idea about how to size these components for your database.*

Getting Necessary Authorizations

You will need authorizations to be granted by the UNIX/Linux or Windows system administrator for you to be able to create file systems on the server. Your Oracle username should be included in the DBA group by the system administrator if you are working on a UNIX or a Linux server. If you are working on a Windows server, the system administrator should give you the appropriate administrative privileges as specified in the Oracle installation manual for Windows.

Setting the Operating System Environment Variables

Before you proceed to create the database, you must set all the necessary operating system environment variables. In Windows systems there is less need to set any specific variables, but in UNIX and Linux environments, you must set the following environment variables:

- *ORACLE_SID*: This is your database's name. For this chapter's purposes, you should set this variable to *remorse*.

- *ORACLE_BASE:* This is the directory at the top of the Oracle software. For this chapter's purposes, this is :/u01/app/oracle.

- *ORACLE_HOME:* This is the directory in which you installed the Oracle software. Oracle recommends you use the following format for this variable: *$ORACLE_BASE/product/release*. For this chapter's purposes, this is /u01/app/oracle/product/9.2.0.1.0.

- *PATH:* This is the directory in which Oracle's executable files are located. Oracle's executables are always located in the $ORACLE_HOME/bin directory. You can add the Oracle's executable files location to the existing PATH value in the following way:

```
Export PATH=$PATH:$ORACLE_HOME/bin
```

- *LD_LIBRARY_PATH:* this variable points out where the Oracle libraries are located. The usual location is the $ORACLE_HOME/lib directory.

Creating the Initialization File

Every Oracle instance needs resources such as memory for the various components of the SGA. In addition, you must sometimes specify or limit how much of the system resources the instance can use. Oracle uses database parameter files, which list the names of the parameters and the values for each. An *initialization parameter* file, known as the init*db_name*.ora, was traditionally the only type of file in which you could store these initialization parameter values. By default, this file is located in the $ORACLE_HOME/dbs directory, and again it's up to you to store it in a place that's helpful to you. When you store the configuration file in any location other than the default location, you must specify the complete location when you start the instance. If the initialization filename and the location follow the default conventions, you don't have to provide the name or location of the configuration file at start-up time.

NOTE *The initialization files are used not only to create the database itself initially, but also to tune its performance later on by modifying parameter values. You can change some of these parameters dynamically while the database is running, but to change the others you'll have to restart your database.*

The initialization file includes parameters that will help tune the instance. It also contains parameters that set limits on certain database resources and parameters that specify the name and location of some important files. The variables that affect performance are called *variable parameters* by Oracle, and these are the variables DBAs are mostly interested in. Once the initialization file is ready, you can start the instance by invoking the file. However, you can dynamically modify several important configuration parameters while the instance is running. These modifications won't be permanent; as soon as you shut down the database, the changes are gone and you're back to the values hard-coded in the init.ora file. If you want to make the dynamic changes permanent so the database will come up with these new values upon a restart, you should use a *server parameter file*, also known as the *SPFILE*. The SPFILE is also an initialization file, but you can't make changes to it directly because it's a binary file, not a text file. Using the SPFILE to manage your instance provides several benefits, as you'll see in the section "The Server Parameter File (SPFILE)" later in the chapter.

In the sections that follow, I group the initialization parameters into sets of related parameters to make it easier to understand the configuration of a new database. My parameter groupings are purely arbitrary and are mainly for exposition purposes. Oracle provides a template to make it easy for you to create your own customized file. This file is located in the $ORACLE_HOME/dbs directory in UNIX systems and in the $ORACLE_HOME/database directory in Windows-based systems. You can copy this init.ora template and name it init*db_name*.ora, and you can then edit it per your own site's requirements. Don't be nervous about trying to make "correct" estimates for the various configuration parameters. Most of the configuration parameters are easily modifiable throughout the life of the database. Just make sure you're careful about the handful of parameters that you can't change without redoing the entire database from scratch.

The interesting thing about the init.ora file is that it contains the configuration parameters for memory and some I/O parameters, but not the database filenames or the tablespaces the data files belong to. The control file holds all that information. The initialization file, though, has the locations of files such as the control files, the redo log files, and the dump directories for error messages. The initialization file also specifies the mode chosen for the undo management, the optimizer mode, and the archiving mode for the redo logs.

NOTE *All the parameters in the initialization file are* optional. *That is, if you don't have any parameters configured in your init.ora file, Oracle will apply default values for all the parameters and your database will be successfully started. For example, I can start a brand-new instance called "remorse" very quickly by using this short init.ora file:*

```
db_name = REMORSE
control_files = (/u01/app/oracle/control1,/u01/app/oracle/control2)
```

As you can imagine, this means you won't have any control over the behavior of the configurable parameters. You should leave parameters out of the init.ora file only after you ascertain that their default values are OK for your database. In general, it's a good idea to use approximate sizes for the important configuration parameters you know well and use a trial-and-error method to decide whether to use newer or never-before-used parameters.

Oracle9*i* is famous for being a highly configurable database, but that benefit also carries with it the need for DBAs to expend the necessary energy to learn how these large numbers of parameters work. Most important, you should learn how the parameters may interact with one another at times, thereby producing a result that is at variance with your initial plans. To give you an elementary example, an increase in the SGA size may increase database performance up to a point. After that, any increase in SGA might actually slow the database down, because the operating system may be induced to swap the higher SGA in and out of real memory. Beware of configuration changes, and always think through the implications of "slight" changes in the parameter file.

Changing the Initialization Parameter Values

You can change the value of any initialization parameter by simply editing the init.ora file. However, for the changes to actually take effect, you have to *bounce* the database, or stop and start it again. As you can imagine, this is not always possible, especially if you are managing a production database. However, you can change several of the parameters "on the fly," and these are called *dynamic* parameters for that reason. The parameters you can change only by restarting the database after changing the init.ora file are called *static* parameters.

You have three ways to change the value of dynamic parameters. You can use the *alter session, alter system,* or *alter system ... deferred* command option to change the parameter values.

Using the Alter Session Command

The *alter session* command enables you to change the dynamic parameter values for the duration of the session that issues the command. Obviously, you are going to use the *alter session* command only to change a parameter's value temporarily. Here is the general syntax for the command:

```
Alter session set parameter_name=value;
```

Using the Alter System Command

The *alter system* command changes the parameter's value for all sessions. However, these changes will be in force only for the duration of the instance; when the database is restarted, these changes will go away unless you modify the init.ora file accordingly or you use the SPFILE. Here is the syntax for this command:

```
Alter system set parameter_name=value;
```

Using the Alter System ... Deferred Command

The *alter system ... deferred* command will make the new values for a parameter effective for all sessions, but not immediately. Only new sessions started after the command is issued are affected. All currently open sessions will continue to use the old parameter values.

```
Alter system set parameter_name deferred;
```

The *alter system ... deferred* command works only for the following parameters: *backup_tape_io_slaves, transaction_auditing, sort_area_retained_size, object_cache_optimal_size, sort_area_size,* and *object_cache_max_size_percent.* Because of the very small number of parameters to whom the "deferred" status applies, you can, for all practical purposes, consider *alter system* a command that applies immediately to all sessions.

Important Oracle9i Initialization Parameters

The following sections present some of the important Oracle initialization parameters you need to be familiar with. For the sake of clarity, I've assigned the parameters to various groups.

Although this list looks long and formidable, it isn't really a complete list of initialization parameters that you can configure for the Oracle9i database—it's a list of only the most commonly used parameters. *Oracle9i has over 250 initialization parameters that DBAs can configure.* Don't be disheartened, though. The basic list of parameters that you need to start your new database could be fairly small and easy to understand. Later on, as you study various topics such as backup and recovery, performance tuning, networking, and so on, you'll have a chance to really understand how to use the more esoteric initialization parameters.

Audit-Related Parameters

An Oracle database can be configured to audit actions by its users, and you can configure this auditing feature according to several criteria. The default behavior of the database is not to audit actions within the database. The following parameters help you audit your database usage.

Audit_File_Dest

The *audit_file_dest* parameter specifies the directory in which you want to save the audit files. You can specify this parameter only if you choose the operating system as the destination for your *audit_trail*.

```
Default: $ORACLE_HOME/rdbms/audit
Type: Static
```

Audit_Trail

You use the *audit_trail* parameter to turn auditing of the database on or off. If you don't want auditing to be turned on, do nothing. If you want auditing turned on, you can set the *audit_trail* parameter to the values *OS*, *DB*, or *true*. If you set the parameter to *OS*, Oracle writes the audit records to an operating system file. If you set the parameter to *true* or *DB*, Oracle records the audit information in the sys.aud$ table. Here are the possible values for the *audit_trail* parameter. The default value for this parameter is *none*.

```
Examples:
Audit_trail = TRUE
Audit_trail = DB
Audit_trail = OS
```

If you choose to set the *audit_trail* parameter to *OS*, audit records will be written to an operating system file. Types of information that will be written to the operating system audit file include audit records from the OS, audit records for the SYS user, and database actions that are always audited. Chapter 11 provides more information about auditing actions within an Oracle database.

 TIP *Even if you don't set the* audit_trail *parameter to any value, Oracle will still write audit information to an operating system file for* all database actions that are audited by default. *On a UNIX system, the default location for this file is the $ORACLE_HOME/rdbms/audit directory. Of course, you can specify a different directory if you wish. See Chapter 11 for more details on this feature.*

Audit_Sys_Operations

This parameter, if set to a value of *true*, will audit all actions of the user SYS and any other user with a SYSDBA/SYSOPER role and write the details to an operating system audit trail. By writing the audit information to a secure operating system location, you remove any possibility of the SYS user tampering with an audit trail that is located within the database.

```
Default: false
Type: static
```

Transaction_Auditing

You can analyze redo logs with the help of a redo log analysis tool. If *transaction_auditing* is set to *true*, Oracle will produce a special redo log record that has session ID, client, and operating system information. By dumping the contents of the redo log file, you can audit specific transactions.

```
Default: true
Type: dynamic – can be changed with the 'alter system … deferred' command.
```

Database Name and Other General Parameters

Most important among the name parameters, of course, is the parameter that sets the name of the database. Let's look at this set of parameters in detail.

Db_Name

The *db_name* parameter sets the name of the database. This parameter can't be changed after the database is created. You can have a *db_name* parameter of up to eight characters.

For the purposes of this chapter, you'll name your database *remorse*, and this will be the *db_name* parameter's value. Note that this parameter is optional; Oracle can get the name of the database from the *create database* statement if this parameter is omitted.

```
Default: false
Type: Static.
```

Db_Domain

The *db_domain* parameter gives a fully qualified name for the database. You'll use the default .world name, so your *db_domain* will be *remorse.world*.

```
Default: false
Type: Static.
```

Instance_Name

The *instance_name* parameter will have the same value as the *db_name* parameter, which is *remorse* for your database.

```
Default: false
Type: Static.
```

Service_Name

The *service_name* parameter provides a name for the database service, and it can be anything you want it to be. Usually, it is a combination of the database name and your database domain.

```
Default: DB_NAME.DB_DOMAIN
Type: Dynamic, can be changed with the 'alter system' command.
```

Compatible

Suppose you upgrade to the Oracle9*i* version, but your application developers haven't made any changes to the Oracle8*i* application. You need to set your compatibility parameter equal to 8*i*, so the untested features of the new version you're using won't hurt your application. Later on, after the application has been suitably upgraded, you can reset the *compatible* initialization parameter to Oracle9*i*.

```
Default: false
Type: Static.
```

Dispatchers

The *dispatchers* parameter configures the dispatcher process if you choose to run your database in the shared server mode.

```
Default: None
Type: Dynamic. 'Alter system' command can be used to reconfigure the dispatchers.
```

Nls_Date_Format

The *nls_date_format* parameter specifies the default date format Oracle will use. Oracle uses this date format when using the to-char or to-date function in SQL. There is a default value, which is derived from the *nls_territory* parameter. For example, if the *nls_territory* format is America, the *nls_date_format* parameter is automatically set to the DD-MON-YY format.

```
Default: Depends on the nls_territory variable and the operating system.
Type: Dynamic. Can be altered by using the 'alter session' command.
```

File-Related Parameters

You can specify several file-related parameters in your init.ora file. Oracle requires you to specify several destination locations for trace files and error messages. The bdump, udump, and cdump files are used by the database to store the alert logs, background trace files, and core dump files. In addition, you need to specify the *utl_file_directory* parameter for using the UTL_FILE package. The following sections cover the key file-related parameters.

Control_Files

Control files are key files that hold information regarding the data file names and locations, and a lot of other important information. The database needs only one control file, but because this is such an important file, you always save multiple copies of it. The way to multiplex the control file is to simply specify multiple locations (two or three, although you can go up to the maximum Oracle allows) for the *control_files* parameter. The minimum number of control files is one. Oracle recommends at least two control files per instance, but three seems to be the number most commonly used by DBAs.

```
Default: false
Type: Static.
```

Db_Files

The *db_files* parameter simply specifies the maximum number of files allowed to be created in the database. This is just a number, and you don't list all the data files for your database here. In fact, the specification of the files and the tablespaces comes during the creation of the database itself. The larger the size of the database, the larger this number should be. For a large warehouse, you can set the value of the *db_files* parameter to 1000 or greater.

```
Default: 200
Type: Static
```

Core_Dump_Dest

The *core_dump_dest* parameter specifies the location where you want the core (error) messages dumped to.

```
Default: Depends on the operating system. You can use any valid directory.
Type: Dynamic, can be changed with the 'alter system' command.
```

User_Dump_Dest

This is the directory where you want Oracle to save error messages from various processes such as PMON and the database writer.

```
Default: Depends on the operating system. You can use any valid directory.
Type:  Dynamic, can be changed with the 'alter system' command.
```

Background_Dump_Dest

This parameter specifies the Oracle alert log location and the locations of some other trace file for the instance.

```
Default:  Depends on the operating system. You can use any valid directory.
Type: Dynamic, can be changed with the 'alter system' command.
```

Utl_File_Directory

You can use the *utl_file_directory* parameter to specify the directory (or directories) Oracle will use to process I/O when you use the Oracle UTL_FILE package to read from or write to the operating system files.

```
Default: None. You can't use the utl_file package
to do any I/O under this scenario.
Type: Static. You can set the utl_file_dir to any OS
directory you want. If you just specify *, instead of any
specific directory name, the utl_file package will read and
 write to and from all the OS directories, and Oracle
recommends against this practice.
```

 CAUTION *Don't use the easy-sounding * as the location for your UTL_FILE directory. You'll need some directory on the server where you have read/write privileges, otherwise the package can't process I/O to the operating system. If you use * as the value for the UTL_FILE parameter, however, users can write to and read from* all *directories for which you have read/write privileges. Obviously, you don't want this to happen!*

Oracle Managed Files Parameters

The test database that you're going to create doesn't use the Oracle Managed Files (OMF) feature, so the parameter will remain blank. If you were to use the OMF feature, however, this is the parameter that you'll need to include to enable your database to use the OMF files. You'll usually need to use two parameters, both of which specify the format of the OMF files when you decide to use the feature. Chapter 17 discusses in detail how to use the initialization parameters dealing with OMF. The following sections cover the OMF-related initialization parameters.

Db_Create_File_Dest

The *db_create_file_dest* parameter denotes the directory where Oracle will create data files and temporary files when you don't specify an explicit location for them. The directory must exist already with the right read/write permissions for Oracle.

```
Default: false
Type: Dynamic, can be changed using either the 'alter system' or
the 'alter session' command.
```

Db_Create_Online_Log_Dest_n

This parameter specifies where you want the OMF online redo log files to be created by default. To multiplex the online redo log files, specify more than one value for the parameter. You can have a maximum of five separate directory locations.

```
Default: false
Type: Dynamic, can be changed using either the 'alter system'
or the 'alter session' command.
```

Process and Session Parameters

Several initialization parameters relate to the number of processes and the number of sessions that your database can handle. The following sections explore the important process and session parameters.

Processes

The value of the *processes* parameter will set the upper limit for the number of operating system processes that can connect to your database concurrently. Both the *sessions* and *transactions* parameters derive their default values from this parameter.

```
Default: 6 (may vary depending on the operating system)
Type: Static.
```

Db_Writer_Processes

The *db_writer_processes* parameter specifies the initial number of database writer processes for your instance. Instances with very heavy data modification may opt for more than the default single process. You can have up to 20 processes per instance.

```
Default: 1
Type: Static.
```

Sessions

The *sessions* parameter sets the maximum number of sessions that can connect to the database simultaneously. Actually, this parameter is redundant, because the *processes* parameter will by default determine the maximum number of sessions also.

```
Default: (1.1 * Processes) + 5
Type: Static.
```

Open_Cursors

The *open_cursors* parameter sets the limit on the number of cursors a single session can have.

```
Default: 50
Type: Static
```

Memory Configuration Parameters

The memory configuration parameters determine the memory allocated to key components of the SGA. There are no hard-and-fast rules regarding the right size for these parameters. You allocate an approximate amount to start with, and based on the performance statistics, you fine-tune the allocations after the database starts operating.

NOTE *Oracle's guidelines regarding the ideal settings for the various components of memory, such as the* db_cache_size *and shared pool, are often vague and not really helpful to a beginner. For example, Oracle states that the* db_cache_size *should be 20 percent to 80 percent of the available memory for a data warehouse database. The shared pool recommendation for the same database is 5 percent to 10 percent.*

Well, the wide ranges make the db_cache_size *recommendations useless. If your total memory is 2GB, you're supposed to allocate 100GB to 200GB of memory for the shared pool. If your total memory allocation is 32GB, your allocation for the shared pool would be between 1.6GB and 3.2GB, according to the "standard" recommendations. The best thing to do is use a trial-and-error method to see if the various memory settings are appropriate for your database.*

The buffer cache and the shared pool are the two main components of Oracle's instance memory, with the other important components being the PGA and the large pool. The buffer cache is the area of Oracle's memory where it keeps the data blocks read in from the disks. The data blocks may be modified here before being written back to disk again. A big enough buffer cache will improve performance by avoiding too many disk accesses, which are much slower than accessing data in memory.

You can set up the buffer cache for your database in units of the standard block size you chose for the database (using the *db_block_size* parameter), or you can use nonstandard block sized buffer caches. If you want to base your buffer cache on the standard block size, you use the *db_cache_size* parameter to size your standard block–based cache. You have to make an educated guess as to the right size of the buffer cache parameter. For larger databases, allocate larger buffer caches. Let's say you want to allocate about 500MB of memory on your system to the buffer cache parameter. The following sections cover the standard block size buffer cache–related initialization parameters.

Db_Cache_Size

This parameter sets the size of the default standard block–sized cache. For example, you can use a number like 1024MB.

```
Default: 48 MB
Type: Dynamic, can be modified with the 'alter system' command.
```

The normal behavior of the buffer pool is to treat all the objects placed in it equally. That is, any object will remain there as long as free memory is available in the buffer cache. Objects are removed or "aged out" only when there is no free space. When this happens, the least recently used (LRU) algorithm is used to remove the oldest unused objects sitting in memory to make space for new objects. The use of two specialized buffer tools, the keep pool and the recycle pool, allows you to specify at object creation time how you want the buffer pool to treat certain objects.

For example, if you know that certain objects don't really need to be kept in memory for long, you can have them assigned to a *recycle pool,* which removes the objects that aren't needed anymore as soon as they're used. Similarly, the *keep pool* always retains an object in memory if it's created with the keep option. The following sections cover the two relevant parameters for configuring *multiple buffer pools.*

Db_Keep_Cache_Size

The *db_keep_cache_size* parameter specifies the size of the keep pool. If you store objects in the keep pool of the buffer cache, Oracle will ensure that they will never age out of the pool.

```
Example: db_keep_cache_size = 5
Default:  0 Megabytes. By default, this is not configured.
Type: Dynamic. Can be changed by using the 'alter system' command.
```

Db_Recycle_Cache_Size

The *db_recycle_cache_size* parameter specifies the size of the recycle pool in the buffer cache. Oracle removes objects from this pool as soon as the objects are used.

```
Example: .db_cycle_cache_size= 20
Default: 0 Megabytes. By default, this is not configured.
Type: Dynamic. Can be changed by using the 'alter system' command.
```

Db_nK_Cache_Size

If you prefer to use nonstandard-sized buffer caches, for each of the nonstandard-sized buffer cache you need to specify the *db_nk_cache_size* parameter, as in the following example: *db_4k_cache_size*=2048MB or *db_8k_cache_size*=4096MB. The range of values for this parameter is 2K, 4K, 8K, 16K, and 32K.

```
Default: 0 Megabytes.
Type: Dynamic. You can change this parameter's value with the
'alter system' command.
```

Shared_Pool_Size

The shared pool is a critical part of Oracle's memory, and the *shared_pool_size* parameter sets the total size of the SGA that is devoted to the shared pool. The shared pool consists of the data dictionary cache and the library cache. The data dictionary cache stores the recently used data dictionary information, so you don't have to constantly hit the disk to access the data dictionary.

Remember that the data dictionary is one of the most frequently consulted parts of any Oracle database. Before any query can execute, the data dictionary is consulted to verify the objects involved, user privileges, and a bunch of other important things. There is no way to separately manipulate the sizes of the two components of the shared pool. If you want to increase the size of either component of the shared pool or both of them at once, you do it through increasing the value of the *shared_pool_size* parameter. Oracle recommends 5 percent to 10 percent of the total memory for the shared pool for a data warehouse and a larger proportion for OLTP databases.

```
Default: 16 Megabytes for non-64 Bit Operating Systems, 64 Megabytes for 64 Bit.
Type: Dynamic. The 'alter system' command can be used to
change it to OS-dependent maximum size.
```

Shared_Pool_Reserved_Size

This parameter sets the amount of space to be reserved in the shared pool for holding large queries or packages.

```
Default: Five percent of shared_pool_size.
Type: Static. You can increase this to half of the total shared_pool size.
```

Pga_Aggregate_Target

Users need areas in memory to perform certain memory-intensive operations, such as sorting, hash joining, bitmap merging, and so on. The *pga_aggregate_target* parameter is the total amount of memory allocated to the instance so it can be assigned to users as "work areas" to perform the previously mentioned memory-heavy jobs. Chapter 5 contains a detailed discussion of the PGA and how to size it. By setting the *pga_aggregate_target* parameter, you let Oracle manage the runtime memory management for SQL execution. The sum of the total PGA memory allocated to all sessions in this instance cannot exceed the value of this parameter.

```
Default: 0
Type: Dynamic. The 'alter system' command can be used to modify this parameter.
```

TIP *You can adjust the* pga_aggregate_target *parameter dynamically using the* alter system *command. The target value should range between 10MB and 4000GB. Oracle recommends that the* pga_aggregate_target *parameter should be between 20 percent and 80 percent of the available memory.*

Log_Buffer

The *log_buffer* parameter indicates the size of the redo log buffer. As you recall, the redo log buffer holds the redo records, which are used to recover a database. The log writer writes the contents of this buffer to the redo log files on disk. The log buffer's size is usually set to a small amount, under about a megabyte or so. The more changes the redo buffers have to process using redo records, the more active the redo logs will be. Instead of adjusting the *log_buffer* parameter to a very large size, you may want to use the *nologging* option to reduce redo operations.

```
Default: Maximum of 512 Kilobytes or 128 Kilobytes * Number of CPUS,
whichever is greater.
Type: Static.
```

Large_Pool

The shared pool can normally take care of the memory needs of shared servers as well as Oracle backup and restore operations and a few other operations. But sometimes this may place a heavy burden on the shared pool, causing a lot of fragmentation in it and also the premature aging-out recycling of important objects from the shared pool due to lack of space.

To avoid these problems, Oracle enables you to use a parameter called *large_pool,* which is used for the previously mentioned specialized operations, thus freeing up the shared pool mostly for caching SQL queries and the data dictionary. If the *parallel_automatic_tuning* parameter is set, the large pool is also used for parallel-execution message buffers. The amount of memory for the large pool in this case depends on the number of parallel threads per CPU and the number of CPUs.

```
Default: Zero if the pool is not required for parallel
execution and DBWR_IO_SLAVES is not set.
Type: Static.
Range: 600K to 2 Gigabytes
```

Java_Pool_Size

Use this parameter only if your database is using Java stored procedures. Otherwise, you can leave it out of the init.ora file.

```
Default: 20000 Bytes
Type: Static.
Range: 1Megabyte to 1Gigabyte
```

Sga_Maximum_Size

You can also set a maximum limit for the memory that can be used by all the components of the SGA with the *sga_maximum_size* parameter. This is an optional parameter, because omitting it just means that the SGA's maximum size will default to the sum of the memory parameters in the SGA.

```
Default: false
Type: Static.
```

Lock_Sga

Setting the value of the *lock_sga* parameter to *true* will lock your entire SGA into the host physical memory. This works only on some operating systems, and you should set this parameter to *true* only after verification. As mentioned in Chapter 5, Oracle doesn't recommend using this parameter under most circumstances.

```
Default: Depends on the values of the component variables.
Type: Static.
```

Db_Cache_Advice

Once you start the instance with an approximate memory sizes, you can have Oracle itself advise you on the best levels for the buffer size based on the cache miss rates for various hypothetical cache sizes. The database will simulate the use of a wide range of buffer cache sizes and store the information. To enable Oracle to do the analysis regarding the ideal value for the database buffer cache size, you must set the *db_cache_advice* parameter to *true* in the init.ora file.

```
Default: Off
Type: Dynamic. 'Alter system' command can be used to switch to off/on.
```

Archive Log Parameters

Oracle gives you the option of archiving your filled redo logs. When you configure your database to archive its redo logs, the database is said to be in an *archivelog mode*. You should always archivelog your production databases unless there are exceptional reasons for not doing so. If you decide to archive the redo logs, you have to specify that in the initialization file by specifying the three parameters described in the following sections.

Log_Archive_Dest_n

This parameter enables you to specify the location (multiple) of the archived logs. You should set this parameter only if you are running the database in archivelog mode. You can do this when you create the database in the next section by specifying the *archivelog* keyword in your *create database* statement. But when you first create the database, there is no need for archiving to be turned on; you will thus not have a need to specify this parameter.

```
Default: None
Type: Dynamic. You can use the 'alter session' or the 'alter
system' command to make changes.
```

Log_Archive_Start

This parameter enables the automatic archiving of the logs. The alternative is to manually archive them, which may not be practical in a busy production system, as you'll see in Chapter 15.

```
Default: false
Type: Static.
```

Log_Archive_Format

This parameter specifies the default filename format for the archived redo log files.

```
Default: Operating system dependent.
Type: Static.
```

Undo Space Parameters

The main parameters to be configured here are the *undo_management* mode and the *undo_tablespace* parameter. The undo management mode will be set to *auto* in your case, because the remorse database will be configured to use the Automatic Undo Management (AUM) option. The *undo_tablespace* will be set to UNDOTBSP_01.

Undo_Tablespace

This parameter determines the default tablespace for undo records. If you don't specify one, the database will use the system rollback segment, and this should be avoided. If you don't specify a value for this parameter when you create the database, and you have chosen AUM, Oracle will create a default undo tablespace with the name UNDOTBS. This default tablespace will have a single 10MB data file that will be automatically extended without any maximum limit.

```
Default: The first undo_tablespace available
Type: Dynamic. You can use the 'alter system' command to
change the default undo tablespace.
```

Undo_Management

If the mode is set to *auto*, then the undo tablespace is used for storing the undo records and Oracle will automatically manage the undo segments.

```
Default: Manual (You need to use rollback segments)
Type: Static. You can use the AUTO value if you want the undo
space management to be automated using the undo tablespace.
```

Undo_Retention

This parameter specifies the amount of redo information to be saved in the undo tablespace before it can be overwritten. The value for this parameter depends on the size of the undo tablespace and the nature of the queries in your database. If the queries aren't huge, they don't need to have large snapshots of data, and you could get by with a low *undo_retention* interval. Similarly, if there is plenty of free space available in the undo tablespace, transactions won't be overwritten, which will cause the failure of queries (the "snapshot too old" problem). If you plan on using the Flashback Query feature extensively, you have to figure out how far back in time your Flashback Queries will go and specify the *undo_retention* parameter accordingly.

```
Default: 900 (seconds)
Type: Dynamic. You can use the 'alter system' command to
increase the value to a practically unlimited time period.
```

Rollback Segment Parameters

These parameters need to be set if you're choosing manual management of undo space. It will then list all the rollback segments that have been configured for the database.

You can switch from an AUM mode to the traditional undo management mode by using the *alter session* statement, as shown here:

```
Alter session set undo_management_mode=manual;
```

Oracle Licensing-Related Parameters

Usage of Oracle software is limited by the license agreement between Oracle and the customer. The total number of "named" (named user licensing policy) or unique users in your database shouldn't exceed the maximum licensed number of users. Once you set the value of this parameter to, for example, 400, the database won't allow you to create more than that many users in the database. Note that the older session-based licensing policy is no longer in vogue.

License_Max_Users

The *license_max_users parameter* specifies the maximum number of users you can create in your database.

```
Default:0
Type: Dynamic. 'Alter system' command can be used to change it.
```

License_Max_Sessions

The *license_max_sessions* initialization parameter states the maximum number of concurrent user sessions in your database.

```
Default: 0
Type: Static.
```

Performance- and Diagnostics-Related Parameters

You can configure several performance-related parameters in the init.ora file. In addition, you can set several parameters through the init.ora file to change the diagnostic capabilities of the database when you're performing activities such as tracing SQL statements.

Optimizer_Mode

This parameter dictates the type of optimization you want Oracle's query optimizer to follow. You can set the optimizer mode to rule-based, *first_rows*, *first_rows_n*, *all_rows*, or *choose*. If you set it to *choose*, Oracle will use the cost-based optimizer if the statistics exist for the tables involved in the query (you can generate these statistics using the *analyze* command or the DBMS_ANALYZE package).

```
Example: optimizer_mode=first_rows
Default: choose
Type: Dynamic. Can be modified by the 'alter session' command.
```

Query_Rewrite_Enabled

This parameter determines whether query rewriting is enabled or disabled, which is of importance mostly when you use materialized views. You can create materialized views only by setting this parameter to *true*.

```
Default: false
Type: Dynamic. Can use 'alter system/alter session' commands
to change the default value to true.
Example: alter session set query_rewrite_enabled=true;
```

Query_Rewrite_Integrity

This parameter sets the level at which query rewriting should be enabled: *enforced,* *trusted,* or *stale tolerated.* The *query_rewrite_integrity* parameter specifies the degree to which Oracle will enforce integrity rules during a query rewrite. Oracle recommends the use of *trusted* as the setting for this parameter. Using *trusted* as the value means that Oracle assumes the materialized view is current. *Enforced,* on the other hand, always uses fresh data, and *stale tolerated* uses materialized views with fresh and stale data.

```
Default: Enforced
Type: 'Alter system/session' commands can be
used to change the value to trusted or stale tolerated.
```

Star_Transformation_Enabled

If you are configuring a data warehouse, this variable is usually set to *true.*

Cursor_Sharing

This is a crucial initialization parameter, as it specifies how Oracle's SQL statements are supposed to share the same cursors. The three possible values are *forced, exact,* and *similar.* You'll learn a lot more about setting this parameter in Chapter 19.

```
Default: Exact.
Type: Dynamic. Both 'alter session' and 'alter system' commands can be used.
```

CAUTION *You have to be extremely careful when using the* cursor_sharing *parameter. As you'll learn in Chapter 19, using the* forced *option will force Oracle to use bind variables, and thus will enhance your application performance. However, there are many caveats, and the wrong option for this parameter can hurt performance. If you're using a stored outline, then* cursor sharing=similar *could cause problems in your application.*

Cursor_Space_For_Time

This parameter specifies whether shared SQL areas are retained in the library cache or deallocated from the library cache. You can set it to *true* or *false.*

```
Default: false
Type: Static.
```

Db_Block_Size

This parameter sets the standard database block size (for example, 4096, a 4KB block size). You can pick anywhere from 2KB to 32KB (2, 4, 8, 16, and 32) as your *db_block_size* value. You always should make the *db_block_size* parameter a multiple of your operating system block size, which you can ascertain from your UNIX or Windows system administrator.

You have to carefully evaluate your application's needs before you pick the correct database block size. Whenever you need to read data from or write data to an Oracle database object, you do so in terms of data blocks.

TIP *Remember that the data block is the smallest unit in the Oracle physical database scheme. So, when you are querying data, the rows aren't fetched individually; rather, the entire block in which the row resides is read into memory in one fell swoop.*

If you're supporting data warehouse applications, it makes sense to have a very large *db_block_size*—say, something between 8KB and 32KB. This will improve database performance when it's reading in huge chunks of data from disk. However, if you're dealing with a typical OLTP application where most of your reads and writes consist of relatively short transactions, a large *db_block_size* would be overkill and could actually lead to inefficiency in input and output operations. Most OLTP transactions read or write a very small number of rows per transaction and conduct numerous transactions with random access I/O (index scans), so you need to have a smaller block size, somewhere between 2KB and 8KB. A large block size for most OLTP applications is going to hurt performance, as the database has to read large amounts of data into memory even when it really needs very small bits of information. A small *db_block_size* for an OLTP database would reduce slowdowns due to *buffer_busy_waits*, of which you'll learn a lot more in Chapter 19. Large data warehouses perform more fill table scans and thus perform more sequential data access than random access I/Os.

```
Default: 2048, range is 2048-32768.
Type: Static.
```

NOTE *If you need to change the* db_block_size *parameter after the database is created, you can't simply change it in the init.ora file. The block size is more or less permanent. However, you can get out of the need to re-create the whole database by creating new tablespaces (all but the System tablespace) with the required block size by using the* blocksize *parameter, which will perform a roundabout change in the block size. Officially, the* db_block_size *parameter will still be at the original value you specified because it can't be changed after the initial database creation. You can then use the online redefinition feature to move tables to the tablespaces you just created with the new block size. You can do this using OEM also.*

Db_File_Multiblock_Read_Count

This parameter specifies the maximum number of blocks Oracle will read during a full table scan. The larger the value, the more efficient your full table scans will be, because Oracle will retrieve multiple blocks of data in a single read. The general principle is that data warehouse operations need high multiblock read counts because of the heavy amount of data processing involved. If you are using a 16KB block size for your database and the multiblock read count parameter is set to 16 also, Oracle will read 256KB in a single I/O. Depending on the platform, Oracle supports I/Os up to 1MB. Note that when you stripe your disks, the stripe size should be a multiple of the I/O size for optimum performance. If you are using an OLTP application, a multiblock read count such as 8 or 16 would be ideal. Large data warehouses could go much higher than this.

```
Default: 8
Type: Dynamic - modifiable with either an 'alter system' or
an 'alter session' command.
```

Oracle_Trace_Enable

This command will *not* start tracing the SQL executed in the database; it just enables the use of the *trace* command in the database or the use of OEM to collect trace data.

```
Default: false
Type: Dynamic. 'Alter session' or 'alter system' can be used to change the value.
```

Sql_Trace

This parameter will turn the SQL trace utility on or off. You can leave this parameter at its default setting of *false*, turning it on (by setting it to *true*) only when you are tuning a specific query or a set of queries. Chapter 18 shows you how to use trace queries and format the trace output to help you in tuning SQL queries.

```
Default: false
Type: Static. You can change it to a value of true to turn SQL tracing on.
```

Parallel_Automatic_Tuning

By setting the *parallel_automatic_tuning* parameter to *true*, you can configure a database for parallel execution. Oracle will configure itself for parallel execution once you choose this option.

```
Default: false
Type: Static.
```

Parallel_Max_Servers

This parameter determines the number of parallel execution processes. Oracle recommends two parallel processes per CPU on larger systems and four processes per CPU on smaller systems.

```
Default: Derived from the values specified for the cpu_count,
parallel-automatic_tuning, and parallel_adaptive_multi_user parameters.
Type: Static.
```

Timed_Statistics

This parameter is used to tell Oracle whether it should collect timing statistics during tracing. If timed statistics are collected, they are used in some dynamic performance views. Timed statistics do impose a certain penalty in terms of higher resource use, and if you have a pretty busy production database you will want to use this parameter sparingly.

```
Default: false
Type: Dynamic. You can use the 'alter system/session' command
 to set the value to true and start collecting timing statistics.
```

Resource_Limit

The *resource_limit* parameter determines whether Oracle will enforce the resource limits of profiles.

```
Default: True. Resource limits are enforced.
Type: Dynamic. The 'alter system' command can be used to change the value to false.
```

Workarea_Size_Policy

This parameter affects the sizing of work areas for individual users. The two possible values are *auto* and *manual*. If you set this parameter to *manual*, you also need to set all the parameters such as *sort_area_size* and *hash_area_size* to manage the PGA. If you set this parameter to *auto*, Oracle will automatically manage the PGA.

```
Default: Auto, provided you have already set the pga_aggregate_target.
Type: Dynamic. You can use the 'alter system/session'
statements to change the value to manual, but Oracle strongly
recommends against it for efficient memory utilization reasons.
```

Recovery-Related Parameters

As you create a database, you'll need to configure several recovery-related parameters. An instance can crash for a number of reasons (e.g., a power failure). When the crash occurs, all the data on disk is safe, but the data stored in the database buffers is wiped out instantaneously. Redo logs are on disk, so they are intact, but the redo log buffers are wiped out. To recover successfully from such a crash, the database needs to be brought to a consistent state. This involves using Oracle's redo logs and undo records from the undo tablespace. The redo log records will help write all the committed data to disk and the undo records will help roll back any uncommitted data that was stored on disk.

All this instance recovery can take a long time—and keep the database out of commission for an unacceptable length of time—if you don't configure any threshold times for how long an instance recovery can take. Yes, you can specify a precise time target for the instance recovery to complete. The database will automatically adjust the frequency of the checkpoints to make sure that at any point in time, there's only a certain maximum amount of redo information to be rolled back when instance recovery is performed. Of course, if you set a very low time target, your instance recovery will be quick, but there's a price to pay for this privilege: The database needs to perform an excessive amount of checkpoints, which will affect performance. Again, there's no one magic number for this target. You have to take into consideration your site's service level agreement and the tolerance for downtime.

Fast_Start_Mttr_Target

The *fast_start_mttr_target* parameter determines the length of time a database needs to recover from an instance crash. The smaller the value, the faster the instance will come up after a crash.

Here's how you set the value of the *fast_start_mttr_target* parameter:

```
Fast_start_mttr_target-120
(the time is in seconds. You can go up to 3600 seconds).
```

Chapter 5 discusses the *fast_start_mttr_target* parameter in detail. The following are its default value and type:

```
Default: 0
Type: Dynamic. You can use the 'alter system' command to change this parameter.
```

Log_Checkpoint_Interval

The *log_checkpoint_interval* parameter determines the frequency of checkpoints by setting the maximum number of redo log database blocks that can accumulate in the redo logs before it is forced to write them to disk.

```
Default: Depends on the operating system, usually 1800 seconds (3 minutes)
Type: Dynamic. You can change the default value using the 'alter system' command.
```

Control_File_Record_Keep_Time

When you use the Recovery Manager for backups, you can choose to use a recovery catalog. If you don't use the recovery catalog, all the backup information is written to the control file. The *control_file_record_keep_time* parameter specifies how long you want the backup records to be saved before they're overwritten.

```
Default: 7 days.
Type: Dynamic. 'Alter system' command can be used.
```

Data Block Verification Parameters

The Oracle9*i* database is equipped with certain features that can check your data blocks on the data files for consistency and data corruption. Turning on these checking parameters will impose a performance penalty on the database, so use these parameters with caution during critical production periods.

Db_Block_Checksum

This parameter checks all the data blocks on disk for the Oracle redo log files. By using checksums written to the data file headers, Oracle can check for corrupted redo logs if you turn this parameter on.

```
Default: true
Type: Dynamic. 'Alter system' command can be used to turn the checking off.
```

Db_Block_Checking

Using this parameter, you can have the database check for corrupted data blocks on all data files, thus preventing data corruption.

```
Default: false
Type: Dynamic. Both 'alter session' and 'alter system' commands can be used.
```

Security-Related Parameters

Several Oracle initialization parameters concern database security, including password authentication.

Os_Authent_Prefix

Oracle uses the value of this parameter as a prefix to the operating system–authenticated usernames. Oracle suggests using double quotes ("") as the value of the parameter to prevent any name prefix from being used at all.

```
Example: os_authent_prefix=""
Default: OPS$
Type: Static.
```

Remote_Login_Passwordfile

The *remote_login_passwordfile* initialization parameter determines whether Oracle will look for a password file for authentication purposes.

```
Default: None
Type: Static. Can be changed to shared or exclusive.
```

> **TIP** *Always ensure that the* remote_login_passwordfile *parameter is set to* shared *or* exclusive. *Otherwise, you'll be exposing the database to a major security weakness.*

Undocumented Initialization Parameters

In addition to the initialization parameters listed in this chapter, Oracle has several undocumented initialization parameters. These parameters are not supposed to be altered in any way by regular users; therefore, they remain undocumented.

The following script shows how to extract the undocumented parameters in an Oracle 9.2 database. Remember that Oracle will not help you troubleshoot several kinds of problems that may occur as a result of using these undocumented and unsupported parameters. Once you gain sufficient experience, though, you will be able to make good use of these parameters. Listing 9-1 shows you how to query for the list of undocumented initialization parameters.

Listing 9-1. Query to List the Undocumented Parameters

```
SQL> select
a.ksppinm parameter,
a.ksppdesc description,
b.ksppstvl session_value,
c.ksppstvl instance_value
FROM
x$ksppi a,
x$ksppcv b,
x$ksppsv c
WHERE
a.indx = b.indx
AND a.indx = c.indx
AND substr(a.ksppinm,1,1) = '_'
ORDER BY a.ksppinm
/
```

This query produces a list of 540 undocumented parameters for the Oracle 9.2.0.1.0 database version.

Viewing the Current Initialization Parameter Values

How do you know what values the numerous initialization parameters on your database are currently set to? You have several ways. You'll examine the different ways to list the parameter values in the following sections.

Reading the Init.ora File (or the SPFILE)

You can always use a file editor such as Windows Notepad to examine init.ora files, not only to view what the settings are for several initialization parameters, but also (at your own risk) to change their values. However, there is a major drawback to doing this: You cannot see the default values of all the initialization parameters. Remember that there are 257 initialization parameters in the 9.2.0.1.0 version, and you will probably not set the values of more than a quarter or so of these parameters explicitly by using your init.ora file.

The V$PARAMETER Table

A good and quick way to find out the initialization settings for your database is to simply query the V$PARAMTER table. You can run the following query to find out the values of all the parameters. The *isdefault* column has a value of *true* if the parameter is the default value and *yes* if you had actually set it to something other than the default value.

```
SQL> select name,value,isdefault
2*    from v$parameter
SQL>
```

When I ran this command on my NT server, the output showed about 250 parameters. Now, if I want to see only one or a set of related parameters and their values, I can do so by adding a *where* clause to my previous SQL query, as shown in the Listing 9-2.

Listing 9-2. Using the V$PARAMETER View to See the Initialization Parameters

```
SQL>   select name,value from v$parameter
2*     where name like '%dump%'
SQL> /
NAME                                VALUE
-----------------------------------------------
shadow_core_dump                    partial
background_core_dump                partial
background_dump_dest                c:\download
user_dump_dest                      c:\oracle9i\admin\remorse\udump
max_dump_file_size                  UNLIMITED
core_dump_dest                      c:\oracle9i\admin\remorse\cdump
6 rows selected.
SQL>
```

The Show Parameter Command

Even though it's easy to query from the V$PARAMETER table, there's a simpler means of querying the database about your initialization parameters. You can just type **show parameter** and you'll see all the initialization parameters with their values. You can limit the vast amount of output shown by passing a keyword to *show parameter*. For example, the keywords *locks, files, log,* and many others can be passed along to the *show parameter* command to get the values of a related set of parameters. Note that the list may not necessarily provide you a set of related parameters, as it just uses a pattern search of the NAME column to pull the values from the V$PARAMETER table. Listing 9-3 shows two examples of the usage of the *show parameter* command.

Listing 9-3. Using the Show Parameter Command

```
SQL> show parameter lock
NAME                                     TYPE        VALUE
---------------------------------------- ----------- ------------------
db_block_buffers                         integer     0
db_block_checking                        boolean     FALSE
db_block_checksum                        boolean     TRUE
db_block_size                            integer     4096
db_file_multiblock_read_count            integer     8
dml_locks                                integer     748
gc_files_to_locks                        string
lock_name_space                          string
lock_sga                                 boolean     FALSE
row_locking                              string      always
SQL>
SQL> sho parameter dump
NAME                                     TYPE        VALUE
---------------------------------------- ----------- -------------
background_core_dump                     string      partial
background_dump_dest                     string      c:\download
core_dump_dest                           string      c:\oracle9i\admin\remorse\cdump
max_dump_file_size                       string      UNLIMITED
shadow_core_dump                         string      partial
user_dump_dest                           string      c:\oracle9i\admin\remorse\udump
SQL>
```

Creating the Database

As I mentioned at the beginning of the chapter, you have several ways to create an Oracle database. One way is to have Oracle itself create a database for you as part of the server software installation.

In the creation of the Oracle9*i* database described in the following sections, I use individual database creation statements, which you can incorporate into a script if you wish. Here, then, are the steps to create an Oracle9*i* database, which you'll call the *remorse* database.

Setting Operating System Variables

You can use the SQL*Plus interface to create the database, either directly from a workstation or through a terminal connected to the server where you want to create the database. Before you log into the SQL*Plus session, you will need to set some operating system–level environment variables to the appropriate values.

First, make sure ORACLE_HOME is set for the session you log into. ORACLE_HOME in this case is designated as follows (using the Korn shell):

```
$ export ORACLE_HOME=/test01/app/oracle/9.2.0.1.0
```

Second, set the Oracle system identifier (Oracle SID) for your database to uniquely identify your database. This will be the same as your *db_name*init.ora parameter value.

```
$ export ORACLE_SID=remorse
```

Ensuring You Have the Privileges to Create Databases

Every Oracle9*i* database has a set of administrative users that comes with the database automatically upon its creation. These include users to manage the database itself and others to monitor various components of the database. Of these default users, two users are special users because these accounts can be used to perform most of the administrative tasks. They are the *SYS* and *SYSTEM* accounts.

The default password for SYS is *change_on_install* and the password for the SYSTEM account is *manager*. In Oracle9*i* version 9.2, you can specify passwords for these two critical accounts as part of your database creation statement, as you'll see shortly. In addition to the two administrative user accounts, most types of Oracle databases come with several other default accounts, usually with default passwords. Please see the section "Changing the Passwords for the Default Users" to learn how to ensure that you change all the default passwords. All users except SYS need to be explicitly granted high-level privileges before they can perform special administrative functions such as creating databases and starting, stopping, and backing them up. The privilege SYSDBA will allow the user SYS to create databases.

The interesting thing about the SYSDBA role is that you don't really need to have the database open or even have a database before you can invoke it. Before you create the database, you'll be creating the instance (SGA + Oracle processes) and the SYSDBA privilege is in effect even at the instance level. You'll be connecting to the database as the superuser SYS and invoking the SYSDBA role as follows:

```
Connect sys as sysdba
```

If the user oracle is made a part of a special group called DBA in the /etc/group file by the system administrator, you can use the following command to log in as the SYS user with the SYSDBA privilege:

```
Connect / as sysdba
```

Creating the Init.ora File

Now you'll create an initialization file with a set of basic parameters for your remorse database. As most of these parameters are easily modifiable later on, the goal isn't to be precise or exhaustive at this point, but rather to get the database up and running quickly. Although the modification of init.ora parameters is not your first or the most important place to do performance tuning, you need to constantly judge performance vis-à-vis all the modifiable parameters. What may be an appropriate setting for an initial database may not be ideal for a much larger database whose needs might also have changed from the time it was conceived and built.

Assume that your remorse database is for supporting an OLTP application. Thus, you won't see most of the typical data warehouse–oriented parameters in your initialization file. Listing 9-4 shows the initialization parameters for the remorse database.

Listing 9-4. Initialization Parameters File for the Remorse Database

```
##  Initialization Parameters for the Remorse Database
##  Database Name and other Related Parameter
db_name=remorse
instance_name=remorse
db_domain=world
##  Files and other Related Parameters
db_files = 500
control_files=(/test02/app/oracle/oradata/
cont1.ora,/test01/app/oracle/oradta/cont2.ora)
db_file_multiblock_read_count = 16
utl_file_dir=/test01/app/oracle/oradata/utldir
##  Memory Configuration Parameters
db_block_size=8192db_cache_size = 25165824
shared_pool_size = 3500000
pga_aggregate_target = 25000000_cache_advice =ON
log_buffer = 512000
##  Process and Session Parameters
processes = 100
open_cursors = 100
## Parallel Processing Parameters
parallel_max_servers = 5
## Diagnostics Related Parameters
oracle_trace_enabled=true
timed_statistics = true
user_dump_dest='/test01/app/oracle/
admin/remorseremorse/udump'
background_dump_dest='/test01/app/oracle
/admin/remorseremorse/bdump'
core_dump_dest = '/test01/app/oracle
/admin/remorseremorse/cdump'
##  Performance and Tuning Related Parameters
Cursor_Sharing = similar
```

```
Optimizer_Mode= Choose
Query_Rewrite_Enabled = True
Query_Rewrite_Integrity = Trusted
Cursor_Space_For_Time = True
## Undo Space related Parameters
undo_tablespace = undotbs
undo_management = auto
undo_retention  = 10800
## Archive Log Related Parameters
# log_archive_start = true
# log_archive_dest = /test02/app/oracle
/oradata/archive
# log_archive_format = "T%TS%S.ARC"
## Recovery Related Parameters
fast_start_mttr_target = 600
##  Database Authorization Related Parameters
os_authent_prefix =" "
remote_login_passwordfile = none
## Data Block Verification Parameters
db_block_checksum = True
```

Once you have your initialization file configured, you are ready
to actually create the database. Make sure you save the initremorse.ora file in
the $ORACLE_HOME/dbs directory, which is the default location for an init.ora
file or an SPFILE on UNIX systems. This way, Oracle will always find it without
your having to specify the complete path of the location.

Starting the Oracle Instance

To create the database, first you must have the instance up and running.
Remember, an instance can exist without any database attached to it. The active
instance makes it possible for you to create the database. The following are the
actual steps.

First, make sure your ORACLE_SID and ORACLE_HOME directories are correctly specified.

Before you can issue the database creation commands, you must first log into
the database through the SQL*Plus interface. Note that you must connect as SYS,
the superuser, with the default password of change_on_install, but due to a quirk
in the way Oracle uses this account, you really can type in *anything* for the
password to get in. It's the slash (/) that's the key to getting in as SYS, not the
password that follows it!

```
Oracle@MYserver [/test01/app/oracle/9.2.0.1.0/dbs]
[remorse] $ sqlplus /nolog
SQL*Plus: Release 9.2.0.1.0 - Production on
Sun Dec 8 14:35:06 2003
© Copyright 2001 Oracle Corporation.  All rights reserved.
```

```
SQL> connect sys as sysdba
Enter password:
Connected to an idle instance.
```

Now you need to start the instance in the nomount mode. Remember that the nomount mode implies that the control files haven't been opened yet. Because you don't have any control files yet for this database, you can only open it in the nomount mode. Remember that an instance consists of all the Oracle background processes in addition to the allocation of memory to Oracle. The instance will be started using the parameters specified in initremorse.ora, which you have stored in the directory /test01/app/oracle/9.2.0.1.0/dbs, which is the ORACLE_HOME directory.

```
SQL> startup nomount
ORACLE instance started.
Total System Global Area  141519848 bytes
Fixed Size                   736232 bytes
Variable Size             113246208 bytes
Database Buffers           25165824 bytes
Redo Buffers                2371584 bytes
SQL>
```

You can see that all the background processes for your database instance have been started at this point by using the *ps –ef* command, as shown in Listing 9-5.

Listing 9-5. The Background Processes for the Remorse Database

```
oracle@Myserver    [/u01/app/oracle]
[remorse] $ ps -ef | grep remorse
oracle  5196   1  0 Dec  4 ?   2:52 ora_qmn0_remorse
oracle  5209   1  0 Dec  4 ?   0:02 ora_d000_remorse
oracle  5074   1  0 Dec  4 ?   2:05 ora_dbw1_remorse
oracle  5141   1  0 Dec  4 ?   0:00 ora_reco_remorse
oracle  5014   1  0 Dec  4 ?   1:15 ora_pmon_remorse
oracle  5090   1  0 Dec  4 ?   4:40 ora_ckpt_remorse
oracle  5084   1  0 Dec  4 ?   2:12 ora_lgwr_remorse
oracle  5055   1  0 Dec  4 ?   2:06 ora_dbw0_remorse
oracle  5115   1  0 Dec  4 ?   1:31 ora_smon_remorse
oracle  5204   1  0 Dec  4 ?   0:04 ora_s000_remorse
oracle 24570 24395  2 09:58:12 pts/2 0:00 grep remorse
oracle  5172      1  0 Dec  4 ? 0:57 ora_cjq0_remorse
oracle@Myserver    [/u01/app/oracle]
```

You can execute a simple query at this stage to verify the version of the database, as shown in Listing 9-6.

Listing 9-6. Determining the Database Version

```
SQL> select * from v$version;
BANNER
---------------------------------------------
Oracle9i Enterprise Edition Release 9.2.0.1.0
- 64bit Production
PL/SQL Release 9.2.0.1.0 - Production
CORE    9.2.0.1.0       Production
TNS for HPUX: Version 9.2.0.1.0 - Production
NLSRTL Version 9.2.0.1.0 - Production
SQL>
```

At this point, go to the location of your bdump directory, /test01/app/oracle/admin/remorseremorse, and look at the alert_remorse.log file. Oracle will always write all the start-up and shutdown information to this file (as I mentioned earlier), as well as any errors during instance creation and routine database operation. Here are the contents of the alertremorse.log file at this point. The alert log lists all the nondefault initialization parameters that you had specified in your initremorse.ora file. Note the starting up of all the Oracle processes: PMON, database writer, log writer, CKPT, SMON, and RECO. As Listing 9-7 shows, this is a clean start-up so far, as there are no errors either on the screen or in the alert log file.

Listing 9-7. The Instance Creation Process in the Alert Log

```
Wed Dec  4 13:00:07 2002
Starting ORACLE instance (normal)
LICENSE_MAX_SESSION = 0
LICENSE_SESSIONS_WARNING = 0
SCN scheme 1
Using log_archive_dest parameter default value
LICENSE_MAX_USERS = 0
SYS auditing is disabled
Starting up ORACLE RDBMS Version: 9.2.0.1.0.
System parameters with non-default values:
  processes               = 50
  timed_statistics        = TRUE
  shared_pool_size        = 50331648
  large_pool_size         = 8388608
  java_pool_size          = 33554432
  control_files           = /test01/app/oracle/CONTROL_01.CTL, /test01/app/orac
.CTL, /test01/app/oracle/CONTROL_03.CTL
  db_block_size           = 8192
  db_cache_size           = 25165824
  compatible              = 9.2.0.0.0
  db_file_multiblock_read_count= 16
  fast_start_mttr_target  = 300
  undo_management         = AUTO
```

```
        undo_tablespace            = UNDOTBS
        undo_retention             = 10800
        db_domain                  = world
        instance_name              = remorse
        dispatchers                = (PROTOCOL=TCP) (SERVICE=realXDB)
        job_queue_processes        = 10
        hash_join_enabled          = TRUE
        background_dump_dest        = /test01/app/oracle/admin/remorse/bdump
        user_dump_dest              = /test01/app/oracle/admin/remorse/udump
        core_dump_dest              = /test01/app/oracle/admin/remorse/cdump
        db_name                    = remorse
        open_cursors               = 100
        star_transformation_enabled= FALSE
        query_rewrite_enabled      = FALSE
        pga_aggregate_target       = 25165824
        aq_tm_processes            = 1
PMON started with pid=2
DBW0 started with pid=3
DBW1 started with pid=4
LGWR started with pid=5
CKPT started with pid=6
SMON started with pid=7
RECO started with pid=8
CJQ0 started with pid=9
QMN0 started with pid=10
Wed Dec  4 13:00:17 2002
starting up 1 shared server(s) ...
starting up 1 dispatcher(s) for network address '(ADDRESS=(PARTTAI=YES)(PROTOCOL
=TCP))'...
```

What do you have so far? Well, you have a running Oracle instance, which is defined as the sum of the Oracle processes and the memory that's allocated for the user oracle. You don't have a database yet; you'll create one from scratch in the next section.

The Create Database Script

The simplest database you can create will have a single tablespace to hold the data dictionary, two redo log files, a default temporary tablespace, and the undo tablespace. Once you have this database going, you can add any number of new tablespaces to it. Let's create your bare-bones Oracle9*i* database with the database name remorse now. Listing 9-8 provides the database creation script for the database remorse.

Listing 9-8. The Create Database Script

```
SQL>  create database remorse
  2  user sys identified by newsys1pass
  3  user system identified by newsystem1pass
  4  maxinstances 1
  5  maxloghistory 1
  6  maxlogfiles 5
  7  maxdatafiles 200
  8  character set US7ASCII
  9  national character set AL16UTF16
 10  datafile '/test01/app/oracle/oradata/remorse/system01.dbf' size 400M
 11  extent management LOCAL
 12  default TEMPORARY tablespace temptbs1
 13  tempfile '/test01/app/oracle/oradata/remorse/temp01.dbf' size 200M
 14  UNDO tablespace undotbs
 15  datafile '/test01/app/oracle/oradata/remorse/undotbs01.dbf' size 100m
 16  autoextend on next 1M maxsize unlimited
 17  LOGFILE group 1 ('/test01/app/oracle/oradata/remorse/redo01.log') size 100M,
 18*         group 2 ('/test01/app/oracle/oradata/remorse/redo02.log') size 100M
SQL> /
Database created.
SQL>
```

Here's a quick review of the *create database* statement:

- Line 1 issues the *create database* command to Oracle. This command prompts the creation of two control files. The locations of these control files are read from the initremorse.ora initialization file. Lines 2 and 3 show how you can specify the passwords for the two key users SYS and SYSTEM, although it isn't mandatory to do so.

- Lines 4 through 7 specify the maximum and minimum for files and instances. These are standard and you can use these same numbers for most of the databases you'll be creating. Lines 8 and 9 specify the character sets used by the database to store the database. Just use these character sets for all the databases you'll be creating, unless you have special needs based on languages other than English.

- Line 10 creates the System tablespace with one data file of size 400MB. The data dictionary is created within this System tablespace. One system rollback segment is also automatically created. Line 11 specifies that the System tablespace should be locally managed, rather than dictionary managed.

- Line 12 creates the default temporary tablespace TEMPTBS1, with one temporary file of size 100MB. All users have to be allotted a temporary tablespace when the users are initially created in the database. If you don't do so, the users will be allocated to the default temporary tablespace TEMPTBS1 automatically. Notice how line 13 specifies that the file used for the temporary tablespace is a *temp file,* not a regular data file. You can't create the temporary tablespace with a normal data file specification.

- Line 14 creates the undo tablespace UNDOTBS, with one data file of size 200MB. Line 15 specifies the location of the data file for the undo tablespace, and line 16 specifies that this file can autoextend.

- Lines 17 and 18 create the minimum pair of redo logs required by Oracle, with one data file for each.

Oracle mounts and opens the database at this stage. As you'll see in the last part of this chapter, mounting a database involves reading the control files, and opening the database enables all users to access the various parts of the new database remorse. Take a peek at the alert log at this point to see what Oracle actually did when the *create database* command was issued. Listing 9-9 provides the relevant portion from the bottom of the alert log, which is located in the $ORACLE_BASE/admin/dbs directory and is named alert_remorse.log.

Listing 9-9. The Database Creation Process in the Alert Log

```
Wed Dec  4 13:30:50 2002
create database remorse
user sys identified by
user system identified by
maxinstances 1
maxloghistory 1
maxlogfiles 5
maxdatafiles 200
character set US7ASCII
national character set AL16UTF16
datafile '/test01/app/oracle/oradata/
remorse/system01.dbf' size 400M
extent management LOCAL
default TEMPORARY tablespace temptbs1
tempfile '/test01/app/oracle/oradata
/remorse/temp01.dbf' size 200M
UNDO tablespace undotbs
datafile '/test01/app/oracle/oradata/
remorse/undotbs01.dbf' size 100m
autoextend on next 1M maxsize unlimited
LOGFILE group 1 ('/test01/app/oracle/oradata/
remorse/redo01.log') size 100M,
        group 2 ('/test01/app/oracle/oradata/
remorse/redo02.log') size 100M
Wed Dec  4 13:30:50 2002
Database mounted in Exclusive Mode.
Wed Dec  4 13:30:56 2002
Successful mount of redo thread 1,
with mount id 3482324042.
Assigning activation ID 3482324042 (0xcf900c4a)
Thread 1 opened at log sequence 1
  Current log# 1 seq# 1 mem# 0: /test01/app/oracle/oradata/remorse/redo01.log
Successful open of redo thread 1.
```

```
Wed Dec  4 13:30:57 2002
SMON: enabling cache recovery
Wed Dec  4 13:30:57 2002
create tablespace SYSTEM datafile  '/test01/app/oracle/oradata/remorse/system01.
dbf' size 400M
   EXTENT MANAGEMENT LOCAL online
Wed Dec  4 13:31:09 2002
Completed: create tablespace SYSTEM datafile
 '/test01/app/or
Wed Dec  4 13:31:09 2002
create rollback segment SYSTEM tablespace SYSTEM
   storage (initial 50K next 50K)
Completed: create rollback segment SYSTEM
 tablespace SYSTEM
Wed Dec  4 13:31:36 2002
CREATE UNDO TABLESPACE UNDOTBS DATAFILE  '/test01/app/oracle/oradata/remorse/und
otbs01.dbf' size 100m
autoextend on next 1M maxsize unlimited
Wed Dec  4 13:31:40 2002
Created Undo Segment _SYSSMU1$
Created Undo Segment _SYSSMU2$
Created Undo Segment _SYSSMU3$
Created Undo Segment _SYSSMU4$
Created Undo Segment _SYSSMU5$
Created Undo Segment _SYSSMU6$
Created Undo Segment _SYSSMU7$
Created Undo Segment _SYSSMU8$
Created Undo Segment _SYSSMU9$
Created Undo Segment _SYSSMU10$
Undo Segment 1 Onlined
Undo Segment 2 Onlined
Undo Segment 3 Onlined
Undo Segment 4 Onlined
Undo Segment 5 Onlined
Undo Segment 6 Onlined
Undo Segment 7 Onlined
Undo Segment 8 Onlined
Undo Segment 9 Onlined
Undo Segment 10 Onlined
Successfully onlined Undo Tablespace 1.
Completed: CREATE UNDO TABLESPACE UNDOTBS
DATAFILE  '/test01/
Wed Dec  4 13:31:42 2002
CREATE TEMPORARY TABLESPACE TEMPTBS1
 TEMPFILE  '/test01/app/oracle/oradata/remor
se/temp01.dbf' size 200M
Completed: CREATE TEMPORARY TABLESPACE
TEMPTBS1 TEMPFILE  '/t
Wed Dec  4 13:31:42 2002
```

```
ALTER DATABASE DEFAULT TEMPORARY TABLESPACE
 TEMPTBS1
Completed: ALTER DATABASE DEFAULT TEMPORARY
 TABLESPACE TEMPTB
Wed Dec  4 13:31:46 2002
SMON: enabling tx recovery
Wed Dec  4 13:31:49 2002
replication_dependency_tracking turned off
 (no async multimaster replication found)
Completed: create database remorse
user sys identified by
us
```

Here are the key steps in the database creation log shown in Listing 9-9:

- The statement *database mounted* means that Oracle has opened the control files you specified in the init.ora files.

- The first redo log file is successfully created and opened for recovery purposes. The *redo thread 1 opened* statement indicates this.

- The System tablespace is successfully created.

- The rollback segment named *system* is created in the System tablespace.

- The undo tablespace, UNDOTBS, is successfully created. Oracle automatically creates ten undo segments and brings them online. This is because you chose *undo_management=AUTO* in the initremorse.ora file.

- The tablespace TEMPTBS1 is first created as a temporary tablespace, using a temp file instead of the regular data files used for permanent tablespaces. After the temporary tablespace is created, the *ALTER DATABASE DEFAULT TEMPORARY TABLESPACE TEMPTBS1* command is used to designate TEMPTBS1 as the default temporary tablespace for this database.

- Finally, Oracle indicates that the remorse database has been successfully created.

Running Oracle Scripts to Create Data Dictionary Objects

Oracle provides two important scripts, catalog.sql and catproc.sql, that you need to run at this point in the database creation. The catalog.sql script populates the database with the data dictionary views, public synonyms, and other objects. The data dictionary base tables, the parents of the V$ views, are the first objects created in the Oracle database. The catproc.sql script creates the Oracle-provided packages and other objects to support the use of PL/SQL code in the database. When you run these scripts, you'll see a lot of information flow past you on the screen indicating that the necessary database objects being created and so on. Just let the two scripts do what they are supposed to do. It should take about half an hour to run these two scripts.

NOTE *Ignore any errors that you see during the execution of the catalog.sql and catproc.sql scripts. These errors mostly state that the object that is to be dropped doesn't exist. If it bothers you to see all those errors, you can reassure yourself by running each script twice. You won't see any errors during execution if you do this.*

Here's how you run the two scripts:

```
Sql> @/test02/app/oracle/product/9.2.0.1.0/rdbms/admin/catalog.sqlPackage created
...
Commit Complete.
Sql>
Sql> @test01/app/oracle//9.2.0.1.0/rdbms/admin/catproc.sql
Package created.
...
Sql>
```

TIP *If you use OMF, you need to specify the location of the data files and log files in the init.ora file. Once you do this, all you need to do is to execute the following statement to create a new database:*

```
SQL> create database remorse;
```

Oracle will automatically create a 100MB autoextensible system file, a pair of redo logs, control files, an undo tablespace, and a temporary tablespace. Simple as that! Chapter 16 shows you this and other interesting features of OMF.

Creating Additional Tablespaces

Now you have a real Oracle9*i* database humming away on your server, although you still can't do a whole lot with it, because it's just a bare-bones database. What's missing? Well, structurally speaking, you have a complete database, but it's of no functional use because you don't have any application code, application objects, or data stored within it. To be able to create objects and load data, you need physical space, and that's what you'll handle next by creating a number of table-spaces.

So how many tablespaces should you create? You don't want thousands of small tablespaces, because you'll have a hard time managing all of them. On the other hand, a very limited number of extra-large tablespaces may lead to contention within your database. First, size the tables, indexes, and other database objects using standard table-sizing guidelines. This will give you an idea of how many tablespaces you'll need to create. Find out from the system administrator what the maximum file size on your system is. Based on all this information, you can come to an approximate idea about the best number of tablespaces to create.

The idea behind tablespaces, of course, is to group similar objects together. If you have a table with a potential of millions of large rows, there's no point in trying to contain it in a 100MB tablespace. Create a large tablespace for these large tables and the associated indexes, which all will tend to be very large. The idea is to have as many tablespaces as necessary to group identical tables together while storing their indexes in separate tablespaces.

For the remorse database, assume you have a small amount of data that will require six tablespaces, each sized at 100MB. Four of the six tablespaces will be for the data and the other two for the associated indexes. It's a good idea to provide a set of data and index tablespaces for each separate application. All the applications in this database will share the single temporary tablespace TEMPTBS1. Listing 9-10 shows the commands necessary to create the tablespaces.

Listing 9-10. Creating Additional Tablespaces

```
SQL> create tablespace sales01 logging
2  datafile '/test02/app/oracle/oradata/remorse/sales01_01.dbf'
3  size 25M autoextend on next 2560k maxsize unlimited
4  extent management local uniform size 16M;
Tablespace created.
SQL> create tablespace saleindx01 logging
2  datafile '/test02/app/oracle/oradata/remorse/saleiindx01_01.dbf'
3  size 25M autoextend on next 2560k maxsize unlimited
4* extent management local uniform size 16M;
Tablespace created.
SQL>
```

Finally, create a general-purpose tablespace that can be assigned to all users as their default tablespace, a tablespace they can use to create specific objects pertaining to their username only that don't belong to any application running on the system. Call this general-purpose tablespace the *users* tablespace and create it as follows:

```
SQL> create tablespace users logging
2  datafile '/test02/app/oracle/oradata/remorse/users01.dbf'
3  size 25M autoextend on next 2560k maxsize unlimited
extent management local uniform size 16M;
Tablespace created.
```

Now, verify the tablespaces in the remorse database:

```
SQL> select tablespace_name from dba_tablespaces;
TABLESPACE NAME
SYSTEM
UNDOTBS
TEMPTBS01
SALES01
SALEINDX01
USERS
6 rows selected.
SQL>
```

Changing the Passwords for the Default Users

One of the first tasks to perform after you create a new database is to change the password for all the default users. The 9.2 version of Oracle9*i* allows you to provide new passwords for both the SYSTEM and SYS users during database creation, as you've seen. Let's see what other default users are in the database by using the following query. The names and number of these default users could differ among databases. For example, if you choose to let Oracle create your database using the Oracle Installer, you could pick a database customized for an OLTP, a DSS, or a hybrid database. Each of these databases has a different group of specialized default users associated with it. Nevertheless, all types of databases will have about three or four common users. In your remorse database, these are the users created as default users:

```
SQL> select username from dba_users;
USERNAME
SYS
SYSTEM
OUTLN
DBSNMP
```

The following are the default passwords for the preceding usernames:

```
Sys        change_on_install
System     manager
Outln      outln
Dbsnmp     dbsnmp
```

You don't have to worry about the SYS and SYSTEM passwords, as you've already changed them during the database creation process. The OUTLN user account is used to provide stored outlines for SQL queries, and the DBSNMP account is for the Oracle Intelligent Agent. The default password for each of these accounts is the same as the username. Change these passwords immediately using the following command, as they represent a potential security problem:

```
SQL> alter user outln identified by 'new_password';
SQL> alter user dbsnmp identified by 'new_password';
```

Changing the Archive Logging Mode

You can configure a database to run in a noarchivelog mode or in an archivelog mode. In noarchivelog mode, Oracle won't archive or save the redo logs it filled up. Instead, it overwrites them after each log switch. In archivelog mode, Oracle will ensure that it first saves the filled up redo log file before permitting it to be overwritten. The distinction between archivelog mode and noarchivelog mode is extremely important. Online redo logs record all changes made to the database.

If you archive all the filled redo logs, you'll have a complete record of the changes made to the database since the last backup. In the event you lose a disk, for example, you can use your backups of the databases along with the archived redo logs to recover the database without losing any committed data. Chapters 14 and 15 deal with the archivelog process and database recovery in detail. Here, I'll show you how to alter the logging mode of a database. You'll need to confirm the archivelog mode of the database by making the following query:

```
SQL> select log_mode from v$database;
LOG_MODE
------------
NOARCHIVELOG
SQL>
```

Now that you've verified that your database is indeed running in the noarchivelog mode, let's see what you need to do to turn archiving on in your new database.

First, make sure that the archivelog-related parameters in your init.ora file (or SPFILE) are set. In my init.ora file, I add (or uncomment) the following parameters:

```
log_archive_start = true
log_archive_dest = /test01/app/oracle/oradata/remorse/arch
log_archive_format = "T%TS%S.ARC"
```

Second, you need to stop and start your database so it can come up with the new archivelog-related information, which wasn't there in the init.ora file or was commented out initially. Note that of the three archivelog-related parameters, only one, the *log_archive_dest* parameter, is a dynamically modifiable parameter. The other two are static, meaning you can't get by with using the *alter system* command to change the archive logging mode of your database; you have to bounce your database.

You have a certain amount of room to maneuver around this limitation: You don't really have to set the two static parameters for archiving to begin. The *log_archive_format* variable just sets the format for the way your archived log files are named. If you don't specify a value, they will take Oracle's default archive log naming convention. The second static parameter, *log_archive_start*, doesn't start archiving—it's the *alter database archivelog* command that starts archiving the redo log files. The *log_archive_start* parameter only determines whether the logs are archived manually or automatically. If you set it to *true*, the filled-up redo logs will be automatically archived by Oracle to the archive destination. If you don't set this parameter, you need to manually archive the logs.

Third, start the database in the mount mode only by using the following command:

```
SQL> startup mount
```

Fourth, use the following command to turn archive logging on:

```
SQL> alter database archivelog;
Database altered.
SQL>
```

Finally, open the database. Your database will now run in the archivelog mode.

```
SQL> alter database open;.
Database altered.
SQL>
```

You can confirm that the database is running in the archivelog mode by using the following command. The result shows you that the database is in the archive mode and automatic archival is enabled.

```
SQL> archive log list;
Database log mode              Archive Mode
Automatic archival             Enabled
Archive destination            /test01/app/oracle/
oradata/remorse/arch
Oldest online log sequence     3
Next log sequence to archive   4
Current log sequence           4
SQL>
```

If the *archive_log_start* parameter is already set to *true* in the init.ora file, or if you don't care whether the archiving has to be done manually for the time being, you can skip the shutdown and start-up parts in the preceding discussion. Instead, you can simply use the following set of *alter system* dynamic commands to set up archive logging immediately and stop logging if it is already in the archivelog mode.

```
SQL> alter system archive log start;
System altered.
SQL> alter system archive log stop;
System altered.
SQL>
```

Running the Pupbld.sql File

You may see errors like the following when new users created by you try accessing the database through SQL*Plus:

```
Error accessing PRODUCT_USER_PROFILEWarning:
  Product user profile information not loaded!
You may need to run PUPBLD.SQL as SYSTEM
```

The product_user_profile table is a table Oracle maintains to control access to the database through SQL*Plus. Chapter 6 discusses how to use the product_user_profile table to restrict operations by certain users in SQL*Plus. Make sure you are logged in as the user System and run the following script to ensure that this table can be accessed properly by all users, so that their SQL*Plus privileges can be checked properly:

```
SQL> @/$ORACLE_HOME/sqlplus/admin/pupbld.sql
DROP SYNONYM  PRODUCT_USER_PROFILE
...
Synonym created.
SQL>
```

What Next?

You've now created the new database, but you still need to do a few things to make remorse a fully functional database (patience—you're almost there!).

At this point, you have the instance up and running and a "first draft" of the physical database based on tentative estimates subject to change later on. To make this database do something useful, you need to *create users*. To empower the users and ensure the security of databases, you'll need to *grant* these users specific roles and privileges. You have to *create objects* such as tables, views, indexes, synonyms, sequences, and so on for the new database based on the requests for the application development team. You also have to create the necessary application code in the database, including stored procedures and packages. Because an empty database with no data won't do anyone much good, you need to *load data* into the database in most cases, from various sources. You have to *establish connectivity* between the database you just created, the users, and other systems that need to access your database. Finally, to secure your database from unexpected failures and malfunctioning systems, you also need to *back up the database* at this point and also put a regular backup schema in place before you go off on your long-awaited and well earned vacation. The remaining chapters of this book address all these important topics in detail.

The Server Parameter File (SPFILE)

The init.ora file is the initialization file where you specify values of all the parameters you intend to use at database creation time. What if you need to change some of the parameters later on? Well, you can do so in two ways: You can change the init.ora parameters, and stop and start the database instance. Or, if the parameter is dynamically configurable (through an *alter system* or *alter session* command), you can change its value while the instance is running. Although being able to dynamically reconfigure database parameters is nice, there are inherent problems with this approach. When you restart the database, dynamically changed parameters are gone, because they weren't part of the init.ora file. So, if you intend to make a change permanent after you dynamically change it, you have to remember to correctly modify the init.ora file so those changes will really become permanent next time the database reads the file when it's restarted. Often, DBAs forget to do this manual chore.

The *server parameter file* (SPFILE) is an alternative (or a complement) to the init.ora file, and it makes the dynamic parameter changes permanent on an ongoing basis. Any parameter changed dynamically using the *alter system* command is stored in the server parameter file, which already consists of all the parameters in the regular init.ora file. After you create the database, you can create the SPFILE from your init.ora file as shown in the next section. If you later use this SPFILE to start your database, all dynamic changes made to the initialization parameters will stay permanent, if you so wish, and become part of your SPFILE. This way, you can ensure that parameter changes will not be lost in between database shutdowns and restarts. The file is called a server file because it is always maintained on the machine where the Oracle database server is located. Oracle recommends the use of the SPFILE to dynamically maintain the database configuration parameters.

The number of dynamically modifiable parameters in Oracle9*i* version 9.2 is quite high, as the following queries show:

```
SQL> select count(*) from v$parameter;
  COUNT(*)
    257
SQL> select count(*) from v$parameter
  2  where ISSYS_MODIFIABLE != 'FALSE';
  COUNT(*)
    120
SQL>
```

Almost half of the initialization parameters are changeable through the *alter system* command, showing why the SPFILE might be a smart way to maintain the list of initialization parameters and their changing values.

In addition to making parameter changes persistent across instance start-ups, SPFILEs also make it simpler to use OEM to start databases remotely. Without an SPFILE, you have to synchronize the local version of the init.ora file with the version of the init.ora file on the server where the database is running. With the SPFILE, there is no need to maintain a local init.ora file. Furthermore, when you use Oracle Real Application Clusters (ORAC), the SPFILE comes in quite handy, because Oracle will *self-tune* several parameter settings in the SPFILE.

When the database is started, unless you specify the type of initialization file and its location explicitly, Oracle will look for the SPFILE first. On UNIX systems, the default location for the SPFILE is $ORACLE_HOME/dbs/SPFILE*db_name*.ora, and on Windows systems it is $ORACLE_HOME\database\SPFILE*db_name*.ora. If the SPFILE is not present, Oracle will look for the init.ora file in the default location, $ORACLE_HOME/dbs.

Creating a Server Parameter File

Oracle still uses the traditional init.ora file (parameter file, or PFILE) as the default configuration file for all the initialization parameters. However, Oracle also recommends that you create and use an SPFILE for all databases. You can create the SPFILE from the init.ora file, and the process is very simple. You must be logged in as a user with SYSDBA or SYSOPER privileges to create the SPFILE from the init.ora file. In the example that follows, PFILE stands for the init.ora file for the remorse database.

```
SQL> create SPFILE from PFILE='/test01/app/oracle/9.2.0.1.0/dbs/initremorse.ora';
File created.
SQL>
```

The previous command will create the SPFILE in the default locations given in the previous section. The file will be name SPFILEremorse.ora. You can also create an SPFILE by giving it an explicit name, as shown in the following example. Any subsequent use of the following command will overwrite the previous SPFILE.

```
SQL> CREATE SPFILE='/u01/app/oracle/product/9.2.0.1.0/dbs/remorse_spfile.ora'
FROM PFILE='/u01/app/oracle/product/9.2.0.1.0/dbs/remorseinit.ora';
```

If you want Oracle to place the PFILE in the default directory, $ORACLE_HOME/dbs, you can simply issue the following command to create the SPFILE from the init.ora file:

```
SQL> create spfile from pfile;
File created.
SQL>
```

You can also create a new init.ora file in the default location by using the following command:

```
SQL> create pfile from spfile;
File created.
SQL>
```

If you bounce the database now, the instance will start up using your new SPFILE. Oracle will look for the initialization parameter list in the following order (note that the default locations for the init.ora file and the SPFILE were explained in the previous section):

1. It looks for the SPFILE$DB_NAME.ora file in the default location.

2. It looks for a file called spfile.ora in the default location.

3. If it doesn't find the SPFILE under either of the possible names, Oracle will simply look for the traditional init.ora file in the default location.

NOTE *You can place the PFILE anywhere, not just in the default location. If you do place it in a nondefault location, you have to specify the location using the SPFILE parameter.*

Creating the SPFILE from the init.ora file doesn't mean that you can't use the init.ora file anymore. If you need to start the instance with the older init.ora file, you can do so as before by specifying it explicitly:

```
SQL> startup pfile='/u01/app/oracle/product/9.2.0.1.0/dbs/initremorse.ora';
```

However, you can't specify the SPFILE instead of the PFILE in the preceding example. Oracle won't allow you to specify the SPFILE directly in a *startup* command, but you can do so indirectly by using a PFILE (init.ora) file, which includes just one initialization parameter: the new SPFILE parameter, as shown in the following example. Note that the init.ora file can have just this one line it. After creating this new init.ora file, you can specify the variable PFILE in the *startup* command.

```
SQL> SPFILE = '/u01/app/oracle/product/9.2.0.1.0/dbs/SPFILEremorse.ora'
```

Listing 9-11 shows the contents of the SPFILE (called SPFILEremorse.ora) that was created from the initfinance1.ora file as a result of the previous command.

Listing 9-11. A Sample SPFILE

```
*.Cursor_Sharing='similar'
*.Cursor_Space_For_Time=True
*.Optimizer_Mode='Choose'
*.Oracle_Trace_Enable=Tru
*.Query_Rewrite_Enabled=True
*.Query_Rewrite_Integrity='Trusted'
*.background_dump_dest='/test01/app/oracle/admin/remorse/bdump'
*.compatible='9.2.0.0.0'
*.control_files='/test02/app/oracle/oradata
remorse/cont1.ora',
'/test01/app/oracle/oradata/remorse/cont2.ora'
*.core_dump_dest='/test01/app/oracle/admin/remorse/cdump'
*.db_block_buffers=500
*.db_block_checksum=True
*.db_block_size=8192
*.db_cache_advice='on'
*.db_file_multiblock_read_count=8
*.db_files=500
*.db_name='remorse'
*.fast_start_mttr_target=600
*.global_names=TRUE
*.instance_name='remorse'
*.log_buffer=512000
*.max_dump_file_size='10240'
*.open_cursors=100
*.os_authent_prefix=' '
*.parallel_max_servers=5
*.pga_aggregate_target=20000000
*.processes=100
*.remote_login_passwordfile='none'
*.shared_pool_size=100000000
*.timed_statistics=true
*.undo_management='auto'
*.undo_retention=3600
*.undo_tablespace='undotbs'
*.user_dump_dest='/test01/app/oracle/admin/remorse/udump'
*.utl_file_dir='/test01/app/oracle/oradata/utldir'
```

CAUTION *You can't modify the contents of an SPFILE like you can an init.ora file. The SPFILE is a binary file, and you may end up corrupting the file if you try to modify it.*

The V$SPPARAMETER dynamic view is comparable to the $PARAMETER view and is used to record all the initialization parameter names and their values when using the SPFILE to run your instance.

TIP *It's customary for DBAs to place comments in the init.ora file. The SPFILE will ignore these comments. However, if you place the comments on the* same line *as the parameter (e.g.,* cursor_sharing=false # comment*) in the init.ora file, the SPFILE will show you all your comments.*

Scope of Dynamic Parameter Changes

You now have an SPFILE that contains all your initialization parameters. Does this mean that all the changes you make to the dynamic initialization parameters now persist automatically? Well, *you* control whether any changes to the initialization parameters persist by getting recorded in the SPFILE or not. Once you create an SPFILE, you can use a special clause called *scope* as part of all your *alter system* commands, and the *scope* clause will determine if the changes persist or not. The *scope* clause can take the following three values:

- SPFILE
- Memory
- Both

When the *scope* clause is set to *memory*, changes are merely temporary and they go away after the database is restarted. When the *scope* clause is set to *both*, all dynamic changes get recorded in the SPFILE, besides being operational in the instance immediately. When the *scope* clause is set to *SPFILE*, changes aren't applied immediately but only get recorded in the SPFILE. When you specify *SPFILE* as the value for the *scope* variable (*scope=SPFILE*), dynamic and static configuration parameters become effective only after the next start-up of the database. Note that for static parameters, *scope=SPFILE* is the only option, because the parameters can't be activated right away by definition. As you can see, you have enormous flexibility in determining how long a change in a dynamically configurable parameter's value will persist. Here are some examples:

```
sql> alter system set log_archive_dest_2='location=/test02/app/oracle/oradata/arch'
SCOPE=SPFILE;
Sql> alter system set log_checkpoint_interval=600
SCOPE=MEMORY;
Sql> alter system set license_max_users=200
SCOPE=BOTH;
```

If the database instance is started with an SPFILE, *scope=BOTH* is the default option used by Oracle.

To reset a parameter's value to its default value, you can use the *alter system reset* command. Note that the "unsetting" of any configuration parameter that you previously altered using the *set* command really means that the parameter will revert to its default value. The following example shows how you can use the *unset* command to restore the default value of the parameter *sort_area_reserved_size*:

```
SQL> alter system reset sort_area_reserved_size scope=spfile
```

If you wish to modify several parameters in the SPFILE, the easiest way to do so is to first create an init.ora file from the SPFILE, make changes in the init.ora file, and create a new SPFILE from it. The simplest way to create an init.ora file from an SPFILE is to issue the following command. Note that the process I described previously would involve a bouncing of the database.

```
Create pfile from spfile;
```

TIP *Always create an SPFILE soon after you create the initial database. You'll be making a lot of initialization parameter changes on a new database, and the SPFILE gives you the chance to make these changes permanent if you so wish. This eliminates a lot of confusion later on when you're making changes to several initialization parameters at once.*

Starting and Shutting Down the Database

You can start up and shut down your Oracle database through different interfaces. You can do so from the OEM interface and the SQL*Plus interface. You can also do so from a Recovery Manager (RMAN) interface. You'll learn how to start up and shut down databases using OEM in Chapter 17, so you'll focus on performing these operations using the SQL*Plus interface in this chapter.

Starting the Database

When you issue the *startup* command, Oracle will look for the initialization parameters in the default location, $ORACLE_HOME/dbs (UNIX). There, Oracle will look for the relevant files in the following order:

```
SPFILE$ORACLE_SID.ora
SPFILE.ora
Init$ORACLE_SID.ora
```

NOTE *Regardless of which file Oracle reads, you don't have to specify the path and location of the file if it's in the default location. If you wish to store your initialization file in a nondefault location, you have to specify the location when you issue the start-up commands, as you'll see shortly.*

You can start the database in several modes. Let's take a quick look at the different options you have while starting up a database.

The Startup Nomount Command

You can start up the database with just the instance running by using the *startup nomount* command. The control files aren't read and the data files aren't opened when you open a database under this mode. The Oracle background processes are started up and the SGA is allocated to Oracle by the operating system. In fact, the instance is running by itself, rather like the engine of a tractor trailer being started with no trailer attached to the cab (you can't do much with either!). Listing 9-12 shows the database after a *startup nomount* command.

Listing 9-12. Using the Startup Nomount Command

```
oracle@hp50.netbsa.org   [/test01/app/oracle]
[remorse] $ sqlplus /nolog
SQL*Plus: Release 9.2.0.1.0 - Production on Sun Dec 8 09:44:51 2002
© Copyright 2001 Oracle Corporation.  All rights reserved.
SQL> connect / as sysdba
Connected to an idle instance.
SQL> startup nomount
ORACLE instance started.
Total System Global Area  156147688 bytes
Fixed Size                   438248 bytes
Variable Size             146800640 bytes
Database Buffers             8388608 bytes
Redo Buffers                 520192 bytes
SQL>
```

What good does it do to have the database instance running without opening the data files for access? Well, sometimes during certain maintenance operations and during recovery times, you can't have the database open for public access. That's when this "partial open" of the database is necessary. During database creation and when you have to re-create control files, you use the *nomount* start-up option.

The Startup Mount Command

The next step in the database start-up process, after the instance is started, is the mounting of the database. This step reads the control file and mounts (i.e., connects) the data files to the database instance. You can do this in two ways. You can either use the *alter database* command to mount an already started instance, or you can use the *startup mount* command in the beginning, as shown in Listing 9-13.

Listing 9-13. The Startup Mount Command

```
Sql> alter database mount;
Database altered.
Sql>
OR,
SQL> startup mount
ORACLE instance started.
Total System Global Area   156147688 bytes
Fixed Size                    438248 bytes
Variable Size              146800640 bytes
Database Buffers             8388608 bytes
Redo Buffers                  520192 bytes
Database mounted.
SQL>
```

During the mount stage, Oracle will associate the instance with the database. Oracle will open and read the control files, and get the names and locations of the data files and the redo log files. You usually need to start up a database in the mount mode when you're doing activities such as performing a full database recovery, changing the archive logging mode of the database, or renaming data files. Note that all three operations mentioned here require Oracle to access the data files, but can't accommodate any user operations in these files. Hence the opening of the database in the mount mode, with access to the general users still cut off.

The Startup Open Command

The last stage of the start-up process is the database open stage. The database is open for all users, not just the DBA. Prior to this stage, the general users can't connect to the database at all. You can bring the database into the open mode by issuing the *alter database* command as follows:

```
Sql> alter database open;
Database altered.
```

When the database is started in the open mode, all valid users can connect to the database and perform database operations. To open the database, the Oracle server will first open all the data files and the online redo log files and verify that the database is consistent. If the database isn't consistent—for example, if the SCNs in the control files don't match some of the SCNs in the data file headers— the background process will automatically perform an instance recovery before opening the database. If media recovery rather than instance recovery is needed, Oracle will signal that a database recovery is called for and won't open the database until you perform the recovery.

NOTE *When you issue the simple* startup *command, Oracle will process all the start-up steps in sequence and will start the instance and open it for public access all at once. Here's the command:*

```
SQL> startup
ORACLE instance started.
Total System Global Area   156147688 bytes
Fixed Size                    438248 bytes
Variable Size              146800640 bytes
Database Buffers             8388608 bytes
Redo Buffers                  520192 bytes
Database mounted.
Database opened.
SQL>
```

NOTE *When you use the* startup *command, the database name isn't needed; it's optional. As long as your ORACLE_SID parameter is set to the right database, you don't need the database name specified in the* startup *command.*

Restricting Database Access

Sometimes when you're performing data loads or an export or import of data, or when you're performing other critical maintenance tasks, you'll want to have the database in an open stage but restrict general users from accessing the database. You can do so in a couple of different ways. First, you can bring up the database in a restrict mode, which will provide you with complete access and prevent general users from connecting, as follows:

```
SQL> startup restrict;
ORACLE instance started.
Total System Global Area   156147688 bytes
Fixed Size                    438248 bytes
Variable Size              146800640 bytes
Database Buffers             8388608 bytes
Redo Buffers                  520192 bytes
Database mounted.
Database opened.
SQL>
```

When you're done with your maintenance or other tasks and wish to open up the database to the general public, use the *alter system* command, as follows:

```
Sql> alter system disable restricted session;
System altered.
Sql>
```

You can also change an open and unrestricted database into a restricted mode operation by using the following command:

```
Sql> alter system enable restricted session;
System altered.
Sql>
```

When you put a database in a restricted mode using the *alter system* command as shown previously, existing users are not hindered in any way. Only new logins are prevented from logging in, unless they have the restricted session privilege. Once you are done with whatever you need to do, you can put the database back in an unrestricted open mode by using the *alter system disable restrict session* command.

Sometimes you may want to use an open database but prevent any changes to the database for the time being. That is, you want to allow only reads (select operations) against the database, but no writes. You may need to do this when you are performing some types of database recovery, for example. Listing 9-14 shows how you can put your database in a read-only mode.

Listing 9-14. Putting the Database in a Read-Only Mode

```
SQL> startup mount
ORACLE instance started.
Total System Global Area  135338868 bytes
Fixed Size                   453492 bytes
Variable Size             109051904 bytes
Database Buffers           25165824 bytes
Redo Buffers                 667648 bytes
Database mounted.
SQL> alter database open read only;
Database altered.
SQL>
```

The read-only mode is usually employed by standby databases, which are copies of production databases designed to relieve the querying load from the parent production database.

Shutting Down the Database

You may need to shut down a database for a number of reasons, for example, for some types of backup, for upgrades of software, and so on. You have several options for shutting down a running database. The option you choose has several implications for the time it takes to shut down the database and any potential need of database instance recovery upon a consequent starting up of the database. The following sections cover the four available shutdown command options for the Oracle9*i* database.

Shutdown Normal

When you issue the *shutdown normal* command to shut the database down, Oracle will wait for all users to disconnect from the database before shutting the database down. That is, if a user goes on vacation for a week after logging into a database and you subsequently issue a *shutdown normal* command, the database will have to keep running until the user returns. The normal mode is Oracle's default mode for shutting down the database. The command is issued as follows:

```
Sql> shutdown normal
OR
Sql> shutdown
```

The *shutdown normal* command involves the following:

- No new user connections can be made to the database.

- Oracle waits for all users to exit their sessions.

- No instance recovery is needed when you restart the database because Oracle will write all redo log buffers and data block buffers to disk before shutting down. Thus, the database will be consistent when it's shut down in this way.

- Oracle closes the data files and terminates the background processes. Oracle's SGA is deallocated.

Shutdown Transactional

If you don't want to wait for a long time for a user to log off, you can use the *shutdown transactional* command. Oracle will wait for all active transactions to complete before disconnecting all users from the database, and then it will shut down the database.

```
Sql> shutdown transactional
```

The *shutdown transactional* command involves the following:

- No new user connections are permitted.

- Existing users can't start a new transaction and will be disconnected.

- If a user has a transaction in progress, Oracle will wait until the transaction is completed before disconnecting the user.

- After all existing transactions are completed, Oracle shuts down the instance and deallocates memory. Oracle writes all redo log buffers and data block buffers to disk.

- No instance recovery is needed because the database is consistent.

Shutdown Immediate

Sometimes, a user may be running a very long transaction when you decide to shut down the database. Both of the previously discussed shutdown modes are worthless to you under such circumstances. Under the *shutdown immediate* mode, Oracle will neither wait indefinitely for users to log off nor wait for any transaction to complete. It simply rolls back all active transactions, disconnects all connected users, and shuts the database down. Here is the command:

```
Sql> shutdown immediate
```

The *shutdown immediate* operation involves the following:

- No new user connections are allowed.

- Oracle immediately disconnects all users.

- Oracle terminates all currently executing transactions.

- For all transactions terminated midway, Oracle will perform a rollback so the database ends up consistent. This rollback process is why the *shutdown immediate* operation is not always *immediate*. This is because Oracle is busy rolling back the transactions it just terminated. However, if there are no active transactions, the *shutdown immediate* command will shut down the database very quickly. Oracle terminates the background processes and deallocates memory.

- No instance recovery is needed upon starting up the database because it is consistent when shut down.

Shutdown Abort

The *shutdown abort* command is a very abrupt shutting down of the database. Currently running transactions are neither allowed to complete nor rolled back. The user connections are just disconnected.

```
Sql> shutdown abort
```

The *shutdown abort* command involves the following:

- No new connections are permitted.

- Existing sessions are terminated, regardless of whether they have an active transaction or not.

- Oracle doesn't roll back the terminated transactions.

- Oracle doesn't write the redo log buffers and data buffers to disk.

- Oracle terminates the background processes, deallocates memory immediately, and shuts down.

- Upon a restart, Oracle will perform an *automatic* instance recovery, because the database isn't guaranteed to be consistent when shut down.

When you shut down the database using the *shutdown abort* command, upon recovery the database has to perform instance recovery to make the database transactionally consistent because there may be uncommitted transactions that need to be rolled back. The critical thing to remember about the *shutdown abort* command is this: The database may be shut down in an inconsistent mode. That's the reason Oracle recommends that you always shut down the database in a consistent mode by using the *shutdown* or *shutdown immediate* command and not the *shutdown abort* command before backing it up. In most cases, you aren't required to explicitly use a *recover* command, because the database will perform the instance recovery on its own.

Listing 9-15 shows what happens when an attempt is made to put a database in a read-only mode after the *shutdown abort* command was used to shut it down first. Note that Oracle won't put the data files in read-only mode until the database is manually recovered. (You'll find a lot more information on recovery in Chapter 15.)

Listing 9-15. The Shutdown Abort Command and Need for Instance Recovery

```
SQL> shutdown abort
ORACLE instance shut down.
SQL> startup mount
ORACLE instance started.
Total System Global Area   135338868 bytes
Fixed Size                    453492 bytes
Variable Size              109051904 bytes
Database Buffers            25165824 bytes
Redo Buffers                  667648 bytes
Database mounted.
SQL> alter database open read only;
alter database open read only
*
ERROR at line 1:
ORA-16005: database requires recovery
SQL> recover database;
Media recovery complete.
SQL>
```

> **NOTE** *In all shutdown modes, upon the issue of the* shutdown *command, all new user connection attempts will fail. Except for the* shutdown abort *command, all the other* shutdown *commands won't require instance recovery upon database start-up.*

Quiescing a Database

Suppose you want to put your database in a restricted mode to perform table reorganization or some other administrative task. Schema changes are especially hard to make while users are conducting live transactions in the database. The same goes for when you have to import data into a large table while users are connected to the database. You have to perform these activities during a "maintenance window" or you have to shut down the database and bring it up in a restricted mode. What if you don't have a maintenance window in which to shut down and restart the database? Or, as it so often happens in practice, the assumed window magically disappears because you encounter some problem in performing your tasks during the allotted time? You are forced to wait for the next weekend, in most cases. *Quiescing* a database gives you the opportunity to put the database in a single-user mode without having to ever shut the database down.

The following are the result of a database being put in a quiesced state by the DBA:

- All inactive sessions are prevented from issuing any database commands until the database is unquiesced.

- All active sessions are allowed to be completed.

- All new login attempts will be queued. A user trying to log in during the time the database is in a quiesced state won't get an error message. Rather, his or her login attempts will seem to "hang."

- Only DBA queries, transactions, and PL/SQL statements will be allowed in the database.

In order for you to put the database in a quiesced mode, the Database Resource Manager feature must have been activated since instance start-up. Oracle uses the Database Resource Manager to prevent new user sessions from starting up. So, wait until you find out how to set up the Database Resource Manager in Chapter 11 before you try out the following command. To place the database into a quiesced state, you use the following *alter system* command as the SYS or SYSTEM user:

```
Sql> alter system quiesce restricted;
```

Later on, when you've finished your administrative tasks, you can allow regular access to the database by issuing the following command:

```
Sql> alter system unquiesce;
```

You'll get an error if you try to put in a quiesced state before the Database Resource Manager feature is activated. Here's how to quickly find out if the Database Resource Manager is activated in your database:

```
SQL>select name,value from v$parameter
  2* where name like 'resource_%'
SQL> /
NAME                          VALUE
-------------------------------
resource_limit                FALSE
resource_manager_plan
SQL>
```

The results of the query tell you that the resource limit is set to its default value of *false* and that there is no Database Resource Manager plan in the database. Chapter 11 shows you how to use these two initialization parameters to activate a Database Resource Manager plan. This involves restarting the database. You will then be able to quiesce your database. Once the database is unquiesced, all the queued logins are allowed into the database and all the inactive transactions are once again allowed to turn active by executing DML statements.

Suspending a Database

If you want to suspend all I/O operations during some special administrative job (an emergency backup of a tablespace, for example), you can suspend the database. All reads from and writes to the data files and control files are prohibited during the time the database is under suspension. Why would you want to suspend a database when even a DBA can't perform reads or writes on the data files? The suspension of activity on a database may be necessary when you want to perform specialized chores such as splitting a mirror, which you can't do in any other way. Use the *resume database* command to bring the database back to a normal mode, as follows:

```
SQL> alter system suspend;
System altered.
SQL> alter system resume;
System altered.
SQL>
```

Using V$VIEWS to Monitor Database Status

The dynamic view V$INSTANCE is useful in monitoring the current status of an instance. The following query tells you that the database is open and no shutdowns are pending:

```
SQL> select instance_name, status,
  2   shutdown_pending,
  3   active_state
  4* from v$instance
SQL> /
INSTANCE  STATUS   SHUTDOWN    ACTIVE
 _NAME             PENDING     STATE
---------------- ------------ --- -----------------------------
remorse   OPEN     NO          NORMAL
SQL>
```

In the preceding code, the active state is *normal*, which means that the database is neither in the process of being quiesced nor in already in a quiesced state. The database status column indicates *open*. A suspended database would have a status of *suspended*.

Summary

This chapter discussed how to create an Oracle9*i* database. I covered the preliminary steps in detail before I discussed the initialization parameters. As I mentioned in the chapter, more than 200 init.ora parameters are available, but you can start off with a basic set and change and increase the number as you learn more about the Oracle database. The initialization parameters are changeable in most cases, and the temptation exists to tinker with them on an ongoing basis. A word of caution here: Don't change an initialization parameter's value or use a new parameter unless you're absolutely sure what the implications are for the database. There are several subtle interactions between a set of initialization parameters, and a small change in one parameter can lead to unwanted repercussions elsewhere.

The use of the SPFILE instead of the traditional init.ora file provides several benefits to the DBA, including the strengthening of database security. I discussed the use of the SPFILE in this chapter, and I provided an example showing its creation from the init.ora file.

This chapter showed you how to create a database from scratch using a series of commands from SQL*Plus. As mentioned earlier, you can simplify the process by using a single script with all the database creation commands included in it. However, for pedagogic purposes, this chapter led you through a command-by-command database creation procedure. Create your own test databases on a Windows or UNIX database—this will enhance your knowledge of the initialization parameters.

The final part of the chapter discussed the various start-up and shutdown modes available to you. There are serious implications, especially for backup and recovery, related to the way you perform a database shutdowns. The chapter showed you all the ways you can shut down your database and pointed out the implications of using the various methods.

Traditionally, Oracle DBAs managing large databases have had trouble performing maintenance operations in a 24/7 environment, or when there was only a narrow window of opportunity to perform the operations. The new restricted modes of operation of a database, quiescing and suspension, offer great help to DBAs in overcoming these problems. As you proceed through this book, you'll see several examples of the usage of the various modes of starting up and shutting down the database.

#### CHAPTER 10

Connectivity and Networking

ONE OF THE DBA's key tasks is to establish and maintain connectivity between the database on the server and the user community. In the traditional client/server model, users connect to the databases on a separate server by using a client. The client/server model is still used in many places to run business functions. Web-based connection models are much more common today as a means of connecting to databases.

Oracle9i provides several methods of connecting database servers to end users. For small sets of users, you can use the Oracle tnsnames.ora file, which is a local file with the server and the database information. Using this file, users can connect to the database.

NOTE *Oracle also provides the "Names" method for organizations with larger client installations. Oracle clearly indicates in its documentation, however, that it will discard the Oracle Names method; therefore, I won't dwell too much on this method of making connections to the Oracle database.*

The most sophisticated connection method provided by Oracle is the directory naming method. You can also use Oracle Internet Directory (OID) for security management and other purposes besides facilitating database connectivity. It's easy to set up OID, and this chapter takes you through all the necessary steps to install and configure OID. You'll also see how you can migrate from a tnsnames.ora naming method to OID using both a GUI-based method and a manual method.

The chapter also provides you a quick introduction to Java Database Connectivity (JDBC). You'll learn how to connect to an Oracle database from within a Java program, and you'll step through a small example that illustrates the basic concepts of Oracle JDBC.

The final section of this chapter deals with testing and troubleshooting Oracle Net Services. Most of the problems you'll encounter when you're troubleshooting networking issues are very easy to fix, and this chapter shows you how to take care of typical connectivity problems.

Oracle Networking and Database Connectivity

After you create the database and the various database objects and load the data, the next big step is to establish connectivity between the database server and the users who will be using it. Oracle Net Services is the set of services that enables connectivity among the database servers, client applications, and the users. You'll use Oracle Net Services to connect to and manage the interaction between the client and the server. Of course, to maintain connectivity, Oracle Net Services components have to "live" on both the client and the server. Typically, Oracle Net Services uses the TCP/IP network protocol to establish network connectivity between clients and the database server.

Oracle Net Services is configured with several important features to make life easier for DBAs. Important among these features are the following:

- *Location Transparency:* Clients need not know the network location or any other privileged information about database services, because you can maintain the information in a centralized repository. Users can be given only the database name, and the connection could be entirely transparent to them.

- *Centralized Configuration:* For large installations, a centralized means of establishing and maintaining connections makes a lot of sense. The LDAP-compliant directory server supported by Oracle provides a very efficient centralized repository for meeting all your networking needs. Network, authentication, and other security information is saved in a central place, and numerous users then access this information. Maintenance is extremely easy, because regardless of the number of clients, you only have to modify the centralized information.

- *Scalability:* Oracle offers a specialized architecture to enhance scalability called the *shared server architecture.* The shared server architecture enables several users to share the same connection process through the use of a dispatcher process. Therefore, a small number of server connections can enable a large number of end users to use the system, thus increasing the scalability of the system. In addition, Oracle provides the Connection Manager feature, which provides connection multiplexing whereby multiple connections are taken care of simultaneously.

Shared Server vs. Dedicated Server Architecture

You can set up a connection architecture where the Oracle server starts a separate server process for each client connection or you can enable several clients to share a single server process. The separate server process uses dedicated connections between each client and the Oracle server, and it is therefore named the *dedicated server architecture.* The *shared server architecture* is the name given to connections where several user processes use same Oracle server connection to perform their work.

Shared Server Architecture

The shared server architecture relies on a dispatcher service to process connection requests from clients. A single dispatcher can service many client connections simultaneously. Thus, a small number of shared server processes can service a large number of clients by using the dispatcher. Dispatchers essentially act as mediators between the clients and the shared servers. Dispatchers are in charge of placing requests from clients in a request queue from which the shared server picks them up.

When you use a dispatcher (i.e., when you use the shared server approach), the listener will not hand off a connection request to the database server directly; it hands the request off to the dispatcher. This is called a *direct hand-off* to the dispatcher. The listener can also redirect a client connection to a dispatcher. In this case, the listener will pass the dispatcher's network address to the client connection. This information enables the client to connect to the dispatcher, whereupon the listener connection is terminated.

Dedicated Server Architecture

Dedicated server processes do not involve any sharing of resources by clients. Each client is assigned a dedicated server connection. The Oracle listener will start up a dedicated server process whenever a client process requests a connection. The listener can also use a redirection of connection to dedicated server processes, wherein it just passes the dedicated server's protocol address back to the client and the client uses that to connect directly to the database server. The listener connection is terminated as soon as it passes the dedicated server's address to the client.

This chapter deals exclusively with the more commonly used dedicated server architecture. To learn how to set up a shared server configuration, please refer to Oracle's manual for networking, the "Net Services Administrator's Guide."

Networking Concepts: How Oracle Networking Works

When you want to open a database session from a client, whether it's a traditional client or a browser-based client, you need to connect to the database across a network. Suppose you're establishing a connection from your desktop to an Oracle9*i* database based on a UNIX server across town. What do you need in order to connect to the database? Well, assume there's a network in place to enable the connection. You need a method of making a connection between your desktop and the Oracle database. You need some kind of an interface to conduct the session. In this example, SQL*Plus will act as the interface.

Now you need to have some way of making a network connection, which involves the use of specialized software that can make the connection. You also need some way of communicating with the industry-standard network protocols such as TCP/IP. Oracle provides a set of software called Oracle Net, which can initiate, establish, and maintain connections between clients and the server. That's why Oracle Net, the connecting software, must be installed on both the client and the server. All servers that host an Oracle database also run a service called the Oracle Net Listener (commonly referred to as just *listener*), whose main function is to listen for requests from client services to log into the Oracle database. The listener, after ensuring that the client service has the matching information for the database (protocol, port, and instance name) passes the client request on to the database. The database will allow the client to log in, provided the username and password are authenticated. Once the listener hands off the user request to the database, the client and the database will be in direct contact, without any help from the listener service.

Oracle provides a number of GUI-based utilities to help configure network connections for your databases. These utilities include Oracle Net Manager and Oracle Net Configuration Assistant. These tools can help you take care of basically all your networking needs. Just click these program icons after you finish reading this chapter and start experimenting with test connections.

In the next sections you'll look at some important terms that are crucial in Oracle networking. How you define the terms in the following sections has a lot to do with how Oracle identifies a database in the network.

Database Instance Name

As you know by now, an Oracle instance consists of the SGA and a set of Oracle processes. The *database instance name* is specified in the initialization file (init.ora) as the *instance_name* parameter. When you talk about the Oracle system identifier (SID), you are simply referring to the Oracle instance. Normally, each database can have only one instance associated with it. In an Oracle Real Application Clusters (ORAC) configuration, however, a single database service could be associated with multiple instances.

Database Service Name

The *database service name* refers the database name, and you can have multiple service names for the same database. A service name consists of two components. The first component is the database name and the second component is the domain name.

You represent the database service name indirectly in the initialization file (or SPFILE) through the specification of the two parameters *database_name* and *domain_name*. The *service_name* parameter defaults to the global database name, which is the default service name of the database and is derived by combining the *database_name* and *domain_name* parameters. You can also specify the service name directly by configuring the *service_name* initialization parameter. Here are some examples:

```
DB_NAME=customer
DB_NAME=sales
DB_DOMAIN=us.national.com
SERVICE_NAME=customer.us.national.com
SERVICE_NAME=sales.us.national.com
```

The database service names in the preceding case would then be customer.us.national.com and sales.us.national.com. Note that the same database can be addressed by more than one service name. Why would you want to have multiple service names for the same database? You may do this when you want different sets of clients to address the (same) database differently to suit their particular needs.

Connect Descriptors

Connect descriptors are nothing more than specifications of network protocols and database identification information. Connect descriptors have two parts: an address portion that shows the protocol address of the listener and a database connection part that specifies the database service name.

To connect to any database in the world from your desktop, you need to know four things: the database name, the server name, the communication protocol, and the port to send the connection request to.

Knowing the communication protocol helps ensure that the networking protocols agree, so you can establish a connection. The standard port number for Oracle connections is 1521 or 1526. The default port on Windows machines is 1521. The standard protocol is TCP/IP or TCP/IP with Secure Socket Layer (SSL). Now you need to worry about identifying your target database in the network. Well, because you can't have more than one database with the same name on any server, an Oracle database name and the server address will uniquely identify and Oracle database in the world. In other words, pairs of database names and machine names are unique by definition.

Here's an example of a typical connect descriptor:

```
(DESCRIPTION
    (ADDRESS=(PROTOCOL=tcp) (HOST=sales-server) (PORT=1521)
    (CONNECT_DATA=(SERVICE_NAME=sales.us.national.com)
```

In this connect descriptor, the address line shows you that the TCP protocol will be used for network communication. Host refers to the UNIX (or Windows) server on which the Oracle listener is listening for any connection requests at a specific port: 1521. The listener knows whether or not it should accept a connection request based on the information provided dynamically by an Oracle database. In other words, upon creation, all Oracle9*i* databases will register themselves with the listener process. Thereafter, the listener will field any requests for connection to that database, which it will pass along to the database server. Once the client and database server hook up in this way through the mediation of the listener, they're in direct communication and the listener won't involve itself any further in the communication process for this client connection.

Connect Identifiers

A *connect identifier* simply maps a service name to a connect descriptor. For example, you can take a service name such as sales and map it to the connect descriptor you saw in the previous section. Here's an example showing the mapping of the connect identifier sales:

```
Sales=
DESCRIPTION
    (ADDRESS=(PROTOCOL=tcp) (HOST=sales-server) (PORT=1521))
    (CONNECT_DATA=(SERVICE_NAME=sales.us.national.com))
```

Connect Strings

When you initiate a connection to the database, you need to use your username and password combination, along with a connect identifier or connect descriptor. The combination of the username/password and the connect identifier is called a *connect string*. Here's an example of using a connect string with a connect identifier:

```
Connect salapati/salapati1@customer
```

Here's an example of how you can connect using a complete connect descriptor:

```
Connect salapati/salapati1@( DESCRIPTION
    (ADDRESS=(PROTOCOL=tcp) (HOST=sales-server) (PORT=1521)
    (CONNECT_DATA=(SERVICE_NAME=customer.us.national.com)))
```

Both of the preceding examples enable me to connect to the customer database, but obviously, I would prefer to use the much simpler connect string (using the connect identifier sales) shown in the first example when I log into the database.

Using the Oracle Net GUI Tools

Oracle Net provides you with several GUI tools to facilitate the configuration of connections between clients and database services. You'll see all these tools under your Oracle Program group on Windows, but they're also available in the UNIX environment. The following are the main network configuration tools in Oracle9*i*:

- *Oracle Net Configuration Assistant (NCA):* This tool enables you to select local, host, names, or directory management options to configure client connectivity. This tool is used mostly to configure network components during installation. This easy-to-use GUI interface enables you to quickly configure client connections under any naming method you choose. On UNIX systems, you can start NCA by typing in **netca** from the $ORACLE_HOME/bin directory.

- *Oracle Net Manager:* Oracle Net Manager allows you to configure various naming methods and listeners. You can use this service on clients and servers. Using Oracle Net Manager, you can configure connect descriptors in local tnsnames.ora files or centralized LDAL OID databases. You can easily add and modify connection methods using this tool. On UNIX systems, you can start this tool by typing in **netmgr** from the $ORACLE_HOME/bin directory.

- *Oracle Directory Manager (OID):* This powerful tool enables you to create the various domains and contexts necessary for using OID. You can also perform password policy management and many Oracle Advanced Security tasks through this tool. On UNIX systems, you can start OID by typing in **oidadmin** from the $ORACLE_HOME/bin directory.

The Listener and Connectivity

The Oracle listener is a service that runs only on the server and performs the task of listening for incoming connection requests. After it verifies the incoming database connection requests, the listener hands them off to the database server. The listener.ora file, whose default location is the $ORACLE_HOME/network/admin directory on UNIX systems and the $ORACLE_HOME\network\admin directory on Windows systems, contains the configuration information for the listener. Because the listener service is run only on the server, there is no listener.ora file on the client machines. Note that all the configuration parameters in listener.ora have a default value. Also note that you don't have to configure a listener service manually anymore. After the first database on the server is created, the listener service automatically starts, and the listener configuration file, listener.ora, is placed in the default $ORACLE_HOME/network/admin (UNIX) directory. Upon the creation of new databases, the databases' network and service information is automatically added to the listener configuration file. Upon database creation, the database registers itself automatically with the listener, and the listener starts listening for connection requests to this new database. Listing 10-1 shows a typical listener.ora file.

Listing 10-1. A Typical Listener Configuration File

```
# LISTENER.ORA Network Configuration File: c:\oracle9i\network\admin\listener.ora
# Generated by Oracle configuration tools.LISTENER =
  (DESCRIPTION_LIST =
    (DESCRIPTION =
      (ADDRESS_LIST -
        (ADDRESS = (PROTOCOL = IPC)(KEY = EXTPROC4))
      )
      (ADDRESS_LIST =
        (ADDRESS = (PROTOCOL = TCP)(HOST = NTL-ALAPATISAM)(PORT = 1521))
      )
    )
  )
```

```
SID_LIST_LISTENER =
  (SID_LIST =
    (SID_DESC =
      (SID_NAME = PLSExtProc)
      (ORACLE_HOME = c:\oracle9i)
      (PROGRAM = extproc)
    )
    (SID_DESC =
      (GLOBAL_DBNAME = remorse.world)
      (ORACLE_HOME = c:\oracle9i)
      (SID_NAME = remorse)
    )
    (SID_DESC =
      (GLOBAL_DBNAME = finance.world)
      (ORACLE_HOME = c:\oracle9i)
      (SID_NAME = finance)
    )  )
```

Automatic Service Registration

As you create new databases, they register themselves with the listener service. The Oracle PMON process is in charge of the dynamic service registration of new Oracle database service names with the listener. The PMON process will update the listener.ora file after each new database service creation on a server. Of course, for all these things to happen, the listener service must be running. Oracle provides a utility called *lsnrctl* to control the listener process. The listener process is vital in Oracle networking—if the listener service isn't up and running, users can't connect to the database.

You can check the status of the listener on the server by using the lsnrctl utility as shown in Listing 10-2. The output shows how long the listener has been up and where the configuration file for the listener service is located. It also tells you the names of the databases for which the listener is "listening" for connect requests.

Listing 10-2. Using the Lsnrctl Utility to Check the Status of the Listener

```
C:\> LSNRCTL status
Connecting to (DESCRIPTION=(ADDRESS=(PROTOCOL=IPC)(KEY=EXTPROC0)))
STATUS of the LISTENER
------------------------
Alias                   LISTENER
Version                 TNSLSNR for 32-bit
Windows: Version 9.2.0.1.0 - Production
Start Date              08-DEC-2002 11:33:14
Uptime                  0 days 0 hr. 0 min. 44 sec
Trace Level             off
Security                OFF
SNMP                    OFF
Listener Parameter File
```

```
C:\oracle\ora92\network\admin\listener.ora
Listener Log File
C:\oracle\ora92\network\log\listener.log
Listening Endpoints Summary...
  (DESCRIPTION=(ADDRESS=(PROTOCOL=ipc)
  (PIPENAME=\\.\pipe\EXTPROC0ipc)))
  (DESCRIPTION=(ADDRESS=(PROTOCOL=tcp)(HOST=NTL-ALAPATISAM.netbsa.org)(PORT=1521
)))
Services Summary...
Service "PLSExtProc" has 1 instance(s).
  Instance "PLSExtProc", status UNKNOWN,
 has 1 handler(s) for this service...
Service "real.world" has 1 instance(s).
  Instance "real", status READY, has
1 handler(s) for this service...
The command completed successfully
C:\>
```

Listener Commands

You can run other important commands besides the *status* command after invoking the lsnrctl utility. For example, the *services* command will let you see what services the listener is monitoring for connection requests. You can see the various commands available by using the *help* command in the lsnrctl interface, as shown in the following listing:

```
C:\> lsnrctl help
LSNRCTL for 32-bit Windows: Version 9.2.0.1.0 -
 Production on 04-DEC-2002 16:48:05
Copyright (c) 1991, 2002, Oracle Corporation.  All rights reserved.
The following operations are available
An asterisk (*) denotes a modifier or extended command:
start            stop              status
services         version           reload
save_config      trace             change_password
quit             exit              set*
show*
C:\>
```

You can start the listener by using the command *start*, and you can stop the listener by using the command *stop* after invoking the lsnrctl utility. If you want to issue these commands from the operating system command line, you may use the commands *lsnrctl start* and *lsnrctl stop* to perform the two tasks. I advise not modifying the listener.ora file unless you absolutely have to. With dynamic, automatic "service registration," there is less need for you to modify the file anyway. Nevertheless, there may be times when you have to change some part of the listener file, which consists of network configuration information for all the services for which the listener is monitoring connection requests.

After you make your changes, one way to put the changes into effect is to restart your listener. The other and safer method is to merely reload the listener information, which includes the newly made changes to the listener configuration file. The *lsnrctl reload* command lets you reload the listener on the fly, without your having to bounce it. Currently connected clients will continue to be connected while the listener is being reloaded (or even bounced) because the listener has already "handed off" the connections to the database and isn't in the loop between the client and the database service.

Listener Management

Although it's quite easy to set up the listener service, you can do several things after the listener is set up to tune up your connection process and to make the listener service secure. You'll explore some of these options in the following sections.

Multiple Listeners

You may have more than one listener service running on the same server, but you'll usually do this when you're using ORAC. If you do use multiple listener services, you can configure the *connect_time_failover* parameter, which determines how long a client connection waits for a connection through a listener before attempting a connection through another listener.

Setting a Queuesize

Sometimes a large volume of simultaneous connection requests from clients may overwhelm a listener service. To keep the listener from failing, you can use the *queuesize* parameter in the listener.ora configuration file to specify how many concurrent connection requests can be made. For most operating systems, the default *queuesize* is a small number such as five. Here's an example:

```
LISTENER=
 (DESCRIPTION=
  (ADDRESS=(PROTOCOL=tcp)(HOST=sales-server)(PORT=1521)(QUEUESIZE=30)))
```

Setting a Password for the Listener

When the listener is first set up, there's no password for getting into the utility. Any user who can get into the operating system can easily stop the listener and thus prevent clients from making new connections by just typing in **lsnrctl stop** at the command prompt. To avoid this security hole, you need to set a password for the listener in the following way. Note that the default password for the listener service is *listener*, and you don't need to use this if you don't change the password.

```
C:\>lsnrctl
LSNRCTL for 32-bit Windows: Version 9.2.0.1.0 -
Production on 08-DEC-2002 11:40:46
Copyright (c) 1991, 2002, Oracle Corporation.  All rights reserved.
```

```
Welcome to LSNRCTL, type "help" for information.
LSNRCTL> change_password
Old password:
New password:
Reenter new password:
Connecting to (DESCRIPTION=(ADDRESS=(PROTOCOL=IPC)(KEY=EXTPROC0)))
Password changed for LISTENER
The command completed successfully
```

After you change the password successfully, notice that you can't stop or start the listener service as before—you need to use your password to do so. You need to use the clause *set password* at the lsnrctl prompt so you can provide the listener your (new) password, and then you'll be able to start and stop the listener service once again. Note that *set password* doesn't set a new password; it's merely asking you for the listener password so you can perform some administrative tasks.

```
LSNRCTL> stop
Connecting to (DESCRIPTION=(ADDRESS=(PROTOCOL=IPC)(KEY=EXTPROC0)))
TNS-01169: The listener has not recognized the password
LSNRCTL> set password
Password:
The command completed successfully
LSNRCTL> stop
Connecting to (DESCRIPTION=(ADDRESS=(PROTOCOL=IPC)(KEY=EXTPROC0)))
The command completed successfully
LSNRCTL>
```

Naming and Connectivity

Remember that you can connect to a database by providing either the complete connect descriptor or just a net service name, which is mapped in some fashion to the connect descriptor. Because providing the complete connect descriptor each time you want to make a connection is very tedious, the use of net service names makes more sense. How does Oracle know if your net service name is valid? Somewhere, you need to maintain a central repository of all the mappings between net service names and the connect description information. Thus, when you type in the following line, the central repository is searched for the connect descriptor for the net service name "customer". Once the connect descriptor is found, a connection is initiated by Oracle Net to the database on the specified server.

```
connect salapati/salapati1@customer
```

The entire issue of naming and connectivity boils down to a very simple question: How do you substitute simple names for complex connect information that includes server names and network addresses? You can have several types of centralized naming repositories. Oracle Net supports five different types of naming methods: local naming, host naming, external naming, Oracle Names, and directory naming. You'll examine these types in detail in the following sections.

Local Naming

Local naming provides the simplest and easiest way to establish Oracle connectivity. For simple installations, you can save the connect information locally, meaning on the client itself. Oracle uses a file with the standard name *tnsnames.ora* to store connection description information. By default, this file is always stored in the $ORACLE_HOME/network/admin directory. Oracle provides a sample tnsnames.ora file for your use, and you can find it in the directory mentioned in the previous sentence. You can think of the tnsnames.ora file as similar to the hosts file in UNIX systems, which contains the networking information for the entire system. The tnsnames.ora file is always present on the client machine. If the database server is also used for client-type connections, there will be a tnsnames.ora file on the server for the other databases you need to connect from that server.

When you initiate a connection by using either the SQL*Plus interface or some other means, you need to pass your username and password for the database you are connecting to. First, Oracle Net has to figure out on which server the database is running. Oracle Net consults the tnsnames.ora file to resolve the network address, the protocol, and the port for the database server. Once it successfully resolves these, it initiates contact with the listener on the machine where the database server is located. Once the listener hands off the connection to the database server, the database authenticates your username and password.

As you can see, several things have to happen before you can successfully log into the target database. First, the tnsnames.ora file should have the net service name mapped to a valid server/database name combination, along with a valid network protocol and valid port number. Next, on the server side, the listener needs to accept the connection and hand it off the database server. Finally, the database server needs to verify your database username and password.

All the users that need to connect to your database should have the Oracle client software installed on their system. Once you install the client piece on the desktop, it will automatically create Oracle's standard directories. You then need to go to the $ORACLE-HOME/network/admin directory and place a copy of the tnsnames.ora file there. You have to do this for every client that wants to connect to your databases. When you add a new database to your system and you need to provide access to this database to all the users of your system, you need to add the connect description database service name mapping to all the users' tnsnames.ora file or send them a new, updated tnsnames.ora file to replace the old one.

Whether it be a connection through SQL*Plus directly or one through an application's logon page, Oracle Net will use the tnsnames.ora file to validate connection requests. As you can imagine, if your user base or the number of database servers grows beyond a certain point, it gets harder and harder to manage database connections using this localized naming method based on a constantly updated tnsnames.ora file.

To configure local naming, you have to edit the tnsnames.ora file provided by Oracle when you create a database. All you need to do is go to the default tnsnames.ora location, $ORACLE_HOME/network/admin, and edit this file to reflect your network and database service name information. Listing 10-3 shows a typical tnsnames.ora file.

Listing 10-3. A Typical Tnsnames.ora File

```
# TNSNAMES.ORA Network Configuration File: c:\oracle9i\network\admin\tnsnames.ora
# Generated by Oracle configuration tools.
FINANCE1 =
  (DESCRIPTION =
    (ADDRESS_LIST =
      (ADDRESS = (PROTOCOL = TCP)(HOST = NTL-ALAPATISAM)(PORT = 1521))
    )
    (CONNECT_DATA =
      (SERVICE_NAME = financ1.world)
    )
  )
salesprod =
  (DESCRIPTION =
    (ADDRESS_LIST =
      (ADDRESS = (PROTOCOL = TCP)(HOST = 172.11.150.1)(PORT = 1521))
    )
    (CONNECT_DATA =
      (SERVICE_NAME = salesprod.world)
    )
  )
custprod =
  (DESCRIPTION =
    (ADDRESS_LIST =
      (ADDRESS = (PROTOCOL = TCP)(HOST = custprod)(PORT = 1521))
    )
    (CONNECT_DATA =
      (SERVICE_NAME = custprod.world)
    )
  )
```

NOTE *Three databases are listed in this tnsnames.ora file on my desktop. All three have different features that distinguish them. The first entry is for the database finance1, which is on my own desktop, NTL-ALAPATISAM. The salesprod database is located in the UNIX server, whose IP address, 172.11.150.1, will enable Oracle Net to connect to it using the port 1521 and the TCP protocol. The last database uses a symbolic name, custprod, instead of the IP address.*

If you add a fourth database, orderprod, to the tnsnames.ora file, you need to add a new connect identifier to the tnsnames.ora file, as shown here:

```
orderprod =
  (DESCRIPTION =
   (ADDRESS_LIST =
     (ADDRESS = (PROTOCOL = TCP)(HOST = 172.16.11.151)(PORT = 1521))
   )
   (CONNECT_DATA =
     (SERVICE_NAME =orderprod.world)
   )
```

Although local naming is quite easy to implement, it is a cumbersome method to use if you have a large number of client installations that need to access the database server directly. You need to maintain a local copy of the tnsnames.ora file on all your local clients. Furthermore, when you change hosts or add databases to your system, you need to be sure to make the changes to all your client tnsnames.ora files. Of course, if you have a small client base, the maintenance of the tnsnames.ora file should not be a problem.

I prefer using NCA to add a new service to my tnsnames.ora file, rather than manually adding it to the file. Like the listener.ora file, the tnsnames.ora file is somewhat tricky, with all its parentheses, and it's easy to make a mistake when you're manually editing the file. Creating new services using the GUI is very easy, with NCA prompting you for your server name, database name, network address, and protocol type. Once you're done configuring the connection, there will be a new or updated tnsnames.ora file in the default location that includes the database services you just added. You must first install the Oracle client software on the client machine, using the Oracle9*i* Client CD. NCA comes bundled with both the server and the client versions of the software. You can start NCA by selecting Programs ➤ Oracle ➤ Configuration and Migration Tools. Once the GUI comes up, you can easily configure a local connection. The only information you need to know is your service name, server name, and protocol type (usually TCP/IP), and you can create a connection and test it too, all in under a minute.

In addition to the tnsnames.ora file, client machines make use of another file called *sqlnet.ora* when they use the local naming method. The sqlnet.ora file is present only on the clients and contains import network configuration parameters. Of course, if a server is used as a client as well, there will be a sqlnet.ora file on the server. Chapter 11 shows how to use the *sqlnet_authentication_services* parameter to configure operating system authentication. Here's a typical sqlnet.ora file:

```
# SQLNET.ORA Network Configuration File:
C:\neworacle\ora9i\network\admin\sqlnet.ora
# Generated by Oracle configuration tools.
NAMES.DEFAULT_DOMAIN = wowcompany.com
SQLNET.AUTHENTICATION_SERVICES= (NTS)
NAMES.DIRECTORY_PATH= (TNSNAMES, ONAMES, HOSTNAME)
```

Host Naming Method

An even easier way to connect to an Oracle database server than the use of the localized tnsnames.ora file is using the host naming method. In this naming method, all you need to do to connect is specify the hostname to connect to the Oracle database. You don't need to have a tnsnames.ora file when you use the host naming method. Perform the following steps if you want to use this simple method of connecting to databases:

1. Make sure the listener is up and running.

2. Make sure the sqlnet.ora file specifies hostnames as the first option for naming methods by using the following line:

   ```
   NAMES-DIRECTORY_PATH=(hostname,tnsnames).
   ```

3. Ask your system administrator to create an entry in the /etc/hosts file specifying your database name as an alias for the server on which the Oracle database is running.

The host naming method makes it possible to connect to the database simply by using the following command, where *custprod* is the database name and an alias for the server in the /etc/hosts file:

```
sqlplus salapati/salapati1@custprod
```

The host naming method works well for simple networks with few users. It is very easy to set up, but you need to meet all the following conditions in order to use the host naming method:

- You must use the TCP/IP communication protocol.

- You must use either the /etc/hosts file or the Domain Name Service (DNS) for resolving server names.

- You can't use the Oracle Connection Manager with the host naming method.

External Naming Method

The external naming method uses external naming services such as the Network Information Service (NIS) to resolve net service names. Sun Microsystems originally developed the NIS name resolution system. NIS systems keep a central database of hostnames and uses a flat name space based on a master server. Here are the steps you need to perform to use the external naming method for name resolution:

1. Have your system administrator configure NIS if it isn't already in place.

2. Create a tnsnames.ora file as you would in the host naming method.

3. Convert the tnsnames.ora file to a tnsnames map, which you'll need for the NIS server later on. You can derive the tnsnames map from the tnsnames.ora file by having your system administrator run the following command:

```
tns2nis tnsnames.ora
```

4. Take the tnsnames map to the server on which the NIS is running.

5. Have the system administrator run the *ypmake* command so NIS can use the tnsnames map. An NIS map is a database built from ASCII files. The data files about hosts are maintained on a central NIS master server. The system administrator will have to convert the tnsnames text file into a format the NIS server can read by using the ypmake program (I am using the HP-UNIX example here). When the tnsnames.ora file is converted into a tnsnames map, two files are created, one ending with .pag and the other with .dir.

6. Edit the sqlnet.ora file as follows:

```
NAMES_DIRECTORY_PATH=(nis, hostname, tnsnames).
```

Again, the order of the list inside the brackets is a random one. The important thing is that the *nis* method should be listed first.

Oracle Names

The Oracle Names method of resolving service names won't be supported in future major releases of the Oracle database, according to Oracle Corporation. Therefore, I'll quickly review this method here, but I won't spend a whole lot of time discussing all the details. The directory naming method, which you'll see next, is a superior alternative to the Oracle Names method.

Oracle Names stores all the service addresses on the network. Clients connect to the Names Server to help resolve service names. The Oracle Names Server accepts the service names passed by clients and resolves them into network addresses. The client uses this network address to connect to the service.

 NOTE *As mentioned at the beginning of the chapter, because the Oracle Names method is on its way out as a naming method, I don't present a detailed discussion of it in this book. If you have a need to learn more about the Oracle Names method, please refer to the relevant sections in the Oracle9i "Net Services Administrator's Guide."*

The Directory Naming Method

When an organization has to deal with a vast amount of data about its networks and databases, it can use a centralized directory to store the information instead of relying on items such as the tnsnames.ora file to store information locally.

Although a centralized setup may seem daunting at first, it is quite easy to set up. The cost may be higher in the beginning, but the cost of managing the information over time will be minimal, as this setup provides a lower cost of ownership. Directories are a must for handling today's heterogeneous and geographically dispersed large networks. In addition to helping clients connect to central networks and databases, directories are valuable for providing enterprisewide security.

Today's Internet-based applications leave many organizations open to huge security risks. Decentralized systems are a constant source of worry for most security professionals. A centralized directory service to authenticate users and enforce security policies enhances the organization's power to safeguard its networked resources.

What Is Oracle Internet Directory (OID)?

Traditionally, network information was stored on multiple servers, often in different formats. Directory services are special-purpose databases designed to enable the storage and efficient retrieval of entry-related information. These directories are relatively low-update databases, with substantial amounts of reads against them. So, retrieval performance is a key factor in the success of a directory service. Directory services provide a centralized means of managing distributed networks. Directory services are huge centralized repositories that contain all the "metadata" pertaining to databases, networks, users, security policies, and so forth. This directory can replace a large number of localized files such as the tnsnames.ora file and provide a single point of name resolution and authentication. Here are some examples of the kinds of data that directories can manage efficiently:

- Usernames and passwords

- User profiles

- Authorization policies

- Network configuration and Net Services information

Many kinds of commercial directory services are available, including Microsoft Internet Directory and Oracle Internet Directory (OID), which can be employed to perform a host of functions for an organization. OID is a Lightweight Directory Access Protocol (LDAP)–compliant directory service. LDAP is a popular protocol for accessing online services, and it is an Internet standard for storage and directory access. OID comes bundled with the Oracle9*i* database and runs as an application based on the database. OID is very scalable because it is implemented on the highly scalable Oracle9*i* database. Thus, a potentially huge amount of directory information can be stored and easily accessed. The data is secure because it is stored in the database, and OID is a high-availability service, just like the Oracle9*i* database. The LDAP specification is also attractive because of the minimal client software it needs.

OID is a general-purpose LDAP v3–based directory, and you can use it for many applications such as address books, security credential repositories, and corporate directory services. Oracle strongly recommends moving to OID as a way of configuring database connectivity. By de-emphasizing the Oracle Names connection methods, Oracle is positioning OID as the main alternative to the traditional localized configuration method, which involves the use of the tnsnames.ora network configuration file that all DBAs are familiar with.

The directory naming method involves the use of a central directory server such as OID or Microsoft Active Directory. This directory will administer the net service names. Clients will contact the directory server and use the net service name entries therein to connect to various databases. In this discussion, I assume the use of OID.

The basic idea behind the use of OID is straightforward. Users connect to OID, which is an application running off an Oracle9*i* database. Users provide OID with an Oracle service identifier (a database name). Oracle Net forwards the service name to the LDAP-based OID. The directory returns the complete connection information—hostname, connection protocol, port number, and database instance name—to the client, which then connects to the database server. The connect identifiers are stored in an Oracle context. An Oracle context contains entries for use with Oracle software, such as database names and service names, for use with OID.

OID is not used just for connecting clients to an Oracle database. Once you create the directory, you can use it for several purposes other than connectivity. Oracle's Advanced Security option uses OID to centrally manage user-related information extensively. The Advanced Security option stores the users' information in the centralized OID, rather than on individual databases. If you are using Oracle's replicated database technology, OID will come in very handy to help manage the complexity involved in managing multiple servers and network protocols.

Although Oracle would like you to convert all your network configurations to OID, it is not clear that OID is worth the extra administrative overhead for most small- to medium-sized enterprises. Remember that OID is not a product meant exclusively for network configuration. Networking database connections is only a small part of the capabilities of OID. The tnsnames-based approach is still meaningful for most organizations because of its simplicity and ease of use.

Having said that, in the following sections I explain in detail how to configure and use OID as a centralized way of name resolution for Oracle databases. For large organizations, the administrative burden of managing dynamic environments is a nightmare sometimes, and OID is perfect for them. Adding new services, relocating servers and networking components, and changing database names all require that system administrators frequently distribute new versions of the configuration files across the organization. On the other hand, if you use OID, there's only an initial cost of time and effort in setting up the system. Once you get the directory service going, management is a snap compared to the old-fashioned localized management of services. The installation, configuration, and setup of the OID infrastructure only *seems* complex—rest assured that it isn't really hard at all. You need to understand the concept of a directory well before you start the installation. That way, you aren't mechanically implementing a directory; rather, you are feeling comfortable with the concept behind a centralized directory. The whole process of installing OID and migrating your tnsnames.ora file or Oracle Names–based name resolution should take no more than a couple of hours at worst.

Installing OID

As mentioned previously, OID comes bundled with the Oracle9*i* software. Note that when you install OID, you're really installing two things: OID and the OID server, which are two different things. The latest version available is OID 3.0.1 from the Oracle 9.2.0.1.0 software release. The following installation steps assume that you already have an Oracle9*i* database up and running to support the use of OID.

Oracle gives you the choice of installing OID in an existing Oracle9*i* database or in a new database all by itself. I would have preferred to install it in a separate database, but to save space on my test server, I first chose to install it in an existing database. However, I kept getting some errors while using OID that prompted me to reinstall it in a small, independent database. Lo and behold, the earlier problems went away, so there, you have your choices. The process of installing OID is similar in UNIX and Windows databases. Note that the installation process first creates OID, after which it gives you the option of starting up the Oracle Internet Directory Configuration Assistant as part of the installation process. Here are the steps for installing OID:

1. Set the DISPLAY variable correctly, so you can use the Oracle Universal Installer.

2. Invoke the Oracle Universal Installer by executing the runInstaller script from the $ORACLE_HOME directory. You'll see a Welcome screen. Click the Next button.

3. When the Installer gets to the Installation Types window, choose Custom, because you're going to install an individual component, Oracle Internet Directory.

4. The Available Products screen appears next, as shown in Figure 10-1. Choose the Oracle9*i* Management and Integration 9.2.0.1.0 option and click Next.

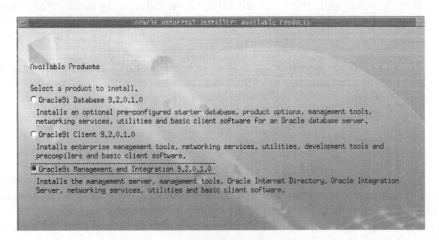

Figure 10-1. Choosing the OID installation option

5. On the Installation Types screen, select Oracle Internet Directory and click Next. Notice that the installation of OID also includes Oracle Directory Manager. Oracle Internet Directory Configuration Assistant is an option that you will be offered toward the end of the OID installation. Don't be alarmed by the 3.3GB or so that the Installer wants you to provide for the OID installation—that's more than it needs for the entire Oracle9*i* installation. Most of the products OID needs are already there from the initial installation of the 9*i* software. The entire OID installation takes up less than 20MB of additional disk space.

6. The next screen is titled "Using an existing instance". The Installer recognizes existing Oracle 9.2.0.1.0 RDBMS software on this server and wants you to confirm that you would like to use the existing database for OID. Click No and proceed to the next screen.

7. The next screen is the Database Identification screen. The installer asks you for the instance SID. Type in the database instance name, which in your case is the SID for the remorse database in which you're installing OID. Oracle next asks you for the database file location.

8. The Summary screen appears next, and you get the installation going by clicking the Install button.

9. After a few minutes, the Installer will prompt you to log in as root and run the root.sh script. The root.sh script takes a few seconds to complete, and it sets file permissions for the Oracle directories created during the installation process. You need to have your system administrator log in at this point and run the root.sh script, which is located in the $ORACLE_HOME directory.

10. At this point, OID is successfully installed in a new database on your server. In my case, I chose *monitor* as the name of the new database. The Installer will create a small database with the name monitor and start it up automatically. In addition, the OID server is installed. OID isn't started, and in the next section you'll see how to manage the OID server. The Installer gives you the option of installing what are called *optional auto-launch configuration tools* (e.g., Oracle Internet Directory Configuration Assistant). Oracle uses the default port information port and SSL port information (389 and 636, respectively). It asks you for the OID superuser oracladmin's password. The default password for oracladmin is *welcome*.

Managing the OID Server

The architecture of OID requires the successful operation of the OID server and a monitor process. The default name of the LDAP Oracle directory server is *oidldapd*. The monitor (or the guardian) daemon process is called the *oidmon* process. The tool that starts and stops the Internet directory service (oidldapad) is *oidctl*. Listing 10-4 shows all the options of the oidctl utility.

Listing 10-4. The Oidctl Utility's Command Options

```
[remorse] $ oidctl
usage: oidctl connect=cc server=ss instance=nn
[configset=cc flags=ff start] | [stop]
options:
connect=cc   The tnsname of the database to connect
to for start/stop.
server=ss    The name of the OID server to be
started/stopped. Server names must be either
oidldapd/oidrepld/odisrv instance=nn The numerical
value of the instance to be started/stopped. Instance
value is mandatory for OIDLDAPD/OIDREPLD/ODISRV.
Instance value MUST be > 0 and <= 1000.
configset=cc   The numerical value of the configuration
set to be used ONLY while starting a OID server.
Configset value MUST be >= 0 and <= 1000.
flags=ff   The flags needed ONLY while starting
the OID server. If the flags consist of UNIX-style
keywords, then, those keyword-value pairs MUST be
separated by spaces.
oracle@hp1   [/test02/app/oracle/product/9.2.0.1.0]
[remorse] $
```

Before you do anything with the Internet directory, you need to start the monitor process. The oidctl tool is used to stop/start the directory server, but it only does so through the oidmon guardian process. The following listing shows the usage of the *oidmon* command:

```
[remorse] $ oidmon
usage: oidmon [connect=cc] [sleep=nn] start | stop
options:
connect=cc   The tnsname of the database to
connect to for start/stop. If connect string is not
provided, it set by default to the value of ORACLE_
SID environment variable.
sleep=nn     The time interval in seconds at which
  the Monitor monitors OID servers. If sleeptime is
  not provided, it is set by default to 10 seconds.
start | stop  Start or Stop the Monitor.
SQL>
```

Here are the commands to start and stop OID on UNIX:

1. Start the OID monitor, the oidmon process. If you have your ORACLE_SID set correctly, you can omit the *connect* keyword:

    ```
    [remorse] $ oidmon  start
    Starting the Monitor process.
    oracle@hp1   [/test02/app/oracle/9.2.0.1.0/bin]
    ```

2.   Start the directory process by invoking oidctl as follows:

```
[remorse] $ oidctl  server=oidldapd instance=1 start
[remorse] ps -ef | grep oid
oracle 16594          1    0  15;17:49   ttyp3    0.30    oidldapd
oracle 16299 12035    0  15:16:17   ttyp4    0.00   grep oid
oracle 16497          1    1  15:16:32   ttyp3    0.01    oidmon
connect=finance1 start
oracle 16586 16497    0    15:17:44  ttyp3    0.06    oidldapd
connect=finance1  -I  1  -
conf  0  key=1081202455
```

To stop the OID server, use the following command:

```
$ oidctl server=oidldapd instance=1 stop
```

You can see there is one process running the monitor process oidmon and two processes for the LDAP server oidldapd. The oidldapd process is a combination of two processes: a listener process and a server process. The listener/dispatch process controls the server process and restarts it if it fails for some reason. But it is the oidmon monitor process that controls the listener/dispatcher process directly.

When you issue a command to stop the directory server (oidldapd) through the oidctl utility, it's the oidmon process that actually stops the server by killing the OID listener/dispatcher process. This in turn brings down the OID server process. Therefore, if the monitor process (oidmon) isn't up, you can't stop and start OID. Always bring the monitor process up first before you try to do anything with the oidctl utility.

Note that you can perform most of the administrative tasks relating to OID using Oracle Directory Manager (on UNIX, you can use the *oidadmin* command to start the Directory Manager). You've already seen how you need to use the oidctl utility to start and stop the OID server. In addition, Oracle provides several command-line tools to help you manage OID. The most important of these tools is the LDAP tool, which uses text files written in LDAP Data Interchange Format (LDIF). Even when you're using GUI tools such as the Oracle Internet Directory Configuration Agent, they're executing LDAP programs such as ldapmodify and other executables in the background. Later in this chapter you'll learn how to use the LDAP tool to add tnsnames.ora entries to OID.

How OID Makes Database Connections

When you use OID to resolve names, remember that the client doesn't have a tnsnames.ora file or a similar file with the name resolution information. The following is a simple explanation of the process of how Net Services clients connect to a database when using directory naming:

1.   When an LDAP client seeks to connect to a databases service, the client types in his or her usual username/password combination, along with a connect identifier. The sqlnet file on the client tells it that it's using OID to resolve names. The Net Services client then hands its request to the OID listener/dispatcher process.

2. The OID listener/dispatcher relays the LDAP request to the Oracle directory server. The directory server connects to the OID database and resolves the connect identifier to the underlying connect descriptor, which has the network, server, and protocol information. It then sends this detailed connect descriptor information to the Net Services client.

3. Once it resolves the connect identifier, the Oracle directory server sends the information to the Oracle Net Listener (or dispatcher, if shared servers are being used).

4. The listener service receives the connection request and, after verifying it, sends it to the database.

The Organization of OID

OID, as you learned earlier, is an LDAP-3–compliant general-purpose directory service. Although in this chapter my emphasis is on using OID for enabling database connectivity, it's also used heavily for ensuring organizational security. A directory contains a set of information about various objects, perhaps employee names and addresses or database service name information (as in this case). The information in a directory is structured hierarchically and is called the Directory Information Tree (DIT).

A directory consists of *entries,* which are collections of information about an object. To identify an entry unambiguously, you need something to tell you where it is located in the directory structure. This unambiguous address locator is the *distinguished name* (DN) of the entry. The DN gives you the complete path from the top of the hierarchy to where an entry is located. Let's use a couple of examples to see how DNs help identify where an entry is located in a DIT. Here's the first example:

```
cn=nina,ou=finance,c=us, o= wowcompany
```

In the preceding DN for entry *nina*, these are what the various nodes stand for:

- *cn*: Common name

- *ou*: Organizational unit

- *c*: Country

- *o*: Organization

Thus, the DN nina.finance.us.wowcompany *uniquely identifies* the person with the name Nina working in the finance department of the U.S. branch of Wow-company. Note that each of the various nodes are called *relative distinguished names* (RDNs), so in essence a DN is nothing more than a string of relative DNs.

There's a *special* RDN of particular significance to you while configuring Oracle networking. This special RDN is called the *Oracle Context*. In the DIT, the Oracle Context RDN is the default location a client uses to look up matching connect descriptors in the directory (for a connect identifier). An Oracle Context in a directory tree would have all the service names underneath it, including complete network and server connection information. In addition to subentries that support directory naming, an Oracle Context contains other entries to support enterprise security. Therefore, if you're trying to connect to a database on a server, the OID server doesn't have to search the directory tree all the way from the root entry to the last node. You have to merely provide it a partial DN going from the top root node to the Oracle Context. The Oracle Context will contain the net service names underneath it, and the net service names (as mentioned previously) will contain the detailed connect information. The administrative context, also known as the *directory naming context,* is a directory entry that contains an Oracle Context. The following simple example demonstrates these sometimes confusing concepts.

The connection information for the database remorse is as follows:

```
Service_name: remorse
Server=hp50
Protocol=TCP/IP
```

The complete DN for the database remorse is the following:

```
dc=com,dc=wowcompany,cn=OracleContext,
cn==remorse,
cn=description,
cn=address,
cn=port,
cn=service_name
```

The important point to note is that because all the connect descriptor information is under the Oracle Context RDN, you don't have to provide the full DN each time you want to look up the connection information for the remorse database. You can replace the preceding lengthy DN with the following generic-looking DN:

```
dc=com,dc=wowcompany,cn=OracleContext
```

Note that *dc* stands for a domain component and *cn* stands for a common name. In this example, *com* and *wowcompany* are both domain components and are therefore at the top of the directory tree. Before you can register service names in an OID database, you need to create an Oracle Context, the jumping-off point in the DIT for Oracle-related information about servers, databases, networks, and so forth. Before you can create the Oracle Context entry, however, you need to create the top-level domain entries for your organization. The next section shows you how to do this.

Creating the OID Directory Structure

Before you can add server information to OID and configure database clients to access it for connect information, you need to do a couple of things. First, you need to set up the OID directory structure, which is a tree-shaped structure. To add or modify information in OID, you need to use Oracle Directory Manager. You can also use a manual method, but Oracle Directory Manager makes the process easy.

NOTE *You can only connect to an already running Oracle directory server using Oracle Directory Manager. You can't stop or start the server itself through Oracle Directory Manager. You can only start and stop the directory server through the command line using the oidctl utility after you have ascertained that the OID monitor (oidmon) is already running.*

Now create a sample OID directory structure using the following steps:

1. Start up Oracle Directory Manager. You can do this on the UNIX server where you created your OID (in the database remorse) or directly from your Windows client. I'm using my Oracle9*i* Windows software for this purpose. Select Programs ➤ Oracle ➤ OraHome ➤ Integrated Management Tools ➤ Oracle Directory Manager.

2. The Oracle Directory Manager Connect Credentials box comes up. Here you need to provide a username and password to get in. Use the username *orcladmin* with the default password *welcome*. You also need to provide the server name on which OID is installed (within the remorse database).

3. You'll now be in Oracle Directory Manager, as shown in Figure 10-2. You need to create new entries in the OID server, so from the menu select Operations ➤ Create Entry. You can also click Create from the toolbar to do the same thing.

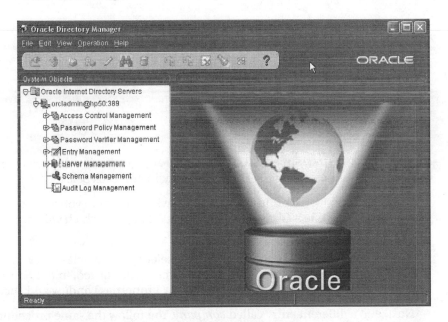

Figure 10-2. Using Oracle Directory Manager

4. You'll see a New Entry window, as shown in Figure 10-3. Before you can do anything, you need to create a DN. I chose dc=org. Click the Add button next to the Object Classes list of choices.

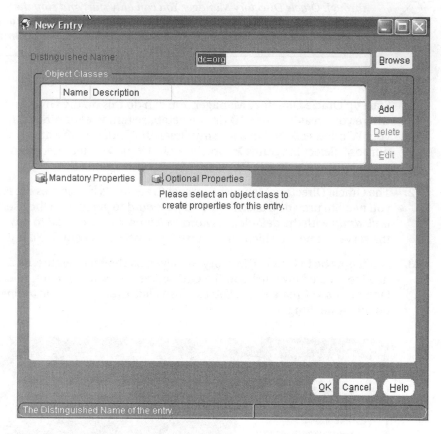

Figure 10-3. The New Entry window

5. A new window, SuperClassSelector, will appear. You need to select only one class here: *Domain*. Highlight Domain and click Select.

6. This brings you back to the New Entry window, where you should see org under the Object Classes window. Click Add again, which will take you back to the SuperClassSelector window.

7. From the SuperClassSelector window, select a second class now: *Top*. Click Select again, and you'll be back where you started, in the New Entry window. Enter the **org** in the Mandatory Properties window and click OK.

Next, add a different entry called *company*. You follow the same procedure as for the entry org, except that in the DN field you enter **dc=company, dc=com**. Add the object classes *Domain* and *Top* to the DN company. In the Mandatory

Properties window, just enter **company** as the value. Now when you click the Entry Management pane, you should see dc=company (in my case, netbsa) under dc=org, as shown in Figure 10-4.

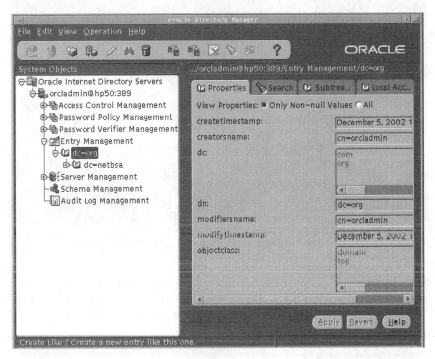

Figure 10-4. Creating a new DN

Creating the Oracle Context

Now that you've created the main domain, you need to create the Oracle Context. As you saw previously, the Oracle Context is a special context for OID users, because all the Oracle connection information will lie underneath the Oracle Context. The entries you made in the previous section when you created the naming context will be helpful in creating the Oracle Context. A naming context is essentially a (contiguous) subtree of the DIT, and the Oracle Context has to be created under this naming context. The Oracle Context is a root entry under which all network connection information is stored. Let's proceed step by step through the creation of the Oracle Context:

1. Bring up the Oracle Net Configuration Assistant (NCA) from the Oracle Program directory (in UNIX, type in **netca** at the command line). Once you get past the Welcome screen, NCA offers you a choice of configuration types. Choose the Directory Usage Configuration option, as shown in Figure 10-5.

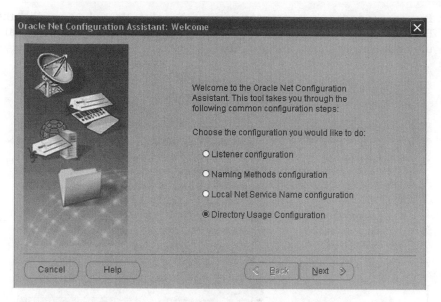

Figure 10-5. Choosing the Directory Usage Configuration option

2. In the next screen, choose the second option, which enables you to select your directory server and configure it for Oracle Context usage after first creating the Oracle Context. Figure 10-6 shows how to select this option.

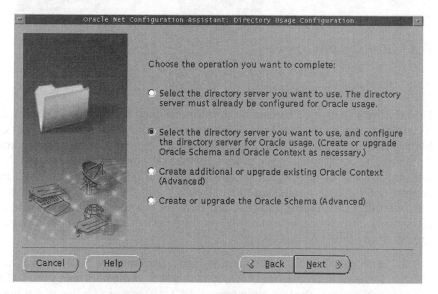

Figure 10-6. Selecting the directory server to configure it for the Oracle Context

3. NCA then asks you which Internet directory server you want to use. Only one option is provided, though: Oracle Internet Directory. Click Next.

4. NCA asks for the host on which you installed the directory server. It also asks you for the port and SSL port information. Just use the default port information provided (ports 339 and 636), unless those ports are already being used on your server.

5. NCA will then ask for your username and password combination. Enter the following default username/password combination and click Next:

   Username: cn=oracladmin

   Password: welcome

6. NCA then asks you where you want your Oracle Context to be created. You're asked to enter the DN of the directory entry under which you want to create your Oracle Context. As you know by now, a DN is the complete path of an entry in the directory tree. Choose the directory you created in the previous section, dc–company,org, as shown in Figure 10-7. (In my case, "company" is netbsa.)

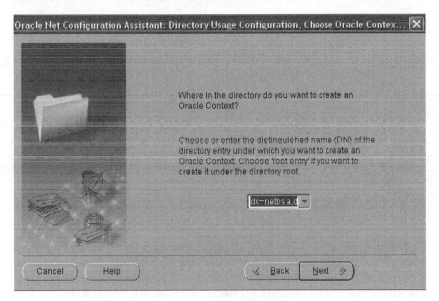

Figure 10-7. Choosing the location for the Oracle Context

7.   The Oracle Context is successfully created, as shown in Figure 10-8.

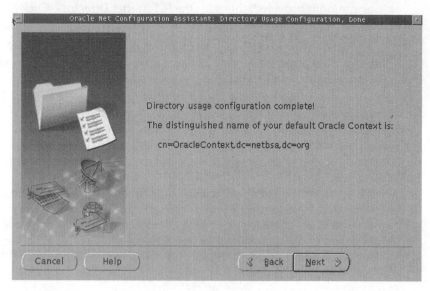

Figure 10-8. Successful creation of the Oracle Context

The user orcladmin is added to the following groups in OID (note that all three of the groups are directly under the Oracle Context entry in the tree hierarchy):

- *OracleDBCreators (cn=OracleDBCreators, cn=OracleContext):* Members can create and modify Oracle Net objects.

- *OracleNetAdmins (cn=OracleNetAdmins,cn=OracleContext):* Members can create and read database services.

- *OracleSecurityAdmins (cn=OracleSecurityAdmins,cn=Oraclecontext):* Members can create and modify enterprise security–related objects.

You can go Oracle Directory Manager and click the Entry Management button to see all the RDNs below the Oracle Context. The database, server, and network information can all be stored under the Oracle Context. Figure 10-9 shows all the new RDNs that are created in OID under the Oracle Context RDN.

Adding Service Names to OID

Once you've configured OID, you're ready to enter Oracle net service names into it. You can use several methods to do so. The easiest method is to add service names using Oracle Net Manager. You can use Oracle Net Manager to add entries individually or you can have a "migration wizard" read your entire tnsnames.ora entries and import them into OID. In this section, for purposes of exposition, you'll first see how you can add a single entry to OID manually. If you have a large number of service names in your existing tnsnames.ora file, do use Oracle Net Manager's easy migration wizards to export all the net service names from your tnsnames.ora file.

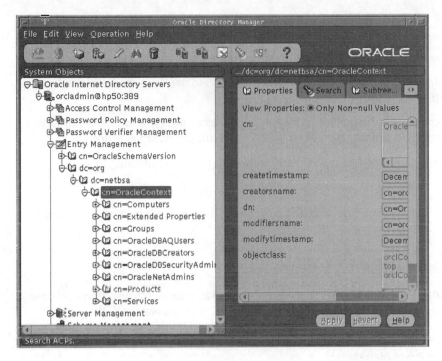

Figure 10-9. Database, server, and network information in OID

Manually Adding Services with the LDAP Command-Line Utility

If you want to manually add net service names to OID, you need to perform the following steps:

1. In the $ORACLE_HOME/network/admin directory, create a text file called the LDIF file, with the name my.ldif, as follows:

```
dn:cn:remorse,cn=OracleContext,cn=company,cn=com
objectclass:  tcp
objectclass: orclnetService
cn: remorse
orclnetDescString: (DESCRIPTION=ADDRESS_LIST=
     (ADDRESS=(PROTOCOL=TCP)(HOST=hp_test)
(PORT=1521)))
(CONNECT_DATA = (SID = remorse)))
```

2. Once you have this file ready, add the new service name, "remorsetest", to OID by using the *ldapadd* command. The *ldapadd* command enters the new service name into OID. The following is a generic *ldapadd* command:

```
ldapadd -h hostname -p portno -D binddn -w password -f  ldif-file
```

In the preceding *ldapadd* command, this is what the various components stand for:

- *hostname* and *portno* are the server name and the default port number.

- *binddn* is the DN to bind to OID. You need to use cn=oracladmin to bind as an administrator.

- *password* is the password for the person executing the *ldapadd* command (for the administrator, of course, the default password is *welcome*).

In your case, the *ldapadd* command would take the following form:

```
ldapadd -h hp50 -p 389 -D cn=oracladmin -W welcome -f my.ldif
```

Once you execute the *ldapadd* command, it enters database service name remorse into OID.

Adding Services with Oracle Net Manager

The manual method of adding service names using the *ldapadd* command-line utility is laborious and prone to syntax errors. The easier way to register your service names in the new OID directory is by using Oracle Net Manager. Let's quickly go through the various steps involved in adding database service names with Oracle Net Manager:

1. Bring up Oracle Net Manager. You'll see that the Oracle Net Configuration option is highlighted, but you still need to choose your naming method. Three naming methods are offered: Directory, Local (tnsnames.ora file), and Oracle Names Server, as shown in Figure 10-10. Choose the directory naming method.

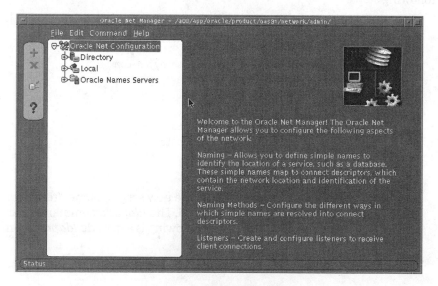

Figure 10-10. Choosing the directory naming method

2. You'll see the Directory entry on the left side of the screen expanding, showing an entry called Service Naming. Click the Service Naming button. You chose the Directory option initially, so OID is where you're going to register your service names. Oracle Net Manager will ask you for a name and password to enter OID. Enter **cn=orcladmin** for the username and **welcome** for the password, as shown in Figure 10-11.

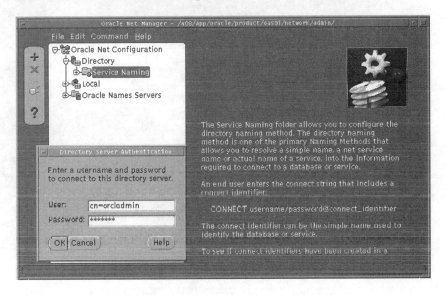

Figure 10-11. Logging into OID using Oracle Net Manager

3. Oracle Net Manager will show you all the database service names that are already registered in OID. You want to add a new entry, so select Edit ➤ Create from the menu at the top. Oracle Net Manager will then ask you for the net service name for the database you want to enter in the OID directory. The first database you want to enter has the database service name *real*.

4. The next screen asks you to choose a network protocol. Choose TCP/IP. Oracle Net Manager asks for the server and port number. It then asks for the service name for the database, which is usually the combination of the database name and its domain. Enter **real.world** here. Oracle Net Manager offers to test the connection. The first attempt fails, because Oracle Net Manager uses the old scott/tiger username/password from earlier Oracle editions, but that user ID may or may not be in your database, depending on the method you used for creating it (manual or DBCA). Once you use the system/password, the connect test is successful. At this point, you need to click Finish to confirm that you want to accept and register the configuration of the new database service real.

5. If you now select Directory ➤ Service Naming ➤ Aliases, you can see all the databases that are part of OID, as shown in Figure 10-12. To connect to any one of these databases, clients in your organization don't need a tnsnames.ora file.

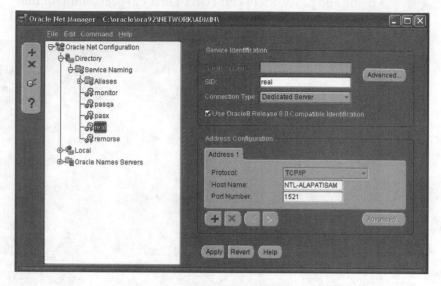

Figure 10-12. Displaying the service names registered in OID

Migrating an Entire Tnsnames.ora File to OID

Once you have tested your OID by entering a few services individually, you are ready to migrate to the new OID naming method. If you have dozens of service names, you may be better off migrating the entire tnsnames.ora entries to the OID directory. Here are the steps:

1. Log into Oracle Net Manager and choose Directory as the (present) naming method.

2. Go to the menu and select Command ➤ Directory ➤ Export Net Service Names.

3. The Directory Migration Wizard will start up next and take you through the steps necessary to migrate your tnsnames.ora file to the OID directory. Click Next.

4. The migration wizard allows you to migrate only one domain at a time. IIf there's more than one domain, the wizard asks you to choose a domain next.

5. The Select Net Service Names page appears next. Highlight one or all the database service names in your tnsnames.ora file at this point. Click Next.

6. The Select Destination Context page appears next. You have to make two choices here: the directory naming context and the Oracle Context. For the directory naming context, choose the top level you created in the

previous sections: dc=company (netbsa in my case),dc=org. For the
Oracle Context, you don't have to enter anything, because the wizard
has already picked the only Oracle Context that you've created in OID:
cn=Oraclecontext,dc=netbsa,dc=org. Figure 10-13 shows how to select
both the directory naming context and the Oracle Context. Click Next.

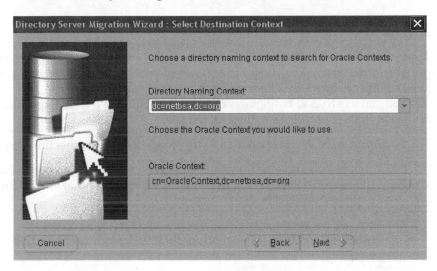

Figure 10-13. Selecting the directory naming context and Oracle Context

7. The Directory Server Update page appears next. This page indicates that
    all the database service names you selected have been migrated from
    your tnsnames.ora file to the OID directory. Click Finish to confirm that
    you want to finalize the migration of all these database services to the OID
    directory. Figure 10-14 shows the Directory Server Update page.

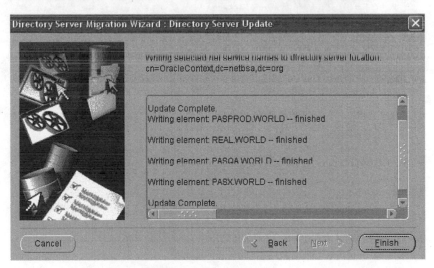

*Figure 10-14. Confirmation of the migration of tnsnames.ora entries
to OID*

Whether you've added a service name manually, used Oracle Net Manager to add one service name, or migrated your entire tnsnames.ora file, you're now configured to use the OID naming method. Now let's turn to the fun part, where you'll see how to enable clients to connect to various databases without a tnsnames.ora file on the client.

Configuring Clients for OID Naming

Any client in your network can now access any net service name stored in OID provided the client has privileges to access the database service. However, you need to first configure the clients for using the OID naming method.

You can use NCA to configure a client to use OID. You'll need to perform the following steps to configure a client for OID use:

1. Bring up NCA and choose Directory usage as your connection choice.

2. You'll see the Directory Server Configuration page. Here, choose the first option, which tells NCA to use your directory server that you've already configured for Oracle. Click Next.

3. NCA will ask you to select the Internet directory to host the service names, but you really don't have to make a choice, as you have only OID installed and no other directories are present in your system. Click Next.

4. The Directory Usage Configuration, Done page appears next, as shown in Figure 10-15. This page indicates that the client is now configured for OID usage.

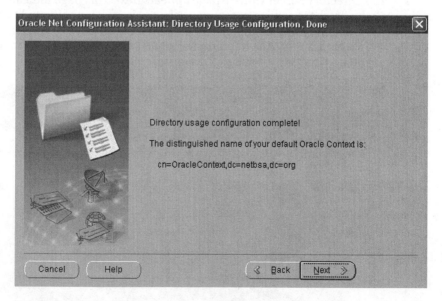

Figure 10-15. Configuring a client for OID usage

The client won't need a tnsnames.ora file to connect to any of the database service names that are part of OID. Make sure the user now has a file named ldap.ora in the $ORACLE_HOME/network/admin directory. Here's a sample ldap.ora file:

```
# LDAP.ORA Network Configuration File:
C:\oracle\ora92\network\admin\ldap.ora
# Generated by Oracle configuration tools.
DEFAULT_ADMIN_CONTEXT = ""
DIRECTORY_SERVERS= (hp50:389:636)
DIRECTORY_SERVER_TYPE = OID
```

The sqlnet.ora file in the same directory should now have the following line:

```
NAMES.DIRECTORY_PATH= (LDAP, TNSNAMES).
```

This line ensures that when a connect request is made, the LDAP directory is searched first for connection information. If the OID server is not up, for example, you can't access the LDAP search, and the tnsnames .ora is consulted in this case. Now, when a user enters the string **username/password@remorse**, OID will perform the name resolution and connect the user to the database.

Oracle and Java Database Connectivity

Frequently, Java programs need to connect to a database to perform data manipulation tasks. Java Database Connectivity (JDBC) is an interface that permits a Java program to connect to a database and issue DML and DDL SQL statements. JDBC allows the use of dynamic SQL statements, where you may not know the number and types of columns until runtime. If you're going to write static SQL, you can use SQLJ, which lets you embed SQL statements in Java. JDBC provides a rich library of routines, which help you open and close connections to databases, as well as process data. In the following sections, you'll see how you can use JDBC to connect to and work with Oracle databases from Java.

Establishing Database Connectivity

Before you can establish database connectivity, you have to select the appropriate drivers. Oracle provides four major kinds of JDBC drivers. Oracle has designed the drivers for specific uses, and you can find all the details in Oracle's JDBC manual. Here is a brief description of Oracle's JDBC drivers:

- *JDBC Thin driver:* This 100 percent pure, Java client–based driver provides a direct connection to the database using the TCP/IP protocol. The driver requires a listener and uses sockets for making connections to databases.

- *JDBC OCI driver:* This driver needs a client installation of Oracle, so it is specific to Oracle. This driver is highly scalable and can use connection pooling to serve large numbers of users.

- *JDBC server-side Thin driver:* Based on the server, this driver connects to remote databases and provides the same functionality as the client-based Thin driver.

- *JDBC server-side internal driver:* As its name indicates, this driver resides on the server and is used by the Java Virtual Machine (JVM) to talk to the Oracle database server.

Once you choose a specific type of JDBC driver, you must include code to indicate the type of driver you want to use for your applications. You can specify the JDBC driver in one of two ways: You can use the static registerDriver() method of the JDBC DriverManager class, or you can use the forName method of the java.lang.class. Here are the two methods of specifying the JDBC driver:

```
DriverManager.registerDriver (new oracle.jdbc.OracleDriver());
```

or

```
Class.forName("oracle.jdbc.driver.OracleDriver")
```

Once you've loaded the JDBC driver, it's time to make the connection to the database, which you can do by using the static getConnection() method of Driver-Manager class. This will create an instance of the JDBC connection class. Here's the code for doing this:

```
Connection conn = DriverManager.getConnection(
"jdbc:oracle:thin:@prod1:1521:finprod", username, passwd);
Here's what the different parts of the connection object stand for:jdbc=protocol
oracle = vendor
thin = driver
prod1=server
1521=port number
finprod=Oracle database
username=database username
password=database password
```

If all your information is valid, you are connected to the database from your Java application. *Conn* indicates that this is an open connection.

Working with the Database

Now that you've learned how to connect to the database using JDBC, it's time to find out how you can process SQL statements in the database through the JDBC connection. You can't execute a SQL directly from your Java program. First you need to create JDBC statements, and then you need to execute your SQL statements. Let's look at these two steps in detail.

Creating the Statement Object

To relay your SQL statements to the database, you need to create a JDBC *Statement object*. This object will associate itself with an open connection and henceforth act as the conduit through which SQL statements are transferred from the Java program to the database for execution. Here's how you create the JDBC Statement object:

```
Statement stmt = conn.createStatement() ;
```

Note that there are no SQL statements associated with the Statement object. However, under the superclass Statement, there is another object called *Prepared-Statement* that always contains a SQL statement in addition to being the channel for the statement's execution. This SQL statement is compiled immediately and can be compiled just once and used many times thereafter, which is a great benefit. For the purpose of simplicity, however, I'll just use the Statement object and not the PreparedStatement object in this discussion. Let's now turn to the execution of SQL statements.

Executing SQL Statements

You can understand JDBC SQL statements if you separate the *select* statements that query the database from all the other statements. *Select* statements don't change the state of the database, whereas the other types of statements change the database. Let's first look at how to deal with *query* statements.

Handling Queries

Select statements use the executeQuery method to get the query results. The method returns the results in the *ResultSet object*. Here's an example:

```
String first_name,last_name,manager;
Number salary;
ResultSet rs = stmt.executeQuery("SELECT * FROM Employees");
    while ( rs.next() ) {
        first_name = rs.getString("first_name");
        last_name = rs.getString("last_name");
        manager = rs.getString("manager");
        salary = rs.getNumber("salary");
        System.out.println(first_name + last_name "works for"
        Manager "salary is:" salary.");
```

Note that *rs* is an instance of the ResultSet object, and it holds the query results. The ResultSet object also provides a cursor, so you can access the results one by one. Each time you invoke the ResultSet method, the cursor moves to the next row in the result set.

Handling DDL and Nonquery DML Statements

Recall that you can use DDL and DML statements through JDBC. Any statement that changes the state of the database—be it a DDL statement or a DML statement such as *insert, update*, or *delete*—is executed using the executeUpdate method. Note that the word "update" indicates that the SQL statement will change something in the database. Here are some examples of the executeUpdate statements:

```
Statement stmt = conn.createStatement();
   stmt.executeUpdate("CREATE TABLE Employees" +
      "(last_name VARCHAR2(30), first_name VARCHAR2(20),
       manager VARCHAR2(30), salary(number" );
   stmt.executeUpdate("INSERT INTO Employees " +
      "VALUES ('Alapati', 'Valerie', 'Shannon', salary)" );
```

The preceding statements create the Statement object, and then they create a table and insert some data into it. All your normal SQL transactions properties such as consistency and durability are maintained when you use JDBC to execute SQL statements. By default, each statement commits after its execution. This is because the value of conn.setAutoCommit is set to *false*, as you can see in the following example. You can ensure that there is a commit after every statement in either of the following ways (if you wish, you may also use the conn.rollback() method to roll back a statement):

```
conn.setAutoCommit(false) ;
```

or

```
conn.commit();
```

Here's a simple example that shows how to use the *commit* and *rollback* statements:

```
conn.setAutoCommit(false);
     Statement stmt = conn.createStatement();
stmt.executeUpdate("INSERT INTO employees
VALUES('Alapati','valerie','Nicholas',50000 )");
     conn.rollback();
stmt.executeUpdate("INSERT INTO employees
VALUES('Alapati','Nina','Nicholas',50000)");
     conn.commit();
```

Error Handling

All programs must have an exception handler built in, especially those DML statements that change the database state. One way to do this is to use the *rollback* statement when you run into an error, so your partial changes are all undone. You can use the SQLException method to catch errors. In Java programs, you use a try code block to generate (or throw) an exception, and the catch block will "catch" the exception thus thrown. Here's a sample Java code block that illustrates these concepts:

```
try {
    conn.setAutoCommit(false) ;
    stmt.executeUpdate("INSERT INTO Sells VALUES " +
    "('Bar Of Foo', 'BudLite', 2.00)") ;
    conn.commit() ;
    conn.setAutoCommit(true) ;

}catch(SQLException ex) {
    System.err.println("SQLException: " + ex.getMessage()) ;
    conn.rollback() ;
    conn.setAutoCommit(true) ;
}
```

A Complete Program

Listing 10-5 shows a sample program that puts together all the concepts of the preceding sections. The example first registers the Oracle Thin driver and connects to the database using it. The program updates some rows in a table and uses the result set to print the data.

Listing 10-5. A Complete Java Program Using JDBC

```
/* import java packages */
import java.sql.* ;
public class accessDatabase{
    public static void main(String[] args)
        throws SQLException {
        Stringfirst_anme,last_name ;
        Number salary ;
        Connection c = null ;
/* register the Oracle Driver */
        try {
            Class.forName("oracle.jdbc.driver.OracleDriver");
            c = DriverManager.getConnection(
                "jdbc:oracle:thin:@prod1:1521:finprod",
                "user", "sammyy1");
/* create the statement object */
            Statement s = c.createStatement() ;
            c.setAutoCommit(false) ;
            s.executeUpdate("CREATE TABLE employees " +
                "(first_name VARCHAR2(30), last_name VARCHAR2(20),salary NUMBER)" )
;
            s.executeUpdate("INSERT INTO employee VALUES " +
                "('nicholas', 'Alapati', 50000 )") ;
            c.commit() ;
            c.setAutoCommit(true) ;
/* the result set */
            ResultSet rs = s.executeQuery("SELECT * FROM Employees") ;
```

```
            while( rs.next() ){
                first_name = rs.getString("first_name");
                last_name = rs.getString("last_name");
                salary = rs.getFloat("salary");
                System.out.println(first_name + last_name + " works for " +
        Manager + " salary is:"  + salary");
            }
    /* exception handler */
        } catch (ClassNotFoundException ex){
            System.out.println(ex);
        } catch (SQLException ex){
            if ( c != null ){
                c.rollback() ;
                c.setAutoCommit(true) ;
            }
            System.out.println("SQLException caught");
            System.out.println("---");
            while ( ex != null ){
                System.out.println("Message    : " + ex.getMessage());
                System.out.println("SQLState   : " + ex.getSQLState());
                System.out.println("ErrorCode : " + ex.getErrorCode());
                System.out.println("---");
                ex = ex.getNextException();
            }
        }
    }
}
```

Connectivity Troubleshooting

Connectivity issues are common, but they're among the easiest problems to fix for experienced DBAs. The most common problem you'll encounter is when a user keeps getting the "ORA-12154: TNS: could not resolve service name" error. The reason for the 12154 error is usually very simple. The service to which the user is attempting the connection is either not listed at all or listed incorrectly in a tnsnames.ora file if you're using local configuration. If you're using OID, the service name is probably not added to the OID database. Of course, you may find that the database service is already in the tnsnames.ora file or has been already added to the OID database. In this case, most likely there's an error somewhere in the syntax or in the specification of the network address or service name. The easiest fix for this is to simply remove the current configuration for the database and add it again. This should fix the ORA-12154 error.

Another common networking error, ORA-12203, is due to the fact that the listener may not be up and running or the service name you provided is wrong. The ORA-12541 states the following: "TNS: no listener". However, you may be confused by this error if your listener is already running and is configured properly. There may be other reasons for this error than the listener being down. For example, you may install a new Oracle database on a new server. If you're using DNS and the new server isn't made a part of your DNS, clients will get the 12541 error. That's why it's important to check the listener, the tnsnames.ora (or ldap.ora and OID), and other network information when you're confronted with any networking errors.

A general approach to Oracle connectivity troubleshooting could use the following approach. First, test connectivity from the client using the telnet or ping utility. This should tell you if the network connection is functioning properly.

Once you've verified the network connection, you can test the tnsnames.ora entries by using the tnsping utility on the client, as shown here:

```
C:\>  tnsping compose
TNS Ping Utility for 32-bit Windows:
Version 9.2.0.1.0 - Production on 07-JAN
03 11:30:05
Copyright (c) 1997 Oracle Corporation.  All rights reserved.
Used parameter files:
C:\neworacle\ora9i\network\admin\sqlnet.ora
Used TNSNAMES adapter to resolve the alias
Attempting to contact (DESCRIPTION =
(ADDRESS_LIST = (ADDRESS = (PROTOCOL = TCP)
(HOST = NTL-ALAPATISAM)(PORT = 1521)))
 (CONNECT_DATA = (SERVER = DEDICATED)
(SERVICE_NAME = compose.world)))
OK (110 msec)
C:\ >
```

Once the tnsping utility shows that the tnsnames.ora file is OK, but you still can't connect to the target database, check to make sure that the SQL*Plus utility works properly and that you have a valid username/password in the target database. Depending on the type of connection you're trying to establish, you may also want to check that the Oracle ODBC driver is correctly installed and configured for database connection.

One of the problems with Oracle networking is its ability to scale beyond certain limits. However, this is not a real problem, as Oracle also provides great solutions to upgrade your ability to connect to a large user population. In this chapter, you've only seen the commonly used dedicated server approach to connectivity. Oracle's shared server approach, where a large number of database connections are channeled through small number of server processes, is one way to increase your connection capacity. Oracle also provides the Connection Manager facility, which you can combine with the shared server approach to "multiplex" sessions, whereby you channel multiple user sessions through a single network connection. In summary, the shared server approach will reduce the number of concurrent client connections, and the multiplexing feature provided by the Connection Manager will enable the multiplexing of multiple client sessions to a single TCP/IP connection.

In a dedicated server approach, large number of users can quickly use up all your physical memory and virtual memory, causing login slowdowns and other related problems. If you have a shortage of memory on your system, then MTS is definitely an option to consider seriously. On average, each dedicated connection takes up 3MB to 4MB each. If you have 4,000 users, that is 12GB to 16GB just for maintaining the user connections whether the connections are active or not. Using a shared server strategy, you can drop total memory usage to about a third of what the dedicated server approach would require.

Summary

This chapter introduced you to the basics of Oracle networking, including Oracle Net and the listener service. You learned how to create a quick database connection using Oracle Network Configuration Assistant. Oracle networking can be very intimidating at first, but rest assured it's indeed simple once you understand the network terminology and the architecture of the different naming methods.

The chapter explained the main service name resolution methods: local naming, host based naming, external naming and, of course, LDAP-based Oracle Internet Directory (OID) naming. The chapter provided you with OID installation examples and showed you how to configure directory access after the installation by creating a naming context. You also learned how to migrate from the traditional tnsnames.ora names to OID.

For most small and medium client loads, you don't need any fancier mechanism than the local naming method using tnsnames.ora files. Nevertheless, Oracle Corporation has been stressing the importance of the LDAP-based OID, and this chapter provided you with a basic understanding of the configuration and use of OID. Installing OID has other payoffs besides enabling client connectivity, as you can use OID for security management.

In the last sections of the chapter, you saw the systematic creation of a Java statement that performs transactions in an Oracle database after connecting via the JDBC protocol. I discussed some common connection problems and I provided troubleshooting advice.

CHAPTER 11

User Management and Database Security

THIS CHAPTER DEALS with database security and user management. You can consider user management a part of overall security management of the Oracle database.

Database security means different things to different people. The essential thing to remember is that in general, the underlying goal of database security is to prevent unauthorized use of the database or its components. Database security also depends on system and network security, but this chapter mostly focuses on how you can provide solid security at the database level.

In this chapter, you'll learn how to create and manage users in an Oracle database. You can grant users system and object privileges directly, but it's far more common to grant these privileges using roles. This chapter shows you how to create and grant roles to users.

This chapter also provides you with a thorough discussion of Oracle profiles and how to manage them. Profiles allow you to set limits on the resources used by each user in the database and also enable you to enforce a password policy for security purposes. The Oracle Database Resource Manager enables you to allocate scarce database and server resources among groups of users according to a resource plan. This chapter provides you with a comprehensive introduction to this tool.

In a production database, it's *always* a good idea to audit database usage. You can audit both the changes made to the data and events such as unsuccessful attempts to log into the database. Triggers based on system events can provide your database with a strong security layer, and this chapter explains how to use these special triggers. Also in this chapter, you'll learn how to use the Database Resource Manager, which lets you "fine-tune" resource use by various users.

The main aspects of Oracle database security management are as follows:

- Controlling access to data (authorization)

- Authenticating users

- Ensuring data integrity

- Auditing users' actions

- Managing enterprise security

Before you can audit users' actions, use a secure directory, or perform other security-related activities, you'll need to have users in the system. The next section deals with Oracle9*i* user management, including creating new users and granting database roles and privileges to those users. After you learn how to perform basic user management tasks, you'll see how you can use the Database Resource Manager to control resource usage in the database.

After you learn about user management, you'll explore various components of Oracle security: authenticating and authorizing users, ensuring data integrity, auditing database usage, and administrating centralized security.

Managing Users

User management is a pretty complex topic because not only does it deal with authorization of entry into the database, but it also touches on vital topics such as security and resource management. The DBA creates the users in the database and sets limits on their access to the various components of the database. The DBA also limits the physical space and system resources that the users can use, usually through the use of database roles and privileges. You'll see later on how to make sure that the default passwords associated with various database users are changed soon after creating a new database.

The first task after you create a new database is to create tablespaces. Once you've created all your tablespaces, you're ready to create the users. When you create a brand-new database, of course, the only users at first will be the application or schema owners. Later on, you'll create the actual end users who will be using the database on a day-to-day basis. For the first set of users, the application owners, you're more concerned with the allocation of sufficient space and other privileges to create objects in the database. For the end users, your primary concern is the users' access rights to the various objects and the limits to their use of resources while accessing the database for their routine uses.

Preliminary Tasks Before Creating Users

When you create a new user, you should always assign the user a default tablespace to store objects he or she may create. As you know, when you create any object in the database, you need to specify a physical location—a tablespace—in which you want to create the object. If you don't specify a tablespace during object creation, the object gets created in the default tablespace of the users. For a really small database, it may be a trivial issue as to where the object is created. However, for a database of any meaningful size, it's important that you place the objects in well-planned locations, so as to maintain a proper grouping of similar objects and also avoid contention down the road.

 CAUTION *If you don't assign a specific tablespace as the default tablespace, the System tablespace becomes your default tablespace. If you create a very large object in the System tablespace, you may take up all the space in it and make it impossible for the superuser SYS to create any new objects in it. In this case, the database will come to a grinding halt. This is the main reason why you should always create a default tablespace for every user.*

In addition to the default tablespace, you should assign a Temporary tablespace for each user. Temporary tablespaces are where the database performs certain operations such as sorting. If you omit mentioning the temporary tablespace, the user is assigned the default temporary tablespace that you chose at database creation time. If you didn't choose one at that time, then the System tablespace becomes the default temporary tablespace. Again, it's important to assign a specific tablespace for fulfilling the temporary tablespace requirement.

Creating a New User

Here is a simple user creation statement:

```
SQL> create user salapati
        Identified by sam1am9
        Default tablespace sales01
        Temporary tablespace  temp;
User created.
SQL>
```

This statement creates a new user, salapati, with the assigned password, sam1Am9. What can this user do in the database? Not a whole lot! You need to give the user a minimal role called *connect*, which will enable the user to simply make a connection to the database and create a *session* in the database:

```
SQL> grant connect to salapati;
Grant succeeded.
SQL>
```

You can also create a new user by using the *grant connect* statement, as shown in the following example:

```
SQL> grant connect to nina identified by nina1;
Grant succeeded.
SQL>
```

User nina is created with the connect system privilege. The default tablespace will be System and the temporary tablespace will be temp.

Let's try to create a new table called xyz1 under user salapati's username (schema):

```
SQL> create table xyz1 (name varchar2(30));
create table xyz1 (name varchar2(30))
*
ERROR at line 1:
ORA-01950: no privileges on tablespace 'SALES01'
SQL>
```

The user salapati was assigned the default tablespace sales01, so that's where Oracle creates the new table, xyz1. However, the user wasn't granted any *quota* on the tablespace. By default, no user is given any space quotas on any tablespace.

Quotas have to be granted explicitly. It's common to assign specific tablespace quotas at user creation time. Here's how you grant a space quota to a user:

```
SQL> alter user salapati
  2  quota 100M on sales01;
User altered.
SQL>
```

 TIP *If you don't want a user to create any objects at all in the database, just don't assign a quota on any tablespace. If it's an existing user with a specific quota on a tablespace, you can use the* alter user *statement to set this quota to 0.*

If you want a user to have no limits on space usage in all tablespaces, you need to grant the user the unlimited tablespace privilege by using the following command:

```
SQL> grant unlimited tablespace to salapati;
Grant succeeded.
SQL>
```

To change the current password of a user, you can use the *alter user* command as shown here:

```
SQL> alter user salapati identified by sammyy1;
User altered.
SQL>
```

If the user wants to change his or her password through SQL*Plus, the user can do so by using the following commands:

```
SQL> password
Changing password for SALAPATI
Old password: *********
New password: *********
Retype new password: *********
Password changed
SQL>
```

User Profiles and Resource Management

In the previous example, you created a new user, assigned the user a set of default and temporary tablespaces, and granted the user the privileges to connect to the database. What is the limit on the amount of resources this user can use? What if this user unwittingly starts a SQL program that guzzles resources like crazy and brings your system to its knees? Of course, there are some third-party tools that include *query governs*, which limit the types of queries that users can use within the database, thus ensuring that the databases is not loaded down by inefficient queries.

Can you limit an individual's usage of resources, so you can allocate resources on a need-to-use basis? You can set the individual resource limits in Oracle by using what are known as *profiles*. You can use profiles to set hard limits on resource consumption by the various users in the database. Profiles help you limit the number of sessions a user can simultaneously keep open, the length of time these sessions can be maintained, and the usage of CPU and other resources. Here, for example, is a profile called "miser" (because it limits the resource usage to a minimum):

```
SQL> create profile miser
  2  limit
  3  connect_time 120
  4  failed_login_attempts 2
  5  idle_time 60
  6* sessions_per_user 2;
Profile created.
  SQL>
```

The miser profile when granted to a user will permit that user to be connected for a maximum of 120 seconds and will log out the user if he or she is idle for more than 1 minute. The user is limited to two sessions at any one time. If the user fails to log in within two attempts, the user's accounts will be "locked" for a specified period or until the DBA manually unlocks them.

Profile Parameters and Limits

Oracle9*i* enables you to set limits on several parameters within a profile. The following sections provide brief explanations of these parameters. You can divide the profile parameters into two broad types: *resource parameters*, which are concerned purely with limiting resource usage, and *password parameters*, which are used for enforcing password-related security policies.

Resource Parameters

As mentioned in the previous section, resource parameters are profile parameters that you can set to control resource usage by users. The main purpose in using resource parameters is to ensure that a single user or a set of users doesn't monopolize the database and server resources. Here are the most important resource parameters that you can set within an Oracle9*i* database:

- *Connect_time:* The total time a session may remain connected to the database.

- *Cpu_per_call:* Limits the CPU used per each call within a transaction (for the parse, execute, and fetch operations).

- *Cpu_per_session:* Limits the total CPU used during a session.

- *Sessions_per_user:* Maximum number of concurrent sessions that can be opened by the user.

- *Idle_time:* Limits the amount of time a session is idle (i.e., nothing is running on its behalf).

- *Logical_reads_per_session:* Total number of data blocks read (memory plus disk reads).

- *Logical_reads_per_call:* Limits the logical reads per each session call (parse, execute, and fetch).

- *Private_sga:* This is a limit applicable only to shared server architecture–based systems. It specifies a session's limits on the space it allocated in the shared pool component of the SGA.

- *Composite_limit:* A composite limit is a sum of several of the previously described resource parameters, measured in service units. These resources are weighted by their importance. Oracle takes into account four parameters to compute a weighted *composite_limit: cpu_per_session, connect_time, logical_reads_per_session,* and *private_sga.* You can set a weight for each of these four parameters by using the *alter resource cost* statement, as shown in the following example:

```
SQL> alter resource cost
  2  cpu_per_session 200
  3  connect_time 2;
Resource cost altered.
SQL>
```

TIP *If you don't use a weight for any of these four parameters, the parameters will be ignored in the computation of the* composite_limit *parameter.*

Password Parameters

Oracle9*i* provides you a wide variety of parameters to manage user passwords. You can set the following password-related profile parameters to enforce your security policies:

- *Failed_login_attempts:* Number of times a user can attempt to log in before being locked out.

- *Password_life_time:* Sets the time limit of using a password. If you don't change the password within this specified time, the password expires.

- *Password_grace_time:* Sets the time period during which you'll be warned that your password has expired. After the grace period is exhausted, you can't connect to the database with that password.

- *Password_lock_time:* number of days a user will be locked out after hitting the maximum number of unsuccessful login attempts.

- *Password_reuse_max:* Determines how many times you need to change your password before you can reuse your current password.

- *Password_verify_function:* Lets you specify your own password verification function if you don't want to use the default Oracle-provided verification function.

As you can see, you can set a number of resource- and password-related parameters to control access to the database and resource usage. What happens if you don't assign a profile to a user? Well, the user will still have a profile assigned called the *default* profile. The default profile, unfortunately, isn't very limiting at all—all the parameters are set to UNLIMITED, meaning there's no limit on resource usage whatsoever. Listing 11-1 shows the results of querying the DBA_PROFILES table regarding the parameters for the profile named default.

Listing 11-1. Resource Limits for the Default Profile

```
SQLselect

RESOURCE_NAME                              LIMIT
-------------------------------    ---------------------------
COMPOSITE_LIMIT                            UNLIMITED
SESSIONS_PER_USER                          UNLIMITED
CPU_PER_SESSION                            UNLIMITED
CPU_PER_CALL                               UNLIMITED
LOGICAL_READS_PER_SESSION                  UNLIMITED
LOGICAL_READS_PER_CALL                     UNLIMITED
IDLE_TIME                                  UNLIMITED
CONNECT_TIME                               UNLIMITED
PRIVATE_SGA                                UNLIMITED
FAILED_LOGIN_ATTEMPTS                      UNLIMITED
PASSWORD_LIFE_TIME                         UNLIMITED
PASSWORD_REUSE_TIME                        UNLIMITED
PASSWORD_REUSE_MAX                         UNLIMITED
PASSWORD_VERIFY_FUNCTION                   NULL
PASSWORD_LOCK_TIME                         UNLIMITED
PASSWORD_GRACE_TIME                        UNLIMITED
16 rows selected.
SQL>
```

 CAUTION *If you don't assign a profile to a user, Oracle assigns that user the default profile. Because the default profile uses a value of UNLIMITED for all parameters, you'll have a serious problem on your hands if the users are assigned this default profile. To avoid this problem, change the default profile's parameters to something more restrictive than UNLIMITED as soon as you get a chance.*

Assigning a Profile

You assign a profile to a user by using the *alter user* statement, as follows:

```
SQL> alter user salapati
  2  profile test;
User altered.
SQL>
```

Altering a Profile

You can alter a profile by using the *alter profile* command, as follows:

```
SQL> alter profile test
  2  limit
  3  sessions_per_user 4
  4* failed_login_attempts 4
SQL> /
Profile altered.
SQL>
```

When Do Profile Changes Go into Effect?

After you alter the profile as shown previously, when does it come into force? That is, when will the user be really restricted to four simultaneous sessions? The surprising answer is . . . *never!* Unless you have an initialization parameter modified from its default value, the profile changes you make will never come into force. The initialization parameter is the *resource_limit* parameter, and its default value is *false*. You need to set it to *true*, either by restarting the database after an init.ora file change or through the use of the *alter system* command, as shown here:

```
SQL> alter system set resource_limit=true;
System altered.
SQL>
```

 TIP *Make sure you have the* resource_limit *parameter set to* true *in order for the resource limits set by the profiles to be enforced. Otherwise, Oracle will ignore the limits set in the* create *or* alter profile *statement.*

Dropping a Profile

Dropping a profile is straightforward, as shown in this example:

```
SQL> drop profile test cascade;
Profile dropped.
SQL>
```

Why use the keyword *cascade* to drop the test profile? The test profile is assigned to some users in the database, and so you are required to use the *cascade* keyword. Note that the users who were assigned the test profile will now be automatically assigned the default profile, which is named DEFAULT.

What Happens When Profile Limits Are Reached?

When a user hits the limits imposed by either a session-level or a call-level resource limit, Oracle rolls back the user's statement that is in progress and returns an error message. If it's a call-level limit (such as *cpu_per_call*), the user's session remains intact and other statements belonging to the current transaction remain valid. Of course, if a session-level limit is reached, the user can't go any further in that session.

How Do You Know What the Profile Limits Should Be?

You have several ways to gather the statistics for the optimal values for several critical resource limits such as *logical_reads_per_session*. If you're too liberal with the value, some users may hog resources, and if you're too conservative, you'll be fielding many calls from irate users who are prevented from completing their jobs. Try to see if you can get some information from any test runs that you've made of a certain job. If you don't have reliable historical data, use the *audit session* statement to acquire baseline data for several parameters such as connect time and logical reads. You can also use Oracle Enterprise Manager (OEM) to gather the data, as you'll see in Chapter 17. In addition, you may have feedback (or complaints!) from the users themselves that their programs are failing due to limits on resource use, or that they need longer connect times to the database server.

Using the Database Resource Manager

Suppose you're managing a production database with the following problems:

- Batch jobs are taking up most of the available resources, which is hurting other, more critical jobs that need to run at the same time.

- Excessive loads at peak times are causing critical processes to run for an unacceptably long period of time.

- You schedule large jobs and really can't predict when they might be launched.

- Some users are using an excessive amount of CPU, causing you to kill their sessions abruptly.

- Some users are using a very high degree of parallelism in their operations, which is hurting the performance of the system as a whole.

- You can't manage active sessions.

- You want to prioritize jobs according to some scheme, but you can't do so using operating system resources.

As you can see, all the problems stem from the inability of the DBA to allocate the limited resources efficiently among competing operations, which leads to lop-sided resource allocation and all the attendant problems, including very high response times for critical jobs.

The Oracle Database Resource Manager is the answer to your problems with resource management vis-à-vis your users. The Database Resource Manager allows you to create resource plans, which specify how much of your resources should go to the various consumer groups. You can now group users based on their resource requirements, and you can have the Database Resource Manager allocate a preset amount of resources to these groups. Thus, you can easily prior-itize among your users and jobs.

The resource plans that you formulate have the directives regarding resource usage, and you can easily modify these plans. Using the Database Resource Manager, it's possible for you to ensure that your critical user groups (called *consumer groups* here) are always guaranteed enough resources to perform their tasks. The resources that the Database Resource Manager can allocate are CPU usage, degree of parallelism, execution time limit, and the undo that can be gen-erated by a consumer group. You can also limit the maximum number of concurrently active sessions allowed in each group.

Using the Database Resource Manager

You manage the Database Resource Manager through executing procedures in the Oracle-supplied DBMS_RESOURCE_MANAGER package. As a DBA, you'll already have privileges to execute any procedure in this package, but you'll have to grant all other users a special system privilege through the DBMS_RESOURCE_MANAGER package. Using the DBMS_RESOURCE_MANAGER package, you create a resource plan for the various consumer groups and finally assign the plans to the consumer groups.

The DBMS_RESOURCE_MANAGER package has several procedures, but you'll focus on a few important ones to learn how to use the package to control resource allocation among database users. The following discussion of the Database Resource Manager is meant to familiarize you with the various steps involved in creating resource plans and enforcing them. The Resource Plan Wizard in the OEM toolset is the best way to quickly create resource plans in your database once you get the hang of the various steps that are involved in creating and maintaining the plans.

Here's the sequence of actions you need to take to start using the Database Resource Manager:

1. Create a pending area.

2. Create a consumer group.

3. Create a resource plan.

4. Create a plan directive.

5. Validate the pending area.

6. Submit the pending area.

Before you can use the Database Resource Manager to allocate resources, you need to create what is called a *pending area* to validate changes before their implementation. The next step is to validate the changes and submit them for implementation. You then need to create resource directives for all the plans.

Creating a Pending Area

Before you can modify an old plan or create a new plan, you need to activate or create a pending area using the Database Resource Manager package in the following manner. All the resource plans you'll create will be stored in the data dictionary, and the following create pending area procedure will enable you to work with resource plans in a staging area before they are implemented:

```
SQL> execute dbms_resource_manager.create_pending_area;
PL/SQL procedure successfully completed.
SQL>
```

You can also clear the pending area anytime you want by using the following procedure:

```
SQL> execute dbms_resource_manager.clear_pending_area;
PL/SQL procedure successfully completed.
SQL>
```

Creating Consumer Groups

Once the pending area is active, you can create the consumer groups to which you'll allocate your users. You can assign users initially to one group, and you can later switch them to other groups if necessary. Now you'll create in your database three consumer groups: local, regional, and national. Listing 11-2 shows how to create your consumer groups.

Listing 11-2. Creating Consumer Groups

```
SQL> execute dbms_resource_manager.create_pending_area;
PL/SQL procedure successfully completed.
SQL> execute dbms_resource_manager.create_consumer_group
    (consumer_group => 'local',-> comment => 'local councils');
PL/SQL procedure successfully completed.
SQL> execute dbms_resource_manager.create_consumer_group
    (consumer_group => 'regional',-> comment => 'regional
    councils');
PL/SQL procedure successfully completed.
SQL> execute dbms_resource_manager. create_consumer_group
    (consumer_group => 'national',-> comment => 'national office');
PL/SQL procedure successfully completed.
SQL>
```

Checking What Groups Exist in Your Database

You can query the DBA_RSRC_CONSUMER_GROUPS view for information relating to what groups currently exist in your database, as shown in Listing 11-3.

Listing 11-3. Querying the DBA_RSRC_CONSUMERS_GROUP View

```
SQL> select consumer_group,status
  2  from dba_rsrc_consumer_groups;
CONSUMER_GROUP                   STATUS
------------------------------   --------
OTHER_GROUPS                     PENDING
DEFAULT_CONSUMER_GROUP           PENDING
SYS_GROUP                        PENDING
LOW_GROUP                        PENDING
OTHER_GROUPS                     ACTIVE
DEFAULT_CONSUMER_GROUP           ACTIVE
SYS_GROUP                        ACTIVE
LOW_GROUP                        ACTIVE
REGIONAL                         PENDING
NATIONAL                         PENDING
LOCAL                            PENDING
11 rows selected.
SQL>
```

Well, what's going on here? You just created three new groups: national, regional, and local. Why does the output in Listing 11-3 show eleven groups? The same query would have given you the following output before you created the three new groups in the pending area:

```
SQL> select consumer_group,status
  2  from dba_rsrc_consumer_groups;
CONSUMER_GROUP                   STATUS
------------------------------   ---
OTHER_GROUPS                     ACTIVE
DEFAULT_CONSUMER_GROUP           ACTIVE
SYS_GROUP                        ACTIVE
LOW_GROUP                        ACTIVE
SQL>
```

The eight groups that you see in the preceding code, in addition to the three you created, are default groups that exist in every Oracle database. Here is a brief explanation of the default groups:

- *Other_groups:* This isn't really a group, because you can't assign users to it. When a resource plan is active, *other_groups* is the catchall term for all sessions that don't belong to this active resource plan.

- *Default_consumer_group:* If you don't assign users to any group, they will, by default, become members of the default group.

- *Sys_group and low_group:* These are part of the default *system_plan* that exists in every database. Oracle supplies three plans for each database, as shown by the output of the following query.

```
SQL> select plan, comments, status from dba_rsrc_plans;
```

PLAN	COMMENTS	STATUS
SYSTEM_PLAN	Plan to give system sessions priority	ACTIVE
INTERNAL_QUIESCE	Plan to internally quiesce the system	ACTIVE
INTERNAL_PLAN	Default plan	ACTIVE
SQL>		

Once you create a pending area, as you saw earlier, you can start creating the different consumer groups. Once you create the groups, you can then validate your pending area. Once the changes are accepted as being correct, you can submit the changes through the Database Resource Manager as follows:

```
SQL> execute dbms_resource_manager.validate_pending_area;
PL/SQL procedure successfully completed.
SQL> execute dbms_resource_manager.submit_pending_area;
PL/SQL procedure successfully completed.
```

If you query the DBA_RSRC_CONSUMER_GROUPS view now, you'll see the four default groups and the three groups you just created, for a total of seven groups. Listing 11-4 shows the various groups that you created.

Listing 11-4. Listing the Consumer Groups

```
SQL> select consumer_group,status
  2  from dba_rsrc_consumer_groups;
```

CONSUMER GROUP	STATUS
OTHER_GROUPS	ACTIVE
DEFAULT_CONSUMER_GROUP	ACTIVE
SYS_GROUP	ACTIVE
LOW_GROUP	ACTIVE
REGIONAL	ACTIVE
NATIONAL	ACTIVE
LOCAL	ACTIVE

Assigning Users to Consumer Groups

Now you'll assign some of your users to the three consumer groups you just created. Normally you'll have several users in each group, but for the purpose of simplicity, you'll assign one user to each of the three groups as follows: Assign *local_user* to *local_consumer_group*, *regional_user* to *regional_consumer_group*, and *national_user* to *national_consumer_group*.

Remember that the three users are already members of a default group, the *default_consumer_group*. Therefore, you need to first grant the three users privileges to switch their groups before you can actually switch them to your new groups. If you just grant the user PUBLIC the privilege to switch groups, you don't have to grant the privilege individually to all the users in the group. If you have a large number of users in each group, it is better to grant the user PUBLIC the privilege to switch groups, so you can avoid granting the privilege individually to each user. Listing 11-5 shows how you can use the DBMS_RESOURCE_MANAGER package to assign and switch users' consumer groups.

Listing 11-5. Assigning Users to Consumer Groups

```
SQL> execute dbms_resource_manager_privs.grant_switch_
     consumer_group ('local_user','local',TRUE);
PL/SQL procedure successfully completed.
SQL> execute dbms_resource_manager.set_
     initial_consumer_group ('local_user','local');
PL/SQL procedure successfully completed.
SQL> execute dbms_resource_manager_privs.grant_
     switch_consumer_group('regional_user','regional',TRUE);
PL/SQL procedure successfully completed.
SQL> execute dbms_resource_manager.set_initial_
     consumer_group ('regional_user','regional');
PL/SQL procedure successfully completed.
SQL> execute dbms_resource_manager_privs.grant_
     switch_consumer_group('national_user','national',TRUE);
PL/SQL procedure successfully completed.
SQL> execute dbms_resource_manager.set_
     initial_consumer_group ('national_user','national');
PL/SQL procedure successfully completed.
SQL>
```

You can verify that the three users have been assigned to the appropriate consumer group by using the query in Listing 11-6.

Listing 11-6. Verifying Consumer Group Membership of Users

```
SQL> select username,initial_rsrc_consumer_group
  2  from dba_users;
USERNAME                 INITIAL_RSRC_CONSUMER_GROUP
------------------------ ------------------------------------
SYS                      SYS_GROUP
SYSTEM                   SYS_GROUP
SALAPATI                 DEFAULT_CONSUMER_GROUP
NATIONAL_USER            NATIONAL
REGIONAL_USER            REGIONAL
LOCAL_USER               LOCAL
6 rows selected.
SQL>
```

Note that superusers SYS and SYSTEM are default members of the *sys_group*. User salapati is a member of the *default_consumer_group*, to which all users in the database are automatically assigned when they are first created.

Creating Resource Plans and Plan Directives

The heart of the Database Resource Manager is its capability to assign resource plans to various groups. You've already created the groups in the previous section, so now you'll create some resource plans that you can assign to these groups.

Creating Resource Plans

Resource plans enable you to set limits on resource use by specifying limits on four variables: CPU, active session pool, degree of parallelism, and the order in which queued sessions will execute. Currently, for all four parameters, only the default levels and methods provided by Oracle can be used. Create your resource plan by invoking the DBMS_RESOURCE_MANAGER package again:

```
SQL> execute dbms_resource_manager.create_pending_area;
PL/SQL procedure successfully completed.
SQL>  execute dbms_resource_Manager.create_plan (plan =>
     'membership_plan', -
     > comment => 'New Membership Recruitment');
PL/SQL procedure successfully completed.
SQL>
```

Creating a Plan Directive

You now have a resource plan, but the plan still doesn't have any resource limits assigned to it. You need to create a *resource plan directive* to assign specific resource limits to your resource plan. Listing 11-7 shows how to create a plan directive.

Listing 11-7. Creating a Plan Directive

```
SQL> execute dbms_resource_manager.create_plan
     _directive (plan => 'membership_plan', -
     > GROUP_OR_SUBPLAN => 'local', COMMENT => 'LOCAL GROUP',-
     > CPU_P1 => 70);
PL/SQL procedure successfully completed.
SQL> execute dbms_resource_manager.create_plan
     _directive (plan => 'membership_plan', -
     > GROUP_OR_SUBPLAN => 'REGIONAL',COMMENT=> 'regional group',-
     > CPU_P1 => 30);
PL/SQL procedure successfully completed.
SQL> execute dbms_resource_manager.create_plan
     _directive (plan => 'membership_plan', -
     > GROUP_OR_SUBPLAN => 'national',comment => 'national group',-
     > CPU_P2 => 100);
PL/SQL procedure successfully completed.
SQL>
```

The plan directive in Listing 11-7 assigns 70 percent of the available CPU at the first level to the local group and the rest, 30 percent, to the regional group. It allocates 100 percent of the CPU at the second level to the national group.

In addition to the preceding three groups, you'll need to add a plan directive for the default *other_groups* for the Database Resource Manager to accept your plan directives.

```
SQL> execute dbms_resource_manager.create
    _plan_directive (plan => 'membership_plan', -
  > GROUP_OR_SUBPLAN => 'OTHER_GROUPS', comment => '
    => 100);
PL/SQL procedure successfully completed.
SQL>
```

TIP *If you don't include a resource directive for* other_groups, *Oracle won't let you use your directives for the other groups if the plan directive is for a primary or* top plan.

You can now validate and submit your new top-level plan, *membership_plan*, in the following manner:

```
SQL>  execute dbms_resource_manager.validate_pending_area;
PL/SQL procedure successfully completed.
SQL> execute dbms_resource_manager.submit_pending_area;
PL/SQL procedure successfully completed.
SQL>
```

You can use the query in Listing 11-8 to determine resource plan directives that are currently in force for various groups.

Listing 11-8. Determining the Status of the Resource Plans

```
SQL> select plan,group_or_subplan,cpu_p1,cpu_p2,cpu_p3, status
  2  from dba_rsrc_plan_directives;
```

PLAN	GROUP	CPU_P1	CPU_P2	CPU_P3	STATUS
SYSTEM_PLAN	SYS_GROUP	100	0	0	ACTIVE
SYSTEM_PLAN	OTHER_GROUPS	0	100	0	ACTIVE
SYSTEM_PLAN	LOW_GROUP	0	0	100	ACTIVE
INTERNAL_QUIESCE	SYS_GROUP	0	0	0	ACTIVE
INTERNAL_QUIESCE	OTHER_GROUPS	0	0	0	ACTIVE
INTERNAL_PLAN	OTHER_GROUPS	0	0	0	ACTIVE
MEMBERSHIP_PLAN	REGIONAL	30	0	0	ACTIVE
MEMBERSHIP_PLAN	NATIONAL	0	100	0	ACTIVE
MEMBERSHIP_PLAN	OTHER_GROUPS	0	0	100	ACTIVE
MEMBERSHIP_PLAN	LOCAL	70	0	0	ACTIVE

```
10 rows selected.
SQL>
```

Enabling the Database Resource Manager

The fact that you created a new plan and plan directives and submitted your pending area doesn't mean that Oracle will automatically enforce the resource plans. It's your job to explicitly activate the Database Resource Manager, either by specifying the initialization parameter *resource_manager_plan* in the init.ora file or by using the *alter system* command in the following manner:

```
SQL> alter system set resource_manager_plan=MEMBERSHIP_PLAN ;
System altered.
SQL> select * from v$rsrc_plan;
NAME
-------------------------------
MEMBERSHIP_PLAN
SQL>
```

If you decide to deactivate the Database Resource Manager, you use the following command:

```
SQL> alter system set resource_manager_plan='';
System altered.
SQL>  select * from v$rsrc_plan;
no rows selected
SQL>
```

At any given time, you can query V$RSRC_CONSUMER_GROUP to see what the resource usage among the consumer groups looks like:

```
SQL> select name,active_sessions,cpu_wait_time, consumed_cpu_time,
     current_undo_consumption
  2  from v$rsrc_consumer_group;
```

NAME	ACTIVE SESSIONS	CPU_ WAIT	CONSUMED_ CPU_TIME	CURRENT UNDO_CONS
REGIONAL	0	0	0	0
NATIONAL	0	0	0	0
OTHER_GROUPS	1	0	74	0
LOCAL	0	0	18017	0

```
SQL>
```

Now that you've sweated through all the error-prone, time-consuming work of creating and enabling resource plans, let me remind you again that OEM's Resource Plan Wizard makes using the Database Resource Manager a snap. Figure 11-1 shows the final step in creating a resource plan using this GUI tool. All the code was created by the wizard in under a minute.

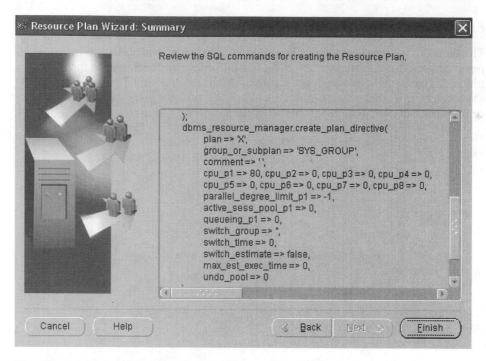

Figure 11-1. Using OEM's Resource Plan Wizard to create resource plans

Managing Access to Data

Once you create users in the database, you need to control their access to the various data objects. To take a simple example, a clerk in the human resources department of an organization may be able to see the salary data of employees, but he or she may not have the authority to change personnel salaries. Oracle uses several means to customize data access. Chief among these methods is the assigning of database privileges and roles to various database users. Let's see how Oracle uses database privileges to control data access.

Privileges in an Oracle Database

The new user that you created in the beginning of this chapter has been assigned a profile, which sets limits on his or her resource use and implements certain password-related limitations. What can this new user do in your database? Nothing at all, other than connect to the database. In Oracle, a user has to be specifically granted the privileges to insert, delete, update, or even select from any table. If the user just needs to execute a procedure or a package, the owner of the package or procedure needs to explicitly grant rights for the user to do so.

Oracle has two types of privileges: *system privileges* and *object privileges*. The following sections cover these two basic types of privileges in some detail.

System Privileges

System privileges grant users the ability to perform operations that may affect the entire database, not just the objects in any particular user's schema. Some of the most common system privileges are analyze any table, audit any, alter database, create database, create any profile, grant any privilege, create role, alter session, alter system, lock any table, insert any table, delete any table, create tablespace, create user, drop user, alter user, and so on. As you can see, system privileges are very powerful, and granting them to the wrong user could have a devastating impact on your database. Therefore, system privileges are not granted to other users besides the DBA-type users in any database.

Note that by default, no user is granted any system privileges except those who have been granted the DBA role. So, when a user attempts to perform an innocuous operation like the following, he or she would get an error:

```
SQL> select username from v$session;
select username from v$session
                 *
ERROR at line 1:
ORA-00942: table or view does not exist
```

The reason for this is simple. The table V$SESSION, of course, exists, but it can't be queried by general users because it's a special table that belongs to the SYS schema. Even if this user has the select any table privilege, the user won't be able to select from any system table.

TIP *Several normal operations require users to query some data dictionary tables routinely. Therefore, it's a good idea to grant your developers on the development databases a set of basic system privileges by granting these users the* select_catalog_role. *This role gives the developers select privileges on all the data dictionary tables (views).*

Object Privileges

Object privileges enable users to query, insert, update, and delete from tables belonging to a specific schema. The owner of any object implicitly has all rights on the object and can grant privileges on the objects to any user in the database. The schema owner has the right to grant these privileges—not the DBA or the SYSTEM or SYS users. There are two other ways, besides being the object's owner, whereby you can grant privileges on an object:

- The user must have the grant any object privilege.

- The user can grant privileges on an object provided the user was given the privilege by the object owner with the grant option.

The schema owner can grant one type or all types of privileges at once on any given object. Listing 11-9 shows some typical examples that illustrate granting various forms of object privileges.

Listing 11-9. Granting Typical Object Privileges

```
SQL> grant select on ods_process to tester;
Grant succeeded.
SQL> grant insert on ods_Process to tester;
Grant succeeded.
SQL> grant all on ods_servers to tester;
Grant succeeded.
SQL> grant insert any table to tester;
grant insert any table to tester
*
ERROR at line 1:
ORA-01031: insufficient privileges
SQL>
```

The user ODS is able to grant all privileges (select, insert, update, and delete) on table ods_servers to the user tester by using the *grant all* command. But ODS fails to successfully grant the insert any table privilege to tester, because this requires a system privilege (insert any table) that ODS does not have. Note that the user System can successfully make this grant, however, as shown here:

```
SQL> connect system/manager@finance1
Connected.
SQL> show user
USER is "SYSTEM"
SQL> grant insert any table to tester;
Grant succeeded.
SQL>
```

If the owner of an object grants an object privilege to a user with the *with grant* clause, the grantee of the privilege is given the right to grant that same object privilege to other users. Here's an example:

```
SQL> grant insert any table to tester with grant option;
```

Column-Level Object Privileges

In the previous discussion, object privileges always implied a right to perform a DML action on an entire table. However, a user can also be granted privileges on only certain column(s) of the table, as shown in the following examples:

```
SQL>  grant insert (product_id) on sales01 to salapati;
Grant succeeded.
SQL> grant update(hostname) on ods_process to tester;
Grant succeeded.
SQL>
```

The Grant Any Object Privilege System Privilege

The *grant any object privilege* is a special system privilege that lets the grantee grant (and revoke) object privileges for objects in any schema. The interesting thing is that when the grantee of this privilege grants any privileges on any object, it appears as if the schema owner granted the privilege if you query the DBA_TAB_PRIVS table. However, if you're auditing the use of the *grant* statement, you'll see the real user who issued this statement. All users with the SYSDBA privilege automatically have the grant any object privilege.

Revoking Privileges

Revoking privileges is analogous to granting privileges. You simply issue the *revoke* statement for each privilege you want to revoke.

```
  SQL> show user
USER is "SYSTEM"
SQL> revoke insert any table from tester;
Revoke succeeded.
SQL> connect ods/ods@finance1;
Connected.
SQL> revoke all on ods_servers from tester;
Revoke succeeded.
SQL> revoke select, insert on ods_process from tester;
Revoke succeeded.
SQL>
```

Note that you can't revoke privileges at a column level, even though the privilege may have been granted at that level. You'll have to use the table level for the revocation of a privilege, regardless of the level at which it was granted, as you can see in the following example:

```
SQL> revoke update(hostname) on ods_process from tester;
revoke update(hostname) on ods_process from tester
                *
ERROR at line 1:
ORA-01750: UPDATE/REFERENCES may only
be REVOKEd from the whole table, not by column
SQL> revoke update on ods_process from tester;
Revoke succeeded.
SQL>
```

Invoker Rights and Definer Rights

When you create a stored procedure in Oracle, it is executed by using the creator's privileges. This is the default behavior, and the procedure is said to have been created with *definer's rights*. When a user executes the procedure, it executes with the creator's (definer) object privileges, not the particular user's. There may be several situations where you don't want all users to be able to execute a procedure with the same rights. You can customize the accessibility of a procedure by crating it with *invoker's rights,* meaning the procedure will execute with the privileges of the user, not the owner, of the procedure.

When you create a procedure with invoker's rights, the procedure will execute under the user's security context, not the owner's security context. Thus, any user who intends to execute a procedure from a different schema should have the object privileges on all the tables that are part of the procedure. All DML privileges on those tables should have been granted directly, not through any role, to the user.

The *authid* clause in a *create procedure* statement indicates that this procedure is being created with user or invoker's rights, not the default owner or definer's rights. Here is an example:

```
SQL>    create or replace procedure delete_emp
  2     ( p_emp_id number )
  3     authid current_user is
  4     begin
  5     delete from emp where
  6     emp_id = p_emp_id;
  7     commit;
  8*    end;
Procedure created.
SQL>
```

In line 3, the *authid* clause specifies that the procedure will execute with the privileges of the *current_user*, the invoker of the procedure. Obviously, the user must have the explicit object privilege on the table, delete on emp, for the procedure to execute successfully.

Roles and Privileges

Although you can fairly easily manage user privileges by directly granting and revoking them, the job can quickly get hairy once you start adding more users and the number of objects keeps increasing. It's very difficult after a while to keep track of each user's current grant of privileges. Oracle uses the concept of *roles,* which are named sets of privileges that can be assigned to users. Think of roles as a set of privileges that you can grant and revoke with a single *grant* or *revoke* command.

 TIP *The DBA role, which is predefined in the Oracle databases, is a set of system privileges with the ADMIN option, meaning the user with this role can grant these privileges to other users as well. In most cases, you grant this role to yourself and any other usernames that need to perform database administration.*

When you create any database, several roles come precreated by Oracle. These include the roles DBA, connect, resource, exp_full_database, imp_full_database, and recovery_catalog_owner. The role DBA is traditionally assigned to all individuals in an organization who perform database administration tasks. Oracle has indicated, however, that it may drop the three predefined roles DBA, connect, and resource, and it recommends that you create your own roles to replace these three roles.

Creating a Role

Assuming you have either the DBA role granted to yourself or a specific system privilege called "create role", you can create a role in the following manner:

```
SQL> create role new_dba;
Role created.
SQL>
```

What does this role contain? Absolutely nothing! You can think of roles as empty vessels into which you can pour any number of system and object privileges. You then simply assign the role to a user and the user will inherit all the privileges contained in the role. Note that the preceding is a simple example, in which you aren't using a password for the role. You can create roles with various kinds of password authorization, a topic you'll explore in the chapter on Oracle security (Chapter 11).

You'll now endow your new_dba role with some privileges. Listing 11-10 shows how to grant various database privileges to your new role.

Listing 11-10. Granting Privileges to a Role

```
SQL> grant connect to new_dba;
Grant succeeded.
SQL> grant select any table to new_dba;
Grant succeeded.
SQl> grant update any table to new_dba;
Grant succeeded.
SQL> grant select_catalog_role to new_dba;
Grant succeeded.
SQL> grant exp_full_database to new_dba;
Grant succeeded.
SQL> grant imp_full_database to new_dba;
Grant succeeded.
SQL>
```

To grant user salapati all the preceding privileges, all you need to do is the following:

```
SQL> grant new_dba to salapati;
Grant succeeded.
SQL>
```

A user can be assigned more than one role, and all of the roles that are granted to that user will be active when the user logs into the database.

The PUBLIC User Group and Roles

If you wish to give a certain privilege or role to all the users in the database, you simply grant this privilege/role to the user group PUBLIC, which exists in every database by default. This is not a recommended way to grant privileges, however, for obvious reasons.

Disabling and Enabling Roles

You can disable a user's role by inserting the appropriate row into the product_user_profile table. Recall that you can use the product_user_profile table to limit users' privileges within the database. One of the attributes that the product_user_profile table can control is a role. Listing 11-11 shows how you insert into the product_user_profile table to disable the role TEST123, which has been assigned to the user TESTER.

Listing 11-11. Disabling a Role Using the Product_User_Profile Table

```
SQL> Insert into
     PRODUCT_USER_PROFILE(PRODUCT,userid,attribute,char_value)
  2*   values('SQL*Plus','TESTER','ROLES','TEST123');
1 row created.
SQL> COMMIT;
Commit complete.
SQL> connect tester/tester@finance1
Connected.
SQL> select * from hr.regions;
select * from hr.regions
              *
ERROR at line 1:
ORA-00942: table or view does not exist
```

As you can see, once the role TEST123 is disabled, user TESTER can't select from the database tables, and an error is issued when the select is attempted. When you want to re-enable the TEST123 role, all you need to do is to delete the appropriate row from the product_user_profile table, as shown here:

```
SQL> delete from product_user_profile
  2  where useRID='TESTER2'
  3* and char_value = 'TEST123'
SQL> /
1 row deleted.
SQL> commit;
Commit complete.
```

Dropping a Role

Dropping a role is simple. Just use the *drop role* command:

```
SQL> drop role test123;
Role dropped.
SQL>
```

Using Secure Application Roles

A secure application role isn't anything like the typical database roles you've seen in the previous sections. *Secure application roles* in Oracle9*i* are roles that are implemented through a package. Using this feature, you create a package that may limit a specific user to a certain IP address only, or only from a specific middle tier. The main function of this security feature is to ensure that users aren't connecting to your database through unauthorized entry points.

Using Views and Stored Procedures to Manage Privileges

In addition to using roles and privileges, Oracle also enables data security through the use of views and stored procedures. You've already seen in Chapter 7 how views on key tables or even table joins can not only hide the complexity of queries, but also provide significant data security.

Fine-grained Data Security

The traditional means of ensuring data security works pretty well, but it has certain limitations. Chief among these limitations is the fact that most security measures are too broad based, with the result that you end up unnecessarily restricting users when your primary goal is to ensure that users freely access information they need. In addition to the traditional concepts of roles and privileges, the Oracle9*i* database provides a lower level security of data using fine-grained data security techniques. Thus, you can allow all users to access a central table such as a payroll table, but transparent to the users you can institute security policies that limit access of an individual user to only those rows in a table, for example, that pertain to his or her department.

Oracle uses two main concepts to enforce fine-grained security within the database: an application context and a fine-grained access control policy. Oracle uses the term *Virtual Private Database* to refer to the implementation of the fine-grained access control policies through application contexts. You'll look at the concept of Oracle's fine-grained data access in detail in the following sections.

Using Virtual Private Databases

Oracle9*i* lets you control row-level access to database objects through the *Virtual Private Database* (VPD). Attaching a security policy directly to a database object, such as a table or a view, enforces this row-level security. No matter which tool the user uses to access the database (SQL*Plus, an ad hoc query tool, or a report writer), the user can't elude this row-level security, which is enforced by the database server. Each user of an application can be limited to seeing only a part of a table's data using the VPD concept.

The VPD concept uses a type of query rewrite to restrict users to certain rows of tables and views. A security policy is attached to the table or tables to which you want to control access. Stored procedures are then written to modify any relevant SQL statements made against the tables(s) in question. When a user issues an *update* statement against a table with such a security policy, Oracle will append a "predicate" to the user's statement, which will modify the user's statement and limit the user's access to that table. For example, if a user belonging to the sales department issues the statement *update employee set salary=salary*1.10*, the security policies attached to the employee table will cause Oracle to add the fine-grained security function to the clause *where dept=SALES* while it is parsing the original *update* statement. The query modification is transparent to the users, hence the name "Virtual Private Database."

Each user can see a different view of the same database by using the VPD feature. Using the VPD concept, you can attach security polices directly at the table level or the view level and the database itself will manage this low-level security. When a user issues a query, Oracle will dynamically modify the query based on a security policy, which is implemented by a function. The security policy will specify the limitations on a user's queries on a table.

How do you implement a VPD? You first have to create what is known as an *application context* and then implement fine-grained access control to enforce the row-level security for database tables and views. The application context helps you create security policies that draw upon certain aspects of a user's session information. To take a simple example, when a user logs into the database, the user's ID tells you who that user is, and based on that piece of information, the application's security policy sets limits on what the user can do within the database. VPD is actually the implementation of an application context with fine-grained access control. In the following sections, you'll examine these two concepts in more detail.

NOTE *A VPD is simply the use of an application context with a fine-grained access control mechanism.*

Application Context

An application context allows you to define a set of attributes that an application can use, so you can control the application's access to the database. Oracle uses a built-in application context "namespace" called USERENV, which has a set of predefined session attributes attached to it. These predefined attributes are then used by Oracle to control access. You can find out session-related information about any user by using the sys_context feature, as shown in Listing 11-12.

Listing 11-12. Using Sys_Context to Find Out Session Information

```
SQL> select sys_context ('USERENV', 'TERMINAL')
  2  from dual;
SYS_CONTEXT('USERENV',''TERMINAL')
----------------------------------------------------------
NTL-ALAPATISAM
SQL>
SQL> select sys_context ('_USERENV', 'CURRENT_USER')
  2  from dual;
SYS_CONTEXT('_USERENV','CURRENT_USER')
----------------------------------------------------------------
SYSTEM
SQL> connect fay/fay1;
Connected.
SQL> select first_name,last_name,employee_id from employees
  2  where upper(last_name)=sys_context('userenv','session_user');
FIRST_NAME      LAST_NAME       EMPLOYEE_ID
------------------- ------------------------ -----------
Pat             Fay             202
1 row selected.
SQL>
```

Besides the terminal and current_user attributes, several other important pre-defined attributes belong to the USERENV namespace. Table 11-1 shows some of the common predefined attributes in the USERENV namespace.

Table 11-1. Common Predefined Attributes in the USERENV Namespace

ATTRIBUTE	DESCRIPTION
Instance	Instance ID
EntryID	Auditing entry identifier
Current_user	Name of the user who started the session
Session_user	Database username by which the current user is authenticated
Proxy_user	Name of the middle tier that opened a session for the session_user
Db_name	Name of the database
Host	Name of the machine on which the database is running
Os_user	Operating system account name
Terminal	Client terminal through which the database is being accessed
Ip_address	IP address of the client machine
External_name	External name of the database user

When a user logs in, you need to be able to identify the type of the user and set some attributes about the user. You can later use this information in the security policies that are attached to the database objects.

The USERENV namespace, of course, is just one of the namespaces that you can use. You'll have to create your own application context so you can define which attributes you want to use in setting your security policies.

Let's now create an application context for the user hr in your finance1 database. You need to take the following two steps to create an application context:

1. Create a package that sets the context.

2. Create an application context that uses the package you just created.

Creating a Package to Set the Context

To set the application context for user hr, you need to create the package hr_context. Listing 11-13 shows you how to create a simple package to set the application context. The package includes a single procedure that selects an employee number.

Listing 11-13. Creating a Package to Set the Application Context

```
SQL> Connect hr/hr
SQL> create or replace package hr_context as
  2  procedure select_emp_no ;
  3* end;
SQL> /
Package created.
SQL> create or replace package body hr_context as
  2  procedure select_emp_no is
  3  empnum number;
  4  begin
  5  select employee_id into empnum from employees where
  6  UPPER( last_name) =
  7  sys_context('userenv','session_user');
  8  dbms_session.set_context('employee_info', 'emp_num', empnum);
  9  end select_emp_no;
 10* end;
SQL> /
Package body created.
SQL>
```

Creating the Context

Once you create the package hr_context, you can go ahead and create the application context for user hr as follows. Note that the user hr uses the package just created in the previous section to create the employee_info application context.

```
SQL> connect system/manager@remorse;
Connected.
SQL> grant create any context to hr;
Grant succeeded.
SQL> connect hr/hr@remorse;
Connected.
SQL> create context employee info using hr.context;
Context created.
SQL>
```

Fine-grained Access Control

Traditionally, security policies were applied to entire applications. Users were given roles or privileges, based on which they could access the tables in the application. This always left open the possibility of users using tools such as SQL*Plus to go around the application's security protocols and modify data in the database tables. Furthermore, application-level security enforcement meant you had to manage a grant/revoke policy for each user in the system for access to all the tables in the database.

Fine-grained access control (FGAC) enables you to restrict Oracle users only to the data that you want them to access and modify. This ability to limit a user's ability to selected portions of the data increases data security. No matter how users access a database, their rights on a table remain the same when you use FGAC. You can use FGAC as an alternative to creating several views on a single table. Note that Oracle uses the term "Virtual Private Database" to refer to the implementation of FGAC. For example, in an employee table, you can restrict a manager to data pertaining to just his or her department. FGAC is facilitated through the use of *policy functions*, which are attached to the tables or views to which you want to have a restricted mode of access. When the SQL statements are parsed, FGAC makes Oracle automatically evaluate the policy functions (there can be more than one attached to a table). After dynamically modifying the query if necessary, Oracle will optimize and execute it.

NOTE *FGAC enables you to implement fine-grained data security. You can enforce a row-level security policy using this feature.*

To illustrate the use of FGAC, I'll use a simple example. Your goal is to create a policy where an employee is only allowed to see data pertaining to him or her, from the employees table.

Creating a Package That Will Access the Context

First, create the package hr_security, which you can use later on to access the application context. Listing 11-14 shows how you create the package hr_security.

Listing 11-14. Creating the Hr_Security Package

```
SQL> create or replace package hr_security as
  2  function empnum_sec (A1 varchar2, A2 varchar2)
  3  return varchar2;
  4  end;
  5*/
Package created.
SQL>  create or replace package body hr_security as
  2    function empnum_sec (A1 varchar2, A2 varchar2)
  3    return varchar2
  4    is
  5    d_predicate varchar2 (2000);
  6    begin
  7    d_predicate := 'employee_id = SYS_CONTEXT
       ("employee_info","emp_num")';
  8    return d_predicate;
  9    end empnum_sec;
 10    end hr_security;
 11* /
Package body created.
SQL>
```

The package you just created, hr_security, will use the context that you created in the previous section, employee_info, to get the emp_num variable. As you can see, the employee_info application context gets the emp_num variable from the USERENV namespace (the session_user attribute of the USERENV namespace).

The d_predicate indicates the predicate that should be applied to any queries made by any employee whose employee_id matches the emp_num variable obtained from the employee_info context. For example, if user salapati issues the following command:

```
SQL> Select * from employees;
```

it will be modified by the predicate as

```
SQL> Select * from employees
  2* Where employee_id =sys_context ('employeee_info','emp_num);
```

Creating the Security Policy

The package you have created, hr_security, lets you to attach dynamic predicates to any SQL statements that can be used by employees whose employee_id matches the emp_num derived by using the employee_info application context. But you still haven't attached a security policy to the employee table. That is, you have to now specify what kinds of statements, and precisely what tables, the hr_security package would be applied to. You can do this by using the DBMS_RLS package provided by Oracle. The DBMS_RLS package helps you apply security policies to tables and views in the database. Execute the statements shown in Listing 11-15 as the user System.

Listing 11-15. Adding the Security Policy Using the DBMS_RLS Package

```
SQL> connect system/manager@finance1

Connected.

SQL> execute  dbms_rls.add_policy('hr','employees','manager_policy','hr',-
'hr_security.empnum_sec','select');
> /
PL/SQL procedure successfully completed.
Note that you could have executed in the following equivalent manner:
 SQL>  begin
  2  sys.dbms_rls.add_policy
  3  (object_schema => 'hr',
  4  object_name     => 'employees',
  5  policy_name     => 'manager_policy',
  6  function_schema => 'hr',
  7  policy_function => 'hr_security.empnum_sec',
  8  statement_types => 'select'
  9  );
 10* end;
SQL> /
```

What did the DBMS_RLS.add_policy procedure accomplish? It created a policy
called manager_policy in the hr schema. The policy is implemented by executing
the function empnum_sec, which is part of the hr_security package that you created
earlier. The SQL operation that this policy applies to is the *select* operation. To put it
simply, manager_policy will ensure that all selects against the hr.employees table
will be limited to viewing only information that pertains to the employee_id of the
user who issued the query.

You can check that the new policy was indeed created successfully by making
the following query:

```
SQL> select object_name,policy_name,sel,ins,upd,del, enable
          from all_policies;
```

OBJECT NAME	POLICY NAME	SEL	INS	UPD	DEL	ENABLED
EMPLOYEES	MANAGER _POLICY	YES	NO	NO	NO	YES

```
SQL>
```

The output of the query indicates that all selects against the employee table
are now controlled by the manager_policy_security policy.

Let's make your security policy functions accessible to the public by making
the following grant:

```
SQL> connect hr/hr@finance1
Connected.
SQL> grant execute on hr_security to public;
Grant succeeded.
```

Now you need to create a trigger such that each user will invoke your hr_context package upon logging into the database:

```
SQL> create or replace trigger hr.security_context
  2  after logon on database
  3  begin
  4  hr_context.select_emp_no;
  5* end;
SQL> /
Trigger created.
SQL>
```

Policy Groups

When you access a table, Oracle looks up the application context (the policy context) to determine which policy group, and therefore which security policy, should be enforced. There is one group called sys_default that can never be dropped from the database, and every policy belongs to this group by default.

Using Oracle Policy Manager

As in the case of using the Database Resource Manager, I strongly recommend using the excellent GUI tools that are a part of OEM to implement and create fine-grained security policies. Oracle Policy Manager will help you effortlessly create complex security policies to enforce fine-grained data security. This definitely beats wrestling with the manual creation of application contexts and security policies. Figure 11-2 shows how Oracle Policy Manager makes it easy to manage the various application contexts in your database.

Label-Based Access Control

Oracle allows you to label parts of your data. Users are then granted privileges to access only data with certain labels. The Oracle Label Security option enables you to enforce label-based access control. The Oracle Label Security feature is built on the same components that help you create a VPD. You can easily construct labels to limit access to rows in a certain table, and use label authorizations and privileges to set up a label-based security policy. Oracle Policy Manager is mainly designed to create and administer Oracle Label Security policies.

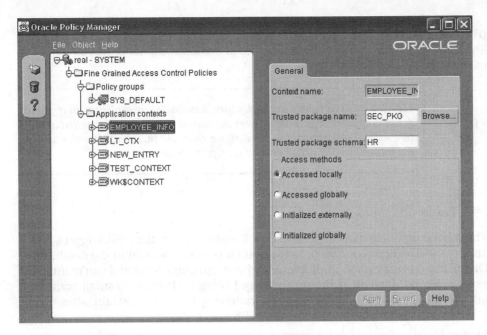

Figure 11-2. Using Oracle Policy Manager

Auditing Database Usage

Databases are used to store critical information, and backups only protect the data from a catastrophe or a mechanical malfunction. What about the intentional altering of important data by unauthorized users? Oracle's built-in auditing features allow you to track the changes being made to the objects within the database. You can audit the granting of privileges within the database, and you can also audit non-DML/DDL changes, such as database start-up and shutdown events. Auditing user activity could potentially lead to a large amount of data to keep track of, but fortunately Oracle offers you a lot of control over what type of activities you want to audit. You can audit just at the session level or at the entire database level.

Customizing Database Auditing with the Help of Triggers

Oracle *triggers* are special blocks of code that are "triggered" or fired off by certain triggering events in the database. Most applications use triggers to update certain tables based on an action in a different table. Triggers help enforce business rules within the database. A trigger could fire off based on DML or DDL statements. You can audit specific actions by users by simply writing triggers or other stored procedures that will log user information into a table when the users perform a specific database operation, such as updating certain tables.

You can create several types of triggers in Oracle9*i*, including DML and DDL triggers, which are based on actions by users on tables and views, and system-level triggers, which are more broad-based. In the following sections you'll examine these types of triggers.

TIP *You don't have to necessarily turn databasewide auditing on if you're solely interested in a specific user's actions or want to audit limited actions in the database. You can write a trigger that will insert information into a log table upon the occurrence of specified events.*

DML-Based Triggers

The most commonly used triggers in Oracle databases are the DML triggers, and applications routinely use them to maintain business rules within the database. Oracle triggers are easy to implement, and you can employ them if you're interested in a modest range of auditing activity. Listing 11-16 shows a small example of how to use a trigger to audit insert operations by users on a certain table.

Listing 11-16. A Typical DML Trigger

```
SQL> create or replace trigger audit_insert
  2  after insert on tester.xyz
  3  for each row
  4  insert into xyz_audit
  5  values (
  6  user,
  7  sysdate);
  8  /
Trigger created.
SQL> connect tester/tester1@finance1
Connected.
SQL> insert into xyz
  2  values
  3  ('sam alapati');
1 row created.
SQL> commit;
Commit complete.
SQL> connect system/manager@finance1
Connected.
SQL> select * from xyz_audit;
USER_NAME                      ACTION_DATE
------------------------------ -----------------
TESTER                         28-NOV-02
SQL>
```

The more actions you want to audit, the larger the space required to hold the audit trail. You have to understand why you are auditing and only audit those activities that are of true significance to your organization.

NOTE *There are no rules regarding the operations you should audit. In some organizations, all DML changes (insert, update, and delete) may have to be audited to ensure that you can track down any unauthorized changes. In other organizations, an audit of just failed logins might suffice.*

System-Level Triggers

Triggers that fire after DML operations such as an insert or a delete are the most commonly used triggers in Oracle databases, but they aren't the only types of triggers you can use. Oracle9*i* provides powerful special triggers such as triggers that can be set to fire after database start-up and before database shutdown. You can also use the user login/logoff-based triggers to audit database usage. The logon/logoff triggers are especially useful for database auditing. The following are the main types of system-level triggers that the Oracle9*i* database offers DBAs:

- *Database start-up triggers:* You can use these triggers mostly to execute code that you want to execute immediately after database start-up. For example, you may create a trigger specifying that certain packages are pinned in the SGA after database start-up.

- *Logon triggers:* These triggers provide you with information regarding the logon times of a user, along with details about the user's session.

- *Logoff triggers:* These triggers are similar to the logon triggers, but they execute right before the user's session logs off.

- *DDL triggers:* You can capture all database object changes with these triggers.

- *Server error triggers:* These triggers capture all major PL/SQL code errors into a special table.

Here's a simple example that shows the potential of the special DBA-type Oracle triggers in auditing users. The example first creates a simple table to hold logon data. Whenever a user logs in, the table captures several pieces of information about the user. Of course, if you also audit the logoff items with another trigger, you can find out how long the user was inside the database on a given day. Listing 11-17 shows the steps involved in creating a logon/logoff auditing system using system-level triggers.

Listing 11-17. Using the Logon and Logoff Triggers

```
First, create test table called logon_audit:
SQL> create table logon_audit (
  2  user_id   varchar2(30),
  3  sess_id   number (10),
  4  logon_time  date,
  5  logoff_time date,
  6* host       varchar2(20));
Table created.
SQL>
Next, create a pair of LOGON and LOGOFF triggers.
SQL> l
  1  create or replace trigger logon_audit_trig
  2  after logon
  3  on database
  4  begin
  5  insert into logon_audit
  6  values
  7  (user,
  8  sys_context('userenv', 'sessionid'),
  9  sysdate,
 10  null,
 11  sys_context('userenv', 'host'));
 12* end;
SQL> /
Trigger created.
SQL> create or replace trigger logoff_audit_trig
  2  after logon
  3  on database
  4  begin
  5  insert into logon_audit
  6  values
  7  (user,
  8  sys_context('userenv', 'sessionid'),
  9  null,
 10  sysdate,
 11  sys_context('userenv', 'host'));
 12* end;
SQL> /
Trigger created.
SQL>
/* Now, You can see your users' login/logout details. */
SQL> select * from logon_audit;
USER_   SESS_ID    LOGON_TIME            LOGOFF          HOST
NAME  -------------------- ----------------TIME-------------NAME
SYSTEM    347     13-DEC-2002 07:00:30                    NTL-ALAPATI
HR        348     13-DEC-2002 07:10:31                    NTL-ALAPATI
HR        348                        13-DEC-2002 07:32:17 NTL-ALAPATI
SQL>
```

The following example shows how you can use a DDL trigger to capture changes made to objects by users, including modification, creation, and deletion of various types of objects. You can capture a large number of attributes of the event and the user that sets off a DDL trigger. Listing 11-18 shows how you can capture some of the important attributes of the user event.

Listing 11-18. Using DDL Triggers to Audit Users

```
First, create the DDL trigger. You must also create a table to log DDL changes.
SQL> create or replace trigger
  2  ddl_log_trig
  3  after ddl on database
  4  begin
  5  insert into ddl_log
  6  (  user_name,
  7     change_date,
  8     object_type,
  9     object_owner,
 10    database
 11  )
 12  values
 13  (  ora_login_user,
 14     sysdate,
 15     ora_dict_obj_type,
 16     ora_dict_obj_owner,
 17     ora_database_name
  16* end;
SQL> /
Trigger created.
As user hr and system, make several DDL-based changes to the database.
Next, query the ddl_log table to see the changes
SQL> select * from ddl_log;
USER      CHANGE     DDL                      OBJECT    DATABASE
NAME      DATE       TYPE                     OWNER     NAME
--------------------------------------------------------------------
HR        13-DEC-02  SYNONYM                  HR        REMORSE
SYSTEM    13-DEC-02  OBJECTPRIVILEGE          SYSTEM    REMORSE
HR        13-DEC-02  TRIGGER                  HR        REMORSE
SQL>
```

Enabling Auditing

In order for you to audit any user activity within the database and even attempts to log into the database, you need to enable auditing by specifying the *audit_trail* parameter in your init.ora file. The *audit_trail* parameter can take a value of *DB* or *OS*. If you want Oracle to write auditing information to an operating system file, specify *DB*. If you want Oracle to write the audit records to an operating system file, specify *OS*. In both cases, there is a default file to which Oracle will write audit data, and you can easily change the location of this file by using the *audit_file_dest* parameter in the init.ora file, as shown here:

```
Audit_trail=DB
Audit_file_dest=/a10/app/oracle/oradata/audit_data
```

If you specify *audit_trail= OS* and you then choose to audit a particular action, the audit trail won't store the audit information in the database. It will instead store the information in the location specified by the *audit_file_dest* parameter. If you omit the *audit_file_dest* parameter, by default the audit information will be written to the $ORACLE_HOME/rdbms/audit/ directory.

TIP *If you specify* audit_trail=DB, *then the audit records will be logged to a special table owned by SYS called the* sys.aud$ *table. The* sys.aud$ *table is located in the System tablespace. If you want to do any kind of serious auditing on your database, the tablespace will quickly run out of space. Make sure you change the storage parameters of the* sys.aud$ *table and add more space to the System tablespace before you turn the auditing on. Otherwise, you run the risk of filling up your System tablespace while auditing the database.*

You don't need to be overly concerned with the filling up of the sys.aud$ table when auditing is turned on. You can always truncate the table after exporting the contents to a different location or when you deem it isn't necessary to store the contents of the audit table any longer.

Oracle Default Auditing

What happens if you don't specify the *audit_trail* parameter at all? Oracle won't write any audit information to either the operating system or the database audit trail, right? Well, even when you don't specify any type of logging, by default Oracle will log three types of database actions under all circumstances. The following actions are audited by Oracle by default and the audit records written to the default $ORACLE_HOME/rdbms/audit directory:

- Connections as SYSOPER or SYSDBA
- Database start-up
- Database shutdown

Listing 11-19 shows a typical default auditing log recorded by the operating system. Notice how the audit file captures the connect, shutdown, and start-up details by the user SYS, who happens to have the SYSDBA privileges.

Listing 11-19. An Operating System Audit Record of SYSDBA Actions

```
Audit file /test02/app/oracle/product/9.2.0.1.0/rdbms/audit/ora_21241.aud
Oracle9i Enterprise Edition Release 9.2.0.1.0 - 64bit Production
With the Partitioning, OLAP and Oracle Data Mining options
JServer Release 9.2.0.1.0 - Production
ORACLE_HOME = /test02/app/oracle/product/9.2.0.1.0
System name:    HP-UX
Node name:      hp5
Release:        B.11.00
Version:        A
Machine:        9000/800
Instance name: monitor
Redo thread mounted by this instance: 1
Oracle process number: 14
Unix process pid: 21241, image: oracle@hp5 (TNS V1-V3)
Thu Dec 12 18:07:24 2002
Unix process pid: 21241, image: oracle@hp5 (TNS V1-V3)
Thu Dec 12 18:07:24 2002
ACTION : 'CONNECT'      /* Connect */
DATABASE USER: '/'
PRIVILEGE : SYSDBA
CLIENT USER: oracle
CLIENT TERMINAL: pts/2
STATUS: 0
Thu Dec 12 18:07:30 2002
ACTION : 'SHUTDOWN'     /* Shutdown */
DATABASE USER: '/'
PRIVILEGE : SYSDBA
CLIENT USER: oracle
CLIENT TERMINAL: pts/2
STATUS: 0
Thu Dec 12 18:07:32 2002
ACTION : 'STARTUP'    /* Startup */
DATABASE USER: '/'
PRIVILEGE : SYSDBA
CLIENT USER: oracle
CLIENT TERMINAL: Not Available
STATUS: 0
```

What if you want to audit *all* actions by the user SYS? You can audit all actions of the user SYS, including all users connecting with the SYSDBA/SYSOPER privileges, by setting the following init.ora parameter. Note that if the following parameter is set, all actions of the SYS user will be audited, *whether you set the* audit_trail *parameter or not.* The parameter has a default value of *false.*

```
audit_sys_operations=true
```

Audit Levels

Oracle9*i* lets you audit database use at three different levels: statement, privilege, and object. A *statement-level audit* specifies the auditing of all actions on any type of object. For example, you can specify that the database audit all actions on tables by using the statement *audit table*. A *privilege-level audit* tracks actions that stem from system privileges. For example, you can audit all actions that involve the use of a granted privilege (e.g., audit all *create any procedure* statements). Finally, an *object-level audit* monitors actions such as update, delete, and insert on a specific table (e.g., audit all deletes on table hr.employees).

For each of the three levels of auditing, you can choose to audit either by *session* or by *access*. If you audit by session, Oracle will log just one record for all similar statements that fall under the purview of auditing. If you audit by access, Oracle writes a record for each access. You can also simply decide to log only whether a certain action failed or succeeded by using the *whenever successful* and the *whenever not successful* auditing options. Why would you want to audit "unsuccessful" selects, inserts, or deletes? When the operation is unsuccessful, usually it's an indication that the user doesn't have privileges to perform the operation. You'll want to know who is attempting such unauthorized operations.

TIP *One of the common arguments against the use of Oracle database auditing is that it will consume a lot of space in the database. Well, if you spend time analyzing why you are auditing, you can limit the amount of data written to the audit trail. By using a focused auditing policy rather than systemwide auditing, you can limit the auditing output to a manageable amount.*

Turning Auditing On

You can start auditing actions at any level by using the appropriate command. Listing 11-20 shows a sampling of commands that turn auditing on at various levels with different options.

Listing 11-20. Turning Auditing On in the Database

```
SQL> audit select on tester.xyz;
Audit succeeded.
SQL> audit delete any table by salapati whenever not successful
Audit succeeded.
SQL> audit update any table;
Audit succeeded.
SQL> audit session by salapati;
Audit succeeded.
SQL> audit select,insert,update,delete
  2  on tester.xyz by access whenever successful;
Audit succeeded.
SQL>
```

Here is a more powerful audit option. This option will ensure the auditing of all privileges. Obviously, the audit trail for this auditing choice will be large if you have many users who have been granted object privileges in the database.

```
SQL> audit all privileges;
Audit succeeded.
SQL>
```

Note that the *audit session* statement does not audit the statements executed during an entire session—it logs the session start time, end time, and the logical and physical I/O resources consumed by this session, among other things.

Turning Auditing Off

To turn auditing off, you use almost an identical statement to the one you used to turn auditing on. The big difference, of course, is you use the keyword *noaudit* in place of *audit*. Here are some examples:

```
SQL> noaudit session;
Noaudit succeeded.
SQL> noaudit delete any table by salapati whenever not successful;
Noaudit succeeded.
SQL>  noaudit delete any table by salapati;
Noaudit succeeded.
```

NOTE *You can use either of the last two statements to turn* delete any table by salapati whenever not successful *off. That is, the* noaudit *keyword, when applied to a more general statement, will turn off lower-level auditing that is subsumed by the general privilege.*

If you want to use all the levels of auditing—statement, privilege, and object—you can do so by using the following three SQL statements:

```
SQL> noaudit all;         /* turns off all statement auditing */
SQL> noaudit all privileges;  /* turns off all privilege auditing */
SQL> noaudit all ondefault;  /* turns off all object auditing */
```

Using Fine-grained Auditing

Suppose you're interested in auditing if users are viewing some data in a table they're not really supposed to. For example, say a manager is supposed to be able see salary-related information for employees working for him. Can you tell if the manager is also looking at the salary information of his superiors? Do you need to audit all the selects done by the manager? That would lead to a colossal amount of audit trail. Fortunately, there's an easy out. Oracle lets you audit actions in the database on the basis on *content*. That is, you can specify that the audit records be written not for all select, insert, update, and delete statements, but only for statements that meet certain criteria. You use the Oracle package DBMS_FGA to enable this fine-grained auditing. Using fine-grained auditing, you can audit only specific rows within a table. You can use this feature to catch employee misuse of data and you can also use it as an intrusion-detection device. Here's an example of how you can use the DBMS_FGA package to enforce fine-grained auditing:

```
SQL> execute sys.dbms_fga.add_policy ( -
> object_schema => 'hr', -
> OBJECT_NAME => 'EMPLOYEES', -
> policy_name => 'chk_hr_emp', -
> audit_condition => 'salary > 10000 ', -
> audit_column => 'salary');
PL/SQL procedure successfully completed.
SQL>
```

Once the DBMS_FGA package is executed as shown previously, all the subsequent *select* statements that query salary information about the sales department would be logged in the audit trail (*OS* or *DB*, depending on what you chose in the init.ora file). You can further narrow the audit criteria by specifying a set of employee names or IDs in the *where* clause of all *select* statements.

TIP *When you use the DBMS_FGA package, the audit records don't go into the standard audit table, the sys.aud$ table, even when you turn on the database audit trail. The audit records go into a special table called the sys.fga_aud$ table.*

Here's a simple example of a query that will log the querying user's information into an audit table in the database. The user tester logs into the database and queries the database to find out who makes more than $20,000 in salary, a query that the user tester isn't authorized to make. Due to your implementation of the fine-grained security policy, however, the user tester's unauthorized enquiries and other information are logged in the audit table (the sys.fga_aud$ table) for fine-grained security audit polices. Listing 11-21 shows how the user tester's actions are logged in the audit table.

Listing 11-21. Using Fine-grained Auditing

```
SQL> select first_name,last_name
  2  from hr.employees
  3  where salary >20000;
FIRST_NAME           LAST_NAME
------------------   -------------------
Nicholas             King
SQL> connect system/password
Connected
SQL> select sessionid, timestamp#, dbuid, osuid,
  2  obj$schema, obj$name
```

```
        3* from sys.fga_log$
SESSION     TIME        DBUID      OSUID    OBJ$      OBJ$NAME
  ID        STAMP                           SCHEMA
========    ========    =======    ======  =======   ==============
  174       12-DEC-02   TESTER     oracle   HR        EMPLOYEES
  172       12-DEC-02   TESTER     oracle   HR        EMPLOYEES
  174       12-DEC-02   TESTER     oracle   HR        EMPLOYEES
  174       12-DEC-02   TESTER     oracle   HR        EMPLOYEES
SQL>
```

The fga_log$ table shows clearly that the user tester overstepped her authority in querying the employee table four different times on December 12. You can find out a lot more about the user tester's unauthorized queries by looking at other columns in the fga_log$ table.

Managing the Audit Trail

As advised earlier, try to keep the audit options to the minimum necessary to meet your audit objectives. As a DBA, you should keep a close watch on the System tablespace and the sys.aud$ table when auditing is turned on. If the sys.aud$ table gets full, further connections and DML activity in the database might come to a standstill. You can always purge the records from the sys.aud$ table and archive all the sys.aud$ table records for future reference.

User Authentication

In the first part of this chapter, you learned how to create users and assign them roles and privileges. The users that you create can, of course, be authenticated by the database itself. *Database authentication* refers to the authentication of the user account and password directly by Oracle. Password management is part of database authentication of users. You'll explore database authentication of users in more detail in the next section, after which you'll briefly review the other means of user authentication.

Database Authentication of Users

Database authentication really means the standard verification of users by using database passwords. If you're relying on the database to authenticate your users, you should have a strong password management policy. Even if you're using other means of authenticating users, you must plug all vulnerabilities created by Oracle passwords.

Password Management

Depending on how you create a database (manually or using the DBCA), Oracle will have several accounts with default passwords. If you create a tablespace manually, you may only have SYS, SYSTEM, DBSNMP (Oracle Intelligent Agent account), and OUTLN (the username for managing the outlines feature). In some cases, the user scott (owner of the old Oracle demo database schema) is also created with the default password *tiger*. A standard database created by the DBCA may have up to 32 default user accounts.

As part of securing the database, you must use all the standard password management techniques, including changing of passwords at set intervals, checking passwords for complexity, and preventing reuse of old passwords.

Let's see how Oracle creates the default user accounts in a new database. The query in Listing 11-22 shows you all the usernames and their status. An account may be open or it maybe locked/expired. An *open* account is one you can log into as long you have a valid password. A *locked* account means that the DBA must explicitly unlock it. For a regular account, it's usually because the user has tried to enter the database with an incorrect password more times than the specified limit allows. An *expired* account means that the password for the account has to be changed, which ensures that the same passwords aren't used forever.

Listing 11-22. Displaying Account Status of All Users

```
SQL> select username, account_status
  2  from dba_users;
USERNAME                   ACCOUNT_STATUS
=========--------------------------------------
SYS                        OPEN
SYSTEM                     OPEN
DBSNMP                     OPEN
SCOTT                      OPEN
OUTLN                      EXPIRED & LOCKED
RMAN                       EXPIRED & LOCKED
SH                         EXPIRED & LOCKED
...
32 rows selected
SQL>
```

If you're using the Oracle 9.2 version, you know that you can't create a new database unless you provide passwords for the SYS and SYSTEM accounts. Thus, these two accounts no longer can be breached using their old passwords (*manager* and *change_on_install*). However, the user accounts DBSNMP and OUTLN have the same passwords as their usernames and are *open*. The DBA should immediately change the passwords for these two accounts after database creation. As you can see, the rest of the accounts are expired and locked.

Account Locking

How do you lock and unlock an account? Any user account that is locked can be unlocked for free access with the following statement:

```
SQL> alter user hr account unlock;
User altered.
SQL>
```

You can make Oracle lock any account after a certain number of failed login attempts. You can use the *create* or *alter profile* statement to do this, as shown in the following code. Note that Oracle lets you specify for how long you want the account to be unlocked after making the specified login attempts to enter the database. After that time is reached, Oracle will *automatically unlock* the account. To close this loophole, simply set the locked time period to *unlimited*. First, create or alter the profile with the new time period for locking the account, and then grant this profile to the user.

```
SQL> CREATE PROFILE TEST_PROFILE
  2  limit FAILED_LOGIN_ATTEMPTS 5
  3* PASSWORD_LOCK_TIME UNLIMITED;
Profile created.
SQL>
```

The database will lock an account once the failed_login_attempts limit is reached. However, the DBA can summarily lock a user's account by using the following command:

```
SQL> alter user hr account unlock;
User altered.
SQL>
```

Password Expiration

Remember how the default accounts in the new database in Listing 11-22 were expired when you first created the database? Password aging policies to ensure that users don't hang onto the same passwords for a long time are a standard part of database security. Once a password expires, the user is forced to change the password. You can make a password expire in a couple of ways, as shown here:

```
SQL> alter user hr identified by hr
     password expire;
User altered.
SQL>
```

or

```
SQL> alter profile test_profile
  2* limit password_life_time 30;
Profile altered.
SQL> alter user hr profile test_profile;
User altered.
SQL>
```

The preceding *alter profile* statement limits the password life to 30 days, and you can gently remind user hr about this by using another clause in your *alter profile* statement, *password_grace_time 7*, which means that the user will be reminded for 7 days prior to the final expiration of the password. After the user's password expires, the password must be changed:

```
SQL> connect hr/hr
ERROR:
ORA-28001: the password has expired
Changing password for hr
New password: **
Retype new password: **
Password changed
Connected.
SQL>
```

The Password File

Oracle will let you choose how you want your privileged users to connect to the database. *Privileged users* are those users who can perform tasks such as starting up and shutting down the database. By default, only the user SYS has the SYSDBA and SYSOPER privileges, both of which are considered high-level privileges. The user SYS can grant these privileges to other users. Of course, any DBA who knows the SYS password can log in as SYS and perform the privileged tasks. However, by granting the critical privileges SYSDBA and SYSOPER explicitly to users, you force them to provide their username and password, which makes it easy to track the actions of privileged users. The value of the initialization parameter *remote_login_passwordfile* determines who can be granted these higher level privileges by the SYS users. Here are the various values the *remote_login_passwordfile* parameter can take:

- *None:* No password file is used. This is the default, and it permits only operating system–authenticated users to perform database administration tasks.

- *Shared:* Creates a shared password file with a single user: SYS. Any user who wants to perform privileged tasks has to log in as SYS.

- *Exclusive:* Uses a password file. Any user can be granted the SYDBA and SYSOPER privileges, and when the user SYS does so, the user is automatically added to the password file.

Oracle strongly recommends that you use the *remote_login_passwordfile=exclusive* option for the highest degree of security. There is a way to manually create a password file and specify which users can have the SYSDBA and SYSOPER privileges, but if you use the *exclusive* option, Oracle will automatically add users to the password file upon their being granted the SYSDBA and SYSOPER privileges. You can use the V$PWFILE_USERS view to see who has been granted these privileges besides the default SYS users by using the following query:

```
SQL> connect sys/life1 as sysdba;
Connected.
SQL> grant sysoper, sysdba to tester;
Grant succeeded.
  SQL> select * from v$pwfile_users;
USERNAME    SYSDB        SYSOP
SYS         TRUE         TRUE
TESTER      TRUE         TRUE
SQL>
```

TIP *Always set the* remote_login_passwordfile *parameter to* exclusive *in the init.ora file (or SPFILE). Once you start the database, the password file will be automatically created, and any new users to whom you grant the SYSDBA and SYSOPER privileges will be automatically added to the file.*

If you don't have a password file and want to create one, you need to use the *orapwd* utility provided by Oracle. If you type **orapwd** at the operating system prompt, this is what you'll see (on both UNIX and Windows platforms):

```
[remorse] $ orapwd
Usage: orapwd file=<fname> password=<password> entries=<users>
  where
    file - name of password file (mand),
    password - password for SYS (mand),
    entries - maximum number of distinct DBA and OPERs (opt),
  There are no spaces around the equal-to (=) character.
oracle@hp1.   [/u01/app/oracle/dba]
[remorse] $
```

The following command creates a new password file called testpwd:

```
[remorse] $ orapwd file=testpwd password=remorse1 entries=20
```

Encrypted Passwords

By default, Oracle user passwords aren't encrypted, and this leaves them vulnerable to unauthorized usage. By setting the following parameters, one on the client and the other on the server, you can ensure that Oracle will always encrypt a password when it's sending it across a network:

```
ora_encrypt_login=true (client)
dblink_encrypt_login=true (server)
```

Database authentication, although it's easy to set up, isn't the only or the best means of authenticating Oracle users. You have a choice of several non-database-dependent means of authenticating users in the database. In the following sections, I discuss the main methods of user authentication that don't use the database itself for performing authentication.

External Authentication

Under the external authentication method, you match the user accounts at the operating system level with the usernames in the database. The advantage to this method is that you'll need only a single username for both the operating system and database connections. This can also help in auditing user actions, as the database names and operating system accounts correspond. To use operating system authentication, first you have to set the configuration parameter *os_authent_prefix* in the init.ora file as follows (the default value for the *os_authent_prefix* parameter is *OPS$*):

```
Os_authent_prefix = ""
```

Note that there should not be a space between the pair of quotes. When you start the database again, you can start using external authentication based on the underlying operating system. To enable operating system authentication, this is how you need to create your users:

```
SQL> create user samalapati identified  externally;
User created.
SQL>
```

Note that the new user isn't given a password—the user doesn't need one. As long as the user can log into the operating system, all he or she will have to do is type the following command to log in:

```
$ sqlplus /
```

All users that need to use the external authentication will log in the same way. Thus, external authentication using the *os_authent_prefix* parameter is a simple way to enable multiple users to connect to the database without creating usernames and passwords for them in the database. All this easy access, of course, means that you're also exposing the security vulnerability of the database.

 NOTE *The well-known OPS$ORACLE account is a simple variation on the preceding example of external authentication. OPS$ is just a prefix Oracle has used since the Oracle 5 version. You can use any prefix or no prefix at all for operating system external authentication. Oracle uses the term* operating system authorize login *for the old term* OPS$ login.

The operating system external authentication described in this section doesn't allow the users to connect over Oracle Net, because it isn't considered very secure. Therefore, shared server configurations that use Oracle Net can't by default use operating system external authentication. To override this default behavior, you have to set the following parameter in your init.ora file:

```
remote_os_authent=true
```

Proxy Authentication

You can use several middle-tier products to facilitate user interaction with the Oracle database. A Web server, for example, such as Oracle's WebDB product or the Oracle 9*i* Internet Application Server (IAS) product, is often used as the middle or application layer connecting the clients to the database. You can choose to have the middle tier authenticate your users or you can have the middle tier pass the username and password to the database for authentication.

Here is an example showing how to authorize a middle tier (WebDB) to proxy a user authenticated by a password:

```
SQL> alter user salapati
  2  grant connect through webdb
  3  authenticated using password
  4  /
User altered.
SQL>
```

The following example illustrates how you can authorize the middle tier to connect as a user:

```
SQL> alter user salapati
  2* grant connect through webdb
SQL> /
User altered.
```

Centralized User Authorization

If you use the Oracle Advanced Security option, you can use a Lightweight Directory Access Protocol (LDAP)–based directory service such as Oracle Internet Directory (OID) to perform user authentication. The directory-based service enables the creation of "enterprise users" who can be granted global roles. Centralized user management enables the use of a *single sign-on*—that is, users have to sign in only once to access all the databases they need to use.

Because Oracle Advanced Security isn't used by every database, I don't provide a detailed explanation of the implementation of centralized user authorization. Please refer to the "Oracle Advanced Security Administrator's Guide" for a detailed explanation of this feature.

Enterprise User Security

Large organizations these days have several applications to manage, both internal and Web based. It quickly becomes an administrative nightmare to manage users and their privileges on all these different applications. Centralized directories are increasingly being seen as the best way to manage multiple systems within an organization. LDAP is a popular industry standard and Oracle has its own implantation of this standard. Information that has been managed in multiple systems and formats can be brought under one umbrella using a directory service like LDAP. You can replace all your tnsnames.ora files on clients and manage user connectivity, authorization, and security with the help of the LDAP directory services. The LDAP directory can provide solid password policy management, data privacy, data integrity, and strong authentication and authorization protocols.

Shared Schemas

When users are registered and maintained in an LDAP repository, they are referred to as *shared schemas* or *schema-independent users*. When an LDAP-registered user connects to a specific database, the database will ask the LDAP server for confirmation of the user's identity and the roles that should be assigned to the user upon connection. Thus, in a database with several hundred users for a certain application, you need to create only one schema to manage the application. The individual user will be registered in the centralized directory, and when the user connects to the database, he or she will be assigned this common schema with all its privileges and roles.

Single Sign-On

If you use the optional Oracle Advanced Security feature, you can use its single sign-on feature, so a user need only log into the system once. Once the user is authenticated, he or she can access all the other applications on the system without having to enter a name and password repeatedly. This automatic authentication is very helpful to system administrators and other key users of systems in an organization.

Data Encryption

Sometimes you may want to *encrypt* data (i.e., encode it so only users who are authorized can understand it). Oracle supports encryption of network data through its Advanced Security feature. For encryption of data, Oracle provides the DBMS_OBFUSCATION_TOOLKIT package, which enables data encryption by using the Data Encryption Standard (DES) algorithm. The DES algorithm is the required standard for many institutions in the United States. The toolkit supports triple DES encryption for the highest level of security. It also supports the use of the MD5 secure cryptographic hash.

Using Oracle Internet Directory for Security Management

In Chapter 10, you learned how to configure Oracle Internet Directory (OID) and manage it. You also learned how to easily configure OID for name resolution by storing network and server information in it. OID provides the functionality to perform effective security management, including the enforcement of strict password policies for security management. OID also helps you maintain a single, global identity for each user across the application environment and helps you centrally store user credentials. An in-depth explanation of the use of OID for security management is beyond the scope of this book; please refer to the Oracle manual "Internet Directory Management" for complete details about using OID for security management.

Enterprise Security Manager (ESM) (not to be confused with the older Security Manager component of OEM) offers you an easy, GUI-based way to manage user and database information in the centralized OID. You must be licensed for the Advanced Security option to use ESM. When you have a large number of databases, ESM helps you register users and roles in OID. It can subsequently manage user access to the databases that have been published to the Oracle Context.

Database Security Do's and Don'ts

A common misunderstanding among DBAs is that once the database is behind a firewall, it's immune to security attacks. This presupposes, of course, that your security threats are always external, when real-life statistics tell you that the majority of security violations are from "insiders." That's why not only do you have to secure database from external threats, but you also have to follow a rock-solid authentication policy and sound data access policies.

You can take several basic steps to enhance the security of your Oracle9*i* database. Most of these steps are based on common sense and prohibit easy entry into the database through well-known back-door access points. Let's quickly review these security guidelines.

User Accounts

Oracle recommends that you *lock and expire* all default user accounts except, of course, the SYS and SYSTEM accounts. If you aren't going to use the Intelligent Agent, you can also lock the DBSNMP account. Unless you're using stored outlines in your database, you should also lock the OUTLN account. The number of default accounts is not limited to these four—the number depends on the kind of database you create and how you create it. For example, creating a database with the help of the DBCA usually results in the creation of a larger number of default accounts.

Passwords

Don't hard-code Oracle user passwords in shell scripts. Use a password file and variables to access the passwords instead. Otherwise, your user passwords can be gleaned by using a simple *ps –ef | grep* command while the process is running.

Use strict password management by forcing users to change passwords in a timely fashion. Use the *failed_login_attempts* option when setting user profiles to limit unsuccessful login attempts to a reasonable number. Accounts should be locked indefinitely (default behavior) if they hit the *failed_login_attempts* ceiling. This way, the DBA will be the only one who can unlock these accounts.

Operating System Authentication

Two initialization parameters enable access to an Oracle database through authentication at the operating system level. One is the well-known *os_authen_prefix* parameter, which many people use to create the OPS$ account for use in shell scripts and other places. Of course, using the OPS$ account implies that you're relying on operating system authentication and security. The other initialization parameter affecting operating system authentication of users is the *remote_os_authent* parameter, which enables users who authenticate themselves not on the server, but on a remote workstation, to gain access to your database. There may be an exceptional circumstance when you want to use this feature. In general, you should leave this parameter at its default value of *false*. A user from a remote system can log in using nonsecure protocols through the remote operating system authorization, and that's a serious violation of security standards.

Audit Your Database

Check the audit trail for logins as SYSDBA to make sure that only authorized people are logging in as SYSDBA users. The audit trail also lets you see if the database was brought up at any time with the auditing feature *disabled*. You should audit all unsuccessful attempts to log in to the database. In addition, you can audit all actions by any user connected as SYSDBA or SYOPER. To enable all SYDBA and SYSOPER operations, you need to set the following initialization parameter:

```
audit_sys_operations=true
```

NOTE *Setting* audit_sys_operations=true *logs all SYDBA and SYSOPER activity to an operating system audit trail, not a database audit trail. Thus, the audit trail will be can't be tampered with by users with powerful privileges within the database.*

Grant Privileges Appropriately

Oracle recommends strongly that you avoid granting *ANY* privileges, as in *Delete ANY table*, to reduce your vulnerability. You can avoid this problem generally by refraining from (carelessly) granting object privileges *directly* to users. In addition, avoid granting privileges with the *ADMIN* privilege. The ADMIN privilege means that the user to whom you granted a privilege can grant the same privilege to other users in turn. This means that you, the DBA, can very well lose control over who is being granted privileges in your database.

Use *roles* rather than grant privileges directly to users. This will help you a whole lot on databases with a large user base, where it is hard to check which user has been granted which privilege if you have been granting them directly to the users.

PUBLIC is sort of a *default role* for every user created in the database. Make sure you don't grant any unnecessary roles or privileges to PUBLIC, because every user will automatically inherit those roles/privileges, including default users such as DBSNMP and OUTLN. What privileges does PUBLIC have? Well, the following query shows that PUBLIC has over 12,000 object-level privileges:

```
SQL> select count(*) from dba_tab_privs
  2  where grantee='PUBLIC';
  COUNT(*)
=========
  12132
SQL>
```

Of the 12,000 or so object privileges that have been granted to PUBLIC, over 100 are privileges to execute DBMS packages such as DBMS_JOB, DBMS_METADATA, DBMS_SNAPSHOT, DBMS_DDL, DBMS_SPACE, and DBMS_OBFUSCATION_TOOLKIT. In addition, PUBLIC can use the UTL_FILE and UTL_HTTP packages by default. The PUBLIC user also has a single system privilege: unlimited tablespace.

Revoke all important execution privileges from PUBLIC. Grant important privileges to users directly through the judicious use of roles.

Set Appropriate Permissions

Set the proper file permissions at the operating system level, as there often can be a security loophole at this level. The default permissions on a newly created file in most UNIX systems are rw-rw-rw. This means that any users that gain admission to the UNIX server can read or copy all files, including your database files. You should set the *umask* variable to 022, so only the Oracle username can read from and write to database files.

Ensure that you remove the *setuid* on all Oracle files immediately. Some of the *setuid* files may allow the execution of scripts as the root user in UNIX systems.

The UTL_FILE package, as you'll see in Chapter 20, enables writing to operating system files from within an Oracle PL/SQL program. When you use the *utl_file_dir* initialization parameter, never use the * value for the parameter, which means that the package could output files to any directory in the operating system's file system. Restrict the directories to some well-known locations exclusively set apart from the UTL_FILE output files.

Remove the PL/SQL EXTPROC functionality unless it is needed. First remove mentions to EXTPROC in both the listener.ora file on the server and the tnsnames.ora file on the client. You then can remove all EXTPROC executables from your $ORACLE_HOME/bin directory. There is usually a pair of executables called extproc and extproc0. The extproc facility gives hackers a way to break into the operating system without any authentication. If you do need to use the extproc functionality, refer to Note 175429.1 on Oracle's MetaLink site.

Make sure you don't allow ordinary users access to your export and import control files, because your passwords may appear in those files.

Safeguard the Network and the Listener

The network and the listener service are vulnerable points of Oracle security, as there are many ways you can inadvertently leave avenues open for attacks on your database. Let's first look at how you can strengthen the listener service.

Securing the Listener

As you learned in Chapter 10, always use a password for the listener to prevent unauthorized users from preventing connections to the database. Once you set a password for the listener, privileged actions such as shutting down or starting up the listener can't be performed unless you provide the right password.

You can also prevent a user from using the *set* command to interfere with listener functions. To do this, you need to add the following line to your listener.ora configuration file. By default, this parameter is set to *false.*

```
admin_retrictions=on
```

You should avoid remote management of the listener service, as its password isn't encrypted over the network. The listener password is stored in the listener.ora file, so you must safeguard this file. Here's a section of the listener.ora file showing the (encrypted) listener password:

```
#----ADDED BY TNSLSNR 09-DEC-2002 13:46:24---
PASSWORDS_LISTENER = 27C3F40B1191F3DF
```

Securing the Network

One of the basic security requirements for today's Internet-based database applications is that you must have a firewall protecting your system from the external world. Once you have a firewall in place, keep it secure by not poking holes in it for any reason.

In addition to having a normal firewall, you can use a feature of Oracle Net to add an additional layer of protection called *server-side access controls.* Server-side access controls limit the capability of an address to connect to your database using the listener service. There are two ways to limit the addresses through which connections can be made. You can either list the *invited* (accepted) address or the *excluded* addresses in the sqlnet.ora file.

Here's the information you have to add to your sqlnet.ora file to enforce server-side access controls. All network addresses in the invited list are allowed to connect and all addresses in the excluded nodes list are denied access. When the listener service starts, it reads the sqlnet.ora file and provides access according to the access controls you specified. Here are the additions that you need to make to your sqlnet.ora file to enforce server-side access controls:

```
tcp.validnode_checking = yes
tcp.invited_nodes = (server1.us.wowcompany.com,
172.14.16.152)
```

or

```
tcp.excluded_nodes = (server1.us.wowcompany.com,
                      172.14.16.152)
```

> **NOTE** *In general, because it's more likely that you know the addresses that are going to connect to your database, using the* tcp_invited_nodes *parameter may be the best way to limit access to your system.*

Denying Remote Client Authentication

As you learned earlier in this chapter, letting remote clients authenticate logins is unsafe, and you should always let the server authenticate clients connecting to your database. You can turn client-based operating system authentication off by setting the following parameter in your init.ora file:

```
remote_os_authent=false
```

Keep Up-to-Date

An important part of security management is keeping up with the latest news about new security vulnerabilities and the patches or workarounds to overcome them. Oracle has a policy of quickly issuing fixes through workarounds or patches for new security problems. Check for the latest security patches on the Oracle MetaLink Web site. You can find regular Oracle security alerts at the following location: http://technet.oracle.com/deploy/security/alerts.htm. You can also find news about security breaches on the MetaLink site in the "News & Notes" section. If you wish, Oracle will send you e-mail security alerts about new issues. You can sign up for this free service by registering at http://otn.oracle.com/deploy/security/alerts.htm.

Use Oracle's Advanced Security Feature

Oracle doesn't require or recommend that you use its Advanced Security feature to secure your Oracle9*i* databases. However, the Advanced Security option provides so many strong security features that you may want to consider using it if your business needs warrant the very highest degree of data and network security. Here are some of the additional security features when you use OAS:

- Encryption of network traffic among clients, application servers, and databases
- Sophisticated authentication methods for users
- Centralized user management
- Support for Public Key Infrastructure (PKI)

Take Care of Application Security

Although all the security guidelines thus far have mostly dealt with preventing unauthorized access to your network and the database, it's extremely important that you review the application security policies to ensure no vulnerabilities exist there. The following sections present some commonsense policies that your organization must enforce to provide strong application security.

Grant Privileges Through Roles

You've already seen in the section on data security how you can use roles to encapsulate privileges rather than granting privileges directly to various users.

Minimize the number of direct object privileges by letting stored code such as procedures and packages be the means through which users can issue DML statements. You just have to grant the user the privilege to execute a certain package or procedure to perform any DML actions. Once the package or procedure completes execution, the users will not have the privilege to perform the DML activity from outside the stored code.

Disable Roles

All application roles should use the *set role* statement to enable the roles granted to users. Application users should be granted roles only for specific purposes, and the roles should be revoked from them when they aren't needed any longer.

Application owners should consider creating *secure application roles,* which are enabled by PL/SQL packages.

Restrict SQL*Plus Usage

One of the first things you should do when turning your database loose to the public is to strictly restrict the ability of users to use the SQL*Plus interface. You can restrict the SQL*Plus capabilities of a user by using the product_user_profile table, which is explained in detail in Chapter 6.

Useful Techniques for Managing Users

In this section you'll examine some simple scripts that can help you manage your users. You'll also learn about some typical problems that you might encounter in this area.

How to Alter a Profile

The following code shows how to alter a user's profile:

```
SQL> alter profile fin_user
  2  limit
  3  failed_login_attempts 5
```

```
   4   password_lock_time 1;
Profile altered.
SQL>
```

How to List User Information

You can use the DBA_USERS view to get quite a bit of information about the user population in your database. Here's a typical query using the DBA_USERS view:

```
SQL> select username, profile, account, status from dba_users;
USERNAME          PROFILE             ACCOUNT_STATUS
-----------------------------------------------------------------
SYS               DEFAULT             OPEN
SYSTEM            DEFAULT             OPEN
OUTLN             DEFAULT             OPEN
DBSNMP            DEFAULT             OPEN
HARTSTEIN         DEFAULT             OPEN
FINANCE           DEFAULT             OPEN
```

How to Find Out the Memory Use for Each Active Session

You can query the V$SESSION table in conjunction with related dynamic performance tables to find out the amount of memory being used by each active session in the database. Listing 11-23 shows the results of a typical query that tells you how memory is being used by all the active sessions in the database.

Listing 11-23. Determining Session Memory Use

```
SQL> SELECT USERNAME,VALUE
  2   FROM V$SESSION V, V$SEssTAT S, V$STATNAME N
  3   WHERE V.SID=S.SID
  4   AND S.STATISTIC# = N.STATISTIC#
  5*  AND N.NAME = 'session uga memory';
USERNAME             VALUE
------------------------------  -----
                     78520
                     78520
                     78520
                     78520
                     143888
                     144040
SYSTEM               274960
SYS                  209560
SYSTEM               209544
9 rows selected.
SQL>
```

What SQL Is a User Currently Executing?

You can use the query shown in Listing 11-24, which joins the V$SESSION and the V$SQLTEXT tables, to give you the text of the SQL currently being used by a user.

Listing 11-24. Finding Out the SQL Being Executed by a User

```
SQL> select a.sid,a.username,
  2  s.sql_text
  3  from v$session a,v$sqltext s
  4  where a.sql_address = s.address
  5  and a.sql_hash_value = s.hash_value
  6  and a.username like 'HR%'
  7* order by a.username,a.sid,s.piece;
   SID       USERNAME           SQL_TEXT
-------------------------------------------------------------
     8         HR          BEGIN dbms_stats.gather_table_stats

                           ('HR','REGIONS'); END;
```

How to Log In As a Different User

Even the Oracle DBA doesn't have access to any user's passwords, which are stored in an encrypted form. You can always change the password of a user and use the new password to get in as that user. How do you change it back to the original password? You can use the encrypted form of a password as a basis for logging in as any user and then resetting the password back. Here's an example:

```
SQL>  select 'alter user tester identified
        by values '||password||';' from dba_users
  2* where username='TESTER';
'ALTERUSERTESTERIDENTIFIED
-----------------------------------------------------------
alter user tester identified by values 1825ACAA229030F1;
```

Now change the password of user tester so you can log in as tester:

```
SQL> alter user tester identified by newpassword;
```

When you're done, change user tester's password back to its original value. Make sure you enclose the encrypted password in single quotes.

```
Sql> alter user tester identified by values '1825ACAA229030F1';
User altered.
SQL>
```

Useful DBA Views to Monitor User Roles and Privileges

Several highly useful data dictionary views can help you see who has what role and what privileges a certain role has. You can also see what system- and object-level privileges have been granted to a certain user. Of course, OEM provides a much easier way to quickly view this information. My point again is that although you can always use OEM for your daily management of the Oracel9*i* database, it is extremely important for you to understand the data sources, the data dictionary views, which underlie OEM and any other GUI management tool. Table 11-2 presents the important data dictionary views for user management.

Table 11-2. Data Dictionary Views for User Management

DATA DICTIONARY VIEW	DESCRIPTION
DBA_COL_PRIVS	Column-level object grants
DBA_ROLE_PRIVS	Users and their roles
DBA_SYS_PRIVS	Users who have been granted system privileges
DBA_TAB_PRIVS	Users and their privileges on tables
ROLE_ROLE_PRIVS	Roles granted to roles
ROLE_SYS_PRIVS	System privileges granted to roles
ROLE_TAB_PRIVS	Table privileges granted to roles
SESSION_PRIVS	Privileges currently enabled for the user
SESSION_ROLES	Roles currently enabled for the users

How to Kill a User's Session

You can use the *alter system* command as shown in the following sample to kill any user's session. You need to first query the V$SESSION view for the values of the SID and serial# of the user. Then using the SID and serial#, you can kill the user's session, as shown in the following SQL commands:

```
SQL> select sid,serial# from v$session
  2* where username='SALAPATI';
     SID    SERIAL#
     ----------------
      10        32
SQL> alter system kill session '10,32';
System altered.
SQL>
```

If the session you want to kill is involved in a long operation such as a lengthy rollback, Oracle will inform you that the session is "marked for kill" and it will be killed after the operation is completed. When Oracle kills a session, it rolls back all ongoing transactions and releases all session locks.

If the UNIX process of the user is killed, the Oracle session will most likely be killed also, but that isn't the most graceful way to end a session. Anyway, if you think you must kill a user's UNIX session, and the Oracle *kill session* command isn't working or it's taking a long time, you can terminate the session rather abruptly by using the UNIX *kill* command as follows. Note that you can use either the *kill* command by itself or with the –9 switch, but in most cases the simple *kill* command will be enough to terminate the UNIX session of your Oracle users.

```
$ kill 345678
```

or

```
$ kill -9 345
```

You can use the following script to derive the process number from the V$SESSION dynamic view (and the SID and serial# as well):

```
SQL> select process,sid,serial# from v$session where
  2* username='&user';
Enter value for user: SALAPATI
old   2: username='&user'
new   2: username='SALAPATI'
PROCESS              SID     SERIAL#
2920:2836             10          34
SQL>
```

Windows systems don't use the concept of processes, of course, but all user "processes" are threads of the same Oracle .exe process. In order to terminate a user's session, you can use the ORAKILL utility, which will kill a specific thread under the Oracle .exe process. Suppose you wish to kill user salapati's session. How do you find out what user salapati's thread is? Listing 11-25 shows how can use a simple query to help you identify any user's thread in a Windows system.

Listing 11-25. Identifying a User's Thread in a Windows System

```
SQL>  select sid, spid as thread, osuser, s.program
  2   from sys.v_$process p, sys.v_$session s
  3*  where p.addr = s.paddr;
     SID THREAD     OSUSER              PROGRAM
       1 1192       SYSTEM              ORACLE.EXE
       2 1420       SYSTEM              ORACLE.EXE
       3 1524       SYSTEM              ORACLE.EXE
       4 1552       SYSTEM              ORACLE.EXE
       5 1528       SYSTEM              ORACLE.EXE
       6 1540       SYSTEM              ORACLE.EXE
       7 1580       SYSTEM              ORACLE.EXE
       8 1680       SYSTEM              ORACLE.EXE
```

```
       9 2948        NETBSA\SAlapati      sqlplusw.exe
      10 4072        NETBSA\SAlapati      sqlplusw.exe
10 rows selected.
SQL>
```

The script in Listing 11-25 will give you the thread numbers associated with each Oracle user. Once you have the thread numbers, you can kill the user's session by using the following command (assuming that the thread number is 2948):

```
C:> orakill 2948
```

Summary

User management is an interesting area for Oracle DBAs, and it's a facet of your job that you'll be dealing with on an ongoing basis, right from the day you create a new database. This chapter provided you with an introduction to Oracle user management, including how to manage the important concepts of roles and profiles.

Resource management in a busy production database isn't always easy. This chapter took you through a complete example where the Oracle Database Resource Manager was used to create user groups and resource plans to efficiently use database resources.

Auditing is an important part of a production databases, for obvious reasons. However, there are alternatives to traditional Oracle auditing, and the use of the Virtual Private Databases (VPDs) and application contexts enables you to audit databases using fine-grained techniques that are more sophisticated than the traditional method of auditing entire sets of actions within a database. In addition to auditing DML activity by users, Oracle9*i* offers you a broad range of auditing features that enable you to audit DDL statements, the SYS user's activities, and system events. This chapter showed you how to use these powerful means of auditing your database.

This chapter also showed you the various means of user authentication in an Oracle database. Database authentication is the most common form of authentication; therefore, you need to have stringent password policies. The chapter discussed various aspects of password management. Database security is an important part of the Oracle DBA's tasks, and this chapter presented a set of guidelines to make your Oracle database secure.

Part Four

Data Loading, Backup, and Recovery

CHAPTER 12

Loading and Transforming Data

ONE OF YOUR most common tasks as a DBA is loading data from external sources. Although you commonly do this when you first populate a database, you're called upon frequently to load data into various tables. Traditionally, the main tool used has been the Oracle-provided SQL*Loader utility, which you can use to load data from flat files into the Oracle database tables. This chapter details the use of SQL*Loader to load data.

SQL*Loader has always been an important tool for loading data into Oracle databases. Oracle has recently started providing another useful way to load tables, the External Table feature. In fact, the chapter illustrates how the use of external tables offers several advantages over SQL*Loader when it comes to the transformation of data during the load.

In many cases, especially in data warehouses, the data that's loaded needs to be transformed or modified. Oracle provides several means of performing data transformation within the database, including the traditional use of SQL and PL/SQL code. In this chapter, you'll learn about the different ways of transforming data, with a special emphasis on the powerful *merge* feature and the use of table functions.

Introduction to Data Loading and Transformation

Before you can run your application on the Oracle9*i* database, you need to populate your database, and one of the most common sources of this data is flat files, with the data either extracted from legacy systems or some other source.

Traditionally, SQL*Loader was the only tool that Oracle provided to load this data from the external files into database tables. SQL*Loader is still technically the only Oracle-supplied utility to load data from external files, but you can also use the new Oracle9*i* External Table feature to perform data loads from external files.

Note that the External Table concept is not a method that bypasses SQL*Loader. You'll see later in this chapter that the External Table concept relies heavily on the SQL*Loader utility. In most data loading, your job is not over after the raw data is loaded into the tables. Because the raw data may contain extraneous information or data in a different format from what your application needs, the data is commonly "transformed" in some way before the database (or data warehouse) can use it for analytical purposes. It's especially common for data warehouses, which extract their data from multiple sources, to perform a transformation of the new data. It's also possible to do some preliminary or basic transformation of the raw data during the SQL*Loader run itself. However, more complex data transformation requires separate steps, and you have a choice of several techniques to manage the transformation process. Oracle9*i* provides new features that facilitate the transformation process.

Large data warehouses are commonly used today for analytical querying purposes. Before you can query the data, you have to load the data into the warehouse, and this is not a trivial issue. Most warehouse data goes through three major steps before you can analyze the data. These three steps or processes are *Extraction, Transformation, Loading* (ETL). You'll examine these steps in the following section.

Loading Data with ETL

As you learned earlier, ETL stands for Extraction, Transformation, Loading. *Extraction* is the identification and extraction of raw data, possibly in multiple formats, from several sources, not all of which may be relational databases. *Transformation* of data is the most challenging and time consuming of the three processes. Transformation of data may involve the application of complex rules to data before it is accepted for loading. Transformation may also include performing operations such as data aggregation and the application of functions to the raw data. *Loading* is the process of placing the data in the database tables. This may also include the task of maintaining indexes and constraints on the tables that are part of the loading process.

Traditionally, organizations have used two different methodologies to perform the ETL process: the *transform-then-load* method and the *load-then-transform* method. In the first method, the data is cleaned or transformed before it's loaded into Oracle tables. Custom-made ETL processes are usually used for the transformation of data. In the transform-then-load method of data cleansing, the Oracle database's capabilities aren't fully extended, as there is dependence on external processes.

In the load-then-transform method, the raw data is first loaded into staging tables and then loaded into other, "final" tables after the data transformation process is performed within the database itself. Intermediate "staging" tables are the key to the load-then-transform method. The drawback to this technique is that you have to maintain multiple types of data in the table, some in a raw and original state and some in a "finished" state.

In addition to its excellent capabilities in the querying area, Oracle9*i* offers terrific ETL capabilities. It is these capabilities that enable Oracle databases to use a newer way to load data into a database: the *transform-while-loading* method. By using the Oracle database to perform all the ETL steps, you can efficiently perform the typically laborious ETL processes. Oracle9*i* provides you with a whole set of complementary tools and techniques to perform ETL tasks. The ETL techniques aim to reduce the time needed to load data into the database while simplifying the work involved. Oracle's ETL solution includes the following components:

- *External tables:* External tables provide a way to merge the loading and transformation processes. Using external tables will enable you to eliminate cumbersome and time-consuming intermediate staging tables during data loading.

- *Multitable inserts:* These provide you a way to insert data simultaneously into multiple tables. This capability eliminates the additional step of first dividing data into separate groupings and then performing data loading. Using the multitable insert feature, you can insert data into more than one table at the same time, using different criteria for the various tables.

- *Upserts:* This is simply a made-up name indicating the technique whereby you can either insert data into a table or just update the rows with a single SQL statement: *merge*. The *merge* statement will insert new data and update data if the rows already exist in the table. This simplifies your loading process because you don't have to worry about whether a table already contains the data.

- *Table functions:* Table functions are a great help when you're doing large and complex transformations.

- *Transportable tablespaces:* These tablespaces provide you with an efficient and speedy way to move data from one database to another. For example, you can migrate data between an OLTP database and data warehouse using transportable tablespaces. Chapter 13 discusses how to use transportable tablespaces.

Loading Data with the Oracle9i Warehouse Builder

You can use Oracle9*i* Warehouse Builder (OWB) to efficiently load data. OWB offers you a wizard-driven facility to load data into the database through SQL*Loader. OWB can load data from an Oracle database or from flat files. In addition, OWB can extract data from other databases such as Sybase, Informix, and Microsoft SQL Server via Oracle Transparent Gateways. OWB combines ETL and design functions in an easy to use format.

NOTE *For more details about OWB, please refer to the excellent white paper titled "Integrated ETL and Modeling," which is available at* http://otn.oracle.com/products/warehouse/pdf/ Oracle9i WB WhitePaper.pdf.

*Microsoft SQL Server's popular Data Transformation Services (DTS) has long been superior to Oracle's SQL*Loader as a data loading and transformation tool. But the arrival of OWB bridges the gap somewhat.*

In the next section you'll learn how to use the SQL*Loader utility to load data from external files. This will help you understand how to use external tables to perform data loading. Toward the end of the chapter, you'll learn how to use various methods of data transformation offered by the Oracle9*i* database.

The SQL*Loader Utility

The SQL*Loader utility comes with the Oracle9*i* database and is a common tool DBAs use to load external data into an Oracle database. The utility works from outside the Oracle database. You invoke the SQL*Loader utility from the operating system with a control file that specifies the data sources and the target table column names, among other things. You can only load data into an Oracle database with the SQL*Loader tool; you can't retrieve data from the database using SQL*Loader. For getting data out of the tables, you can use the export utility, which is discussed in the next chapter. You can also write a SQL statement to extract data out of an Oracle table and spool the output to a file.

Essentially, SQL*Loader is a tool to load data from one or more operating system flat files into one or more Oracle database tables. Although using the SQL*Loader utility is straightforward, it's an immensely powerful tool that's capable of performing more than just a data load from text files. You can use SQL*Loader to transform data before it's loaded into the database. You can also perform selective loading based on the record values. You'll generally load data from operating system text files, but if necessary, you can also load data from tapes.

A number of third-party tools are available to help you extract data out of Oracle tables. For example, DT/Studio from Embarcadero Technologies is a good tool. (You can find out more about this tool at http://www.embarcadero.com/.) For data loading, however, Oracle's free SQL*Loader utility may be all you'll ever need. The SQL*Loader utility is an old standby of DBAs, and it can do really amazing things in terms of data loading and basic data manipulation. Here's a quick list of the utility's capabilities:

- You can load data from multiple sources: disk, tape, and named pipes.

- You can selectively load from the input file based on conditions.

- You can load all or part of a table.

- You can perform simultaneous data loads. You can transform the data during the data load itself (limited capabilities).

- You can automate the load process, so it runs at scheduled times.

- You can load complex object-relational data.

Different Methods of Data Loading

You can use the SQL*Loader utility to perform several types of data loading: conventional data loading, direct path loading, and the newer external data loading, which uses the External Table concept.

Under *conventional* data loading, SQL*Loader reads multiple rows at a time and stores them a bind array. SQL*Loader will subsequently insert this whole array at once into the database and commit the operation.

The *direct path* loading method doesn't use the SQL *insert* statement to load the data into Oracle tables. Column array structures are built from the data to be loaded, and these structures are used to format Oracle data blocks that are then written directly to the database tables.

The new External Table feature of Oracle9*i* relies on the functionality of SQL*Loader to access data that in external files as if it is part of the database tables. Because the External Table capability has many interesting features, I have devoted a separate section in this chapter to it, although you can technically consider it to be a part of the SQL*Loader utility.

The conventional and direct path loading methods offer their own benefits and drawbacks. Because the direct path loading method bypasses the Oracle SQL mechanism, it is much faster than the conventional loading method. However, when it comes to the data transformation capabilities, the conventional loading method is much more powerful than direct path loading, because it allows a full range of functions to be applied to the table columns during the load. The direct path loading method supports a far more limited number of transformations during the load. Oracle recommends that you use the conventional loading method for small data loads and the direct path loading method for larger loads.

NOTE *In the following explanation of SQL*Loader features, I use the conventional loading method. Later on in this chapter, I include a separate discussion of using SQL*Loader with the direct path loading option.*

Loading data using the SQL*Loader utility involves the following steps:

1. Select the data file to be loaded. The data file always ends with the extension .dat and contains the data you want to load. The data could be in several formats.

2. Create a control file. The control file tells SQL*Loader how to map the data fields to an Oracle table and specifies if the data needs to be transformed in some way. The control file always ends with the extension .ctl.

The control file will provide the mapping of the table columns to the data fields in the input file. There is no requirement that you have a separate data file for the load. If you wish, you can include the data in the control file itself, after you specify the load control information such as the field specification and so on. The data can be supplied in fixed-length fields or in free format, separated by a character such as a comma (,) or a pipe (|).

SQL*Loader will create several files during the load process, including the log file, the bad file, and the discard file. You'll find details about these files in the "Command-Line Parameters in the Control File" section later in this chapter. In the next section you'll study the all-important control file in more detail.

The SQL*Loader Control File

The SQL*Loader control file is a simple text file that you create in which you specify the location of the source data file and the name and columns of the target table(s). The control file is the place where you map the data files to the table columns. You can also specify any transformation during the load process within the control file. The control file contains the names of the log files for the load and files for catching "bad" and "rejected" data. The control file instructs SQL*Loader regarding the following aspects of the SQL*Loader session:

- The source of the data to be loaded into the database
- The column specification of the target table
- The nature of the input file formatting
- The mapping of the input file fields to the table columns
- Data transformation rules (applying SQL functions)
- The locations for the log files and error files

Listing 12-1 shows a typical SQL*Loader control file. Note that you can also use a separate file for the data. In this example, you are seeing the control information followed by in-line data, as shown by the use of the *INFILE* * specification in the control file. This specification indicates that the data for the load will follow the control information for the load. If you are doing a one-time data load, it is probably better to keep things simple and place the data in the control file itself. The keyword BEGINDATA tells SQL*Loader where the data portion of the control file starts.

*Listing 12-1. A Typical SQL*Loader Control File*

```
LOAD DATA
INFILE *
BADFILE test.bad
DISCARDFILE test.dsc
INSERT
INTO TABLE tablename
FIELDS TERMINATED BY ',' OPTIONALLY ENCLOSED BY""
(column1   position (1:2) char,
column2   position (3:9) integer external,
column3    position (10:15) integer external,
column4   position (16:16) char
)
  BEGINDATA
    AY3456789111111Y
/*   Rest of the data here …*/
```

You can specify numerous variables in the control file, and you can informally sort them into the following groups:

- Loading-related clauses
- Data file–related clauses
- Table- and field-mapping clauses
- Command-line parameters in the control file

In the sections that follow you'll study in detail the different parameters that can help you configure your data loads by specifying them in the control file.

 TIP *If you aren't sure which parameters you can use for your SQL*Loader run, just type* **sqlldr** *at the operating system prompt and the SQL*Loader Help screen will pop up. You can see a complete list of all the parameters and their operating system–specific default values (if any exist).*

Loading-Related Clauses

The keyword *load data* starts off a control file. This simply means that the data is to be loaded from the input data file to the Oracle tables using the SQL*Loader utility.

The *into* table clause indicates what table the data will be loaded into. If you're loading into several tables at once, the same input record is processed several times. If you're loading into *n* tables simultaneously, you'll need *n* times *into* table statements.

The keywords *insert*, *replace*, and *append* instruct the database how the load will be done. If it is an insert, the table is assumed to be empty, otherwise, the load will error out. The *replace* clause will truncate the table and start loading new data. You'll often see that a load job using the *replace* option seems to hang initially—this is because Oracle is busy truncating the table before it starts the load process. The *append* clause will add the new rows to existing table data.

Data File–Related Clauses

You can use several clauses to specify the locations and other characteristics of the data file(s) from which you're going to load data using SQL*Loader. The following sections cover the important data file–related clauses.

Data File Specification

You specify the input data file name and location by using the *infile* parameter, as in

```
INFILE='/a01/app/oracle/oradata/load/consumer.data'
```

If you don't want to use the *infile* specification, you can include the data in the control file itself. When you include the data in the control file instead of a separate input file, you omit the file location and use the * notation, as follows:

```
INFILE = *
```

If you choose to have the data in the control file itself, you must use the following clause before your data starts:

```
BEGINDATA
Thomas Mannino,243 New Highway,12345
...
```

Physical and Logical Records

Every physical record in the source data file is equivalent to a logical record by default, but the control file can specify that more than one physical record be combined into a single logical record. For example, in the following input file there are three physical records that are also considered three logical records:

```
Thomas Mannino,243 New Highway, Irving, TX 12345
John Starks, 1234 Elm Street, Fort Worth, TX 98765
Nina Alapati, 2629 Skinner Drive, Flower Mound, TX 75028
```

You can transform these three physical records by using either of two parameters in the control file: the *concatenate* clause or the *continueif* clause.

For example, *concatenate 3* will concatenate three records into one logical record. The *continueif* parameter lets you merge two or more records into one logical record by specifying a character in a specified location. Let's go through a couple of examples to see how to use these two important clauses.

If your input is in the fixed format, you can specify the number of rows of data to be read for each logical record in the following way:

```
concatenate 4
```

This *concatenate* clause will combine four rows of data. If each row of data has 80 characters, then the total number of characters in the new logical record that is created will be 320. Therefore, when you use the *concatenate* clause, you should also specify a record length (*reclen*) clause along with it. In this case, the record length clause is as follows:

```
Reclen 240
```

The *continueif* clause lets you combine physical records into logical records by specifying one or more characters in a specified location. Let's look at the following example:

```
Continueif this (1:4) = 'next'
```

In this line, the *continueif* clause means that if SQL*Loader finds the four letters "next" at the beginning of a line, it should treat the data that follows as a continuation of the previous line (the four characters and the word "next" are arbitrary—continuation indicators can be any arbitrary character[s]). If you are using fixed format data, the *continueif* character may be placed in the very last column, as shown in the following example:

```
Continueif last = '&'
```

This line means that if SQL*Loader encounters the ampersand (&) character at the end of a line, it will treat the following line as a continuation of the preceding line.

TIP *Using either* continueif *or* concatenate *will slow down SQL*Loader, so map physical and logical records one-to-one. You should do this because when you join more than one physical record to make a single logical record, SQL*Loader has to scan the input data, which takes more time.*

Record Format

How does SQL*Loader know where a record ends and where a new one begins? There is no clause for specifying the record format, but you may specify a record format in one three ways: stream record format, variable record format, or fixed record format.

Stream record format is the most common record format, where you include a record terminator to indicate the end of a record. When SQL*Loader scans the input file, it knows that it reached the end of a record when it encounters this "terminator string." If no terminator string is specified, the last character defaults to a newline character or a linefeed (carriage return followed by a linefeed on Windows) character. This is the most common format in which input files are formatted. The set of three records in the previous example use this record format.

If you use the *variable record format*, you explicitly specify the length of each record at the beginning of the record, as shown in the following example:

```
infile 'example1.dat'   "var 2"
06sammyy12johnson,1234
```

There are two records in this line, the first with six characters (sammyy) and the second with a length of twelve characters (johnson,1234). *Var 2* indicates that the data records are of variable size, with a size field of length 2 before every new record.

With the *fixed record format*, you specify that all records are some specified, fixed size. Here's an example:

```
infile 'example1.dat'   "fix 12"
sammyy,1234
johnso,1234
```

Table- and Field-Mapping Clauses

During a load session, SQL*Loader takes the data fields in the data records and converts them into table columns. The following set of clauses pertains to the mapping process between data fields and table columns. The control file provides the following details about fields.

Table Column Name

Each column in the table is specified clearly, with the position and data type of the matching field value in the input file. You don't have to load all the columns in the table. If you omit any columns in the control file, they're set to null.

Position

SQL*Loader must have a way of knowing the location of the various fields in the input file. The *position* clause specifies exactly where in the data record the various fields are. You have two ways to specify the location of the fields: relative and absolute.

Relative position implies that you specify the position of a field with respect to the position of the preceding field, as shown in the following example:

```
Employee_id  POSITION (*) number
external 6
Employee_name  POSITION(*) char 30
```

In this example, the load starts with the first field, employee_id. SQL*Loader then expects employee_name to start in position 7 and continue for 30 characters. It will look for the next field starting for position 37 and so on.

When you use the *position* clause in an *absolute position* sense, you just specify the position at which each field starts and ends, as follows:

```
Employee_id POSITION(1:6) number external
Employee_name POSITION(7:36) char
```

Data Types

The *data types* used in the control file refer to the input records only and aren't the same as the column data types within the database tables. The following are the main data types used in SQL*Loader control files:

```
Integer(n) : Binary integer, where n can be 1, 2,4, or 8.
Smallint
char
Integer external
Float external
Decimal external
```

Delimiters

After each column's data type is specified, you can specify a *delimiter*, which indicates how the field should be delimited. You can delimit data by using one of the following two clauses: *terminated by* or *enclosed by*.

Terminated by limits the field to the character specified and denotes the end of a field. Here are a couple of examples:

```
TERMINATED BY WHITESPACE
TERMINATED BY ","
```

The first example indicates that the field is terminated by the first blank that is encountered and the second example simply indicates that the fields are separated by commas.

The *enclosed by* "" delimiter specifies that the field is enclosed by a pair of quotation marks. Here is an example:

```
FIELDS TERMINATED BY ',' OPTIONALLY ENCLOSED BY '"'
```

Data Transformation Parameters

You can apply SQL functions to the field data before loading it into table columns. Only SQL functions that return single values can be used for transforming field values, in general. The field should be denoted inside the SQL string as field_*name*. You specify the SQL function(s) after you specify the data type for the field, and you enclose the SQL string in double quotation marks, as shown in the following examples:

```
Field_name  CHAR TERMINATED BY "," "SUBSTR(:field_name, 1, 10)"
Employee_name position 32-62 char  "UPPER(:ename)"
Salary position 75 char "TO_NUMBER(:sal,'$99,999.99')"
Commission integer external "":commission * 100"
```

As you can see, the application of SQL operators and functions to field values before they are loaded into tables helps you transform the data at the same time you are loading it. This is a nice feature to have.

Command-Line Parameters in the Control File

SQL*Loader allows you to specify a number of runtime parameters at the command line when you invoke the SQL*Loader executable. What if you have to type in a number of parameters over and over again during SQL*Loader runs? You can use the *options* clause of the control file to specify all these runtime parameters inside the control file.

 TIP *You can always specify a number of runtime parameters while invoking SQL*Loader, but you're better off using the* options *clause to specify them inside the control file.*

The following sections cover some of the important parameters you can control using the *options* clause in the control file.

Userid

The *userid* parameter specifies both the username and the password of the user in the database that has the privileges for the data load:

```
Example: Userid = salapati/sammyy1
```

Control

The *control* parameter specifies the name of the control file for the SQL*Loader session. The control file may include the specifications for all the load parameters. Of course, you can load data using manual commands, but the use of a control file gives you more flexibility and enables the automation of the load process.

Example: CONTROL='/test01/app/oracle/oradata/load/finance.ctl'

Data

This parameter simply refers to the input data file. The default file extension is .dat. Note that the data doesn't necessarily have to be inside a separate data file. If you wish, you can include the data at the end of the control file load specifications.

Example: DATA='/test02/app/oracle/oradata/load/finance.dat'

Bindsize and Rows

You can use the two parameters *bindsize* and *rows* to specify a conventional path bind array. Recall that SQL*Loader in the conventional path mode doesn't insert data into the table row by row. Rather, it inserts a set of rows at a time, and that set of rows, called the *bind array*, is sized based on either of two parameters: *bindsize* or *rows*.

The *bindsize* parameter sets the bind array size in bytes. On my system, the default bind size is 256000 bytes.

Example: Bindsize = 512000

The *rows* parameter does not set any limit on the number of bytes in the bind array. It imposes a limit on the number of rows in each bind array, and SQL*Loader multiplies this value in the *rows* parameter with its estimate of the size of each row in the table. This indirectly derives the bind array's size in bytes by multiplying the number of rows and the row size. The default number of rows under conventional method on my system is 64.

Example: rows=64000

 NOTE *If you specify both the* bindsize *and* rows *parameters, SQL*Loader uses the smaller of the two values for the bind array.*

Direct

If you specify *direct=true*, then SQL*Loader will load using the direct path method, instead of the conventional method. Later in this chapter (in the "Setting Options for Direct Loads" section), you'll find a detailed discussion of the direct method of data loading. The default for this parameter is *direct=false*, meaning the conventional method is the default method used.

Example: DIRECT=true

Errors

This parameter specifies the maximum number of errors that can occur before the SQL*Loader job is terminated. The default for it on most systems is 50. If you don't want to tolerate any errors, here's what you do:

Example: ERRORS=0

Load

Using the *load* parameter, you can set the maximum number of logical records to be loaded into the table. The default, when you don't use this parameter, is to load all the records in the input data file.

Example: LOAD = 10000

Log

The *log* parameter specifies the name of the log file. The SQL*Loader log file, as you'll see shortly, provides a lot of information about your SQL*Loader session.

Example: LOG='/u01/app/oracle/admin/finance/logs/financeload.log'

Bad

The *bad* parameter specifies the name and location of the "bad file." If any records are rejected due to formatting errors, SQL*Loader will write the record to the bad file. For example, a field could exceed its specified length and be rejected by SQL*Loader. If you don't explicitly name a bad file, Oracle will create one and use a default name with the control file name as a prefix.

Example: bad = '/u01/app/oracle/load/financeload.bad'

Discard

Discarded data records are those that passed through the SQL*Loader checks but failed some database checks. The discard file contains all records rejected during the load because they didn't meet the record selection criteria (e.g., they didn't meet a unique constraint requirement). The default is to not have a discard file. If you don't specify a discard file, Oracle will create one just as in the case of a bad file.

Example: discard='test01/app/oracle/oradata/load/finance.dsc'

NOTE *Both the "bad" and "discard" files contain records in the original format. Therefore, it's easy, especially during large loads, to just edit these files and use them for a load of the data that was left out during the first load run.*

Parallel

The *parallel* parameter specifies whether SQL*Loader can run multiple sessions of the loader when you're employing the direct path loading method. Obviously, you need a server with multiple CPUs if you wish to use the parallel load feature.

```
Example: parallel=true
Example:  sqlldr userid=salapati/sammyy1
               control=load1.ctl direct=true parallel=true
```

Resumable

Using the *resumable* parameter, you can turn on Oracle's Resumable Space Allocation feature. By default, the *resumable* parameter is set to *false* and Resumable Space Allocation is therefore disabled.

```
Default: = n
Example: RESUMABLE = true
```

Resumable_Name

The *resumable_name* parameter enables you to identify a specific resumable statement when you use the Resumable Space Allocation feature.

```
Default: user username, session (sessionid) instance (instanceid)
Example: resumable_name = finance1_load
```

Resumable_Timeout

The *resumable_timeout* parameter can be set, of course, only when the *resumable* parameter is set to *true*. The timeout is the maximum length of time for which an operation can be suspended when it runs into a space-related problem. If the space-related problem is not fixed within this interval, the operation will be aborted.

```
Default: 7200 (seconds).
Example: RESUMABLE_TIMEOUT = 3600
```

Skip

What if your SQL*Loader job fails to complete its run due to some errors, but it has already committed some rows in a table? The *skip* parameter is very useful in situations like this, because it lets you skip a specified number of records in the input file when you run the SQL*Loader job the second time. The alternative, of course, is to truncate the table and restart the SQL*Loader job from the beginning—not a great idea if a large number of rows has already been loaded into the database tables.

```
Example: SKIP = 235550 (assuming the first job
failed after loading 235549 records successfully. You can find out
this information from the log file for the load,
or query the table directly).
```

Generating Data During the Load

The SQL*Loader utility enables you to generate data to load columns. This means that you can do a load without ever using a data file. More commonly, however, you generate data for one or more columns of the data when you are loading from a data file. The following different types of data can be generated by SQL*Loader:

- *Constant values:* You can set a column to a constant value by using the following syntax in the control file:

  ```
  Loaded_by     constant  "sysadm"
  ```

  All the rows populated during this run will have the value sysadm in the loaded_by column.

- *Data file record number:* You can set a column's value to the record number that loaded that row by using the recnum column specification:

  ```
  Record_num RECNUM
  ```

- *sysdate:* You can use the *sysdate* variable to set a column to the date you're loading the data:

  ```
  Example: Loaded_date    sysdate
  ```

- *sequence:* You can generate unique values to load a column by using the *sequence* function. In the following example, the current maximum value of the loadseq sequence is incremented by one each time a row is inserted:

  ```
  Example: Loadseq    SEQUENCE(max,1)
  ```

Invoking SQL*Loader

You can invoke the SQL*Loader utility in a number of ways from the operating system. The simplest way is to type the following string of commands at the operating system prompt:

```
$sqlldr userid=salapati/sammyy1 control=/u01/app/oracle/admin/finance/finance.ctl
data=/u01/app/oracle/oradata/load/finance.dat log=
/u01/aapp/oracle/admin/finance/log/finance.log
errors=0 direct=true skip=235550 resumable=true resumable_timeout=7200
```

As you can see, the more parameters you want to use, the more information you need to provide at the command line. There are two problems with this approach. First, if you make typing or other errors, you'll have a mess on your hands. Second, there may be a limit on some operating systems regarding how many characters you can input at the command prompt. Not to worry, though, as you can run the same SQL*Loader job shown previously with the following command, which is a lot less complicated:

```
$ sqlldr parfile=/u01/app/oracle/admin/finance/load/finance.par
```

What is this "parfile," and where are all the other parameters that you need for this load? Well, the command-line parameter *parfile* stands for *parameter file*, which is a file where you can specify values for all your command parameters. For example, in your present load, the parameter file or parfile looks like the following:

```
USERID=nicholas/nicholas1
CONTROL = '01/app/oracle/admin/finance/finance.ctl'
DATA = '/app/oracle/oradata/load/finance.dat'
LOG= '/u01/aapp/oracle/admin/finance/log/finance.log'
ERRORS=0
DIRECT=true
SKIP=235550
RESUMABLE=true
RESUMABLE_TIMEOUT=7200
```

Using the parfile is more elegant than typing out all the parameters at the command line, and it is a logical approach for regularly run jobs that use the same options. Any option that you specify at the command line will override the value specified for that parameter inside a parameter file.

If you want to use the command line but you don't want to type the password where someone can easily see it, you can invoke SQL*Loader in the following manner:

```
$ sqlldr control=control.ctl
```

SQL*Loader will then prompt you for your username/password combination.

What's in the Loader Log File?

The SQL*Loader log file offers a host of information regarding a SQL*Loader run, whether it is partially or completely successful. It unambiguously tells you how many records were supposed to be loaded and how many actually got loaded. It tells you which records failed to get loaded and why. It also describes the field columns provided in the SQL*Loader control file. Listing 12-2 shows a typical SQL*Loader log file.

*Listing 12-2. A Typical SQL*Loader Log File*

```
SQL*Loader: Release 9.2.0.1.0 - Production on Wed Dec 18 08:47:44 2002
/*File Location Section: Provides all the file names and their locations
, in case you specified them.*/
 Control File:   /u01/app/oracle/admin/fnfactsp/load/fndata.ctl
 Data File:      /ffp01/ffacts/import/gtrhstco803030402.001
 Bad File:       /u01/app/oracle/admin/fnfactsp/load/gtrhstco803030402.bad
 Discard File:  none specified
  (Allow all discards)
Number to load: ALL
Number to skip: 0
Errors allowed: 0
Bind array:     64 rows, maximum of 65536 bytes
Continuation:    none specified
Path used:      Conventional
Table TBLSTAGE1, loaded when ACTIVITY_TYPE != 0X48(character 'H')
                 and ACTIVITY_TYPE != 0X54(character 'T')
Insert option in effect for this table: APPEND
TRAILING NULLCOLS option in effect
    Column Name             Position   Len  Term Encl Datatype
-------------------------------- ---------- ----- ---- ---- --------------------
COUNCIL_NUMBER                   FIRST      *    ,        CHARACTER
COMPANY                          NEXT       *    ,        CHARACTER
ACTIVITY_TYPE                    NEXT       *    ,        CHARACTER
RECORD_NUMBER                    NEXT       *    ,        CHARACTER
FUND_NUMBER                      NEXT       *    ,        CHARACTER
BASE_ACCOUNT_NUMBER              NEXT       *    ,        CHARACTER
FUNCTIONAL_CODE                  NEXT       *    ,        CHARACTER
DEFERRED_STATUS                  NEXT       *    ,        CHARACTER
CLASS                            NEXT       *    ,        CHARACTER
 UPDATE_DATE                                             SYSDATE
UPDATED_BY                                               CONSTANT
    Value is 'sysadm'
BATCH_LOADED_BY                                          CONSTANT
    Value is 'sysadm'
/*Discarded Records Section: Gives you the complete list of discarded
records, including reasons why they were discarded.*/
Record 1: Discarded - failed all WHEN clauses.
Record 1527: Discarded - failed all WHEN clauses.
```

```
Table TBLSTAGE1:
/*Number of Rows: Gives you the number of rows
 successfully loaded and the number of rows not
loaded due to errors or because they failed the
 WHEN conditions, if any. Here, two records failed the WHEN condition*/
  1525 Rows successfully loaded.
  0 Rows not loaded due to data errors.
  2 Rows not loaded because all WHEN clauses were failed.
  0 Rows not loaded because all fields were null.
/* Memory Section: Gives the bind array size chosen for the data load*/
Space allocated for bind array:                  63540 bytes(6 rows)
Space allocated for memory besides bind array:       0 bytes
/* Logical Records Section: Gives you the total records, number of rejected
 and discarded records.*/
Total logical records skipped:          0
Total logical records read:          1527
Total logical records rejected:         0
Total logical records discarded:        2
/*Date Section: Gives the Day and Date of the data load.*/
Run began on Wed Mar 06 08:47:44 2002
Run ended on Wed Mar 06 08:47:46 2002
/*Time section: Gives you the time taken for completing the data load.*/
Elapsed time was:      00:00:02.21
CPU time was:          00:00:00.50
```

Using Return Codes

The log file provides a wealth of information about the load, but Oracle also allows you trap the exit code after each load run. This enables you to check the results of the load when you run it through a cronjob and a shell script. For a Windows server, you may use the at command to schedule the load job. Here are the key exit codes for the UNIX operating system:

```
EX_SUCC 0: Indicates that all the rows were loaded successfully
EX_FAIL 1 : Indicates that there were command line or syntax errors
EX_WARN 2: Indicates that some or all rows were rejected
EX_FTL 3: Indicates operating system errors
```

Using the Direct Load Option

So far, you have looked at the SQL*Loader utility from the point of view of a conventional load. As you recall, the conventional loading method uses SQL *insert* statements to insert the data into the tables one bind array size at a time. The direct path loading option doesn't use the SQL *insert* statement to put data into the tables; rather, it formats Oracle data blocks and writes them directly to the database files (hence the name "direct path loading"). This direct write process eliminates much of the overhead involved in executing SQL statements to load tables.

For larger data loads, a direct path is the best, and it may be the only viable method of loading data into tables for the simple reason that a conventional load may require so much time that it simply won't fit into the available window of time. You can't use the direct path loading method if you're using clustered tables or if you're loading parent and child tables together. You can't load VARRAYS or BFILE columns using the direct path loading option. Direct path loads have another serious limitation: You can't do them across heterogeneous platforms using Oracle Net.

If you want to apply SQL functions during the load, you have to use the conventional loading method. In a direct load, you can't use any SQL functions. If you need to perform a large data load and also transform the data during the load, you have a problem. The conventional data load will let you use SQL functions to transform data, but the method is very slow compared to the direct load. Thus, for large data loads, you may very well be forced to consider using one of the newer load/transform techniques such as the use of external tables and table functions, which you'll learn about later in this chapter. Here's a list of the advantages of using the direct path loading method as opposed to the conventional loading method:

- The load is much faster than in the conventional loading method because you aren't using SQL *insert* statements for the load.

- The direct load uses multiblock asynchronous I/O for database writes, so the writing is fast.

- You have the option of presorting data using efficient sorting routines with the direct load.

- By setting the *unrecoverable=Y* parameter, you can avoid the writing of any redo during a direct load.

- By using temporary storage, you can build indexes better during a direct load than using the conventional load.

 NOTE *A conventional load will always generate redo entries, whereas the direct path load will generate redo only under specific conditions. A direct load also won't fire any insert triggers, unlike the conventional load, which fires the triggers during the load. Users can't make any changes when a table is being loaded using a direct load, unlike in a conventional load.*

Besides the obvious advantages of a shorter load time, direct loading also helps you rebuild indexes and presort table data. Some SQL*Loader options are specific to the direct load method. Let's see how you can specify options during a direct load.

Setting Options for Direct Loads

Several SQL*Loader options are intended especially for use with the direct load option or are more significant for direct loads than conventional loads. The following sections contain a brief description of the each of the options relevant to the direct load method.

Direct

The *direct* clause has to be set to *true* in order for you to use the direct load method.

Example. DIRECT=true.

Rows

The *rows* parameter is crucial because you can use it to specify how many rows SQL*Loader will read from the input data file before saving the inserts to the tables. You use the *rows* parameter to set the ceiling on the amount of data lost if the instance fails during a long SQL*Loader run. Oracle recommends that you set the *rows* parameter such that data is saved to the table every 15 minutes. When SQL*Loader reads the number of rows specified in the *rows* parameter, it will stop loading data until all of the data buffers are successfully written to the data files. This process is called a *data save*. So if you want to set the *rows* parameter to where the data saves occur every 15 minutes, your *rows* parameter will be computed as shown in the following example (assume that SQL*Loader can load about 10,000 rows per minute):

Example: ROWS= 15*10000 = 150000 (rows)

Unrecoverable

If you want to minimize the use of the redo log, you can do so by using the *unrecoverable* parameter during a direct load.

Example: UNRECOVERABLE=true

Skip_Index_Maintenance

The *skip_index_maintenance* parameter, when turned on, instructs SQL*Loader not to bother maintaining the indexes during the load.

Default: false
Example: skip_index_maintenance=true

Columnarrayrows

This parameter determines the number of rows loaded before the building of the stream buffer. The size of the direct path column array is thus determined by this parameter. The default value for this parameter on my UNIX server is 5000.

```
Example: columnarrayrows = 100000
```

Streamsize

The *streamsize* parameter lets you set the size of the stream buffer. The default on my server, for example, is 256000, and I can increase it using the *streamsize* parameter.

```
Example: streamsize=512000
```

Multithreading

Under *multithreading,* the conversion of column arrays to stream buffers and the stream buffer loading are performed in parallel. On machines with multiple processors, the default for a direct load is to have multithreading turned on.

 CAUTION *While you're doing a direct load, sometimes the instance may fail halfway through, or SQL*Loader may run out of space that it needs to update the index or it may encounter duplicate values for the index keys. In such cases, the indexes will be unusable upon instance recovery. This situation is referred to as the* indexes left unusable condition. *In such cases, it may be better to create the indexes after the load is complete.*

Direct Loads and Constraint/Trigger Management

The direct path loading method inserts data directly into the data files by formatting the data blocks. By bypassing the *insert* statement mechanism, the table constraints and triggers aren't systematically applied during a direct load. All triggers are disabled and so are several integrity constraints. SQL*Loader automatically disables all foreign keys and check constraints. The not null, unique, and primary key constraints are still maintained by SQL*Loader. Upon completion of the SQL*Loader run, the disabled constraints are automatically enabled by SQL*Loader if the *reenable* clause has been specified. Otherwise, the disabled constraints have to be manually re-enabled. The disabled triggers are automatically enabled after the load is completed.

Tips for Optimal Use of SQL*Loader

The following list of tips will help you optimize SQL*Loader during data loads, especially when the data loads are large and/or you have multiple indexes and constraints on the tables in your database.

- Try to use the direct path loading method as much as possible. It's much faster than conventional data loading.

- Use the *UNRECOVERABLE=true* option wherever possible (in direct loads). This will save you considerable time, because the newly loaded data doesn't have to be logged in the redo log file. Media recovery is still in force for all the other users of the database, and you can always start a new SQL*Loader run if there's a problem.

- Keep the use of the *nullif* and *defaultif* parameters to a minimum. These clauses have to be tested for every single row on which they're used.

- Minimize the number of data type and character set conversions, as they slow processing down.

- Wherever possible, use positional fields rather than delimited fields. SQL*Loader can move from field to field much faster if it's given the position of the field.

- Map physical and logical records on a one-to-one basis.

- Disable constraints before the load, as the constraints will slow down the loading. Of course, you may sometimes end up with errors while enabling the constraints, but it's a small price to pay for a much faster data load, especially for large tables.

- If you're using the direct path loading method, specify the *sorted indexes* clause. This will optimize the load performance.

- If you're doing large data loads, it's smart to drop the indexes on the tables before the load. Index maintenance will slow down your SQL*Loader session. If it isn't possible to drop the indexes, you can make them unusable and use the *skip_unusable_indexes* clause during the load. If it's a direct load, use the *skip_index_maintenance* clause.

Using External Tables to Load Data

Up until now, you've seen how you can load data from an external file into an Oracle table using the SQL*Loader utility. For many years, Oracle DBAs have used SQL*Loader almost exclusively for loading data from outside sources, using either the conventional loading method or the direct path loading method. Oracle9*i*'s External Table feature goes one step further: It enables you to access data stored in operating system files without ever loading the data into a real Oracle table. Using the External Table feature, you can visualize external data "as if" it's stored in an Oracle table. When you "create" an external table, the columns are listed the same way as they are when you create a regular table. However, the data fields in the external file are merely "mapped" to the external table columns, not actually loaded into them.

The big difference between using external tables and the traditional SQL*Loader to load data from external sources is that the external tables are read-only. In addition, you can't have indexes and the standard table constraints on an external table. Yes, these are major differences from a regular table, and therefore external tables may not be an ideal replacement for SQL*Loader in many instances. But there are times when external tables are definitely the way to go. External tables offer a wonderful advantage. You can query data in the external data files, without loading the data into a staging table.

The following are the general advantages that the External Table method of loading offers in comparison with the SQL*Loader method:

- You can query data in the external files *before* it's loaded into the tables.

- External tables eliminate the need for staging tables.

- You may choose to perform data transformation at the same time you're loading data into the tables. This is called the *pipelining* of the two phases. When you use SQL*Loader to load directly into the tables, you can't perform anything other than the most minimal data transformation at load time. Consequently, major transformations have to be done in a separate step from that of data loading.

- External tables are suitable for large data loads that may have a one-time use for your database.

- External tables save the time involved in creating real database tables and then aggregating the data dimensions for loading into other tables.

- External tables eliminate the need to create staging or temporary tables, which are almost a must if you're using SQL*Loader to load the data from external sources.

- You don't need any physical space even for the largest external table. Once the data files are loaded into the operating system, you can create your external tables and start executing SQL queries against them.

TIP *External tables don't exist anywhere in the real sense inside or outside the database. The term "external table" implies that a given table structure is mapped to a data file that's located in an operating system file. When you create an external table, the only thing that happens in the database is the creation of new metadata entries in the data dictionary for the new table. Note that you can't change the data file's contents in any way while you're accessing its contents from within the database. In other words, you can only use the* select *command, not the* insert, update, *or* delete *commands when you're dealing with external tables.*

External tables are in no way as versatile as your regular database tables, because they're read-only tables. Furthermore, external tables suffer from the limitation that you can't index them. Therefore, high-powered query work with these tables is impractical. The real benefit of the external tables is mostly in data warehousing environments or in situations where you need to load and transform huge amounts of data when you first load an application's data.

NOTE *Here's an interesting article on Oracle Corporation's Web site that gives you more details about the External Table feature:* http://otn.oracle.com/products/oracle9i/daily/sept19.html.

Using External Tables for Data Loading

The external table description is also called the *external table layer,* and it is basically a description of the columns in your external table. This external table layer, along with the access driver, maps the data in the external file to the external table definition.

Suppose you have an external data file named sales.data that contains detailed information about your firm's sales data for last year. Your firm wants to perform product and time cost analysis based on this raw data. You create a table to do this analysis called the cost table. Now, the sales.data file contains a lot of detailed information on costs, but only in an aggregated form; your company wants the data to be aggregated, where distribution channels or regions break down the raw data. External tables are excellent for this kind of analysis, where you have large amounts of raw data available, but you only need certain transformed parts of this data loaded into your database tables. Let's discuss how to proceed in this case.

First, create an external table that includes providing the access parameters. The *create* statement for an external table is very similar to that of a regular table, except that in addition to the column definitions, you must provide the mapping for the columns to the data fields in the external data file. Also, the external table location must, of course, provide the operating system location of the external data file. The *access parameters* describe the external data in the data files. The *access driver* ensures that the external data is processed to match the description of the external table. So, first you need to describe the external table, and then you have to list the access parameters, in that order. Listing 12-3 shows how to create an external table.

Listing 12-3. Creating an External Table

```
SQL>    CREATE TABLE sales_ext(
  2      product_id number(6),
  3      sale_date date,
  4      store_id  number(8),
  5      quantity_sold number(8),
  6      unit price number(10,2))
  7      ORGANIZATION external (
  8      TYPE oracle_loader
  9      DEFAULT DIRECTORY ext_dat_dir
 10      ACCESS PARAMETERS
 11      (RECORDS DELIMITED BY NEWLINE CHARACTERSET US7ASCII
 12      BADFILE log_file_dir:'sales.bad_xt'
 13      LOGFILE log_file_dir:'sales.log_xt'
 14      fields terminated by "|" ldrtrim
 15      missing field values are null )
 16      LOCATION   ( '/u01/app/oracle/sales/load/sales.data'  ))
 17*     reject limit unlimited
SQL> /
Table created.
SQL>
```

Let's analyze this statement in detail. The statement *create table sales_ext (...)* describes the external table structure, with the *organization external* clause that follows it indicating that this isn't going to be a regular Oracle table, but rather an external table.

The *access parameters* clause is similar to the SQL*Loader control file, and it indicates the various options chosen as well as the location of the bad file and log file.

You can't place the external data files in any random operating system directory for obvious security reasons. You need to first create what is called a *directory object,* and then grant rights to specific users on this directory object:

```
SQL> create directory ext_dat_dir as '/usr/apps/datafiles';
Directory created.
SQL> grant read on directory ext_dat_dir to salapati;
Grant succeeded.
SQL>
```

Once you create *ext_dat_dir* and grant the proper rights, you can then use this as the default directory for placing all the external data files. The *location* parameter simply names the external data file, which is located in the default directory.

Next, create the new fact table called costs, which needs to have the aggregate inserted into it from the external data file (external table):

```
SQL> create table costs
  2  (sale_datee,
  3  product_id number(6),
  4  unit_cost number (10,2),
  5  unit_price number(10,2)
  6* );
Table created.
```

Now you're ready to insert the necessary aggregate data from the external table into the new costs table. Here's the code to do so:

```
SQL> insert /*append */ into costs
  (
  transaction_date,
  product_id, unit_cost,unit_price
  )
SELECT
  Transaction_date,
  Product_id,
  Sum(unit_cost),
  Sum(unit_price)
FROM sales_transactions_ext
GROUP BY time_id, prod_id;
SQL>
```

Note that you can insert only part of the columns in the external table if you choose, and you can transform the data *before* it's even loaded into your tables. This is one of the key differences between using external tables and SQL*Loader to load data into Oracle9*i* tables. I'm aware that the SQL*Loader tool permits you to do data transformation, but its capabilities in that area are extremely limited, as you saw earlier in this chapter.

Important Access Parameters for External Tables

When you create an external table by using the *organization external* clause, there are several external table parameters that you can use to specify the format of the data. Important among them are the following access parameters:

- *Record_format_info clause:* This is an optional clause and the default is *records delimited by newline.*

- *Fixed length:* When you specify a fixed length, you're indicating that all records in the external file are of the same length:

  Example: ACCESS PARAMETERS (RECORD FIXED 20 FIELDS (…))

- *Variable length:* The variable size indicates that each record may be a different size, the size being indicated by a number of digits before the beginning of each record.

  ```
  Example: ACCESS PARAMETERS (RECORDS VARIABLE 2)
  ```

  When you use the variable length parameters as shown previously, every record in this data set will have the following format, with the first two bytes indicating the length of the record:

  ```
  22samalapati1999dallastx
  ```

- *Delimited by:* This clause indicates the character that terminates each record. The most common delimiters are the pipe (|) and the comma (,).

- *Load when:* This clause indicates the conditions that may have to be satisfied before a record can be loaded into a table:

  ```
  Example: Load When (job != MANAGER)
  ```

- *Log file, bad file, discard file:* These are optional parameters, but a log file is always created by default. The bad file and the discard file are created only if data is rejected or data fails to meet a load-when condition.

- *Condition:* This variable compares all or part of a field against an arbitrarily chosen constant string:

Using SQL*Loader to Generate External Table Creation Statements

As you saw in the previous sections, creating external tables correctly and choosing the right access parameters can be a tedious task. Fortunately, there is an easier way to do all this: You can have SQL*Loader *generate* the entire DDL for creating the external tables and all the SQL statements to load the tables directly, without using SQL*Loader. The SQL*Loader parameter *external_table=generate_only* will allow you to generate the DDL for creating all your external tables. When you use this parameter, the SQL*Loader utility does not load any data from the external files. It instead outputs the following information in the SQL*Loader log file:

- A *create directory* statement

- A complete *create table* statement for the external table, with all necessary access parameters

- All *insert* statements needed for loading the internal tables

- The *delete* statements for the directory and the external table

Let's look at an example that illustrates how to generate the external table creation statements with the help of the SQL*Loader utility. In the following example, these are the names of the component fields and tables:

- The internal table name is test_emp.

- The control file for SQL*Loader is test_ctl.

- The SQL*Loader-generated external table name is sys_sqlldr_x_ext_test_emp.

- The control file for the load is called test.ctl, and it looks like this:

```
load data
infile *
into table test_emp
fields terminated by ',' optionally enclosed by '"'
(employee_id,first_name,last_name,hire_date,salary,manager_id)
begindata
12345,"sam","alapati",sysdate,50000,99999
23456,"mark","potts",sysdate,50000,99999
```

Invoke the SQL*Loader utility with test.ctl as your control file. Note that you're only generating the *create table* and *insert* statements—you aren't actually loading the tables.

```
[remorse] $ sqlldr userid=system/remorse1
control=test.ctl external_table=generate_only
SQL*Loader: Release 9.2.0.1.0 - Production on Sat Jan 4 10:43:34 2003
Copyright (c) 1982, 2002, Oracle Corporation.  All rights reserved.
[remorse] $
```

The log file for the preceding run, test.log, will have all the information in it now, including the external directory and table creation statements, and the actual *insert* statements to load the data into those tables. You can create the external table and then load the data directly using SQL without having to use the SQL*Loader utility again. Listing 12-4 shows the log file generated using the *external_table=generate_only* parameter.

*Listing 12-4. Using SQL*Loader to Generate the External Table Creation Statements*

```
SQL*Loader: Release 9.2.0.1.0 - Production on Sat Jan 4 10:43:34 2003
Copyright (c) 1982, 2002, Oracle Corporation.  All rights reserved.
Control File:   test.ctl
Data File:      test.ctl
  Bad File:     test.bad
  Discard File: none specified
 (Allow all discards)
Number to load: ALL
Number to skip: 0
Errors allowed: 50
Continuation:    none specified
```

```
Path used:      External Table
Table TEST_EMP, loaded from every logical record.
Insert option in effect for this table: INSERT
   Column Name                      Position  Len  Term Encl Datatype
   ------------------------------   --------- ---- ---- ---- --------------------
   EMPLOYEE_ID                      FIRST      *   ,   O(") CHARACTER
   FIRST_NAME                       NEXT       *   ,   O(") CHARACTER
   LAST_NAME                        NEXT       *   ,   O(") CHARACTER
   HIRE_DATE                        NEXT       *   ,   O(") CHARACTER
   SALARY                           NEXT       *   ,   O(") CHARACTER
   MANAGER_ID                       NEXT       *   ,   O(") CHARACTER
CREATE DIRECTORY statements needed for files
CREATE DIRECTORY SYS_SQLLDR_XT_TMPDIR_00000 AS '/u01/app/oracle/dba'
CREATE TABLE statement for external table:
CREATE TABLE "SYS_SQLLDR_X_EXT_TEST_EMP"
(
EMPLOYEE_ID NUMBER(6),
  FIRST_NAME VARCHAR2(20),
  LAST_NAME VARCHAR2(25),
  HIRE_DATE DATE,
  SALARY NUMBER(8,2),
  MANAGER_ID NUMBER(6)
)
ORGANIZATION external
(
  TYPE oracle_loader
  DEFAULT DIRECTORY SYS_SQLLDR_XT_TMPDIR_00000
  ACCESS PARAMETERS
  (
    RECORDS DELIMITED BY NEWLINE CHARACTERSET US7ASCII
    BADFILE 'SYS_SQLLDR_XT_TMPDIR_00000':'test.bad'
    LOGFILE 'test.log_xt'
    READSIZE 1048576
    SKIP 6
    FIELDS TERMINATED BY "," OPTIONALLY ENCLOSED BY '"' LDRTRIM
    REJECT ROWS WITH ALL NULL FIELDS
    (
      EMPLOYEE_ID CHAR(255)
        TERMINATED BY "," OPTIONALLY ENCLOSED BY '"',
      FIRST_NAME CHAR(255)
        TERMINATED BY "," OPTIONALLY ENCLOSED BY '"',
      LAST_NAME CHAR(255)
        TERMINATED BY "," OPTIONALLY ENCLOSED BY '"',
      HIRE_DATE CHAR(255)
        TERMINATED BY "," OPTIONALLY ENCLOSED BY '"',
      SALARY CHAR(255)
        TERMINATED BY "," OPTIONALLY ENCLOSED BY '"',
      MANAGER_ID CHAR(255)
        TERMINATED BY "," OPTIONALLY ENCLOSED BY '"'
```

```
      )
    )
    location
    (
      'test.ctl'
    )
)REJECT LIMIT UNLIMITED
INSERT statements used to load internal tables:
INSERT /*+ append */ INTO TEST_EMP
(
  EMPLOYEE_ID,
  FIRST_NAME,
  LAST_NAME,
  HIRE_DATE,
  SALARY,
  MANAGER_ID
)
SELECT
  EMPLOYEE_ID,
  FIRST_NAME,
  LAST_NAME,
  HIRE_DATE,
  SALARY,
  MANAGER_ID
FROM "SYS_SQLLDR_X_EXT_TEST_EMP"
statements to clean up objects created by previous statements:
DROP TABLE "SYS_SQLLDR_X_EXT_TEST_EMP"
DROP DIRECTORY SYS_SQLLDR_XT_TMPDIR_00000
Run began on Sat Jan 04 10:43:34 2003
Run ended on Sat Jan 04 10:43:35 2003
```

You can see that it's a lot easier to generate the *create table* statements for the external tables this way, rather than creating them from scratch.

Transforming Data

As you saw in the beginning of this chapter, in most cases, especially in data warehouse environments, data needs to be transformed to make it more meaningful for analysis. Several third-party tools are designed to perform various kinds of data transformation. In this chapter, though, I stress learning about how the Oracle9*i* database can help you perform sophisticated and efficient data transformation within the database itself, without your having to rely on external processes or tools. You have several ways of performing data transformations in Oracle9*i*, the most commonly used being the following:

- *Derive the data from existing tables:* You can use joins or aggregations of data from tables in the same database. Or you can gather the data from tables located in external Oracle or non-Oracle databases.

- *Use PL/SQL to transform data:* You can use PL/SQL procedural techniques to perform complex data transformations.

- *Use SQL to transform data:* The Oracle9*i* database offers several exciting techniques such as the *merge* statement, table functions, and multiple-table inserts to transform data during the loading process.

NOTE *The External Table feature of Oracle9i lets you use SQL and PL/SQL code to transform data. You have several other ways to perform data transformation. You'll examine the main Oracle9i data transformation techniques in more detail in the following sections.*

Deriving the Data from Existing Tables

It's common to derive your new transformed data from pre-existing tables in your database or other databases. You have two basic methods you can use to derive data from another table. If you're creating the table for the very first time, you can use the *create table as select * from* (CTAS) method to create new tables that meet your specifications. If the table already exists in your database or another database, you can use the *insert /* append */ as select* method.

If the tables are in external databases, you can still use the CTAS method by using database links. Using the CTAS method simply means that you create a new table, which is derived from an existing table. While you're creating the new table, you can apply certain SQL functions to the source table's columns, thereby transforming the data in the process. The following is a simple example showing the use of the CTAS method:

```
SQL> create table new_employees
  2  as
  3  select * from hr.employees;
Table created.
SQL>
```

The next example shows how to load data into an existing table from another table. The use of the *nologging* and *parallel* options in the example make the bulk insert run extremely fast.

```
SQL> insert /* append nologging parallel */
     into sales_data
     Select product id, customer_id, TRUNC(sales_date), 'S',
     discount_rate, sales_quantity, sale_price
     from  sales_history;
SQL>
```

Note that even though you used the parallel *hint* in the preceding *insert* statement, Oracle may not execute your *insert* statement in parallel because your session, by default, is in the *disable parallel mode*. You first have to use the following statement so any DML statements you issue can be considered for parallel execution:

```
SQL> alter session enable parallel dml;
Session altered.
SQL>
```

Once you have enabled parallel DML in your session, you can use the *parallel* hint in your DML statements and Oracle will parallelize its execution. There are several restrictions on the use of parallel DML. For example, you can't use parallel DML on a table that has triggers. Please refer to Oracle's documentation to see all the conditions that may preclude the use of the parallel DML feature.

Using PL/SQL to Transform Data

PL/SQL is an extremely functional language, and you can always write code to perform complex data transformations. The real issue here is whether you have the time and expertise at your disposal to code the transformation. In addition, when you're dealing with very large data sets, the use of PL/SQL is not very efficient when you compare it to some alternatives.

Using SQL to Transform Data

It's common to use SQL statements to perform various kinds of data transformations. In the following sections, you'll explore some of the common ways of using SQL to transform your data before loading.

Using the Update Statement

You can transform data by using simple *update* statements, although they could take a considerable time to execute in large tables. For smaller transactions in OLTP databases, the *update* statement is adequate when you have to transform data in a column based on some criteria.

Using the Merge Statement

The *merge* statement is a powerful means of transforming data, because it provides the functionality of checking the data to see if an update is indeed required for a given row. Suppose you're loading data from a data source into your table. You want to insert customer data only if the customer is a new customer. If the customer's data is already present in your table, you don't want to reload the data, of course, but you may want to merely update the customer's information based on the new data you just received. How would you go about doing this?

You could do this in SQL by doing a *two-pass* operation. In the first pass, you *insert* all rows that don't have a matching customer_id in your table. In the second pass, you *update* all rows that have matching customer_ids in the table. However, both methods are fairly tedious and take a long time.

The following listings show the traditional two-step insert/update method using separate *insert* and *update* statements. First, here's the update:

```
SQL> UPDATE catalog c
    SET
    (catalog_name, catalog_desc,catalog_category,
    catalog_price) =
    select (catalog_name, catalog_desc,catalog_category,
    catalog_price)
    from catalog_data where c.catalog_id=d.catalog_id;
```

Second, here's the insert:

```
INSERT INTO catalog cc
Select * from catalog_data d
Where c.catalog_id NOT IN
(select catalog_id from catalog_data);
```

You could do the preceding work using a lengthy PL/SQL code piece. The PL/SQL procedures have to match each input row against the table to see if it already exists. Based on the results of the checks, code that will either insert or update rows is executed. Whether you use SQL or PL/SQL, you can't avoid the inefficient multiple processing of the same data to complete your update/insert processing.

The *merge* statement, sometimes referred to as the *upsert* statement (because it does *both* an update and an insert using a single SQL statement), is a much more efficient way of performing traditionally multiple-pass operations such the one previously described. The *merge* statement enables you to perform both the update and insert operations in one pass. It's almost like using if-then-else logic. Listing 12-5 shows the same insert and update process, this time using the *merge* statement. The *merge* statement in Listing 12-5 indicates that if customer_id exists, *then update, else insert* into the table.

Listing 12-5. Using the Merge Statement to Perform an Update/Insert

```
SQL> merge into target  t
    using source s
    on (t.product_id=s.product_id)
    when matched then update set
    t.price=s.price,
    t.discount=s.discount
    when NOT matched then insert
    (product_id, product_code, product_desc,
    product_price, product_discount)
    values
    (s.product_id, s.product_code s.product_desc,
    s.product_price, s.product_discount);
```

Using Multitable Inserts

Suppose you need to insert data from the source table into several target tables. Further, you want this loading to be based on various conditions: If condition A, then load into table X, if condition B, then load into table Y, and so on. What is the best way to do this? Normally, you're forced to write several *insert* statements for inserting from the source into the target tables. If the data is very large, of course, this would slow down the data loading. Alternatively, you could write PL/SQL-based code to do the same thing, but that would also slow the process down.

Now there's a new type of SQL statement called a *multitable insert* that enables you to do fast conditional loads of data from one source into multiple table simultaneously. Because it's still a normal SQL statement, you can parallelize the operation to make the operation even faster. Multitable inserts can be either *unconditional* or *conditional*. You can also have a multitable insert that is a mix of conditional and unconditional inserts. The structure of the multitable insert varies depending on whether all or only some of the source table's rows are being loaded into the target tables. You'll look at examples of each type in the sections that follow.

NOTE *The performance gain from using a multitable insert is directly proportional to the complexity of the data and the number of target tables. Oracle claims that you can achieve a processing speed gain of 400 percent or more.*

Loading All the Rows from the Source Table

In the following example, the source table is a table called sales_activity, the data from which is loaded at the same time into two tables, sales and cost. When you load all rows of a table, you can use either an *unconditional all row insert* or a *conditional all row insert*. Let's look at the difference between the conditional and unconditional inserts.

The unconditional insert example uses the keywords *insert all*, meaning that all the source rows (sales_activity) are loaded into the sales and cost tables. After the *insert all* keywords, there can be several *into* keywords, each denoting an insert into a separate table. Notice that the *select* statement contains all the necessary columns required by both *into* statements for inserting into the two tables, sales and cost. The following code shows you how to perform an unconditional all row insert:

```
SQL> insert all
    Into target1 values (product_id,customer_id,sysdate,product_quantity)
    Into target2 values
    (product_id,sysdate,product_price,product_discount)
    Select s.product_id,s.customer_id,sysdate,s.product_quantity,
    s.product_price,s.product_discount
    from source s;
```

The conditional insert of all rows from the source table is very similar to the previous statement for an unconditional insert, except that you replace the first part of the *insert* statement with this statement. The keyword *when* indicates the conditions under which the inserts will be made. You are still inserting all the rows from sales_data because you are using the key phrase *insert all*. The following example shows how to perform a conditional all row insert:

```
SQL> insert all
    When product_id in (select product_id from primary) then
    Into target1 values (product_id,customer_id,sysdate,product_quantity)
    When product_id in (select product_id from secondary) then
    Into target2 values
    (product_id,sysdate,product_price,product_discount)
    Select s.product_id,s.customer_id,sysdate,s.product_quantity,
    s.product_price,s.product_discount
    from source s;
```

Loading Select Rows from the Source Table

Sometimes, you're interested in loading only some rows from a table, whether based on a condition or unconditionally. You can do this in a multitable insert by using the key phrase *insert first*. Listing 12-6 shows a how only some of the source table's rows are loaded into each target table, based on a separate condition for each table.

Listing 12-6. Partial Loading of Rows from the Source Table

```
SQL> INSERT FIRST
WHEN (quantitysold > 10 AND product id <1000)
THEN
     INTO targetA VALUES
     (sysdate,product_id,customer_id, quantity_sold))
WHEN quantity_sold <= 10 and product_id >10000 THEN
     INTO targetB VALUES
(sysdate,product_id,customer_id, quantity_sold)
    ELSE
    INTO targetC VALUES
    (time_id, cust_id, prod_id, sum_quantity_sold)
SELECT s.time_id, s.cust_id, s.prod_id, p.prod_weight_class,
SUM(amount_sold) AS sum_amount_sold,
SUM(quantity_sold) AS sum_quantity_sold
     FROM sales s, products p
WHERE s.prod_id = p.prod_id
And s.time_id = TRUNC(sysdate)
GROUP BY s.time_id, s.cust_id, s.prod_id, p.prod_weight_class;
```

Using Table Functions for Data Transformation

You can use Oracle9*i*'s table functions to perform efficient data transformations. Table functions produce a collection of transformed rows that can be queried just like a regular table's data. Oracle table functions are an excellent example of Oracle's sophisticated transform-while-loading paradigm. Table functions can take a set of rows as input and return a set of rows. When you query a table function in a statement, the function returns a collection type instance representing the rows in a table. The collection types can be either a varray or a nested table. Table functions allow you to use PL/SQL, C, or Java with SQL without any problems.

Table functions make the traditional use of staging tables redundant. You don't have to create any intermediate tables to perform data transformations before loading data into the final data warehouse tables. Three features make table functions a powerful means of performing fast transformation of data sets: streaming, parallel execution, and pipelining.

Streaming refers to the direct transmission of results from one process to the other without any intermediate steps. The way in which a table function orders or clusters rows that it fetches from cursor arguments is called *data streaming*.

Parallel execution, of course, is the concurrent execution of the functions on multiprocessor systems.

Pipelining lets you see the results of a query iteratively, instead of waiting for the entire result set to be batched and returned. Pipelining can thus help table functions reduce the response time by sending results as soon as they are produced in batches. You also have the option of having the table function immediately return rows from a collection by using pipelining. The elimination of (sometimes multiple) staging tables and the lack of need for any manual coding of parallel processing makes the "pipelined parallel processing" provided by table functions very attractive during large-scale data loading and transformation.

Here's a brief summary of the tasks that table functions can help you perform. A table function can do the following:

- Return a set of rows

- Return a result set incrementally, so you can process the results gradually

- Accept a cursor as an input

- Return results continuously while the transformation is taking place

- Be parallelized

It's easy to understand what a table function is when you think about a regular Oracle function. An Oracle function such as SUBSTR or TRANSLATE transforms data. For example, you can use the SUBSTR function to cut out a portion of a string, as shown in the following example:

```
SQL> select sysdate from dual;
SYSDATE
========
20-DEC-02
SQL> select substr(sysdate,4,3) from dual;
SUBSTRING(SYSDATE)
==================
DEC
SQL>
```

Table functions work the same way as regular Oracle functions that transform data. The only difference is that the table functions can be much more complex, and they can take cursors as inputs and return multiple rows after transforming them.

Where can you use table functions? Suppose you need to load data from a table using an *insert* statement. Also suppose that you don't need the data to be in the same format as the data in the source table. You can easily use the *insert* statement with one additional (automatic) step: You can use a table function to transform the data after it extracts the rows from the source and before the data gets inserted into your target table. So, your *insert* statement will look like the following. Instead of the normal statement

```
insert into target_table
select * from source_table;
```

you'll use the following *insert* statement:

```
insert  into target_table
select * from (Table Function(source_table));
```

Using a Table Function

Now you'll create a table function to illustrate how to use a table function to efficiently transform data. The table function uses a REF CURSOR to fetch the input rows. It then transforms the data and sends it out interactively (i.e., it pipelines the data).

Table sales_data is your original table. This table shows a holding company's stores and their sales figures for two years, 2001 and 2002. Your goal is to extract data from this table to a target table with a different format.

```
SQL> select * from sales_data;
STORE_NAME          SALES_2001    SALES_2002
------------------------- ---------- ----------------------------------
shoe city                               500000
trinkets galore     1400000       1500000
modern tools        1000000       1200000
toys and toys                           800000
SQL>
```

The new table is named yearly_store_sales, and it lists the company sales figures differently—each company's sales figure is listed year-wise. For example, in the original table, the store "modern tools" showed two yearly sales numbers in the same row: 1000000 and 1200000. In the new transformed table, these numbers should appear in different rows—that is, the data should show the store/sales_year combinations. To do this, the company name may have to appear more than once in this table:

```
SQL> create table yearly_store_sales
  2  (store_name    varchar2(25),
  3  sales_year   number,
  4* total_sales    number);
Table created.
```

Because table functions return *sets* of records, you need to create some special object structures to use table functions to transform data. The first object you need to create is an *object type* called yearly_store_sales_row, which reflects the records Note that the structure of this type is the same as your target table, yearly_store_sales.

```
SQL> create type yearly_store_sales_row as
  2  object(
  3  store_name     varchar2(25),
  4  sales_year number,
  5* total_sales number)
SQL> /
Type created.
```

The next step is to create a *table type* named yearly_store_sales_table. This table type is based on the object type you just created.

```
SQL> create type yearly_store_sales_table
  2  as
  3  table of yearly_store_sales_row;
Type created.
```

The package creation statement shown in Listing 12-7 is somewhat complex and it is the heart of the table function feature.

Listing 12-7. Creating the Table Function

```
SQL> create or replace package sales_package
  2  as
  3  type sales_cursor_type is REF CURSOR
  4  return sales_data%ROWTYPE;
  5  function modify_sales_data
  6  (inputdata in sales_cursor_type)
  7  return yearly_store_sales_table
  8  pipelined;
  9* end;
SQL> /
```

```
Package created.
SQL>
  1   create or replace package body sales_package
  2   as
  3   function modify_sales_data(
  4   inputdata IN sales_cursor_type)
  5   RETURN yearly_store_sales_table
  6   PIPELINED IS
  7   inputrec sales_data%rowtype;
  8   outputrow_2001 yearly_store_sales_row :=
      yearly_store_sales_row(null,null,null);
  9   outputrow_2002 yearly_store_sales_row :=
      yearly_store_sales_row(null,null,null);
 10   BEGIN
 11      LOOP
 12        fetch inputdata into inputrec;
 13        exit when inputdata%NOTFOUND;
 14        IF INPUTREC.SALES_2001 IS NOT NULL THEN
 15          outputrow_2001.store_name := inputrec.store_name;
 16          outputrow_2001.sales_year := 2001;
 17          outputrow_2001.total_sales:= inputrec.sales_2001;
 18          pipe row (outputrow_2001);
 19        end if;
 20        if INPUTREC.SALES_2002 is not null then
 21           outputrow_2002.store_name := inputrec.store_name;
 22          outputrow_2002.sales_year := 2002;
 23          outputrow_2002.total_sales:= inputrec.sales_2002;
 24          pipe row (outputrow_2002);
 25        end if;
 26      end loop;
 27      return;
 28   end;
 29*  end;
SQL> /
Package body created.
SQL/
```

Let's look at each part of the package carefully:

- In order to return sets of rows from the source table as inputs to the table function, you need to create a REF CURSOR based on the source table rows. The REF CURSOR in the example is named sales_cursor.

- The function modify_sales_data is your table function. It has one input parameter, the REF CURSOR sales_cursor. The function returns data in the format of your source table, yearly_store_sales.

- The keyword *pipelined* at the end means that data flows through the data transformation process. As the input data is processed, the transformed results are continuously fed into the target table.

- The package body shows the details of the function modify_sales_data. The function will transform the original structure of data in the source table into the desired format and insert it into the target table.

In the following *insert* statement, the function modify_sales_data is used in an *insert* statement. Note how the function is applied to the row data from the original table sales_data. The data is transformed before it is inserted into the yearly_store_sales table.

```
SQL> insert into yearly_store_sales t
  2  select *
  3  from table(sales_package.modify_sales_data(
  4  cursor(select store_name,sales_2001,sales_2002
  5  from sales_data)))
  6  /
6 rows created.
SQL> commit;
Commit complete.
```

Listing 12-8 shows the data in the new table. Note how the original data in the sales_data table has been transformed into a different format by the table function.

Listing 12-8. The Transformed Table

```
SQL> select * from yearly_store_sales;
STORE_NAME            SALES_YEAR    TOTAL_SALES
------------------------- ---------- -----------
shoe city             2002           500000
trinkets galore       2001          1400000
trinkets galore       2002          1500000
modern tools          2001          1000000
modern tools          2002          1200000
toys and toys         2002           800000
6 rows selected.
SQL>
```

The final *select* statement from the yearly_store_sales table shows a different layout of data from that of the original table, sales_data. Now each store has a new column and year, and the yearly sales data is now in separate rows. This makes it easier to see how the yearly sales figures of the various stores stack up. The example you see here is a trivial one, but it clearly illustrates how you can use table functions to easily transform data during the process of loading it into another table.

Using Table Functions to Mine Web Services Data

Web services are self-contained, modular applications that can be published and invoked on the Web. Web services can perform complex business processes or serve as information providers (e.g., a weather information service or a stock market ticker service). Let's see how table functions can help you mine the stock market information that is published on the Web to provide a stock price alert system. Due to space considerations, I'm only providing the outline of the system. Here is the stock price alert system process:

1. A private Web service run by a stock market information services is accessed to collect the stock price information.

2. A table function, using a REF CURSOR of stock symbols as inputs, calls a Java stored procedure to gather the stock information from the Web service. The table function converts the necessary stock price information into relational table data. The table function processes the information in the REF CURSOR one row at a time, and loads it into the table in a streamed fashion. You can have this information updated at regular intervals.

3. You can then use SQL and PL/SQL code to "mine" the stock data you collected in step 2. For example, the following is a typical SQL statement that uses the Web services data you downloaded into your database table(s):

```
SQL> SELECT avg(price), min(price),max(price)
     FROM
     TABLE(stock_service_pack.TO_TABLE
     (CURSOR(SELECT stock_symbol FROM stocks )));
SQL>
```

Some Useful SQL*Loader Data-Loading Techniques

Using SQL*Loader is a lot of fun and it's a fast means of loading data, but it's not without its share of headaches. This section contains some techniques to perform special types of operations during data loads.

Using the When Clause During Loads

You can use *when* clauses during data loads to limit the load to only those rows that match certain conditions. For example, in a data file, you can pick up only those records that have a field matching certain criteria. Here's an example that shows how to use the *when* clause in a SQL*Loader control file:

```
LOAD DATA
INFILE *
INTO table stagetbl
APPEND
 WHEN (activity_type <>'H') and  (activity_type <>'T')
FIELDS TERMINATED BY ','
TRAILING NULLCOLS
(Table columns Here …)
BEGINDATA
/* Data Here …*/
```

The *when* condition will reject all records where the data record field matching the activity_type column in table stagetbl is neither H nor T.

Loading the Username into a Table

You can use the *user* pseudo-variable to load the username into a table during the load. The following example illustrates the use of this variable. Note that the target table stagetbl should have a column called loaded_by so SQL*Loader can insert the username into that column.

```
LOAD DATA
INFILE *
INTO table stagetbl
INSERT
(loaded_by    "USER"
the table columns and the data follow ...)
```

Loading Large Data Fields into a Table

If you try to load any field larger than 255 bytes into a table, even if the table column is defined as varchar2(2000) or a CLOB, SQL*Loader won't be able to load the data. You'll get an error informing you that the "Field in data file exceeds maximum length". How do you get around this problem? Well, to manage the load of the large field, you have to specify the size of the table column in the control file when you're matching table columns to the data fields. Here's an example. Suppose you have a table column called text, which is defined as varchar2(2000). You won't be able to load this column normally if the data field is larger than the default maximum size of 255 bytes. Here's what you do:

```
Load data
Infile '/u01/app/oracle/oradata/load/testload.txt'
Insert into table test123
Fields terminated by ','
(text char(2000))
```

TIP *Even though your table column is defined as varchar2(2000), you must use char(2000) to overcome the default limit of 255 bytes for field sizes.*

Loading a Sequence Number into a Table

Suppose you have a sequence named test.seq, and you want this sequence to be incremented each time you load a data record into your table. Here's how to do it:

```
Load data
Infile '/u01/app/oracle/oradata/load/testload.txt'
Insert into table test123
   (test.seq.nextval,…)
```

Loading Data from a Table into an ASCII File

You may sometimes want to get data out of the database table into flat files. You can later use this data to load data into Oracle tables in a different location, for example. You can write complex scripts to do the job if there are a number of tables, but if there are few tables to load, you can use the following simple method of extracting data using SQL*Plus commands:

```
Set termout off
Set pagesize 0
Set echo off
Set feed off
Set head off
Set linesize 100
Column customer_id format 099999990
Column first_name format a15
Column last_name format a25
Spool test.txt
Select customer_id,first_name,last_name from customer;
Spool off
```

You may also use the UTL_FILE package (see Chapter 21) to load data into text files.

Identifying and Removing Duplicate Data

A typical problem encountered by DBAs while performing data loads is the existence of duplicate rows in a table. How do you quickly eliminate duplicate rows from your tables? You have to first identify if there are duplicate rows in a table. Then you need to remove the duplicate rows from the table. You have several ways to remove the duplicate rows, and Appendix A shows you the details.

Dropping Indexes Before Bulk Data Loads

There are two major reasons why you should seriously consider dropping indexes on a large table before performing a direct path load using the *nologging* option. First, it may take you a longer time to do the load with the indexes included with the table data. Second, if you leave indexes on, there will be redo records generated by the changes that will be made to the index structure during the load.

 TIP *Even if you choose to load data using the* nologging *option, there will be considerable redo generated to mark the changes being made to the indexes. In addition, of course, there will always be some redo to support the data dictionary, even during a* nologging *data load operation. The best strategy here is to drop the indexes and rebuild them after the tables are created first.*

Loading into Multiple Tables

You can use the same SQL*Loader run to load into multiple tables. Here's an example that shows how to load data into two tables simultaneously:

```
Load data
Infile *
Insert
Into table emp
(employee_id        position (1:8) integer external,
first_name          position (9:18) char,
last_name           position (19:37) char)
into table emp_address
(street_name        position(38:53) char
(house_no           position(54-60) integer external)
```

Trapping Error Codes from SQL*Loader

Here's a simple example of how you can trap the process error codes issued by SQL*Loader:

```
$ sqlldr parfile=test.par
retcode=$?
If [[retcode !=2 ]]
    Then
      mv ${ImpDir}/${Fil} ${InvalidLoadDir}/.${Dstamp}.${Fil}
      WriteLog $func "Load Error" "load error:${retcode} on file ${Fil}"
      Else
      Sqlplus / ___EOF
      /* You can place any SQL statements to process the successfully loaded data */
___EOF
```

Loading XML Data into an Oracle XML Database

SQL*Loader supports the XML data type for columns. If a column is of this type, you can use SQL*Loader to load the XML data into a table. SQL*Loader treats the XML columns as CLOBs. Oracle also lets you load the XML data either from a primary data file or from an external LOBFILE. You can use fixed-length fields or delimited fields. The contents of the entire file could also be read into a single LOB field.

Summary

This chapter introduced you to the powerful SQL*Loader utility. The SQL*Loader utility has been the tried-and-trusted companion of Oracle DBAs for efficiently loading large amounts of data into the database. In this chapter you learned how to invoke the SQL*Loader utility in different ways, and you learned the key options and parameters for executing data loads. The chapter also showed you how to use the direct path loading method to optimize data loads. All in all, SQL*Loader is one of the Oracle DBA's best friends, and you'll probably use it often not only for initially populating databases, but also for refreshing or modifying data in your Oracle9*i* tables.

Oracle9*i* provides you alternatives or complements to SQL*Loader, such as the new External Table feature, to load data into your tables. I included a detailed explanation of the External Table feature in this chapter. The *merge* function and the new *table functions* feature of Oracle9*i* are very powerful means of transforming data. They do require that you get deeper into SQL and PL/SQL, but the payoff is big, because you can do things with these features that previously took much more programming time and effort.

This chapter concluded by showing you how to handle several interesting situations you're likely to encounter during a data load.

Using the Export and Import Utilities

THE EXPORT AND import utilities are some of the most useful and frequently used tools in the Oracle DBA's toolkit. The SQL*Loader tool can only load data into the tables from external files, whereas the export utility can extract data out of the database in order to import it into another database or another table in the same database. Oracle's export and import utilities are highly flexible tools, and you can use them from the table level to the database level.

The import and export tools provide you with an efficient and easy way of getting data in and out of Oracle databases. You always use the export and import utilities in combination, because only the import utility can read export dumps produced by the export utility.

An interesting feature of the Oracle export/import facility is that you can export data from an Oracle database on the Windows platform to another Oracle database on the UNIX or any other platform. This feature helps you with migrating test databases from a small Windows SQL Server database, for example, to a large UNIX-based database.

This chapter begins with a detailed discussion of the export and import utilities. Next, it covers the topic of transportable tablespaces, which are a highly efficient and sophisticated means of transporting large amounts of data from one database to another. The chapter concludes with a discussion of several ways to optimize the export and import utilities, as well as some of the typical problems you may encounter while using these tools.

Exporting and Importing Data

When you export data out of database tables, you're sending it to a dump file, which the import utility can then use to load the data into tables in another database. As you saw in the previous chapter, the SQL*Loader tool can only load data into tables; you can't use it to extract data from tables. The export/import pair of tools can both load and unload data. This is a great functionality to have, as you'll need partial or full copies of the data in your table for many reasons. Here are some of the main uses of the export and import utilities:

- Migrating databases from development to test or production.

- Copying test data from development/testing databases to production or vice versa.

- Transferring data between Oracle databases on different operating system platforms.

- Backing up important tables before you make any changes to them.

- Backing up databases, although this isn't a perfect backup in the sense that you won't have up-to-the-minute data in the export file when a disaster occurs. Also, you can't easily back up huge databases using the export utility.

- Moving database objects from one tablespace to another.

- Transporting tablespaces between databases.

- Reorganizing fragmented table data.

- Extracting the DDL for tables and other objects such as stored procedures and packages.

As you'll see, the export and import utilities are extremely easy to use and versatile. You can export just the DDLs of objects if you wish, or you can export and import the objects with the data. You also have the choice of exporting and importing a single table (or even a part of a single table), all the tables in a table-space, an entire schema, or even an entire database.

You'll first examine the export utility in detail, after which you'll have a chance to look at the import utility. If you need to refer to the default values of some of the export/import parameters and see all the available parameters you can set, just type **exp help=y** at the command line. Oracle will print a complete menu of export and import parameters on the screen.

 NOTE *Performing an export or import of data using manual methods is tedious and error-prone. OEM provides excellent export and import wizards that let you quickly perform an export or import. You can also schedule these jobs using OEM. Before you can use the OEM's wizards, however, it's good to go through the manual processes to understand what's involved in using the export and import utilities.*

Using the Export Utility

You can use the export utility at the table, tablespace, user, or database level to create dump files of the tables, with or without the data, and a number of other objects such as indexes, synonyms, sequences, stored code, and so on. The output of the export utility is the export dump file, which can only be read by the import utility, to load data into a different table or a different database. You have several ways to use the export utility—for example, command line invocation and the use of a parameter file. But no matter which method you use, the parameters you can specify are the same, and they determine how the export is actually performed. The following section covers the set of export parameters.

Export Parameters

When you run the export utility, you can pretty much leave out most of the parameters that you'll see shortly—Oracle will use the default values for these parameters. You therefore need to know what the parameters are and what their default values are in order to control your exports.

> **TIP** *The only parameter that you must have is the* userid *parameter. If you invoke the export utility with just the* userid *parameter, by default Oracle will perform an export of the specified user's schema. That is, if you type* **exp userid=hr/hr**, *all of hr's tables will export to the default dump file* expdat.dmp.

In the following sections you'll examine in detail the parameters that you can specify when you invoke the export utility.

Userid

The format of the *userid* parameter is *userid=username/password*. You can use any user's name, but a user will be able to export only his or her schema by default. To be able to export the whole database, the user must be assigned the *export full database* role granted explicitly to the user. The role DBA is granted the export full database role.

```
Example: exp  userid = hr/hr
```

The *userid* parameter has several variations. You can specify this parameter in the following ways:

```
Userid = system/manager
Userid = system/manager as sysdba
Userid = system/manager@finance1
Userid= system/manager@finance1 as sysdba
```

Export Mode Parameters

You can specify that the export be performed at four different levels: table, tablespace, schema, or database. In the following sections you'll look at some examples of an export at various levels.

Table Level

When you use the export utility at the *table* level, you need to supply the list of tables as follows:

```
Example: $exp  userid=system/manager  tables = (employees,jobs,regions)
```

You can also use the following notation:

```
Example: $exp userid=system/manager  tables = (owner.pattern%)
```

The latter notation enables you to export a set of tables that share a common pattern, such as sysadm.hr or sysadm.finance. This makes it easy to export tables belonging to an entire application or a subset of an application.

Tablespace Level

The *tablespace* level option lets you export all the tables within a tablespace or a set of tablespaces. You don't have to specify the table names.

```
Example: $ exp userid=system/manager  tablespaces = (users)
```

The *tablespaces* parameter will export all the tables included in a tablespace or a list of tablespaces. The indexes associated with the tables are also exported. If a partitioned table has at least one partition in a tablespace, the entire partitioned table will be exported automatically.

NOTE *Only a DBA can perform a tablespace-level export for obvious reasons: A tablespace can potentially include objects belonging to more than one user in the database.*

Schema Level

Using the *owner* parameter, you can export an entire schema (user). Schema-level exports are especially useful when you want to migrate all the objects and/or data that belongs to a specific user in the database.

```
Example: exp userid=system/manager  owner = (sysadm)
```

Database Level

The parameter *full* will let you export the entire database. The syntax is as follows:

```
Example: $ exp=system/manger  full=y
```

NOTE *Only the DBA is allowed to perform a full database export. Chapter 14 shows how you can use a full export as a form of backup for your databases. The full database export mode further entitles you to specify an incremental export. An incremental export is an export that covers only the changes since the last export.*

Only the DBA can export another user's tables. A regular user can't export another user's tables. So, a regular user can't use the *full=y* option and the *owner=usr* option when the user isn't the exporter.

File Parameters

Several export parameters deal with files. These include the specification of the export dump file and other files such as the log files and the all-important parameter file, which is used to specify the export parameters. Let's look at the file parameters in detail.

File

The *file* parameter specifies the name of the export dump file. It defaults to expdat.dmp if you don't specify a dump filename.

```
Default: expdat.dmp
Example: $ exp userid = hr/hr  File = finance1.dmp
```

Log

The parameter *log* enables you to specify a log file for the export run. It's very important to have this file in case you need to troubleshoot the export. Besides, the log file will capture a lot of information: the tables exported, a summary of other types of objects exported, and so forth.

```
Default: no log file
Example: $ exp userid = hr/hr  log = finance1.log
```

Parfile

Instead of specifying all your parameters at the command line, you can do so inside a file called the *parameter file*, or *parfile.* You can then use *parfile=filename* as an option at the command line. If you're going to perform the same export many times, it's useful to place all the export parameters in the parfile, so you don't have to specify them explicitly each time you need to export the same set of data.

```
Default: none
Example: $ exp userid = hr/hr  parfile=finance1.par
```

Export Options

The export utility allows you to specify several options for your exports by using various parameters for the export. The following sections cover the important export parameters.

Compress

The *compress* option directs Oracle to consolidate all the data in an object into the first extent. So, if your table has 50 extents before the export, after the export you can import the table back and it will have one large extent. The default is to compress the extents.

```
Default: Yes
Example: $ exp userid = hr/hr   compress = Y
```

Rows

The *rows* option directs Oracle to export the data along with the table structure, and that's the default behavior of the export utility. Sometimes you may wish to extract just the DDL of the objects and not the data, in which case you set the *rows* parameter to *no*.

```
Default: y
Example: $ exp userid = hr/hr    rows=n
```

Query

The *query* clause enables the export of only parts of a table. The *query* clause involves the use of a *where* condition, which limits the export to only a subset of the table.

```
Default: none
Example: $ exp userid = hr/hr   tables = sales_data   query =
 \"Where sale_date \> sysdate -5\
```

The *query* clause in the preceding example will export only that part of table sales_data where the sale_date is not older than 5 days.

NOTE *You can specify the* query *parameter only during a table mode export. You can't use it during a full or user mode export. The* query *parameter forces you to export only a single table at a time.*

You can't specify the *query* parameter for tables that have nested tables. You also can't use the *query* parameter and the direct path option together. As you know, the direct path option bypasses SQL processing completely, whereas you need to use SQL processing to make the *query* parameter get you a subset of the table's data.

When you use the *query* parameter for a table export, the statistics exported with it become questionable. You're advised to recalculate the statistics after the import is completed. The reason for this, of course, is that the statistics were originally computed for the entire table, and the *query* clause exports only a subset of this table, thus making the use of the statistics questionable.

Direct

The *direct* option bypasses the buffer that evaluates expressions and writes directly to the export file. When you use the *direct* option, you're skipping the SQL layer, also called the *evaluation layer*.

```
Default: n
Example: $ exp userid = hr/hr  direct=Y
```

Recordlength

If you're using the direct path to export, you specify the buffer size that the export utility uses by specifying the *recordlength* parameter. The larger the buffer size, the more data that export will hold in memory before writing it all at once to disk. Obviously, the larger the buffer, the more efficient the writes to disk. Oracle recommends that the *recordlength* parameter be a multiple of the *db_block_size* parameter or the operating system block size. The maximum value of this parameter is limited to 64KB.

```
Default: operating-system dependent. Maximum size is 64K.
Example: : $ exp userid = hr/hr  recordlength=32000
```

Feedback

If you turn *feedback* on, the export process will indicate its progress on the screen. The progress is indicated in the form of a period for every *n* number of rows exported. In the next example, Oracle outputs a period onto the screen after every 1,000 rows exported.

```
Default: none
Example: $exp userid = hr/hr  feedback = 1000
```

Statistics

The *statistics* parameter directs Oracle to generate a specific type of statistics— computed or estimated—at import time.

```
Default: none
Example: $exp userid = hr/hr  statistics = compute
```

Indexes, Constraints, Grants, and Triggers

These four parameters determine whether these objects are exported along with the data in the tables. By default, all four (indexes, constraints, grants, and triggers) are exported automatically.

```
Default: y
Example: $exp  userid = hr/hr  indexes = n constraints = n grants = n triggers = n
```

Consistent

The *consistent* parameter ensures that the data being exported is consistent with a point in time and isn't being changed while export is running. The default is to export in a consistent mode.

```
Default: y
Example: $exp  userid = hr/hr  consistent = No.
```

Resumable Operation Parameters

Three export parameters are related to Oracle's Resumable Space Allocation feature. A brief description of the three parameters follows.

Resumable

The *resumable* parameter must be set to *yes* for the other two parameters, *resumable_name* and *resumable_timeout*, to be used. The default for this parameter is *no*, so you'll need to first set the parameter correctly for the other two resumable parameters to work.

```
Default: n
Example:  $ exp userid = hr/hr    resumable=y
```

Resumable_Name

The *resumable_name* parameter identifies the *resumable* statement.

```
Default: user=userid  session=sessionid  instance=instanceid
Resumable_name = 'nightly_consumer_data_load'
```

Resumable_Timeout

The *resumable_timeout* parameter specifies the time you have to fix the problem that caused the resumable operation to be stopped.

```
Default: 7200 seconds (2 hours)
Example: $exp userid = hr/hr  resumable_timeout = 14400
```

Flashback-Related Parameters

You need to set two special parameters if you're using Oracle's Flashback Query feature.

Flashback_Scn

If you set the *flashback_scn* parameter, the export utility will ensure that the data exported is consistent with this SCN.

Flashback_Time

If you specify the *flashback_time* parameter, the export utility will find the SCN closest to the time specified, and Oracle will use that SCN to enable flashback.

Default: none

Invoking the Export Utility

You can run the export utility interactively or through the command line. You'll look at both alternatives in detail in the sections that follow.

Interactive Use of Export

The interactive use of export is the easiest to understand for beginners, although it has several limitations. All you need to do to export data using the interactive method is type **exp** at the command line. The utility will then take over, prompting you for values of various parameters. Listing 13-1 shows a typical interactive export session.

Listing 13-1. An Interactive Export Session

```
Oracle@hp1  [/u01/app/oracle/admin/remorse/export
[remorse] $ exp
Export: Release 9.2.0.1.0 - Production on Sat Dec 21 10:37:23 2002
Copyright (c) 1982, 2002, Oracle Corporation.  All rights reserved.
Username: hr
Password:
Connected to: Oracle9i Enterprise Edition Release 9.2.0.1.0 - 64bit Production
With the Partitioning, OLAP and Oracle Data Mining options
JServer Release 9.2.0.1.0 - Production
Enter array fetch buffer size: 4096 >
Export file: expdat.dmp > hr.dmp
(2)U(sers), or (3)T(ables): (2)U > u
Export grants (yes/no): yes >
Export table data (yes/no): yes >
Compress extents (yes/no): yes >
Export done in US7ASCII character set and AL16UTF16 NCHAR character set
. exporting pre-schema procedural objects and actions
. exporting foreign function library names for user HR
. exporting PUBLIC type synonyms
. exporting private type synonyms
. exporting object type definitions for user HR
About to export HR's objects ...
. exporting database links
. exporting sequence numbers
. exporting cluster definitions
. about to export HR's tables via Conventional Path ...
. . exporting table                     COUNTRIES          25 rows exported
. . exporting table                     DEPARTMENTS        27 rows exported
```

```
. . exporting table                   EMPLOYEES     107 rows exported
. . exporting table                        JOBS      19 rows exported
. . exporting table                 JOB_HISTORY      10 rows exported
. . exporting table                   LOCATIONS      23 rows exported
. . exporting table                     REGIONS       4 rows exported
. exporting synonyms
. exporting views
. exporting stored procedures
. exporting operators
. exporting referential integrity constraints
. exporting triggers
. exporting indextypes
. exporting bitmap, functional and extensible indexes
. exporting posttables actions
. exporting materialized views
. exporting snapshot logs
. exporting job queues
. exporting refresh groups and children
. exporting dimensions
. exporting post-schema procedural objects and actions
. exporting statistics
Export terminated successfully without warnings.
oracle@hp1  [/u01/app/oracle/admin/remorse/export
```

In this export example, the user HR chose to export the entire schema (a user-level export). All the objects and the data in them are exported to the dump file called hr.dmp. As you can see, there isn't a whole lot to the interactive use of the export utility. The problem, however, is that the interactive mode won't let you modify many of the default parameters. Out of all the parameters you learned about in the previous section, only a handful of them—*buffer, filename, grants, compress*, and *rows*—can be chosen explicitly by the user. The level of export is limited to table, schema (user), or the entire database. You can't perform tablespace-level exports using the interactive mode. You also can't use a log file to capture information regarding the export run. By definition, you can't, of course, automate an interactive export.

Using the Command Line to Perform Exports

With all of its previously mentioned weaknesses, the interactive method is extremely limited. You can use the interactive mode for quick-and-dirty export and import of small amounts of data. The command-line invocation of the export utility gives you the opportunity to specify all the parameters you want, so you aren't forced to take the default values for several important parameters. Here's an example of how to invoke the export utility from the command line:

```
$exp  userid=/system/manager  rows=n tablespace=(users)
 log=finance.log statistics=n
```

As the number of parameters grows, the command line use of the export utility quickly becomes unwieldy. As in the case of SQL*Loader, you can use a parameter file to run the exports. The parameter file will include all the parameter values you want to specify, and you can invoke the export utility itself as follows:

```
$ exp  parfile=finance.par
```

The finance.par file looks like the following:

```
Userid=system/manager
Rows=n
Tablespace=(users)
Log=finance.log
Statistics=n
```

Messages and Error Codes for Exports

If the export is completely successful, the message at the end of the dump file is "Export terminated successfully without warnings" and the error code is EX_SUCC 0. If there are some recoverable errors, the message is "Export terminated successfully with warnings" and the error code is EX_OKWARN 0. If there are fatal errors, the message is "Export terminated unsuccessfully" and the error code is EX_FAIL 1.

What Is the Export Dump File?

The output of the export utility is the export dump file, which can only be read by the import utility to load data into a different table or a different database. The export dump file is not operating system–specific, so you can, for example, export a Windows-based Oracle database and use the resulting dump file to import into a UNIX-based Oracle database. The file itself is in a binary format, which you can view with an editor such as Notepad, but you may not edit it before an import, because that could corrupt the binary file.

The export dump file contains the DDL statements *create tablespace, create table, create index, create user, grants,* and so on, along with the table data. Listing 13-2 shows the partial contents of an export dump file.

Listing 13-2. Export Dump File Contents

```
EXPORT:V09.02.00
UHR
RUSERS
Sat Dec 21
 10:37:49 200  hr.dmp
BEGIN
sys.dbms_logrep_imp.instantiate_schema(schema_name=>'HR',
export_db_name=>'REMORSE.WORLD', inst_scn=>'1346809');
COMMIT; END;
CREATE SEQUENCE "DEPARTMENTS_SEQ" MINVALUE 1 MAXVALUE
 9990 INCREMENT BY 10 START WITH 280 NOCACHE NOORDER NOCYCLE
TABLE "COUNTRIES"
```

```
CREATE TABLE "COUNTRIES" ("COUNTRY_ID" CHAR(2) CONSTRAINT
 "COUNTRY_ID_NN" NOT NULL ENABLE, "COUNTRY_NAME"
 VARCHAR2(40), "REGION_ID" NUMBER,   CONSTRAINT
 "COUNTRY_C_ID_PK" PRIMARY KEY ("COUNTRY_ID") ENABLE )
 ORGANIZATION INDEX  PCTFREE 10 INITRANS 2 MAXTRANS 255
 STORAGE(INITIAL 65536 FREELISTS 1 FREELIST GROUPS 1)
 TABLESPACE "USERS" LOGGING NOCOMPRESS PCTTHRESHOLD 50
 INSERT INTO "COUNTRIES" ("COUNTRY_ID", "COUNTRY_NAME",
 "REGION_ID") VALUES Argentina AU  Australia BE Belgium BR  Brazil
 CREATE TABLE "DEPARTMENTS" ("DEPARTMENT_ID" NUMBER(4, 0), "
 INSERT INTO "DEPARTMENTS" ("DEPARTMENT_ID", "DEPARTMENT
 ALTER TABLE "LOCATIONS" ENABLE CONSTRAINT "LOC_C_ID_FK"
 ENDTABLE
 EXIT
 EXIT
```

Using the Import Utility

Only the import utility can read the export file dump to load data into your tables.
Import parameters and the invocation of the import utility are analogous to the
use of the export utility. In practice, however, the import part is where you are
going to have most of your problems. Existence of constraints, especially, is an
issue that could pose problems during imports.

Other issues exist, such as whether you should bring in the original table's statistics when you do the import. Note that unlike the SQL*Loader utility, the import
utility doesn't give you too many options when it comes to loading pre-existing
tables. You have to manually truncate or drop any existing tables before running
the import; otherwise, the data will be appended to the existing data. If constraints
don't permit the insertion of duplicate rows, for example, you'll get Oracle errors
during the import process.

The Order of Importing

The export file contains the exact sequence in which various objects are imported
into the database. First the table is created (if it isn't already present in the target
database). The table data is imported next, followed by all the indexes on that
table. Any constraints on the table are imported next. Finally, special indexes such
as the bitmap, functional, and domain indexes are imported.

Import Parameters

Just as in the case of the export utility, the import utility comes with a set of
parameters you can modify. Again, remember that if you don't set any parameter,
it stays at its default level. To see a complete list of parameters quickly, type
imp help=y at the operating system prompt. The following sections cover the
important import parameters.

Userid

This is the username and password combination for the user doing the import. Only a DBA can import a file exported by another DBA. This means that if you did the export as the user System, you need to do the import again with the user System or someone who possesses the DBA role. In addition, only a DBA can import another user's objects.

The *userid* parameter has several variations. You can specify the parameter in the following ways:

```
Userid = system/manager
Userid = system/manager as sysdba
Userid = system/manager@finance1
Userid= system/manager@finance1 as sysdba
```

File-Related Parameters

Like the export utility, the import utility has several file-related import parameters. You'll examine the important ones in the following sections.

File

The *file* parameter refers to the input file where the export dump is created. The default name for it is expdat.dmp if no filename has been explicitly specified during the export.

```
Default: expdat.dmp
Example: imp userid=system/manager  file=hrexport.dmp
```

Log

The *log* parameter enables you to specify a log file for the import. All import log files automatically receive a .log suffix.

```
Default: none
Example: imp userid=system/manager  log==hrexport
```

Parfile

If you choose to use a parameter file to specify all your parameters for the import, you need to use the *parfile* parameter.

```
Default: none
Example: imp  userid=system/manager  parfile=salesimp.par
```

Specifying Objects to Be Imported

Several parameters enable you to specify whether or not you wish to import certain objects during the import process. These objects include grants, indexes, and constraints. In addition, you can specify whether you want the data itself (i.e., the rows in the tables) to be imported or just the table and index definitions. The following sections cover the important object-related import parameters.

Grants

The *grants* parameter specifies whether or not you want to import the object grants. By default, this parameter is always set to *y*.

```
Default: y
Example: : $imp userid = hr/hr  grants=n
```

Indexes

The *indexes* parameter specifies whether or not you want indexes to be imported. The default for this parameter is *y*. If you have any indexes in an unusable state, you should also set the *skip_unusable_indexes* parameter to *y*. Otherwise, the import utility will issue errors when it tries to update the unusable indexes.

```
Default: y
Example: indexes=n
```

Rows

The *rows* parameter specifies whether or not you want the table rows to be imported.

```
Default: y
Example: rows=y
```

Constraints

The *constraints* parameter specifies whether or not you want the object constraints to be imported. The default is *y*. If a table has referential constraints pointing to another table, you may run into some problems during the import. For example, in the sales table, the column product references the product column in table product. If you import the sales table before you import the product table, the import utility will issue an error because the sales table's product must first exist in the product column. One way to avoid this is to disable the referential integrity constraints. Another way is to switch the order and import the product table before the sales table is imported.

```
Default: y
Example: imp userid = hr/hr constraints=n
```

Import Mode Parameters

You can perform an import at three different levels, with each level corresponding to a similar level on the export side.

- *Full:* The full mode imports an entire database, and you'll normally use it when you're setting up several versions of a database or you're importing a test database into a production version.

- *Schema level:* By specifying the *fromuser* and the *touser* parameters, you can import an entire schema (user). You're allowed to do import only your own schema, unless you're a DBA or you've been granted the import full database privilege. You use the *fromuser* and *touser* parameters in the following way (note that the *touser* parameter is necessary only if you're importing objects into a different schema than the one they were exported from):

  ```
  Example: $ imp userid=system/manager  fromusr=hr tousr=salapati
  ```

  In the preceding example, user hr's schema is imported into user salapati's schema. If no *touser* parameter is offered, then the import will be performed into the user specified in the *fromuser* parameter (in this case, hr).

- *Table:* In the table mode, a specified set of tables can be imported into the target database.

  ```
  Example: imp userid=system/manager  full=y
              Imp userid=system/manager  fromuser=hr  touser=hr
              Imp userid=system/manager  tables=(employees,jobs)
  ```

You can export all the tables in a tablespace by specifying the *tablespaces* parameter during an export. However, while importing, the *tablespaces* parameter doesn't work in a corresponding way. That is, you just can't use the *tablespaces* parameter to import all the objects in the export dump file into the target tablespace. You have to use the *full=y, tables= (table list)*, or *fromuser=touser* option to perform the import of the tables in the tablespace. Of course, you can transport the entire tablespace by using the *transport_tablespace* parameter, in which case the metadata belonging to the tablespace is imported. When you use the *tablespaces* parameter after specifying the *transport_tablespace* parameter, the tables in the tablespaces can be imported. You can see this in detail in the section "Transportable Tablespaces" later on in this chapter. Just as in the case of export, you have several options that you can specify for the import process. You'll look at the important import options in the next section.

Import Options

In addition to specifying parameters such as the *userid* and filenames, you can also specify several options that control various aspects of the import process, such as the memory allocated to it. You can also tell the import utility what to do if the object it's trying to create and load already exists in the database. Proper selection of import options will prevent errors and make the process more efficient. Let's look at some of the import parameters of Oracle9*i*.

Buffer

The *buffer* parameter indicates the size of the insert data buffer while performing the import. The higher the value of the *buffer* parameter, the more rows in each array-insert during the import process. If you're importing long data, too small of a buffer size will result in errors and slow down your import considerably. A buffer size that's too large may lead to memory problems for the operating system (e.g., paging and swapping). Use a trial-and-error method and increase the buffer size by a little each time.

```
Default: operating system dependent
Example: imp userid = hr/hr  buffer=64000
```

NOTE *The import utility performs a commit only after loading the entire table; this is its default behavior. If you want the commits to be done more often, you need to specify the* commit=Y *option in combination with the* buffer *parameter. This way, import will commit after each array-insert, the length of which is specified by the* buffer *parameter.*

Feedback

The *feedback* parameter is purely an import progress indicator parameter. If you set *feedback=Y*, the import utility will display a dot each time a specified number of rows have been successfully imported into the tables. In the example that follows, the *feedback* option asks the import utility to output a dot to the screen after the import of every 10,000 rows. This is the easiest way to monitor how fast your import process is loading rows into the tables.

```
Default: none
Example: imp userid=system/manager  feedback=10000
```

Show

When you specify the *show* parameter by typing **show=y**, the import utility will show you all the SQL statements that are part of the export dump file. It won't perform any actions based on the statements. This gives you a good idea of exactly what objects the import utility is going to create during the import process. Listing 13-3 shows the partial output from the *show* option.

Listing 13-3. Using the Show Option

```
Example: $ imp userid=system/manager fromuser=hr touser=hr show=y
oracle@hp1.  [/test01/app/oracle/export]
[finance1] $imp userid=system/manager file=hrexport.dmp show=y
 fromuser=hr touser=hrImport: Release 9.2.0.1.0
- Production on Sat Dec 21 10:10:46 2002
(c) Copyright 2001 Oracle Corporation.  All rights reserved.
```

```
Connected to: Oracle9i Enterprise Edition Release 9.0.1.0.0 - 64bit Production
With the Partitioning option
JServer Release 9.2.0.1.0 - Production
Export file created by EXPORT:V09.00.01 via conventional path
import done in US7ASCII character set and AL16UTF16 NCHAR character set
. importing HR's objects into HR ALTER SESSION SET CURRENT_SCHEMA= "HR""
 "CREATE SEQUENCE "DEPARTMENTS_SEQ" MINVALUE 1
MAXVALUE 9990 INCREMENT BY 10 "
 "START WITH 280 NOCACHE NOORDER NOCYCLE"
  "9999 INCREMENT BY 1 START WITH 207 NOCACHE NOORDER NOCYCLE"
 "CREATE TABLE "COUNTRIES" ("COUNTRY_ID" CHAR(2)
 CONSTRAINT "COUNTRY_ID_NN" NOT NULL ENABLE, "COUNTRY_NAME"
 VARCHAR2(40), "REGION_ID" NUMBER,  CONSTRAINT
"COUNTRY_C_ID_PK" PRIMARY KEY ("COUNTRY_ID") ENABLE )
 ORGANIZATION INDEX " " PCTFREE 10 INITRANS 2 MAXTRANS 255
 STORAGE(INITIAL 16777216 FREELISTS 1 FREELIST GROUPS 1)
 TABLESPACE "USERS" LOGGING NOCOMPRESS PCTTHRESHOLD 50"
 "COMMENT ON COLUMN "EMPLOYEES"."DEPARTMENT_ID" IS
 'Department id where employee works; foreign key to department_id
column of the departments table'"
 "CREATE TABLE "JOBS" ("JOB_ID" VARCHAR2(10)
, "JOB_TITLE" VARCHAR2(35) CONSTR"
 "AINT "JOB_TITLE_NN" NOT NULL ENABLE, "MIN_SALARY"
NUMBER(6, 0), "MAX_SALARY"
 "" NUMBER(6, 0))  PCTFREE 10 PCTUSED 40 INITRANS 1 MAXTRANS 255 STORAGE(INIT"
 "IAL 16777216 FREELISTS 1 FREELIST GROUPS 1)
 TABLESPACE "USERS" LOGGING"
 "GRANT SELECT ON "JOBS" TO "TESTER2""
 "ALTER TABLE "DEPARTMENTS" ENABLE CONSTRAINT "DEPT_LOC_FK""
 "ALTER TABLE "LOCATIONS" ENABLE CONSTRAINT "LOC_C_ID_FK""
Import terminated successfully without warnings.
oracle@hp1   [/test01/app/oracle/export]
```

Indexfile

The *indexfile* parameter gives you a handy way to capture all the *create index* statements in a file, the index file. Why would you want to use the *indexfile* option? You may decide to just load the tables and not the indexes during the import to make the process quicker. In such a case, you can specify the *indexes=n* option and use the index file to create the indexes after you complete the import.

```
Default: none
Example: imp  userid=system/manager  full=y indexfile= salesindex.sql
```

Listing 13-4 shows an excerpt from the index file you just created, the salesindex.sql file.

NOTE *All non–index creation statements are marked as comments (by using the REM before the line). Thus, if you just execute salesindex.sql in SQL*Plus, you can create all the indexes in the target database. As you can see, the use of the index file makes the extraction of the index creation statements a simple matter.*

Listing 13-4. An Index File Generated by the Import Utility

```
CREATE UNIQUE INDEX "REPOWNER"."EXUPD_PK" ON "VBZ$EX_UPDATES" ("DB_OBJ_ID"
, "VERSION_NO" ) PCTFREE 10 INITRANS 2 MAXTRANS 255 STORAGE(INITIAL 65536
FREELISTS 1 FREELIST GROUPS 1) TABLESPACE "OEM_REPOSITORY" LOGGING ;
REM  ALTER TABLE "REPOWNER"."VBZ$EX_UPDATES" ADD CONSTRAINT "EXUPD_PK"
REM  PRIMARY KEY ("DB_OBJ_ID", "VERSION_NO") USING INDEX PCTFREE 10
REM  INITRANS 2 MAXTRANS 255 STORAGE(INITIAL 65536 FREELISTS 1 FREELIST
REM  GROUPS 1) TABLESPACE "OEM_REPOSITORY" LOGGING ENABLE ;
REM  CREATE TABLE "REPOWNER"."VBZ$HISTORY" ("HISTORY_ID" NUMBER NOT NULL
REM  ENABLE, "ACTION_OWNER" VARCHAR2(256), "OBJECT_TYPE" NUMBER,
REM  "OBJECT_OWNER" VARCHAR2(256), "OBJECT_NAME" VARCHAR2(50),
REM  "OBJECT_VERSION" NUMBER, "OPERATION" NUMBER, "OPERAND_1"
REM  VARCHAR2(64), "OPERAND_2" VARCHAR2(64), "STATUS" NUMBER, "MONITORED"
REM  NUMBER, "START_DATE" DATE, "END_DATE" DATE, "REP_OBJ_ID" NUMBER)
REM  PCTFREE 10 PCTUSED 40 INITRANS 1 MAXTRANS 255 STORAGE(INITIAL 65536
REM  FREELISTS 1 FREELIST GROUPS 1) TABLESPACE "OEM_REPOSITORY" LOGGING
REM  NOCOMPRESS ;
REM  ... 0 rows
CREATE UNIQUE INDEX "REPOWNER"."HIST_PK" ON "VBZ$HISTORY" ("HISTORY_ID" )
PCTFREE 10 INITRANS 2 MAXTRANS 255 STORAGE(INITIAL 65536 FREELISTS 1
FREELIST GROUPS 1) TABLESPACE "OEM_REPOSITORY" LOGGING ;
CREATE INDEX "REPOWNER"."OTS_INDEX" ON "VBZ$HISTORY" ("OBJECT_OWNER" ,
"OBJECT_TYPE" , "STATUS" ) PCTFREE 10 INITRANS 2 MAXTRANS 255
STORAGE(INITIAL 65536 FREELISTS 1 FREELIST GROUPS 1) TABLESPACE
"OEM_REPOSITORY" LOGGING ;
CREATE INDEX "REPOWNER"."TS_INDEX" ON "VBZ$HISTORY" ("OBJECT_TYPE" ,
"STATUS" ) PCTFREE 10 INITRANS 2 MAXTRANS 255 STORAGE(INITIAL 65536
FREELISTS 1 FREELIST GROUPS 1) TABLESPACE "OEM_REPOSITORY" LOGGING ;
```

Destroy

When you're importing, the import utility will create any tablespaces that are necessary. If you specify *destroy=y*, the utility will overwrite any files with the same name as the data file names in the export dump file, on the server. The *destroy* option is set to *n* by default, and it may be judicious to leave it that way, unless you really have a need to change it to *y*.

```
Default: n
Example: imp userid = hr/hr destroy=y
```

Ignore

The import utility will attempt to create all database objects such as tables and indexes by default. If the table already exists, even if it's empty, the import utility will issue an error because of the object's existence and not import any data into the object. By using the *ignore=y* option, you can tell the import utility to overlook the object's prior existence and go ahead and load data into it.

```
Default: n
Example: imp userid=system/manager  ignore=y
```

Optimizer Statistics

The import utility offers you several choices regarding the table statistics that are automatically exported by the export utility. It may not be smart to always use these statistics, though. As you saw in the "Using the Export Utility" section earlier in this chapter, a partial export of a table using the *query* parameter may not accurately reflect the statistics gathered by Oracle for the entire table. It's better in such circumstances to not import these statistics; rather, you should compile them afresh after the import.

Here the options you have regarding importing table statistics:

- *Always:* this is the default behavior of the import utility. It will import all statistics under all circumstances.

- *None:* No statistics are imported.

- *Safe:* Import statistics only if they aren't questionable. Oracle tags the statistics if they're questionable.

- *Recalculate:* Recalculate the statistics while performing the import.

Resumable Parameters

The Resumable Space Allocation feature applies to the import utility and the export utility. Sometimes while you're performing an import, you'll run out of space. Setting the resumable parameters will prevent your import process from aborting, as you have a predetermined amount of time to fix the problem (usually by allocating additional space to the database) and resume the import process from where it stopped. The three parameters described in the following sections pertain to the Resumable Space Allocation feature.

Resumable

You specify the *resumable* parameter to turn Resumable Space Allocation on and off. By default, this feature is turned off.

```
Default: n
Example: imp=system/manager  resumable=y
```

Resumable_Name

If the *resumable* parameter is set to *y*, then you may use the *resumable_name* parameter to specify a name for the resumable operation.

```
Default: n
Example:. imp userid = hr/hr resumable_name=test_resumable
```

Resumable_Timeout

The *resumable_timeout* parameter specifies the time within which the error that stopped an export (due to space problems) is fixed. You can use this parameter, of course, only if you've already set the *resumable=y* option.

```
Default: 7200 seconds (2 hours)
Example: imp  system/manager  resumable=y  resumable_timeout=14400
```

Invoking the Import Utility

You can invoke the import utility from the command line and use it interactively, or you can perform the entire process using a parameter file, with no interaction with the utility. As with the export utility, the interactive use of the import utility seriously limits the number of parameters that you can explicitly choose—you're forced to accept several default parameters. Using the command line is a far better approach, and using parameter files will make it easy for you to run the import utility and enable automatic import scheduling.

An Import Example

Listing 13-5 shows a typical import session. The import was done at the user level. First, the hr schema is dropped from the remorse database. Then, the user hr is re-created. Using the export dump file, user hr's objects and data are imported into the database. Note that you are given a choice of importing the objects without any data. The utility also asks you whether it should ignore errors due to the objects being already present in the database. The import utility always attempts to create the tables and other objects before inserting rows into them. If a table already exists, you must specify the *ignore=yes* option, and the import utility won't issue any errors.

Listing 13-5. An Import Session

```
oracle@hp5   [/u01/app/oracle/admin/remorse/export
[remorse] $ imp
Import: Release 9.2.0.1.0 - Production on Sat Dec 21 11:22:29 2002
Copyright (c) 1982, 2002, Oracle Corporation.  All rights reserved.
Username: hr
Password:
Connected to: Oracle9i Enterprise Edition Release 9.2.0.1.0 - 64bit Production
```

```
With the Partitioning, OLAP and Oracle Data Mining options
JServer Release 9.2.0.1.0 - Production
Import file: expdat.dmp > hrnew.dmp
Enter insert buffer size (minimum is 8192) 30720>
Export file created by EXPORT:V09.02.00 via conventional path
import done in US7ASCII character set and AL16UTF16 NCHAR character set
List contents of import file only (yes/no): no >
Ignore create error due to object existence (yes/no): no >
Import grants (yes/no): yes >
Import table data (yes/no): yes >
Import entire export file (yes/no): no >
Username: hr
Enter table(T) or partition(T:P) names. Null list means all tables for user
Enter table(T) or partition(T:P) name or . if done:
. importing HR's objects into HR
. . importing table                "COUNTRIES"          25 rows imported
. . importing table                "DEPARTMENTS"        27 rows imported
. . importing table                "EMPLOYEES"         107 rows imported
. . importing table                     "JOBS"          19 rows imported
. . importing table                "JOB_HISTORY"        10 rows imported
. . importing table                "LOCATIONS"          23 rows imported
. . importing table                  "REGIONS"           4 rows imported
About to enable constraints...
Import terminated successfully without warnings.
oracle@hp5   [/u01/app/oracle/admin/remorse/export
    [remorse] $
```

Messages and Error Codes for Imports

If the import is completely successful, you'll see the message "Import terminated successfully without any errors" at the end of your import. The exit code for this is EX_SUCC 0. If there are some unrecoverable errors, such as the import trying to create already existing objects, errors are issued but the rest of the import will continue. You'll get the message "Import terminated successfully with warnings" with the resulting error code EX_OKWARN 0. Finally, if there are fatal errors, the import utility will abort with the message "Import terminated unsuccessfully". This results in an error code of EX_FAIL.

Transportable Tablespaces

Oracle's transportable tablespaces feature offers you an easy way to move large amounts of data between databases efficiently by simply moving data files from one database to the other. Instead of re-creating the objects, transportable tablespaces enable you to move large objects effortlessly in a fraction of the time it takes to re-create them manually in a database. Oracle recommends strongly that you use the transportable tablespaces feature wherever applicable, because of its superiority to other methods of moving data between databases.

Why do I discuss the transportable tablespaces feature in a chapter covering the export and import utilities? Transporting tablespaces involves copying all the data files belonging to the source database to the target database and importing the data dictionary information about the tablespaces from the source database to the target database. Thus, the export and import utilities are part of the transportable tablespaces feature, and that's why I include coverage of this feature in this chapter. You can also transport the index tablespaces pertaining to the tables, which makes the entire data transfer extremely fast. The whole operation will only take a little longer than the time it takes for you to copy the data files belonging to the tablespace to the new location, either by using FTP, remote copy, or some other method (e.g., using a tape copy).

An important limitation of the transportable tablespaces feature, unlike the use of the export and import utilities, is that all the databases involved in the transport of the tablespaces should be on the same operating system platforms. Furthermore, you can't transport any materialized views under this method.

Uses of Transportable Tablespaces

Transportable tablespaces are used mainly in the context of data warehouse, but they can be used fruitfully in any kind of database. The following are some of the important uses of the transportable tablespaces feature:

- Moving data from a staging database into a data warehouse

- Moving data from a data warehouse to a data mart

- Moving data from OLTP databases to a decision support data warehouse

- Performing tablespace point-in-time recovery (PITR)

- Archiving historical data

Transporting a Tablespace

Let's quickly go through the steps involved in transporting a tablespace between two databases. Note that the tablespace you're transporting must not already exist in the target database.

Select the Tablespaces to Be Transported

The primary condition you have to meet for transporting tablespaces is that the set of candidate tablespaces must be *self-contained*. For example, if the tables in the tablespaces have any indexes, they should be contained in one of the tablespaces in the set you're transporting. Referential integrity constraints for objects inside the tablespace being transported must not refer to objects outside the tablespace.

You must meet a few other conditions when you're importing tablespaces containing partitioned tables (please refer to the "Oracle9*i* Database Administrator's Guide" for the complete set of conditions). One way to verify that your set of tablespaces meets the self-contained criteria is by using the DBMS_TTS package as follows:

```
SQL> execute sys.dbms_tts.transport_set_check('sales01,sales02',true);
PL/SQL procedure successfully completed.
SQL>
```

The procedure *transport_set_check* returns no errors, indicating that the two tablespaces in your transportable tablespaces set, sales01 and sales02, are self-contained and therefore are eligible candidates for transporting. You can further confirm this by querying the transport_set_violation table. The transport_set_violation table lists all the partially contained tables in a tablespace and any references between objects belonging to different tablespaces.

```
SQL> select * from sys.transport_set_violation
no rows selected
SQL>
```

Generate the Transportable Tablespace Set

Before you can transport your tablespaces to the target database, you must generate a *transportable tablespace set*. The transportable tablespace set consists of all the data files in the tablespaces plus the export dump file, which contains the structural data dictionary information about the tablespaces.

The first thing you need to do before transporting a tablespace is to put the tablespaces in a *read-only* mode. If there are active transactions modifying the tables, you can't transport the tablespace. If your objective is to export a very large table or a part of a very large table, then create a new tablespace where you can create a new table that holds the data you are interested in. You can then transport this new tablespace to a different database.

```
SQL> alter tablespace sales01 read only;
Tablespace altered.
SQL> alter tablespace sales02 read only;
Tablespace altered.
SQL>
```

Once you've put both tablespaces that you want to transport in the read-only mode, you have two things left to do to generate your transportable tablespaces set. First, you must use the export utility to generate the data dictionary metadata for the two tablespaces, sales01 and sales02. Second, you must physically copy all the data files in the two tablespaces and the export dump file to a directory that the target database can access. The next two sections show you how to perform these steps.

Export the Dictionary Information for the Tablespaces

The first step in creating the transportable tablespaces set is to perform the export of the tablespaces you want to export. Here's the interesting part about the transportable tables feature: No matter how large the tablespace is, this step gets done very quickly because all you're exporting is the data dictionary information (metadata) about the objects in the tablespace. No table rows are being exported here. You also have the option of using the parameter *tts_full_check=y*, in which case the export utility will ensure that the tablespaces being exported are fully contained. However, you've already ascertained this in the previous step, so you can leave this parameter off. Listing 13-6 shows the export of the metadata for the pair of tablespaces.

Listing 13-6. Exporting the Dictionary Metadata for the Tablespaces

```
[remorse] $ exp transport_tablespace=y tablespaces=sales01,sales02
 triggers=y constraints=y grants=y file=sales.dmp
Export: Release 9.2.0.1.0 - Production on Sun Dec 22 11:20:44 2002
Copyright (c) 1982, 2002, Oracle Corporation.  All rights reserved.
Username: sys/remorse1 as sysdba
Connected to: Oracle9i Enterprise Edition Release 9.2.0.1.0 - 64bit Production
With the Partitioning, OLAP and Oracle Data Mining options
JServer Release 9.2.0.1.0 - Production
Export done in US7ASCII character set and AL16UTF16 NCHAR character set
Note: table data (rows) will not be exported
About to export transportable tablespace metadata...
For tablespace SALES01 ...
. exporting cluster definitions
. exporting table definitions
. . exporting table                      SALES01
For tablespace SALES02 ...
. exporting cluster definitions
. exporting table definitions
. . exporting table                      SALES02
. exporting referential integrity constraints
. exporting triggers
. end transportable tablespace metadata export
Export terminated successfully without warnings.
oracle@hp1  [/u01/app/oracle/admin/remorse/export
[remorse] $
```

TIP *Don't specify the* userid *parameter when you use the* transport_tablespace *parameter. Omit the* userid *parameter and the export utility will prompt you for the username. Connect by using the string "connect SYS/password as SYSDBA" to perform the* transport_tablespace *export.*

Note that the export you just performed didn't export any rows of the tables in your tablespaces. The export is done only to specify which tablespaces are going to be part of your transportable tablespaces set. Only metadata (table and index definitions) is exported to the export dump file. The export dump file sales.dmp will be very small, because it contains just the table definitions, column descriptions, and so forth that will help identify the objects in the tablespace when you export them to the target database.

Copy the Export File and the Tablespace Files to the Target

The next step in generating the transportable tablespaces set is the physical copying of the data files contained in the tablespaces and the export dump file containing the metadata about the tablespaces to the target location. Before you can start importing the export dump file to the target database, make sure that the block size of the tablespace is the same as the standard block size of the target tablespace. If it isn't, then the target database must have a nonstandard block size specified in its init.ora file of the same size as the block size of the tablespace you want to export.

You must now copy the export dump file, sales.dmp, to the target database using FTP, remote copy (or copy, if you're using Windows), or some other means. You also copy all the data files that are part of the two tablespaces sales01 and sales02 to the target location so they're accessible to the target database for importing.

Perform the Tablespace Import

Next, run the import utility, which will plug in the tablespaces and incorporate information about them in the data dictionary of the target database. Because the export dump file doesn't have any data, all you'll be importing is the metadata about the objects. The target database will simply use the copied data files from the source database as the data files for the transported tablespaces. All you're doing is plugging the tablespaces into the target database. Here are the import commands you need to use:

```
$ imp transport_tablespace=y tablespaces=sales01,sales02  file=sales.dmp
  datafiles='/test01/app/oracle/oradata/sales01_01.dbf',
  '/test01/app/oracle/oradata/sales02_021.dbf'
```

Listing 13-7 shows the import process. As you can see, there are two parts to the import of the transportable tablespaces. First, the import utility will extract the metadata of the transportable tablespaces from the export dump file. After this, it will extract the various objects (tables and indexes) definitions from the dump file into the target database. No data rows are actually imported into the database at this time. The data is already in the data files of the tablespaces, and you've already "plugged in" those tablespaces into the target database. Notice how the import log shows that the two tables, sales_data and price_data, are being imported into the target database, but unlike in a normal import process, you don't see the number of rows being imported.

Listing 13-7. Performing the Transportable Tablespaces Import

```
$  imp transport_tablespace=y tablespaces=sales01,sales02
   file=salesnew.dmp
datafiles='c:\oracle\oradata\real\sales01.dbf','c:\oracle\ora
data\real\sales02.dbf'
Import: Release 9.2.0.1.0 - Production on Sun Dec 22 12:29:23 2002
Copyright (c) 1982, 2002, Oracle Corporation.  All rights reserved.
Username: sys/monitor1 as sysdba
Connected to: Oracle9i Enterprise Edition Release 9.2.0.1.0 - Production
With the Partitioning, OLAP and Oracle Data Mining options
JServer Release 9.2.0.1.0 - Production
Export file created by EXPORT:V09.02.00 via conventional path
About to import transportable tablespace(s) metadata...
import done in WE8MSWIN1252 character set and AL16UTF16 NCHAR character set
. importing SYS's objects into SYS
. importing SYSTEM's objects into SYSTEM
. . importing table                  "SALES_DATA"
. . importing table                  "PRICE_DATA"
Import terminated successfully without warnings.
$
```

Or, you can use the *fromuser* and *touser* parameters to change ownership of the tables and other objects. In Listing 13-7, these are omitted, so when the import is done, you should have a user matching the user that owned the objects in the original source database.

As you can see from this simple example, the transportable tablespaces feature is very powerful, because it will let you move entire tablespaces between databases by merely copying the data files and the data dictionary information from one database to another. This is a much a faster and more efficient means of transferring very large objects compared to any of the traditional methods.

Some Export and Import Techniques

When your export or import completes, always look at the line in the log file or on the screen where the export or import's progress is displayed. This last line should read "Export (import) terminated successfully *without* warnings". This is the only unambiguous means of verifying that the entire export/import ran correctly. Sometimes you may see a similar statement that reads "Export/import terminated successfully *with* warnings". This is usually an indicator that all did not go well during the export or import.

The export (and the import) utility considers certain errors as recoverable errors. When the utility encounters these kinds of errors, it won't abort midway into the export. Instead, it skips the particular partition or table with the problem and continues with the export of the other tables in the list. At the end, you get the following message: "Export finished successfully with warnings". You must go into the log file and rerun the export for the tables whose failure to get exported caused the warning message to be displayed. Of course, if a completely nonrecoverable error such as an I/O problem occurs, export will abort immediately and issue the message "Export terminated unsuccessfully".

Avoiding Common Export/Import Errors

One of the most common export/import errors is the case when Oracle informs you that "Export views are not installed" (EXP-00024). The *export views* are a set of necessary objects that are installed automatically most of the time when you run the catproc.sql script during database installation. Anyway, if you're getting this message, you need to run the script catexp.sql, which is located in the $ORACLE_HOME/rdbms/admin directory, before you attempt to use the export or import utility.

A typical export-related problem occurs when the export dump file ends up being larger than the free space available on the disk where the dump file is being created. Make sure you specify an export dump file location on a disk with plenty of free space. If even an entire disk is insufficient to hold your dump file, then you may want to consider using the UNIX *compress* command. You may also have to specify multiple files using the *file* parameter and specify a file size for each file to get around the large export dump file problem.

If tables already exist, make sure you choose the *ignore=y* option. Otherwise, Oracle will issue an error and refuse to do the import. Also, remember that import will append data to existing tables. If that's not your intention, make sure the tables are empty before you perform the import. Otherwise, you'll usually end up with the ORA-00001 error "Unique constraint ... violated" due to the import utility's attempt to insert duplicate rows. If you don't use the *ignore=y* option and the object exists, Oracle will issue the IMP-00015 error: "Following statement failed because the object already exists". This is so because the import utility is designed to create all tables and other objects based on the dump file created by the export. If the object already exists, it makes sense to ask the import utility to ignore any errors due to the object's existence and continue on with the load.

There's an easy way to move tables to different tablespaces during imports. Just remove the quota the schema owner had on the original tablespace and change the default tablespace to the tablespace you want the tables to be moved into. Import will naturally place the objects in the user's new default tablespace.

Using the Statistics Parameter Appropriately

Be wary of the statistics that are imported from another database when you're using the *query* option to export/import only a part of a table, or when you're exporting/importing only a partition of a partitioned table. The statistics are all-important from the query optimizer's point of view. The default for the *statistics* parameter during exports is *estimate*, which could give you a misleading idea about the distribution of table values, especially for very large tables. While doing the import, the default for the statistics parameter is *always*, meaning that statistics are imported, however unrepresentative they are, as a matter of course. Set the value of the statistics parameter to *never* or *recalculate*, depending on the availability of time. The *recalculate* value will lengthen the import process, because it calculates the statistics at import time.

Understanding the Limitations of the Export and Import Utilities

If you're using Oracle's Workspace Manager, remember that you can't import a version-enabled table if the database you're importing the table into doesn't have the Workspace Manager set up.

If you're attempting to import fine-grained access polices or fine-grained audit policies, you need to have execute privileges on the DBMS_RLS and DBMS_FGA packages, respectively, for your import to be successful.

Performing an Efficient Database Migration

You can use the export and import utilities to perform database migrations. You usually do this when you're migrating a test database to production, and sometimes a production database into development. Even assuming you have the disk capacity to perform the export without problems, there's the element of time to worry about. Exports and imports typically are very time-consuming for large databases with large numbers of rows and several indexes. Probably the best means of doing the migration is to simply clone the database by creating a new control file, as shown in Chapter 15. The best way to perform these migrations, if export and import are your choices, is to break up or partition both the export and the import. This gives you the option of running several smaller jobs in parallel, which will cut back on the time it takes to complete the job. The following example illustrates how to partition export and import for a large database.

The following example shows you how to perform a database migration. Assume that you have three schemas in your database: finance, hr, and sales.

1. Do a database-level export without any data, tables, or indexes. All you're getting are the table definitions and the stored packages and procedures stored in the database. Note that you're not exporting any table data (*rows=n*), indexes, or triggers.

   ```
   $ exp system/manager file=fulldb.dmp rows=n indexes=n triggers=n
   ```

2. As soon as the preceding full export is done (no data is exported yet), run the following full import:

   ```
   $ imp system/manager file=fulldb.dmp
   ```

3. Run three different export streams simultaneously from different screens, as follows:

   ```
   $ exp system/manager owner=finance file=finance.dmp
   $ exp system/manager owner=hr file=hr.dmp
   $exp system/manager owner=sales file=sales.dmp
   ```

4. Once the preceding exports complete, run parallel imports of the three schemas as follows. The parameters should be set to *y*, because the full import has already created all the tables. You're instructing the import utility to ignore any consequent errors and import the rows into the existing tables and then the indexes.

```
$ imp system/manager  fromuser=finance  touser=finance  ignore=y
$ imp system/manager  fromser=hr  touser=hr  ignore=y
$imp system/manager  fromuser=sales  touser=sales  ignore=y
```

Restoring a Database Using the Export and Import Utilities

You can't perform an up-to-the-minute recovery with the export and import utilities, but you can restore your database to the point when the export was made. Here are the procedures to restore your database:

1. Create a simple database, with only the System tablespace.

2. Perform the import with the export dump as the source. The import will create the users, tablespaces, tables, indexes, and any other necessary objects. If your export was an incremental export, you'll have to use the appropriate set of export files to perform a complete import.

Exporting and Importing Large Databases

You're probably better off using cloning techniques instead of using the export and import utilities for copying large databases. However, if for some reason you choose to use the export utility to move a very large database, you can use the *files* parameter to specify multiple files. While importing, you can similarly specify multiple files under the *files* parameter. Here's an example of the usage of multiple files:

```
$ exp  userid=system/manager
  FILE=/a01/app/oracle/expdmp1,/a02/app/oracle/expdmp2,
  /a03/app/oracle/expdmp3 FILESIZE 500m.
```

The export utility will write the first 500MB to the first file, the next 500MB to the second export file on a different disk, and so on. The corresponding import parameters will look like this:

```
$ imp  userid=system/manager  FILE=/a01/app/oracle/expdmp1,/
  a02/app/oracle/expdmp2,
  /a03/app/oracle/expdmp3 FILESIZE 500M
```

The import utility will read from the three data files, one after the other. You have to specify the *filesize* parameter while performing an import if you've specified more than one file for the export.

UNIX Shell Script to Automate Exports

It's quite common for DBAs to include their export and import command files within a UNIX shell script so they can schedule the process to run at specified times. Listing 13-8 shows a simple UNIX shell script you can use to perform an export. An import script would be very similar to the export shell script.

Listing 13-8. A UNIX Export Script

```
#! /bin/ksh
INSTANCE=$1
export ORACLE_SID=finance1
DIR=/finance1/app/oracle/
export DIR
FILE=${DIR}/oradata/exports/${ORACLE_SID}-`date +%d` .dmp.gz;
export FILE;
LOG=${DIR}/oradata/exports//${ORACLE_SID}-`date +%d` .log;
export LOG
PIPEFILE={DIR}/fiinance1_pipe.dmp;
export PIPE
if  [! -p ${PIPEFILE}  ]
then mknod    p  $DIR/PIPEFILE
cat $PIPEFILE | gzip  > ${FILE}
exp   userid=system/manager       log=${LOG}
file=${PIPEFILE} | compress < ${PIPEFILE} >
$DIR/ exp${ORACLE_SID}_full_export.Z
```

This script will use *compress* and UNIX pipes to export the entire database.

Ensuring the Validity of the Exports

The Oracle9*i* export facility is indeed very efficient and reliable, but it isn't infallible. You have to exercise proper caution to make sure that you always have a *usable* export dump. By painstakingly checking every time you take an export, you can avoid nasty surprises when you're trying to perform an import for a critical task, only to see it come to an untimely stop well before it should.

As you learned elsewhere in this chapter, you do have to make sure that every export of a user (or table or the database) ends with the comment "Export terminated successfully without warnings". However, to ensure that you can indeed use the export dump's contents every time without a problem, you can quickly run the following test:

```
Imp userid=salapati/sammyy1/ full=y file=expdat.dmp indexfile=testindex.sql
```

By running the preceding import with the *indexfile* option, you aren't going to import either data or DDL. You just want the import utility to successfully create the index file. If it does so without issuing any errors ("Import terminated successfully without warnings"), you are home free. This isn't a 100 percent guarantee against any problems later on, but it's a quick-and-dirty verification method that can reassure you as to the validity of your exports, especially if you're relying on the export and import utilities as part of your backup strategy.

Optimizing Exports and Imports

Oracle9*i* offers you several ways to optimize your exports and imports. Optimization of the export and import processes is almost mandatory when you're dealing with large data sets. The following list presents some of the ways you can make the export and import processes faster:

- Use the direct path option while exporting by setting the *direct* parameter to *y*. The direct export is much faster than the default conventional exports.

- You can reduce the total time taken by the import by not archiving your redo logs. You'll need to turn archiving off for this to take effect. Imports generate considerable redo activity and you really don't need to run the database in the archivelog mode during the course of the import. You have the source data in the export dump file in case you lose data for some unexpected reason. This also means that you should pick times when there are no users or very few users on your system.

- The import run also uses the rollback segments, so if you're using manual undo management, use a very large rollback segment and turn smaller rollback segments offline to avoid errors during the import.

- For large table, it's better, in general, not to export and import the indexes. Just import the tables with the rows, and using the index file or other index creation scripts, re-create the index after the imports are done.

- If you're exporting a large database with many schemas, you can reduce the total time taken for the export by performing several simultaneous exports at the schema level. When you import this database, you can do so with several parallel streams of imports.

- Use a very large buffer while you do the export and import. For example, on my UNIX system, the default size for export is 4KB and the default size for import is 8KB. I recommend setting the sizes much higher for large exports and imports. Of course, you're constrained by the amount of memory available to your system as a whole in setting the *buffer* parameter. As with the SGA, too high a buffer size will induce paging at the operating system level.

- While you're performing an import, use *commit=n*, which will force Oracle to commit only after each object is fully imported, rather than commit after every batch of data (array) is loaded. This will make the import run faster.

- As mentioned earlier in the chapter, use a high value for the *recordlength* parameter to make the export run faster, and use a high value for the *buffer* parameter to speed up the import process.

- The default behavior of the import utility is to always import the statistics for the optimizer. You're better off choosing not to bring the statistics at import time. This should make the imports complete sooner. You can always analyze the table later on.

- The *analyze* option will cost you a considerable amount of time, so use *analyze=n* during the import. You can always analyze the data later on. Both exports and imports will complete much faster if they use disks rather than tapes.

- It helps to place the dump file for imports on a disk that's separate from the Oracle data files. This reduces contention during the import process, because the database must be open for an import run.

Summary

This chapter provided you with a quick introduction to the use of the export and import utilities. The export and import utilities are extremely useful and are used often in a DBA's day-to-day work, as well as for periodic database or schema migration. The *files* parameter enables you to specify several files for the export dump, thereby making it possible to export large databases.

The import utility is analogous to the export utility, and it's very dependable, though it can be tricky when you're importing tables with dependencies such as referential integrity constraints.

The transportable tablespaces feature uses export and import utilities to transport metadata involving the tablespaces being transported. Because you're only exporting and importing metadata, the time used for export and import is minimal in these cases. That's why the transportable tablespaces feature is a highly efficient means of moving large tables or entire schemas between databases.

This chapter ended by covering several complex issues that you can solve through the use of the export and import utilities.

Backing Up Databases

THIS CHAPTER DEALS with the crucial topic of backing up Oracle databases. One of the most fundamental tasks of the Oracle DBA is to ensure that the databases are backed up on a regular basis. Backups provide the basis of all database recoveries—no backup, no recovery. One of the best things you can do to help yourself as a DBA is to focus on a tried-and-tested strategy for backing up the database, because the more time you spend planning backups, the less time you'll spend recovering the database from a mishap.

There are two different ways to perform backups: You can use Oracle's Recovery Manager (RMAN) and you can use the operating system utilities to perform database backups. I give RMAN-based backups much more attention in this chapter because of the many benefits they offer you compared to operating system–based backups. I explain RMAN in detail, including its configuration and the various types of commands that you can use within it. You'll see examples of how to make different types of backups using RMAN. I also include a brief discussion of user-managed database backups using operating system utilities.

Tape devices are commonly used in Oracle backups, both because of the convenience they offer compared to disks and the ease with which you can archive tape backups for safekeeping. If you want to use RMAN with tape devices, you need to use a Media Management Layer (MML) supplied by a third-party vendor to facilitate communication between the tape devices and RMAN. You can also back up Oracle with a number of third-party backup tools, but Oracle Corporation endorses products made by Legato and supplies a scaled-down version of their storage product, Legato Single Server Version (LSSV), free with the Oracle server. In this chapter, you'll learn how to install, configure, and integrate LSSV with RMAN to perform sophisticated backups of the Oracle database.

You have to consistently check and verify backups to make sure they're correct and they're usable during a recovery. The latter part of this chapter is devoted to a review of database corruption and the many ways to test for it.

Let's begin with an overview of the backup process for Oracle databases.

Backing Up Oracle Databases

Database backups are used to avoid the loss of data. Any number of things can result in data loss, so it's essential to have a backup system in place. Backups involve keeping copies of the various database files so the database can be re-created, if necessary, wholly or partially. Oracle backups refer to physical copies of the key Oracle database files. These usually consist of all the data files, the control files, and the redo log files (both online and archived). You can run an Oracle database in two different modes: archivelog and noarchivelog. If you run the database in archivelog mode, Oracle will archive (save) all redo logs before overwriting them. Noarchivelog mode doesn't keep track of the changes made to the database by saving all the changes made to the database (archiving the logs).

I can't really think of any firm that doesn't care if it loses valuable business data. So just about all production databases are run in archivelog mode. Although I do discuss backing up noarchivelog mode databases in this chapter, I concentrate on backing up databases operating in archivelog mode. If the database is being run in noarchivelog mode, I'm going to assume that it's a "scratch" or development database whose loss wouldn't really matter, or that it's a non-real-time data warehouse that could be reconstructed relatively easily from source data. By contrast, production databases are the lifeblood of organizations, and you owe it to your employer to know the backup procedures backward and forward.

Important Backup Terms

Backing up databases is a critical operation, and the types of backup you make and the conditions under which you make the backups can have an important bearing on the recoverability of the database. A focused and clear understanding of the types of backups and a conceptual understanding of backups is extremely important for successful recovery. The next sections cover important terminology related to Oracle database backups.

Archivelog and Noarchivelog Modes

Oracle writes all changes to the data blocks in memory to the online redo logs, usually before they are written to the database files. During a recovery process, Oracle will use the changes recorded in the redo log files to bring the database up-to-date. Oracle can manage the redo log files in two ways. In *archivelog mode,* Oracle saves (archives) the filled redo logs. Thus, no matter how old the database backup is, if you are running in archivelog mode, you can recover the database to any point in time using the archived logs.

In *noarchivelog mode,* the filled redo logs are overwritten and not saved. The noarchivelog mode thus implies that you can only restore the backup, and you'll lose all the changes made to the database after the backup was performed. The noarchivelog mode of operation means that you can only recover from a crash of the database instance. If there is a media failure (e.g., a loss of a disk), a database in noarchivelog mode may be restored from a backup, but it will lose all changes made to the database since the backup was made.

Production systems are usually run in archivelog mode. There may be exceptions where the database is being backed up very frequently using a snapshot technology–based tool such as Hewlett Packard's Business Copy, when you may be able to get away without running in archivelog mode. If you're running in noarchivelog mode, the implication is that the data can be restored from other sources, or it's just a test or development database and you don't need to have up-to-the-minute recoverability. Only the archivelog mode operation ensures the following:

- You can recover completely from an instance failure as well as media failure.

- You can completely recover all your data in the event of a damaged disk drive.

- You can maintain high availability because a database run in archivelog mode doesn't have to be shut down in order to be backed up. You can perform online backups in this mode, thus keeping the database open for any length of time you wish.

- You can perform open backups—that is, backups while the database is running—only if the database is operating in archivelog mode.

- You have to run your database in archivelog mode to perform a tablespace point-in-time recovery. A recovery to a point in time is possible only if the database is in archivelog mode.

 NOTE *Because archivelog mode is the mode virtually all production databases run in, the discussion on backups in this chapter doesn't focus on databases running in noarchivelog mode.*

Whole and Partial Database Backups

You can back up either an entire database or part of it, such as a tablespace or a data file. Note that you can't back up a partial database if the database is running in noarchivelog mode, unless all the tablespaces and files in the partial backup are in read-only mode. You can make a whole database backup in either archivelog or noarchivelog mode.

The most commonly performed backup is the whole database backup, and it consists of all the data files and one other important file: the control file. Without the control file, Oracle will not open the database, so you need the latest backup of the control file along with all the data file backups for recovery.

Consistent and Inconsistent Backups

The difference between consistent and inconsistent backups is simple. A *consistent backup* doesn't need to go through a recovery process. When a backup is used to recover a database or a part of a database (such as a tablespace or a data file), first you need to restore the backup and then you recover the database. In the case of a consistent backup, there's no need for this recovery process. An *inconsistent backup*, on the other hand, always needs to undergo a recovery.

Oracle assigns every committed transaction a unique System Change Number (SCN). Each commit, for example, will advance the SCN forward. Each time Oracle performs a checkpoint, all the changed data in the online data files is written to disk. And each time there is a checkpoint, the thread checkpoint in the control file is updated by Oracle. During this thread checkpoint, Oracle makes all the read/write data files and the control files consistent to the same SCN. A consistent database means that the SCNs stored in all the data file headers are identical and are also the same as the data file header information held in the control files. The important thing is this: *The same SCN number must appear in all the data files and the control file(s).*

To make a consistent backup, either the database needs to be closed (with a normal *shutdown* or *shutdown transactional* command, not a *shutdown abort* command) or it needs to be in a mount position after being started (again, after a clean shutdown).

Open and Closed Backups

Online or *open* (or *hot/warm*) backups are backups you make while the database is open and accessible to users. You can make an online backup of the entire database (or a tablespace or data file) as long as the database is being run in archivelog mode. You cannot make an online backup if the database is running in noarchivelog mode.

A closed backup of a database, also called a *cold* backup, is made while the database is shut down. A closed backup is always consistent, as long as the database wasn't shut down with the *shutdown abort* command.

TIP *An important fact to remember is that if the backup is online or if it closed (offline) but inconsistent, you may need to apply archived redo logs to make the database consistent.*

The decision about whether you should make a closed (cold) backup or an open (hot or warm) backup is a decision that is dependent on business requirements. Business requirements would dictate the uptime levels, which are then encapsulated in the service level agreement (SLA). If your SLA requires that your database be up 24/7, you have to make online hot backups. On the other hand, if your organization allows you a backup "window" that will enable you to bring the database down, you can schedule closed backups. The frequency of closed backups and the number of redo logs produced by the database are both factors in the time it takes to recover the database. If you are performing closed backups on a weekly basis, then you may have up to 6 days' worth of archived logs to apply to the database backup during recovery (in the worst case).

Backup Strategies

You can't have a great backup policy without at least a basic strategy regarding your database backups. You can take it for granted that there will be data losses of some kind over time. You need to have a strategy so you can be ready for this eventuality.

Your backup strategy will depend heavily on the type of SLA you have in place. It is common for most IT departments today to draw up formal SLAs with their clients. SLAs are ways to formalize expectations regarding the availability and performance of the database as well as other components such as the network. SLAs usually include factors such as the following:

- Maintenance windows

- Upgrade schedules

- Backup and recovery procedures

- Response times for certain key database operations

- Database and server downtime parameters

SLAs specify the uptime for the databases in clear terms. They also specify maintenance windows and the planned recovery time under several identifiable downtimes (e.g., due to a disk failure). The concept of *uptime* is pretty tricky—with a 99 percent uptime, you are still down almost 4 entire days during the year. Whether your organization can handle this or would like a 99.999 percent uptime, which implies only a 5-minute downtime, is something you have to nail down in clear terms.

A typical SLA for database operations may look like the following (a partial agreement is shown here):

```
Standard  Processing Services. The Provider shall furnish and
allow access to the processing environments listed below:
a. Mid tier processing.
(1) Applications to be processed:
Financial Information Systems (FIS) to include:
LIST OF FIS APPLICATIONS
Other Departmental Applications
(2) Hours of Availability.
Interactive:      Monday-Friday*           07:00-17:00*
                           Saturday, Sunday, & Holidays Not Applicable
* Application will be a web-based 24 x 7x 365 system WITH the
exception of the scheduled maintenance periods (see below)
Batch: Not applicable
Maintenance: Monthly, 4th Weekend of every month
(3) Standard Processing/Service Requirements.
All of the systems/applications listed in
paragraph (1) above are required to be operational
98% of the total time listed in
paragraph (2) above. The Information Systems Department
will provide a method for the Department of Finance
to monitor operational percentages.(4)  Processing of data will be
limited to the functionality/processing that was being
conducted at the time of handing over the operations to the
Information Services Department.
```

NOTE *SLAs also specify the cause of possible service interruptions and the expectations regarding the resumption of normal service. If the disruption of service is not due to a database failure (e.g., the loss of a data file), obviously other factors come into play, such as the network and the UNIX or Windows servers. You should, however, list the potential reasons for a database failure and the time it will take to recover from each of those failures. The total time taken for any recovery, of course, will include the time taken to restore the lost or damaged files and the time to recover the database. Chapter 15 goes into the recovery process in detail.*

Why is clarifying uptime so important? The type of backup and recovery strategy you want to adopt depends very much on the level of uptime specified in your SLA. By specifying the uptime levels, you are stating how quickly you must recover from a failure. If the SLA states that you may take a whole day to restore and recover your database, then you may not need to do a nightly online backup.

You can get by with a once-a-week cold backup (if you're allowed the downtime for it). If your SLA specifies a 99.999 percent uptime, you may want to invest in Oracle Real Application Clusters (ORAC), for example. Usually, you'll find that uptime and cost are directly proportional to each other. What happens if you find out you can't make your main production server function for a very long time? Maybe you should have a standby database in place to take over from the main database in such a case. Note that your backup strategy will depend on the recovery expectations specified in your SLA.

Backup Guidelines

Regardless of your SLA and your recovery requirements, some general guidelines regarding backup processes will help you *avoid* a recovery in most cases. After all, the best strategy for recovery is to avoid having to do one by having an ironclad backup and data protection system in place. The guidelines are as follows:

- Build redundancy into your systems by using RAID-based storage systems, which will let you mask individual disk failures.

- Perform backups at frequent intervals to reduce your recovery time.

- Maintain offsite storage of your backups with a reliable vendor. The tapes that you store offsite should be part of a regular recovery testing program.

- Always run any database deemed to contain useful data for the organization in archivelog mode. If you choose to run the database in noarchivelog mode, you're clearly assuming that you don't care about the up-to-the-minute recoverability of the data.

- Always multiplex the control files on separate disk drives managed by different disk controllers. *Multiplexing* means that Oracle will automatically maintain more than one copy of a file. For example, when you specify three copies of the Oracle control file, Oracle will write to all three of the control files. Mirror the control files in addition to using the multiplexing offered by

Oracle. Do the same with the redo logs. Even when the database files are mirrored, it's important to use Oracle multiplexing for both archive logs and control files.

- After every major structural change, back up the control file. The control file backup takes so little space anyway that you can schedule a job that will do a "back up the control file to trace" every hour or so on a production machine with a heavy amount of activity.

- Take advantage of the archivelog multiplexing option and set the *min succeed DEST* option to at least 2 or more to ensure you have multiple sets of good archived logs.

- Always make more than one copy of the database when it's being backed up to tape, because the tapes can be defective and you may not be aware of it.

- Always make regularly scheduled copies of the initialization file, the network files, and the password files and save them in a secure location. Normal backups involve only data files, redo log files, and control files. But you may sometimes need these "other files" to restore and recover a damaged database.

- Keep the use of the unrecoverable and no logging options to a minimum, for obvious reasons. If there's a problem, you won't have those objects in the redo logs and you won't be able to recover them.

- Use the Recovery Manager (RMAN) tool, which is provided free of cost from Oracle, to perform your backups and recovery. RMAN maintains a log of all the backup and recovery actions performed, so it's very easy to keep track of those operations.

- Make at least two copies of the archived redo logs, and keep one on disk for a short recovery time if there's a media problem.

- Keep older copies of backups for added protection. It's not a good idea to overwrite your tapes too soon to save a little money. If the current backups turn out to be unusable for some reason, you end up losing all of your data. This could happen more often than you believe. Always know how many archived backups you have and where your archived backups are and safe-guard them.

- Your backup scripts should write to a log file or a log table, which should be examined for any problems that might have occurred during the backups.

- Ensure that your applications are separated in independent tablespaces, so you don't have to take more than one application offline if you have a major media problem.

- Consider using snapshot technology–based storage system backup techniques for fast backups of large databases.

- Use the export utility to provide supplemental protection.

TIP *Always try to keep a redundancy set online so you can recover faster. A redundancy set is defined as the last backup of all data files, copies of the current redo log files and the control file, and all the archived redo logs since the last backup. You may also include the server parameter file (SPFILE) or the init.ora, listener.ora, and tnsnames.ora files in this file. Make sure you save the redundancy set on completely separate physical volumes and RAID systems than those on which the database is located.*

Testing Your Backups

Too often, the first encounter a DBA has with a defective backup strategy occurs during a frustrating recovery session of a production database. You can attribute the vast majority of problems encountered during recovery to inadequate or even nonexistent planning and testing of the backup and recovery strategy. The time to find out whether your database is recoverable is most definitely not when you are trying to recover a production database in the dead of night. To avoid a catastrophic recovery experience, every DBA should have established and tested backup and disaster recovery plans. Here are some guidelines regarding testing your database backups:

- Test all backup files. Always validate your backups and make sure that the backups are actually readable. Check for corrupted blocks in the backed-up files, so recovery doesn't become impossible due to bad files. The RMAN utility and user-managed backups both offer ways to check for data block corruption. I discuss these features in detail toward the end of this chapter.

- Make periodic restoration tests mandatory for all key databases.

- Test the integrity of the backups by using utilities such as dbverify and DBMS_REPAIR (I discuss these utilities later in this chapter) so you aren't surprised during a recovery.

Protecting Against a Single Point of Failure

A loss of an active redo log file could be a *single point of failure*, which will result in the loss of data. To avoid such an event, Oracle strongly recommends that you multiplex the redo log file. The same advice applies to the control files. When you multiplex the redo log file, even if one of the files is corrupted or lost, Oracle will continue writing to its copy. A mirrored strategy may not be appropriate here, as both copies might be corrupted at the same time, thus making the extra copy just as useless as the original.

NOTE *Unlike in the case of the online redo log file, the Oracle instance will shut down if one of the multiplexed control files can't be written to.*

Backing Up the "Other" Files

Though the data files, log files, and control files are indeed the key files needed for recovery, there are other files you should back up and put away safely on a routine basis. These include the init.ora parameter file, the sqlnet.ora file, the tnsnames.ora file, and the password file. You can always reconfigure each of these files in case you lose them, but this wastes a lot of critical time and you might very well end up making mistakes in the process. These "other" files take very little space to store, and you should get into the habit of archiving them on a regular basis.

A Summary of Backup Methods

Whether you perform an online or offline backup, or a full or partial backup, you have two ways you can perform the backup. The first method is called *user-managed backups,* wherein the DBA or the system administrator uses either the operating system utilities or a third-party backup tool to perform the backup of the database (or parts of the database). The other method is the use of the Oracle Recovery Manager (RMAN) tool, which is part of your Oracle9*i* server software. This chapter focuses on using RMAN to perform backups because of its vast superiority over user-managed backups. I present a quick review of user-managed backups later on, but first you'll learn more about the highly utilitarian RMAN tool.

The following list presents a summary of the consequences of the various types of database backups that you can perform: whole and partial, closed and open, and consistent and inconsistent:

- If a database is shut down with the *shutdown abort* command, it may not be consistent.

- If the database is open during a backup, it will always be inconsistent.

- If you're running the database in archivelog mode, you can do an open backup that's always inconsistent and a closed backup that's either consistent or inconsistent, depending on how the database was shut down.

- If you're running the database in noarchivelog mode, you can only perform a closed recovery.

- If you're running the database in noarchivelog mode, you can only perform whole database backups. To be able to back up a data file or tablespace, in most cases, you should be running the database in the archivelog mode of operation.

Oracle Recovery Manager

As mentioned earlier, you can perform Oracle database backups in one of two ways. The first is the traditional user-managed backup method, which consists simply of using the operating system commands to copy the relevant files to a different location and/or to a tape device. The other method is RMAN, which is bundled with the database itself. With RMAN, you back up the database files from *within* the database.

NOTE *Is using RMAN better than using the traditional user-managed backup and recovery methods? Most "old-school" Oracle DBAs will be familiar with operating system commands, but newer DBAs may be better off focusing on the use of RMAN, which offers ease of use, safety, and features that the traditional methods don't have.*

Despite its sophistication, RMAN has some limitations. You can't, for example, read from or write directly to a tape device using RMAN. You would have to use what's known as a third-party *Media Management Layer* (MML) to make tape backups if you use the RMAN utility for backups.

In the long run, however, RMAN could simplify the backup procedures by enabling the use of powerful yet easy-to-write backup and recovery scripts. RMAN also offers features such as corruption detection within the data blocks and the ability to back up only the changed blocks in the database. You can save RMAN's scripts in the database and use them right from there, without your needing to write operating system–based scripts. RMAN automatically ensures the backup of all the database files, which eliminates the human-error component that is present in operating system–based backups.

Benefits of RMAN

RMAN provides an array of benefits compared to user-managed backup methods. Here's a list of the benefits offered by the use of RMAN as compared to the use of traditional operating system backup utilities:

- You can perform incremental backups using RMAN. The size of the backups doesn't depend on the size of the database; rather, it depends on the activity level within the database, because unchanged blocks are skipped during incremental backups. You can't perform incremental backups any other way. You can perform incremental exports, but that isn't considered a real backup for all databases.

- Human error is minimized because RMAN, not the individual DBA, keeps track of all the filenames and locations. Once you understand the use of the RMAN utility, it's easy for you take over the backup and recovery of databases from another DBA.

- A simple command such as *backup database* can back up an entire database, without the need for complex scripts.

- It's easy to automate the backup and recovery process through RMAN. RMAN can also automatically parallelize your backup and recovery sessions.

- RMAN can perform error checking during backups and recovery, thus ensuring that the backed-up files aren't corrupt. RMAN has the capability to recover any corrupted data blocks without taking the data file offline.

- During online backups, no redo is generated, unlike when online backups are performed using the operating system utilities. Thus, the overhead is low for online backups.

- If you use the recovery catalog, you can store backup and recovery scripts directly in it.

- RMAN can perform simulated backups and restores.

- RMAN enables you to make *image copies*, which are similar to operating system–based backups of files.

- RMAN can be easily integrated with powerful third-party media management products to make tape backups effortless.

- RMAN is integrated well with the OEM backup functionality, so you can schedule backup jobs easily for a large number of databases through a common management framework.

- You can easily clone databases and maintain standby databases using the RMAN functionality.

NOTE *As the preceding list clearly shows, it's no contest when it comes to the question of whether you should be using operating system–based backup and recovery (user-managed backup and recovery) or RMAN. Therefore, you'll see quite a bit of discussion about RMAN in this chapter and the next, which deals with recovering databases. Oracle maintains that both RMAN and traditional user-managed backup and recovery methods are equally valid and effective, but it prefers the use of RMAN.*

RMAN Architecture

RMAN is provided free of charge with the Oracle server software. The utility works by opening server sessions with the *target* database, which is the database you want to back up or recover. The collection of information about the target database, such as its schema information, backup copy information, configuration settings, and backup and recover scripts, is called the *RMAN repository*. RMAN uses this metadata about the target databases to perform its backup and recovery activities. The next sections cover how RMAN manages the all-important repository.

The Recovery Catalog

You have a choice of two locations for storing the RMAN repository. You can let RMAN store it in the target database control file, or you can configure and use the optional *recovery catalog* to manage the metadata. The objections you'll hear regarding using the recovery catalog is that it's too complex to maintain and that it needs another database to manage it. There are some commands that you can use only when you use the recovery catalog. If you use the control file, you run the risk of getting some of the historical data overwritten, but the recovery catalog will safeguard all such data. One recovery catalog in your system can perform backup, restore, and recovery activities for dozens of Oracle databases. Thus, you can centralize and automate backup and recovery operations by using the recovery catalog. Oracle recommends that you use a dedicated database for running the recovery catalog, but it isn't absolutely necessary.

 NOTE *You're strongly advised to use the recovery catalog so you can take advantage of the full range of features provided by RMAN. The discussions of RMAN's features in this chapter and the next assume the existence of the recovery catalog.*

The Media Management Layer

You can make backups to your operating system disks using RMAN. If you want to make backups to tape, you'll need additional MML software, such as the Net-Worker product supplied by Legato Systems. Later on in this chapter, I show you how to use an MML to back up your database to tape. Although you'll see the manual use of RMAN in this chapter, you can also use OEM to make your backups through RMAN.

Connecting to RMAN

You can connect to RMAN by simply typing **rman** at the operating system prompt. This will get you the Recovery Manager prompt, at which point you can type in the various commands. Or, you can specify the commands after you invoke RMAN. You can also use the RMAN commands in batch mode or through pipes by using Oracle's DBMS_PIPE package.

   The following sections contain some examples of how you can connect to RMAN. Note that you must have SYSDBA privileges to connect to other databases through RMAN. You don't need to be a SYSDBA privilege holder to just connect to the RMAN catalog—you can do so with the special rman account and password. As you'll see in the section "Creating the Recovery Catalog," the user rman is the owner of the catalog. You can connect to RMAN through database password authentication by using the SYS username. You can also connect to the database using operating system authentication.

Connecting to RMAN Through Database Authentication

You can log into the RMAN utility by using your database credentials. You need to have SYSDBA privileges to use RMAN. The following examples use the SYS user account to log into RMAN.

```
[monitor] $ rman
Recovery Manager: Release 9.2.0.1.0 - 64bit Production
Copyright (c) 1995, 2002, Oracle Corporation.  All rights reserved.
RMAN> connect target sys/monitor1
connected to target database: MONITOR (DBID=2029096430)
RMAN> exit
Recovery Manager complete.
oracle@hp50.netbsa.org   [/u01/app/oracle]
[monitor] $
```

The following sequence of steps is equivalent to the preceding commands. In both cases, you are connecting to the target database named *monitor.* Once you connect to the target database, you can then issue the appropriate backup/recovery commands. The *exit* command will take you out of the RMAN environment.

```
[monitor] $ rman target sys/monitor1
Recovery Manager: Release 9.2.0.1.0 - 64bit Production
Copyright (c) 1995, 2002, Oracle Corporation.  All rights reserved.
connected to target database: MONITOR (DBID=2029096430)
RMAN> exit
Recovery Manager complete.
oracle@hp50.netbsa.org   [/u01/app/oracle]
[monitor] $
```

Connecting to RMAN Using Operating System Authentication

You can also log into RMAN using operating system authentication. In this case, you don't need to use the SYS account and password. Here's how you do this:

```
[monitor] $ rman target /
Recovery Manager: Release 9.2.0.1.0 - 64bit Production
Copyright (c) 1995, 2002, Oracle Corporation.  All rights reserved.
connected to target database: MONITOR (DBID=2029096430)
RMAN>
```

As in the case of database authentication, you can also connect to RMAN by typing **rman** first and then connecting to the target database and the recovery catalog database separately, as shown here:

```
[monitor] $ rman
Recovery Manager: Release 9.2.0.1.0 - 64bit Production
Copyright (c) 1995, 2002, Oracle Corporation.  All rights reserved.
RMAN> connect target sys/monitor1
connected to target database: MONITOR (DBID=2029096430)
RMAN>
```

Connecting to the Recovery Catalog

In the preceding login examples, you are connecting directly to the target database without a recovery catalog. Once you configure the recovery catalog, you have the option of connecting to the recovery catalog first and performing all your backup/ recovery actions with the help of it. This is also the option Oracle strongly recommends because of the critical benefits provided by the use of the (optional) recovery catalog. Here's how you can connect when using the recovery catalog. (In the following example, the recovery catalog is in the database named *monitor*. The target database, which is to be backed up, is called *remorse*.)

```
[remorse] $ rman  target  remorse catalog  rman/rman1@monitor
Recovery Manager: Release 9.2.0.1.0 - 64bit Production
Copyright (c) 1995, 2002, Oracle Corporation.  All rights reserved.
target database Password:
connected to target database: REMORSE (DBID=3482335306)
connected to recovery catalog database
RMAN>
```

Scripting with RMAN

You'll see several examples later in this chapter that use simple manual commands such as backup *database and list obsolete*. However, manual commands aren't the only or the best way to give directives to RMAN. RMAN comes with an operating system–independent scripting language, which is highly powerful and lets you encapsulate common backup tasks easily. Oracle provides several well-documented scripts for performing backup and recovery using RMAN. You can find these scripts in the $ORACLE_HOME/rdbms/demo directory. Four scripts are in this directory, and all end with the .rcv extension.

All scripts in RMAN have the format *run {script}*, as the following example shows. The RMAN scripts do look a bit cryptic at first, but they are highly effective and easy to write. A script is always executed with the *run* command, and the script's contents are always enclosed within a pair of curly brackets { }.

When you have to use a large number of configuration parameters for a particular backup, it's much easier to use a script. RMAN scripts thus perform the same function as regular scripts in UNIX or SQL: They make it easier to store and rerun long sets of commands. Here's a simplified nightly backup script that performs a full database backup. Note that by using the keyword SQL, you can include regular SQL commands within your RMAN backup script.

```
RMAN> create script test_script {
2> allocate channel c1 type disk;
3> backup database format '/u01/app/oracle/%u';
4> SQL 'alter database backup controlfile to trace';
5> }
created script test_script
RMAN>
```

Now that you have created the script nightly_backup, all you have to do to run the full backup is to simply execute the script as follows:

```
RMAN> run {execute script nightly_backup;}
executing script: night_backup
allocated channel: c1
channel c1: sid=19 devtype=DISK
...
RMAN>
```

RMAN scripting is very powerful and flexible—it enables you to perform complex tasks in a few short lines. The following script uses two tape devices to perform a full database backup. The script allocates the two channels, completes the backup in a specified format, and releases the channels.

```
RMAN> run {
2> allocate channel c1 type 'sbt_tabpe';
3> allocate channel c2 type 'sbt_tape';
4> backup
5> format 'full d%d_u%u'
6> gfilesperset 10
7> database;
8> release channel c1;
9> release channel c2;
10> }
```

Important RMAN Terms

Several terms, which are defined in the following sections, are exclusive to RMAN. To use RMAN effectively, you need a good understanding of the following terms.

Backup Piece

A *backup piece* is an operating system file containing the backup of a data file, a control file, or archived redo log files.

Backup Set

A *backup set* is a logical concept that consists of one or more backup pieces. If you back up a database, data file, tablespace, or archive log, the complete set of relevant backup pieces together are grouped into a backup set. When the *backup* command is issued, RMAN creates the backup set to hold the output. A backup set is a file or set of files in a proprietary format that only RMAN can understand. Thus, only RMAN is able to use the backup sets to recover the database.

Image Copy

Image copies are similar to the copies you can make of operating system files with the *cp* command in UNIX or the *copy* command in DOS. You can make image copies of data files, control files, and archived redo log files. RMAN image copies can only be made to disk; they can't be made to tape. Really, there's no difference between RMAN image copies and normal copies made with the *cp* command, for example, except that image copies are made through the RMAN tool, and so the information regarding them is already written to the control file or the recovery catalog, if it's being used. In fact, you can use a manually copied data file during a recovery if you first use the *catalog* command to register the file with RMAN. You can then use the *restore* and *switch* commands to use these user-made copies of data files.

Proxy Copy

RMAN can also perform a special kind of backup called the *proxy copy*, wherein the media manager is given control of the copying process.

Channel

An RMAN session has to use some kind of a connection to the server to perform backup and recovery work, and *channels* represent those connections. Channels specify the specific device, disk or tape, that will be used for the backup/recovery action. You can either have preconfigured channels (somewhat like default channels) or specify the channel manually in the RMAN run blocks. The following sections present examples of channel allocation.

Automatic Channel Configuration

In the following examples, the default device is set to a tape device in the first case and to disk in the second case. These devices are made part of the RMAN configuration, and until they are changed again through the use of the *configure* command, they remain the default device types for all RMAN sessions.

```
rman> CONFIGURE DEFAULT DEVICE TYPE TO sbt; (tape device)
rman> CONFIGURE DEFAULT DEVICE TYPE TO disk; (using the OS file system)
```

Manual Channel Allocation

The following example shows how you can manually set the channel type by using the *allocate channel* command. The following command sets the device to *sbt*, which indicates a sequential tape device:

```
rman>  RUN
{ ALLOCATE CHANNEL  a1 DEVICE TYPE TO sbt;
backup database;
}
```

RMAN Commands

You need to be familiar with a limited set of commands to use the RMAN utility for performing backups. You'll encounter the specific commands pertaining to restoring and recovering databases in Chapter 15. The commands can be grouped into the following types:

- Backup commands
- Job commands
- Copy commands
- Reporting commands
- Listing commands
- Validating commands

In the following sections you'll examine the various RMAN commands.

Backup Commands

The most important backup command is the obvious *backup* command. You can either specify a channel manually at backup time or let RMAN allocate a default channel. You can use the *backup* command to back up the database in different ways. You can choose to back up the entire database, a tablespace, or just a single data file. You also use the *backup* command to back up archived redo logs. Here are some examples showing how to use the *backup* command:

```
RMAN> backup database;
RMAN> backup tablespace sales01;
RMAN> backup datafile '/test01/app/oracle/oradta/help/user01.dbf';
```

Incremental Backups

All the *backup* commands in the preceding section are *full backup* commands. You can also perform incremental backups using RMAN, and in fact, this is one of the big advantages of using RMAN in the first place. An *incremental backup* will only back up those parts of the database that have changed since the last level 0 backup or the last incremental backup. A *level 0* backup is similar to a full backup, and it copies all data blocks. However, if you want to use incremental backups, you have to explicitly perform a level 0 backup to server as the basis for all incremental backups. All incremental backups back up the changed data blocks only. The following is the syntax for an incremental backup. The first command performs a level 0 incremental backup, and the second command performs a level 1 incremental backup.

```
RMAN> backup incremental level 0 database;
RMAN> backup incremental level 1 database;
```

If you're running the database in archivelog mode, you can perform a closed or open database backup. If you're running the database in noarchivelog mode, you can only perform a closed database backup.

Job Commands

You can't use the *allocate channel* and *switch* commands as stand-alone commands. You must use them with the *run* command, as follows:

```
RMAN> run
{
3> allocate channel c1 device type sbt4> PARMS='ENV={NSR_GROUP=default)';
5> backup datafile 1;
6> }
allocated channel: c1
channel c1: sid=11 devtype=SBT_TAPE
channel c1: MMS Version 2.2.0.1
The switch command is similar to the alter database rename datafile command,
 and it lets you replace a data file with file copy made by RMAN.
```

Copy Command

The *copy* command in RMAN makes a plain copy of a data file. These image copies are identical to the copies made by using operating system utilities. The following illustrates the use of the *copy* command:

```
RMAN>  copy datafile 1 to 'c:\oraclent\admin\goal\df1.copy';
Starting copy at 24-DEC--02
starting full resync of recovery catalog
full resync complete
allocated channel: ORA_DISK_1
channel ORA_DISK_1: sid=11 devtype=DISK
channel ORA_DISK_1: copied datafile 1
output filename=C:\ORACLENT\ADMIN\GOAL\DF1.COPY recid=9 stamp=462981532
Finished copy at 24-DEC-02
RMAN>
```

Reporting Commands

RMAN provides useful reporting commands that enable you to check your backup and recovery processes. You can query RMAN to see which files need backup and which files are obsolete and can be removed.

The *report schema* command tells you what tablespaces and data files are part of the target database, as shown here:

```
RMAN> report schema;
Report of database schema
File K-bytes    Tablespace    RB segs    Datafile Name
---- ---------- -------------------- ------- ------------------
```

```
1   332800      SYSTEM      ***     /test02/app/oracle/oradata/help/system01.dbf
2   204800      UNDOTBS     ***     /test02/app/oracle/oradata/help/undotbs01.dbf
3   51200       USERS       ***     /test02/app/oracle/oradata/help/users01.dbf
4   204800      RMANAGER    ***     /test02/app/oracle/oradata/help/rman01.dbf
RMAN>
```

The *report obsolete* command displays all the backups rendered obsolete based on the retention policy you choose (more on this later on in the chapter):

```
RMAN> report obsolete;
RMAN retention policy will be applied to the command
RMAN retention policy is set to recovery window of 14 days
no obsolete backups found
RMAN>
```

The *report need backup* command lists any data files that need backup to conform with the retention policy chosen:

```
RMAN> report need backup;
RMAN retention policy will be applied to the command
RMAN retention policy is set to redundancy 1
Report of files with less than 1 redundant backups
File# bkps               Name
---- -----  ------------------------------------------
2     0      C:\ORACLENT\ORADATA\HELPME\UNDOTBS01.DBF
7     0      C:\ORACLENT\ORADATA\HELPME\TOOLS01.DBF
8     0      C:\ORACLENT\ORADATA\HELPME\USERS01.DBF
RMAN>
```

Listing Commands

The *list backup* command shows you all the completed backups registered by RMAN. Listing 14-1 shows the output of the *list backup* command.

Listing 14-1. Using the List Backup Command

```
RMAN> list backup;
List of Backup Sets
BS Key  Type LV Size        Device Type Elapsed Time Completion Time
37      Full    195M        DISK         00:00:49     24-DEC-02
        BP Key: 38   Status: AVAILABLE   Tag: TAG20021224T140642
        Piece Name: /test02/app/oracle/product/9.2.0.1.0/dbs/02eb5b3j_1_1
   Controlfile Included: Ckp SCN: 1626964      Ckp time: 24-DEC-02
   List of Datafiles in backup set 37
File LV Type Ckp SCN    Ckp Time   Name
1       Full 1626966    24-DEC-02
/test01/app/oracle/oradata/remorse/system01.dbf
 2      Full 1626966    24-DEC-02
 /test01/app/oracle/oradata/remorse/undotbs01.dbf
...
```

```
67      30K      DISK        00:00:01    24-DEC-02
         BP Key: 68   Status: AVAILABLE   Tag: TAG20021224T140742
         Piece Name: /test02/app/oracle/product/9.2.0.1.0/dbs/03eb5b5e_1_1
   List of Archived Logs in backup set 67
   Thrd Seq    Low SCN   Low Time    Next SCN   Next Time
   1    12     1626931   24-DEC-02 1627030    24-DEC-02
216     Full    984K      DISK        00:00:08      24-DEC-02
         BP Key: 221   Status: AVAILABLE   Tag:
         Piece Name: /test02/app/oracle/product/9.2.0.1.0/
dbs/c-3482335306-20021225-01
   SPFILE Included: Modification time: 24-DEC-02
RMAN>
```

The *list copy* command is analogous to the *list backup* command. It gives you the complete list of all the copies made using RMAN.

```
RMAN> list copy;
List of Archived Log Copies
Key     Thrd Seq    S Low Time  Name
------- ---- ------- - --------- ----
6       1    10      A 24-DEC-02
/test02/app/oracle/oradata/archive/T0001S0000000010.ARC
```

Validating Commands

You can use the *validate backupset* command to validate backup sets before you use them from a recovery:

```
RMAN> validate backupset 5;
allocated channel: ORA_DISK_1
channel ORA_DISK_1: sid=24 devtype=DISK
allocated channel: ORA_DISK_2
channel ORA_DISK_2: sid=25 devtype=DISK
RMAN-00571: ===========================================================
RMAN-00569: =============== ERROR MESSAGE STACK FOLLOWS ===============
RMAN-00571: ===========================================================
RMAN-03002: failure of validate command at 01/11/2003 14:50:32
RMAN-06160: no backup pieces found for backup set key: 5
RMAN>
```

In the preceding example, the *validate* command results in an error because RMAN could not find any component pieces for backupset 5. In the following example, the *validate* command successfully validates the existence of backupset 2:

```
RMAN> validate backupset 2;
using channel ORA_DISK_1
using channel ORA_DISK_2
channel ORA_DISK_1: starting validation of datafile backupset
channel ORA_DISK_1: restored backup piece 1
piece handle=/test02/app/oracle/product/9.2.0.1.0/dbs
```

```
/02eb5b3j_1_1 tag=TAG20021224T140642 params=NULL
channel ORA_DISK_1: validation complete
RMAN>
```

You can also use the *crosscheck* command to make sure that a backup is indeed present and is usable. You'll see an example of this command in the section on "Detecting Data Block Corruption" later in this chapter.

Configuring RMAN

RMAN comes with several configuration parameters, and these are set to their default values when you first use RMAN. Type the command **show all**, as shown in Listing 14-2, to see what the configurable parameters are.

Listing 14-2. The Show All Command

```
RMAN> show all; RMAN configuration parameters are:
CONFIGURE RETENTION POLICY TO REDUNDANCY 2;
CONFIGURE BACKUP OPTIMIZATION ON;
CONFIGURE DEFAULT DEVICE TYPE TO DISK;
CONFIGURE CONTROLFILE AUTOBACKUP ON;
CONFIGURE CONTROLFILE AUTOBACKUP FORMAT
 FOR DEVICE TYPE DISK TO '%F'; # default
CONFIGURE DEVICE TYPE DISK PARALLELISM 4;
CONFIGURE DATAFILE BACKUP COPIES FOR DEVICE
 TYPE DISK TO 1; # default
CONFIGURE ARCHIVELOG BACKUP COPIES FOR DEVICE
 TYPE DISK TO 1; # default
CONFIGURE MAXSETSIZE TO UNLIMITED; # default
CONFIGURE SNAPSHOT CONTROLFILE NAME TO
 '/test02/app/oracle/product/9.2.0.1.0/dbs/snapcf_remorse.f'; # default
RMAN>
```

Note that you can list the current configuration values of various RMAN parameters by using the following command, which is based on the V$RMAN_CONFIGURATION view:

```
SQL> select * from v$rman_configuration
```

You can use the *configure* command to change the values of these RMAN configuration parameters. Let's take a closer look at some of the important configurable parameters and how you can change them.

Retention Policy

A backup retention policy is used to tell RMAN when to consider backups of data files and log files *obsolete*. Note that that when you tell RMAN to consider a backup file obsolete after a certain time period, RMAN only marks the file as obsolete—it does not delete it. You must go in and delete the obsolete files.

You can set a retention policy by using either of two methods: the default redundancy option or the retention window option. I describe these options in the following sections.

Using the Redundancy Option

The *redundancy* option lets you specify how many copies of the backups you want retained. The default for retention policy redundancy is 1. You set the retention policy by using the following command:

```
RMAN> configure retention policy to redundancy 2;
old RMAN configuration parameters:
CONFIGURE RETENTION POLICY TO REDUNDANCY 1;
new RMAN configuration parameters:
CONFIGURE RETENTION POLICY TO REDUNDANCY 2;
new RMAN configuration parameters are successfully stored
starting full resync of recovery catalog
full resync complete
RMAN>
```

Using the Recovery Window Option

Setting the backup retention policy using the *recovery window* option enables you to specify how far back in time you want to recover from, when your database is affected by a media failure. RMAN will keep all backups of data files and log files, which are one backup older than the recovery window time period. For example, if the recovery window is 7 days, RMAN will save all backups starting from the backups done immediately before the 7-day period. You set the recovery window as follows:

```
RMAN> configure retention policy to recovery window of 14 days;
old RMAN configuration parameters:
CONFIGURE RETENTION POLICY TO REDUNDANCY 2;
new RMAN configuration parameters:
CONFIGURE RETENTION POLICY TO RECOVERY WINDOW OF 14 DAYS;
new RMAN configuration parameters are successfully stored

 starting full resync of recovery catalog
full resync complete
RMAN>
```

As you can see in this example, you can set the redundancy number or a recovery window, but not both. A change in the value of either of the two options will supersede the values of the existing option.

The Report Obsolete Command

You can use the *report obsolete* command to see which of the backups do not meet the retention policy that you set for the database backups. The following listing shows the output of the *report obsolete* command:

```
RMAN> report obsolete;
RMAN retention policy will be applied to the command
RMAN retention policy is set to redundancy 1
Report of obsolete backups and copies
Type           Key  Completion Time       Filename/Handle
------------   ----- -----------------   ----------------------------------------
Backup Set     1    24-DEC-02
Backup Piece   1    24-DEC-02             /test01/app/oracle/9.2.0.1.0/dbs/02doetml_1_1
Backup Set     2    24-DEC-02
Backup Piece   2    24-DEC-02             /test01/app/oracle/9.2.0.1.0 /dbs/04dof0q1_1_1
Archive Log    1    24-DEC-02             /test02/app/oracle/oradata/arch/T0001S00005.ARC
RMAN>
```

Once you see that there are obsolete backups in the repository, you can delete them with the *delete obsolete* command, as shown here:

```
RMAN> delete obsolete;
RMAN retention policy will be applied to the command
RMAN retention policy is set to redundancy 1
allocated channel: ORA_DISK_1
channel ORA_DISK_1: sid=11 devtype=DISK
 Deleting the following obsolete backups and copies:
Type           Key  Completion Time  Filename/Handle
---------------   ----- -----------------  --------------------
Backup Set     1     24-DEC-02
Backup Piece   1     24-DEC-02  /test01/app/oracle/9.2.01.0/dbs/02doetml_1_1
...
Archive Log    3     24-DEC-02  /test02/app/oracle/oradata/arch/T0001S000007.ARC
 Do you really want to delete the above objects (enter YES or NO)? y
deleted backup piece
...
 Deleted 11 objects
RMAN>
```

You'll need to verify that all the obsolete backups have been deleted from the repository, whether in the control file or the recovery catalog:

```
RMAN> report obsolete;
RMAN retention policy will be applied to the command
RMAN retention policy is set to redundancy 1
no obsolete backups found
RMAN>
```

If you notice a discrepancy between the recovery catalog entries and the actual backups on disk, RMAN will continue to issue errors whenever you try to perform a backup or recovery. To get rid of entries in the recovery catalog that aren't valid anymore, you have to use the *delete* command with the *force* option, as shown in the following output:

```
RMAN> delete force noprompt archivelog sequence 40;
released channel: ORA_DISK_1
…
List of Archived Log Copies
Key     Thrd Seq    S   Low Time         Name
------- ---- ------- - --------- ------------------------------
72      1    40      A   10-JAN-03 /test01/app/oracle/oradata
remorse/arch/T0001S0000000040.ARC
deleted archive log
archive log filename=/test01/app/oracle/oradata/remorse/
arch/T0001S0000000040.ARC recid=33 stamp=482939840
Deleted 1 objects
RMAN>
```

Default Device Type

The default device for backups is disk. That is, RMAN will automatically make backups to a file system on your server. If you want the backup to be made to tape, you have to configure the default device type to sbt. All tape destinations are referred to as sbt. Here's an example that shows how to configure the default device to a tape:

```
RMAN> configure default device type to sbt;
new RMAN configuration parameters:
CONFIGURE DEFAULT DEVICE TYPE TO 'SBT_TAPE';
new RMAN configuration parameters are successfully stored
starting full resync of recovery catalog
full resync complete
RMAN>
```

If you wish to switch the default device back to disk, you can do so with the following command:

```
RMAN> configure default device type to disk;
old RMAN configuration parameters:
CONFIGURE DEFAULT DEVICE TYPE TO 'SBT_TAPE';
new RMAN configuration parameters:
CONFIGURE DEFAULT DEVICE TYPE TO DISK;
new RMAN configuration parameters are successfully stored
starting full resync of recovery catalog
full resync complete
RMAN> remove obsolete
```

Degree of Parallelism

The *degree of parallelism* (the default degree is 1) denotes the parallel channels that RMAN can open up during a backup or recovery. The time taken to complete the backup or recovery will decrease as you increase the degree of parallelism.

```
RMAN> configure device type disk parallelism 4;
new RMAN configuration parameters:
CONFIGURE DEVICE TYPE DISK PARALLELISM 4;
new RMAN configuration parameters are successfully stored
starting full resync of recovery catalog
full resync complete
released channel: ORA_DISK_1
RMAN>
```

Configuring Channels

Channels are the means by which RMAN conducts its backup and recovery operations, and they represent a single stream of data to a particular device (e.g., a tape). If you have four channels configured, four connections will be made to the target database to open up four separate server sessions.

What if you don't have enough space in one directory for your backup? You don't need to worry on this account, as you can set several disks as the backup target by configuring the *channels* parameter. In the following example, I configure two channels, with channel 1 backing up to the backup directory under /test01 and channel 2 backing up to the backup directory under /test02:

```
RMAN> confgure channel 1 device type disk format
 '/test01/app/oracle/oradata/backup/%U';
new RMAN configuration parameters:
CONFIGURE CHANNEL 1 DEVICE TYPE DISK FORMAT'/test01/app/oracle/oradata/backup/%U';
new RMAN configuration parameters are successfully stored
RMAN> configure channel 2 device type disk format
 '/test02/app/oracle/oradata/backup/%U';new RMAN configuration parameters:
CONFIGURE CHANNEL 2 DEVICE TYPE DISK
FORMAT'/test02/app/oracle/oradata/backup/%U';new RMAN configuration
parameters are successfully stored
```

TIP *The degree of parallelism parameter and the configure channel parameter are related to each other. For example, if the degree of parallelism is 4 and you have specified only two or even no channels at all, RMAN will open up four generic channels. If, on the other hand, you have manually configured six channels but set the degree of parallelism to 1, RMAN will use only the first channel and ignore the other five.*

Backup Optimization

The *backup optimization* feature, when turned on, will ensure that backups of files are skipped if identical versions of the file have already been backed up. Here is how you turn the parameter on:

```
RMAN> configure backup optimization on;
new RMAN configuration parameters:
CONFIGURE BACKUP OPTIMIZATION ON;
new RMAN configuration parameters are successfully stored
starting full resync of recovery catalog
full resync complete
RMAN>
```

Control File Parameters

RMAN has some configuration parameters that deal with control file backups. The following sections cover the important control file parameters.

Control File Autobackup

If you set the *controlfile autobackup* feature to *on*, each time you do a backup of your data files, the control file is automatically backed up along with the SPFILE, as shown in the following example:

```
RMAN> configure controlfile autobackup on;
old RMAN configuration parameters:
CONFIGURE CONTROLFILE AUTOBACKUP ON;
new RMAN configuration parameters:
CONFIGURE CONTROLFILE AUTOBACKUP ON;
new RMAN configuration parameters are successfully stored
starting full resync of recovery catalog
full resync complete
RMAN>
```

Now, if you use any *backup* command, the control file and the SPFILE are both automatically backed up, as shown in the following example:

```
RMAN> backup tablespace users;
Starting backup at 26-DEC-02
allocated channel: ORA_DISK_1
channel ORA_DISK_1: sid=17 devtype=DISK
...
Finished backup at 26-DEC-02
Starting Control File and SPFILE Autobackup at 26-DEC-02
piece handle=/test02/app/oracle/product/9.2.0.1.0
/dbs/c-3482335306-20021225-01 comment=NONE
Finished Control File and SPFILE Autobackup at 26-DEC-02
RMAN>
```

Control File Backup Location and Format

You can use the control file *autobackup format* parameter to specify the location and format of the control file backups. Here's an example:

```
RMAN> configure controlfile autobackup format for device type disk to
 '/test01/app/oracle/oradta/backup/cf_%F';
new RMAN configuration parameters:
CONFIGURE CONTROLFILE AUTOBACKUP FORMAT FOR
DEVICE TYPE DISK TO '/test01/app/oracle/oradata
/backup/cf_%F'; new RMAN configuration parameters
are successfully stored
RMAN>
```

Using the recovery catalog is purely optional, as Oracle can use the control file to store the RMAN repository data (metadata). However, as explained at the beginning of this chapter, it's a good idea to spend the little time it takes to create and use the recovery catalog. The recovery catalog is assumed to exist in all the discussions of RMAN in this and the next chapter. In the next section you'll learn what the recovery catalog is and how to create and manage it.

TIP *Make sure that the database in which the recovery catalog is being created runs in archivelog mode. This ensures that you can always perform a point-in-time recovery.*

Creating the Recovery Catalog

To create the recovery catalog, connect to the database in which you want to create the recovery catalog. You need to create a new schema called rman, grant the necessary privileges to it, and then create the recovery catalog. Once you create the catalog, you can register databases in it. Make sure you first create the rmantbs tablespace for the user rman.

NOTE *If you create your Oracle9i database using the Oracle Database Configuration Assistant (ODCA), you don't have to manually create the user rman. The rman schema will be already a part of the database and will have the recovery_catalog_owner role. The user rman's account, however, will be "locked and expired" when you create the database. You have to unlock the account and change the password to change the account status to open. Just make sure that the default tablespace for rman, tools, has adequate free space.*

Create the Recovery Catalog Schema

The following code shows how to create the recovery catalog schema:

```
Sql> CREATE USER rman IDENTIFIED BY rman1
     TEMPORARY TABLESPACE temp
     DEFAULT TABLESPACE rmantbs
     QUOTA UNLIMITED ON rmantbs;
User created.
SQL>
```

Make the Necessary Grants to User Rman

The following code shows how to make the necessary grants to user rman:

```
SQL> grant connect,resource to rman;
Grant succeeded.
SQL> grant recovery_catalog_owner to rman;
Grant succeeded.
SQL>
```

Connect As Rman

Before you actually make the connection, make sure that your database, if it is a brand-new one, is added to your tnsnames.ora file:

```
oracle@hp50.netbsa.org   [/u01/app/oracle/dba]
[monitor] $ rman
Recovery Manager: Release 9.2.0.1.0 - 64bit Production
Copyright (c) 1995, 2002, Oracle Corporation.  All rights reserved.
RMAN> connect catalog rman/rman1
connected to recovery catalog database
RMAN>
```

Create the Recovery Catalog

You are now ready to create the recovery catalog. If you want to drop the catalog later, the command you use to do so is just as easy as the one you use for creating it. The *drop catalog* command will remove the recovery catalog.

```
RMAN> create catalog
recovery catalog created
RMAN>
```

Note that if you're using a database where the user rman was created during database creation, you don't need to create the recovery catalog. The catalog already exists, and when you try to create it, it will give you the following error:

```
RMAN> create catalog
recovery catalog already exists
RMAN>
```

Registering a Database

For RMAN to do its job, you need to register to the target database you want to back up and recover. First, connect to the target database. In the following example, the rman credentials are entered at the command line. As you'll see, not only can you issue RMAN commands once you connect to the database, but you can also issue regular database administration commands for starting and shutting down the database.

```
oracle@hp50.netbsa.org    [/test02/app/oracle/product/9.2.0.1.0/network/admin]
[remorse] $ rman target remorse catalog rman/rman1@monitor
Recovery Manager: Release 9.2.0.1.0 - 64bit Production
Copyright (c) 1995, 2002, Oracle Corporation.  All rights reserved.
target database Password:
connected to target database: REMORSE (DBID=3482335306)
connected to recovery catalog database
RMAN>
```

TIP *Make sure the ORACLE_SID is set to the target database SID before you perform the following step. Otherwise, when you specify target, you'll connect not to the target database, but to the database whose instance name matches the ORACLE_SID of your UNIX session.*

Now that you're connected to the target database remorse, you're ready to register this database in the recovery catalog that exists on the database named monitor. Once you register the database, RMAN will automatically get all the relevant metadata pertaining the target database and store it in its own schema. Here's how you register a database:

```
RMAN> register database;
database registered in recovery catalog
starting full resync of recovery catalog
full resync complete
RMAN>
```

The target database remorse is now successfully registered in the recovery catalog, which is located in monitor. Now use the *list* command to see if the registration was successful. The output of the following *list schema* command should show all the data files of the target database:

```
RMAN> report schema;
Report of database schema
File Kbytes Tablespace  RB segs     Datafile Name
1   102400  UNDOTBS     YES   /test02/app/oracle/od/remorse/undotbs01.dbf
2   512000  SYSTEM      YES   /test02/app/oracle/odremorse/system02.dbf
3   25600   DATA01      NO    /test02/app/oracle/od/remorse/data01.dbf
4   25600   CUSTOM1     NO    /test02/app/oracle/od/remorse/custom0101.dbf
5   25600   SALEINDX01  NO    /test02/app/oracle/od/remorse/saleiindx01.01.dbf
...
12  512000  TEMP        NO    /test02/app/oracle/od/temp_01.dbf
```

You can also issue the following command to check the incarnation of the database:

```
RMAN> list incarnation;
List of Database Incarnations
DB Key  Inc Key  DB Name    DB ID       CUR Reset   SCN  Reset Time
-----   -------  -------    ----------- ----------- ---- -----------
  1       2      REMORSE    3482335306     YES       1   04-DEC-02
RMAN>
```

Changes made to the target database structure aren't automatically propagated to the recovery catalog. The *backup* and *copy* commands automatically perform a resync each time you perform a backup or copy. But you may need to manually resynchronize the recovery catalog under two circumstances: when your target database may have just undergone a number of physical changes and when the target database may be performing a very large number of log switches in between the backups.

During a resync operation, RMAN reads the target database's control file to update the information it keeps regarding data file, log switches, physical schema, and so forth. You issue the *resync* catalog command as follows, after you connect to the target database as shown previously:

```
RMAN> resync catalog;
starting full resync of recovery catalog
full resync complete
RMAN>
```

Backing Up the Recovery Catalog

You should always back up the recovery catalog right after you back up the target database. This ensures that you have all the latest information on the target database backed up safely. Backing up the recovery catalog becomes even more critical if you're using a single recovery catalog to store the metadata of all the databases in your system. The recovery catalog information is saved to the control file of the database in which the recovery catalog is created. You should follow these principles to afford the maximum possible security to the recovery catalog database:

- Never store the recovery catalog in the target database. You could end up losing the target database and the recovery catalog at the same time if there's a media failure.

- Make multiple copies of the recovery catalog backup, preferably to tape, in addition to disk backups.

- Set the retention policy value to greater than 1.

- Set *controlfile autobackup* on.

- Set a very high value for *control_file_record_keep_time* so the control file won't be overwritten quickly and thereby wipe out your recovery catalog information.

Backing up the recovery catalog safely tends to be a confusing task at first, but here are the salient points. First, back up the target database, remorse, with the RMAN utility with the recovery catalog enabled, as shown in Listing 14-3.

Listing 14-3. Backing Up the Target Database Using the Recovery Catalog

```
oracle@hp1[/test01/app/oracle/9.2.0.1.0/dbs]RMAN> backup database plus archivelog;
Starting backup at 11-JAN-03
current log archived
using channel ORA_DISK_1
using channel ORA_DISK_2
Starting backup at 11-JAN-03
current log archived
using channel ORA_DISK_1
using channel ORA_DISK_2
channel ORA_DISK_1: starting archive log backupset
channel ORA_DISK_1: specifying archive log(s) in backup set
input archive log thread=1 sequence=122 recid=115 stamp=483033990
channel ORA_DISK_1: starting piece 1 at 11-JAN-03
channel ORA_DISK_1: finished piece 1 at 11-JAN-03
piece handle=/test02/app/oracle/product/9.2.0.1.0/dbs/20ecl0s8_1_1 comment=NONE
channel ORA_DISK_1: backup set complete, elapsed time: 00:00:03
Finished backup at 11-JAN-03
...
Starting Control File and SPFILE Autobackup at 11-JAN-03
piece handle=/test02/app/oracle/product/9.2.0.1.0/
dbs/c-3482335306-20030111-00 comment=NONE
Finished Control File and SPFILE Autobackup at 11-JAN-03
RMAN>
```

The recovery catalog will now hold information about the backups of the target database.

Now that your recovery catalog database backup repository is going to be saved in its control file (because you are using it with the *nocatalog* option), back up the recovery catalog database (the monitor database) control file. The easiest way to do this is to turn the *controlfile autobackup* feature *on*, so RMAN will automatically back up your control file after every RMAN command that involves a backup or copy.

```
oracle@hp1  [/test02/app/oracle/product/9.2.0.1.0/network/admin]
[monitor] $ rman target /
Recovery Manager: Release 9.2.0.1.0 - 64bit Production
Copyright (c) 1995, 2002, Oracle Corporation.  All rights reserved.
connected to target database: MONITOR (DBID=2029096430)
RMAN> configure controlfile autobackup on;
using target database controlfile instead of recovery catalog
new RMAN configuration parameters:
CONFIGURE CONTROLFILE AUTOBACKUP ON;
new RMAN configuration parameters are successfully stored
RMAN>
```

Next, use RMAN to back up the recovery catalog database itself (the help database). When you perform this backup, don't use the recovery catalog. Enter RMAN with the *nocatalog* option.

```
[monitor] $ rman target /
Recovery Manager: Release 9.2.0.1.0 - 64bit Production
Copyright (c) 1995, 2002, Oracle Corporation.  All rights reserved.
connected to target database: MONITOR (DBID=2029096430)
RMAN> backup database plus archivelog;
Starting backup at 24-DEC-02
using target database controlfile instead of recovery catalog
...
Finished backup at 24-DEC-02
Starting Control File and SPFILE Autobackup at 24-DEC-02
piece handle=/test02/app/oracle/product/9.2.0.1.0
/dbs/c-2029096430-20021224-01 comment=NONE
Finished Control File and SPFILE Autobackup at 24-DEC-02
RMAN>
```

Note that RMAN backs up both the control file and the SPFILE as part of a full backup of the database with the recovery catalog.

Examples of Various Backups Using RMAN

The following sections take you through a few examples of various kinds of backups you can perform using RMAN.

Backing Up an Entire Database

If you want to back up the entire database, you use the *backup database* command, as shown here:

```
RMAN> BACKUP DATABASE;
Starting backup at 24-DEC-02
using channel ORA_DISK_1
using channel ORA_DISK_2
using channel ORA_DISK_3
using channel ORA_DISK_4
channel ORA_DISK_1: starting full datafile backupset
channel ORA_DISK_1: specifying datafile(s) in backupset
input datafile fno=00002 name=/test01/app/oracle/oradata/remorse/undotbs01.dbf
...
channel ORA_DISK_4: finished piece 1 at 24-DEC-02
piece handle=/test02/app/oracle/product/9.2.0.1.0/dbs/0beb836f_1_1 comment=NONE
channel ORA_DISK_4: backup set complete, elapsed time: 00:00:28
Finished backup at 24-DEC-02
Starting Control File and SPFILE Autobackup at 24-DEC-02
piece handle=/test02/app/oracle/product/9.2.0.1.0/
dbs/c-3482335306-20021225-02 comment=NONE
Finished Control File and SPFILE Autobackup at 24-DEC-02
RMAN>
```

Backing Up the Archived Logs

You can use the *backup archivelog all* command to back up all archived logs that have not been backed up already. Here's what the *backup archivelog all* command output looks like:

```
RMAN> BACKUP ARCHIVELOG ALL;
Starting backup at 24-DEC-02
current log archived
using channel ORA_DISK_1
...
channel ORA_DISK_3: backup set complete,
 elapsed time: 00:00:01
channel ORA_DISK_4: finished piece 1 at 24-DEC-02
Starting Control File and SPFILE Autobackup at 24-DEC-02
piece handle=/test02/app/oracle/product/9.2.0.1.0
/dbs/c-3482335306-20021225-03 comment=NONE
Finished Control File and SPFILE Autobackup at 24-DEC-02
RMAN>
```

Backing Up the Control File

The *backup current controlfile* command backs up the control file, as shown in
Listing 14-4.

Listing 14-4. Backing Up the Control File

```
RMAN> backup current controlfile;
Starting backup at 24-DEC-02
using channel ORA_DISK_1
channel ORA_DISK_1: starting full datafile backupset
channel ORA_DISK_1: specifying datafile(s) in backupset
including current controlfile in backupset
channel ORA_DISK_1: starting piece 1 at 24-DEC-02
channel ORA_DISK_1: finished piece 1 at 24-DEC-02
piece handle=/test02/app/oracle/product/9.2.0.1.0/dbs/05eb5dkf_1_1 comment=NONE
channel ORA_DISK_1: backup set complete, elapsed time: 00:00:01
Finished backup at 24-DEC-02
Starting Control File and SPFILE Autobackup at 24-DEC-02
piece handle=/test02/app/oracle/product/9.2.0.1.0
/dbs/c-2029096430-20021224-02 comment=NONE
Finished Control File and SPFILE Autobackup at 24-DEC-02
RMAN>
```

If you had already configured the control file with autobackup on, you can
back up the entire database—data files, log files, and the control file—with the
following command:

```
RMAN> BACKUP DATABASE PLUS ARCHIVELOG;
```

Backing Up a Tablespace

You can back up individual tablespaces if you are operating the database in
archivelog mode:

```
RMAN> backup tablespace rmantbs;
Starting backup at 24-DEC-02
using channel ORA_DISK_1
...
Finished backup at 24-DEC-02
Starting Control File and SPFILE Autobackup at 24-DEC-02
piece handle=/test02/app/oracle/product/9.2.0.1.0
/dbs/c-2029096430-20021224-03 comment=NONE
Finished Control File and SPFILE Autobackup at 24-DEC-02
RMAN>
```

Performing Incremental Backups

Incremental backups are much faster than backing up the database each time.
Incremental backups will back up only those data blocks that changed since the last
level 0 backup. To perform a level 1 incremental backup, you must first have a base
level 0 backup. RMAN provides two types of incremental backups: differential and
cumulative. Listing 14-5 illustrates how you can get a level 0 backup to start with.

Listing 14-5. Getting the Level 0 Backup

```
RMAN> backup incremental level=0 database;
Starting backup at 24-DEC-02
using channel ORA_DISK_1
using channel ORA_DISK_2
using channel ORA_DISK_3
using channel ORA_DISK_4
channel ORA_DISK_1: starting incremental level 0 datafile backupset
channel ORA_DISK_1: specifying datafile(s) in backupset
input datafile fno=00002 name=/test01/app/oracle/oradata/remorse/undotbs01.dbf
...
channel ORA_DISK_4: finished piece 1 at 24-DEC-02
piece handle=/test02/app/oracle/product/9.2.0.1.0/dbs/0leb83l7_1_1 comment=NONE
channel ORA_DISK_4: backup set complete, elapsed time: 00:00:32
Finished backup at 25-DEC-02
Starting Control File and SPFILE Autobackup at 24-DEC-02
piece handle=/test02/app/oracle/product/9.2.0.1.0/dbs
/c-3482335306-20021225-04 comment=NONE
Finished Control File and SPFILE Autobackup at 24-DEC-02
RMAN>
```

Once you have the level 0 backup, you perform a level 1 *differential* incremental backup using the backup command shown in Listing 14-6.

Listing 14-6. Getting the Level 1 Backup

```
RMAN> backup incremental level=1 database;
Starting backup at 24-DEC-02
using channel ORA_DISK_1
channel ORA_DISK_1: starting incremental level 1 datafile backupset
channel ORA_DISK_1: specifying datafile(s) in backupset
input datafile fno=00001 name=/test02/app/oracle/oradata/help/system01.dbf
input datafile fno=00002 name=/test02/app/oracle/oradata/help/undotbs01.dbf
input datafile fno=00004 name=/test01/app/oracle/oradata/recover.dbf01_COPY
channel ORA_DISK_1: starting piece 1 at 24-DEC-02
channel ORA_DISK_1: finished piece 1 at 24-DEC-02 with 2 copies
piece handle=/test01/app/oracle/oradata/backup/1idopc0h_1_1 comment=NONE
piece handle=/test01/app/oracle/oradata/backup/1idopc0h_1_2 comment=NONE
channel ORA_DISK_1: backup set complete, elapsed time: 00:00:26
Finished backup at 24-DEC-02
RMAN>
```

A *cumulative* incremental backup at level *n* will perform a backup of all changed blocks since the last backup at level *n-1* or lower. So, if you perform the cumulative incremental backup at level 2 as shown in Listing 14-7, it will back up all data blocks changed since level 0 or level 1.

Listing 14-7. Making a Cumulative Incremental Backup

```
RMAN> backup cumulative incremental level=2 cumulative database;
Starting backup at 24-DEC-02
using channel ORA_DISK_1
channel ORA_DISK_1: starting incremental level 2 datafile backupset
channel ORA_DISK_1: specifying datafile(s) in backupset
input datafile fno=00001 name=/test02/app/oracle/oradata/help/system01.dbf
input datafile fno=00002 name=/test02/app/oracle/oradata/help/undotbs01.dbf
input datafile fno=00004 name=/test01/app/oracle/oradata/recover.dbf01_COPY
channel ORA_DISK_1: starting piece 1 at 24-DEC-02
channel ORA_DISK_1: finished piece 1 at 24-DEC-02 with 2 copies
piece handle=/test01/app/oracle/oradata/backup/1kdopc29_1_1 comment=NONE
piece handle=/test01/app/oracle/oradata/backup/1kdopc29_1_2 comment=NONE
channel ORA_DISK_1: backup set complete, elapsed time: 00:00:36
Finished backup at 24-DEC-02
RMAN>
```

Using RMAN to Perform Online Backups

The RMAN utility performs online backups in a more efficient manner than the normal user-managed backups, besides providing many extra benefits that make the backups far easier and safer. For one thing, you don't have to place the tablespaces being backed up into the begin backup and end backup modes. In addition, only the used space in the database is backed up, not the entire allocated space. The problem of fractured blocks is also taken care of, because RMAN will continue to read the blocks until it gets a consistent read.

Listing 14-8 is a typical script that performs online backups using RMAN, assuming you are backing up to disk. Assume also that the RMAN's recovery catalog is being used.

Listing 14-8. Performing an Online Backup with RMAN

```
RMAN> run {
# backup the database to disk
allocate channel d1 type disk;
allocate channel t2 type disk;
allocate channel t3 type disk;
#backup the whole db
backup
tag whole_database_open
format '/a10/oradata//backups/db_%t_%s_p%p'
database;
```

```
# switch the current log file
sql 'alter system archive log current';
#backup the archived logs
backup
archivelog all
format '/a11/oradata/backups/al_%t_%s_p%p';
# backup a copy of the controlfile
backup
current controlfile
tag = cf1
format '/a12/oradata/backups/cf_%t_%s_p%p';
release channel d1;
release channel d2;
release channel d3;
        }
RMAN>
```

> **NOTE** *Just as with user-managed backups, you can monitor RMAN's backups using several important data dictionary views. The V$BACKUP_CORRUPTION and V$COPY_CORRUPTION views provide information about corrupt blocks.*

Using a Media Management Layer with RMAN

It's not uncommon these days to see Oracle databases that are hundreds of giga-bytes in size. Backing up large mission-critical databases poses challenges to the DBA in terms of the techniques to be used and the longer time periods involved in performing backups. In recent years, several advances in technology have con-tributed to easing the DBA's burden in this area. Today's leading solutions do provide an array of choices, in terms of both strategy and third-party tools, to make the backup process extremely efficient and safe. Traditional backup methods mostly involved the use of UNIX scripts, which are laborious to write and maintain. The time factor becomes critical as the databases get larger all the time.

Manually tracking backup files and backup operations also starts hitting the point of diminishing returns after a while. Even if you use RMAN, a large number of databases make it imperative to work with a third-party tool to manage the backup schedules and to automate the media devices. It's very common for most firms that have a meaningful number of databases to use third-party tools to streamline their backups and automate pretty much the entire process. Oracle maintains the Oracle Backup Solutions Program (BSP), which is a team of vendors whose media-management products are designed to work with RMAN. Some of the important players in the field are Legato Systems (NetWorker) and VERITAS (NetBackup). For a complete list of the BSP members, please visit
http://otn.oracle.com/deploy/availability/htdocs/bsp.htm#MMV.

The Legato NetWorker product offered by Legato Systems is strongly sup-ported by Oracle Corporation and is intertwined with RMAN. NetWorker provides an automated way of performing backups that includes monitoring all the backups in addition to scheduling them. NetWorker also has the capability to perform parallel backups to multiple tape systems simultaneously, thereby cutting down on the time needed for backups of extremely large databases. Dedicated storage servers and autochanger-based tape drives are used by Legato as well as other similar private-party offerings. Basically, NetWorker accepts data through RMAN, saves it on tape, and provides archiving and indexing services for the tapes. Products such as NetWorker are configured to provide much better I/O performance than the traditional operating system utilities.

Another interesting third-party product is HP Business Copy XP, which is offered by Hewlett-Packard in support of their HP line of UNIX machines. Business Copy XP is an array-based mirroring strategy that enables you to make copies online in a fraction of the time it normally takes. You can even run background processes on the copied data without adversely affecting production. This reduction in the time taken for backups enables more frequent backups.

Using Legato Single Server Version with RMAN

Although you can use the RMAN utility to manually perform backups and recovery, there are limitations to that method. If you're using tape backups, you should use a data storage management system, which will automatically load and unload tapes for you, among other things. Oracle used to bundle the Legato Storage Manager (LSM), a third-party media manager, with its 8*i* and 9*i* (release 1) server software. In the Oracle 9.2 version, Oracle includes the new Legato Single Server Version (LSSV) product, which is actually a "light" version of the Legato NetWorker product (http://www.legato.com).

LSSV serves as an interface between your RMAN backups and the storage devices used to store the backups. You can initiate a backup using RMAN, and then LSSV receives the backup data from RMAN and stores it on backup media. Similarly, during a recovery, you issue a recovery command through RMAN, and it's LSSV again that fetches necessary data from the appropriate tape storage volumes and passes it to RMAN. In the discussion that follows, I use LSSV as an example of a third-party MML. All MML products are similar in the way they are integrated with the RMAN utility. Therefore, even if you're using other MML products, the discussion that follows should help you understand how a typical MML works, which is your real goal.

As stated previously, LSSV is an example of a third-party media manager. It performs actions such as loading and unloading the tape drives and scheduling the backups. The media manager can also control tape libraries that can control a large number of tape drives. LSSV takes care of both the storage devices attached to your Oracle server and the storage volumes (tapes) used by the devices. During a recovery, LSSV knows which tape has the data you're looking for. The LSSV software is integrated with the Oracle server, so when you issue a backup or restore command, the server redirects the command to the media manager (LSSV) to back up or read files from sequential storage such as tape drives. This automation of the backup and recovery process makes tools like LSSV an indispensable part of your backup and recovery system. In this section, you'll take a look at how to install, configure, and use LSSV to manage the backups made through RMAN.

LSSV is a lighter version of Legato's NetWorker product, and it provides an entry-level MML to RMAN. As such, it doesn't have all the capabilities of a full-fledged storage management system, such as autochangers and scheduled backups. Further, it's capable of using only a maximum of four tapes. You can integrate LSSV (as well as NetWorker) with OEM and perform offline backups, online backups, and recovery with it. You may want to explore the possibility of purchasing a comprehensive storage product such as NetWorker or Omniback if your organization's needs warrant it. For example, the NetWorker systems can manage 32 or more tapes simultaneously. So, if you're using RMAN, you can specify 32 or more channels for simultaneous backup and recovery. The full-fledged systems also provide the capability to back up server file systems. Even if you're planning on using other types of storage systems, LSSV gives you an introduction to the use of those complex systems.

In the following discussion of the use of LSSV, assume that RMAN is being used with the recovery catalog option. If you aren't using the recovery catalog, LSSV can't perform some types of recovery (e.g., point-in-time recovery).

NOTE *Typically, MML tools can support the backup of Oracle data files, control files, and redo log files. You can't use them to support backups of any other files on the server.*

The LSSV Architecture

The LSSV software is installed on the server, and it has two components: an LSSV server and an LSSV Administrator GUI component that you can use to manage the LSSV server. Tasks you can perform with the LSSV Administrator GUI program you can also perform using the LSSV character-based interface, which is called the *nsradmin* program. In addition, you can enter individual LSSV commands at the operating system command line. You can run the LSSV Administrator GUI program on the server machine or from your Windows workstation.

RMAN *doesn't deal with the media directly* when you use an MML such as Legato NetWorker. RMAN simply sends a named stream of bytes, and it's the MML's job to copy it to the tape devices. All the tape loading and unloading commands are the responsibility of the MML. The MML server administers the required configurations as a set of internal resources. For example, resources would be items such as devices, clients, and schedules. You administer the MML by manipulating the values of these resources, and you can use the command line or a GUI to manage the resources. The following main resources are configurable by the LSSV server:

- *NSR:* This is the LSSV server resource. Its attributes control the authorization of administrators, among others.

- *NSR client:* The client usually is the target Oracle database. Its attributes include the files to be saved, the schedules to be used, and the client group.

- *NSR device:* This is the actual storage device used in the backup and recovery. The attributes include the device name, the media type, and the name of the volume currently being used.

- *NSR pool:* A *pool* refers to a collection of backup volumes. The pool determines the volume the backups should be stored on.

- *NSR policy:* The policy controls the lifetime of the backups. The policy attributes are part of the index management process.

- *NSR label template:* The label templates are names for the pools of backup volumes.

- *NSR schedule:* You can set schedules for your backups through LSSV. The backup levels are determined by the schedule attributes.

The resource information is kept in the form of text files on the server. You can use the *nsradmin* tool or the *nwadmin* tool to configure the resources. You configure an individual resource by modifying its attributes. The configuration of the previously listed resources determines how the MML interacts with your Oracle server. Here is an example of what a resource file looks like:

```
Type:              NSR schedule;
Action:            incr incr incr incr full incr, incr;
Administrator:     root, oracle;
Name:              hp1;
Period:            week;
```

LSSV maintains two online files, the *client index* and the *media index,* in which it stores information to help manage all Oracle backups. Users can browse this index information.

Installing LSSV

I performed my installation of LSSV on an HP-UX 11–based UNIX server. The procedure changes only slightly among servers. Complete documentation for installing and managing LSSV is available at http://www.legato.com/lssv. The LSSV installation process installs the necessary files in the /opt/networker directory by default. To start the installation, a user with the root privilege must log into the server. Here are the installation steps:

1. Mount the Oracle9*i* CD-ROM and go to the /stage/Components/lgto directory.

2. Type the following command to invoke the Legato Installer:

    ```
    $> . /lsminst lgto
    ```

3. From the window that appears, select Legato Single Server Version as the software you want to install.

4. At the Action prompt, enter **Install**.

5. The installation starts. After it is finished, click Complete and exit the Software Selection window.

6. Update your MANPATH variable to $MANPATH:/opt/networker/bin. Update your PATH variable to $PATH:/opt/networker/bin.

7. Start the LSSV Administrator by typing in **nwadmin**. This command works
   on a Windows server too, if you choose to install the LSSV software on it.
   In Windows, you can also access the LSSV administrator by going to Start
   ➤ Programs ➤ NetWorker Group ➤ NetWorker Administrator. Then type
   Registration at the Server prompt. In the Registration window, click
   create. In the Enabler Code window, type in the code provided in the
   installation manual, which is **fa577c-126e3f-d26553**. Click Apply.

You can confirm that LSSV has been correctly installed on your server by
typing the following command (you should be logged in as the root user):

```
root@hp1:/ #/usr/sbin/swlist |grep -i lssv
NetWorker              nw_lssv.Build.71 NetWorker for HP-UX 11.XX (32-bit)
```

Note that *swlist* is an HP UNIX command that lists installed software on the
system.

Using LSSV

You can use LSSV either through operating system–level commands or through
the character-based administrative tool nsradmin. In addition, you can invoke
LSSV in a GUI mode. The GUI mode, of course, is a lot easier to use. The UNIX
system administrator must log into LSSV first and grant you administrative rights
to use LSSV. The root user needs to invoke the LSSV administrator screen by using
the command *nsradmin* at the command prompt. Once the Storage Manager
administrative screen comes up, the system administrator should add the Oracle
DBA's operating system name to the list of administrators.

Once you are made a part of the administrative group, you can invoke
the administrator tool for LSSV by typing in either **nsradmin** or **nwadmin** at the
command prompt. The *nsradmin* command will bring up a character-based window
through which you can manage LSSV. Figure 14-1 shows the nsradmin window.

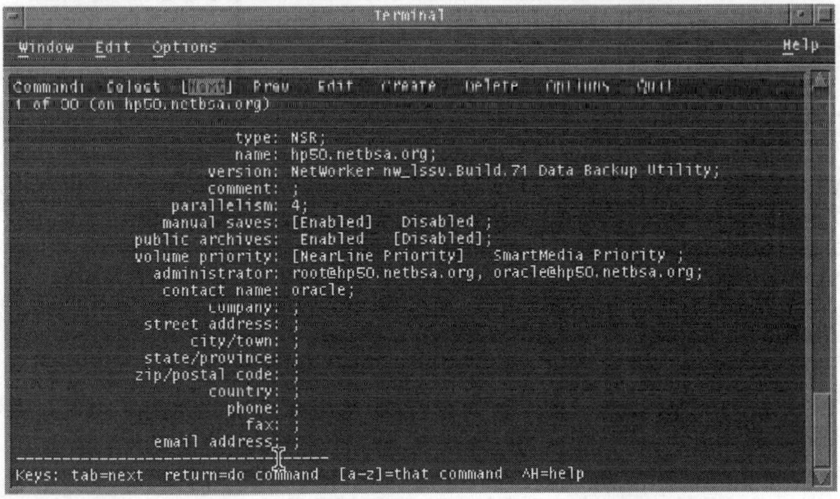

Figure 14-1. The nsradmin window

Typing **nwadmin** will bring up the LSSV Administrator window. Using the GUI LSSV Administrator, you can modify resources such as servers, clients, devices, pools, and policies. Figure 14-2 shows the LSSV GUI interface invoked by the *nwadmin* command at the operating system command line. LSSV has two GUI utilities that you can invoke with the commands *nwbackup* and *nwrecover* to perform operating system file backup and restores. LSSV provides complete media management capabilities, including the ability to tape labels, track media, and manage retention policy.

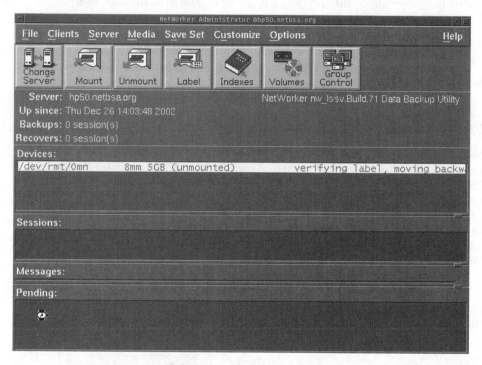

Figure 14-2. The LSSV GUI interface

LSSV and its full-blown version, Legato NetWorker, are sophisticated products that take some work to master. Your main goal in this chapter, though, is seeing how RMAN interacts with an MML like LSSV, and this will also be the focus of the next chapter. Once you get comfortable with LSSV, it's a simple step to upgrade to the full-featured Legato NetWorker. The tape formats of LSSV are compatible with those of NetWorker, and all the backups you make using the "light" version are fully usable with NetWorker as well.

LSSV and RMAN

To do tape backups, you need to configure some third-party MML such as LSSV. After you install the MML, you should first do a couple of operating system–level backups using the MML to make sure it has been installed properly. After you have verified that the MML software has been correctly installed, you can do database backups to tapes using RMAN.

Listing 14-9 shows an example where RMAN is used to back up the system data file to tapes managed by LSSV.

Listing 14-9. Using LSSV and RMAN

```
oracle@hp1   [/test01/app/oracle/9.2.0.1.0]
[help] $ rman catalog /
Recovery Manager: Release 9.2.0.1.0 - 64bit Production
(c) Copyright 2001 Oracle Corporation.  All rights reserved.
connected to target database: HELP (DBID=3588476182)
RMAN> run
2> {
3> allocate channel c1 device type sbt
4> PARMS='ENV={NSR_GROUP=default)';
5> backup datafile 1;
6> }
allocated channel: c1
channel c1: sid=11 devtype=SBT_TAPE
channel c1: MMS Version 2.2.0.1
Starting backup at 26-DEC-02
channel c1: starting full datafile backupset
channel c1: specifying datafile(s) in backupset
input datafile fno=00001 name=/test02/app/oracle/oradata/help/system01.dbf
channel c1: starting piece 1 at 26-DEC-02
channel c1: finished piece 1 at 26-DEC-02
piece handle=0sdoml43_1_1 comment=API Version 1.1,MMS Version 2.2.0.1
channel c1: backup set complete, elapsed time: 00:10:16
Finished backup at 26-DEC-02
Starting Control File Autobackup at 26-DEC-02
piece handle=c-3588476182-20020517-00 comment=API Version 1.1,MMS Version 2.2.0.1
Finished Control File Autobackup at 26-DEC-02
released channel: c1
RMAN>
```

In this example, it doesn't matter if your default backup device is disk or tape. The *allocate channel* command overrides the default configuration. The device type is specified as sbt, which indicates a tape device (operating system files would be denoted by keyword *disk*). Whenever you use a tape device, you are expected to provide RMAN with a set of characteristics of the device by using the PARMS keyword. The PARMS line includes the NSR GROUP resource, which tells RMAN that LSSV is being used to manage the tape devices. The *backup datafile 1* command will back up the first file—the system file—in the database named *help*. Channel 1 is opened and then closed automatically after the backup.

> **TIP** *RMAN doesn't necessarily indicate problems it might have with the tape devices. For example, if your tape driver isn't mounted for use, RMAN will still try to use the MML and perform the backup. It just sits there, without issuing any error messages. If you monitor the progress of the backup by using the GUI tool, you can see problems like this clearly and troubleshoot them.*

In the previous example, the *run* command used the PARMS keyword to describe the tape device. You can make the *run* command a lot simpler, if you always intend to use this tape device, by configuring it as the default device. Listing 14-10 shows an example.

Listing 14-10. Configuring a Tape Device As the Default Device

```
RMAN> show device type;
RMAN configuration parameters are:
CONFIGURE DEVICE TYPE DISK PARALLELISM 1;
RMAN> configure channel device type sbt
2> PARMS='ENV(NSR_GROUP=default)' ';
new RMAN configuration parameters:
CONFIGURE CHANNEL DEVICE TYPE 'SBT_TAPE' PARMS  'ENV(NSR_GROUP=default)';
new RMAN configuration parameters are successfully stored
RMAN> backup datafile 2;
Starting backup at 26-DEC-02
configuration for DISK channel 2 is ignored
allocated channel: ORA_DISK_1
channel ORA_DISK_1: sid=10 devtype=DISK
channel ORA_DISK_1: starting full datafile backupset
channel ORA_DISK_1: specifying datafile(s) in backupset
input datafile fno=00002 name=/test02/app/oracle/oradata/help/undotbs01.dbf
channel ORA_DISK_1: starting piece 1 at 26-DEC-02
channel c1: finished piece 1 at 26-DEC-02
piece handle=0sdoml43_1_1 comment=API Version 1.1,MMS Version 2.2.0.1
channel c1: backup set complete, elapsed time: 00:2:35
Finished backup at 26-DEC-02
released channel: c1
RMAN>
```

In this example, you have to manually configure the tape channel by using the *allocate channel* command. If you want to use the same configuration in the future, you can simplify matters by using the *configure channels* command as follows to avoid having to allocate the channels each time you do a backup:

```
RMAN> configure default device type to sbt;
old RMAN configuration parameters:
CONFIGURE DEFAULT DEVICE TYPE TO DISK;
new RMAN configuration parameters:
CONFIGURE DEFAULT DEVICE TYPE TO 'SBT_TAPE';
```

```
new RMAN configuration parameters are successfully stored
starting full resync of recovery catalog
full resync complete
RMAN> backup database;
```

In this example, RMAN automatically connects to the MML (LSSV, in this case) to back up to the tape device, provided you've already specified the MML when you defined the tape devices by using the *CONFIGURE CHANNEL DEVICE TYPE 'SBT_TAPE' PARMS 'ENV (NSR_GROUP=default)'* command.

You can also parallelize your backup sessions when you use LSSV with RMAN. As noted previously, you can have a maximum of four tape devices for simultaneous use during a backup or recovery when you use LSSV. The following are the steps for parallelizing the backup and recovery operations using LSSV and RMAN:

1. Configure the degree pf parallelization by selecting nwadmin ➤ Server Setup ➤ Parallelism. Choose 4, which is the maximum number of tape devices you can have.

2. Select nwadimin ➤ Media ➤ Devices ➤ Target Sessions. Set this to 1.

Now you are set up for parallelization of your backup stream to more than one tape device. If you intend to use all four tape devices, your backup script would look like the following:

```
RMAN> rman {
allocate channel  t1  type 'sbt_tape';
allocate channel  t2  type 'sbt_tape';
allocate channel  t3  type 'sbt_tape';
allocate channel  t4  type 'sbt_tape';
backup
format 'dbfull_weekend_s%s_t%t'
tab 'weekly full backup'
(database);
}
RMAN>
```

As you can see, RMAN integrates well with an MML, thereby allowing the use of tape devices for your backups. The preceding discussion used a scaled-down version of NetWorker, and you should have no problem using that product or a similar product, as you now have an understanding of how RMAN integrates with an MML in general. The combination of storage management products, such as LSSV with RMAN, makes it possible for you to make backups to any storage medium very easily.

Creating Backups with Operating System Commands

You can make completely valid backups yourself, without the use of RMAN, by using the operating system copy commands such as *cp* and *dd* in UNIX and the *copy* command in Windows systems. You can also connect to a media manager if you want to make tape backups. The big difference is, of course, that you have to keep track of all the backups, check their validity, and also decide which of the backups you'll need during a recovery session. This is the reason Oracle calls this method *user-managed backups*. RMAN offers you many advantages over a manual user-managed backup system, but you still need to know how to back up your databases using the traditional user-managed backup (and recovery) techniques. After all, your RMAN utility might fail to work someday for some strange reason, and what do you do then? The next sections briefly examine the operating system methods to back up databases and their components.

Making Whole Database Backups

You can make a backup of the entire database when the database is closed or when it's open, provided you're operating in archivelog mode. If you're using noarchivelog mode, you can only make a closed database backup, as long as the database was shut down cleanly through a normal, immediate, or transactional shutdown. The backups taken when the database is open are called *hot backups* or sometimes *warm backups*. If the database is backed up after it's shut down cleanly, the backup is termed a *cold backup*. So, you can make a hot or cold backup of a database run in archivelog mode, but only a cold backup of a database run in noarchivelog mode. Note that the procedure for making a cold backup is similar for both archivelog and noarchivelog mode databases. In both cases, the database has to be shut down cleanly and a backup made of all the database files.

You can perform user-managed backups of archivelog databases with the database either open or closed. You can choose to shut down the database completely and copy the relevant files to disk or tape, or you can back up a running database's data files. Obviously, the backups of a running database, the online backups, are more cumbersome and more likely to need troubleshooting in general. If your organization can afford the downtime involved (which may be under an hour for a small-to-medium database and up to several hours for a large database), then the offline backup is a sensible approach. If you can't bring the database down frequently (on at least a daily or weekly basis, depending on the volume of transactions), then you have no choice but to make online backups.

Making a Whole Closed Backup

You need to back up the entire set of files necessary to restore the database: the data files, online redo log files, and control files. Technically, you need only one control file to restore the database, but because the init.ora file or the SPFILE will refer to multiple control files, you might as well back up all the multiplexed copies of the control files. You first get a list of the files in each category, and you then copy the files to the target. In the following sections you'll learn how you can do the backup of the three main types of files involved in a whole closed backup.

Backing Up the Data Files

You can get the list of all the data files in your database by using the following query:

```
SQL> select file_name from dba_data_files;
FILE_NAME
----------------------------------------------
C:\ORACLENT\ORADATA\HELPME\SYSTEM01.DBF
C:\ORACLENT\ORADATA\HELPME\UNDOTBS01.xB
C:\ORACLENT\ORADATA\HELPME\CWMLITE01.DBF
C:\ORACLENT\ORADATA\HELPME\DRSYS01.DBF
C:\ORACLENT\ORADATA\HELPME\EXAMPLE01.DBF
C:\ORACLENT\ORADATA\HELPME\INDX01.DBF
C:\ORACLENT\ORADATA\HELPME\TOOLS01.DBF
C:\ORACLENT\ORADATA\HELPME\USERS01.DBF
8 rows selected.
SQL>
```

You can then use the UNIX *cp* command (or the Windows *copy* command) to copy these data files to whatever location you want. You may first copy them to an operating system file and later on copy those files to a tape device, so you can store them off-site. For example, in UNIX, you may use the following command to back up the files:

```
$ cp /u01/oradata/data/data_01.dbf  /u09/oradata/data/data_01.dbf
 (copying to a UNIX file system)
```

Backing Up the Online Redo Log Files

You'll need to back up all the online redo log files when you perform a closed backup. You can get the list of online redo files by making the following query:

```
SQL> select member from v$logfile;
MEMBER
--------------------------------------------------
C:\ORACLENT\ORADATA\HELPME\REDO03.LOG
C:\ORACLENT\ORADATA\HELPME\REDO02.LOG
C:\ORACLENT\ORADATA\HELPME\REDO01.LOG
SQL>
```

Backing Up the Control Files

You can find the control file names and their location by querying the V$CONTROLFILE view:

```
SQL> select name from v$controlfile;
NAME
--------------------------------------------------
C:\ORACLENT\ORADATA\HELPME\CONTROL01.CTL
C:\ORACLENT\ORADATA\HELPME\CONTROL02.CTL
C:\ORACLENT\ORADATA\HELPME\CONTROL03.CTL
SQL>
```

A Simple Cold Backup Script

Scripts for cold backups are fairly simple. Because you're doing a backup while the database is shut down, the backup process boils down to copying all the necessary files using the operating system copy utilities.

```
#!/bin/ksh
ORACLE_SID=$1
export ORACLE_SID
export ORAENV_ASK=NO
BACKUP_DIR=/test01/app/oracle
. oraenv
sqlplus -s   system/remorse1 << EOF
set head off feed off echo off trimspool on linesize 200
spool  /u01/app/oracle/dba/cold_backup.ksh
select  'cp ' ||file_name||    ' ${BACKUP_DIR}' from sys.dba_data_files;
select  'cp ' ||name ||  ' ${BACKUP_DIR}'  from V$controlfile;
select  'cp ' ||member||  ' ${BACKUP_DIR}' from V$logfile;
spool off;
exit;
EOF
```

When you run the preceding commands, the output will be cold_backup.ksh, which you can then make into an executable script and schedule for regular execution using cron.

Making a Whole Open Backup

There's a world of difference between making closed backups and open backups. Open backups imply that users are changing data while you're backing up, and this leads to more complex mechanisms on behalf of the Oracle server to perform the backups.

You need to back up all the data files, control files, and archived redo logs for a complete online database backup. You use the normal operating system copy commands to achieve this, but because the database is actually running, you need to add some other commands to make the backups valid and consistent. To understand this, it's necessary to understand the anatomy of online backups, or what happens within the database during an online backup.

What Happens While an Online Backup Is Being Performed?

When you first prepare the tablespace for the backup by issuing the *begin backup* command, Oracle notes the SCNs in the data file headers and "freezes" them. In other words, the data file header checkpoint SCNs will remain constant at their old values until the backup is completed and the command *end backup* is issued. Does this mean that the data file isn't being written to by Oracle during the backup process? Not at all! Oracle will continue writing all the changes to the data files and to the redo log files. The redo log files get filled up pretty fast in most cases, because Oracle will be writing the entire data block instead of just the changes made by individual transactions, as is done during normal operation. As users are modifying the data during the online backup, checkpoints will occur as normal and data blocks will keep being written to disk as usual. Once the backup is completed for the entire tablespace, Oracle will advance the checkpoint SCN for each file to the latest actual SCN value.

The crucial idea in the hot backup process is that should a crash of the database occur during recovery before the end of the backup, recovery can be performed based on the checkpoint that was noted when the tablespace was first put in backup mode. The SCN that is frozen in the file headers is placed there right after a checkpoint, which flushes all the modified records in the buffer to the data files. There is a considerable amount of redo log activity during hot backups, mostly to handle what is known as the *split block* problem. Note that the while the online backup is being made of a particular Oracle block, the block could be in the process of being written to. Consequently, a backed-up copy could conceivably end up with *inconsistent* data, with part of the data from before the change was made and the rest from after the change. The inconsistent block thus produced is called a split block. Oracle copies the entire block to the redo log file to make sure that it can create a consistent version of the block later on if it indeed has been split during the hot backup process.

How to Perform a Hot Backup

Performing a hot (online) backup involves certain unique commands due to the fact that the database is operating while you are making copies of the data files. The following is the basic hot backup process:

1. The following is the command you issue to perform hot backups. You'll repeat the command for all the tablespaces in the database:

   ```
   SQL> alter tablespace proddata_01 begin backup;
   ```

2. Copy all the data files that are part of the proddata_01 tablespace. The operating system *copy* command is invoked at this point to perform the physical copy of all the data files.

   ```
   SQL> host cp /u10/app./oracle/oradata/remorse/users01.dbf
                /u01/app/oracle/remorse/backup
   ```

3. End the tablespace backup after the copying of all the files is completed with the following statement:

   ```
   SQL> alter tablespace proddata_01 end backup;
   ```

The *end backup* command instructs Oracle to take the concerned tablespace out of backup mode.

 TIP *RMAN doesn't put the tablespaces in the begin backup and end backup modes. The Oracle server session checks the data block header and footer to see if the data block is "fractured." If it is, the RMAN server simply reads the data block again to get a consistent view of it.*

When you perform an online whole backup of an archivelog database, you must back up the control file using the special *backup to 'filename'* command, as shown here:

```
SQL> alter database backup controlfile to
     'c:\oraclent\oradata\helpme\';
```

During a recovery, you need to use the backup of the control file derived in the previous manner to avoid problems you may encounter if you try to use the normal operating system copy of the control file.

You've seen how the online backup mechanism works. You'll now move on to examine a complete online backup script. Listing 14-11 contains a complete online backup script that will dynamically pick up all the tablespaces in the databases and back them up to disk, from where they can be copied to a tape later on.

Listing 14-11. An Online Backup Script

```ksh
#!/bin/ksh
ORACLE_SID=$1
export  ORACLE_SID
export ORACLE_ASK=NO
   BACKUP_DIR=/u01/app/oracle/backup
   export BACKUP_DIR
   . oraenv
set linesize 200
set head off
set feed off
sqlplus -s "sys/password as sysdba" << EOF
spool /u01/app/oracle/dba/hot_backup.ksh
BEGIN
 for f1 in (select tablespace_name ts
                    from dba_tablespaces)
      loop
            dbms_output.put_line ('alter tablespace '||f1.ts|| '
            begin backup;');
               for f2 in (select file_name fn
                          from sys.dba_data_files
                          where tablespace_name=f1.ts)
            loop
                  dbms_output.put_line( 'host cp
                  '||f2.fn||  ' $BACKUP_DIR');
            end loop;
            dbms_output.put_line ('alter tablespace ' ||f1.ts|| '
            end backup;');
      end loop;
     dbms_output.put_line('alter database backup
 controlfile to        '|| ' $BACKUP_DIR/control'|| ';');
     dbms_output.put_line('alter system switch logfile;');
END;
/
```

```
spool off;
exit
EOF
```

The spooled script hot_backup.sh looks like this:

```
alter tablespace SYSTEM begin backup;
host cp C:\NEWORACLE\ORA9I\ORADATA\COMPOSE\SYSTEM01.DBF $BACKUP_DIR
alter tablespace SYSTEM end backup;
alter tablespace UNDOTBS1 begin backup;
host cp C:\NEWORACLE\ORA9I\ORADATA\COMPOSE\UNDOTBS01.DBF $BACKUP_DIR
alter tablespace UNDOTBS1 end backup;
…  /* all the other tablespace and datafile backup statements follow */
alter database backup controlfile to  $BACKUP_DIR/control;
alter system switch logfile;
```

As in the case of your cold backup script, you can make the hot backup script a part of a shell script and run it at the specified backup time.

Partial Database Backups

You don't always have to back up the entire database at one time. You can back up a part of the database—for instance, a tablespace or just a single data file. Understand that you can do a partial backup of a database only if the database is running in archivelog mode. There are a couple of exceptions to this: If a database in noarchivelog mode has some read-only or offline-normal tablespaces, they can be backed up by themselves. You can make a tablespace backup with the tablespace either online or in an offline status, depending on your needs. Here's an example of an offline backup of a tablespace. You first take the tablespace offline and then you back up the files comprising the tablespace.

```
SQL> select file_name from dba_data_files
  2  where tablespace_name = 'USERS';
C:\ORACLENT\ORADATA\HELPME\USERS01.DBF
SQL> alter tablespace users offline;
SQL> host copy
C:\ORACLENT\ORADATA\HELPME\USERS01.DBF  C:ORACLENT\ORADATA\users01.dbf_copy
SQL> alter tablespace users online;
SQL>
```

In the following case, you're backing up a tablespace that's online. As you recall, during the open database whole backup, you had to put the tablespaces in "begin backup" mode before backing up the data files. That's the same thing you have to do here, as shown in the following example:

```
SQL> alter database open;
SQL> select file_name from dba_data_files
  2  where tablespace_name='EXAMPLE';
FILE_NAME
-------------------------------------------------------------------
```

```
C:\ORACLENT\ORADATA\HELPME\EXAMPLE01.DBF
SQL> alter tablespace example begin backup;
Tablespace altered.
SQL> host copy C:\ORACLENT\ORADATA\HELPME\EXAMPLE01.DBF c:\oraclent\oradata\helpme
SQL> alter tablespace example end backup;
Tablespace altered.
SQL>
```

Monitoring User-Managed Online Backups

Several dynamic performance tables (rather, the views on those tables) can help you monitor the online backups and troubleshoot the process. Online backups could take a considerable amount of time depending on the size of the database, and it's not unheard of for the backup process to fail or hang up before it completes. As a DBA, you should be aware of the steps you need to take under those circumstances to prevent major problems. Table 14-1 lists the critical V$ views that help monitor and diagnose problems in backups.

Table 14-1. V$ Views for Monitoring Backups

V$BACKUP	This table is of great help in determining if any of the data files are still in backup mode. Hot backups sometimes get "hung up," and you can query the status column of this table to find out if any file shows ACTIVE as the status. If a file does show this status, and the backup is supposed to have been finished based on the schedule, something obviously went wrong and you need it to get the file(s) out of hot backup mode.
V$DATAFILE	The V$DATAFILE table, of course, helps in listing all the data files that belong to all the tablespaces that need to be backed up.
V$LOG	This view displays all the online redo logs for the database.
V$ARCHIVED_LOG	This view displays historical archived log information from the control file.
V$LOG_HISTORY	This view displays the redo logs that have been archived.

Enhanced Data Protection for Disaster Recovery

The backup techniques you've seen in this chapter will protect your database from unexpected disk and other hardware failures. If you have a well-designed mirroring and/or a RAID-configured disk system, you'll have built enough redundancy into your system to survive ordinary disasters. However, even the most stringent backup systems are no guarantee that you have a high availability system in place. A natural or other disaster could easily put your organization data resources out of commission, causing severe service interruptions. For events like those, you need more than the ordinary backup systems in place—you need a *high availability strategy* in place. A high availability system will ensure almost continuous data availability in the face of disasters of just about any kind. The key to providing such high availability, of course, is to have *multiple* data systems using various architectures. Oracle provides several alternatives, with the most important being the following:

- *Oracle Real Application Clusters (ORAC):* ORAC uses multiple Oracle instances on multiple nodes (servers) to connect to a single database. In the event of a node failure due to any reason, the surviving nodes recover the failed instance while providing continuous service to the users, who aren't aware that anything went wrong. ORAC is good for providing high availability, and under some circumstances it can also enhance performance and provide scalability. However, if the single database goes, everything goes with it, the multiple nodes notwithstanding.

- *Oracle Replication:* Oracle's Replication feature provides high availability by maintaining a distributed database system. Changes from the primary database are captured and sent to other databases located in a remote location. High availability is assured because the failure of one site means customers are switched over to a different site and can continue selecting and updating data as before.

- *Oracle Data Guard and standby databases:* Oracle provides the standby database concept, wherein you can have your production database update a secondary database in a different location on a continuous basis. If you wish, you may also use the secondary database for reporting purposes. When the primary database service goes down for some reason, you can switch to the secondary service and designate it as the production database service. You can do this with minimal or even no data loss whatsoever, depending on how you configure your databases. Oracle Data Guard is the management infrastructure for the standby database feature of Oracle9*i*. Oracle Data Guard helps you administer sophisticated standby database setups so you can quickly switch from one database to another.

Oracle Data Guard and standby databases offer a very effective means of providing disaster recovery, data protection, and high availability. You'll take a closer look at these useful tools in the next section.

Oracle Data Guard and Standby Databases

Oracle Data Guard uses standby databases to protect against disasters, human errors, and any other problems that threaten continued service. The standby database feature has been provided by Oracle for many years. Oracle Data Guard is the management and monitoring layer through which the standby databases are maintained. The standby databases are kept up-to-date by propagating changes from the primary server continuously.

In the event of a disaster, a standby database is activated and brought online as the primary database. Besides providing you protection against a total destruction of the primary database, the standby database can also be used for reporting purposes. The databases maintained in an Oracle Data Guard configuration can be in the same LAN-based location, or they could be in a much wider WAN-supported network. LAN-based local standby databases offer faster failure capabilities, and WAN-based databases are a better bet against a catastrophic disaster affecting your data center or local sites. You can configure a primary database and several standby databases. You can reduce downtime to less than a minute by choosing the proper protection level when you set up the standby databases. Here is a brief summary of the many benefits of using the Oracle Data Guard standby databases feature:

- High availability

- Protection against disasters

- Protection against physical data corruption

- Protection against user errors

- Failover and switchover capabilities, which can be used for both planned and unplanned switching of production and standby databases

- Geographical separation of primary and secondary servers through Oracle Net

Oracle provides you the excellent Oracle Data Guard Broker to help create and manage the Oracle Data Guard configurations. The Oracle Data Guard Broker can support up to nine databases (one primary and eight secondary) at a time. Log application, log transportation, and switchover or failover from primary to secondary are examples of tasks managed by the Oracle Data Guard Broker. The Oracle Data Guard Broker offers two interfaces: a command-line interface and a GUI-based interface called the Data Guard Manager.

The Oracle Data Guard Broker is a great tool, in that it automates the many tasks involved in creating, configuring, and maintaining complex standby database groupings. It also automates the often complex networking aspects of maintaining standby databases. However, your goal in this book is to understand the conceptual underpinnings behind the various features provided by Oracle; thus, you will not see the Oracle Data Guard Broker used in this chapter. What you will see, though, is the step-by-step creation and maintenance of an Oracle Data Guard standby database. The manual procedure, while tedious, has the benefit of acquainting you with the techniques used in maintaining standby databases.

 TIP *Oracle Data Guard isn't meant for maintaining a very low downtime. It's meant to serve in a disaster-protection capacity and as an alternative database during scheduled maintenance of the production database.*

Physical and Logical Standby Databases

Standby databases come in two flavors: physical and logical. Even the logical database, contrary to what its name implies, is a real standby database. Logical and physical standby databases are maintained in the same fashion: by propagating changes from the main production (primary) database to the standby database.

Physical standby databases are updated by continuously applying the primary database's archived logs. Physical standby databases are identical on a block-per-block basis to the production database. A physical standby database has to undergo a constant recovery process for it to be in tune with the production database.

Logical standby databases, on the other hand, use the same archived logs to derive transaction information, which is applied to the standby database using SQL statements.

The big difference between the two standby databases is this: You can't use a physical standby database for reporting while it's being updated by performing recovery. However, you can continuously access a logical database for reporting and querying, even while you're performing recovery on it. You can have a maximum of nine logical and physical standby databases in one Oracle Data Guard configuration.

Both logical and physical standby databases have their own benefits and drawbacks. The physical standby database is the traditional Oracle standby database, and it is based on applying archived redo logs from the production server to recover. There are no data limitations—all types of DML and DDL can be propagated mechanically with the application of the redo logs.

Protection Modes

You can choose three data protection modes when you use the Oracle Data Guard feature to maintain standby databases. The protection modes are a reflection of the tradeoff between availability and performance.

As you'll see in the following sections, each method is designed to provide either a greater amount of performance or a greater amount of data protection, and it's up to the individual organization to make a choice between them depending on the firm's needs.

Maximum Protection Mode

The *maximum protection mode*, also called the *double failure protection mode*, offers you the highest level of protection. This mode ensures that no transaction data is lost, even if there are two simultaneous failures. The cost of this high degree of protection is the maintenance of two standby databases. In addition, to avoid a single network failure from affecting all three databases, there should be independent networks among the three databases. This mode is ideal for organizations dealing with high-value transactions where a loss is intolerable. Even if one of the standby databases fails, the primary database will keep logging changes to the other standby server.

Maximum Availability Mode

This mode is also known as *instant protection mode*. It offers you protection from the failure of the primary production database. You could lose your primary database, your standby database, or the network connection connecting the two without losing any data under this data protection mode. If you lose connection to the standby database, the primary server stops shipping changes to it. There is a drawback with this method: The transactions must be shipped to the standby database before they are committed on the production database.

Maximum Performance Mode

If you don't need protection against a zero loss of data, but you would like to keep the production database's performance at its peak level, then this is the mode of protection you should choose. The primary database doesn't wait for confirmation from the secondary database before committing its changes. If the primary database fails, the standby database might miss some changes that were already committed on the primary.

Database Corruption and Testing Backups

Regular backups of a production database are imperative, but the backups won't do you any good if they turn out to be unusable, partly or entirely, for some reason. Testing of backups is an often-ignored area of backup and recovery, its necessity being realized too often under painful circumstances. Backed-up database files may become useless during recovery for several reasons: corrupt data files and redo logs; accidentally written-over files; unreadable, defective tapes; and even nonexistent files. You must get into the habit of regularly testing your production backups according to a schedule. This will help you catch any data corruption. I use the term "corruption" to indicate the fact that the data is inconsistent with what it should be. You are concerned here basically with what is known as *block corruption*, which could be logical or physical.

Oracle Data Block Corruption

First I'll briefly summarize the different types of corruption that could occur in an Oracle database. "Corruption" here refers to the presence of inconsistent data structures, usually due to media defects. Media corruption can be caused by myriad factors, ranging from user error to bugs in the operating system software to bad disks to a Logical Volume Manager (LVM) error to faulty memory chips. Media defects could lead to corruption in the control files, redo logs, data dictionary, or table and index data. Your detection of media corruption anywhere in the database involves using scripts to monitor your alert logs on a regular basis and using some Oracle features that enable early detection of problems. You can almost completely prevent redo log and control file corruption by using multiplexing, at both the operating system level and the Oracle level. Owing to its sheer size and the fact that its files are not multiplexed as a matter of course, data block corruption is of most concern to DBAs. Again, try and catch the corruption messages in your alert logs early on, and seek Oracle Worldwide Support's help in fixing any type of corruption issues in your database.

Data block corruption occurs when you have inconsistent data in tables or indexes, and you usually end up losing a significant amount of data if you can't fix the corrupted blocks of data. Because you need to perform some kind of a recovery most of the time to fix the corrupted data blocks, it's appropriate to cover it in this chapter. Although you may take several steps to prevent corruption, early detection of corrupted data files will help you in two ways. First, it will enable you to find quick ways of salvaging all or as much of the affected data as possible by using the techniques I discuss in the following sections. Second, it will save you surprises during a recovery from media errors. Early detection of corruption always will minimize the problem, because it will enable you to offline the files and reduce the potential damage.

Detecting Data Block Corruption

You have several methods to detect data block corruption. You shouldn't take these methods to be mutually exclusive; rather, you should use them as complements to each other, as each has its own appealing feature. First of all, there are a few initialization parameters you can set to trap corrupted block information. Also, you can use utilities such as dbverify and DBMS_REPAIR and the *analyze* command to enable you to detect data block corruption. The following sections cover the use of each of these techniques in detail.

Initialization Parameters

You can set the initialization parameter *db_block_checksum* to *true* to force Oracle to perform *checksumming*, which involves the computation of checksums for every data block and their storage in the data block header. When the data is read, the checksums are compared and corrupt data blocks are identified. The new *db_block_checking* parameter is more sophisticated, and it checks data and index blocks only when the blocks are actually changed. It also detects corruption before the data blocks are marked corrupt. You can set this feature into play by making the following changes in the init.ora file. You can also change this parameter dynamically by using the *alter session* statement.

```
db_block_checking=true (In the init.ora file)
```

or

```
SQL> alter session set db_block_checking=true;
```

The Analyze Command

You can use the easy-to-use *analyze* command to catch corrupted data blocks. The following command verifies each data block in the customer table, and if it finds any corrupted blocks, it adds the suspect rows to the invalid_rows table. In addition to checking for block corruption, the command will make sure that the index data corresponds to the table data.

```
SQL> analyze table customer validate structure;
```

The Dbverify Utility

When you suspect data block corruption, you can use the Oracle-provided dbverify utility. The dbverify program, which has been around for a long time, is used from the operating system level. It checks the structural integrity of the database files for corruption. Dbverify's big drawback is that the data files have to be offline for you to be able to use it. In other words, if you have a 24/7 operation, you just can't use dbverify.

To illustrate the use of dbverify, the following example verifies a file on a Windows platform (the command works exactly the same way on UNIX platforms). You can easily write a script that will perform the data file verification and use the crontab to schedule it on a regular basis.

```
C:\>dbv file= \oraclent\oradata\users01.dbf_copy blocksize=4096
DBVERIFY: Release 9.0.1.1.1 - Production on Sun DEC 22 14:15:49 2002
(c) Copyright 2001 Oracle Corporation.  All rights reserved.
DBVERIFY - Verification starting : FILE = \oraclent\oradata\users01.dbf_copy
DBVERIFY - Verification complete
Total Pages Examined         : 6400
Total Pages Processed (Data) : 0
Total Pages Failing   (Data) : 0
Total Pages Processed (Index): 0
Total Pages Failing   (Index): 0
Total Pages Processed (Other): 16
Total Pages Processed (Seg)  : 0
Total Pages Failing   (Seg)  : 0
Total Pages Empty            : 6384
Total Pages Marked Corrupt   : 0
Total Pages Influx           : 0
C:\>
```

This example shows a simplified use of the dbverify utility, which is invoked by the command *dbv* on the UNIX platform and the Windows platform. The keyword *file* indicates the data file to be checked and *db blocksize* is the Oracle block size of the database. As you can see, the total pages marked corrupt are 0, which means the data file is free of any structural integrity problems—it is corruption-free.

The DBMS_REPAIR Utility

Though the dbverify utility is simplicity itself, it's severely limited by the fact that the file has to be offline before it's checked. In Oracle8*i*, a new utility, DBMS_REPAIR, was introduced. This utility can detect data block corruption while the data files are online. To use this utility, you first need to log in as the user SYS and then create a pair of tables, the first of which needs to be prefixed with repair_. The second table is called the orphan_key table.

Once you create the table repair_table, you're ready to run the DBMS_REPAIR utility. The table repair_table will log all the information about corrupt data. The *check_object* procedure of the DBMS_REPAIR package detects corrupted data blocks and recommends fixes. After the execution of the *check_object* procedure, the table repair_table1 is queried on the columns object_name and corrupt_description to identify if and what type of data block corruption exists.

I discuss various ways of fixing data block corruption in the next chapter, which covers recovering the Oracle database, because one of the ways to fix the problem involves restoring the database from backups.

Verification of RMAN Backups

You have several ways to ensure the backups made using RMAN are actually useful during a recovery. These include the use of the *crosscheck* feature to test for the existence of the copied files or tapes. You can also verify the accuracy of the backups using the *validate* command. The following sections examine the *crosscheck* feature and the *validate* command.

Cross-Checking Backups Made with RMAN

RMAN provides the extremely useful *crosscheck* feature to enable you to check that the backup sets and image copies listed in the recovery catalog actually do exist in their specified locations and have not been accidentally deleted or written over. Besides verifying the existence of the backup files, RMAN also verifies the headers and ensures the files can be read. Using the *crosscheck* feature can thus test both the existence and the readability of the backups. Here's an example of the use of the *crosscheck* command in RMAN:

```
RMAN> crosscheck backupset 326;
allocated channel: ORA_DISK_1
...
channel ORA_DISK_4: sid=21 devtype=DISK
crosschecked backup piece: found to be 'AVAILABLE'
backup piece handle=/test02/app/oracle/product/9.2.0.1.0
/dbs/c-3482335306-20021225-04 recid=22 stamp=481562313
Crosschecked 1 objects
RMAN>
```

As you can see, RMAN has crosschecked the backup piece and found it to be AVAILABLE, which confirms that the backup files do exist and can be used for a recovery.

Using the RMAN Validate Command

RMAN helps detect both physical and logical corruption. Whenever corrupt blocks of either kind are encountered during the backup process, the information is logged to the control file and the recovery catalog. The *validate* command helps you ensure that the backed-up files exist in the proper locations, and that they are readable and free from any logical and physical corruption. You simply issue the following command to test any particular backup set:

```
RMAN> validate backupset 9;
```

To test the entire database and archived log backup sets, you issue the following command:

```
RMAN> backup validate database archivelog all;
```

If the backup set does not exist, RMAN will let you know that the file does not exist. If the command does not result in any errors, you can assume that the specified backup set exists and can be used in the recovery process.

Oracle's HARD Initiative

RAID ensures only that the data storage drives are redundant, so you can withstand the loss of some disks without losing any data. What if you have mirrored system, but the data that's being written to a mirrored pair is corrupted? Both the disks in the mirrored pair, of course, will hold corrupted data. Oracle has recently instituted a new initiative, the Hardware Assisted Resilient Data (HARD) Initiative, to prevent data corruption before it occurs. Oracle will incorporate special data validation algorithms inside the storage devices sold by participating vendors in the HARD Initiative, thus *preventing* corrupted data from being written permanently to disk. The HARD Initiative is designed to address problems of the following nature:

- Operating system overwrites of Oracle data

- Partially written blocks and lost writes

- Physically and logically corrupt blocks being written

- Blocks being written to the wrong locations

Techniques and Troubleshooting

Backup and recovery pose a lot of problems for the Oracle DBA. A sound understanding of the concepts and thorough testing of the procedures will help you become proficient in using the techniques.

Monitoring RMAN

When you're using RMAN, how do you monitor the pace of the backup? If you're looking at the screen from where you launched RMAN, you really can't tell much. You need to use the V$SESSION_LONGOPS table as follows:

```
SQL> Select to_char (start_time,'DD-MON-YY HH24:MI') "Start of

    Backup"'Sofar, totalwork,
    Elapsped_seconds/60 "ELAPSED TIME IN MINUTES",
    Round(sofar/totalwork*100,2) "Percentage Completed so far"
    From v$session_longops
    Where opname='prod1_dbbackup';
```

The output will tell you how far the backup has been completed.

The ORA_00257 Error

The error message is this: "Archiver error. Connect internal only, until freed".
What this message is saying is that your archive log directory is full and users
can't connect to the database anymore. Existing users can continue to query
the database, but no DML can be executed because Oracle can't archive the logs.
If you quickly move some of the files in the archive log directory to a different
location, the database is free to continue its normal operations. If you have a
script monitoring the free space on your archive log directory, you shouldn't have
this problem.

Summary

Proper production database backup is probably the single most important task of
the Oracle DBA. A lot of thought needs to go into framing a good backup strategy.
As a DBA, you need to understand the service level agreement (SLA) and the
uptime expectations of your organization, and plan the backups around those
constraints. Because good backups reduce problems at the recovery stage, time
spent coming up with solid strategies is time well spent.

The importance of backup testing can't be overstressed. It's very important
not only to have a good backup plan in place, but also to periodically verify and
test the backups, probably by simulating recoveries under different scenarios.

RMAN has its learning curve, but you can do several things with it that you
can't do with the manual backup and recovery methods. These advantages include
the ability to perform incremental backups, the ability to validate and check
backups, and more efficient online backups.

Although this chapter focused on using RMAN for backing up databases, it
also showed you how to perform offline and online backups using operating
system copy utilities.

It's common in most large organizations to use third-party tools for database
backup management. In this chapter you learned how to install and use LSSV, a
tool that is very similar to the Legato NetWorker product.

Database corruption is always a potential danger, and this chapter provided
you with various ways of detecting block corruption in Oracle. In the next chapter
you'll learn ways to fix database block corruption. The next chapter also presents
several Oracle database recovery techniques.

Database Recovery

DATABASE RECOVERY IS the topic many DBAs dread most. A database could be unavailable for use for a number of reasons, including a system crash, a network failure, a media failure, or a natural disaster. If the downtime is due to something like a power failure, Oracle will recover itself—there's no need for you to do anything special. You'll see how you can set a bound on the time taken for crash recovery using Oracle9*i*'s new features. In cases where a disk becomes nonfunctional, for example, you have to perform media recovery. This involves two steps. First, you restore the database from backups, and second, you bring the database up-to-date with the help of archived redo logs. The keys to a successful recovery, of course, are solidly tested backups and regular recovery drills using those backups.

Besides media recovery, you may also be confronted with data corruption, where data blocks could be corrupted, sometimes leading to an irretrievable loss of critical data. There are some steps you can take to prevent corruption, and you can salvage most of the noncorrupted data from the data blocks using special Oracle-provided packages. You'll learn how to use these techniques in the latter part of this chapter.

Recovery is a process in which mistakes could be very expensive in terms of data loss. Your success during a recovery process is directly related to the degree that you understand the backup and recovery concepts, as well as your knowledge of which techniques to apply under different kinds of media losses. At the very end of this chapter, you'll examine a set of recovery scenarios that outline the steps to be followed during these various types of recovery.

Types of Database Failures

As a DBA, your most important task is to safeguard the enterprise data and enable users to access it with as few disruptions as possible. In the previous chapter you learned how important it is to have a proper backup and recovery process in place. Too often, organizations don't have formal backup and recovery procedures in place. In firms where the policies do exist, sometimes there isn't adequate testing of those plans to avoid catastrophic misjudgments, faulty backup scripts, or any number of potential pitfalls that could make recovery hazardous when media problems occur. Your database could stop functioning for a number of reasons, some of them mechanical and others due to user errors or natural disasters.

System Failure

The most common system failures are hardware-related failures. A disk drive controller may fail, or the disk head could be defective. Some of the system peripherals or controllers can also malfunction. You may have problem with a

CPU on your system or the memory chips may turn out to be defective. Of course, you could always end up with a power supply–related failure, especially if you aren't using systems to provide an uninterrupted supply of power. Software-related problems could be the result of problems on both the operating system side and the Oracle server side. Sometimes, the database might crash without any notice upon hitting a server bug. In addition, the network could fail or problems might spring from the middle-tier software.

If your entire system goes down, there's really not a whole lot you can do if you have only one instance running. If you have mission-critical systems, you can avoid the downtime by using a clustered approach. Clustering uses several nodes, thus avoiding a single point of failure. Oracle offers Oracle Real Application Clusters (ORAC), which involves running several instances from different servers connecting to a single database. When one node or server goes down, the others can take over within seconds, without any noticeable disruption in service. Oracle also offers the Transparent Application Fail-over feature, which you can use in tandem with ORAC to failover clients transparently from one sever to the other.

Fast-Start Fault Recovery

Using Oracle's *fast-start fault recovery* functionality, you can substantially reduce the downtime resulting from system-related outages by specifying the approx-imate number of seconds crash recovery should take. As you know, when the database suddenly crashes, not all the committed transactions will have been written to disk. The online redo logs have committed data that needs to be written to disk upon starting up the instance, a process called *roll-forward*. In addition, all the uncommitted changes that were written to disk have to be undone based on the redo log contents, a process called *rollback*. If your database is fairly large, and the redo log files are therefore also large, it can take an exorbitantly long period of time for the roll-forward and rollback to complete.

The roll-forward phase of a crash recovery uses the redo logs to see what changes need to be applied to disk. Redo application begins at a point in the redo logs known as the *thread checkpoint redo byte address*. This is the point at which a checkpoint was last done before the crash occurred. Because all the data in the buffers is written to disk during a checkpoint, you'll only need to look beyond this last checkpoint position to perform a recovery. *Fast-start checkpointing* is the fre-quent writing of the dirty database buffers in the cache to disk by the database writer (DBWn). You can control the time taken for crash recovery by advancing the checkpoint position often. Oracle uses a two-pass technique. The first pass deter-mines which blocks in the redo logs need recovery, and the second pass applies the required changes. This process involves the use of the following two initial-ization configuration parameters:

- *Log_checkpoint_interval:* This parameter specifies the maximum number of redo records to be read (in the first pass). These records, of course, will be the ones between the last checkpoint and the end of the log.

- *Fast_start_io_target:* This parameter specifies the number of data blocks to be recovered (in the second pass).

You can explicitly set targets for the preceding two parameters, or you can implicitly set the values for them by configuring yet another parameter called the *fast_start_mttr_target* (FSMT) parameter. The FSMT parameter allows you to specify the time a recovery should take. Internally, Oracle will translate this into targets for the *log_checkpoint_interval* and *fast_start_io_target* parameters. For example, you can specify that any crash recovery will take no longer than 1 minute in the following manner:

```
fast_start_mttr_target=60 (seconds).
```

Your target of 60 seconds in the preceding example may not be exactly met by Oracle the very first time during a crash recovery. This is because Oracle uses only an estimate of the I/O rates on your systems in the beginning to calculate values for its two components, *log_checkpoint_interval* and *fast_start_io_target*. Oracle will constantly monitor your system to measure the actual I/O rates, and it uses this information over time to estimate the recovery time more precisely. Every 30 seconds Oracle estimates the current Mean Time to Recover (MTTR) and places this value in the V$INSTANCE_RECOVERY table. You can query this table to see what Oracle's current estimated MTTR is and adjust your FSMT value accordingly.

```
SQL> select recovery_estimated_ios,estimated_mttr,
  2  target_mttr from v$instance_recovery;
   RECOVERY_ESTIMATED_IOS     ESTIMATED_MTTR     TARGET_MTTR
   --------------- --  ---------------  -------------
               994                20               52
SQL>
```

Using fast-start fault recovery can dramatically lower your crash recovery times to less than a minute. Although there is a concern that more frequent check-pointing has a performance cost, studies have shown that the performance hit is negligible.

Data Center Disasters

Data center disasters could range from a tornado to a fire to a terrorist attack. I discussed the Oracle Data Guard feature based on standby databases in Chapter 14. Standby databases provide good protection against a data center disaster. Your business will continue to run without any interruption, because all the changes made to your operational database are sent over to a duplicate standby database over the network. In a disaster recovery situation, you just turn the duplicate database into your main production database, with almost no disruption and no loss of data. You can also use Oracle's Advanced Replication, whereby you maintain a distributed database system so a remote distributed database can take over from the primary production system if the latter suffers a total failure due to a disaster.

Human Error

People can and do make mistakes when it comes to using and managing systems. DBAs and/or system administrators could make critical errors that might put their databases in jeopardy. For example, you could accidentally run the wrong batch job, producing data that is meaningless or wrong. If you have entered wrong data into a table or deleted some data in error, you have several mechanisms available to get you out of the jam. You can use Oracle's Flashback Query feature to query old data, which enables you to replace the lost or wrongly entered data without bringing the database offline. You can also use the LogMiner tool provided by Oracle to read your redo logs to undo changes to the database. You can use export and import to replace the affected tables, but you may lose some data in the process. Or, you can perform what is called a *point-in-time recovery* (PITR) to recover the database or a tablespace to a point in time before the problem occurred. A simple way to re-create an inadvertently dropped table is to use the export and import utilities. You do not have to suffer any downtime all.

Media Failures

The most serious recovery issues are those related to media problems. Damage to disks that prevent the disk from being read from or written to is the most serious type of scenario in which you'll have to depend on your backup copies of the database and log files to make the database current and not lose any of the data in the database permanently. If your data files or control files are on the media that is inaccessible, you'll most likely end up doing a recovery. In some situations, you may perform a recovery even if there's no media damage—for instance, when there's a serious case of user error. If you have to restore a backed-up data file or you take a file offline using the *offline immediate* option, you'll need to perform a media recovery. Two factors are critical when disasters occur: the magnitude of the data that becomes unavailable and needs to be replaced from backups, and the amount of time it might take to replace the data.

When users can't perform read or write operations against the database, the magnitude of the failure is clearly larger than when there's a database "failure" that doesn't quite interrupt the interaction of the users with the database. Some of these "other" errors are user statement errors, process failures, and instance failures. User statement errors called by faulty syntax or constraint violations, for example, result only in the failure of the particular user's statement. Instance failures really don't need the intervention of a DBA. When you address the conditions that caused the instance failure (e.g., a power failure), the database starts humming away on its own. As you may recall from Chapter 5, the background process PMON will automatically perform instance recovery upon start-up of the database. You can consider these "other" failures as unimportant in terms of the steps you need to take to fix them. Focus on the really important type of database failure—media failure—because this is where you need to use your conceptual skills to restore the database and, when necessary, to recover it to the point when failure occurred.

The key idea to remember is this: If the failure is a system-related failure, such as a hardware failure or an operating system or database crash, Oracle automatically recovers the database without any loss of data that was already committed. If you have data failure, say, due to the loss of a disk, Oracle can't automatically recover from it. You need to perform explicit database recovery to avoid data loss. You can perform this media recovery with the help of Recovery Manager (RMAN) or by using manual recovery commands directly by using SQL*Plus.

You need the following four items to perform a complete media recovery:

- A full backup of all data files

- Archived redo logs since the full backup

- A control file copy

- Current online redo logs

Oracle media recovery ensures the recovery of up-to-the-minute data provided you have a copy of a recent backup along with archived redo logs. The archived logs are transaction journals and have the complete set of committed data since the last backup. Thus, using the archived redo logs, you can bring your database forward from the time the backups were taken.

You'll see quite a bit of discussion on recovering databases from a media failure in this chapter. In addition, you'll learn about fine-grained recovery techniques and how to recover from database corruption.

Extent of Database Failure and Types of Recovery

It's important early on to remember that a database failure or even a disaster need not involve the entire database. Users can very well continue to work away on most parts of the database while a part of it is being repaired with the help of backups, much like you don't have to have all the inhabitants of a multistory building leave the premises while construction or repairs are going on in one floor of the building. Replacing lost data files, entire tablespaces, or even the whole database with backup versions is termed *restoring the database*. For example, if a database failure hits your organization on a Wednesday morning and you have a backed-up version of the database from last Friday night, then you can copy all those data files to restore the database. If you don't have all the changes since that last backup until now somewhere, you can't proceed any further, of course. If you do have the changes in the form of archived redo logs, then you can recover the database and bring the restored database up-to-date.

When you need only address a part of the database to recover from failure, you can continue to run the database as usual, with service interruption only for those transactions that involve the damaged part of the database. This procedure is called an *open recovery*. A *closed recovery* is what its name implies: You need to shut down the database completely to perform the recovery. You'll need to use closed recovery when your entire database needs to be recovered and also when your system or rollback data files are damaged.

Restoring vs. Recovering a Database

Restoring a database involves copying the database files from a period in the past. Because recovering the damaged database to the most recent time period may involve the application of logs, a database running in noarchivelog mode can only be restored from a backup.

Time Needed for Recovery

How long does it take to recover the database? If you're a DBA with production databases under your supervision, sooner or later the answer to this question becomes critical. It's quite common for all your superiors, sometimes including the CEO of the company, to line up outside your office, asking you a host of questions about when you think you'll finish the recovery and be able to reconnect the users. It's kind of intimidating to perform your critical database recovery operations under such tense and charged circumstances, but that's how it goes in the real world. The key to making it successfully through these circumstances is adherence to the simple admonition "Be prepared." Be prepared by having the right backups, which you know have passed a rigorous (and recent) testing process.

The other dimension of the "being prepared" philosophy is to get your recovery concepts crystal clear in your head. Although you can pore over the books and manuals and probably figure out the right sequence of actions (eventually) for any DBA task, I don't recommend that course of action in the case of database recovery for a number of reasons. First, there's enormous psychological pressure to bring the database "up" as soon as possible. Second, your normal tranquil work circumstances are transformed rather suddenly and rudely, as your cubicle turns into an overcrowded war room of edgy and frustrated managers—not exactly a great time to be hitting the books. Third, you need to conserve as much time as you can by knowing the drill ahead of time to any number of typical potential problem situations. And fourth, database recovery is one of those areas where sometimes the decisions you make and the commands you execute aren't retractable. You'll be traversing a one-way street during those times, and any errors you make in haste or ignorance tend to cost you dearly.

The time it will take you to perform a recovery depends on the following factors:

- On what media do you have your archived redo logs in case they're necessary? If the logs are all on tape, it will take much longer to perform the recovery than if they're on disk. It's a good idea to keep an extra copy of the logs on disk somewhere.

- Are you using the parallel recovery feature? Parallel recovery, when it can be implemented, will cut back on the time needed to recover the database.

- Do you need replacement of the disks right away, or can you get away with just moving the data files to a different good location on the UNIX machine?

- What's your service contract for replacement and repair of parts on the UNIX machine? Some companies have a response time as short as 45 minutes from the initial call. Some may have a 24-hour turnaround. Make sure you know and understand the implications of your company's service contract with the vendor of your system.

- How frequently do you perform backups? The more infrequently you perform backups, the more logs need to be applied, and the longer the recovery time.

Complete and Incomplete Recovery

If you have a disk go bad on you and consequently force you to restore and recover from backup, naturally your goal will be a full recovery up to the time the problem occurred. On the other hand, if you're recovering your database due to user errors (e.g., incorrect data entry), your goal may be to remove the errors from your database by only recovering until the point when the incorrect data began to be input into the tables of the database. This is typically called *incomplete recovery*, and as you'll see later on, you make the decision about exactly when to stop recovering the database based on different criteria.

Complete recovery simply means a recovery with no loss of data. All the changes in the online and archived redo logs are applied to the most recent backup of the database during a complete recovery. Thus, the database is brought up-to-date with the current point in time. You may perform a complete recovery at the database, tablespace, or data file level.

Incomplete recovery implies data loss, because you restore only part of the data that existed when the database failure occurred. That is, you apply only some of the archived and current log records to the database. Therefore, your database after recovery is consistent but it's not an up-to-date version. You could have several reasons for wanting to do an incomplete recovery, including user error, loss of necessary archived log files, and loss of an online redo log or a current control file. When you perform an incomplete recovery, you always open the database after resetting your redo log sequence to 1. This will, in effect, give you a new version or incarnation of the database. You can make an incomplete recovery only at the database level, not at the tablespace or data file level.

In real life, most recoveries are complete recoveries, with a 100 percent data recovery being the goal almost always. But it's nice to know that if you ever need to recover to a prior point in time, you can do so for whatever reason. Because most recoveries are 100-percent recoveries, you'll focus your energies in that direction in this chapter.

Open and Closed Recovery

Open recovery is when you perform recovery on a part of the database—a tablespace or a data file—while users are continuing to access the rest of the database normally. *Closed* database recovery is when you can mount the database but not open it.

Reducing Your Vulnerability

No aspect of the job is more dreadful or even downright scary to an Oracle DBA than recovering databases. War stories and horror stories aside, what's really the problem and how do you protect against it? I'm not asking what techniques you need to understand to recover a database. You'll learn those techniques later on in this chapter. My focus is rather on the question of how to reduce your vulnerability.

The most common errors on a day-to-day basis are hardware related. Disks or the controllers that manage them fail on a regular basis. The larger the database, the greater the likelihood that on any given day, a service person from the server vendor is fixing or replacing a faulty part. Because it is a well-known fact that the entire disk system is a vulnerable point, you must provide redundancy in your database. Either a mirrored system or a RAID 5–based disk system, or a combination of both, will give you the redundancy you need.

In case your whole site goes down, you can start without a noticeable disruption if you have a distributed replication database or standby database in place. Otherwise, know that your uptime will be seriously compromised by a major problem at the production data center.

Keep a complete set of the redundancy set on disk somewhere on the production server. This *redundancy set* should consist of the latest database backups, the archived redo logs since that backup, and a multiplexed copy of the online redo log files and the control file. You may also include the "other" Oracle files, such as the init.ora or SPFILE, tnsnames.ora or ldap.ora, and the listener.ora file, in the redundancy set.

In the rest of this chapter, I explain several techniques for restoring and recovering databases. Many more techniques are enumerated in the Oracle manuals. It's sometimes bewildering to see the types of recovery situations you can encounter. But here's a simple thought: If you have a good set of backups and you're running your database in archivelog mode, you can recover without data loss from the loss of any data file or control file. The only situation in which you might have data loss is if your online redo log files are lost. So, if you multiplex your online redo log files and also mirror them, there's very little chance you'll ever lose any data, even with a major problem involving your disk drives. Well, if all your drives are inaccessible, mirrored and otherwise, you do have a disaster on your hands, and you need to have an alternative database to switch over to, or at least you need to have an off-site disaster recovery system in place.

In the examples of various scenarios of database recovery that follow, I only deal with the recovery of a database running in archivelog mode. The reason is obvious: Just about all critical databases are run in archivelog mode. If you understand the recovery procedures in the following sections, you can perform the recovery (rather, the *restoration*) of a noarchivelog mode database very easily. For details about procedures that aren't covered here, please refer to "Oracle9*i* User-Managed Backup and Recovery Guide" and "Oracle9*i* Recovery Manager User's Guide."

Performing Recovery with RMAN

As in the case of backups, you can make your recovery tasks a lot easier with the help of RMAN. It's critical to have the right log files during a recovery, and RMAN, with its automatic maintenance of all the needed files, will help you tremendously. In addition to being able to perform all types of recovery that you can perform with user-managed recovery techniques, RMAN provides several other benefits.

Why RMAN Is Best for Recovery

As mentioned in the previous section, RMAN provides some undeniable benefits when compared to the traditional user-managed recovery methods. Here's a summary of the advantages provided by RMAN during a database recovery:

- RMAN does away with the manual selection and application of the necessary data and log files during recovery.

- RMAN automatically selects the most recent backup sets and image copies to recover with.

- Only RMAN gives you the ability to perform recovery at the data block level with the block media recovery feature. This feature can cut the recovery time dramatically.

- Only RMAN provides *restore optimization,* a great timesaving feature that enables you to bypass data files that are OK during the recovery process. RMAN has the ability to check the files that need to be restored and avoid recovering those that are good.

- RMAN provides the *duplicate* command, which lets you easily create clones of your production database for testing purposes or create standby databases for your production database.

- RMAN provides you with the ability to recover through unrecoverable operations when using the incremental backups.

 NOTE *If you don't use the RMAN recovery catalog, you can't perform a PITR. The recovery catalog, as you learned in Chapter 14, provides so many other benefits that you should plan on using one if RMAN is a central part of your backup and recovery strategy.*

RMAN performs the restoration of the data files from backups and applies the necessary archived redo logs to bring it up-to-date. RMAN knows, by looking into its recovery catalog, all the files and logs needed to recover the database. Gone is the extremely labor-intensive and error-prone manual intervention that you had to use in a typical user-managed recovery.

Here's an example of recovering an entire database. First, make sure you're connected to both the target database and the recovery catalog:

```
RMAN> run {
  2>  allocate channel t1 type sbt_tape;
  3>  restore database;
  4>  release channel t1;
      }
```

RMAN can recover the entire database or only a part of it (e.g., a tablespace or a data file). The following set of commands shows you how to recover just a tablespace (note the use of regular SQL commands within the RMAN script):

```
SQL > startup mount
RMAN> sql 'alter tablespace data_01 offline immediate';
RMAN> restore tablespace data_01
RMAN> recover tablespace data_01
RMAN> sql 'alter tablespace data_01 online';
SQL> open database;
```

As the preceding generic examples show, you first put the database in the mount position if it's a full database recovery, and you then restore the data files and recover them before bringing the database online again for the users.

When you use RMAN to perform backup and recovery tasks, it's easy to verify that a certain backup exists and that it's usable. In the example shown in Listing 15-1, the command *list backupsets* indicates what backups have been performed by RMAN. The next command, *validate backups*, ensures that the backups are usable for recovery.

Listing 15-1. The List Backupset Command

```
RMAN> list backupset;
List of Backup Sets
===================
BS Key  Type   LV Size       Device Type Elapsed Time Completion Time
------- ----   -- ----------  ----------- ------------ ---------------
677     Full   229M              DISK        00:00:40     29-DEC-02
        BP Key: 714    Status: AVAILABLE   Tag:
        Piece Name: /test01/app/oracle/9.2.0.1.0/dbs/0bdof1mk_1_1
   List of Datafiles in backup set 677
   File Type Ckp SCN Ckp Time  Name
   ---- ------- ------- ------ ----
    1 Full 82272 29-DEC-02 /test02/app/oracle/odata/help/sys01.dbf
    2 Full 82272 29-DEC-02 /test02/app/oracle/odata/help/und01.dbf
    3 Full 82272 29-DEC-02 /test02/app/oracle/odata/help/usr01.dbf
    4 Full 82272 29-DEC-02 /test01/app/oracle/odata/reer.dbf01_COPY
   RMAN> validate backupset  677;
using channel ORA_DISK_1
channel ORA_DISK_1: starting validation of datafile backupset
channel ORA_DISK_1: restored backup piece 1
piece handle=/test01/app/oracle/oradata/backup/1odp3oi2_1_1 tag=null params=NULL
channel ORA_DISK_1: validation complete
RMAN>
```

User-Managed Recovery of a Database

As in the case of backups, you can use operating system–based or user-managed techniques to restore and recover a database. It's my firm belief that RMAN is vastly superior to the old-fashioned manual method. However, most of you need to be aware of both methods, just in case you need to use both of them someday. One of the interesting things about the user-managed recovery method is that you can learn a lot about how the recovery proceeds by watching the different steps that Oracle goes through during a recovery.

You should use the following general procedure during the user-managed recovery of archivelog mode databases. Specific situations demand different strategies to recover, but the essential technique is same, no matter what type of file (control file, system tablespace file, data file, and so forth) was lost due to, say, media damage.

1. Restore the affected data files to their original location if possible or to an alternate location after renaming them.

2. Use the *restore database*, *restore tablespace*, or *restore datafile* command depending on the situation to recover the entire database, a tablespace, or a data file, respectively.

3. At this point, Oracle will ask you to supply the archived redo logs, and you can recover up until the point of failure for a complete recovery. It's assumed that you have all the necessary archived logs, and that you do want to recover to the point of failure.

4. Open the database after the recovery is complete and let the users log back into the system.

If you don't want to recover to the point of failure—for instance, due to previous user errors or missing necessary archived redo logs—you can only perform an incomplete recovery.

In the next section, you'll explore the specific types of media losses that could occur in a database and how you go about recovering in each situation.

Typical Media Recovery Scenarios

The steps you take during a database recovery depend on the extent of the recovery and which of the files (data files, control files, online and archived redo logs) are missing due to a media problem. The following sections take you through several common recovery scenarios, first using RMAN and later on operating system–based user-managed recoveries.

Complete Recovery of a Whole Database

You may have to perform a complete recovery of the whole database when you lose several or all of your data files. Before you recover the database, you must restore the backup files. After this, you need to apply all the available archived redo logs to the database. In the following sections, you'll learn how to do this with RMAN and with user-managed techniques.

Using RMAN

Assume that all the data files in your database are inaccessible due to a media malfunction. What to do? If you have all your archived redo logs, you can restore your backups and do a complete recovery without any loss of data. To recover an entire database, first start the database but leave it in the mount position, as shown in Listing 15-2. Thus, the database is not open to users while you're restoring files and recovering the database.

Listing 15-2. Using RMAN to Start the Database

```
oracle@hp50.netbsa.org   [/a08/app/oracle/product/oas9i/network/admin]
[remorse] $ rman target / catalog rman/rman1@monitor
Recovery Manager: Release 9.2.0.1.0 - 64bit Production
Copyright (c) 1995, 2002, Oracle Corporation.  All rights reserved.
connected to target database: REMORSE (DBID=3482335306)
connected to recovery catalog database
RMAN> startup mount
connected to target database (not started)
Oracle instance started
database mounted
Total System Global Area      156147688 bytes
Fixed Size                       438248 bytes
Variable Size                 146800640 bytes
Database Buffers                8388608 bytes
Redo Buffers                     520192 bytes
RMAN>
```

Next, restore the data files that are lost. Because this is the recovery of an entire database, you ask RMAN to restore all the data files from backup sets. The command is very simple: *restore database*. RMAN knows where the backed-up files are on disk, and it copies them to their default locations. Listing 15-3 shows the output of the *restore database* command.

Listing 15-3. The RMAN Restore Database Command

```
RMAN> restore database;
Starting restore at 28-DEC-02
configuration for DISK channel 2 is ignored
allocated channel: ORA_DISK_1
channel ORA_DISK_1: sid=10 devtype=DISK
channel ORA_DISK_1: starting datafile backupset restore
channel ORA_DISK_1: specifying datafile(s) to restore from backup set
restoring datafile 00001 to /test02/app/oracle/oradata/remorse/system01.dbf
...
restoring datafile 00011 to /test02/app/oracle/oradata/temp_01.dbf
channel ORA_DISK_1: restored backup piece 1
piece handle=/test01/app/oracle/oradata/backup/27dop960_1_1 tag=null params=NULL
channel ORA_DISK_1: restore complete
Finished restore at 27-DEC-2002
RMAN>
```

Once the data files are all restored, they have to be synchronized using the archived redo logs. The *recover database* command applies the archived logs to the restored files and synchronizes the SCNs for all the data files and the control file. Listing 15-4 shows the output of the *recover database* command.

Listing 15-4. The RMAN Recover Database Command

```
RMAN> recover database;
Starting recover at 27-DEC-2002
using channel ORA_DISK_1
starting media recovery
archive log thread 1 sequence 66 is already on disk as file
/test02/app/oracle/oradata/archive/T0001S0000000066.ARC
...
archive log filename=/test02/app/oracle/oradata/archive
/T0001S0000000069.ARC thread=1 sequence=69
media recovery complete
Finished recover at 27-DEC-02
RMAN>
```

Finally, you bring the database online so users can access it once again:

```
RMAN> alter database open;
database opened;
RMAN>
```

Note that you can simplify the preceding steps for recovering the whole database by using the following script:

```
RMAN> run {
        shutdown immediate;
        startup mount;
        restore database;
        recover database;
        alter database open;
      }
RMAN>
```

User-Managed Recovery

The user-managed complete database recovery process starts with the restoration of all lost or damaged data files from the backup. You then recover the database by using the *recover database* command. Oracle will ask for the necessary archived log files and perform the recovery by applying the archived log files. It's easier to let Oracle apply the relevant archived log file than to attempt to do it yourself manually.

You can automate the application of the archived redo log files in two ways. Before you use the *recover database* command, you can use the command *set autorecovery on*. The other way is to specify the keyword *automatic* in the *recover* command, as in *recover database automatic*.

The following is a summary of steps for a complete recovery of your database:

1. Restore the data files from backup.

2. Start up the database in the mount mode:

   ```
   SQL> Startup mount
   ```

3. Use the *recover database* command to start recovering the database. The keyword *automatic* tells Oracle to automate the application of the archived redo logs. In this example, I'm assuming that you're placing the archived redo logs in the default location specified in the init.ora or SPFILE. If you've placed them in a different location, you'll have to supply the location to Oracle when it can't find the archived redo log files in the default location.

```
SQL> recover database automatic
```

4. Open the database once you're sure Oracle has completed media recovery:

```
 Media recovery complete.
SQL> alter database open;
```

Recovering a Tablespace

You need to perform a tablespace recovery usually when you lose one or more data files that belong to the tablespace and you don't have a mirrored copy of the files. The recovery may be open or closed, and it may be a full recovery or a point-in-time recovery, as explained at the beginning of this chapter. You can recover using either RMAN or user-managed techniques. In the next section you'll look at how you can use RMAN to perform database recovery.

Using RMAN

Sometimes you may have to recover a tablespace or a set of tablespaces. You can use the restore and recover commands at the tablespace level for these situations. Here's an example:

1. Start up the database in the mount state. Once you start the database, don't open it, because you need to restore and recover the files that are part of the tablespace.

2. Restore the tablespace using the *restore tablespace* command, as follows:

```
RMAN> restore tablespace users;
Starting restore at 11-JAN-03
allocated channel: ORA_DISK_1
channel ORA_DISK_1: sid=14 devtype=DISK
allocated channel: ORA_DISK_2
channel ORA_DISK_2: sid=15 devtype=DISK
allocated channel: ORA_DISK_3
channel ORA_DISK_3: sid=16 devtype=DISK
allocated channel: ORA_DISK_4
channel ORA_DISK_4: sid=17 devtype=DISK
channel ORA_DISK_1: starting datafile backupset restore
channel ORA_DISK_1: specifying datafile(s) to restore from backup set
restoring datafile 00016 to
```

```
/test01/app/oracle/oradata/remorse/users01.dbf
channel ORA_DISK_1: restored backup piece 1
piece handle=/test02/app/oracle/product/9.2.0.1.0/dbs/25ecl0vu_1_1 tag=
TAG20030111T160828 params=NULL
channel ORA_DISK_1: restore complete
Finished restore at 11-JAN-03
RMAN>
```

3. The next step is to recover the tablespace, as follows:

```
RMAN> recover tablespace users;
Starting recover at 11-JAN-03
using channel ORA_DISK_1
using channel ORA_DISK_2
using channel ORA_DISK_3
using channel ORA_DISK_4
channel ORA_DISK_1: starting incremental datafile backupset restore
channel ORA_DISK_1: specifying datafile(s) to restore from backup set
destination for restore of datafile 00016: /test01/app/oracle
/oradata/remorse/users01.dbf
channel ORA_DISK_1: restored backup piece 1
piece handle=/test02/app/oracle/product/9.2.0.1.0/dbs/2becl1at_1_1 tag-
TAG20030111T161419 params=NULL
channel ORA_DISK_1: restore complete
starting media recovery
media recovery complete
Finished recover at 11-JAN-03
RMAN>
```

4. Finally, open the database as follows:

```
RMAN> alter database open;
RMAN> database opened
RMAN>
```

Suppose your database is still open and the only data file of tablespace test01 Is lost. All user transactions that access the other tablespaces can continue unhindered while you recover the tablespace test01. The following code shows the RMAN tablespace recovery script to do this:

```
RMAN> run {
allocate channel s1 type 'sbt_tape';
allocate channel s2 type 'sbt_tape';
sql "alter tablespace test01 offline immediate";
restore tablespace test01;
recover tablespace test01;
sql "alter tablespace test01 online";
release channel s1;
release channel s2;
}
```

User-Managed Recovery

Say your database is online, and a file(s) belonging to it is damaged. If the database write can't write to the damaged files, Oracle will take the file(s) offline automatically. Users continue to access the database at this time. To perform a recovery of the contents of the tablespace containing the damaged data file(s), you must first take the tablespace offline. You need to restore the damaged data files and perform a recovery after that. Here's a summary of the recovery process:

1. Take the affected tablespace offline:

   ```
   SQL> alter tablespace sales01 offline temporary;
   ```

2. Restore the damaged file(s):

   ```
   SQL> host cp /u01/app/oracle/backup/remorse/sales_01.dbf
                     /u01/app/oracle/oradata/remorse/sales_01.dbf
   ```

3. Recover the offlined tablespace:

   ```
   SQL> recover tablespace sales01;
   ```

4. Bring the tablespace you just recovered online:

   ```
   Sql> alter tablespace sales01 online;
   ```

Recovering a Data File

The procedures for recovering from the loss of a data file depend on the type of tablespace the data file belonged to. The following discussion deals with the loss of a data file from a normal tablespace.

Using RMAN

The recovery process using RMAN is remarkably simpler than the user-managed recovery technique. First of all, you don't need to tell RMAN where to get the backup file from—it gets the correct file to restore from its recovery catalog. All you have to do is tell RMAN to restore and recover the necessary tablespace. You may want to put the tablespace offline because your database is open. Listing 15-5 shows how RMAN recovers a lost data file. First, RMAN restores the data files(s). Then it recovers the data files by using the archived redo logs. RMAN knows what archived logs to apply to the restored data file.

Listing 15-5. Recovering a Data File Using RMAN

```
RMAN> run {
2> sql "alter tablespace sales01 offline";
3> restore datafile '/test01/app/oracle/oradata/remorse/sales_01.dbf';
4> recover datafile '/test01/app/oracle/oradata/remorse/sales_01.dbf';
5> SQL "alter tablespace sales01 online";
6> }
```

```
sql statement: alter tablespace sales01 offline
starting full resync of recovery catalog
full resync complete
Starting restore at 28-DEC-02
using channel ORA_DISK_1
...
channel ORA_DISK_1: starting datafile backupset restore
channel ORA_DISK_1: specifying datafile(s) to restore from backup set
restoring datafile 00022 to /test01/app/oracle/oradata/remorse/sales_01.dbf
channel ORA_DISK_1: restored backup piece 1
piece handle=/test02/app/oracle/product/9.2.0.1.0/dbs/0leb83l7_1_1 tag=
TAG20021225T151758 params=NULL
channel ORA_DISK_1: restore complete
Finished restore at 28-DEC-02Starting recover at 28-DEC-02
using channel ORA_DISK_1
...
starting media recovery
archive log thread 1 sequence 25
 is already on disk as file
/test01/app/oracle/oradata/remorse/arch/T0001S0000000025.ARC
...
archive log filename=/test01/app/oracle/oradata/remorse/arch/
T0001S0000000025.ARC thread=1 sequence=25
...
media recovery complete
Finished recover at 28-DEC-02
sql statement: alter tablespace sales01 online
starting full resync of recovery catalog
full resync complete
RMAN>
```

User-Managed Recovery

To recover from the loss of a data file with the user-managed method while the database is open, you must first put the affected tablespace offline. You must then restore the data file from a backup and recover the tablespace. Here's a summary of the commands you need to use:

```
SQL> alter  tablespace sales01 offline immediate;
SQL > host cp /test01/app/oracle/backup/sales01.dbf
    /test01/app/oracle/oradata/remorse/sales01.dbf;
SQL> recover tablespace sales01;
SQL> alter tablespace sales01 online;
```

The *alter tablespace* offline/online commands ensure that users don't access the tablespace during the recovery process.

Incomplete Recovery

The previous examples deal with complete recovery scenarios. The database or the tablespace, as the case may be, are fully recovered and there's no loss of data. You use incomplete recovery in situations where you want to recover to a previous point in time, perhaps because an error was made in data entry or an online redo log was lost. After recovery, you end up with a database that's not current to the latest point in time. In the next sections you'll look at how to perform incomplete recovery using RMAN and user-managed recovery procedures.

Using RMAN

You can perform three types of incomplete recovery using RMAN. Your recovery type choice depends on the type of problem that prompts the incomplete recovery.

- *Time-based recovery:* This type of recovery enables you to recover the database up to a point in time. This is helpful if you know that a problem, such as the accidental dropping of a table, occurred around a certain point in time.

- *Change-based SCN:* You can perform the recovery up to a specific SCN if you know it.

- *Log sequence recovery:* You can recover until a particular log sequence number.

Let's look at an example of a recovery based on time. Assume that table test was dropped accidentally around 10:00 A.M. Listing 15-6 shows the time-based recovery process.

Listing 15-6. A Time-Based Incomplete Recovery Using RMAN

```
RMAN> startup mount
connected to target database (not started)
Oracle instance started
database mounted
Total System Global Area    120548208 bytes
Fixed Size                     736112 bytes
Variable Size                88080384 bytes
Database Buffers             29360128 bytes
Redo Buffers                  2371584 bytes
RMAN> run
2> { set until time 'Jan 11 2002 16:00:00';
3> restore database;
4> recover database;
5> }
executing command: SET until clause
restoring datafile 00024 to /test02/app/oracle/oradata/temp_01.dbf
channel ORA_DISK_1: restored backup piece 1
```

```
piece handle=/test01/app/oracle/oradata/backup
/2ddp387s_1_1 tag=null params=NULL
channel ORA_DISK_1: restore complete
Finished restore at 22-DEC-02
Starting recover at 22-DEC-02
using channel ORA_DISK_1
starting media recovery
media recovery complete
Finished recover at 22-DEC-02
RMAN> alter database open resetlogs;
Database opened.
RMAN>
```

In Listing 15-6, the database is first mounted, but not opened. RMAN is asked
to restore the database (meaning it is asked to get the backed-up data files that are
necessary for this restore). It then is asked to recover the database. RMAN knows
what the necessary archived redo logs are based on the information about backups
stored in its recovery catalog. RMAN applies the archived redo logs and finishes
the recovery process. You can then open the database with the *alter database open
resetlogs* command. This is a PITR, and you need to make sure that the database
doesn't apply the old redo logs by mistake. You ensure this by resetting or reinitial-
izing the redo log files.

Here's the entire script to perform a tablespace PITR using RMAN:

```
RMAN> Run {
Allocate channel s1 type 'sbt_tape';
Allocate channel s2 type 'sbt_tape';
Set until time '28-DEC-02 04:00:00';
Restore database;
Recover database;
Sql "alter database open reset logs";
Release channel s1;
Release channel s2;
}
```

What Is Resetlogs?

Note that after you perform any kind of incomplete recovery, the logs are always
reset. Essentially, the *resetlogs* option reinitializes the redo log files, erasing all
the redo information they currently have, and resets the log sequence number
to 1. This is done to ensure that Oracle won't mistakenly try to apply the outdated redo information in the log files—all the redo information applied during an
incomplete recovery is removed from the logs. To apply any archived redo logs
to a data file, the SCNs and timestamps in the database files have to match the
SCNs and timestamps in the headers of the archived redo log files. When you
perform a *resetlogs* operation, the data files are stamped with new SCN and
timestamp information, making it impossible for the older archived redo logs to
be applied to them by mistake.

The *resetlogs* option is used under these circumstances:

- When you use a backup control file to recover

- When you perform an incomplete recovery, rather than a complete recovery

- When you recover using a control file created with the *resetlogs* option

Always remember to perform a backup right after you use the *resetlogs* option because you can't use the old redo logs that you archived. The old backups that you have can't recover the database past the point where the *resetlogs* command was used.

If you were to do the incomplete recovery using an SCN number, the *set until* command would be modified as *set until scn nnnn*. If you were to use an archived log sequence number, the command would be *set until logseq=nnnn thread=nnnn*, where *logseq* is the log you want to recover until.

Incomplete Recovery with User-Managed Techniques

Assume that your database is open and you decide that you have to perform an incomplete recovery—that is, you want to take the database back to a previous point. All changes since then are gone, whether you want it that way (e.g., due to a user error) or you're forced to do so (e.g., you might not have all the archived redo logs needed for up-to-date recovery). Here's a brief summary of the steps you must take to perform an incomplete recovery:

1. Shut down the database immediately:

    ```
    SQL> shutdown abort;
    ```

2. Restore all the data files and make sure all of them are online.

3. Once you restore all the data files, you're ready for recovery using the archived redo logs. You may choose one of the following three commands, depending upon your situation:

    - *Cancel-based recovery:* Here, you let Oracle apply the archived redo logs until you cancel the recovery process. You may use this method, for example, when there is a gap in your archived redo logs.

        ```
        SQL> Recover database until cancel;
        ```

    - *Time-based recovery:* You have to specify the point in time to which you want the database to be recovered.

        ```
        SQL> Recover database until time '2002-12-30:12:00:00';
        ```

        Or, if you're using a backed-up control file, you should use the following command instead of the preceding command:

        ```
        Sql>  Recover database until time

              '2002-12-30:12:00:00'using  backup controlfile;
        ```

- *Change-based recovery:* In the change-based method, you need to find out what SCN number you want to go back to.

```
SQL> Recover until change 27845;
```

4. No matter which of the three methods you use to perform your recovery, you must issue the following command when the recovery is complete, as this is an incomplete recovery:

```
SQL> alter database reset logs;
```

Recovering from the Loss of Control Files

The following case studies show how to recover from a situation where all your control files are lost. You'll have to recover using a backup control file.

Using RMAN

In this section you'll simulate a control file loss by deleting both the control files. Make sure you have a backup of the database, including the control files, before you do this. Next, shut down the database and try to start it up. The instance will come up and try to mount the database, but it doesn't find the control files with which to mount all the data files of the database. The database thus fails to mount. You can avoid the following error messages if you use the alternative command *startup nomount.*

```
RMAN> startup
Oracle instance started
RMAN-00571:
RMAN-00569: ERROR MESSAGE STACK FOLLOWS
RMAN-00571:
RMAN-03002: failure of startup command at 01/11/2003 17:18:05
ORA-00205: error in identifying controlfile, check alert log for more info
RMAN>
```

Issue the *restore controlfile* command so RMAN can copy the control file backups to their default locations specified in the init.ora file. Listing 15-7 shows how you can recover from the loss of control files using RMAN.

Listing 15-7. Using RMAN to Recover from the Loss of Control Files

```
RMAN> restore controlfile;
Starting restore at 11-JAN-03
allocated channel: ORA_DISK_1
channel ORA_DISK_1: sid=14 devtype=DISK
...
channel ORA_DISK_1: starting datafile backupset restore
channel ORA_DISK_1: restoring controlfile
output filename=/test01/app/oracle/CONTROL_01.CTL
channel ORA_DISK_1: restored backup piece 1
```

```
piece handle=/test02/app/oracle/product/9.2.0.1.0
/dbs/c-3482335306-20030111-02 tag=null params=NULL
channel ORA_DISK_1: restore complete
replicating controlfile
input filename=/test01/app/oracle/CONTROL_01.CTL
output filename=/test01/app/oracle/CONTROL_03.CTL
Finished restore at 11-JAN-03
RMAN>
```

After the restore has finished successfully, mount the database as follows:

```
RMAN> alter database mount;
database mounted
RMAN>
```

Next, recover the database:

```
RMAN> recover database;
Starting recover at 11-JAN-03
using channel ORA_DISK_1
using channel ORA_DISK_2
datafile 23 not processed because file is read-only
starting media recovery
archive log thread 1 sequence 125 is already on disk as file
/test01/app/oracle/oradata/remorse/arch/T0001S0000000125.ARC
...
archive log filename=/test01/app/oracle/oradata/remorse/redo04.log
 thread=1 sequence=128
archive log filename=/test01/app/oracle/oradata/remorse/redo03.log
 thread=1 sequence=129
media recovery complete
Finished recover at 11-JAN-03
RMAN>
```

Because the control files are restored from the RMAN backups, you have to open the database with the *resetlogs* option:

```
RMAN> alter database open resetlogs;
database opened
new incarnation of database registered in recovery catalog
starting full resync of recovery catalog
full resync complete
RMAN>
```

User-Managed Recovery

If you've lost all your control files, you can create a brand-new control file by using the *create controlfile* command. You can also use a new control file when you need to change the name of a database, clone a database in a different location, or increase the maximum number of files you specified when you first created the control file. It's a good practice to back up your control file on a regular basis by using the *backup controlfile to trace* command, as shown here:

```
SQL> alter database backup controlfile to trace;
Database altered.
SQL>
```

You can use the *backup controlfile to directory name* command to achieve the same result as the preceding command—it will produce a file that has the *create controlfile* statement in it.

 TIP *Even if you don't have a control file backup, you can easily create a new one provided you have a complete list of all the data files and the redo log files that are part of the database.*

Listing 15-8 shows a typical control file creation statement that was derived by using the *create controlfile to trace* command. After you issue the command, you can get the following file from your trace directory, which is typically the udump directory.

Listing 15-8. Recovering Lost Control with User-Managed Techniques

```
Dump file c:\oraclent\admin\remorse\udump\ORA02220.TRC
Thu DEC28 08:14:38 2002
ORACLE V9.2.0.1.0 - Production vsnsta=0
vsnsql=10 vsnxtr=3
Windows 2000 Version 5.0 Service Pack 2, CPU type 586
Oracle9i Enterprise Edition Release V9.2.0.1.0 - Production
With the Partitioning option
JServer Release V9.2.0.1.0 - Production
Windows 2000 Version 5.0 Service Pack 2, CPU type 586
Instance name: remorse
Redo thread mounted by this instance: 1
Oracle process number: 12
Windows thread id: 2220, image: ORACLE.EXE
*** SESSION ID:(7.1128) 2002-12-23 08:14:38.000
*** 2002-12-23 08:14:38.000
# The following commands will create a new control file and use it
# to open the database.
# Data used by the recovery manager will be lost. Additional logs
# may  be required for media recovery of offline data files.
# Use this only if current version of all online logs are available
STARTUP NOMOUNT
CREATE CONTROLFILE REUSE DATABASE "REMORSE" NORESETLOGS ARCHIVELOG
    MAXLOGFILES 50
    MAXLOGMEMBERS 5
    MAXDATAFILES 100
    MAXINSTANCES 1
```

```
     MAXLOGHISTORY 113
LOGFILE
  GROUP 1 'C:\ORACLENT\ORADATA\REMORSE\REDO01.LOG'  SIZE 100M,
  GROUP 2 'C:\ORACLENT\ORADATA\REMORSE\REDO02.LOG'  SIZE 100M,
  GROUP 3 'C:\ORACLENT\ORADATA\REMORSE\REDO03.LOG'  SIZE 100M
# STANDBY LOGFILE
DATAFILE
  'C:\ORACLENT\ORADATA\REMORSE\SYSTEM01.DBF',
...
  'C:\ORACLENT\ORADATA\REMORSE\USERS01.DBF'
CHARACTER SET WE8MSWIN1252
;
# Recovery is required if any of the datafiles are restored backups,
# or if the last shutdown was not normal or immediate.
RECOVER DATABASE
# All logs need archiving and a log switch is needed.
ALTER SYSTEM ARCHIVE LOG ALL;
# Database can now be opened normally.
ALTER DATABASE OPEN;
#
```

As you can see, you could make up your own *create controlfile* statement, with the catch being that you need to have an accurate record of all the component files of your database. Let's take a closer look at the control file creation script.

Start up the database in nomount mode. Obviously, if you don't have the control files, you can't mount the database. The very first line, which includes the *create controlfile* statement, is the most critical one in the script. If you have all your redo log files intact, you have to specify the *noresetlogs* option so the existing logs can be used. If you specify *resetlogs*, the redo logs don't have to exist. Oracle will create new redo files in this case, or if they exist, Oracle will reinitialize them, essentially creating a new set of redo log files. The *reuse* parameter asks Oracle to overwrite any of the old control files if they exist in their default location.

Listing 15-9 shows how to use the control file creation statement described previously.

Listing 15-9. Creating New Control Files

```
SQL> startup nomount
ORACLE instance started.
Total System Global Area  118255568 bytes
Fixed Size                   282576 bytes
Variable Size              83886080 bytes
Database Buffers           33554432 bytes
Redo Buffers                 532480 bytes
SQL> CREATE CONTROLFILE REUSE DATABASE "REMORSE" NORESETLOGS ARCHIVELOG
```

```
...
Control file created.
SQL> recover database;
ORA-00283: recovery session canceled due to errors
ORA-00264: no recovery required
SQL> alter system archive log all;
System altered.
SQL> alter database open;
Database altered.
SQL>
```

Recovering a Data File Without a Backup

Suppose you add a new data file and users consequently create some objects in it. Before you back up your database over the weekend, the new file is damaged and you need to recover the data. How do you get your data back? Well, the archived redo logs since the last backup will contain the information regarding the lost file and will enable you to recover the lost data. The following sections an example that illustrates the procedures involved.

Using RMAN

You first notice the problem when you access the lost or damaged file and get the following error:

```
SQL> create table x(name varchar2(30));
create table x(name varchar2(30))
*
ERROR at line 1:
ORA-01116: error in opening database file 5
ORA-01110: data file 5: '/test02/app/oracle/oradata/finance1/test01.dbf'
```

The first step to fix the problem is to take the affected data file offline:

```
RMAN> SQL "alter database datafile
    2> ''/test01/app/oracle/oradata/remorse/sales_01.dbf'' offline";
      sql statement: alter database datafile
      ''/test01/app/oracle/oradata/remorse/sales_01.dbf'' offline
RMAN>
```

Then, create a new data file with the same name as the damaged offline data file:

```
RMAN> sql "alter database create datafile
    2> ''/test02/app/oracle/oradata/remorse/sales01.dbf'' ";
      sql statement: alter database create datafile
      ''/test02/app/oracle/oradata/remorse/sales01.dbf"
RMAN>
```

Next, recover the new data file. RMAN will retrieve data from the archived redo logs, so the new data file is identical to the one that was lost.

```
RMAN> recover datafile '/test01/app/oracle/oradata/remorse/sales_01.dbf';
Starting recover at 11-JAN-03
using channel ORA_DISK_1
using channel ORA_DISK_2
using channel ORA_DISK_3
using channel ORA_DISK_4
starting media recovery
media recovery complete
Finished recover at 11-JAN-03
RMAN>
```

Finally, after recovery, bring the new data file online:

```
RMAN> sql "alter database datafile
2> ''/test02/app/oracle/oradata/finance1/test01.dbf'' online";
   sql statement: alter database datafile
   ''/test02/app/oracle/oradata/remrose/sales01.dbf'' online
RMAN>exit
```

User-Managed Method

The procedure for recovering a file that was never backed up is very straight-forward, again assuming you have all the archived redo logs available. You first create a new file with the same name as the lost file and use the archived logs (if necessary) to recover the data that was in that file.

Cloning a Database

DBAs are routinely asked to refresh their development and test databases from production. They may also have to create clone databases for other purposes. You may need to clone databases to test your backup and recovery strategies. Note that the main purpose behind closing databases in not to serve as a failover database during a crisis—you use standby databases for that purpose. If you have a small database, a simple export/import will suffice, but most databases are not amenable to this procedure because of their vast size. You can produce a clone database either through RMAN by using the *duplicate* command or through SQL*Plus by manually performing the copy. The RMAN method is amazingly simple, and once you get past the initial hiccups (which are natural when you use a sophisticated tool like RMAN), your gain in productivity is simply phenomenal. The following sections take you through an example using both methods.

Using RMAN

RMAN provides the *duplicate* command, which uses the backups of the source database to create a new database. The files are restored to the target database, after which an incomplete recovery is performed and the new database is opened with the *open resetlogs* command. The good thing about using RMAN is that all the preceding steps are performed automatically, without any user intervention. The duplicate database may be an exact replica of the original, or it may contain only a subset of it. The following steps are involved in cloning a database:

1. Create a new init.ora file for the auxiliary database. The init.ora file should have the following parameters, with the data files and log file parameters to ensure that the original database files aren't used for the new database but are instead renamed:

   - *Db_file_name_convert:* This parameter transforms the target data file names to the duplicate database data file names.

   - *Log_file_name_convert:* This parameter converts the target database redo log file names to the duplicate database file names.

2. Start the target database. You must start the target database where you're going to copy the source database to in nomount mode.

3. Connect the recovery catalog to the target database (primary) and the auxiliary database, as follows:

   ```
   RMAN> rman target / catalog rman/rman1@catalog_db  auxiliary
           sys/password@auxiliary_db
   ```

4. Issue the RMAN *duplicate* command, as follows:

   ```
   RMAN> Duplicate target database to
           auxiliary_db (actual name of auxiliary databs here)
           pfile =/test01/app/oracle/9.2.0.1.0/dbs/init_auxiliary_db;
   ```

   This statement is a simple illustration of the *duplicate* command.

Many other details may be relevant to your case, and you should look up Oracle's Recovery Manager manuals for the details. RMAN will shut down the auxiliary database and start it up again. It then copies all the backed-up files of the target database to the destination auxiliary database.

A Simple Example of Duplicating a Database with RMAN

Here's a simple step-by-step example of how to duplicate a database using RMAN. Note that three databases are involved in the operation because I'm using a specialized database to run RMAN with the recovery catalog. The three databases are as follows:

- *Manager* is the database where RMAN's recovery catalog is located.

- *Remorse* is the target database, which is being duplicated.

- *Goal* is the database to which the remorse target database is being duplicated.

To duplicate a database with RMAN, start up the database you want to be the new duplicate database—in this case, the database named goal. You need to start it up in the nomount state. The database will not have any files yet, because you are going to duplicate the target database, called remorse, to the duplicate database named goal. All of the target database's data files will be renamed and copied to the duplicate database. You have to use a password file to set the privileged users password. (See Chapter 11 for information on how to create a password file.) Here is a sample initialization file for the duplicate database:

```
Db_name=remorse (this is the target database_name)
Db_file_name_convert=('/oraclehome/oradata/target/', '/tmp/')
 Note: The above lets you convert the target database
data files to a different name
Log_file_name_convert=
('/oraclehome/oradata/target/redo', '/tmp/redo')
 Note: The above lets you convert the target database redo log files to a
 different name.
Lock_name_space= remorse(you have to use this parameter,
 and it must be the same as db_name)
Instance_name=aux
Control_files=/tmp/control1.ctl
Compatible=9.2.0
Db_block_size=8192
```

Next, connect to all three databases, as shown here:

```
[remorse] $ rman
Recovery Manager: Release 9.2.0.1.0 - 64bit Production
Copyright (c) 1995, 2002, Oracle Corporation.  All rights reserved.
RMAN> connect target sys/remorse1@remorse
connected to target database: REMORSE (DBID=2852692821)
RMAN> connect catalog rman/rman1@monitor
connected to recovery catalog database
RMAN> connect auxiliary sys/goal1 @goal
connected to auxiliary database: goal (not mounted)
```

Now you'll issue the *rman duplicate* command. The command asks RMAN to copy the remorse database to the new goal database. Listing 15-10 shows the output of the *duplicate* command. Notice how the *duplicate* command does the following:

- Copies the database files over to the new locations

- Creates a new control file

- Completes database recovery for the new database

- Opens the new clone database named goal

Listing 15-10. Cloning a Database with the RMAN Duplicate Command

```
RMAN> duplicate database target to goal
   2> nofilenamecheck;
Starting Duplicate Db at 27-DEC-02
allocated channel: ORA_AUX_DISK_1
channel ORA_AUX_DISK_1: sid=9 devtype=DISK
printing stored script: Memory Script
    {
   set until scn  417967;
   set newname for datafile  1 to
 "C:\ORACLENT\ORADATA\REMORSE\SYSTEM01.DBF";
   set newname for datafile  2 to
 "C:\ORACLENT\ORADATA\REMORSE\UNDOTBS01.DBF";
"C:\ORACLENT\ORADATA\REMORSE\TOOLS01.DBF";
   set newname for datafile  8 to
 "C:\ORACLENT\ORADATA\REMORSE\USERS01.DBF";
   restore
   check readonly
   clone database;
       }
executing script: Memory Script
executing command: SET until clause
executing command: SET NEWNAME
executing command: SET NEWNAME
Starting restore at 27-DEC-02
using channel ORA_AUX_DISK_1
channel ORA_AUX_DISK_1: starting datafile backupset restore
...
restoring datafile 00008 to C:\ORACLENT\ORADATA\REMORSE\USERS01.DBF
channel ORA_AUX_DISK_1: restore complete
Finished restore at 27-DEC-02
sql statement: CREATE CONTROLFILE REUSE SET DATABASE "goal" RESETLOGS ARCHIVELOG
...

{
   set until scn  417967;
   recover
   clone database
   ;
}
executing script: Memory Script
executing command: SET until clause
Starting recover at 27-DEC-02
using channel ORA_AUX_DISK_1
starting media recovery
...
media recovery complete
Finished recover at 27-DEC--02
```

```
printing stored script: Memory Script
{
   shutdown clone;
   startup clone nomount ;
}
executing script: Memory Script
database dismounted
Oracle instance shut down
connected to auxiliary database (not started)
Oracle instance started
Total System Global Area     30174764 bytes
Fixed Size                     282156 bytes
Variable Size               25165824 bytes
Database Buffers             4194304 bytes
Redo Buffers                  532480 bytes
...
{
   Alter clone database open resetlogs;
}
executing script: Memory Script
database opened
Finished Duplicate Db at 27-DEC-02
RMAN>
```

An RMAN Script for Cloning a Database

Although the preceding explanation of database cloning using RMAN seems tedious, you really can simplify matters quite a bit with an RMAN cloning script. Once you understand the entire process of cloning described previously, you can perform the entire operation with the following script:

```
#!/bin/ksh
STRING1="sys/remorse1@remorse"
STRING2="rman/rman1@monitor"
STRING3="sys/goal1@goal"
rman target $STRING1\
     catalog $STRING2\
     auxiliary $STRING3
run
{duplicate database target to goal
nofilename check;
}
```

Cloning a Database Manually

To clone a database manually, you need to first use the operating system to make a copy of all the source database files to the target location. If you are on the same server, you have to change the name of the database. If you are on a different server, you can keep the same name for the databases if you so wish. You back up the target database control file to trace and, using that, create a new database. Here's a summary of the steps involved in manually cloning a database. The procedure is simple, with most of the time being consumed by copying the database files from source to target. Assume that your production database is the source base and is named prod. Your destination database is named test.

1. Copy the prod database files to the target location.

2. Prepare an ASCII text-based file for the creation of a control file for the new database on the source database as follows:

   ```
   SQL> alter database backup controlfile to trace;
   ```

3. On the target location, create all the directories for the various files.

4. Copy the following four sets of files from the production (source) to the target database: parameter files, control files, data files, and redo log files.

5. Make sure you change the production database name to the database name test in all the clone database files.

6. Once the database files have been copied, you are ready to run the *create database* statement, which you have prepared with the *alter database backup controlfile to trace* statement.

7. Create the test database using the following statement:

   ```
   SQL> create controlfile reuse set database "TEST" resetlogs
        noarchivelog
   ```

   You'll now have a new database called test that has a new control file pointing to the copied files of the production database.

8. Run the following command after you get the prompt back from the previous command:

   ```
   SQL> Alter database open resetlogs using backup controlfile;
   ```

9. Finally, change the global name of the database you just created by running the following command:

   ```
   Sql> Update global_name set global name='test. World';
   ```

Techniques for Granular Recovery

The techniques you've seen thus far, both RMAN and user-managed recovery strategies, are reliable methods to restore databases when there's a media-related problem. However, suppose you have a problem where you only need to undo some changes in the database. Do you still need to resort to these recovery techniques? Even the incomplete recoveries, though they remove unwanted changes, will lead to a loss of data. In addition, sometimes you can't determine exactly when a change was made, and consequently, you can't make a precise incomplete recovery. You may have to close the database during the recovery process and you'll probably have to reset the redo logs.

Sometimes, due to the complexity involved, the DBA may decide to just do a complete recovery, even though it may not be called for. The result would be, of course, a limited or complete unplanned downtime. Besides, every real database recovery is fraught with danger, as you have to follow the steps pretty carefully.

Fortunately, you can use several other more granular recovery methods when your needs are more precise. The tablespace point-in-time recovery (TSPITR) method enables you to recover a database until a specified point of time in the past. The LogMiner utility, which Oracle provides free of charge, enables you to perform extremely precise recovery based on a reading of the changes recorded in the redo logs. In addition, you can use the Flashback Query feature to identify and recover lost data or wrongly committed incorrect data. Depending on your needs, you may find one of these alternatives a better way to fix data loss problems than having to restore and recover every time you have a media problem.

Tablespace Point-in-Time Recovery

Suppose you or one of the users of your database has dropped a table by mistake. Or, as it happens sometimes, you truncated the wrong table or you wrongly deleted (or inserted) data into a table. You don't have to recover the entire database when you need to bring back the table's contents. You can use Oracle's *tablespace point-in-time recovery* (TSPITR) technique to recover the tablespace containing the lost table to a point in time that's different from the rest of the database.

You can perform TSPITR using RMAN, or you can manage the whole process manually. Essentially, you have to use an auxiliary database so you can recover the tablespace (or tablespaces) to the desired point in time before the damaging action occurred. Once the tablespace is recovered to that "clean" point, it is brought back to the main database. RMAN makes it very easy for you to do the TSPITR-type recovery. The next section covers how you can use RMAN to perform a TSPITR.

Using RMAN for TSPITR

You recover the tablespaces from the main database (the target database) by first performing the PITR in a temporary instance called the *auxiliary database,* which is created solely to serve as the staging ground for the recovery of the tablespaces.

Here's how to use RMAN to perform a TSPITR. First, create the auxiliary database. Use a skeleton initialization parameter file for the temporary auxiliary instance along the lines of the following:

```
Db_name=help1 (this is the target database_name)
Db_file_name_convert=('/oraclehome/oradata/target/', '/tmp/')
/* Note: Lets you convert the target database data files to a different name */
Log_file_name_convert=('/oraclehome/oradata/target/redo', '/tmp/redo')
/* Note: Lets you convert the target database redo log files
to a different name. */
```

```
Instance_name=aux
Control_files=/tmp/control1.ctl
Compatible=9.0.1
Db_block_size=8192
```

Next, start up the auxiliary database in the nomount mode:

```
$ sqlplus /nolog
SQL> connect sys/oracle@aux as sysdba
SQL> startup nomount pfile=/tmp/initaux.ora
```

Now generate some archived redo logs and back up the target database. You can use the *alter system switch logfile* command to produce the archived redo log files. Connect to all three databases—the catalog, target, and auxiliary databases—as follows:

```
$ rman target sys/password@remorse catalog rman/rman1@help
  auxiliary system/oracle@aux
```

Perform a PITR. If you want to recover until a certain time, for example, you can use the following statement (assuming your nls_date format is of the following format mask: *Mon DD YYYY HH24:MI:SS*):

```
RMAN> recover tablespace users until time ('Dec 24 2002 12:00:00');
```

This is a deceptively simple step, but RMAN performs a number of tasks in this step. It restores the data files in the users tablespace to the auxiliary database and recovers them to the time you specified. It then exports the metadata about the objects in the tablespaces from the auxiliary to the target database, finance1. RMAN also uses the *switch* command to point the control file to the newly recovered data files.

Now that the recovery is complete, bring the user tablespace online:

```
$ rman target sys/password@finance1
RMAN> SQL "alter tablespace users online";
RMAN> Exit;
```

The last step is to remove the auxiliary instance. You can now shut down the auxiliary instance and remove all the control files, redo log files, and data files pertaining to the database.

Using LogMiner for Precision Recovery

Oracle provides the excellent LogMiner utility along with server software. LogMiner can read the redo logs, which opens the door to a number of possibilities, including the ability to restore a database to a precise point in time. Remember that only redo logs hold the information about the history of the changes made to the database. Although you can use LogMiner's capability to read redo logs for security and auditing purposes, your interest in it here is solely for database recovery. Previously, DBAs could fix any user errors only with a PITR in most cases, thereby losing valuable data in the process. LogMiner obviates the need for a full recovery while you are trying to undo a minor change to the data. In cases where you need to undo a committed change to just one table, you can do so with the help of LogMiner by identifying the exact transaction from reading the redo log files and then undoing the changes that were incorrectly made. If you need to recover from a massive error, LogMiner can still help by pinpointing the time to which you need to recover from backups. You can then perform a time-based or change-based recovery.

LogMiner helps you avoid a traditional restore and recover for tables when users make data errors. Using the tool, it is easy to perform fine-grained recovery by rolling back the unwanted changes from a table. In addition to serving as a fine-grained recovery tool, the LogMiner utility can help you to reconstruct SQL statements to help in auditing as well as debugging. Also, you can use this tool to discover when you suspect logical corruption in the database.

LogMiner uses the DBMS_LOGMNR and the DBMS_LOGMNR_D packages supplied by Oracle (a couple of other, less important packages are used also) to extract the information from the redo logs. In addition, LogMiner uses several dynamic performance views to help analyze the information contained in the redo logs. You can give regular users access to the SYS-owned packages by granting them the role execute_catalog_role. To enable LogMiner to match its object IDs with actual database object names, you have to specify a data dictionary to use, and the easiest thing to do here is assign LogMiner the normal data dictionary that belongs to the database. The V$LOGMNR_CONTENTS view holds a wealth of information that LogMiner uses to help remove unwanted changes in table data. Here is a brief list of the types of information recorded in the V$LOGMNR_CON-TENTS view:

- Timestamp

- Username

- Type of action (insert, update, delete, or DDL)

- The transaction and SCN numbers

- The tables involved in the transaction

- A reconstruction of the SQL that made the changes

- SQL that will undo the change, if necessary

How the LogMiner Utility Works

LogMiner reads redo log files and puts the information that it extracts in the V$LOGMNR_CONTENTS view, which you can then query to find out details about transactions you're interested in. Because the information in the redo logs is in the form of internal object identifiers and data in hex bytes form, Oracle recommends you provide LogMiner access to the data dictionary so it can translate the contents of the redo log file into a form you can readily understand. You can provide access to the data dictionary to LogMiner in three different ways. First, you can extract the data dictionary to a flat file. Second, you can have a dictionary snapshot placed in the redo logs themselves. Third, you can do away with the extraction of the data dictionary and direct LogMiner to just use the online data dictionary itself. Note that LogMiner doesn't show you all the SQL statements in the redo log, just the end statement that would need to be applied to the database to undo the unwanted changes.

Supplemental Logging

Before you start using the LogMiner utility, be aware that starting with Oracle9*i* version 9.2, you must turn on supplemental logging to take full advantage of the LogMiner functionality. As its name indicates, *supplemental logging* logs more information about transactions in the redo logs. If you don't have supplemental logging turned on, direct path inserts aren't supported. The SQL undo and SQL redo will contain the primary key information if you use supplemental logging. Supplemental logging enables you to capture the before image of the rows. You can turn supplemental logging on at the table level or the database level.

Although supplemental logging is strongly recommended by Oracle if you want to avail yourself of all the features of the LogMiner utility, it does inflict a heavy burden on the system. It affects performance if you choose the more expansive databasewide supplemental logging.

You can turn supplemental logging on for any single table by using *log groups*. These log groups contain a set of the table columns, and you can have a restrictive or a more general log group. If you want the before images of these columns to be always logged, even if none of the columns were changed, then you use an *unconditional log group*. Here's an example:

```
SQL> alter table hr.employees
  2* add supplemental log group key_info (empno, ename) from
     hr.employees always;
SQL>
```

The *alternative log group* is a conditional log group that logs the before images of all the specified columns in the group only if one of them changes. Here's an example:

```
SQL> alter table hr.employees
  2* add supplemental log group key_info (empno,ename) from
     hr.employees;
  SQL>
```

If you would rather turn on supplemental logging for the entire database, keep in mind that it could impose a performance penalty on your database. If you must use supplemental logging at the database level, use the *minimal supplemental logging*, which is an option designed to put the least amount of stress on your database. That said, minimal supplemental logging still provides the information you need to identify and group the operations associated with various DML operations. Oracle strongly recommends you have at least this level of supplemental logging turned on for LogMiner to be really effective. To turn minimal data-basewide supplemental logging on, use the following command:

```
SQL> alter database add supplemental log data;
```

Extracting the Data Dictionary

As mentioned previously, you have three ways to extract the data dictionary information for LogMiner's use: using a flat file, extracting the dictionary to the redo logs, or using the online data dictionary. When you start LogMiner, it builds its own internal data dictionary from the dictionary extracted by using one of the preceding three methods. Of the three methods, the easiest one is using the existing data dictionary. The problem with this method, though, is that it isn't valid with an important option of LogMiner, the *ddl_dict_tracking* option. Without this option, you can't track changes to DDL. Also, you can't track DML operations performed on tables created after the dictionary was extracted. The problem with the extraction of the dictionary to a flat file is that you can't guarantee that it's always consistent, because DDL operations could be changing the database structure while the dictionary is being extracted to the flat file. During the extraction of the dictionary to the redo logs, on the other hand, DDL statements aren't allowed, thus ensuring the consistency of the dictionary that's being extracted. So, extract the data dictionary to the redo logs because it gives you a consistent version of the data dictionary and enables DDL tracking at the same time.

A LogMiner Session

Before you invoke the LogMiner utility, make sure you create a separate tablespace for LogMiner's data, because the default location for that is the System tablespace. Also make sure you have a minimal databasewide logging turned on, as explained in the "Supplemental Logging" section.

Here's an illustration of a simple LogMiner session with minimal supplemental logging already turned on. Note that the two packages you'll be using, DBMS_LOGMNR and DBMS_LOGMNR, are owned by SYS. First, extract the data dictionary to the redo logs. The DBMS_LOGMNR_D package builds the data dictionary and stores it in the online redo logs.

```
SQL> execute sys.DBMS_LOGMNR_D.build( -
   > options => sys.DBMS_LOGMNR_D.store_in_redo_logs);
PL/SQL procedure successfully completed.
SQL>
```

Next, you specify the logs to be included in the LogMiner analysis. Because you chose to use the redo logs to extract the data dictionary, you must specify the redo logs that contain the data dictionary in addition to the other redo logs you're interested in, using the DBMS_LOGMNR.add_logfile procedure. Your first file that is added should use the DBMS_LOGMNR.newfile procedure and all the other ones should use the DBMS_LOGMNR.addfile procedure.

How do you know which of the redo log files the data dictionary was extracted to when you invoked the DBMS_LOGMNR_D.build procedure? You use the V$ARCHIVED_LOG view to find out. The columns dictionary_begin and dictionary_end will tell you in which redo log files your data dictionary is contained. Here's the query:

```
SQL> SELECT SEQUENCE#,DICTIONARY_BEGIN,DICTIONARY_END
  2 FROM V$ARCHIVED_LOG;
    SEQ#   DIC   DIC
           BEG   END
    ----   ----- -----
     2     NO    NO
    24     YES   YES
    25     NO    NO
    26     NO    NO
    27     NO    NO
    28     NO    NO
SQL>
```

From the output, you can see that the dictionary_begin and dictionary_end columns are both contained in archived redo log number 24. You include this in your list of log files, as follows:

```
SQL> EXECUTE DBMS_LOGMNR.ADD_LOGFILE( -
   > LOGFILENAME => 'C:\ORACLENT\RDBMS\ARC00024.001', -
   > OPTIONS => DBMS_LOGMNR.NEW);
PL/SQL procedure successfully completed.
```

In addition, you add the following files you're interested in to the add_logfile procedure in the DBMS_LOGMNR package:

```
SQL> EXECUTE DBMS_LOGMNR.ADD_LOGFILE( -
   > LOGFILENAME => 'C:\ORACLENT\RDBMS\ARC00025.001' , -
   > OPTIONS => DBMS_LOGMNR.ADDFILE);
PL/SQL procedure successfully completed.
SQL> EXECUTE DBMS_LOGMNR.ADD_LOGFILE( -
   > LOGFILENAME => 'C:\ORACLENT\RDBMS\ARC00026.001', -
   > OPTIONS => DBMS_LOGMNR.ADDFILE);
PL/SQL procedure successfully completed.
```

Note that you can also add log files without the options line, as follows:

```
SQL> EXECUTE DBMS_LOGMNR.ADD_LOGFILE( -
   > LOGFILENAME => 'C:\ORACLENT\RDBMS\ARC00027.001');
PL/SQL procedure successfully completed.
```

Once you've specified the redo log files, it's time to start the LogMiner utility. In this case, in addition to specifying that LogMiner uses the redo logs as a source of the data dictionary, you also enable DDL tracking (DDL tracking is turned off by default):

```
SQL>  EXECUTE DBMS_LOGMNR.START_LOGMNR(OPTIONS => -
   >  DBMS_LOGMNR.DICT_FROM_REDO_LOGS + -
   >  DBMS_LOGMNR.DDL_DICT_TRACKING );
PL/SQL procedure successfully completed.
SQL>
```

Using LogMiner to Analyze Redo Logs

Now that you've successfully started LogMiner, you can issue commands against the V$LOGMR_CONTENTS table to get information about various DML and DDL statements encompassed by the set of redo log files you included earlier by using the DBMS_LOGMNR.addfile procedure. Whenever you query the V$LOGMNR_CONTENTS view, all the redo log files you specified will be read sequentially and the information will be loaded into the V$LOGMNR_CONTENTS view. Listing 15-11 shows a simple example.

Listing 15-11. Analyzing the V$LOGMNR_CONTENTS View

```
SQL> SELECT SQL_REDO
  2  FROM V$LOGMNR_CONTENTS
  3* WHERE USERNAME='HR';
                          SQL_REDO
-------------------------------------------------------------------
set transaction read write;
select * from "SYS"."DUAL" where ROWID = 'AAAADdAABAAAANnAAA' for update;
commit;
set transaction read write;
delete from "HR"."REGIONS" where "REGION_ID" = '5'
and "REGION_NAME" =
'northern  europe' and ROWID = 'AAAHrNAAFAAAAESAAE';
delete from "HR"."REGIONS" where "REGION_ID" = '6'
and "REGION_NAME" =
'pacific region' and ROWID = 'AAAHrNAAFAAAAESAAF';
update "HR"."REGIONS" set "REGION_NAME" = 'eastern europe' where
"REGION_NAME" = 'northern africa' and ROWID = 'AAAHrNAAFAAAAESAAG';
commit;
10 rows selected.
SQL>
```

You can see that user HR has deleted two rows and updated one row. You can thus use LogMiner to retrieve DML from a previous period. There's an additional bonus to using LogMiner: It will give you the SQL to undo the preceding DML statements, as shown in the following example.

```
SQL> SELECT SQL_UNDO
  2 FROM V$LOGMNR_CONTENTS
  3* WHERE USERNAME='HR';
                            SQL_UNDO
----------------------------------------------------------------------
insert into "HR"."REGIONS"("REGION_ID","REGION_NAME")
values ('5','northern europe');
insert into "HR"."REGIONS"("REGION_ID","REGION_NAME")
values ('6','pacific region');
update "HR"."REGIONS" set "REGION_NAME" = 'northern africa' where
 "REGION_NAME"= 'eastern europe' and ROWID = 'AAAHrNAAFAAAAESAAG';
10 rows selected.
SQL>
```

LogMiner provides you with SQL you can use to undo the changes if necessary. The inserts replace the deletes and the *update* statement reverses the changes made. Note that SQL*Plus indicates that ten rows were selected in response to your query, although only the three DML operations executed by user HR are displayed.

As you can see, the SQL_UNDO column contains statements that are ready to be used in SQL, semicolon and all. However, the statements aren't very easy to read when they're long and complex. LogMiner provides a procedure to make the LogMiner output appear less cluttered. The procedure DBMS_LOGMNR.print_pretty_sql enables you to print easy-to-read output.

If you want to continuously analyze data using LogMiner, you don't have to keep adding files manually. You can just add the DBMS_LOGMNR.continuous_mine procedure by using the keyword *options*, and LogMiner will keep adding any redo log files that are archived to the list of files to be analyzed each time you query the V$LOGMNR_CONTENTS view.

Because you started LogMiner with the DDL tracking option turned on, the following query will tell you, for example, all the DDL changes made by user SYS:

```
SQL> select sql_undo
  2   from v$logmnr_contents
  3   where username='SYS'
  4* AND operation='DDL'
SQL>
```

When you've finished using LogMiner, end your session with the DBMS_LOGMNR.end_logmnr procedure, as follows:

```
SQL> execute DBMS_LOGMNR.end_logmnr ();
PL/SQL procedure successfully completed.
SQL>
```

Using Flashback Query for Recovery

Flashback Query isn't really a recovery tool per se, but you can use it effectively for fine-grained recovery under some circumstances. The tool is designed for application developers to provide self-service error correction capabilities without the need for a DBA's intervention. Flashback Query lets you query the database about committed changes that occurred at some previous point in time or a previous SCN. Using this tool, you can recover lost data or undo unwanted changes to the database. You simply execute a query to see the deleted changes and reinsert them into your tables, for example. Flashback Query enables you to see the contents of a database table as they were some time ago. Even committed changes will not be shown in this "flashback" to the past. Not only can you view the "old" data, but you can also retrieve that data into a current table.

As you may surmise, the Flashback Query feature does depend on the undo content saved in the undo tablespace. Oracle prefers you use Automatic Undo Management (AUM) rather than rollback segments to maintain the necessary read consistency. The following list contains the prerequisites to enable the Flashback Query feature in your database and get the most benefit out of it:

- Use AUM (*undo_management=auto*). This isn't mandatory, but it's highly recommended if you wish to use the Flashback Query feature.

- Set a fairly large size for the *undo_retention* initialization parameter.

- Grant execute privileges on the DBMS_FLASHBACK package to the users who will be using this feature.

- If a non-DBA user is performing an undo operation, he or she needs to be given the flashback any table privilege.

 NOTE *Chapter 8 explains how to start using the Flashback Query feature and provides a simple example of its use.*

In the next section you'll learn how you can use the Flashback Query feature to restore lost data in a table. In Chapter 8 you saw how to use the *as of* clause to select data from a past point in time. In this chapter you'll learn how to use another method to retrieve data from the past.

Before you start using the Flashback Query feature, make sure you're running in AUM mode. The following is an introduction to Flashback Query techniques.

You can use a timestamp or the SCN to tell Oracle the point in time it needs to go back to. This example presents the use of a SCN. This is how you can get the SCN:

```
SQL> variable old_scn number;
SQL>  execute :old_scn:= sys.DBMS_FLASHBACK. -
     get_system_change_number; .
The PL/SQL procedure is successfully completed.

SQL>
```

Now let's see how you can use the Flashback Query technique to get back the deleted rows without your having to perform an export/import or a TPITR. It's convenient to use PL/SQL to create a simple code block that does the job, as shown in Listing 15-12.

Listing 15-12. Using the DBMS_FLASHBACK Package to Insert Old Data

```
SQL> declare
  2  cursor old_cursor is
  3  select * from test1;
  4  old_rec old_cursor%rowtype;
  5  begin
  6  delete from test1;
  7  commit;
  8  dbms_flashback.enable_at_system_change_number(:old_scn);
  9  open old_cursor;
 10  dbms_flashback.disable;
 11  loop
 12     fetch old_cursor into old_rec;
 13     exit when old_cursor%NOTFOUND;
 14     insert into test1
 15     values
 16     (old_rec.employee_id,
 17      old.rec.first_name,
 18      old_rec.last_name
 19      old rec.hire_date,
 20      old_rec.salary);
 21  end loop;
 22  close old_cursor;
 23  commit;
 24* end;
/
PL/SQL procedure successfully completed.
SQL>
```

This is what the code in Listing 15-12 does:

1. It first enables the Flashback Query feature by using the *enable_at_system_change_number* procedure.

2. The cursor old_data is opened so it can retrieve and hold the needed data from an older version (the same table at a previous point in time) of the table employees.

3. It disables the Flashback Query feature by using the disable feature of the DBMS_FLASHBACK package.

4. Using old_cursor, the code then fetches row data from old_cursor and inserts it into the table employees.

5. The Flashback Query feature is activated at the SCN old_scn (DBMS_FLASHBACK.enable_at_system_change_number).

6. Old_cursor is opened and the Flashback Query feature is deactivated (DBMS_FLASHBACK.disable). Note that you can't insert, delete, or update data while the Flashback Query feature is turned on.

7. The original data in old_cursor is inserted into test1.

Now, if you query test1, you'll see that all 107 rows in it have magically reappeared, thanks to the Flashback Query feature:

```
SQL> select count(*) from test1;
    COUNT(*)
    --------
       107
SQL>
```

As I mentioned previously, in this chapter you'll only see the use of the SCN as a reference point for the DBMS_FLASHBACK package. Chapter 8 used the timestamp as a starting point for Flashback Query. When you use a system time to tell Flashback Query how far to go back in time, you use the following syntax to enable Flashback Query:

```
SQL1> dbms_flashback.enable_at_time(to_timestamp
    ('28-DEC-2002 03:00:00','DD-MON-YYYY HH:MI:SS'))
```

Repairing Data Corruption and Trial Recovery

As you saw in Chapter 14, Oracle provides several means of detecting data block corruption. These methods include the use of the *analyze* command, the *dbverify* command, and the *db_block_checking* initialization parameter. Oracle also provides the excellent DBMS_REPAIR package, which not only detects corruption, but also helps you fix it. Using this package, you can analyze and repair block corruption in Oracle tables and indexes. As Chapter 14 explains, you can use the *validate* command to check for data corruption in addition to verifying the backup data files.

Block Media Recovery

Although data file recovery will let users continue to access the rest of the database, you're still making an entire data file(s) unavailable while you're recovering data. Even if a few data blocks are being recovered, the entire data file has to brought offline for this type of recovery.

RMAN can help you recover from data block corruption by enabling *block media recovery* (BMR). Only RMAN allows BMR. RMAN's *blockrecover* command recovers blocks marked corrupt in the V$BACKUP _CORRUPTION and V$COPY_CORRUPTION views. With BMR, your smallest recoverable unit of data is the data block instead of the data file. RMAN restores from backups only those data blocks that need recovery. Redo application time is vastly reduced because you need to recover only certain data blocks, not entire data files. The database continues to be available to users while the corrupted blocks are being recovered. Only the specific data blocks you are recovering will be unavailable to the users. Thus, BMR helps you achieve the following goals:

- Faster recovery time

- Increased database availability

Data block corruption could lead to the following types of messages in your alert log:

```
ORA_11578: ORACLE data block corrupted (file# 9, block# 21)
ORA=01110:  data file 9: /u01/app/oracle/oradata/remorse/users_01.dbf'
```

Once you find the data file number and the corrupt block number, you use the following *blockrecover* command to recover the corrupted block:

```
RMAN> blockrecover datafile 9 block 21;
```

The *blockrecover* command determines the backups from which it needs to get the necessary data blocks to perform recovery. It then reads the backups and collects the necessary data blocks into memory buffers. The *blockrecover* command may use an older backup if it finds that the most recent backup contains corrupt data blocks. The *blockrecover* command then starts and manages the BMR session. It reads any necessary archived redo logs from the backed-up archived logs. Note that the *blockrecover* command always results in a complete recovery; you can't perform a PITR using this command.

If you think you have database block corruption, the best course of action is to get in touch with Oracle Worldwide Support, which has access to specialized tools that can help you extract data from corrupted data blocks. Oracle may charge you extra for these services, but if your data is critical, it may be well worth the expense.

Trial Recovery

While you're recovering databases, the recovery process may encounter corrupt data blocks somewhere along the line. When a situation like this occurs, the recovery process will stop, leaving the database in a consistent state. Although it's possible to recover the database to a point before the corruption occurred, this could be a time-consuming process. To accurately determine the extent of the damage before you start recovery, you can use a *trial recovery*. Depending on the amount of corruption you find, you can then decide if you'll use an incomplete recovery or continue recovery beyond the corrupted block by using the recovery option *allow n corruption*. For example, if you want to ignore a minor amount of corruption, you can use the following command, which can find one data corrupt data block yet continue the recovery process. If there is a larger number of data blocks, you will have to perform a PITR, with significant data loss. In this example, you can see how Oracle will let you allow for corruption.

```
SQL> recover database allow 1 corruption;
```

Trial recovery lets you *simulate* the recovery process—it neither does a real recovery wherein updated blocks are written to disk nor does it fix data corruption. It lets you know if there is corruption and, if there is, the extent of the corruption. Trial recovery proceeds in the same way as real data recovery by applying the redo changes. However, trial recovery changes the data blocks only in memory, not permanently on disk. After the test, it rolls back all its changes, leaving only any possible error messages in the alert log file. Here are the typical trial recovery commands:

```
SQL> recover database until cancel TEST;
ORA-10574: Test recovery did not corrupt any data block
ORA-10573: Test recovery tested redo from change 9948095 to 9948095
ORA-10570: Test recovery complete
/*  The following statement would recover a tablespace  */
SQL> recover tablespace users TEST;
```

Troubleshooting Recovery

Recovery management is prone to more errors and needs more troubleshooting than any other part of Oracle database administration. If a production recovery is being bogged down by Oracle errors, it gets to be an even more stressful event. You could conceivably run into numerous different problems over the years. This section covers a few common error messages issued during a recovery session.

The ORA-01194 Error

When you're trying to start up a database after a database cloning, you'll usually end up with the ORA-01194 error. Listing 15-13 shows the sequence of Oracle messages and your responses.

Listing 15-13. The ORA-01194 Error

```
SQL> startup
ORACLE instance started.
Total System Global Area  118255568 bytes
Fixed Size                   282576 bytes
Variable Size              83886080 bytes
Database Buffers           33554432 bytes
Redo Buffers                 532480 bytes
Database mounted.
ORA-01589: must use RESETLOGS or NORESETLOGS option for database open
SQL> alter database open noresetlogs;
alter database open noresetlogs
*
ERROR at line 1:
ORA-01588: must use RESETLOGS option for database open
SQL> alter database open resetlogs;
alter database open resetlogs
*
ERROR at line 1:
ORA-01194: file 1 needs more recovery to be consistent
ORA-01110: data file 1: 'C:\ORACLENT\ORADATA\MANAGER\SYSTEM01.DBF'
SQL> recover database until cancel using backup controlfile;
ORA-00279: change 405719 generated at 05/26/2002 15:51:04 needed for thread 1
```

```
ORA-00289: suggestion : C:\ORACLENT\RDBMS\ARC00019.001
ORA-00280: change 405719 for thread 1 is in sequence #19
Specify log: {<RET>=suggested | filename | AUTO | CANCEL}
ORA-01547: warning: RECOVER succeeded but OPEN RESETLOGS would get error below
ORA-01194: file 1 needs more recovery to be consistent
ORA-01110: data file 1: 'C:\ORACLENT\ORADATA\MANAGER\SYSTEM01.DBF'
SQL>
```

Oracle keeps issuing the error message 1194, and even using the "recover database using backup controlfile until cancel" (with which you can mimic a recovery) does not succeed in stopping it. The problem is that the changes needed for recovery are in the very last online redo log, not in any archived redo log Oracle might be suggesting to you. When you apply this online redo log, Oracle will finish recovery successfully, as shown here:

```
SQL> recover database until cancel using backup controlfile;
ORA-00279: change 405719 generated at 01/26/2003 15:51:04 needed for thread 1
ORA-00289: suggestion : C:\ORACLENT\RDBMS\ARC00019.001
ORA-00280: change 405719 for thread 1 is in sequence #19
Specify log: {<RET>=suggested | filename | AUTO | CANCEL}
C:\ORACLENT\ORADATA\MANAGER\REDO03.LOG
Log applied.
Media recovery complete.
SQL> alter database open resetlogs;
Database altered.
SQL>
```

The ORA-01152 Error

The ORA-01152 error ("File # was not restored from a sufficiently old backup") bedevils quite a few recovery sessions. Here is an interesting situation (that I owe to my colleague Lance Parkes) whose solution is similar to the preceding example. The recovery session was provided all the archived redo logs that it asked for, but in the end, Oracle came up with the following error messages:

```
...
ORA-00289: suggestion :
/u01/app/oracle/admin/pasedu/arch/pasedu/_0000012976.arc
ORA-00280: change 962725326 for thread 1 is in sequence #12976
ORA-00278:
logfile'/u01/app/oracle/admin/pasedu/arch/pasedu/_0000012975.arc'
no longer needed for this recovery
Specify log: {<RET>=suggested | filename | AUTO | CANCEL}
ORA-01547: warning: RECOVER succeeded but OPEN RESETLOGS would get error below
ORA-01152: file 1 was not restored from a sufficiently old backup
ORA-01110: data file 1: '/pase16/oradata/pasedu/system_01.dbf'ORA-01112:
media recovery not started
```

In response to the preceding errors, the following recovery command was used:

```
SQL> recover database until cancel using backup controlfile;
ORA-00279: change 962726675 generated at 01/19/2003 04:32:48 needed for thread 1
ORA-00289: suggestion :
/u01/app/oracle/admin/pasedu/arch/pasedu/_0000012977.arc
ORA-00280: change 962726675 for thread 1 is in sequence #12977
```

Oracle's response was to ask for an archived redo log file, but because the recovery process has already indicated that it doesn't need any more archived redo logs, you can ignore this misleading request and provide Oracle with the name of your restored *online redo log files*, starting with the first one. One of those redo log files will have the change number the recovery process is looking for. Just provide Oracle your redo log files, one member from each redo log group. Here's the rest of this recovery process:

```
Specify log: {<RET>=suggested | filename | AUTO | CANCEL}
/pase04/oradata/pasedu/redo01a.rdo
ORA-00279: change 962746677 generated at 01/19/2003 04:33:52 needed for thread 1
ORA-00289: suggestion :
/u01/app/oracle/admin/pasedu/arch/pasedu/_0000012978.arc
ORA-00280: change 962746677 for thread 1 is in sequence #12978
ORA-00278: log file '/pase04/oradata/pasedu/redo01a.rdo'
no longer needed for this recovery
Specify log: {<RET>=suggested | filename | AUTO | CANCEL}
/pase04/oradata/pasedu/redo02a.rdo
Log applied.
Media recovery complete.
SQL>
```

The ORA-00376 Error

Another common error that could bedevil you is the ORA-00376 error, which indicates that a certain files(s) cannot be read. The error results in the following messages:

```
ORA-00376: file 10 cannot be read at this time
ORA-01110: data file 10: '/u01/app/oracle/remorse/data_01.dbf'
```

The ORA-00376 is usually caused by a data file or tablespace being offline. By bringing the tablespaces or data file online, you can fix the problem easily. Sometimes, the error is because the data file doesn't exist at the tablespace level. In this case, you have to take the tablespace offline, re-create it with the correct data file name and bring it online.

Summary

This is one of the most important chapters in this book, at least in the sense that you need to have a solid understanding of the concepts and the techniques of recovery, so you don't encounter any surprises when you perform a production recovery.

Remember that to get good at recovering databases, it's not enough to understand the theoretical concepts well. It will do you a world of good if you install a small database on a UNIX or a Windows-based server and go through the various recovery scenarios described in the Oracle manuals. Many times, you'll encounter errors in the implementation of these recovery methods, but at least you aren't under the gun, recovering a critical production database in the middle of the night and trying to get help from an Oracle support person halfway around the world.

In this chapter you learned how to recover a database under various scenarios. Copying or cloning databases offers you a good chance to regularly test your backup and restore mechanisms, and you learned how to clone a database using both RMAN and user-managed recovery techniques.

Although it's important to understand how to use various recovery techniques, chances are you'll more frequently restore just a table or a set of tables at a point in time. Granular recovery techniques are useful in this regard, and you learned how to use the LogMiner utility to perform fine-grained recovery of object data. You also learned how to use the DBMS_FLASHBACK package to retrieve accidentally lost or deleted data, without the need for an incomplete point-in-time recovery (PITR), which is much more complex to perform.

Handling database corruption issues is an important part of your job, and you saw how to use trial recovery to judge the extent of block corruption. You also learned how to perform block media recovery with the help of RMAN.

Part Five

Managing the Operational Oracle Database

CHAPTER 16

Managing the Operational Database

THIS CHAPTER DEALS with the operational aspects of a running Oracle database. Several components of the database require constant monitoring and changes. You can manage your database efficiently by understanding how these components work. The goal of the new features provided by Oracle9*i* is to make the database as self-managing as possible. Several areas of the Oracle9*i* database server help achieve this goal, and you'll review some of the important features in some detail in this chapter.

Space management in Oracle9*i* has become considerably simpler than in the past versions of the database. In this chapter, you'll see how you can set up automatic space management in your databases. You'll also revisit locally managed tablespaces to learn how you can set up a fully locally managed database.

Dynamic memory management is another feature that will help you immensely in your day-to-day administration of complex production databases. The online table redefinition feature will help you perform several routine tasks without reducing the availability of the tables to your users. This chapter's detailed discussion of Oracle Managed Files (OMF) explains how this feature helps you build databases quickly without your having to manage the database files.

You'll also learn about Oracle's improved file management and I/O topology for intelligent storage arrays. Transaction management is a big part of the Oracle server's tasks, and you'll review the concepts of Automatic Undo Management (AUM) and Resumable Space Allocation. Dynamic shared memory management is an important tool in managing the Oracle database, and you'll explore topics such as self-tuning SQL execution memory and self-tuning direct I/O.

Earlier chapters introduced several of the topics that you're going to see here, and this chapter's goal is to tie together the various aspects of the Oracle9*i* database that make the DBA's job easier. Two areas, automatic database management features and online management features, are highlighted in this chapter. In addition to these two areas, various other topics, such as mapping Oracle files to physical devices, managing online redo logs, and managing remote database links, are also explained here.

Oracle's Automatic Management Features

Oracle has been emphasizing that its latest 9*i* database automates management to such an extent that it refers to the database as a *self-managing* database. Well, this is at least partially true, as several traditional time-consuming and error-prone tasks are now made redundant due to new ways of organizing space and managing memory, transactions, and resources, in addition to improvements in backup and recovery techniques.

But the DBA is just as essential as ever. If anything, the DBA's role has become even more central because of the new features' added complexity in the latest version of the Oracle database. One of the most useful innovations in recent years has been the concept of locally managed tablespaces and the uses of Oracle managed undo segments. In the next section you'll explore how adopting these new features can make day-to-day database management easier.

Fully Locally Managed Databases

Space management has been one of the most time-consuming Oracle DBA tasks for many years. DBAs used to constantly worry about tablespace fragmentation, and they devoted considerable time to reorganizing database objects to coalesce fragmented free space in tablespaces. The use of locally managed databases (see Chapters 5 and 7) frees up DBAs from routine space management tasks and improves the performance of DML and certain DDL operations.

Oracle9*i* Release 2 lets you choose locally managed tablespaces even for the System tablespace, thus enabling you to create fully locally managed databases. Analysis of locally managed tablespaces indicates that even with a larger number of extents than dictionary managed tablespaces, their performance is as good as or better than that of dictionary managed tablespaces. When you couple this information with the fact that you need to spend hardly any time managing locally managed tablespaces, you have a very easy decision to make regarding how you manage extents in the database.

The choice of locally managed tablespaces over the alternative dictionary managed tablespaces frees up DBAs to work on issues other than space management. If you currently have dictionary managed tablespaces, you can convert to locally managed tablespaces using Oracle's DBMS_SPACE_ADMIN package.

Automatic Extent Allocation

In the 9.2 version of the Oracle9*i* database server, you can create locally managed tablespaces by default. The *create database* statement for a locally managed System tablespace will look like the following statement. In Chapter 9, the database creation statement uses the *extent management local* clause to create a database that can have only locally managed tablespaces. In the following statement, the *extent management local* clause specifies that the System tablespace is locally managed. If the System tablespace is locally managed, all other tablespaces in that database have to be locally managed as well—you can't create any dictionary managed tablespaces in that database.

```
SQL> Create database test
...
datafile '/test01/app//oracle/test/system01.dbf' size 500M reuse
EXTENT MANAGEMENT LOCAL
...
SQL>
```

You can specify that the tablespaces be traditional tablespaces by using the *extent management dictionary* clause or by omitting the *extent management local* clause. Eventually, Oracle will do away completely with dictionary managed tablespaces in future versions, and you are strongly urged to choose locally managed tablespaces for your databases.

If your database has been created with the System tablespace in a dictionary managed tablespace, you can convert the System tablespace into a locally managed tablespace using the following statement:

```
SQL> execute sys.dbms_space_admin.tablespace_migrate_to_local('SYSTEM');
```

Traditionally, database fragmentation has been a serious issue for Oracle DBAs. Fragmentation occurs when there are chunks of free space in the tablespace that are too small to be used by tables and indexes. The *autoallocate* feature of the *create tablespace* statement ensures that Oracle will automatically allocate space without wasting free space.

Automatic Segment Space Management

If you use locally managed tablespaces, Oracle lets you choose between the traditional manual segment space management and the newer Automatic Segment Space Management feature. As you recall from the discussion in Chapter 7, manual segment space management means that you specify FREELISTS and other traditional parameters for the objects you create in that tablespace. FREELISTS, for example, keep track of the blocks in the objects that have room for inserting new rows. Automatic Segment Space Management does away with setting and manually managing the old space management parameters—Oracle uses bitmaps to keep track of the free space in the data blocks.

In addition to FREELISTS, you don't have to set the value of the FREELIST GROUPS and PCTUSED parameters. Bitmaps are more accurate in estimating the available free space in the data blocks and significantly improve the performance of concurrent DML operations.

Here is a simple example of using the Automatic Segment Space Management feature of the 9*i* database:

```
SQL> create tablespace auto_example
  2  datafile 'C:\ORACLENT\ORADATA\MANAGER\EXAMPLE02.dbf'
  3  size 20M
  4  extent management local
  5* segment space management AUTO;
Tablespace created.
SQL>
```

If you examine the DBA_TABLESPACES view, you'll see the following under the segment_space_management column:

```
SQL> select segment_space_management
  2  from dba_tablespaces
  3* where tablespace_NAME= 'AUTO_EXAMPLE';
SEGMEN
------
AUTO
SQL>;
```

The specification of AUTO segment space management mode for the table-space auto_example eliminates the need to specify the parameters FREELISTS, FREELISTS GROUPS, and PCTUSED for any objects you may create in that tablespace.

 NOTE *If you do use the FREELISTS, FREELISTS GROUPS, and PCTUSED parameters during the creation of any object in a tablespace that uses the Automatic Segment Space Management feature, Oracle will simply ignore those parameters.*

Automatic Undo Management

"Undo" refers to the before image of data as it existed before the start of a transaction. All the concurrent transactions running in your database need to be able to fit into the undo space allocated for them, or you're going to have transaction failures. Rollback segment contention and space management used to be big database management issues, but with the new Automatic Undo Management (AUM) mode, you don't have to worry about these problems anymore.

You can still choose the traditional rollback segment option instead of AUM. If you wish to manually manage the rollback segments, you have to worry about specifying large segments for large transactions to avoid "Snapshot too old" errors. In addition, you have to worry about contention for rollback segments, proper sizing of the segments, and the correct number of segments. When you choose AUM mode, you simply create a dedicated undo tablespace, select the undo retention period, and Oracle will do the rest.

Oracle still uses rollback segments, but they are now internally created and referred to as *undo segments*. Oracle will handle issues such as the number and size of the rollback segments, block contention, and maintenance of read consistency. When you create the undo tablespace during database creation, a set of ten undo segments is created automatically. Each of these ten segments consists of two segments of 16KB each. The size of the extents is automatically increased by Oracle according to an internal algorithm. The *undo_retention* parameter enables you to set how long Oracle should retain the undo information.

Undo Management Concepts

Undo records contain information about transactions that you can use to roll back transactions, recover databases, and provide read consistency. Undo records are stored automatically by Oracle in the undo tablespace you set up during database creation. Undo tablespaces are created in uniform bitmapped tablespaces, with one or more data files within the undo tablespace, whereas ten undo segments are automatically created when you choose AUM. You cannot alter or drop these undo segments.

Whenever the system monitor (SMON) process determines that space is getting low, the undo segments are shrunk. In any case, SMON performs a shrink every 12 hours to reclaim space from unused undo segments. New undo segments are automatically created and brought online by Oracle as the need arises. The AUM method transfers undo space dynamically between extents. If the undo tablespace can't extend existing segments due to lack of space in the undo tablespace, idle free space is stolen from other undo segments. If Oracle determines that some undo segments aren't needed any longer, those segments are taken offline and their space reclaimed.

Implementing Automatic Undo Management

You learned how to set up AUM in Chapter 9. You specify the undo tablespace at database creation time, and you can specify several tablespaces to hold the undo tablespace. However, Oracle will only use only one undo tablespace at a time.

Creating Undo Tablespaces

You can specify undo tablespaces either at database creation time or after database creation time. If you specify an undo tablespace at database creation time, you need to insert the line *undo tablespace = tablespace_name* right after the *create database* statement, as shown earlier in this book. If you want to create or drop an undo tablespace later on, you can do that as well. Here is the *undo tablespace* command:

```
SQL> create undo tablespace undotbs2
  2  datafile 'C:\ORACLENT\ORADATA\MANAGER\UNDOTBS2_03.DBF'
  3* size 100m;
Tablespace created.
SQL>
```

Once you create the undo tablespace, you can drop it or add data files to it just as you would a regular tablespace.

Specifying the Undo Retention Period

The *undo_retention* parameter determines the length of time Oracle will retain undo information from a transaction. If you leave this parameter out of the init.ora file, Oracle will retain undo for 30 seconds (the default value for the *undo_retention* parameter). You can change this value dynamically with the *alter system* command, as shown here:

```
SQL> alter system set undo_retention=3600;
System altered.
SQL>
```

How do you know what the ideal amount of space for the undo tablespace is? Obviously, the size of the undo tablespace depends on the nature of transactions in your database. The more undo information generated by your database, the larger the undo tablespace should be. Oracle provides a very easy way to estimate the correct size for the undo tablespace through Oracle Enterprise Manager

(OEM). You can get to this Undo Space Advisor by selecting Database ➤ Configuration ➤ Undo in the OEM window. The Advisor will provide an estimate of the undo tablespace size required by the database based on both the average and maximum amounts of undo generation. Figure 16-1 shows the Undo Space Advisor in action.

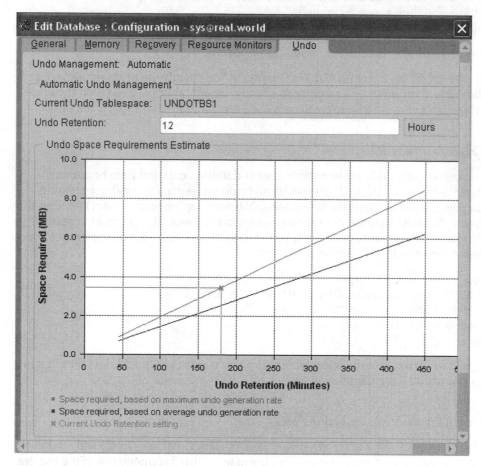

Figure 16-1. Using the Undo Space Advisor

Switching Undo Tablespaces

If you have more than one undo tablespace, you can switch from one undo tablespace to another by using the following command. You can easily switch undo tablespaces online, which provides you with great flexibility.

```
SQL> alter system set undo_tablespace=undotbs2;
System altered.
SQL>
```

If you want to unassign an undo tablespace, you can use the following command:

```
SQL> alter system set undo_tablespace=undotbs1;
System altered.
SQL>
```

Monitoring Undo Tablespaces

You can query the V$UNDOSTAT view to find out how transactions are using the undo space. This view gives you a good idea about whether your *undo_retention* parameter is set appropriately. You can also receive information about the maximum length of queries, the maximum duration of transactions, and the maximum number of concurrent transactions. Listing 16-1 shows the output of a simple query based on the V$UNDOSTAT table.

Listing 16-1. Monitoring the Undo Tablespace

```
SQL>  select begin_time,
  2  end_time,
  3  undoblks,
  4  txncount,
  5  maxquerylen,
  6  maxconcurrency
  7* from v$undostat;
```

Begin time	End time	Undo blks	Txn Count	Max Query	Max Concur
05/Jan/03 064724:pm	05/Jan/03 065724:pm	4	104	3	1
05/Jan/03 063724:pm	05/Jan/03 064724:pm	6	104	4	1
05/Jan003 062724:pm	05/Jan/03 063724:pm	4	102	3	1
05/Jan/03 061724:pm	05/Jan/03 062724:pm	7	104	3	1
05/Jan/03 060724:pm	05/Jan003 061724:pm	3	104	4	1
05/Jan/03 055724:pm	05/Jan/03 060724:pm	6	102	3	1
05/Jan/03 054724:pm	05/Jan003 055724:pm	3	104	4	1
05/Jan/03 053724:pm	05/Jan003 054724:pm	8	104	3	2
05/Jan/03 052724:pm	05/Jan003 053724:pm	2	102	2	1
05/Jan03 051724:pm	05/Jan/03 052724:pm	7	104	3	2
05/Jan/03 050724:pm	05/Jan/03 051724:pm	1	104	3	2

```
SQL>
```

Undo Quota

The DBA can control the undo space used by transactions by using a *resource plan directive*. If you have the Database Resource Manager configured and running, you can use the *undo_pool* parameter to ration the undo space among your resource groups. If a resource group reaches the maximum of the total undo space allocated to it, no further *insert, delete,* and *update* statements are processed. If the resource group exceeds the *undo_quota* limit during a transaction, the DML statement is aborted. The transaction can only run after others release some undo space in the resource group, unless you decide to increase the resource group's undo quota.

CAUTION *One of the main drawbacks of the AUM feature, as compared to the older manual specification of rollback segments, is that Oracle will use only one undo tablespace at any given time. This could lead to a physical I/O contention because all the undo segment headers are in the same data file for all the undo segments.*

TIP *If you are already using rollback segments, and the number and length of your transactions are high, you may want to experiment cautiously with the AUM feature because of its limited flexibility.*

Resumable Space Allocation

When you run large batch jobs or huge data loads, there is always a risk that you will inadvertently run out of space. When that happens, the operation is terminated with an error and you have to redo the whole process to get the job done. If a transaction managed to insert almost a million rows before failing, all those rows may have to be rolled back and the operation started from the beginning. The result is frustration all around, as an out-of-space error is something that can and should be avoided. After all, these are not inevitable errors, but these types of errors unfortunately happen quite a bit in many operations.

Oracle9*i*'s Resumable Space Allocation feature ensures that your jobs are not aborted due to a lack of space. Instead of abruptly terminating the job when an error condition is reached, Oracle will notify you and wait for a specified length of time before erroring out. This wonderful feature is going to save you quite a bit of frustration when jobs fail to complete due to space-related errors.

Essentially, the Resumable Space Allocation feature provides you with intervention time, so the statements don't error out automatically. If you take care of the space problem within the allotted time, the statements automatically resume execution as though the initial error never occurred.

You can turn on the Resumable Space Allocation feature by using the *alter session* statement, as shown here:

```
SQL> alter session enable resumable;
```

You can use the *alter session enable resumable* statement before the start of all your major transactions, thus removing the anxiety associated with space-related errors. At the very end of the transaction, you can include the *alter system disable resumable* statement to turn off this feature.

NOTE *Chapter 8 shows you in detail how to set up and use the Resumable Space Allocation feature.*

A Resumable Space Allocation Example

In this section you'll go through a simple example to demonstrate how the Resumable Space Allocation feature works. First, make sure you turn on the Resumable Space Allocation feature by using the following *alter session* command:

```
SQL> alter session enable resumable timeout 600;
Session altered.
```

The *alter session* statement set the Resumable Space Allocation time to 10 minutes (600 seconds). Any space-related error will cause the operation generating it to be suspended for 5 minutes, after which the operation will error out.

Next, create a test tablespace with a very small data file:

```
SQL> create tablespace test_resume
  2* datafile '/test01/app/oracle/remorse/test1.dbf' size 100k;
Tablespace created.
SQL>
```

Then create a test table that you'll use to perform a large insert operation:

```
SQL> create table test_resume
  2  (employee_id number,
  3  first_name varchar2(20),
  4  last_name varchar2(30),
  5  hiredate date,
  6  salary number)
  7* tablespace test_resume;
Table created.
SQL>
```

Now insert a very large amount of data into the new test_resume table. The goal is to force an out-of-space error condition.

```
SQL> insert into test_resume
  2  select employee_id,first_name,last_name,hire_date,
  3* salary from hr.employees;
```

Your insert transaction just hangs, and after exactly 10 minutes, it gives you the following error message:

```
SQL> insert into test_resume
  2  select * from test_resume;
insert into test_resume
            *
ERROR at line 1:
ORA-30032: the suspended (resumable) statement has timed out
ORA-01653: unable to extend table SYS.TEST_RESUME by 8 in tablespace
TEST_RESUME
SQL>
```

You can also see the space allocation error in the alert log file, where you'll find the following statement:

```
Fri Jan 17 05:48:16 2003
statement in resumable session 'User SYS(0),
Session 12, Instance 1' was suspended due to
ORA-01653: unable to extend table SYS.TEST_RESUME

 by 8 in tablespace TEST_RESUME
```

If no action is taken within the 10 minutes, you have to resume the insert operation. If you don't resume the insert operation, it will error out for good, as shown in the alert log:

```
Fri Jan 17 05:58:18 2003
statement in resumable session 'User SYS(0), Session 12, Instance 1' was timed out
Fri Jan 17 05:59:02 2003
ORA-1652: unable to extend temp segment by 8 in tablespace            TEST_RESUME
```

However, if you add a data file to the test_resume tablespace before the allowable resumable operation time is up, the statement will resume and the insert will complete without any errors. The alert log will then show the following sequence of events:

```
Fri Jan 17 06:14:25 2003
alter tablespace test_resume
add datafile '/test01/app/oracle/remorse/test_resume_02.dbf' size 50M
Fri Jan 17 06:14:27 2003
statement in resumable session 'User SYS(0), Session 12, Instance 1' was resumed
Fri Jan 17 06:14:28 2003
```

Types of Resumable Statements

Oracle9*i* lets you use the Resumable Space Allocation feature for the categories of conditions described in the following sections.

Maximum Extents–Related Errors

If a table or index reaches the maximum number of extents specified during its creation, the object can't go any further for new insertions of data. The statement that's trying to do the insert will fail in such a case. The following are the typical extent limit–related Oracle errors:

```
ORA-1631 maximum extents reached for  a table
ORA_1654 maximum extents reached for an index
```

You can increase the number of extents in a table or index segment using the following statement:

```
SQL> alter table A storage (max extents unlimited);
```

More often than not, however, the maximum extents–related errors don't give you enough time to run the preceding statement, and the SQL statement that's inserting data will fail. One of your options in this case is to rebuild the index.

Note that under locally managed tablespaces, the *maxextents storage* clause for objects is ignored at object creation time. In fact, if you create locally managed tablespaces, the terms DEFAULT STORAGE, NEXT, PCTINCREASE, MINEXTENTS, and MAXEXTENTS aren't valid any longer. Look at the following example:

```
SQL> CREATE table fn_data2 (product_id number,
  2  price number,
  3  product_desc varchar2(100))
  4* storage (initial 2m  maxextents 500);
Table created.
SQL>  select initial_extent ,extents ,next_extent, max_extents
       from dba_segments where segment_name='FN_DATA2';
INITIAL_EXTENT    EXTENTS NEXT_EXTENT   MAX_EXTENTS
-------------- ---------- ----------- -----------
    16384             1               2147483645
SQL>
```

As you can see, Oracle ignores the initial_extent and max_extents values that you specified in the *table creation* statement. The max_extents value is set to 2147483645, which is the same as the value of the "unlimited" *maxextents* clause. If you try to change any of the storage parameters of this table, you'll get the following error:

```
SQL> alter table fin_data
  2  storage (next 50m);
alter table fin_data
*
ERROR at line 1:
ORA-25150: ALTERING of extent parameters not permitted
SQL>
```

This error is the result of an attempt to alter the storage parameters of a segment in a locally managed tablespace, regardless of whether it has the uniform or autoallocate extent allocation policy.

The reason for this digression from the discussion of the Resumable Space Allocation feature is to point out that you don't really have to worry about running out of extents if you use locally managed tablespaces. However, if for some reason you're still using the traditional dictionary managed tablespaces, this is a clear and present danger to any busy production system with numerous tables.

Out-of-Space Errors

The table or index may be well under its *maxextents* limit, but it still may not be able to grow if there simply isn't enough room in the tablespace for throwing the new extent. The following are the typical extent limit–related Oracle errors:

```
ORA-1653 out of space error for a table
Ex. ORA-01653: unable to extend table FNADM.TBLARCHIVE
by 8091 in tablespace FNDATA01
ORA-1654 out of space error for an index
```

Once you reach an out-of-space condition, any SQL statements that are trying to insert new rows to the table will fail abruptly.

User's Space Quota–Related Errors

When a user runs out of the space that has been allocated to him or her, any attempt to create or expand an object's size in that user's tablespace will fail. You can use the Resumable Space Allocation feature to prevent such space-related failures.

Resumable Operations

Any *select, insert, update,* and *delete* statements are candidates for resumable operations. An import and export process is also resumable if you set the *resumable = y* parameter. By default, SQL*Loader operations aren't resumable, but you can make a SQL*Loader session resumable by using the *resumable=yes* parameter value.

In addition to DML statements, the following DDL statements are eligible for the Resumable Space Allocation feature:

- *Create table as select*

- *Alter table … move partition*

- *Create materialized view*

- *Create index*

- *Alter index … rebuild*

Automating and Monitoring Recovery Time

Oracle is capable of recovering from an unexpected database crash without losing any data. Remember that when the database crashes, there are two phases to the ensuing recovery:

- *Redo or roll-forward phase:* In the first phase, the database applies to the data files any committed updates that haven't been made a part of the data files. These committed transactions are recovered from the redo log.

- *Undo or rollback phase:* In the second phase, all uncommitted transactions that are already part of the data files are undone.

After a crash, the database can't be opened unless it performs recovery. However, here's the interesting part: Oracle lets you open the database before the second phase is completed. As soon as the redo or roll-forward phase is over, the database is opened for the users, while the SMON process performs the undo in the background. When a user's process runs into a transaction locked for rollback, it rolls back the transaction quickly. These intermittent rollbacks don't have a discernible impact on the user's query performance. This means that the database is open far quicker after a crash than if you waited for both phases of recovery to complete.

How long does the second phase (the rollback) take to complete? It depends on how much undo information you have to roll back. In Chapter 5, I explained the fast start time–based recovery concept, wherein you can set an upper limit on the *Mean Time to Recover* (MTTR), which is the average time it will take a database to recover from an instance crash. Oracle automatically recovers the database from an instance crash without the involvement of the DBA. Once you set the MTTR by using the *fast_start_mttr_target* (FSMT) initialization parameter, Oracle will automatically enforce the limits on database recovery times. (Please see Chapter 5 for more information about how fast start time–based recovery works.) Essentially, Oracle does this by internally translating the MTTR into the appropriate values for the parameters involved in recovery: *log_checkpoint_timeout_interval* and *fast_start_io_target*.

NOTE *As you may recall from Chapter 5, there is an inherent tradeoff between database performance and the MTTR time limit. At each checkpoint, Oracle writes the contents of the data block buffers to the data files. Simply put, the more frequently checkpointing occurs within the database, the faster the recovery, because only the changes after the latest checkpoint have to be recovered after a crash. However, database checkpointing imposes an overhead on the database, and checkpointing too frequently will hurt database performance because of the additional physical I/Os necessary for writing the checkpointing information. The quicker the recovery you wish to specify, the higher the cost in terms of performance, because the data files have to be updated more frequently.*

You can use the V$INSTANCE_RECOVERY view to monitor the estimates of the current MTTR that Oracle calculates every 30 seconds. You can thus see how close the MTTR is to the target set by the FSMT parameter using the following simple query:

```
SQL> select target_mttr,
  2    estimated_mttr
  3    from v$instance_recovery;
TARGET_MTTR      ESTIMATED_MTTR
----------       ----------------
      82               50
SQL>
```

NOTE *Notice that in the V$INSTANCE_RECOVERY view, the column ckpt_block_writes is inversely related to your MTTR target. An abnormal increase in the checkpoint block writes means that you are setting the MTTR value too low.*

Oracle provides the MTTR Advisor to show you quickly the tradeoff between performance and instance recovery time. You can get to the MTTR Advisor page in OEM by selecting Database ➤ Instance ➤ Resource Advisors ➤ MTTR Advisor. The MTTR Advisor shows the change in total I/O for various MTTR values. Thus, you can easily see how your MTTR setting affects system performance. Figure 16-2 shows the MTTR Advisor.

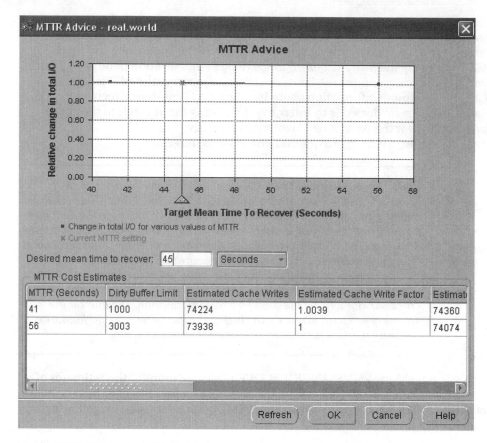

Figure 16-2. Using the MTTR Advisor

In Figure 16-2, you can see the inverse relationship between the MTTR and the change in I/O caused by the more frequent updating of the data files following checkpoints. You can change the MTTR dynamically by simply using the *alter system* command, as shown here:

```
SQL> alter system set fast_start_mttr_target=6000;
System altered.
SQL>
```

Easy File Management with OMF

Oracle Managed Files (OMF) makes managing data files, control files, and redo log files a lot easier than doing it manually. Normally, if you drop a data file, the database won't have any references to the data file, but the physical file still exists in the old location. You'll have to explicitly remove the physical file yourself. If you use OMF, Oracle will remove the file for you when you drop it from the database. As I mentioned in an earlier chapter, Oracle Corporation recommends limiting the use of the OMF feature to small test or development databases. Oracle Corporation also recommends that you stripe the files in the OMF system and make them as large as possible.

You have to use operating system–based files if you want to use the OMF feature; you can't use raw files. You do lose some control over the placement of data in your storage system when you use OMF files. Even with these limitations, the benefits of OMF file management could outweigh its limitations under some circumstances.

Benefits of Using OMF

You can create tablespaces with OMF-based files. You can also specify that your online redo log files and your control files are in the OMF format. OMF files offers several advantages over user-managed files:

- Oracle automatically creates and deletes OMF-based files.

- You don't have to worry about coming up with a naming convention for the files. Oracle has its own unique naming scheme for the files.

- It's easy to drop data files by mistake when you're managing them. With OMF files, you don't run the risk of accidentally deleting database files. Also, you can't specify the same OMF file twice by mistake, because Oracle ensures each file is uniquely named.

- Oracle automatically deletes a file when it's no longer needed. The typical accumulation of older files taking up unnecessary space in the file system is gone with the use of OMF files.

- Interestingly, you can have a mix of traditional files and OMF-based files in the same database.

You have to use operating system–based files if you want to use OMF; you can't use raw files. In the following sections you'll explore the OMF feature in some detail. I present a quick explanation of how OMF files are created by Oracle. Most of the commands you use for managing the normal data files and redo log files apply to OMF files as well.

Creating Oracle Managed Files

You can create OMF files when you create the database, or you can add them later on to your traditionally created database. Either way, you need to set some initialization parameters to enable OMF file creation.

Initialization Parameters for OMF

You need to set two initialization parameters to enable the use of OMF files. You can use each of these parameters to specify the file destination for different types of OMF files, as shown here:

- *Db_create_file_dest:* This parameter specifies the location of data files, online redo log files, and temp files. You may specify a control file location also if you wish. Unfortunately, the *db_create_file_dest* parameter can take only a single directory as its value; you can't specify multiple file systems for the parameter. What do you do if the assigned directory for file creation fills up? Because the *db_create_file_dest* parameter is dynamic, you can always specify a new directory, which enables you to place Oracle data files anywhere in the file system without any limits whatsoever.

- *Db_create_online_log_dest_n:* You can use this parameter to specify the location of online redo log files and control files. In this parameter, *n* refers to the number of redo log files you want created. If you want to multiplex your online redo log files as Oracle recommends, you should set *n* to 2.

If you don't specify these two initialization parameters in your init.ora file or SPFILE, you can still use the *alter system* command to dynamically enable the creation of OMF files, as shown in the following example:

```
SQL> alter system set db_create_file_dest =
  2  '/test01/app/oracle/oradata/finance1';
System altered.
SQL>
```

As long as you specify the *db_create_file_dest* parameter, you can have Oracle create OMF files for you and you can use both the user-managed and Optimal Flexible Architecture (OFA) files simultaneously without a problem.

File Naming Conventions

Oracle uses the OFA standards in creating filenames, so filenames are unique and data files are easily identifiable as belonging to a certain tablespace. Table 16-1 shows the naming convention for various kinds of OMF files and an example of each type. Note that the letter *t* stands for a unique tablespace name, *g* stands for an online redo group, and *u* is an 8-character string.

Table 16-1. OMF File Naming Convention

OMF FILE TYPE	NAMING CONVENTION	EXAMPLE
Data file	ora_t%_u.dbf	ora_data_Y2ZV8P00.dbf
Temp file (default size is 100MB)	ora_%t_u.tmp	ora_temp_Y2ZWGD00.tmp
Online redo log file (default size is 100MB)	ora_%g_%u.log	ora_4_Y2ZSQK00.log
Control file	ora_u%. ctl	ora_Y2ZROW00.ctl

Different Types of Oracle-Managed Files

You can use OMF to create all three types of files that the Oracle9*i* database requires: control files, redo log files and, of course, data files. However, there are interesting differences in the way OMF requires you to specify (or not specify) each of these types of files. The following sections cover how Oracle creates the three different types of files.

Control Files

As you have probably noticed already, there is no specific parameter that you need to include in your init.ora file to specify the OMF format. If you specify the control files parameter, you will, of course, have to specify a complete file location for those files, and obviously they will not be OMF files—they are managed by you. If you do not specify the control files parameter and you use either the *db_create_file_dest* or *db_create_online_log_dest_n* parameter, your control files will be OMF files.

If you are using a traditional init.ora file, you need to add the control file locations to it. If you are using an SPFILE, Oracle automatically adds the control file information to it.

Redo Log Files

OMF redo log file creation is along the same lines as control file creation. If you don't specify a location for the redo log files and you set either the *db_create_file_dest* or the *db_create_online_log_dest_n* parameter in the init.ora file, Oracle automatically creates OMF-based redo log files.

Data Files

If you don't specify a data file location in the *create* or *alter* statements for a regular data file, or a temporary tablespace temp file or an undo tablespace data file, but instead specify the *db_create_file_dest* parameter, all these files will be OMF files.

Simple Database Creation Using OMF

Let's use a small example to see how OMF files can really simplify database creation. When you create a new database, you need to specify the control file, redo log file, and data file locations to Oracle. You specify some file locations in the initialization file (e.g., control file locations) and some file locations at database creation (e.g., redo log locations). However, if you use OMF-based files, database creation can be a snap, as you'll see in the sections that follow.

Setting Up File Location Parameters

For your new database, named ora_omf, first set the locations for the files in the init.ora file as follows:

```
undo_management=AUTO
db_create_file_dest = '/test01/app/oracle/oradataora_omf/omfDATA'
db-create_online_log_dest_1='/test01/app/oracle/oradata/ora_omf/finLOGS'
db_create_online_log_dest_2='/test02/app/oracle/oradata/ora_omf/finLOGS'
```

Of course, you need the usual memory and other configuration parameters specified in the init.ora file. Once you add the preceding parameters to your init.ora initialization file, you are ready to create an OMF-based database.

Starting the Instance

Using the simple init.ora file you just created with the OMF file location parameters, start an instance as follows:

```
SQL> connect sys/remorse1 as sysdba
Connected to an idle instance.
SQL> startup nomount
     pfile=
      '/test02/app/oracle/product/9.2.0.1.0/dbs/initremorse.ora'
ORACLE instance started.
Total System Global Area  120548208 bytes
Fixed Size                    736112 bytes
Variable Size               88080384 bytes
Database Buffers            29360128 bytes
Redo Buffers                 2371584 bytes
SQL>
```

Creating the Database

You can create the database now with this simple command:

```
SQL> create database ora_omf   2 default temporary tablespace temp;
Database created.
SQL>
```

That's it! Just those two simple lines are all you need to create a functional database with the following structures:

- A System tablespace

- Two duplexed redo log files

- Two copies of the control file

- A default temporary tablespace

- An undo tablespace managed by Oracle

Where Are the OMF Files?

You can see the various files within the database by looking at the alert log for the ora_omf database. Here's what you'll find in the alert log.

At the very outset, Oracle creates the control files and places them in the location you specified for the *db_create_online_log_dest_n* parameter.

```
create database ora_omf
default temporary tablespace temp
Sat Jan  4 22:37:45 2003
Created Oracle managed file
/test01/app/oracle/oradata/ora_omf/finLOGS/ora_yj5md98t.ctl
Created Oracle managed file
/test02/app/oracle/oradata/ora_omf/finLOGS/ora_yj5md9dz.ctl
Database mounted in Exclusive Mode.
```

The next step is the creation of the duplexed online redo log file. Oracle creates the minimum number of groups necessary (two) and duplexes them, again as specified by the *db_create_online_log_dest_n* parameter.

```
Created Oracle managed file
/test01/app/oracle/oradata/ora_omf/finLOGS/ora_1_yj5md9jo.log
Created Oracle managed file
/test02/app/oracle/oradata/ora_omf/finLOGS/ora_1_yj5mdf5s.log
Created Oracle managed file
/test01/app/oracle/oradata/ora_omf/finLOGS/ora_2_yj5mdjsj.log
Created Oracle managed file
/test02/app/oracle/oradata/ora_omf/finLOGS/ora_2_yj5mdocg.log
```

The System tablespace is created next, in the location you specified for the *db_create_file_dest* parameter.

```
create tablespace SYSTEM datafile /* OMF datafile */
default storage (initial 10K next 10K) EXTENT MANAGEMENT DICTIONARY online
Sat Jan  4 22:38:04 2003
Created Oracle managed file /test01/app/oracle/oradata/ora_omf
/omfDATA/ora_system_yj5mdio2.dbf
Completed: create tablespace SYSTEM datafile /* OMF datafile
```

Then the undo tablespace is created with the default name UNDOTS in the location specified by the *db_create_file_dest* parameter. The temporary tablespace is also created in the same directory.

```
CREATE UNDO TABLESPACE SYS_UNDOTS DATAFILE SIZE 10M AUTOEXTEND ON
Created Oracle managed file
/test01/app/oracle/oradata/ora_omf/finDATA/ora_sys_undo_yj5mg123.dbf
...
Successfully onlined Undo Tablespace 1
Completed: CREATE UNDO TABLESPACE SYS_UNDOTS DATAFILE  SIZE 1
Sat Jan  4 22:38:45 2003
CREATE TEMPORARY TABLESPACE TEMP TEMPFILE
Created Oracle managed file
/test01/app/oracle/oradata/ora_omf/finDATA/ora_temp_yj5mg592.tmp
Completed: CREATE TEMPORARY TABLESPACE TEMP TEMPFILE
```

Adding Tablespaces

Adding other tablespaces and data files is easy. All you have to do is invoke the *create tablespace* command without the *datafile* keyword. Oracle will automatically create the data files for the tablespace in the location specified in the *db_create_file_dest* parameter. The example that follows shows how to create the tablespace:

```
SQL> alter system set db_create_file_dest =
  2  '/test01/app/oracle/ora_omf/finance1';
System altered.
SQL> create tablespace omftest;
Tablespace created.
```

```
SQL> select file_name from dba_data_files
  2 where tablespace_name='OMFTEST';
FILE_NAME
-----------------------------------------------------------
/test01/app/oracle/oradata/ora_omf/ora_omftest_yj7590bm.dbf
SQL>
```

Compare this OMF tablespace creation statement with the typical tablespace creation statement, and you'll see how OMF simplifies database administration. Adding data files is also simple with the OMF, as shown by the following example:

```
SQL> alter tablespace omftest add datafile;
```

Online Capabilities of Oracle9*i*

In addition to the automatic database management features, Oracle9*i* offers you unprecedented opportunities to perform many common tasks online, thus reducing the work that you could previously perform only after the database was shut down or an object was taken offline. In some cases (e.g., the *move* command), DML operations were prevented until the table was moved. The new features offer you continuous online availability, making it easier for you to perform the reorganization tasks. Several of these features are new, and a lot of the older online techniques have been further refined. In the sections that follow, you'll examine some of the important online capabilities of the Oracle9*i* database.

Online Data Reorganization

Oracle provided several online reorganization features, such as the ability to create partitions, move tables, and add constraints, in older versions of its software. The 9*i* version goes much further and provides more online options for DBAs. Let's look at some of the important online features of Oracle9*i*.

Using OEM to Perform Online Reorganization

If you've configured OEM (see Chapter 17), you can easily perform offline or online reorganization of database objects. Many times, you'll see a need to change the storage attributes of a table or index. OEM makes it easy to perform these reorganizations. I'm not going to go through the whole sequence of steps, but I'll show you a couple of the screens in the reorganization process. You access the Reorganization Wizard by choosing Tools ➤ Tuning Pack ➤ Reorg Wizard. Figure 16-3 shows you the first step of the reorganization process, which displays the cases where reorganization can help you.

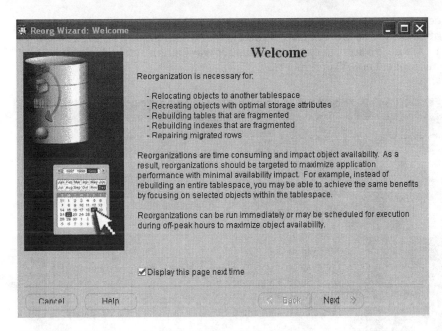

Figure 16-3. Using the Reorganization Wizard

Step 4 of the reorganization process (see Figure 16-4) offers you a choice of reorganization methods. You can choose either offline or online reorganization. Online reorganization is slower, but it provides access to the objects being reorganized.

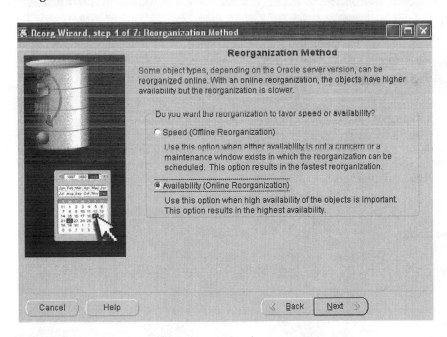

Figure 16-4. Choosing online reorganization.

Once you choose the online reorganization method, OEM will ask you for the list of objects to be reorganized. It then generates an impact report and job summary, which is a summary of the actual reorganization script. Figure 16-5 shows the Impact Report screen.

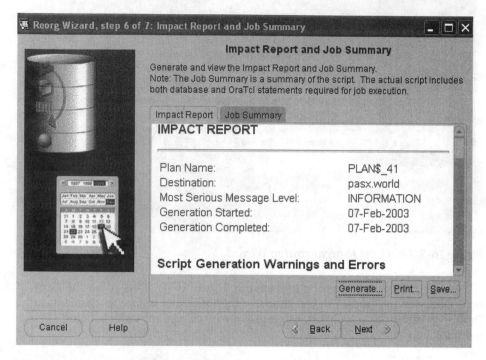

Figure 16-5. The Impact Report screen

In the next step, you decide whether to perform the online reorganization right away or schedule it for some other time.

Online Analyze Validate

The online analyze validate feature enables you to validate the structure of an object while users are making changes to the table. The following example shows the use of this online feature:

```
SQL> analyze table jobs
  2* validate structure online;
Table analyzed.
SQL>
```

Online Index Rebuilds

You can rebuild indexes online, thus improving the availability of large database tables. Note that while users can change the table data, they can't use the parallel DML options during an online index rebuild. Users can, however, perform normal DML operations against the base table. You can rebuild many kinds of indexes, including function-based indexes and reverse-key indexes, online. You can't rebuild a bitmap index online, though.

Online Table Redefinition

Oracle offers the online table redefinition feature, which lets you redefine a table online, while users continue read/write access to the table. You can use the online feature to create new tables with more efficient physical storage parameters, move tables to different tablespaces, reduce fragmentation in tables, and change a heap table into an index organized table and vice versa.

The online table redefinition feature can enhance both data availability and disk usage. The table that is being redefined will be locked for a short period of time, which enables simultaneous access for both reads and writes by all users. Both the newly redefined table and the original table continue to exist together until the DBA decides to switch over to the newly redefined table. The switching process is independent of the size of the table being redefined and the complexity of the redefinition.

During the redefinition process, local materialized logs are maintained, and changes to the master table are tracked using snapshot logs. If you have materialized views and materialized logs defined on a table, you can't redefine them online.

What Can Online Redefinition Do?

You can use online redefinition to perform a number of tasks that would have necessitated taking tables offline in previous versions of Oracle. Using the online table redefinition feature, you can

- Add, drop, or rename columns.

- Transform table data.

- Change data types of the columns.

- Rename table constraints.

- Change the original storage parameters.

- Reduce fragmentation in tables.

- Create a partitioned table out of a regular table online.

- Create an index-organized table (IOT) out of a regular table.

- Move a table to a different tablespace.

The list of tasks you can perform using online redefinition is truly impressive, because you don't have to keep users from accessing the tables while you're performing these common tasks.

The online table redefinition follows a simple sequence of steps:

1. Determine if a table is a good candidate for redefinition.

2. Decide on the structure of the new table and create a new image of the table.

3. Start the redefinition process by using the DBMS_REDEFINITION package.

4. Create necessary constraints and triggers on the new table.

5. Perform periodic synchronization and validation of data in the new table.

6. Complete the redefinition of the table.

You can perform online table redefinition using one of two methods: a primary key method and a ROWID method. The ROWID method is more complex, and Oracle recommends you use the easier primary key method, which requires that the original and the redefined tables have the same primary key columns. In the following sections you'll perform online table redefinition using the default primary key method.

An Online Table Redefinition Example

In this example you'll reorganize the table employees in the HR schema. You'll create a temporary table with all the new attributes that you want. In your case, you'll want to drop the salary column in the employees table. The goal here is to add the salary column to the employees table (with the data) and partition the table using a range scheme based on the employee_id column. Once you have completed the online redefinition, you can drop the temporary table. The employees will have the attributes of the temporary table.

 TIP *It may seem simpler for the DBA account to perform the online redefinition, but granting the schema owner the requisite privileges on the DBMS_REDEFINITION and the system privileges described in the following section turned out to be a lot easier in practice.*

Verifying Eligibility of the Table

The first step in the online redefinition process is to ensure that the table employees is a candidate for the process. By using the DBMS_REDEFINITION package, you can verify whether or not the employees table is a candidate. If your table is not eligible, Oracle will issue an error message. The following procedure shows the use of the package for verifying the employees table:

```
SQL> BEGIN
  2    dbms_redefinition.can_redef_table('hr','employees');
  3    END;
  4  /
PL/SQL procedure successfully completed.
SQL>
```

In the DBMS_REDEFINITION.can_redef_table procedure, you can specify the method of online redefinition as the third parameter in addition to the schema owner name (hr) and the table name (employees). This third parameter is called the *options_flag*, and it can take two possible values: DBMS_REDEFINITION.cons_use_pk if you want to use the primary key method or DBMS_REDEFINITION.cons_use_rowid if you want to use ROWIDs to do the redefinition. Because you're using the default primary key method, you don't have to specify this third parameter for your procedure. Note that a table doesn't need a primary key for it to be eligible for online redefinition.

Now that the employees table has indeed been verified as an eligible candidate for redefinition, you'll move to the next step, where you'll create an interim table.

Creating the Temporary Table

The next step is to create an interim table. Why an interim table? Well, if you're redefining a production table, you don't want to change the table directly. It's a lot less risky if you can view the results and finally OK the redefinition. At this point, you swap the interim table for the existing production table. In your case, the interim table will have the new column salary. It will also be partitioned on the employee_id column, as shown in Listing 16-2.

Listing 16-2. Creating the Temporary Table for Online Redefinition

```
SQL>  create table hr.employees_temp
  2    (employee_id       number(6),
  3    first_name         varchar2(20) not null,
  4    last_name          varchar2(25) not null,
  5    email              varchar2(25) not null,
  6    phone_number       varchar2(20),
  7    hire_date          date not null,
  8    job_id             varchar2(10) not null,
  9    salary             number(8,2),
 10    commission_pct     number(2,2),
 11    manager_id         number(6),
 12    department_id      number(4))
 13    PARTITION BY RANGE(employee_id)
 14    (partition employees1 values less than (100) tablespace example,
 15*  partition employees2 values less than (300) tablespace example);
Table created.
SQL>
```

Redefining the Table

You can now start the redefinition process by using the DBMS_REDEFINITION.start_redef_table procedure as shown in Listing 16-3. The *start_redef_table* procedure has the following parameters:

- *Uname* is the schema name (hr).

- *Orig_table* is the table you're redefining (employees).

- *Int_table* is the name of the interim table.

- *Col_mapping* shows the mapping between the interim and the original table's columns. If you don't supply any values for the column mapping parameter, then all the columns of the original table will be included in the interim table.

- *Options_flag* indicates the method of redefinition. In this example, because you're using the default primary key method, you can omit this parameter.

 TIP *When you perform table redefinition, you should be logged in as the schema owner. Make sure the schema owner is granted execute privileges on the DBMS_REDEFINITION package. The schema owner should also be granted the privileges to select, create, alter, drop, and lock any table. Otherwise, you'll encounter the "ORA-01031 insufficient privileges" error.*

Listing 16-3. Starting the Online Redefinition Process

```
SQL> begin
  2  dbms_redefinition.start_redef_table('hr','employees',
  3  'employees_interim',
  4  'employee_id employee_id,
  5  first_name first_name,
  6  last_name last_name,
  7  email email,
  8  phone_number phone_number,
  9  hire_date hire_date,
 10  job_id job_id,
 11  commission_pct commission_pct,
 12  manager_id manager_id,
 13  department_id department_id')
 14  ;
 15  end;
 16  /
PL/SQL procedure successfully completed.
```

Make sure the interim and master tables have the same number of rows by running the following queries:

```
SQL> select count(*) from employees_interim;
  COUNT(*)
-----------
    107
SQL> select count(*) from employees;
  COUNT(*)
----------
    107
SQL>
```

Using the DBMS_REDEFINITION package is easy, but a lot is going on behind the scenes. When you execute the DBMS_REDEFINITION.start_redef_table procedure, two new tables are created: a temporary table and a permanent table. The temporary table is called RUPD$_Employee, and it lasts for the duration of the session. The permanent table is a snapshot table that holds all the changes made to the master employees table once you execute the *start_redefinition_table* procedure. The master table's rows are copied to the interim table, and users will be able to update the master table during this process. The changes made by the users are logged in the materialized log during this process.

Here's a query on usr_object that shows that your new table has been partitioned based on your redefinition. The query also shows the two new tables created during the online redefinition process.

```
SQL> select object_type,object_name
  2  from user_objects
  3  where object_name like '%EMPLOYEES%';
OBJECT_TYPE          OBJECT_NAME
------------------   --------------------
TABLE                EMPLOYEES
TABLE PARTITION      EMPLOYEES_INTERIM
TABLE PARTITION      EMPLOYEES_INTERIM
TABLE                EMPLOYEES_INTERIM
TABLE                EMPLOYEES_NEW
SEQUENCE             EMPLOYEES_SEQ
TABLE                MLOG$_EMPLOYEES
TABLE                RUPD$_EMPLOYEES
TRIGGER              SECURE_EMPLOYEES
9 rows selected.
SQL>
```

Creating Constraints and Triggers on the Interim Table

You're now ready to create any necessary constraints, triggers, or indexes on the interim table. During the final redefinition step, the constraints, triggers, indexes, and grants on the interim table will replace those in the original table. Foreign key constraints that you create on the interim table must be disabled. These constraints will be automatically re-enabled when the online redefinition is completed.

Synchronizing the Interim and Source Tables

This is an optional step where you use the *sync_interim_table* procedure to synchronize the data in the interim and the source table. Here's how you execute the procedure:

```
SQL> execute dbms_redefinition.sync_interim_table('hr', -
   > 'employees','employees_interim');
PL/SQL procedure successfully completed.
SQL>
```

You should use this procedure only if you have reason to believe that a large number of updates have taken place on the source table after you started the redefinition process, by executing the *start_redef_table* procedure. By using the *sync_interim_table* procedure, you save time in the last phase of the process, when a large number of updates have taken place. Otherwise, you can ignore this step safely, because the last procedure you run, the *finish_redef* procedure, will perform the synchronization anyway.

Completing the Redefinition Process

Once you're done creating triggers and constraints and granting privileges on the interim table, it's time to complete the process by running the following *finish_redef_table* procedure. The interim table at this point has all the data of the source table, employees. However, the employees table still has its old structure. In your case, the employees table is still not partitioned, and it doesn't contain the salary column yet.

```
SQL> execute DBMS_REDEFINITION.FINISH_REDEF_TABLE('hr', -
   > 'employees', 'employees_interim');
PL/SQL procedure successfully completed.
```

When you run the *finish_redef_table* procedure, the following things happen:

- Oracle reads the materialized log on the master table so the contents can be added to the interim table.

- The employees table is redefined so it has all the attributes, indexes, constraints, and grants of the interim table employees_interim.

- Any referential constraints involving the employees_interim table are enabled.

- Any new triggers that you defined on the employees_interim table are on the newly redefined table and are enabled.

- The two tables are briefly locked in the exclusive mode to make the necessary changes in the data dictionary.

- The materialized view and the log are dropped.

The following output shows you the contents of the employees table:

```
SQL> desc hr.employees
    Name                Null?           Type
   -------            ---------       -------------
  EMPLOYEE_ID         NOT NULL        NUMBER(6)
  FIRST_NAME                          VARCHAR2(20)
  LAST_NAME           NOT NULL        VARCHAR2(25)
  EMAIL               NOT NULL        VARCHAR2(25)
  PHONE_NUMBER                        VARCHAR2(20)
  HIRE_DATE           NOT NULL        DATE
  JOB_ID              NOT NULL        VARCHAR2(10)
  SALARY                              NUMBER(8,2)
  COMMISSION_PCT                      NUMBER(2,2)
  MANAGER_ID                          NUMBER(6)
  DEPARTMENT_ID                       NUMBER(4)
SQL> select object_type,object_name
  2  from user_objects
  3* where object_name='EMPLOYEES';
OBJECT_TYPE          OBJECT_NAME
------------------   -------------
TABLE PARTITION      EMPLOYEES
TABLE PARTITION      EMPLOYEES
TABLE                EMPLOYEES
SQL>
```

As you can see in the preceding output, the employees table now has the salary column. In addition, it is a partitioned table now. The table is locked in an exclusive mode only for a very small amount of time, regardless of how many rows it has or what kinds of redefinitions you perform.

You can now drop the employees_interim table. When you drop the interim table, all the indexes, triggers, and constraints on the original table are dropped also, because the original table has become the interim table.

If you see any major errors during the preceding process, it is easy to abort the redefinition process by using the DBMS_REDEFINITION.abort_redef_table procedure. This procedure drops the temporary table and logs created during the preceding process. You can then manually drop the interim table.

Dynamic Resource Management

Traditionally, once any user started a transaction in the database, he or she had to be given the same priority as all the other sessions in the database. This would sometimes lead to a single user hogging the database resources and consequently slowing down the database. In Chapter 8, you saw how the Database Resource Manager can help you control resource use within the database by using resource groups and resource plans to allocate critical resources.

In addition to its resource allocation capabilities, the Database Resource Manager has the following features. These features help you dynamically alter the performance of active transactions (please refer to Chapter 8 to learn how to set up and use the Database Resource Manager).

- You can automatically move a long-running operation from a high-priority consumer group to a low-priority group.

- You can limit the number of concurrent long transactions.

- You can prevent any transaction from running if its estimated time for completion exceeds a preset execution limit set by the DBA.

The following sections cover how you can perform each of the previously mentioned tasks using the Database Resource Manager.

Switching Long-Running Transactions

The Database Resource Manager lets you use *plan directives* with which you can specify limits on resource usage. Plan directives include the following parameters, which you can use to shift the priority of consumer groups:

- *Switch_time*

- *Switch_group*

- *Switch_estimate*

A user will be assigned to a certain consumer group at the beginning of a transaction. If the user's transaction is active for more than a certain number of seconds as specified by the *switch_time* parameter, the transaction is automatically switched to a lower priority group denoted by the *switch_group* parameter.

You can have the Database Resource Manager determine whether it should switch a user session, even *before* an operation starts, by setting the *switch_estimate* parameter to *true*. In this case, the Database Resource Manager will *estimate* the time it will take for the operation to complete, and based on that time estimate, the Database Resource Manager will determine if it should switch the user's consumer group right away.

Limiting Number of Long Transactions with Operation Queuing

When you create resource consumer groups using the Database Resource Manager, you can set the active session pool for each group. An *active session* is one where a transaction or a select operation is currently active. Once the consumer group's active session pool limit is reached, new sessions belonging to the group can't become active. They're queued by the Database Resource Manager and allowed to become active as the current active sessions complete.

You can set an optional time-out period for the queued sessions in each group. If a session is queued past this time-out period, it will abort with an error message. The user then has the choice of resubmitting the job or ignoring it.

Limiting Maximum Execution Times for Transactions

All DBAs dread the possibility of a very large job that could take up most of the database's resources and bring it to its knees. Most times, you're left to decide if you should kill the long-running job. The Database Resource Manager avoids such stressful situations by allowing you to set limits on the execution times of operations. To be accurate, the Database Resource Manager allows you to run only those jobs that fall within a maximum runtime limit that you set. You have two ways to limit the execution times of a transaction in the Oracle9*i* database.

NOTE *You can use the DBMS_APPLICATION.set_session_longops procedure to track long-running operations. The procedure will populate the V$SESSION_LONGOPS virtual table. Chapter 20 shows you how to use the procedure.*

Using the Max_Estimated_Exec_Time Resource Plan Directive

You can limit the maximum execution times for transactions by using the resource plan directive *max_estimated_exec_time.* When you set this parameter, the Database Resource Manager will estimate the operation's execution time and will abort the operation if it exceeds the maximum estimated execution time set by you.

Using the Undo Pool Resource Plan Directive

You can control long-running transactions by limiting the amount of undo space that a resource consumer group can use. Long-running transactions in general tend to need a large amount of undo space to maintain a consistent image of the old data and to enable the session to roll back the transaction. By default, an active session can use an unlimited amount of undo space. You can specify a limit to the undo space for a consumer group by using the resource plan directive *undo_pool.* Once all the sessions in a consumer group use up the allotted undo space specified by the *undo_pool* parameter, all insert, update, and delete transactions on behalf of any session transaction within that group will abort with an error.

Online Database Block Changes

Suppose you have a tablespace that has a block size of 8KB, as shown in the following example:

```
SQL> select name, value from V$Spparameter
  2 where name='db_block_size';
    NAME            VALUE
--------------------------------
db_block_size      8192
SQL>
```

Because the block size is 8KB and you have only a single block size, all your tablespaces are created with this default block size of 8KB. Suppose that you now want to create a tablespace with a higher block size—for example, 32KB. Can you do this? Creating a tablespace with varying block sizes is easy in Oracle9*i*. As I explained in Chapters 5 and 7, you can have several cache sizes (a total of five—the default block size plus up to four other block sizes) by using the *db_Nk_cache_size* parameter. Each of the tablespace block sizes in the database should correspond to a *cache_size* in the buffer cache. Thus, if you want five differently sized (block sizes, I mean) tablespaces, then you must have all five of the buffer cache sizes configured.

In Listing 16-4, which shows the results of a query in my test database, you don't see any values under any of the five possible *db_Nk_cache_size* parameters. This is because I chose only one block size, the standard block size of 8KB, and none of the other optional cache sizes. My total *db_cache_size* value is shown as 25MB (2516824 bytes) in the listing, and it's composed of the standard 8KB blocks.

Listing 16-4. The Buffer Cache Nk Size Components

```
SQL> select name, value
  2  from v$parameter
  3* where name like '%cache_size%';
     NAME                         VALUE
--------------------------------------
db_keep_cache_size                   0
db_recycle_cache_size                0
db_2k_cache_size                     0
db_4k_cache_size                     0
db_8k_cache_size                     0
db_16k_cache_size                    0
db_32k_cache_size                    0
db_cache_size                 25165824
8 rows selected.
SQL>
```

You can easily create a new buffer cache size of 16KB online and create a new tablespace with that block size. You can then create your objects in this new tablespace or move any existing objects into this tablespace, all online. Here's what you have to do. First, create a new 16KB buffer cache, so you can create a tablespace with a 16KB block size.

```
SQL> alter system set db_16K_cache_size=1024m;
System altered.
SQL>
```

Now you can create your new tablespace with the 16KB block size because you have a matching 16KB buffer cache size. Here's the *create tablespace* statement:

```
SQL> create tablespace Big_block
  3 datafile '/test01/app/oracle/big_block_01.dbf' size 1000M
  4*blocksize 16K;
Tablespace created.
SQL>
```

If you have a table that you want to move to the new big_block tablespace with the 16KB block size, all you have to do is use the *move* command:

```
SQL> alter table why move tablespace big_block;
Table altered.
SQL>
```

Of course, you can also use the online table redefinition method to move your table to the new tablespace.

Dynamic Memory Reconfiguration

One of the biggest problems regarding memory management in the earlier versions was that you had to bounce the database when you needed to make any change in the shared pool or buffer cache configurations. Oracle9*i* lets you configure memory dynamically, and this makes it easier for you to quickly respond to a recently discovered need to modify the memory parameters belonging to the buffer cache, shared pool, or large pool.

Dynamic Reconfiguration of the SGA

You use the *alter system* command to add or subtract memory from the System Global Area (SGA) without having to modify the init.ora file and restart the database. You can add memory to the SGA, as long as you don't exceed the value of the initialization parameter *sga_max_size*. You add memory in units called *granules*. Each granule is 4MB if your total SGA is less than 128MB. For larger SGAs, each granule is 16MB. Here are some examples showing the usage of the *alter system* command to modify memory allocation:

```
SQL> alter system set db_cache_size = 32M;
System altered.
SQL> alter system set shared_pool_size = 32M;
System altered.
SQL>
SQL>
```

Using dynamic memory reconfiguration, you can reduce memory allocated to the buffer cache to the shared pool and vice versa based on the performance of the database. You can use the V$DB_CACHE_ADVICE view to get recommendations about the ideal size of the SGA and have any changes implemented immediately, which increases the availability of your database. The V$DB_CACHE_ADVICE view has the following structure:

```
SQL>   desc v$db_cache_advice
 Name                      Null?        Type
 ------------------------------------------------
 ID                                     NUMBER
 NAME                                   VARCHAR2(20)
 BLOCK_SIZE                             NUMBER
 ADVICE_STATUS                          VARCHAR2(3)
```

```
         SIZE_FOR_ESTIMATE                      NUMBER
         SIZE_FACTOR                            NUMBER
         BUFFERS_FOR_ESTIMATE                   NUMBER
         ESTD_PHYSICAL_READ_FACTOR              NUMBER
         ESTD_PHYSICAL_READS                    NUMBER
SQL>
```

The key columns in the V$DB_CACHE_ADVICE view are as follows:

- Size_for_estimate is the cache size you want to use in the prediction, in megabytes.

- Buffers_for_estimate is the cache size you want to use in terms of buffers.

- Estd_physical_reads is the estimated number of physical reads for the cache size you choose.

You'll want to increase your *buffer_cache* parameter value when the buffer cache hit ratio (see Chapter 5) falls below a level that's unacceptable to you. You can use the query in Listing 16-5 to see the relationship between an increase in the buffer size and the decrease in the amount of physical reads. Obviously, if an increase in the buffer size isn't bringing forth a further lowering of physical reads, you have reached a plateau, and you shouldn't increase your buffer size.

Listing 16-5. Estimating the Correct Buffer Size Using V$DB_CACHE_ADVICE

```
SQL> select
  2   size_for_estimate,
  3   buffers_for_estimate,
  4   estd_physical_reads
  5* from v$db_cache_advice;
```

SIZE_FOR_ ESTIMATE	BUFFERS_FOR ESTIMATE	ESTD_PHYSICAL READS
4	496	7949
8	992	7797
12	1488	7751
16	1984	7714
20	2480	7683
24	2976	1552
28	3472	1518
32	3968	1518
36	4464	1515
40	4960	1403
44	5456	1394
48	5952	1394
52	6448	1394

```
SQL>
```

An easier way to find out the ideal buffer size configuration is to use the GUI-based Buffer Cache Size Advisor that is part of the OEM toolkit. Figure 16-6 shows the Buffer Cache Size Advisor. You can access the Advisor by going to OEM ➤ Databases ➤ Instance ➤ Resource Advisors ➤ Buffer Cache Advisor. In Figure 16-6, you can see that after a total buffer cache allocation of 136MB, there is no decrease in physical reads.

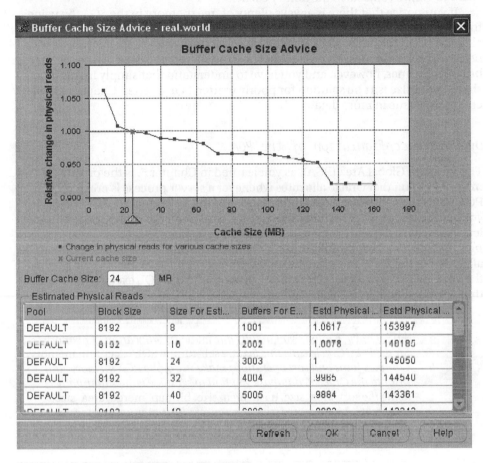

Figure 16-6. *The OEM Buffer Cache Advisor*

Dynamic Reconfiguration of the Shared Pool

In Oracle 9.2 you can dynamically change the memory allocated to the shared pool component of the SGA. You can increase or decrease the amount of memory allocated as long as you don't go over the *max_sga* limit. You can use the V$SHARED_POOL_ADVICE view or OEM's Shared Pool Size Adviser to help you configure the ideal amount of shared pool memory. The Shared Pool Size Adviser will estimate the impact of altering the shared pool size on the total amount of parsing activity in the database.

The V$SHARED_POOL_ADVICE view indicates the estimated parse time savings for various levels of the shared pool memory. Remember that one of the main reasons for using the shared pool is to keep parsed versions of SQL and PL/SQL in memory so they can be reused. If you have sufficient shared pool memory for retaining a parsed query, you save the time it takes to reparse it. You can also use the V$LIBRARY_CACHE_MEMORY view to view the memory allocated to various objects in the library cache.

If you notice that there is always plenty of free memory in the SGA (by using the V$SGA view), it's a safe bet that you can decrease your shared pool memory allocation. On the other hand, if you notice that the library cache hit ratio is way below the high nineties, it's time to increase the shared pool size. These are very broad guidelines, however, and you have to understand that simply increasing shared pool size isn't he solution for poorly written SQL queries. Chapter 19 discusses this issue in more detail.

Dynamic Reconfiguration of the PGA

The Program Global Area (PGA), as you learned in Chapter 5, is the private memory region that Oracle allocates whenever a server process is created. The PGA holds the control and data information for the individual server process. If you set the initialization parameter *worksize_area_policy* to *auto*, Oracle automatically adjusts the PGA dynamically. In addition, you have to set the *pga_aggregation_target* initialization parameter to control the total memory to be allocated to the PGA, and it can be anywhere between 10MB and 4TB. In general, if the V$PGASTAT view shows that are too many multipass SQL executions, it means that you need to increase your PGA allocation.

 NOTE *Oracle9i allows you to fully automate the allocation of memory for the PGA. Oracle calls this feature* self-tuning SQL execution memory. *Complex joins and sort operations make use of the PGA memory, and prior to the Oracle9i database you had to set these values manually using the* sort_area_size, hash_area_size, bitmap_merge_area_size, *and* create_bitmap_area_size *parameters. This manual management was often tricky, and you had to use trial-and-error to arrive at a decent configuration of these parameters.*

As you learned in Chapter 5, by setting two parameters in your init.ora file, an aggregate value for the PGA memory (by setting the *pga_aggregate_target* parameter) and choosing *auto* as the value for the *workarea_size_policy* parameter, you let Oracle automatically tune the SQL area execution memory. This is truly a self-tuning feature, as Oracle will make optimal use of memory and enhance database performance without any intervention from the DBA.

Prior to the Oracle9*i* database version, once you allocated a certain amount of PGA memory to a process, Oracle wouldn't yield the memory back, even when the process wasn't actually using it. Oracle9*i* yields the PGA memory back to the operating system when a process isn't using it for SQL execution.

Using Database Quiescing for Online Maintenance

Suppose you want to change the schema of a table. If a transaction is currently using this table, you can't perform this task. If the procedure is later updated to reflect the change in the schema, users currently trying to execute the procedure will receive an error. Fortunately, Oracle has a great feature called *quiescing the database,* whereby you don't have to shut down the database first and open it in the restricted mode. (A reviewer thought I was making up the phrase "quiesced database." I don't know how Oracle decided on this name, but it does describe its functionality rather cogently.) You use this feature when you need to perform actions that require no active transactions running in the database. Users will continue to be logged in and execute their requests during the time the database is the quiesced state.

The database, however, will block all transactional requests except those made by the users SYS and SYSTEM. Users can continue to query the database, thereby increasing the availability of the database when compared to a database in the restricted mode. Quiescing thus puts the database in a partially available state, without your having to shut it down and bring it up again in a restricted mode. When you take the database out of the quiesced state, the requests of the users are processed. You must configure the Database Resource Manager for the quiesce feature to work. The Database Resource Manager blocks the actions of all the nonsystem users during the quiesced state. It is easy to put the database in a quiesced state and later take it out of that mode. The following commands perform the quiescing and unquiescing of the database:

```
Sql> alter system quiesce restricted;
Sql> alter system unquiesce;
```

NOTE *Not every user with DBA privileges can quiesce the database. Only the SYS and SYSTEM users can use the feature.*

Users can continue to log into the system unless you're using the shared server architecture. Typical maintenance operations that can use the quiesce database feature are those that need the exclusive use of an object, such as an alter table, drop table, or create procedure operation. Any DDL statement that a DBA might want to execute in a live database will need exclusive locks, and it will fail if other transactions are using this table.

During the time the database is in the quiesced state, the following statements are true:

- Users other than SYS and SYSTEM won't be able to start any new transactions or queries.

- Any inactive session won't be able to become active.

- Oracle waits for all transactions and queries to commit or rollback.

- The database waits for the release of all shared resources such as enqueues.

- Upon unquiescing the database, all the blocked actions will be allowed to proceed to execution.

Users won't get any error messages during this process. When they try to execute a transaction on a quiesced database, their transaction hangs until the database is put into a normal mode again.

Suspending the Database

In addition to the restricted start-up and database quiesce modes, you can run the database in the suspend mode to perform certain tasks (say, a backup) without any user activity. You use the following commands to use the database suspend feature:

```
SQL> alter system suspend;
System altered.
SQL> alter system resume;
System altered.
```

When you suspend a database, currently executing transactions are allowed to complete. All other transactions that come in for execution will be suspended until the database resumes normal operation mode.

The ability to suspend a database comes in handy when you need to back up a database using a mirrored set of disks. You can suspend the database, split the mirror, and back up the database. You don't have to contend with I/O during the online backup of the split mirror.

Managing the Online Redo Logs

The online redo logs are Oracle's means of ensuring that all the changes made by the users are logged in case there's a failure before those changes are all written to permanent storage. Thus, redo logs are fundamental for the recovery process. The redo log buffer's contents are written to the online redo logs. When an instance goes down abnormally, there may be information in the redo logs that isn't yet written to the data files.

Oracle organizes its redo log files in *redo log groups*. Each group has at least one redo log. You need to have at least two different groups of redo logs (also called *redo threads*), each with at least one member in it. You need to have at least two redo groups, because the log writer should be able to write to an active redo log in case the other log is being archived. Although your database will run just fine with just one member in each redo log group, Oracle strongly recommends that you multiplex your online redo logs. *Multiplexing* simply means that you maintain more than one member in each of your redo log groups. All the members of a redo log group are identical. When you multiplex the online redo log files, the log writer writes simultaneously to all the members of a group.

TIP *Always multiplex the online redo log, as you can lose data if one of the active online redo logs is lost due to a disk problem. The multiplexed redo logs should ideally be located on different disk drives under different disk controllers.*

Hardware Mirroring vs. Oracle Multiplexing

If your system is mirrored at the hardware level, where is the need for multiplexing redo logs from within Oracle? Well, the mirroring will protect you from a disk failure, but it will not protect you against an accidental deletion of files. Multiplexing ensures that your files are protected soundly against such errors. In addition, if there are problems in writing to one member of a multiplexed group of redo logs, the writes to the other members continue unhindered.

Creating Online Redo Log Groups

You create online redo log groups when you create a database for the first time. Here's an example showing the redo log creation statement as part of the database creation process. Note that the three redo log groups each have only a single member—they are not multiplexed at this point.

```
SQL> create database
...
logfile
    group 1 '/u10/app/oracle/oradata/remorse/log01.dbf' size 50M,
    group 1 '/u20/app/oracle/oradata/remorse/log01.dbf' size 50M,
    group 1 '/u30/app/oracle/oradata/remorse/log01.dbf' size 50M,
database created
SQL>
```

Adding Redo Log Groups

Although you need a minimum of two online redo log groups, the ideal number of online redo logs for your database can only be known by the transaction activity in your database.

TIP *Start with two or three online redo groups and monitor your alert log for any redo log errors. If the alert log frequently shows that the log writer was waiting to write to an online redo log, you have to increase the number of redo groups.*

The following statement adds a new group of redo logs to your database:

```
SQL> alter database add logfile GROUP 3
  2  ('C:\ORACLENT\ORADATA\MANAGER\LOG1D.RDO',
  3  'C:\ORACLENT\ORADATA\MANAGER\LOG2D.RDO')
  4* SIZE 10m;
Database altered.
SQL>
```

In the example in the previous section, you created three online log groups, but each of them had only a single member. To duplex those groups to provide you additional safety, you need to add a member to each group. To add a single member to an existing group, you use the *add logfile* statement:

```
SQL>  alter database add logfile member
  2  'C:\ORACLENT\ORADATA\MANAGER\LOG4b.rdo'
  3  to group 4;
Database altered.
SQL>
```

Renaming Redo Log Files

If you need to rename your redo log file, follow these steps:

1. Shut down the database and start it up in the mount mode:

   ```
   SQL> startup mount
   ```

2. Move the files using an operating system command to the new location:

   ```
   SQL> host! mv /u10/app/oracle/oradata/remorse/log01.dbf'
              /a10/app/oracle/oradata/remorse/log01.dbf
   ```

3. Use the *alter database rename datafile to* command to rename the file name within the control file:

   ```
   SQL> alter database rename
           '/u10/app/oracle/oradata/remorse/log01.dbf'' to
           '/a10/app/oracle/oradata/remorse/log01.dbf';
   SQL>
   ```

Dropping Online Redo Logs

You can drop an entire redo log group by using the following command:

```
SQL> Alter database drop logfile group 3;
```

To drop a single member of an online redo log group, use this command:

```
SQL> alter database drop logfile member
        '/u01/app/oracle/oradata/remorse/log01.dbf'
```

If the redo log file you want to drop is active, Oracle won't let you drop it. You need to use the following command to first switch the log file, after which you drop it:

```
SQL> alter system switch logfile;
```

Online Redo Log Corruption

You can set *db_block_checksum* on to make sure Oracle checks for corruption in the redo logs before they're archived. If the online redo logs are corrupted, the file can't be archived, and one solution is to just drop and re-create them. But if there are only two log groups, you can't do this, as Oracle insists on having a minimum of two online redo log groups at all times. This means you can't drop one of the two existing redo log groups. However, you can create a new (third) redo log group, and then drop the corrupted redo log group. You can't also drop an online redo log file if the log file is part of the current group. Your strategy then would be to reinitialize the log file by using the following statement:

```
SQL> Alter database clear logfile group 1;
```

If the log group has not been archived yet, you can use the following statement:

```
SQL> Alter database clear unarchived logfile group 1;
```

Monitoring the Redo Logs

You can use two key dynamic views, V$LOG and V$LOGFILE, to monitor the online redo logs. The V$LOG view gives detailed information about the size and status of the redo logs, and the V$LOGFILE view provides the full file name of the redo logs. Listing 16-6 shows the results of queries on these two views.

Listing 16-6. Obtaining Redo Log Information

```
SQL> select * from v$logfile;
  GROUP #    STATUS    TYPE           MEMBER
  --------   --------  -------  ---------------------------------
     3       STALE     ONLINE   C:\ORACLENT\ORADATA\MANAGER\REDO03.LOG
     2                 ONLINE   C:\ORACLENT\ORADATA\MANAGER\REDO02.LOG
     1                 ONLINE   C:\ORACLENT\ORADATA\MANAGER\REDO01.LOG
3 rows selected.
SQL>  select group#,sequence#,bytes,archived,members,status
  2* from v$log;
```

GROUP#	SEQUENCE#	BYTES	ARCHIVED	MEMBERS	STATUS
1	8	104857600	NO	1	INACTIVE
2	10	104857600	NO	1	CURRENT
3	7	104857600	NO	1	INACTIVE
4	9	10485760	NO	3	INACTIVE

```
SQL>
```

Managing the Archived Logs

Production databases that can't tolerate any data loss must use archived logs. Besides protecting against data loss, archived logs have significant additional benefits: You don't have to shut down your database during backups, and you can set up a standby database using the archived redo logs. You learned how to set up the automatic archiving process in earlier chapters. The focus of this section is on managing various types of failures during the archiving process.

If your archiving destination fills up, the database will hang and users won't be able to make any DML changes to the data. When you clear some space in the directory, the database will resume normal operation.

By default, Oracle will only write to one archive log destination. You may, however, use the optional *log_archive_min_succeed_dest=n=n* initialization parameter to force Oracle to write successfully to multiple archive log destinations. If Oracle can't write to the specified number of destinations, it won't overwrite the online redo logs. You can specify the *reopen* attribute of the *log_archive_min_succeed_dest=n=n* parameter to specify if and for how long Oracle will attempt to re-archive to a failed destination. The parameter can be set to a maximum value of 300 seconds, and the default is 0. If you specify the *reopen* parameter and there's a failure in logging to a mandatory destination, the database hangs. You can either drop or change the destination. You can also manually archive the logs to the destination if it's usable.

Managing a Database Link

A *database link* is a way to connect to a remote database through a local database. For example, if you want to connect to the database monitor from the database remote, you can do so via a database link. Database links are useful when you want to query a table in a distributed database or even insert the data from another database table into a local table.

You can create three basic types of database links: private, public, and global. Global database links are networkwide links and are used by Oracle Names servers. In the following sections you'll look at examples of how to create private and public database links.

Creating a Private Database Link

A *private* database link is owned by the user that creates the link. The following statement creates a private database link. The user hr will connect to the remote database monitor using hr's username and password in that database (monitor). To create this private database link, a user must have the create private database link privilege on the local database and the create session privilege on the remote database. After I create the link (as user SYSTEM), I can query the hr.employees table in the remote database monitor.

```
SQL> connect system/remorse1;
Connected.
SQL>
SQL> create database link monitor
  2  connect to hr identified by hr
  3  using 'monitor.world';
Database link created.
SQL> select count(*) from hr.employees@monitor;
  COUNT(*)
----------
    107
SQL>
```

In this statement, note that the database link's name is monitor, which is the same as the remote database's name, but it could be anything you want. The *connect to … identified by …* clause means that the user of this database link will use that user ID/password to enter the remote database. The *using 'monitor. world'* clause simply specifies the global name of the remote database.

Because this is a private database link, only the user SYSTEM can use this link. When the user hr tries to use this link to a remote database, this is what happens:

```
SQL> connect hr/hr;
Connected.
SQL> select count(*) from hr.employees@dblink1;
select count(*) from hr.employees@dblink1
                                 *
ERROR at line 1:
ORA-02019: connection description for remote database not found
SQL>
```

Creating a Public Database Link

A *public* database link, unlike a private database link, enables any user or any PL/SQL program unit to access the remote database objects. The creation statement is very similar to that of a private database link. You just add the keyword *public* to the create database link statement, as shown here:

```
SQL> connect system/remrose1 as sysdba;
Connected.
SQL> create public database link monitor
  2  connect to hr identified by hr
  3  using 'monitor.world';
Database link created.
SQL> connect tester/tester1;
Connected.
SQL> select count(*) from hr.employees@monitor;
  COUNT(*)
----------
    107
SQL>
```

NOTE *Notice how the user tester can access the remote database, even if a user with the same name isn't present in the remote database. The user tester can do this because he or she is using a public database link, which enables any user to use user hr's account/password combination to access the remote database.*

Mapping Oracle Files to Physical Devices

How do you know where exactly your data files reside in your storage system? Most organizations use Logical Volume Managers (LVMs) and RAID-based storage systems. If you're interested in finding out where your hot files are located in the storage system, you're normally out of luck. If your files are merely operating system files or you're using a raw file system, it's no big deal to map data files to the devices that host them. If you aren't mapping UNIX mount points directly to physical disks, it's hard to tell where in the disk system a particular Oracle data file is located.

You can use the V$DATAFILE and V$TABLESPACE dynamic views, along with some other views, to glean information about data files. When you're using host-based LVMs and RAID-based storage systems, you'll quickly find out that an I/O on a data file can involve multiple storage devices that are part of a complex storage system. As a DBA, it's impossible for you tell where your objects are located in I/O stack.

For the first time, using Oracle9*i*, you can come up with the physical mapping of all the data files in your database with the new Oracle file-mapping feature. Oracle provides storage mapping APIs, which are used by the storage vendors to provide corresponding mapping libraries. These vendor-specific mapping libraries provide a complete mapping of the data files. Using the new file-mapping feature, you can link data files to the logical devices and the physical drives. You can also map individual objects, including their file and specific blocks on which they reside. This kind of detailed information helps you really understand and evaluate I/O performance. In the following sections you'll discover how Oracle's file-mapping interface works.

Architecture of File Mapping

When you use the file-mapping feature of Oracle9*i*, there will be a new Oracle background process, FMON, that will run as part of you instance. This FMON process will run only if you specify the new initialization parameter *file_mapping=true* in the init.ora file or SPFILE. You can set this parameter dynamically by using the *alter system* statement. The FMON process starts an operating system process called FMPUTL, which communicates with mapping libraries that contain detailed information about where the files are located. Vendors of the storage systems provide mapping libraries, although Oracle does provide the mapping library for storage systems made by EMC, a leading storage vendor. The FMPUTL process supplies FMON with the mapping information for various levels of I/O stack, and FMON stores this information in the Oracle data dictionary.

Oracle uses mapping structures to map data files with their physical counterparts. At the foundation of the mapping structure are components that Oracle calls *elements*. Elements can be RAID 0, RAID 1, or RAID 5 configured disks or just whole disks. The FMON process gathers information about files and their elements through the FMPUTL process. It saves this information in the SGA and some data dictionary views. Whenever you add, drop, or change the size of a data file, FMON changes the information in the SGA and in the related V$ tables.

Setting Up File Mapping

Now let's look at the various steps that are necessary to trace file mapping in your database.

Providing the Mapping Library

You must first have the mapping library from your storage system vendor, if it is not EMC. EMC's mapping library is supplied by Oracle. The mapping library path and the vendor name should be added to the filemap.ora file, which is located in the $ORACLE_HOME/rdbms/filemap/etc directory. You should edit the file in the following way:

```
lib:vendor_name:mapping_library_path
```

For example, you may have the following line for the VERITAS mapping library:

```
Lib=VERITAS:/opt/VRTSdbed/lib/libvxoramap_32.so
```

Once you edit the filemap.ora file, either start the database or use the *alter system* command to set the initialization parameter *file_mapping* to *true*.

```
SQL> alter system set file_mapping=true;
```

Starting the File Mapping

When you use the initialization parameter *file_mapping=true*, Oracle doesn't automatically start mapping the files. You do this by invoking the DBMS_STORAGE_MAP package. If you invoke the *map_all* procedure in this package, mapping information about all the data files in your database will be collected. You can also use the *restore()* procedure of the package to restore the information after you restart the instance. Three dynamic performance tables, VMAP_FILE, VMAP_ELEMENT, and V$MAP_FILE_IO_STACK, can then be joined to see the mapping between Oracle data files and physical elements in the storage system. You can see the storage hierarchy all the way from an individual table down to a disk in any storage system.

> **NOTE** *This is the one feature in Oracle 9.2 that I couldn't test successfully, either on my Windows server or a UNIX server. First of all, the filemap.ora file isn't where the Oracle manual says it should be. I failed to bring up the FMON process, as it needs the filemap.ora file, even if it's empty. I found the filemap.ora file in the $ORACLE_HOME/Inventory/filemap.ora directory, but all my attempts thus far to spawn the FMON processes have failed.*

Tips and Troubleshooting

This section presents a few common problems you may encounter when you quiesce databases and perform online table redefinition. Some unexpected problems during the online rebuilding of indexes are also discussed.

Problems During Quiescing a Database

When you want to quiesce a database, be sure you have the Database Resource Manager continuously on. Otherwise, you can't put the database in the quiesced state. Here's the error you get when you try to quiesce a database that doesn't have the Database Resource Manager continuously on:

```
SQL> alter system quiesce restricted;
alter system quiesce restricted
*
ERROR at line 1:
ORA-25507: resource manager has not been continuously on
SQL>
```

The reason for the preceding error is that quiescing a database depends entirely on the existence of the Database Resource Manager. When you issue the command for the database to be activated, the internal_quiesce plan in the Database Resource Manager is turned on. Therefore, if the Database Resource Manager is not continuously on, your quiesce request can't be fulfilled. The Database Resource Manager blocks the inactive sessions from becoming active during the time the database is in the quiesced state. The internal_quiesce resource plan sets the *active_sess_pool_p1* parameter to 0 for all users except SYS and SYSTEM.

Failed Online Table Redefinitions

The table redefinition feature is powerful, but it does get messy at times. If you fail to redefine a table online for some reason, make sure you wipe the state clean before your next attempt. To do this, use the following procedure from the DBMS_REDEFINITION package:

```
SQL> execute dbms_redefinition.abort_redef_table;
```

Problems During Online Index Rebuilds

Although the very reason for using the online index rebuild feature is to increase the availability of the database, there are some hidden problems behind the use of the online index rebuild feature while there is high level of DML in the database. Even Oracle Corporation points out that while you can use the *alter index rebuild online* command during DML operations, it is preferable to not do so.

Problems that might occur due to the use of the *alter index ... rebuild online* command include unexpected locking of the index, thereby causing problems to the users. In addition, you may end up with index corruptions under some circumstances. Any kind of an unexpected shutdown of the database due to a *shutdown abort* command or due to process or instance failure during the online rebuild will increase the possibility of index corruption.

You can check for index corruption using the following command, which will issue the ORA-14909 error if the table and index data don't match due to corruption in the index:

```
SQL> analyze table Customers validate structure cascade;
```

In general, it's a good a good idea to simply drop and re-create indexes when you suspect a corruption in the indexes. Because of the problems discussed here, it may also be a good idea to avoid the *alter index ... rebuild online* command in general and use the humble but much safer *alter index rebuild* command as much as possible. This command, unlike the *alter index ... rebuild online* command, will prevent concurrent DML against the table while the index is being built.

Summary

This chapter brought together a number of Oracle9*i*'s features that make database management easier than ever before. Especially beneficial are the new features that enable you to perform more administrative tasks without shutting down the database. Oracle9*i* does have excellent self-management capabilities, and in this chapter, I covered these topics to show how you can use the features to make your job easier. New features always come with caveats, so be sure to try these features out on small databases first, and see what the drawbacks are for your own situation (if any).

Features such as the new online table redefinition process improve your productivity and the availability of your database. Automatic Undo Management (AUM) is an attractive feature, but you need to check it out thoroughly before you get rid of your trusted traditional rollback segments. Dynamic memory management is a good example of how you can respond immediately to a performance problem. Take advantage of as many new features as you can implement in your system. You saw how OMF-managed files make the management of tablespaces and data files a snap, and under the right circumstances, they may be ideal for certain types of databases.

Oracle provides several useful resource advisors that you can use to quickly figure out the ideal size for the various SGA components, such as the buffer cache. In addition, the advisors help you choose the right undo tablespace size, as well as the Mean Time to Recover (MTTR). Although you still need to know how to use the important data dictionary and dynamic performance views, try to make OEM's powerful features a part of your repertoire for database management and tuning.

Although Oracle9*i* does have excellent self-management features and automated capabilities, you learned in this chapter that it takes quite a bit of skill and experience to configure and troubleshoot these features. You are far from being a member of an endangered species—Larry Ellison's (chairman of Oracle Corporation) remark that the Oracle9*i* database will make the DBA redundant notwithstanding.

CHAPTER 17

Using Oracle9*i* Enterprise Manager

ORACLE ENTERPRISE MANAGER (OEM) has been a part of the Oracle server software for many years, and Oracle Corporation has substantially improved it over time. OEM is Oracle's GUI-based, comprehensive database management toolset. It provides a wide array of services, including reporting features and event notification through e-mail and pagers.

You can manage your databases with the help of homegrown SQL and PL/SQL scripts, but OEM gives you an attractive console-based client framework to help you perform almost all of your day-to-day management activities, including tasks such as backup, recovery, export, import, and data loading.

OEM isn't widely used by the Oracle DBA community because of its perceived difficulty of installation and use. The installation of components, such as the Management Server, the repository, and the Intelligent Agent, were substantially more complex in previous versions and kept users from enthusiastically adopting the OEM suite of products. The latest versions of OEM are quite user-friendly when compared to their predecessors.

In this chapter you'll learn how to install and configure OEM in the shortest amount of time possible. You'll also learn how to set up events and jobs, customized reporting, and alert notification. If you aren't comfortable with using scripts, OEM is ideal for you because it comes with all the essential scripts to manage a database and other services. You'll discover how to use OEM to monitor your databases and the nodes on which they're running. The modern Oracle DBA should strive to master the OEM tool and use its powerful functionality to enhance the depth and breadth of his or her database management.

Oracle Enterprise Manager

Traditionally, Oracle DBAs have used a variety of scripts to manage their databases. You can either write a script yourself or you can get just about any script you want at one of the many fine DBA help sites on the Internet (I listed some of them in the Introduction). Scripts are either SQL based or a combination of SQL*Plus and UNIX shell scripts, and they can perform monitoring and performance diagnostics. You can manually monitor the system or schedule the scripts to provide automated monitoring and notification through pages and/or e-mail. Most DBAs also use operating system–based tools such as HP's Glance, sar, vmstat, and iostat.

If you have a single database with few users, you can probably manage it with a few automated scripts and some occasional manual monitoring. If you have to manage several databases, you're in a completely different ballgame and you should be looking at automated tools to help you manage the databases proactively. You can use automated tools to perform object creation, security maintenance, database monitoring and alerts, event management, backup, recovery, and data loading. A number of excellent tools are available that are marketed by companies such as Quest (http://www.quest.com) and Embarcadero Technologies (http://www.embarcadero.com). However, your focus here is to maximize the potential of the tool that is already at your disposal: OEM.

OEM is installed automatically with the Oracle Enterprise Edition data server, and you can choose to install it as a stand-alone product using the Oracle Installer. OEM is designed to be a tool that will help you establish a robust "lights-out" database management system. If you configure this tool carefully and use it correctly, it can enable you to manage more nodes (the servers on which your databases are running) effectively. OEM is designed to be highly scalable, as you can increase the number of databases managed by a DBA without hurting performance.

Monitoring database performance is not the only benefit of using OEM. Proactive event management helps you set thresholds for various database parameters for event notification. Job scheduling makes the traditional crontab seem antiquated. You can even perform some reverse engineering of the schema and application tuning with OEM. Finally, you can perform many DBA tasks such as backup, recovery, data loading, online table reorganization, and replicating databases (Data Guard) much more easily using OEM. You can even publish trend charts about the database performance, uptime, and capacity planning.

There is a learning curve involved in understanding the architecture, configuration, and use of OEM, but with the latest version of OEM (version 9.2.0.1.0), you should be able to overcome the initial hiccups without too much frustration. The configuration of the system is easy, although there is always a possibility of your running into some glitches regarding connections to the server or functioning of the HTTP server. OEM is really an amazing tool, for both the breadth and depth of its coverage. You can use the tool to perform virtually all of your tasks as an Oracle9*i* DBA.

The OEM console can be overwhelming in the beginning, because you have several ways to access the same tool—you can access several components through the menu or through an icon. Beginners may also be initially overwhelmed by the sheer number of components, especially if you include the optional specialized management packs. I don't cover any of the management packs in this chapter; rather, I cover the management packs in relevant chapters throughout the book. For example, I describe the Diagnostics and Tuning Packs in detail in Chapters 18 and 19.

My goal in this chapter is to show how you can quickly configure a full-fledged OEM setup with the Management Servers and Intelligent Agents, and start scheduling jobs and events and monitoring your databases. Once you start using OEM, your skill level will increase as you explore the various areas of the tool. You'll be much more effective as a DBA, and you'll significantly reduce the time taken by important but tedious tasks such as checking logs and monitoring various components of the database. Therefore, my advice is to persevere and you'll have a delightful tool you can use to become a much more effective DBA.

Benefits of Using OEM to Manage Databases

OEM offers you several features that make it an attractive tool for managing Oracle databases. The complete toolset of OEM enables you to monitor databases, analyze databases, improve database performance, and create useful reports. In the following sections you'll take a look at the various benefits OEM provides.

Out-of-the-Box Management

OEM offers you a true out-of-the box solution to complete systems monitoring and management. I do cover the "configuration" of the various components of OEM later in this chapter, but there really isn't any heavy-duty configuration as such necessary to get going with OEM. OEM is automatically installed with the Oracle9*i* server, or you can use custom installation to install the tool separately. The HTTP server is part of the Oracle installation as well. All you have to do is start up the HTTP server and then configure the Management Server. Once the Management Server is up and running, you need to discover the services in your environment, and you're ready to go. All told, you should be up and running within a couple of hours or less. Once OEM is installed, it will monitor databases from different Oracle versions and disparate operating system platforms, thus making your management tasks easier to handle.

Web-Based Management

You can view the OEM console on your workstation or access it through your Web server. OEM uses Secure Sockets Layer (SSL), so database security isn't compromised when you access your databases through the Internet. All tiers of OEM communicate via HTTP, so they can go through any firewall that the HTTP communications are allowed to go through. The Web-based OEM console has all the features of the regular console, so all you need is a Web browser to access your databases from anywhere, at any time.

Real-Time Monitoring

OEM provides excellent real-time monitoring in addition to its capability to provide reports on the database. You can use the Instance Manager, for example, to see what's going on in your database right now. Without OEM, you're forced to use SQL scripts, and the information isn't always quick in coming. Locking scripts, especially, can take a long time to finish. Using OEM, you can immediately see all the locks in the database. Similarly, OEM helps you identify the waits in the system and find out what's causing them while they're occurring.

Complete Environment Monitoring

As most of you know already, a poorly performing (or unavailable) database could be the result of a problem anywhere in the application stack—in the database, in the Web servers, or in the server that's hosting any of the components of the application. OEM monitors the performance of all the components of this stack, not just the Oracle database. Now, you can quickly figure out why the database is performing poorly all of a sudden. Maybe you have a Web server that isn't able to process the connect requests efficiently for some reason, while your database is performing just fine. The following list provides a sampling of the items that OEM can monitor and report on:

- The entire platform

- End user experience

- Systems and Web application availability

- The extended network components

- Business transactions

- Historical data analysis and change tracking

Application Performance Monitoring

OEM provides Application Performance Monitoring (APM) tools, which provide you with an easy way to diagnose system problems and monitor database performance. APM tools gather and report not only the status, but also the response times of all the databases in your system. This information helps you proactively manage your databases and prevent problems from happening.

When DBAs use OEM's alert systems and notifications, they can quickly inform managers about poorly performing system components. These alerts thus help you resolve bottlenecks before the database becomes completely unavailable to users.

APM performs the following functions:

- Monitors performance and availability of the system

- Indicates outages and bottlenecks throughout the application system

- Analyzes the root cause of performance problems

- Diagnoses performance with drill-downs

- Minimizes application downtime through the use of efficient problem resolution tools

Scalable Management Capability

OEM is a highly scalable tool, and you don't need additional resources to monitor an ever-growing enterprise. All you need to do when you add new servers to your system is start up the Intelligent Agent on the new node. The Intelligent node will help you gather all pertinent information about servers and databases.

Consolidated Database Management

OEM provides you with a quick top-level view of the entire environment—servers, databases, application servers, and so forth—through its home pages. Each managed target has a home page that provides a concise overall view of system health and performance. By summarizing key information on the home pages, OEM helps you quickly identify the root cause of any system problems.

OEM also enables you to efficiently query for the latest code patches for all the Oracle products installed in your enterprise. If new patches are available, you can download and install them easily with OEM.

Centralized Console for a Single Point of Management

You can use the OEM console to perform your routine database administration tasks, such as creating and dropping users. If you want, you can access the OEM console through a Web browser, which means that you don't have to install the OEM software on your workstation.

Use of the Web-based OEM console has some limitations. For example, you can't use the Oracle Diagnostics Pack and the Oracle Tuning Pack through the browser. You can, however, perform all other administrative functions, and using the Web-based console is a great way to monitor your OEM reports. I show you how to run the OEM console through a Web browser in the section "Running the Console from a Web Browser" later in this chapter.

Integrated Systems Management

You can easily integrate OEM with a systemwide monitoring tool such as HP OpenView. This integration of the database and server management tools lets you view both the database and system events from a single browser. The two products essentially act like a single integrated management suite. OEM uses the Smart Plug-in (SPI) to provide the integration of OEM and OpenView operations.

You can view OEM as a set of integrated systems. In the next section you'll look at OEM from this point of view.

The Various Systems of OEM

You can look at OEM as a coordinated set of "systems," each concentrating on a specific part of database operation. The main OEM systems are as follows:

- Job system

- Event system

- Notification system

- Reporting system

- Security system

You'll examine the various OEM systems in detail in the following sections.

The Job System

The *job system* lets you schedule either OEM's predefined jobs or your own customized scripts, on single or multiple nodes. You can choose to save the jobs in a library and view the job history through the Jobs pane in the main Console window.

The Event System

You can use your console to set up threshold parameters concerning various targets such as databases, servers, and the network, such that when a critical event occurs, you are notified automatically. The events are defined with the help of *tests*, which are a set of event conditions polled on a scheduled basis.

The *event system* consists of several preconfigured events, but you could also easily create user-defined events to suit your specific needs. If you have a set of good database-monitoring scripts, you can plug them into OEM's event system, thus availing yourself of all of the tool's functionality.

The Notification System

The *notification system* enables you to be notified by e-mail or pager when certain events take place. You can also be notified when specific jobs complete or fail to run to completion. The OEM tool also lets you black out the notifications (i.e., suspend them) if you are getting repetitive notifications about a problem that is already being attended to.

The Reporting System

When you install the Management Server component, a default HTTP server is automatically installed. In addition, other reporting components such as the reporting Web site are automatically installed and properly configured for use with the repository and the Management Server. You will, however, have to configure the Management Server so it can communicate with the reporting Web site, but this is an easy process, as you'll see later in this chapter.

The Security System

OEM allows for a "superadministrator" account, which is used to control the security settings of all the other administrators. If you wish, you can create more than one superadministrator account.

The OEM Architecture and Components

OEM uses an Intelligent Agent and a Java-based console to monitor database events and performance. The heart of OEM is a component called the *Management Server,* which enables you to perform management functions called *jobs* and *events.* The *Intelligent Agents* run on the various nodes (servers) and collect the information about databases, listeners, and Web servers. This information is sent to a central Management Server. You communicate with the Management Server through a GUI-based console. This console-based administration makes it possible to easily manage a large number of systems running in heterogeneous environments. The Management Server is ideally used with a *repository* to store all of its data. This repository is simply a set of tables on any database accessible by the Management Server. The Management Server assigns tasks such as database monitoring and backup and recovery to the Intelligent Agents, and takes its instructions either manually through the console or through scheduled jobs.

Let's take a closer look at the three main components of OEM.

The Console

The *console* is the means through which you monitor your databases, nodes, and listeners. You can access the console through the OEM software installed on your workstation or through a Web browser.

The console is the user interface to OEM, but it's capable of much more than simply enabling you to monitor a database. In addition to facilitating routine administrative tasks, the console serves two other important functions. You can administer several integrated applications through the console, including the Oracle LogMiner Viewer, the Enterprise Security Manager, Oracle Directory Manager, Oracle Data Guard Manager, Oracle Net Manager, and Oracle Form Server Manager. Through the console, you can also use Oracle's management packs: Change Management Pack, Diagnostics Pack, and Tuning Pack.

The Management Server

The Management Server is a separate process from the console, and it usually runs on a middle tier. The Management Server isn't a mandatory component of OEM. OEM gives you the option of using it without the Management Server. Go ahead and configure it, because without it you can use a limited amount of OEM's functionality. The Management Server requires you to create a repository in a database. You can create the repository automatically when you configure the Management Server. The Management Server will automatically update the repository tables with the data collected by the Intelligent Agents. The repository is owned by a separate schema, and it's entirely under the control of the Management Server. The repository has the complete listing of all the nodes, services, and administrators. All job and event information flows through the repository as well. Note that the Management Server's administrative account isn't the same as the SYS or SYSTEM user account on the database.

The Management Server gets information about the nodes, databases, and services with the help of the Intelligent Agents, which run on each node covered by OEM. The server stores this information in the OEM repository and makes it available to requests made through the OEM console.

TIP *You can and should deploy multiple Management Servers to provide fault tolerance.*

The Intelligent Agents

Intelligent Agents are the real workers of OEM. You can use them to monitor targets, which can include not just databases, but also servers, databases, application servers, and Web servers. Whether it's a scheduled or an impromptu task, it's the Intelligent Agents that perform the execution of the tasks. The Intelligent Agents run the OEM jobs, collect the output, and check for events.

Intelligent Agents are autonomous processes running on remote nodes (e.g., a UNIX server) that you want to monitor. If you have a half a dozen servers, you'll start Intelligent Agent services on all six servers so they can perform services for the Management Server, which is relaying requests from the administrative console. The Intelligent Agents support the Simple Network Management Protocol (SNMP), thus making it possible for third-party tools using SNMP to receive information from the Agent.

NOTE *An important fact to remember is that the Intelligent Agent runs independently of the console and the Management Server. It is a dedicated process that continues to run even after you shut down the Management Server and the console.*

Configuring OEM

Although OEM is installed along with the Oracle9*i* Database Server Enterprise edition, you do need to perform a considerable amount of configuration to use it to its full potential. You can use OEM right out of the box, with little or no configuration, but you can't use the powerful Management Server and the OEM repository without configuring them. You can use a simple configuration that connects directly to the databases to perform a set of limited administrative tasks. If you have just a single database, you may not want to go the trouble of configuring the Management Server. However, a simple configuration without the Management Server and the Intelligent Agents won't let you do any reporting or generate notifications and proactively monitor your databases.

The real power of OEM lies in using it with the Management Server and the Intelligent Agents in place. So, let's go ahead and configure the full-fledged OEM, with all the bells and whistles.

Configuring the Intelligent Agent

You should be aware of three configuration files concerning the Intelligent Agent: snmp_ro.ora, snmp_rw.ora, and services.ora. The first two files are located in the

$ORACLE_HOME/network/admin directory and the third file is located in the $ORACLE_HOME/network/agent directory. The snmp.rw file has some user-configurable parameters, such as setting agent trace levels.

The Intelligent Agent doesn't need any special configuration. If you correctly installed your Oracle software, all the necessary files for the Intelligent Agent are automatically installed. On Windows servers, you start the Intelligent Agent by going to Control Panel ➤ Administrative Tools ➤ Services and clicking the Oracle-OraHomeAgent line. On UNIX servers, you use the agentctl utility to start, stop, restart, and check the status of the Intelligent Agent process. Figure 17-1 shows you how to start up the Intelligent Agent on a UNIX server. You can replace the start command with the stop, restart, or status command to manage the Intelligent Agent.

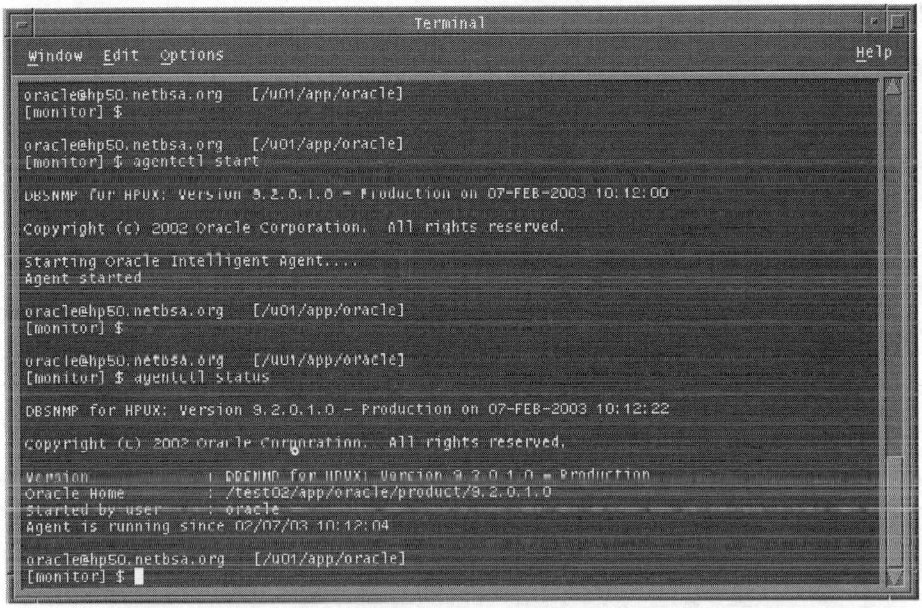

Figure 17-1. Starting the Intelligent Agent on a node

Once you've started the Intelligent Agent, you're home free with regard to receiving information about the databases and other services to be monitored. The Intelligent Agent has a built-in autodiscovery feature that automatically collects information about all the databases and other services running on the node where the agent is started. There is a small difference in how the agent gathers information on UNIX and Windows servers. On Windows servers, the agent looks in the Windows registry, the listener.ora file, and the tnsnames.ora file. On UNIX, it first looks in the /etc/oratab file for the database names, and then the listener.ora and tnsnames.ora files. From the tnsnames.ora file it gathers the service names to match the database names in the /etc/oratab file.

Configuring the Management Server

Configuring the Management Server will take the most time, because you have to create a repository for the Management Server in either an existing database or a brand-new database. Here are the important steps that you need to follow during the creation of the all-important Management Server.

You can start the configuration of the Management Server by typing the command **emca**, either at a Windows command prompt or a UNIX command prompt. On Windows, you can also start the process by choosing the Enterprise Manager Configuration Assistant from the OEM program area. Here's the step-by-step process for installing the Management Server:

1. The first screen is the Welcome screen, which consists of a brief explanation of the Management Server. Click Next.

2. The next screen gives you several options regarding the choice of a Management Server, as shown in Figure 17-2. Click the "Configure local Oracle Management Server" option.

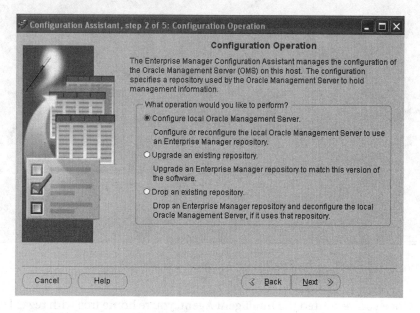

Figure 17-2. Management Server configuration options

Choosing Repository Creation

When the next screen comes up (see Figure 17-3), ask the Configuration Assistant to create a repository for your Management Server.

In the Create New Repository Options screen (see Figure 17-4), choose the Custom option to let Oracle create a new repository for you. You are using a preexisting database for this example, but you can have the Configuration Assistant build a brand-new database just for installing the repository by clicking the Typical option. The guideline regarding the use of a database is simple: Pick a database that is not among the list of databases you are planning to monitor with the help of the Management Server.

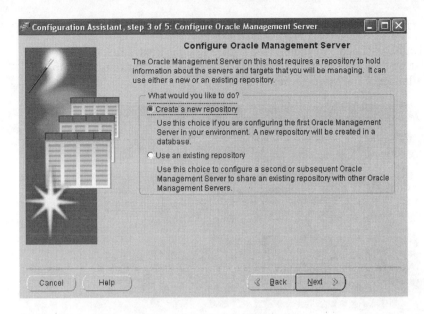

Figure 17-3. Choosing to create a new repository

 TIP *Always create the repository, even though it is an optional choice. There is no way you can configure OEM to use its full functionality without the repository.*

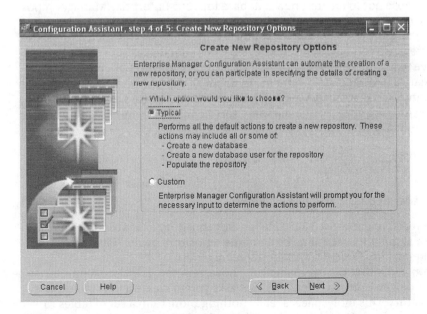

Figure 17-4. New repository creation options

Choosing the Database for the Management Server

The Select Database Location screen (see Figure 17-5) is next. Click the "In another existing database" option because you are using a preexisting database for the installation of the Management Server.

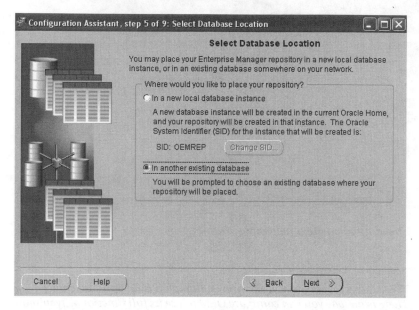

Figure 17-5. Selecting the repository database location

If you choose not to create a new database for your Enterprise Manager repository, Oracle can create the repository in an existing database. Pick a database that you can treat as production grade—you don't want to lose all the good stuff in your repository because you have chosen a development database that's never backed up. You have to log into the repository database as a user with DBA privileges so you can create a new repository schema. In the next screen, you need to enter a valid username and password, along with the database service name. Note that if you can't log in using your regular database service name (in my case, manager), you can log in using the following format:

```
Host:port:sid.
For example: hp1:1521:manager.
```

Choosing the Repository Username

Now you're ready to choose a username for the repository user account. The only requirement is that this username be a unique repository owner. Figure 17-6 shows the Repository Login Information screen.

After you verify that the username you chose, repman, is indeed a unique database name, the Configuration Assistant asks you to create a new tablespace for the repository. This tablespace is really nothing more than a set of tables to store the Management Server data about the nodes and services it's helping monitor and manage. Click Next after you choose a new tablespace name for holding the repository information.

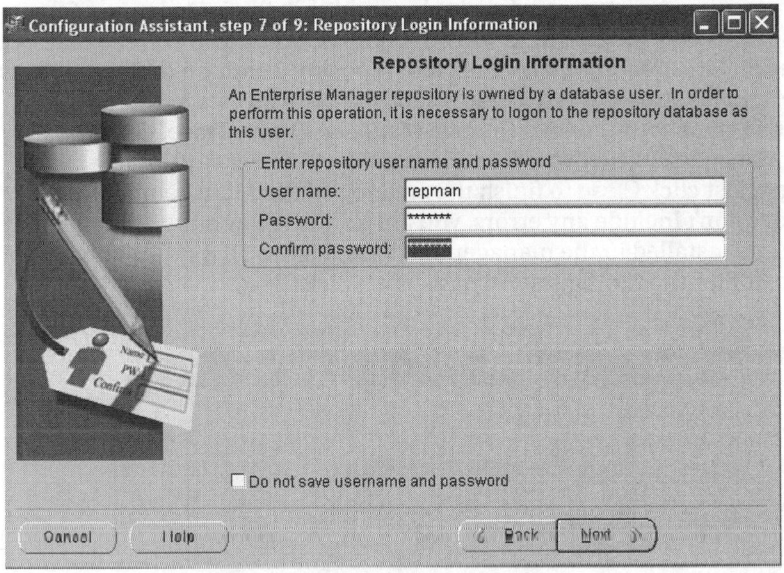

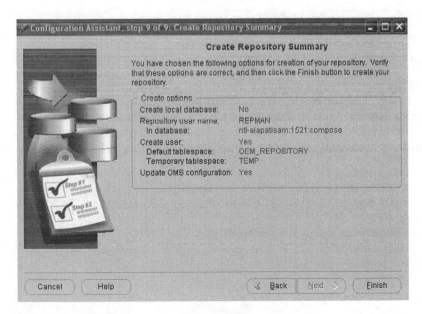

Figure 17-6. Choosing the repository owner name

Creating the Repository Tablespace

Oracle will create the repository tablespace named OEM_repository in the manager tablespace. It will then show you a summary of the attributes you picked for confirmation before it creates the repository. Figure 17-7 shows the summary screen for the repository creation. Confirm the attributes by clicking Finish.

Figure 17.7. Summary of repository creation

The Configuration Assistant will finally show you that the installation of the Management Server was successful. If you click Show Details, you will see that the Configuration Assistant populates the OEM repository with predefined reports after creating it. Interestingly, it also creates separate repositories in the same tablespace for all OEM components: Change Manager, Oracle Trace, Oracle Performance Manager, Oracle Expert, Oracle LogMiner Viewer, and Oracle Data Guard Manager. Just click Close to finish the creation of the Management Server.

If the details don't include any errors, you are home free and the Management Server is correctly installed in the manager database. Figure 17-8 shows the progress indicator for the Configuration Assistant. Click Close.

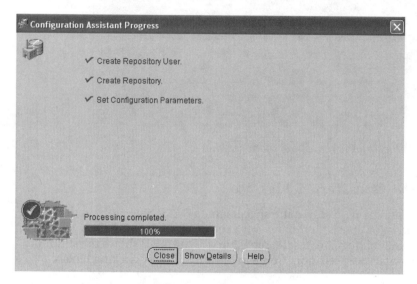

Figure 17-8. Successful creation of the Management Server

Monitoring the Management Server

If you look in the Services window (select Control Panel ➤ Administrative Tools ➤ Services) on the Windows server, you should now see a new service called OracleHomeManagementServer. You can switch the start-up type from manual to automatic at this point. You can also start or stop the OMS manually at the UNIX or Windows command prompt by using the oemctl utility as follows:

```
C:\> oemctl start oms
The OracleOraHome92ManagementServer service is starting..........
The OracleOraHome92ManagementServer service was started successfully.
C:\>oemctl stop oms
OEMCTL for Windows NT: Version 9.2.0.1.0 Production
Copyright (c) 1998, 2002, Oracle Corporation.  All rights reserved.
Stopping the Oracle Management Server...
C:\>
```

To check the status of the OEM server, use the command *oemctl status oms*, as shown in Listing 17-1. The output of the command indicates that the Management Server is up and functioning properly.

Listing 17-1. Checking the Status of the Management Server

```
C:\>oemctl status oms
OEMCTL for Windows NT: Version 9.2.0.1.0 Production
Copyright (c) 1998, 2002, Oracle Corporation.  All rights reserved.
The Oracle Management Server on host [ntl-alapatisam.netbsa.org] is functioning
properly.
   The server has been up for 0 22:26:42.351
   Target database session count: 1 (session sharing is off)
   Operations queued for processing: 1
   Number of OMS systems in domain: 1 (ntl-alapatisam.netbsa.org)
   Number of administrators logged in: 1
   Repository session pool depth: 15
   Repository session count: 8 in-use and 3 available, pool efficiency: 100%
C:\>
```

If you want to see if the Management Server is running, use the *ping* command as follows:

```
C:\>oemctl ping oms
OEMCTL for Windows NT: Version 9.2.0.1.0 Production
Copyright (c) 1998, 2002, Oracle Corporation.  All rights reserved.
The management server is running.
C:\>
```

Of course, you can also check the status of the Management Server on a Windows machine by selecting Control Panel ➤ Administrative Tools ➤ Services. If the status of the OracleOraHomeManagementServer is listed as "started," then the Management Server is running.

TIP *When you first log into the Management Server, the username/password combination it requests belong to neither the Oracle SYS user nor the repository owner rman, which you created previously. You got in by using the default superadministrator of the Management Server, SYSMAN with the password* oem_temp. *SYSMAN is analogous to the "root" user in UNIX systems. The Management Server will force you to change the default password at subsequent logins.*

Configuring the OEM Console

As I explained before, it makes sense to use the console with the Management Server connection, although you can use it in a limited way without the Management Server. Powerful OEM features such as proactive monitoring, notification, and task scheduling are available only when you have configured the Management Server.

The console is ready to use when you access it after installing OEM. After you configure and start the Management Server, start the console by clicking the OEM console button in the OEM programs area (select Programs ➤ Oracle_Home ➤ Enterprise Manager Console). You will see the login screen shown in Figure 17-9, where you should choose to connect to the Management Server by using the SYSMAN superadministrator account.

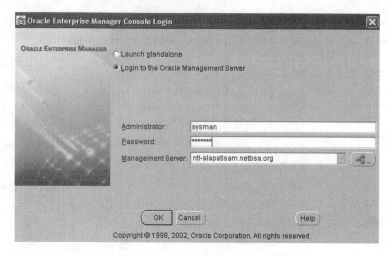

Figure 17-9. Logging into the Management Server

Once your credentials are verified, you're connected to OEM console. You'll see the Console Administrator screen shown in Figure 17-10.

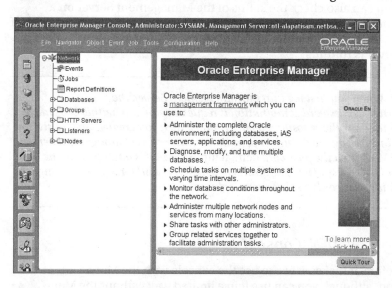

Figure 17-10. The OEM Console Administrator screen

From the menu, click the Navigator button and ask OEM to Discover Nodes. You are asked to specify your server name. In the example in Figure 17-11, I entered the workstation name where I installed the Management Server.

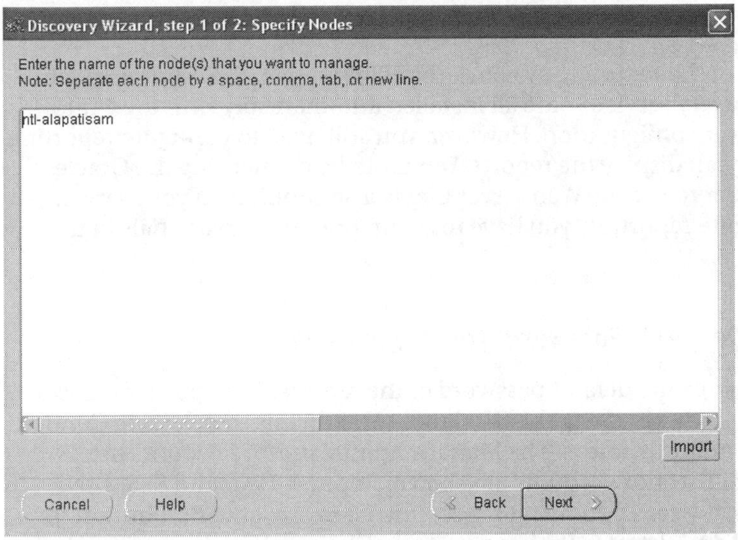

Figure 17-11. Specifying the node for discovery

The Console Navigator will look for all the nodes on your server. Once the discovery process is completed, you'll get a confirmation, as shown in Figure 17-12. Note that the discovery process will automatically register databases, listeners, HTTP servers, and the nodes themselves with the Management Server. In fact, this is one of the attractive features of OEM, in that you just install the Intelligent Agent on the server and leave it to OEM to gather all the information about the various services automatically. Thus, you are ready to monitor all your services in a very short time.

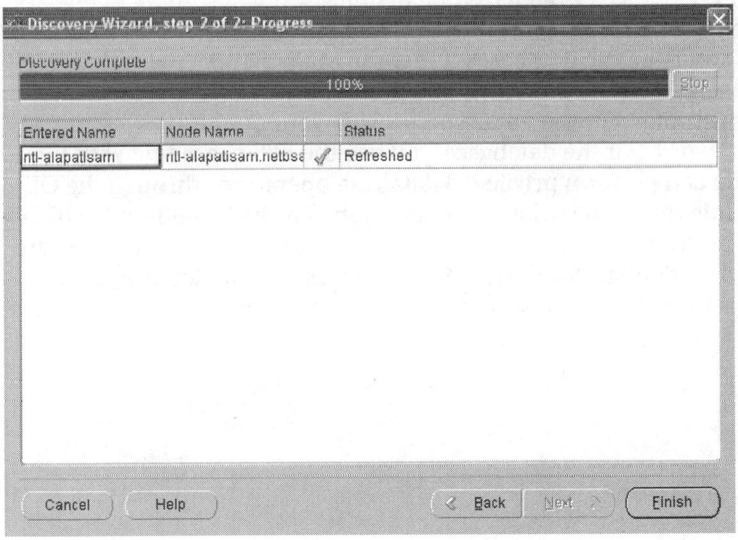

Figure 17-12. Completion of node discovery

Configuring Reporting

The components of the reporting system—the HTTP server, the reporting Web site, and the necessary servlets—are all installed automatically with the Oracle Management Server configuration. However, you still need to configure reporting so the Web server can display the reports. You do so by configuring the Oracle Management Server to use the Web server that is also running on your server. Before you configure reporting, you have to set up preferred credentials in the OEM console.

Changing the Default Password for Reports_User

Make sure you change the default password of the reports user you created who owns the reports produced using the OEM tools. You do this by selecting Configuration ➤ Manage Administrators. The Manage Administrator Accounts box appears. Two administrator accounts are shown: Reports_User and SYSMAN. Choose the Reports_User administrator account. Next, click the Edit button to move to the Edit Administrator Preferences page. Change the password for the Reports_User account and confirm your changes.

Setting Up Preferred Credentials

To perform many important database activities (e.g., backup and recovery) and to view the reports, you should configure OEM's preferred credentials. The establishment of preferred credentials makes it easy for the Intelligent Agent to authenticate the administrators for all the jobs and events that are set up. To set up preferred credentials, choose the Administrator Preferred Credentials property sheet (see Figure 17-13), which you access by selecting Configuration ➤ Preferences ➤ Edit Administrator Preferences ➤ Preferred Credentials.

Click the Preferred Credentials tab and you'll be taken to the Administrator Preferences page, where all the databases under the Management Server's purview are listed, as are the listener, HTTP server, and the node on which the Management Server is running. For the node, you provide your operating system username and password. For the databases, you use the SYS username with the SYSDBA role so you can perform privileged database operations through the OEM console and schedule those operations through a job. For the job at hand, which is the configuration of the Management Server to work with the Web server, be sure to set the preferred credentials for the OEM supplied username Reports_User. Figure 17-14 shows the selection of administrator preferences.

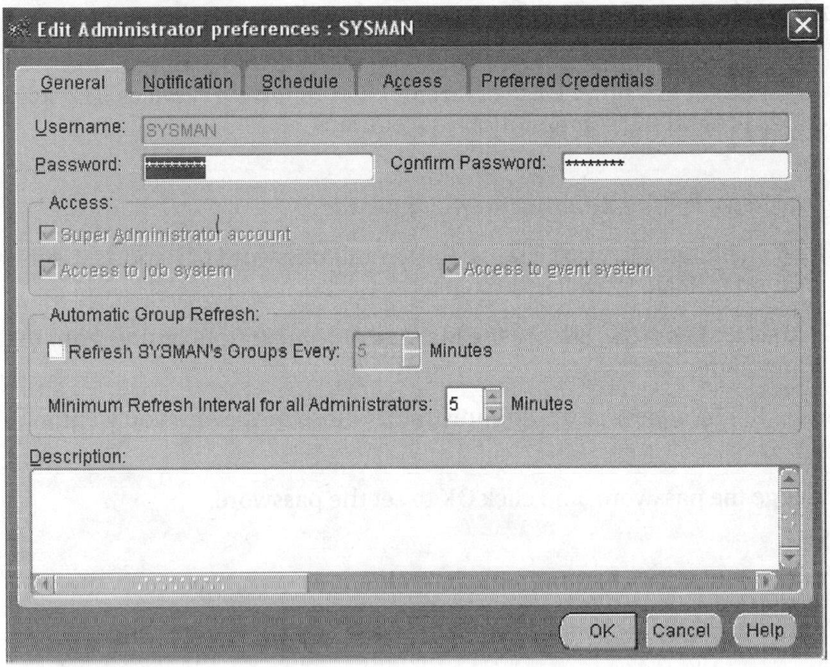

Figure 17-13. The Administrator Preferred Credentials sheet

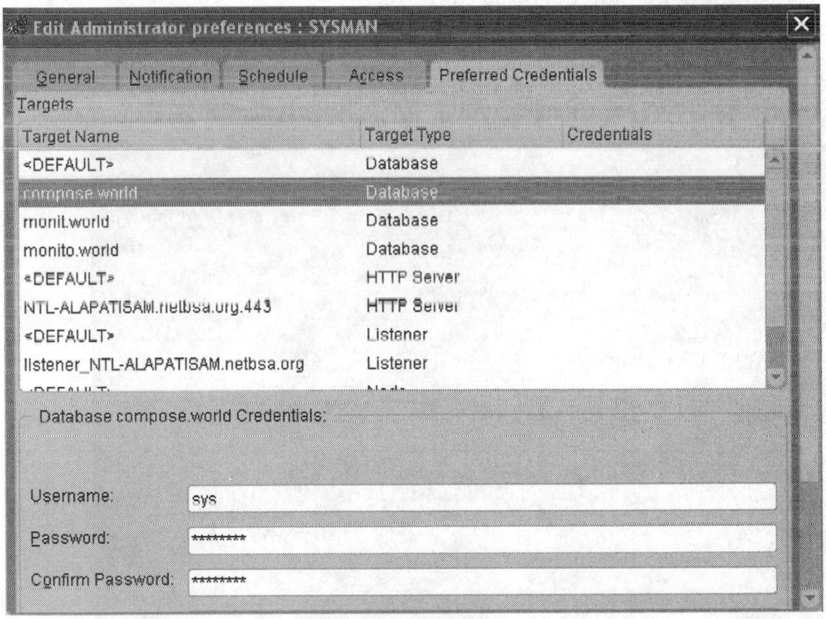

Figure 17-14. Setting preferred credentials

Configuring the Web Server for Enterprise Manager Reporting

Once you've assigned the preferred credentials, you're ready to configure the default Web server (or any other Web server) for OEM reporting services. The following sections present the configuration procedure.

Changing the Reports_User Administrator Password

Before you do anything, you must change the default password of Reports_User or the configuration will fail. Here are the steps:

1. On the OEM console, choose the Manage Administrators option from the Configuration menu.

2. Select Reports_User as the administrator whose properties you want to edit.

3. Change the password, and click OK to set the password.

Running the Oemctl Utility to Configure the Web Server

Go the command prompt of your server and run the following command:

```
C:\ oemctl configure rws
```

Figure 17-15 shows the output from the preceding command on my Windows server, where my Management Server is running.

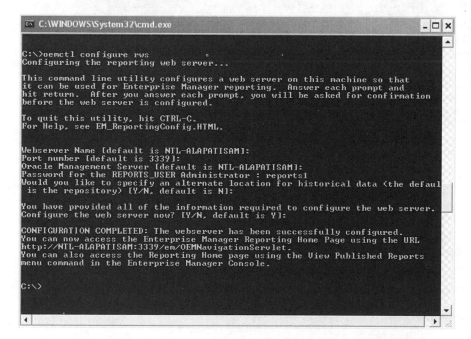

Figure 17-15. Configuring the Web server with the oemctl utility

Your Management Server is now talking to your Web server, and you're ready to go! The message in Figure 17-15 informs you that you can access the reports through either the console (*view published reports* command) or through a URL based on your server name (in my case, `http://ntl-alapatisam:3339/em/OEMNavigationServlet`).

Running the Console from a Web Browser

It's very easy to run the OEM console and the OEM reports through a Web browser. You need to have a Web server running on the server where the Management Server is installed. If you don't have one, not to worry—the Management Server configuration process includes the installation of a default HTTP server (Apache). Check to make sure that the HTTP server is running (through the Services window on your workstation), and invoke the OEM console and OEM reports through the URL `http://yourserver:portnumber`. The default port number of the Oracle HTTP server is 3339, and on my Windows server, the URL for the OEM console is `http://ntl-alapatisam:3339`. You'll log into the access screen shown in Figure 17-16.

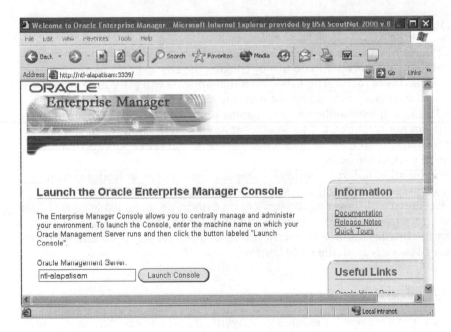

Figure 17-16. A browser-based OEM console

In Figure 17-16, you can see that you can launch a console or just access the Enterprise Manager reports. The advantage of accessing the OEM console or the OEM reports through the browser, of course, is that you don't have to have OEM installed on the your workstation. The drawback to using the Web-based console is that some parts of OEM, such as the Diagnostics Pack, the Tuning Pack, and Oracle Directory Manager, can't be used with it.

TIP *The Web-based OEM console will fail to come up, even after you have properly configured your HTTP server and the Management Server, if you don't have the JInitiator plug-in installed on your client machine. Just click the Download Plug-in link (in the Useful Links section) shown on the right side of the OEM Welcome Page to start downloading and installing the Oracle JInitiator plug-in.*

Using the OEM Console

The OEM console is the interface you'll use to monitor the databases and other services on various nodes. You've seen how you can access the console through a desktop installation or through a Web browser. However you invoke the console, its functionality remains the same. In the following sections, you'll learn how to use console to manage databases. First you'll explore how to add all the databases you want to cover to the console's list of services.

Discovering Services

The first thing you need to do is provide OEM with a list of all the nodes (servers) you want to be monitored. You do this by clicking the Discover Nodes option under the Navigator menu. The first screen that appears will ask you to type in the name of the node you want monitored. You can specify either the IP address (172.14.15.11) or the symbolic name (ntl-samalapati) of the server. Once you type in your list of nodes, click OK. The Intelligent Agents on the nodes will start gathering information about all the databases, listeners, and HTTP servers that are running on each of the nodes.

Once the information gathering is completed, the Discover Nodes screen shows a message indicating that it successfully discovered all services and the nodes. If it failed to discover all the services on a node, the most likely cause is that you don't have the Intelligent server up and running on that node. Usually, after you start the Intelligent node correctly, you shouldn't have any problems with the discovery of services from the OEM console.

The Services.ora File

When a node is discovered, the Intelligent Agent on that node is contacted. The Agent sends the service names listed in its services.ora file to the OEM console. The services.ora file is located in the $ORACLE_HOME/agent directory on the server where you have the Intelligent Agents running. Thus, the registration of the databases you want to monitor is extremely easy. You ask the console to discover a node, and the rest is automatic.

Database Management Through OEM

OEM is designed for both monitoring and managing databases. Although the reporting and other features enable reporting, OEM provides excellent support for performing the myriad tasks that a typical Oracle9i DBA's task list consists of, including creating users, performing backups, managing instances, adding space to tablespaces, and managing objects (e.g., tables and indexes).

The Databases folder has all the databases that are located on the various nodes. You can also access the databases through the Nodes folder, but you'll see only the databases on each node that way. When you click one of the listed databases, the console asks you for a valid username/password combination to enter the database. Once you get in, you'll see that you have access to five instance objects under the database selected: instance, schema, security, storage, and replication (see Figure 17-17). Note that when you successfully log into the database, your username/password combination is saved in the preferred credentials category automatically.

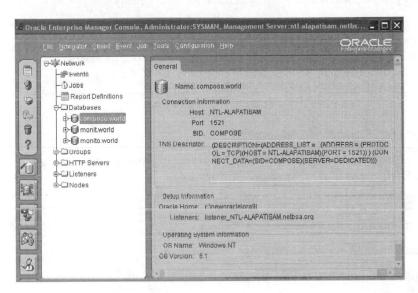

Figure 17-17. The console database page

OEM provides great functionality to simplify a DBA's tasks including, but not limited to, the following:

- Performing instance management, including starting up and shutting down the database

- Performing complex backup and recovery tasks

- Using RMAN without having to write RMAN scripts

- Managing users

- Managing space in tablespaces and administering data files, control files, and redo log files

- Managing schema objects such as tables and indexes

- Monitoring and managing memory, including dynamically adjusting the SGA components

- Analyzing objects

- Exporting and importing data

- Producing database health reports

In the following sections you'll look at how you can perform all the preceding tasks using OEM. OEM provides several key components: instance management, schema management, storage management, security management, warehouse management, distributed management, workspace management, and XML databases to help you perform a wide variety of database tasks easily.

 NOTE *If a non-DBA user needs to use DBA functionality through OEM (e.g., analyze or export/import), the DBA needs to grant this user the select any dictionary privilege.*

Database Instance Management

The Instance object under databases lets you perform the following tasks in an operational Oracle instance:

- Enable starting up and shutting down the database instance.

- Perform backup and recovery.

- Use the resource advisors to manage the instance.

- Modify the init.ora file/SPFILE parameter configuration.

- Monitor session information, including locked session details.

- Manage the resource plan and resource group information.

- Monitor long-running transactions.

Figure 17-18 shows how you can elect to use the various components of instance management. Note that you can check the status of user sessions and lock statistics through the Instance Manager.

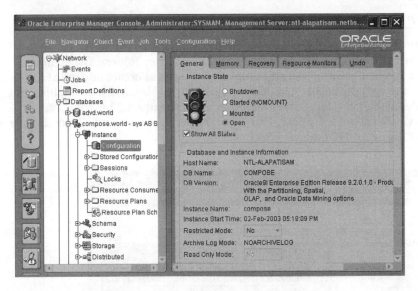

Figure 17-18. The instance management components

Database Schema Management

The Schema Management object helps you manage the schema objects: tables, indexes, packages, procedures, materialized views, and so on. You can, for example, click tables and see table definitions and the number of rows in each table without having to perform a single query. You can also use the Schema Management object (also known as the *Schema Manager*) to generate DDL scripts for the objects in the database. You can look at the source code for the various packages and procedures through the Schema Manager. Figure 17-19 shows the various objects you can manage through the Schema Manager.

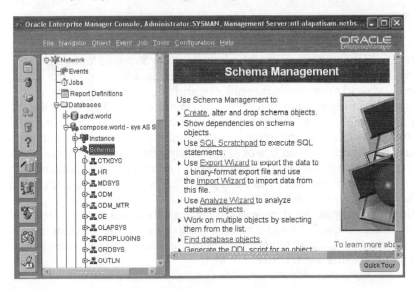

Figure 17-19. The Schema Manager

Database Security Management

The Security Management object (also known as the *Security Manager*) is used mostly to perform user management functions. It has three folders: Users, Roles, and Profiles. You can easily create and drop users as well as create and grant roles and profiles through the Security Manager. The Security Manager also enables you to change the default and temporary tablespaces for the users. The Security Manager is your best bet for quickly looking up a user's roles and privileges. Figure 17-20 shows the Security Manager screen.

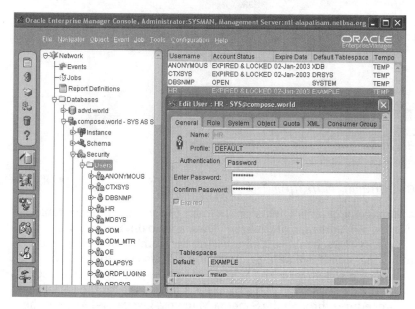

Figure 17-20. The Security Manager

Database Storage Management

Using the Storage Management object (also known as the *Storage Manager*), you can administer storage objects such as tablespaces, data files, and redo logs. You can create and drop the storage objects, and add space to existing tablespaces and data files. You can also bring objects online or offline using the Storage Manager. You can click the Controlfile tab to see detailed control file record information without having to issue any kind of query. Figure 17-21 shows you how you can easily change the size of data file using the Storage Manager without ever having to log into the database directly and execute the standard *alter datafile resize* command. After you change the size of the data file, just click Apply and the data file size is changed.

In addition to managing the storage of tablespaces, data files, and control files, you can manage the redo logs and archived redo logs through the Storage Manager. If you are managing an Oracle 9.2 version database, you can also view the storage layout by using the Schema Manager.

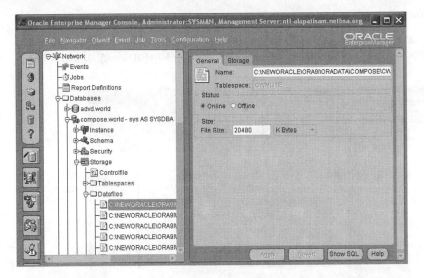

Figure 17-21. Changing a data file's size through the OEM console

Distributed Database Management

OEM provides complete distributed database management capabilities. OEM supports data replication and messaging technologies to support distributed database systems. The main uses of the distributed database management capability are as follows:

- Using advanced replication to replicate live data or a snapshot of data among a set of databases

- Checking two-phase commit transactions

- Using advanced queues to integrate applications through messaging technologies

- Creating database links between databases

- Using Oracle Streams to replicate data over a network of databases

Warehouse Management

OEM provides you two major capabilities to help with warehouse management. The OLAP (Online Analytical Processing) folder helps with complex analysis of warehouse data. The Summary Management folder helps improve the performance of the warehouse by using summaries. Let's look at these two components of OEM's Warehouse Management feature in more detail.

OLAP Management

You can create and manage OLAP metadata objects such as Cubes, Dimensions, and Measure. Figure 17-22 shows how you can pull up the topology of any cube.

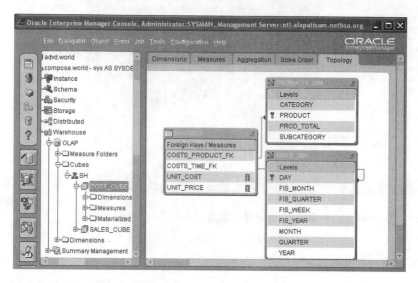

Figure 17-22. Using the OLAP Manager

Summary Management

Summary Management helps you create materialized views to improve the warehouse query performance. Following are the main capabilities of the Summary Management feature:

- Creating materialized views (with the Summary Advisor)

- Managing materialized view logs

- Using refresh groups to keep materialized views consistent with each other

Workspace Management

Workspaces in Oracle9*i* enable the versioning of databases by letting users share a virtual environment to make changes to the version-enabled tables. You learned how to use versioning in Chapter 8. OEM's Workspace Management object (also known as the *Workspace Manager*) provides an interface to easily enable and disable table versioning. You can also effortlessly create, edit, or delete a workspace using the Workspace Manager. This saves you the headache of repeatedly executing complex DBMS packages to manage the workspaces.

XML Database Management

Oracle supports the XML database, which is based on the XML data model. Using the XML database, you can efficiently store, retrieve, and update XML objects. Using OEM, you can configure XML databases and create tables and schemas based on the XML schema.

Groups

The Groups folder lets you group your nodes and the various services in them into regional groups, if you so wish. The Groups folder is useful only if you have a large, geographically spread out set of nodes to manage.

Listeners

The Listeners folder contains the Oracle listeners on all the nodes and the databases they are listening for. The folder displays the status of all Oracle listeners on every node. If the user has the proper credentials, the listener can also be stopped are started from here.

HTTP Servers

The Servers folder lists the names and status of the HTTP servers on all of the nodes. Although start and stop buttons are presented for all the servers on all nodes, you need to have the right permissions to bounce the servers.

Nodes

The Nodes folder lists the nodes that have been discovered by the OEM console. From this folder, you can see what nodes the Management Server is currently monitoring. You can request that OEM discover all the services on the nodes or refresh its database if you think there may be new services on the nodes.

Using the OEM Wizards

In addition to the database Instance, Schema, Security, and Storage Managers, OEM provides a set of useful wizards that enable you to execute jobs without having to manually enter the commands. For example, the Export Wizard and the Import Wizard make it a snap to get data into and out of databases, without your having to worry about writing parameter files and executing them at the command line. You can employ these wizards to eliminate the drudgery that you experience in repeatedly performing simple database management tasks. Let's take a quick trip through the main database wizards.

You can invoke the database wizards in any of the following ways:

- In the console, select Tools ➤ Database Tools ➤ Backup Management (or Data Management or Analyze).

- In the console, select Object ➤ Backup Management (or Data Management or Analyze).

- From the Console Navigator tree, click the Schema Container. The Schema Manager window on the right side has links to the Export and Import Wizards and the Backup wizard.

- On the far left side of the OEM console, you'll see various icons. Click the Database Tools icon to access the Backup, Import, and Export Wizards.

- You can highlight any database name in the Navigator tree and right-click it to get to all the database wizards.

The Export and Import Wizards

In Chapter 13, you learned how to use the export and import utilities. In that chapter, you performed the exports and imports using either the command line or a shell script that included an export parameter file. OEM provides you an easier way to perform exports and imports without having to create any parameter files. The Export and Import Wizards perform fast data extraction and loading into Oracle databases. You can export and import at the database, user, or table level. You can use the wizards to easily pick the objects to be exported/imported and specify the parameters for the operations. Figure 17-23 shows the Export Wizard in action.

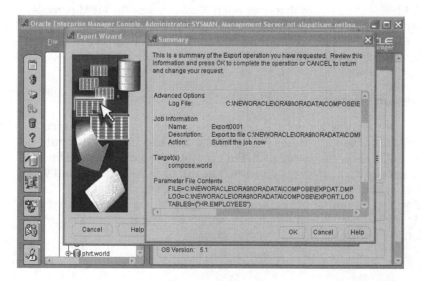

Figure 17-23. Using the Export Wizard

The Export and Import Wizards let you specify whether you want the operation to run immediately or you would like to schedule it for a specific time, as shown in Figure 17-24.

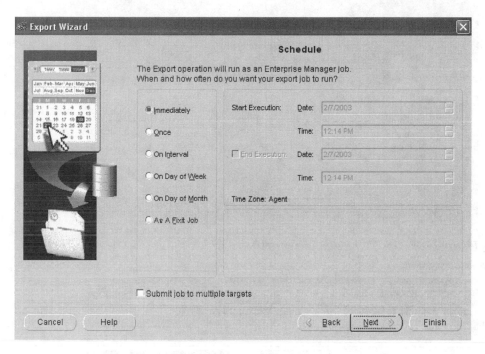

Figure 17-24. Scheduling an export

The Analyze Wizard

The Analyze Wizard helps you analyze tables and indexes, or entire schemas at once. You can use the *analyze* statement by itself or as part of the DBMS_STATS package. After you invoke the Analyze Wizard, you have to specify the options, after which you are asked to pick the tables or schemas, and the analyze operation will begin. You can specify that the analyze operation is done immediately or you can schedule it on an ongoing basis. Figure 17-25 shows how you choose among the various options for the analyze operation.

After you submit the job using the Analyze Wizard, go the Navigator pane and click the Jobs interface. There you'll see a list of all the jobs that have been submitted through the OEM console or through a scheduled job. To see the status of the job, click your analyze job. Figure 17-26 shows the status window.

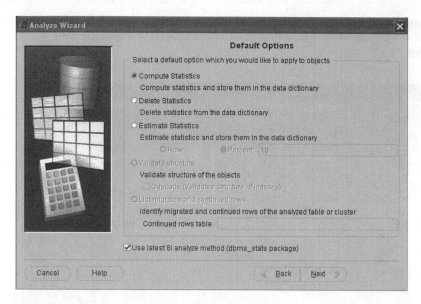

Figure 17-25. Specifying analyze parameters

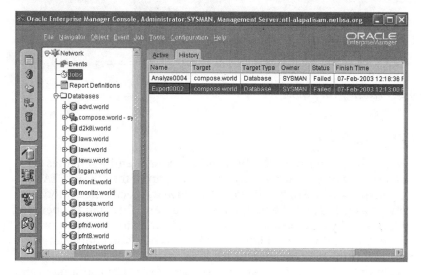

Figure 17-26. Analyze status window

The Backup Wizard

The Backup Wizard helps you make easy backups of data files, tablespaces, or whole databases, with or without the archive logs. You can also perform database recovery. You can employ user-managed backup and recovery, or you can use RMAN with or without a recovery catalog. Figure 17-27 shows you how to back up a single data file using the Backup Wizard.

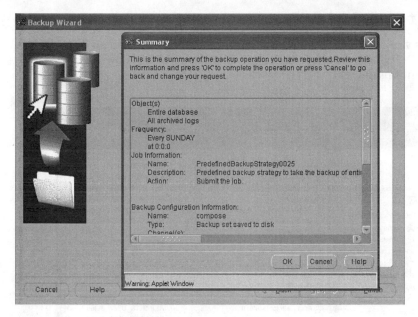

Figure 17-27. Using the Backup Wizard

Using the OEM Reporting Features

As a DBA, you'll have to produce reports on an ongoing basis, some for an analysis of database performance and general health and others for a long-term analysis of capacity, uptime, and other features. In addition, your organization's management may want you to produce certain custom made reports on the servers, databases, and network on a regular basis. OEM provides a set of prebuilt templates you can use to schedule reports, or you can customize the reports to suit your own purposes. If you have a great monitoring script, you can run it and view the output in the form of a nice-looking report on the Web. The OEM reporting system provides reports on all the monitored systems, and you can either schedule the reports or generate them on an ad hoc basis.

NOTE *If you are using UNIX scripts for reporting, be sure to include a return code in your scripts that indicates the success or failure of the script. If there is no return code, OEM indicates every job's status as "completed."*

Even if you don't have a single script on hand, OEM's prebuilt reports put a wealth of information at your fingertips, touching all the vital aspects of database management: storage, schema, instance, users, and performance.

Prebuilt and Custom Reports

OEM offers you several prebuilt report definitions. You can see them by clicking
the Report Definitions interface in the console. Figure 17-28 shows the standard
report definitions in OEM.

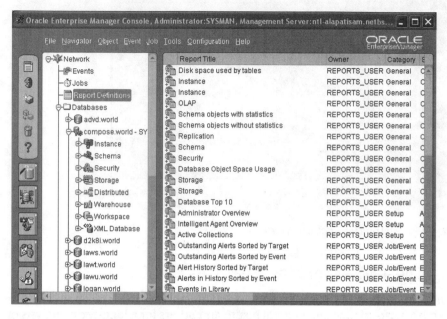

Figure 17-28. Standard OEM report definitions

If the prebuilt report definitions are inadequate for your purposes, you can
create customized report definitions easily.

Accessing the Reporting Web Site

If you want, you can publish any report to the OEM reporting Web site. This Web
site is automatically installed with the OEM software when you install the Oracle9*i*
server. A big advantage of using the Web site for reports, of course, is that a large
number of managers, system administrators, and DBAs can access it for the same
reports. You reach this Web site by using a URL in this form:
`http://your_servername: 3339/em/OEMGenerationservlet? reportName=EM-REPORTING_`
`HOMEPAGE`. To get there easily, just click Access Reports on your OEM Web page.
Figure 17-29 shows you the reporting Web site home page.

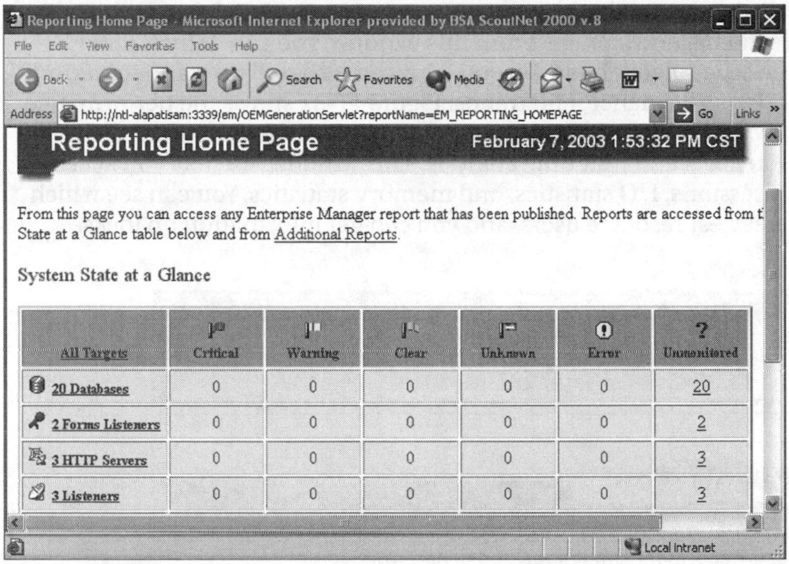

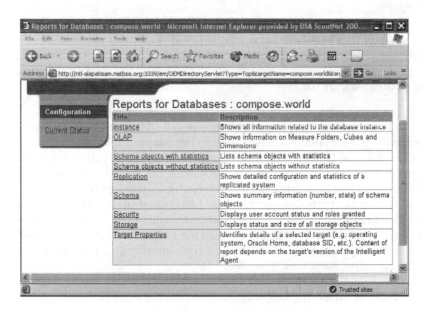

Figure 17-29. The reporting Web site home page

To see all the published reports for a given service, say a database, click the particular target under the All Targets column. You'll get a list of all the databases that are being managed, and when you click the database you're interested in, you'll see a screen similar to the one shown in Figure 17-30.

Figure 17-30. Available database reports by category

As you can see, the database reports cover a wide variety of topics, including the instance, schema, and storage. From this window, you can launch other windows to see scheduled jobs and events. You can also pull up standard reports on service levels, performance, and trends. Figure 17-31 shows the performance reports window. You can get an overview of performance here, in addition to response time reports and wait time analysis. This window also lets you access reports on top sessions, I/O statistics, and memory statistics. You can see which users are the heaviest resource users, and you can get information on locks.

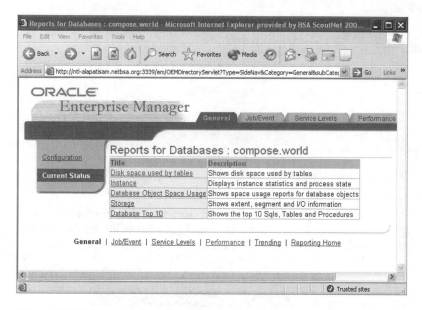

Figure 17-31. Standard performance reports

Managing Jobs with OEM

The ability to create and schedule jobs is one of the most useful features of the OEM toolset. You can run standard tasks such as export and import, backup, and analyze through the wizards that you saw earlier in the chapter. You can also run SQL scripts and shell scripts with operating system commands, or you can use one of the many predefined job tasks provided by OEM. The Jobs feature lets you test for some conditions before launching the job. For example, you can schedule a cold backup only after verifying that the database has been shut down cleanly. You can even schedule the database start-up and shutdown with OEM itself. The Intelligent Agent running on the various nodes runs all the jobs. You don't even have to be connected to the Management Server once a job is submitted, as long as the Intelligent Agent is up on the nodes.

The procedure for creating and scheduling jobs is easy once you go through the exercise a couple of times. The following sections describe the OEM job process.

The Job Detail View

You can view the main Job Detail view by clicking the Jobs icon in the OEM console. The Job Detail view lists all active jobs by default, and you can view older jobs by clicking the History tab. Figure 17-32 shows a typical Job Detail view. The Jobs icon in the menu will let you create, edit, and remove jobs.

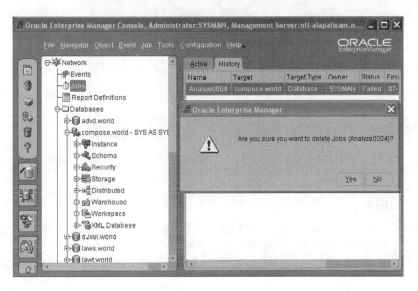

Figure 17-32. The Job Detail view

Creating a Job

Now you'll go through the steps involved in creating a job through the OEM console. The entire process is extremely easy, and it provides you with a convenient and powerful alternative to using the *crontab* or *at* commands discussed in Chapter 3 of this book.

Choosing the Database and Naming the Job

First, click the Jobs icon in the menu. Choose the Create a Job option and choose a database. Give the job a name so you can identify it, and provide a brief description of it. Because you can't submit the job without building the job itself, don't submit it yet, but choose the Add to Library option so your job name and description can be stored in the library. Figure 17-33 shows the General tab of the Jobs option.

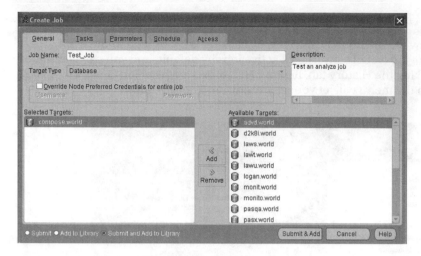

Figure 17-33. The Jobs General tab

Choosing a Task

After you name the job and save it, you are given a list of all the available tasks on the Tasks tab. You can choose a predefined task (such as export) or create your own task. I picked the Run SQL*Plus Script option, as shown in Figure 17-34. Click the Parameters tab next.

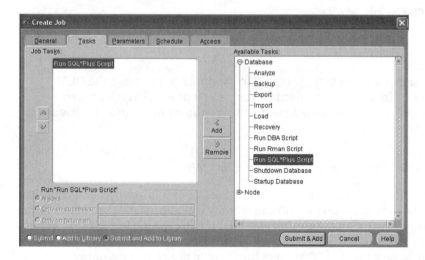

Figure 17-34. Choosing the job tasks

Choosing the Script for the Job

You can either type in your SQL script in the Script Text box or click Import if you want to use a stored script on your workstation. Figure 17-35 shows the Jobs Parameters tab.

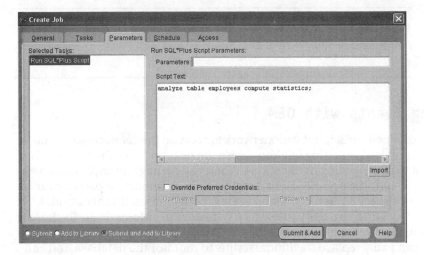

Figure 17-35. Choosing the job parameters

Scheduling and Submitting the Job

Once you have selected the script for the job, you are ready to submit it. Go the scheduling page by clicking the Schedule tab. You can choose to execute the job immediately or you can schedule the job for daily or weekly execution. Figure 17-36 shows how my test job has been scheduled to run daily at midnight. Once you have determined the schedule, click the Submit radio button (or the Submit and Add to Library radio button) and your job will be successfully submitted.

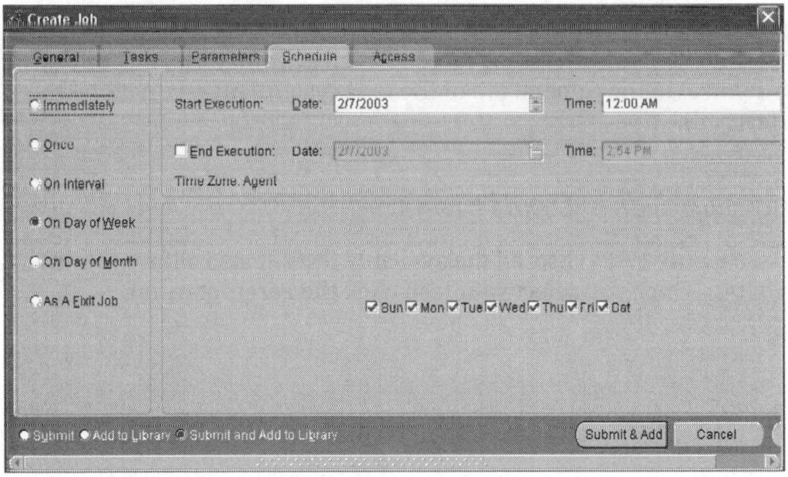

Figure 17-36. Scheduling a job

NOTE *You can manage the job library by selecting the Jobs option from the menu and clicking Job Library.*

Managing Events with OEM

Events, as explained earlier, test your network for certain predetermined conditions, say an archive log getting full. You devise the tests and pick the thresholds for the event to start sending notifications. When you manage multiple databases on multiple servers, the events system could be truly an important part of your arsenal as an Oracle DBA. You can set up events for databases, listeners, nodes, and Web servers. OEM also lets you use its *fixit* feature to automatically fix the problem, but only for certain events.

Events can easily replace traditional scripts to monitor the database. You can put in your own scripts if you wish, but OEM comes with the typical set of events preconfigured already. All you have to do is provide the parameters and thresholds for the events, and you can schedule them in minutes (literally). You can use events to set up a system of management by exception, where you are notified only if something doesn't work or run, thereby saving you the trouble of wading through numerous status reports and logs each day.

The way you administer OEM's events feature is very similar to the way you manage the job system. In the following sections you'll walk through an event example, where the event is defined as your archive logs directory filling up.

Creating Events

From the console's menu, pick the Events option and click Create Event. You'll be asked to name your event and select the target, which is a database in your case. The screen is identical to the General tab of the Jobs system. After you name the event, go the Tests tab.

Specifying the Test Conditions

The Tests tab (see Figure 17-37) lists all the available tests. It also allows you to create your own test. Once you select your test, click the Parameters tab.

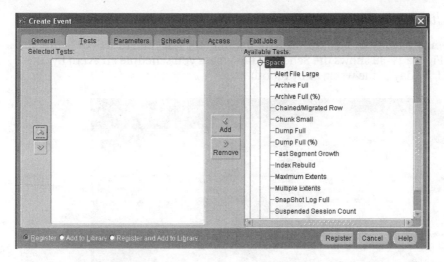

Figure 17-37. Specifying a test

Selecting the Test Criteria

On the Parameters tab, you are allowed to either choose the default thresholds or modify them according to your needs. Figure 17-38 shows the Parameters tab.

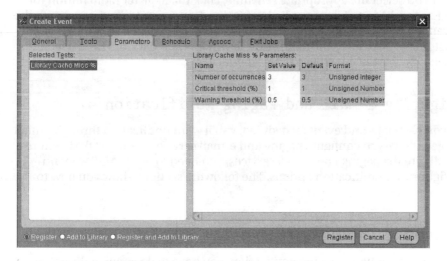

Figure 17-38. Specifying test parameters

Scheduling the Event

Once you are ready with your threshold parameters, it is time to schedule the event. Figure 17-39 shows the Schedule tab where you schedule an event by interval, by day of the week, or by month.

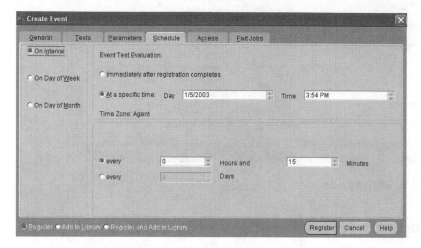

Figure 17-39. Scheduling an event

After you select the appropriate schedule, click the Register radio button (or the Register and Add to Library radio button), and your event is registered with the Intelligent Agent on the node where the database is running. As in the case of the Jobs system, you can go to the main console window and click the Events icon to see the status of events that have been scheduled.

Configuring E-mail and Paging Notification

When you have jobs and events scheduled, you'll want notification through e-mail or a pager. It's easy to configure paging and e-mail services through OEM. Before you configure the paging and e-mail services, you need to use the OEM menu to configure your notification options. The following sections show you how to do this.

Configuring Paging Notification

Before you can configure paging notification, you have to do some preliminary work. You have to start a paging service and let OEM register that paging service.

Starting the Paging Service

You have to first start the paging server on your server by using either of two methods. You may start it from the Windows Services panel by clicking the Start button, selecting Settings ➤ Control Panel ➤ Services, and starting the

Oracle<ORACLE_HOME>PagingService. You can also start the paging server from the command line by using the following command:

```
C:\> oemctl start paging
The OracleoraHome9iPagingServer service is Starting …..
The OracleoraHome9iPagingServer service was started successfully.
C:\>
```

You can check the status of your paging server from the OEM console by selecting Configuration ➤ Configure Paging/Email and pinging your paging server.

Adding the Paging Server to OEM

After you've started the paging server, it's time to let OEM know that the service is ready for use. Go to the main menu of your OEM console and use the Discover Nodes option to register the new paging server with OEM. You can also choose to just refresh the node, rather than discover it.

Setting Notification Preferences

You'll now have to set notification preferences by selecting System ➤ Preferences ➤ Notification and choosing the Paging configuration. Enter your pager PIN number and go the Schedule tab. Here you can schedule the times when you want pages to be sent to your PIN number. Figure 17-40 shows a typical notification schedule for e-mail and paging.

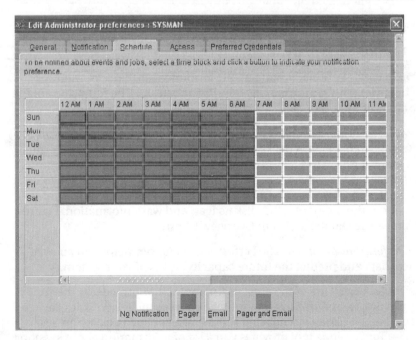

Figure 17-40. Setting the schedule for paging and e-mail

Configuring E-mail Notification

E-mail notification is very straightforward. All you need is the name of your SMTP Mail Gateway, which you find out by looking it up on your system. On my Exchange Server, I found it by selecting Services ➤ Properties ➤ Microsoft Exchange Server. Just go into the Notification area as you did with the paging service and set up and specify the times you want to receive e-mail. If you prefer, you can choose to get e-mail and page notifications for a given job. Once you choose the notification times, you'll be notified of every event and job automatically.

Oracle Management Packs

You have thus far seen the standard OEM toolset's functionality. You can extend the power of the toolset even further by using the Oracle management packs, which are like a set of accessory packs for OEM. The OEM management packs take you beyond systems monitoring and management to more complex issues such as performance tuning, resource optimization, and change management in the organization. The following are the important Oracle management packs. You'll find an in-depth discussion of the Oracle Diagnostics Pack in this chapter. The other packs are discussed in more detail in Chapters 18 and 19.

- The Oracle Diagnostics Pack

- The Oracle Tuning Pack

- The Oracle Change Management Pack

Oracle Diagnostics Pack

The Oracle Diagnostics Pack helps you find performance bottlenecks, monitor user session behavior, and perform many other related tasks. The following are the main components of the Diagnostics Pack:

- *The Oracle Performance Manager:* The Performance Manager ships with other Oracle management packs besides the Diagnostics Pack. The Performance Manager provides real-time monitoring, which facilitates diagnosis of bottlenecks in the system. The Performance Manager enables you to get a Database Health Overview Chart for your instance that summarizes information about the memory, CPU, disk usages, and wait information. Figure 17-41 shows the Database Health Overview Chart.

- *Oracle Performance Planner:* The Performance Planner helps you analyze historical data and predict the future capacity needs of your system.

- *Oracle TopSessions:* One of the most useful tools OEM provides is the Top Sessions database monitoring tool, which is part of the Diagnostics Pack. You access TopSessions by choosing Tools ➤ Diagnostic Pack ➤ Top Sessions. The TopSessions tool provides you a lot of information about sessions currently logged into a database. You get all the information captured by the V$SESSION table and resource use statistics such as disk reads and writes, memory consumption, CPU usage, and so on. With TopSessions, it is very easy to see how your users are consuming various resources within the database. You can choose to sort information according to various criteria, such as logical reads, total parses, and so forth. Figure 17-42 shows the TopSessions main screen.

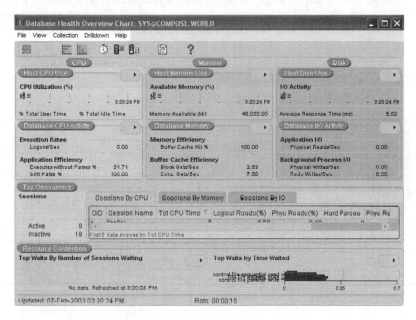

Figure 17-41. The Database Health Overview Chart.

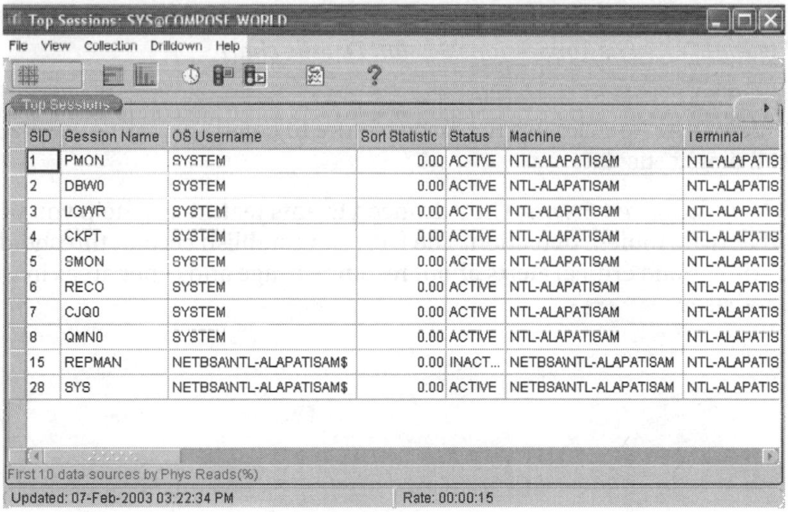

Figure 17-42. The Oracle TopSessions main screen

You can effectively use TopSessions to monitor the users in a database and kill user sessions, if necessary. The Drilldown option provides you two very useful charts. The first is the Current SQL chart, which lets you identify the SQL statement a particular user is currently executing. If you wish, you can tune the SQL directly from this chart. If you want detailed information about an individual session, you can drill down to the Session Details chart. This chart is truly impressive in the amount of information it provides regarding a session. You get detailed metrics about the I/O, memory, and CPU usage. In addition, you can see exactly what SQL statement is being currently executed, and you can view an analysis of the top wait events in the session. Figure 17-43 shows the Session Details chart.

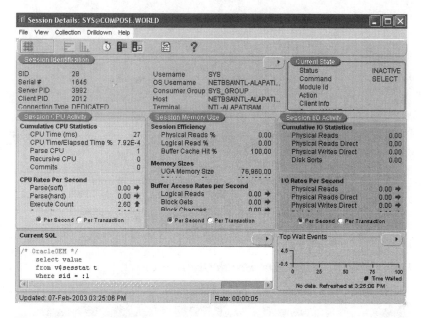

Figure 17-43. The TopSessions Session Details chart

- *Oracle Trace:* You can use the Trace feature to collect performance statistics and diagnostic data.

- *Oracle Advanced Events:* The Advanced Events feature will help you with proactive problem detection. The DBA can establish certain thresholds for warnings and critical alerts about resource usage and other areas in the databases.

Oracle Tuning Pack

The Oracle Tuning Pack contains several self-contained applications to help you tune various aspects of your database performance. The following are the main components of the Tuning Pack:

- *Oracle Expert:* This feature provides expert tuning recommendations based on the performance data it collects.

- *Outline Management:* You can create and manage stored outlines with this feature of OEM.

- *Oracle Tablespace Map:* This feature provides a comprehensive picture of space usage in a tablespaces at the segment and extent level.

- *Oracle Index Tuning Wizard:* This wizard advises you regarding the usefulness of old and proposed indexes. It can both report on the tables needing indexes and implement the recommendations by creating the indexes.

- *Oracle SQL Analyze:* This feature analyzes SQL statement performance and helps you modify statements to make them optimal.

- *Reorg Wizard:* This wizard helps you reorganize tables, indexes, and tablespaces, and fix chained and migrated rows.

Oracle Change Management Pack

The Change Management Pack provides support for managing the change process when you are changing software and application versions. Tracking and implementing changes in the server software and the database objects is very complex and time-consuming. The Change Management Pack provides several tools to make the transition process efficient.

Troubleshooting OEM

I've been using OEM in one way or another for a number of years now. I must be honest and tell you that at times, using OEM has been a frustrating experience because the tool has in general been very "clunky" throughout its life. Having unburdened myself of that part of my experience with OEM, let me say that the latest OEM that Oracle9*i* provides you is the best version thus far and actually is a pleasant surprise from the initial installation down to the configuration of its fanciest features. However, like most software programs, OEM has its own set of problems.

Here is some basic advice to help cope with some OEM problems. The Oracle MetaLink site can help you with most of the problems you'll encounter with OEM. Once in a while, you'll notice that you can start the OEM console from your client machine but not from the Web. Check to make sure you have the Oracle JInitiator plug-in installed, because you can't access OEM through the Web without it. Sometimes, the OEM console just won't start through the Web site, and your best bet is to restart your client server. If your console isn't able to "see" the target services, it's most likely because the Intelligent Agent is running on *each* of the nodes you want to monitor.

Summary

Oracle Enterprise Manager (OEM) is a truly useful and powerful tool, especially if you have a large number of databases, nodes, and HTTP servers to monitor. Its event management feature notifies you immediately when things go wrong. You can use its job system in a proactive way to prevent many things from going bad in the first place.

In this chapter you learned how easy it is to produce jobs and create events. You learned how to set up paging and e-mail notifications with ease. If you have homegrown scripts, you can incorporate them within OEM very easily, with no changes.

The latest version of OEM is remarkably easy to configure and use. You may have some frustrating moments setting it up, but it's a small price to pay for a useful tool to manage your databases with.

Part Six

Performance Tuning and Troubleshooting the Production Database

Improving Database Performance: SQL Query Optimization

PERFORMANCE TUNING IS the one area where the Oracle DBA will probably spend the most of his or her time, whether the DBA is working with a development or a production database. Performance tuning could be proactive as well as reactive. If you're a DBA helping developers to tune their SQL, you can improve performance by suggesting more efficient queries or table- and index-organization schemes. If you're a production DBA, you'll be dealing with user perceptions of a "slow" database, batch jobs taking longer and longer to complete, and so on.

Performance tuning focuses primarily on writing efficient SQL, allocating appropriate computing resources, and analyzing wait events and contention in the system. This chapter focuses on SQL query optimization in Oracle. You'll learn the important principles that underlie efficient code. You'll also learn about the initialization parameters you can tune to optimize performance. I present a detailed discussion of the various tools, such as the Explain Plan and SQL Trace utilities, with which you analyze SQL and find ways to improve performance.

Oracle provides several options to aid performance, such as partitioning large tables, using materialized views, storing plan outlines, and many others. This chapter examines how DBAs can use these techniques to aid developers' efforts to increase the efficiency of their application code.

I begin the chapter with a discussion of how to approach performance tuning. More than the specific performance improvement techniques you use, it's your approach to performance tuning that determines your success in tuning a recalcitrant application system.

An Approach to Oracle Performance Tuning

Performance tuning is the 800-pound gorilla that is constantly menacing you and that requires every bit of your ingenuity, knowledge, and perseverance to keep out of harm's way. Your efforts to increase performance or to revive a bogged-down database can have a major impact on your organization, and your results will be monitored and appreciated by users and management.

Unlike several other features of Oracle database management, performance tuning is not a cut-and-dried subject with clear prescriptions and rules for every type of problem you may face. This is one area where your technical knowledge must be used together with constant experimentation and observation. Practice does make you better, if not perfect, in this field.

Frustrating as it is at times, performance tuning is a rewarding part of the Oracle DBA's tasks. You can automate most of the mundane tasks such as backup, export and import, and data loading—the simple, everyday tasks that can take up so much of your valuable time. Performance tuning is one area that requires a lot of detective work on the part of application programmers and DBAs to see why some process is running slower than expected, or why you can't scale your application to a larger number of users without problems.

A Systematic Approach to Performance Tuning

It's important to follow a systematic approach to tuning database performance. It's very common for performance problems to come to the fore only after a large number of users starts working on a new production database. The system seems fine during development and rigorous testing, but it slows down to a crawl when it goes to production. This could be because the application isn't easily scalable for a number of reasons.

The seeds of the future performance potential of your database are planted when you design your database. You need to know the nature of the applications the database is going to support. The more you understand your application, the better you can prepare for it by creating your database with the right configuration parameters. If major mistakes were made during the design stage, and the database is already built, you are left with tuning application code on one hand and the database resources such as memory, CPU, and I/O on the other. Oracle suggests a specific approach to tune your database performance. The steps are as follows:

1. Design the application correctly.

2. Tune the application SQL code.

3. Tune memory.

4. Tune I/O.

5. Tune contention and other issues.

Reactive Performance Tuning

Although the preceding performance tuning steps suggests that you can follow the sequence in an orderly fashion, the reality is completely different. Performance tuning is an iterative process, not a sequential process where you start at the top and end up with a fully tuned database as the product. As a DBA, you may be involved in a new project from the outset, when you have just the functional requirements of the project. In this case, you have an opportunity to be involved in the tuning effort from the beginning stages of the application, a phase that is somewhat misleadingly dubbed *proactive tuning* by some. Alternatively, you may come in after the application has already been designed and implemented, and currently is in production. In this case, your performance efforts are categorized as *reactive performance tuning.* Of course, what you can do to improve the performance of the database will depend on the stage at which you can have input and the nature of the application itself.

In general, developers are responsible for writing the proper code, but the DBA has a critical responsibility to ensure that the SQL is optimal. Developers and QA testers may test the application conscientiously, but the application may not scale well when exposed to heavy-duty real-life production conditions. Consequently, DBAs are left scrambling to find solutions to a poorly performing SQL statement after the code is placed in production. Especially stressful is the time right before your application goes into production, when performance issues come up for the very first time in most cases. Reactive performance tuning comprises most of the performance tuning done by most DBAs, for the simple reason that most problems come to light only after real users start using the application.

In many cases, you're administering a production instance that was designed and coded long ago, and is currently experiencing performance problems. Try to fix the SQL statements first if that's at all possible. Many people have pointed out that if the application is seriously flawed, you can do little to improve the overall performance of the database, and they're probably correct. Still, you can make a significant difference to performance, even when the suboptimal code can't be changed for one reason or another. You can't just say, "It's the application's fault, therefore don't expect me to improve the performance." You can use several techniques to improve performance, even when the code is deemed poorly written but can't be changed in the immediate future. The same analysis, more or less, applies to performance tuning packaged systems such as PeopleSoft and SAP, where you really can't delve into the code that underlies the system. Yet you as a DBA must be able to improve the performance of these systems as well. *Instance tuning*, which is the topic of this chapter, is how you improve the performance in both of the aforementioned situations. In the next chapter, you'll learn how to tune database resources such as memory, disks, and CPU.

SQL Coding Practices

If you're a member of a team that's building a new application, you can contribute to a well-performing database by suggesting good SQL coding practices. If, on the other hand, the application is already built, there's a lot less scope for you to help improve the SQL code itself. If your organization is using one of the ERP packages that uses canned code, you're also not going to be able to touch the code.

In this chapter, I discuss the principles behind designing high-performance applications and writing efficient SQL and PL/SQL code. You can use these principles to your advantage, especially if you're serving as a design or development DBA, helping developers come up with a well-tuned application. You'll also learn about the initialization parameters that you can change to improve SQL performance. I include a detailed discussion on using various tools for determining efficient SQL execution plans.

Optimizing Oracle Query Processing

When a user starts a data-retrieval operation, the user's SQL statement goes through several sequential steps. All the steps involved in retrieving information from the database together constitute *query processing*. One of the great benefits of using SQL language is that it isn't a procedural a language where you have to specify the steps to be followed to achieve the statement's goal. In other words, you don't have to state how to do something; rather, you just state what you need from the database.

Query processing is the transformation of your SQL statement into an efficient execution plan and the execution of this plan to return the requested data from the database. *Query optimization* is the process of choosing the efficient execution plan. The goal is to achieve the result with the least cost in terms of resource usage. This also means that the goal is to reduce the total execution time of the query, which is simply the sum of the execution times of all the component operations of the optimized query. This optimization of throughput may not be the same as minimizing response time. If you want to minimize the time it takes to get the first *n* rows of a query instead of the entire output of the query, the optimizer may choose a different plan. If you choose to minimize the response time for all the query data, you may also choose to parallelize the operation.

A user's SQL statement goes through the *parse, optimize,* and *execution* stages. If the SQL statement is a query, data has to be retrieved, so there's an additional *fetch* stage before the SQL statement processing is complete. In the next sections you'll examine what Oracle does during each of these steps.

Parsing

Parsing primarily consists of the checking of the syntax and semantics of the SQL statements. The end product of the parse stage of query compilation is the creation of the *parse tree*, which represents the query's structure.

The SQL statement is decomposed from a SQL query into a relational algebra query. The query is analyzed to see that it is syntactically correct. The query then undergoes semantic checking. The data dictionary is consulted to ensure that the tables and the individual columns that are referenced in the query do exist in the data dictionary and that all the object privileges also exist. In addition, the column types are checked to ensure that data matched column definitions. The statement is normalized so it can be processed more efficiently. The query is semantically analyzed and it is rejected if it is incorrectly formulated. Once the parse tree passes all the syntactic and semantic checks, it is considered a valid parse tree, and it is sent to the logical query plan generation stage. All these operations take place in the library cache portion of the SGA.

Optimization

During the optimization phase, Oracle will use its optimizer—usually a cost-based optimizer (CBO)—to choose the best access method for retrieving data for the tables and indexes referred to in the query. The optimization process results in the creation of an execution plan for optimal execution of the SQL query. Using statistics that you provide and any hints specified in the SQL queries, the CBO will produce an optimal execution plan for the SQL statement.

The optimization phase described in the last paragraph can be divided into two distinct parts: the query rewrite phase and the physical execution plan generation phase. Let's look at these two optimization phases in detail.

Query Rewrite Phase

In this phase, the parse tree is converted into an abstract logical query plan. This is an initial pass at an actual query plan, and it contains only a general algebraic reformulation of the initial query. The various nodes and branches of the parse tree are replaced by operators of relational algebra.

Execution Plan Generation Phase

During this phase, Oracle transforms the logical query plan into a physical query plan. The optimizer may be faced with a choice of several algorithms to resolve a query. It needs to choose the most efficient algorithm to answer a query. In addition to choosing the type of operations to perform, the optimizer needs to determine the most efficient way to implement the operations. In addition to deciding on the best operational steps, the optimizer determines the order in which it will perform these steps. For example, the optimizer may decide that a join between table A and table B is called for. It needs to then decide on the type of join and the order in which it performs the table join.

The most important part of query optimization is the choice of execution plans for the individual steps of the execution plan, which is the same as the physical query plan. The physical query plan takes into account the following factors:

- The various operations (e.g., joins) to be performed during the query

- The order in which the operations are performed

- The algorithm to be used for performing each operation

- The best way to retrieve data from disk or memory

- The best way to pass data from one operation to another during the query

The optimizer may generate several valid physical query plans, all of which are potential execution plans. How does it choose among the various possible physical query execution plans? The optimizer does so by estimating the cost of each possible physical plan based on the table and index statistics available to it and selecting the plan with the lowest estimated cost. This evaluation of the possible physical query plans is called *cost-based optimization*. The cost of executing a plan is directly proportional to the amount of resources necessary to execute the proposed plan. The cost includes resources such as I/O, memory, and CPU. The optimizer passes this low-cost physical query plan to Oracle's query execution engine. The next section presents a simple example to help you understand the principles of cost optimization.

An Example of Cost Optimization

Time for an example. Let's say you want to run the following query, which seeks to find all the supervisors who work in Dallas. The query looks like this:

```
SQL> select * from employee e, dept d
where e.dept_no = d.dept_no
and(e.job = 'SUPERVISOR'
and d.city = 'DALLAS');
SQL>
```

Now, you have several ways to arrive at the list of the supervisors. You'll consider three ways to arrive at this list, and you'll also compute the "cost" of accessing the results in each of the three ways.

Make the following simplifying assumptions for your cost computations:

- You can only read and write data one row at a time (in the real world, you do I/O at the block level, not the row level).

- The database writes each intermediate step to disk (again, this may not be the case in the real world).

- There are no indexes on the tables.

- The employee table has 2,000 rows.

- The dept table has 40 rows. The number of supervisors is also 40 (one for each department).

- There are 10 departments in the city of Dallas.

In the following sections, you'll see three different queries that retrieve the same data, but use different access methods. For each query, a crude cost is calculated, so you can compare how the three queries stack up in terms of resource cost. The first query uses a Cartesian join.

Query 1: A Cartesian Join

First, form a Cartesian product of the employee and dept tables. Next, see which of the rows in the Cartesian product will satisfy the requirement *where e.job=supervisor AND d.dept=operations and e.dept_no=d.dept_no*.

The following would be the total cost of performing the query:

The Cartesian product of employee and dept requires a read of both tables: 2,000 + 40 = 2,040 reads

Creating the Cartesian product: 2,000 * 40 = 80,000 writes

Reading the Cartesian product to compare against the select condition: 2,000 * 40 = 80,000 reads

Total I/O cost: 2,040 + 80,000 + 80,000 = 16,2040

Query 2: A Join of Two Tables

The second query uses a join of the employee and dept tables. First, join the employee and dept tables on the dept_no column. From this join, select all rows where *e.job=supervisor* and *city=Dallas.*

The following would be the total cost of performing the query:

Joining the employee and dept tables first requires a read of all the rows in both tables: 2,000 + 40 = 2,040

Creating the join of the employee and dept tables: 2,000 writes

Reading the join results costs: 2,000 reads

Total I/O cost: 2,040 + 2,000 + 2,000 = 6,040

Query 3: A Join of Reduced Relations

The third query also uses a join of the employee and dept tables, but not all the rows in the two tables—only selected rows from the two tables are joined. Here's how this query would proceed to retrieve the needed data. First, read the employee table to get all supervisor rows. Next, read the dept table to get all Dallas departments. Finally, join the rows you derived from the employee and the dept tables.

The following would be the total cost of performing the query:

Reading the employee table to get the supervisor rows: 2,000 reads

Writing the supervisor rows derived in the previous step: 40 writes

Reading the dept table to get all Dallas departments: 40 reads

Writing the Dallas department rows derived from the previous step: 10 writes

Joining the supervisor rows and department rows derived in the previous steps of this query execution results in a total of 40 + 10 = 50 writes

Reading the join result from the previous step: 50 reads

Total I/O cost: 2,000 + 2(40) + 10 + 2(50) = 2,190

This example, simplified as it may be, shows you that Cartesian products are more expensive than more restrictive joins. Even a selective join operation, the results show, is more expensive than a selection operation. Although there is a join operation in query 3, it is a join of two reduced relations: The size of the join was much smaller than the join in query 2. Query optimization often involves early selection (picking only some rows) and projection (picking only some columns) operations to reduce the size of the resulting outputs or row sources.

Heuristic Strategies for Query Processing

The use of the cost-based optimization technique isn't the only way to perform query optimization. Cost-based optimization is a very systematic way to approximate the cost of query processing and thus arrive at the most efficient form of processing a query. A database can also use less systematic techniques, known as *heuristic strategies*, for query processing. A join operation is called a *binary* operation, and an operation such as selection is called a *unary* operation. A successful strategy in general is to perform the unary operation early on, so the more complex and time-consuming binary operations will use smaller operands. Performing as many of the unary operations as possible first reduces the row sources of the join operations. Here are some of the common heuristic query-processing strategies:

- Perform selection operations early so you can eliminate a majority of the candidate rows early in the operation. If you leave most rows in until the end, you're going to do needless comparisons with the rows that you're going to get rid of later anyway.

- Perform projection operations early so you limit the number of columns you have to deal with.

- If you need to perform consecutive join operations, perform the operation that produces the smaller join first.

- Compute common expressions once and save the results.

Query Execution

During the final stage of query processing, the optimized query (the physical query plan that has been selected) is executed. If it is a *select* statement, the rows are returned to the user. If it is an *insert*, *update*, or *delete* statement, the rows are modified. It is the SQL execution engine that takes the execution plan provided by the optimization phase and executes it.

Of the three basic steps involved in SQL statement processing, the optimization process is the crucial one because it determines the all-important question about how fast your data will be retrieved. Understanding how the optimizer works is at the heart of query optimization. It is important to know what the common access methods, join methods, and join orders are in order to write efficient SQL. The next section presents a detailed discussion of the all-powerful Oracle CBO.

Query Optimization and the Oracle Cost-Based Optimizer

In most cases, you have multiple ways to execute a SQL query. You can get the same results from doing a full table scan or using an index. You can also retrieve the same data by accessing the tables and indexes in a different order. The job of the optimizer is to find the optimal or best plan to execute your DML statements such as *select*, *insert*, *update*, and *delete*. Oracle uses the *cost-based optimizer* (CBO) to help determine efficient methods to execute queries.

The CBO uses statistics on tables and indexes, the order of tables and columns in the SQL statements, available indexes, and any user-supplied access hints to pick the most efficient way to access them. The most efficient way, according to the CBO, is the least costly access method, "cost" being defined in terms of the I/O and the CPU expended in retrieving the rows. Accessing the necessary rows means Oracle will read the database blocks on the file system into the buffer pool. The resulting I/O cost is the most expensive part of SQL statement execution because it involves reading from the disk. You can examine these access paths by using tools such as the explain plan. The following sections cover the tasks you need to perform to ensure that the optimizer will function efficiently.

Choosing Your Optimization Mode

Although Oracle offers an additional rule-based optimization mode, it strongly recommends using the CBO method, where the cost is in units of resource use, such as CPU and I/O cost.

The rule-based optimization approach mainly exists to support older Oracle applications. Under this approach, Oracle uses a heuristic method to select among several alternative access paths with the help of certain rules. All the access paths are assigned a rank and the path with the lowest rank is chosen. The operations with a lower rank usually execute faster than those with a higher rank. For example, a query that uses the ROWID to search for a row will have a cost of 1. This is expected because identifying a row with the help of the ROWID, an Oracle pointer like mechanism, is the fastest way to locate a row. On the other hand, a query that uses a full table scan will have a cost of 19, the highest possible cost under rule-based optimization. The CBO method almost always performs better than the rule-based approach because, among other things, it takes into account the latest statistics about the database objects.

Providing Statistics About the Objects to the Optimizer

You can provide the necessary statistics to the optimizer by using the DBMS_STATS package, which you'll learn about later on in this chapter. The DBMS_STATS package makes sure the optimizer has information on the number of rows in tables and indexes, as well as how the column data is distributed. The optimizer also has information about the levels in the index B-trees and the degree of selectivity in the tables. You can generate these statistics by using the *analyze* command, but you're better off using the DBMS_STATS package to do this, as you'll see in the section "Providing Statistics to the CBO." Here's a short list of the main types of statistics provided by using the DBMS_STATS package or the *analyze* command:

- The number or rows in a table

- The number of rows per database block

- The average row length for the table

- The total number of database blocks occupied by the table

- The number of levels in each index on the table

- The number of leaf blocks in each index

- The number of distinct values of each column value

- The number of distinct index keys

- The selection cardinality (the number of columns with similar values for each column)

- The minimum and maximum values for each column

The key to the CBOs capability to pick the best possible query plan is its capability to correctly estimate the cost of the individual operations of the query plan. These cost estimates are derived from the knowledge about the I/O, CPU, and memory resources needed to execute each operation, the table and index information you saw earlier, and additional information regarding the operating system performance.

NOTE *Oracle doesn't automatically maintain or update the database statistics. You are the one responsible for the range and frequency of statistics collection. Fortunately, using the DBMS_STATS package makes collecting sophisticated statistics a snap. After you initially configure the statistics collection package, you can automate the whole process for subsequently updating the statistics. The optimizer will then choose the best access method among the alternatives available. "Cost-based optimization" refers to the fact that the optimizer will seek to pick the access method that has the least cost in terms of physical I/O calls. The optimizer calculates the number of physical I/O calls for all the access methods and chooses the method with the least cost for its execution plan. To use the CBO, you have to set certain initialization parameters, as shown in the next section.*

Setting the Optimizer Mode

Oracle will optimize the throughput of queries by default. *Throughput* refers to the total number of times it takes to retrieve all the rows. You can also ask Oracle to optimize the response time, which usually means using the least amount of resources to get the first (or first *n*) row(s).

You can use the following three modes for the optimizer, all of which involve the CBO. The rule-based optimizer is going to be a deprecated product, and I do not even mention it here.

- *Choose:* This is the default optimizer mode, and it directs Oracle to use the CBO if there are statistics (derived by running the *analyze* command or using the DBMS_STATS package) on any of the tables involved in a query. If no statistics are available for any of the tables involved in a query, Oracle will use the rule-based optimizer.

- *First_rows:* The *first_rows* mode uses the CBO, regardless of whether you have statistics or not. You use this option when you want the first few rows to come out quickly so response time can be minimized. This mode is retained for backward compatibility only, with the *first_rows_n* mode being the latest version of this mode.

- *First_rows_n:* This optimizing mode uses cost optimization regardless of the availability of statistics. The goal is the fastest response time for the first n number of rows of output, where n can takes the value of 10, 100, or 1000.

- *All_rows:* This mode uses the CBO, whether you have statistics or not, with the express goal of maximizing throughput rather than minimizing resource cost of the operation.

Setting the Optimizer Level

You can set the optimizer mode at the instance, session, or statement level. You set the optimizer mode at the instance level by using the initialization parameter *optimizer_mode* to either *choose, first_rows_n,* or *all_rows,* as explained in the previous section.

You can set the optimizer mode for a single session by using the following statement:

```
SQL> alter session set optimizer_goal = first_rows;
Session altered.
SQL>
```

To determine the current optimizer mode for your database, you can run the following query:

```
SQL> select name,value
     from v$parameter
     where name ='optimizer_mode';
```

Any SQL statement can override the instance or session-level settings with the use of *hints,* which are directives to the optimizer in choosing the optimal access method.

What Does the Optimizer Do?

The CBO performs several intricate steps to arrive at the optimal execution plan for a user's query. The original SQL statement will most likely be transformed, and it evaluates alternative access paths (e.g., full table or index-based scans). If table joins are necessary, the optimizer evaluates all possible join methods and join orders. The optimizer evaluates all the possibilities and arrives at the execution plan it deems the cheapest in terms of resource usage.

SQL Transformation

Your query is hardly ever executed in its original form by Oracle. If the CBO determines that a different SQL formulation will achieve the same results more efficiently, it transforms the statement before executing it. The purpose of statement transformation by the optimizer is to transform the statement into an equivalent but more efficient expression. A good example is where you submit a query with an OR condition, and the CBO transforms it into a statement using UNION or UNION ALL. Or, your statement may include an index, but the CBO might transform the statement so it can do a full table scan, which can be more efficient under some circumstances. In any case, it is good to remember that the query a user wishes to be executed may not be executed in the same form by Oracle but, of course, the query's results will still be the same. The following are some of the common transformations performed by the Oracle CBO:

- Transform IN into OR statements.

- Transform OR into UNION or UNION ALL statements.

- Transform noncorrelated nested selects into the more efficient joins.

- Transform outer joins into more efficient inner joins.

- Transform complex subqueries into joins, semijoins, and antijoins.

- Star transformation for data warehouse tables based on the star schema.

- Transform BETWEEN to greater than or equal to and less than or equal to statements.

Choosing the Access Path

Oracle can often access the same data through different paths. For each query, the optimizer evaluates all the available paths and picks the least expensive one in terms of resource usage. The following sections present a summary of the common access methods available to the optimizer. If joins are involved, then the join order and the join method are evaluated to finally arrive at the best execution plan. You'll take a brief look at the steps the optimizer goes through before deciding on its choice of execution path.

Full Table Scans

Oracle will scan the entire table during a full table scan. Oracle reads each block in the table sequentially, so the full table scan can be efficient if the *multi_block_read_count* initialization parameter is set high enough. However, for large tables, full table scans will be inefficient in general.

Table Access by ROWID

Accessing a table by ROWID will retrieve rows by using unique ROWIDs. ROWIDs in Oracle specify the exact location in the data file and the data block where the row resides, so ROWID access is the fastest way to retrieve a row in Oracle. Often, Oracle obtains the ROWID through an index scan of the table's indexes. Using these ROWIDs, Oracle will swiftly fetch the rows.

Index Scans

An index stores two things: the column value of the column on which the index is based and the ROWID of the rows in the table that contain that column value. An index scan retrieves data from an index using the values of the index columns. If the query requests only the indexed column values, Oracle will return those values. If the query requests other columns outside the indexed column, Oracle will use the ROWIDs to get the rows of the table.

Choosing the Join Method

When you need to access data that is in two or more tables, Oracle will join the tables based on a common column. However, there are several ways to join the row sets returned from the execution plan steps. For each statement, Oracle will evaluate the best join method based on the statistics and the type of unique or primary keys on the tables. After Oracle has evaluated the join methods, the CBO picks the join method with least cost.

The following are the common join methods used by the CBO:

- *Nested-loop join:* A nested loop join involves the designation of one table as the *driving table* (also called the *outer table*) in the join loop. The other table in the join is called the *inner table*. Oracle will fetch all the rows of the inner table for every row in the driving table.

- *Hash join:* When you join two tables, Oracle uses the smaller table to build a hash table on the join key. Oracle will then search the larger table and return the joined rows from the hash table.

- *Sort-merge join:* If both the tables in a join are sorted on the join key, the sorted lists are merged together.

Choosing the Join Order

Once the optimizer chooses the join method, it determines the order in which the tables are joined. The goal of the optimizer is to always join tables in such a way that the driving table will eliminate the largest number of rows. A query with four tables has a maximum of 4!=24 possible ways in which the tables can be joined. Each such join order would lead to a number of different execution plans, based on the available indexes and the access methods. Because the search for an optimal join strategy could take a long time in a query with a large number of tables, Oracle depends on an adaptive search strategy to limit the time it takes to find the best execution plan. Simply put, an *adaptive search strategy* means that the time taken for optimization will always be a small percentage of the total time that will be taken for execution of the query itself.

Drawbacks of the CBO

The CBO is systematic, but it's ultimately based on heuristics, which don't guarantee that the optimizer will follow the same plan in every similar case. Like all good weapons, the CBO has its drawbacks. However, as you'll see, you have ways to overcome these deficiencies. The following is a brief discussion of typical things to watch out for:

- The CBO is not fixed across Oracle versions. Execution plans can change over time, as versions change. Later in this chapter, you'll see how to use stored outlines to maintain plan stability, so the optimizer always uses a known plan.

- Application developers may know more than the CBO when it comes to choosing the best access path. Application developers know the needs of the users, which the CBO is completely unaware of. This could lead to a situation where the CBO may be optimizing through, let's say, when the users would rather have a quick set of results on their screen. By using hints such as *first_rows*, you can overcome this drawback in the CBO.

- The CBO depends enormously on correct statistics gathering, whether it be with the DBMS_STATS package or the *analyze* command. If the statistics are absent or outdated, the optimizer can make some very poor decisions.

Providing Statistics to the CBO

The CBO can follow optimal execution paths only if it has detailed knowledge of the database objects. You provide statistics to the optimizer with the DBMS_STATS package. You can also use the traditional *analyze* statement, but Oracle prefers you use the DBMS_STATS package to do the job. The statistics collected by the DBMS_STATS package include the average row length, the number of empty blocks, the number of distinct values in a column, the number of nulls, the average leaf blocks per index key, the number of distinct index keys, and so on.

You can collect statistics on the entire schema or an individual table. In addition to statistics on tables, indexes, and clusters, the DBMS_STATS package can collect system performance statistics. You can gather both CPU and I/O performance and utilization statistics. Remember that the accuracy of the optimizer's cost estimation depends on the amount and recency of the statistics stored in the data dictionary. You don't really need to update the statistics on a constant basis to keep up with the inserts, deletes, and updates in your database. However, your statistics collection interval should reflect the changes being made to table data. If you have a table with 100 million rows, and over a week only a few thousand rows are modified, deleted, or inserted, your old statistics are still highly relevant. If, on the other hand, a significant proportion of the rows in a table are undergoing change on a daily basis, you may have to analyze that table on a daily basis.

NOTE *If you are using the CBO but you don't provide any statistics on a table or tables, Oracle will use the rule-based optimization approach.*

Using DBMS_STATS to Collect Statistics

Oracle provides the DBMS_STATS package to facilitate statistics collection for database objects such as tables and indexes. Using this package, you can ask Oracle to compute statistics based on all the data in the tables and indexes, or estimate statistics based on a sample. You can also use the parallel option to complete the statistics collection quickly.

 TIP *For large tables, Oracle recommends just sampling the data, rather than looking at all the data. Oracle lets you specify row or block sampling, and it sometimes seems to recommend sampling sizes as low as 5 percent. The default sampling size for estimate is very low too. Oracle also recommends using the DBMS_STATS automatic sampling procedure. However, statistics gathered with sampled data are not reliable. The difference between an* analyze *command with the estimate at 30 percent and 50 percent (an estimate of 50 percent or more could lead to a full or compute analyze of the table anyway) is startling at times in terms of performance. Always fully compute your statistics, even if the frequency is not as high as it could be if you just sample the data.*

The following sections show you how to use the DBMS_STATS package to gather statistics.

Creating the Statistics Table

You must first invoke the DBMS_STATS package to create a table to hold the statistics. The procedure *create_stat_table* is used and three parameters are passed to it: the schema owner, the statistics table to be created, and the tablespace in which to create the table. The following example shows how to use the procedure for the hr schema. The statistics table is named stat_tab, and it is to be created in the example tablespace.

```
SQL> execute dbms_stats.create_stat_table('hr','stat_tab','example');
PL/SQL procedure successfully completed.
SQL>
```

Collecting the Schema Statistics

The DBMS_STATS package has several procedures that let you collect data at different levels. The main data collection procedures are as follows:

- *Gather_database_statistics* gathers statistics for all objects in the database.

- *Gather_schema_statistics* gathers statistics for an entire schema.

- *Gather_table_stats* gathers statistics for a table and its indexes.

- *Gather_index_stats* gathers statistics for an index.

Let's use the DBMS_STATS package to collect statistics first for a schema, and then for an individual table.

- Collecting statistics at the schema level:

```
SQL> execute dbms_stats.gather_schema_stats(ownname => 'hr');
PL/SQL procedure successfully completed.
SQL>
```

- Collecting statistics at the table level:

```
SQL> execute dbms_stats.gather_table_stats('hr','employees');
PL/SQL procedure successfully completed.
SQL>
```

Note that in both of the examples shown here, the statistics are computed for all the data in the tables and indexes. If for some reason you wish to use only a sample and not all the rows of a large table for gathering statistics, you can use the DBMS_STATS.auto_sample_size procedure, as shown here:

```
SQL> execute dbms_stats.gather_schema_stats(ownname =>
        'hr',estimate_percent => dbms_stats.auto_sample_size);
PL/SQL procedure successfully completed.
SQL>
```

Gathering System Statistics

You can use the DBMS_STATS package to provide system performance statistics to the CBO. The package collects these statistics for both CPU usage and I/O performance. You use the *gather_system_stats* procedure of the DBMS_STATS package to gather system statistics. The procedure has the following parameters:

- *Gathering_mode:* If you want to gather statistics over a specified period of time, you can use either the interval or the start/stop values for *gathering_mode*. If you don't have a specific workload, then just indicate *noworkload* and the package will collect system statistics in general.

- *Interval:* You use this parameter only if you specify *interval* as the value for the *gathering_mode* parameter.

- *Stattab:* This parameter identifies the table in which the system statistics are gathered.

- *Statown:* This is the name of the schema owner where the statistics table is located (only if it is not in the current schema).

The following example illustrates how you can collect system statistics using the DBMS_STATS package:

```
SQL> BEGIN
  2    DBMS_STATS.GATHER_SYSTEM_STATS (
  3               gathering_mode => 'interval',
  4               interval => 60,
```

```
     5                    stattab => 'stat_tab',
     6                    statown => 'HR');
     7   END;
     8   /
PL/SQL procedure successfully completed.
SQL>
```

 TIP *Make sure you have the initialization parameter* job_queue_processes *set to a positive number. If this parameter is not set, it takes the default value of 0, and your DBMS_STATS.gather_system_stats procedure will not work. You can do this dynamically, for example, by issuing the command* alter system set job_queue_processes = 20.

Using the Analyze Command

Oracle strongly recommends using the DBMS_STATS package rather than the traditional *analyze* command to gather statistics for the CBO. However, in some cases where you need to use the *validate* option, you can only use the *analyze* command. In addition, the *analyze* command is really easy to use, especially if you are gathering statistics for just a couple of tables.

Note that you can use the *estimate* or *compute* options for statistics collection. Using the *compute* option will force Oracle to use all the rows of the table or index to calculate the statistics. The *estimate* clause, contrary to what Oracle Corporation claims, doesn't always provide accurate estimates. Thus, even though the *compute* option takes much longer, try not to use *estimate* as an option for collecting statistics. Here's how you use the *analyze* command to gather statistics:

```
SQL> analyze table emp compute statistics;
Table analyzed.
SQL>
```

The *validate index* command enables you to collect detailed data about index structures. The *validate* command populates the index_stats table, which contains only one row at a time—the statistics of the last index that you analyzed with the *validate index* command.

You can use the *validate index* command to decide when to rebuild an Oracle index. When you delete rows from an Oracle table, Oracle will reuse the vacated space for newer rows. However, the corresponding deletions in index structures are only logical; the pointers to the index rows are removed, but the physical space continues to be occupied by the deleted index information. Oracle won't reuse the deleted index space unless you explicitly rebuild the index.

When indexes get very large and undergo numerous deletions, they become inefficient and take up much more storage than necessary. As indexes grow in size, new index nodes are created at the same level as a full node, thereby widening the index-tree structure, which reduces performance. In addition, a node that undergoes a high level of inserts may create new levels without other nodes doing the same, thus making the index unbalanced.

You can use the *analyze index index_name validate structure* statement to populate the index_stats table, as shown in the following example. Note how index_stats is empty before you run the *analyze … validate structure* statement. Thereafter, it will always have one row, which happens to be from the most recently run *validate structure* command.

```
SQL> select count(*) from index_stats;
  COUNT(*)
----------
        0
SQL> analyze index sh.cust_orders_bji validate structure;
Index analyzed.
SQL> select count(*) from index_stats;
  COUNT(*)
----------
        1
SQL>
```

Once you run the *validate index* or the *analyze index … validate structure* command, your index_stats table will be populated. Note that the table will hold only one row, and each time you run one of the preceding commands, the table will be repopulated.

The following query on index_stats will help you identify unbalanced indexes that need to be rebuilt:

```
SQL> select name, height,
  2  lf_rows, del_lf_rows,
  3  (del_lf_rows * 100) /lf_rows delete_pct
  4  from index_stats;
```

In the preceding example, the following is what the different columns of the index_stats table stand for:

- *Height:* This is the maximum number of levels in the index.

- *Lf_rows:* This is the number of leaf nodes in the index.

- *Del_lf_rows:* This is the number of leaf rows marked deleted as a result of deletions in table row data.

- *Delete_pct:* If this is more than 20–25 percent, the index may be a candidate for a rebuild.

Now you'll take an actual index and decide if you should rebuild it. Here are the results of the query on the index_stats table:

```
SQL>   select name, height,
  2    lf_rows, del_lf_rows,
  3    del_lf_rows * 100) /lf_rows delete_pct
  4*   from index_stats;
NAME        HEIGHT    LF_ROWS    DEL_LF_ROWS    DELETE_PCT
------      ------    -------    -----------    ----------
PERSON_PK      3      17636866   71784          .407011087
SQL>
```

The *delete_pct* value is over 40 percent, which is way above the rule of thumb of 20–25 percent, so the person_pk index is a good candidate for a rebuild. After you rebuild the index, look at the index_stats table again:

```
SQL> alter index person_pk rebuild online;
Index altered.
SQL>  select name, height,
  2    lf_rows, del_lf_rows,
  3    del_lf_rows * 100) /lf_rows delete_pct
  4* from index_stats;
NAME            HEIGHT     LF_ROWS   DEL_LF_ROWS    DELETE_PCT
----            ------    ---------  ------------   ----------

PERSON_PK          3      17565082        0              0
SQL>
```

After the person_pk index is rebuilt, the *del_lf_rows* total is 0. The total *lf_rows*, 1,7565,082, is now smaller by the number of *del_lf_rows* (71,784) that have been removed during the rebuild of the index.

Writing Efficient SQL

One of the trickiest and most satisfying aspects of a DBA's job is helping improve the quality of SQL code in the application. You can use some standard guidelines to ensure efficient SQL code. Efficient code means fast performance, and an easy way to decrease the I/O your query requires is to try to lower the number of rows that the optimizer has to examine. The optimizer is supposed to find the optimal plan based on your query. There are two problems with this. First, the optimizer will not rewrite an inefficiently written query—it only produces the execution plan for that query. Second, even if your query is efficiently written, the optimizer may not always end up producing the "best" execution plan. You have better knowledge of your application and data than the optimizer, and you can, with hints, force the optimizer to use that knowledge. The following sections cover some of the best guidelines for writing good SQL.

Efficient Where Clauses

Selective criteria in your *where* clauses can dramatically decrease the amount of data Oracle has to consider during a query. You can follow some simple principles to ensure that the structure of your SQL statements is not inherently inefficient. Your join methods may be fine, but overlooking some of these principles could doom your statement from a performance point of view.

Careful specification of where conditions can have a significant bearing on whether the optimizer will choose existing indexes. The principle of *selectivity*, the number of rows returned by a query as a percentage of the total number of rows in a table, is the key idea here. A low percentage means high selectivity and a high percentage means the reverse. Because more selective *where* clauses mean fewer

I/Os, the CBO will tend to prefer to choose those kinds of *where* clauses over others in the same query. The following example makes this clear:

```
SQL> select * from national_employees
     where ss_number = 515086789
     and city='DALLAS';
```

There are two *where* clauses in this example, but you can see that the first *where* clause that uses ss_number will require fewer I/Os. The column ss_number is the primary key and is highly selective—there is only one row with that ss_number in the entire table. The optimizer determines the selectivity of each of the two columns in the query by looking at the index statistics, which tell it how many rows in the table contain each of the two column values in the query. If neither of the columns has an index, Oracle will use full table scans of both tables to retrieve the answer to the query. If both of them have indexes, it will use the more selective and hence more efficient index on the ss_number column.

If you think that the optimizer should have used an index instead of doing a full table scan, then perform the following steps:

1. Make sure the table is being analyzed thoroughly by using the *estimate* parameter instead of the *sample* parameter.

2. Views in a query sometimes prevent the use of indexes. Check to make sure that the execution plan shows that the correct indexes are being used.

3. If you think there is heavy data skew in the table, use histograms to provide Oracle with a more accurate representation of the data distribution in the table. The CBO assumes a uniform distribution of column data. The CBO may forego the use of an index even when a column value is very selective, because the column itself is unselective in nature. Histograms help by providing the CBO with an accurate picture of the column data distribution.

4. If Oracle is still refusing to use the index, force it to do so by using an index hint, as explained in the section "Using Hints to Influence the Execution Plan" later in this chapter.

 NOTE *It isn't always obvious why Oracle doesn't use an index. For example, Oracle may not use an index because the indexed columns are part of an IN list and the consequent transformation prevents the use of an index.*

If you use a *where* clause such as *where last_name like '%MA%'*, the optimizer might just decide to skip the index and do a full scan of the table because it needs to perform a pattern match of the entire last_name column to retrieve data. The optimizer correctly figures that it will just go ahead and look up just the table, instead of having to read both the index and the table values. For example, if a table has 1,000 rows placed in 200 blocks, and you perform a full table scan assuming a *db_file_multiblock_read_count* of 8, you'll incur a total of 25 I/Os to read in the entire table. If your index has a very low selectivity, most of the index has to be read first. If your index has 40 leaf blocks and you have to read 90 percent of them to first get the indexed data, your I/O is already at 32. On top of this, you'll have to incur additional I/O to read the table values. However, a full table scan costs you only 25 I/Os, making that a far more efficient choice than using the index. Be aware that the mere existence of an index on a column doesn't guarantee that it will be used all the time.

You'll look at some important principles to make your queries more efficient in the following sections.

Using SQL Functions

If you use SQL functions—for example, the SUBSTR and INSTR, TO_DATE, and TO_NUMBER functions—in the *where* clause, the Oracle optimizer will ignore the index on that column. Make sure you use a function-based index if you must use a SQL function in the *where* clause.

Using the Right Joins

Most of your SQL statements will involve multitable joins. Often, improper table joining strategies doom a query. Here are some pointers regarding joining tables wisely:

- Using the *equijoin* leads to a more efficient query path than otherwise. Try to use equijoins wherever possible.

- Performing filtering operations early reduces the number of rows to be joined in later steps. Fop example, a *where* condition applied early reduces the row source that needs to be joined to another table. The goal is to use the table that has the most selective filter as the driving table, because this means fewer rows are passed to the next step.

- Join in the order that will produce the least amount of rows as output to the parent step.

Using the Case Statement

When you need to calculate multiple aggregates from the same table, avoid writing a separate query for each aggregate. With separate queries, Oracle will have to read the entire table for each query. It is more efficient to use the *case* statement in this case, as it will enable you to compute multiple aggregates from the table with just a single read of the table.

Efficient Subquery Execution

Subqueries perform better when you use IN rather than EXISTS. Oracle recommends using the IN clause if the subquery has the selective *where* clause. If the parent query contains the selective *where* clause, use the EXISTS clause rather than the IN clause.

Using Where Instead of Having

Wherever possible, use the *where* clause instead of the *having* clause. The *where* clause will restrict the number of rows retrieved at the very outset. The *having* clause will force the retrieval of a lot more rows than necessary. It then also incurs the additional overhead of sorting and summing.

Minimizing Table Lookups

One of the primary mottos of query writing is "Visit the data as few times as possible." This means getting rid of SQL that repeatedly accesses a table for different column values. Use multicolumn updates instead.

Using Hints to Influence the Execution Plan

The assumption that underlies the use of the CBO is that the optimizer knows best. That is, by evaluating the various statistics, the CBO will come to the best decision in terms of choosing the optimal execution plan. However, the optimizer is based on rules, and a good application developer has knowledge about the application and data that the CBO can't exploit. You can provide *hints* to the optimizer to override the CBO's execution plans. For example, if you know that a certain index is more selective than another, you can force Oracle to use that index by providing the hint in your query.

Hints can alter the join method, join order, or access path. You can also provide hints to parallelize the SQL statement operations. The following are some of the common hints that you can use in SQL statements:

- *All_rows:* The all_rows hint instructs Oracle to optimize throughput (i.e., minimize total cost), not the response time of the statement.

- *First_rows (n):* The first_rows (n) hint dictates that Oracle return the first *n* rows quickly. Low response time is the goal of this hint.

- *Full:* The full hint requires that a full scan be done on the table, ignoring any indexes that may be present. You would want to do this when you have reason to believe that using an index in this case will be inefficient compared to a full table scan. To force Oracle to do a full table scan, you use the full hint.

- *Ordered:* This hint forces the join order for the tables in the query.

- *Index:* This hint forces the use of an index scan, even if the optimizer was going to ignore the indexes and do a full table scan for some reason.

- *Index_ffs:* An index fast full scan (index_ffs) hint forces a fast full scan of an index, just as if you did a full table scan that scans several blocks at a time. Index_ffs will scan all the blocks in an index using multiblock I/O, the size of which is determined by the *db_file_multiblock_read_count* parameter. And like a full table scan, you can also parallelize an index_ffs hint and it is generally preferable to a full table scan.

Selecting the Best Join Method

Choose a join method based on how many rows you expect to be returned from the join. The optimizer generally tries to choose the ideal join condition, but it may not do so for various reasons. It's up to you to see what join method the optimizer will adopt and change it if necessary. The following guidelines will help you when you're analyzing output produced by an explain plan.

Avoiding Cartesian Joins

Cartesian joins usually aren't the result of intentional planning; rather, they happen due to logical mistakes in the query. Cartesian joins are produced when your joins don't have any *where* clauses. If you're joining several tables, make sure that each table in the join is referenced by a *where* condition. Even if the tables being joined are small, avoid Cartesian joins because they're very inefficient. For example, if the table employee has 2,000 rows and table dept has 100 rows, a Cartesian join of employee and dept will have 2,000 * 100 = 200,000 rows.

Nested Loops

If you're joining small subsets of data, the nested loop (NL) method is ideal. If you're returning fewer than, say, 10,000 rows, the NL join may be the right join method. If the optimizer is using hash joins or full table scans, force it to use the NL join method by using the following hint:

Example: Select /*+ USE_NL (TableA, TableB) */

Hash Joins

If the join will produce large subsets of data or a substantial proportion of a table is going to be joined, use the hash join hint if the optimizer indicates it is not going to use it.

Example: Select /* USE_HASH */

Merge Join

If the tables in the join are being joined with an inequality condition (not an equijoin), the merge join method is ideal.

Example: Select /*+ USE_MERGE (TableA, TableB) */

Using Bitmap Join Indexes

Bitmap join indexes (BJIs) *prestore* the results of a join between two tables in an index, and thus do away with the need for an expensive runtime join operation. BJIs are specially designed for data warehouse star schemas, but any application can use them as long as there is a primary key/foreign key relationship between the two tables.

Typically, in a data warehouse setting, the primary key will be in a dimension table and the fact table will have the foreign key. For example, customer_id in the customer dimension table will be the primary key, and customer_id in the fact table will be the foreign key. Using a BJI, you can avoid a join between these two tables because the rows that would result from the join are already stored in the BJI. Let's look at a simple example of a BJI here.

Say you expect to use the following SQL statement frequently in your application:

```
SQL> Select sum(s.quantity)
     from sales s, customers c
     where s.customer_id = c.customer_id
     and c.city = 'DALLAS';
```

In this example, table sales is the fact table with all the details about product sales and table customers is a dimension table with information about your customers. The column cust_id acts as the primary key for the table customers and as the foreign key for the table sales, so the table meets the basic requirement for creating a BJI.

The following statement will create the BJI. Notice line 2, where you are specifying the index on sales (c.cust_id). This is how you get the join information to place in the new BJI. Because table sales is partitioned, you're using the clause *local* in line 5 to create a locally partitioned index.

```
SQL> create BITMAP INDEX cust_orders_BJI
  2  on sales (c.cust_id)
  3  from sales s, customers c
  4  where c.cust_id = s.cust_id
  5  LOCAL
  6* tablespace users;
Index created.
SQL>
```

You can confirm that the intended index has been created with the help of the following query. The first index is the new BJI index you just created.

```
SQL> select index_name, index_type, join_index from user_indexes
  2* where table_name='SALES';
INDEX_NAME                      INDEX_TYPE                  JOI
------------------------------- --------------------------- ---
CUST_ORDERS_BJI                 BITMAP                      YES
SALES_CHANNEL_BIX               BITMAP                      NO
SALES_CUST_BIX                  BITMAP                      NO
3 rows selected.
 SQL>
```

Being a bitmap index, of course, the new BJI will be extremely efficient space usage–wise. However, the real benefit of using this index is that when you need to find out the sales for a given city, you don't need to join the sales and customers tables. You only need to use the sales table and the new BJI that holds the join information already.

Selecting the Best Join Order

When your SQL statement includes a join between two or more tables, the order in which you join the tables is extremely important. The driving table in a join is the first table that comes after the *where* clause. The driving table in the join should contain the filter that will eliminate the most rows. Choose the join order that will give you the least number of rows to be joined to the other tables. That is, if you are joining three tables, the one with the more restrictive filter should be joined first to one of the other two tables. Compare various join orders and pick the best one after you consider the number of rows returned by each join order.

Indexing Strategy

An index is a data structure that takes the value of one or more columns of a table (the key) and returns all rows (or the requested columns in a row) with that value of the column quickly. The efficiency of an index comes from the fact that it lets you find necessary rows without having to scan all the rows of a table. As a result, indexes are more efficient in general, because they need fewer disk I/Os than if you had to scan the table.

 NOTE *For a quick summary of indexing guidelines, please refer to the section "Guidelines for Creating Indexes" in Chapter 7.*

Developers are content when an explain plan indicates that a query was using indexes. However, there's more to query optimization than simply using an index for speeding up your queries. If you don't use good indexes, your queries could slow down the database significantly. Important things to consider are whether you have the right indexes or even if the index is necessary in a certain query. In the next sections you'll look at some of the issues you should consider regarding the use of indexes.

 CAUTION *A common problem is that an index that performs admirably during development and testing phases simply won't perform well on a production database. Often, this is due to the much larger amounts of data in the "real" system than in the development system. Ideally, you should develop and test queries on an identical version of the production database.*

When to Index

You need to index tables only if you think your queries will be selecting a small portion of the table. If your query is retrieving rows that are greater 10 or 15 percent of the total rows in the table, you may not need an index. Remember that using an index will prevent a full table scan, and so it is inherently a faster means to traverse a table's rows. However, each time you want to access a particular row in an indexed table, Oracle will have to first look up the column referenced in your query in its index. From the index, Oracle obtains the ROWID of the row, which is the logical address of its location on disk.

If you choose to enforce uniqueness of the rows in a table, you can use a *primary index* on that table. By definition, a column that serves as a primary index must be non-null and unique. In addition to the primary index, you can have several *secondary indexes*. For example, the attribute last_name may serve as a primary index. However, if most of your queries include the city column, you many choose to index the city column as well. Thus, the addition of secondary indexes would enhance query performance. However, there is a cost associated with maintaining additional secondary indexes. In addition to the additional disk space required for large secondary indexes, remember that all inserts and updates to the table require that the indexes also be updated.

If your system involves a large number of inserts and deletes, understand that too many indexes may be detrimental, because each DML would result in changes in the table and its indexes. Therefore, an OLTP-oriented database ought to keep its indexes to a minimum. A data warehouse, on the other hand, can have a much larger number of indexes, because there is no penalty to be paid, as the data warehouse is a purely query-oriented database, not a transactional database.

What to Index

There are no hard-and-fast rules on what columns in a table should be indexed, but you can safely use the following guidelines. Your goal should be to use as few indexes as possible to meet your performance criteria. There is a price to be paid for having too many indexes, especially in OLTP databases. Each *insert, update,* and *delete* statement causes changes to be made to the underlying indexes of a table and can slow down an application in some cases. The following are some broad guidelines you can follow to make sure your indexes help the application instead of hindering it:

- Index columns with high selectivity. "Selectivity" here means the percentage of rows in a table with a certain value. High selectivity, as you learned earlier in this chapter, means that there are few rows with identical values.

- Index all important foreign keys.

- Index all predicate columns.

- Index columns used in table joins.

Proper indexing of tables involves careful consideration of the type of application you are running, the number of DML operations, and the response time expectations. Here are some additional tips that can aid you in selecting appropriate indexes for your application:

- Try to avoid indexing columns that consist of long character strings, unless you're using the Oracle Context feature.

- Wherever possible, use *index-only plans,* meaning a query that can be satisfied completely by just the data in the index alone. This requires that you pay attention to the most common queries and create any necessary composite indexes (indexes that include more than one column attribute).

- Use secondary indexes on columns frequently involved in *order by* and *group by* operations, as well as sorting operations such as *union* or *distinct.*

Using Appropriate Index Types

The B-tree index (sometimes referred to as the B*tree index) is the default or normal type of Oracle index. You're probably going to use it for almost all the indexes in a typical OLTP application. Although you could use the B-tree index for all your index needs, you'll get better performance by using more specialized indexes for certain kinds of data. Your knowledge of the type of data you have and the nature of your application should determine the index type. In the next few sections, you'll see several alternative types of indexes.

Bitmap Indexes

Bitmap indexes are ideal for column data that has a *low cardinality,* which means that the indexed column has very few distinct values. The index is compact in size and performs better than the B-tree index for these types of data. However, the bitmap index is going to cause some problems if there is a lot of DML going on in the column being indexed.

Index-Organized Tables

Index-organized tables (IOTs) are explained in Chapter 7. The traditional Oracle tables are called heap-organized tables, wherein data is stored in the order in which it is inserted. Indexes enable fast access to the rows. However, indexes also mean more storage and the need for accessing both the index and the table rows for most queries (unless the query can be selected just by the indexed columns themselves). IOTs placed all the table data in its primary key index, thus eliminating the need for a separate index.

IOTs are actually more akin to B-tree indexes (the regular table and index structure in Oracle) than tables. The data in an IOT is sorted, and rows are stored in primary key order. This type of organization of row values gives you faster access in addition to saving space. To limit the size of the row that is stored in the B-tree leaf blocks, IOTs use an overflow area to store infrequently accessed nonkey columns, which leads to lower space consumption in the B-tree. For a quick summary of the benefits of using Oracle9*i*'s IOTs, please read the article "Oracle9*i* IOTs—Faster, More Available and Scalable Than Ever" (http://otn.oracle.com/products/oracle9i/daily/may08.html).
Another good resource is "Index-Organized Tables Technical Whitepaper" (http://otn.oracle.com/products/oracle9i/pdf/iot_twp.pdf).

Concatenated Indexes

Concatenated or composite indexes are indexes that include more than one column and are excellent for improving the selectivity of the *where* predicates. Even in cases where the selectivity of the individual columns is poor, concatenating the index will improve selectivity. If the concatenated index contains all the columns in the *where* list, you're saved the trouble of looking up the table, thus reducing your I/O. However, you have to pay particular attention to the order of the columns in the composite index. If the *where* clause doesn't specify the leading column of the concatenated index first, Oracle may not use the index at all.

Up until recently, Oracle used a composite index only if the leading column of the index was used in the *where* clause or if the entire index was scanned. Oracle 9.2 introduces the new *index skip scan* feature, which lets Oracle use a composite index even when the leading column is not used in the query. Obviously, this is a nice feature that eliminates many full table scans that would have resulted in previous versions of Oracle. For a quick summary of the index skip scan feature, please read the Oracle paper found at http://otn.oracle.com/products/oracle9i/daily/aug19.html.

Function-Based Indexes

As you know by now, if you have functions on any of your columns in the *where* predicate, Oracle will ignore any indexes on those columns. A better strategy is to use function-based indexes, which will enable you to safely index functions. Function-based indexes are efficient in frequently used statements that involve functions on columns. For example, the following function-based index will let you search for people based on the last_name column (in all uppercase letters):

```
SQL create index upper_lastname_idxidx ON employees (UPPER(last_name));
```

If you wish to use function-based indexes, you need to set the initialization parameter *query_rewrite_enable=true* (the default is *false*). In addition, you need to set the value of the initialization parameter *query_rewrite_integrity* to its default value of *enforced*, so Oracle can use function-based indexes to evaluate SQL expressions.

Reverse Key Indexes

If you're having performance issues in a database with a large number of inserts, you should consider using reverse key indexes. These indexes are ideal for insert-heavy applications, although they suffer from the drawback that they can't be used in index range scans. A reverse key index looks like this:

Index value	Reverse_Key Index Value
9001	1009
9002	2009
9003	3009
9004	4009

When you're dealing with columns that sequentially increase, the reverse key indexes provide an efficient way to distribute the index values more evenly and thus improve performance.

Partitioned Indexing Strategy

As you saw in Chapter 7, partitioned tables can have several types of indexes on them. Partitioned indexes can be local or global. In addition, they can be prefixed or nonprefixed indexes. The following is a very brief summary of important partitioned indexes:

- *Local partitioned indexes* correspond to the underlying partitions of the table. If you add a new partition to the table, you also add a new partition to the local partitioned index.

- *Global partitioned indexes* do not correspond to the partitions of the local table.

- *Prefixed indexes* are partitioned on a left prefix on the index columns.

- *Nonprefixed indexes* are indexes that are not partitioned on the left prefix of the index columns.

In general, local partitioned indexes are a good indexing strategy if the table has been indexed primarily for access reasons. If your queries include columns that aren't a part of the partitioned table's key, global prefixed indexes are a good choice. Using global prefixed indexes is a good indexing strategy if the table has been indexed primarily for access reasons. Local nonfixed indexes are good if you're using parallel query operations.

Using the OEM Index Tuning Wizard

When you change your applications or the response time for queries is slow, you can use OEM's Index Tuning Wizard to proactively tune your indexes. The Index Tuning Wizard creates virtual indexes and tests these potential indexes before you actually create them. Note that you can only access the Index Tuning Wizard on a console displayed directly on your server, not through a Web browser. If you're using the Web-based console, you can't access the Index Tuning Wizard.

If you're using the OEM console on your Windows server, you can access the index wizard by selecting Tools ➤ Tuning Pack ➤ Index Tuning Wizard. You can access the Index Tuning Wizard by selecting Programs ➤ OEM ➤ Enterprise Manager Packs ➤ Tuning ➤ SQL Analyze.

Once you're in the SQL Analyze Wizard GUI, you first enter a typical SQL statement that involves the table for which you're currently evaluating indexes. From the icons, select Index Tuning Wizard. This wizard will take you through a couple of steps where you're asked to make some basic choices about the type of index you want to test. The Index Tuning Wizard will run your query through the CBO and show you the explain plans for your SQL query before and after the creation of the new "virtual" index.

Figure 18-1 shows the Explain Plan Comparison screen of the Index Tuning Wizard.

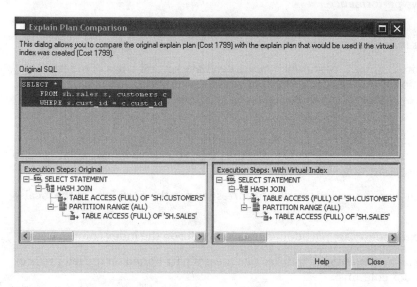

Figure 18-1. Comparing explain plans with the Index Tuning Wizard

From the comparison, you can see that the projected cost improvement, if any, from using the new index(es). You can see from the comparison that the cost of the query with or without the new indexes would be the same at 1799. Thus, you can conclude that there is no benefit to adding any new indexes to the table in question.

Monitoring Index Utilization

You may have several indexes on a table, but that in itself is no guarantee that they're being used in queries. If you aren't using indexes, you might as well get rid of them, as they just take up space and time to manage them. Oracle9i provides the V$OBJECT_USAGE view, which provides index utilization information. Here's the structure of the V$OBJECT_USAGE view:

```
SQL> desc v$object_usage
    Name                 Null?         Type
    ------------         --------      -----------
    INDEX_NAME           NOT NULL      VARCHAR2(30)
    TABLE_NAME           NOT NULL      VARCHAR2(30)
    MONITORING                         VARCHAR2(3)
    USED                               VARCHAR2(3)
    START_MONITORING                   VARCHAR2(19)
    END_MONITORING                     VARCHAR2(19)
SQL>
```

Removing Unnecessary Indexes

The idea of removing indexes may seem surprising in the beginning, but you aren't being asked to remove just any index on a table. By all means, keep the indexes that are being used and that are also selective. If an index is being used but it's a very nonselective index, you may be better off in most cases getting rid of it, because the index will slow down the DML operations without significantly increasing performance. In addition, unnecessary indexes just waste space in your system.

Using Similar SQL Statements

As you know by now, reusing already parsed statements will lead to a performance improvement, besides conserving the use of the shared pool area of the SGA. The catch however, is that the SQL statements must be identical in all respects, white space and all.

Reducing SQL Overhead via "Inline" Functions

Inline stored functions can help improve the performance of your SQL statements. Here's a simple example to demonstrate how you can use an inline function to reduce the overhead of a SQL statement. The following code chunk shows the initial SQL statement without the inline function:

```
SQL> Select r.emp_id,
    e.name, r.em>p_type,t.type_des,
    count(*)
    from employees e, emp_type t, emp_records r
    where r.emp_id = e.emp_id
    and r.emp_type = t.emp_type
    group by r. emp_id, e.name, r.emp_type, t.emp_des;
```

You can improve the performance of the preceding statement by using an inline function call. First, you create a couple of functions, which you can later on call from within your SQL statement. The first function is called select_emp_desc, and it fetches the employee description if you provide emp_type as an input parameter. Here's how you create this function:

```
SQL> create or replace function select_emp_desc (type IN) number)
    return varchar2
  2  As
  3  desc varchar2(30);
  4  cursor a1 is
  5   select emp_desc from emp_type
  6   where emp_type = type;
  7   begin
  8   open a1;
  9   fetch a1 into desc;
 10   close a1;
 11  return (NVL(desc,'?'));
 12  end;
 13* /
Function created.
SQL>
```

Next, create another function, select_emp, that will return the full name of an employee once you pass it employee_id as a parameter:

```
SQL> create or replace function select_emp (emp IN number) return
    varchar2
  2  as
  3  emp_name varchar2(30);
  4  cursor a1 is
  5  select name from employees
  6  where employee_id = emp;
  7  begin
  8  open a1;
  9          fetch a1 into emp_name;
 10  close a1;
 11  return (NVL(emp_name,'?'));
 12  end;
 13*/
Function created.
SQL>
```

Now that you have both of your functions, it's a simple matter to call them from within a SQL statement, as the following code shows:

```
SQL> select r.emp_id, select_emp(r.emp_id),
  2  r.emp_type, select_emp_desc(r.emp_type),
  3  count(*)
  4  from emp_records  r
  5* group by r.emp_id, r.emp_type;
SQL>
```

Using Bind Variables

The parsing stage of query processing consumes resources, and ideally you should parse just once and use the same parsed version of the statement for repeated executions. Parsing is a much more expensive operation than executing the statement. You should use bind variables in SQL statements instead of literal values to reduce the amount of parsing in the database. Bind variables should be identical in terms of their name, data type, and length. Failure to use bind variables leads to heavy use of the shared pool area and, more often than not, contention for latches and a general slowing down of the database when a large number of queries are being processed. Sometimes your application may not be changeable into a form where bind variables are used.

In Chapter 19, you'll see how to use new Oracle configuration parameters to force statements that fail to use bind variables to do so.

Avoiding Improper Use of Views

Views have several benefits to offer, but faster performance may not necessarily be one of them. Views are useful when you want to present only the relevant portions of a table to an application or a user. Whenever you query a view, it has to be instantiated at that time. Because the view is just a SQL query, it has to perform this instantiation if you want to query the view again. If your query uses joins on views, it could lead to a substantial time to execute the query.

Avoiding Unnecessary Full Table Scans

Full table scans can occur sometimes, even when you have indexed a table. The use of functions on indexed columns is a good example when you unwittingly can cause Oracle to skip indexes and go to a full table scan. You should avoid the use of inequality and the greater than or equal to predicates, as they may also bypass indexes.

NOTE *For an excellent summary of Oracle's approach to query opti-mization, please refer to the paper "Query Optimization in Oracle9i"* (http://otn.oracle.com/products/bi/pdf/o9i_optimization_twp.pdf).

How the DBA Can Help Improve SQL Processing

Performance tuning involves the optimization of SQL code and the calibration of the resources used by Oracle. SQL tuning is generally performed by the developers, and the DBA merely facilitates their tuning efforts by setting the relevant initialization parameters, turning tracing on, and so on. Nevertheless, the DBA can implement several strategies to help improve SQL processing in his or her database.

In some cases, you and the developers might be working together to optimize the application. What if you can't really modify the code, as is the case when you're dealing with packaged applications? Or what if even the developers are aware that major code changes are needed to improve performance, but time and budget constraints make the immediate revamping of the application difficult? There are several ways you can help without having to change the code itself.

It's common for DBAs to bemoan the fact that the response times are slow because of poorly written SQL. I've heard this in every place I've worked, so I assume this is a universal complaint of DBAs who have to manage the consequences of bad code. Well, my attitude in these matters is a practical one: Assuming that the application is poorly written, what can I, the DBA, do right now to improve performance? A perfectly designed and coded application with all the right joins and smart indexing strategies would be nice, but that perfect state of affairs more often than not doesn't happen. The theory of the "next best" option dictates that you should do everything you can to optimize within the limitations imposed by the application design.

That said, let's look at some of the important ways in which you can help improve query performance in an application, even when you can't change the code right away.

Using Partitioned Tables

Partitioned tables usually lead to tremendous improvements in performance, and they're very easy to administer. By partitioning a table into several subpartitions, you are in essence limiting the amount of data that needs to be examined to satisfy your queries. If you have very large tables, running into tens of millions of rows, consider partitioning the tables.

There are four different partitioning schemes available to you in Oracle9*i*, and they are explained in Chapter 7. You can index partitioned tables in a variety of ways, depending on the needs of application. Partition maintenance is also easy, and it is well worth the additional effort when you consider the tremendous gains partitioned tables provide.

Using Compression Techniques

The Oracle9*i* database lets you use *table compression* to compress tables, table partitions, and materialized views. Table compression helps reduce space requirements for the tables and enhances query performance. Oracle compresses the tables by eliminating the duplicate values in a data block and replacing those values with algorithms to re-create the data when necessary. The table compression technique is especially suitable for data warehouse and OLAP databases, but OLTP databases can also use the technique fruitfully. The larger the table that is compressed, the more benefits you'll achieve with this technique. For a quick review of this feature, please see the whitepaper "Table Compression in Oracle9*i* Release 2" (http://otn.oracle.com/products/bi/pdf/o9ir2_compression_twp.pdf). Here's a simple table compression statement:

```
SQL>  create table sales_compress
  2  compress
  3* as select * from sh.sales;
Table created.
SQL>
```

You can also use *index key compression* to compress the primary key columns of IOTs. This compression will not only save you storage space, but also enhance query performance. The way index compression works is by removing duplicate column values from the index.

To compress an index, all you have to do is add the keyword *compress* after the index creation statement, as shown here:

```
SQL> create index item_product_x
  2  on order_items(product_id)
  3  tablespace order_items_indx_01
  4* compress;
Index created.
SQL>
```

Perform some tests to confirm the space savings and the time savings during the creation statements. Later, you can test query performance to measure the improvement.

For an interesting explanation of how table compression works and some TPC performance benchmarks, please read the excellent paper by Meikel Poess of the Oracle Corporation titled "Table Compression in Oracle9*i* Release 2: A Performance Analysis," which is available at

http://otn.oracle.com/products/bi/pdf/o9ir2_compression_performance_twp.pdf.

Using Materialized Views

If you're dealing with large amounts of data, you should seriously consider using materialized views to improve response time. *Materialized views* are objects with data in them—usually summary data from the underlying tables. Expensive joins can be done beforehand and saved in the materialized view. When users query the underlying table, Oracle will automatically rewrite the query to access the materialized view instead of the tables.

Materialized views reduce the need for several complex queries because you can precalculate aggregates with them. Joins between large tables and data aggregation are very expensive in terms of resource usage, and materialized views significantly reduce the response time for complex queries on large tables. If you aren't sure which materialized views to create, not to worry—you can use the DBMS_OLAP package supplied by Oracle to get recommendations on ideal materialized views. For a fuller discussion of how to create and use materialized views in Oracle9*i*, please refer to the "Using Materialized Views" section in Chapter 7.

Using Stored Outlines to Stabilize the CBO

As I mentioned earlier in this chapter, the CBO doesn't always use the same execution strategies. Changes in Oracle versions or changes in the initialization parameters concerning memory allocation may force the CBO to modify its plans. For example, changing the values of initialization parameters such as *sort_area_size* and *bitmap_merge_area_size* may sometimes cause Oracle to change its access paths. What if you like an existing execution plan and don't want the CBO to change it on its own? You can use Oracle's plan stability feature to ensure that the execution plan remains stable regardless of any changes in the database environment.

The plan stability feature uses stored outlines to preserve the current execution plans, even if the statistics and optimizer mode are changed. The CBO will use the same execution plan with identical access paths each time you execute the same query. The catch is that the query must be exactly identical each time if you want Oracle to use the stored plan.

On the face of it, the stored outline feature doesn't seem impressive. Let's consider a simple example to see how stored outline could be useful in a real production environment.

CAUTION *When you use stored outlines to preserve a currently efficient execution plan, you're basically limiting Oracle's capability to dynamically modify its execution plans based on changes to the database environment and changes to the statistics. Make sure you use this feature for valid purposes, such as maintaining similar plans for distributed applications.*

Suppose you have a system that is running satisfactorily and, due to a special need, you add an index to a table. The addition of the new index could unwittingly modify the execution plans of the CBO, and your previously fast-running SQL queries may slow down. It could conceivably take a lot of effort, testing, and time to fix the problem by changing the original query. However, if you had created stored outlines, these kinds of problems would not arise. Once Oracle creates an outline, it stores it until you remove it. In the next section you'll examine how to implement planned stability in a database.

When to Use Outlines

Outlines are very useful when you're planning migrations from one version of Oracle to another. The CBO could behave differently in between versions, and you can cut your risk down by using stored outlines to preserve the application's present performance. You can also use them when you're upgrading your applications. Outlines ensure that the execution paths the queries used in a test instance will successfully carry over to the production instance.

Stored plan outlines can be public, in which case all users can use them. If, on the other hand, they're private, only selected users can use them. Unless you remove them explicitly, all stored outlines are stored permanently in the data dictionary.

Stored outlines are especially useful when the users of an application have information about the environment that the Oracle CBO doesn't possess. By enabling the direct editing of stored outlines, Oracle9*i* lets you tune SQL queries without changing the underlying application. This is especially useful when you're dealing with packaged applications where you can't get at the source code.

Implementing Plan Stability

Implementing plan stability is a simple matter. You have to ensure that the following initialization parameters are consistent in all the environments. The value of the three following parameters must be set to *true*:

- *Query_rewrite_enabled*

- *Star_transformation_enabled*

- *Optimizer_features_enable*

Creating Outlines

The outlines themselves are managed through the DBMS_OUTLN and DBMS_OUTLN_EDIT Oracle packages. To create outlines for all your current SQL queries, you simple set the initialization parameter *create_stored_outlines* to *true*.

You must have noticed a user called OUTLN, who is part of the database when it is created. The OUTLN user owns the stored outlines in the database. The outlines are stored in the table OL$. Listing 18-1 shows the structure of the OL$ table.

Listing 18-1. The OL$ Table

```
SQL> desc OL$
 Name               Null?        Type
 -------------------- ------------ ------
 OL_NAME                          VARCHAR2(30)
 SQL_TEXT                         LONG
 TEXTLEN                          NUMBER
 SIGNATURE                        RAW(16)
 HASH_VALUE                       NUMBER
 HASH_VALUE2                      NUMBER
 CATEGORY                         VARCHAR2(30)
 VERSION                          VARCHAR2(64)
 CREATOR                          VARCHAR2(30)
 TIMESTAMP                        DATE
 FLAGS                            NUMBER
 HINTCOUNT                        NUMBER
 SPARE1                           NUMBER
 SPARE2                           VARCHAR2(1000)
SQL>
```

The sql_text column has the SQL statement that is outlined. In addition to the OL$ table, the user OUTLN uses the OL$HINTS and OL$NODES tables to manage stored outlines.

Create a special tablespace for the user OUTLN and the tables OL$, OL$HINTS, and OL$NODES. By default, they are created in the System tablespace. After you create a new tablespace for user OUTLN, you can use the export/import utilities to move the tables.

Creating Outlines at the Instance Level

If you want outlines for all the SQL statements to be stored automatically, make the following changes in your initialization file, init.ora:

```
Create_Stored_Outlines=TRUE
```

You can also have Oracle create stored outlines for the entire database by issuing the following command:

```
SQL> alter system set create_stored_outlines = true;
System altered.
SQL>
```

Creating Outlines for Specific Statements

You can create outlines for a specific statement or a set of statements by altering the session or system in the following manner:

```
SQL> alter session set create_stored_outlines = true;
Session altered.
SQL>
```

Any statements you issue after the *alter session* statement is processed have outlines stored for them.

If you want to create a stored outline for a specific SQL statement, you can do so by using the *create outline* statement. The user issuing this command must have the create outline privilege. The following set of statements show to create and drop a simple outline for a select operation on table employees:

```
SQL>  create outline test_outline
  2* on select employee_id,last_name from hr.employees;
Outline created.
SQL> drop outline test_outline;
Outline dropped.
SQL>
```

Using the Stored Outlines

After you create the stored outlines, Oracle won't automatically start using them. You have to use the *alter session* or *alter system* command *use_stored_outlines* to enable the use of the stored outlines, as shown here:

```
SQL> alter system set use_stored_outlines=true;
System altered.
SQL>
```

Editing Stored Outlines

What if you, the DBA, *know* that there's a better access path than what's stored in a certain plan outline? You can easily change the stored access paths while using the plan stability feature. You can use either the DBMS_OUTLN_EDIT package or OEM to perform the changes. Chapter 20 shows you how to use the DBMS_OUTLN_EDIT package to modify stored outlines. The next section discusses how to use OEM's Outline Manager, which includes the capability to edit and modify stored outlines.

Using the OEM Outline Manager

Instead of creating outline manually, you can use OEM's Outline Manager. You can access the Outline Manager by selecting Tools ➤ Tuning Pack ➤ Outline Management from the OEM console menu. The first screen you'll see is the view shown in Figure 18-2. There are no user created outlines in this figure, with outlines owned by the user SYS being the only outlines in the database at first.

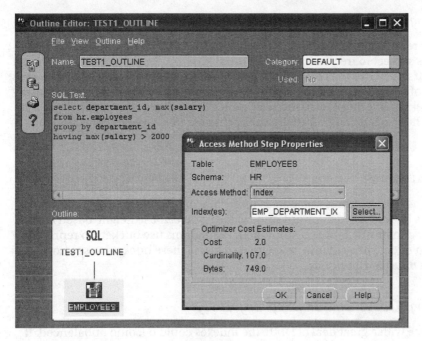

Figure 18-2. Using the OEM Outline Manager

In the Outline Management screen, you can use the icons shown on the left to delete, edit, or refresh stored outlines. When you click the Create icon, an Outline Editor screen will pop up in which you can enter the text of your new outline. You can access the Outline Editor from this window, which will enable you to modify stored outlines. You can change access paths and the indexes you want the optimizer to use. The outline management feature of the OEM makes it easy to create and manage outlines without fuss.

Using Parallel Execution

Parallel execution of statements can make SQL statements run in a shorter period of time, and it's especially suitable for large warehouse type databases. You can set the parallel option at the database or table level. If you increase the degree of parallelism of a table, Oracle could decide to more full table scans instead of using an index, because the cost of a full table scan may now be lower than the cost of an index scan. If you want to use parallel operations in an OLTP environment, make sure you have enough processors on your machine so the CPU does not become a bottleneck.

Other DBA Tasks

The DBA must perform certain tasks regularly to optimize the performance of the application. Some of these tasks fall under the routine administrative chores of the DBA. The following sections cover some of the important DBA tasks pertaining to performance tuning.

Refreshing Statistics Frequently

Frequently refreshing statistics is extremely important if you're using the CBO and your data is subject to frequent changes.

How often you run the DBMS_STATS package to collect statistics depends on the nature of your data. For applications with a moderate number of DML transactions, a weekly gathering of statistics will suffice. If you have reason to believe that your data changes substantially daily, then schedule the statistics collection on a daily basis.

Using Histograms

Normally, the CBO assumes that data is uniformly distributed in a table. If the table data is heavily skewed toward some values, you can use height-based histograms for a more efficient access method. Histograms use buckets to represent distribution of data in a column, and Oracle can use these buckets to see how skewed the data distribution is.

Rebuilding Tables and Indexes Regularly

In a database with a great deal of DML, the indexes could become unbalanced. It is important to regularly rebuild such indexes so queries can run faster. You may want to rebuild an index to change its storage characteristics or to consolidate it and reduce fragmentation. Use the *alter index ... rebuild* statement, because the old index will be accessible while you are re-creating it. (The alternative is to drop the index and re-create it.)

When you rebuild the indexes, include the *compute statistics* statement so you don't have to gather statistics after the rebuild. Of course, if you have a 24/7 environment, you can use the *alter index ... rebuild online* statement so that user access to the database won't be affected. Just make sure that your tables aren't going through a lot of DML operations while you're rebuilding online, because the online feature may not work as advertised under such circumstances, and it might even end up unexpectedly preventing simultaneous updates by users.

Caching Small Tables in Memory

If the application doesn't reuse a table's data for a long period, it might be aged out of the SGA and need to be read by from disk. You can safely pin small tables in the shared pool by using the following statement:

```
SQL> alter table hr.employees cache;
Table altered.
SQL>
```

SQL Performance Tuning Tools

SQL performance tuning tools are extremely important, both for development databases and production instances. Developers can use the tools to examine good execution strategies, and in a production database they are highly useful for reactive tuning. The tools can give you a good estimate of resource use by queries. The basic SQL tools are the Explain Plan, SQL Trace, and Autotrace utilities. The output of the Explain Plan tool goes into a table, usually called plan_table, where it can be queried to determine the planned execution plan of statements. In addition, you can use GUI tools, such as OEM or TOAD, to get the execution plan for your SQL statements without any fuss. In OEM, you can view the explain statements from the following locations:

- OEM Instance Management folder

- TopSessions charts

- TopSQL charts

- Performance Manager Overview charts

Using the Explain Plan

The Explain Plan facility helps you tune SQL by letting you see the execution plan for various formulations of a SQL query. During SQL tuning, you may have to rewrite your queries and experiment with optimizer hints. The Explain Plan tool is great for this experimentation, as it immediately lets you know how the query will perform with each change in the code. Because the utility gives you the execution plan without actually executing the code, you save yourself from having to run untuned software to see if the changes were beneficial or not.

A walk-through of an explain plan output takes you through the steps (to be) undertaken by the CBO to execute the SQL statement. The Explain Plan tool indicates clearly whether the optimizer is actually using an index, for example. It also tells you the order in which tables are being joined and helps you understand your query performance. More precisely, an explain plan output shows the following:

- The tables used in the query and the order in which they were accessed.

- The operations performed on the output of each step of the plan. For example, these could be sorting and aggregation operations.

- The specific access and join methods used for each table mentioned in the SQL statement.

- The cost of each operation.

Prerequisites for Using the Explain Plan

Before you can start using the Explain Plan tool to help identify the best execution plan, you have to take care of a couple of preliminaries. First, make sure utlxplan.sql, which is located in the $ORACLE_HOME/rdbms/admin directory, has been run in the database. The script will, among other things, create a table called plan_table, where the output of the Explain Plan utility will be stored for your viewing. You are free to rename this table.

Creating the Explain Plan

To create an explain plan for any SQL data manipulation language statement, you use the statement shown in Listing 18-2.

Listing 18-2. Creating the Explain Plan

```
SQL> explain plan
  2  set statement_id = 'test1'
  3  into plan_table
  4  for select p.product_id,i.quantity_on_hand
  5  from oe.inventories i,
  6  oe.product_descriptions p,
  7  oe.warehouses w
  8  where p.product_id=i.product_id
  9  and i.quantity_on_hand > 250
 10* and w.warehouse_id = i.warehouse_id;
Explained.
SQL>
```

Producing the Explain Plan

You can't select the columns out of plan_table easily because of the hierarchical nature of relationships among the columns. Listing 18-3 shows the code that you can use so the explain plan output is printed in a form that is readable and shows clearly how the execution plan for the statement looks.

Listing 18-3. Producing the Explain Plan

```
SQL>  SELECT lpad(' ',level-1)||operation||' '||options||' '||
  2          object_name "Plan"
  3  FROM plan_table
  4  CONNECT BY prior id = parent_id
  5          AND prior statement_id = statement_id
  6  START WITH id = 0 AND statement_id = '&1'
  7  ORDER BY id;
Enter value for 1: test1
old   6:    START WITH id = 0 AND statement_id = '&1'
new   6:    START WITH id = 0 AND statement_id = 'test1'
Plan
------------------------------------------------------------------------
SELECT STATEMENT
 HASH JOIN
  NESTED LOOPS
   TABLE ACCESS FULL INVENTORIES
   INDEX UNIQUE SCAN WAREHOUSES_PK
  INDEX FAST FULL SCAN PRD_DESC_PK
6 rows selected.
SQL>
```

Interpreting the Explain Plan Output

Reading explain plans is somewhat confusing in the beginning, and it helps to remember these simple principles:

- Each step in the plan will return output in the form of a set of rows to the "parent" step.

- If two operations are at the same level, read the top one first.

- The numbering of the steps in the plan is misleading. Start reading the explain plan output from the inside out. That is, read the *least indented* operation first.

In the previous example, then, Oracle uses the inventories table as its driving table and uses the following execution path:

1. Oracle performs an index unique scan of the warehouses table using its primary key index.

2. Oracle does a full table scan of the inventories table.

3. Oracle performs a nested loops operation to join the rows from steps 1 and 2.

4. Oracle performs an index fast full scan of the product_descriptions table using its primary key, prd_desc_pk.

5. In the final step, Oracle performs a hash join of the set from step 3 and the rows resulting from the index full scan of step 4.

Using the output of the explain plan, you can quickly see why some of your queries are taking much longer than anticipated. Armed with this knowledge, you can fine-tune a query until an acceptable performance threshold is reached. The wonderful thing about the explain plan is that you never have to actually execute any statement in the database to trace the execution plan of the statement. The next section presents a few examples so you can feel more comfortable using the Explain Plan utility.

More Plan Examples

In this section, you'll learn how to interpret various kinds of execution plans derived by using the Explain Plan utility.

In the first example, consider what happens when you use a function on an indexed column. The index is completely ignored by Oracle!

```
SQL> EXPLAIN PLAN set statement_id = 'example_plan1' FOR
  2  SELECT last_name from hr.employees
  3* where upper(last_name) = 'FAY';
Explained.
SQL>
example_plan1
--------------------------------------------------
```

```
SELECT STATEMENT
 TABLE ACCESS FULL EMPLOYEES
SQL>
```

The next example is a query similar to the last, but without the upper function on last_name. This time, Oracle uses the index on the last_name column.

```
SQL> explain plan set  statement_id = 'example_plan1'
  2  for
  3  select last_name from hr.employees
  4* where last_name='FAY';
Explained.
SQL>
example_plan1
------------------------------
SELECT STATEMENT
 INDEX RANGE SCAN EMP_NAME_IX
SQL>
```

In the third example, two tables (customers and orders) are joined to retrieve the query results.

```
SQL> explain plan set statement_id 'newplan1'
  2  for
  3  select o.order_id,
  4  o.order_total,
  5  c.account_mgr_id
  6  from customers c,
  7  orders o
  8  where o.customer_id=c.customer_id
  9* and o.order_date > '01-DEC-99'
Explained.
SQL>
```

Listing 18-4 shows the explain plan from the plan table.

Listing 18-4. Another Explain Plan Output

```
 SQL> select  lpad(' ',level-1)||operation||' '||options||' '||
  2          object_name "newplan"
  3          from plan_table
  4           connect by prior id = parent_id
  5          and prior statement_id = statement_id
  6          start with id = 0 AND statement_id = '&1'
  7*         order by id;
Enter value for 1: newplan1
old   6:    START WITH id = 0 AND statement_id = '&1'
new   6:    START WITH id = 0 AND statement_id = 'newplan1'
newplan
SELECT STATEMENT
 HASH JOIN                                              /* step 4 */
```

```
TABLE ACCESS FULL CUSTOMERS                 /* step 3 */
TABLE ACCESS BY INDEX ROWID ORDERS    /* step 2 */
 INDEX RANGE SCAN ORD_ORDER_DATE_IX /* step 1 */
Elapsed: 00:00:00.01
SQL>
```

In step 1, the query first does an index range scan of the orders table using the ord_order_date_x index. Why an index range scan? Because this index is nonunique—it has multiple rows with the same data value. Thus, the optimizer has to scan these multiple rows to get the data it is interested in. If the indexed column is a primary key, for example, it will be unique by definition, and you'll see the notation *Unique Scan* in the explain plan statement.

In step 2, the query accesses the orders table by index_rowid using the ROWID it derived in the previous step. This step gets you the order_id, customer_id, and order_total columns from the orders table for the date specified.

In step 3, the customers table is accessed through a full table scan, because account_manager_id in that table, which is part of the *where* clause, isn't indexed.

In step 4, the rows from the orders table are joined with the rows from the customers table based on the join condition *where o.customer_id=c.customer_id*.

As you can see from the preceding examples, the explain plan facility provides you with a clear idea as to the access methods used by the optimizer. You can do this, of course, without having to run the query itself. Often, the explain plan will provide you with a quick answer as to why your SQL may be performing poorly. The plan's output can help you determine how selective your indexes are and let you experiment with quick changes in code.

Using Autotrace

The Autotrace facility enables you to automatically produce explain plans when you execute a SQL statement in SQL*Plus. You automatically have the privileges necessary to use the Autotrace facility when you log in as SYS or SYSTEM.

First, if you plan to use Autotrace, you should create a plan table in your schema. Once you create this plan table, you can use it for all your future executions of the Autotrace facility. If you don't have this table in your schema, you'll get an error when you try to use the Autotrace facility, as shown here:

```
SQL> set autotrace on explain
SQL> select * from emp;
no rows selected
ERROR:
ORA-00942: table or view does not exist
SP2-0612: Error generating AUTOTRACE EXPLAIN report
SQL>
```

You can create the plan_table table by using the *create table* statement, as shown in Listing 18-5. You can also create this table by executing the $ORACLE_HOME/rdbms/admin/utlxplan.sql script.

Listing 18-5. Manually Creating the Plan Table

```
SQL>  CREATE TABLE PLAN_TABLE
 (  2  STATEMENT_ID     VARCHAR2(30), TIMESTAMP       DATE,
    3  REMARKS          VARCHAR2(80), OPERATION       VARCHAR2(30),
    4  OPTIONS          VARCHAR2(30), OBJECT_NODE     VARCHAR2(128),
    5  OBJECT_OWNER     VARCHAR2(30), OBJECT_NAME     VARCHAR2(30),
    6  OBJECT_INSTANCE  NUMERIC,      OBJECT_TYPE     VARCHAR2(30),
    7  OPTIMIZER        VARCHAR2(255),SEARCH_COLUMNS  NUMBER,
    8  ID               NUMERIC,      PARENT_ID       NUMERIC,
    9  POSITION         NUMERIC,      COST            NUMERIC,
   10  CARDINALITY      NUMERIC,      BYTES           NUMERIC,
   11  OTHER_TAG        VARCHAR2(255),PARTITION_START VARCHAR2(255),
   12  PARTITION_STOP   VARCHAR2(255),PARTITION_ID    NUMERIC,
   13  OTHER            LONG,         DISTRIBUTION    VARCHAR2(30));
Table created.
SQL>
```

Second, the SYS or SYSTEM user needs to grant you the plustrace role. If the plustrace role doesn't already exist in the database, the SYS user needs to run the script in Listing 18-6 to create the plustrace role.

Listing 18-6. Creating the Plustrace Role

```
SQL> @ORACLE_HOME/sqlplus/admin/plustrce.sql
SQL> drop role plustrace;
drop role plustrace
          *
ERROR at line 1:
ORA-01919: role 'PLUSTRACE' does not exist
SQL> create role plustrace;
Role created.
SQL>
SQL> grant select on v_$sesstat to plustrace;
Grant succeeded.
SQL> grant select on v_$statname to plustrac;
Grant succeeded.
SQL> grant select on v_$session to plustrace;
Grant succeeded.
SQL> grant plustrace to dba with admin option;
Grant succeeded.
SQL> set echo off
SQL>
```

Third, the user who intends to use Autotrace should be given the plustrace role, as shown here:

```
SQL> grant plustrace to salapati;
Grant succeeded.SQL>
```

The user can now set the Autotrace feature on and view the explain plan for any query that is used in the session. The Autotrace feature can be turned on with different options:

- *Set Autotrace on explain:* This will generate the execution plan only and will not actually execute the query itself.

- *Set Autotrace on statistics:* This shows only the execution statistics for the SQL statement.

- *Set Autotrace on:* This shows both the execution plan and the SQL statement execution statistics.

All SQL statements issued after the Autotrace feature is turned on will generate the execution plans (until you turn off the Autotrace facility with the command *set autotrace off*) as shown in Listing 18-7.

Listing 18-7. Using the Autotrace Utility

```
SQL> set autotrace on;
SQL> select * from emp;
no rows selected
Execution Plan
    0        SELECT STATEMENT Optimizer=CHOOSE (Cost=2 Card=1 Bytes=74)
    1    0   TABLE ACCESS (FULL) OF 'EMP' (Cost=2 Card=1 Bytes=74)
Statistics
          0   recursive calls
          0   db block gets
          3   consistent gets
          0   physical reads
          0   redo size
        511   bytes sent via SQL*Net to client
        368   bytes received via SQL*Net from client
          1   SQL*Net roundtrips to/from client
          0   sorts (memory)
          0   sorts (disk)
          0   rows processed
SQL>
```

Examples Using Autotrace

This section presents a few simple examples to show how Autotrace helps you optimize SQL queries. In the following examples, the same query is used again in the table courses, once without an index and once with an index. After the table is indexed, you run the query before you analyze the table. The results are very instructive.

In the first example, whose output is shown in Listing 18-8, you run the test query before you create an index on the table courses.

Listing 18-8. The Execution Plan for a Query Without an Index

```
SQL> set autotrace on
SQL> select count(*) from courses
  2  where course_subject='medicine'
  3* and course_title = 'fundamentals of human anatomy';
  COUNT(*)
   98304
Execution Plan
---------------------------------------------------------------
   0      SELECT STATEMENT Optimizer=CHOOSE
   1   0    SORT (AGGREGATE)
   2   1      TABLE ACCESS (FULL) OF 'COURSES'
Statistics
---------------------------------------------------------------
        0   recursive calls
        0   db block gets
      753   consistent gets
      338   physical reads
        0   redo size
      381   bytes sent via SQL*Net to client
      499   bytes received via SQL*Net from client
        2   SQL*Net roundtrips to/from client
        0   sorts (memory)
        0   sorts (disk)
        1   rows processed
SQL>
```

As you can see, the query used a full table scan, because there are no indexes. There were a total of 338 reads. Note that the total number of rows in the table courses is 98,384. Out of this total, the courses with medicine as the course subject were 98,304. That is, the table values are not distributed evenly among the courses at all. Now let's see what happens when you use an index.

The next example uses a query with an index (no analyze of the tables and index). When you create an index on the courses table and run the same query, you'll see some interesting results. Listing 18-9 tells the story.

Listing 18-9. The Execution Plan for a Query with an Index

```
SQL> create index title_idx on courses (course_title);
Index created.
SQL> select count(*) from courses
  2  where course_subject='medicine'
  3  and course_title = 'fundamentals of human anatomy';
  COUNT(*)
    98304
Execution Plan
---------------------------------------------------------------
   0      SELECT STATEMENT Optimizer=CHOOSE
   1   0    SORT (AGGREGATE)
```

```
 2    1      TABLE ACCESS (BY INDEX ROWID) OF 'COURSES'
 3    2        INDEX (RANGE SCAN) OF 'TITLE_IDX' (NON-UNIQUE)
Statistics
-----------------------------------------------------------
         0  recursive calls
         0  db block gets
      1273  consistent gets
      1249  physical reads
         0  redo size
       381  bytes sent via SQL*Net to client
       499  bytes received via SQL*Net from client
         2  SQL*Net roundtrips to/from client
         0  sorts (memory)
         0  sorts (disk)
         1  rows processed
SQL>
```

After you created the index, the physical reads went from 338 to 1,249! The explain plan shows that Oracle is indeed using the index, so you would expect the physical reads to be lower when compared to the "no index" case. What happened here? Well, remember that the fact that even if a table has an index, this doesn't mean that it's always good to use it under all circumstances. The CBO always figures the "best" way to get a query's results, with or without using the index. In this case, the query has to look at almost all the rows of the table, so using an index isn't the best way to go. However, you haven't analyzed the table and the index, so Oracle has no way of knowing the distribution of the actual data in the courses table. Lacking any statistics, it falls back to a rule-based approach (the *choose* option uses the CBO only if there are statistics). Under a rule-based optimization, using an index occupies a lower rank and therefore indicates that this is the optimal approach here. Let's see the results after analyzing the table.

The third example is a query with an index, after analyzing the table. Once you analyze the table, Oracle has the complete statistics, and it uses the CBO this time around. The CBO will decide to use an index only if the cost of using the index is lower than the cost of a full table scan. The CBO decides that it won't use the index, because the query will have to read 98,304 out of a total of 98,384 rows. It rightly decides to do a full table scan instead. The results are shown in Listing 18-10.

Listing 18-10. The Execution Plan with an Index, After Analyzing the Table

```
SQL> analyze table courses compute statistics;
Table analyzed.
SQL> select count(*) from courses
  2  where course_subject='medicine'
  3  and course_title = 'fundamentals of human anatomy';
  COUNT(*)
-----------
     98304
Execution Plan
-----------------------------------------------------------
```

```
     0        SELECT STATEMENT Optimizer=CHOOSE (Cost=74 Card=1 Bytes=39)
     1     0    SORT (AGGREGATE)
     2     1      TABLE ACCESS (FULL) OF 'COURSES' (Cost=74 Card=24596 Bytes=959244)
Statistics
-----------------------------------------------------------
       290  recursive calls
         0  db block gets
       792  consistent gets
       334  physical reads
         0  redo size
       381  bytes sent via SQL*Net to client
       499  bytes received via SQL*Net from client
         2  SQL*Net roundtrips to/from client
         6  sorts (memory)
         0  sorts (disk)
         1  rows processed
SQL> /
```

Using SQL Trace and TKPROF

SQL Trace is an Oracle utility that helps you trace the execution of SQL statements. TKPROF is also an Oracle utility that helps you output the trace files output by SQL Trace into a readable form. Although the Explain Plan facility will give you the expected execution plan, the SQL Trace tool will give you the actual results of an expected SQL query. Sometimes, you may not be able to identify the exact code, say, for dynamically generated SQL. SQL Trace files can capture the SQL for dynamic SQL as well. Among other things, SQL Trace will enable you to track the following variables:

- CPU and elapsed times

- Parsed and executed counts for each SQL statement

- Number of physical and logical reads

- Execution plan for all the SQL statements

- Library cache hit ratios

 TIP *If your application has a lot of dynamically generated SQL, the SQL Trace utility is ideal for tuning the SQL statements.*

Although the Explain Plan tool is important for determining the access path that will be used by the optimizer, SQL Trace gives you lot of "hard" information on resource use and the efficacy of the statements. You'll get a good idea of whether your statement is being parsed excessively. The statement's execute and fetch counts illustrate its efficiency. You get a good sense of how much CPU time is consumed by your queries and how much I/O is being performed during the execution phase. This will help you identify the resource-guzzling SQL statements in your application and tune them. The explain plan, which is an optional part of SQL Trace, will give the rows counts for the individual steps of the explain plan, helping you pinpoint at what step the most work is being done. By comparing resource use with the number of rows fetched, you can easily determine how productive a particular statement is.

In the next sections you'll use SQL Trace to trace a simple SQL statement and interpret it with the TKPROF utility. You start by setting a few initialization parameters to ensure tracing.

Setting the Trace Initialization Parameters

Collecting trace statistics imposes a performance penalty, and consequently the database doesn't automatically trace all sessions. Tracing is purely an optional process that you turn on for a limited duration to capture metrics about the performance of critical SQL statements. You need to look at four initialization parameters to correctly set up Oracle for SQL tracing. You have to restart the database after checking that the following parameters are correctly configured. Three of these parameters are dynamic session parameters, and you can change them at the session level.

Statistics_Level

The *statistics_level* parameter can take three values. The value of this parameter has a bearing on the *timed_statistics* parameter. You can see this dependency clearly in the following summary:

- If the *statistics_level* parameter is set to *typical* or *all*, timed statistics are collected automatically for the database.

- If *statistics_level* is set to *basic*, then *timed_statistics* must be set to *true* for statistics collection.

- Even if *statistics_level* is set to *typical* or *all*, you can keep the database from tracing by using the *alter session* parameter to set *timed_statistics* to *false*.

Timed_Statistics

The *timed_statistics* parameter is *false* by default. To collect performance statistics such as CPU and execution time, set the value of the *timed_statistics* parameter to *true* in the init.ora file or SPFILE, or use the *alter system set timed_statistics = true* statement to turn timed statistics on instancewide. You can also do this at the session level by using the *alter session* statement as follows:

```
SQL> alter session set timed_statistics = true;
Session altered.
SQL>
```

CAUTION *Make sure that you turn the* timed_statistics *parameter on only for brief periods while tracing SQL statements. The continuous use of the parameter can impose an overhead that could be significant for some operating systems.*

User_Dump_Dest

User_dump_dest is the directory on your server where your SQL Trace files will be sent. Normally the dump destination given is $ORACLE_HOME/admin/*database_name*/udump. If you want non-DBAs to be able to read this file, make sure the directory permissions authorize reading by others. Alternatively, you can set the parameter *trace_files_public=true* to let others read the trace files on UNIX systems. Make sure the destination points to a directory that has plenty of free space to accommodate large trace files. Because *user_dump_dest* is a dynamic parameter, you can also change it using the *alter system* command as follows:

```
SQL> alter system set user_dump_dest='c:\oraclent\oradata';
System altered.
SQL>
```

Max_Dump_File_Size

Some traces could result in very large trace files in a big hurry, so make sure your *max_dump_file_size* initialization parameter is set to a very high number. The default size of this parameter may be too small for some traces. If the trace fills the dump file, it won't terminate, but the information in file will be truncated.

Enabling SQL Trace

To use SQL Trace and TKPROF, you need to first enable the Trace facility. You can do at the instance level by using the *alter session* statement or the DBMS_SESSION package. You can trace the entire instance (this isn't recommended, because it will generate a huge amount of tracing information, most of which will be useless for your purpose) by either including the line *sql_trace=true* in your init.ora file or SPFILE or by using the *alter system* command to set *sql_trace* to *true*. The statement that follows shows how to set tracing on from your session using the *alter session* statement:

```
SQL> alter session set sql_trace=true;
Session altered.
SQL>
```

The following example shows how you set *sql_trace* to *true* using the DBMS_SESSION package:

```
SQL> execute sys.dbms_session.set_sql_trace(true);
PL/SQL procedure successfully completed.
SQL>
```

Often, users request the DBA to help them trace their SQL statements. You can use the DBMS_SESSION.set_sql_trace_in_session procedure to set tracing on in another user's session. Once the *alter session set sql_trace* statement or the DBMS_SESSION package are used to start tracing in a user's session, all statements are traced until you use the *alter session* statement or the DBMS_SESSION package to turn tracing off (replace *true* with *false* in either of the preceding statements). Alternatively, when the user logs off, tracing is automatically stopped for that user.

Interpreting the Trace Files with TKPROF

The trace files of a *sql_trace* command are output to the (udump) directory specified by the *user_dump_dest* parameter in your init.ora file or SPFILE. The filename has the format *db_name_ora_nnnnn.trc*, where *nnnnn* is usually a four- or five-digit number. For example, the example trace file is named *monitor_ora_10423.trc*. If you go to the user dump destination directory immediately after a trace session is completed, the most recent file is usually the file output by the *sql_trace* command.

You can also differentiate the trace file put out by the *sql_trace* command from the other files by its size—these trace files are much larger in general than the other files output to the directory. These trace files are very detailed and complex. Fortunately, the easy-to-run TKPROF utility will format the output into a very readable format. The TKPROF utility uses the trace file as the input, along with several parameters you can specify.

Table 18-1 shows the main TKPROF parameters you can choose to produce the format that suits you. If you type in **tkprof** at the command prompt, you'll see a complete listing of all the parameters that you can specify when you invoke TKPROF.

Table 18-1. TKPROF Command-Line Arguments

PARAMETER	DESCRIPTION
Filename	The input trace file produced by SQL Trace
Explain	The explain plan for the SQL statements
Record	Creates a SQL script with all the nonrecursive SQL statements
Waits	Records a summary of wait events
Sorts	Sorts the statements in descending order
Table	The name of the tables into which the TKPROF utility temporarily puts the execution plans
Sys	Enables and disables listing of SQL statements issued by SYS
Print	Lists only a specified number of SQL statements instead of all statements
Insert	Creates a script that stores the trace information in the database

Let's trace a session by a user who is executing two *select* statements, one using tables with indexes and the other using tables without any indexes. In this example, you are using only a few parameters, choosing to run TKPROF with default sort options. The first parameter is the name of the output file and the second is the name for the TKPROF-formatted output. You're specifying that you don't want any analysis of statements issued by the user SYS. You're also specifying that the explain plan for the statement be shown in addition to the other statistics.

```
[monitor] $ tkprof monitor_ora_10423.trc  test.prf
           sys=no  explain =y
TKPROF: Release 9.2.0.1.0 - Production on Fri Jan 24 04:09:50 2003
Copyright (c) 1982, 2002, Oracle Corporation.  All rights reserved.
oracle@hp50.netbsa.org   [/a08/app/oracle/admin/monitor/udump]
[monitor] $
```

Examining the Formatted Output File

TKPROF will format the output of the SQL trace session in the test.prf file that you specified. Listing 18-11 shows the top portion of the test.prf file, which explains the key terms used by the utility.

Listing 18-11. The TKPROF-Formatted Trace File

```
TKPROF: Release 9.2.0.1.0 - Production on Fri Jan 24 04:09:50 2003
Copyright (c) 1982, 2002, Oracle Corporation.  All rights reserved.
Trace file: monitor_ora_10423.trc
Sort options: default
********************************************************
count    = number of times OCI procedure was executed
cpu      = cpu time in seconds executing
elapsed  = elapsed time in seconds executing
disk     = number of physical reads of buffers from disk
query    = number of buffers gotten for consistent read
current  = number of buffers gotten in current mode (usually for update)
rows     = number of rows processed by the fetch or execute call
**********************************************************************
```

Each TKPROF report shows the following information for each SQL statement issued during the time the user's session was traced:

- The SQL statement

- Counts of parse, execute, and fetch (for *select* statements) calls

- Count of rows processed

- CPU seconds used

- I/O used

- Library cache misses

- Optional execution plan

- Row source operation listing

- A report summary analyzing how many similar and distinct statements were found in the trace file

Let's analyze the formatted output created by TKPROF. Listing 18-12 shows the parts of the TKPROF output showing the parse, execute, and fetch counts.

Listing 18-12. The Parse, Execute, and Fetch Counts

```
SQL> select e.last_name,e.first_name,d.department_name
     from teste e,testd dwhere e.department_id=d.department_id;
```

call	count	cpu	elapsed	disk	query	current	rows
Parse	1	0.00	0.00	0	0	0	0
Execute	1	0.00	0.00	0	0	0	0
Fetch	17322	1.82	1.85	3	136	5	259806
total	17324	1.82	1.85	3	136	5	259806

```
Misses in library cache during parse: 0
Optimizer goal: CHOOSE
Parsing user id: 53
```

In Listing 18-12,

- *CPU* stands for total CPU time in seconds.

- *Elapsed* is the total time elapsed in seconds.

- *Disk* denotes total physical reads.

- *Query* is the number of consistent buffer gets.

- *Current* is the number of DB block gets.

- *Rows* is the total number rows processed for each type of call.

From Listing 18-12, you can draw the following conclusions:

- The SQL statement shown previously was parsed once, so a parsed version was not available in the shared pool before execution. The parse column shows that this operation took less than 0.01 seconds. Note that the lack of disk I/Os and buffer gets indicates that there were no data dictionary cache misses during the parse operation. If the parse column showed a large number for the same statement, it would be an indicator that bind variables were not being used.

- The statement was executed once and execution took less than 0.01 seconds. Again, there were no disk I/Os or buffer gets during the execution phase.

- It took me a lot longer than 0.01 seconds to get the results of the *select* statement back. Why the delay, if execution took less than 0.01 seconds? The fetch column answers this question: It shows that that the operation was performed 17,324 times and took up 1.82 seconds of CPU time.

- The fetch operation was performed 17,324 times and fetched 259,806 rows. Because the number of rows is far greater than the number of fetches, you can deduce that Oracle used array fetch operations.

- There were three physical reads during the fetch operation. If there is a large difference between CPU time and elapsed time, it can be attributed to time taken up by disk reads. In this case, the physical I/O has a value of only 3, and it matches the insignificant gap between CPU time and elapsed time. The fetch required 136 buffer gets in the consistent mode and only 5 DB block gets.

- The CBO was being used, because the optimizer goal is shown as *choose*.

The following output shows the execution plan that was explicitly requested when TKPROF was invoked. Note that instead of the cost estimates that you get when use the Explain Plan tool, you get the number of rows output by each step of the execution.

```
Rows      Row Source Operation
-------   -----------------------
259806    MERGE JOIN
  1161    SORT JOIN
  1161    TABLE ACCESS FULL TESTD
259806    SORT JOIN
```

Finally, TKPROF summarizes the report, stating how many SQL statements were traced. Here's the summary portion of the TKPROF-formatted output:

```
Trace file: ORA02344.TRC
Trace file compatibility: 9.00.01
Sort options: default
    2  sessions in tracefile.
   18  user  SQL statements in trace file.
  104  internal SQL statements in trace file.
   72  SQL statements in trace file.
   33  unique SQL statements in trace file.
18182  lines in trace file.
```

The TKPROF output makes it very easy to identify inefficient SQL statements. TKPROF can order the SQL statements by elapsed time (time taken for execution), which tells you which of the SQL statements you should focus on for optimization.

The SQL Trace utility is a very powerful tool in tuning SQL, because it goes far beyond the explain plan statements and provides you with hard information about the number of the various types of calls made to Oracle during statement execution and how the resource use was allocated to the various stages of execution.

Using V$SQLAREA to Find Inefficient SQL

The V$SQLAREA view is an invaluable tool in tracking down wasteful SQL code in your application. The V$SQLAREA view gathers information from the shared pool area on every statement's disk reads and memory reads, as well as other important information. The view holds all the SQL statements executed since instance start-up, but there is no guarantee that it will hold every statement until you shutdown the instance. Due to space reasons, the older statements are aged out of the V$SQLAREA view. It is a good idea for you to grant your developers select rights on this view directly if you haven't already granted them the select any catalog role. You can use the V$SQLAREA view to perform ad hoc queries on disk and CPU usage, but remember that the Statspack report includes summaries of this information.

The V$SQLAREA view includes, among other things, the following columns, which help in assessing how much resources a SQL statement consumes:

- *Rows_processed* gives you the total number of rows processed by the statement.

- *Sql_text* is the text of the SQL statement (first 1,000 characters).

- *Buffer_gets* gives you the total number of logical reads (indicates high CPU use).

- *Disk_reads* tells you the total number of disk reads (indicates high I/O).

- *Sorts* gives the number of sorts for the statement (indicates high sort ratios).

- *Cpu_time* is the total parse and execution time.

- *Elapsed time* is the elapsed time for parsing and execution.

- *Parse_calls* is the combined soft and hard parse calls for the statement.

- *Executions* is the number of times a statement was executed.

- *Loads* is the number of times the statement was reloaded into the shared pool after being flushed out.

- *Sharable_memory* is the total shared memory used by the cursor.

- *Persistent_memory* is the total persistent memory used by the cursor.

- *Runtime_memory* is the total runtime memory used by the cursor.

Finding SQL That Is Using Most of Your Resources

You can query the V$SQLAREA view to find out high resource SQL. You can determine resource-intensive SQL on the basis of the number of logical reads or buffer gets, or high disk reads, high parse calls, large number of executions, or combinations of these factors. It's obvious that a high number of disk reads are inefficient, because a high amount of physical I/O could slow query performance. However, a high number of memory reads (buffer gets) are also expensive because they consume CPU resources. You normally have high buffer gets because you are using the wrong index, the wrong driving table in a join, or a similar SQL-related error. One of the primary goals of SQL tuning should be to lower the number of unnecessary logical reads. If buffer gets and disk reads are at identical levels, it could be an indication of a missing index. The reasoning is this: If you don't have an index, Oracle is forced to do a full table scan. However, full table scans can't be kept in the SGA for too long, because they might force a lot of other data to be cleared out of there. Consequently, the full table won't get to stay in the SGA for too long, unless it's a small table.

The following simple query shows how the V$SQLAREA view can pinpoint problem SQL statements. In the following query, both high disk reads and high logical reads are used as the criteria for flagging down poor SQL statements captured by the V$SQLAREA view:

```
SQL> SELECT hash_value, executions, buffer_gets, disk_reads,
  2  parse_calls
  3  FROM V$SQLAREA
  4  WHERE buffer_gets > 100000
  5  OR disk_reads > 100000
  6* ORDER BY buffer_gets + 100*disk_reads DESC;
HASH_VALUE   EXECUTIONS    BUFFER_GETS   DISK_READS PARSE_CALLS
----------   ----------    -----------   ---------- -----------

1091038690      726216     1615283234       125828        2077
1742065543       34665     1211625422      3680242           4
2307064662       70564      152737737      7186125        3863
3991501940       37849       96590083      5547319        5476
3618066162     5163242       33272842      6034715         606
SQL>
```

The following query is a slight variation on the preceding query. It seeks to find out the number of rows processed for each statement.

```
SQL> SELECT hash_value, rows_processed,
  2   buffer_gets, disk_reads, parse_calls
  3  FROM V$SQLAREA
  4  WHERE buffer_gets > 100000
  5  OR disk_reads > 100000
  6* ORDER BY buffer_gets + 100*disk_reads DESC;
HASH_VALUE ROWS_PROCESSED  BUFFER_GETS DISK_READS PARSE_CALLS
---------- --------------  ----------------------------------

1091038690      9659       1615322749     125830        2078
1742065543      3928       1214405479    3680515           4
2307064662     70660        152737737    7186125        3863
3991501940     37848         96590083    5547319        5476
3618066162    5163236        33272842    6034715         606
SQL>
```

The V$SQLAREA view helps you find out which of your queries have high *logical I/O* (LIO) and high *physical I/O* (PIO). By also providing the number of rows processed by each statement, it tells you if a statement is efficient or not. By providing the disk reads and the number of executions per statement, the view helps you determine if the number of disk reads per execution is reasonable. If CPU usage is your concern, look at the statements that have a high number of buffer gets. If I/O is your primary concern, focus on the statements with the highest number of disk reads. Once you settle on the statement you want to investigate further, use the hash_value of the SQL statement to get its full text from the V$SQLTEXT view.

Using Other Dictionary Views for SQL Tuning

The new Oracle9*i* views V$SQL_PLAN and V$SQL_PLAN_STATISTICS are highly useful for tracking the efficiency of execution plans. Chapter 20 shows you examples of how to use these two views. The V$SQL view always provided excellent information about SQL query performance, but now in the Oracle9*i* Release 2 version it has some new columns added that let you quickly identify your worst performing SQL queries. Here's a query that sorts the top five queries that are taking the most CPU time and the most elapsed time to complete:

```
SQL> select hash_value, executions,
  2  round (elapsed_time/1000000, 2) elapsed_seconds,
  3  round(cpu_time/1000000, 2) cpu_secs from
  4  (select * from v$sql order by elapsed_time desc)
  5* where rownum <6;
HASH_VALUE    EXECUTIONS ELAPSED_SECONDS   CPU_SECS
...........   ..........  ...............   .........
 238087931        2283       44.57           43.04
2963598673       14132       19.74           20.52
3460529092        9132        9.95           9
2964743345       14132        5.26           5.81
3223513021        2284        4.13           4.43
SQL>
```

You should be wary of quick changes in code to fix even the worst performing query in the system. Let's say you create an extra index on a table or change the order of columns in a composite key in order to fix this problem query. How do you know these aren't going to adversely impact other queries in the application? This happens more often than you think, and therefore you must do your due diligence to rule out unintended consequences of your fixes.

Using GUI Tools in Tuning

The Explain Plan and SQL Trace utilities are not the only tools you have available to tune SQL statements. Several GUI-based tools provide the same information much faster. Just make sure that statistics collection is tuned on the initialization file before you use these tools.

Figure 18-3 illustrates the use of one such tool, the free version of TOAD software, which is marketed by Quest Software (http://www.quest.com). From this tool you get not only the execution plan, but also memory usage, parse calls, I/O usage, and a lot of other useful information, which will help you tune your queries.

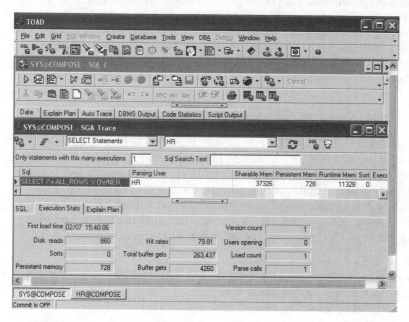

Figure 18-3. Using TOAD to get the explain plan for a SQL statement

The use of GUI tools helps you avoid most of the drudgery involved in producing and reading explain plans. Note that whether you use GUI tools or manual methods, the dynamic performance views that you use are the same. It is how you access them and use the data that makes the difference in the kind of tool you use.

Using the OEM Tuning Pack

OEM provides an excellent set of management packs, one of which is the Tuning Pack. You can use the Tuning Pack to create explain plan diagrams, analyze SQL, and produce indexing recommendations, among other things. I present two of the important Tuning Pack components, the SQL Analyze and Oracle Expert applications, in the following sections. For a useful summary of the OEM Tuning Pack, please refer to the data sheet for the Oracle Tuning Pack, which is available at http://otn.oracle.com/products/oracle9i/datasheets/oem_tuning/tuning.html.

SQL Analyze

SQL Analyze provides many functions designed to help you create optimal SQL statements. You can get explain plans using SQL Analyze and also perform "as-if" index creation exercises. SQL Analyze provides you with useful statistics on high-resource-usage SQL statements, as shown in Figure 18-4. Statements that consume the most resources in general or those that consume the most resources per row are obvious candidates for further investigation. It is especially beneficial to tune frequently used statements that are highly resource intensive. Your application could execute literally thousands of statements during the course of a day in a production database. Your goal should be to narrow down your focus to the top five or ten most resource-intensive SQL statements to see if you can improve their performance.

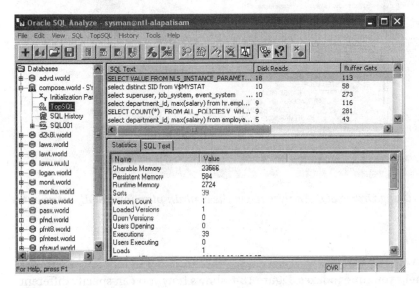

Figure 18-4. Using Oracle SQL Analyze to investigate resource-intensive SQL

Other tasks you can perform using SQL Analyze include the following:

- Maintain a history of the SQL statements executed in the database.

- View a potential statement's join order and join methods.

- Provide index recommendations.

- Add hints to SQL statements if necessary.

- Check your SQL and provide alternative statements to improve them if necessary.

The SQL Analyze tool provides you with three very easy-to-use wizards:

- The Virtual Index Wizard lets you simulate the effects of creating new indexes on key tables by showing you the before and after explain plans.

- The Hint Wizard helps you create various hints for your SQL queries.• The SQL Tuning Wizard checks for inefficiencies in your SQL code and suggests improvements by generating alternative code. It also shows your potential performance gains after the improvements.

Figure 18-5 shows how you can use SQL Analyze to produce explain plans for SQL statements.

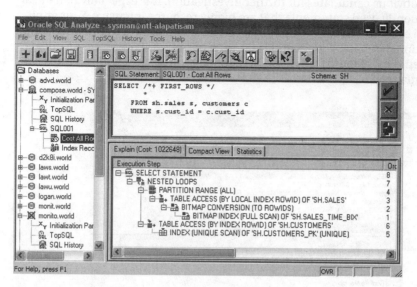

Figure 18-5. Using Oracle SQL Analyze to get the explain plan for a SQL statement

Oracle Expert

Oracle Expert helps you tune instance parameters and other database structures. It can also help you tune indexes. Figure 18-6 shows how you can specify different items in the tuning scope.

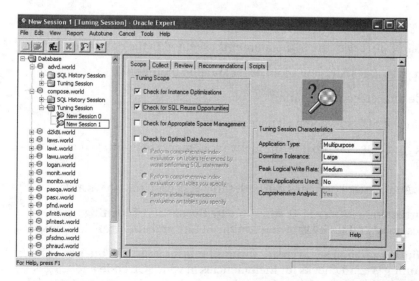

Figure 18-6. Using Oracle Expert to collect database performance statistics

Here's a summary of the various steps involved in using Oracle Expert to tune a database or instance:

1. Create a tuning session. You can specify either the database or instance, or you can have Oracle Expert look at all of the tunable parameters at once. Figure 18-7 shows this screen.

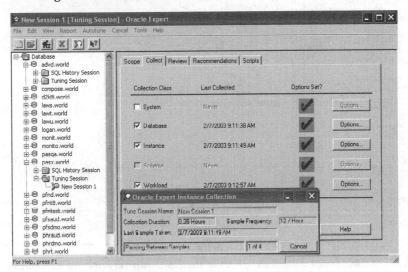

Figure 18-7. Oracle Expert in action

2. Let Oracle Expert collect the data. Depending on the size of the database, Oracle Expert will take some time to collect the data.

3. Review Oracle Expert's tuning recommendations. After Oracle Expert has finished collecting the instance and database data, it provides you with a set of recommendations. These recommendations are surprisingly effective, catching many of the mistakes you made while creating and tuning the database.

4. Generate an analysis report. You can optionally ask Oracle Expert to create an analysis report, an example of which is shown in Figure 18-8. The report is very detailed and provides you with useful information about your database and the recommended Oracle best practices.

5. Generate the scripts for implementing recommendations. You can next ask Oracle Expert to generate and apply scripts to implement its recommendations.

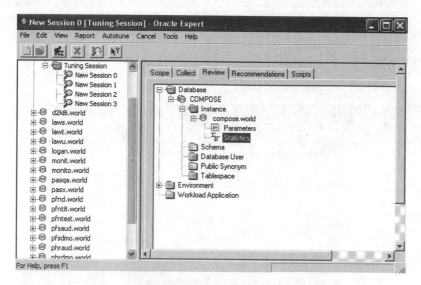

Figure 18-8. Oracle Expert summary report

 NOTE *For a good summary of the OEM Tuning Pack, which includes both the SQL Analyze and Oracle Expert tools, please read the Oracle Tuning Pack data sheet, which is available at* http://otn.oracle.com/products/oracle9i/datasheets/oem_tuning/ 9iR2_DS_EMTunePck.html.

A Simple Approach to Tuning SQL Statements

Whether you use manual methods such as Explain Plan, SQL Trace, and TKPROF, or more sophisticated methods such as OEM's SQL Analyze wizards, you need to understand that optimizing SQL statements can improve performance significantly. In the following sections, I summarize a simple methodology you can follow to tune your SQL statements.

Identify Problem Statements

This chapter has shown you many ways you can identify your slow-running or most resource-intensive SQL statements. For example, you can use dynamic performance views such as V$SQLAREA to find out your worst SQL statements, as shown earlier. Statements with high buffer gets are the CPU-intensive statements and those with high disk reads are the high I/O statements. Obviously, you want to start (and maybe end) with the tuning of these problem statements.

Locate the Source of the Inefficiency

The next step is to locate the inefficiency in the SQL statements. To do this, you need to collect information on how the optimizer is executing the statement. That is, you must first walk through the explain plan for the statement. This step will help you find out if there are any obvious problems such as full table scans due to missing indexes.

In addition to analyzing the explain plan output or using the V$SQL_PLAN view, collect the performance information, if you can, by using the SQL Trace and TKPROF utilities.

Review the explain plans carefully to see that the access and join methods and the join order are optimal. Specifically, check the plans with the following questions in mind:

- Are there any inefficient full table scans?

- Are there any unselective range scans?

- Are the indexes appropriate for your queries?

- Are the indexes selective enough?

- If there are indexes, are all of them being used?

- Are there any later filter operations?

- Does the driving table in the join have the best filter?

- Are you using the right join method and the right join order?

- Do your SQL statements follow basic guidelines for writing good SQL statements (see the section "Writing Efficient SQL" in this chapter)?

In most cases, a structured analysis of the query will reveal the source of the inefficiency.

Tune the Statement

Use OEM's Index Tuning Wizard to get index tuning recommendations. Review the access path for the tables in the statement and the join order. Consider the use of hints to force the optimizer to use a better execution plan. You can also use the SQL Analyze tool to get improved SQL statements.

Compare Performance

Once you generate alternative SQL, it's time to go through the first three steps again. Use explains plans and performance statistics to compare the new statement with the older one. After you ensure that your new statements perform better, it's time to replace the inefficient SQL.

Summary

Performance tuning is a skill that you will improve as you gain more experience working with Oracle databases. None of the requirements of the Oracle DBA's job are as fascinating or as demanding as performance tuning. In this chapter, you focused on SQL performance tuning. Optimizing SQL statements goes a long way toward making a well-tuned application, and as a DBA, you can do a lot to make your SQL code optimal. In this chapter, you learned how the cost-based optimizer (CBO) determines access paths. You also learned the importance of choosing the right indexes, the right hints, and the right join methods to help the CBO find the most efficient execution plan.

SQL tuning is an area where there are not cut-and-dried techniques, and lot of tedious trial and error is often required to come up with efficient code. Tools such as the Explain Plan, Autotrace, and SQL Trace are valuable allies in writing efficient SQL code. Learning how to interpret an explain plan or the results of a SQL Trace takes some time. Understanding the crucial dynamic performance tables such as V$SYSSTAT, V$SQLAREA, and the V$SQL_TEXT will help you easily figure out which of your SQL statements need optimization.

This chapter also introduced you to the excellent performance tools included in the OEM toolset, such as Oracle Expert and SQL Analyze. Finally, the chapter showed you how to follow a simple approach to tune SQL statements.

CHAPTER 19

Performance Tuning: Tuning the Instance

IN THE PREVIOUS chapter, you learned how to tune an application by writing efficient SQL in order to maximize its performance. The use of optimal SQL, efficient design of the layout of the database objects, and so on are all part of a planned or proactive tuning effort. This chapter focuses on the efficient use of the resources Oracle works with: memory, CPU, and storage disks.

The chapter discusses how to monitor and optimize memory allocation for the Oracle instance. In this context, you'll learn about the traditional database hit ratios, such as the buffer cache hit ratios. However, focusing on the hit ratios isn't the smartest way to maintain efficient Oracle databases, as you need to focus on the user's response time. Investigating factors that are causing processes to spend excessive time waiting for resources is a better approach to performance tuning. This chapter provides you with a solid introduction to Oracle wait events and tells you how to interpret them and reduce the incidence of these wait events in your system.

A fairly common problem in many production systems is that of a database *hang*, when things seem to come to a standstill for some reason. The chapter explores several potential showstoppers and shows you ways to avoid the occurrence of database hangs.

To tune the instance, you need to collect the relevant instance statistics. In this chapter you'll learn how to use the useful Oracle Statspack to collect performance data. The chapter explains the key dynamic performance tables that you need to be familiar with to understand instance performance issues. You'll also see how the OEM Diagnostics Pack can help you monitor and tune instance performance.

Although it's nice to be able to proactively design a system for high performance, more often than not, the DBA has to deal with proactive tuning when performance is unsatisfactory and a fix needs to be found right away. The final part of this chapter deals with a simple methodology to follow when your system performance deteriorates and you need to fine-tune the Oracle instance.

I begin this chapter with a short introduction to instance tuning and then turn to cover in detail the tuning of crucial resources such as memory, disk, and CPU usage. Later on in the chapter, I review the important Oracle wait events, which will help you get a handle on several kinds of database performance issues.

An Introduction to Instance Tuning

Oracle doesn't give anything but minimal and casual advice regarding the appropriate settings of key resources such as total memory allocation or the sizes of the components of memory. Oracle has some general guidelines about the correct settings for several key initialization parameters that have a bearing on performance. However, beyond specifying wide ranges for the parameters, the company's guidelines aren't very helpful to DBAs deciding on the "optimal" levels for these parameters.

Oracle says this is because all these parameters are heavily application dependent. All of this means that you as a DBA have to find out what the optimal sizes of resource allocations and the ideal settings of key initialization parameters are, through trial and error. You have to be resourceful when it comes to memory sizing: If you need more shared pool memory, first see if you can drop the buffer cache some, and vice versa. In this chapter, I provide some guidelines for figuring out the optimal sizes of memory and other configuration parameters.

As a DBA, you're often called in to tune the instance when users perceive a slow response, which is in turn caused by a bottleneck somewhere in the system. This bottleneck is the result of either an excessive use of or insufficient provision of one of the resources such as memory, CPU, or disks. In addition, database locks and latches may cause a slowdown. You have to remember, though, that in most cases, the solution isn't to simply increase the resource that seems to be getting hit hard—that may be the symptom, not the cause of a problem. If you address the performance slowdown by "fixing" the symptoms, the root causes will remain potential troublemakers.

Performance tuning an Oracle database instance involves tuning memory and I/O, as well as operating system resources such as CPU, the operating system kernel, and the operating system memory allocation. In the previous chapter, you saw how tuning the application leads to faster response times and more throughput. Application code changes, however, are incremental, and once the application is in production, instance tuning takes center stage in the tuning efforts.

When you receive calls from the help desk or other users of the system complaining that the system is running slowly, you can only change what is under your direct control—mainly, the allocation of memory and its components, and some dynamic initialization parameters that have a bearing on instance performance. Depending on what the various indicators tell you, you may adjust the shared pool and other components of memory to improve performance. You can also change the operating system priority of some processes, or quickly add some disk drives to your system.

One of the main reasons for a slow response time in a production system is the waiting time incurred by user processes. Oracle provides several ways of monitoring these waits, but you need to understand their significance in your system. Long wait times are not the problem themselves; they're symptoms of deep-seated problems. The DBA should be able to connect different types of waits with possible causes in the application or in the instance.

Although some manuals will tell you that you should do performance tuning before application tuning—before you proceed to tuning areas such as memory, I/O, and contention—real life isn't so orderly. Most of the time, you don't have the opportunity to have the code revised, even if there are indications that it isn't optimal. Instead of being an orderly process, tuning databases is an iterative process, where you may have to go back and forth between stages.

More often than not, DBAs are forced to do what they can to fix the performance problem that is besetting them at that moment. In this sense, most performance tuning is a reactive kind of tuning. Nevertheless, DBAs should endeavor to understand the innards of wait issues and seek to be proactive in their outlooks.

There are two big advantages to being in a proactive mode of tuning. First, you have fewer sudden performance problems that force hurried reactions. Second, as your understanding of your system increases, so does your familiarity with the various indicators of poor performance and the likely causes for them, so you can resolve problems that do occur much faster.

If you're fortunate enough to be with an application during its design stages, you can improve performance by performing several steps, including choosing automatic space management and setting correct storage options such as PCTFREE for your tables and indexes. Sizing the table and indexes correctly doesn't hurt, either. If you're stuck with a database that has a poor design, however, all is not lost. You can still tune the instance using techniques that I show later in this chapter to improve performance.

When response time is slower than usual, or when throughput falls, you'll notice that the Oracle instance isn't performing at its usual level. If response times are higher, obviously there's a problem somewhere in one of the critical resources Oracle uses. If you can rule out any network slowdowns, that leaves you with memory (Oracle's memory and the system's memory), the I/O system, and CPUs. One of these resources is usually the bottleneck that's slowing down your system.

In the next few sections, you'll learn how to tune key system resources such as memory and CPU to improve performance. You'll also see how to measure performance, detect inefficient waits in the system, and resolve various types of contention in an Oracle database. The next section presents a discussion of how tuning Oracle's memory can help improve database performance.

Patches and New Versions of Software

Oracle Corporation, like the other software vendors, releases periodic *patches* or *patch sets*, which are a set of fixes for bugs discovered by either Oracle or its customers. When you get in touch with Oracle technical support, one of the things the technical support representative will commonly ask you to do is make sure you have applied the latest patch set to your Oracle software. Similarly, UNIX operating systems may have their own patch sets that you may have to apply to fix certain bugs.

Each of Oracle's patch sets could cover fixes for literally hundreds of bugs. My recommendation is to apply a patch set as soon as it is available. One of the primary reasons for this is to see if your bug is unique to your database, or if a general solution has already been found for the problem. When you ask Oracle technical support to resolve a major problem caused by a bug, Oracle will usually provide you with a workaround. Oracle recommends that you upgrade your database to the latest versions and patch sets, because some Oracle bugs may not have any workarounds or fixes. Oracle will continue to support older versions of its server software throughout their support life cycle, which is usually about 2 to 3 years after the release of the next major release. Many organizations see no urgency to move to newer versions, as Oracle continues to support the older versions after the release of the new versions.

The question regarding how fast you should convert to a new version is somewhat tricky to answer. Traditionally, people have shied away from being early adopters of new Oracle software versions. Oracle, like most other software companies, has a reputation for very buggy initial releases of their major software versions (such as the 9.0 version of the 9*i* server software). Therefore, DBAs and managers in general prefer to wait a while until a "stable version" comes out. Although the logic behind this approach is understandable, you must also figure in the cost of not being able to use the many powerful features Oracle introduces in each of its major releases.

Because nobody likes to jeopardize the performance of a production system, the ideal solution is to maintain a test server where the new server is tested thoroughly and then move into production as early as possible. Oracle does provide support for a version for several years after its release, so companies have no urgent reason to migrate to uncertain new versions. However, don't wait forever to move to a new version—by the time some companies move to the new version, an even newer Oracle version is already out!

One of the best ways to improve performance is to move aggressively to the newer versions and take advantage of the powerful features they offer. For example, the new cursor-sharing features of Oracle8*i* and 9*i* have improved performance tremendously when compared to the older versions. I haven't met anybody yet who complains that his or her system is slower with the newer version. Of course, there's a caveat here: Some of your good SQL statements may not be so good after you migrate to a new version, due to the way a hint might behave in the new version, for example. That's why it's extremely important to test the whole system on the new version before cutting over production systems.

A smart strategy is to collect a set of performance statistics that can serve as a baseline, before you make any major changes in the system. These system changes may include the following:

- Migrating or upgrading a database

- Applying a new database or operating system patch set

- Adding a new application to your database

- Substantially increasing the user population

Tuning Oracle Memory

A well-known fact of system performance is that fetching data that's stored in memory is a lot faster than retrieving data from disk storage. Given this, Oracle tries to keep as much of the recently accessed data as possible in its SGA. In addition to data, shared parsed SQL code and necessary data dictionary information are cached in memory for quick access. Memory allocated to Oracle is highly configurable and is one of the easiest things to adjust, especially with the new Oracle9*i* version.

There is a two-way relationship between memory configuration and the application's use of that memory. The correct memory allocation size depends on the nature of your application, the number of users, and the size of transactions. If there is not enough memory, the application will have to perform time-consuming disk I/Os, but the application itself might be using memory unnecessarily, and throwing more memory at it may not be the right strategy.

As a DBA, you must not view memory and its sizing in isolation—this can lead to some poor choices, as you address the symptoms instead of the causes for what seems like insufficient memory. The tendency on a DBA's part is to allocate as much memory as possible to the shared pool, hoping that doing so will resolve the problem, but sometimes this only exacerbates the problem. It is wise to manage the database with as little memory as necessary, and no more. The system can always use the free memory to ensure there is no swapping or paging, which can slow down your application. Performance slowdowns caused by paging outweigh the benefits of a larger SGA under most operating systems.

The SGA has several components. Of these components, the redo log buffer and the Java pool are relatively small components. You need to allocate the Java pool only for applications that use Java. The main components of the SGA that you have to worry about are the following:

- Shared pool

- Buffer cache

- Large pool

- Redo log buffer

- Process-private memory

The total size of the SGA is the sum of all its components, as shown in the following query:

```
SQL> select * from v$sga;
NAME                      VALUE
-------------------- ----------
Fixed Size               736304
Variable Size         117440512
Database Buffers       33554432
Redo Buffers            2371584
SQL>
```

In this listing, the database buffers column shows the database buffer cache memory, and the variable size column consists mostly of the shared pool component. As shown in Chapter 16, you can dynamically change the settings of all the SGA components except the redo log buffer and the Java pool. That is, you don't have to restart the instance if you need to adjust the important components of the SGA.

In the following sections you'll look at each of these memory components in detail.

TIP *The* max_sga_size *initialization parameter is purely optional. However, if you don't set it, the maximum size will be the sum of all its components that you explicitly set. If you want to dynamically increase one component, you're forced to decrease some other component to make room for it in the SGA. To avoid this dilemma, always set the* max_sga_size *parameter to a value larger than the sum of its components.*

Tuning the Shared Pool

In a production database, the shared pool is going to command most of your attention because of its direct bearing on application performance. The shared pool is a part of the SGA that holds almost all the necessary elements for execution of the SQL statements and PL/SQL programs. In addition to caching program code, the shared pool caches the data dictionary information that Oracle needs to refer to often during the course of program execution.

Proper shared pool configuration leads to dramatic improvements in performance. An improperly tuned shared pool leads to problems such as the following:

- Fragmentation of the pool

- Increased latch contention with the resulting demand for more CPU resources

- Greater I/O because executable forms of SQL are not present in the shared pool

- Higher CPU usage because of unnecessary parsing of SQL code

The general increase in shared pool waits and other waits observed during a severe slowdown of the production database is the result of SQL code that fails to use bind variables. As the number of users increases, so does the demand on shared pool memory and latches, which are internal locks for memory areas. The result is a higher wait time and a slower response time. Sometimes the entire database seems to "hang."

The shared pool consists of two major areas: the library cache and the data dictionary cache. You can't allocate or decrease memory specifically for one of these components. If you increase the total shared pool memory size, both components will increase in some ratio that is determined by Oracle. Similarly, when you decrease the total shared pool memory, both components will decrease in size. Let's look at these two important components of the shared pool in detail.

The Library Cache

The *library cache* holds the parsed and executable versions of SQL and PL/SQL code. As you may recall from Chapter 18, all SQL statements undergo the following steps during their processing:

- *Parsing,* which includes syntactic and semantic verification of the statements and checking necessary object privileges to perform the actions.

- *Optimization,* where the Oracle optimizer evaluates how to process the statement with the least cost, after it evaluates several alternatives.

- *Execution,* where Oracle uses the optimized physical execution plan to perform the action stated in the SQL statement.

- *Fetching,* which only applies to *select* statements where Oracle has to return rows to you. This step isn't necessary, of course, in any nonquery-type statements.

Parsing is a very resource-intensive operation, and if your application needs to execute the same SQL statement repeatedly, having a parsed version of the same in memory will reduce contention for latches, CPU, I/O, and memory usage. The first time Oracle parses a statement, it creates a *parse tree.* The optimization step is necessary only for the first execution of a SQL statement. Once the statement is optimized, the best access path is encapsulated in the *access plan.* Both the parse tree and the access plan are stored in the library cache before the statement is executed for the first time. Future invocation of the same statement will need to go through only the last stage, execution, which avoids the overhead of parsing and optimizing as long as Oracle can find the parse tree and access plan in the library cache. Of course, if the statement is a SQL query, the last statement will be the fetch operation.

The library cache, being limited in size, will discard aged SQL when there is no more room for new SQL statements. The only way you can use a parsed statement repeatedly for multiple executions is if all the SQL statements are identical. Two statements are considered identical if they have exactly the same code, *including case and spaces.* The reason for this is that when Oracle compares a new statement to existing statements in the library cache, it uses simple string comparisons. In addition, any bind variables used must be similar in *data type and size.* Here are a couple of examples that show you how picky Oracle is when it comes to considering whether two SQL statements are identical.

In the following example, the statements are not considered identical because of an extra space in the second statement:

```
select * from employees;
select *  from employees;
```

In this example, the statements are not considered identical because of the different case used for the table Employees in the second statement. The two versions of "employees" are termed *literals* because they are literally different from each other.

```
Select * from employees;
Select * from Employees;
```

Hard Parsing and Soft Parsing

You may recall from the last chapter that all SQL code goes through the parse, optimize, and execute phases. When an application issues a statement, Oracle will first see if a parsed version of the statement already exists. If it does, the result is a so-called soft parse and is considered a library cache hit. If, during a parse phase or the execution phase, Oracle is not able to find the parsed version or the executable version of the code in the shared pool, it will perform a *hard parse*, which means that the SQL statement has to be reloaded into the shared pool and parsed completely.

During a hard parse, Oracle performs syntactic and semantic checking, checks the object and system privileges, builds the optimal execution plan, and finally loads it into the library cache. A hard parse involves a lot more CPU usage and is inefficient compared to a soft parse, which depends on reusing previously parsed statements. Hard parsing involves building all parse information from scratch, and therefore it is more resource intensive. Besides involving a higher CPU usage, hard parsing involves a large number of latch gets, which may increase the response time of the query. The ideal situation is where you parse once and execute many times.

 CAUTION *High hard parse rates lead to severe performance problems, so it's critical that you reduce hard parse counts in your database. Later sections in this chapter show you how to do this.*

A soft parse simply involves checking the library cache for an identical statement and reusing it. The major step of optimizing the SQL statement is completely omitted during a soft parse. There's really no parsing (as done during a hard parse) during a soft parse, because the new statement is hashed and its hash value is compared with the hash values of similar statements in the library cache. During a soft parse, Oracle only checks for the necessary privileges. For example, even if there's an identical statement in the library cache, your statement may not be executed if Oracle determines during the (soft) parsing stage that you don't have the necessary privileges.

Here are some very rough figures listed by Oracle as general guidelines to determine if there's excessive parsing in your database:

- If the hard parse rate is more than 100/second, it's excessive.

- If the soft parse rate is more than 300/second, you need to examine the reasons for it.

Using SQL Trace and TKPROF to Examine Parse Information

One of the most useful pieces of information the SQL Trace utility provides concerns the hard and soft parsing information for a query. The following simple example demonstrates how you can derive the parse information for any query:

1. Enable tracing in the session by using the following command:

    ```
    SQL> alter session set sql_trace=true;
    Session altered.
    SQL>
    ```

    To make sure none of your queries were parsed before, flush the shared pool, which removes all SQL statements from the library cache:

    ```
    SQL> alter system flush shared_pool;
    System altered.
    SQL>
    ```

2. Use the following query to create a trace in the user dump directory:

    ```
    SQL> select * from bsa_orgs where created_date >sysdate-5;
    ```

    The sql_trace output shows the following in the output file:

    ```
    PARSING IN CURSOR #1 len=63 dep=0 uid=21 oct=3
    lid=21 tim=1326831345 hv=71548308
    select * from bsa_orgs where created_date > sysdate-:"SYS_B_0"
    END OF STMT
    PARSE #1:c=4,e=4,p=0,cr=57,cu=3,mis=1,r=0,dep=0,og=0,tim=1326831345
    ```

    Note that *mis=1* indicates a hard parse because this SQL isn't present in the library cache.

3. Use a slightly different version of the previous query next. The output will be the same, but Oracle won't use the previously parsed version, because the statements in steps 2 and 3 aren't identical.

    ```
    SQL> select * from bsa_orgs where created_date > (sysdate -5);
    ```

    Here's the associated sql_trace output:

    ```
    PARSING IN CURSOR #1 len=77 dep=0 uid=21 oct=3 lid=21 tim=1326833972
    select /* A  Hint */ * from bsa_orgs where
     created_date > sysdate-:"SYS_B_0"
    END OF STMT
    PARSE #1:c=1,e=1,p=0,cr=0,cu=0,mis=1,r=0,dep=0,og=0,tim=1326833972
    ```

    Again, there is a hard parse, indicated by *mis=1*, showing a library cache miss. This isn't a surprise, as this statement isn't identical to the one before, so it has to be parsed from scratch.

4. Use the original query again. Now, Oracle will perform only a soft parse, because the statements here and in the first step are the same. Here's the sql_trace output:

    ```
    PARSING IN CURSOR #1 len=63 dep=0 uid=21 oct=3 lid=21 tim=1326834357
    select * from bsa_orgs where created_date > sysdate-:"SYS_B_0"
    END OF STMT
    PARSE #1:c=0,e=0,p=0,cr=0,cu=0,mis=0,r=0,dep=0,og=4,tim=1326834357
    ```

The statement is step 4 is identical in all respects to the statement in step 1, so Oracle reuses the parsed version, hence *mis=0* indicating there wasn't a hard parse but merely a soft parse, which is a lot cheaper in terms of resource usage.

If you now look at the TKPROF output (see Chapter 18 for details on how to use the TKPROF utility to format sql_trace output in a meaningful format), you'll see the following section for the SQL statements in step 2 and step 4 (identical statements):

```
******************************************************
select *from national_orgs where created_date > sysdate- 5
call    count    cpu    elapsed    disk    query    current    rows
-------  ------  --------  ----------  ----------  ----------  ----------  ----------
Parse   2       0.03    0.01      0       1        3         0
Execute 2       0.00    0.00      0       0        0         0
Fetch   4       0.07    0.10      156     166      24        10
total   8       0.10    0.11      156     167      27        10
Misses in library cache during parse: 1
******************************************************
```

As you can see, there was one miss in the library cache when you first executed the statement. The second time around, there was no hard parse and hence no library cache miss.

Measuring Library Cache Efficiency

You can use simple ratios to see if your library cache is sized correctly. The V$LIBRARYCACHE data dictionary view provides you all the information you need to see if the library cache is efficiently sized. Listing 19-1 shows the structure of the V$LIBRARYCACHE view.

Listing 19-1. The V$LIBRARYCACHE View

```
SQL> desc v$librarycache
 Name                                      Null?    Type
 ---------------------------------------- -------- -------------
 NAMESPACE                                          VARCHAR2(15)
 GETS                                               NUMBER
 GETHITS                                            NUMBER
 GETHITRATIO                                        NUMBER
 PINS                                               NUMBER
 PINHITS                                            NUMBER
 PINHITRATIO                                        NUMBER
 RELOADS                                            NUMBER
 INVALIDATIONS                                      NUMBER
 DLM_LOCK_REQUESTS                                  NUMBER
 DLM_PIN_REQUESTS                                   NUMBER
 DLM_PIN_RELEASES                                   NUMBER
 DLM_INVALIDATION_REQUESTS                          NUMBER
 DLM_INVALIDATIONS                                  NUMBER
SQL>
```

The following is the formula that provides you with an indicator of the library cache hit ratio:

```
SQL> Select sum(pinhits)/sum(pins)  Library_cache_hit_ratio
  2  From v$librarycache;
LIBRARY_CACHE_HIT_RATIO
------------------------
      .993928013
SQL>
```

The formula indicates that the library cache currently has a higher than 99 percent hit ratio, which is considered good. However, be cautious about relying exclusively on high hit ratios for the library cache and the buffer caches like the one shown here. You may have a hit ratio such as 99.99 percent, but if there are significant waits caused by events such as excessive parsing (both hard and soft), you are going to have a slow database. Always keep an eye on the wait events in your system, and do not rely blindly on high hit ratios like these.

Listing 19-2 shows how to determine the number of reloads and pinhits of various statements in your library cache.

Listing 19-2. Determining the Efficiency of the Library Cache

```
SQL>  SELECT namespace,pins,pinhits,reloads
  2   FROM V$LIBRARYCACHE
  3   ORDER BY namespace;
```

NAMESPACE	PINS	PINHITS	RELOADS
BODY	25	12	0
CLUSTER	248	239	0
INDEX	31	0	0
JAVA DATA	6	4	0
JAVA RESOURCE	2	1	0
JAVA SOURCE	0	0	0
OBJECT	0	0	0
PIPE	0	0	0
SQL AREA	390039	389465	14
TABLE/PROCEDURE	3532	1992	0
TRIGGER	5	3	0

```
11 rows selected.
SQL>
```

If the reloads column of the V$LIBRARYCACHE view shows large values, it means that many SQL statements are being reloaded into the library pool after they've been aged out. You might want to increase your shared pool, but this still may not do the trick if the application is large and the number of executions is large or the application doesn't use bind variables. If the SQL statements aren't exactly identical and/or they use constants instead of bind variables, more hard parses will be performed, and hard parses are inherently expensive in terms of resource usage. You can force the executable SQL statements to remain in the library cache component of the shared pool by using the Oracle DBMS_SHARED_POOL package. The package has *keep* and *unkeep* procedures, using which you can retain and release objects in the shared pool.

 NOTE *The section "Pinning Objects in the Shared Pool" later in this chapter shows you how to pin objects in the shared pool. Chapter 21 explains the DBMS_SHARED_POOL package in more detail.*

You can use the V$LIBRARY_CACHE_MEMORY view to determine the number of library cache memory objects currently in use in the shared pool and to determine the number of freeable library cache memory objects in the shared pool. The V$SHARED_POOL_ADVICE view provides you information about the parse time savings you can expect for various sizes of the shared pool.

Optimizing the Library Cache

Other than mechanically increasing the size of the library cache, is there anything you can do to improve the performance of this critical component of Oracle's memory? Fortunately, the answer is yes. You can configure some important initialization parameters so the library cache areas are used efficiently. You'll look at some of these initialization parameters in the following sections.

Using the Cursor_Sharing (Literal Replacement) Parameter

The key idea behind optimizing the use of the library cache is to reuse previously parsed or executed code. One of the easiest ways to do this is to use bind variables rather than literal statements in the SQL code. *Bind variables* are like placeholders—they allow binding of application data to the SQL statement. Each time a SQL statement is presented to Oracle, it will have to be parsed by Oracle. If a parsed version of the SQL statement already exists in the shared pool, Oracle can skip the parsing phase.

Because parsing is expensive, you should make every attempt to reduce the amount of parsing your application goes through. Using bind variables enables Oracle to reuse statements when the only thing changing in the statements are the values of the input variables. Bind variables enable you to reuse the cached parsed versions of queries and thus speed up your application. Here's an example of the use of bind variables. The following code sets up a bind variable as a number type:

```
SQL> variable bindvariable number;
SQL> begin
  2   :bindvariable := 1200;
  3   end;
  4   /
PL/SQL procedure successfully completed.
SQL> select last_name from persons where person_id = :bindvariable;
```

Once you set up your bind variable in the preceding fashion, all identical SQL statements that follow will use the parsed version of the query, thus cutting down on the total time taken to retrieve data. For example, all the following statements can use the parsed version of the query. Each time, once Oracle sees the parsed statement in the shared pool, it will replace person_id with the new bind variable value.

```
select last_name from persons where person_id =  98765;
select last_name from persons where person_id = 1010101;
select last_name from persons where person_id = 9999999;
```

A better way is to use bind variables, which transform each of the previous literal statements into the following statement:

```
select last_name from persons where person_id =  :b;
```

You can execute this statement multiple times with different values for the bind variable *b*. The statement will be parsed only once and execute many times. Unfortunately, in too many applications, literal values rather than bind values are used, which leads to a heavy amount of hard parsing and consequent latch contention for shared pool areas. The application is already in implementation and there is no way to rewrite code, replacing literal values with bind variables. What are you to do? You can take the easy way out of the problem by setting up the following initialization parameter:

```
Cursor_sharing=force
```

or

```
Cursor_sharing=similar
```

By default, the *cursor_sharing* initialization parameter is set to *exact*, meaning that only statements that are identical in all respects will be shared among different executions of the statement. Either of the alternative values for the *cursor_sharing* parameter, *force* or *similar*, will ensure Oracle will reuse statements even if they are not identical in all respects.

For example, if two statements are identical in all respects and differ only in the value of their literal values for some variables, using *cursor sharing=force* will enable Oracle to reuse the parsed SQL statements in cache. Literal values will be replaced by bind values to make the statements identical. The *cursor_sharing=force* option will literally force the use of bind variables under all circumstances, whereas the *cursor sharing=similar* option will do so only when Oracle thinks doing so won't adversely affect optimization. Oracle recommends the use of *cursor_sharing=similar* rather than *cursor_sharing=force* because of possible deterioration in the execution plans. However, in reality, the benefits provided by the *cursor_sharing=force* parameter far outweigh any possible damage to the execution plans. You can improve the performance of your database dramatically when you notice a high degree of hard parsing due to the failure to use bind variables by moving from the default *cursor_sharing=exact* option to the *cursor_sharing=force* option. You can change the value of this parameter in the init.ora file or SPFILE, or you can do so dynamically by using the *alter system* (instancewide) statement or the *alter session* (session-level) statement.

By allowing users to share statements that differ only in the value of the constants, the *cursor_sharing* parameter enables the Oracle database to scale easily to a large number of users who are using similar, but not identical, SQL statements. This major innovation started in the Oracle8*i* version.

Sessions with a High Number of Hard Parses

The query in Listing 19-3 enables you to find out how the hard parses compare with the number of executions since the instance was started. It also tells you the session ID for the user using the SQL statements.

Listing 19-3. Determining Sessions with a High Number of Parses

```
SQL> SELECT pa.sid, pa.value "Hard Parses",
  3  ex.value "Execute   Count"
  3  FROM v$sesstat s, v$sesstat t
  4  WHERE s.sid=t.sid
  5  AND s.statistic#=(select statistic#
  6  FROM v$statname where name='parse count (hard)')
  7  AND t.statistic#=(select statistic#
  8  FROM v$statname where name='execute count')
  9* AND s.value>0;
     SID Hard Parses Execute Count
    ---- ----------- -------------
       5          12          1122
       6           1            39
      11           6           189
      12         136          5475
      15           4            69
      17           1            37
6 rows selected.
SQL>
```

Using the Cursor_Space_For_Time Parameter

By default, cursors can be deallocated even when the application cursors are not closed. This forces an increase in Oracle's overhead because of the need to check if the cursor is flushed from the library cache. The parameter that controls whether this deallocation of cursors takes place is the *cursor_space_for_time* initialization parameter, whose default value is *false*. If you set this parameter to *true*, you ensure that the cursors for the application cannot be deallocated while the application cursors are still open. The initialization parameter in the init.ora file should be as follows:

```
Cursor_space_for_time=true
```

TIP *Of course, if you want to set this parameter, make sure that you have plenty of free shared pool memory available, because this parameter will use more shared pool memory for saving the cursors in the library cache.*

Using the Session_Cached_Cursors Parameter

Ideally, an application should have all the parsed statements available in separate cursors, so that if it has to execute a new statement, all it has to do is to pick the parsed statement and change the value of the variables (if you're using bind variables). If the application reuses a single cursor with different SQL statements, it still has to pay the cost of a soft parse. After opening a cursor for the first time, Oracle will parse the statement, and then it can reuse this parsed version in the future. This is a much better strategy than re-creating the cursor each time the database executes the same SQL statement. If you can cache all the cursors, you'll retain the server-side context, even when clients close the cursors or reuse them for new SQL statements.

You'll appreciate the usefulness of the *session_cached_cursors* parameter in a situation where users repeatedly parse the same statements, as happens in an Oracle Forms-based application when users switch among various forms. Using the *session_cached_cursors* parameter will prevent the closed cursors from being cached at the session level, so any new calls to parse the same statements will avoid the parsing overhead. Using the initialization parameter *session_cached_cursors* and setting it to a high number will make the query processing more efficient. Although soft parses are cheaper than hard parses, you can reduce even soft parsing by using the *session_cached_cursors* parameter and setting it to a high number.

The perfect situation is where a SQL statement is soft parsed once in a session and executed multiple times. For a good explanation of bind variables, cursor sharing, and related issues, please read the Oracle white paper "Efficient use of bind variables, cursor_sharing, and related cursor parameters" (http://otn.oracle.com/deploy/performance/pdf/cursor.pdf).

Parsing and Scaling Applications

When the number of users keeps increasing, some systems have trouble coping. Performance slows down dramatically in many systems as a result of trying to scale to increased user populations. When your user counts are increasing, focus on unnecessary parsing in your system. A high amount of parsing leads to latch contention, which will slow down the system. Here are some guidelines that help summarize the previous discussion about the library cache, parsing, and the use of special initialization parameters:

- A standard rule is to put as much of the code as possible in the form of stored code—packages, procedures, and functions—so you don't have the problems caused by ad hoc SQL. Use of ad hoc SQL could wreak havoc with your library cache, and it's an inefficient way to run a large application with many users. Using stored code guarantees that code is identical and thus reused, thereby enhancing scalability.

- Lower the number of hard parses, as they could be very expensive. One way to convert a hard parse to a soft parse is to use bind variables, as you saw earlier in this chapter. Reducing hard parsing will reduce shared pool latch contention.

- If bind variables aren't being used in your system currently, you can use the *cursor_sharing=force* parameter to force the sharing of SQL statements that differ only in the value of literals.

- Pay attention to the *amount* of soft parsing, not the *per unit* cost, which is much lower than that of a hard parse. A high amount of soft parsing will increase contention for the library cache latch and could lead to a slow-performing database.

- Use the *session_cached_cursors* initialization parameter to reuse the open cursors in a session. This, as you've seen, will reduce the amount of soft parsing. Set the value of this parameter to somewhere between the value of the *open_cursors* initialization parameter and the number of cursors that are being used in the instance.

- Use the *cursor_space_for_time* initialization parameter (set it to *true*) to prevent the early deallocation of cursors. If you don't mind the extra cost of using more memory, this feature will enhance your application's scalability level.

- Reduce the amount of session logging on/off activity by the users, as this will reduce scalability due to the increased amount of parsing that results. Each time a session logs off, the SQL it uses has to be reparsed, leading to a waste of time and resources. Furthermore, the users may be spending more time trying to log into the system than actually executing their SQL statements. Frequent logging off and logging back on might also cause contention for the Web server and other resources and increase the time it takes to log into your system.

The Dictionary Cache

The dictionary cache, as mentioned earlier, caches data dictionary information. This cache is much smaller than the library cache, and to increase or decrease it you modify the shared pool accordingly. If your library cache is satisfactorily configured, chances are that the dictionary cache is going to be fine too. You can get an idea about the efficiency of the dictionary cache by using the following query:

```
SQL> select (sum(gets - getmisses - fixed)) / sum(gets)
  2* "data dictionary hit ratio" from v$rowcache;
data dictionary hit ratio
-------------------------
      .936781093
SQL>
```

Usually, it's a good idea to shoot for a dictionary hit ratio as high as 95 to 99 percent. To do so in the preceding example, you need to increase the shared pool size for the instance.

Sizing the Shared Pool

You can estimate the size of the total shared pool by trial and error. Start with a moderate amount and watch the library cache and dictionary cache hit ratios. If the hit ratios are high (99 percent and above for the library cache, and 85 to 90 percent for the dictionary cache), you *do* have enough shared pool memory in the SGA. How do you know if you have too much memory allocated to the shared pool? You can easily find out if you have too much shared pool memory by querying the V$SGASTAT view in the following manner:

```
SQL>  select bytes from v$sgastat
   2  where pool='shared pool'
   3* and name = 'free memory';
       BYTES
    ----------
    123647628
SQL>
```

If you consistently see a lot of free memory, obviously your shared pool allocation is excessive and you can reduce it. On the other hand, if the free memory is consistently hovering around 1MB to 5MB, it is an indication that the shared pool memory is too low and you need to raise it. A very low amount of free memory in the shared pool is usually seen along with heavy fragmentation of the shared pool.

Another way you can decide the minimum size of your shared pool memory is by looking at a pair of key dynamic performance views, V$DB_OBJECT_CACHE and V$SQLAREA. Chapter 21 discusses both of these views in detail. Here, let me show you how to use these views to help you size the shared pool.

The V$DB_OBJECT_CACHE view has information on all objects that are presently cached in the library cache, including tables, indexes, views, procedures, functions, packages, and triggers. An important column is sharable_mem, which is the amount of memory used by a particular object.

The V$SQLAREA view contains information about parsed SQL statements that are ready for execution. In this view, the column sharable_mem shows the total amount of shared memory used by a cursor, including all its child cursors.

Another key column is users_opening, which shows the number of users who have any child cursors open. Obviously, any amount of memory in your library cache should be enough to enable the execution of all SQL and PL/SQL statements that are currently executing in your database. Using these two dynamic performance views, you can use the query shown in Listing 19-4, which indicates what the minimum (not the ideal) amount of your shared pool ought to be.

Listing 19-4. Determining the Correct Shared Pool Size

```
SQL> select to_number (value)
  2  shared_pool_size,
  3  sum_obj_size,
  4  sum_sql_size,
  5  sum_user_size,
  6  (sum_obj_size + sum_sql_size + sum_user_size) *
  7  1.2  min_shared_pool
  8  from
  9  (select sum(sharable_mem) sum_obj_size
 10  from v$db_object_cache),
 11  (select sum(sharable_mem) sum_sql_size
 12  from v$sqlarea),
 13  (select sum(250 * users_opening) sum_user_size
 14  from v$sqlarea), v$parameter
 15* where name='shared_pool_size';
SHAR_POOL_SIZ  SUM_OBJ_SIZ  SUM_SQL_SIZ  SUM_USR_SIZ  MIN_SHAR_POOL
---------------  ------------  ------------  ----------  --------------
   900000000      328233570    306795453     26035125     793276978
1 row selected.
SQL>
```

In Listing 19-4, the minimum shared pool is calculated as the sum of the following three major areas that use the library cache:

- *Sum_obj_size* indicates the total amount of memory used by all objects cached in the library cache.

- *Sum_sql_size* is the total memory used by all the SQL cursors in the library cache.

- *Sum_user_size* is the total amount of memory in the library cache allocated to all the users who have cursors open in the library cache.

In this case, the query indicates that the database needs a minimum of about 800MB. Because the database already has 900MB, you have a little more memory in the shared pool than you need.

Pinning Objects in the Shared Pool

If code objects have to be repeatedly hard-parsed and executed, database performance will deteriorate eventually. Your goal should be to see that as much of the executed code remains in memory as possible, so compiled code can be re-executed. You can avoid repeated reloading of objects in your library cache by pinning objects using the DBMS_SHARED_POOL package. Listing 19-5 shows how you can determine the objects that should be pinned in your library cache (shared pool).

Listing 19-5. Determining the Objects to Be Pinned in the Shared Pool

```
SQL>  select
   2    type,
   3    count(*)  objects,
   4    sum(decode(kept, 'YES', 1, 0))  kept,
   5    sum(loads) - count(*)  reloads
   6    from
   7    v$db_object_cache
   8    group by
   9    type
  10    order by
  11*   objects desc;
```

TYPE	OBJECTS	KEPT	RELOADS
NOT LOADED	43245	0	498
CURSOR	22482	0	3548
TABLE	1373	0	908
PUB_SUB	534	0	280
SYNONYM	331	0	85
PACKAGE	165	0	106
PACKAGE BODY	158	0	63
TRIGGER	125	0	128
SEQUENCE	82	0	0
VIEW	66	0	140
FUNCTION	17	0	28
INDEX	15	0	0
PROCEDURE	8	0	1
PIPE	7	0	0
NON-EXISTENT	6	0	5
CLUSTER	5	5	0

```
16 rows selected.
SQL>
```

If the number of reloads in the output shown in Listing 19-5 is high, you need to make sure that the objects are pinned using the following command:

```
SQL> execute sys.dbms_shared_pool.keep(object_name, object_type);
```

You can use the following statements to first pin a package in the shared pool and then remove it:

```
SQL> execute sys.dbms_shared_pool.keep(NEW_EMP.PKG, PACKAGE);
SQL> execute sys.dbms_shared_pool.unkeep(NEW_EMP.PKG,PACKAGE);
```

Of course, if you shut down and restart your database, the shared pool won't retain the pinned objects. That's why most DBAs use scripts with all the objects they want to pin in the shared pool, which they schedule to run right after every database start. Exactly what and how many objects should you pin in your shared pool? Well, if you realize the point that most of the objects usually are very small, there's no reason to be too conservative in this regard. For example, I pin all my packages, including Oracle-supplied PL/SQL packages.

Look at the following example, which gives you an idea about the total memory taken up by a large number of packages. This query shows the total number of packages in my database:

```
SQL>  select COUNT(*)
  2  from v$db_object_cache
  3* where type='PACKAGE';
  COUNT(*)
---------------
     167
1 row selected.
```

The following query shows the total amount of memory needed to pin all my packages in the shared pool:

```
SQL>  select sum(sharable_mem)
  2  from v$db_object_cache
  3* where type='PACKAGE';
  SUM(SHARABLE_MEM)
-----------------
      4771127
SQL>
```

As you can see, pinning every single package in my database will take up less than 5MB of a total of several hundred megabytes of memory allocated to the shared pool.

Using the Shared Pool Advisor

"Eyeballing" the free memory through the V$SGASTAT view and the collection of cache hit ratios for the shared pool is helpful, but it doesn't really tell you whether the configuration of your shared pool is optimal. Oracle provides an excellent Shared Pool Advisor as part of the OEM toolset to help you figure out the optimal amount of shared pool memory allocation. Chapters 5 and 16 explore the Shared Pool Advisor in detail.

Tuning the Buffer Cache

When users request data, Oracle reads the data from the disks (in terms of Oracle blocks) and stores it in the buffer cache so it may access the data easily if necessary. As the need for the data diminishes, eventually Oracle removes the data from the buffer cache to make room for newer data. Note that some operations do not use the buffer cache (SGA); rather, they read directly into the PGA area. Direct sort operations and parallel reads are examples of such operations.

How to Size the Buffer Cache

You use a process of trial and error to set the buffer cache size. You assign an initial amount of memory to the pool and watch the buffer cache hit ratios to see how often the application can retrieve the data from memory, as opposed to going to disk. The terminology used for calculating the buffer hit ratio can be somewhat confusing on occasion. Here are the key terms you need to understand:

- *Physical reads:* These are the data blocks that Oracle reads from disk. Reading data from disk is much more expensive than reading data that's already in Oracle's memory. When you issue a query, Oracle will always first try to retrieve the data from memory—the database buffer cache—and not disk.

- *DB block gets:* When Oracle finds the required data in the database buffer cache, it checks whether the data in the blocks is up-to-date. If a user changes the data in the buffer cache but hasn't committed those changes yet, new requests for the same data can't show these interim changes. If the data in the buffer blocks is up-to-date, each such data block retrieved is counted as a DB block get.

- *Consistent gets:* Sometimes Oracle finds the necessary data blocks in the buffer cache, but some of the data has been changed by other users. Oracle then applies rollback information from the undo segments to maintain the read consistency principle (see Chapter 8 for more information about read consistency). These data blocks are part of the consistent gets category.

- *Logical reads:* Every time Oracle is able to satisfy a request for data by reading it from the database buffer cache, you get a logical read. The logical reads include both DB block gets and consistent gets.

- *Buffer gets:* This term refers to the number of database cache buffers retrieved. This value is the same as logical reads described earlier.

Here's a query on the V$BUFFER_POOL_STATISTICS view that indicates how the physical and logical reads stack up:

```
SQL> select name,value from v$sysstat
  2  where name in ('physical reads','db block gets', 'consistent gets');
NAME                                   VALUE
----------------------------------- ----------
db block gets                          31641879
consistent gets                        827618230
physical reads                         52805579
3 rows selected.
SQL>.
```

The following formula gives you the buffer cache hit ratio. Note that you need to subtract the number of *physical_reads_direct* from *physical_reads* to get a more accurate measure of total disk reads, because direct physical reads bypass the buffer cache and use the PGA instead. I am assuming there are no large objects (LOBs) in this application. If you have LOBs, you need to modify the formula slightly.

```
Buffer cache hit ratio=1–(physical reads – physical_reads_direct) /
(db block gets + consistent gets _ physical_reads_direct)
```

For example, the following calculation shows that the buffer cache hit ratio for my database is a little over 95 percent:

```
1 - (66755055-2003269) / (43026759+1338792226-2003269) = .953072149
```

As you can see from the formula for the buffer cache hit ratio, the lower the ratio of physical reads to the total logical reads, the higher the buffer cache hit ratio.

In addition, you can use the Buffer Cache Advisory, which you learned about in Chapter 5, to help you get an idea about what an optimal buffer cache size may be. To use this advisory, first set the *db_cache_advisor* parameter on. You can then examine the V$DB_CACHE_ADVICE view to see how much you need to increase the buffer cache to lower the physical I/O by a certain amount. Essentially, the output of the V$DB_CACHE_ADVICE view shows you how much you can increase your buffer cache memory before the gains in terms of a reduction in the amount of physical reads (estimated) will be insignificant. The Buffer Cache Advisory simulates the miss rates in the buffer cache for caches of different sizes, both higher and lower than the current buffer cache size. In this sense, the Buffer Cache Advisory can keep you from throwing excess memory in a vain attempt at lowering the amount of physical reads in your system.

 TIP *Oracle may decide to keep only part of the large table in the buffer cache to avoid having to flush out its entire buffer cache. If your application involves many full table scans for some reason, increasing the buffer cache size isn't going to improve performance. Some DBAs are obsessed about achieving a very high cache hit ratio, such as 99 percent or so. Well, a high buffer cache hit ratio is no guarantee that your application response time and throughput will be high also. If you have a large number of full table scans or if your database is more of data warehouse rather than an OLTP system, your buffer cache may be well below 100 percent, and that's not a bad thing. If your database consists of inefficient SQL, there will be an inordinately high number of logical reads, making the buffer cache hit ratio look very good (say 99.99 percent), but this may not mean your database is performing efficiently. Please read the interesting article by Cary Millsap titled "Why a 99% Database Buffer Cache Hit Ratio Is Not OK" (*http://www.hotsos.com*).*

Using Multiple Pools for the Buffer Cache

You don't have to allocate all the buffer cache memory to a single pool. As Chapter 5 showed you, you can use three separate pools: the *keep* buffer pool, the *recycle* buffer pool, and the *default* buffer pool. Although you don't have to use the keep and default buffer pools, it's a good idea to configure all three pools so you can assign objects to them based on their access patterns. In general, you follow these rules of thumb when you use the multiple buffer pools:

- Use the recycle cache for large objects that are infrequently accessed. You don't want these objects to unnecessarily occupy a large amount of space in the default pool.

- Use the keep cache for small objects that you want in memory at all times.

- Oracle automatically uses the default pool for all objects not assigned to either the recycle or keep cache.

Since version 8.1, Oracle has used a concept called *touch count* to measure how many times an object is accessed in the buffer cache. This algorithm of using touch counts for managing the buffer cache is somewhat different from the traditional modified LRU algorithm that Oracle used to employ for managing the cache. Each time a buffer is accessed, the touch count is incremented. If you have large objects that have a low touch count but occupy a significant proportion of the buffer cache, you can consider them ideal candidates for the recycle cache. Listing 19-6 contains a query that shows you how to find out which objects have a low touch count. The touch count column is in the x$bh table owned by the user SYS.

Listing 19-6. Determining Candidates for the Recycle Buffer Pool

```
SQL>   select
   2   obj object,
   3   count(1)  buffers,
   4   (count(1)/totsize) * 100 percent_cache
   5      from x$bh,
   6            (select value totsize
   7             from v$parameter
   8   where name ='db_block_buffers')
   9   where tch=1
  10   or (tch = 0 and lru_flag <10)
  11            group by obj, totsize
  12*            having (count(1)/totsize)  *  100 > 5
     OBJECT    BUFFERS  PERCENT_CACHE
---------- ---------- ---------------
      1386     14288    5.95333333
      1412     12616    5.25666667
    613114     22459    9.35791667
```

The preceding query shows you that three objects, each with a low touch count, are taking up about 20 percent of the total buffer cache. Obviously, they are good candidates for the recycle buffer pool. In effect, what you are doing is limiting the number of buffers these three infrequently accessed tables can use up in the buffer cache.

The following query on DBA_OBJECTS gives you the names of the objects:

```
SQL> select object_name from dba_objects
   2  where object_id in (1386,1412,613114);
OBJECT_NAME
--------------------------------------------
EMPLOYEES
EMPLOYEE_HISTORY
FINANCE_RECS
SQL>
```

You can then assign these three objects to the reserved buffer cache pool. You can use a similar criterion to decide which objects should be part of your keep buffer pool. Say you want pin all objects in the keep pool that occupy at least 25 buffers and have an average touch count of more than 5. Listing 19-7 shows the query that you should run as the user SYS.

Listing 19-7. Determining Candidates for the Keep Buffer Cache

```
SQL> select obj object,
  2  count(1) buffers,
  3  avg(tch) average_touch_count
  4  from x$bh
  5  where lru_flag = 8
  6  group by obj
  7  having avg(tch) > 5
  8*    and count(1) > 25;
   OBJECT    BUFFERS AVERAGE_TOUCH_COUNT
---------- ---------- -------------------
   1349785         36                  67
4294967295         87           57.137931
SQL>
```

Again, querying the DBA_OBJECTS view provides you with the names of the objects that are candidates for the keep buffer cache pool.

Here's a simple example to show how you can assign objects to specific buffer caches (keep and recycle). First, make sure you configure the keep and recycle pools in your database by using the following set of initialization parameters:

```
db_cache_size=33554432
db_keep_cache_size=10000000
db_recycle_cache_size=10000000
```

In this example, the keep and recycle caches are 10MB each. The rest of the buffer cache, about 13MB, will remain the default buffer cache. Once you create the keep and recycle pools, it's easy to assign objects to these pools. All tables are originally in the default buffer cache, where all tables are cached automatically unless specified otherwise in the object creation statement.

You can use the *alter table* statement to assign any table or index to a particular type of buffer cache. For example, you can assign the following two tables to the keep and recycle buffer caches:

```
SQL> alter table test1 storage (buffer_pool keep);
Table altered.
SQL> alter table test2 storage (buffer_pool recycle);
Table altered.
SQL>
```

NOTE *For details about Oracle's touch count buffer management, please read Craig A. Shallahamer's interesting paper "All About Oracle's Touch Count Data Block Buffer Management" at* http://www.orapub.com. *You need to get a free membership to OraPub.com before you can download this and other papers.*

Tuning the Large Pool

You mainly use the large pool, an optional component of the SGA, for providing memory for backup and restores, and shared server processes. Oracle recommends the use of the large pool if you are using shared server processes so you can keep the shared pool fragmentation low. If you are using shared server configurations or the Recovery Manager, you should configure the large pool.

NOTE *You size the large pool based on the number of active simultaneous session in a shared server environment. Remember that if you're using the shared server configuration and you don't specify a large pool, Oracle will allocate memory to the shared sessions out of your shared pool.*

Tuning PGA Memory

Each server process is allocated a private memory area, the PGA, most of which is dedicated to memory-intensive tasks such as group by, order by, rollup, and hash joins. Operations such as in-memory sorting and building hash tables need specialized work areas. The memory you allocate to the PGA determines the size of these work areas for specialized tasks, such as sorting, and determines how fast the system can finish them. In the following sections you'll examine how you can decide on the optimal amount of PGA for your system.

Automatic PGA Memory Management

The management of the PGA memory allocation is easy from a DBA's point of view. You can set a couple of basic parameters and let Oracle automatically manage the allocation of memory to the individual work areas. You need to do a couple of things before Oracle can automatically manage the PGA: You need to use the *pga_aggregate_target* parameter to set the memory limit and you need to use the V$PGA_TARGET_ADVICE view to tune the target's value. In the next sections I discuss those tasks.

Using the Pga_Aggregate_Target Parameter

The *pga_aggregate_target* parameter in the init.ora file sets the maximum limit on the total memory allocated to the PGA. Oracle offers the following guidelines on sizing the *pga_aggregate_target* parameter:

- For an OLTP database, the target should be 16 to 20 percent of the total memory allocated to Oracle.

- For a DSS database, the target should be 40 to 70 percent of the total memory allocated to Oracle.

Using the V$PGA_TARGET_ADVICE View

Once you've set the initial allocation for the PGA memory area, you can use the V$PGA_TARGET_ADVICE view to tune the target's value. Oracle will populate this view with the results of its simulations of different workloads for various PGA target levels. You can then query the view as follows:

```
SQL>  SELECT round(PGA_TARGET_FOR_ESTIMATE/1024/1024) target_mb,
  2    ESTD_PGA_CACHE_HIT_PERCENTAGE cache_hit_perc,
  3    ESTD_OVERALLOC_COUNT
  4*  FROM v$pga_target_advice;
```

Using the estimates from the V$PGA_TARGET_ADVICE view, you can then set the optimal level for PGA memory. Chapters 5 and 16 provide you with more detailed explanations of PGA memory and how to use the V$PGA_TARGET_ADVICE view.

Evaluating System Performance

The instance tuning efforts that you undertake from within Oracle will have only a limited impact (they may even have a negative impact) if you don't pay attention to the system performance as a whole. System performance includes the CPU performance, disk I/O, and memory usage at the operating system level. In the following sections you'll look at each of these important resources in more detail.

CPU Performance

You can use operating system utilities such as sar (system activity reporter) or vmstat to find out how the CPU is performing. Don't panic if your processors seem busy during peak periods—that's what they're there for, so you can use them when necessary. If the processors are showing a heavy load during low usage times, you do need to investigate further. Listing 19-8 shows a *sar* command output indicating how hard your system is using the CPU resources right now.

Listing 19-8. Sar Command Output Showing CPU Utilization

```
[finance1] $ sar -u 10 5
HP-UX finance1  B.11.00 A 9000/800    01/28/03
13:39:17    %usr      %sys       %wio     %idle
13:39:27    34        23          7        36
13:39:37    37        17          8        38
13:39:47    34        18          6        41
13:39:57    31        16          9        44
13:40:07    38        19         11        32
Average     35        19          8        38
oracle@finance1.netbsa.org   [/u01/app/oracle/dba]
[finance1] $
```

In the preceding listing, the four columns report on the following CPU usage patterns:

- *%usr* shows the proportion of total CPU time taken up by the various users of the system.

- *%sys* shows the proportion of time the system itself was using the CPU.

- *%wio* indicates the percent of time the system was waiting for I/O.

- *%idle* is the proportion of time the CPU was idle.

If the %wio or %idle percentages are near zero during nonpeak times, it's an indication of a CPU-bound system.

Remember that a very intensive CPU usage level may mean that an operating system process is hogging CPU, or an Oracle process may be doing the damage. If it is Oracle, a background process such as PMON may be the culprit, or an Oracle user process may be running some extraordinarily bad ad hoc SQL query on the production box. You may sometimes track down such a user and inform the person that you are killing the process in the interest of the welfare of the entire system. Imagine your surprise when you find that the user's Oracle process is hale and hearty, while merrily continuing to devastate your system in the middle of a busy day. This could happen because a child process or a bequeath process continued to run even after you "killed" this user. It pays to double-check that the user is gone—lock, stock, and barrel—instead of assuming that the job has been done.

That said, let's look at some of the common events that could cause CPU-related slowdowns on your system.

The Run Queue Length

One of the main indicators of a heavily loaded CPU system is the length of the run queue. A longer run queue means that more processes are lined up, waiting for CPU processing time. Occasional blips in the run queue length are not bad, but prolonged high run queue lengths indicate that the system is CPU bound.

CPU Units Used by Processes

You can determine the number of CPU units a UNIX process is currently using by using the simple process (*ps*) command, as shown here:

```
oracle@finance1   [/u01/app/oracle/dba]
[finance1] $ ps -ef | grep f60
   UID   PID  PPID C   STIME TTY   TIME   CMD
 oracle 20108  4768  0  09:11:49 ?   0:28  f60webm
 oracle   883  4768  5 17:12:21  ?   0:06  f60webm
 oracle  7090  4768 16 09:18:46  ?   1:08  f60webm
 oracle 15292  4768 101 15:49:21 ?   1:53  f60webm
 oracle 18654  4768  0 14:44:23  ?   1:18  f60webm
 oracle 24316  4768  0 15:53:33  ?   0:52  f60webm
```

The key column to watch is the fourth one from the left, which indicates the CPU units of processing each process is using. If each CPU on a server has 100 units, the Oracle process with PID 15292 (the fourth in the preceding list) is occupying more than an entire CPU's processing power. If you have only two processors altogether, you should worry about this process and why it is so CPU intensive.

Finding High CPU Users

If the CPU usage levels are high, you need to find out which of your users are among the top CPU consumers. Listing 19-9 shows how you can easily identify those users.

Listing 19-9. Identifying High CPU Users

```
SQL>  select n.username,
  2    s.sid,
  3    s.value
  4    from v$sesstat s,v$statname t, v$session n
  5    where s.statistic# = t.statistic#
  6    and n.sid = s.sid
  7    and t.name='CPU used by this session'
  8    ORDER BY s.value desc;
USERNAME            SID     VALUE
------------------------------- ----------
JOHLMAN             152     20745
NROBERTS            103      4944
JOHLMAN             167      4330
LROLLINS             87      3699
JENGMAN             130      3694
JPATEL               66      3344
NALAPATI             73      3286
SQL>
```

Listing 19-9 shows that CPU usage is not uniformly spread across the users. You need to investigate why one user is using such a significant amount of resources. If you need to, you can control CPU usage by a single user or a group of users by using the Database Resource Manager, as explained in Chapter 11. You can also find out session-level CPU usage information by using the V$SESSION_STAT view, as shown in Listing 19-10.

Listing 19-10. Determining Session-Level CPU Usage

```
SQL> select sid, s.value "Total CPU Used by this Session"
  2  from v$sesstat s
  3  where s.statistic# = 12
  4* order by s.value desc;
     SID Total CPU Used by this Session
   ----- ------------------------------
     496                          27623
     542                          21325
     111                          20814
     731                          17089
     424                          15228
SQL>
```

Using OEM to Track CPU Usage

Instead of running SQL scripts, you can simply use OEM to analyze CPU usage in your database. Select Tools ➤ Diagnostic Pack ➤ Performance Overview in the OEM console. You can see all the active sessions ordered by physical reads, logical reads, and total CPU time used. You can also review CPU usage through OEM's TopSessions, as shown in Chapter 17.

What Is the CPU Time Used For?

It would be a mistake to treat all CPU time as equal. CPU time is generally understood as the processor time taken to perform various tasks, such as the following:

- Loading SQL statements into the library cache

- Searching the shared pool for parsed versions of SQL statements

- Parsing the SQL statements

- Querying the data dictionary

- Reading data from the buffer cache

- Traversing index trees to fetch index keys

The total CPU time used by an instance (ora session) can be viewed as the sum of the following components:

```
Total CPU Time = Parsing CPU usage + Recursive CPU usage + Other CPU usage
```

Ideally, your total CPU usage numbers should show a very small proportion of the first two categories of CPU usage—parsing and recursive CPU usage. For example, for a sessionwide estimate of CPU usage, you can run the query shown in Listing 19-11.

Listing 19-11. Decomposition of Total CPU Usage

```
SQL> select name,value from v$sysstat
  2  where name in ('CPU used by this session',
  3                 'recursive cpu usage',
  4*                'parse time cpu')
NAME                                            VALUE
---------------------------------------------- ----------
recursive cpu usage                               4713085
CPU used by this session                         98196187
parse time cpu                                     132947
3 rows selected.
SQL>
```

In this example, the sum of recursive CPU usage and parse time CPU usage is a small proportion of total CPU usage. You need to be concerned if the parsing or recursive CPU usage is a significant part of total CPU usage. Let's see how you can go about reducing the CPU usage attributable to these various components.

NOTE *In the following examples, you can examine CPU usage at the instance level by using the V$SYSSTAT view or at an individual session level by using the V$SESSTAT view. Just remember that the column "total CPU used by this session" in the V$SYSSTAT view refers to the* sum *of the CPU used by all the sessions combined.*

Parse CPU Usage

As you learned at the beginning of this chapter, parsing is an expensive operation that you should reduce to a minimum.

In the following example, the parse time CPU usage is quite low as a percentage of total CPU usage. The first query tells you that the total CPU usage in your instance is 49159124:

```
SQL> select name, value from v$sysstat
  2* where name like '%CPU%';
NAME                                            VALUE
------------------------------------------------ --------
CPU used when call started                     13220745
CPU used by this session                       49159124
2 rows selected.
SQL>
```

The next query shows the parse time CPU usage at 96431, which is an insignificant proportion of total CPU usage in your database:

```
SQL> select name, value from v$sysstat
  2  where name like '%parse%';
NAME                               VALUE
parse time cpu                     96431
parse time elapsed                295451
parse count (total)              3147900
parse count (hard)                 29139
4 rows selected.
SQL>
```

Listing 19-12 shows an example of a session whose CPU usage is predominantly due to a high amount of parse time CPU usage.

Listing 19-12. Determining Parse Time CPU Usage

```
SQL  select  a.value  " Tot_CPU_Used_This_Session",
  2  b.value "Total_Parse_Count",
  3  c.value "Hard_Parse_Count",
  4  d.value "parse_time_cpu"
  5  from v$sysstat a,
  6  v$sysstat b,
  7  v$sysstat c,
  8  v$sysstat d
  9  where a.name = 'CPU used by this session'
 10  and b.name = 'parse count (total)'
 11  and c.name - 'parse count (hard)'
 12* and d.name = 'parse time cpu';
Tot_CPU_Used  Total_Parse_Count  Hard_Parse_Count  Parse_Time_CPU
This_Session
------------------------------ ------------------ -----------------
2240                53286                281                1486
SQL>
```

Parse time CPU in the preceding example is fully two-thirds of the total CPU usage. Obviously, you need to be concerned about the high rates of parsing, even though most of the parses are soft parses. The next section shows you what you can do to reduce the amount of parsing in your database.

Reducing Parse CPU Usage

If parse time CPU is the major part of total CPU usage, you need to reduce this by performing the following steps:

1. Use bind variables and remove hard-coded literal values from code, as explained in the "Optimizing the Library Cache" section earlier in this chapter.

2. Make sure you aren't allocating *too much memory* for the shared pool. Remember that even if you have an exact copy of a new SQL statement in your library cache, Oracle has to find it by scanning all the statements in the cache. If you have a zillion relatively useless statements sitting in the cache, all they're doing is slowing down the instance by increasing the parse time.

3. Make sure you don't have latch contention on the library cache, which could result in increased parse time CPU usage.

4. If your TKPROF output or one of the queries shown previously indicates that total parse CPU time is as high as 90 percent or more, check to make sure all the tables in the queries have been analyzed recently. If you don't have statistics on some of the tables, the parsing process generates the statistics, but the parse CPU usage time goes up dramatically.

Recursive CPU Usage

Recursive CPU usage is mostly for data dictionary lookups and for executing PL/SQL programs. Thus, if your application uses a high number of packages and procedures, you'll see a significant amount of recursive CPU usage.

In the following example, there's no need for alarm, because the percentage of recursive CPU usage is only about 5 percent of total CPU usage.

```
SQL>  select name,value from v$sysstat
  2  where name in ('CPU used by this session',
  3*               'recursive cpu usage');
NAME                                              VALUE
------------------------------------------------- ----------
recursive cpu usage                               4286925
CPU used by this session                          84219625
2 rows selected.
SQL>
```

If the recursive CPU usage percentage is a large proportion of total CPU usage, you may want to make sure the shared pool memory allocation is inadequate. However, a PL/SQL-based application will always have a significant amount of recursive CPU usage.

 NOTE *A very high number of recursive SQL statements indicates that Oracle is busy with space management activities such as allocating extents. This has a detrimental effect on performance and you can avoid this problem by increasing the extent sizes for your database objects. Of course, this is another good reason to choose locally managed tablespaces, which really cut down on the number of recursive SQL statements.*

Disk I/O

The way you configure your disk system has a profound impact on your I/O rates. You have to address several issues when you are planning your disk system. Important factors that have a bearing on your I/O are as follows:

- *Choice of RAID configuration:* Chapter 3 covered RAID systems configuration in detail. Just remember that a RAID 5 configuration doesn't give you ideal I/O performance if your application involves a large number of writes. For faster performance, use a RAID 1 configuration, in which you mirror all the disks.

- *Raw devices or operating system file systems:* Under some circumstances, you can benefit by using raw devices, which bypass the operating system buffer cache. Raw devices have their own drawbacks, including limited backup features, and you want to be sure the benefits outweigh the drawbacks. Raw devices in general provide faster I/O capabilities and give better performance for a write-intensive application. You might also want to consider alternative file systems such as Veritas VxFsS, which helps large I/O operations through its direct I/O option.

- *I/O size:* I/O size is in terms of the Oracle block size. The minimum size of I/O depends on your block size, and the maximum size depends on the *multi_block_read_count* initialization parameter. If your application is OLTP based, the I/O size needs to be small, and if your application is oriented toward a DSS, the I/O size needs to be much larger.

- *Logical volume stripe sizes:* Stripe size (or stripe width) is a function of the stripe depth and the number of drives in the striped set. If you stripe across multiple disks, your database's I/O performance will be higher and its load balancing will be enhanced. Make sure that the stripe size is larger than the average I/O request; otherwise, you'll be making multiple I/Os for a single I/O request by Oracle. If you have multiple concurrent I/O requests, your stripe size should be much larger than the I/O size. Most modern LVMs can dynamically reconfigure the stripe size.

- *Number of controllers and disks:* The number of spindles and the number of controllers are both important variables in determining disk performance. Even if you have a large number of spindles, you could conceivably run into contention at the controller level.

- *Distribution of I/O:* Your goal should be to avoid a lopsided distribution of I/O in your disk system. If you are using an LVM or using striping at the hardware level, you don't have a whole lot to worry about in this area. If you aren't using an LVM or using striping at the hardware level, however, you should manually arrange your data files on the disks such that the I/O rate is fairly even across the system. Note that your tables and indexes are usually required to be in different tablespaces, but there is no rule that they can't be placed on different disks. Because the index is read before the table, they can coexist on the same disk.

Measuring I/O Performance

You have a choice of several excellent tools to measure I/O performance. The operating system utility is easy to use and gives you information about how busy your disks are. Iostat and sar are two of the popular operating system utilities that measure disk performance. Figure 19-1 shows the partial output of a typical *sar* command.

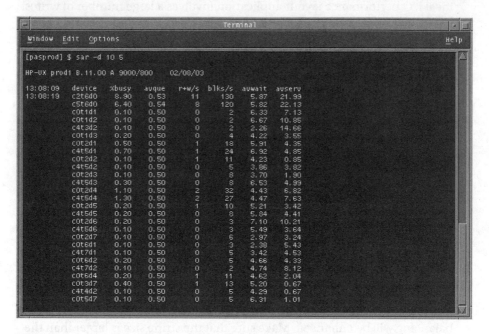

Figure 19-1. Output of the sar command showing disk usage statistics

Figure 19-1 shows the execution of the *sar* command five times at intervals of 10 seconds, and the columns have the following meaning:

- *Device* is the name of the physical device.

- *%busy* is the percentage of time the device was busy.

- *Avque* is the average number of wait requests for a device.

- *R+w/s* is the total number of reads and writes.

- *Blks/s* is the number of blocks.

- *Avwait* is the average wait time for the device.

- *Avserv* is the average service time for this device.

Is the I/O Optimally Distributed?

From the *sar* output, you can figure out if you're using the storage subsystem heavily. If the number of waits is higher than the number of CPUs, or if the service times are high (say, greater than 20ms), then your system is facing contention at the I/O level. One of the most useful pieces of information from using the *sar –d* command is finding out if you are using any of your disks excessively compared to other disks in the system. Once you identify such hot spots, you can move the data files to less busy drives, thereby spreading the load more evenly.

The following is the output of a *sar –d* command that shows extremely high queue values. Even at peak levels, the avque column value should be less than 2. Here, it is 61.4. Obviously, something is happening on the file system c2t6d0 that is showing up as a high queue value.

```
[finance1 $ sar -d 10 5
HP-UX finance1 B.11.00 A 9000/800    02/02/03
11:27:13  device  %busy  avque   r+w/s  blks/s  avwait  avserv
11:27:23  c2t6d0  100    61.40   37     245     4.71    10.43
          c5t6d0  20.38  0.50    28     208     4.92    9.54
          c2t6d0  100    61.40   38     273     4.55    9.49
          c5t6d0  18.28  0.50    27     233     4.46    7.93
          c0t1d0  0.10   0.50    4      33      4.99    0.81
$
```

The Statspack output has a section on I/O distribution. If you want an ad hoc picture of the same, you can obtain it by using the query in Listing 19-13.

Listing 19-13. Determining I/O Distribution in the Database

```
SQL> select d.name,
  2  f.phyrds reads,
  3  f.phywrts wrts,
  4  (f.readtim/ decode(f.phyrds,0,-1,f.phyrds)) readtime,
  5  (f.writetim / decode(f.phywrts,0,-1,phywrts)) writetime
  6  from
  7  v$datafile d,
  8  v$filestat f
  9  where
 10  d.file# = f.file#
 11  order by
 12* d.name;
NAME                            READS    WRTS   READTIME    WRITETIME
-----------------------------------------------------------------------
/pa01/oradata/pa/lol_i_17.dbf   23       9      .608695652  .222222222

/pa01/oradata/pa/lol_i_18.dbf   18       7      .277777778           0

/pa02/oradata/pa/pli_i_17.dbf   121816   9      .234066133  .111111111

/pa02/oradata/pa/ptr_d_02.dbf   27       5      0                    0
```

```
/pa04/oradata/pa/m_01_01.dbf    355689   5    .108594868           0

/pa10/oradata/pa/pe_d_09.dbf    800759   5    .204540942           0
SQL>
```

 CAUTION *Excessive reads and writes on some disks indicate that there might be disk contention in your I/O system.*

Reducing Disk Contention

If there is sever I/O contention in your system, you can undertake some of the following steps, depending on your present database configuration:

- Increase the number of disks in the storage system.

- Separate the database and the redo log files.

- For a large table, use partitions to reduce I/O.

- Stripe the data either manually or by using a RAID disk-striping system.

- Invest in cutting-edge technology, such as file caching, to avoid I/O bottlenecks.

The Oracle SAME Guidelines for Optimal Disk Usage

Oracle recently published the *Stripe and Mirror Everything* (SAME) guidelines for optimal disk usage. This methodology advocates striping all files across all disks and mirroring all data to achieve a simple, efficient, and highly available disk configuration. Striping across all the available disks aims to spread the load evenly and avoid hot spots. The SAME methodology also recommends placing frequently accessed data on the outer half of the disks. The goal of the SAME disk storage strategy is to eliminate I/O hot spots and maximize I/O bandwidth. For more details about the SAME guidelines, please refer to the article "Optimal Storage Configuration Made Easy," by Juan Loaiza, which is available at `http://otn.oracle.com/deploy/availability/pdf/OOW2000_same_ppt.pdf`.

Collecting Instance Performance Statistics with Statspack

You can collect instance performance information in a couple of ways. You can use Oracle's excellent Statspack tool to capture and store performance information. The Statspack tool lets you create quick instance performance reports, which enable you to figure out what events are causing waits in the system, for example.

You can also directly query important dynamic performance views to see how the instance is performing. You can use OEM's Diagnostics Pack to quickly get summary information about current instance performance.

No matter which of the two methods you use, the dynamic performance views underlie the computation of the statistics. In this section, you'll look at the use of the Statspack tool to collect and report performance statistics. In this way, you'll get a chance to understand exactly what factors contribute to database performance at a very detailed level. Statspack also provides a way for you to maintain baseline information and compare current database performance statistics with the baseline numbers to see what's happening within the database.

Statspack is essentially a set of SQL scripts provided by Oracle to help gather and store performance statistics. When you're trying to determine which of your SQL statements is using the most resources, the Statspack data is very useful, with its precalculated cache hit ratios and a number of other statistics. Statspack collects instance performance data between two periods (called *snapshots*), and based on the time interval it computes a number of timed performance statistics.

Installing Statspack

To start using Statspack, you must first create a new user named sqlplus sysqlplus, who will own all the statistics tables. To create the perfstat user and install Statspack, you'll first connect as SYS and run the installation scripts from the $ORACLE/HOME/rdbms/admin directory. To install Statspack, you need to run three scripts: spcuser.sql, spctab.sql, and spcpkg.sql. You can call of them from within one script, spcreate.sql, but I have found that if you use the three scripts, Oracle is less prone to erroring out. The three scripts perform the following tasks:

- Spcuser.sql creates the perfstat user.

- Spctab.sql creates the necessary tables and other objects to store the statistics.

- Spcpkg.sql creates the Statspack package.

 NOTE *Although the Oracle manuals don't make this obvious, you need to run the three scripts under different schemas. You must run the first script, spcusr.sql, under the SYS schema, and you must run the next two as the Statspack user perfstat.*

Listing 19-14 shows the sequence of the Statspack creation steps.

Listing 19-14. Installing Statspack

```
SQL> connect sys/mark1@mark1 as sysdba
Connected.
SQL> @%ORACLE_HOME%\rdbms\admin\spcreate
... Installing Required Packages
```

```
Package created.
... Creating PERFSTAT user...
Choose the PERFSTAT user's password.
Not specifying a password will result in the installation FAILING
Specify PERFSTAT password
Enter value for perfstat_password: perfstat1
Specify PERFSTAT user's temporary tablespace.
Enter value for temporary_tablespace: TEMP
Using TEMP for the temporary tablespace
PL/SQL procedure successfully completed.
User altered.
NOTE:
SPCUSR complete. Please check spcusr.lis for any errors.
SQL> @?/rdbms/admin/spctab
SQL> Rem $Header: spctab.sql 16-feb-2003.14:54:46 vbarrier Exp $
SQL> Rem spctab.sql
If this script is automatically called from spcreate (which is
the supported method), all STATSPACK segments will be created
in the PERFSTAT user's default tablespace.
Using EXAMPLE tablespace to store Statspack objects
... Creating STATS$SNAPSHOT_ID Sequence
Sequence created.
Synonym created.
... Creating STATS$... tables
Table created.
Synonym created.
...
Synonym created.
NOTE:
SPCTAB complete. Please check spctab.lis for any errors.
SQL>SQL> @?/rdbms/admin/spcpkg
SQL> Rem $Header: spcpkg.sql 17-feb-2003.16:59:10 vbarrier Exp $
Creating Package STATSPACK...
Package created.
No errors.
Creating Package Body STATSPACK...
Package body created.
No errors.
NOTE:
SPCPKG complete. Please check spcpkg.lis for any errors.
SQL>
```

NOTE *If you run into problems during the installation of Statspack, simply use the spdrop.sql script to drop the perfuser schema and start over.*

Using Statspack

The key to using Statspack is taking a snapshot of the instance at a given time, which involves gathering vital instance statistics and storing them in the Statspack tables. This will serve as your baseline for comparison with later snapshots. This snapshot is compared with the snapshot taken after a specified time elapses, and the changes in the instance are evaluated with reference to the time elapsed. How long should the all-important snapshot interval be? Well, there's no point in collecting statistics all day long if your key "spikes" in system activity last for only a few minutes. Just turn on statistics collection for short intervals—say 15 to 30 minutes.

You need to have the initialization parameter *timed_statistics* turned on so Statspack can capture useful information. You can ensure that the *timed_statistics* parameter is turned on in any of the following ways:

- *Timed_statistics=true* (in the init.ora file)

- *Statistics_level=typical* (in the init.ora file)

- *Statistics_level=all* (in the init.ora file)

- *Alter session set timed_statistics=true* (at the session level)

Note that the *statistics_level=typical* is the default level, and it provides you with a broad array of statistics with the least amount of overhead. The *statistics_level=full* setting gives you more details, but it's much more expensive to run in terms of a performance hit. By querying the V$STATISTICS_LEVEL view, you can get detailed information about all the statistics that are being currently captured in your instance. Before you actually take the snapshots, which will collect performance data, you need to decide on two things: the level at which you want to collect the statistics and the threshold for the SQL statements. You'll look at each of these issues in the following sections.

Snapshot Levels and SQL Thresholds

Oracle gives you a lot of flexibility in choosing the level at which you want Statspack to gather statistics. You need to specify a higher level for progressively more detailed performance data. You can summarize the snapshot levels as follows.

Level 0 collects the following general performance information:

- Wait statistics

- System statistics

- System events

- Session events

- Lock and latch statistics

- Rollback segment data

- SGA, buffer pool, and row cache statistics

Level 5 collects all the statistics gathered in the lower levels, plus SQL statement statistics that exceed a high resource usage threshold. The SQL statement statistics include parse calls, disk reads, buffer reads, and the number of executions. You can specify thresholds at the time you take the snapshots. The snapshot examples presented later on in this chapter show you how to set thresholds.

Level 6 collects all the statistics gathered in the lower levels, plus the execution plans for SQL statements, which will help you determine if the plans changed over time.

Level 7 statistics help you optimize the physical layout of your disks by providing information on segment-level access and contention. You get all the statistics from the lower levels, plus the following statistics:

- Top five segments by logical reads

- Top five segments by physical reads

- Top five segments by buffer busy waits

Levels 10 and above are for gathering specialized latch information, and you should set them only upon the recommendation of Oracle support personnel.

NOTE *The higher the snapshot level you choose, the more data Statspack collects. Level 5 is the default level. At present, the only valid levels are levels 0, 5, 6, 7, and 10. Please review the Oracle document spdoc.txt, which is in the $ORACLE_HOME/rdbms/admin directory on your server, for detailed information about the various snapshot levels and other information about the Statspack utility.*

Collecting Statspack Data

The first step in collecting data is to capture the initial snapshot of the instance, which you can do in several ways. You can do it manually, you can use the DBMS_JOB package, or you can use the crontab (in Windows, the *at* facility) to automate statistics collection. You need to take at least one other snapshot later so you can make comparisons and derive performance statistics. In the following sections you'll look at examples of the three methods.

TIP *Statspack depends on the V$ dynamic performance tables for its data. This means that if you restart the database in between two snapshots, the results will be meaningless. Each time the database is shut down, the data in the dynamic performance tables is completely lost.*

Method 1: Collecting Statistics Manually

You can start the statistics collection process by executing the *statspack.snap* procedure (as the perfstat user) both to start and stop data collection, as shown here:

```
SQL> show user
USER is "PERFSTAT"
SQL> execute statspack.snap;
PL/SQL procedure successfully completed.
SQL>
```

To get the snap_id of the snapshot you just captured, you need to execute the following procedure:

```
SQL> variable snap_num number;
SQL> begin
  2  :snap_num := statspack.snap;
  3  end;
  4  /
PL/SQL procedure successfully completed.
SQL> print snap_num
    SNAP_NUM
    ----------
        2
SQL>
```

After you let some time elapse (how much time depends on how long you want to capture statistics for), repeat the two steps:

```
SQL> begin
  2  :snap_num := statspack.snap;
  3  end;
  4  /
PL/SQL procedure successfully completed.
SQL> print snap_num
    SNAP_NUM
    ----------
        4
SQL>
```

Method 2: Using the DBMS_JOB Package to Automate Statspack

When you create the perfstat user, the DBMS_JOB package is created for scheduling jobs through Oracle. Chapter 21 presents a detailed explanation of the DBMS_JOB package, but the scheduling is really a simple matter, as you can see in Listing 19-15.

Listing 19-15. Automating Statspack Execution

```
SQL>  declare
  2   job_number integer;
  3   begin
  4   dbms_job.submit(
  5   job_number,
  6   'statspack.snap',
  7   sysdate + (1/48),
  8   'sysdate + (1/48)',
  9   true);
 10*  end;
SQL> /
PL/SQL procedure successfully completed.
SQL>
```

The job to run the *statspack.snap* procedure is scheduled to run every half hour in this example.

Method 3: Using the Crontab or the At Command to Schedule Statistics Collection

You can just use the crontab or the Windows *at* command to schedule the *snapshot.snap* procedure periodically. Chapter 3 shows you how to use the *crontab* (UNIX and Linux) and *at* (Windows) commands to schedule database jobs.

Deleting Statspack Data

Oracle provides an easy-to-use script, sppurge.sql (which is located in the $ORACLE_HOME/rdbms/admin directory), to remove unnecessary Statspack data. Once you execute this script, it asks you for an upper and lower bound of snapshot IDs, and it removes all the data that belongs to the snapshot IDs within. There is an even faster way to get rid of all Statspack data that you have collected: Simply execute the sptrunc.sql script (also located in the $ORACLE_HOME/rdbms/admin directory). Remember to log in as the user perfstat when you want to purge or truncate data using the Oracle-provided scripts.

Obtaining Statspack Reports

All you need to generate the all-important Statspack report are a pair of snapshot IDs, which will serve as the beginning and ending values for the time over which you want the reporting to be done. If you have taken many snapshots, you can have Statspack report over any specific period of time you wish.

NOTE *All wait events are shown in microseconds, rather than 10 milliseconds, as in the previous Oracle versions.*

You can run two types of Statspack reports: a general database health report called *spreport.sql* and a more specific report on single SQL statements. Let's see how you can run obtain a simple database health report from the two Statspack snapshots you gathered in the previous section. In the following output, note that you have to provide the *begin* and *end* snapshot IDs that you have created through using the *snapshot.snap* procedure (see the earlier section "Method 1: Collecting Statistics Manually"). Listing 19-16 shows the report.

Listing 19-16. The Statspack Report

```
SQL> sho user
USER is "PERFSTAT"
SQL> @?/rdbms/admin/spreport
Current Instance
~~~~~~~~~~~~~~~~

DB Id        DB Name      Inst Num   Instance
----------- ------------ -------- ------------
 1672169339   MANAGER       1        manager
Instances in this Statspack schema
~~~~~~~~~~~~~~~~~~~~~~~~~~~~~~~~~~~~~~~

   DB Id    Inst Num   DB Name     Instance      Host
----------- -------- ------------ ------------ ------------
  1672169339    1        MANAGER     manager     ALAPATISAM
Using 1672169339 for database Id
Using          1 for instance number
Completed Snapshots
                        Snap              Snap
Instance    DB Name      Id   Snap Started   Level Comment
----------- ------------ ----- ----------------- ----- --------

manager     MANAGER        1 19 Jan 2003 13:44    5
                           2 19 Jan 2003 14:55    5
                           3 19 Jan 2003 15:12    5
                           4 19 Jan 2003 15:13    5
Specify the Begin and End Snapshot Ids
~~~~~~~~~~~~~~~~~~~~~~~~~~~~~~~~~~~~~~~~

Enter value for begin_snap: 2
Begin Snapshot Id specified: 2
Enter value for end_snap: 4
End   Snapshot Id specified: 4
Specify the Report Name
~~~~~~~~~~~~~~~~~~~~~~~~~

The default report file name is sp_2_4. To use this name,
press <return> to continue, otherwise enter an alternative.
Enter value for report_name: statspack.rep1_Jan192003
Using the report name statspack.rep1_Jan192003
STATSPACK report for
DB Name   DB Id      Instance   Inst Num  Release  Cluster  Host
-------- ----------- --------- -------- --------- ------- ----------

MANAGER   1672169339  manager     1      9.2.0.1.0   NO    ALAPATISAM
```

	Snap Id	Snap Time	Sessions	Curs/Sess	Comment
	-------	------------------	--------	---------	----------
Begin Snap:	2	19-Jan-03 14:55:40	21	5.4	
End Snap:	4	19-Jan-03 15:13:58	22	5.3	
Elapsed:		18.30 (mins)			

Cache Sizes (end)
~~~~~~~~~~~~~~~~~~

Buffer Cache:	32M	Std Block Size:	4K
Shared Pool Size:	136M	Log Buffer:	512K

The Load Profile section (see Listing 19-17) gives you an idea about the logical and physical reads and writes per second and per transaction. The per-second load figures give you an indication of the throughput ("Is the database performing more work per second?") of the instance. The per-transaction figures tell you how the application transaction characteristics are changing over time. One of the items you need to watch carefully is the hard parse rate per second. If the hard parse rate is over 100 per second, the system is going to slow down noticeably because of the increased need for shared pool and library cache latches.

Listing 19-17. The Load Profile Section of the Statspack Report

	Per Second	Per Transaction
	------------	----------------
Redo size:	860.77	2,213.41
Logical reads:	18.36	47.21
Block changes:	2.94	7.56
Physical reads:	0.19	0.48
Physical writes:	0.11	0.29
User calls:	6.17	15.88
Parses:	1.44	3.71
Hard parses:	0.02	0.04
Sorts:	2.18	5.62
Logons:	0.00	0.00
Executes:	1.73	4.44
Transactions:	0.39	

% Blocks changed per Read:	16.01	Recursive Call %:	45.65
Rollback per transaction %:	40.98	Rows per Sort:	7.31

The Instance Efficiency section of the Statspack report (see Listing 19-18) indicates how good the shared pool and buffer cache hit ratios are.

Listing 19-18. The Instance Efficiency Section of the Statspack Report

Buffer Nowait %:	99.99	Redo NoWait %:	100.00
Buffer Hit %:	98.98	In-memory Sort %:	100.00
Library Hit %:	98.70	Soft Parse %:	98.86
Execute to Parse %:	16.51	Latch Hit %:	100.00
Parse CPU to Parse Elapsd %:	10.98	% Non-Parse CPU:	99.90

Shared Pool Statistics	Begin	End
	------	------

```
        Memory Usage %:    21.15    21.53
   % SQL with executions>1:   49.16    49.31
% Memory for SQL w/exec>1:   49.66    51.08
```

The Top 5 Timed Events section gives you the top five (timed) wait events and the CPU usage (if it ranks in the top five events) during the period the statistics collection was going on. These top five events may include the CPU usage time, but the CPU time only indicates CPU usage, *not* a CPU wait event. The idle wait events are omitted from the list. Note that the low hard parse rates (shown in the Load Profile section) mean that there will not be a significant wait event for latches in this section. Listing 19-19 shows the Top 5 Timed Events list.

Listing 19-19. The Top 5 Timed Events

```
Top 5 Timed Events
```

Event	Waits	Time (s)	% Total Ela Time
control file sequential read	162	2	26.58
db file sequential read	132	2	21.13
log file sync	254	2	16.73
control file parallel write	356	1	13.74
db file parallel write	42	1	7.89

In the example here, the Top 5 Timed Events section shows only wait events. If you see a Top 5 Timed Events section such as the one shown in Listing 19-20, you'll notice that about two-thirds of the total elapsed time is due to CPU usage, not wait events. Thus, you don't have to query the V$SYSSTAT view to determine if high CPU usage or high wait events are responsible for delays in your system.

Listing 19-20. A Different Set of Top 5 Timed Events

```
Top 5 Timed Events
```

Event	Waits	Time (s)	% Total Ela Time
CPU time		4	66.78
log file parallel write	83	1	14.87
control file parallel write	246	1	12.93
db file sequential read	65	0	4.06
db file scattered read	4	0	.44

The next two sections in the Statspack report show you all the wait events for the instance, including the background wait events. Listing 19-21 shows these wait events.

Listing 19-21. All Wait Events in the Database

```
Wait Events
-> s  - second
-> cs - centisecond -     100th of a second
-> ms - millisecond -    1000th of a second
-> us - microsecond - 1000000th of a second
-> ordered by wait time desc, waits desc (idle events last)
                                        Avg
                             Tot Wait  wait  Waits
Event                   Waits Timouts  Time  (ms)  /txn
----------------------- ------------ ---------- ----------
log file parallel write   783      0     1     1   195.8
control file parallel write 246    0     1     3    61.5
db file sequential read    65      0     0     4    16.3
db file scattered read      4      0     0     7     1.0
control file sequential read 228   0     0     0    57.0
...
Background Wait Events
-> ordered by wait time desc, waits desc (idle events last)
                                          Avg
                             Total Wait  wait    Waits
Event                   Waits Timeouts  Time (s) (ms)   /txn
----------------------- ------------ ---------- ---------- ---
log file parallel write   783      0     1     1   195.8
control file parallel write 246    0     1     3    61.5
db file sequential read    42      0     0     3    10.5
control file sequential read 100   0     0     0    25.0
```

The next section in the report gives you all the SQL statements that were executed in the database during the statistics collection interval. The SQL statements are ordered by the number of buffer gets. Listing 19-22 shows the SQL statements in the report.

Listing 19-22. SQL Statements Ordered by Buffer Gets

```
SQL ordered by Gets
-> End Buffer Gets Threshold:    10000
-> Note that resources reported for PL/SQL includes the resources used by
   all SQL statements called within the PL/SQL code.  As individual SQL
   statements are also reported, it is possible and valid for the summed
   total % to exceed 100
                                          CPU  Elapsd
Buffer Gets Executions Gets per Exec  %Total Time  Time  Hash Value
--------------- ------------ --------------- ------ -------- --------
  10,038         24          418.3          63.3   1.15  1.11  238087931
select count(*) from sys.job$ where (next_date > sysdate) and (n
ext_date < (sysdate+5/86400))
```

You can also review the instance activity statistics, which tells you how the CPU was being used by the instance. Listing 19-23 shows the instance activity statistics.

Listing 19-23. The Instance Activity Statistics

```
Instance Activity Stats
Statistic                       Total   per Second  per Trans
--------------------------      -------  ----------- ----------
CPU used by this session      *  420        0.6        105.0
CPU used when call started       417        0.6        104.3
DBWR checkpoint buffers written  199        0.3         49.8
SQL*Net roundtrips to/from client 100       0.1         25.0
consistent changes             1,128        1.5        282.0
consistent gets                9,636       12.7      2,409.0
data blocks consistent reads-un 1,128       1.5        282.0
db block changes               7,872       10.4      1,968.0
db block gets                  6,214        8.2      1,553.5
deferredCURRENT)block cleanout 1,010        1.3        252.5
dirty buffers inspected            5        0.0          1.3
```

In addition to the preceding information, the Statspack report also provides you with the following details (note that the Statspack data was collected at Level 5, which is the default level):

- Tablespace I/O stats

- File I/O stats

- Buffer pool statistics and the Buffer Pool Advisory for the instance

- Instance recovery statistics

- PGA aggregate target statistics

- Undo segment statistics

- Latch activity and library cache activity

NOTE *For a more on the Statspack utility, please refer to the Oracle paper "Diagnosing Performance Using Statspack"* (http://otn.oracle.com/deploy/performance/pdf/statspack.pdf).

Once you learn how the Statspack utility works, you may want to invest in a GUI-based tool through which you can launch Statspack statistics collection, create customized charts and reports, and get expert tuning advice. For one such tool, please visit the Statspack Viewer Professional page (http://www.statsviewer.narod.ru/sppro.html).

Using the OEM Diagnostics Pack to Monitor Performance

You can use a number of dynamic performance table–based scripts to check database performance. However, there are several drawbacks to the use of scripts. First, it just takes too much time to run all the scripts manually. Second, it takes an even longer time to pore over the reports and come up with meaningful conclusions. For these reasons, the use of a GUI-based tool is mandatory to get a quick visual idea of how well the database is performing. OEM has a specialized Diagnostics Pack that lets you capture operating system, middle-tier, and application and instance performance data. You can thus easily diagnose system problems, and detect and analyze the cause of problems while they are occurring. This is difficult to achieve by exclusively using SQL and operating system scripts.

 NOTE *The current version of OEM's Diagnostics Pack has very useful and powerful performance-monitoring features. Oracle recommends using this tool for database monitoring and tuning. In fact, Oracle recommends using Statspack only if you don't have the Diagnostics Pack. Remember that OEM also has a built-in capability to collect operating system statistics.*

The Diagnostics Pack uses the same V$ tables as the other performance evaluation methods such as Statspack, but it saves the data and makes efficient use of it. You can launch the Diagnostics Pack from the OEM console using either the menu or an icon. You can also select Programs ➤ Oracle Enterprise Manager ➤ Diagnostics Pack if you wish. For a feature review of the Oracle Diagnostics Pack, please read the white paper "Oracle Diagnostics Pack" (http://otn.oracle.com/products/oem/pdf/DP_9iR2_FO.pdf).

The Performance Manager

The Performance Manager component of the Diagnostics Pack provides you with an excellent interface for a real-time study of how key resources such as memory, I/O, and the CPU are performing. You can access the Database Health Overview Chart of the Performance Manager from the OEM console by selecting Tools ➤ Diagnostics Pack ➤ Performance Manager. Figure 19-2 shows the main screen of the Performance Manager, the Database Health Overview Chart.

The Database Health Overview Chart helps you track down the causes for deterioration in the I/O, memory, and CPU resources while the problem is manifesting itself. You can also get summary wait information for the instance from this chart. You can drill down into any one of these resources and find the exact SQL statement responsible for the problem. This is powerful, because you can quickly get to the problem SQL and start analyzing it.

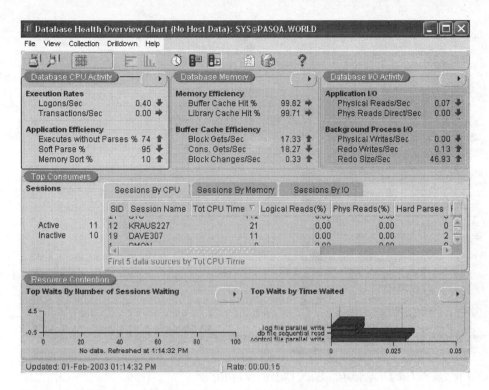

Figure 19-2. The Database Health Overview Chart of the OEM Performance Manager

The Capacity Planner

The Capacity Planner is another Diagnostics Pack component that you can use to obtain excellent statistics of database performance. You can use this OEM feature to obtain historical performance data that you can store in a history database, so you can plan future requirements of CPU and I/O.

Figure 19-3 shows the Capacity Planner application of the OEM Diagnostics Pack. You can either use Oracle's recommended collection of performance statistics or specify your own metrics. You can select the scope, frequency, and the length of time you want the data to be saved. Historical data collection should be a priority for any Oracle DBA, because it's hard to figure out *what* the instance statistics should look like if you haven't collected any data over time.

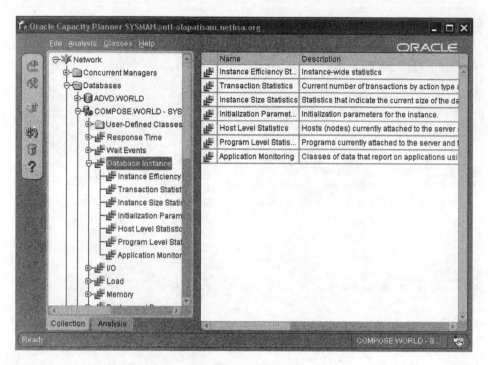

Figure 19-3. The Diagnostics Pack Capacity Planner

Measuring Instance Performance

One of the trickiest parts of the DBA's job is to accurately judge the performance of the Oracle instance. Trainers and the manuals advise you to perform diligent proactive tuning, but in reality most tuning efforts are reactive—they're intensive attempts to fix problems such as a perceptibly slow database that's causing user complaints to increase. You look at the same things whether you're doing proactive or reactive tuning, but proactive tuning gives you the luxury of making decisions in an unhurried and low-stress environment. Ideally, you should spend over two-thirds of your total tuning time on proactive planning. As you do so, you'll find that you're reacting less and less over time to sudden emergencies.

There are statistics that you can look at to see how well the database is performing. These statistics fall into two groups: database hit ratios and database wait statistics. The hit ratios tell you how well the different parts of the SGA memory are configured. If you are consistently seeing numbers in the high 90s for the various hit ratios you saw earlier in this chapter, there is no need to add any more memory to these components.

However, the big question is this: Do high ratios automatically imply a perfectly tuned and efficient database? The surprising answer is no. To understand this confusing fact, you need to look at what hit ratios really indicate. The following sections examine the two main groups of performance statistics.

Database Hit Ratios

Database hit ratios are the most commonly used measures of performance. These include the buffer cache hit ratio, the library cache and dictionary cache hit ratios, the latch hit ratio, and the disk sort ratios. These hit ratios don't really indicate how well your system is performing. They're very broad indicators of proper SGA allocation, and they may be very high even when the system as a whole is performing poorly. The thing to remember is that the hit ratios just measure ratios such as how physical reads compare with logical reads and how much of the time a parsed version of a statement is found in memory. As to whether the statements themselves are efficient or not, the hit ratios can't tell you anything. When your system is slow due to bottlenecks, the hit ratios are of little help and you should turn to a careful study of wait statistics instead.

 CAUTION *Even if you have a 99.99 percent buffer cache hit ratio, you may still have major inefficiencies in your application. What if you have an extremely high number of "unnecessary" logical reads? This will make your buffer cache hit ratio look really good, as that hit ratio is defined as physical reads over the sum of logical reads. Although you may think your application should run faster because you're doing most of your reads from memory instead of disk, this may very well not happen. The reason is that even if you're doing logical reads, you're still burning up the CPU units to do the unnecessary logical reads. In essence, by focusing zealously on the buffer cache hit ratio to relieve the I/O subsystem, you could be an unwitting party to a CPU usage problem. Please read Cary Millsap's interesting article, "Why You Should Focus on LIOs instead of PIOs" (http://www.hotsos.com), which explains why a high logical I/O level could be a major problem.*

As you're aware by now, high buffer cache hit ratios don't necessarily mean that the application is well tuned. All a high buffer cache hit ratio is telling you is that your physical reads are very small when compared to the total logical reads from the buffer cache. It's entirely possible for you to have a 99.0 buffer cache hit ratio and still have a database slowdown.

When faced with a slow-performing database or a demand for shorter response times, Oracle DBAs have traditionally looked to increase their database hit ratios and tune the database by adjusting a host of initialization parameters (such as spin count and so on). More recently, there's awareness that the key area to focus on is clearing up database bottlenecks that contribute to a lower response time.

The total response time for a query is the time Oracle takes to execute it plus the time the process spends waiting for resources such as latches, data buffers, and so on. For a database instance to perform well, ideally your application should spend very little time waiting for access to critical resources.

Let's now turn to examine the critical wait events in your database, which can be real showstoppers on a busy day in a production instance.

Database Wait Statistics

When your users complain that the database is crawling and they can't get their queries returned fast enough, there is no use in your protesting that your database is showing high hit ratios for the shared pool and the buffer cache (and the large pool and redo log buffer as well). If the users are waiting for long periods of time to complete their tasks, then the response time will be slow, and you can't say that the database is performing well, the high hit ratios notwithstanding.

NOTE *For an interesting review of the Oracle wait analysis (the wait interface), please read the article "Yet Another Performance Profiling Method (or YAPP-Method),"by Anjo Kolk, Shari Yamaguchi, and Jim Viscusi, which is available at* http://www.dbatoolbox.com/WP2001/tuning/08I_tuning_method.htm.

An Oracle process, once it starts executing a SQL statement, doesn't always get to "work" on the execution of the statement without any interruptions. Often, the process has to pause or wait for some resource to be released before it can continue its execution. Thus, an active Oracle process is doing one of the following at any given time:

- The process is executing the SQL statement.

- The process is waiting for something (e.g., a resource such as a database buffer or a latch). It could be waiting for an action such as a write to the buffer cache to complete.

That's why the response time—the total time taken by Oracle to finish work—is correctly defined as follows:

```
Response time = service time + wait time.
```

When you track the total time taken by a transaction to complete, you may find that only part of that time was taken up by the Oracle server to actually "do" something. The rest of the time, the server may have waiting for some resource to be freed up or waiting for a request to do something. This busy resource may be a slow log writer or database writer process. The wait event may also be due to unavailable buffers or latches. The wait events in the V$SYSTEM_EVENT view (instance-level waits) and the V$SESSION_EVENT view (session-level waits) will tell you what the wait time is due to (full table scans, high number of library cache latches, and so on). Not only will the wait events tell you what the wait time in the database instance is due to, but they will also tell you a lot about bottlenecks in the network and the application.

NOTE *It is very important to understand that the wait events are only the symptoms of problems, most likely within the application code. The wait events show you what is slowing down performance, but not why a certain wait event is showing up in large numbers. It is up to you to investigate the SQL code to find out the real cause of the performance problems.*

Three dynamic performance views contain wait information: V$SYSTEM_EVENT, V$SESSION_EVENT, and V$SESSION_WAIT. These three views list just about all the events the instance was waiting for and the duration of these waits. Understanding these wait events is essential for resolving performance issues.

Let's look at the common wait events in detail in the following sections. Remember that the three views I mentioned previously show similar information but focus on different aspects of the database, as you can see from the following summary. The wait events are most useful when you have timed statistics turned on. Otherwise, the wait events will only have the number of times they occurred, not the length of time they consumed. Without timing the events, you really can't tell if a wait event was indeed a contributing factor in a system slowdown.

Using V$ Tables for Wait Information

The three key dynamic performance tables for finding wait information are the V$SYSTEM_EVENT, V$SESSION_EVENT, and V$SESSION_WAIT views. The first two views show the waiting time for different events.

The V$SYSTEM_EVENT view shows the total time waited for all the events for the entire system since the instance started up. The view does not focus on the individual sessions experiencing waits, and therefore it gives you a high-level view of waits in the system. You can use this view to find out what the top instancewide wait events are. You can calculate the top *n* waits in the system by dividing the event's wait time by the total wait time for all events.

The three key columns of the V$SYSTEM_EVENT view are total_waits, which gives the total number of waits; time_waited, which is the total wait time per session since the instance started; and average_wait, which is the average wait time by all sessions per event.

The V$SESSION_EVENT view is similar to the V$SYSTEM_EVENT view, and it shows the total time waited per session. By querying this view, you can find out the specific bottlenecks encountered by each session.

The third dynamic view is the V$SESSION_WAIT view, which shows the current waits or just completed waits for sessions. The information on waits in this view changes continuously based on the type of waits that are occurring in the system. The real-time information in this view provides you tremendous insight into what is holding up things in the database *right now*. The V$SESSION_WAIT view provides detailed information on the wait event, including details such as file number, latch numbers, and block number. This detailed level of information provided by the V$SESSION_WAIT view enables you to probe into the exact bottleneck that is currently slowing down the database. The low-level information helps you zoom in on the root cause of performance problems.

Listing 19-24 shows you the structure of the important V$SESSION_WAIT view.

Listing 19-24. The V$SESSION_WAIT View

```
SQL> desc v$session_wait
 Name                 Null?    Type
 -------------        -------- --------------
 SID                           NUMBER
 SEQ#                          NUMBER
 EVENT                         VARCHAR2(64)
 P1TEXT                        VARCHAR2(64)
 P1                            NUMBER
 P1RAW                         RAW(4)
 P2TEXT                        VARCHAR2(64)
 P2                            NUMBER
 P2RAW                         RAW(4)
 P3TEXT                        VARCHAR2(64)
 P3                            NUMBER
 P3RAW                         RAW(4)
 WAIT_TIME                     NUMBER
 SECONDS_IN_WAIT               NUMBER
 STATE                         VARCHAR2(19)
SQL>
```

The following columns from the V$SESSION_WAIT view are important for troubleshooting performance issues:

- *Event:* These are the different wait events described in the next section (e.g., latch free and buffer busy waits).

- *P1, P2, P3:* These are the additional parameters that represent different items, depending on the particular wait event. For example, if the wait event is *db_file_sequential_read*, P1 stands for the file number, P2 stands for the block number, and P3 stands for the number of blocks. If the wait is due to a latch-free event, P1 stands for the latch address, P2 stands for the latch number, and P3 stands for the number of attempts for the event.

- *Wait_time:* This is the wait time in seconds if the state is *waited known time*.

- *Seconds_in_wait:* This is the wait time in seconds if the state is *waiting*.

- *State:* The state could be *waited short time, waited known time*, or *waiting*, if the session is currently waiting for an event.

You can start analyzing the wait events in your system by first querying the V$SYSTEM_EVENT view to see if there are any significant wait events currently occurring in the database. You can do this by running the query shown in Listing 19-25.

Listing 19-25. Using the V$SYSTEM_EVENT View to View Wait Events

```
select event, time_waited, average_wait
 2  from v$system_event
 3  group by event, time_waited, average_wait
 4* order by time_waited desc;
EVENT                           TIME_WAITED         AVERAGE_WAIT
-----------------------------------------------------------------
rdbms ipc message                 24483121           216.71465
SQL*Net message from client       18622096           106.19049
PX Idle Wait                      12485418           205.01844
pmon timer                         3120909           306.93440
smon timer                         3093214         29459.18100
PL/SQL lock timer                  3024203          1536.68852
db file sequential read             831831              .25480
db file scattered read              107253              .90554
free buffer waits                    52955            43.08787
log file parallel write              19958             2.02639
latch free                            5884             1.47505
...
58 rows selected.
SQL>
```

This example shows a very simple system with hardly any waits other than the idle type of events and the SQL*Net wait events. There aren't any significant I/O-related or latch contention–related wait events in this database. However, if your query on a real-life production system shows significant numbers for any "nonidle" wait event, it's probably a good idea to find out the SQL statements that are causing the waits. After all, the SQL statements are causing the high waits, so that's where you have to focus your efforts to reduce the waits. You have different ways to obtain the associated SQL for the waits, as explained in the following section.

Obtaining Wait Information

Obtaining wait information is as easy as querying the related dynamic performance tables. For example, if you wish to quickly find out the types of waits different user sessions (session-level wait information) are facing and the SQL text of the statements that they are executing, you can use the following query:

```
SQL> select s.username,
     t.sql_text, w.event
     from v$session s, v$sqltext t, v$session_wait w
     where s.sql_hash_value = t.hash_value
     and s.sql_address       = t.address
     and s.type          <> 'BACKGROUND'
     and s.sid           = w.sid
     order by s.sid,t.hash_value,t.piece;
```

NOTE *You need to turn on statistics collection by either setting the initialization parameter* timed_ statistics *to* true *or setting the initialization parameter* statistics_level *to* typical *or* all.

If you want quick instancewide wait event status, showing which events are the biggest contributors to total wait time, you can use the query shown in Listing 19-26 (there will be several "idle" events listed in the output, but don't show them here).

Listing 19-26. Instance-wide Waits Sorted by Total Wait Time

```
SQL> select event, total_waits,time_waited from V$system_event
  2  where event NOT IN
  3  ('pmon timer', 'smon timer', 'rdbms ipc reply', 'parallel deque wait',
  4  'virtual circuit', '%SQL*Net%', 'client message', 'NULL event')
  5* order by time_waited desc;
EVENT                       TOTAL_WAITS        TIME_WAITED
------------------------    -------------      -------------
db file sequential read     35051309           15965640
latch free                  1373973            1913357
db file scattered read      2958367            1840810
enqueue                     2837               370871
buffer busy waits           444743             252664
log file parallel write     146221             123435
SQL>
```

It's somewhat confusing in the beginning when you're trying to use all the wait-related V$ views, which all look very similar. Here's a quick summary of how you go about using the key wait-related Oracle9*i* dynamic performance views.

First, look at the V$SYSTEM_EVENT view and rank the top wait events by the total amount of time waited, as well as the average wait time for that event. Start investigating the top waits in terms of the percentage of total wait time. You can also look at any Statspack reports you may have, because Statspack also lists the top five wait events in the instance.

Next, find out more details about the specific wait event that's at the top of the list. For example, if the top event is buffer busy waits, look in the V$WAITSTAT view to see which buffer block is causing the busy buffer waits (a simple *select* * from V$WAITSTAT will get you all the necessary information). For example, if the undo block buffer waits make up most of your buffer busy waits, then it's the undo segments that are at fault, not the data blocks.

Finally, use the V$SESSION_WAIT view to find out the exact objects that may be the source of a problem. For example, if you have a high amount "db file scattered reads"–type waits, the V$SESSION_WAIT view will give you the file number and block number involved in the wait events. In the following example, the V$ views V$SESSION and V$SESSION_WAIT are used to find out who is doing the full table scans showing up as the most important wait events right now:

```
SQL> select S.sid, s.sql_address, s.sql_hash_value
    from V$SESSION s, V$SESSION_WAIT w
    where w.event like '%scattered read'
    and w.sid = s.sid;
```

You can also use the V$SQLAREA view to find out which SQL statements are responsible for high disk reads. If latch waits predominate, you should be looking at the V$LATCH view to gain more information about the type of latch that's responsible for the high latch wait time.

Looking at Segment-Level Statistics

Whether you use the Statspack tool or the wait-related V$ views, you're going to find no information about where a certain wait event is occurring. For example, you can see from the V$SYSTEM_EVENT view that buffer busy waits are your problem, and you know that you reduce these waits either by increasing the I/O bandwidth or by modifying the table storage parameters and adjusting parameters such as FREELISTS and INITTRANS. However, neither Statspack nor the V$ view indicates which tables or indexes you should be looking at to fix the high wait events. Oracle 9.2 provides three new V$ views to help you drill down to the *segment level.*

The new segment level dynamic performance views are V$SEGSTAT_NAME, V$SEGSTAT, and V$SEGMENT_STATISTICS. Now you can find out which of your tables and indexes are being subjected to high resource utilization or high waits. Once you are aware of a performance problem due to high waits, you can use these segment-level views to find out exactly which table or index is the culprit and fix that object to reduce the waits and increase database performance.

The V$SEGMENT_NAME view provides you with a list of all the segment levels that are being collected, and tells you whether the statistics are sampled or not. Listing 19-27 shows you a query on the V$SEGSTAT_NAME view that gives you all the events for which segment-level information is being collected since the instance started.

Listing 19-27. Events for Which Segment-Level Data Is Available

```
SQL> select * from v$segstat_name;
    STATISTIC       # NAME                              SAMPLED
---------- -------------------------------------------- -------
        0           logical reads                       YES
        1           buffer busy waits                   NO
        2           db block changes                    YES
        3           physical reads                      NO
        4           physical writes                     NO
        5           physical reads direct               NO
        6           physical writes direct              NO
        8           global cache cr blocks served       NO
        9           global cache current blocks served  NO
       10           ITL waits                           NO
       11           row lock waits                      NO
11 rows selected.
SQL>
```

Let's see how you can use these segment-level views to your advantage when you're confronted by a high number of wait events in your system. Say that you look at the V$SYSTEM_EVENT view and realize that there are a large number of buffer busy waits. You should now examine the V$SEGMENT_STATISTICS view with a query such as the following to find out which object is the source of the high buffer busy waits. You can then decide on the appropriate corrective measures for this wait event, as discussed in the section "Important Oracle Wait Events" later in this chapter.

```
SQL> select owner, object_name, object_type, tablespace_name
  2  from v$segment_statistics
  3  where statistic_name='buffer busy waits'
  4  order by value desc ;
```

Collecting Detailed Wait Event Information

Selecting data from V$ dynamic performance views and interpreting them meaningfully isn't always so easy to do. Because the views are dynamic, the information that they contain is constantly changing, with Oracle updating the underlying tables for each wait event. Also, the wait-related dynamic performance views you just examined don't provide crucial data such as bind variable information. For a more detailed level of wait information, you can use one of the three methods described in the following sections. The first method is simple to use and should suffice for most cases.

Method 1: Using the Oracle Event 10046 to Trace SQL Code

You can get all kinds of bind variable information by using a special trace called the 10046 Trace, which is much more advanced than the SQL Trace you saw in Chapter 18. The use of this trace will cause an output file to be written to the trace directory. You can set the 10046 Trace in many ways by specifying various levels, with each higher level providing you with more detailed information. (Level 12 is used in the following case as an example only—it may give you much more information than necessary. Level 4 will give you detailed bind value information, and Level 8 will give you wait information.)

You can use the *alter session* statement as follows:

```
SQL> alter session set events '10046 trace name context forever, level 12';
Session altered.
SQL>
```

You can also incorporate the following line in your init.ora file:

```
Event=  10046 trace name context forever, level 12
```

Method 2: Using the Oradebug Utility to Perform the Trace

You can use the oradebug utility as shown in the following example:

```
SQL> oradebug setmypid
Statement processed.
SQL> oradebug event 10046 trace name context forever, level 8;
Statement processed.
SQL>
```

In this example, *setmypid* indicates that you want to trace the current session. If you want a different session to be traced, you replace this with *setospid <Process Id>*.

Method 3: Using the DBMS_SYSTEM Package to Set the Trace

The syntax for this package is shown in Chapter 18. Also, Chapter 21 explains the DBMS_SYSTEM package in more detail. Using the *set_ev* procedure of the DBMS_SYSTEM package, so you can set tracing on in any session, as shown in the following example:

```
SQL> execute sys.dbms_system.set_ev (9,271,10046,12,'');
PL/SQL procedure successfully completed.
SQL>
```

Important Oracle Wait Events

The wait events listed in the sections that follow have a significant impact on system performance by increasing response times. Each of these events (and several other events) indicates an unproductive use of time because of an excessive demand for a resource or contention for Oracle structures such as tables or the online redo log files.

NOTE *The V$EVENT_NAME view will give you the complete list of all Oracle wait events and their description.*

Buffer Busy Waits

The *buffer busy waits* event occurs in the buffer cache area when several processes are trying to access the same buffer in the buffer cache area. One session is waiting for another session's read of a buffer into the buffer cache. This wait could also occur when the buffer is in the buffer cache, but another session is changing the buffer.

You should observe the V$SESSION_WAIT view while this wait is occurring to find out exactly what type of block is causing the wait. If the waits are primarily on data blocks, try increasing the PCTFREE parameter to lower the number of rows in each data block. You may also want to increase the INITRANS parameter to reduce contention from competing transactions. If the waits are mainly in segment headers, increase the number of FREELISTS or FREELIST GROUPS for the segment in question, or consider increasing the extent size for the table or index.

Buffer busy waits can occur for several types of buffers, including data block and header blocks buffers for tables and undo segments. However, if you are using Automatic Undo Management (AUM), the undo segments won't have this problem, leaving table and index data block buffers as the main problem areas. The following query clearly shows that in this database, the buffer busy waits are really in the data block:

```
SQL> select class,count from v$waitstat
  2  where count > 0
  3* order by count desc;
CLASS                    COUNT
------------------   ----------
data block               519731
undo block                 5829
undo header                2026
segment header               25
SQL>
```

If data block buffer waits are the main problem, this could be a problem caused by poorly chosen indexes that are leading to large index range scans. Tuning the SQL statements is necessary to fix these waits. Oracle maintains that if you use AUM instead of traditional rollback segments, the two types of buffer busy waits, undo block and undo header, will go away. However, that's not the case in practice, as the following example from a database with AUM shows:

```
CLASS                    COUNT
------------------   ----------
undo header              29891
data block                  52
segment header               1
```

Once in a while, you may have a situation where the buffer busy waits spike suddenly, seemingly for no reason. The sar utility (*sar –d*) might indicate high request queues and service times. This often happens when the disk controllers get saturated by a high amount of I/O. Usually, you see excessive core dumps during this time in your core dump directory. If core dumps are choking your I/O subsystem, do the following:

- Move your core dump directory to a less busy file system, where it resides by itself.

- Use the following init.ora/SPFILE parameters to control core dumps in your system. Setting these parameters' values could reduce the size of a core dump to a few megabytes from a gigabyte or more.

```
Shadow_core_dump = partial /* or none */
Background_core_dump = partial /* or none */
```

- Investigate the core dumps and see if you can fix them by applying necessary Oracle and operating system patch sets.

Checkpoint Completed

The *checkpoint completed* wait event means that a session is waiting for a checkpoint to complete. This could happen when you're shutting the database down or during normal checkpoints.

DB File Scattered Read

The *DB file scattered read* wait event indicates that full tables scans (or index fast full scans) are occurring in the database. During full table scans or index fast full scans, the table data blocks are read into scattered rather than contiguous buffers. The number of blocks read at one time by Oracle is set by the initialization parameter *db_file_multiblock_read_count*. Although Oracle will read in multiblock chunks, it scatters them into noncontiguous cache buffers. If the full table scans are not high in number, and if they mainly consist of smaller tables, don't worry about it.

However, if this event is showing up as an important wait event, you need to look at it as an I/O-related problem—the database isn't able to cope with an excessive request for physical I/Os. There are two possible solutions. You can either reduce the demand for physical I/Os or increase the capacity of the system to handle more I/Os. You can reduce the demand for physical I/O by drilling down further to see if one of the following solutions will work:

- Add missing indexes on key tables (unlikely in a production system).

- Optimize SQL statements if they aren't following an efficient execution plan currently.

If you don't see any potential for reducing the demand for physical I/O, you're left with no choice but to increase the number of disks on your system. You also need to make sure you're reducing the hot spots in your system by carefully distributing the heavily hit tables and indexes across the available disks. You can identify the data files where the full table or index fast full scans are occurring with the help of a query using the V$FILESTAT view. In this view, two columns are of great use:

- *Phyrds:* The number of physical reads done

- *Phyblkrd:* The number of physical blocks read

Obviously, if the amount of phyrds is equal to or close to the amount of phyblkrds, almost all reads are single block reads. If the column phyrds shows a much smaller value than the phyblkrds column, Oracle is reading multiple blocks in one read—a full table scan or an index fast full scan, for example. Here's a sample query on the V$FILESTAT view:

```
SQL> select file#, phyrds,phyblkrd
  2  from v$filestat
  3* where phyrds != phyblkrd;
     FILE#     PHYRDS   PHYBLKRD
---------- ---------- ----------
         1       4458      36533
         7      67923     494433
        15      28794     378676
        16      53849     408981
SQL>
```

DB File Sequential Read

The *DB file sequential read* wait event signifies that a single block is being read into the buffer cache. This event occurs when you're doing an indexed read and you're waiting for a physical I/O call to return. This is nothing to be alarmed about, because the database has to wait for file I/O. However, you should investigate disk I/O if this statistic seems extraordinarily high. Because the very occurrence of this event proves that your application is making heavy use of an index, you really can't do much to reduce the demand for physical I/Os in this case, unlike in the case of the DB file scattered read event. You should see whether increasing the FREELISTS for the indexes would reduce the sequential reads. Increasing the number of disks and striping indexes across them may be your best bet to reduce DB file sequential read waits.

Direct Path Read and Direct Path Write

The *direct path read* and *direct path write* events are waits during performing a direct read or write into the PGA, bypassing the SGA buffer cache. Direct path reads indicate that sorts are being done on disk instead of in memory. They could also result from a busy I/O system. If you use automatic PGA tuning (see Chapters 5 and 7), you shouldn't encounter this problem too often.

Automatic tuning of the PGA by Oracle should reduce your disk sorts due to a low PGA memory allocation. Another solution may be to increase the number of disks, as this problem also results in an I/O system that can't keep up with the increased requests for reading blocks into the PGA. Of course, tuning the SQL statements themselves to reduce sorting wouldn't hurt in this case.

Free Buffer Waits

Free buffer waits usually show up when the database writer process is slow. The database writer process is simply unable to keep up with the requests to service the buffer cache. All buffers are dirty (modified) and the database writer process is trying to write their contents to disk. The number of dirty buffers in cache waiting to be written to disk is larger than the number of buffers the database writer process can write per batch. Meanwhile, sessions have to wait because they can't get free buffers to write to. You need to first rule out that the buffer cache is not too small, and check the I/O numbers on the server, especially the write time, using an operating system tool. A check of the database buffer cache and a quick peek at OEM's Buffer Cache Advisor may tell you that you're below your optimal buffer cache level, in which case you can increase the size of the buffer cache.

The other reason for a high number of buffer busy waits in your system is that the number of database writer processes is inadequate to perform the amount of work your instance needs to get done. As you know, you can add additional database writer processes to the default single DBWR0 process. You can reduce these waits in most cases by increasing the number of database writer processes using a value that is in between 2 and 10 for the *db_writer_processes* initialization parameter. Oracle recommends that you use one database writer process for every four CPUs on your system. You can't change this variable on the fly, so you'll need to perform a system restart to change the number of database writer processes.

Enqueue Waits

Enqueues are similar to locks in that they are internal mechanisms that control access to resources. High enqueue waits indicate that a large number of sessions are waiting for locks held by other sessions. You can query the dynamic performance view V$ENQUEUE_STAT to find out which of the enqueues have the most wait times reported. You can do this by using the cum_wait_time column of the view.

Note that the use of locally managed tablespaces will eliminate several types of enqueues such as space transactions (ST) enqueues. In a system with a massive concurrent user base, most common enqueues are due to infrequent commits (or rollbacks) by transactions that force other transactions to wait for the locks held by the early transactions. In addition, there may be a problem with too few interested transactions list (ITL) slots, which will also show up as a transaction (TX) enqueues. You can increase the value of the INITTRANS or MAXTRANS parameter for the key tables in your system that undergo a large number DML operations.

Latch Free

Latches are internal serialization mechanisms used to protect shared data structures in Oracle's SGA. You can consider latches as a type of lock that is held for an extremely short time period. Oracle has several types of latches, with each type guarding access to a specific set of data. The *latch-free* wait event is incremented when a process can't get a latch on the first attempt. If a required Oracle latch is not available, the process requesting it keeps spinning and retrying for the access (the spinning is limited by the spin count initialization parameter). The continuous spinning will increase the wait time and increase the CPU usage in the system. There are about 200 latches used by Oracle, but two of the important latches that show up in wait statistics are the *shared pool latch* (and the library cache latches) and the *cache buffers LRU chain*. It's normal to see a very high number of latch-free events in an instance. You should worry about this wait event only if the total time consumed by this event is high.

High latch waits will show up in your Statspack reports, or you can use the query shown in Listing 19-28 to find out your latch hit ratio.

Listing 19-28. Determining the Latch Hit Ratio

```
SQL> select  a.name "Latch Name",
        a.gets "Gets (Wait)",
        a.misses "Misses (Wait)",
        (1 - (misses / gets)) * 100 "Latch Hit Ratio %"
FROM   v$latch a
WHERE  a.gets    != 0
UNION
SELECT a.name "Latch Name",
        a.gets "Gets (Wait)",
        a.misses "Misses (Wait)",
        100 "Latch Hit Ratio"
FROM   v$latch a
WHERE  a.gets    = 0
ORDER BY 1;
SQL>
```

If the ratio is not close to 1, it's time to think about tuning the latch contention in your instance. There is only one shared pool latch for the database, and it protects the allocation off memory in the library cache. The library cache latch regulates access to the objects present in the library cache. Any SQL statement, PL/SQL code, procedure, function, or package needs to acquire this latch before execution. If the shared pool and library cache latches are high, more often than not that's because the parse rates in the database are high. The high parse rates are due to the following factors:

- An undersized shared pool (or an oversized shared pool)

- Failure to use bind variables

- Using dissimilar SQL statements and failing to reuse statements

- Users frequently logging off and logging back into the application

- Failure to keep cursors open after each execution

- Using a shared pool size that is too large

The *cache buffers LRU chain* latch-free wait is caused by very high buffer cache throughput either due to full table scans or the use of unselective indexes, which lead to large index range scans. Unselective indexes can also lead to yet another type of latch-free wait: the *cache buffer chain* latch-free wait. The cache buffer chain latch waits are often due to the presence of hot blocks, so you need to investigate why that might be happening. If you see a high value for row cache objects latch waits, it indicates contention for the dictionary cache, and you need to increase the shared pool memory allocation.

In most instances, latch waits tend to show up as a wait event, and DBAs sometimes are alarmed by their very presence in the wait event list. As with the other Oracle wait events, ask yourself this question: "Are these latch waits a significant proportion of my total wait time?" If the answer is no, don't worry about it—your goal isn't to try and eliminate all waits in the instance, because you can't do it.

Log Buffer Space

The *log buffer space* wait event indicates that a process waited for space in the log buffer. Either the log buffer is too small or the redo is being written faster than the log writer process can write it to the redo log buffer. If the redo log buffer is already at a large size, then investigate the I/O to the disk that houses the redo log files. There is probably some contention for the disk, and you need to work on reducing that. This type of wait usually shows up when the log buffer is too small, in which case you increase the log buffer size. A large log buffer will tend to reduce the redo log I/O in general. Note that Oracle's default value for this parameter could be as high as 4MB (for a 32-CPU system). Don't be afraid to set a fairly large size for this parameter, although Oracle claims that about 1MB should be sufficient.

The other way to attack this problem is to increase the number of log writer processes. You can configure more log writer processes in addition to the initial log writer process. You may have to do this if you determine the log writer process is unable to keep up with the amount of work.

Log File Switch

The *log file switch* wait event can occur when a session is forced to wait for a log file switch because the log file hasn't yet been archived. It can also occur because the log file switch is awaiting the completion of a checkpoint.

If the problem isn't due to the archive destination getting full, it means that the archive process isn't able to keep up with the rate at which the redo logs are being archived. In this case, you need to increase the number of archiver (ARCHn) processes to keep up with the archiving work. The default for the ARCHn process is 2, and this is a static parameter, so you can't use this fix to resolve a slowdown right away.

You also need to investigate whether too-small redo log files are contributing to the wait for the log file switch. If the log file switch is held up pending the completion of checkpoint, obviously the log files are too small and hence are filling up too fast. You need to increase the size of the redo log files in this case. Redo log files are added and dropped online, so you can consider this a dynamic change.

If you see high values for *redo log space requests* in V$SYSSTAT, that means that user processes are waiting for space in the redo log buffer. This is because the log writer process can't find a free redo log file to empty the contents of the log buffer. Resize your redo logs, with the goal of having a log switch every 15 to 30 minutes.

Log File Sync

You'll see a high number of waits under the *log file sync* category if the server processes are frequently waiting for the log writer process to finish writing committed transactions (redo) to the redo log files from the log buffer. This is usually the result of too-frequent commits, and you can reduce it by adopting batch commits instead of a commit after every single transaction. This wait event may also be the result of an I/O bottleneck.

Idle Events

You can group some wait events under the category *idle events*. Some of these wait events may be harmless in the sense that they just indicate that an Oracle process was waiting for something to do. These events don't indicate database bottlenecks or contention for Oracle's resources. For example, the system may be waiting for a client process to provide SQL statements for execution. The following list presents some common idle events:

- *Rdbms ipc message:* Used by the background process like the log writer process and PMON to indicate they are idle.

- *SMON timer:* The SMON process waits on this event.

- *PMON timer:* The PMON process idle event.

- *SQL*Net Message from Client:* User process idle event.

You should ignore many idle events during your instance performance tuning. However, some events, such as the SQL*Net Message from Client, may indicate that your application may not be using a very efficient database connection strategy. In this case, you need to see how you can reduce these waits, maybe by avoiding frequently logging on and off the applications.

 NOTE *An excellent article that shows you how to follow a structured approach to performance tuning is "Oracle9i Performance Management: The Oracle Method," by Mughees A. Minhas (*http://otn.oracle.com/ products/manageability/database/pdf/OWPerformanceMgmtPaper.pdf)*. For a useful set of Oracle best practices to ensure high performance, please refer to the paper "Oracle9i Database Administration Best Practices," also by Mughees A. Minhas (*http://otn.oracle.com/products/ manageability/database/pdf/BestPractices9i.pdf)*.

Know Your Application

Experts rely on hit ratios or wait statistics, or sometimes both, but there are situations where both the hit ratios and the wait statistics can completely fail you. Imagine a situation where all the hit ratios are in the 99 percent range. Also, imagine that the wait statistics don't show any significant waiting for resources or any contention for latches. Does this mean that your system is running optimally?

Well, your system is doing what you asked it to do extremely well, but there's no guarantee that your SQL code is processing things efficiently. If a query is performing an inordinate number of logical reads, the hit ratios are going to look wonderful. The wait events also won't show you a whole lot, because they don't capture the time spent while you were actually using the CPU. However, you'll be burning a lot of CPU time, because the query is making too many logical reads.

This example shows why it's important not to rely on just the hit ratios or the wait statistics, but also to look at the major consumers of resources on your instance with an intense focus—for example, why is this query doing a billion logical reads? Check the top session list (sorted according to different criteria) on your instance and see if there's justification for them to be in that list.

Above all, try not to confuse the symptoms of poor performance with the causes of poor performance. If your latch rate is high, there are initialization parameters that you might want to adjust right away—after all, isn't Oracle a highly configurable database? Well, you may succeed sometimes by relying solely on adjusting the initialization parameters, but it may be time to pause and question why exactly the latch rate is so high. More than likely, the high latch rate is due to application coding issues, rather than a specific parameter setting. Similarly, you may notice that your system is CPU bound, but the reason may not be slow or too few CPU resources. Your application may again be the likely culprit, because it is doing too many unnecessary I/Os, even if they're mostly from the database buffer cache and not disk.

When you are examining wait ratios, please understand that your goal is not make all the wait events go away, because that will never happen. Learn to ignore the unimportant and routine, unavoidable wait events such as the control file parallel wait event. As you saw in the previous section, wait events such as the SQL*Net Message from Client event reflect waits outside the database, so don't attribute these waits to a poorly performing database. Focus on the total wait time rather than the number of wait events that show up in your performance tables and Statspack reports. Also, if the wait events make up only a small portion of response time, there's no point in fretting about the waits. That is, if the response time is 20 minutes and the waits are 20 seconds, what's the point of wasting your time investigating the wait events any further? As Einstein might say, the significance of wait events is relative—relative to the total response time and relative to the total CPU execution time.

In addition to the hit ratios and the wait event statistics, you need to monitor other areas of the database for possible performance implications. Among other things, you should try to achieve the following goals to maximize the performance of your database:

- Minimize row chaining and migration.

- Check for blocking locks in your system.

- Make sure that the redo log space requests are kept low by tuning your database writer process. If the number of requests is high, it means the database is slowing down due to an inadequate number/size of redo logs.

- Monitor checkpoint intervals to optimize their frequency.

Recently, there has been a surge in publications that expound the virtues of a wait event analysis–based performance approach (also called the *wait interface* approach). If you use this method for performance tuning, how important are the traditional hit ratios? Well, you can always use the buffer hit ratios and the other ratios for a general idea about how the system is using Oracle's memory and other resources, but an analysis of wait events is still a better bet in terms of improving performance. If you take care of the wait issues, you'll have taken care of the traditional hit ratios as well anyway. For example, if you want to fix a problem that is the result of a high number of free buffer waits, you may need to increase the buffer cache. Similarly, if latch-free wait events are troublesome, one of the solutions is to check if you need to add more memory to the shared pool. You may fix a problem due to a high level of waits caused by the direct path reads by increasing the value of the *pga_aggregate_target* parameter.

Operating System Memory Management

You can use the vmstat utility, as explained in Chapter 3, to find out if there is enough free memory on the system. If the system is paging and swapping, database performance will deteriorate and you need to investigate the causes. If the heavy consumption of memory is due to a non-Oracle process, you may want to move that process off the peak time for your system. You may also want to consider increasing the size of the total memory available to the operating system. You can use the *vmstat* command to monitor virtual memory on a UNIX system. The UNIX tool *top* shows you CPU and memory use on your system.

When a Database Hangs

So far in this chapter, you've looked at ways to improve performance—how to make the database go faster. Sometimes, however, your problem is not the more mundane one of tweaking extra performance from a database, but something much more serious: The database all of a sudden seems to have stopped! What do you do in such a circumstance? Performance was acceptable on a Friday, but Monday morning your manager comes to you to ask why users are complaining about a slow database. What to do? The following sections describe the most important reasons for a hanging or an extremely slow performing database and how you can fix the problem ASAP.

One of the first things I do when the database seems to freeze is check and make sure that the archiver process is doing its job. The following sections describe the archiver process.

Handling a Stuck Archiver Process

If your archive log destination is full and there isn't room for more redo logs to be archived, the archiver process is said to be *stuck*. The database doesn't merely slow down—it freezes in its tracks. As you are aware, in an archive log mode the database simply won't overwrite redo log files until they're archived successfully. Thus, the database starts hanging when the archive log directory is full. It stays in that mode until you move some of the archive logs off that directory manually.

How the Archiver Process Works

The archiver process is in charge of archiving the filled redo logs. The archiver process reads the control files to find out if there are any unarchived filled redo logs. The archiver process checks the redo log headers and blocks to make sure they're valid before archiving them. You may have archiving-related problems if you're in the archivelog mode but the archiver process isn't running for some reason. In this case, you need to start the archiver process by using the following command:

```
SQL> alter system archive log start;
```

If the archiver process is running but the redo logs aren't being archived, then you may have a problem with the archive log destination, which may be full. This will cause the archiver process to become stuck, as you'll learn in the next section.

What If the Archiver Process Is Stuck?

When the archiver process is stuck, all database transactions that involve any changes to the tables can't proceed any further. You can still perform select operations, because they don't involve the redo logs.

If you look in the alert log, you can see the Oracle error messages indicating that the archiver process is stuck due to lack of disk space. You can also query the V$ARCHIVE view. This view holds information about all the redo logs that need archiving. If the number of these logs is very high and increasing quickly, you know your archiver process is stuck and that you need to manually clear it. Listing 19-29 shows the error messages you'll see when the archiver process is stuck.

Listing 19-29. Database Hang Due to Archive Errors

```
[monitor] $ sqlplus system/monitor1
SQL*Plus: Release 9.2.0.1.0 - Production on Thu Jan 23 11:12:42 2003
Copyright (c) 1982, 2002, Oracle Corporation.  All rights reserved.
ERROR:
ORA-00257: archiver error. Connect internal only, until freed.
oracle@hp50.netbsa.org   [/u01/app/oracle]
[monitor] $ oerr ora 257
00257, 00000, "archiver error. Connect internal only, until freed."
//*Cause: The archiver process received an error while trying to
// archive a redo log.  If the problem is not resolved soon, the
// database will stop executing transactions. The most likely cause
// of this message is the destination device is out of space to
// store the redo log file.
// *Action:  Check archiver trace file for a detailed description
// of the problem. Also verify that the device specified in the
// initialization parameter ARCHIVE_LOG_DEST is set up properly for // archiving.
oracle@hp50.netbsa.org   [/u01/app/oracle]
[monitor] $
```

You can do either of the following in such a circumstance:

- Redirect archiving to a different directory.

- Clear the archive log destination by removing some archive logs. Just make sure you back up the archive logs to tape before removing them.

Once you create more space in the archive log directory, the database resumes normal operations and you don't have to do anything further. If the archiver process isn't the cause of the hanging or frozen database problem, then you need to look in other places to resolve the problem.

If you see too many "checkpoint not complete" messages in your alert log, then the problem isn't being caused by the archiver process. Your slowdown is being caused by the redo logs, which are unable to keep up with the high level of updates. You can increase the size of the redo logs online to alleviate the problem.

System Utilization Problems

You need to check several things to make sure there are no major problems with the I/O subsystem or with the CPU usage. Here are some of the important things you need to examine:

- Make sure your system isn't suffering from a severe paging and swapping problem, which could result in a slower performing database.

- Use top, sar, vmstat, or similar operating system–level tools to check resource usage. Large queries, sorting, and space management operations could all lead to an increase in CPU usage.

- Runaway processes and excessive SNP processes could gobble excessive CPU resources. Monitor any replication (snapshot) processes or DBMS_JOB processes, because they both use resource-hungry SNP processes. If CPU usage spikes, make sure there are no unexpected jobs running in the database. Even if there aren't any jobs executing currently, the SNP processes consume a great deal of CPU because they have to constantly query the job queue.

- High runqueues indicate that the system is CPU bound, with processes waiting for an available processor.

- If your disk I/O is close to or at 100 percent and you've already killed several top user sessions, you may have a disk controller problem. For example, the 100 percent busy disk pack might be using a controller configured to 16-bit, instead of 32-bit like the rest of the controllers, causing a severe slowdown in I/O performance.

Excessive Contention for Resources

Usually when people talk about a database hang, they're actually mistaking a severe performance problem for a database hang. This is normally the case when there's severe contention for internal kernel-level resources such as latches and pins.

If your database is performing an extremely high number of updates, contention for resources such as undo segments and latches could potentially be a major source of databasewide slowdowns, making is seem sometimes like the database is hanging. In the early part of this chapter, you learned how to analyze database contention and wait issues using the V$SESSION_WAIT view and the Statspack output. On Windows servers, you can use the Performance Monitor and Event Monitor to locate possible high resource usage.

Check for excessive library cache contention also if you're confronted by a databasewide slowdown.

Locking Issues

If a major table or tables are locked unbeknownst to you, the database could slow down dramatically in very short order. Try running a command such as *select * from persons*, for example, where *persons* is your largest table and is part of just about every SQL statement. If you aren't sure which tables (if any) might be locked, you can run the following statement to identify the table or index that's being locked, leading to a slow database:

```
SQl> select l.object_id,l.session_id,
  2  l.oracle_username,l.locked_mode,
  3  o.object_name
  4  from v$locked_object l,
  5  dba objects o
  6* where o.object_id=l.object_id;
OBJECT_ID  SESSION_ID ORACLE_USERNAME  LOCKED_MODE  OBJECT_NAME
  6699        22         NICHOLAS           6         EMPLOYEES
SQL>
```

As the preceding query and its output show, user Nicholas has locked up the Employees table. If this is preventing other users from accessing the table, you have to quickly remove the lock by killing the locking user's session. You can get the session_id from the preceding output and the V$SESSION view will give you the serial# that goes with it. Using the *alter system kill ...* command, you can kill the offending session. The same analysis applies to a locked index, which will prevent users from using the base table. For example, an attempt to create an index or rebuild it when users are accessing the table can end up inadvertently locking up the table.

If there is a table or index corruption, that could cause a problem with accessing that object(s). You can quickly check for corruption by running the following statement:

```
SQL> analyze table employees validate structure cascade;
Table analyzed.
SQL>
```

Abnormal Increase in Process Size

On occasion, there might be a problem because of an alarming increase in the size of one or more Oracle processes. You have to be cautious in measuring Oracle process size, because traditional UNIX operating system–based tools can give you a misleading idea about process size. The following sections explain how to measure Oracle process memory usage accurately.

What Is Inside an Oracle Process?

An Oracle process in memory has several components:

- *Shared memory:* This is the SGA that you are so familiar with.

- *The executable:* Also known as TEXT, this component consists of the machine instructions. The TEXT pages in memory are marked read-only.

- *Private data:* Also called DATA or heap, this component includes the PGA and the UGA. The DATA pages are writable and aren't shared among processes.

- *Shared libraries:* These can be private or public.

When a new process starts, it requires only the DATA (heap) memory allocation. Oracle uses the UNIX implementation of shared memory. Shared memory means that all processes attach to shared memory segments. The SGA and TEXT are visible to and shared by all Oracle processes, and they aren't part of the cost of creating new Oracle processes. If 1,000 users are using Oracle Forms, only one set of TEXT pages is needed for the Forms executable.

Unfortunately, most operating system tools such as ps and top give you a misleading idea as to the process size, because they include the common shared TEXT sizes in individual processes. Sometimes they may even include the SGA size. Solaris's pmap and HP's glance are better tools from this standpoint, as they provide you with a more accurate picture of memory usage at the process level.

 NOTE *Even after processes free up memory, the operating system may not take the memory back, indicating larger process sizes as a result.*

Measuring Process Memory Usage

As a result of the problems you saw in the previous section, it's better to rely on Oracle itself for a true indication of its process memory usage. If you want to find out the total DATA or heap memory size (the biggest nonsharable process memory component), you can do so by using the following query:

```
SQL> select value, n.name|| '('||s.statistic#||')' , sid
    from v$sesstat s, v$statname n
    where s.statistic# = n.statistic# ,
    and n.name like '%ga memory%'
    order by value;
```

If you want to find out the total memory allocated to the PGA and UGA memory together, you can issue the following command. The query reveals that a total of over 367MB of memory is allocated to the processes. Note that this memory is in addition to the SGA memory allocation, so you need to make allowances for both types of memory to avoid paging and swapping issues.

```
SQL> select sum(value)
    from v$sesstat s, v$statname n
    where s.statistic# = n.statistic#
    and n.name like '%ga memory%';
SUM(VALUE)
---------------
3674019536
1 row selected.
SQL>
```

If the query shows that the total session memory usage is growing abnormally over time, you might have a problem such as a memory leak. A telltale sign of a memory leak is when Oracle's memory usage is way outside the bounds of the memory you've allocated to it through the initialization parameters. The Oracle processes fail to return the memory to the operating system in this case. If the processes continue to grow in size, eventually they may hit some system memory barriers and fail with the ORA-4030 error:

```
[finance1] $ oerr ora 4030
04030, 00000, "out of process memory when trying to allocate %s bytes (%s,%s)"
// *Cause:  Operating system process private memory has been exhausted
[finance1] $
```

Note that Oracle tech support may request that you collect a *heap dump* of the affected Oracle processes (using the oradebug tool) to fix the memory leak problem.

If your system runs out of swap space, the operating system can't continue to allocate any more virtual memory. Processes will fail when this happens, and the best way to get out of this mess is to see if you can quickly kill some of the processes that are using a heavy amount of virtual memory.

Delays Due to Shared Pool Problems

Sometimes, database performance deteriorates dramatically because of inadequate shared pool memory. Low shared pool memory relative to the number of stored procedures and packages in your database could lead to objects constantly aging out of the shared pool and having to be executed repeatedly.

Problems Due to Bad Statistics

As you know by now, the Oracle cost-based optimizer (CBO) needs up-to-date statistics so it can pick the most efficient method of processing queries. It is common for most DBAs to analyze tables and indexes on a regular basis. Of course, you can also analyze the tables in a more efficient way by using the DBMS_STATS package.

If you don't execute the DBMS_STATS package (or run the *analyze* command) regularly while lots of new data is being inserted into tables, your old statistics will soon be out of whack, and the performance of critical SQL queries could head south. DBAs are under time constraints to finish the analyze of table overnight or over a weekend. Sometimes, they may be tempted to use the *estimate* option to analyze the tables. As I advised earlier in this chapter, always do a full analyze of tables, with the *compute* option. The *estimate* option is totally unreliable, and it leads to the generation of bad statistics. The database could slow down considerably as a result.

Collecting Information During a Database Hang

It sometimes can be downright chaotic when things crawl down to a standstill in the database. You might be swamped with phone calls and anxious visitors to your office who are wondering why things are slow. Oftentimes, especially when serious unknown locking issues are holding up database activity, it's tempting to just bounce the database because usually it clears up the problem. Unfortunately, you really don't know what caused the problem, so when it happens again, you're still just as ignorant as you were the first time around regarding the cause of the problem. Bouncing the database also means that all the users currently connected will be forced out of the database, which may not always be a smart strategy.

It's important that you collect some information quickly for two reasons. First, you might be able to prevent the problem next time or have someone in Oracle tech support (or a private firm) diagnose the problem using their specialized tools and expertise in these matters. Second, most likely a quick shutdown and restart of the database will fix the problem for sure (as in the case of some locking situations, for example). But a database bounce is too mighty a weapon to bring to bear on every similar situation. If you diagnose the problem correctly, simple measures may prevent the problem or help you fix it when it does occur. The following sections describe what you need to do to collect information on a very slow or hanging database.

Gathering Error Messages

The first thing you do when you find out the database suddenly slowed down or is hanging is to look in some of the log files where Oracle might have sent a message to. Quickly look in the alert log file to see if there are any Oracle error messages or any other information that could pinpoint any problems. You can check the background dump directory (bdump) for any other trace files with error messages in them. I summarize these areas in the following discussion.

Getting a Systemstate Dump

A systemstate dump is simply a trace file that is output to the user dump directory. Oracle (or a qualified expert) can analyze these dumps and tell you what was going on in the database when the hanging situation occurred. For example, if logons are very slow, you can do a systemstate dump during this time, and it may reveal that most of the waits are for a particular type of library cache latch. These dumps tend be very large, so make sure your *user_dump_dest* parameter is bumped up to a large value (such as 200MB) if it is set to a small value right now. To get a systemstate dump, run the following command:

```
SQL> alter session set events 'immediate trace name systemstate, level 10';
```

CAUTION *Oracle Corporation strongly warns against customers setting events on their own. You may end up causing more severe problems when you set events sometimes. Please contact Oracle technical support before you set any event. For example, the event 10235 has been known to cause heavy latch contention.*

You can send the resulting output to Oracle so they can analyze it for you. Note that at this stage, you need to open a technical assistance report (TAR) with Oracle technical support through MetaLink (http://metalink.oracle.com) (The hanging database problem will get you a priority level 1 response, so you should hear from an analyst within minutes.) Oracle technical support may ask you for more information, such as a core dump, and ask you to run a debugger or another diagnostic tool and FTP the output to them.

Using the Hanganalyze Utility

The systemstate dumps, while useful, have several drawbacks, including the fact that they dump out too much irrelevant information and take too much to complete the dump, leading to inconsistencies in the dump information. The newer hanganalyze utility is more sophisticated than a systemstate dump. Hanganalyze provides you with information on resources each session is waiting for and what is blocking access to those resources. The utility also provides you with a dependency graph among the active sessions in the database. This utility is not meant to supplant the systemstate dumps; rather, you should use it to help make systemstate dumps more meaningful. Again, use this utility in consultation with Oracle technical support experts. Here is a typical *hanganalyze* command:

```
SQL> alter session set events 'immediate trace name HANGANALYZE level 3';
```

The Promise and the Performance

The Immigration and Naturalization Service (INS) of the United States government created a new $36 million Student and Exchange Visitor Information System (SEVIS) to replace the old paper-based methods the INS had used for years to track foreign students in U.S. educational institutions. More than 5,400 high schools, colleges, and universities have to use SEVIS to enter the necessary information about enrolled students from other countries.

The INS had imposed a deadline of January 31, 2003, by which all educational institutions had to switch over fully to the SEVIS system. However, it extended the deadline by at least 2 weeks amidst several complaints about the system working slowly, if at all. Here are a few of those complaints from users across the country:

- Some employees in Virginia could enter data only in the mornings, before the West Coast institutions logged onto the system. In the afternoons, the system slowed to a crawl.

- From the University of Minnesota came complaints that that the officials were "completely unable" to use the system at all. The users mentioned that the system "was really jammed with users trying to get on." They also complained that the system was "unbelievably slow." An INS spokesperson admitted that the system had been "somewhat sluggish" and that schools were having trouble using the SEVIS system.

- The University of North Carolina complained that the situation, if it continued any further, was going to be "a real nightmare" and that it was already "starting to cause some problems."

- One worker at a college in Michigan was quoted as saying this in frustration: "Please tell me what I'm doing wrong, or I am going to quit."

The INS realized the colleges and universities weren't going to meet the deadline, and they announced a grace period after saying that "upgrades to the system" had greatly improved performance.

Why am I discussing INS's problem in this chapter? Well, behind the SEVIS system is an Oracle9*i* database, which was performing awfully slowly. The system apparently couldn't scale well enough. When large number of users got on, it basically ground to a halt. Obviously, the system wasn't configured to handle a high number of simultaneous operations. Was the shared server approach considered, for example? How were the wait statistics? I don't know the details. I do know that the Oracle9*i* database is fully capable of meeting the requirements of an application such as this. I picked this example to show that even in high-profile cases, DBAs sometimes have to eat humble pie when the database isn't tuned properly and consequently performance doesn't meet expectations.

A Simple Approach to Instance Tuning

Most of the instance tuning that DBAs perform is in response to a poorly performing database. Although a well-designed system with well-written SQL code might avoid many performance issues, here you are, on a busy day, with your customers complaining about slow performance. What do you do? The following sections present a brief summary of how you can start analyzing the instance to find out where the problem lies.

First, examine all the major resources such as the memory, CPUs, and storage subsystem to make sure your database isn't being slowed down by bottlenecks in these critical areas.

NOTE *Collecting baseline data about your database statistics, including wait events, is critically important for troubleshooting performance issues. If you don't have baseline numbers, what are you going to compare the present system data with? If you have baseline data, you can immediately check if the current resource usage patterns are consistent with the load on the system.*

What's Happening in the Database?

It isn't rare for a single user's SQL query to cause an instancewide deterioration in performance if the query is bad enough. SQL statements are at the root of all database activity, so you should look at what's going on in the database right now. The following are some of the key questions you need to find answers to:

- Who are the top users in your TopSessions display?

- What are the exact SQL statements being executed by these users?

- Is the number of users unusually high compared to your baseline numbers for the same time period?

- Is the load on the database higher than what your baseline figures show for the time of the day or the time of the week or month? You can judge loads fairly quickly by using the V$SYSSTAT view to find out the number of logical reads, physical reads and writes, parse counts (hard and soft), DB block changes, and the size of the undo that is being generated.

- What top waits can you see in the V$SESSION_WAITS view? This is a real-time wait event view that shows the wait events that are happening right now or have just happened in the instance. You have already seen how you can find out the actual users responsible for the waits by using other V$ views.

My colleague Don Rios correctly points out that a critical question here is whether the performance problem du jour is something that is "sudden" without any forewarnings or if it is caused by factors that have been "gradually" creeping up on you. Under the latter category are things such as a growing database, a larger number of users, and a larger of number of DML operation updates than what you had originally designed the system for. These types of problems may mean that you need to redesign at least some of your tables and indexes, with different storage and other parameters such as FREELISTS. If, on the other hand, the database has slowed down suddenly, you need to focus your attention on a separate set of items.

Are There Any Long-Running Transactions?

You can use the V$SQL view as shown in the following example to find out which of the SQL statements in the instance are currently taking the most time to finish and are the most resource intensive. The query ranks the transactions on the total number of elapsed seconds. You can also rank the statements according to CPU seconds used.

```
SQL> select hash_value, executions,
  2  round (elapsed_time/1000000, 2) total_time,
  3  round (cpu_time/1000000, 2) cpu_seconds from (
  4  select * from v$sql order by elapsed_time desc);
HASH_VALUE EXECUTIONS   TOTAL_TIME  CPU_SECONDSS
---------- ----------   ----------  ------------
 238087931    168          9.51        9.27
1178035321    108          4.98        5.01
...
SQL>
```

Once you have the value for the hash_value column from the query you just ran, it's a simple matter to find out the execution plan for this statement, which is in your library cache. The following query uses the V$SQL_PLAN view to get you the execution plan for your longest running SQL statements.

```
SQL> select * from V$SQL_PLAN where hash_value = 238087931;
```

You can also use the hash value from the previous example to get a Statspack SQL report. To get the SQL report, you need to execute the sprepsql.sql script, which is located in the $ORACLE_HOME/rdbms/admin directory. The script will prompt you for the *begin* and *end* snapshot IDs (2 and 4 in the snapshot example), as well as the hash value for a single SQL statement. Statspack will provide you with the execution plan used by the SQL statement and a detailed accounting of the resources used during the execution of the statement. Statspack will place the output in a report for you. Here's an example:

```
STATSPACK SQL report for Hash Value: 238087931
DB Name         DB Id      Instance       Inst Num Release  Cluster Host
----------- ----------- ------------- -------- ----------- ------- -
MONITOR      2029096430 monitor            1    9.2.0.1.0    NO     hp5
 Start Id  Start Time        End Id   End Time       Duration(mins)
--------- ------------------- --------- ------------------- --------
     1    7-Feb-03 09:13:45    2    17-Feb-03 09:26:24    12.65
```

The report then provides detailed execution statistics for the SQL statement you specified, as shown here:

```
-> CPU and Elapsed Time are in seconds (s) for Statement Total and in
   milliseconds (ms) for Per Execute

                                                    % Snap
                     Statement Total   Per Execute   Total
                     ---------------   -----------   ------
       Buffer Gets:           10,038         418.3   63.33
        Disk Reads:                0           0.0     .00
    Rows processed:              528          22.0
     CPU Time(s/ms):              1           47.9
 Elapsed Time(s/ms):              1           46.4
             Sorts:              0             .0
       Parse Calls:             24            1.0
     Invalidations:              0
     Version count:              1
    Sharable Mem(K):            23
```

The SQL report will also show you the execution plan for the SQL statement that was found in the library cache during the begin and end snapshots of Statspack.

Is Oracle the Problem?

Just because your database users are complaining, you shouldn't be in a hurry to conclude that the problem lies within the database. After all, the database doesn't work in a vacuum—it runs on the server and is subject to the resource constraints and bottlenecks of that server. If the non-Oracle users on the server are using up critical resources such as CPU processing and disk I/O, your database may be the victim of circumstances, and you need to look for answers outside the database. That's why it's critical that DBAs understand how to measure general system performance, including memory, the disk storage subsystem, the network, and the processors. In the following sections you'll take a look at the system resources you should focus on.

Is the Network Okay?

One of the first things you need to do when you're investigating slowdowns is to rule out network-related problems. Quite often, users complain of their being unable to connect to or being abruptly disconnected from the system. Check your round-trip ping times and the number of collisions. Your network administrator should check the Internet connections and routers.

On the Oracle end, you can check the following dynamic views to find out if there is a slowdown due to a network problem. The V$SESSION_EVENT view shows the average amount of time Oracle waits between messages, in the average wait column. The V$SESSION_WAIT view, as you've seen, shows what a session is waiting for, and you can see if waits for network message transport are higher than normal.

If the time for SQL round-trips is extremely long, it could reflect itself as a high amount of network-related wait time in the V$ views. Check to see if your ping time for network round-trips has gone up appreciably. You should discuss with your network administrator what you can do to decrease the waits for network traffic.

You may explore the possibility of setting the parameter *tcp.nodelay=true* in your sqlnet.ora file. This will result in TCP sending packets without waiting, thus increasing response time for real-time applications.

If the network seems like one of your constant bottlenecks, you may want to investigate the possibility of using the shared server approach instead of the dedicated server approach for connecting users to your database. This will help your application scale more efficiently to very large user bases.

Is the System CPU Bound?

Check the CPU performance to make sure a runaway process or a valid Oracle process is not hogging one or more processes and contributing to the system slowdown. Often, killing the runaway processes or the resource-hogging sessions will bring matters to a more even keel. Using OEM, you can get a quick idea about the breakdown of CPU usage among parse, recursive, and other usage components, as shown in Figure 19-4.

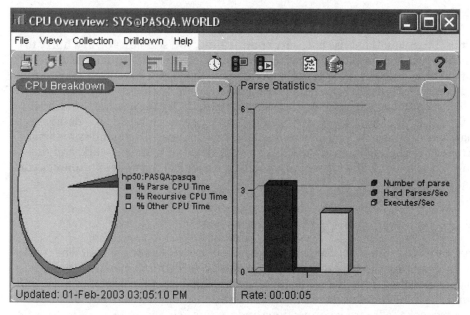

Figure 19-4. Using OEM to analyze CPU usage

Normally, you should expect to see no more than 20 to 25 percent of total CPU usage by the system itself, and about 60 to 65 percent usage by the Oracle application. If the system usage is close to 50 percent, it is an indication that there are too many system calls, for example, which leads to excessive use of the processors.

As you learned earlier in this chapter, the V$SESSTAT view shows CPU usage by session. Using the following query, you can find out the top CPU-using Oracle sessions. You may want to look into the actual SQL that these sessions are executing.

```
SQL> select a.sid,a.username,
  2   s.sql_text
  3   from v$session a,v$sqltext s
  4   where a.sql_address = s.address
  5   and a.sql_hash_value = s.hash_value
  6   and a.username  = '&USERNAME'
  7   AND A.STATUS='ACTIVE'
8*  order by a.username,a.sid,s.piece;
```

You can also view the Oracle Performance Manager's Database Health Overview Chart to examine CPU usage and see if a few users are using up most of the available processing resources. As indicated in earlier sections of this chapter, you should break down the CPU usage into parse, recursive, and other types of usage. If the parse usage is predominant, for example, you know that the database is performing excessive parsing for some reason. High CPU usage is not necessarily a problem; it is the type of use the CPU is being put to that is more important. Figure 19-5 shows a database that has a large number of waits, with the total wait time outweighing the total CPU time taken to execute the queries in the database.

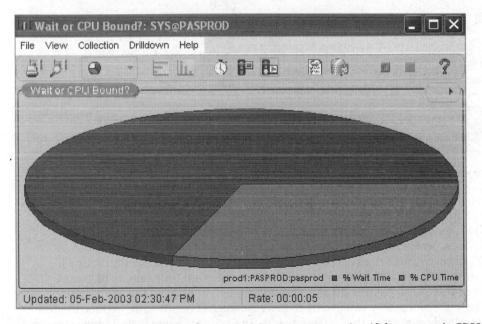

Figure 19-5. Using the OEM Performance Manager to examine if the system is CPU or wait bound

Is the System I/O Bound?

Before you go any further analyzing other wait events, it's a good idea to rule out that you are not limited by your storage subsystem by checking your I/O situation. Are the read and write times on the host system within the normal range? Is the I/O evenly distributed, or are there hot spots with one or two disks being hit really hard? If your normal, "healthy" I/O rates are 40–50/ms and you're seeing an I/O rate of 80/ms, obviously something is amiss. Figure 19-6 shows how you can view I/O times (disk read and disk write) times by data file. This will usually tip you off about what might be causing the spike. For example, if the temporary tablespace data files are showing up in the high I/O list often, that's usually an indication that disk sorting is going on, and you need to investigate that further.

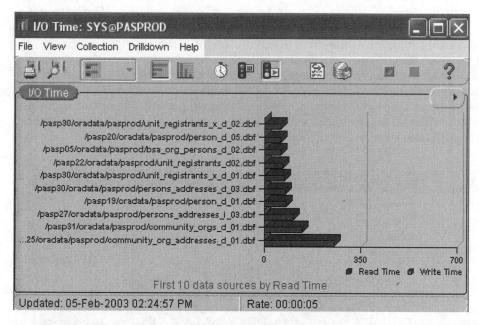

Figure 19-6. Top ten I/O sources in the database

Too often, a batch program that runs into the daytime could cause spikes in the I/O rates. Your goal is to see if you can rule out the I/O system as the bottleneck. Several of the wait events that occur in the Oracle database, such as the DB file sequential read and DB file scattered read waits, can be the result of extremely heavy I/O in the system. If the average wait time for any of these I/O related events is significant, you should focus on improving the I/O situation. There are two things you can do to increase the I/O bandwidth: Reduce the I/O workload or increase the I/O bandwidth. In Chapter 18 you learned how you can reduce physical I/Os by proper indexing strategies and the use of efficient SQL statements.

Improving SQL statements is something that can't happen right away, so there are other things you need to do to help matters in this case. This means you need to increase to increase the I/O bandwidth by doing either or both of the following:

- Make sure that the key database objects that are used heavily are spread evenly on the disks.

- Increase the number of disks.

Storage disks are getting larger and larger in terms of their capacity, but the I/O rates aren't quite keeping up with the increased disk sizes. Thus, servers are frequently I/O bound in environments with large databases. Innovative techniques such as file caching might be one solution to a serious I/O bottleneck. The idea behind the file cache accelerators is simple: Because on average, about 50 percent of I/O activity involves less than 5 percent of the total data files in your database, why not cache these limited number of "hot files"? Caching gives you the benefit of read/write operations at memory speeds, which could be 200 times faster than a mechanical disk. What are good candidates for the list of hot files? You can include your temp, redo log, and undo tablespace files as well as the most frequently used table and index data files on file cache accelerators. For a state-of-the-art file caching accelerator, please visit the Imperial Technology Web site (`http://www.imperialtech.com`).

Checking Memory-Related Issues

As you saw earlier in this chapter, high buffer cache and shared pool hit ratios are not guarantees of efficient instance performance. Sometimes, an excessive preoccupation with hit ratios can lead you to allocate too much memory to Oracle, which opens the door to serious problems such as paging and swapping at the operating system level. Make sure that the paging and swapping indicators don't show anything abnormal. High amounts of paging and swapping will slow down everything, including the databases on the server.

Due to the virtual memory system used by most operating systems, a certain amount of paging is normal and to be expected. If physical memory isn't enough to process the demand for memory, the operating system will go the disk to use its virtual memory, and this results in a page fault. Processes that result in high page faults are going to run very slowly.

When it comes to Oracle memory allocation, don't forget to pay proper attention to PGA memory allocation, especially if you're dealing with a DSS-type environment. The database will self-tune the PGA, but you still have to ensure that the *pga_aggregate_target* value is high enough for Oracle to perform its magic.

See if you can terminate a few of the top sessions that seem to be consuming inordinate amounts of memory. It's quite possible that some of these processes are orphan or runaway processes.

Is the System Wait Bound?

If none of the previous steps indicated any problems, chances are that your system is suffering from a serious contention for some resource such as library cache latches. Check to see if there is contention for critical database resources such as locks and latches, for example. Contention for these resources manifests itself in the form of wait events. The wait event analysis earlier in this chapter gave you a detailed explanation of various critical wait events. You can use the output of the Statspack utility to see what the top wait events in your database are. A quick-and-dirty way to find out what waits are causing the system slowdown is to run the query shown in Listing 19-30.

Listing 19-30. Current Wait Events in the Instance

```
SQL>  select event,count(*) from v$session_wait
  2*  group by event;
EVENT                                        COUNT(*)
-----------------------------------------------------------------
PL/SQL lock timer                                  1
SQL*Net message from client                      569
SQL*Net message to client                          2
SQL*Net more data from client                      2
buffer busy waits                                  1
db file scattered read                             2
db file sequential read                            7
latch free                                         1
8 rows selected.
SQL>
```

An even more efficient method of viewing current waits in the system is to use OEM's Performance Manager. For example, if the Latch Analysis Chart shows much more than 1 percent latch contention in the system, you may have some type of latch issue. Figure 19-7 shows how to use OEM's Performance Manager to examine the latch wait levels in your database.

You can also use the Performance Manager to view the Wait Analysis Overview tool, which shows you summary information on various wait events in the database. You can view a chart showing the number of sessions currently waiting for a specific event. You can also look at charts that show the top five wait events that have finished waiting for the sample period. OEM's wait analysis screen will also show you the top waits by time waited, as shown in Figure 19-8.

Eliminating the Contention

Once you identify wait events due to contention in the system, you need to remove the bottleneck. Of course, this is easier said than done in the short run. You may be able to fix some contention problems right away, whereas you may need more time with others. Problems such as high DB file scattered read events, which are due to full table scans, may indicate, as you have seen, that the I/O workload of the system needs to be reduced. However, if the reduction in I/O requires creating new indexes and rewriting SQL statements, obviously you can't fix the problem right away. You can't add disks and rearrange objects to reduce hot spots right away either. Similarly, most latch contention requires changes at the application level. Just make sure you don't perform a whole bunch of changes at once—you'll never be able to find out what fixed the problem (or in some cases, what made it worse!).

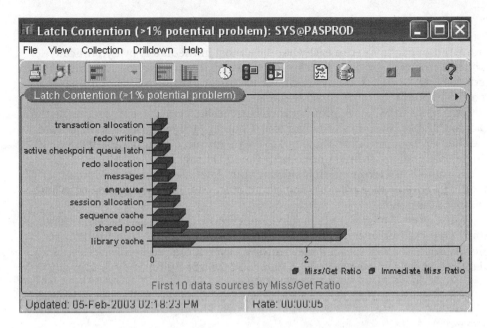

Figure 19-7. Using the Performance Manager to examine latch waits

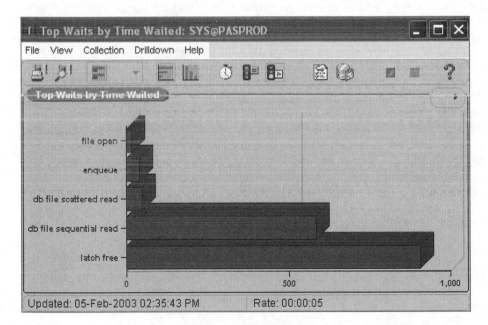

Figure 19-8. Top Waits by Time Waited analysis

The trick, as usual, is to go after the problems you can fix in the short run. Problems that you can fix by changing the memory allocation to the shared pool or the buffer cache you can easily handle almost immediately by dynamically adjusting the cache values. You can also take care of any changes that concern the redo logs right away. If you notice one or two users causing a CPU bottleneck, it may be a smart idea to kill those sessions so the database as whole will perform better. As you know, prevention is much better than a cure, so consider using the Oracle Database Resource Manager tool (Chapter 11 shows you in detail how to use the Database Resource Manager) to create resource groups and prevent a single user or group from monopolizing the CPU usage.

If intense latch contention is slowing your database down, you probably should be setting the *cursor_sharing* parameter's value to force or similar to ameliorate the situation.

Most other changes, though, may require more time-consuming solutions. Some changes may even require major changes in the code or the addition or modification of important indexes. However, even if the problem isn't fixed immediately, you have learned your craft, and you're on the right path to improving instance performance.

Summary

In an operational database, the scope for SQL tuning is extremely limited in most cases, unless the poor SQL code is bringing the entire system to a standstill. Most of the time, you have to work your way around less-than-optimal SQL code. As a DBA, you can impact instance performance considerably, however, and it's important to know how to evaluate system performance.

This chapter provided you with detailed analyses of database hit ratios and Oracle wait events. The issue of whether you should use the traditional hit ratios or the more sophisticated wait ratio analysis isn't hard to resolve. You need to look at both the hit ratios and wait ratios to assess performance problems. In some cases, the problem may be elusive, even when you employ both of these performance indicators. A better methodology is sometimes to simply focus on the top resource-consuming SQL statements in your system and see if you can tune them. Remember that in order to reduce the response time of your users, you'll need to bring down the wait time involved. If high wait times are causing response times to go down, you need to focus intensely on the type of waits and what's causing them. Just make sure you don't mistake the symptoms of high wait times for the maladies themselves.

The chapter showed you how to handle a database hang and offered a systematic methodology for you to follow when your database response times are slow.

#### CHAPTER 20

The Oracle Data Dictionary and the Dynamic Performance Views

THE ORACLE DATA dictionary is the heart of the Oracle database management system. The data dictionary holds all the necessary information for the database to function. Oracle needs this metadata to verify users, objects, privileges, and roles in the database. Understanding the data dictionary well is of paramount importance for an Oracle DBA.

The dynamic performance tables provide you with detailed information about the functioning of the database. You can query these tables to find information about database hit ratios, wait statistics, and other important indicators of database performance.

All database monitoring, whether manual or GUI based, relies on the data dictionary and the dynamic performance views to provide an accurate picture of how the database is performing. The dynamic performance tables capture all the important indicators of instance performance such as I/O rates and memory. The first part of this chapter discusses the important data dictionary static views with which every DBA should be familiar. The second part deals with the equally important dynamic performance tables, which underlie instance management and performance tuning of the database.

The Oracle Data Dictionary

Every Oracle database contains a set of read-only tables, which contain *metadata* (information about the various component of the database). The Oracle data dictionary is the heart of the database management system, and mastery of it will take you far in your quest to become an expert DBA. If you understand the data dictionary well, you can easily perform database management tasks.

As I pointed out earlier, the data dictionary tables are read-only for all the database users except the user SYS. The tables are located in the System tablespace. The SYS user updates the data dictionary when any database objects or user information changes (any DDL changes in the database will modify the data dictionary). Some of the key objects the data dictionary provides information for are the following:

- User information

- Object information (tables, indexes, packages, and so on)

- Roles and privileges

- Constraint information

- Storage information (data files and tablespaces)

- Auditing information

- Operational information (backups, log files, archived log files, and so on)

Oracle doesn't allow you to directly access the internal data dictionary tables. It creates views on the base dictionary tables and creates public synonyms for these views so users can access them. There are three sets of data dictionary views: user, others, and dba. Each set is very similar to the others. The views in each category are prefixed by the keywords "USER," "ALL," or "DBA." Each of these sets of views shows only the information the user is granted privileges to access.

- *USER:* The user views show a user only those objects that the user owns. These views are useful to users, especially developers, to see the owner's objects, grants, and so on.

- *ALL:* The others views show you information about objects you have been granted privileges. The views with the prefix ALL include information on the user's objects and all other objects on which privileges have been granted, directly or through a role.

- *DBA:* The DBA views are the most powerful in their range. Users who have been assigned the DBA role can access information about any object or any user in the database. The DBA-prefixed dictionary views are the ones you will use to monitor and administer the database.

How Is the Data Dictionary Created?

The data dictionary is created automatically when you create the database. Well, almost automatically, anyway, because you do have to manually run the catalog.sql script (located in the $ORACLE_HOME/rdbms/admin directory) if you are not using the Database Configuration Assistant. The catalog.sql script creates the data dictionary tables, views, and synonyms, and they are the first set of objects to populate the database. The data dictionary, once created, will have to remain in the System tablespace.

In the rest of the chapter, you'll see detailed references to the DBA data dictionary tables only, because your focus is database management. There are many data dictionary tables and views. You'll examine the most useful of the data dictionary views in the next few sections.

Using the Data Dictionary Static Views

How does Oracle use its vast array of data dictionary tables? How can you use the data dictionary to manage the database? No matter if you do it manually or use sophisticated GUI-based management tools, the data dictionary (along with the dynamic performance tables) provides you with detailed information about the database. Because there are literally hundreds of data dictionary views, I obviously can't cover every one of them in this chapter, but you'll look into how you can use the important views to manage your database.

For convenience, I divide the key data dictionary views into the following categories:

- General views

- User management–related views

- Audit-related views

- Storage-related views

- Views for monitoring transactions

- Constraint- and index-related views

- Views for managing database objects (such as sequences and synonyms)

- Views for managing tables and views

The following sections cover the most important data dictionary views of the Oracle9*i* database. You will first examine the structure of each of these views, and then you will see how you can query them to find out useful things about the various aspects of the database.

General Views

A collection of general dictionary views provides information on the global name and instance parameters. For example, the view GLOBAL_NAME shows the global name of the database. The DBA_CATALOG view contains the names of all tables, views, synonyms, and sequences in the database. The following sections cover some of the more useful general data dictionary views.

Dict

Dict is short for "dictionary," and it is a view that has all the dictionary table names and their descriptions. Because Dict includes the USER-, ALL-, and DBA-prefixed tables, it includes over 1,200 tables, but if you ever forget the name of a data dictionary table, you can use Dict to find out the table's name. The following code shows the results of a query using the Dict view:

```
SQL> select * from dict
  2* where table_name like '%LINKS%'
```

```
TABLE_NAME                                          COMMENTS
-------------------------------------------------------------------------------
ALL_DB_LINKS                                        Database links accessible to the user
DBA_DB_LINKS                                        All database links in the database
USER_DB_LINKS                                       Database links owned by the user
SQL>
```

PRODUCT_COMPONENT_VERSION

The PRODUCT_COMPONENT_VERSION view shows you at a glance the version number of all the major components of your Oracle database components. The following is a typical query on this view:

```
SQL> select * from product_component_version;
PRODUCT                          VERSION              STATUS
-------------------------------- -------------------- ----------------------
NLSRTL                           9.2.0.1.0            Production
Oracle9i Enterprise Edition      9.2.0.1.0            Production
PL/SQL                           9.2.0.1.0            Production
TNS for 32-bit Windows:          9.2.0.1.0            Production
4 rows selected.
SQL>
```

DBA_REGISTRY

The DBA_REGISTRY view provides information about the different Oracle components that are installed, along with their version number, schema, and other details. Listing 20-1 shows the contents of the DBA_REGISTRY view.

Listing 20-1. Querying the DBA_REGISTRY View

```
SQL> col comp_id format a15
SQL> col comp_name format a30
SQL> col version format a12
SQL> column schema format a12
SQL> column startup format a12
SQL>  select comp_id,
  2   comp_name,
  3   version,
  4   status,
  5   startup
  6*  from dba_registry;
```

COMP_ID	COMP_NAME	VERSION	STATUS	STARTUP
CATALOG	Oracle9i Catalog Views	9.2.0.1.0	VALID	SYS
CATPROC	Oracle9i Packages and Types	9.2.0.1.0	VALID	SYS
OWM	Oracle Workspace Manager	9.2.0.1.0	VALID	WMSYS
JAVAVM	Server JAVA Virtual Machine	9.2.0.1.0	VALID	SYS
XML	Oracle XDK for Java	9.2.0.2.0	VALID	SYS
CATJAVA	Oracle9i Java Packages	9.2.0.1.0	VALID	SYS
ORDIM	Oracle interMedia	9.2.0.1.0	LOADED	ORDSYS
SDO	Spatial	9.2.0.1.0	LOADED	MDSYS
CONTEXT	Oracle Text	9.2.0.1.0	VALID	CTXSYS
XDB	Oracle XML Database	9.2.0.1.0	VALID	XDB
WK	Oracle Ultra Search	9.2.0.1.0	VALID	WKSYS
ODM	Oracle Data Mining	9.2.0.1.0	LOADED	ODM
APS	OLAP Analytic Workspace	9.2.0.1.0	LOADED	SYS
XOQ	Oracle OLAP API	9.2.0.1.0	LOADED	SYS
AMD	OLAP Catalog	9.2.0.1.0	VALID	OLAPSYS

```
15 rows selected.
SQL>
```

NLS_DATABASE_PARAMETERS

The NLS_DATABASE_PARAMETERS dictionary view shows you the database settings of the various NLS parameters, such as the NLS_DATE_FORMAT. The related NLS_INSTANCE_PARAMETERS and NLS_SESSION_PARAMETERS views are identical to the NLS_DATABASE_PARAMETERS view, but they show the instance-level and session-level NLS values. Listing 20-2 shows an abbreviated output of a query on the NLS_DATABASE_PARAMETERS view.

Listing 20-2. Querying the NLS_DATABASE_PARAMETERS View

```
SQL> select * from nls_database_parameters;
PARAMETER                         VALUE
-------------------------------   ----------------
NLS_LANGUAGE                      AMERICAN
NLS_TERRITORY                     AMERICA
NLS_CURRENCY                      $
NLS_ISO_CURRENCY                  AMERICA
NLS_NUMERIC_CHARACTERS            .,
NLS_CHARACTERSET                  WE8MSWIN1252
NLS_CALENDAR                      GREGORIAN
NLS_DATE_FORMAT                   DD-MON-RR
NLS_DATE_LANGUAGE                 AMERICAN
NLS_SORT                          BINARY
NLS_TIME_FORMAT                   HH.MI.SSXFF AM
```

Plan_Table

Plan_table is the well-known name for the table that holds the execution plans of SQL statements. If you can't describe this table, it means you have to run the utlxplan.sql script from the $ORACLE_HOME/rdbms/admin directory. You can use a different name if you wish for the plan_table. Chapter 19 reviews the use of the Explain Plan utility.

DBA_SOURCE

How do you know what is in the body of a package owned by a certain schema? The DBA_SOURCE dictionary view is great for situations when you need to know what the source code of a database object looks like. The DBA_SOURCE view stores the complete text of all functions, procedures, packages, types, and Java source. The following code describes the DBA_SOURCE view:

```
SQL> desc dba_source
 Name
 --------
 OWNER
 NAME
 TYPE
 LINE
 TEXT
SQL>
```

The following is a query using the DBA_SOURCE view that gets you the text of a type in the OE schema:

```
SQL> select TEXT
  2  FROM dba_source
  3  where owner='OE'
  4  and name='WAREHOUSE_TYP';
                         TEXT
----------------------------------------------------
TYPE warehouse_typ

                                    AS OBJECT

   ( warehouse_id        NUMBER(3)
   , warehouse_name      VARCHAR2(35)
   , location_id         NUMBER(4)
   ) ;
6 rows selected.
SQL>
```

DBA_JOBS

If you have created any jobs within your database using the DBMS_JOB package (Chapter 21 shows you how to do this), you can query the DBA_JOBS view to monitor the job status. Listing 20-3 shows a typical query against the DBA_JOBS view.

Listing 20-3. Querying the DBA_JOBS View

```
SQL> select
  2  job,        /* Job Identifier */
  3  last_date, /* last time the job was successfully run */
  4  this_date, /* data when the job started executing */
  5  next_date, /* next time the job is scheduled to run *?
  6  broken,     /Y=an attempt will not be made to run it.
                 No=attempt will be made*/
  7  interval, /* the next NEXT_DATE */
  8  failures, /* Number of failures since last success */
  9  what        /*Text of the PL/SQL code that the job will execute*/
 10 from dba_jobs;
```

DBA_OBJECTS

The DBA_OBJECTS view contains information about all the objects in the database, including tables, indexes, packages, procedures, functions, dimensions, materialized views, resource plans, types, sequences, synonyms, triggers, views, and table partitions. As you can surmise, this view is very useful when you need to know general information regarding any database object. Listing 20-4 shows a query designed to find out the created time and the last_ddl_time (the last time the object was modified). This type of query often helps you identify when a certain object was modified.

Listing 20-4. Querying the DBA_OBJECTS View

```
SQL> col object_name format a20
SQL> col object_type format a12
col created format a18
col last_ddl_time format a18
SQL> select object_name,
  2  object_type,
  3  created,
  4  last_ddl_time,
  5  from dba_objects
  6  where owner ='PERFSTAT'
  7* and object_type like 'PACKAGE';
OBJECT_NAME    OBJECT_TYPE    CREATED      LAST_DDL_TIME
----------     -----------    -------      -------------
STATSPACK      PACKAGE        2003-03-19    2003-03-19
SQL>
```

User Management-Related Views

How do you know if a user has a certain privilege on a table? A large set of data dictionary views deals with the management of users, profiles, roles, and system and object privileges. In the following sections you'll look at some of the important user management views.

DBA_USERS

DBA_USERS is your main user-related view. It contains information about the database user's name, profile, expiry date, default and temporary tablespaces, and the date of creation. Listing 20-5 shows the structure of the DBA_USERS view.

Listing 20-5. The DBA_USERS View

```
SQL> desc dba_users
 Name                                      Null?    Type
 ----------------------------------------- -------- --------------
 USERNAME                                  NOT NULL VARCHAR2(30)
 USER_ID                                   NOT NULL NUMBER
 PASSWORD                                           VARCHAR2(30)
 ACCOUNT_STATUS                            NOT NULL VARCHAR2(32)
 LOCK_DATE                                          DATE
 EXPIRY_DATE                                        DATE
 DEFAULT_TABLESPACE                        NOT NULL VARCHAR2(30)
 TEMPORARY_TABLESPACE                      NOT NULL VARCHAR2(30)
 CREATED                                   NOT NULL DATE
 PROFILE                                   NOT NULL VARCHAR2(30)
 INITIAL_RSRC_CONSUMER_GROUP                        VARCHAR2(30)
 EXTERNAL_NAME                                      VARCHAR2(4000)
SQL>
```

You can use the DBA_USERS view to find out the profile, temporary tablespace, or default tablespace assigned to users. Although there's a password column, you *can't* find out the password, because the password is encrypted. What do you do when you have to log in as a user and you don't know the user's password? There are two ways to get in as the user. First, you can just change the user's password by using the *alter user* command. However, this will permanently change the user's password, which may not be what you want to do. The following example shows the other way to log in as a different user without knowing that user's password.

Suppose you want to log in as user hr, and you don't know user hr's password. First, find out the encrypted version of hr's password:

```
SQL> select password from dba_users
  2 where username='HR';
PASSWORD
------------------------------
4C6D73C3E8B0F0DA
SQL>
```

Second, alter hr's password:

```
SQL> alter user hr identified by new_pass;
User altered.
```

Third, when you're done using hr's username and you want to change the password to its original (unknown) version, use the following statement:

```
SQL> ALTER USER HR IDENTIFIED BY VALUES '4C6D73C3E8B0F0DA';
User altered.
```

DBA_PROFILES

The DBA_PROFILES view provides information on user profiles. You're going to find out that this view is one of your most important aids in managing user resource allocation. Two important values under the column resource_type are kernel and password. Here's the structure of this view:

```
SQL> desc dba_profiles
 Name                                      Null?    Type
 ----------------------------------------- -------- -----------------
 PROFILE                                   NOT NULL VARCHAR2(30)
 RESOURCE_NAME                             NOT NULL VARCHAR2(32)
 RESOURCE_TYPE                                      VARCHAR2(8)
 LIMIT                                              VARCHAR2(40)
```

The following simple example shows how you can query the DBA_PROFILES view to find out what a user's password profile looks like. Listing 20-6 shows the results of the query.

Listing 20-6. Querying the DBA_PROFILES View

```
SQL> select resource_name,limit
  2  from dba_Profiles p,
  3  dba_users u
  4  where p.profile=u.profile
  5  and u.username='HR'
  6* and p.resource_type='PASSWORD';
RESOURCE_NAME                        LIMIT
------------------------------------ -------
FAILED_LOGIN_ATTEMPTS                UNLIMITED
PASSWORD_LIFE_TIME                   UNLIMITED
PASSWORD_REUSE_TIME                  UNLIMITED
PASSWORD_REUSE_MAX                   UNLIMITED
PASSWORD_VERIFY_FUNCTION             NULL
PASSWORD_LOCK_TIME                   UNLIMITED
PASSWORD_GRACE_TIME                  UNLIMITED
7 rows selected.
SQL>
```

ROLE_ROLE_PRIVS

The ROLE_ROLE_PRIVS dictionary view shows the roles that have been granted to roles. For example, the DBA role is granted to all database administrator accounts. If you query the ROLE_ROLE_PRIVS view, you'll see the roles that are granted to you through the DBA role that you already have. Listing 20-7 shows the query's output.

Listing 20-7. Querying the ROLE_ROLE_PRIVS View

```
SQL> select granted_role from role_ROLE_privs
   2 where role='DBA';
GRANTED_ROLE
----------------------------
OLAP_DBA
XDBADMIN
JAVA_ADMIN
JAVA_DEPLOY
WM_ADMIN_ROLE
EXP_FULL_DATABASE
IMP_FULL_DATABASE
DELETE_CATALOG_ROLE
SELECT_CATALOG_ROLE
EXECUTE_CATALOG_ROLE
GATHER_SYSTEM_STATISTICS
11 rows selected.
SQL>
```

The DBA_ROLES view just lists all the roles in the database, along with a column stating whether the grantee can grant this role to others or not.

ROLE_TAB_PRIVS

How do you find out what types of table privileges a role has? The ROLE_TAB_PRIVS view comes in handy in situations like this, with its listing of roles and their corresponding table privileges. Here's the structure of the ROLE_TAB_PRIVS view:

```
SQL> desc role_tab_privs
 Name              Null?    Type
 ----------------------------------------
 ROLE              NOT NULL VARCHAR2(30)
 OWNER             NOT NULL VARCHAR2(30)
 TABLE_NAME        NOT NULL VARCHAR2(30)
 COLUMN_NAME                VARCHAR2(30)
 PRIVILEGE         NOT NULL VARCHAR2(40)
 GRANTABLE                  VARCHAR2(3)
SQL>
```

You can find out the specific table privileges of a user by issuing the query shown in Listing 20-8.

Listing 20-8. Querying the ROLE_TAB_PRIVS View

```
  SQL> select table_name,privilege
    2  from role_tab_privs
    3* where role='HR_SELECT';
```

```
TABLE_NAME                    PRIVILEGE
----------------------------  ----------
JOBS                          SELECT
REGIONS                       SELECT
COUNTRIES                     SELECT
EMPLOYEES                     SELECT
LOCATIONS                     SELECT
DEPARTMENTS                   SELECT
JOB_HISTORY                   SELECT
7 rows selected.
SQL>
```

ROLE_SYS_PRIVS

You can grant a role two kinds of privileges: object and system. The ROLE_SYS_PRIVS view lets you find out what system privileges have been given to a role. Here's the structure of the ROLE_SYS_PRIVS view:

```
SQL> desc role_sys_privs
 Name                  Null?     Type
 --------------------  --------  ------------
 ROLE                  NOT NULL  VARCHAR2(30)
 PRIVILEGE             NOT NULL  VARCHAR2(40)
 ADMIN_OPTION                    VARCHAR2(3)
SQL>
```

Listing 20-9 shows the output of a query using the ROLE_SYS_PRIVS view.

Listing 20-9. Querying the ROLE_SYS_PRIVS View

```
SQL> select role,privilege  from role_sys_privs
  2* where role='DBA';
ROLE                          PRIVILEGE
----------------------------  ---------------
DBA                           AUDIT ANY
DBA                           DROP USER
DBA                           RESUMABLE
DBA                           ALTER USER
DBA                           ANALYZE ANY
DBA                           BECOME USER
DBA                           CREATE ROLE
DBA                           CREATE RULE
DBA                           CREATE TYPE
DBA                           CREATE USER
DBA                           CREATE VIEW
139 rows selected.
SQL>
```

DBA_SYS_PRIVS

The DBA_SYS_PRIVS view contains the privileges granted to both users and roles. The following code describes this view:

```
SQL> desc dba_sys_privs
 Name
 --------------
 GRANTEE
 PRIVILEGE
 ADMIN_OPTION
```

The following query shows how to use the view to get information about privileges granted to a user:

```
SQL> select * from dba_sys_privs
  2  where grantee='OE';
GRANTEE          PRIVILEGE               ADM
------------------------------- --------------
OE               QUERY REWRITE           NO
OE               CREATE SNAPSHOT         NO
OE               UNLIMITED TABLESPACE    NO
SQL>
```

DBA_TAB_PRIVS

The DBA_TAB_PRIVS view shows the various table-level privileges that have been granted to users. The query in Listing 20-10 shows the grantees and the exact privileges they have on each table.

Listing 20-10. Querying the DBA_TAB_PRIVS View

```
SQL> col grantee format a10
SQL> col owner format a10
SQL> col table_name format a30
SQL> col privilege format a10
SQL> select
  2   grantee,
  3   owner,
  4   table_name,
  5   privilege
  6   from DBA_TAB_PRIVS
  7* where grantee='OE';
GRANTEE    OWNER      TABLE_NAME             PRIVILEGE
---------- ---------- ---------------  ------------------
OE         SYS        DBMS_STATS             EXECUTE
OE         SYS        DBMS_REDEFINITION      EXECUTE
OE         HR         COUNTRIES              SELECT
OE         HR         COUNTRIES              REFERENCES
OE         HR         LOCATIONS              SELECT
```

OE	HR	LOCATIONS	REFERENCES
OE	HR	DEPARTMENTS	SELECT
OE	HR	JOBS	SELECT
OE	HR	EMPLOYEES_INTER	SELECT

DBA_COL_PRIVS

Sometimes you may want to give a user privileges on just one or two columns in the table, and Oracle will let you do so when you use the *grant* command. The DBA_COL_PRIVS view provides you the details of all users in the database who are grantees of these column-level object privileges. The following example shows how to grant column-level objects to the OE user on a table that belongs to the user hr:

```
SQL>  grant select,update (salary)
   2  on hr.employees
   3  to oe;
Grant succeeded.
SQL>
```

The next query shows how to query the DBA_COL_PRIVS view to see which users have column privileges and on what objects:

```
SQL>  select grantee,
   2  table_name,
   3  column_name,
   4  privilege
   5* from dba_col_privs
GRANTEE    TABLE_NAME      COLUMN_NAME    PRIVILEGE
---------- --------------- -------------- ----------
   OE      EMPLOYEES       SALARY         UPDATE
SQL
```

DBA_POLICIES

The DBA_POLICIES view shows all the security policies in the database. You can find out what operations (select, insert, update, and delete) are in the policy and whether the package is enabled. Listing 20-11 shows a typical query on the DBA_POLICIES view. Note that in this example, there are no user-created polices. The sys_default group, of course, is the default policy group for all policies.

Listing 20-11. Querying the DBA_POLICIES View

```
SQL> select policy_name,
   2  policy_group,
   3  object_name,
   4  sel,ins,upd,del,
   5  enable
   6* from dba_policies;
```

POLICY_NAME	POLICY_GROUP	OBJECT_NAME	SEL	INS	UPD	DEL	ENABLE
SERVLET_xdbrls_del	SYS_DEF	SERVLET	NO	NO	NO	YES	YES
SERVLET_xdbrls_sel	SYS_DEF	SERVLET	YES	NO	NO	NO	YES
ftp-log14__xdbrls_del	SYS_DEF	ftp-log14_TAB	NO	NO	NO	YES	YES
ftp-log14__xdbrls_sel	SYS_DEF	ftp-log14_TAB	YES	NO	NO	NO	YES
http-log20_xdbrls_del	SYS_DEF	http-log20_TAB	NO	NO	NO	YES	YES
http-log20_xdbrls_sel	SYS_DEF	http-log20_TAB	YES	NO	NO	NO	YES

```
SQL>
```

DBA_OUTLINES

The DBA_OUTLINES view provides information on all outlines in the database. You can use this view or the DBA_OUTLINE_HINTS view to view the hints in the outlines. Here's the structure of the DBA_OUTLINES view:

```
SQL> desc dba_outlines
 Name                    Null?      Type
 -------------           -------------------------
 NAME                               VARCHAR2(30)
 OWNER                              VARCHAR2(30)
 CATEGORY                           VARCHAR2(30)
 USED                               VARCHAR2(9)
 TIMESTAMP                          DATE
 VERSION                            VARCHAR2(64)
 SQL_TEXT                           LONG
SQL
```

DBA_RSRC_PLANS

The DBA_RSRC_PLANS view contains information on all the resource plans. Chapter 8 covers in detail how to use the Database Resource Manager to implement resource plans in your database. The query in Listing 20-12 shows how to use the DBA_RSRC_PLANS view.

Listing 20-12. Querying the DBA_RSRC_PLANS View

```
SQL> col plan format a20
SQL> col cpu_method format a12
SQL> col comments format a50
SQL> col status format a10
SQL> col mandatory format a3
SQL> select
  2  plan,
  3  cpu_method,
  4  comments,
  5  status,
  6  mandatory
  7* from dba_rsrc_plans;
```

PLAN	CPU_METHOD	COMMENTS	STATUS	MANDAT
SYSTEM PLAN	EMPHASIS	Plan to give system priority	ACTIVE	NO
INTERNAL QUIESCE	EMPHASIS	Plan to internally quiesce system	ACTIVE	YES
INTERNAL PLAN	EMPHASIS	Default Plan	ACTIVE	YES

```
SQL>
```

Audit-Related Views

A small set of data dictionary views helps you maintain the auditing feature of Oracle9*i*. When you start auditing activity in an Oracle database, a table called sys.aud$, also known as audit_trail, is used to hold the audit information. This is the default location for audit information, although you can choose an operating system file to store the audit details. Let's quickly look at the important audit-related data dictionary tables.

DBA_AUDIT_TRAIL

Listing 20-13 shows the structure of the DBA_AUDIT_TRAIL dictionary view.

Listing 20-13. The DBA_AUDIT_TRAIL View

```
SQL> desc dba_audit_trail
 Name                                      Null?    Type
 ----------------------------------------- -------- ----------------
 OS_USERNAME                                        VARCHAR2(255)
 USERNAME                                           VARCHAR2(30)
 USERHOST                                           VARCHAR2(128)
 TERMINAL                                           VARCHAR2(255)
 TIMESTAMP                                 NOT NULL DATE
 OWNER                                              VARCHAR2(30)
 OBJ_NAME                                           VARCHAR2(128)
 ACTION                                    NOT NULL NUMBER
 ACTION_NAME                                        VARCHAR2(27)
 NEW_OWNER                                          VARCHAR2(30)
 NEW_NAME                                           VARCHAR2(128)
 OBJ_PRIVILEGE                                      VARCHAR2(16)
 SYS_PRIVILEGE                                      VARCHAR2(40)
 ADMIN_OPTION                                       VARCHAR2(1)
 GRANTEE                                            VARCHAR2(30)
 AUDIT_OPTION                                       VARCHAR2(40)
 SES_ACTIONS                                        VARCHAR2(19)
 LOGOFF_TIME                                        DATE
 LOGOFF_LREAD                                       NUMBER
```

```
LOGOFF_PREAD                                        NUMBER
LOGOFF_LWRITE                                       NUMBER
LOGOFF_DLOCK                                        VARCHAR2(40)
COMMENT_TEXT                                        VARCHAR2(4000)
SESSIONID                              NOT NULL NUMBER
ENTRYID                                NOT NULL NUMBER
STATEMENTID                            NOT NULL NUMBER
RETURNCODE                             NOT NULL NUMBER
PRIV_USED                                           VARCHAR2(40)
CLIENT_ID                                           VARCHAR2(64)
SESSION_CPU                                         NUMBER
SQL>
```

DBA_AUDIT_OBJECT

The DBA_AUDIT_OBJECT view holds all the audit records for the objects in the database. The query in Listing 20-14 traps the audited information on user HR's tables.

Listing 20-14. Querying the DBA_AUDIT_OBJECT View

```
SQL> select username,
  2  timestamp,
  3  obj_name,
  4  action_name
  5  from dba_audit_object
  6* where owner='HR';
USERNAME   TIMESTAMP      OBJ_NAME       ACTION_NAME
---------- ------------   ------------   ---------------------
HR         26-jun-2002    EMPLOYEES        SELECT
           08:39:56 am
OE         26-jun-2002    EMPLOYEES        SELECT
           08:40:18 am
SQL>
```

DBA_AUDIT_SESSION

The DBA_AUDIT_SESSION view contains information on only the *connect* and *disconnect* statements issued in the database.

DBA_AUDIT_STATEMENT

The DBA_AUDIT_STATEMENT dictionary view captures all audit trail records that involve an *alter system, grant, revoke, audit,* or *noaudit* statement issued in the database.

Storage-Related Views

Several important data dictionary views relate to space and storage issues. When you want to monitor or change storage at the data file or the tablespace level, you will most likely use one or a combination of these views. In the following sections you'll look at how you can use these views to manage space in the database.

DBA_EXTENTS

Extents are a collection of contiguous Oracle data blocks, and they are the smallest unit in which you can allocate space to various database objects. The DBA_EXTENTS view is extremely useful for finding out the number of extents your database objects have and also for getting alerts before you hit a maximum extents barrier. Listing 20-15 shows the structure of the DBA_EXTENTS view.

Listing 20-15. The DBA_EXTENTS View

```
SQL> desc dba_extents
 Name                    Null?      Type
 ------------------------------------------------
 OWNER                              VARCHAR2(30)
 SEGMENT_NAME                       VARCHAR2(81)
 PARTITION_NAME                     VARCHAR2(30)
 SEGMENT_TYPE                       VARCHAR2(18)
 TABLESPACE_NAME                    VARCHAR2(30)
 EXTENT_ID                          NUMBER
 FILE_ID                            NUMBER
 BLOCK_ID                           NUMBER
 BYTES                              NUMBER
 BLOCKS                             NUMBER
 RELATIVE_FNO                       NUMBER
SQL>
```

You can use the DBA_EXTENTS view in combination with several other data dictionary views to help manage extent issues, as shown in the query in Listing 20-16. The results of the query indicate that there is no segment with more than 20 extents in it. The number 20 is arbitrary—you can replace it with any reasonable number of extents.

Listing 20-16. Using the DBA_EXTENTS View

```
SQL> select x.segment_name,
  2  x.segment_type,
  3  sum(x.bytes/1024/1024) megabytes,
  4  count(x.bytes) count,
  5  x.tablespace_name
  6  from dba_extents x,
  7  dba_tables t,
  8  dba_indexes i
```

```
 9   where x.segment_name in ('TABLE','INDEX')
10   and x.owner = t.owner(+)
11   and x.owner=i.owner(+)
12   group by
13.  x.OWNER,x.SEGMENT_NAME,x.SEGMENT_TYPE,x.TABLESPACE_NAME
14   having count(x.bytes) >= 20
15*  order by 1,2;
no rows selected
SQL>
```

DBA_FREE_SPACE

The DBA_FREE_SPACE view tells you how much free space you have in the database at any given moment. The following code shows the columns in the DBA_FREE_SPACE view:

```
SQL> desc dba_free_space
 Name
 -----------------
 TABLESPACE_NAME
 FILE_ID
 BLOCK_ID
 BYTES
 BLOCKS
 RELATIVE_FNO
```

You can use the query in Listing 20-17 to find out how much free space your tablespaces have in them.

Listing 20-17. Querying the DBA_FREE_SPACE View

```
SQL> select tablespace_name,sum(bytes) from dba_free_space
  2* group by tablespace_name
SQL> /
TABLESPACE_NAME                   SUM(BYTES)
------------------------------    ----------
CWMLITE                            11141120
DRSYS                              10813440
EXAMPLE                              262144
INDX                               26148864
ODM                                11206656
SYSTEM                              4325376
TOOLS                              4128768
UNDOTBS1                          202047488
USERS                              26148864
XDB                                  196608
10 rows selected.
SQL>
```

DBA_SEGMENTS

As you are aware, the Oracle database contains several kinds of segments: table, index, undo, and so on. The DBA_SEGMENTS view provides you with detailed information on the various segments in the database.

As an example, you can use the code shown in Listing 20-18, which joins several data dictionary tables, to gather detailed segment information about specific database segments.

Listing 20-18. Querying the DBA_SEGMENTS View

```
SQL> col tablespace_name format a20
SQL> col segment_name format a30
SQL> col segment_type format a10
SQL> col extents format 9999
SQL> col blocks format 9999
SQL> col bytes format 99,999,999
SQL> SELECT
  2        tablespace_name,
  3        segment_name,
  4        segment_type,
  5        extents,        /*Number of extents in the segment*/
  6        blocks,         /*Number of db blocks in the segment*/
  7        bytes           /*Number of bytes in the segment*/
  8        FROM dba_segments
  9*       where owner = 'HR';
TABLESPACE_NAME SEGMENT_NAME       SEGMEN EXTENTS BLOCKS     BYTES
--------------- ------------------ ------ ------- ------ -----------
EXAMPLE         REGIONS            TABLE       1      8     65,536
EXAMPLE         LOCATIONS          TABLE       1      8     65,536
EXAMPLE         DEPARTMENTS        TABLE       1      8     65,536
EXAMPLE         JOBS               TABLE       1      8     65,536
EXAMPLE         EMPLOYEES          TABLE       1      8     65,536
EXAMPLE         JOB_HISTORY        TABLE       1      8     65,536
EXAMPLE         REG_ID_PK          INDEX       1      8     65,536
EXAMPLE         COUNTRY_C_ID_PK    INDEX       1      8     65,536
EXAMPLE         LOC_ID_PK          INDEX       1      8     65,536
EXAMPLE         DEPT_ID_PK         INDEX       1      8     65,536
EXAMPLE         DEPT_LOCATION_IX   INDEX       1      8     65,536
...
25 rows selected.
SQL>
```

DBA_DATA_FILES/DBA_TEMP_FILES

The DBA_DATA_FILES data dictionary view is yet another extremely useful view that you'll refer to often while managing the space in your database. You can query the view to find out the names of all the data files, the tablespaces they belong to, and file information such as the number of bytes and blocks and the relative file number. The DBA_TEMP_FILES view shows the temporary tablespace file information. A simple query on the DBA_DATA_FILES view will show all your data files, as shown in Listing 20-19.

Listing 20-19. Querying the DBA_DATA_FILES View

```
SQL> col file_name format a70
SQL> col tablespace_name format a20
SQL> select file_name,tablespace_name from dba_data_files;
FILE_NAME                                                      TABLESPACE_NAME
-------------------------------------------------------------- -------
C:\ORACLENT\ORADATA\MANAGER\SYSTEM01.DBF                       SYSTEM
C:\ORACLENT\ORADATA\MANAGER\UNDOTBS01.DBF                      UNDOTBS
C:\ORACLENT\ORADATA\MANAGER\CWMLITE01.DBF                      CWMLITE
C:\ORACLENT\ORADATA\MANAGER\DRSYS01.DBF                        DRSYS
C:\ORACLENT\ORADATA\MANAGER\EXAMPLE01.DBF                      EXAMPLE
C:\ORACLENT\ORADATA\MANAGER\INDX01.DBF                         INDX
C:\ORACLENT\ORADATA\MANAGER\TOOLS01.DBF                        TOOLS
C:\ORACLENT\ORADATA\MANAGER\USERS01.DBF                        USERS
8 rows selected.
SQL>
```

The data files view is especially useful when you join it with another data dictionary view, as the example in Listing 20-20 illustrates.

Listing 20-20. Querying the DBA_TABLESPACES View

```
SQL>  select f.tablespace_name,a.total,u.used,f.free,
  2  round((u.used/a.total)*100)
  3  "%used",round((f.free/a.total)*100) "% Free" from
  4  (select tablespace_name, sum(bytes/(1024*1024))
  5  total from dba_data_files group
  6  by tablespace_name
  7  (select tablespace_name, round(sum(bytes/(1024*1024)))
  8  "used" from dba_extents
  9  group by tablespace_name
 10  (select tablespace_name, round(sum(bytes/(1024*1024)))
 11  "free" from dba_free_space group by tablespace_name
 12  WHERE a.tablespace_name = f.tablespace_name
 13  and a.tablespace_name   = u.tablespace_name;
TABLESPACE_NAME     TOTAL  USED    FREE   % used    % Free
------------------- -----  ----   ----   ------    ------
CWMLITE                40     6      34       15        85
DRSYS                  20     8      12       40        60
EXAMPLE               230   230       0      100         0
OEM_REPOSITORY         75    74       1       99         1
SYSTEM                325   255      70       78        22
UNDOTBS               200     4     196        2        98
UNDOTBS2              100     1      99        1        99
USERS                  25     6      19       24        76
8 rows selected.
SQL>
```

DBA_TABLESPACES

You can use the DBA_TABLESPACES dictionary view to find out important information about a tablespace, including the following:

- Initial extent size
- Next extent size
- Default maximum number of extents
- Status (online, offline, or read-only)
- Contents (permanent, temporary, or undo)
- Type of extent management (DICTIONARY or LOCAL)
- Segment space management (AUTO or MANUAL)

To see what the names and default storage parameters are for all the tablespaces in the database, you can use the query in Listing 20-21.

Listing 20-21. Querying the DBA_TABLESPACES View

```
SQL> select tablespace_name,
  2  initial_extent,
  3  next_extent,
  4  min_extents
  5  from dba_tablespaces;
TABLESPACE_NAME INITIAL_EXTENT NEXT_EXTENT  MIN_EXTENTS
--------------- -------------- -----------  --------------
SYSTEM                   12288 12288                  1
UNDOTBS                  65536                         1
CWMLITE                  65536                         1
DRSYS                    65536                         1
EXAMPLE                  65536                         1
INDX                     65536                         1
TEMP                   1048576 1048576                1
TOOLS                    65536                         1
USERS                    65536                         1
OEM_REPOSITORY           65536                         1
UNDOTBS2                 65536                         1
AUTO_EXAMPLE             65536                         1
12 rows selected.
SQL>
```

Views for Monitoring Transactions

There are many data dictionary and dynamic performance views that you can use to monitor transactions. The main dictionary views in this regard are the DBA_LOCKS, DBA_WAITERS, and DBA_UNDO_EXTENTS views. In the following sections you'll take a closer look at each of these views.

DBA_LOCKS

The DBA_LOCKS view tells you what locks and latches are currently being held in the database. It also informs you about outstanding locks and latch requests. Listing 20-22 describes the DBA_LOCKS view.

Listing 20-22. The DBA_LOCKS View

```
SQL> desc dba_locks
 Name                        Null?      Type
 -------------------------   --------   ------------
 SESSION_ID                             NUMBER
 LOCK_TYPE                              VARCHAR2(26)
 MODE_HELD                              VARCHAR2(40)
 MODE_REQUESTED                         VARCHAR2(40)
 LOCK_ID1                               VARCHAR2(40)
 LOCK_ID2                               VARCHAR2(40)
 LAST_CONVERT                           NUMBER
 BLOCKING_OTHERS                        VARCHAR2(40)
SQL>
```

Another lock-related view, DBA_WAITERS, shows you the sessions that are waiting for locks.

DBA_UNDO_EXTENTS

If you are using Automatic Undo Management (AUM), the DBA_UNDO_EXTENTS view contains detailed information on the various undo extents, including their status. The status column shows the transaction status of the undo in the extents and can take the following three values:

- Active

- Unexpired

- Expired

Listing 20-23 shows the output of a query using the DBA_UNDO_EXTENTS view.

Listing 20-23. Querying the DBA_UNDO_EXTENTS View

```
SQL>  select segment_name,tablespace_name,
  2   bytes,status
  3*  from dba_undo_extents;
SEGMENT_NAME          TABLESPACE_NAME       BYTES       STATUS
-------------------   ----------------   ----------   --------
_SYSSMU1$             UNDOTBS1              57344       UNEXPIRED
_SYSSMU1$             UNDOTBS1              65536       UNEXPIRED
_SYSSMU1$             UNDOTBS1              65536       UNEXPIRED
_SYSSMU1$             UNDOTBS1              65536       UNEXPIRED
```

```
_SYSSMU1$        UNDOTBS1              65536      EXPIRED
_SYSSMU1$        UNDOTBS1              65536      EXPIRED
_SYSSMU2$        UNDOTBS1              57344      UNEXPIRED
_SYSSMU2$        UNDOTBS1              65536      UNEXPIRED
_SYSSMU2$        UNDOTBS1              65536      UNEXPIRED
...
55 rows selected.
SQL>
```

DBA_RESUMABLE

The DBMS_RESUMABLE Oracle-supplied package populates the DBA_RESUMABLE view with details about the start time, end time, and error messages related to the resumable statements in the database. The following simple query finds out what statements are currently resumable in the database:

```
SQL> select
  2   start_time,
  3   suspend_time,
  4   resume_time,
  5   name,sql_text
  6* from dba_resumable;
```

Constraint- and Index-Related Views

How do you find out what constraints exist on a table's columns? When a process fails with the message "Referential integrity constraint violated", what's the best way to find out what the constraint and the affected tables are? The constraint- and index-related data dictionary views are critical for resolving problems similar to these. In the following sections you'll examine the key constraint- and index-related views.

DBA_CONSTRAINTS

The DBA_CONSTRAINTS view provides information on all types of table constraints in the database. You can query this view when you need to figure out what type of constraints a table has. The view lists several types of constraints, as shown by the following query:

```
SQL> select distinct constraint_type from dba_constraints;
Constraint_type
---------------
       C         /* stands for check constraints */
       P         /* primary key constraint */
       R         /* referential integrity (foreign key constraint) */
       U         /* unique key constraint */
SQL>
```

The following query lets you know what, if any, constraints are in the table testd. The response indicates that the table has a single check constraint defined on it. The SYS prefix in the name column shows that constraint_name is a default name, not one that was explicitly named by the owner of the table.

```
SQL> select constraint_name, constraint_type
  2  from dba_constraints
  3* where table_name='TESTD'
   CONSTRAINT_NAME    CONSTRAINT_TYPE
-------------------   ---------------
_   SYS_C005263            C
SQL>
```

Note that if you want to see the particular referential constraints and the delete rule, you have to use a slight variation on the preceding query:

```
SQL>  select CONSTRAINT_NAME,CONSTRAINT_TYPE,
        r_constraint_name,delete_rule
  2  from dba_constraints
  3* where table_name='ORDERS'
CONSTRAINT_NAME         TYPE    R_CONSTRAINT_NAME    DELETE_RULE
-----------------------------  -  ------------------------------
ORDER_DATE_NN           C
ORDER_CUSTOMER_ID_NN    C
ORDER_MODE_LOV          C
ORDER_TOTAL_MIN         C
ORDER_PK                P
ORDERS_SALES_REP_FK     R       EMP_EMP_ID_PK        SET NULL
ORDERS_CUSTOMER_ID_FK   R       CUSTOMERS_PK         SET NULL
7 rows selected.
SQL>
```

DBA_CONS_COLUMNS

The DBA_CONS_COLUMNS view provides the column name and position in the table on which a constraint is defined. Here's the view:

```
SQL> desc dba_cons_columns
  Name
  -----------------
  OWNER
  CONSTRAINT_NAME
  TABLE_NAME
  COLUMN_NAME
  POSITION
SQL>
```

DBA_INDEXES

You can use the DBA_INDEXES dictionary view to find out just about everything you need to know about the indexes in your database. Listing 20-24 shows the output of a simple query using this view.

Listing 20-24. Using the DBA_INDEXES View

```
SQL> select index_NAME,table_name,status,last_analyzed from
  2   dba_indexes
  3*  where owner='HR';
INDEX_NAME                  TABLE_NAME        STATUS    LAST_ANALYZED
--------------------------- ----------------- --------  ------------
COUNTRY_C_ID_PK             COUNTRIES         VALID     22-jan-2003 01:33:07 pm
DEPT_ID_PK                  DEPARTMENTS       VALID
DEPT_LOCATION_IX            DEPARTMENTS       VALID
LOC_ID_PK                   LOCATIONS         VALID
LOC_STATE_PROVINCE_IX       LOCATIONS         VALID
REG_ID_PK                   REGIONS           VALID
STAT_TAB                    STAT_TAB          VALID
SQL
```

DBA_IND_COLUMNS

The DBA_IND_COLUMNS view is very similar to the DBA_CONS_COLUMNS view in structure, and it provides information on all the indexed columns in every table. This is very important during SQL performance tuning when you notice that an index is being used by the query, but you aren't sure exactly on what columns the index is defined. The query in Listing 20-25 may reveal that the table has indexes on the wrong columns after all.

Listing 20-25. Querying the DBA_IND_COLUMNS View

```
SQL> select index_name,
  2   table_name,
  3   column_name,
  4   column_position
  5   from dba_ind_columns
  6*  where table_owner='OE'
INDEX_NAME                  TABLE_NAME    COLUMN_NAME     COLUMN_POSITION
--------------------------- ------------- --------------- --------
CUST_ACCOUNT_MANAGER_IX     CUSTOMERS     ACCOUNT_MGR_ID  1
CUST_LNAME_IX               CUSTOMERS     CUST_LAST_NAME  1
CUST_EMAIL_IX               CUSTOMERS     CUST_EMAIL      1
INVENTORY_PK                INVENTORIES   PRODUCT_ID      1
INVENTORY_PK                INVENTORIES   WAREHOUSE_ID    2
INV_PRODUCT_IX              INVENTORIES   PRODUCT_ID      1
ORDER_PK                    ORDERS        ORDER_ID        1
ORD_SALES_REP_IX            ORDERS        SALES_REP_ID    1
ORD_CUSTOMER_IX             ORDERS        CUSTOMER_ID     1
```

> **TIP** *You can identify composite keys easily by looking in the index_name column. If the same index_name entry appears more than once, it is a composite key, and you can see the columns that are part of the key in the column_name column. For example, inventory_pk is the primary key of table inventories and is defined on two columns: product_id and warehouse_id. You can glean the order of the two columns in a composite key by looking at the column_position column.*

INDEX_STATS

The INDEX_STATS view is useful for seeing how efficiently an index is using its space. Large indexes have a tendency to become unbalanced over time if there are many deletions in the table (and therefore, index) data. Your goal is to keep an eye on those large indexes, with a view to keep them balanced.

Note that the INDEX_STATS view will be populated only if the table has been analyzed by using the *analyze* command, as follows:

```
SQL> analyze index hr.EMP_NAME_IX validate structure;
Index analyzed.
```

The query in Listing 20-26 using the INDEX_STATS view helps determine if you need to rebuild the index. In the query, you should focus on the following columns in the INDEX_STATS view to determine if your index is a candidate for a rebuild:

- *Height:* This column refers to the height of the B-tree index, and it's usually at the 1, 2, or 3 level. If large inserts push the index height beyond a level of 4, it's time to rebuild, which flattens the B-tree.

- *Del_lf_rows:* This is the number of leaf nodes deleted due to the deletion of rows. Oracle doesn't rebuild indexes automatically and, consequently, too many deleted leaf rows can lead to an unbalance B-tree.

- *Blks_gets_per_access:* You can look at the blks_gets_per_access column to see how much logical I/O it takes to retrieve data from the index. If this row shows a double-digit number, you should probably start rebuilding the index.

Listing 20-26. Using the INDEX_STATS View to Determine Whether to Rebuild an Index

```
SQL> select height,        /*Height of the B-Tree*/
  2    blocks,             /* Blocks in the index segment */
  3    name,               /*index name */
  4    lf_rows,            /* number of leaf rows in the index */
  5    lf_blks,            /* number of leaf blocks in the index */
  6    del_lf_rows,        /* number of deleted leaf rows
                              in the index */
  7    rows_per_key        /* average number of rows
                              per distinct key */
```

```
  8  blks_gets_per_access  /* consistent mode block reads (gets)  */
  8  from index_stats
  9* where name='EMP_NAME_IX';
HEIGHT BLOCK LF_ROWS  LF_BLKS DEL_LF_ROWS ROWS_PER_KEY  BLK_GETS
---------- ---------- -------------------- ---------- ----------
16    EMP_NAME_IX  107       1          0          1          1
SQL>
```

Views for Managing Database Objects

In this section, you'll look at the important data dictionary views that help you
manage *nondata* objects (i.e., objects other than tables and indexes). The table-
and index-related views are dealt with in separate sections in this chapter. The following is a list of the important data dictionary views for looking up various
database objects:

- *DBA_SYNONYMS:* Information about database sequences

- *DBA_TRIGGERS:* Information about triggers

- *DBA_SEQUENCES:* Information about user-created sequences

- *DBA_DB_LINKS:* Information about database links

Views for Managing Tables and Views

You manage objects such as tables and views by referring to the data dictionary
views such as DBA_TABLES and DBA_VIEWS. There are also separate views for
partitioned tables. Let's look at the key table- and index-related dictionary views.

DBA_TABLES

The DBA_TABLES view is your main reference for finding out storage information,
the number of rows in the table, logging status, buffer pool information, and a
host of other information. Listing 20-27 shows a simple query on the DBA_TABLES
view.

Listing 20-27. Querying the DBA_TABLES View

```
SQL> select tablespace_name,table_name
     from dba_tables;
TABLESPACE_NAME                 TABLE_NAME
------------------------------- ----------------
  EXAMPLE                       DEPARTMENTS
EXAMPLE                         EMPLOYEES_INTERI
EXAMPLE                         EMPLOYEES_NEW
EXAMPLE                         JOBS
EXAMPLE                         JOB_HISTORY
EXAMPLE                         TEST
6 rows selected.
SQL>
```

DBA_TAB_PARTITIONS

The DBA_TAB_PARTITIONS view is similar to the DBA_TABLES view, but it provides detailed information on table partitions. You can get information on the partition name, partition high values, partition storage information, and partition statistics, plus all the other information that is available from the DBA_TABLES view. Listing 20-28 shows a simple query using the DBA_TAB_PARTITIONS view.

Listing 20-28. Querying the DBA_TAB_PARTITIONS View

```
SQL> select table_name, partition_name,
  2  high_value,
  3* from dba_tab_Partitions;
TABLE_NAME    PARTITION_NAME            HIGH_VALUE
------------  ------------------------  -------------------------------
SALES         SALES_Q2_1998   TO_DATE(' 1998-07-01 00:00:00')
SALES         SALES_Q3_1998   TO_DATE(' 1998-10-01 00:00:00')
SALES         SALES_Q4_1998   TO_DATE(' 1999-01-01 00:00:00')
SALES         SALES_Q1_1999   TO_DATE(' 1999-04-01 00:00:00')
SALES         SALES_Q2_1999   TO_DATE(' 1999-07-01 00:00:00')
SALES         SALES_Q3_1999   TO_DATE(' 1999-10-01 00:00:00')
SALES         SALES_Q4_1999   TO_DATE(' 2000-01-01 00:00:00')
EMPLOYEES     EMPLOYEES1                      100
EMPLOYEES     EMPLOYEES2                      300
SQL>
```

DBA_PART_TABLES

The DBA_PART_TABLES view provides information about the type of partition scheme and other storage parameters for partitions and subpartitions. You can find out the partition type of each partitioned table using the following query:

```
SQL> select table_name,partitioning_type,
  2  def_tablespace_name
  3  from dba_part_tables;
TABLE_NAME                    PARTITION_TYPE  DEF_TABLESPACE_NAME
----------------------------  --------------- ----------
EMPLOYEES                     RANGE           EXAMPLE
EMPLOYEES_INTERIM             RANGE           EXAMPLE
COSTS                         RANGE           EXAMPLE
SALES                         RANGE           EXAMPLE
SQL>
```

DBA_TAB_COLUMNS

Suppose you want to find out the average length of each row in a table or the default value of each column (if there is one). The DBA_TAB_COLUMNS view is an excellent way to quickly get detailed column-level information on schema tables, as shown in Listing 20-29.

Listing 20-29. Using the DBA_TAB_COLUMNS View

```
SQL> col column_name format a30
SQL> col avg_col_len format 999
SQL> col data_type format a12
SQL> col data_length format a10
SQL> col nullable format a3
SQL> select COLUMN_name,
  2  avg_col_len,
  3  data_type,
  4  data_length,
  5  nullable,
  6  from dba_tab_columns
  7* where owner='OE';
COLUMN_NAME              AVG_COL_LEN DATA_TYPE    DATA_LENGTH NULL
------------------------------------------------------------------
CUSTOMER_ID                       4 NUMBER                22 N
CUST_FIRST_NAME                   7 VARCHAR2              20 N
CUST_LAST_NAME                    8 VARCHAR2              20 N
CUST_ADDRESS                        CUST_ADDRESS_T         1 Y
PHONE_NUMBERS                       PHONE_LIST_T         147 Y
PRODUCT_NAME                        VARCHAR2              50 Y
PRODUCT_DESCRIPTION                 VARCHAR2            2000 Y
ORDER_DATE                          TIMESTAMP(6)          11 N
                                    WITH LOCAL
                                    TIME ZONE
TRANSLATED_DESCRIPTION          245 NVARCHAR2           4000 N
PRODUCT_DESCRIPTION             123 VARCHAR2            2000 Y
WARRANTY_PERIOD                   5 INTERVAL YEA           5 Y
SQL>
```

DBA_VIEWS

As you know, views are the product of a query on some database table(s). How do you know what the query behind a view is? The DBA_VIEWS dictionary view provides you with the SQL query that underlies the views. Listing 20-30 shows how to get the text of a view, OC_CUSTOMERS, owned by user OE.

TIP *To ensure you see the whole text of the view when you use the DBA_VIEWS view, set the long variable to a large number (e.g., set long 2000). Otherwise, you'll see only the first line of the view definition.*

Listing 20-30. Getting the Source for a View Using the DBA_VIEWS View

```
SQL> set long 2000
SQL> select text
  2  from dba_views
  3  where view_name ='OC_CUSTOMERS'
  4* and owner = 'OE';
TEXT
----------------------------------------
SELECT c.customer_id, c.cust_first_name,
 c.cust_last_name, c.cust_address,
          c.phone_numbers,c.nls_languag
e,c.nls_territory,c.credit_limit, c.cust_email,
  CAST(MULTISET(SELECT o.order_id, o.order_mode,
    MAKE_REF(
oc_customers,o.customer_id),
   o.order_status,o.order_t
otal,o.sales_rep_id,
  CAST(MULTISET(SELECT l.order_id,l.line_item_id,
     l.unit_price,l.quantity,
       MAKE_REF(oc_product_information,
          l.product_id)
FROM order_items l
WHERE o.order_id = l.order_id)
AS order_item_list_typ)
FROM orders o
WHERE c.customer_id = o.customer_id)
AS order_list_typ)
FROM customers c
SQL>
```

DBA_MVIEWS

The DBA_MVIEWS dictionary view tells you all about the materialized views in your database, including whether the query rewrite feature is enabled or not on the views. Listing 20-31 shows you how to use this view.

Listing 20-31. Using the DBA_MVIEWS View

```
SQL> col mview_name format a25
SQL> col query format a50
SQL> col updatable format a3
SQL> col rewrite_enabled format a3
SQL> col refresh_mode format a10
SQL> col refresh_method format a10
SQL> select
  2  mview_name,
  3  query,
  4  updatable,
```

```
5  rewrite_enabled,    /* whether query rewrite is enabled */
6  refresh_mode,       /* demand,commit or never */
7  refresh_method      /* complete,force,fast or never */
8* from dba_mviews
MVIEW_NAME               QUERY                     UPD REW  REFR REFRESH_ME
------------------------ ------------------------- ------------------------
MONTH_SALES_MV  SELECT t.calendar_month_desc N   Y  DEMAND FORCE
PCAT_SALES_MV   SELECT t.week_ending_day      N   Y  DEMAND COMPLETE
SQL>
```

Using the Dynamic Performance Tables

The data dictionary views are static in the sense that they hold information about various components of the database but don't change continuously while the database operates. Oracle updates the dictionary tables only when a DDL transaction takes place. The other set of tables (or views, rather) that the DBA uses are dynamic, because they're updated continuously while the database is running. Thus, the views provide a valuable window into the performance characteristics and are vital to database management. As in the case of the data dictionary, even the DBA has only read access to the views defined on the dynamic performance tables. The views themselves have the prefix "V_$", but Oracle creates synonyms for those whose prefix is just "V$"—thus the alternative name V$ tables or views for the dynamic performance tables.

TIP *Be aware that the dynamic performance or V$ tables and views get their information solely from the operational instance. If the instance is shut down and restarted, the tables lose all the data and Oracle will repopulate the tables. When you interpret statistics, especially performance data, let the database reach a steady state before you start interpreting the results.*

As I did with the data dictionary views, I group the dynamic performance views into related areas:

- Memory-related views

- Backup-related views

- Session- and user-related views

- Redo log– and archive log–related views

- Recovery-related views

- Performance monitoring views

- SQL-related views

- Operational performance–related views

- General views

- Storage- and file-related views

Memory-Related Views

Not surprisingly, there is a large group of views that helps you monitor or modify memory allocation to the instance. You can even use some of these views to get recommendations on the ideal size of the various SGA components. In the next sections you'll take a look at some of the important memory-related dynamic performance views.

V$SGA

The V$SGA view is very useful in determining how much total memory is allocated to the various components of the SGA. The following simple query gives you a summary of the SGA memory usage by the current instance:

```
SQL> select * from v$sga
NAME                      VALUE
--------------------- ----------
Fixed Size                453492
Variable Size          109051904
Database Buffers        25165824
Redo Buffers              667648
SQL>
```

In the preceding listing, variable size includes the shared pool memory and the database buffers that contain the buffer cache. Redo buffers, of course, is the redo log buffer cache.

V$SGASTAT

The V$SGASTAT view gives you the breakdown of the SGA memory. Suppose you allocate 50MB of memory to a small database. Why does the previous listing show a total of 109MB as variable size memory? Using the V$SGASTAT view, it is easy to see how the variable size component of the summary view, V$SGA, is computed.

The total memory you allocate to the shared pool, 50MB, is allocated in the following way:

```
SQL> select sum(bytes) from v$sgastat
  2  where pool='shared pool'
  3  and name in ('dictionary cache','library cache','free memory');
 SUM(BYTES)
------------
   50751544
SQL>
```

The 109MB you saw under the variable size component of SGA consists of three subcomponents: the memory that you allocated, the extra memory that Oracle allocates based on the number of processes and other initialization parameters and, finally, the amount of free memory in the large pool and the Java pool.

V$SGA_DYNAMIC_COMPONENTS

The V$SGA_DYNAMIC_COMPONENTS view lets you find out details about the memory granule sizes and the minimum and maximum size of the SGA. Here's the output of a query using this dynamic view:

```
SQL> select min_size,max_size,
  2  granule_size,current_size
  3* from v$sga_dynamic_components
  MIN_SIZE    MAX_SIZE  GRANULE_SIZE  CURRENT_SIZE
---------- ---------- ------------ ------------
  50331648    50331648      4194304     50331648
   8388608     8388608      4194304      8388608
  25165824    25165824      4194304     25165824
```

V$BUFFER_POOL

The V$BUFFER_POOL view shows you multiple buffer pool information. By default there is just one pool, named the "default" pool, but you can configure other pools called the "recycle" and "keep buffer" pools. The following query uses the V$BUFFER_POOL view:

```
SQL> select
  2  name,             /* name of pool - recycle,keep or default */
  3  current_size,     /* size in megabytes */
  4  buffers           /* number of buffers */
  5* from v$buffer_pool
NAME                  CURRENT_SIZE   BUFFERS
-------------------- ------------ ----------
DEFAULT                        24       3000
SQL>
```

V$DB_CACHE_ADVICE

If you have set the initialization parameter *db_cache_advice* on, the Buffer Cache Advisory is turned on. The advisory is also automatically turned on if you set the initialization parameter *statistics_level* to *typical* or *all*. In either case, the V$DB_CACHE_ADVICE view enables the prediction of behavior with different database cache sizes. Listing 20-32 shows how to use the V$DB_CACHE_ADVICE view to get estimates of the buffer size.

Listing 20-32. Using the V$DB_CACHE_ADVICE View

```
SQL> col name format a10
SQL> col size_for_estimate format 99999
SQL> col size_factor format 99.9999
SQL> col buffers_for_estimate format 99999
SQL> col estd_physical_read_factor format 99.9999
SQL> col estd_physical_reads format 999999
```

```
SQL> select name,    /* buffer pool name */
  2  size_for_estimate,  /* cache size for prediction   */
  3  size_factor,
  4  buffers_for_estimate,   /* cache_size for prediction */
  5  estd_physical_read_factor,/* ratio of estimated physical reads
     to number of reads   */
  6  estd_physical_reads      /* estimated number of physical reads
     for this cache size  */
  7* from v$db_cache_advice;
NAME SIZE_FOR_EST SIZE BUFF_FOR_EST  PHYS_READ_FACTOR  PHYS_READS
-----------------------------------------------------------------
DEFAULT     4   .1667    500            2.4000          4486
DEFAULT     8   .3333   1000            1.0696          1999
DEFAULT    12   .5000   1500            1.0435          1950
DEFAULT    16   .6667   2000            1.0000          1869
DEFAULT    20   .8333   2500            1.0000          1869
DEFAULT    24  1.000    3000            1.0000          1869
SQL>
```

The V$SHARED_POOL_ADVICE view is similar to the V$DB_CACHE_ADVICE view, and it presents the estimated savings in parse time (in seconds) for a specified increase in the shared pool size. Thus, you can see the estimated impact of calibrating the size of the shared pool without having to actually change it.

V$LIBRARYCACHE

You'll probably find the V$LIBRARYCACHE view most useful when you have to deal with contention the shared pool. The dictionary or the row cache usually doesn't give you any problems—it's the library cache where most of the critical shared memory problems will occur. Chapter 19 shows you how to compute library cache hit ratios using data from the V$LIBRARYCACHE view.

V$ROWCACHE

You saw the V$ROWCACHE view in Chapter 19 as part of the discussion of the data dictionary cache. The row cache, also known as the *dictionary cache,* captures all data dictionary activity. Chapter 19 also includes a formula for computing the data dictionary hit ratio, which indicates if the sizing of the row cache is appropriate for your instance.

V$DB_OBJECT_CACHE

The V$DB_OBJECT_CACHE view lets you see all objects, such as tables, procedures, triggers, packages, and so on, that are cached in the library cache. This is a highly useful view that indicates, for example, if an object is being reloaded multiple times because it can't be cached in the shared pool. The script shown in Listing 20-33 illustrates how you can get information on the number of executions, and whether an object is "kept" in the shared pool.

Listing 20-33. Using the V$DB_OBJECT_CACHE View

```
SQL> select name,
    executions,
    sharable_mem,
    kept
    from v$db_object_cache
    where type='PACKAGE'
    and owner='&OWNER'    ORDER BY EXECUTIONS DESC;
  NAME            EXECUTIONS  SHARABLE_MEM  KEPT
  -----------     ----------  ------------  ----
  SALARY_PKG        10149        23169       NO
  NEW_PKG            9111        19858       NO
  STD_PKG            7550        32964       NO
  SEL_PKG            4537        21549       NO
SQL>
```

V$PGASTAT

The V$PGASTAT view is analogous the V$SGASTAT view. It shows the usage of the PGA memory. If you have the *pga_aggregate_target* initialization parameter set, the view will also show information about the automatic PGA memory manager. Listing 20-34 shows the contents of the V$PGASTAT view.

Listing 20-34. Querying the V$PGASTAT View

```
SQL> select * from v$pgastat;
  NAME                                  VALUE      UNIT
  ------------------------------------------------------------------
  aggregate PGA target parameter        25165824   bytes
  aggregate PGA auto target             15141888   bytes
  global memory bound                    1257472   bytes
  total PGA inuse                        8346624    bytes
  total PGA allocated                    12263424   bytes
  maximum PGA allocated                  20016128   bytes
  total freeable PGA memory              0          bytes
  PGA memory freed back to OS            0          bytes
  total PGA used for auto workareas      0          bytes
  maximum PGA used for auto workareas    147456     bytes
  total PGA used for manual workareas    0          bytes
  maximum PGA used for manual workareas  0          bytes
  over allocation count                  0
  bytes processed                        90370048   bytes
  extra bytes read/written               0          bytes
  cache hit percentage                   100
16 rows selected.
SQL>
```

V$PGA_TARGET_ADVICE

If you have set the *pga_aggregate_target* initialization parameter, you can use the V$PGA_TARGET_ADVICE view to figure out the optimal size of the PGA memory. The view contains a prediction of the cache-hit performance for various hypothetical values of the *pga_aggregate_target* parameter.

Backup-Related Views

You should be very familiar with several backup-related dynamic performance tables. Some of them just list the available backup devices and backup control file and data file names. Others provide more critical information (e.g., if a data file is currently in backup mode). The following sections introduce you the most essential backup-related dynamic performance views.

V$BACKUP_DEVICE

The V$BACKUP_DEVICE view provides information on available devices for performing backups, but it essentially includes only tape devices. The disk system is always available as a potential backup device, so no mention is made of it in this view. Here's the output of a simple query using the V$BACKUP_DEVICE view:

```
SQL> select * from v$backup_device;
DEVICE_TYPE      DEVICE_NAME
---------------- -----------------
SBT_TAPE         Tape1
SQL>
```

V$BACKUP

The V$BACKUP view indicates which of your database files are currently in backup mode. In Listing 20-35, if the status column shows ACTIVE, the data file is currently undergoing a backup.

Listing 20-35. Using the V$BACKUP View

```
SQL> select file#,status
  2  from v$backup;
      FILE#  STATUS
      -----  --------
          1  NOT ACTIVE
          2  NOT ACTIVE
          3  NOT ACTIVE
          4  NOT ACTIVE
          5  NOT ACTIVE
          6  NOT ACTIVE
          7  NOT ACTIVE
          8  NOT ACTIVE
```

```
        9 NOT ACTIVE
       10 NOT ACTIVE
10 rows selected.
SQL>
```

V$BACKUP_PIECE

The V$BACKUP_PIECE view shows the control file information about the various backup pieces. Listing 20-36 shows the output of a query on the V$BACKUP_PIECE view. The last column, deleted, can have two values: YES or NO. If the value is YES, the file has been deleted already.

Listing 20-36. Querying the V$BACKUP_PIECE View

```
SQL> select piece#,
  2  status,
  3  start_time,
  4  deleted
  5* from v$backup_piece;
   PIECE# STATUS     START_TIME DELETED
   -- - --------------------------------
        1 A May 23 2002 15:35:19 NO
        1 A May 23 2002 15:36:06 NO
        1 A May 23 2002 16:56:06 NO
        1 A May 23 2002 16:56:44 NO
        1 A May 25 2002 15:13:33 NO
        1 A May 25 2002 15:13:34 NO
        1 A May 25 2002 15:51:56 NO
        1 A May 25 2002 15:51:58 NO
8 rows selected.
SQL>
```

V$RMAN_CONFIGURATION

Contrary to what this view's name indicates, it contains only the *persistent* RMAN configuration settings. The output of a query using this view, shown in the following code, shows that currently only the *controlfile autobackup* is persistently configured. All the other configuration parameters, such as *backup device*, *retention policy*, and so on, have to be configured before RMAN can be used to perform a backup.

```
SQL> select * from v$rman_configuration
     CONF#               NAME                VALUE
     -------       ----------------------   -------
        1          CONTROLFILE AUTOBACKUP      ON
SQL>
```

Session- and User-Related Views

Data dictionary views such as DBA_USERS, ROLE_ROLE_PRIVS, and ROLE_TAB_PRIVS help you find out who the users are and what their privileges are. However, those views don't help you find out what the users are doing in the database right now—you need the session-related dynamic views for that. These views are some of the most useful ones you'll be using on a day-to-day basis for monitoring user sessions.

V$PWFILE_USERS

If you want to find out which of your users has been granted the SYSOPER or the SYSDBA role, you can do so by using the V$PWFILE_USERS view, as follows:

```
SQL> select *
  2* from  v$pwfile_users;
USERNAME                            SYSDBA  SYSOPER
----------------------------------- ------  ---------
SYS                                 TRUE    TRUE
SQL>
```

V$SESSION_CONNECT_INFO

The V$SESSION_CONNECT_INFO view shows you the session authentication details for users. The following code details the V$SESSION_CONNECT_INFO view:

```
SQL> desc v$session_connect_info
          Name
 --------------------------
 SID
 AUTHENTICATION_TYPE
 OSUSER
 NETWORK_SERVICE_BANNER
SQL>
```

The important column is authentication_type, which could hold the following values:

- *Database*, if the authentication is through the database

- *OS*, if you are using the operating system external authentication

- *Network*, if you are using the network protocol or ANO authentication

Listing 20-37 shows the contents of the V$SESSION_CONNECT_INFO view.

Listing 20-37. Using the V$SESSION_CONNECT_INFO View

```
SQL> select * from v$session_connect_info
 SID AUTHENTICATION OSUSER     NETWORK_SERVICE_BANNER
------------------------------------------------------------------
7     DATABASE      SYSTEM
8     DATABASE      SYSTEM
9     DATABASE      salapati  Windows NT TCP/IP NT Protocol
                              Adapter for 32-bit Windows:
                              Version 9.2.0.1.0  Production
9     DATABASE      salapati  Oracle Advanced Security:
                              Encryption service for 32-bit
                              Windows: Version 9.2.0.1.0 Production
9     DATABASE      salapati  Oracle Advanced Security:
                              crypto-checksumming service for 32-
                              bit Windows: Version 9.2.0.1.0 Produ
SQL>
```

V$SESSION

The V$SESSION view gives you a wealth of information about the users, including their operating system username, terminal name, whether they are actively executing a transaction or just connected to the database, and how long their connection has been in place. Listing 20-38 shows a typical query using the V$SESSION view.

Listing 20-38. Using the V$SESSION View

```
SQL> select username,osuser,terminal,logon_time,
  2  status from v$session
  3  where status='ACTIVE';
```

USERNAME	OSUSER	TERMINAL	LOGON_TIM	STATUS
		NTL-POTTSMARK	27 JUN 02	ACTIVE
		NTL-POTTSMARK	27-JUN-02	ACTIVE
		NTL-POTTSMARK	27-JUN-02	ACTIVE
		NTL-POTTSMARK	27-JUN-02	ACTIVE
		NTL-POTTSMARK	27-JUN-02	ACTIVE
		NTL-POTTSMARK	27-JUN-02	ACTIVE
		NTL-POTTSMARK	27-JUN-02	ACTIVE
		NTL-POTTSMARK	27-JUN-02	ACTIVE
SYSTEM	salapati	NTL-ALAPATISAM	27-JUN-02	ACTIVE

```
9 rows selected.
SQL>
```

In Listing 20-38, the username and osuser columns are empty for eight of the nine processes—these are Oracle processes such as LGWR, DBWR, PMON, SMON, and so on.

V$SESS_IO

The V$SESS_IO view provides session I/O statistics. Here are the columns in this view:

```
SQL> desc v$sess_io
 Name
 --------------------
 SID
 BLOCK_GETS
 CONSISTENT_GETS
 PHYSICAL_READS
 BLOCK_CHANGES
 CONSISTENT_CHANGES
SQL>
```

V$SESSION_LONGOPS

The V$SESSION_LONGOPS view shows the status of all operations that run for a long time (more than 6 seconds in absolute time). The columns sofar and time_remaining indicate how much of the work is done and how long the operation has to go before completing. The following is a sample query using the view:

```
SQL  select sid,opname,sofar,totalwork,
  2  start_time,time_remaining
  3* from v$sessioN_longops;
```

You can use either the V$SESSION_LONGOPS or V$RECOVERY_PROGRESS view, which is a subview of the former, to monitor the progress of a backup. The following listing shows the structure of the V$RECOVERY_PROGRESS view:

```
SQL> desc v$recovery_progress
 Name
 -------------------------------------------
 TYPE    /* type of recovery operation  */
 ITEM    /* the item name */
 SOFAR  /* Work completed so far */
 TOTAL  /* Total expected amount of work  */
SQL>
```

Redo Log- and Archive Log-Related Views

The dynamic performance views are excellent for monitoring the redo log and the archived log usage. The following sections present some of the key performance views relating to logs, both online and archived.

V$LOG

The V$LOG view provides detailed information on the online redo logs. It is very useful for finding out two important things: the log status and whether it has been archived. Log status could take one of the following values:

- *Unused:* The log is either new or it is right after a reset logs operation.

- *Current:* The current, active redo log.

- *Active:* An active log, but not one currently in use.

- *Inactive:* Instance recovery doesn't need this log.

Here's the output of a query using the V$LOG view:

```
SQL> select group#, thread#, sequence#, archived,
  2* status from v$log;
    GROUP#    THREAD#  SEQUENCE# ARC STATUS
---------- ---------- ---------- --- ----------------
         1          1         11 NO  CURRENT
         2          1          9 NO  INACTIVE
         3          1         10 NO  INACTIVE
SQL>
```

V$LOGFILE

The V$LOGFILE view provides information about each redo log file, including its name and whether the file is valid or not. The status column has the following values:

- *Invalid* if the file is not accessible

- *Stale* if the contents are incomplete

- *Blank* if it is currently in use

- *Deleted* if the file is not used any longer

The following is a query on the V$LOGFILE view showing the status and name of the redo log files. Because its status column is blank, group 1 (with one member) is the currently used redo log group.

```
SQL> select * from v$logfile;
GROUP# STATUS TYPE    MEMBER
---------- ------- ------- --------------------------------
    3     STALE   ONLINE C:\ORACLE\ORADATA\MARK1\REDO03.LOG
    2     STALE   ONLINE C:\ORACLE\ORADATA\MARK1\REDO02.LOG
    1             ONLINE C:\ORACLE\ORADATA\MARK1\REDO01.LOG
SQL>
```

The V$LOG_HISTORY view shows you all the logs from the beginning log to the latest one, along with the high and low SCNs in each redo log.

V$ARCHIVED_LOG

The V$ARCHIVED_LOG view is essential when you are looking at information regarding what archived logs you have access to. The view contains one entry for every log that your database archives. When you restore an archived log, the operation will insert one row into the view for each archived log. Listing 20-39 show the output of a query using the view.

Listing 20-39. Querying the V$ARCHIVED_LOG View

```
SQL> select name,thread#,sequence#,
  2  archived,applied,deleted,completion_time
  3* from v$archived_log;
NAME                          THREAD# SEQ#  ARC  APP  DEL  COMPLETIO
----------------------------------------------------------------------
C:\ORACLENT\RDBMS\ARC00001.001  1     1    YES  NO   NO   03-JUN-02
C:\ORACLENT\RDBMS\ARC00002.001  1     2    YES  NO   NO   05-JUN-02
C:\ORACLENT\RDBMS\ARC00003.001  1     3    YES  NO   NO   05-JUN-02
C:\ORACLENT\RDBMS\ARC00004.001  1     4    YES  NO   NO   05-JUN-02
C:\ORACLENT\RDBMS\ARC00005.001  1     5    YES  NO   NO   05-JUN-02
C:\ORACLENT\RDBMS\ARC00006.001  1     6    YES  NO   NO   05-JUN-02
C:\ORACLENT\RDBMS\ARC00007.001  1     7    YES  NO   NO   07-JUN-02
SQL>
```

V$ARCHIVE_DEST

As its name indicates, the V$ARCHIVE_DEST view shows you all the archived log destinations and their status. This view has a large number of columns, and you need to pay special attention to the following columns:

- *Status:* This column could take several values, but the important values are valid, inactive, deferred, disabled, full, and alternate.

- *Binding:* A value of mandatory means that the archival must be successful. A value of optional indicates that depending on the value of the *log_archive_min_succeed_dest* initialization parameter, you don't have to successfully archive logs to this destination every time.

- *Target:* If the target column shows primary, it is referring to the local destination, and if it shows standby, it is pointing to a remote destination.

Listing 20-40 shows a typical query using the V$ARCHIVE_DEST dictionary view.

Listing 20-40. Using the V$ARCHIVE_DEST View

```
SQL> select dest_name
  2  from v$archive_dest;
DEST_NAME
-------------------
LOG_ARCHIVE_DEST_1
```

```
LOG_ARCHIVE_DEST_2
LOG_ARCHIVE_DEST_3
LOG_ARCHIVE_DEST_4
LOG_ARCHIVE_DEST_5
LOG_ARCHIVE_DEST_6
LOG_ARCHIVE_DEST_7
LOG_ARCHIVE_DEST_8
LOG_ARCHIVE_DEST_9
LOG_ARCHIVE_DEST_10
10 rows selected.
SQL>
```

The V$ARCHIVE_DEST_STATUS view provides runtime information about the archived log destinations, as shown here:

```
SQL> select dest_id,database_mode,
  2  destination,
  3* from v$archive_dest_status;
  DEST_ID DATABASE_MODE    RECOVER DESTINATION
--------- ---------------- ------- -----------------
        1 OPEN             IDLE    c:\oraclent\RDBMS
        2 OPEN             IDLE
        3 OPEN             IDLE
        4 OPEN             IDLE
        5 OPEN             IDLE
SQL>
```

Recovery-Related Views

When you are performing any kind of recovery activity, the dynamic views pertaining to recovery are indispensable. In the following sections I discuss the most important of these recovery views.

V$INSTANCE_RECOVERY

As you know by now, the Oracle9*i* database allows you to set a limit on instance recovery time when you set parameters such as *fast_start_mttr_target*. The V$INSTANCE_RECOVERY view monitors the number of blocks set as target and records ongoing estimates of the Mean Time to Recover (MTTR). Here's a typical query using the V$INSTANCE_RECOVERY view:

```
SQL> select recovery_estimated_ios,
       /*No. of dirty buffers in the buffer cache*/
  2  actual_redo_blks,
     /* No. of redo blocks needed for recovery */
  3  target_redo_blks,
     /*Target no. of redo blocks to be processed*/
  4  target_mttr,
     /* mean time to recover target value */
```

```
  5 estimated_mttr
     /* current estimated mean time to recover */
  6* from v$instance_recovery;
REC_EST_IOS ACTUAL_REDO  TARGET_REDO  TARGET_MTTR  ESTIMATED_MTTR
----------------  ----------------  ----------------  -----------
      983            2422         18432          47              38
SQL>
```

V$RECOVER_FILE

The V$RECOVER_FILE view provides information on all files that need recovery. The following is the structure of the V$RECOVER_FILE view:

```
SQL> desc v$recover_file
Name                                    Null?    Type
---------------------------------------- -------- ----------------
 FILE#                                            NUMBER
 ONLINE                                           VARCHAR2(7)
 ONLINE_STATUS                                    VARCHAR2(7)
 ERROR                                            VARCHAR2(18)
 CHANGE#                                          NUMBER
 TIME                                             DATE
SQL>
```

Performance Monitoring Views

You can use all V$ views to monitor various aspects of the database instance, including its performance. However, some specific views are instrumental in judging the performance of the instance. You learned about some of these views in detail in Chapters 18 and 19, therefore I don't discuss those in detail here. The performance monitoring views you've already seen are V$SYSTEM_EVENT, V$SESSION_EVENT, V$SESSION_WAIT, V$SQLAREA, V$SQL_PLAN, and V$SQLTEXT. The V$EVENT_NAME view provides the names of all wait events in the instance. The V$WAIT_STAT view provides information on the various types of block contention, including undo block contention.

V$SYSSTAT

The V$SYSSTAT view provides you with all the major system statistics: parse, execution rates, and full table scans and other indices performance. The V$SYSSTAT view provides you the buffer cache hit ratios and number of other hit ratios. Listing 20-41 shows a summary of the main classes of statistics contained in the V$SYSSTAT view.

Listing 20-41. The V$SYSSTAT View

```
SQL> select * from V$sysstat;
STATISTIC#   NAME                               CLASS       VALUE
----------   -------------------------------------------------------
        1 logons current                          1           9
        4 user commits                            1           3
        5 user rollbacks                          1           0
        9 session logical reads                   1     2487612
       12 CPU used by this session                1         541
       13 session connect time                    1  3075787237
       20 session pga memory                      1    12353212
       40 db block gets                           8       97322
       41 consistent gets                         8     1514391
       42 physical reads                          8        2313
       43 db block changes                        8     1392911
       44 consistent changes                      8      246421
       45 recovery blocks read                    8          96
       46 physical writes                         8        6110
       49 DBWR checkpoint buffers written         8        6027
       79 free buffer inspected                   8           0
       97 physical reads direct                   8          54
       98 physical writes direct                  8          30
      114 redo entries                            2      702571
      115 redo size                               2   150629028
      116 redo buffer allocation retries          2           2
      117 redo wastage                            2     8335572
      183 table scans (short tables)             64      142400
      184 table scans (long tables)              64      193935
      190 table fetch by rowid                   64      383338
      200 index fast full scans (full)           64           0
      203 index fetch by key                    128      363856
      230 parse time cpu                         64        1309
      231 parse time elapsed                     64        4306
      232 parse count (total)                    64      109354
      233 parse count (hard)                     64         353
      235 execute count                          64      238933
      242 sorts (memory)                         64       47225
      243 sorts (disk)                           64           0
      244 sorts (rows)                           64       50862
```

SQL-Related Views

The three main SQL-related dynamic views are VSQL, VSQLAREA, and V$SQLTEXT. You can join these and other views such as the V$SESSION view to find out information relating to current SQL usage in the database (e.g., the SQL being executed currently in the database). Here's one such query that lets you see a user's SQL statement:

```
SQL> select a.sid,a.username,
    s.sql_text
    from v$session a,v$sqltext s
    where a.sql_address = s.address
    and a.sql_hash_value = s.hash_value
    and a.username like '&user'
    order by a.username,a.sid,s.piece;
```

Operational Performance-Related Views

You can use several views to monitor the status of the database. Using some of these views, you can check on any resource contention (e.g., the existence of locks and latches).

V$INSTANCE

The V$INSTANCE view gives you the status of your instance. It provides you with the hostname, the database name and version, and the status of the database. Listing 20-42 shows the output of a simple query using the V$INSTANCE view. Note that the status could be one of the following: started, mounted, open, or open migrated. The possible values for the active_state column are normal, quiesced, and quiescing.

Listing 20-42. Using the V$INSTANCE View

```
SQL> col instance_name  format a8
SQL> col host_name format a16
SQL> col version format a9
SQL> col startup time format a12
SQL> col status format a8
SQL> col database_status format a10
SQL> col active_status format a4
SQL> select instance_name,host_name,version,
  2  startup_time,status,database_status,active_state
  3* from v$instance
INSTANCE  HOST         VERSION    STARTUP      STATUS    DB_STATUS  ACTIVE_ST
--------  ------------ ---------- ------------ --------  ---------  ---------
mark1 NTL-POTTSMARK 9.2.0.1.0 27-JUN-02  OPEN      ACTIVE     NORMAL
SQL>
```

The following script gives you the SID and serial number of a user, in case you want to kill the session for some reason:

```
SQL> select sid, serial#,
  2  username from v$session
  3  where username ='&username'
Enter value for username: HR
old   3: where username ='&username'
new   3: where username ='HR'
     SID   SERIAL#    USERNAME
---------- ---------- --------------
      22     19167       HR
```

V$LOCK

The V$LOCK view indicates the session holding the lock and the type of lock that is being held or requested. The two key columns in this view are the lmode column, which tells you the mode in which a session holds the lock, and the request column, which specifies the mode in which a different process requests the lock. For both the lmode and the request columns, you should translate the numerical lock mode according the following list, which orders the locks from least to most restrictive:

- Lock Mode 0: None

- Lock Mode 1: Null (NULL)

- Lock Mode 2: Row lock shared (SS)

- Lock Mode 3: Row lock exclusive (SX)

- Lock Mode 4: Shared lock (S)

- Lock Mode 5: Shared lock row exclusive (SSX)

- Lock Mode 6: Exclusive (X)

Here's the output of a query using the V$LOCK view:

```
SQL> select sid,type,
  2  lmode,request from v$lock;
     SID TY       LMODE  REQUEST
------ -- ---------- ----------
       2 MR           4          0
       2 MR           4          0
       2 MR           4          0
       2 MR           4          0
       2 MR           4          0
       3 RT           6          0
       5 TS           3          0
7 rows selected.
SQL>
```

V$LOCKED_OBJECT

Suppose you want to create an index on a database table that is already in use. You issue the *create index* command and get the following message:

```
SQL>  CREATE INDEX neims_history_idx on
    2  neims_history(nsaorg_id);
  NEIMS_HISTORY (NSAORG_ID)
   *
ERROR at line 2:
ORA-00054: resource busy and acquire with NOWAIT specified
SQL>
```

You can't begin to create the index until you find out the session that's locking the table seims_history, and either ask the user to log off or kill the session as a last resort. You can use the V$LOCKED_OBJECT view to help you get rid of the session locking up the table. First, go to the DBA_OBJECTS data dictionary view and get the object_id of the table seims_history. Once you have the object_id for the locked table, you can query the V$LOCKED_OBJECTS view as shown in the following listing. Once you have the username and serial number, you can use the V$SESSION view to get the corresponding username and kill the session, thus releasing the lock that is preventing you from creating the index.

```
SQL> select object_id,session_id,oracle_username
     from v$locked_object;
```

V$LATCH

The V$LATCH view shows latch statistics since the beginning of the instance. The statistics are grouped by latch name. This view is usually joined with the V$LATCHNAME view to give you the statistics associated with each latch request that occurs in the current instance. ·

V$LATCHNAME

The V$LATCHNAME and V$LATCH views have an intimate relationship. The V$LATCHNAME view gives you the name of each type of latch requested since the instance began, and the V$LATCH view provides the statistics for each of those latches. Every row in the V$LATCHNAME view corresponds to a row in the V$LATCH view, and usually you join these two views to get information on the latches being held in the instance.

V$PROCESS

The V$PROCESS view shows all the active processes in the instance. The latchwait column indicates the latches the process is waiting for. If there are latch waits, the column latchwaits will be NULL. Listing 20-43 shows how to query the V$PROCESS view.

Listing 20-43. *Querying the V$PROCESS View*

```
SQL> select username,serial#,latchwait,
  2* program from v$process;
USERNAME          SERIAL# LATCHWAI PROGRAM
--------------- ---------- -------- ----------------------------
                       0            PSEUDO
SYSTEM                 1            ORACLE.EXE
SYSTEM                 1            ORACLE.EXE
SYSTEM                 1            ORACLE.EXE
SYSTEM                 1            ORACLE.EXE
SYSTEM                 1            ORACLE.EXE
SYSTEM                 1            ORACLE.EXE
SYSTEM                 1            ORACLE.EXE
SYSTEM                 5            ORACLE.EXE
SQL>
```

V$TRANSACTION

The V$TRANSACTION view lists information about the active transactions in the database. The following query shows you the physical and logical I/Os incurred by the transaction:

```
SQL> select start_time, status,log_io,phy_io
  2 from v$transaction;
```

V$RSRC_PLAN and V$RSRC_CONSUMER_GROUP

The V$RSRC_PLAN view shows you all the active resource plans in the database. You can join this to the V$RSRC_CONSUMER_GROUP view, which provides the resource usage statistics for all the resource plans in the database. Listing 20-44 shows the V$RSRC_CONSUMER_GROUP view.

Listing 20-44. *The V$RSRC_CONSUMER_GROUP View*

```
SQL> desc v$rsrc_consumer_group
 Name                                      Null?    Type
 ----------------------------------------- -------- --------------
 NAME                                               VARCHAR2(32)
 ACTIVE_SESSIONS                                    NUMBER
 EXECUTION_WAITERS                                  NUMBER
 REQUESTS                                           NUMBER
 CPU_WAIT_TIME                                      NUMBER
 CPU_WAITS                                          NUMBER
 CONSUMED_CPU_TIME                                  NUMBER
 YIELDS                                             NUMBER
 QUEUE_LENGTH                                       NUMBER
 CURRENT_UNDO_CONSUMPTION                           NUMBER
SQL>
```

General Views

Several dynamic performance views provide general information about the database, such as the version of the database, the database name, the initialization parameters specified in the initialization file, and the default parameters. These views are very useful for quickly finding out the value of an initialization parameter, for example, instead of having to look into the init.ora file or the SPFILE.

V$LICENSE

The V$LICENSE view contains your Oracle licensing information and informs you about the maximum number of concurrent users or sessions that your license will allow. The following listing describes the V$LICENSE view:

```
SQL> desc v$license
          Name
------------------------------------------------------------------
SESSIONS_MAX         /*max no. of permissible concurrent sessions */
SESSIONS_WARNING     /* warn limit for concurrent sessions limit */
SESSIONS_CURRENT     /* current concurrent sessions */
SESSIONS_HIGHWATER   /*max no. of concurrent sessions at a time */
USERS_MAX            /* maximum number of named users */
```

V$VERSION

If you want to quickly find out the version of your database software and its various components, use the query shown here:

```
SQL> SELECT * from v$version;
BANNER
----------------------------------------------------------
Oracle9i Enterprise Edition Release 9.2.0.1.0 - Production
PL/SQL Release 9.2.0.1.0 - Production
CORE    9.2.0.1.0        Production
TNS for 32-bit Windows: Version 9.2.0.1.0 - Production
NLSRTL Version 9.2.0.1.0 - Production
SQL>
```

V$DATABASE is another important view that provides information about the status of the running instance. The following is the output of a typical query using the V$DATABASE dynamic view:

```
SQL> select name,created,
  2  log_mode,open_mode,protection_mode,
  3* database_role from v$database;
NAME     CREATED    LOG_MODE    OPEN_MODE  PRO_MODE    DATABASE_ROLE
-------- --------- ------------ ---------- ------------------- ---
MARK1    18-JUN-02 NOARCHIVELOG READ WRITE MAX PERF    PRIMARY
SQL>
```

The V$DATABASE view is very useful when you're dealing with standby databases. The view contains information on the protection mode, switchover status, protection level, guard status, and other critical information that you need to manage standby databases.

The V$DISPATCHER view provides information on the dispatcher processes in the instance.

V$OPTION

How do you know if your database includes the partitioning option? If you want to find out what options are enabled in your database, you can query the V$OPTION dynamic view. Listing 20-45 shows a (partial) query using the V$OPTION view.

Listing 20-45. The V$OPTION View

```
SQL> select * from v$option;
 PARAMETER                              VALUE
-------------------------------------------------------------
 Partitioning                           TRUE
Objects                                 TRUE
Real Application Clusters               FALSE
Advanced replication                    TRUE
Bit-mapped indexes                      TRUE
Connection multiplexing                 TRUE
Connection pooling                      TRUE
Database queuing                        TRUE
Incremental backup and recovery         TRUE
Instead-of triggers                     TRUE
Parallel backup and recovery            TRUE
Online Redefinition                     TRUE
File Mapping                            TRUE
...
48 rows selected.
SQL>
```

V$SYSTEM_PARAMETER

The V$SYSTEM_PARAMETER dynamic view lists all the initialization parameters that are in effect for the current instance. The V$SYSTEM_PARAMETER2 view is similar, except that it lists multiple values of parameters in case they exist.

V$PARAMETER

The V$PARAMETER view shows you the initialization parameters that are currently in effect for a given session. The view inherits all the parameter values from the instance view, V$SYSTEM_PARAMETER. There is also a V$PARAMETER2 view, and it is the counterpart of the V$SYSTEM_PARAMETER2 view. Listing 20-46 describes the V$PARAMETER view.

Listing 20-46. Querying the V$PARAMETER View

```
SQL> desc v$parameter
 Name
 ------------------------------------------------------------------
 NUM
 NAME               /* name of the parameter */
 TYPE
 VALUE              /* value of the parameter */
 ISDEFAULT          /* if TRUE, the parameter is set to default */
 ISSES_MODIFIABLE   /*can  be modified using alter session command? */
 ISSYS_MODIFIABLE   /*can  be modified using alter system command? */
 ISMODIFIED         /* has been modified since instance startup? */
 ISADJUSTED         /* has Oracle adjusted  user-set value ? *?
 DESCRIPTION        /* description of the parameter */
 UPDATE_COMMENT
SQL>
```

V$SPPARAMETER

The V$SPPARAMETER view is useful only if you are using the SPFILE instead of the init.ora file. The view indicates the names of all parameters whether you are using an SPFILE or not, but the value column will be populated only if you are using an SPFILE.

V$NLS_PARAMETERS

The V$NLS_PARAMETERS view contains the name and current value of all NLS parameters. Listing 20-47 shows you some of the common NLS parameters and their values.

Listing 20-47. Using the V$NLS_PARAMETERS View

```
SQL> select * from v$nls_parameters;
PARAMETER                   VALUE
---------------------------------------------
NLS_LANGUAGE                AMERICAN
NLS_TERRITORY               AMERICA
NLS_CURRENCY                $
NLS_ISO_CURRENCY            AMERICA
NLS_NUMERIC_CHARACTERS      .,
NLS_CALENDAR                GREGORIAN
NLS_DATE_FORMAT             DD-MON-RR
NLS_DATE_LANGUAGE           AMERICAN
NLS_CHARACTERSET            WE8MSWIN1252
NLS_SORT                    BINARY
NLS_TIME_FORMAT             HH.MI.SSXFF AM
```

V$STATISTICS_LEVEL

You can set the initialization parameter *statistics_level* at different levels to control the statistics your instance collects. The V$STATISTICS_LEVEL view provides you the present level of all statistics and advisories based on the *statistics_level* configuration value. Listing 20-48 shows the list of all statistics currently being collected or not collected in the system.

Listing 20-48. Querying the V$STATISTICS_LEVEL View

```
SQL> select
  2  STATISTICS_NAME,
  3  SESSION_STATUS,
  4  SYSTEM_STATUS,
  5  STATISTICS_VIEW_NAME,
  6* from v$statistics_level;
STAT_NAME                    SESS_STAT SYS_STAT STAT_VIEW_NAME
---------------------------  --------- -------- ----------------------
Buffer Cache Advice          ENABLED   ENABLED  V$DB_CACHE_ADVICE
MTTR Advice                  ENABLED   ENABLED  V$MTTR_TARGET_ADVICE
Timed Statistics             ENABLED   ENABLED
Timed OS Statistics          DISABLED  DISABLED
Segment Level Statistics     ENABLED   ENABLED  V$SEGSTAT
PGA Advice                   ENABLED   ENABLED  V$PGA_TARGET_ADVICE
Plan Execution Statistics    DISABLED  DISABLED V$SOL_PLAN_STATISTICS
Shared Pool Advice           ENABLED   ENABLED  V$SHARED_POOL_ADVICE
8 rows selected.
SQL>
```

V$OBJECT_USAGE

You can ask Oracle to monitor the usage of an index to determine if you need the index after all. The V$OBJECT_USAGE dynamic view holds the results of the index usage monitoring. You need to use the SYS.OBJECT_STATS package to enable Oracle to monitor index use. Chapter 21 shows you how to use this package.

The following listing shows the structure of the V$OBJECT_USAGE view. You need to watch the key column used to see if a certain index is being used or not during the monitoring period.

```
SQL> desc v$object_usage
 Name
 -----------------------
 INDEX_NAME
 TABLE_NAME
 MONITORING
 USED
 START_MONITORING
 END_MONITORING
```

Storage- and File-Related Views

When you are dealing with issues such as I/O distribution among your data files, for example, the dynamic views pertaining to storage objects are quite useful. In the following sections you'll look at the main storage-related dynamic views.

V$DATAFILE

The V$DATAFILE view contains information on the data file name, the tablespace number, the status, the timestamp of the last change, and so on. The V$TEMPFILE view shows you particulars about the temporary tablespace files. The V$DATAFILE view provides important information when you join it to the V$FILESTAT view.

V$FILESTAT

The V$FILESTAT view provides you with detailed data on file read/write statistics, including the number of physical reads and writes, the time taken for that I/O, and the average read and write times in milliseconds. The V$TABLESPACE view provides information on the tablespaces. Listing 20-49 shows how you can join the V$DATAFILE, V$TABLESPACE, and V$FILESTAT views to obtain useful disk I/O information.

Listing 20-49. Getting Disk I/O Information

```
SQL> SELECT d.name,t.name,f.phyrds,f.phywrts,
  2  f.readtim,f.writetim
  3  from v$datafile d,
  4  v$filestat f,
  5  v$tablespace t
  6  where f.file# = d.file#
  7* and d.ts# = t.ts#;
```

NAME	NAME	PHYRDS	PHYWRTS	READTIM	WRITETIM
C:\ORACLEN T\ORADATA\ MANAGER\SY STEM01.DBF	SYSTEM	46180	98697	29637	473716
C:\ORACLEN T\ORADATA\ MANAGER\UN DOTBS01.DBF	UNDOTBS	330	140887	801	165629
C:\ORACLEN T\ORADATA\ MANAGER\DR SYS01.DBF	DRSYS	649	23	515	0
C:\ORACLEN T\ORADATA\ MANAGER\IN DX01.DBF	INDX	34	23	4	0

```
SQL>
```

V$CONTROLFILE

The V$CONTROLFILE dynamic view gives you the names of all the control files. The status column will remain empty if the name can be found. If the control file name can't be found, you'll see the value INVALID in the status column. Here's the output of a query on the V$CONTROLFILE view:

```
SQL> select * from v$controlfile;
STATUS                     NAME
-----------    -----------------------------------------
               C:\ORACLE\ORADATA\MARK1\CONTROL01.CTL
               C:\ORACLE\ORADATA\MARK1\CONTROL02.CTL
               C:\ORACLE\ORADATA\MARK1\CONTROL03.CTL
SQL>
```

V$CONTROLFILE_RECORD_SECTION

The control file carries information in *record sections*. Information pertaining to data files, for example, will come under the data file record section. The V$CONTROLFILE_RECORD_SECTION view contains information about all control file record sections.

Summary

This chapter gave you a quick introduction to a large number of the most useful data dictionary views that you can use to find out just about anything you want to know about what's going on in your database.

A good way to familiarize yourself with the numerous Oracle features is to use the data dictionary views and dynamic performance views to make simple queries that show you the database's physical structure and its performance dynamics.

I can't overemphasize the importance of mastering the data dictionary, both the static views and the dynamic views. Your understanding of the way the database works will increase in direct proportion to your understanding of the data dictionary views described in this chapter.

CHAPTER 21

Using Oracle PL/SQL Packages

ORACLE SUPPLIES A large number of both PL/SQL and Java packages, and this chapter focuses on the PL/SQL packages that DBAs can use to extend database functionality. Oracle implements most of the special features of the database with these PL/SQL packages. The number of Oracle-supplied PL/SQL packages is growing with each version of the software, as the trend is clearly moving toward helping DBAs automate the database as much as possible. Several packages are available for you to use to manage database tasks. There are other packages that you need to use only occasionally to perform special tasks. This chapter will help you get familiar with the most important packages. They're mostly easy to use, and they help you avoid reinventing the wheel by having to write code to perform the same tasks. Some specialized packages, such as UTL_FILE and UTL_SMTP, enable you to easily perform tasks such as reading operating system files or sending pages, without your having to write hardly any code.

You've used Oracle packages in earlier chapters. In this chapter, you'll look at the important Oracle PL/SQL packages that help you manage the database. You'll begin with an overview of the Oracle-supplied packages. Then, you'll review the key PL/SQL packages in detail, including examples of their use. Don't be intimidated by the many procedures and functions that are part of most of these packages. In most cases, you'll probably need to use just a couple of the key procedures.

Overview of the Oracle-Supplied PL/SQL Packages

Oracle-supplied packages have the same kind of functionality as the packages that you can create in the database. They have the same specification and body structure, and can include several functions and procedures. The biggest advantage to using packages, of course, is the reusability of code, the ability to overload procedures and functions, and an efficient organization of stored program code. Oracle PL/SQL packages exploit all the standard benefits of the regular user-created packages.

Who Creates the Oracle Packages?

The Oracle PL/SQL packages are automatically created when you run the script catproc.sql (from the $ORACLE_HOME/rdbms/admin directory), right after the creation of the database. You do need to create some special packages manually, but most of the packages are created along with the database.

The user SYS owns all these packages, and the DBA has the privileges to execute any of these packages. The Oracle packages usually have synonyms, but if you can't execute a PL/SQL package, remember to put the SYS schema before the package name (e.g., SYS.DBMS_SYSTEM).

How Do You Use the Oracle Packages?

Almost all the Oracle-supplied PL/SQL packages consist of a set of procedures that together provide the functionality for which the package is designed. At any given time, you are usually executing a procedure from the packages. For example, the well-known package DBMS_OUTPUT has the procedure *put_line*, which you need to use to see the output of PL/SQL code on your screen.

In the following discussion of important Oracle packages, first you'll learn the important procedures that make up each package. Later on, you'll see how to use the package to perform relevant tasks.

In the following sections, when you review all the important packages, you'll see that an easy way to list all the procedures and functions within an Oracle package is to simply use the familiar *describe* command in SQL*Plus. For each package, the *describe* command shows the following columns:

- *Procedure/function_name:* This column indicates whether the component is a procedure or a function and provides you with the component's name.

- *Argument_name:* This column provides you with the name of each argument in a procedure/function.

- *Type:* This column contains the argument type (Boolean, date, and so forth).

- *In/out:* This column indicates whether the argument is an IN or OUT parameter.

- *Default?:* This column indicates whether there is a default value for the column. If the default column is empty, the default value is NULL. If there is a default value, you'll see the word DEFAULT instead.

In the following sections, you'll see all the important Oracle-supplied PL/SQL packages that are part of Oracle 9.2. You can roughly divide the packages into two types: a set of general database management utilities and a set of specialized packages for implementing certain features of the Oracle database. The first part of the discussion deals with the general PL/SQL packages, and the second section reviews the features of the specialized packages. The specialized packages are used extensively in various chapters in this book, as noted in the relevant sections. Some important DBMS packages such as DBMS_SQL aren't covered here, because this chapter's focus is on the most useful packages for DBAs. To save space, I may not list all the procedures and functions in every package when I describe it. You can either describe the package in SQL*Plus to view all the components of any package, or you can look it up in the Oracle manual titled "Oracle9*i* Supplied PL/SQL Packages and Reference."

DBMS_JOB

DBMS_JOB is one of the most widely used Oracle-supplied packages. The package is used to schedule and maintain automated user jobs from within Oracle itself. Many times, you'll need to schedule a program to run on a regular basis, and the DBMS_JOB package lets you do this without recourse to the operating system utilities. Listing 21-1 shows the contents of the DBMS_JOB package.

Listing 21-1. The DBMS_JOB Package

```
SQL> desc dbms_job
Argument Name                    Type                    In/Out Default?
-------------------------------- ----------------------- ------ --------
FUNCTION BACKGROUND_PROCESS RETURNS BOOLEAN
PROCEDURE BROKEN
 JOB                             BINARY_INTEGER          IN
 BROKEN                          BOOLEAN                 IN
 NEXT_DATE                       DATE                    IN     DEFAULT
PROCEDURE CHANGE
 JOB                             BINARY_INTEGER          IN
 WHAT                            VARCHAR2                IN
 NEXT_DATE                       DATE                    IN
 INTERVAL                        VARCHAR2                IN
 INSTANCE                        BINARY_INTEGER          IN     DEFAULT
 FORCE                           BOOLEAN                 IN     DEFAULT
PROCEDURE INSTANCE
 JOB                             BINARY_INTEGER          IN
 INSTANCE                        BINARY_INTEGER          IN
 FORCE                           BOOLEAN                 IN     DEFAULT
PROCEDURE INTERVAL
 JOB                             BINARY_INTEGER          IN
 INTERVAL                        VARCHAR2                IN
PROCEDURE ISUBMIT
 JOB                             BINARY_INTEGER          IN
 WHAT                            VARCHAR2                IN
 NEXT_DATE                       DATE                    IN
 INTERVAL                        VARCHAR2                IN     DEFAULT
 NO_PARSE                        BOOLEAN                 IN     DEFAULT
PROCEDURE REMOVE
 JOB                             BINARY_INTEGER          IN
PROCEDURE RUN
 JOB                             BINARY_INTEGER          IN
 FORCE                           BOOLEAN                 IN     DEFAULT
PROCEDURE SUBMIT
 JOB                             BINARY_INTEGER          OUT
 WHAT                            VARCHAR2                IN
 NEXT_DATE                       DATE                    IN     DEFAULT
 INTERVAL                        VARCHAR2                IN     DEFAULT
 NO_PARSE                        BOOLEAN                 IN     DEFAULT
```

INSTANCE	BINARY_INTEGER	IN	DEFAULT
FORCE	BOOLEAN	IN	DEFAULT
...			
PROCEDURE WHAT			
JOB	BINARY_INTEGER	IN	
WHAT	VARCHAR2	IN	

Using the DBMS_JOB Package

You use various procedures in the DBMS_JOB package to create and schedule jobs. The *submit* procedure lets you submit a new job. The *submit* procedure has several parameters, which I explain in more detail in the following section. These parameters are as follows:

- *Job:* This parameter stands for the job ID.

- *What:* This is the code to be executed, and it can be plain SQL or a PL/SQL module.

- *Next_date:* This parameter indicates the next time the job is to be run.

- *Interval:* This parameter indicates the next time to execute the job after *next_date*.

- *No_parse:* This parameter's default is *false*. If it is set to *true*, Oracle will parse the statement when it is run for the first time.

- *Instance:* This parameter specifies the instance that runs the jobs.

- *Force:* This parameter's default is *false*, which means that the instance must be running for the job to be scheduled.

Listing 21-2 shows the use of the *submit* procedure to create and schedule a new job.

Listing 21-2. Using the Submit Procedure

```
SQL> declare
  2  v_job number;
  3  v_what   varchar2(1000) := 'insert into test values (9999);';
  4  begin
  5  dbms_job.submit(job => v_job,
  6                  what => v_what,
  7                  next_date => sysdate,
  8                  interval => 'sysdate + 1/24'
  9                  );
 10  commit;
 11  end;
12* /
PL/SQL procedure successfully completed.
SQL>
```

As you can see from Listing 21-2, you need to pass a minimum of only one parameter, *what*, to schedule a job. However, it is important to pass the *next_date* and *interval* parameters instead of taking the default values.

TIP *If you don't specify the* next_date *parameter explicitly, the job will run only once. Note that you also need to use an explicit* commit *after your DBMS_JOB.submit procedure.*

To make sure your job is scheduled correctly, you can query the DBA_JOBS dictionary view, as shown here:

```
SQL> select job,
  2  next_date,
  3  what
  4  from
  5* dba_jobs;
JOB     NEXT_DATE                        WHAT
-----  -----------------------------    ----------------------------------
  2     04-jul-2002 03:38:54 pm          insert into test values (9999);
SQL>
```

Other DBMS_JOB Procedures

The *remove* procedure lets you remove a job and the *change* procedure enables you to change the parameters of an existing job. The *interval* parameter in the *submit* procedure species how often your job will run. It is very simple to figure out how to set the interval. Refer to the following list to set your interval. Remember that dividing sysdate by a number sets the interval.

- If you want the job to run every 6 hours, use the interval *sysdate + 1/4*.

- If you want the job to run every hour, use the interval *sysdate + 1/24*.

- If you want the job to run every half hour, use the interval *sysdate + 1/48*.

- If you want the job to run every 15 minutes, use the interval *sysdate + 1/96*.

- If you want the job to run every minute, use the interval *sysdate + 1/1440*.

DBMS_APPLICATION_INFO

The DBMS_APPLICATION_INFO package enables you to track the names of transactions or modules that the database is executing currently. When you're performing application tuning, it's often important to know exactly how each module is performing. The DBMS_APPLICATION_INFO package lets you register an application in the database and track its actions. The V$SESSION and the V$SQLAREA dictionary views will have the registered application's name and actions. Listing 21-3 shows the contents of the package.

Listing 21-3. The DBMS_APPLICATION_INFO Package

```
SQL> desc dbms_application_info
Argument Name                    Type                    In/Out Default?
------------------------------   ---------------------   ------ --------
PROCEDURE READ_CLIENT_INFO
 CLIENT_INFO                     VARCHAR2                OUT
PROCEDURE READ_MODULE
 MODULE_NAME                     VARCHAR2                OUT
 ACTION_NAME                     VARCHAR2                OUT
PROCEDURE SET_ACTION
 ACTION_NAME                     VARCHAR2                IN
PROCEDURE SET_CLIENT_INFO
 CLIENT_INFO                     VARCHAR2                IN
PROCEDURE SET_MODULE
 MODULE_NAME                     VARCHAR2                IN
 ACTION_NAME                     VARCHAR2                IN
PROCEDURE SET_SESSION_LONGOPS
 RINDEX                          BINARY_INTEGER          IN/OUT
 SLNO                            BINARY_INTEGER          IN/OUT
 OP_NAME                         VARCHAR2                IN     DEFAULT
 TARGET                          BINARY_INTEGER          IN     DEFAULT
 CONTEXT                         BINARY_INTEGER          IN     DEFAULT
 SOFAR                           NUMBER                  IN     DEFAULT
 TOTALWORK                       NUMBER                  IN     DEFAULT
 TARGET_DESC                     VARCHAR2                IN     DEFAULT
 UNITS                           VARCHAR2                IN     DEFAULT
```

The *set_module* procedure is your key DBMS_APPLICATION_INFO procedure. It is with this procedure that you set a module's name and actions. You can incorporate this package in your code, so that you can track the performance of the code easily using the V$SESSION and V$SQLAREA dictionary views. Without the DBMS_APPLICATION_INFO package, you'll have a harder time tracking down the exact piece of code in the application that's causing a particular performance problem.

NOTE *Before you can use the DBMS_APPLICATION_INFO package, the owner SYS should grant execute privileges on the package:*

```
SQL> grant execute on dbms_application_info to hr;
Grant succeeded.
SQL>
```

Listing 21-4 shows how to use the *set_module* procedure.

Listing 21-4. Using the Set_Module Procedure

```
SQL>  CREATE or replace PROCEDURE delete_employee(
  2   name VARCHAR2)
  3   AS
  4   BEGIN
  5   DBMS_APPLICATION_INFO.SET_MODULE(
  6      module_name => 'delete_employee',
  7      action_name => 'delete from emp');
  8   delete from employees
  9   where last_name=name;
 10 END;
 11* /
Procedure created.
SQL>
```

User HR can execute this procedure as follows:

```
SQL> execute delete_employee('Zlotsky');
PL/SQL procedure successfully completed.
SQL>
```

You can query the V$SESSION view to see that the DBMS_APPLICATION_INFO.set_module procedure did indeed do its job:

```
SQL> select username, module, action
  2  from v$session
  3  where username =HR;
USERNAME          MODULE              ACTION
----------------------------- ----------------------
HR                delete_employee     delete from emp
SQL>
```

You can also query the V$SQLAREA view to see the sql_text associated with the module delete_employee, as follows:

```
SQL> select sql_text
  2  from v$sqlarea
  3  where module=delete_employee;
SQL_TEXT
-------------------------------------------------------------------
  DELETE from employees    where last_name=:b1
  select /*+ all_rows */ count(1) from HR.DEPARTMENTS where MANAGER_ID = :1
  update OE.CUSTOMERS set ACCOUNT_MGR_ID = null where ACCOUNT_MGR_ID = :1
SQL>
```

DBMS_SESSION

You're well aware of the *alter session* command and how you can use it to set or change several important parameters at the session level. You're also very familiar with the allocation of privileges to users through the use of roles. Suppose, however, that you need to grant a role or issue an *alter session* from within a PL/SQL program unit. How do you do that? The DBMS_SESSION package is ideal for situations where normal DDL commands won't work. The package helps control the session-specific parameters, hence the name DBMS_SESSION. Listing 21-5 shows the components of the DBMS_SESSION package.

Listing 21-5. The DBMS_SESSION Package

```
SQL> desc dbms_session
Argument Name                         Type                    In/Out Default?
PROCEDURE FREE_UNUSED_USER_MEMORY
PROCEDURE SET_CLOSE_CACHED_OPEN_CURSORS
 CLOSE_CURSORS                        BOOLEAN                 IN
PROCEDURE SET_CONTEXT
 NAMESPACE                            VARCHAR2                IN
 ATTRIBUTE                            VARCHAR2                IN
 VALUE                               VARCHAR2                IN
 USERNAME                             VARCHAR2                IN     DEFAULT
 CLIENT_ID                            VARCHAR2                IN     DEFAULT
PROCEDURE SET_ROLE
 ROLE_CMD                             VARCHAR2                IN
PROCEDURE SET_SQL_TRACE
 SQL_TRACE                            BOOLEAN                 IN
PROCEDURE SWITCH_CURRENT_CONSUMER_GROUP
 NEW_CONSUMER_GROUP                   VARCHAR2                IN
 OLD_CONSUMER_GROUP                   VARCHAR2                OUT
 INITIAL_GROUP_ON_ERROR               BOOLEAN                 IN
SQL>
```

In the following sections you'll look closely at some of the important procedures of the DBMS_SESSION package.

Set_Role

The *set_role* procedure enables you to set a role for a user from within a PL/SQL module. You can either grant or revoke a rule using this procedure. Here's an example of the use of this procedure:

```
SQL> EXECUTE DBMS_SESSION.SET_ROLE('dba');
PL/SQL procedure successfully completed.
SQL>
```

Set_Sql_Trace

You can use the *set_sql_trace* procedure to trace the current session of a user. The procedure accepts the Boolean values of *true* and *false*. Developers must first be granted the execute privilege on the DBMS_SESSION package. The developers can incorporate the *set_sql_trace* procedure anytime they want to debug their code or assess its performance. The output of the trace file will be sent to the directory (usually the dump directory) specified in the init.ora parameter file. Listing 21-6 illustrates the use of this procedure.

Listing 21-6. Using the Set_Sql_Trace Procedure

```
SQL> CREATE or replace PROCEDURE delete_employee(
  2      name VARCHAR2)
  3      AS
  4  BEGIN
  5  dbms_SESSION.SET_SQL_TRACE(TRUE);
  6      delete from employees
  7      where last_name=name;
  8  DBMS_SESSION.SET_SQL_TRACE(FALSE);
  9  END;
 10  /
Procedure created.
SQL> execute delete_employee('Zlotsky');
PL/SQL procedure successfully completed.
SQL>
```

Switch_Current_Consumer_Group

The *switch_current_consumer_group* procedure takes three parameters—the new group, the old group, and a parameter in case of an error—and enables the user to switch the resource group. You can use this procedure while running large jobs, for example, so the new group can give you access to more resources. The syntax of the procedure is as follows:

```
EXEC DBMS_SESSION.switch_current_consumer_group (
    new_consumer_group       IN  VARCHAR2,
    old_consumer_group        OUT VARCHAR2,
    initial_group_on_error   IN  BOOLEAN);
```

For example, you can switch yourself to a new group, finance, from your current group, admin, by using the following statement:

```
declare
begin
EXEC DBMS_SESSION.SWITCH_CURRENT_CONSUMER_GROUP('sales', 'admin' false);
end;
```

DBMS_SYSTEM

Oracle includes the DBMS_SYSTEM package, which you can use to manipulate other user sessions, gather event information, and so on. It is similar in some respects to the DBMS_SESSION package but, unlike the DBMS_SESSION package, which focuses on current sessions, you can use the DBMS_SYSTEM package to modify any session's behavior. For example, you can use this package if you want to set tracing on for a user from a different session. Thus, you can trace a developer's session from your session.

TIP *The DBMS_SYSTEM package is fairly well known, but it's an undocumented package. You won't find references to it in the manuals. Oracle doesn't support the use of this package, and you use it at your own risk. Not to worry—the most useful procedures of this package work just fine all the time.*

Listing 21-7 shows the components of the DBMS_SYSTEM package.

Listing 21-7. The DBMS_SYSTEM Package

```
SQL> desc dbms_system
Argument Name                    Type                     In/Out Default?
------------------------------   ----------------------   ------ --------
PROCEDURE READ_EV /* Get the level of events in the current session */
 IEV                             BINARY_INTEGER           IN
 OEV                             BINARY_INTEGER           OUT
PROCEDURE SET_BOOL_PARAM_IN_SESSION
 SID                             NUMBER                   IN
 SERIAL#                         NUMBER                   IN
 PARNAM                          VARCHAR2                 IN
 BVAL                            BOOLEAN                  IN
PROCEDURE SET_EV /* Set an event in a session */
 SI                              BINARY_INTEGER           IN
 SE                              BINARY_INTEGER           IN
 EV                              BINARY_INTEGER           IN
 LE                              BINARY_INTEGER           IN
 NM                              VARCHAR2                 IN
PROCEDURE SET_BOOL_PARAM_IN_SESSION
 SID                             NUMBER                   IN
 SERIAL#                         NUMBER                   IN
 PARNAM                          VARCHAR2                 IN
 BVAL                            BOOLEAN                  IN
PROCEDURE SET_INT_PARAM_IN_SESSION /* Set integer_type init
parameters in a session */
 SID                             NUMBER                   IN
 SERIAL#                         NUMBER                   IN
 PARNAM                          VARCHAR2                 IN
 INTVAL                          BINARY_INTEGER           IN
PROCEDURE SET_SQL_TRACE_IN_SESSION /* Trace any user session */
 SID                             NUMBER                   IN
 SERIAL#                         NUMBER                   IN
 SQL_TRACE                       BOOLEAN                  IN
PROCEDURE WAIT_FOR_EVENT /* Puts the current session
in a wait mode for a wait event */
 EVENT                           VARCHAR2                 IN
 EXTENDED_ID                     BINARY_INTEGER           IN
 TIMEOUT                         BINARY_INTEGER           IN
SQL>
```

The next sections present the most useful procedures in the DBMS_SYSTEM package.

Set_Sql_Trace_In_Session

You probably are aware that you can use the *alter session set trace in session* statement to turn the tracing of SQL statements on (and off). What do you do when a developer wants you to trace his or her session? Or, how can you find out from the V$ views that a certain user is performing an extraordinarily large number of disk reads and you want to see what the user's SQL looks like?

The *set_sql_trace_in_session* procedure is ideal for turning tracing on and off in sessions other than your own. The following example shows how to use the *set_sql_trace_in_session* procedure. The first statement uses the *true* flag to turn tracing on. The second statement shows how to turn tracing off once you no longer need it. Oracle will trace any SQL statements that are run by the user while the tracing is on, and you can get the trace file from the user_dump_dest directory, as is the case when you use the SQL Trace utility.

```
SQL> execute sys.dbms_system.set_sql_trace_in_session ( 9,271,true);
PL/SQL procedure successfully completed.
SQL> execute sys.dbms_system.set_sql_trace_in_session ( 9,271,false);
PL/SQL procedure successfully completed.
SQL>
```

Set_Int_Param_In_Session

The *set_int_param_in_session* procedure is another very useful procedure for managing active user sessions from your session. It lets you alter the initialization parameters (integer valued parameters only) for a certain session. Its effects are similar to the use of the following statement:

```
SQL> alter session set parameter_name = xxx;
```

For example, you can set the sort area size in a user's session using the *set_int_param_in_session* procedure, as shown here:

```
SQL> exec sys.dbms_system.SET_INT_PARAM_IN_SESSION
(999, 8888, 'sort_area_size', 5000000);
```

Set_Bool_Param_In_Session

When you want to set parameters such as tracing on and off in another user's session, you can use the *set_bool_param_in_session* procedure, as shown in the following example. Unlike the *set_sql_trace_in_session* procedure, this procedure will enable you to set other Boolean (true/false) parameters as well.

```
SQL> exec sys.dbms_system.Set_Bool_Param_in_Session(9,271,'sql_trace',true);
PL/SQL procedure successfully completed.
SQL> exec sys.dbms_system.Set_Bool_Param_in_Session(9,271,'sql_trace',false);
PL/SQL procedure successfully completed.

SQL>
```

Set_Ev

It is common for Oracle technical support or other Oracle experts to ask you to set an event in a session so you can gather information to debug or tune code. You use the *set event* statement to set an event. Note that the event 10046 denotes *sql_trace*. The level could be anything from 1 to 12, with each level producing more detailed output than the one below it. Level 12 is the most detailed level at which you can collect trace statistics, and it includes all wait events and the bind variables. As usual, the trace information is output to the udump directory. The *set event* statement looks like this:

```
SQL> alter session set events '10046 trace name context forever, level 8';
Session altered.
SQL>
```

You can achieve the same result using the *set_ev* procedure, except that you can set events for any session without logging into it yourself. The following example illustrates the use of the *set_ev* procedure. Note that you can leave the fourth parameter, *NM*, blank.

```
SQL> execute sys.dbms_system.set_ev (9,271,10046,8,'');
PL/SQL procedure successfully completed.
SQL>
```

DBMS_OUTPUT

When you're testing PL/SQL code embedded in procedures and packages, it's nice to have some way of knowing how long it will be until the program finishes executing. If the code fails, you would like to know what parts it completed successfully before failing. The DBMS_OUTPUT package helps you by enabling output to be sent from within procedures and packages. You can use the package to send messages to other packages or triggers, or you can have it output debugging information straight to your screen. Listing 21-8 shows the components of the DBMS_OUTPUT package.

Listing 21-8. The DBMS_OUTPUT Package

```
SQL> desc dbms_output
Argument Name                      Type                     In/Out Default?
--------------------------------   ----------------------   ------ --------
PROCEDURE DISABLE
PROCEDURE ENABLE
 BUFFER_SIZE                       NUMBER(38)               IN     DEFAULT
PROCEDURE GET_LINE
 LINE                              VARCHAR2                 OUT
 STATUS                            NUMBER(38)               OUT
PROCEDURE GET_LINES
 LINES                             TABLE OF VARCHAR2(255)   OUT
 NUMLINES                          NUMBER(38)               IN/OUT
PROCEDURE NEW_LINE
 P
```

```
ROCEDURE PUT
 A                              VARCHAR2              IN
PROCEDURE PUT
 A                              NUMBER                IN
PROCEDURE PUT_LINE
 A                              VARCHAR2              IN
PROCEDURE PUT_LINE
 A                              NUMBER                IN
SQL>
```

I'll present some simple examples to show how to use the important procedures in this package.

You can use the *put_line* and *put* procedures to send output to the screen or to the buffer. The *put_line* procedure puts an entire line into the buffer at one time, and the *put* procedure will build the line piece by piece. The maximum size of the buffer is 1,000,000 bytes. Listing 21-9 shows how to use the *put_line* procedure to print output to the screen so you can see the results of executing your PL/SQL code.

21-9. Using the DBMS_OUTPUT Package

```
SQL> set serveroutput on
SQL> declare
  2  v_lastname hr.employees.last_name%type;
  3  v_firstname hr.employees.first_name%type;
  4  v_salary hr.employees.salary%type;
  5  v_maxsalary hr.employees.salary%type;
  6  begin
  7  select max(salary) into v_maxsalary from hr.employees
  8  ;
  9  select first_name into v_firstname from hr.employees
 10  where salary=v_maxsalary ;
 11  select last_name into v_lastname from hr.employees
 12  where salary=v_maxsalary ;
 13  dbms_output.put_line(' The person with the highest salary is
 14  '||v_firstname  ||v_lastname||' and the salary is :'||  v_maxsalary);
 15* end;
SQL> /
The person with the highest salary is
Susan Mavris and the salary is : 65000
PL/SQL procedure successfully completed.
SQL>
```

NOTE *You won't see the output on your screen unless you use the command* set serveroutput on *first in SQL*Plus. The default value for this is* off, *so you won't see any output if you forget to turn it* on.

DBMS_REPAIR

The DBMS_REPAIR package enables you to detect and repair block corruption in database tables and indexes. When you suspect block corruption, of course, you can drop and re-create the object, but it may not always be feasible to do so. You can perform media recovery if the corruption is extensive. You may also create a new table by selecting out all the "good" rows from the table. The DBMS_REPAIR package offers you a better way to tackle block corruption without the need to take the objects offline. The procedures in this package will help you detect corruption and fix it with ease, while users continue to use the database as usual. Listing 21-10 shows the components of the DBMS_REPAIR package.

Listing 21-10. The DBMS_REPAIR Package

```
SQL> desc dbms_repair
Argument Name                    Type                      In/Out Default?
------------------------------   ----------------------    ------ --------
PROCEDURE ADMIN_TABLES
 TABLE_NAME                      VARCHAR2                   IN     DEFAULT
 TABLE_TYPE                      BINARY_INTEGER             IN
 ACTION                          BINARY_INTEGER             IN
 TABLESPACE                      VARCHAR2                   IN     DEFAULT
PROCEDURE CHECK_OBJECT
 SCHEMA_NAME                     VARCHAR2                   IN
 OBJECT_NAME                     VARCHAR2                   IN
 PARTITION_NAME                  VARCHAR2                   IN     DEFAULT
 OBJECT_TYPE                     BINARY_INTEGER             IN     DEFAULT
 REPAIR_TABLE_NAME               VARCHAR2                   IN     DEFAULT
 FLAGS                           BINARY_INTEGER             IN     DEFAULT
 RELATIVE_FNO                    BINARY_INTEGER             IN     DEFAULT
 BLOCK_START                     BINARY_INTEGER             IN     DEFAULT
 BLOCK_END                       BINARY_INTEGER             IN     DEFAULT
 CORRUPT_COUNT                   BINARY_INTEGER             OUT
PROCEDURE DUMP_ORPHAN_KEYS
 SCHEMA_NAME                     VARCHAR2                   IN
 OBJECT_NAME                     VARCHAR2                   IN
 PARTITION_NAME                  VARCHAR2                   IN     DEFAULT
 OBJECT_TYPE                     BINARY_INTEGER             IN     DEFAULT
 REPAIR_TABLE_NAME               VARCHAR2                   IN     DEFAULT
 ORPHAN_TABLE_NAME               VARCHAR2                   IN     DEFAULT
 FLAGS                           BINARY_INTEGER             IN     DEFAULT
 KEY_COUNT                       BINARY_INTEGER             OUT
PROCEDURE FIX_CORRUPT_BLOCKS
 SCHEMA_NAME                     VARCHAR2                   IN
 OBJECT_NAME                     VARCHAR2                   IN
 PARTITION_NAME                  VARCHAR2                   IN     DEFAULT
 OBJECT_TYPE                     BINARY_INTEGER             IN     DEFAULT
 REPAIR_TABLE_NAME               VARCHAR2                   IN     DEFAULT
```

FLAGS	BINARY_INTEGER	IN	DEFAULT
FIX_COUNT	BINARY_INTEGER	OUT	

...

PROCEDURE SKIP_CORRUPT_BLOCKS

SCHEMA_NAME	VARCHAR2	IN	
OBJECT_NAME	VARCHAR2	IN	
OBJECT_TYPE	BINARY_INTEGER	IN	DEFAULT
FLAGS	BINARY_INTEGER	IN	DEFAULT

Using the DBMS_REPAIR Package

This section presents a simple example to show the functionality of the DBMS_REPAIR package. The first step is to create a pair of tables called repair_table and orphan_key_table to hold the corrupt blocks if any are found during the investigation. You use the procedure *admin_tables* to create the repair table, whose default name is repair_table. Listing 21-11 shows the execution of the *admin_tables* procedure.

Listing 21-11. Using the DBMS_REPAIR Package to Detect Block Corruption

```
SQL> BEGIN
  2    DBMS_REPAIR.ADMIN_TABLES (
  3        TABLE_NAME => 'REPAIR_TABLE',
  4        TABLE_TYPE => dbms_repair.repair_table,
  5        ACTION     => dbms_repair.create_action,
  6        TABLESPACE => 'USERS');
  7 END;
  8* /
PL/SQL procedure successfully completed.
SQL> BEGIN
  2    DBMS_REPAIR.ADMIN_TABLES (
  3        TABLE_NAME => 'ORPHAN_KEY_TABLE',
  4        TABLE_TYPE => dbms_repair.orphan_table,
  5        ACTION     => dbms_repair.create_action,
  6        TABLESPACE => 'USERS');
  7  END;
  8*/
  PL/SQL procedure successfully completed.
SQL>
```

What is the repair table? Listing 21-12 shows the columns of the repair_table you just created. The table gives you the object_id and the block_id for the corrupt block. It also gives you a description of the corruption and the repair that fixed the corrupt block.

Listing 21-12. Describing the Repair_Table

```
SQL> desc repair_table
 Name
 --------------------
 OBJECT_ID
 TABLESPACE_ID
 RELATIVE_FILE_ID
 BLOCK_ID
 CORRUPT_TYPE
 SCHEMA_NAME
 OBJECT_NAME
 BASEOBJECT_NAME
 PARTITION_NAME
 CORRUPT_DESCRIPTION
 REPAIR_DESCRIPTION
 MARKED_CORRUPT
 CHECK_TIMESTAMP
 FIX_TIMESTAMP
 REFORMAT_TIMESTAMP
SQL>
```

After you create the two tables, repair_table and orphan_keys_table, it's time to check for block corruption using the *check_object* procedure, as shown in Listing 21-13.

Listing 21-13. Using the DBMS_REPAIR.Check_Object Procedure

```
SQL>  declare num_corrupt int;
  2    begin
  3    num_corrupt := 0;
  4    dbms_repair.check_object(
  5    schema_name => 'HR',
  6    object_name => 'EMPLOYEES',
  7    repair_table_name => 'REPAIR_TABLE',
  8    corrupt_count => num_corrupt);
  9    end;
 10   /
PL/SQL procedure successfully completed.
SQL>
```

Fixing Block Corruption

If the *check_object* procedure populates any rows into your repair table (repair_table), then it's time to fix it using the procedure *fix_corrupt_blocks*. Listing 21-14 shows how to use the *fix_corrupt_blocks* procedure.

Listing 21-14. Using the DBMS_REPAIR.Fix_Corrupt_Blocks Procedure

```
SQL>  declare num_fix int;
  2    begin
  3    num_fix := 0;
  4    dbms_repair.fix_corrupt_blocks(
  5    schema_name => 'HR',
  6    object_name => 'EMPLOYEES',
  7    object_type => dbms_repair.table_object,
  8     repair_table_name => 'REPAIR_TABLE',
  9    fix_count => num_fix);
 10    end;
 PL/SQL procedure successfully completed.
SQL>
```

DBMS_OUTLN and DBMS_OUTLN_EDIT

The DBMS_OUTLN and DBMS_OUTLN_EDIT packages are used to manage stored plan outlines, thereby helping to stabilize the cost-based optimizer (CBO). The packages contain several procedures, as shown in Listing 21-15.

Listing 21-15. The DBMS_OUTLN Package

```
SQL> desc dbms_outln
Argument Name                         Type                       In/Out Default?
------------------------------------  -------------------------  ------ --------
PROCEDURE CLEAR_USED
 NAME                                 VARCHAR2                   IN
PROCEDURE DROP_BY_CAT
 CAT                                  VARCHAR2                   IN
PROCEDURE DROP_COLLISION
PROCEDURE DROP_UNUSED
PROCEDURE EXACT_TEXT_SIGNATURES
PROCEDURE CREATE_EDIT_TABLES
PROCEDURE DROP_EDIT_TABLES
SQL>
```

Using the DBMS_OUTLN Package to Manage Stored Outlines

You need to take a couple of preliminary steps before you can use the DBMS_OUTLN package to manage outlines. First, you need to grant certain privileges to the user who wants to use the outlines. Next, you should enable the creation of outlines by using either an initialization parameter or the *alter session* command.

In the following example, you'll make all the changes in the parameters at the session level by using the *alter session* command. Listing 21-16 demonstrates all the necessary commands to enable the creation of plan outlines.

Listing 21-16. Setting the Parameters for Using Stored Outlines

```
SQL> grant create any outline to HR;
Grant succeeded.
SQL> alter session set create_stored_outlines =true;
Session altered.
/* Run the application, so you can capture the stored outlines */
SQL> alter session set create_stored_outlines = false;
/* The above statement will suspend the generation of outlines */
Session altered.
SQL> alter session set use_stored_outlines = true;
Session altered.
SQL>
```

Oracle will save the outlines of all SQL statements that the user HR executes after the *create_stored_outlines* parameter is set to *true*. The outlines are stored in the OUTLN user's schema. The following example shows the main tables in the user OUTLN's schema. The default location for the user OUTLN's tables is the System tablespace. Using the outlines in the OUTLN tables OL$ and OL$HINTS, Oracle will populate the dictionary views USER_OUTLINES and USER_OUTLINES_HINTS.

```
SQL> select table_name from dba_tables
  2  where owner ='OUTLN';
TABLE_NAME
-----------
OL$
OL$HINTS
OL$NODES
SQL>
```

Tracking the Outlines in the Database

You can use the USER_OUTLINES (or DBA_OUTLINES) and USER_OUTLINE_HINTS views to get information about the stored outlines in your database. The following code shows the output of such a query:

```
SQL> select name, used,
  2* timestamp,sql_text from user_outlines;
NAME                           USED      TIMESTAMP
------------------------------ --------- ---------
SQL_TEXT
------------------------------------------------------------
SYS_OUTLINE_020705102225483    USED      05-JUL-02
select * from employees
SQL>
```

In order for Oracle to use stored outlines consistently, you need to turn the *use_stored_outlines* parameter on by setting its value to *true*. By doing this, you are ensuring that the CBO will be stable, without changing its plans over time. If the System tablespace is being filled up with too many stored outlines, you can drop some of the outlines by using the DBMS_OUTLN.drop_unused procedure. This procedure, which doesn't need any parameters, removes all literal SQL outlines from the OUTLN tables. The DBMS_OUTLN_EDIT.create_edit_tables procedure creates tables in a user's schema if you need to edit any private outlines. The DBMS_OUTLN_EDIT.drop_tables procedure enables you to drop the outlined editing tables.

DBMS_SPACE

The DBMS_SPACE package is useful for finding out how much space is used and how much free space is left in various dataset segments such as table, index, and cluster segments. Recall that the DBA_FREESPACE dictionary view lets you find out free space information in tablespaces and data files, but not in the database objects. Unless you use the DBMS_SPACE package, it is hard to find out how much free space there is in the segments allocated to various objects in the database. The DBMS_SPACE package enables you to answer questions such as the following:

- How much free space can I use before a new extent is thrown?

- How many data blocks are above the high watermark?

- How many data blocks are in the FREELISTS?

The DBA_EXTENTS and the DBA_SEGMENTS dictionary views do give you a lot of information about the size *allocated* to objects such as tables and indexes, but you really can't tell what the *used* and free space usage is from looking at those views. If you have been analyzing the tables, the blocks column will give you the "high watermark"—the highest point in terms of size that the table has ever reached. However, if your tables are undergoing a large number of inserts and deletes, the high watermark is not an accurate indictor of the real space used by the tables. The DBMS_SPACE package is ideal for finding out the used and free space left in objects.

The DBMS_SPACE package has three procedures, as shown in Listing 21-17. The *unused_space* procedure gives you information about the unused space in an object segment, the *free_blocks* procedure gives you information about the number of free blocks in a segment, and the *space usage* procedure gives you details about space usage in the blocks.

Listing 21-17. Describing the DBMS_SPACE Package

```
SQL> desc dbms_space
Argument Name                    Type                    In/Out Default?
-----------------------------    --------------------    ------ --------
PROCEDURE FREE_BLOCKS
 SEGMENT_OWNER                   VARCHAR2                IN
 SEGMENT_NAME                    VARCHAR2                IN
 SEGMENT_TYPE                    VARCHAR2                IN
 FREELIST_GROUP_ID               NUMBER                  IN
 FREE_BLKS                       NUMBER                  OUT
 SCAN_LIMIT                      NUMBER                  IN     DEFAULT
 PARTITION_NAME                  VARCHAR2                IN     DEFAULT
```

```
PROCEDURE SPACE_USAGE
 SEGMENT_OWNER                  VARCHAR2              IN
 SEGMENT_NAME                   VARCHAR2              IN
 SEGMENT_TYPE                   VARCHAR2              IN
 UNFORMATTED_BLOCKS             NUMBER               OUT
 UNFORMATTED_BYTES              NUMBER               OUT
 FS1_BLOCKS                     NUMBER               OUT
 FS1_BYTES                      NUMBER               OUT
 FS2_BLOCKS                     NUMBER               OUT
 FS2_BYTES                      NUMBER               OUT
 FS3_BLOCKS                     NUMBER               OUT
 FS3_BYTES                      NUMBER               OUT
 FS4_BLOCKS                     NUMBER               OUT
 FS4_BYTES                      NUMBER               OUT
 FULL_BLOCKS                    NUMBER               OUT
 FULL_BYTES                     NUMBER               OUT
 PARTITION_NAME                 VARCHAR2             IN    DEFAULT
PROCEDURE UNUSED_SPACE
 SEGMENT_OWNER                  VARCHAR2              IN
 SEGMENT_NAME                   VARCHAR2              IN
 SEGMENT_TYPE                   VARCHAR2              IN
 TOTAL_BLOCKS                   NUMBER               OUT
 TOTAL_BYTES                    NUMBER               OUT
 UNUSED_BLOCKS                  NUMBER               OUT
 UNUSED_BYTES                   NUMBER               OUT
 LAST_USED_EXTENT_FILE_ID       NUMBER               OUT
 LAST_USED_EXTENT_BLOCK_ID      NUMBER               OUT
 LAST_USED_BLOCK                NUMBER               OUT
 PARTITION_NAME                 VARCHAR2             IN    DEFAULT
SQL>
```

Let's look at the *unused_space* procedure closely and see how you can use it to get detailed unused space information. Note that the procedure has three IN parameters (a fourth one is a default parameter) and seven OUT parameters. Listing 21-18 shows the output from the use of the *unused_space* procedure.

Listing 21-18. Using the DBMS_SPACE.Free_Space Procedure

```
SQL> declare
  2  v_total_blocks          number;
  3  v_total_bytes           number;
  4  v_unused_blocks         number;
  5  v_unused_bytes          number;
  6  v_last_used_extent_file_id      number;
  7  v_last_used_extent_block_id     number;
  8  v_last_used_block               number;
  9  begin
 10  dbms_space.unused_space (segment_owner   => 'OE',
 11    segment_name     => 'PRODUCT_DESCRIPTIONS',
 12    segment_type     => 'TABLE',
```

```
13    total_blocks      => v_total_blocks,
14    total_bytes       => v_total_bytes,
15    unused_blocks     => v_unused_blocks,
16    unused_bytes      =>  v_unused_bytes,
17    last_used_extent_file_id   => v_last_used_extent_file_id,
18    last_used_extent_block_id  => v_last_used_extent_block_id,
19    last_used_block              => v_last_used_block,
20    partition_name               => NULL);
21    dbms_output.put_line ( 'Number of Total Blocks  :
      '||v_total_blocks);
22    dbms_output.put_line ( 'Number of Bytes         :
      '||v_total_bytes);
23    dbms_output.put_line ('Number of Unused Blocks :
      '||v_unused_blocks);
24    dbms_output.put_line ('Number of unused Bytes  :
      '||v_unused_bytes );
25    end;
Number of Total Blocks  : 384
Number of Bytes         : 3145728
Number of Unused Blocks : 0
Number of unused Bytes  : 0
PL/SQL procedure successfully completed.
SQL>
```

DBMS_SPACE_ADMIN

Contrary to what its name suggests, this package will not help you administer space within the Oracle database. You use the DBMS_SPACE_ADMIN package mostly to manage the locally managed tablespaces. You can migrate dictionary managed tablespaces to locally managed tablespaces using the DBMS_SPACE_ADMIN package. Make sure you first follow all the requirements before you perform the actual migration of the tablespaces. The package has several procedures, as shown in Listing 21-19.

Listing 21-19. Describing the DBMS_SPACE_ADMIN Package

```
SQL> DESC dbms_space_admin
Argument Name                    Type                    In/Out Default?
------------------------------   ---------------------   ------ --------
PROCEDURE SEGMENT_CORRUPT
 TABLESPACE_NAME                 VARCHAR2                IN
 HEADER_RELATIVE_FILE            BINARY_INTEGER          IN
 HEADER_BLOCK                    BINARY_INTEGER          IN
 CORRUPT_OPTION                  BINARY_INTEGER          IN     DEFAULT
PROCEDURE SEGMENT_DROP_CORRUPT
 TABLESPACE_NAME                 VARCHAR2                IN
 HEADER_RELATIVE_FILE            BINARY_INTEGER          IN
 HEADER_BLOCK                    BINARY_INTEGER          IN
```

```
PROCEDURE TABLESPACE_MIGRATE_FROM_LOCAL
 TABLESPACE_NAME                 VARCHAR2              IN
PROCEDURE TABLESPACE_MIGRATE_TO_LOCAL
 TABLESPACE_NAME                 VARCHAR2              IN
 UNIT_SIZE                       BINARY_INTEGER        IN      DEFAULT
 RFNO                            BINARY_INTEGER        IN      DEFAULT
PROCEDURE TABLESPACE_RELOCATE_BITMAPS
TABLESPACE_NAME                  VARCHAR2              IN
 FILNO                           BINARY_INTEGER        IN
 BLKNO                           BINARY_INTEGER        IN
PROCEDURE TABLESPACE_VERIFY
 TABLESPACE_NAME                 VARCHAR2              IN
 VERIFY_OPTION                   BINARY_INTEGER        IN      DEFAULT
SQL>
```

You can use the DBMS_SPACE_ADMIN package to migrate dictionary managed tablespaces to locally managed tablespaces. The following example shows how to use the *tablespace_migrate_to_local* procedure to perform the tablespace migration. There is also a *tablespace_migrate_from_local* procedure that converts a locally managed tablespace into a dictionary managed tablespace.

```
SQL> execute dbms_space_admin.tablespace_migrate_to_local('TEST1');
PL/SQL procedure successfully completed.
SQL>
```

NOTE *The DBMS_SPACE_ADMIN.tablespace_migrate_to_local procedure has three parameters, but you can leave out the* allocation unit *and the* relative file number *parameters in most cases.*

DBMS_PROFILER

The DBMS_PROFILER package lets you gather performance data on your applications. Each time your PL/SQL code executes in the database, performance data is stored in database tables. You start the profiler, run your PL/SQL code, and stop the profiler. Repeated executions of several variations of the code will give you a good idea about where your performance problems lie.

A Useful Package for Developers

As programs get larger and more complex, and developers are seriously in pursuit of fulfilling the functional specifications, code performance becomes harder to improve. The DBMS_PROFILER packages helps you catch inefficient PL/SQL code and eliminate bottlenecks in your code. All you need to do to take advantage of the DBMS_PROFILER package is the following:

- Enable the profiler data collection.

- Execute the test code.

- Analyze the profiler data and trap inefficient code.

- Execute new code until performance meets acceptable standards.

Installing the DBMS_PROFILER Package

The DBMS_PROFILER is a useful package for DBAs, but it isn't automatically created like all the other DBMS packages when you run the catalog.sql and catproc.sql scripts after installing the database. You need to run a special installation script manually, as shown in Listing 21-20. The example here shows the execution of the script in a Windows Oracle9*i* database. On a UNIX system, the script is located in the /$ORACLE_HOME/rdbms/admin directory. You need to be logged in as the user SYS to execute this script.

Listing 21-20. Installing the Profiler

```
SQL> show user
USER is "SYS"
SQL> @c:\oraclent\rdbms\admin\profload.sql
Package created.
Grant succeeded.
Synonym created.
Library created.
Package body created.
Testing for correct installation
SYS.DBMS_PROFILER successfully loaded.
PL/SQL procedure successfully completed.
SQL>
```

Using the DBMS_PROFILER Package

Once you have created the DBMS_PROFILER package, grant the execute privilege on it to the user who needs to use the package, as shown here (you can also grant the privilege to PUBLIC if you wish):

```
SQL> grant execute on dbms_profiler to OE;
Grant succeeded.
SQL>
```

Next, log in as user OE and execute the proftab.sql script, which is located in the $ORACLE_HOME/rdbms/admin directory. This creates the necessary tables in user OE's schema, where the performance details of the PL/SQL code runs can be stored. The following code shows the results of the script execution by user OE:

```
SQL> connect oe/oe@manager
Connected.
SQL> @c:\oraclent\rdbms\admin\proftab.sql
drop table plsql_profiler_data cascade constraints
   ...
```

```
Table created.
Comment created.
...
Sequence created.
SQL>
```

Oracle provides sample code that you can use to learn how the DBMS_PRO-
FILER package works. Go to the $ORACLE_HOME/plsql/demo directory and
study the script profdemo.sql. The script creates the following objects:

- A pair of test tables in the OE schema called the profdemo_tab_1 and
  profdemo_tab_2, to demo the DBMS_PROFILER package

- A type named prof_demo_typ

- A trigger that inserts data into the second table after each insert into the first
  table

- A package that inserts data into the two demo tables

Next, the script executes the DBMS_PROFILER.start_profiler procedure to
start the profiling session. It then executes the package it just created and, finally,
it executes the DBMS_PROFILER.stop_profiler procedure to stop the collection of
performance data.

Once the profiler is done, the script will execute the profsum.sql script, which
generates a report of the profiler session for you. The code execution profile
includes the number of times each line of your code was executed and the total
amount of time taken to execute each line. The report also indicates the minimum
and maximum amounts of time taken to execute each line. Armed with such
information, you can quickly get an idea about where the performance bottlenecks are in your code. For example, you may find that using bulk binds might
improve the code performance figures tremendously. Listing 21-21 shows the
main procedures and functions that are part of the DBMS_PROFILER package.

Listing 21-21. The DBMS_PROFILER Package

```
SQL> desc dbms_profiler
Argument Name                   Type                    In/Out Default?
-----------------------------   ----------------------  ------ --------
PROCEDURE FLUSH_DATA
/* Flushes the performance data to the storage tables */
PROCEDURE START_PROFILER
/* Starts the profiler */
 RUN_COMMENT                    VARCHAR2                IN     DEFAULT
 RUN_COMMENT1                   VARCHAR2                IN     DEFAULT
 RUN_NUMBER                     BINARY_INTEGER          OUT
PROCEDURE STOP_PROFILER
/* Stops the profiler */
SQL>
```

Note that you can also use the DBMS_PROFILER in a much more intuitive
fashion by using the GUI-based TOAD software distributed by Quest Software
(http://www.quest.com).

UTL_FILE

How do you write to operating system text files from within a PL/SQL program unit? Is there any way to read data directly from a text file into a PL/SQL code block? The wonderful UTL_FILE package enables you to easily write to and read from operating system files. The UTL_FILE package provides you with a restricted version of standard operating system stream file I/O.

Listing 21-22 shows you the main procedures and functions in the UTL_FILE package. The procedures let you open, read from, write to, and close the operating system files. Oracle also uses a client-side text I/O package, the TEXT_IO package, as part of the Oracle Procedure Builder.

Listing 21-22. Describing the UTL_FILE Package

```
SQL> desc utl_file
Argument Name                      Type                    In/Out Default?
------------------------------     --------------------    ------ --------
FUNCTION FOPEN RETURNS RECORD
/* Opens a file for input/output */
    ID                             BINARY_INTEGER          OUT
    DATATYPE                       BINARY_INTEGER          OUT
 LOCATION                          VARCHAR2                IN
 FILENAME                          VARCHAR2                IN
 OPEN_MODE                         VARCHAR2                IN
PROCEDURE FCLOSE
/* Closes a file */
 FILE                              RECORD                  IN/OUT
    ID                             BINARY_INTEGER          IN/OUT
    DATATYPE                       BINARY_INTEGER          IN/OUT
PROCEDURE FFLUSH
/* Writes all pending output to a file */
 FILE                              RECORD                  IN
    ID                             BINARY_INTEGER          IN
    DATATYPE                       BINARY_INTEGER          IN
 FILE                              RECORD                  IN
    ID                             BINARY_INTEGER          IN
    DATATYPE                       BINARY_INTEGER          IN
 BUFFER                            VARCHAR2                OUT
PROCEDURE NEW_LINE
 /* Writes an end of line terminator */
 FILE                              RECORD                  IN
    ID                             BINARY_INTEGER          IN
    DATATYPE                       BINARY_INTEGER          IN
 LINES                             BINARY_INTEGER          IN     DEFAULT
PROCEDURE PUT
/* Writes a line to a file */
 FILE                              RECORD                  IN
    ID                             BINARY_INTEGER          IN
    DATATYPE                       BINARY_INTEGER          IN
 BUFFER                            VARCHAR2                IN
```

```
PROCEDURE PUT_LINE
/* Writes a single line to the file, and includes a line terminator */
FILE                          RECORD                  IN
   ID                         BINARY_INTEGER          IN
   DATATYPE                   BINARY_INTEGER          IN
 BUFFER                       VARCHAR2                IN
SQL>
```

Using the UTL_FILE Package

It is easy to use the UTL_FILE directory to read from and write to the operating system files. In many cases, you may need to create a report on something, and the UTL_FILE package is ideal for creating the file, which you can send to an external source using the FTP utility. The following sections take you through a simple example that illustrates the use of this utilitarian package.

Create the File Directory

The first step in using the UTL_FILE directory is to create the directory where you want to place the operating system files. You need to create a special directory for this purpose using the following command:

```
SQL> create directory utl_dir as 'C:\oraclent\oradata\mark1';
     /*the directory could be named anything you want - utl_dir
     is just an example*/
Directory created.
SQL>
```

> **TIP** *The* utl_file_dir *initialization parameter is still valid, but Oracle doesn't recommend using it anymore. Oracle recommends that you use the new* create directory *command instead. Using the* create directory *approach is better because you don't have to restart the database (when you want to add the* utl_file_dir *parameter).*

Grant Privileges to Users

You have to grant your users privileges to read and write files in the utl_dir directory that you just created. You can do this by executing the following command:

```
SQL> grant read, write on directory utl_dir to public;
Grant succeeded.
SQL>
```

UTL_FILE Procedures in Detail

The UTL_FILE package uses its many procedures and functions to perform file manipulation and text writing/reading activities. The next sections briefly cover the key procedures and functions in the UTL_FILE package.

UTL_FILE.File_Type

UTL_FILE.file_type is a file handle data type, and you use it for all the procedures and functions of the UTL_FILE package. Anytime you use the UTL_FILE package within a PL/SQL anonymous code block or a procedure, you must first declare a file handle of UTL_FILE.file_type, as you'll see later.

Opening an Operating System File

You use the FOPEN function to open an operating system file for input and output. You can open a file in three modes: read (r), write (w), or append (a).

Reading from a File

To read from a file, you first specify the read (r) mode when you open a file using the FOPEN function. The *get_line* procedure enables you to read a line of text at a time from the specified operating system file.

Writing to a File

To write to a file, you must open the file in the write (w) or append (a) mode. The append (a) mode will just add to the file, and the write (w) mode will overwrite the file if it already exists. If the file doesn't already exist in the UTL_FILE directory, the UTL_FILE utility will first create the file and then write to it. Note that you don't have to create the file manually—the FOPEN function will take care of that for you.

When you want to write a line to the file, you can use the *put* procedure. After the package writes a line, you can ask it to go to a new line by using the *new_line* procedure. Better yet, you can just use the *put_line* procedure, which is like a combination of the *put* and *new_line* procedures, to write to the text file.

Closing a File

When you finish reading from and/or writing to the file, you need to use the FCLOSE procedure to close the operating system file. If you have more than one file open, you may use the *fclose_all* procedure to close all the open files at once.

Exceptions

Whenever you use the UTL_FILE package in a PL/SQL procedure or block, make sure you have an exception block at the very end to account for all the possible errors that may occur while you're using the package. For example, your directory location may be wrong, or a "no data found" error is raised within the procedure. You may have a read or write error due to a number of reasons. The UTL_FILE package comes with a large number of predefined exceptions, and I recommend using all the exceptions at the end of your procedure or code block to facilitate debugging. If you use *raise_application_error* to assign an error number and a message with the exceptions, you'll have an easier time debugging the code.

A Simple Example Using the UTL_FILE Package

The following anonymous PL/SQL code uses the UTL_FILE package to write password-related information using the DBA_USERS and the DBA_PROFILES dictionary views. Your goal is to produce an operating system file listing user names, their maximum login attempts, their password lifetime, and their password lock time. Listing 21-23 shows the code block.

Listing 21-23. Using the UTL_FILE Package to Perform Text Input and Output

```
DECLARE
        v_failed  dba_profiles.limit%TYPE;
        v_lock     dba_profiles.limit%TYPE;
        v_reuse    dba_profiles.limit%TYPE;
        /* the fHandle declared here is used every time
        the OS file is opened /*
        fHandle UTL_FILE.FILE_TYPE;
        vText varchar2(10);
        v_username dba_users.username%TYPE;
        cursor users is
select username from dba_users;
BEGIN
        /* Open  utlfile.txt file for writing, and get its file handle */
        fHandle := UTL_FILE.FOPEN('/a01/pas/pasp/import','utlfile.txt','w');
/* Write a line of text to the file utlfile.txt */
UTL_FILE.PUT_LINE(fHandle,'USERNAME'||'ATTEMPTS'||'LIFE'||'LOCK'||);
/* Close the utlfile.txt file */
UTL_FILE.FCLOSE(fHandle);
/* Open the utlfile.txt file for writing, and get its file handle */
    fHandle := UTL_FILE.FOPEN('/a01/pas/pasp/import','utlfile.txt','a');
    open users;
      LOOP
      FETCH users INTO v_username;
      EXIT when users%NOTFOUND;
SELECT p.limit
      INTO v_failed
      FROM dba_profiles p, dba_users u
      WHERE p.resource_name='FAILED_LOGIN_ATTEMPTS'
      AND p.profile=u.profile
      AND u.username=v_username;
SELECT p.limit
      INTO v_life
      FROM dba_profiles p, dba_users u
      WHERE p.resource_name='PASSWORD_LIFE_TIME'
      AND p.profile=u.profile
      AND u.username=v_username;
SELECT p.limit
      INTO v_lock
      FROM dba_profiles p, dba_users u
```

```
        WHERE p.resource_name='PASSWORD_LOCK_TIME'
        AND p.profile=u.profile
        AND u.username=v_username;
        vtext :='TEST';
        /* Write a line of text to the file utlfile.txt */
        UTL_FILE.PUT_LINE(fHandle,v_username||v_failed||_life||v_lock);
        /* Read a line from the file utltext.txt */
       UTL_FILE.GET_LINE(fHandle,v_username||v_failed||v_life||v_lock);
        /* Write a line of text to the Screen */
        UTL_FILE.PUT_LINE(v_username||_failed||v_life||v_lock);
    END LOOP;
    CLOSE users;
      /* Close the utlfile.txt file */
      UTL_FILE.FCLOSE(fHandle);
    /* this is the exception block for the Utl_File errors */
    EXCEPTION
      WHEN UTL_FILE.INVALID_PATH THEN
RAISE_APPLICATION_ERROR(-20100,'Invalid Path');
WHEN UTL_FILE.INVALID_MODE THEN
        RATSE_APPLICATION_ERROR(-20101,'Invalid Mode');
WHEN UTL_FILE.INVALID_OPERATION then
        RAISE_APPLICATION_ERROR(-20102,'Invalid Operation');
      WHEN UTL_FILE.INVALID_FILEHANDLE then
        RAISE_APPLICATION_ERROR(-20103,'Invalid Filehandle');
      WHEN UTL_FILE.WRITE_ERROR then
        RAISE_APPLICATION_ERROR(-20104,'Write Error');
      WHEN UTL_FILE.READ_ERROR then
        RAISE_APPLICATION_ERROR(-20105,'Read Error');
      WHEN UTL_FILE.INTERNAL_ERROR then
        RAISE_APPLICATION_ERROR(-20106,'Internal Error');
      WHEN OTHERS THEN
        UTL_FILE.FCLOSE(fHandle);
END;
```

UTL_SMTP

The UTL_SMTP package is useful for sending e-mail messages from a PL/SQL program. This package has too many low-level primitives, and it's therefore too cumbersome to be thought of as an interactive e-mail client.

Why would you need to send e-mails from a PL/SQL package? You may want to alert people when specific events take place in the database. You can send e-mail, pages, and even text messages over a cell phone using the UTL_SMTP package. Your e-mail can also have attachments.

Procedures in the UTL_SMTP Package

The UTL_SMTP package is named after the Simple Mail Transfer Protocol (SMTP), which can send or receive e-mail using TCP/IP. The UTL_TCP package can send

data through the TCP/IP protocol, and the UTL_SMTP package uses this functionality of the UTL_TCP package to send e-mails from the database. Listing 21-24
shows the main procedures and functions included in the UTL_SMTP package.

Listing 21-24. The UTL_SMTP Package

```
SQL> desc utl_smtp
FUNCTION OPEN_CONNECTION RETURNS RECORD
/* Opens the SMTP connection */
 Argument Name                   Type                       In/Out Default?
 ------------------------------  -------------------------  ------ --------
    CODE                         BINARY_INTEGER             OUT
    TEXT                         VARCHAR2(508)              OUT
 HOST                            VARCHAR2                   IN
 PORT                            BINARY_INTEGER             IN      DEFAULT
 C                               RECORD                     OUT
    HOST                         VARCHAR2(255)              OUT
    PORT                         BINARY_INTEGER             OUT
    TX_TIMEOUT                   BINARY_INTEGER             OUT
    PRIVATE_TCP_CON              RECORD                     OUT
      REMOTE_HOST                VARCHAR2(255)              OUT
      REMOTE_PORT                BINARY_INTEGER             OUT
      LOCAL_HOST                 VARCHAR2(255)              OUT
      LOCAL_PORT                 BINARY_INTEGER             OUT
      CHARSET                    VARCHAR2(30)               OUT
      NEWLINE                    VARCHAR2(2)                OUT
      TX_TIMEOUT                 BINARY_INTEGER             OUT
      PRIVATE_SD                 BINARY_INTEGER             OUT
    PRIVATE_STATE                BINARY_INTEGER             OUT
 TX_TIMEOUT                      BINARY_INTEGER             IN      DEFAULT
PROCEDURE DATA
/* specified the body of the Email message */
 C                               RECORD                     IN/OUT
   HOST                          VARCHAR2(255)              IN/OUT
   PORT                          BINARY_INTEGER             IN/OUT
   TX_TIMEOUT                    BINARY_INTEGER             IN/OUT
   PRIVATE_TCP_CON               RECORD                     IN/OUT
     REMOTE_HOST                 VARCHAR2(255)              IN/OUT
     REMOTE_PORT                 BINARY_INTEGER             IN/OUT
     LOCAL_HOST                  VARCHAR2(255)              IN/OUT
     LOCAL_PORT                  BINARY_INTEGER             IN/OUT
     CHARSET                     VARCHAR2(30)               IN/OUT
     NEWLINE                     VARCHAR2(2)                IN/OUT
     TX_TIMEOUT                  BINARY_INTEGER             IN/OUT
     PRIVATE_SD                  BINARY_INTEGER             IN/OUT
   PRIVATE_STATE                 BINARY_INTEGER             IN/OUT
 BODY                            VARCHAR2                   IN
PROCEDURE HELO
/* After making the connection, will initiate the contact with the SMTP server */
 C                               RECORD                     IN/OUT
```

HOST	VARCHAR2(255)	IN/OUT
PORT	BINARY_INTEGER	IN/OUT
TX_TIMEOUT	BINARY_INTEGER	IN/OUT
PRIVATE_TCP_CON	RECORD	IN/OUT
REMOTE_HOST	VARCHAR2(255)	IN/OUT
REMOTE_PORT	BINARY_INTEGER	IN/OUT
LOCAL_HOST	VARCHAR2(255)	IN/OUT
LOCAL_PORT	BINARY_INTEGER	IN/OUT
CHARSET	VARCHAR2(30)	IN/OUT
NEWLINE	VARCHAR2(2)	IN/OUT
TX_TIMEOUT	BINARY_INTEGER	IN/OUT
PRIVATE_SD	BINARY_INTEGER	IN/OUT
PRIVATE_STATE	BINARY_INTEGER	IN/OUT

PROCEDURE MAIL

/* Initiates the mail transaction with the SMTP server */

C	RECORD	IN/OUT	
HOST	VARCHAR2(255)	IN/OUT	
PORT	BINARY_INTEGER	IN/OUT	
TX_TIMEOUT	BINARY_INTEGER	IN/OUT	
PRIVATE_TCP_CON	RECORD	IN/OUT	
REMOTE_HOST	VARCHAR2(255)	IN/OUT	
REMOTE_PORT	BINARY_INTEGER	IN/OUT	
LOCAL_HOST	VARCHAR2(255)	IN/OUT	
LOCAL_PORT	BINARY_INTEGER	IN/OUT	
CHARSET	VARCHAR2(30)	IN/OUT	
NEWLINE	VARCHAR2(2)	IN/OUT	
TX_TIMEOUT	BINARY_INTEGER	IN/OUT	
PRIVATE_SD	BINARY_INTEGER	IN/OUT	
PRIVATE_STATE	BINARY_INTEGER	IN/OUT	
SENDER	VARCHAR2	IN	
PARAMETERS	VARCHAR2	IN	DEFAULT

PROCEDURE RCPT

/* Specifies the recipient of the Email message */

C	RECORD	IN/OUT	
HOST	VARCHAR2(255)	IN/OUT	
PORT	BINARY_INTEGER	IN/OUT	
TX_TIMEOUT	BINARY_INTEGER	IN/OUT	
PRIVATE_TCP_CON	RECORD	IN/OUT	
REMOTE_HOST	VARCHAR2(255)	IN/OUT	
REMOTE_PORT	BINARY_INTEGER	IN/OUT	
LOCAL_HOST	VARCHAR2(255)	IN/OUT	
LOCAL_PORT	BINARY_INTEGER	IN/OUT	
CHARSET	VARCHAR2(30)	IN/OUT	
NEWLINE	VARCHAR2(2)	IN/OUT	
TX_TIMEOUT	BINARY_INTEGER	IN/OUT	
PRIVATE_SD	BINARY_INTEGER	IN/OUT	
PRIVATE_STATE	BINARY_INTEGER	IN/OUT	
RECIPIENT	VARCHAR2	IN	
PARAMETERS	VARCHAR2	IN	DEFAULT

Using the UTL_SMTP Package

The UTL_SMTP package essentially performs the following steps to send messages from the database:

1. Establish the connection to the SMTP server using the *open_connection* function and the *helo* procedure.

2. Initiate a mail transaction using the *mail* function.

3. Specify the recipients of the e-mail message using the *rcpt* function.

4. Provide the e-mail message using the *data* function.

5. Terminate the SMTP connection and disconnect using the *quit* function.

Listing 21-25 presents a simple example demonstrating how you can send e-mail from a PL/SQL program using the UTL_SMTP package. The simple message doesn't have any headers indicating who sent the message.

Listing 21-25. Using the UTL_SMTP Package to Send Mail from PL/SQL

```
Declare
 v_connection utl_Smtp.connection;
BEGIN
     V_connection := Utl_Smtp.Open_Connection (smtp.server.xyz.com);
      Utl_smtp.hel(v_connection, xyz.com);
      Utl_smtp.mail(v_connection, program@xyz.com);
      Utl_smtp.rcpt(v_connection, oracle_dba@xyz.com);
      Utl_smtp.data(v_connection, Just a SMTP Test Message );
      Utl_smtp.quit(v_connection);
END;
```

DBMS_SHARED_POOL

The DBMS_SHARED_POOL package enables you to find out the size of the stored PL/SQL objects and either pin them or unpin them from the shared pool. The package is especially useful when you're trying to invoke large PL/SQL objects and you can't increase your shared pool size by much right away.

The introduction of the large package may push a large number of necessary packages out of the shared pool. Or, you may even have a problem loading the large package into the shared pool, because there's no large contiguous area of shared pool available due to excessive fragmentation of the pool. In both cases, you can use this package to use your shared pool memory area more efficiently. Listing 21-26 describes the procedures in the DBMS_SHARED_POOL package.

Listing 21-26. The DBMS_SHARED_POOL Package

```
SQL> desc sys.dbms_shared_pool
Argument Name                    Type                      In/Out Default?
-----------------------------    ----------------------    ------ --------
PROCEDURE ABORTED_REQUEST_THRESHOLD
  THRESHOLD_SIZE                 NUMBER                    IN
PROCEDURE KEEP
  NAME                           VARCHAR2                  IN
  FLAG                           CHAR                      IN     DEFAULT
PROCEDURE SIZES
  MINSIZE                        NUMBER                    IN
PROCEDURE UNKEEP
  NAME                           VARCHAR2                  IN
  FLAG                           CHAR                      IN     DEFAULT
SQL>
```

If you're having a problem with shared pool fragmentation, you should consider pinning almost all the commonly used stored procedures and packages in the shared pool upon starting the instance. Pinning packages in the shared pool will reduce fragmentation in the shared pool and consequently keep the pool from running out of space when a new object is trying to enter it.

The following code shows how to use the DBMS_SHARED_POOL package to pin and unpin packages in the shared pool component of the SGA:

```
SQL> execute sys.dbms_shared_pool.keep ('QS_ADM.QS_APPLICATIONS','P');
PL/SQL procedure successfully completed.
SQL> execute sys.dbms_shared_pool.unkeep ('QS_ADM.QS_APPLICATIONS','P');
PL/SQL procedure successfully completed.
SQL>
```

You can query the V$DB_OBJECT_CACHE view to see if the object is indeed pinned, as shown in Listing 21-27.

Listing 21-27. Querying the V$DB_OBJECT_CACHE View

```
SQL> select name,type,kept
  2  from
  3  v$db_object_cache
  4  where owner='QS_ADM';
      Name                   Type            Kept
----------------------   --------------   ------
QS_APPITCATTONS          PACKAGE          YES
QS_APPLICATIONS          PACKAGE BODY     YES
ORDER_TYP                NOT LOADED       NO
ORDERITEMLIST_VARTYP     NOT LOADED       NO
SQL>
```

The *sizes* procedure gives you the size of all the packages that are larger than a threshold you specify. You can use this procedure to decide which procedures you may want to pin to the shared pool. Here's an example of the use of the *sizes* procedure:

```
SQL> set serveroutput on
SQL> execute sys.dbms_shared_pool.sizes(8000);
PL/SQL procedure successfully completed.
```

DBMS_LOGSTDBY

If you create logical standby databases, you need to use the DBMS_LOGSTDBY package to set up and modify certain parameters during the creation of the logical database. For example, you need to use the *guard_bypass_on* procedure to bypass the database guard and allow modifications to the logical standby database tables. The *unskip* procedure lets you verify that the database links are correctly configured between the primary and standby databases. Listing 21-28 shows some of the important procedures of the DBMS_LOGSTDBY package.

Listing 21-28. The DBMS_LOGSTDBY Package

```
SQL> desc dbms_logstdby
Argument Name                  Type                     In/Out Default?
-----------------------------  -----------------------  ------ --------
PROCEDURE GUARD_BYPASS_ON

/* Lets you bypass the dataguard manager and directly modify
 the standby database tables */
PROCEDURE SKIP
 STMT                          VARCHAR2                 IN
 SCHEMA_NAME                   VARCHAR2                 IN
 OBJECT_NAME                   VARCHAR2                 IN
 PROC_NAME                     VARCHAR2                 IN
PROCEDURE SKIP_ERROR

/* specifies the operation in the primary database that will not
be applied to the standby database */
 STMT                          VARCHAR2                 IN
 SCHEMA_NAME                   VARCHAR2                 IN
 OBJECT_NAME                   VARCHAR2                 IN
 PROC_NAME                     VARCHAR2                 IN
PROCEDURE UNSKIP
 STMT                          VARCHAR2                 IN
 SCHEMA_NAME                   VARCHAR2                 IN
 OBJECT_NAME                   VARCHAR2                 IN
SQL>
```

Oracle Packages in Earlier Chapters

You've seen how to use the following Oracle-supplied packages in earlier chapters. Consequently, I don't provide any examples of the use of these packages in this chapter. In the following sections, I briefly discuss the packages that you've reviewed elsewhere in this book.

The DBMS_STATS Package

The DBMS_STATS package is a highly useful Oracle package that you use to enable statistics collection for the Oracle optimizer. Listing 21-29 shows the important procedures of the DBMS_STATS package.

Listing 21-29. The DBMS_STATS Package

```
Sql> Describe dbms_stats
Argument Name                    Type                      In/Out Default?
-------------------------------- ------------------------- ------ -------------
PROCEDURE CREATE_STAT_TABLE
 OWNNAME                         VARCHAR2                  IN
 STATTAB                         VARCHAR2                  IN
 TBLSPACE                        VARCHAR2                  IN     DEFAULT
PROCEDURE EXPORT_SCHEMA_STATS
 OWNNAME                         VARCHAR2                  IN
 STATTAB                         VARCHAR2                  IN
 STATID                          VARCHAR2                  IN     DEFAULT
 STATOWN                         VARCHAR2                  IN     DEFAULT
PROCEDURE GATHER_DATABASE_STATS
 ESTIMATE_PERCENT                NUMBER                    IN     DEFAULT
 BLOCK_SAMPLE                    BOOLEAN                   IN     DEFAULT
 METHOD_OPT                      VARCHAR2                  IN     DEFAULT
 DEGREE                          NUMBER                    IN     DEFAULT
 GRANULARITY                     VARCHAR2                  IN     DEFAULT
 CASCADE                         BOOLEAN                   IN     DEFAULT
 STATTAB                         VARCHAR2                  IN     DEFAULT
 STATID                          VARCHAR2                  IN     DEFAULT
 OPTIONS                         VARCHAR2                  IN     DEFAULT
 OBJLIST                         DBMS_STATS                OUT
 STATOWN                         VARCHAR2                  IN     DEFAULT
 GATHER_SYS                      BOOLEAN                   IN     DEFAULT
 NO_INVALIDATE                   BOOLEAN                   IN     DEFAULT
 GATHER_TEMP                     BOOLEAN                   IN     DEFAULT
 GATHER_FIXED                    BOOLEAN                   IN     DEFAULT
PROCEDURE GATHER_SYSTEM_STATS
 GATHERING_MODE                  VARCHAR2                  IN     DEFAULT
 INTERVAL                        NUMBER(38)                IN     DEFAULT
 STATTAB                         VARCHAR2                  IN     DEFAULT
 STATID                          VARCHAR2                  IN     DEFAULT
 STATOWN                         VARCHAR2                  IN     DEFAULT
```

```
PROCEDURE GET_TABLE_STATS
   OWNNAME                        VARCHAR2              IN
   TABNAME                        VARCHAR2              IN
   PARTNAME                       VARCHAR2              IN    DEFAULT
   STATTAB                        VARCHAR2              IN    DEFAULT
   STATID                         VARCHAR2              IN    DEFAULT
   NUMROWS                        NUMBER                OUT
   NUMBLKS                        NUMBER                OUT
   AVGRLEN                        NUMBER                OUT
   STATOWN                        VARCHAR2              IN    DEFAULT
```

Chapter 18 shows how to use the *create_stat_table*, *gather_schema_stats*, *gather_table_stats*, and *gather_system_stats* procedures to collect instance and system performance data.

DBMS_RLS

In Chapter 11, you saw how you could use the DBMS_RLS package to create security policies when you're implementing fine-grained access control (FGAC). You can use the DBMS_RLS package to administer FGAC. Listing 21-30 shows the important procedures and functions that are part of the DBMS_RLS package.

Listing 21-30. The DBMS_RLS Package

```
SQL> desc Dbms_Rls
Argument Name                     Type            In/Out Default?
--------------------------------------------------------------------------------
PROCEDURE ADD_POLICY
/* Adds a fine-grained access control policy to a database object */
   OBJECT_SCHEMA                  VARCHAR2              IN    DEFAULT
   /* if NULL, default schema */
   OBJECT_NAME                    VARCHAR2              IN
   POLICY_NAME                    VARCHAR2              IN
   FUNCTION_SCHEMA                VARCHAR2              IN    DEFAULT
   /* if NULL, current default schema */
   POLICY_FUNCTION                VARCHAR2              IN
   STATEMENT_TYPES                VARCHAR2              IN    DEFAULT
   UPDATE_CHECK                   BOOLEAN               IN    DEFAULT
   ENABLE                         BOOLEAN               IN    DEFAULT
   STATIC_POLICY                  BOOLEAN               IN    DEFAULT
PROCEDURE ADD_POLICY_CONTEXT
/* Adds the Context for the Application */
   OBJECT_SCHEMA                  VARCHAR2              IN    DEFAULT
   OBJECT_NAME                    VARCHAR2              IN
   NAMESPACE                      VARCHAR2              IN
   ATTRIBUTE                      VARCHAR2              IN
PROCEDURE CREATE_POLICY_GROUP
   OBJECT_SCHEMA                  VARCHAR2              IN    DEFAULT
   OBJECT_NAME                    VARCHAR2              IN
   POLICY_GROUP                   VARCHAR2              IN
```

```
PROCEDURE REFRESH_POLICY
 OBJECT_SCHEMA                    VARCHAR2                IN      DEFAULT
 OBJECT_NAME                      VARCHAR2                IN      DEFAULT
 POLICY_NAME                      VARCHAR2                IN      DEFAULT
SQL>
```

DBMS_FGA

The DBMS_FGA package provides fine-grained auditing functionality to the DBA. Chapter 11 contains a full description of fine-grained auditing using the DBMS_FGA package. Listing 21-31 shows the component procedures of the DBMS_FGA package.

Listing 21-31. The DBMS_FGA Package

```
SQL> desc dbms_fga
Argument Name                    Type                    In/Out Default?
-------------------------------------------------------------------------
PROCEDURE ADD_POLICY
 OBJECT_SCHEMA                    VARCHAR2                IN      DEFAULT
 OBJECT_NAME                      VARCHAR2                IN
 POLICY_NAME                      VARCHAR2                IN
 AUDIT_CONDITION                  VARCHAR2                IN      DEFAULT
 AUDIT_COLUMN                     VARCHAR2                IN      DEFAULT
 HANDLER_SCHEMA                   VARCHAR2                IN      DEFAULT
 HANDLER_MODULE                   VARCHAR2                IN      DEFAULT
 ENABLE                           BOOLEAN                 IN      DEFAULT
PROCEDURE DISABLE_POLICY
 OBJECT_SCHEMA                    VARCHAR2                IN      DEFAULT
 OBJECT_NAME                      VARCHAR2                IN
 POLICY_NAME                      VARCHAR2                IN
PROCEDURE DROP_POLICY
 OBJECT_SCHEMA                    VARCHAR2                IN      DEFAULT
 OBJECT_NAME                      VARCHAR2                IN
 POLICY_NAME                      VARCHAR2                IN
PROCEDURE ENABLE_POLICY
 OBJECT_SCHEMA                    VARCHAR2                IN      DEFAULT
 OBJECT_NAME                      VARCHAR2                IN
 POLICY_NAME                      VARCHAR2                IN
 ENABLE                           BOOLEAN                 IN      DEFAULT
SQL>
```

DBMS_RESOURCE_MANAGER

The DBMS_RESOURCE_MANAGER package helps you administer the Database Resource Manager, which is useful in allocating resources to the consumers. With the DBMS_RESOURCE_MANAGER package, you can create, drop, and switch consumer groups and manage the resource plans.

Chapter 11 contains an extensive review of the use of the DBMS_RESOURCE_MANAGER package.

DBMS_RESUMABLE

You can use the DBMS_RESUMABLE package to manage Oracle's Resumable Space Allocation feature, whereby the database will suspend operations that encounter out-of-space errors instead of aborting them. Chapter 8 discusses the use of the DBMS_RESUMABLE package in detail. Listing 21-32 shows the important procedures in the DBMS_RESUMABLE package.

Listing 21-32. The DBMS_RESUMABLE Package

```
SQL> desc dbms_resumable
Argument Name                      Type                       In/Out Default?
--------------------------------   -----------------------    ------ ------
PROCEDURE ABORT
/* Aborts a suspended resumable space allocation */
 SESSIONID                         NUMBER                      IN
FUNCTION GET_SESSION_TIMEOUT RETURNS NUMBER
/* Returns current timeout value of resumable space allocations */
 SESSIONID                         NUMBER                      IN
FUNCTION GET_TIMEOUT RETURNS NUMBER
/* Returns current timeout value in seconds */
PROCEDURE SET_SESSION_TIMEOUT
/* Used to set the timeout for resumable space allocation */
 SESSIONID                         NUMBER                      IN
 TIMEOUT                           NUMBER                      IN
PROCEDURE SET_TIMEOUT
/* used to set the timeout for current session */
 TIMEOUT                           NUMBER                      IN
FUNCTION SPACE_ERROR_INFO RETURNS BOOLEAN
/* function returns TRUE if it finds space-related errors, FALSE otherwise */
 ERROR_TYPE                        VARCHAR2                    OUT
 OBJECT_TYPE                       VARCHAR2                    OUT
 OBJECT_OWNER                      VARCHAR2                    OUT
 TABLE_SPACE_NAME                  VARCHAR2                    OUT
 OBJECT_NAME                       VARCHAR2                    OUT
 SUB_OBJECT_NAME                   VARCHAR2                    OUT
SQL>
```

DBMS_OLAP

The DBMS_OLAP package is indispensable when you create materialized views in your database. The package recommends and evaluates candidates for materialized views. The package is also useful in maintaining a repository and for reporting on the materialized views. Among other things, the DBMS_OLAP package provides information on the following:

- Size of the summary tables
- Workload filtering information

- Materialized view recommendations

- Scripts to implement the recommendations

- Materialized view utilization statistics

- Verification of relationships in dimensions

- Recommendations of the Summary Advisor

Once you enable query rewriting in your database, Oracle will use the materialized views transparently, which improves the query response times. Chapter 7 shows you how to use the DBMS_OLAP package to create materialized views. For the DBMS_OLAP package to recommend and evaluate materialized views, you need to provide it the workload information. The package can also use workload information provided through the SQL cache or the Oracle Trace utility.

Listing 21-33 shows the most important procedures and functions of the DBMS_OLAP package.

Listing 21-33. The DBMS_OLAP Package

```
SQL> desc dbms_olap
Argument Name                    Type                    In/Out Default?
------------------------------   ----------------------  ------ --------
PROCEDURE ADD_FILTER_ITEM
/* Creates a filter to restrict the workload analysis */
 FILTER_ID                       NUMBER                  IN
 FILTER_NAME                     VARCHAR2                IN
 STRING_LIST                     VARCHAR2                IN
 NUMBER_MIN                      NUMBER                  IN
 NUMBER_MAX                      NUMBER                  IN
 DATE_MIN                        VARCHAR2                IN
 DATE_MAX                        VARCHAR2                IN
PROCEDURE ESTIMATE_MVIEW_SIZE
/* Estimates the size of the materialized view in bytes */
 STMT_ID                         VARCHAR2                IN
 SELECT_CLAUSE                   VARCHAR2                IN
 NUM_ROWS                        NUMBER                  OUT
 NUM_BYTES                       NUMBER                  OUT
PROCEDURE ESTIMATE_SUMMARY_SIZE
/* Estimates the summary size */
 STMT_ID                         VARCHAR2                IN
 SELECT_CLAUSE                   VARCHAR2                IN
 NUM_ROWS                        NUMBER                  OUT
 NUM_BYTES                       NUMBER                  OUT
PROCEDURE EVALUATE_MVIEW_STRATEGY
/* Measures utilization of a materialized view */
 RUN_ID                          NUMBER                  IN
 WORKLOAD_ID                     NUMBER                  IN
 FILTER_ID                       NUMBER                  IN
```

```
PROCEDURE GENERATE_MVIEW_REPORT
/* Generates a HTML report on the Summary Advisor results */
 FILENAME                          VARCHAR2                    IN
 ID                                NUMBER                      IN
 FLAGS                             NUMBER                      IN
PROCEDURE RECOMMEND_MVIEW_STRATEGY
/* Provides materialized view recommendations */
 RUN_ID                            NUMBER                      IN
 WORKLOAD_ID                       NUMBER                      IN
 FILTER_ID                         NUMBER                      IN
 STORAGE_IN_BYTES                  NUMBER                      IN
 RETENTION_PCT                     NUMBER                      IN
 RETENTION_LIST                    VARCHAR2                    IN
 FACT_TABLE_FILTER                 VARCHAR2                    IN
SQL>
```

DBMS_MVIEW

You can use the DBMS_MVIEW package to refresh materialized views that aren't part of the same group and to understand the rewrite capability of materialized views. Chapter 7 explains the use of the DBMS_MVIEW package for managing materialized views. Listing 21-34 shows the important procedures of the DBMS_MVIEW package.

Listing 21-34. The DBMS_MVIEW Package

```
SQL> desc dbms_mview
Argument Name                     Type                    In/Out Default?
------------------------------    --------------------    ------ --------
PROCEDURE EXPLAIN_MVIEW
/* Explains the possibilities of a materialized view -
 the results are written to the mv_capabilities_table by default. */
 MV                                VARCHAR2                    IN
 STMT_ID                           VARCHAR2                    IN     DEFAULT
PROCEDURE EXPLAIN_REWRITE
/* Tells you why a query failed to rewrite */
 QUERY                             VARCHAR2                    IN
 MV                                VARCHAR2                    IN     DEFAULT
 STATEMENT_ID                      VARCHAR2                    IN     DEFAULT
PROCEDURE REFRESH
/* Refreshes a list of materialized views,
all of which may not be members of the same group */
 LIST                              VARCHAR2                    IN
 METHOD                            VARCHAR2                    IN     DEFAULT
 ROLLBACK_SEG                      VARCHAR2                    IN     DEFAULT
 PUSH_DEFERRED_RPC                 BOOLEAN                     IN     DEFAULT
 REFRESH_AFTER_ERRORS              BOOLEAN                     IN     DEFAULT
 PURGE_OPTION                      BINARY_INTEGER              IN     DEFAULT
```

PARALLELISM	BINARY_INTEGER	IN	DEFAULT
HEAP_SIZE	BINARY_INTEGER	IN	DEFAULT
ATOMIC_REFRESH	BOOLEAN	IN	DEFAULT

PROCEDURE REFRESH_ALL_MVIEWS
/* refreshes all the materialized views that meet certain conditions */

NUMBER_OF_FAILURES	BINARY_INTEGER	OUT	
METHOD	VARCHAR2	IN	DEFAULT
ROLLBACK_SEG	VARCHAR2	IN	DEFAULT
REFRESH_AFTER_ERRORS	BOOLEAN	IN	DEFAULT
ATOMIC_REFRESH	BOOLEAN	IN	DEFAULT

SQL>

DBMS_METADATA

The DBMS_METADATA package can be useful in situations where you need to retrieve the database definitions (metadata) of an object or the entire schema. The package also helps you get the XML representation of Oracle tables.

Chapter 7 shows you how to use the DBMS_METADATA package to retrieve the DDL for a database table.

DBMS_REDEFINITION

You can use the DBMS_REDEFINITION package to perform an *online* reorganization of a table. Listing 21-35 describes the component procedures of the DBMS_REDEFINITION procedure. Chapter 16 provides a complete example of the online reorganization of a table using the DBMS_REDEFINITION package.

Listing 21-35. The DBMS_REDEFINITION Package

```
SQL> desc dbms_redefinition
Argument Name                   Type                        In/Out Default?
---------------------------------------------------------------------------
PROCEDURE ABORT_REDEF_TABLE
 UNAME                          VARCHAR2                     IN
 ORIG_TABLE                     VARCHAR2                     IN
 INT_TABLE                      VARCHAR2                     IN
PROCEDURE CAN_REDEF_TABLE
/* Determines if a table can be a candidate for an online redefinition */
 UNAME                          VARCHAR2                     IN
 TNAME                          VARCHAR2                     IN
 OPTIONS_FLAG                   BINARY_INTEGER               IN     DEFAULT
PROCEDURE FINISH_REDEF_TABLE
/* Competes the redefinition */
 UNAME                          VARCHAR2                     IN
 ORIG_TABLE                     VARCHAR2                     IN
 INT_TABLE                      VARCHAR2                     IN
```

```
PROCEDURE START_REDEF_TABLE
/* Starts the table redefinition */
  UNAME                           VARCHAR2              IN
  ORIG_TABLE                      VARCHAR2              IN
  INT_TABLE                       VARCHAR2              IN
  COL_MAPPING                     VARCHAR2              IN      DEFAULT
  OPTIONS_FLAG                    BINARY_INTEGER        IN      DEFAULT
PROCEDURE SYNC_INTERIM_TABLE
/* Uses the information in the interim table to capture
  all the DML performed during the redefinition process */
  UNAME                           VARCHAR2              IN
  ORIG_TABLE                      VARCHAR2              IN
  INT_TABLE                       VARCHAR2              IN
  SQL>
```

DBMS_FLASHBACK

The DBMS_FLASHBACK package enables you to look at the database at a previous point in time or at some previous SCN. Of course, you use the undo segments to go back (or flash back) to a previous version of the database. The value of the *undo_retention* parameter sets the limit on how far you can go back in time. Chapters 8 and 15 provide you with complete examples on using the DBMS_FLASHBACK package. Listing 21-36 shows the contents of the package.

Listing 21-36. The DBMS_FLASHBACK Package

```
SQL> desc dbms_flashback
Argument Name                     Type                 In/Out Default?
------------------------------ ---------------------- ------ --------
PROCEDURE DISABLE
/* Disables flashback for the entire session */
PROCEDURE ENABLE_AT_SYSTEM_CHANGE_NUMBER
/* Enables flashback starting at the specified SCN */
  QUERY_SCN                       NUMBER               IN
PROCEDURE ENABLE_AT_TIME
/* Enables flashback for the entire session,
using query_time to find the closest SCN */
  QUERY_TIME                      TIMESTAMP            IN
FUNCTION GET_SYSTEM_CHANGE_NUMBER RETURNS NUMBER
/* Returns the current SCN */
SQL>
```

DBMS_WM

You can use the Oracle Workspace Manager facility to manage long transactions. The Workspace Manager lets you version the database (i.e., hold multiple versions of the database in various workspaces). The DBMS_WM package lets you create and manage the workspaces needed for database versioning. Chapter 8 provides a detailed example illustrating the use of the DBMS_WM package. Listing 21-37 shows the main procedures included in the package.

Listing 21-37. The DBMS_WM Package

```
SQL> desc dbms_wm
Argument Name                      Type                    In/Out Default?
-----------------------------------------------------------------------
PROCEDURE CREATEWORKSPACE
/* Creates a New Workspace */
 WORKSPACE                         VARCHAR2                IN
 DESCRIPTION                       VARCHAR2                IN      DEFAULT
 AUTO_COMMIT                       BOOLEAN                 IN      DEFAULT
PROCEDURE GRANTWORKSPACEPRIV
/* grants workspace-level privileges to users and roles */
 PRIV_TYPES                        VARCHAR2                IN
 WORKSPACE                         VARCHAR2                IN
 GRANTEE                           VARCHAR2                IN
 GRANT_OPTION                      VARCHAR2                IN      DEFAULT
 AUTO_COMMIT                       BOOLEAN                 IN      DEFAULT
PROCEDURE DISABLEVERSIONING
/* Deletes the Workspace Manager Infrastructure after creating the workspace */
 TABLE_NAME                        VARCHAR2                IN
 FORCE                             BOOLEAN                 IN      DEFAULT
 IGNORE_LAST_ERROR                 BOOLEAN                 IN      DEFAULT
PROCEDURE MERGEWORKSPACE
/* Merges changes in the workspace with the parent workspace */
 WORKSPACE                         VARCHAR2                IN
 CREATE_SAVEPOINT                  BOOLEAN                 IN      DEFAULT
 REMOVE_WORKSPACE                  BOOLEAN                 IN      DEFAULT
 AUTO_COMMIT                       BOOLEAN                 IN      DEFAULT
PROCEDURE REFRESHWORKSPACE
/* Applies changes made in the parent workspace to the child workspace */
 WORKSPACE                         VARCHAR2                IN
 AUTO_COMMIT                       BOOLEAN                 IN      DEFAULT
PROCEDURE REMOVEWORKSPACE
/* Deletes the workspace */
 WORKSPACE                         VARCHAR2                IN
 AUTO_COMMIT                       BOOLEAN                 IN      DEFAULT
PROCEDURE ROLLBACKWORKSPACE
/* Rolls back the changes made to version-enabled tables in the workspace */
 WORKSPACE                         VARCHAR2                IN
 AUTO_COMMIT                       BOOLEAN                 IN      DEFAULT
```

DBMS_LOGMNR

The LogMiner tool lets you "mine" or analyze online and archived redo logs. You can use the tool to either undo changes made to the database without having to perform a formal recovery or audit user sessions. The DBMS_LOGMNR package provides the functionality for the LogMiner tool. The package lets you specify the redo logs and the SCN or calendar time from which to start the analysis. You can view the results of the execution of the DBMS_LOGMNR package by selecting from the dictionary view V$LOGMNR_CONTENTS. Chapter 15 reviews in detail the use of the LogMiner utility and the DBMS_LOGMNR package. Listing 21-38 shows the procedures that are part of the DBMS_LOGMNR package.

Listing 21-38. The DBMS_LOGMNR Package

```
SQL> desc dbms_logmnr
Argument Name                   Type                    In/Out Default?
PROCEDURE ADD_LOG_FILE
/* Adds a redo log file to the list of files to process */
LOGFILENAME                     VARCHAR2                IN
 OPTIONS                        BINARY_INTEGER          IN      DEFAULT
FUNCTION COLUMN_PRESENT RETURNS BINARY_INTEGER
/* Determines if undo or redo column values exist in the log files */
SQL_REDO_UNDO                   RAW                     IN
 COLUMN_NAME                    VARCHAR2                IN      DEFAULT
PROCEDURE END_LOGMNR
/* Ends the LogMiner session */
FUNCTION MINE_VALUE RETURNS VARCHAR2
/* Returns undo or redo column values if they exist */
 SQL_REDO_UNDO                  RAW                     IN
 COLUMN_NAME                    VARCHAR2                IN      DEFAULT
PROCEDURE START_LOGMNR
/* Starts the LogMiner session */
 STARTSCN                       NUMBER                  IN      DEFAULT
 ENDSCN                         NUMBER                  IN      DEFAULT
 STARTTIME                      DATE                    IN      DEFAULT
 ENDTIME                        DATE                    IN      DEFAULT
 DICTFILENAME                   VARCHAR2                IN      DEFAULT
 OPTIONS                        BINARY_INTEGER          IN      DEFAULT
SQL>
```

DBMS_REFRESH

If you're using materialized views, you'll need to refresh those views on a regular basis, and the DBMS_REFRESH package contains procedures to perform a refresh of groups of materialized views. Listing 21-39 shows the main procedures of the DBMS_REFRESH package.

Listing 21-39. The DBMS_REFRESH Package

```
SQL> desc dbms_refresh
Argument Name                   Type                    In/Out Default?
 PROCEDURE ADD
/*Adds materialized views to a refresh group */
 NAME                           VARCHAR2                IN
 LIST                           VARCHAR2                IN
 LAX                            BOOLEAN                 IN      DEFAULT
 SITEID                         BINARY_INTEGER          IN      DEFAULT
 EXPORT_DB                      VARCHAR2                IN      DEFAULT
```

PROCEDURE CHANGE
/* Changes the refresh interval for a group */

NAME	VARCHAR2	IN	
NEXT_DATE	DATE	IN	DEFAULT
INTERVAL	VARCHAR2	IN	DEFAULT
IMPLICIT_DESTROY	BOOLEAN	IN	DEFAULT
ROLLBACK_SEG	VARCHAR2	IN	DEFAULT
PUSH_DEFERRED_RPC	BOOLEAN	IN	DEFAULT
REFRESH_AFTER_ERRORS	BOOLEAN	IN	DEFAULT
PURGE_OPTION	BINARY_INTEGER	IN	DEFAULT
PARALLELISM	BINARY_INTEGER	IN	DEFAULT
HEAP_SIZE	BINARY_INTEGER	IN	DEFAULT

PROCEDURE DESTROY
/* Removes the refresh group and the materialized views within it */

NAME	VARCHAR2	IN

PROCEDURE MAKE
/*Creates the refresh group and specifies the members and the refresh intervals */

NAME	VARCHAR2	IN	
LIST	VARCHAR2	IN	
NEXT_DATE	DATE	IN	
INTERVAL	VARCHAR2	IN	
IMPLICIT_DESTROY	BOOLEAN	IN	DEFAULT
LAX	BOOLEAN	IN	DEFAULT
JOB	BINARY_INTEGER	IN	DEFAULT
ROLLBACK_SEG	VARCHAR2	IN	DEFAULT
PUSH_DEFERRED_RPC	BOOLEAN	IN	DEFAULT
REFRESH_AFTER_ERRORS	BOOLEAN	IN	DEFAULT
PURGE_OPTION	BINARY_INTEGER	IN	DEFAULT
PARALLELISM	BINARY_INTEGER	IN	DEFAULT
HEAP_SIZE	BINARY_INTEGER	IN	DEFAULT

PROCEDURE REFRESH
/* Manually refreshes a group */

NAME	VARCHAR2	IN

PROCEDURE SUBTRACT
/* Removes materialized views from a refresh group */

NAME	VARCHAR2	IN	
LIST	VARCHAR2	IN	
LAX	BOOLEAN	IN	DEFAULT

SQL>

DBMS_TTS

In order to use the transportable tablespaces feature, you need to first use the DBMS_TTS package to verify if the tablespaces are eligible for the transport operation. The procedures in the packages check to make sure that your candidate tablespaces are self-contained. Chapter 13 shows you how to use the transportable tablespaces feature. To transport tablespaces, you need to invoke the DBMS_TTS package. Listing 21-40 shows the components of the DBMS_TTS package.

Listing 21-40. The DBMS_TTS Package

```
SQL> desc dbms_tts
Argument Name                        Type                In/Out Default?
---------------------------------------------------------------------------
PROCEDURE DOWNGRADE
/* Downgrades data relating to transportable tablespaces */
FUNCTION ISSELFCONTAINED RETURNS BOOLEAN
 TS_LIST                             VARCHAR2            IN
 INCL_CONSTRAINTS                    BOOLEAN            IN
 FULL_CHECK                          BOOLEAN            IN
PROCEDURE KFP_CKCMP
PROCEDURE TRANSPORT_SET_CHECK
/* Checks if the tablespace or list of tablespaces
can be transported without any violations */
 TS_LIST                             VARCHAR2            IN
 INCL_CONSTRAINTS                    BOOLEAN            IN      DEFAULT
 FULL_CHECK                          BOOLEAN            IN      DEFAULT
SQL>
```

DBMS_UTILITY

The DBMS_UTILITY package provides procedures that perform various database tasks. Important tasks that you can perform using this package include analyzing a schema or a database, compiling a schema, and converting a comma-delimited list of names into a PL/SQL table of names and vice versa. Listing 21- 41 shows the important procedures that are part of the DBMS_UTILITY package.

Listing 21-41. The DBMS_UTILITY Package

```
SQL> desc dbms_utility
Argument Name                        Type                In/Out Default?
---------------------------    ---------------------- ------ --------
PROCEDURE ANALYZE_DATABASE
/* Analyzes all the tables, indexes and clusters in the database */
 METHOD                              VARCHAR2            IN
 ESTIMATE_ROWS                       NUMBER             IN      DEFAULT
 ESTIMATE_PERCENT                    NUMBER             IN      DEFAULT
 METHOD_OPT                          VARCHAR2            IN      DEFAULT
PROCEDURE ANALYZE_PART_OBJECT
/* Analyzes a partition of a table */
 SCHEMA                              VARCHAR2            IN      DEFAULT
 OBJECT_NAME                         VARCHAR2            IN      DEFAULT
 OBJECT_TYPE                         CHAR               IN      DEFAULT
 COMMAND_TYPE                        CHAR               IN      DEFAULT
 COMMAND_OPT                         VARCHAR2            IN      DEFAULT
 SAMPLE_CLAUSE                       VARCHAR2            IN      DEFAULT
```

PROCEDURE ANALYZE_SCHEMA
/* Analyzes all the tables, indexes and clusters belonging to a schema */

SCHEMA	VARCHAR2	IN	
METHOD	VARCHAR2	IN	
ESTIMATE_ROWS	NUMBER	IN	DEFAULT
ESTIMATE_PERCENT	NUMBER	IN	DEFAULT
METHOD_OPT	VARCHAR2	IN	DEFAULT

PROCEDURE COMMA_TO_TABLE
/* Converts a comma-delimited list of names into a PL/SQL table of names */

LIST	VARCHAR2	IN
TABLEN	BINARY_INTEGER	OUT
TAB	TABLE OF VARCHAR2(227)	OUT

PROCEDURE TABLE_TO_COMMA
/* Converts a PL/SQL table of names into a comma-delimited list of names */

TAB	TABLE OF VARCHAR2(227)	IN
TABLEN	BINARY_INTEGER	OUT
LIST	VARCHAR2	OUT

PROCEDURE COMPILE_SCHEMA
/* Compiles an entire schema */

SCHEMA	VARCHAR2	IN	
COMPILE_ALL	BOOLEAN	IN	DEFAULT

PROCEDURE EXEC_DDL_STATEMENT
/* Executes a given DDL statement */

PARSE_STRING	VARCHAR2	IN

SQL>

DBMS_STORAGE_MAP

The Oracle9*i* Server version 2 provides a file-mapping interface that enables the mapping of Oracle files to the underlying logical volume partitions and the physical volumes. The background process FMON builds the mapping information, provided you first set the initialization parameter *file_mapping* to *true*. The DBMS_STORAGE_MAP package contains the procedures that will start the mapping operations and cause the mapping data to be placed in the dictionary views such as V$MAP_FILE and the V$MAP_ELEMENT. Chapter 16 provides more information on the file-mapping topic and Listing 21-42 shows the important procedures in the DBMS_STORAGE_MAP package.

Listing 21-42. The DBMS_STORAGE_MAP Package

```
SQL> desc dbms_storage_map
Argument Name                    Type                     In/Out Default?
------------------------------   ----------------------   ------ --------
PROCEDURE MAP_ALL
/* Builds mapping information for all types of Oracle files */
 MAX_NUM_FILEEXTENT              NUMBER                   IN     DEFAULT
 DICTIONARY_UPDATE               BOOLEAN                  IN     DEFAULT
PROCEDURE MAP_ELEMENT
/* Builds mapping information for the specified element */
 ELEMNAME                        VARCHAR2                 IN
 CASCADE                         BOOLEAN                  IN
 DICTIONARY_UPDATE               BOOLEAN                  IN     DEFAULT
PROCEDURE MAP_FILE
 /* Builds mapping information for the specified file */
 FILENAME                        VARCHAR2                 IN
 FILETYPE                        VARCHAR2                 IN
 CASCADE                         BOOLEAN                  IN
 MAX_NUM_FILEEXTENT              NUMBER                   IN     DEFAULT
 DICTIONARY_UPDATE               BOOLEAN                  IN     DEFAULT
PROCEDURE MAP_OBJECT
/* Builds mapping information for the specified object */
 OBJNAME                         VARCHAR2                 IN
 OWNER                           VARCHAR2                 IN
 OBJTYPE                         VARCHAR2                 IN
```

Summary

This chapter briefly touched on several of the most important packages provided by Oracle to enhance the functionality of the database. Most DBAs are content to use just a couple of the packages on a regular basis, without realizing the hidden potential of many of these powerful packages.

You should make every attempt to use as many of the Oracle-supplied packages as possible, so you can take advantage of the additional functionality made possible by them.

CHAPTER 22

Managing Oracle Databases on Windows and Linux Systems

THIS CHAPTER SHOWS you how to manage the Oracle9*i* Release 2 database on the Windows and Linux operating system. For the most part, there's no difference in the way the SQL or database administration commands work in the UNIX, Linux, and Windows operating systems. The main differences relate to the way the database instance runs under the two operating systems.

In this chapter, you'll learn how to install, configure, and manage an Oracle9*i* database on a Windows 2000 server. In the last part of the chapter, I briefly discuss using Oracle9*i* on a Linux operating system.

 NOTE *Please bear in mind that this is more of an overview chapter than a detailed discussion about the management of Oracle on Windows and Linux systems. The primary goal of the chapter is to look at the differences between the UNIX system and the Windows and Linux-based systems.*

You'll begin this chapter with a review of the special features of Oracle9*i* Release 2 on the Microsoft Windows platform.

Oracle9*i* and Windows

Oracle was the first major database vendor to provide a commercial database for Microsoft SQL Server (in 1993). Microsoft SQL Server has recently overtaken Oracle as the leading database (in terms of the installed software base and number of purchased licenses) on the Windows platform, but when it comes to functionality and performance, Oracle9*i* Release 2 is way ahead of SQL Server—and any other database, for that matter.

The Oracle9*i* Release 2 version provides features and capabilities that make it the premier database for sophisticated, enterprisewide Internet-based applications. The following sections explain some of the more powerful features of the Oracle9*i* database on the Windows platform. The Oracle databases on Windows have essentially the same functionality as the UNIX versions, but Oracle modifies the software in order to accommodate Windows operating system features.

Database Access Methods

Oracle9*i* provides multiple data access methods for applications, including COM and .NET data access. Thus, a vast number of developers are able to access the database using the method that best suits their needs. Here is a summary of the Oracle9*i* data access methods:

- *Oracle ODBC:* This is the traditional Oracle data access method for Windows-based applications, wherein you use Oracle ODBC drivers to access the database.

- *Oracle Objects for OLE:* The Oracle Objects for OLE (OO4O) are COM-based Oracle native drivers that provide superior performance when compared to ODBC. OO4O is architected as thin layer sitting on top of the Oracle Call Interface (OCI), which performs the database access. OO4O is popular with programmers because it's easy to use and it's easily accessible from all popular scripting languages.

- *Oracle OLE DB:* OLE DB is the well-known Microsoft data access specification, and the Oracle OLE DB provider is optimized for Oracle9*i* database access. Other third-party Oracle OLE DB providers are available, but Oracle Corporation's OLE DB provider provides superior data access features and better performance.

- *COM Automation Feature:* This feature enables developers to access COM Automation servers. Developers access these servers by using PL/SQL and Java packages, procedures, and functions. The COM objects you can thus access can be local or external to the database in which they are accessed by using the Distributed Component Object Model (DCOM).

 NOTE *The Oracle ODBC and OLE DB providers access the database through a middle layer: the automation layer Microsoft ActiveX Data Objects (ADO).*

Oracle Support for .NET

Oracle9*i* Release 2 makes it easy for developers to write applications for the .NET platform. Oracle9*i* provides .NET data access through OLE DB .NET and ODBC .NET. Using these interoperability layers, you can access the Oracle9*i* database from .NET languages such as C#, Visual Basic .NET, and ASP.NET.

The new Oracle Data Provider for .NET (ODP .NET) enables you to access an Oracle9*i* database from any .NET language and is far more efficient than using OLE DB .NET or ODBC .NET. The big difference is that ODP .NET doesn't need a data access bridge like Microsoft ADO to access the database, because it's a native driver. This direct access capability makes ODP .NET more stable and far more scalable.

Integration with Windows Services

The Oracle9*i* Release 2 database provides tight integration between the database and the Windows operating system to help support highly scalable and secure applications. The following sections discuss the most important Oracle features that help integration with the Windows server.

Oracle Fail Safe

The Oracle Fail Safe feature is exclusive to the Windows-based Oracle database. The Fail Safe feature guarantees that if one of your clustered nodes fails, the database and the applications automatically make the transition from that node to one of the other functioning nodes.

The Oracle Fail Safe feature works in conjunction with the Microsoft Cluster Service (MSCS). You can currently have a maximum of four servers in a cluster. You can also implement Oracle's Logical or Physical Standby feature along with the Fail Safe feature, thus providing both enhanced disaster protection and higher availability at the same time.

The Oracle Services for Microsoft Transaction Server

Microsoft Transaction Server (MTS) serves as an application server for COM objects and transactions under distributed environments. To coordinate transactions among the distributed resource managers, MTS uses a Distributed Transaction Coordinator (DTC).

The Oracle Services for MTS coordinate the work of the DTC with the database. These services enable the use of the database to coordinate transactions. The Oracle Services for MTS run on a Windows server, but you can use them with an Oracle database on any operating system platform.

Oracle9i and Windows Security Features

Oracle9*i* enhances the Windows security model by providing two new features that use the Oracle Public Key Infrastructure (PKI) in an improved manner. These features are the use of Oracle Wallets in the Windows Registry and the Microsoft Certificate Store integration.

Oracle Wallets

The Oracle9*i* Release 2 version lets you store Oracle Wallets in the Windows Registry, thus providing an additional layer of security for Wallets. The PKI security is enhanced by storing the Oracle Wallets in the Registry. You can use both the Oracle Wallet Manager and the Oracle Enterprise Login Assistant to provide single sign-on for Oracle PKI applications.

Microsoft Certificate Store Integration

Oracle's PKI applications are designed to work with Oracle products. However, by integrating with the Microsoft Certificate Store, Oracle's PKI credentials for public key security services can be used by non-Oracle applications using Microsoft PKI.

Oracle and Windows Active Directory

In Chapter 11, you saw that the LDAP-compliant Oracle Internet Directory (OID) facilitates the management of database connectivity management in addition to serving other purposes. You also saw how a centralized directory eliminated the administrative overhead that is involved in managing large groups of database users.

You can use the Windows Active Directory to perform the same tasks as OID. Oracle provides native authentication through the use of Windows authentication mechanisms, which enables the use of single sign-on features and Windows operating system authentication of users.

Essential Differences in Managing Oracle on Windows and UNIX

What is the difference between managing Oracle9*i* on a Windows system and managing it on a UNIX operating system? Well, surprisingly, there is little or no difference in the database administration commands between the two operating systems. The SQL and PL/SQL code is the same across all operating systems. If you learn to manage Oracle9*i* on one operating system, you can move to the other operating system and continue to use the same commands and techniques.

The real difference between using Oracle on the two types of operating systems is in the architecture of Oracle, the way the environmental variables are configured, and the way you start up and shut down the database instance. The differences are thus minor, with one caveat: It is much easier going from a UNIX-based system to an Oracle database running on Windows than the other way around. The reason, of course, is that most people are already familiar with Windows systems, but UNIX systems require specialized study. To make matters more complex, the vi editor and shell scripting are not terribly intuitive to people who are just moving to the UNIX world. The UNIX-based DBA who is trying to implement Oracle on Windows also has some hurdles to clear, but they are not nearly as difficult to overcome.

In the following sections I summarize the essential differences in installing and managing the Oracle9*i* database management system on Windows and UNIX systems.

Processes vs. Threads

Remember the various processes, such as the database writer and the log writer, that start when the Oracle instance starts? In UNIX, these processes run as separate entities, each with its own process identifier (PID). In Windows, there is just one process for the entire instance: the Oracle Service. If you have three Oracle database instances running on your Windows server, you'll have three Oracle Services running also. In fact, you could have two services for each instance, as shown here:

- *OracleServiceSID* is the mandatory Windows service for each Oracle instance.

- *OracleStartSID* is an optional service that will run only if you configure your databases to start automatically upon a server reboot.

In a UNIX-based Oracle instance, all Oracle processes, including the background processes, are separate. In Windows, all Oracle processes are threads of a single Oracle process, the oracle.exe process. All Oracle background processes (log writer, database writer, and so on) and all dedicated servers spawned for each user connection are threads of the same single Oracle process. This multithreaded architecture enables a Windows-based Oracle database to perform fast context switches, because all threads share the resources of a common Oracle process.

How do you know what background processes are running in a Windows Oracle instance, if all the processes are threads of the main Oracle Service process? You can query the V$BGPROCESS view, as shown in Listing 22-1. The V$BGPROCESS view provides the names and descriptions for all background processes.

Listing 22-1. Viewing the Oracle Processes

```
SQL> select b.name,
  2  p.program,
  3  p.spid
  4  from v$session s,
  5  v$process p,
  6  v$bgprocess b
  7  where b.paddr = p.addr
  8* and p.addr = s.paddr;
NAME        PROGRAM        SPID
-----       ------------   ----------
PMON        ORACLE.EXE     3200
DBWO        ORACLE.EXE     2132
LGWR        ORACLE.EXE     3236
CKPT        ORACLE.EXE     3264
SMON        ORACLE.EXE     3316
RECO        ORACLE.EXE     2288
ARCO        ORACLE.EXE     3276
7 rows selected.
SQL>
```

Because you can't use the Windows Task Manager to kill the (only) Oracle process, Oracle provides the special orakill utility to help you kill a single thread within the MAIN Oracle process. If, for some reason, you want to terminate a (nonessential) user's process, you can use the *orakill* command from the command line, as shown in Figure 22-1. You can also shut down and restart your database to get rid of stubborn processes, but that may be a luxury that you can't afford in a database that must be online. Using the orakill utility will get rid of the unnecessary user connections.

```
C:\WINDOWS\System32\cmd.exe                                              _□×

C:\>orakill

Usage:  orakill sid thread

  where sid    = the Oracle instance to target
        thread = the thread id of the thread to kill

  The thread id should be retrieved from the spid column of a query such as:

        select spid, osuser, s.program from
        v$process p, v$session s where p.addr=s.paddr

C:\>orakill compose 2224

Kill of thread id 2224 in instance compose successfully signalled.

C:\>
```

Figure 22-1. Using the orakill command

Of course, as in the case of UNIX-based Oracle databases, you can kill a user's session by using the following command. Note that the user's session may still show up in the session monitor, because the background process may still be busy rolling back the transaction for the session you just killed.

```
SQL> alter system kill session 'sid, serial#'
```

Using the preceding command will kill the user's session, but not the user's thread (akin to a process in UNIX-based systems), which represents the user's connection to the Windows server. The orakill utility will mercifully kill the user's thread.

 CAUTION *Exercise care before you use the* orakill *command. Killing a background process by mistake will bring the database down.*

You can use the following query to ensure you are killing a user's unwanted session, not an important background process:

```
SQL> select p.spid "Windows Thread",
     b.name "Username", s.osuser, s.program
     from v$process p, v$session s, v$bgprocess b
     where p.addr = s.paddr
     and p.addr = b.paddr
     UNION ALL
     select p.spid "Windows Thread",
     s.username "Username", s.osuser, s.program
     from v$process p, v$session s
     where p.addr = s.paddr  and s.username is not null;
Windows        Username      OSUSER          PROGRAM
Thread
-----------------------------------------------------------------
300            PMON          SYSTEM          ORACLE.EXE
1396           DBWO          SYSTEM          ORACLE.EXE
2052           LGWR          SYSTEM          ORACLE.EXE
2068           CKPT          SYSTEM          ORACLE.EXE
2080           SMON          SYSTEM          ORACLE.EXE
...
2484           SYS           MYPC\SAlapati   sqlplus.exe
  SQL>
```

This script will reveal all shadow processes with the thread IDs. Now you can make sure that you aren't killing off a background process inadvertently.

Oracle Service Threads

Each Oracle instance linked to the oracle.exe binary will have several threads that are part of it. The following list presents the most common threads under each Oracle service:

- *Thread 0:* This is the dispatcher thread, and it mainly handles the input from the listener process.

- *Thread 1:* This thread executes the requests made by thread 0. On a dedicated server, this means launching a thread on behalf of the new connections.

- *Thread 2:* This is the PMON thread.

- *Thread 3:* This is the database writer thread.

- *Thread 4:* This is the log writer thread.

- *Thread 5:* This is the checkpoint thread.

- *Thread 6:* This is the SMON thread.

- *Thread 7:* This is the recoverer thread.

You can also get information about the various threads by querying the V$BGPROCESS view, as shown in Listing 22-2.

Listing 22-2. Querying the V$BGPROCESS View for Thread Information

```
SQL> col paddress format a20
SQL> col name format a20
SQL> col description format a40
SQL> col error format 9999999
SQL> select * from v$bgprocess where paddr <> '00';
     PADDR          NAME          DESCRIPTION              ERROR
---------------    ----    -----------------------         ------
C000000096EC50B0   PMON       process cleanup               0
C000000096EC54E0   DBWO       db writer process            0
C000000096EC5910   LGWR       Redo etc.                     0
C000000096EC5D40   CKPT       checkpoint                    0
C000000096EC6170   SMON       System Monitor Process        0
C000000096EC65A0   RECO       distributed recovery          0
C000000096EC69D0   SNP0       Job Queue Process             0
C000000096EC6E00   SNP1       Job Queue Process             1
C000000096EC7230   SNP2       Job Queue Process             2
C000000096EC7660   SNP3       Job Queue Process             3
10 rows selected.
SQL>
```

If you have a large number of users, the Windows resource limits will be hard to overcome, unless you use the Multi-Threaded Server (MTS) and connection pooling. This is a major difference between the Windows and UNIX systems. Contrary to all the hype, Windows systems do have a scalability problem. One other way you can scale up Windows systems is by using server clusters and using the Oracle Real Application Clusters (ORAC). Although Oracle claims that you can have databases as large as 4PB on a Windows system, there are serious limitations on the number of processors you can have on single systems. Oracle does maintain that you can have up to 10,000 separate user connections for a single server.

Services and Daemons

Windows Services are the closest things to the daemons on UNIX servers. All Windows Services run under the operating system username (osuser) SYSTEM. Don't confuse this SYSTEM user with the default user SYSTEM in the Oracle database.

Table 22-1 shows a list of typical Oracle services created in a Windows server when you install Oracle 9.2 software and create a new database.

Table 22-1. Typical Oracle Windows Services

SERVICE NAME	FUNCTION
OracleService<SID>	Created for the database instance SID
Oracle<ORACLE_HOME>TNSListener	Listens for incoming connection requests
Oracle<ORACLE_HOME>agent	Performs job and event requests by OEM
Oracle<ORACLE_HOME> ManagementServer	Gathers data about databases for OEM

Table 22-1. Typical Oracle Windows Services (Continued)

SERVICE NAME	FUNCTION
Oracle<ORACLE_HOEM>HTTPServer	The Oracle HTTP server service
Oracle<ORACLE_HOME>PagingServer	Used by OEM to send external pages

Tuning Memory Resources

As Windows systems don't have the large number of processes that you see in UNIX systems, you need less memory for running the instance. In UNIX-based systems, the root user may have to reconfigure the kernel after adjusting the SHMMAX parameter, which sets the maximum size of a shared memory segment. The UNIX administrator may also have to modify the SEMMNS parameter, which sets the maximum number of semaphores available in the system.

Oracle provides the orastack utility to modify the amount of stack that's reserved for each thread in the Oracle server. The default stack size of 1MB may be excessive, and using orastack, you can drop it to around 500KB. You can serve larger user populations by reducing the stack of every session created in the Oracle executable. For example, if you have 100 users in your system, dropping the stack from 1MB to 0.5MB will free up 500MB of the address space for other purposes. Oracle recommends that you not drop the stack below 350KB per process.

Figure 22-2 provides information on the orastack utility.

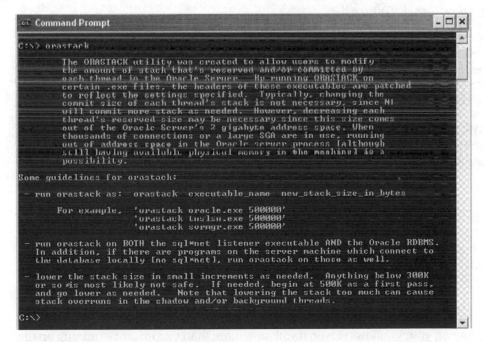

Figure 22-2. Using the orastack utility

Oracle has been gradually increasing the capabilities of its database servers on the Windows platform. For example, Oracle9*i* Release 2 permits an allocation of up to 64GB as database buffer cache, up from a limit of only 3GB in earlier Windows versions. New API calls named the Windows Address Windowing Extensions (AWEs) enable Oracle to access more than the traditional limit of 4GB of RAM.

CPU and Memory Considerations

One of the first things you'll notice on a Windows server is that invariably the number of processes is much smaller than on a typical UNIX server. It is not uncommon for UNIX servers to have 16 and 24 processors, whereas Windows-based systems are limited usually to 4, and sometimes 6 processors. Thus, UNIX-based systems scale much more effectively than Windows-based systems.

Automatic Start-up and Shutdown

On UNIX systems, you can use the well-known *dbshut* and *dbstart* scripts to cleanly shut down your database on system shutdown and start it up at system boot-up. In a Windows system, there is no need for a special file. The automatic start-up and shutdown is determined by settings in the Windows Registry.

You can use the oradim utility, which you'll learn more about later in this chapter, to configure automatic start-up of the database.

Users and Groups

You may recall that under the UNIX system, the root user has to create an Oracle group, and the DBA should be part of this Oracle group. When you install Oracle server software, you do so as the oracle user, not as the root user. In a Windows system, the Oracle installer needs to a member of the Administrators group. When a member of the Administrators group installs Oracle, that username is automatically added to the ORA_DBA group, which confers the SYSDBA privilege to all its members. Thus, any user who is part of the ORA_DBA group can connect to the database as a privileged user by simply using the *connect / as sysdba* command, as shown here:

```
C:\ sqlplus /nolog
SQL*Plus: Release 9.2.0.1.0 - Production on Tue Feb 4 06:54:43 2003
Copyright (c) 1982, 2002, Oracle Corporation.  All rights reserved.
SQL> connect / as sysdba
Connected.
SQL> sho user
USER is "SYS"
SQL>
```

If you wish, you can have an ORAS_SID_OPER group and an ORA_SID_DBA group on your Windows server, if you have more than one instance running on the server.

The File Systems

A UNIX system can support a number of file systems, including the Journal File System (JFS). Under a Windows system, you have a choice of the FAT and NTFS file systems. The essential difference between them from a DBA's point of view is that the NTFS file system has much better file-level security than the FAT file system. The maximum file size is also much larger under the NTFS file system than under the FAT file system. Use the FAT file system for the boot partition and the Oracle executables. You should use the NTFS files system for the Oracle database and log files. Windows systems support database files up to 64GB in size.

In addition to the NTFS and FAT file systems, Windows systems also support raw files, as in the UNIX systems. Thus, if you want to install ORAC on a Windows system, you can do so without problems, because raw partitions are an absolute requirement for sharing files among the databases in the cluster. If you use raw files, you are subject to the limitation that you can create only a single file per partition. In UNIX, you need to use the dd utility to back up and restore raw files. The Windows counterpart is the OCOPY command.

The Windows Copy Utilities

In a UNIX system, the common copy commands such as *cpio* and *tar* can copy files to disk or to tape without a problem. However, the Windows OCOPY command can't copy files to tape directly. You have to first copy the files to disk, and then transfer them to tape from there using NT Backup or a similar copy utility.

Also note that that the NT Backup utility can't back up files that are in use, so it can't perform a hot Oracle database backup, which must be done while the database is running. Only the OCOPY utility can copy open files during a hot backup.

Differences in the Use of the GUI

On a Windows server, you can have only one interactive GUI session. Of course, if you are using a service such as Citrix, Carbon Copy, or the Microsoft Terminal Server, you can have more than one GUI session simultaneously. UNIX servers have no inherent limitation on the number of GUI sessions that you can start from a single server.

Automating Jobs

On UNIX system, you usually use the crontab facility to schedule jobs. On Windows, you use the *at* command (which is also available in UNIX systems) to automate jobs. If you want to perform a hot backup, you must use the Windows OCOPY command to first copy the online data files to disk. From there, you can copy the files to tape using third-party tools.

Diagnostic Tools

Because you can't use utilities such as sar and vmstat on a Windows system, you need other tools to diagnose performance and monitor system resources. Fortunately, the Windows operating system comes with several built-in monitoring tools such as the well-known Task Manager, Event Viewer, User Manager, and Oracle Performance Monitor. In addition, Windows 2000 comes with the Microsoft Management Console (MMC), which you can use to perform specialized management tasks.

Installing Oracle9*i* on a Windows System

In this section you'll take a quick look at installing the Oracle 9.2 software on a Windows XP system. Installing Oracle server software on a Windows system is very similar to installing Oracle on a UNIX-based system. Please see Chapter 4 for the screen views of the installation process. Here are the installation steps:

1. The installer asks you for the location of the Oracle home directory. Note that you can have multiple Oracle home directories.

2. The Available Product window appears. You have a choice of the type of product you want to install. Because you want to install the database server, choose the Oracle9*i* Database 9.2.0.1.0 option.

3. The Installation Types window now appears. Enterprise Edition is the version you want to install on your server, as it has the capability to support high-end applications.

4. In the next window, you choose the type of database: OLTP, data warehouse, or a hybrid. In most cases, you may not want Oracle to create a database for you because you have the database creation scripts already. You need to choose the "Software only" option in those cases.

5. In the newer Windows systems, the Oracle MTS Recovery Service is automatically installed with the Oracle Services for MTS. The next window provides the default port number (2030) for the recovery service. Click Next to accept this port number.

6. The next window asks you to provide the name of your database. Of course, if you choose to install just the software, this screen won't display. In my case, I chose *manager* as the Oracle SID. If you choose the Global Database Name with a domain, Oracle will make this global name the Oracle SID.

7. Next is the Select Database Character Set window, after which you'll see the Database File Location screen. Select a directory name where you want your Oracle database files.

8. The next screen summarizes the choices you've made so far. Once you confirm the summary information by clicking the Install button, the Oracle installation will start. The installation takes about an hour or so, at the end of which Oracle will automatically start the Net Configuration and Database Configuration agents for you. At this point, your Oracle server is installed, but there is no database yet. Oracle will now create and start the Oracle instance. It will then create the sample database by creating the database files. The Database Configuration Assistant screen will show the progress of the database creation process.

9. The Password Management screen appears and asks you to provide the passwords for the two database management accounts, SYSTEM and SYS.

10. Finally, you'll see the End of Installation screen, which indicates that your installation and database creation have completed successfully, without any errors.

The Windows Registry

The Windows Registry holds a central place in the configuration of Oracle. The Windows Registry contains all the permanent configuration parameters and environment variables for all Oracle databases running on the server. Windows-based Oracle databases use the Registry in much the same way as UNIX-based Oracle databases use the shell environment variables. The registry information is stored in a tree format, with keys at the head of branches and parameters under the various keys. The keys are shown in the left pane of the Windows Registry window, and the parameter values are shown in the right pane.

Using the Registry

You enter the Registry by typing the command **Regedit** after invoking the *run* command. Click HKEY_LOCAL_MACHINESOFTWARE. You will see the Oracle key on the left side of the Registry Editor. The following sections cover the important registry keys for your Oracle installation.

HOMEID

The HOMEID key is under HKEY_LOCAL_MACHINE/SOFTWARE. It is the most important Oracle Registry key, as it contains the most important Oracle environment variables on your system. There are as many HOMEID keys as there are databases on your Windows system. The HOMEID subkey contains the values for most of your configuration parameters. The first database that you create on your server will have its registry entries located in the HKEY\LOCAL_MACHINE\ SFTWARE\Oracle\HOME0 subkey. Additional databases will have the subkeys HOME1, HOME2, and HOME3, for example. Table 22-2 presents some of the important subkeys of the HOMEID key.

Table 22-2. Important Oracle Entries in the Windows Registry

ENTRY	FUNCTION
Oracle_Sid	Specifies the name of the Oracle instance on your server.
Oracle_Home	Specifies the directory in which you install all Oracle products (e.g., C:\oracle\).
Oracle_Home_Name	Any name for the Oracle_Home variable (e.g., ORAHOME).
Oracle_Base	Specifies the top-level Oracle directory under which ORACLE_HOME and all the other directories are located.
Ora_Sid_Autostart	Starts the Oracle instance when the OracleServiceSID service starts.
Ora_Sid_Shutdown	Shuts down the Oracle instance when the OracleServiceSID service stops.
Sqlpath	Specifies the location of SQL scripts. If you place your SQL scripts in this directory, you don't have to specify the full path when you invoke them from SQL*Plus. The default location is $ORACLE_HOME\database.

ALL_HOMES

The ALL_HOMES subkey provides information about all the Oracle home directories on your Windows server. The key has values for the default home, the last installed Oracle home, and the number of Oracle homes on your server.

Managing Oracle on Windows Systems

Surprisingly, there is very little difference between managing a Windows system Oracle server and a UNIX system Oracle server. That said, let me clarify that I am referring only to the database commands and database features. You use exactly the same commands for all the database activities, and there is no need to learn new commands when you switch operating systems. The management differences relate mainly to starting and stopping services, some backup commands, and how you monitor the instance. In the following sections you'll look at some of the important elements of managing Oracle databases on Windows servers.

Oracle Services

When you create a new Oracle9*i* database on a Windows server, a number of services are started for the instance by the Windows operating system. You can access the Services window by selecting Settings ➤ Control Panel ➤ Administrative Tools ➤ Services.

To log into a database to perform tasks such as start-up and shutdown, you need to log in as a user with the SYSDBA role in SQL*Plus. For example, this is the way the user SYS can log into the database named Shannon:

```
connect sys/password@shannon as sysdba
```

The following sections describe the important Oracle services that you can manage from the Services window. You can configure each service as manual or automatic, with "automatic" meaning the service will come up by itself upon the Windows server starting up.

The Oracle Service

This is the main Oracle Service, and without it you can't access the database. This service runs the main Oracle executable, oracle.exe. The Oracle Service has the naming convention *OracleServiceSID* (e.g., OracleService*Manager*, where *Manager* is the name of the database). If the Oracle Service is not up for some reason and you try to connect to the database, you'll get an Oracle error, as shown here:

```
ERROR:
ORA-12500: TNS:listener failed to start a dedicated server process
```

If you try to start the database from the command line while the Oracle Service is down, you'll get the ORA-12571 error, as shown here:

```
SQl > startup
ORA-12571:  INS: packet writer failure
```

Starting and Stopping the Oracle Service

You can start the main Windows service, Oracle Service, in one of two ways. You can go the Services window through the Control Panel and click the Start or Stop button of the Oracle Service entry. Optionally, you can go the command line and use the *net start* or *net stop* commands, as shown in Figure 22-3.

Figure 22-3. Starting and stopping the Oracle Service with the net start and net stop commands

Automatic Start-up of Oracle Databases

Your Oracle databases will start up automatically when the Windows server is rebooted. On occasion, however, your databases may surprise you by not starting up with system start-up. A common cause of this start-up failure is when the *remote_login_passwordfile* parameter isn't set in the init.ora file or the SPFILE.

Accessing the Database from the Command Prompt

You can also start the database from the command prompt or access it after it has started, but be careful to set your ORACLE_SID variable at the command prompt or make sure it's part of your environment. If the database name is set in neither of the previously mentioned two ways, you'll get the following error:

```
C:\>sqlplus /nolog
SQL*Plus: Release 9.2.0.1.0 - Production on Tue Feb 4 05:27:32 2003
Copyright (c) 1982, 2002, Oracle Corporation.  All rights reserved.
SQL> connect sys/compose1 as sysdba;
ERROR:
ORA-12560: TNS:protocol adapter error
```

You can avoid the preceding error by setting the ORACLE_SID variable as follows:

```
C:\>set ORACLE_SID=compose
C:\>sqlplus /nolog
SQL*Plus: Release 9.2.0.1.0 - Production on Tue Feb 4 05:28:07 2003
Copyright (c) 1982, 2002, Oracle Corporation.  All rights reserved.
SQL> connect sys/compose1 as sysdba;
Connected.
SQL>
```

Instead of setting the environment variable for the ORCLE_SID variable each time you want to log into the database from the command line, you can set it permanently by adding an environment variable for ORACLE_SID. To do this, go to Control Panel ➤ System ➤ Advanced ➤ Environment Variables. Here, you can use the Edit button to enter the new environment variable ORACLE_SID and its value. You can set the environment variable for a single user or you can set it systemwide.

Oracle Listener

The Oracle listener service, similar to the listener utility on UNIX servers, is responsible for listening to requests from new connections. You can't connect to the instance using the *username/password@net_service name* format if the listener service is down. The listener service has the naming format *OracleHOME_NAMETNSListener*. You'll get the ORA-12541 error if you try to connect to a database when the listener service is down, as shown here:

```
ERROR
ORA-12541: TNS:no listener
```

To restart the listener service, you can use the Services window by going to Control Panel ➤ Administrative Services ➤ Component Services ➤ Services (Local) and starting the OracleOraHome9iTNSListener service. Alternatively, you can use the lsnrctl utility, as shown in Figure 22-4. Note that a single listener service can serve all the database instances on your server.

Figure 22-1. Using the lsnrctl utility to start the listener service

Oracle Agent

The Oracle Agent is a service that needs to run on every server where you have a database or other services such as listeners and HTTP servers running. The Oracle Agent is the same as the Intelligent Agent that you need to execute jobs and events through the Enterprise Manager utility. The service has the format *OracleHOME_NAMEAgent*.

HTTP Server

If you want to configure reporting through OEM, you'll need an HTTP server. You'll also need the HTTP server if you want to configure the *i*SQL*Plus utility on your Windows server. The HTTP service has the format *OracleHOME_NAMEHTTP Service*.

Management Server

The Management Server, as you know, sits between the Intelligent Agent and the OEM console and manages the Intelligent Agent. If you want a full-powered OEM installation, you'll need to install the Management Server, which you can start from the Services window or from the command line, as shown in Chapter 17.

Starting Up and Shutting Down the Oracle Database

In a UNIX operating system, starting up and shutting down an Oracle9*i* database is straightforward. You perform the start-up and shutdown operations by going into SQL*Plus and running the commands *startup* and *shutdown* after you log in as user with the SYSDBA privilege. In the Windows operating system, you have several ways to start up and shut down your database instance, as the following sections show.

Use the Services Window

You can go to the Services window by following these steps:

1. Click the Start button and select Settings ➤ Control Panel.

2. Double-click the Administrative Tools icon.

3. Double-click the Services icon.

4. Highlight the OracleServiceManager entry, and click the Start or Stop button.

5. Click OK and exit the Services window.

Using the SQL*Plus Utility

You can use SQL*Plus, as in UNIX, to start and stop an Oracle9*i* instance. The sequence of steps to perform is as follows:

1. Go the command prompt and invoke the SQL*Plus utility by typing in the following:

   ```
   C:\> sqlplus   / nolog
   ```

2. Connect to the database as a user with the SYSDBA privilege, as follows:

   ```
   SQL> connect sys/managerm@manager as sysdba
   Connected.
   ```

3. Once you are connected, you can start up or shut down the database by using the appropriate commands.

Administering the Instance with the Oradim Utility

You can use the Windows oradim utility to create, delete, and modify databases. You can also perform the same activities using the Database Configuration Assistant. Let's see how you can use the oradim utility to start and stop services.

The oradim utility is very easy to use, but unfortunately it doesn't provide adequate information on its activities. The utility provides a log of its activity, and the log is located in the $ORACLE_HOME\database directory under the name "oradim."

TIP *The oradim utility doesn't let you know whether a specific command failed or succeeded. It returns the prompt in either case, and you can't rely on the absence of an error message as an indication that everything is working fine. Make sure you read the oradim log file after each invocation of the utility.*

When the Oracle Service starts, it will start the database automatically by default. You may use the oradim utility to configure the Oracle Service to start, with or without the Oracle instance. Note that if your Registry settings point to an automatic start of the Oracle instance, the instance will come up when you start the Oracle Service. Let's look at some examples of how to use the oradim utility to manage the Oracle Service and the database instance.

NOTE *Don't confuse the Oracle Service with the Oracle instance. The Oracle Service is merely the Windows process that denotes that the Oracle server executable, oracle.exe, has been invoked. Starting the Oracle instance, on the other hand, includes starting well-known processes such as the database writer and the log writer.*

In the following examples, assume that the instance name is Manager.

Starting a Service

You can start just a service by itself, or you can start a service along with a database instance. To start the service by itself, use oradim as follows:

```
C:> oradim –startup  -sid  manager
```

Depending on your Registry settings, this command will also bring up your database instance. If you want to ensure that the instance also comes up, use the following command:

```
C:> oradim  -startup  -sid  manager  -starttype srvc, inst
```

If your initialization parameter file is not in its default location ($ORACLE_HOME\dbs), you need to add a parameter called *pfile* to the previous command to specify the location of the initialization parameter file.

Stopping a Service

You can stop either the service or the instance, or both, using the oradim utility. If you don't specify either one, the values specified in your Windows Registry will be used as the default values. The following are a couple of variations of the use of the oradim utility to stop a service/database:

```
C:> oradim  -shutdown -sid  manager
C:> oradim  -shutdown -sid  manager  -shuttype srvc, inst
```

Creating a Service

When you use the Oracle Database Configuration Assistant to create a database for you, whether at the time you install the software or later on, Oracle will use the oradim utility to create the service for you. When you create a database manually in UNIX, there is no need to create a separate "service" for it. You just go into SQL*Plus and start the database instance. In Windows systems, however, you need to specifically create the database service after you create the database. You use the oradim utility to manually create the service. The following example illustrates how to create the instance for the Manager database:

```
C:> oradim -new -sid  manager -srvc OracleserviceManager
     -intpwd  newpass1  -startmode auto
```

 NOTE *Again, I am assuming that the initialization file is in the default location; otherwise, you need to use the* pfile *parameter and provide the complete path for the file.*

Modifying a Service

If you need to change some of the important values such as the instance name or the start-up mode, you can use the oradim utility with the *edit* command, as shown here:

```
C:> oradim -edit   -sid  manager -newsid newmanager
```

Deleting a Service

Finally, you can delete an instance using the oradim utility, as shown in the following examples:

```
C:> oradim –delete -sid   manager
```

or

```
C:> oradim  -delete  -srvc  manager
```

Using the Oracle Administration Assistant for NT

The Oracle9*i* 9.2 version provides you with a graphical tool called the Oracle Administration Assistant for Windows NT, which makes it easy for you to configure users, administrators, and their roles. In addition, you can use the Administration Assistant to start and stop the databases. The Oracle Administration Assistant for Windows NT appears as part of the MMC window on your Windows server.

The following brief list present the tasks you can perform with the help of the Oracle Administration Assistant for Windows NT:

- Create local and external operating system database roles to Windows domain users and global groups without a password.

- Create and grant local and external operating system database roles to users and groups.

- Configure Windows DBAs and operators to access the database without a password.

- Start and stop the Oracle Service.

- Configure automatic start-up and shutdown of the Oracle database along with the Oracle Service.

- Modify the Oracle home Windows Registry parameters without using Regedit or Regedit32.

You'll look at the Oracle Administration Assistant for Windows NT in detail in the following sections.

Starting the Oracle Administration Assistant for Windows NT

You can start the Oracle Administration Assistant for Windows NT by clicking the Start button and selecting Programs ➤ Oracle ➤ Configuration and Migration Tools ➤ Administration Assistant for Windows NT. Once the Administration Assistant GUI shows up, you can choose Oracle Managed Objects ➤ Computers ➤ *Your_Computer_Name* ➤ Databases. When you click a database name, you can create and modify settings for several important variables. Figure 22-5 shows the Oracle Administration Assistant for Windows NT window. You can choose to modify or add database administrators, database operators, and Oracle homes from here.

Viewing Process Information

The Oracle Administration Assistant for Windows NT lets you view the process information for your Oracle database. It also enables you to kill a specified process. Figure 22-6 shows the Process Information screen.

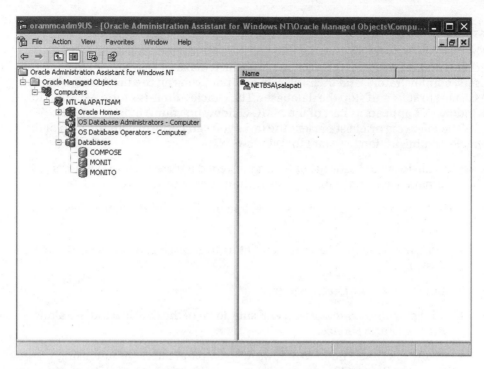

Figure 22-5. The Oracle Administration Assistant for Windows NT GUI

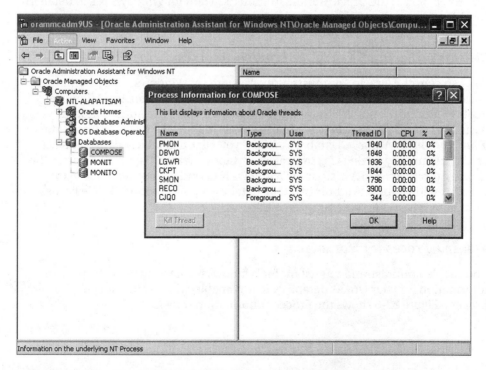

Figure 22-6. The Oracle Administration Assistant for Windows NT Process
Information screen

Starting and Stopping the Oracle Service and the Database

You can use the Oracle Administration Assistant for Windows NT to start and stop the database instance, the Oracle Service, or both. You can also alter the settings that determine if your database will come up automatically along with the service. Figure 22-7 shows how to stop and start services using the Administration Assistant.

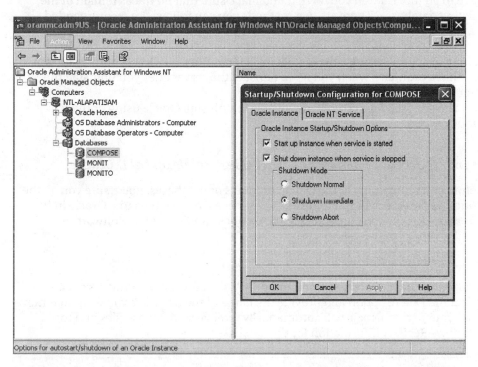

Figure 22-7. *Managing the Oracle Service with the Oracle Administration Assistant for Windows NT*

Changing the Oracle Home Registry Settings

You can also use the Oracle Administration Assistant for Windows NT to modify the Windows Registry settings for your Oracle home. The Registry settings for the Oracle_Home variable are located in the HKEY_LOCAL_MACHINE\SOFTWARE\ORACLE\HOMEID key. By clicking the Oracle Home snap-in in the Administration Assistant for Windows NT window, you can add, modify, and delete the parameters under the Oracle Homes key in the Registry.

Uninstalling Oracle on Windows

Suppose you need to uninstall an Oracle installation on your server, either because you are encountering some insurmountable problems or because you just want to start fresh with a new installation. How do you uninstall Oracle? If you are going to uninstall the Oracle server software, it means that your databases have to go too. How do you do that and make sure that no traces remain of the existing databases? There are two methods you can follow: the recommended way (using the Oracle Universal Installer) and the manual method. Do not use the manual method, which involves the removal of database files as the first course of action, because the Installer will remember the Oracle home, and you may have problems when you try to reinstall the server after you uninstall the Oracle software.

The next sections cover in detail how to uninstall Oracle using both techniques.

Using the Oracle Universal Installer to Uninstall Oracle

Before you remove any of the Oracle products or databases, make sure you go the Windows Services window and stop any service that has the name Oracle in it. After you do this, you can uninstall the database and the server software.

Uninstalling the Database

Invoke the Oracle Database Configuration Assistant from the Programs screen. Select the Delete option and provide the name of the database you want to remove from your server. Oracle will automatically remove all database files and the Windows Registry information for the database.

Uninstalling Other Services

Apart from the database, you need to remove other services, including the Oracle listener, OID, and any other services that may have been installed for your database. Stop each of the services first, and then manually remove them from the Windows Registry.

Uninstalling the Oracle Software

Now you can use the Oracle Universal Installer to remove the server software. After you start the Installer, choose the Deinstall Products option and check the boxes of all the components you want to uninstall. In this case, if you want to remove the entire installation, you can check everything on this screen and choose Yes to uninstall the component when the confirmation window appears. Your Oracle software will be uninstalled in a short time.

Uninstalling Oracle Manually

To completely remove all traces of the Oracle database and software, you need to do a couple more things. First, stop all services that have the word "Oracle" in their service name. Next, go to Windows Explorer and delete all the directories under the Oracle home directory, including the software installation directories and the database files for all the databases on your server. Finally, go the Windows Registry and remove any key that starts with "Oracle" or "ORCL," starting at HKEY_CLASSES_ROOT, and reboot your computer.

Oracle9*i* and Linux

Linux is a multiuser, multitasking X Window–using operating system. If it sounds very much like someone is describing UNIX, well, it's no surprise, because Linux and UNIX are essentially the same. Linux is a descendent of the UNIX software, and its main claim to fame is that it's open source, free software. Of course, if you want a firm like Red Hat to hold your hand while you install and manage Linux, you have to pay of course!

Red Hat's version or not, Linux is red-hot right now, and many major businesses are already using it for everything except their core mission-critical applications. For example, a major Wall Street firm uses Linux for everything except its main live customer databases. Increasingly, firms are finding that they can use Linux for mission-critical applications. The main draw of Linux is that it's much cheaper than proprietary UNIX servers, and that it's not a Microsoft product. Linux is the fastest growing operating system platform, and total sales are projected to grow to $5.9 billion by the year 2006, according to the IDC consulting firm. Oracle9*i* is the leading commercial database on the Linux operating system. Also according to IDC, Linux now owns 27 percent of the server operating system market, up from a meager 1 percent as recently as 1995.

If you know UNIX, you know Linux as well, because the commands are similar. The main kernel parameters, such as the shared memory and semaphores, are handled similarly in both Linux and UNIX. The differences between the two relate to the installation process, where you may have more difficulty, especially with noncertified versions of Linux. In addition, some of the smaller Linux distributions may not be as stable as UNIX software sold by Sun Microsystems and HP.

Several versions of Linux are available, some totally free and some available at a price that is a fraction of what Sun Microsystems and HP charge for their UNIX software. Although this is essentially true, do understand that a feature-laden Linux operating system with technical support worth mentioning will cost you some serious money. In the end, you may save anywhere between 20 percent and 60 percent of what you'll spend on a well-known UNIX brand. Are these savings significant enough to warrant letting go of the established, battle-proven UNIX servers from Sun Microsystems and HP? This is a question that each individual organization has to answer based on the types of needs they have and their expectations regarding performance. For example, a research institution would be more justified in plunging headlong into the Linux world than a commercial financial service providing online services to a large number of customers.

Despite all the hype, do remember that Linux is still busy gradually incorporating features that have been well established in UNIX servers for years. These features include improving I/O throughput and memory utilization, as well as Symmetric Multi-Processor (SMP) scalability.

Oracle's Commitment to Linux

Oracle was the first major commercial database available on the Linux platform. Oracle supports and certifies many products, including the Oracle9*i* database server software, on several major Linux distributions. Oracle9*i*'s Linux version can support all the options supported by the UNIX and Windows versions. Oracle Corporation itself uses Linux-based systems to run all its outsourcing business and its application demo systems.

Although Oracle is working with many Linux distributors, it has a special relationship with the Red Hat version of Linux, and has been helping Red Hat to enhance the Linux kernel's functionality. In fact, Oracle and Red Hat's collaborative efforts in improving performance and reliability have resulted in the development of Red Hat Linux Advanced Server. Oracle provides Red Hat Linux users support for both the Oracle database *and* the operating system. The only requirement is that clients should be running Red Hat Linux Advanced Server on specific hardware platforms such as Dell and HP that are certified by Oracle. Red Hat Linux Advanced Server includes many powerful performance features that are commonly seen in regular UNIX software. Oracle also works closely with the SuSE distribution of Linux. Oracle is backing the soon-to-be-released UnitedLinux version of Linux, which is the result of collaboration among SuSE, the SCO Group, Turbolinux, and Connectiva.

Oracle provides support for the Oracle Real Application Clusters (ORAC)–based systems running on Linux, and because of the inexpensive outlays for Linux servers, they may be an alternative to traditional UNIX software for several organizations. The Linux Kernel 2.4 distribution supports ORAC just as well as the established UNIX severs. The new cluster file system that Oracle has developed for Linux is easier to work with than the standard raw disks you have to use for an ORAC configuration.

Oracle Corporation foresees the industry migrating in large numbers to Linux-based systems, and Oracle is involved in many such migrations using enterprise-ready Linux distributions such as Red Hat Linux Advanced Server. Oracle has taken over the responsibility of being the main Linux technical support group for Red Hat/Oracle customers to ensure that Oracle performs as well on Linux as it does on the UNIX platform. In fact, Oracle wishes to see Linux supplant UNIX as the main Oracle database platform.

Ensuring You Have a Stable Version of Linux

Unlike commercial UNIX software, Linux is well known as open source software, meaning that new versions are often released to the public at frequent intervals, and therefore tend to have more bugs than officially tested and certified software. For someone planning to implement Linux, it is critically important to distinguish between the two "types" of Linux software releases: *stable* and *beta* releases. Stable versions aren't likely to crash unexpectedly and you may encounter minor bugs. You can expect bug fixes to be released to fix the defects. Beta versions are aimed at developers, and they may be unstable and tend to crash frequently. You can expect newer releases to focus more on adding new features. Here's how you can tell which Linux version is stable and which one isn't:

- The generic version number for a Linux distribution is *r.x.y*, where *r* is the release number. If *x* is an even number, it's a stable version (e.g., Release 2.2.15).

- If *x* is an odd number, it's a beta version (e.g., Release 2.3.99).

Managing Oracle on Linux

As far as managing the database goes, there isn't much difference between running Oracle databases on a UNIX server and running them on a Linux-based server. Some commands such as *ps* may show slightly different things under the two systems, so make sure you check the Linux documentation for such differences. The main difference between the two systems is in the installation of the operating system itself. The installation of the Oracle9*i* software is remarkably similar across all operating system platforms, and that is one of the strengths of the Oracle RDBMS. Once you learn your craft on one type of operating system, you can ply it on any other type with ease. All your UNIX scripts will still work in the Linux operating system.

The key to a successful installation of the Oracle9*i* database on Linux is careful installation and tuning of the Linux server itself. For help with installing Red Hat Linux Advanced Server, please read the excellent white paper titled "Tips for Installing and Configuring Oracle9*i* Database on Red Hat Linux" (http://technet.oracle.com).

Summary

This chapter provided you with a quick review of the management of Oracle9*i* databases on a Windows platform. Though the Oracle software provides the same functionality on all platforms, you learned about certain nuances and some limitations are specific to the Windows platform.

One of the goals of this chapter was to introduce you to some of the main differences between managing an Oracle9*i* database on a UNIX platform and a Windows server. As it turns out, the administrative commands and the SQL queries are identical in the two operating systems. The differences lie in the way you monitor the database in the two operating systems. If you are managing Oracle databases on a Windows server, you need to be familiar with Windows tools such as the Oracle Administration Assistant for Windows NT.

The chapter concluded with a discussion of the management of Oracle9*i* databases on the Linux platform.

A Brief Oracle9*i* SQL and PL/SQL Primer

I'M SURE MOST of you are already familiar with SQL to some extent. However, I present in this appendix a quick review of Oracle9*i* SQL and its programmatic cousin, PL/SQL, so it may provide a starting point to learning Oracle's programmatic aspects for newcomers to the Oracle database. If you're already quite familiar with Oracle SQL, you may benefit from focusing on the newer additions to SQL and PL/SQL made in the Oracle9*i* database. My goal here is simply to present a short summary of the classic DML and DDL commands and then discuss the newer SQL and PL/SQL concepts in greater detail.

NOTE *You might consider reading another Apress book,* Oracle9*i* PL/SQL: A Developer's Guide, *by Bulusu Lakshman, if you're interested in an up-to-date PL/SQL book oriented toward developers. You can download a sample chapter of the book from* http://www.apress.com/book/bookDisplay.html?bID=142.

How much SQL or PL/SQL do you as a DBA need to know? The answer, of course, depends on the type of DBA you are: a production support DBA or a DBA assisting in developmental efforts. Regardless of the type of DBA you are, though, increasingly it's becoming more important for DBAs to learn a number of advanced SQL and PL/SQL concepts, including the new Java and XML-based technologies. The reason is simple: Even when you aren't developing applications yourself, you're going to be assisting people who are doing so, and it helps to know what they're doing.

Oracle9*i* makes several powerful and innovative changes to both SQL and PL/SQL. This appendix aims to summarize some of the most important features, so you and the developers you work with can take advantage of these new features. Oracle SQL and PL/SQL represent an enormously broad topic, so this appendix lightly covers several important topics without attempting any detailed explanation due to space considerations. The primary goal of this appendix is to give you a very general understanding of the Oracle9*i* SQL and PL/SQL language concepts.

The Oracle9*i* Sample Schemas

The examples in this appendix use the demo tables provided by Oracle as part of the Oracle9*i* server software. Ideally, you should install the Oracle demo schemas in a test database and practice the parts of SQL you aren't familiar with. Oracle has a new manual called "Sample Oracle Schemas" in its documentation. If you've installed the starter database as part of your Oracle software installation, these schemas will most likely be part of your new starter database. If you've chosen to not create the starter database (by selecting a "Software only" installation option), first you must create a small Oracle9*i* database. Toward the end of the database creation process, make sure you unlock the same schema accounts.

After you create the database, you can proceed to the following steps to install the sample Oracle schemas. The main Oracle9*i* sample schemas are the HR, OE, PM, QS, and SH schemas. The last schema, SH, can't be installed if you don't have the partitioning option as part of your database server.

Also, you *must* create the schemas in the order that follows because of dependencies that exist among the schema objects. You may get errors if you create the schemas in the wrong order. Each of the scripts will create the necessary schema users, tables, indexes, and constraints, and will load data into the tables. The scripts perform all this by calling other scripts in the same directory.

1. Go to the $ORACLE_HOME/demo/schema/human_resources directory and run the script hr_main.sql to create the human resources (HR) schema.

2. Go to the $ORACLE_HOME/demo/schema/order_entry directory and run the script oe_main.sql to create the order entry (OE) schema.

3. Go to the $ORACLE_HOME/demo/schema/product_media directory, and run the script pm_main.sql to create the product media (PM) schema.

4. Go to the $ORACLE_HOME/demo/schema/shipping directory and run the script qs_main.sql to create the queued shipping (QS) schema.

5. Go to the $ORACLE_HOME/demo/schema/sales_history directory and run the script sh_main.sql to create the sales history (SH) schema.

6. You're now ready to use the various schemas to practice your SQL and PL/SQL commands. If you need to reset the schemas to their initial state, all you have to do is run the following command in SQL*Plus:

```
@?/demo/schema/mksample systempwd syspwd hrpwd oepwd pmpwd qspwd shpwd
```

In the preceding command, the seven variables after the *mksample* keyword should be replaced with the actual passwords for the SYSTEM and SYS users, and the passwords for the HR, OE, PM, QS, and SH schemas.

Here's a brief description of the five main sample schemas:

- The HR schema is the most commonly used schema, with its familiar employees and dept tables. The schema uses scalar data types and simple tables with basic constraints.

- The OE schema covers a simple order-entry system and includes regular relational objects as well as object-relational objects. Because the OE schema contains synonyms for HR tables, you can query HR's objects from the OE schema.

- The PM schema covers content management. You can use this schema if you're exploring Oracle's *inter*Media option. The tables in the PM schema contain audio and video tracks, images, and documents.

- The QS schema is a group of schemas that hosts message queues. This sample schema is designed for use with Oracle's Advanced Queuing feature.

- The SH schema is the largest sample schema. You can use it for testing examples with large amounts of data. The schema contains partitioned tables, an external table, and Online Analytical Processing (OLAP) features. The fact tables sales and costs contain 750,000 rows and 250,000 rows, respectively, as compared to 107 rows in the employees table from the HR schema.

Now that you've successfully created your sample schemas, let's start the SQL review.

Basic SQL

In Chapter 7 you saw how Oracle SQL statements include DDL, DML, and other types of statements. This appendix focuses on Oracle DML statements almost exclusively. The idea is to quickly review elementary Oracle SQL and then focus on the newer Oracle9*i* additions to SQL. Let's begin with a review of the most basic of all SQL statements, the *select* statement.

The Select Statement

The *select* statement is the most common SQL statement. The selection operation is also called a *projection*. A *select* statement will retrieve all or some of the data in a table, based on the criteria that you specify.

The most basic *select* statement is one that retrieves all the data in the table:

```
SQL> select * from employees;
```

If you want to retrieve only certain columns from a table, you specify the column names after the keyword *select*, as shown in the following example:

```
SQL> select first_name,last_name,hiredate from employees;
```

If you want only the first ten rows of a table, you can use the following statement:

```
SQL> select * from employees where rownum <11;
```

If you want just a count of all the rows in the table, you can use the following statement:

```
SQL> select count (*) from employees;
```

If a table has duplicate data, you can use the *distinct* clause to eliminate the duplicate values, as shown in the following example:

```
SQL> select distinct username from v$session;
```

The optional *where* clause in a *select* statement uses conditions that help you specify that only certain rows be returned. Here are some of the common conditions that you can use in a *where* clause:

```
= Equal
> Greater Than
< less Than
<+ Less than or equal to
>= greater than or equal to
<> or ! not equal to
```

Here are some examples of using the *where* clause:

```
SQL> select employee_id where salary=50000;
SQL> select employee_id where salary < 50000;
SQL> select employee_id where salary > 50000;
SQL> select employee_id where salary <= 50000;
SQL> select employee_id where salary >= 50000;
SQL> select employee_id where salary ! 50000;
```

The Like Condition

The *like* condition uses pattern matching to restrict rows in a *select* statement. Here's an example:

```
SQL> select employee_Id, LAST_NAME from employees
  2* where last_name like 'Fa%';
EMPLOYEE_ID    LAST_NAME
-----------    ----------
    109        Faviet
    202        Fay
SQL>
```

The pattern that you want the *where* clause to match should be enclosed in single quotes (' '). The percent sign (%) indicates that the letters *Fa* can be followed by any character string. Thus, the percent sign acts as a wildcard for one or more characters, performing the same job as the asterisk (*) in many operating systems. Note that a single underscore character (_) acts as a wildcard for one and only one character.

The Insert Statement

The *insert* statement enables you to add new data to a table. The *insert* statement lets you add duplicate data if there are no unique requirements enforced by a primary key or an index. The general form of the *insert* statement is as follows:

```
Insert into <table> [(<column i, …, column j>)]
Values (<value i,…,value j>);
```

Here is an example of the *insert* command:

```
SQL> insert into employees(
  2  employee_id,last_name,email,hire_date,job_id)
  3  values
  4* (56789,'alapati','salapati',sysdate,98765);
1 row created.
SQL>
```

In the preceding list, you had to specify the column names, because only some columns were being populated in the row you inserted. The rest of them are left blank, which is OK, provided the column isn't defined a "not null" column.

If you're inserting values for all the columns of a table, you can use the simpler *insert* statement shown here:

```
SQL> insert into department (dept_id, dept_name,
     dept_type, dept_city)
     values
     (34567, 'payroll', 'headquarters', 'dallas');
  1 row created.
SQL>
```

If you want to insert all the columns of a table into another table, you can use the following *insert* statement:

```
SQL> insert into b select * from a
     where city='DALLAS';
```

If table b doesn't exist, you can use the *create table as select * from* (CTAS) command, as shown here:

```
SQL> create table b as select * from a;
```

The Delete Statement

You use the *delete* statement to remove rows from a table. The *delete* statement has the following structure:

```
delete from <table> [where ,condition>];
```

For example, if you want to delete employee Fay's row from the employees table, you use the following *delete* statement:

```
SQL>  delete from employees
  2* where last_name='Fay';
1 row deleted.
```

If you don't have a limiting *where* condition, *delete from X* will result in the removal of all the rows in the table, as shown here:

```
SQL> Delete from X;
```

You can also remove all rows in a table using the *truncate* command, but the big difference, of course, is that you can't undo or roll back the *truncate* command's effects. You can undo a delete, on the other hand, by using the *rollback* statement:

```
SQL> rollback;
```

The Update Statement

The *update* statement changes the value (or values) of one or more columns of a row (or rows) in a table. The general structure of the *update* statement is as follows (note that the elements in square brackets are optional):

```
update <table>
set <column i> = <expression i>,…, <column j> = <expression j>
[where  <condition> ];
```

In the *update* statement, the expression to which a column is being set or modified can be a constant, an arithmetic or string operation, or the product of a *select* statement.

If you want to change or modify a column's values for all the rows in the table, you use an *update* statement without a *where* condition, as shown here:

```
SQL> update persons set salary=salary*0.10;
```

If you want to modify only some rows, you need to use the *where* clause in your *update* statement, as follows:

```
SQL> update persons set salary = salary * 0.10
    where review_grade > 5;
```

Filtering Data

The *where* clause in a *select, insert, delete,* or *update* statement lets you filter data. That is, you can restrict the number of rows on which you want to perform a SQL operation. Here's a simple example:

```
SQL> insert into a
    select * from b
    where city='DALLAS';
```

Sorting the Results of a Query

Frequently, you'll have to sort the results of a query in some order. The *order by* clause enables you to sort the data based on the value(s) of one or more columns. You can choose the sorting order and you can choose to sort by column aliases. You can also sort by multiple columns. I explain the Oracle *order by* clause in the following sections.

The Order By Clause

The *order by* clause lets you sort the results of a query based on one or more columns' values. You can sort the results in an ascending or descending order. Here's an example:

```
SQL>  select employee_id, salary from employees
    order by salary;
```

Sorting Order

Be default, an *order by* clause sorts in ascending order. If you want to sort in descending order, you need to specify the keyword *desc,* as shown here:

```
SQL>  select employee_id, salary from employees
    order by salary desc;
```

Sorting by Multiple Columns

You can sort results based on the values of more than one column. The following query sorts on the basis of two columns, salary and dept.

```
SQL>  select employee_id, salary from employees
    order by salary, dept ;
```

Operators

SQL provides you with a number of operators to perform various tasks, such as comparing column values and performing logical operations. In the following sections you'll look at the important SQL operators.

Comparison Operators

Comparison operators compare a certain column value with several other column values. Here are the main comparison operators:

- *Between:* Tests whether a value is between a pair of values

- *In:* Tests whether a value is in a list of values

- *Like:* Tests whether a value follows a certain pattern, as shown here:

```
SQL> select employee_id from employees
where dept like 'FIN%';
```

Logical Operators

The *logical operators*, also called *Boolean operators*, logically compare two or more values. The main logical operators are AND, OR, NOT, GE (greater than or equal to), and LE (less than or equal to). Here's an example that illustrates the use of some of the logical operators:

```
SQL> select last_name, city
    where salary GT 100000 and LE 200000;
```

When there are multiple operators within a single statement, you need certain rules of precedence. Oracle always evaluates arithmetical operations such as multiplication, division, addition, and subtraction before it evaluates conditions. The following is the order of precedence of operators in Oracle, with the most important being listed first:

=, !=, <, >, <=, >=

IS NULL, LIKE, BETWEEN, IN, EXISTS

NOT

AND

OR

The Set Operators

Sometimes your query may need to combine results from more than one SQL statement. In other words, you need to write a compound query. *Set operators* facilitate compound SQL queries. Here are the important Oracle set operators:

- *Union:* The *union* operator combines the results of more than one *select* statement after removing any duplicate rows. Oracle will sort the resulting set of data.

```
SQL> select emp_id from old_employees
            UNION
            select emp_id from new_employees;
```

- *Union all:* The *union all* operator is similar to *union*, but it doesn't remove the duplicate rows. Oracle doesn't sort the result set in this case, unlike in the case of a *union* operation.

- *Intersection:* The *intersection* operator gets you the common values in two or more result sets derived from separate *select* statements. The result set is distinct and sorted.

- *Minus:* The *minus* operator returns the rows returned by the first query that isn't in the second query's results. The result set is distinct and sorted.

SQL Functions

Oracle functions manipulate data items and return a result. Built-in Oracle9i functions help you perform many transformations quickly, without your having to do any coding. In addition, you can create your own user-built functions. You can separate functions into several groups, as explained in the following sections.

Single-Row Functions

Single-row functions are typically used to perform tasks such as converting a lowercase word to uppercase or vice versa, or replacing a portion of text in a row. Here are the main Oracle single-row functions:

- *CONCAT:* The CONCAT function concatenates or puts together two or more character strings into one string.

- *LENGTH:* The LENGTH function gives you the length of a character string.

- *LOWER:* The LOWER function transforms uppercase into lowercase, as shown in the following example:

```
SQL> select LOWER('SHANNON ALAPATI') from dual;
LOWER('SHANNONALAPATI')
-----------------------
shannon alapati
SQL>
```

- *SUBSTR:* The SUBSTR function gives you part of a string.

- *INSTR:* The INSTR function returns a number indicating where in a string a certain string value starts.

- *LPAD:* The LPAD function returns a string after padding it for a specified length on the left.

- *RPAD:* The RPAD function pads a string on the right side.

- *TRIM:* The TRIM function trims a character string.

- *REPLACE:* The REPLACE function replaces every occurrence of a specified string with another specified replacement string.

Aggregate Functions

You can use *aggregate functions* to compute things such as averages and totals of a selected column in a query. Here are the important aggregate functions:

- *MIN:* Returns the smallest value

```
select min(join_date) from employees;
```

- *MAX:* Returns the largest value

- *AVG:* Computes the average value of a column

- *SUM:* Computes the sum of a column

```
SQL> select sum(bytes) from dba_free_space;
```

- *COUNT:* Returns the total number of columns

- *COUNT(*):* Returns the number of rows in a table

Number and Date Functions

Oracle9*i* includes a number of number functions. The data functions help you format dates and times in different ways. Here are some of the important number and date functions:

- *ROUND:* This function returns a number rounded to the specified number of integer places to the right of the decimal point.

- *TRUNC:* This function returns the result of a date truncated in the specified format.

- *SYSDATE:* This commonly used function returns the current date and time.

```
SQL> select sysdate from dual;
SYSDATE
--------------------
08/FEB/2003 04:05:18
SQL>
```

- *TO_TIMESTAMP:* This function converts a char or varchar(2) data type to a timestamp data type.

- *TO_DATE:* You can use this function to change the current date format. The standard date format in Oracle is DD-MON-YYYY, as shown in the following example:

```
20-FEB-2003
```

The TO_DATE format accepts a character string that contains valid data and converts it into the default Oracle date format. The TO_DATE function can change the date format, as shown here:

```
SQL> select to_date ('February 20, 2003', 'MonthDD,YYYY') from dual;
TO_DATE('FE
-----------
20-FEB-2003
SQL>
```

- *TO_CHAR:* This function converts a data into a character string, as shown in the following example:

```
SQL> select sysdate from dual;
SYSDATE
-----------
20-FEB-2003
SQL>
SQL> select to_char(sysdate,'dd/mon/yyyy') from dual;
TO_CHAR(SYSDATE,'DD/MON/YYYY')
------------------------------------------------------
20/FEB/2003
SQL>
```

- *TO_NUMBER:* This function converts a character string to a number format.

General Functions and Conditional Expressions

Oracle9*i* provides some very powerful general functions and conditional functions that enable you to extend the power of simple SQL statements into something similar to a traditional programming language construct. The conditional functions help you decide among several choices. Here are the important general and conditional Oracle9*i* expressions:

- *NVL:* The NVL function replaces the value in table column with the value after the comma if the column is null. Thus, the NVL function takes care of column values "just in case" the column values are null and converts them to non-null values:

```
SQL> select  last_name, title,
      salary * NVL (commission_pct,0) / 100 COMM
      from employees;
```

- *COALESCE:* This function is similar to NVL, but it returns the first non-null value in the list:

```
coalesce (region1, region2, region3, region4)
```

- *DECODE:* This function is used to incorporate basic if-then functionality into SQL code. The following example assigns a party name to all the voters in the table based on the value in the affiliation column. If there is no value under the affiliation column, the voter is listed as an independent.

```
SQL> select  decode (affiliation, 'D', 'Democrat',
        'R', 'Republican', 'Independent') from voters;
```

- *CASE:* This function provides the same functionality as the DECODE function, but in a much more intuitive and elegant way. Here's a simple example of using the CASE statement, which helps you incorporate if-then logic into your code:

```
SQL> SELECT ename,
     (CASE deptno
     WHEN 10 THEN 'Accounting'
     WHEN 20 THEN 'Research'
     WHEN 30 THEN 'Sales'
     WHEN 40 THEN 'Operations'
     ELSE 'Unknown'
     END) department
     FROM employees;
```

SQL Analytical Functions

Oracle's SQL analytical functions are powerful tools for business intelligence applications. Oracle claims a potential improvement of 200 to 500 percent in query performance with the use of the SQL analytical functions. The purpose behind using analytical functions is to perform complex summary computations without using a lot of code. Here are the main SQL analytical functions of the Oracle9*i* Release 2 database:

- *Ranking functions* enable you to rank items in a data set according to some criteria. Oracle9*i* has several types of ranking functions, including rank, dense rank, cume_dist, percent_rank, and ntile. The following code shows a simple example of how a ranking function can help you rank some sales data:

```
SQL> SELECT sales_type,
       TO_CHAR(SUM(amount_sold), '9,999,999,999') SALES,
       RANK() OVER (ORDER BY SUM(amount_sold) ) AS original_rank,
       RANK() OVER (ORDER BY SUM(amount_sold)
       DESC NULLS LAST) AS derived_rank
     FROM sales, products, customers, time_frame, sales_types
     WHERE sales.prod_id=products.prod_id AND
      sales.cust_id=customers.cust_id AND
      sales.time_id=time_frame.time_id AND
```

```
        sales.sales_type_id=sales_types.sales_type_id AND
         timeframe.calendar_month_desc IN ('2003-01', '2003-02')
        AND country_id='INDIA'
        GROUP BY sales_type;
SALES_TYPE                  SALES    ORIGINAL_RANK DERIVED_RANK
-------------------- -------------- ------------ -----------
Direct Sales             5,744,263           5           1
Internet                 3,625,993           4           2
Catalog                  1,858,386           3           3
Partners                 1,500,213           2           4
Tele Sales                 604,656           1           5
SQL>
```

- *Moving-window aggregates* provide cumulative sums and moving averages.

- *Period-overperiod comparisons* let you compare two periods (e.g., "How does the first quarter of 2002 compare with the first quarter of 2003 in terms of percentage growth?").

- *Ratio-to-report comparisons* make it possible to compare ratios (e.g., "What is August's enrollment as a percentage of the entire year's enrollment?").

- *Statistical functions* calculate correlations and regression functions so you can see cause and effect relationships among data.

- *Inverse percentiles* help you find the data corresponding to a percentile value (e.g., "Get me the names of the salespeople who correspond to the median sales value.").

- *Hypothetical ranks and distributions* help you figure out how a new value for a column fits into existing data in terms of its rank and distribution.

- *Histograms* return the number of the histogram data appropriate for each row in a table.

- *First/last aggregates* are appropriate when you are using the *group by* clause to sort data into groups. These aggregate functions let you specify the sort order for the groups.

Hierarchical Retrieval of Data

If a table contains hierarchical data (i.e., data that can be grouped into levels, with the parent data at higher levels and child data at lower levels), you can use Oracle's hierarchical queries. Hierarchical queries typically use the following structure:

- The *start with* clause denotes the root row or rows for the hierarchical relationship.

- The *connect by* clause specifies the relationship between parent and child rows, with the *prior* operator always pointing out the parent row.

Listing 1 shows a hierarchical relationship between the employees and manager columns. The *connect by* clause describes the relationship. The *start with* clause specifies where the statement should start tracing the hierarchy.

Listing 1. A Hierarchical Relationship Between Data

```
SQL> select employee_id, last_name, manager_id
     from employees
     start with manager_id = 100
     connect BY PRIOR employee_id = manager_id;
 EMPLOYEE_ID  LAST_NAME       MANAGER_ID
 -----------  --------------  ----------
         101  Reddy                  100
         108  Greenberg              101
         109  Faviet                 108
         110  Colon                  108
         111  Chowdhary              108
         112  Urman                  108
         113  Singh                  108
         200  Whalen                 101
SQL>
```

Selecting Data from Multiple Tables

So far, you've mostly seen how to perform various DML operations on single tables, including using SQL functions and expressions. However, in real life, you'll mostly deal with query output retrieved from several tables or views. When you need to retrieve data from several tables, you need to join the tables. A *join* is a query that lets you link data that's in two or more tables into a single query result. In the following sections you'll look at the various types of Oracle table joins. Note that a table can be joined to other tables or to itself.

The Cartesian Product

The *Cartesian product* or *Cartesian join* is simply a join of two tables without a selective *where* clause. Therefore, the query output will consist of all rows from both tables. Cartesian products of two large tables are almost always the result of a mistaken SQL query that omits the join condition. Here's an example of a Cartesian join:

```
SQL> select * from employees, dept;
```

When you use a join condition when you're combining data from two or more tables, you can limit the number of rows returned, as you will learn in the following section.

The Four Types of Oracle Joins

Oracle offers you four major types of joins based on the way you combine rows from two or more tables or views. The next sections discuss the four types of Oracle joins.

Equi-join

With an *equi-join,* the tables are joined based on an equality condition between two columns. In other words, the same column has the same value in all the tables that are being joined, as shown in the following example:

```
SQL> select e.last_name, d.dept
     from emp e, dept d where e.emp_id = d.emp_id;
```

You can also use the following new syntax for the preceding join statement:

```
SQL> select e.last_name, d.dept
     from emp e JOIN dept d
     USING (emp_id);
```

If you want to join multiple columns, you can do so by using a comma-delimited list of column names, as in *USING (dept_id, emp_name).*

Natural Join

A *natural join* is an equi-join where you don't specify any columns to be matched for the join. Oracle will automatically determine the columns to be joined, based on the matching columns in the two tables, before performing the join. Here's an example:

```
SQL> select e.last_name, d.dept
     from emp e NATURAL JOIN dept d;
```

In the preceding example, the join is based on identical values for the last_name column in both the emp and dept tables.

Self Join

A *self join* is a join of a table to itself through the use of table aliases. The following is a simple example of a self join. The table employees is joined to itself using an alias. The query deletes duplicate rows in the employees table.

```
SQL> delete from  employees X where ROWID >
  2  (select MIN(rowid) from employees Y
  3  where X.key_values = Y.key_values);
```

Inner Join

An *inner join* returns all rows that satisfy the join condition. The traditional Oracle inner join syntax used the *where* clause to specify how the tables were to be joined. Here's an example:

```
SQL> select e.flast_name, d.dept
     from emp e, dept d where e.emp_id = d.emp_id;
```

The newer Oracle9*i* inner joins (or simply *joins*) specify join criteria with the new *on* or *using* clause. Here's a simple example:

```
SQL> Select distinct nvl(dname, 'No Dept'),
     count(empno) nbr_emps
     from emp JOIN DEPT
     ON emp.deptno = dept.deptno
     where emp.job in ('MANAGER', 'SALESMAN', 'ANALYST')
     group by dname;
```

Outer Join

An *outer join* returns all rows that satisfy the join condition, *plus* some or all of the rows from the table that doesn't have matching rows that meet the join condition in the other table. There are three types of outer joins: left outer join, right outer join, and full outer join. Usually, the word "outer" is omitted from the join statement. Oracle9*i* also provides the Oracle outer join operator wherein you use a plus sign (+) to indicate missing values in one table, but it recommends the use of the newer ISO/ANSI joins. Here's a typical query using the full outer join:

```
SQL> select distinct nvl(dept_name, 'No Dept') deptname,
     count(empno) nbr_emps
     from emp full join dept
     on dept.deptno = emp.deptno
     group by dname;
```

Grouping Operations

Oracle provides several clauses that enable you to group the results of a query according to various criteria. The *group by* clause enables you to consider a column value for all the rows in the table fulfilling the select condition. Normally, you use the *group by* clause so you can perform an aggregate function.

A *group by* clause commonly uses aggregate functions to summarize each group defined by the *group by* clause. The data is sorted on the *group by* columns, and the aggregates are calculated. Here's an example:

```
SQL>   select department_id, max(salary)
  2    from employees
  3*   group by department_id;
```

```
DEPARTMENT_ID   MAX(SALARY)
-------------   -----------
           10          4400
           20         13000
           30         11000
           40          6500
           50          8200
5 rows selected.
    SQL>
```

Nesting Group Functions

Oracle allows you to nest group functions. The following query gets you the minimum average budget for all departments:

```
SQL> SELECT min(AVG(budget))
     FROM dept_budgets
     GROUP BY dept_no;
```

The Group By Clause with a Rollup Operator

You've seen how you can derive subtotals with the help of the *group by* clause. The *group by* clause with a *rollup* clause gives you subtotals and total values. You can thus build subtotal aggregates at any level. In other words, the *rollup* clause gets you the aggregates at each *group by* level. The subtotal rows and the grand total row are called the *superaggregate rows*. Listing 2 shows an example of using the *rollup* clause.

Listing 2. A Group By with a Rollup Clause

```
SQL> SELECT Year,Country,SUM(Sales) AS Sales
     FROM Company_Sales
     GROUP BY ROLLUP (Year,Country);
  YEAR          COUNTRY        SALES
  --------      --------      --------
    1997        France         3990
    1997        USA           13090
    1997                      17080
    1998        France         4310
    1998        USA           13900
    1998                      18210
    1999        France         4570
    1999        USA           14670
    1999                      19240
                              54530    /*This is the grand total */
SQL>
```

The Group By Clause with a Cube Operator

You can consider the *cube* operator to be an extension of the *rollup* operator, as it helps extend the standard Oracle *group by* clause. The *cube* operator computes all possible combinations of subtotals in a group by operation. In the previous example, the *rollup* operator gave you yearly subtotals. Using the *cube* operator, you can get countrywide totals in addition to the yearly totals. Here's a simple example:

```
SQL> select department_id, job_id,  sum(salary)
  4   from employees
  5   group by CUBE (department_id, job_id);
DEPARTMENT_ID   JOB_ID        SUM(SALARY)
------------- ---------- -----------------
     10         AD_ASST          44000
     20         MK_MAN          130000
     20         MK_REP           60000
     30         PU_MAN          110000
     30         PU_CLERK        139000
...
SQL>
```

The Group By Clause with a Grouping Operator

As you've seen, the *rollup* function gets you the superaggregate subtotals and grand totals. The *grouping* function in a *group by* clause helps you distinguish between superaggregated subtotals and the grand total column from the other row data.

The Group By Clause with a Grouping Sets Operator

The *grouping sets* operator lets you group multiple sets of columns when you're calculating aggregates such as sums. Here's an example that shows how you can use this operator to calculate aggregates over three groupings: (year, region, product), (year, product), and (region, product). The *grouping sets* operator eliminates the need for inefficient *union all* operators.

```
SQL> select year, region, product, sum(sales)
     from regional_sales
     group by
     grouping sets (( year, region, item),
     (year, item), (region, item));
```

The Having Clause

The *having* clause lets you restrict or exclude the results of a *group by* operation, in essence putting a *where* condition on the *group by* clause's result set. In the following example, the *having* clause restricts the query results to only those departments that have a maximum salary greater than 20,000:

```
SQL> select department_id, max(salary)
  2  from employees
  3  group by department_id
  4* having max(salary)>20000;
DEPARTMENT_ID MAX(SALARY)
------------- -----------
     90           24000
SQL>
```

Writing Subqueries

Subqueries resolve queries that have to be processed in multiple steps. The answer to a query depends on the results of a child or subquery to the main query. If you put a subquery in the *where* clause of a *select* statement, it's called an *inline view*. If the subquery occurs in the *where* clause of the statement, it's called a *nested subquery*. The following sections show you how to use a subquery to rank the values in a column.

Top N Analysis

The following query gives you the top ten employees in a firm ranked by salary. You can just as easily retrieve the bottom ten employees by using the *order by* clause instead of the *order by desc* clause.

```
SQL> SELECT Emp_id, emp_name, Job, Manager, Salary
     FROM
     (SELECT Emp_id, emp_name, Job, Manager, Salary,
     RANK() OVER
     (ORDER BY SALARY Desc NULLS LAST) AS Employee_Rank
     FROM Employees
     ORDER BY SALARY Desc NULLS LAST)
     WHERE Employee_Rank < 5;
```

Subqueries can be single-row or multiple-row SQL statements. Let's take a quick look at both types of subqueries.

Single-Row Subqueries

Subqueries are useful when you need to answer queries on the basis of as yet unknown values. Subqueries help you answer questions such as the following: Which employees have a salary higher than the employee with the employee ID 9999? To answer such a question, a subquery or inner query is executed first (and only once). The result of this subquery is then used by the main or outer query. Here's the resulting query:

```
SQL> SELECT first_name||last_name,dept
  2  FROM  employee
  3 WHERE sal >
  4 (SELECT sal
  5 FROM  emp
  6 WHERE empno= 9999);
```

Multiple-Row Subqueries

A multiple-row subquery returns multiple rows in the output, so you need to use multiple-row comparison operators such as IN, ANY, and ALL. Using a single-row operator with a multiple-row subquery returns this common Oracle error:

```
ERROR:
ORA-01427: single-row subquery returns more than one row
```

Multiple-Column Subqueries

Multiple-column subqueries are queries where the inner query retrieves the values of more than one column. The rows in the subquery are then evaluated in the main query in pair-wise comparison, column by column and row by row.

Advanced Subqueries

Correlated subqueries are more complex than regular subqueries and answer questions such as the following: What are the names of all employees whose salary is below the average salary of their department? The inner query computes the average salary and the outer or main query gets the employee information. However, for each employee in the main (outer) query, the inner query has to be computed because department averages depend on the department number of the employee in the outer query.

The Exists and Not Exists Operators

The *exists* operator tests for the existence of rows in the inner or subquery when you're using subqueries. The *not exists* operator tests for the nonexistence of rows in the inner query. In the following statement, the *exists* operator will be *true* if the subquery returns at least one row:

```
SQL> SELECT department_id
     FROM departments d
     WHERE EXISTS
     (SELECT * FROM employees e
     WHERE d.department_id
     = e.department_id);
```

Abstract Data Types

In this section you'll briefly review the important Oracle9*i* features that facilitate object-oriented programming. *Abstract types,* also called *object types,* are at the heart of Oracle's object-oriented programming. Unlike a normal data type, an abstract data type contains a data structure along with the functions and procedures needed to manipulate the data; thus, data and behavior are coupled.

Object types are like other schema objects, and they consist of a name, attributes, and methods. Object types are similar to the concept of classes in C++ and Java. The Oracle9*i* support of object-oriented features such as types makes it feasible to implement object-oriented features such as encapsulation and abstraction while modeling complex real-life objects and processes. Oracle9*i* also supports single inheritance of user-defined SQL types.

The Create Type Command

Object types are created by users and stored in the database like Oracle data types such as varchar2, for example. The *create type* command lets you create an abstract template that corresponds to a real-world object. Here's an example:

```
SQL> create type person as object
  2  (name varchar2(30),
  3  phone varchar2(20))
  4  /
Type created.
SQL>
```

Object Tables

Object tables contain objects such as the person type you created in the previous section. Here's an example:

```
SQL> create table person_table of person;
Table created.
SQL>
```

Here's the interesting part. The table person_table doesn't contain single value columns like a regular Oracle table—its columns are types, which can hold multiple values. You can use object tables to view the data as a single-column table or a multi-column table that consists of the components of the object type. Here's how you would insert data into an object table:

```
SQL> insert into person_table
  2  values
  3  ('john smith', '1-800-555-9999');
1 row created.
SQL>
```

Collections

Collections are ideal for representing one-to-many relationships among data. Oracle9*i* offers you two main types of collections: varrays and nested tables. You'll look at these two types of collections in more detail in the following sections.

Varrays

Varrays are stored in the database as RAW or BLOB objects. A varray is simply an ordered collection of data elements. Each element in the array is identified by an index, which is used to access that particular element. Here's how you declare an array type:

```
CREATE TYPE prices AS VARRAY (10) OF NUMBER (12,2);
```

Nested Tables

A *nested table* consists of an ordered set of data elements. The ordered set can be of an object type or an Oracle built-in type. Here's a simple example:

```
CREATE TYPE lineitem_table AS TABLE OF lineitem;
```

To access the elements of a collection with SQL, you can use the *table* operator, as shown in the following example. Here, history is a nested table and courses is the column you want to insert data into.

```
SQL> Insert into
     TABLE(SELECT courses FROM department WHERE name = 'History')
     VALUES('Modern India');
```

Type Inheritance

You can create not just types, but also *type hierarchies,* which consist of parent supertypes and child subtypes connected to the parent types by inheritance. Here's an example of how you can create a subtype from a supertype. First, create the supertype:

```
SQL> create type person_t as object (
    name varchar2(80),
    social_sec_no number,
    hire_date date,
    member function age() RETURN number,
    member function print() RETURN varchar2) NOT FINAL;
```

Next, create the subtype, which will inherit all the attributes and methods from its supertype:

```
SQL> create type employee_t UNDER person_t
    ( salary number,
    commission number,
    member function wages () RETURN number,
    OVERRIDING member function print () RETURN varchar2);
```

The Cast Operator

The *cast* operator enables you to do two things. First, it lets you convert built-in data types. Second, the *cast* operator lets you convert a collection-type value into another collection-type value.

Here's an example of using *cast* with built-in data types:

```
SQL> SELECT product_id,
    CAST(description AS VARCHAR2(30))
    FROM product_desc;
```

The sample schema OE has the following types. Use these types for the *cast* example that follows.

```
CREATE TYPE address_book_t AS TABLE OF cust_address_typ;
CREATE TYPE address_array_t AS VARRAY(3) OF cust_address_typ;
```

Using the *cast* operator, you can convert a varray into a nested table, as shown here:

```
SQL> SELECT CAST(s.addresses AS address_book_t)
    FROM states s
    WHERE s.state_id = 111;
```

Using PL/SQL

Although SQL is easy to learn and has a lot of powerful features, it doesn't allow procedural constructs of third-generation languages such as C. PL/SQL is Oracle's proprietary extension to SQL, and it provides you the functionality of a serious programming language. One of the big advantages of using PL/SQL is that you can use program units called *procedures* or *packages* in the database, thus increasing code reuse and performance.

The Basic PL/SQL Block

A PL/SQL *block* is an executable program. A PL/SQL code block, whether encapsulated in a program unit such as a procedure or specified as a free-form anonymous block, consists of the following structures, with a total of four key statements, only two of which are mandatory:

- *Declare:* In this optional section, you declare the program variables and cursors.

- *Begin:* This mandatory statement indicates that SQL and PL/SQL statements will follow it.

- *Exception:* This optional statement specifies error handling.

- *End:* This mandatory statement indicates the end of the PL/SQL code block.

Here's an example of a simple PL/SQL code block:

```
declare
    isbn     number (9)
begin
    isbn := 123456789;
    insert into book values (isbn, 'databases', 59.99);
    commit;
end;
```

Declaring Variables

You can declare both variables and constants in the *declare* section. Before you can use any variable, you must first declare the variable. A PL/SQL variable can be a built-in type such as date, number, varchar2, or char, or it can be a composite type such as varray. In addition to the varchar2, char, number, and date data types, PL/SQL uses the binary_integer and Boolean data types. Here are some common PL/SQL variable declarations:

```
Hired_date    DATE;
Emp_name      varchar 2(30);
```

In addition to declaring variables, you can also declare constants, as shown in the following example:

```
tax_rate    constant    number := 0.08;
```

You can also use the %TYPE attribute to declare a variable that is of the same type as a specified table's column, as shown here:

```
Emp_num       employee.emp_id%TYPE;
```

The %ROWTYPE attribute specifies that the record (row) is of the same data type as a database table. In the following example, the DeptRecord record has all the columns contained in the department table, with identical data types and length:

```
Declare
V_DeptRecord        department%ROWTYPE;
```

Writing Executable Statements

After the *begin* statement, you can enter all your DML statements. These look just like your regular SQL statements, but notice the difference in how you handle a *select* statement and an *insert* statement in the following sections.

A Select Statement in PL/SQL

When you use a *select* statement in PL/SQL, you need to store the retrieved values in variables, as shown here:

```
declare
name   varchar2(30);begin
     Select employee_name into name from employees where emp_id=99999;
end;
/    .
```

DML Statements in PL/SQL

Any *insert*, *delete*, or *update* statements in PL/SQL work just as they do in regular SQL. You can use the *commit* statement after any such operation, as shown here:

```
Begin
     Delete from employee where emp_id = 99999;
     Commit;
End;
/
```

Handling Errors

In PL/SQL, an error or a warning is called an *exception*. PL/SQL has some internally defined errors and you can also define your own error conditions. When any error occurs, an exception is raised, and program control is handed to the exception handling section of the PL/SQL program. If you define your own error conditions, you have to raise exceptions by using a special *raise* statement.

The following example shows the use of one such exception handler using the *raise* statement:

```
DECLARE
   acct_type INTEGER := 7;
BEGIN
   IF acct_type NOT IN (1, 2, 3) THEN
      RAISE INVALID_NUMBER;  -- raise predefined exception
   END IF;
EXCEPTION
   WHEN INVALID_NUMBER THEN
   ROLLBACK;
END;
/
```

PL/SQL Control Structures

PL/SQL offers you several types of control structures, which enable you to perform iterations of code or conditional execution of certain statements. You'll look at the various types of control structures in PL/SQL in the following sections.

Conditional Control

The main type of conditional control structure in PL/SQL is the *if* statement, which enables conditional execution of statements. Here's a simple example. You can use the *if* statement in three forms: *if-then*, *if-then-else*, and *if-then-elsif*. Here's an example of a simple *if-then-elsif* statement:

```
BEGIN
   ...
   IF total_sales > 100000 THEN
      bonus := 5000;
   ELSIF total_sales > 35000 THEN
      bonus := 500;
   ELSE
      bonus := 0;
   END IF;
   INSERT INTO new_payroll VALUES (emp_id, bonus, ...);
END;
/
```

PL/SQL Looping Constructs

PL/SQL loops provide a way to perform iterations of code for a specified number of times or until a certain condition is *true* or *false*. The following sections cover the basic types of looping constructs.

The Simple Loop

The simple loop construct encloses a set of SQL statements in between the keywords *loop* and *end loop*, as shown in the following example. Note that the *exit* statement ends the loop. You use the simple loop construct when you don't know how many times the loop should execute. The logic inside the *loop* and *end loop* statements decides when the loop is terminated. In the following example, the loop will be executed until a quality grade of 6 is reached:

```
loop
   ...
   if quality_grade > 5   then
   ...
   exit;
   end if;
end loop;
```

Another simple loop type is the *loop ... exit ... when* construct, which controls the duration of the loop with a *when* statement. A condition is specified for the *when* statement, and when this condition becomes true, the loop will terminate. Here's a simple example:

```
Declare
   count_num   number(6);
Begin
   count_num := 1;
   Loop
   dbms_output.put_line(' This is the current count  '|| count_num);
   count_num := count_num + 1;
   Exit when count num > 100;
   End loop;
End;
```

The While Loop

The *while* loop specifies that a certain statement be executed while a certain condition is true. Note that the condition is evaluated outside the loop. Each time the statements within the *loop* and *end loop* statements are executed, the condition is evaluated. When the condition no longer holds true, the loop is exited. Here's an example of the *while* loop:

```
WHILE total <= 25000 Loop
   ...
   SELECT sal INTO salary FROM emp WHERE ...
   total := total + salary;
END Loop;
```

The For Loop

The *for loop* is used when you want a statement to be executed for a certain number of times. The *for* loop emulates the classic *do* loop that exists in most programming languages. Here's an example of the *for* loop:

```
Begin
    For count_num in 1..100
    Loop
      Dbms_output.put_line('The current count is :  '|| count_num);
    End loop;
End;
```

Cursors

An Oracle *cursor* is an area in memory that holds the result set of a SQL query, enabling you to individually process the rows in the result set. An Oracle cursor is actually a handle to an area of memory that Oracle uses to execute code and store information. Oracle uses implicit cursors for all DML statements. Explicit cursors are created and used by application coders.

Implicit Cursors

Implicit cursors are automatically used by Oracle every time you use a *select* statement in PL/SQL. You can use implicit cursors in statements that return just one row. If your SQL statement returns more than one row, an error will result. In the following PL/SQL code block, the *select* statement makes use of an implicit cursor:

```
Declare
  Emp_name  varchar2(40);
  Salary    float;
Begin
  select  emp_name, salary from employees
  where  employee_id=9999;
  dbms_output.put_line('employee_name : '||emp_name||'
  salary :'||salary);
End;
/
```

Explicit Cursors

Explicit cursors are created by the application developer, and they facilitate operations with a set of rows, which can be processed one by one. You always use explicit cursors when you know your SQL statement will return more than one row. Notice that you have to *declare* an explicit cursor in the *declare* section at the beginning of the PL/SQL block, unlike an implicit cursor, which you never refer to in the code. Once you declare your cursor, the explicit cursor will go through these steps:

1. The *open* clause will identify the rows that are in the cursor and make them available for the PL/SQL program.

2. The *fetch* command will retrieve data from the cursor into a specified variable.

3. The cursor should always be explicitly closed after your processing is completed.

Listing 3 shows how a cursor is created first and later used within a loop.

Listing 3. Using an Explicit Cursor

```
Declare
/* The cursor select_emp is explicitly declared */
      cursor select_emp is
      select emp_id, city
      from employees
      where city = 'DALLAS';
      v_empno   employees.emp_id%TYPE;
      v_empcity employees.city%TYPE;
Begin
  /* The cursor select_emp is opened */
   Open select _emp;
    Loop
  /* The select_emp cursor data is fetched into v_empno variable */
     Fetch select_emp into v_empno;
     Exit when select_emp%NOTFOUND;
     Dbms_output.put_line(v_empno|| ','||v_empcity);
    End loop;
      /* The cursor select_emp is closed */
   Close select_emp;
End;
/
```

Cursor Attributes

In the example shown in Listing 3, a special cursor attribute, %NOTFOUND, is used to indicate when the loop should terminate. Cursor attributes are very useful when you're dealing with explicit cursors. Here are the main cursor attributes:

- %ISOPEN is a Boolean attribute that evaluates to *false* after the SQL statement completes execution. It returns *true* as long as the cursor is open.

- %FOUND is a Boolean attribute that tests whether the SQL statement matches any row—that is, whether the cursor has any more rows to fetch.

- %NOTFOUND is a Boolean attribute that tells you that the SQL statement doesn't match any row, meaning there are no more rows left to fetch.

- %ROWCOUNT gives you the number of rows the cursor fetched so far.

Cursor For Loops

Normally when you use explicit cursors, cursors have to be opened, the data has to be fetched, and finally the cursor needs to be closed. A *cursor for loop* automatically performs the open, fetch, and close procedures, which simplifies your job. Listing 4 shows an example that uses a *cursor for loop* construct.

Listing 4. Using the Cursor For Loop

```
Declare
  Cursor emp_cursor is
  Select emp_id, emp_name,salary
  From employees;
  V_emp_info    employees%RowType;
Begin
  For emp_info IN emp_cursor LOOP
  Dbms_output.put_line ('Employee id : '||emp_id||'Employee
  name : '|| emp_name||'Employee salary :'||salary);
  End LOOP;
End;
/
```

PL/SQL Records

Records in PL/SQL let you treat related data as a single unit. Records contain fields, with each field standing for a different item. You can use the %ROWTYPE attribute to declare a table's columns as a record, or you can create your own records. Here's a simple example of a record:

```
DECLARE
      TYPE MeetingTyp IS RECORD (
      date_held DATE,
      location  VARCHAR2(20),
      purpose   VARCHAR2(50));
```

To reference an individual field in a record, you use the dot notation, as shown here:

```
meetingtyp.location
```

Cursor Variables

Cursor variables point to the current row in a multirow result set. Unlike a regular cursor, though, a cursor variable is dynamic—that is, you can assign new values to a cursor variable and pass it other procedures and functions. Let's see how you can create cursor variables in PL/SQL.

First, define a REF CURSOR type, as shown here:

```
declare
type EmpCurTyp IS ref cursor return dept%ROWTYPE;
```

Next, declare cursor variables of the type DeptCurTyp in an anonymous PL/SQL code block or in a procedure (or function), as shown in the following code snippet:

```
DECLARE
    TYPE EmpRecTyp IS RECORD (
        Emp_id NUMBER(9),
        emp_name VARCHAR2(30),
        sal    NUMBER(7,2));
    TYPE EmpCurTyp IS REF CURSOR RETURN EmpRecTyp;
    emp_cv EmpCurTyp;  -- declare cursor variableProcedures
```

A PL/SQL procedure can be used to perform various DML operations. The following is a simple Oracle procedure:

```
create or replace procedure new_employee (emp_id number,
last_name varchar(2), first_name varchar(2))
is
begin
    insert into employees values ( emp_id, last_name, first_name);
end new_employee;
/
```

Functions

Unlike a PL/SQL procedure, a *function* returns a value, as shown in the following example:

```
create or replace function sal_ok (salary REAL, title VARCHAR2) return BOOLEAN IS
    min_sal REAL;
    max_sal REAL;
begin
    SELECT losal, hisal INTO min_sal, max_sal FROM sals
        WHERE job = title;
    RETURN (salary >= min_sal) AND (salary <= max_sal);
end sal_ok;
```

Packages

Oracle *packages* are objects that usually consist of several procedures and functions. These procedures and functions are related to each other, and the package usually is designed to perform an application function by invoking all the related procedures and functions within the package. Packages are extremely powerful, because large amounts of functional code can be stored on the server and repeatedly executed by several users.

A package usually has two parts: a package specification and a package body. The *package specification* declares the variables, cursors, and subprograms (procedures and functions) that are part of the package. The *package body* contains the actual cursors and subprogram code. Listing 5 shows a simple Oracle package.

Listing 5. A PL/SQL Package

```
/* First, the Package Specification /*
 create or replace package emp_pkg as
 type list is varray (100) of number (5);
 procedure new_employee  (emp_id number, last_name
 varchar 2, first_name varchar2);
 procedure salary_raise ( emp_id number, raise number);
end emp_pkg;
/
/* The Package Body follows */
create or replace package body emp_pkg as
procedure new_employee  (emp_id number,
last_name varchar(2), first_name varchar(2) is
  begin
    insert into employees values ( emp_id, last_name, first_name);
  end new_employee;
  procedure salary_raise ( emp_num number, raise_pct real)  is
  begin
    update employees set salary = salary * raise_pct
    where emp_id = emp_num;
  end salary_raise;
end emp_pkg;
/
```

If you want to use emp_pkg to award a raise to an employee, all you have to do is execute the following:

```
SQL> execute em_pkg.salary_raise(99999, 0.15);
```

Oracle XML DB

A typical organization has information stored in multiple formats, some of which may be organized in relational databases, but most of which is stored outside the database. The nondatabase information may be stored in application-specific formats, such as an Excel spreadsheet. Storing the nondatabase information in XML format makes it easier to access and update nonstructured organizational information.

Oracle XML DB isn't really a special type of database for XML. It simply refers to the set of built-in XML storage and retrieval technologies in Oracle9*i* Release 2 for the manipulation of XML data. Oracle9*i* XML DB provides the advantages of object-relational database technology and XML technology. For example, one of the major problems involved in dealing with XML data from within a relational database is the fact that most XML data is hierarchical in nature, whereas the Oracle database is based on the relational model. Oracle9*i* manages to deal effectively with the hierarchical XML data by using special SQL operators and methods. Using these operators, you can easily query and update XML data stored in an

Oracle9*i* database. Oracle XML DB builds the XML Document Object Model (DOM) into the Oracle kernel. Thus, most XML operations are treated as part of normal database processing.

Oracle XML DB provides the ability to view both structured and nonstructured information as relational data. You can now view data as either rows in a table or nodes in an XML document. Here is a brief list of the benefits offered by Oracle XML DB:

- You can access XML data using regular SQL queries.

- You can use Oracle's OLTP, data warehousing, test, spatial data, and multimedia features to process XML data.

- You can generate XML from an Oracle SQL query.

- You can transform XML into HTML format easily.

Storing XML in Oracle XML DB

Oracle9*i* uses a special native data type called XMLType to store and manage XML data in a relational table. XMLType and XDBUriType, which is another built-in type for XML data, enable you to leave the XML parsing, storage, and retrieval to the Oracle database. You can use the XMLType data type just as you would the usual data types in an Oracle database. You can now store a well-formed XML document in the database as an XML test using the CLOB base data type. Here's an example of using the XMLType data type:

```
SQL> create table sales_catalog_table
  2  (sales_num  number(18),
  3  sales_order xmltype);
Table created.
SQL> desc sales_catalog_table
 Name                          Null?      Type
 ------------------------------------- --------
 SALES_NUM                                NUMBER(18)
 SALES_ORDER                              XMLTYPE
SQL>
```

The XMLType data type comes with a set of XML-specific methods, which you use to work with XMLType objects. You can use these methods to perform common database operations such as checking for the existence of a node and extracting a node. The methods also support several operators that enable you to access and manipulate XML data as part of a regular SQL statement. These operators follow the emerging SQL/XML standard. Using the well-known XPath notation, the SQL/XML operators traverse XML structures to find the node or nodes on which they should use the SQL operations. Here are some of the important SQL/XML operators:

- Extract() extracts a subset of the nodes contained in the XMLType.

- ExistsNode() checks whether a certain node exists in the XMLType.

- Validating() validates the XMLType contents against an XML schema.

- Transform() performs an XSL transformation.

- ExtractValue() returns a node corresponding to an XPath expression.

XML is in abstract form compared to the normal relational table entries. How does Oracle optimize and execute statements that involve XML data? Oracle uses a query-rewrite mechanism to transform an XPath expression into an equivalent regular SQL statement. The optimizer then processes the transformed SQL statement like any other SQL statement.

You can store XML in Oracle XML DB in the following ways:

- You can use SQL or PL/SQL to insert the data. Using XMLType constructors, you must first convert the sourced data into an XMLType instance.

- You can use the Oracle XML DB repository to store the XML data.

Here's a simple example using the table sales_catalog_table to demonstrate how to perform SQL-based DML operations with an XML-enabled table. In the following section, you'll learn how to use the Oracle XML DB repository to load XML data into a table. In Listing 6, an XML document is inserted into the sales_catalog_table table.

Listing 6. Inserting an XML Document into an Oracle Table

```
SQL>   insert into sales_catalog_table
  2    values (123456,
  3    XMLTYPE(
  4    '<SalesOrder>
  5    <Reference>Alapati - 200302201428CDT</Reference>
  6    <Actions/>
  7    <Reject/>
  8    <Requestor>Nina U. Alapati</Requestor>
  9    <User>ALAPATI</User>
 10    <SalesLocation>Dallas</SalesLocation>
 11    <ShippingInstructions/>
 12    <DeliveryInstructions>Bicycle Courier</DeliveryInstructions>
 13    <ItemDescriptions>
 14       <ItemDescription  ItemNumber="1">
 15       <Description>Expert Oracle DB Administration</Description>
 16       <ISBN Number="1590590228"Price="59.95"Quantity="5"/>
 17       </ItemDescription>
 18    </ItemDescriptions>
 19* </SalesOrder>'));
1 row created.
SQL>
```

You can query the sales_catalog_table table's sales_order column, as shown in Listing 7, to view the XML document in its original format.

Listing 7. Viewing XML Data Stored in an Oracle Table

```
SQL> select sales_order from
  2 sales_catalog_table;
    <SalesOrder>
  <Reference>Alapati - 200302201428CDT</Reference>
  <Actions/>
  <Reject/>
  <Requestor>Sam R. Alapati</Requestor>
  <User>ALAPATI</User>
  <SalesLocation>Dallas</SalesLocation>
  <ShippingInstructions/>
  <DeliveryInstructions>Bicycle Courier</DeliveryInstructions>
  <ItemDescriptions>
    <ItemDescription ItemNumber="1">
      <Description>Expert Oracle DB Administration</Description>
      <ISBN Number="9999990228" Price="59.95" Quantity="2"/>
    </ItemDescription>
  </ItemDescriptions>
</SalesOrder>
SQL>
```

Once you create the table sales_catalog_table, it's very easy to retrieve data using one of the methods I just described. The following example shows how to query the table using the extract() method. Note that the query includes XPath expressions and the SQL/XML operators *extractValue* and *existsNode* to find the requestor's name where the value of the node */SalesOrder/SalesLocation/text()* contains the value *Dallas*.

```
  1  select extractValue(s.sales_order,'/SalesOrder/Requestor')
  2  from sales_catalog_table s
  3  where existsNode(s.SALES_ORDER,
  4* '/SalesOrder[SalesLocation="Dallas"]') = 1;
EXTRACTVALUE(S.SALES_ORDER,'/SALESORDER/REQUESTOR')
----------------------------------------------------
Nina U. Alapati
SQL>
```

The Oracle XML DB Repository

The best way to process XML documents in Oracle XML DB is to first load them into a special repository called the *Oracle XML DB repository*. The XML repository is hierarchical, like most XML data is, and it enables you to easily query XML data. The paths and URLs in the repository represent the relationships among the XML data, and a special hierarchical index is used to traverse the folders and paths within the repository. The XML repository can hold non-XML data such as JPEG images, Word documents, and more.

You can use SQL and PL/SQL to access the XML repository. XML authoring tools can directly access the documents in the XML repository using popular

Internet protocols such as HTTP, FTP, and WebDAV. For example, you can use Windows Explorer, Microsoft Office, and Adobe Acrobat to work with the XML documents that are stored in the XML repository. XML is by nature document-centric, and the XML repository provides applications a file abstraction when dealing with XML data.

Setting Up an XML Schema

Before you can start using Oracle XML DB to manage XML documents, you need to perform the following tasks:

1. Create an XML schema. For example, SalesOrder, shown in Listing 6, is a simple XML schema that reflects a simple XML document. Within the SalesOrder schema are elements such as ItemDescription, which provides details about the attributes of the component items.

2. Register the XML schema. After the XML schema is created, you must register it with the Oracle9*i* database using a PL/SQL procedure. When you register the XML schema, Oracle will create the SQL objects and the XMLType tables that are necessary to store and manage the XML documents. In the previous example, registering the XML schema created a table called SalesOrder automatically, with one row in the table for each SalesOrder document loaded into the XML repository. The XML schema is registered under the URL `http://localhost:8080/home/SCOTT/xdb/salesorder.xsd` and contains the definition of the SalesOrder element.

Creating a Relational View from an XML Document

Even if a developer doesn't know much XML, he or she can use the XML documents stored in the Oracle database by creating relational views based on the XML documents. In the following example, you'll see how to map nodes in an XML document to columns in a relational view called salesorder_view:

```
SQL> create or replace view salesorder_view
  2  (requestor,description,sales_location)
  3  as select
  4  extractValue(s.sales_order,'/SalesOrder/Requestor'),
  5  extractValue(s.sales_order,'/SalesOrder/Sales_Location')
  6* from sales_Catalog_Table s ;
 View created.
SQL>
```

You can then query salesorder_view like you would any other view in an Oracle database, as shown here:

```
SQL> select requestor,sales_location from salesorder_view;
REQUESTOR
SALES_LOCATION
Aparna Alapati
Dallas
SQL>
```

Oracle9i and Java

You can use both PL/SQL and Java to write applications that need Oracle9*i* database access. Although PL/SQL has several object-oriented features, the Java language is well known as an object-oriented programming language. If your application needs heavy database access and must process large amounts of data, PL/SQL is probably a better bet. However, for open distributed applications, Java-based applications are more suitable.

The Oracle9*i* database contains a Java Virtual Machine (JVM) to enable the interpretation of Java code from within the database. Just as PL/SQL enables you to store code on the server and use it multiple times, you can also create Java stored procedures and store them in the database. These Java stored procedures are in the form of Java classes. You make Java files available to the Oracle JVM by loading them into the Oracle database as schema objects.

Using Java with Oracle

You can use the Java programming language in several ways in Oracle9*i*. You can invoke Java methods in classes that are loaded in the database in the form of Java stored procedures. You can also use two different application programming interfaces (APIs), Java Database Connectivity (JDBC) or SQLJ, to access the Oracle9*i* database from a Java-based application program. In the sections the follow, you'll briefly look at the various ways you can work with Java and the Oracle database.

Java Stored Procedures

Java stored procedures are, of course, written using Java, and they facilitate the implementation of data-intensive business logic using Java. These procedures are stored within the database like PL/SQL stored procedures. Java stored procedures can be seen as a link between the Java and non-Java environments.

You can execute Java stored procedures just as you would PL/SQL stored procedures. Here's a summary of the steps involved in creating a Java stored procedure. You can invoke the Java stored procedure after you complete the following steps.

1. Define the Java class.

2. Using the Java compiler, compile the new class.

3. Load the class into the Oracle9*i* database. You can do this by using the *loadjava* command-line utility.4. Publish the Java stored procedure.

JDBC

JDBC is a popular method used to connect to an Oracle database from Java. Chapter 11 contains a complete example of a Java program. JDBC provides a set of interfaces for querying databases and processing SQL data in the Java programming language. Listing 8 shows a simple JDBC program that connects to an Oracle database and executes a simple SQL query.

Listing 8. A Simple JDBC Program

```
import java.sql.*;
public class JDBCExample {
  public static void main(String args[]) throws SQLException
/* Declare the type of Oracle Driver you are using */
    {DriverManager.registerDriver(new oracle.jdbc.driver.OracleDriver());
/* Create a database connection for the JDBC program */
Connection conn=
DriverManager.getConnection(
                "jdbc:oracle:thin:@nicholas:1521:aparna","hr","hr");
Statement stmt = conn.createStatement();
/* Pass a query to SQL and store the results in the result set rs */
ResultSet rs =
stmt.executeQuery("select emp_id, emp_name,salary from employees");
/* Using the while loop, result set rs is accessed row by row */
while(rs.next()){
int number = rs.getInt(1);
String name= rs.getString(2);
System.out.println(number+" "+name+" "+salary);
        }
/* Close the JDBC result set and close the database connection */
rs.close();
conn.close();
        }
}
```

JDBC is ideal for dynamic SQL, where the SQL statements aren't known until runtime.

SQLJ

SQLJ is a complementary API to JDBC, and it's ideal for applications in which you're using static SQL (i.e., SQL that's known before the execution). Being static, SQLJ enables you to trap errors before they occur during runtime. Do understand that even with SQLJ, you still use JDBC drivers to access the database. There are three steps involved in executing a SQLJ program:

1. Create the SQLJ source code.

2. Translate the SQLJ source code into Java source code using a Java compiler.

3. Execute the SQLJ runtime program after you connect to the database.

Listing 9 contains a simple SQLJ example that shows how to execute a SQL statement from within Java.

Listing 9. A Simple SQLJ Program

```
import java.sql.*;
import sqlj.runtime.ref.DefaultContext;
import oracle.sqlj.runtime.Oracle;
/* Declare the variables here */
/* Define an Iterator type to store query results */
#sql iterator ExampleIter (int emp_id, String emp_name,float salary);
public class MyExample
/* The main method */
   { public static void main (String args[]) throws SQLException
   {
/* Establish the database connection for SQLJ */
   Oracle.connect
    ("jdbc:oracle:thin:@shannon:1234:nicholas1", "hr", "hr");
/* Insert a row into the employees table */
   #sql { insert into employees  (emp_id, emp_name, salary)
       values (1001, 'Nina Alapati', 50000) };
/* Create an instance of the iterator ExampleIter */
  ExampleIter iter;
/* Store the results of the select query in the iterator ExampleIter */
  #sql iter={ select emp_id, emp_name, salary from  employees };
/* Access the data stored in the iterator, using the next() method */
  while (iter.next()) {
      System.out.println
      (iter.emp_id,()+" "+iter.emp_name()+" "+iter.salary());
       }
  }
}
```

As you can see from the SQLJ example in Listing 9, SQLJ is nothing more than embedded SQL in a Java program. Using SQLJ, you can easily make calls to the database from Java. For a wealth of information on Oracle9*i* and Java, please visit Oracle's Java Center Web site (http://otn.oracle.com/tech/java/content.html).

Summary

This appendix provided you with a brief review of the most commonly used SQL and PL/SQL in the Oracle9*i* database. As a DBA, you may not be expected to be a master of high-level SQL and PL/SQL. However, because developers use programming languages such as these on a daily basis, it's helpful for you to be familiar with as much SQL and PL/SQL as you possible can.

Java and XML play increasingly important roles in the Oracle database. This appendix provided you with an introduction into how Java and XML are integrated with Oracle9*i*.

Index

O